The Children of Immigrants in Schools

With an Introductory Essay by
Francesco Cordasco
Professor of Education
Montclair State College

Volume III

Scarecrow Reprint Corporation
Metuchen, N. J.   1970

61st Congress 3d Session	SENATE	Document No. 749

REPORTS OF THE IMMIGRATION COMMISSION

THE CHILDREN OF IMMIGRANTS IN SCHOOLS

(IN FIVE VOLUMES: VOL. III)

GENERAL TABLES

DETROIT, DULUTH, FALL RIVER, HAVERHILL, JOHNSTOWN,
KANSAS CITY, MO., LOS ANGELES, LOWELL, LYNN,
MANCHESTER, AND MERIDEN

PRESENTED BY MR. DILLINGHAM

DECEMBER 5, 1910.—Referred to the Committee on Immigration
and ordered to be printed, with illustrations

WASHINGTON
GOVERNMENT PRINTING OFFICE
1911

THE IMMIGRATION COMMISSION.

Senator WILLIAM P. DILLINGHAM, Chairman.
Senator HENRY CABOT LODGE.
Senator ASBURY C. LATIMER.[a]
Senator ANSELM J. McLAURIN.[b]
Senator LE ROY PERCY.[c]

Representative BENJAMIN F. HOWELL.
Representative WILLIAM S. BENNET.
Representative JOHN L. BURNETT.
Mr. CHARLES P. NEILL.
Mr. JEREMIAH W. JENKS.
Mr. WILLIAM R. WHEELER.

Secretaries:
MORTON E. CRANE.   W. W. HUSBAND.
C. S. ATKINSON.

Chief Statistician:
FRED C. CROXTON.

Extract from act of Congress of February 20, 1907, creating and defining the duties of the Immigration Commission.

That a commission is hereby created, consisting of three Senators, to be appointed by the President of the Senate, and three Members of the House of Representatives, to be appointed by the Speaker of the House of Representatives, and three persons to be appointed by the President of the United States. Said commission shall make full inquiry, examination, and investigation, by subcommittee or otherwise, into the subject of immigration. For the purpose of said inquiry, examination, and investigation said commission is authorized to send for persons and papers, make all necessary travel, either in the United States or any foreign country, and, through the chairman of the commission, or any member thereof, to administer oaths and to examine witnesses and papers respecting all matters pertaining to the subject, and to employ necessary clerical and other assistance. Said commission shall report to Congress the conclusions reached by it, and make such recommendations as in its judgment may seem proper. Such sums of money as may be necessary for the said inquiry, examination, and investigation are hereby appropriated and authorized to be paid out of the "immigrant fund" on the certificate of the chairman of said commission, including all expenses of the commissioners, and a reasonable compensation, to be fixed by the President of the United States, for those members of the commission who are not Members of Congress; * * *

---

[a] Died February 20, 1908.
[b] Appointed to succeed Mr. Latimer, February 25, 1908. Died December 22, 1909.
[c] Appointed to succeed Mr. McLaurin, March 16, 1910.

II

LIST OF REPORTS OF THE IMMIGRATION COMMISSION.

THE CHILDREN OF IMMIGRANTS IN SCHOOLS.

GENERAL TABLES FOR DETROIT, DULUTH, FALL RIVER, HAVERHILL, JOHNSTOWN, KANSAS CITY, LOS ANGELES, LOWELL, LYNN, MANCHESTER, AND MERIDEN.

The present volume, containing a portion of the general tables collected in the school inquiries under the direction of the Immigration Commission, by Roland P. Falkner, expert special agent, forms Volume III of the general report of the Commission on The Children of Immigrants in Schools.

IV

CONTENTS.

INTRODUCTION.

The tables printed in these volumes are intended to supply the material for the detailed study of the schools of the several cities included in the scope of the investigations of the Immigration Commission, and of the races found in such schools. All the material collected and tabulated for each city is assembled here under the name of the city, the cities being arranged in alphabetical order.

The material here printed is divided into four groups: (1) General tables public school pupils, (2) special tables public school pupils, (3) tables for public school teachers, and (4) general tables parochial school pupils.

THE GENERAL TABLES FOR PUPILS OF PUBLIC SCHOOLS.

The general tables for public school pupils result mainly from the general investigation. This was conducted by means of a grade record, which was filled out by every grade teacher in the public schools of the cities investigated. This record noted the grade and sex, race and age of pupils present on a given day early in December, 1908. The sheet was divided vertically into two sections, one for boys and the other for girls. Each line of the sheet was devoted to the pupils of a given race determined by the race of the father. The sheet was also ruled vertically, and each column was given to the pupils of a given age, the pupils of each race being entered according to the numbers at the different ages. Added horizontally, the sheet gave the total for each race for boys and girls separately; added vertically, it gave the total for each age for boys and girls separately.

These sheets for all the schools of the city were sorted by grades, and all sheets for each grade were added together to give the total for each grade in the city. This was the fundamental tabulation, the results of which appear in Table 3. For convenience of studying the facts herein revealed certain rearrangements of them are made in the other tables presented in this volume.

Similar tables were constructed for the public schools of seven cities where information was gathered by means of cards for each pupil. While the method of assembling the general results for the city as a whole were quite different, the resulting tables were identical in every respect. For convenience of reference these tables are referred to throughout this volume as the tables of the general investigation.

For the public schools of each city there are six of these general tables, as follows:

*Table 1.—Grade and age—Number of pupils of each age in each grade, by sex.—*This table shows for each grade and for each year of the high school and also for the kindergarten and special schools the number of boys and the number of girls of each age. The age entered is the age at last birthday. The pupils are not classified by race.

*Table 2.—Race, sex, and grade—Number of pupils of each sex in each grade, by general nativity and race of father of pupil.—*This table shows by sex the number of pupils in each grade or year of school work. The information is presented by general nativity and race of father of pupil. The age of the pupils is not shown. From this table are computed the percentages showing "race distribution" in Table 5 and the percentages showing "grade distribution" in Table 6.

Table 3.—Race, sex, and age, by grade—Number of pupils of each age in each grade, by sex and by general nativity and race of father of pupil.— This table takes up separately the kindergarten, each of the elementary grades, each year of the high school, and the special grades. For each grade or year of school work the table shows the number of boys and the number of girls of each age at last birthday. The data are presented by general nativity and race of father of pupil.

Table 4.—Race and grade, by age—Number of pupils of each specified age in each grade, by general nativity and race of father of pupil.— In this table the pupils of each age are taken up separately. The table shows the distribution throughout the grades or years of school work. Boys and girls are shown separately, and the information is presented by general nativity and race of father of pupil. This table presents, differently arranged, the same information which is shown in Table 3.

Table 5.—Race distribution in each grade—Percentages.—This table shows for the kindergarten, for each of the grades, for each year of the high school, and for the special schools, the proportion of pupils whose fathers were of each specified general nativity and race.

The table shows for the public schools of Pittsburg, for instance, the following proportion of races among the pupils in the first grade:

	Per cent.		Per cent.
Children of native-born—		Children of foreign-born—Con.	
White fathers	43.0	Irish fathers	5.8
Negro fathers	7.3	North Italian fathers	3.0
Children of foreign-born—		South Italian fathers	5.0
Canadian fathers (other than French)	.4	Magyar fathers	.6
English fathers	3.8	Polish fathers	2.7
French fathers	.2	Russian fathers	.4
German fathers	7.7	Scotch fathers	1.0
German Hebrew fathers	.7	Slovak fathers	1.3
Polish Hebrew fathers	1.4	Swedish fathers	.7
Roumanian Hebrew fathers	1.6	Welsh fathers	.9
Russian Hebrew fathers	10.0	Fathers of other races	2.4
Hebrew fathers other than those specified	1.1		

Only races represented in the public schools of the city by 100 or more pupils are shown in detail; all others are shown under "Other races" in this table.

Table 6.—Grade distribution of each race—Percentages.—This table shows for the pupils of each race the proportion in the kindergarten, in each of the elmentary grades, in each year of the high school, and in the special schools. In the public schools of Pittsburg, for instance, of the 3,626 pupils present who are children of Russian Hebrew fathers the table shows the following percentages in the various grades:

	Per cent.		Per cent.
Kindergarten	5.3	Seventh grade	4.9
First grade	23.4	Eighth grade	3.4
Second grade	17.2	First year high school	2.2
Third grade	13.6	Second year high school	1.6
Fourth grade	11.4	Third year high school	1.0
Fifth grade	8.2	Fourth year high school	.4
Sixth grade	7.4		

Only races represented in the public schools of the city by 100 or more pupils are shown in detail; all others are shown under "Other races" in this table.

The object of the first table is to obtain a general characterization of the pupils in the city schools. From it we learn the grade distribution of the pupils, and can group them, if so desired, according to types of schools, kindergarten, elementary, with divisions into primary and grammar grades, and secondary schools. From it we learn also the age distribution of the pupils and can form some idea of the ages at which pupils enter the schools and when they leave them. From the combination of grades and ages which the table presents can be deduced figures showing the extent of retardation. This can be expressed as the number of pupils in a given grade who are over age or the number of pupils of a given age who are under grade.

Table 2 gives the details of racial distribution among the pupils, while Tables 5 and 6 réduce the facts of the table to convenient percentages. These tables not only show the whole number and per cent of pupils of each race in the schools as a whole, but give this information by grades. From them can be gathered in convenient form information regarding the number and proportion of pupils of the different races in the secondary as compared with the elementary schools, or in upper grades compared with the lower ones.

Tables 3 and 4 bring the facts of race into connection with those of age as well as grade. From Table 3 a combined grade and age, similar to Table 1, can be derived for each race. Such a derived table will lend itself for the particular race concerned to a convenient study of grade distribution, age distribution, and retardation in its several aspects. If the question is as to the retardation of a particular race in a given grade, the answer can be obtained directly from Table 3. If the question is as to the retardation of pupils of a particular race at a given age, the answer can be obtained directly from Table 4. It may be suggested that a short method of comparing the relative standing of the different races would be to determine from Table 1 the grade which had the maximum retardation and from Table 3 the retardation in this grade of the several races. Table 4 can be used in a similar manner to determine relative retardation at a given age, but care should be exercised to choose a year of age before there is any considerable dropping off of pupils, as otherwise the numbers of the individual races may be too small to furnish a broad enough basis for the calculation of proportions.

SPECIAL TABLES FOR PUPILS OF PUBLIC SCHOOLS.

The special tables for public school pupils are the result of an intensive investigation carried on in seven cities and in selected schools of five cities included in the general investigation. The procedure adopted was to secure from each pupil an individual card upon which were given not only the facts of sex, race, grade, and age, but a variety of other facts concerning birthplace of the pupil and parents, the social environment and school history of the pupil. On the receipt of the cards they were sorted first by grade and sex, and then by race. A further sorting of the cards by ages furnished the material from which the general tables were derived.

The age sort permitted a grouping of the cards in three groups of children under 8 years of age to whom the criterion of retardation does not apply, those 8 years and over who were of normal age or under with reference to their grades, and those of 8 years and over who were retarded. The cards were then sorted in these groups with respect to the various other facts for which the cards gave information. What these are can be conveniently shown by a description of the special tables resulting from these operations.

In each of these tables the pupils are classified according to general nativity and race of father. A grouping of foreign races also classifies the children of foreign-born fathers according to English-speaking and non-English-speaking races. Each of the twenty-four tables shows data relative to retardation of pupils. A list of the tables follows:

Table 1.—Birthplace of pupils, by general nativity and race of father.—In this table all of the pupils included in the investigation are divided according to place of birth into three groups, as follows:

    1. Those born in the city in which they lived at the time of the investigation.
    2. Those born in the United States, but elsewhere than in the city in which they lived at the time of the investigation.
    3. Those born abroad.

Under each of the three groups are shown the number and per cent of pupils 8 years of age or over who are retarded.

Table 2.—School attendance of pupils born in the United States, but elsewhere than in the city in which they lived at the time of the investigation, by general nativity and race of father.—In this table the pupils included are divided into two groups:

    1. Those having attended school elsewhere.
    2. Those not having attended school elsewhere.

Under each of the above groups are shown the number and per cent of pupils 8 years of age or over who are retarded.

Table 3.—Age of foreign-born pupils at time of arrival in the United States, by race of father.—In this table all foreign-born pupils are separated into four groups according to age at time of arrival in the United States:

    1. Those who were under 6 years of age.
    2. Those who were 6 or 7 years of age.
    3. Those who were 8 or 9 years of age.
    4. Those who were 10 years of age or over.

The proportion of pupils 8 years of age or over retarded is shown under each of the above groups.

Table 4.—School attendance abroad of foreign-born pupils who were 6 years of age or over at time of arrival in the United States, by race of father.—This table separates all foreign-born pupils who were 6 years of age or over at time of arrival in the United States into two groups, as follows:

    1. Those having attended school abroad.
    2. Those not having attended school abroad.

Under each of the above groups is shown the proportion of pupils 8 years of age or over who are retarded.

Table 5.—Age of pupils at time of entering public school in the United States, by general nativity and race of father.—By entrai . 3 into public school is meant entrance into the grades, and no account is taken of kindergarten. The table separates the pupils into six groups according to age at time of entering public school in the United States, as follows:

1. Those who were 5 years of age or under.
2. Those who were 6 years of age.
3. Those who were 7 years of age.
4. Those who were 8 years of age.
5. Those who were 9 years of age.
6. Those who were 10 years of age or over.

The proportion of pupils 8 years of age or over retarded is shown under each of the groups.

Table 6.—Age of pupils at time of entering public school in the United States, by race of father; foreign-born pupils only.—This table is similar to Table 5 in every respect except that it relates only to foreign-born children.

Table 7.—Grade entered by pupils, by general nativity and race of father.—This table refers to the grade entered in public school. No account is taken of entrance into kindergarten. The table separates the pupils into five groups according to grade first entered, as follows:

1. Those who entered first grade.
2. Those who entered second grade.
3. Those who entered third grade.
4. Those who entered fourth grade.
5. Those who entered fifth grade or above.

Under each of the groups is shown the proportion of pupils 8 years of age or over retarded.

Table 8.—Grade entered by pupils, by race of father; foreign-born pupils only.—This table is similar to Table 7 in every respect except that it relates only to foreign-born children.

Table 9.—Grade entered by pupils 8 years of age or over at time of entering, by general nativity and race of father.—This table refers to the grade entered in public school, and no account is taken of entrance into kindergarten. The pupils included in the table are separated into eight groups according to grade entered, as follows:

1. Those who entered first grade.
2. Those who entered second grade.
3. Those who entered third grade.
4. Those who entered fourth grade.
5. Those who entered fifth grade.
6. Those who entered sixth grade.
7. Those who entered seventh grade.
8. Those who entered eighth grade or above.

Table 10.—Grade entered by pupils 8 years of age or over at time of entering, by race of father; foreign-born pupils only.—This table is similar to Table 9 in every respect except that it relates only to foreign-born pupils.

Table 11.—Rate of progress of pupils and time in school in the United States, by general nativity and race of father.—In this table the pupils are separated into three groups according to progress in school, as follows:

1. Those who have been in school in the United States a less number of years than the number of the grade.
2. Those who have been in school in the United States the same number of years as the number of the grade.
3. Those who have been in school in the United States a greater number of years than the number of the grade.

Under each of these groups is shown the proportion of pupils 8 years of age or over who are retarded.

Table 12.—Rate of progress of pupils and time in school in the United States, by general nativity and race of father; foreign-born pupils only.—This table is similar to Table 11 in every respect except that it relates only to foreign-born pupils.

Table 13.—Ability to speak English of foreign-born fathers of pupils, by race of father.—This table includes only non-English-speaking races. The pupils included are separated into two groups as follows:

1. Those whose fathers speak English.
2. Those whose fathers do not speak English.

Under each of the two groups is shown the proportion of pupils 8 years of age or over who are retarded.

Table 14.—Ability to speak English of foreign-born fathers of pupils, by race of father; foreign-born pupils only.—This table is similar to Table 13 in every respect except that it relates only to foreign-born pupils.

Table 15.—Citizenship of foreign-born fathers of pupils, by race of father.—The pupils included in this table are separated into two groups, as follows:

1. Those whose fathers have either first or second naturalization papers.
2. Those whose fathers have neither first nor second naturalization papers.

Under each of the two groups is shown the proportion of pupils 8 years of age or over who are retarded.

Table 16.—Citizenship of foreign-born fathers of pupils, by race of father; foreign-born pupils only.—This table is similar to Table 15 in every respect except that it relates only to foreign-born pupils.

Table 17.—Length of residence in the United States of foreign-born fathers of pupils, by race of father.—The pupils included in this table are separated into four groups, as follows:

1. Those whose fathers first came to the United States less than 5 years ago.
2. Those whose fathers first came to the United States from 5 to 9 years ago.
3. Those whose fathers first came to the United States from 10 to 19 years ago.
4. Those whose fathers first came to the United States 20 or more years ago.

Under each of the groups is shown the proportion of pupils 8 years of age or over who are retarded.

Table 18.—Length of residence in the United States of foreign-born fathers of pupils, by race of father; foreign-born pupils only.—This table is similar to Table 17 in every respect except that it relates only to foreign-born pupils.

Table 19.—Home language—Pupils of foreign-born fathers of non-English-speaking races, by race of father.—The pupils included in this table are separated into two groups according to home language, as follows:

1. Those in homes where English is used.
2. Those in homes where English is not used.

Under each of the groups is shown the proportion of pupils 8 years of age or over who are retarded.

Table 20.—Home language—Pupils of foreign-born fathers of non-English-speaking races, by race of father; foreign-born pupils only.—This table is similar to Table 19 in every respect except that it relates only to foreign-born pupils.

Table 21.—Proportion of term attended, by general nativity and race of father.—This table shows, separately, data for primary grades (grades 1 to 4) and for grammar grades (grades 5 to 8) and also data for all elementary grades combined. The meaning of "term" as used in this table is the period from the beginning of the school year to December 31, 1908. The pupils are separated into four groups according to proportion of "term" attended, as follows:

1. Those who attended nine-tenths or more of the time.
2. Those who attended three-fourths and less than nine-tenths of the time.
3. Those who attended one-half and less than three-fourths of the time.
4. Those who attended less than one-half of the time.

For the purpose of showing the data relative to retardation the first and second groups and the third and fourth groups are combined, and under each of these two resulting groups is shown the proportion of pupils 8 years of age or over who are retarded.

Table 22.—Proportion of term attended, by race of father; foreign-born pupils only.—This table is similar to Table 21 in every respect except that it relates only to foreign-born pupils.

Table 23.—Access to present grade, by general nativity and race of father.—By "Access to present grade" is meant how the pupil was admitted in the fall of 1908 to the class he was in at the time the investigation was made. The pupils are separated into five groups, as follows:

1. Those who were admitted to the grade in "regular course," that is, either by promotion from a lower grade in the same school or as a pupil entering school for the first time.
2. Those who were admitted by transfer from another public school in the same city.
3. Those who were admitted by transfer from a public school elsewhere than in the city in which they lived at the time of the investigation.
4. Those who were admitted by transfer from a "private" school. "Private" school, as here used, includes all kinds of schools other than public schools.
5. Those who had failed of promotion at the end of the previous school year.

In the section of the table relating to retardation, groups 2, 3, and 4 are combined under the heading "By transfer." Under each of the three groups which remain is shown the proportion of pupils 8 years of age or over who are retarded.

Table 24.—Access to present grade, by race of father; foreign-born pupils only.—This table is similar to Table 23 in every respect except that it relates only to foreign-born pupils.

The purpose of these tables is to give more details in regard to the personal and school history of the children and their home environment, and to bring these facts into relation with the question of school progress. The former appears in the various items tabulated in the successive tables; the latter is accomplished by the distinction of the children of 8 years of age and upward into the normal and retarded groups.

The shifting of the population from which the school children are drawn is reflected in Table 1, which deals with the birthplace of pupils. From it can be learned the number and proportion of the children who are natives of the city in which they were attending school.

Table 2 shows for those who were born elsewhere in the United States how far the changing residence of the parents has affected the school history of the children. It may be assumed that the children born elsewhere, but not having attended school elsewhere, were young when the change of residence occurred and have not been influenced in their school life by it. Those who have been to school elsewhere and whose education has therefore been interrupted by a change of schools are, in some instances, a considerable proportion of the group.

The foreign-born pupils are a class by themselves. Their promise of satisfactory progress in the American schools depends in large measure upon their age at the time of arrival, concerning which information is given in the third table, supplemented by the fourth which shows whether the children of school age at the time of arrival in the United States had attended school in the land of their birth.

Tables 5 to 10 throw light upon the important questions of when children enter school, and the effect of age upon school progress. They show the ages at which all children entered the graded schools, in which matter there is considerable divergence between the records in the different cities. They show that though compulsory education begins with 8 years of age, but a very small proportion of children defer entrance till they have attained this age. These tables also show that the number of pupils entering school at 8 years of age or over is largely accounted for by the pupils of foreign birth. They show that very few pupils enter school above the first grade, though this is relatively more frequent among pupils of foreign than of native birth. In view of the statements sometimes heard in educational discussion that pupils entering late frequently enter grades higher than the first, a special test is made in Tables 9 and 10 which are devoted to the grades entered by older pupils. The tables are so constructed that as far as possible the influence of the foreign-born pupil in swelling the number of pupils who enter school late is eliminated.

Educational circles have been discussing for some time whether age with reference to grade is a proper criterion of retardation. Those who oppose this view take the ground that the only proper test is whether a child has taken longer to reach a given point in school work than the regular program provides. Tables 11 and 12 are designed to show the mutual relations of these different standpoints. Information is here given as to the number of pupils who have progressed more rapidly than the school program, those who have kept pace with it, and those who have lagged behind.

Certain conditions of home environment among pupils whose parents were born abroad find expression in Tables 13 to 20. Here we can ascertain the facts concerning the ability of fathers to speak English, length of residence in the United States, citizenship, and home language.

The remaining tables, 21 to 24, deal with the school history of the pupil, relating, as they do, to the regularity of attendance and access to the present grade.

The general purposes which these tables serve being thus indicated, it should be noted that throughout the pupils are divided by racial groups and distinct races. Every combination of facts possible for the pupils as a whole is therefore possible for each group or race noted. It should, however, be remarked that for some of the special races the number of cases to which the figures apply is very small, and care should be exercised lest too sweeping conclusions be drawn from a too narrow basis of fact.

The value of these tables is enhanced by the special mention in each case of the retarded group. By this means it is designed to give some indication of the general influence of these factors successively exhibited by the tables upon the school progress of the children. The analysis of these figures in detail can not fail to be illuminating in this respect. But, as before stated, for some of the details considered the recorded facts in a given city are often meager, and in such cases a combination of figures from several cities is advisable.

TEACHERS IN PUBLIC SCHOOLS.

In those cities where information concerning public school pupils was obtained by means of the grade record sheets, certain information was collected in regard to the teachers. Besides the grade taught and the sex of the teacher, questions were asked as to country of birth, years in the United States if born abroad, country of birth and race of father, and the number of years engaged in teaching. This information was not asked in the high schools, because in those institutions the sheets were as a rule filled out by the principals and not by the individual teachers. The facts brought out by these inquiries have been summarized in the general tables as follows:

Table 1.—Number of teachers in each grade, by sex and general nativity and race.—This table shows for the kindergarten and for each of the elementary grades the number of male and the number of female teachers of each race.

Table 2.—Number of teachers engaged in teaching each specified number of years, by sex and general nativity and race.—This table shows for the teachers of each race the number who have been engaged in teaching—

Less than 5 years.
5 to 9 years.
10 to 14 years.
15 to 19 years.

20 to 24 years.
25 to 29 years.
30 years or over.

The general purpose of this investigation was to secure information regarding the racial actecedents of the teachers. From the tables considerable interesting information can be gathered. The distribution of the number of teachers by grades naturally follows that of the pupils, though in some cases it might be found that there were interesting variations in the size of the average class by grades. Of wider interest is the distribution of the teachers by race in the several grades. The second table gives information as to the length of service. Contrary to the general belief that few teachers have a long term of service, it is found generally that at least half of them have served in the profession ten years or more. The division by race affords an opportunity of discovering whether there is any difference with respect to racial composition between the older and the younger groups of teachers.

PUPILS IN PAROCHIAL SCHOOLS.

Through the courtesy of the church authorities an investigation was made of the pupils in parochial schools, parallel to the general investigation of the pupils in public schools. The same schedules were used to collect the information, the same methods were employed to tabulate the returns, and the results are presented in these volumes in statistical tables of the same form. A general description of these tables and an account of the uses to which they may be put has already been given in connection with the general tables for pupils in public schools, to which the reader is referred.[a]   It would seem needless to repeat the statement here.   These tables give a wealth of detailed information in regard to the parochial schools and permit the test of the same aspects of school life as in the case of the public schools.

The division of the pupils by race in particular lends itself not only to an interesting comparison of the two sets of schools, but the combination of the two permits an admirable survey of the racial composition of the population of school age.   The parochial schools draw upon a somewhat different constituency than the public schools, and without them an incorrect view of the general status of the races would be obtained.   It seems proper also to remark that, though designed primarily to supplement the information gathered with respect to the races in public schools, the statistics of parochial schools here published are, for the areas to which they relate, the most detailed statements which have been made public concerning schools of this category.

SUMMARY.

A bird's-eye view of the contents of these volumes of general tables for the school investigation can best be obtained from a statement by cities of the information gathered in each.   The fol' wing table shows the number of pupils or teachers comprehended in the several investigations conducted by the Commission.   It shows where each investigation was carried on and, conversely, shows for each city what information is available concerning it.

---

[a] See pp. VII–IX.

Character and extent of school inquiries.

No.	City.	Public schools.				Parochial schools.
		General tables. Number of pupils.	Special tables. Number of pupils.	Special tables, selected schools. Number of pupils.	Teachers' tables. Number of teachers.	General tables. Number of pupils.
1	Baltimore, Md.	59,876			1,805	10,181
2	Bay City, Mich.	5,474	5,148			
3	Boston, Mass.	91,443			1,997	11,009
4	Buffalo, N. Y.	49,111		2,453	1,320	
5	Cedar Rapids, Iowa	2,231	2,200			
6	Chelsea, Mass.	3,903	3,810			
7	Chicago, Ill.	235,452		7,272	6,340	
8	Cincinnati, Ohio	33,621			859	
9	Cleveland, Ohio	58,941		5,540	1,596	12,156
10	Detroit, Mich.	42,760			1,436	13,449
11	Duluth, Minn.	10,895			460	1,008
12	Fall River, Mass.	13,926			413	5,722
13	Haverhill, Mass.	4,264	4,128			1,737
14	Johnstown, Pa.	5,320	5,073			
15	Kansas City, Mo.	27,159			672	983
16	Los Angeles, Cal.	33,422			1,147	2,200
17	Lowell, Mass.	11,011			285	4,412
18	Lynn, Mass.	9,583			219	2,959
19	Manchester, N. H.	5,078			268	1,489
20	Meriden, Conn.	4,014			99	1,594
21	Milwaukee, Wis.	38,650			1,195	6,999
22	Minneapolis, Minn.	38,578			1,083	1,392
23	Newark, N. J.	44,605		7,836	1,186	9,403
24	New Bedford, Mass.	8,435	8,067			
25	New Britain, Conn.	4,718	4,614			1,444
26	New Orleans, La.	30,199			985	4,211
27	New York, N. Y.	569,163			14,904	72,887
28	Philadelphia, Pa.	145,285			3,958	45,604
29	Pittsburg, Pa.	45,378		5,090	1,142	
30	Providence, R. I.	25,260			1,000	3,296
31	St. Louis, Mo.	70,928			1,876	
32	San Francisco, Cal.	33,547			1,055	3,156
33	Scranton, Pa.	16,157			447	3,382
34	Shenandoah, Pa.	3,519			88	486
35	South Omaha, Nebr.	4,246			120	
36	Worcester, Mass.	18,226			823	
37	Yonkers, N. Y.	10,841			289	
	Total	1,815,217	33,040	28,191	49,067	221,159

The quantity of information gathered prohibits its publication in a single volume. Since, however, the cities are arranged alphabetically and all information relative to any city is assembled in one place, it should not be difficult for the inquirer to find conveniently in the series of volumes the places in which he is especially interested. The present volume contains the tables for the following cities: Detroit, Duluth, Fall River, Haverhill, Johnstown, Kansas City, Los Angeles, Lowell, Lynn, Manchester, and Meriden.

DETROIT, MICHIGAN.

INTRODUCTORY NOTE.
PUBLIC SCHOOL PUPILS—GENERAL INVESTIGATION.
PUBLIC SCHOOL TEACHERS IN ELEMENTARY GRADES
  AND KINDERGARTEN.
PAROCHIAL SCHOOL PUPILS—GENERAL INVESTIGATION.

LIST OF TABLES.

3

DETROIT.

The tables here presented for the schools in the city of Detroit are those of the general investigation covering pupils in the public schools, those with regard to teachers in the public schools, and those relating to children in the parochial schools. Both in the public and parochial schools the inquiry was conducted in this city by means of the grade record sheets. Those used in the public schools gave certain information in regard to the teachers as well as the pupils. The methods of the inquiry, the general character of the tables resulting from them, and the purposes which such tables serve. are explained in full in the introduction to this volume.[a]

PUBLIC SCHOOL PUPILS—GENERAL INVESTIGATION.

The whole number of public school pupils enumerated in Detroit was 42,760. This number represents those actually present in the schools on a day early in December, 1908. During the school year 1908–9 the average annual attendance in the schools of Detroit was 41,600. It is not to be expected that the number of the pupils on a given day should coincide exactly with the annual average, but the close approximation of the two figures, the number secured by the Immigration Commission, being slightly higher than the average annual attendance, leaves no room for doubt that the inquiry in Detroit was comprehensive and complete and that the figures resulting therefrom furnish a representative picture of conditions in the public schools of the city.

The distribution of pupils in the public schools by grades is as follows:

Kindergarten	3,101	Eighth grade	2,143
First grade	6,765	First year high school	1,418
Second grade	5,204	Second year high school	926
Third grade	5,409	Third year high school	709
Fourth grade	4,945	Fourth year high school	530
Fifth grade	4,616	Special and ungraded school	298
Sixth grade	3,660		
Seventh grade	3,036	Total	42,760

This table shows, as is generally the case, that the number of pupils in the first grade considerably exceeds that in any other grade. From the second to the fourth grade the numbers reported are not far from equal. The fifth, sixth, and seventh grades show successively a slight decrease in numbers, while the eighth grade is markedly inferior in number to any of those which precede it, containing only about two-thirds of the number in the seventh grade and less than one-half the number in the fifth grade. The diminution in the number of pupils between the eighth grade and the first year in the high school is not more conspicuous than that between the seventh and eighth grades of the elementary schools.

a See pp. VI to XVII.

For convenience of comparison of the upper and lower schools the numbers in the grades are grouped in the statement following, which divides the elementary grades into two groups, grades 1 to 4 being designated for convenience as primary, while 5 to 8 are designated grammar grades.

Class of school.	Number.	Per cent.
Kindergarten	3,101	7.3
Primary grades, 1 to 4	22,323	52.6
Grammar grades, 5 to 8	13,455	31.7
High school	3,583	8.4
Total	42,462	100.0

Including the kindergarten, six-tenths of the pupils in the Detroit schools are in the lower grades, or the first five years of school, the remaining four-tenths being in the upper grades, or the last eight years of the school course.

An examination of the ages of the pupils as shown in Table 1 indicates that the pupils in the Detroit public schools attend school at a comparatively early age. There are 2,226 pupils at 5 years of age, and 4,042 pupils at 6 years of age. The number at succeeding ages remains somewhat near the mark 4,000, until the thirteenth year is reached. In the thirteenth year of age there are 3,885 pupils, but this number drops at the age of 14 to 3,049, and at the age of 15 suffers a further diminution to 2,015, or about one-half as many as in any year of age between 6 and 13.

Table 1 also affords an opportunity for the study of the relation which exists between the ages of the pupils and the grades in which they are found. From such a study the number of pupils in each grade who are older than the age appropriate to that grade can be ascertained, and conversely one can determine the number of pupils of each age who are in grades lower than those appropriate to their age. The first group may be designated as "overage," the second as "undergrade," pupils, one expression being the complement of the other. Both of these figures are used to designate the number of backward or retarded pupils. The usual form of expressing retardation is to give the number and percentage of the pupils in the grades who can be designated as "overage" for their respective grades. The number of pupils in each grade, the normal age, and the number above normal age in each grade, together with the totals for all the elementary grades, are given in the following table:

Grade.	Number in grade.	Retarded pupils.		
		Age.	Number.	Per cent of all pupils.
First	6,765	8 years and over	1,239	18.3
Second	5,204	9 years and over	1,453	27.9
Third	5,409	10 years and over	2,008	37.1
Fourth	4,945	11 years and over	2,221	44.9
Fifth	4,616	12 years and over	2,197	47.6
Sixth	3,660	13 years and over	1,654	45.2
Seventh	3,036	14 years and over	1,170	38.5
Eighth	2,143	15 years and over	715	33.4
Total	35,778		12,657	35.4

In the aggregate of the elementary grades 12,657 pupils, or 35.4 per cent of the whole number, are older than the age appropriate for their respective grades. The percentage of retardation is less than this average in the first and second grades, which contain the younger pupils. But with the third grade the average for the school system is attained, and the proportion of retarded children increases until the fifth grade is reached, where it has a maximum of 47.6 per cent. After this point it declines, and in the eighth grade falls slightly below the general average. The table shows the diminution of pupils in the upper grades and also shows that this diminution is more rapid among the retarded pupils.

From Table 1 can also be derived a statement of retardation by ages, showing for each age the number of children who are below the appropriate grade for that age. The following table, drawn from Table 1, gives such figures for the ages 10, 11, and 12 years:

Age.	Number of pupils of this age.	Normal grade.	Retarded, or below normal grade.	
			Number.	Per cent.
10 years	4,151	4	1,593	38.4
11 years	4,045	5	1,785	44.1
12 years	4,032	6	2,041	50.6
Total	12,228		5,419	44.3

It appears from this table that at 10 years of age 38.4 per cent of the pupils in the Detroit schools are retarded or below their normal grade, and that this proportion increases with the years, so that at 12 years of age one-half of the pupils can be deemed behind in their work. The average is calculated here for the purpose of establishing a standard with which to compare the different elements which compose the population of the schools. Some of these are so small in number that one might go wrong in establishing relationships based on single years of age, and in order to obviate accidental variation the average of the three years, 10 to 12, is therefore taken.

The principal object of the researches of the Immigration Commission was to throw light upon any possible variations which might exist among the different races which form the population of the schools. The inquiry as to race was fundamental to its investigations. The main results of this inquiry are shown in the table following, which gives the larger racial groups as well as the individual races which had a representation of at least 200 children in the public schools of the city.

General nativity and race of father of pupil.	Number.	Per cent.	General nativity and race of father of pupil.	Number.	Per cent.
Native-born:			Foreign-born—Continued.		
White	19,409	45.4	Hebrew, German	416	1.0
Negro and Indian	520	1.2	Hebrew, Russian	1,505	3.5
			Irish	694	1.6
Total native-born	19,929	46.6	Italian, North	420	1.0
			Italian, South	215	.5
Foreign-born:			Polish	1,284	3.0
Bohemian and Moravian	292	.7	Scotch	864	2.0
Canadian, French	657	1.5	All others	1,511	3.5
Canadian, Other	4,817	11.3			
English	1,920	4.5	Total foreign-born	22,831	53.4
French	296	.7			
German	7,940	18.6	Grand total	42,760	100.0

The children of native-born fathers form 46.6 per cent, or somewhat less than one-half, of the whole number of children in the schools. Disregarding the comparatively small number of negroes, the contrast furnished by the tables is between 45.4 per cent of the children having native white fathers and 53.4 per cent having foreign white fathers. Among the latter the most numerous group were the Germans, with 18.6 per cent of the total number, and the Canadians, other than French, who form 11.3 per cent of the whole number of children in the schools. The proximity of Detroit to Canada gives it a comparatively large population which is of foreign origin but of English speech. The English-speaking elements noted in this table—the Canadian, the English, the Irish, and the Scotch—make up together 18.4 per cent of the total school population, a figure almost identical with that for the Germans. The other groups which stand out somewhat prominently in the aggregate are the Poles and the Russian Hebrews.

It will be noted that a not inconsiderable group of children is included under the designation "All others," which comprises a variety of races having fewer than 200 representatives each, and for which a calculation of the percentages would have been impracticable. A list of these races, however, with the numbers of each, is necessary to a complete understanding of the racial diversity of the pupils in the public schools. These races are: Arabian (2), Armenian (4), Bulgarian (13), Chinese (5), Croatian (5), Cuban (1), Danish (125), Dutch (184), Finnish (5), Flemish (151), Greek (3), Hebrew, Polish (188), Hebrew, Roumanian (68), Hebrew, Other (157), Japanese (3), Lithuanian (39), Malay (102), Negro (8), Norwegian (49), Roumanian (11), Russian (72), Ruthenian (5), Scotch-Irish (6), Slovak (23), Slovenian (1), Spanish (2), Spanish-American (11), Swedish (114), Syrian (22), Turkish (3), and Welsh (51).

The general tables are so constructed that for the two groups, native and foreign, as well as for many individual races, the same analysis as respects ages and grades can be made for the pupils in the aggregate. Without carrying this analysis into all the details of which it is capable, it may be well to note some of the main results. The table following exhibits the distribution of the children by grades under the same grouping into kindergarten, primary grades, grammar grades, and high school, as has previously been done for the aggregate school population.

General nativity and race of father of pupil.	Number of pupils.					Per cent.			
	Kinder-garten.	Pri-mary.	Gram-mar.	High.	Total.	Kinder-garten.	Pri-mary.	Gram-mar.	High.
Native-born:									
White..................	1,365	9,583	6,381	2,010	19,339	7.1	49.6	33.0	10.4
Negro and Indian........	26	295	160	30	511	5.1	57.7	31.3	5.9
Total native-born......	1,391	9,878	6,541	2,040	19,850	7.0	49.8	33.0	10.3
Foreign born:									
Bohemian and Moravian.	21	159	101	11	292	7.2	54.5	34.6	3.8
Canadian, French........	47	376	193	33	649	7.2	57.9	29.7	5.1
Canadian, Other.........	292	2,375	1,647	488	4,802	6.1	49.5	34.3	10.2
English..................	116	891	715	189	1,911	6.1	46.6	37.4	9.9
French..................	19	166	90	20	295	6.4	56.3	30.5	6.8
German.................	612	4,383	2,492	380	7,867	7.8	55.7	31.7	4.8
Hebrew, German........	11	187	150	66	414	2.7	45.2	36.2	15.9
Hebrew, Russian........	49	1,019	360	71	1,499	3.3	68.0	24.0	4.7
Irish....................	61	308	242	79	690	8.8	44.6	35.1	11.4
Italian, North...........	98	284	35	3	420	23.3	67.6	8.3	.7
Italian, South...........	24	147	33	....	204	11.8	72.1	16.2	....
Polish..................	172	920	100	18	1,210	14.2	76.0	8.3	1.5
Scotch.................	56	380	325	100	861	6.5	44.1	37.7	11.6
All others..............	132	850	431	85	1,498	8.8	56.7	28.8	5.7
Total foreign-born.....	1,710	12,445	6,914	1,543	22,612	7.6	55.0	30.6	6.8
Grand total...........	3,101	22,323	13,455	3,583	42,462	7.3	52.6	31.7	8.4

Comparing the children of native white parents with those of foreign white parents, it will be observed that the former have larger proportions in the grammar grades and high school, and the latter larger proportions in the kindergarten and the primary grades. Thus the primary grades contain 49.6 per cent of all the pupils of native white parentage as contrasted with 55 per cent of the pupils of foreign white parentage. Among the latter group it is noticeable that the Canadians other than French have practically the same proportion in the primary grades as have the native white, while the English, the Scotch, the Irish, and the German Hebrews have an even smaller percentage of their pupils in these grades. The races which rise most conspicuously above the average in the proportion of pupils in the primary grades are the Russian Hebrews, Poles, and Italians. In contrast with the primary grades, the high schools contain 10.4 per cent of all the pupils of native white parentage, but only 6.8 per cent of the pupils of foreign white parentage. Among the latter it will be noticed that the proportion of Canadians in the high school is almost identical with that of the native white, while on the other hand the Irish, Scotch, and especially the German Hebrews, show a larger proportion of pupils in the high school than do the native whites. In contrast with these races the numbers of Poles and Italians in the high schools are quite insignificant. How far this may be due to the fact that children of the high-school ages may be comparatively few in the community at large in these two races can not be determined from any figures which are now available.

Applying to the different racial groups and to the more numerous individual races the same tests of retardation which have already been discussed in connection with the whole number of pupils, the following table results.

General nativity and race of father of pupil.	All elementary pupils.			Pupils 10, 11, and 12 years of age.		
	Number.	Retarded, overage.	Per cent retarded.	Number.	Retarded, under-grade.	Per cent retarded.
Native-born:						
White........................	15,964	4,994	31.3	5,324	2,041	38.3
Negro and Indian..................	455	244	53.6	179	110	61.5
Total native-born.................	16,419	5,238	31.9	5,503	2,151	39.1
Foreign-born:						
Bohemian and Moravian............	260	105	40.4	102	51	50.0
Canadian, French.............	569	264	46.4	184	106	57.6
Canadian, Other.................	4,022	1,478	36.7	1,421	632	44.5
English.......................	1,606	604	37.6	583	245	42.0
French.......................	256	116	45.3	95	57	60.0
German........................	6,875	2,520	36.7	2,453	1,143	46.6
Hebrew, German................	337	93	27.6	108	36	33.3
Hebrew, Russian............	1,379	558	40.5	473	276	58.4
Irish........................	550	202	36.7	207	92	44.4
Italian, North................	319	142	44.5	90	76	84.4
Italian, South................	180	93	51.7	62	48	77.4
Polish.......................	1,020	507	49.7	201	163	81.1
Scotch.......................	705	253	35.9	266	104	39.1
All others...................	1,281	484	37.8	480	239	49.8
Total foreign-born...............	19,359	7,419	38.3	6,725	3,268	48.6
Grand total....................	35,778	12,657	35.4	12,228	5,419	44.3

In the first section of the table, which gives the retardation of all elementary pupils, we observe that the number of overage pupils among the native white (31.3 per cent of the whole number) is somewhat below the average already noted, while that for the children of foreign white parents (38.3 per cent) rises above the average. Comparing the different races a wide diversity appears. One of them—the German Hebrew—exhibits less retardation than the native white. Canadian, English, Irish, and Scotch children have a comparatively small degree of retardation, larger indeed than the native white but less than the average for the foreign group. On the other hand, children of Polish, Italian, and French Canadian fathers show a degree of retardation which is markedly in advance of the general average for the group.

The indication has already been given that the differences among races may be due in part to the fact that some of them contain a relatively larger number of younger children or a relatively larger number of older children when compared with one another. In order to eliminate the disturbing effect of this difference in the ages the second part of the table refers to children of the same ages throughout. By being confined to three years of life it deals necessarily with smaller, though perhaps more exactly comparable, numbers. A consideration of this table shows as between the children of native parentage and those of foreign parentage a retardation of 38.3 per cent in the first case and 48.6 per cent in the second. Contrasting the different races which form the foreign element, we find again that the German Hebrews have notably less retardation than the native white, but that some other races, especially the Poles and Italians, have a very excessive retardation as compared with the foreign white group. Inasmuch, however, as our figures are distinguished by parentage only and not by nativity, it should be taken into consideration that the Italians and Poles of the ages 10 to 12 years undoubtedly contain a larger proportion of children born abroad, and therefore comparatively unused to American ways, than do most of the other races named.

PUBLIC SCHOOL TEACHERS.

In the kindergarten and elementary grades of the Detroit public school system there were employed 1,436 teachers. Only six were men, and these, with one exception, were employed in the ungraded and special schools. In the statement following these teachers are classified by general nativity and race:

	Number.	Per cent.
Native white of native fathers	643	44.8
Native negro of native fathers	2	0.1
Native white of foreign fathers	655	45.6
Foreign white	136	9.5
Total	1,436	100.0

Approximately 45 per cent of the teachers of the Detroit schools were of wholly native antecedents, and an equal number were born in this country, though of foreign fathers. In this group the most important single race is the Irish, representing 14.2 per cent of all the teachers. If to the latter we add the other teachers of English-speaking races, we find that they aggregate 34.1 per cent of the whole number of teachers leaving only 11.5 per cent as the proportion of teachers who were of native birth, but whose linguistic antecedents were not English. Nearly 10 per cent of the teachers are of foreign birth, and among these again those of the English-speaking races predominate.

With respect to the positions occupied by the teachers of different extractions the following table gives information:

	Kindergarten and primary.	Grammar and special.	Total.	Per cent in grammar grades.
Native white, native fathers	398	245	643	38.1
Native negro, native fathers	2		2	
Native white, foreign fathers	395	260	655	39.7
Foreign white	78	58	136	42.6
Total	873	563	1,436	39.2

While on the average 39.2 per cent of the teachers are employed in the grammar and special grades, it is noticed that the proportions for the groups "native white of foreign fathers" and "foreign white" are somewhat larger than for those of purely native origin. Of these teachers 1,430 reported the length of their service in the public schools as follows.

Under 5 years	303	From 25 to 29 years	74
From 5 to 9 years	399	30 years and over	69
From 10 to 14 years	249		
From 15 to 19 years	209	Total	1,430
From 20 to 24 years	127		

The youngest teachers are the most numerous, as those with less than ten years' service constitute very nearly one-half of all the teachers. The proportion of teachers who had a length of service of twenty years or more was slightly less than one-fifth of the whole number. The length of service of the teachers, as distinguished by racial groups, is summarized in the following statement:

Race and nativity of teachers.	Length of service, in years.			
	Under 10.	10 to 19.	20 and over.	Total.
Native white, native fathers	322	202	118	642
Native negro, native fathers	1	1		2
Native white, foreign fathers	321	216	113	650
Foreign white	58	39	39	136
Total	702	458	270	1,430
Percentages—all teachers	49.1	32.0	18.9	100.0

These figures show that the proportions of younger and older teachers are very nearly the same among the different racial groups.

PUPILS OF THE PAROCHIAL SCHOOLS.

Figures were collected in the parochial schools of the city of Detroit for 13,449 pupils. The only records with which it is possible to compare these figures with a view to estimating their completeness are those given in the official directory of the Roman Catholic Church, which states the total enrollment of the parochial schools of the city of Detroit as 16,079. There is always a divergence between enrollment figures and attendance figures, oftentimes greater than that here noted. It is therefore reasonable to assume that the figures available include practically all of the children who were in attendance in the parochial schools of Detroit in December, 1908, when the record was made. The division of these pupils, by grades, is as follows:

First grade	2,738	First year high school	142
Second grade	2,327	Second year high school	66
Third grade	2,079	Third year high school	31
Fourth grade	1,991	Fourth year high school	28
Fifth grade	1,746	Commercial school	91
Sixth grade	1,073		
Seventh grade	762	Total	13,449
Eighth grade	375		

The figures here given show, as usual, a large number of pupils in grade 1. In grades 2 and 5 there is comparatively little difference between the numbers reported, although each grade is slightly less in number than that immediately preceding it. Between the fifth and sixth grades there is a considerable loss in the number of pupils, and the sixth grade contains only one-half as many pupils as are found in grades 2 or 3. This rapid decrease continues until the eighth grade is reached, which contains less than one-fourth as many pupils as are found in the earlier grades.

The concentration of pupils in the lower grades is brought out more clearly by the table following, which contrasts primary and grammar grades.

	Number.	Per cent.
Grades 1 to 4	9,135	68.4
Grades 5 to 8	3,956	29.6
High school	267	2.0
Total	13,358	100.0

It appears that over two-thirds of the pupils are in the primary grades, while the high school comprises only 2 per cent of the whole number of pupils in the parochial schools.

The ages of the pupils as revealed in Table 1 show relatively fewer young pupils than are in the public schools. At the age of 6 years there are 411 pupils; at the age of 8, 1,461. The number of pupils increases with advancing age until it reaches 2,149 at the age of 12 years. There is a slight falling off at the age of 13, and at the age of 14 there are only 601 pupils in schools of this class.

The relation of the grades and ages, showing the number of retarded pupils in each grade, is exhibited in the table following.

Grade.	Number in grade.	Retarded pupils.		
		Age.	Number.	Per cent of all pupils.
First	2,738	8 years and over	1,446	52.8
Second	2,327	9 years and over	1,545	66.4
Third	2,079	10 years and over	1,400	67.3
Fourth	1,991	11 years and over	1,400	70.3
Fifth	1,746	12 years and over	1,120	64.1
Sixth	1,073	13 years and over	496	46.2
Seventh	762	14 years and over	260	34.1
Eighth	375	15 years and over	151	40.3
Total	13,091		7,818	59.7

This table shows that in the parochial schools 59.7 per cent of the pupils, or nearly six-tenths, are retarded. A high percentage of retardation is characteristic of all the grades, as even in the first grades more than one-half of the children are backward. It reaches its maximum in the fourth grade, where 70 per cent of the pupils are in the retarded class. From this point on the ratio of retardation diminishes, and the sixth, seventh, and eighth grades show smaller ratios than the general average, pointing clearly to the more rapid elimination of retarded than of normal pupils.

If we examine the question from the standpoint of the somewhat older scholars we find in the ages 10, 11, and 12 years the following number of ungraded or retarded children.

Age.	Number of pupils of this age.	Normal grade.	Retarded, or below normal grade.	
			Number.	Per cent.
10 years	1,894	4	1,274	67.3
11 years	1,935	5	1,327	68.5
12 years	2,149	6	1,589	73.9
Total	5,978	....	4,190	70.1

This table shows that at the age of 10 years there are more than two-thirds of the children retarded, a proportion which increases to nearly three-fourths at the age of 12. The distribution, by race, of the pupils in the parochial schools is shown in the table next presented.

General nativity and race of father of pupil.	Pupils.		General nativity and race of father of pupil.	Pupils.	
	Number.	Per cent.		Number.	Per cent.
Native-born:			Foreign-born—Continued.		
White	3,914	29.1	Irish	584	4.3
Negro and Indian	6	....	Italian, North	109	.8
			Italian, South	159	1.2
Total native born	3,920	29.1	Polish	5,456	40.6
			All others	389	2.
Foreign-born:					
Canadian, French	461	3.4	Total foreign-born	9,529	70.9
Canadian, Other	424	3.2			
French	163	1.2	Grand total	13,449	100.0
German	1,784	13.3			

Of the pupils of the parochial schools practically three-tenths are of native origin and seven-tenths of foreign origin. Among the latter by far the most numerous race is the Polish, which is represented by by 40.6 per cent of the whole number of children in these schools. The Germans, with 13.3 per cent, are also numerous, but other races are represented by comparatively small numbers.

The group "All others" has so many component elements that it is not practical to calculate the percentages for all of them. The numbers throw further light upon the racial diversity of the parochial school children. The races represented are: Arabian (1), Bohemian and Moravian (61), Bulgarian (6), Chinese (6), Danish (4), Dutch (69), English (98), Finnish (1), Flemish (2), Greek (3), Hebrew, race not specified (16), Lithuanian (3), Magyar (47), Norwegian (4), Roumanian (11), Scotch (23), Slovak (8), Slovenian (2), Spanish-American (4), Swedish (3), Syrian (14), and Welsh (2).

The general tables are so constructed that for the foreign races most numerously represented the same studies in regard to grade distribution and retardation can be made as for the schools as a whole.

PUBLIC AND PAROCHIAL SCHOOLS COMBINED.

Considered in conjunction, the figures for the public schools and the parochial schools give an admirable picture of the population of school age in the city of Detroit. The combined figures are as follows:

General nativity and race of father of pupil.	Pupils by schools.			Per cent of all pupils.
	Public schools.	Parochial schools.	Total.	
Native-born:				
White	19,409	3,914	23,323	41.5
Negro and Indian	520	6	526	.9
Total native-born	19,929	3,920	23,849	42.4
Foreign-born:				
Bohemian and Moravian	292	61	353	.6
Canadian, French	657	461	1,118	2.0
Canadian, Other	4,817	424	5,241	9.3
English	1,920	98	2,018	3.6
French	296	163	459	.8
German	7,940	1,784	9,724	17.3
Hebrew, German	416	....	416	.7
Hebrew, Russian	1,505	....	1,505	2.7
Irish	694	584	1,278	2.3
Italian, North	420	109	529	.9
Italian, South	215	159	374	.7
Polish	1,284	5,456	6,740	12.0
Scotch	864	23	887	1.6
All others	1,511	207	1,718	3.1
Total foreign-born	22,831	9,529	32,360	57.6
Grand total	42,760	13,449	56,209	100.0

It is probable that these figures give a substantially accurate picture of all the school children in Detroit, inasmuch as the number of children attending private schools is always a very small fraction of the whole number of children of the school age. In this table it appears that 41.5 per cent of the school children in Detroit have native parents and 57.6 per cent have foreign parents. Among the latter the largest individual groups are the German with 17.3 per cent, the Polish with 12 per cent, and the Canadian other than French with 9.3 per cent, of the whole school population. No other single race has as many as one-half the number of the Canadians. A comparison of the two columns shows plainly that the parochial schools contain a somewhat larger proportion of the foreign-born than do the public schools. If attention is given to individual races it will be noted that in spite of the fact that the parochial school system contains less than one-third as many pupils as the public school system, the parochial schools comprise large proportions of the French Canadians and Irish, while the Poles in the parochial schools are more than four times as numerous as in the public schools.

GENERAL TABLES.

PUBLIC SCHOOL PUPILS: GENERAL INVESTIGATION.

TABLE **1.**—*Grade and age—Number of pupils of each age in each grade, by sex.*

BOYS.

Age.	Kinder-garten.	Elementary grades.								
		1.	2.	3.	4.	5.	6.	7.	8.	Total.
years	11									
4 years	1,109	42	1							43
5 years	468	1,588	38							1,626
76 years	14	1,223	858	58	4					2,143
8 years	2	465	1,052	684	66					2,267
9 years		132	491	925	495	46	3			2,092
10 years	1	52	225	593	746	413	60	1		2,090
11 years		18	70	297	588	693	335	66	2	2,069
12 years		6	30	135	349	551	575	312	56	2,014
13 years		5	13	56	174	415	497	523	237	1,920
14 years		4	2	34	86	175	287	416	369	1,373
15 years			1	9	21	37	85	170	261	584
16 years					3	3	15	38	82	141
17 years							1	5	13	19
18 years									1	1
19 years								1		1
20 years or over					2			1		3
Total	1,605	3,535	2,781	2,791	2,534	2,333	1,858	1,533	1,021	18,386

Age.	High school.					Special and un-graded school.	Grand total.
	First year.	Second year.	Third year.	Fourth year.	Total.		
4 years							11
5 years						3	1,155
6 years						1	2,095
7 years						9	2,166
8 years						8	2,277
9 years						13	2,105
10 years						20	2,111
11 years						20	2,039
12 years	6				6	34	2,054
13 years	56	6	1		63	59	2,042
14 years	173	29	8	1	211	52	1,636
15 years	264	119	47	5	435	31	1,050
16 years	133	134	95	25	387		528
17 years	43	84	107	75	309		328
18 years	11	35	56	80	182		183
19 years	1	9	26	40	76		77
20 years or over	2	2	7	11	22		25
Total	689	418	347	237	1,691	250	21,932

TABLE 1.—*Grade and age—Number of pupils of each age in each grade, by sex*—Contd.

GIRLS.

Age.	Kinder-garten.	Elementary grades.									
		1.	2.	3.	4.	5.	6.	7.	8.	Total.
4 years	20		1							1
5 years	1,034	36	1							37
6 years	420	1,493	30	1						1,524
7 years	19	1,144	833	77						2,054
8 years	1	382	937	730	59	2				2,110
9 years		103	378	926	546	60				2,013
10 years	2	43	160	517	808	479	49	2		2,058
11 years		16	58	214	524	726	380	54	4	1,976
12 years		8	14	102	302	544	604	375	56	2,005
13 years		2	7	38	136	473	533	274		1,787
14 years		3	3	12	27	111	233	351	430	1,170
15 years			1	1	9	25	53	146	269	504
16 years						12	8	37	75	132
17 years							2	5	12	19
18 years									2	2
19 years										
20 years or over										
Total	1,496	3,230	2,423	2,618	2,411	2,283	1,802	1,503	1,122	17,392

Age.	High school.					Special and un-graded school.	Grand total.
	First year.	Second year.	Third year.	Fourth year.	Total.		
4 years						1	22
5 years							1,071
6 years						3	1,947
7 years						4	2,077
8 years						6	2,117
9 years						4	2,017
10 years						6	2,066
11 years						4	1,980
12 years	7	2			7	3	2,015
13 years	47	2			49	7	1,843
14 years	187	50	3		240	3	1,413
15 years	262	161	31	5	459	2	965
16 years	162	158	103	27	450	4	586
17 years	50	90	132	89	361	1	381
18 years	9	38	75	97	219		221
19 years	3	8	15	56	82		82
20 years or over	2	1	3	19	25		25
Total	729	508	362	293	1,892	48	20,828

TABLE 1.—*Grade and age—Number of pupils of each age in each grade, by sex*—Contd.

TOTAL.

Age.	Kindergarten.	Elementary grades.								
		1.	2.	3.	4.	5.	6.	7.	8.	Total.
4 years	31		1							1
5 years	2,143	78	2							80
6 years	888	3,081	68	1						3,150
7 years	33	2,367	1,691	135	4					4,197
8 years	3	847	1,989	1,414	125	2				4,377
9 years		235	869	1,851	1,041	106	3			4,105
10 years	3	95	385	1,110	1,554	892	109	3		4,148
11 years		34	128	511	1,112	1,419	715	120	6	4,045
12 years		14	44	237	651	1,095	1,179	687	112	4,019
13 years		7	20	94	310	739	970	1,056	511	3,707
14 years		7	5	46	113	286	520	767	799	2,543
15 years			2	10	30	62	138	316	530	1,088
16 years					3	15	23	75	157	273
17 years							3	10	25	38
18 years									3	3
19 years								1		1
20 years or over					2			1		3
Total	3,101	6,765	5,204	5,409	4,945	4,616	3,660	3,036	2,143	35,778

Age.	High school.					Special and ungraded school.	Grand total.
	First year.	Second year.	Third year.	Fourth year.	Total.		
4 years						1	33
5 years						3	2,226
6 years						4	4,042
7 years						13	4,243
8 years						14	4,394
9 years						17	4,122
10 years						26	4,177
11 years						24	4,069
12 years	13				13	37	4,069
13 years	103	8	1		112	66	3,885
14 years	360	79	11	1	451	55	3,049
15 years	526	280	78	10	894	33	2,015
16 years	295	292	198	52	837	4	1,114
17 years	93	174	239	164	670	1	709
18 years	20	73	131	177	401		404
19 years	4	17	41	96	158		159
20 years or over	4	3	10	30	47		50
Total	1,418	926	709	530	3,583	208	42,760

TABLE 2.—Race, sex, and grade—Number of pupils of each sex in each grade, by general nativity and race of father of pupil.

General nativity and race of father of pupil	Kindergarten	Elementary grades									High school					Special and ungraded schools	Grand total
		1.	2.	3.	4.	5.	6.	7.	8.	Total.	First year.	Second year.	Third year.	Fourth year.	Total.		
Native-born:																	
White—																	
Male	708	1,449	1,202	1,205	1,069	1,015	875	739	499	8,053	374	236	200	127	937	52	9,750
Female	657	1,356	1,061	1,160	1,081	1,027	858	782	586	7,911	410	279	214	170	1,073	18	9,659
Total	1,365	2,805	2,263	2,365	2,150	2,042	1,733	1,521	1,085	15,964	784	515	414	297	2,010	70	19,409
Negro—																	
Male	14	35	27	30	34	27	27	15	10	205	2	2			4	9	232
Female	12	53	31	39	45	28	24	20	9	249	6	10	6	2	24		285
Total	26	88	58	69	79	55	51	35	19	454	8	12	6	2	28	9	517
Indian—																	
Male			1							1							1
Female											2				2		2
Total			1							1	2				2		3
Total native-born—																	
Male	722	1,484	1,230	1,235	1,103	1,042	902	754	509	8,259	376	238	200	127	941	61	9,983
Female	669	1,409	1,092	1,199	1,126	1,055	882	802	595	8,160	418	289	220	172	1,099	18	9,046
Total	1,391	2,893	2,322	2,434	2,229	2,097	1,784	1,556	1,104	16,419	794	527	420	299	2,040	79	19,929
Foreign-born:																	
Bohemian and Moravian—																	
Male	9	18	31	13	18	22	14	10	6	132	3		3	2	8		149
Female	12	20	15	20	24	20	12	14	3	128	1	1		1	3		143
Total	21	38	46	33	42	42	26	24	9	260	4	1	3	3	11		292
Bulgarian—																	
Male	2				1	1			4	6							8
Female		1			1					2	2	1			3		5
Total	2	1			2	1			4	8	2	1			3		13
Canadian, French—																	
Male	19	58	40	42	36	35	30	21	11	273	5	2	5	1	13	8	313
Female	28	58	36	58	48	34	25	23	14	296	10	6	2	2	20		344
Total	47	116	76	100	84	69	55	44	25	569	15	8	7	3	33	8	657
Canadian, Other—																	
Male	149	360	294	292	317	274	231	183	116	2,067	84	55	50	35	224	13	2,453
Female	143	317	222	295	278	305	214	179	145	1,955	94	77	49	44	264	2	2,364
Total	292	677	516	587	595	579	445	362	261	4,022	178	132	99	79	488	15	4,817
Danish—																	
Male	3	7	7	14	6	2	7	4	3	50	5	1	1		7		60
Female	5	6	5	2	10	15	8	7	3	56	1	1	2		4		65
Total	8	13	12	16	16	17	15	11	6	106	6	2	3		11		125

Race and sex	1	2	3	4	5	6	7	8	9	10	11	12	13	14	15	16	17
Dutch— Male	93		4		1		3	82	5	8	6	8	16	14	14	11	7
Female	91		2				2	74	5	3	3	7	19	13	15	9	15
Total	184		6		1		5	156	10	11	9	15	35	27	29	20	22
English— Male	958	7	84	12	21	28	22	811	52	83	83	121	129	128	109	106	56
Female	962	2	105	24	12	28	43	795	60	81	114	121	102	114	93	110	60
Total	1,920	9	189	36	33	55	65	1,606	112	164	197	242	231	242	202	216	116
Flemish— Male	76	1	2			2	6	71		4	5	3	17	8	13	21	3
Female	75		1			1	4	66	2	2	3	8	17	8	11	15	7
Total	151	1	3			3	10	137	2	6	8	11	34	16	24	36	10
French— Male	152	1	11	2	4	1		132	5	11	12	16	14	22	18	34	8
Female	144		9		1	2		124	4	8	14	20	20	22	16	20	11
Total	296	1	20	2	5	3		256	9	19	26	36	34	44	34	54	19
German— Male	4,225	61	200	35	29	39	97	3,634	196	280	337	503	520	575	530	693	330
Female	3,715	12	180	19	39	50	72	3,241	186	235	336	419	477	486	482	620	282
Total	7,940	73	380	54	68	89	169	6,875	382	515	673	922	997	1,061	1,012	1,313	612
Hebrew, German— Male	235	2	43	6	10	14	13	185	14	17	21	26	24	19	32	32	5
Female	181		23	3	8	4	8	152	15	19	21	17	18	19	18	25	6
Total	416	2	66	9	18	18	21	337	29	36	42	43	42	38	50	57	11
Hebrew, Polish— Male	94		12	1	1	3	7	80	13	8	7	11	10	5	16	10	1
Female	94	1	11	3	2	4	2	82	11	1	6	15	23	10	5	11	1
Total	188	1	23	4	3	7	9	162	24	9	13	26	33	15	21	21	2
Hebrew, Roumanian— Male	40	1						37	3	6	2	4	5	6	2	9	2
Female	28							25		3	2	3	3	4	1	9	3
Total	68	1						62	3	9	4	7	8	10	3	18	5
Hebrew, Russian— Male	762	5	40	6	6	10	18	693	14	37	71	68	89	136	131	147	24
Female	743	1	31	6	3	7	15	686	17	32	37	84	93	127	133	163	25
Total	1,505	6	71	12	9	17	33	1,379	31	69	108	152	182	263	264	310	49
Hebrew, Other— Male	89	4	4	1	2			78	6	8	11	14	13	12	8	6	3
Female	68	3	1			1	1	63	3	6	4	12	10	13	7	8	1
Total	157	7	5	1	2	1	1	141	9	14	15	26	23	25	15	14	4
Irish— Male	348	3	30	3	5	8	14	290	20	27	21	51	31	53	36	51	25
Female	346	1	49	7	14	11	17	260	18	22	38	45	35	43	27	32	36
Total	694	4	79	10	19	19	31	550	38	49	59	96	66	96	63	83	61
Italian, North— Male	234		2			2	2	176	1	4	4	9	24	39	36	59	56
Female	186		1			1	1	143	2	4	1	10	17	27	35	47	42
Total	420		3			3	3	319	3	8	5	19	41	66	71	106	98
Italian, South— Male	113	7						91	3	3	5	5	6	10	22	37	15
Female	102	4						89	2	2	7	6	7	10	19	36	9
Total	215	11						180	5	5	12	11	13	20	41	73	24

TABLE 2.—*Race, sex, and grade—Number of pupils of each sex in each grade, by general nativity and race of father of pupil*—Continued.

General nativity and race of father of pupil	Kindergarten	Elementary grades									High school					Special and ungraded schools	Grand total
		1	2	3	4	5	6	7	8	Total	First year	Second year	Third year	Fourth year	Total		
Foreign-born—Continued.																	
Lithuanian—																	
Male	10	6	7	2	5	1				21			1		1		32
Female	1	3	2	1						6							7
Total	11	9	9	3	5	1				27			1		1		39
Magyar—																	
Male	3	14	7	10	1	5		2	2	41	1				1		45
Female	12	19	8	11	1	4		1		44		1			1		57
Total	15	33	15	21	2	9		3	2	85	1	1			2		102
Norwegian—																	
Male		4	2	5	6	3	7	4		31	1				1		32
Female	2	1	2	3	3	1	2	1		13	1	1			2		17
Total	2	5	4	8	9	4	9	5		44	2	1			3		49
Polish—																	
Male	100	291	117	61	55	34	21	7	2	588	8	1	1	1	11	71	770
Female	72	218	115	42	21	16	13	7		432	6			1	7	3	514
Total	172	509	232	103	76	50	34	14	2	1,020	14	1	1	2	18	74	1,284
Roumanian—																	
Male	1			4		2	1		1	8							9
Female				1			1			2							2
Total	1			5		2	2		1	10							11
Russian—																	
Male	8	2	9	5	5	3	4	1	1	30		1			1		39
Female	4	4	6	6	3	3	3		1	26		1		1	2	1	33
Total	12	6	15	11	8	6	7	1	2	56		2		1	3	1	72
Scotch—																	
Male	25	40	43	62	54	48	48	39	25	359	15	10	7	4	36	3	423
Female	31	44	36	55	46	43	49	41	32	346	28	22	9	5	64		441
Total	56	84	79	117	100	91	97	80	57	705	43	32	16	9	100	3	864
Slovak—																	
Male	2	2		1						3	2				2		7
Female	5	4	2	4	1					11							16
Total	7	6	2	5	1					14	2				2		23
Spanish-American—																	
Male	2			1						1	1				1		4
Female				2			2		2	6				1	1		7
Total	2			3			2		2	7	1			1	2		11
Swedish—																	
Male	2	14	5	6	17	7	6	8	2	65	1	2		1	4	1	72
Female	3		5	6	7	9	4	4	2	37	2				2		42
Total	5	14	10	12	24	16	10	12	4	102	3	2		1	6	1	114

Syrian—																	
Male	1	1	......	5	2	3	1	......	......	12	......	......	......	......	......	......	13
Female	1	4	1	2	......	1	......	......	......	8	......	......	......	......	......	......	9
Total	2	5	1	7	2	4	1	......	......	20	......	......	......	......	......	......	22
Welsh—																	
Male	3	2	3	4	3	4	......	1	3	20	4	1	......	1	6	......	29
Female	......	2	3	8	1	2	......	1	1	18	1	1	1	1	4	......	22
Total	3	4	6	12	4	6	......	2	4	38	5	2	1	2	10	......	51
Other races—a																	
Male	13	15	17	2	7	6	1	4	4	56	1	1	......	......	2	1	72
Female	6	15	9	8	1	8	4	2	1	48	2	2	......	1	5	......	59
Total	19	30	26	10	8	14	5	6	5	104	3	3	......	1	7	1	131
Total foreign-born—																	
Male	883	2,051	1,551	1,556	1,431	1,291	956	779	512	10,127	313	180	147	110	750	189	11,949
Female	827	1,821	1,331	1,419	1,285	1,228	920	701	527	9,232	311	219	142	121	793	30	10,882
Total	1,710	3,872	2,882	2,975	2,716	2,519	1,876	1,480	1,039	19,359	624	399	289	231	1,543	219	22,831
Grand total—																	
Male	1,605	3,535	2,781	2,791	2,534	2,333	1,858	1,533	1,021	18,386	689	418	347	237	1,691	250	21,932
Female	1,496	3,230	2,423	2,618	2,411	2,283	1,802	1,503	1,122	17,392	729	508	362	293	1,892	48	20,828
Total	3,101	6,765	5,204	5,409	4,945	4,616	3,660	3,036	2,143	35,778	1,418	926	709	530	3,583	298	42,760

a Other races include 2 Arabian, 4 Armenian, 5 Chinese, 5 Croatian, 1 Cuban 5 Finnish, 3 Greek, 3 Japanese, 8 Negro, 5 Ruthenian (Russniaks), 6 Scotch-Irish, 1 Slovenian, 2 Spanish, 3 Turkish, and 78 not specified.

TABLE 3.—*Race, sex, and age, by grade—Number of pupils of each age in each grade, by sex and by general nativity and race of father of pupil.*

KINDERGARTEN.

BOYS.

General nativity and race of father of pupil.	Number of pupils of each age.							Total.
	4.	5.	6.	7.	8.	9.	10.	
Native-born:								
White	6	514	184	4				708
Negro		9	5					14
Total native-born	6	523	189	4				722
Foreign-born:								
Bohemian and Moravian		6	3					9
Canadian, French	1	17	1					19
Canadian, Other	1	103	45					149
Danish		2	1					3
Dutch		3	4					7
English		42	12	2				56
Flemish		1	2					3
French		5	3					8
German	3	220	104	1	2			330
Hebrew, German		4	1					5
Hebrew, Polish		1						1
Hebrew, Roumanian		1	1					2
Hebrew, Russian		17	7					24
Hebrew, Other		2	1					3
Irish		20	5					25
Italian, North		34	20	2				56
Italian, South		12	3					15
Lithuanian		5	5					10
Magyar		2	1					3
Polish		52	43	4			1	100
Roumanian			1					1
Russian		4	4					8
Scotch		18	6	1				25
Slovak		2						2
Swedish		2						2
Syrian			1					1
Welsh		3						3
Other races a		8	5					13
Total foreign-born	5	586	279	10	2		1	883
Grand total	11	1,109	468	14	2		1	1,605

a "Other races" includes races having less than 10 representatives in this city and pupils whose race is not reported.

TABLE 3.—*Race, sex, and age, by grade—Number of pupils of each age in each grade, by sex and by general nativity and race of father of pupil—Continued.*

KINDERGARTEN—Continued.

GIRLS.

General nativity and race of father of pupil.	Number of pupils of each age.							Total.
	4.	5.	6.	7.	8.	9.	10.	
Native-born:								
White	11	474	170	2				657
Negro		6	6					12
Total native-born	11	480	176	2				669
Foreign-born:								
Bohemian and Moravian		7	5					12
Bulgarian		2						2
Canadian, French		23	5					28
Canadian, Other	3	101	39					143
Danish		4	1					5
Dutch		13	2					15
English	1	48	7	2			2	60
Flemish		6	1					7
French		9	2					11
German	2	193	83	4				282
Hebrew, German		4	2					6
Hebrew, Polish		1						1
Hebrew, Roumanian		2		1				3
Hebrew, Russian		15	10					25
Hebrew, Other		1						1
Irish	1	22	13					36
Italian, North		28	14					42
Italian, South		7	2					9
Lithuanian			1					1
Magyar	1	6	5					12
Norwegian		2						2
Polish	1	27	36	7	1			72
Russian		1	2	1				4
Scotch		21	9	1				31
Slovak		3	2					5
Spanish-American		2						2
Swedish		2	1					3
Syrian		1						1
Other races[a]		3	2	1				6
Total foreign-born	9	554	244	17	1		2	827
Grand total	20	1,034	420	19	1		2	1,496

[a] "Other races" includes races having less than 10 representatives in this sex and age and pupils whose race is not reported.

TABLE 3.—*Race, sex, and age, by grade—Number of pupils of each age in each grade, by sex and by general nativity and race of father of pupil*—Continued.

KINDERGARTEN—Continued.

TOTAL.

General nativity and race of father of pupil.	Number of pupils of each age.							Total.
	4.	5.	6.	7.	8.	9.	10.	
Native-born:								
White	17	988	354	6				1,365
Negro		15	11					26
Total native-born	17	1,003	365	6				1,391
Foreign-born:								
Bohemian and Moravian		13	8					21
Bulgarian		2						2
Canadian, French	1	40	6					47
Canadian, Other	4	204	84					292
Danish		6	2					8
Dutch		16	6					22
English	1	90	19	4			2	116
Flemish		7	3					10
French		14	5					19
German	5	413	187	5	2			612
Hebrew, German		8	3					11
Hebrew, Polish		2						2
Hebrew, Roumanian		3	1	1				5
Hebrew, Russian		32	17					49
Hebrew, Other		3	1					4
Irish	1	42	18					61
Italian, North		62	34	2				98
Italian, South		19	5					24
Lithuanian		5	6					11
Magyar	1	8	6					15
Norwegian		2						2
Polish	1	79	79	11	1		1	172
Roumanian			1					1
Russian		5	6	1				12
Scotch		39	15	2				56
Slovak		5	2					7
Spanish-American		2						2
Swedish		4	1					5
Syrian		1	1					2
Welsh		3						3
Other races *a*		11	7	1				19
Total foreign-born	14	1,140	523	27	3		3	1,710
Grand total	31	2,143	888	33	3		3	3,101

a "Other races" includes races having less than 10 representatives in this sex and age and pupils whose race is not reported.

TABLE 3.—*Race, sex, and age, by grade—Number of pupils of each age in each grade, by sex and by general nativity and race of father of pupil—Continued.*

FIRST GRADE.

BOYS.

General nativity and race of father of pupil.	Number of pupils of each age.										Total.
	5.	6.	7.	8.	9.	10.	11.	12.	13.	14.	
Native-born:											
White	24	729	501	146	33	11	3	1	1	....	1,449
Negro	....	10	12	5	3	2	3	....	....	....	35
Total native-born	24	739	513	151	36	13	6	1	1	....	1,484
Foreign-born:											
Bohemian and Moravian	......	8	4	4	1	1	....	....	....	....	18
Canadian, French	......	24	18	12	3	1	....	....	....	....	58
Canadian, Other	7	172	124	46	6	5	....	....	....	....	360
Danish	......	4	2	1	....	....	....	....	....	....	7
Dutch	......	6	3	1	....	....	....	....	....	1	11
English	......	46	39	14	4	1	2	....	....	....	106
Flemish	1	6	7	1	1	4	....	....	1	....	21
French	......	15	10	7	2	....	....	....	....	....	34
German	4	275	263	102	33	13	2	....	1	....	693
Hebrew, German	......	15	11	4	....	....	....	1	....	1	32
Hebrew, Polish	......	9	......	1	....	....	....	....	....	....	10
Hebrew, Roumanian	......	6	1	2	....	....	....	....	....	....	9
Hebrew, Russian	......	78	46	17	2	1	....	1	1	1	147
Hebrew, Other	1	2	3	....	....	....	....	....	....	....	6
Irish	1	23	23	4	....	....	....	....	....	....	51
Italian, North	1	26	17	5	6	....	2	....	1	1	59
Italian, South	......	10	11	9	3	2	1	1	....	....	37
Lithuanian	......	1	3	1	....	....	....	1	....	....	6
Magyar	......	3	7	1	2	1	....	....	....	....	14
Norwegian	......	2	2	....	....	....	....	....	....	....	4
Polish	2	88	89	68	31	9	3	1	....	....	291
Roumanian	......	1	....	....	....	....	....	....	....	....	1
Russian	......	1	1	....	....	....	....	....	....	....	2
Scotch	1	17	17	4	....	1	....	....	....	....	40
Slovak	......	......	1	....	....	....	1	....	....	....	2
Swedish	......	8	3	2	1	....	....	....	....	....	14
Syrian	......	......	......	....	....	....	1	....	....	....	1
Welsh	......	1	......	1	....	....	....	....	....	....	2
Other races *a*	......	2	5	7	1	....	....	....	....	....	15
Total foreign-born	18	840	710	314	96	39	12	5	4	4	2,051
Grand total	42	1,588	1,223	465	132	52	18	6	5	4	3,535

a "Other races" includes races having less than 10 representatives in this city.and pupils whose race is not reported.

TABLE 3.—*Race, sex, and age, by grade—Number of pupils of each age in each grade, by sex and by general nativity and race of father of pupil*—Continued.

FIRST GRADE—Continued.

GIRLS.

General nativity and race of father of pupil.	\multicolumn{10}{c}{Number of pupils of each age.}										Total.
	5.	6.	7.	8.	9.	10.	11.	12.	13.	14.	
Native-born:											
White	17	707	492	108	25	7	....	....	....	....	1,356
Negro	....	18	18	12	2	1	2	....	....	....	53
Total native-born	17	725	510	120	27	8	2	....	....	....	1,409
Foreign-born:											
Bohemian and Moravian	....	12	8	....	....	....	....	....	....	....	20
Bulgarian	....	....	1	....	....	....	....	....	....	....	1
Canadian, French	1	28	16	7	4	2	....	....	....	....	58
Canadian, Other	1	155	115	37	7	1	1	....	....	....	317
Danish	....	3	3	....	....	....	....	....	....	....	6
Dutch	1	2	2	2	....	1	....	1	....	....	9
English	2	58	37	12	....	1	....	....	....	....	110
Flemish	....	3	9	1	1	1	....	....	....	....	15
French	....	9	8	....	2	....	....	....	1	....	20
German	5	258	236	91	21	6	2	....	....	1	620
Hebrew, German	....	11	8	3	....	1	2	....	....	....	25
Hebrew, Polish	....	7	3	....	1	....	....	....	....	....	11
Hebrew, Roumanian	....	5	2	1	....	1	....	....	....	....	9
Hebrew, Russian	3	72	54	19	5	3	1	4	1	1	163
Hebrew, Other	....	5	3	....	....	....	....	....	....	....	8
Irish	1	16	12	2	....	1	....	....	....	....	32
Italian, North	....	17	14	8	2	4	....	1	....	1	47
Italian, South	....	10	10	6	2	3	3	2	....	....	36
Lithuanian	....	2	1	....	....	....	....	....	....	....	3
Magyar	....	5	5	3	2	4	....	....	....	....	19
Norwegian	....	....	1	....	....	....	....	....	....	....	1
Polish	2	56	71	55	27	3	4	....	....	....	218
Russian	2	....	....	....	1	....	1	....	....	....	4
Scotch	....	25	10	7	1	1	....	....	....	....	44
Slovak	....	....	2	1	....	1	....	....	....	....	4
Syrian	....	2	1	1	....	....	....	....	....	....	4
Welsh	....	1	....	1	....	....	....	....	....	....	2
Other races a	1	6	2	5	....	1	....	....	....	....	15
Total foreign-born	19	768	634	262	76	35	14	8	2	3	1,821
Grand total	36	1,493	1,144	382	103	43	16	8	2	3	3,230

a "Other races" includes races having less than 10 representatives in this city and pupils whose race is not reported.

TABLE 3.—*Race, sex, and age, by grade—Number of pupils of each age in each grade, by sex and by general nativity and race of father of pupil*—Continued.

FIRST GRADE—Continued.

TOTAL.

General nativity and race of father of pupil.	Number of pupils of each age.										Total.
	5.	6.	7.	8.	9.	10.	11.	12.	13.	14.	
Native-born:											
White	41	1,436	993	254	58	18	3	1	1	....	2,805
Negro	....	28	30	17	5	3	5	....	....	....	88
Total native-born	41	1,464	1,023	271	63	21	8	1	1	....	2,893
Foreign-born:											
Bohemian and Moravian	....	20	12	4	1	1	....	....	....	....	38
Bulgarian	....	....	1	....	....	....	....	....	....	....	1
Canadian, French	1	52	34	19	7	3	....	....	....	....	116
Canadian, Other	8	327	239	83	13	6	1	....	....	....	677
Danish	....	7	5	1	....	....	....	....	....	....	13
Dutch	1	8	5	3	....	1	....	1	....	1	20
English	2	104	76	26	4	2	2	....	....	....	216
Flemish	1	9	16	2	2	5	....	....	1	....	36
French	....	24	18	7	4	....	....	....	1	....	54
German	9	533	499	193	54	19	4	....	1	1	1,313
Hebrew, German	....	26	19	7	....	1	2	1	....	1	57
Hebrew, Polish	....	16	3	1	1	....	....	....	....	....	21
Hebrew, Roumanian	....	11	3	3	....	1	....	....	....	....	18
Hebrew, Russian	3	150	100	36	7	4	1	5	2	2	310
Hebrew, Other	1	7	6	....	....	....	....	....	....	....	14
Irish	2	39	35	6	....	1	....	....	....	....	83
Italian, North	1	43	31	13	8	4	2	1	1	2	106
Italian, South	....	20	21	15	5	5	4	3	....	....	73
Lithuanian	....	3	4	1	....	....	....	1	....	....	9
Magyar	....	8	12	4	4	5	....	....	....	....	33
Norwegian	....	2	3	....	....	....	....	....	....	....	5
Polish	4	144	160	123	58	12	7	1	....	....	509
Roumanian	....	1	....	....	....	....	....	....	....	....	1
Russian	2	1	1	....	1	....	1	....	....	....	6
Scotch	1	42	27	11	1	2	....	....	....	....	84
Slovak	....	....	3	1	....	1	1	....	....	....	6
Swedish	....	8	3	2	1	....	....	....	....	....	14
Syrian	....	2	1	1	....	....	1	....	....	....	5
Welsh	....	2	....	2	....	....	....	....	....	....	4
Other races a	1	8	7	12	1	1	....	....	....	....	30
Total foreign-born	37	1,617	1,344	576	172	74	26	13	6	7	3,872
Grand total	78	3,081	2,367	847	235	95	34	14	7	7	6,765

a "Other races" includes races having less than 10 representatives in this city and pupils whose race is not reported.

TABLE **3.**—*Race, sex, and age, by grade—Number of pupils of each age in each grade, by sex and by general nativity and race of father of pupil*—Continued.

SECOND GRADE.

BOYS.

General nativity and race of father of pupil.	Number of pupils of each age.												Total.
	4.	5.	6.	7.	8.	9.	10.	11.	12.	13.	14.	15.	
Native-born:													
White	...	...	15	413	469	206	77	17	4	1	...	...	1,202
Negro				3	10	7	5	2			...	...	27
Indian								1			...	...	1
Total native-born	...	...	15	416	479	213	82	20	4	1	...	...	1,230
Foreign-born:													
Bohemian and Moravian				9	14	6	1		1				31
Canadian, French				9	16	7	4	2	2				40
Canadian, Other			7	97	117	47	20	4	2				294
Danish				3	4								7
Dutch				5	5	2	1	1					14
English			1	29	48	18	9	2	2				109
Flemish				2	5	4		2					13
French			1	3	7	4	2	1					18
German			7	161	193	93	53	14	5	4			530
Hebrew, German			2	16	11		3						32
Hebrew, Polish			1	10	3	1	1						16
Hebrew, Roumanian					1	1							2
Hebrew, Russian			2	38	44	22	11	4	7	1	2		131
Hebrew, Other				4	3	1							8
Irish		1	1	9	11	10	3	1					36
Italian, North				6	11	8	5	3	1	2			36
Italian, South				3	9	2	3	2	2			1	22
Lithuanian				1		2	1	2		1			7
Magyar				3	1	3							7
Norwegian						1				1			2
Polish			1	15	36	29	19	12	4	1			117
Russian					1	6	1			1			9
Scotch				10	23	8	2						43
Spanish-American				2									2
Swedish					5								5
Welsh					1	1	1						3
Other races *a*				7	4	2	3			1			17
Total foreign-born	...	1	23	442	573	278	143	50	26	12	2	1	1,551
Grand total	...	1	38	858	1,052	491	225	70	30	13	2	1	2,781

a "Other races" includes races having less than 10 representatives in this city and pupils whose race is not reported.

TABLE 3.—*Race, sex, and age, by grade—Number of pupils of each age in each grade, by sex and by general nativity and race of father of pupil*—Continued.

SECOND GRADE—Continued.

GIRLS.

General nativity and race of father of pupil.	Number of pupils of each age.												Total.
	4.	5.	6.	7.	8.	9.	10.	11.	12.	13.	14.	15.	
Native-born:													
White			20	422	398	158	46	11	3	1	1	1	1,061
Negro			1	8	12	4	3	3					31
Total native-born			21	430	410	162	49	14	3	1	1	1	1,092
Foreign-born:													
Bohemian and Moravian				4	5	4	1		1				15
Canadian, French				12	13	6	4	1					36
Canadian, Other	1		1	83	94	24	13	6					222
Danish				1	2	1	1						5
Dutch				4	8	2	1						15
English			1	29	45	12	6						93
Flemish				4	4	1		1	1				11
French				5	7	1		1	2				16
German			3	158	187	81	38	10	3	2			482
Hebrew, German				11	6	1							18
Hebrew, Polish				2	2	1							5
Hebrew, Roumanian					1								1
Hebrew, Russian			3	33	46	23	14	9	1	2	2		133
Hebrew, Other				2	4	1							7
Irish				9	12	5	1						27
Italian, North			1	8	17	3	2	1	1	2			35
Italian, South				4	4	5	4	1	1				19
Lithuanian						1		1					2
Magyar				1		3	2	2					8
Norwegian				1	1								2
Polish		1		15	45	26	17	10	1				115
Russian				1	2	1	1	1					6
Scotch				12	14	8	2						36
Slovak							2						2
Spanish-American					1	1							2
Swedish				2	2		1						5
Syrian					1								1
Welsh				1	2								3
Other races *a*				1	2	5	1						9
Total foreign-born	1	1	9	403	527	216	111	44	11	6	2		1,331
Grand total	1	1	30	833	937	378	160	58	14	7	3	1	2,423

a "Other races" includes races having less than 10 representatives in this city and pupils whose race is not reported.

66083°—VOL 31—12——4

TABLE 3.—*Race, sex, and age, by grade—Number of pupils of each age in each grade, by sex and by general nativity and race of father of pupil*—Continued.

SECOND GRADE—Continued.

TOTAL.

General nativity and race of father of pupil.	Number of pupils of each age.												Total.
	4.	5.	6.	7.	8.	9.	10.	11.	12.	13.	14.	15.	
Native-born:													
White			35	835	867	364	123	28	7	2	1	1	2,263
Negro			1	11	22	11	8	5					58
Indian								1					1
Total native-born			36	846	889	375	131	34	7	2	1	1	2,322
Foreign-born:													
Bohemian and Moravian				13	19	10	2		2				46
Canadian, French				21	29	13	8	3	2				76
Canadian, Other	1		8	180	211	71	33	10	2				516
Danish				4	6	1	1						12
Dutch				9	13	4	2	1					29
English			2	58	93	30	15	2	2				202
Flemish				6	9	5		3	1				24
French			1	8	14	5	2	2	2				34
German			10	319	380	174	91	24	8	6			1,012
Hebrew, German			2	27	17	1	3						50
Hebrew, Polish			1	12	5	2	1						21
Hebrew, Roumanian					2	1							3
Hebrew, Russian			5	71	90	45	25	13	8	3	4		264
Hebrew, Other				6	7	2							15
Irish		1	1	18	23	15	4	1					63
Italian, North			1	14	28	11	7	4	2	4			71
Italian, South				7	13	7	7	3	3			1	41
Lithuanian				1		3	1	3		1			9
Magyar				4	1	6	2	2					15
Norwegian				1	1	1							4
Polish		1	1	30	81	55	36	22	5	1			232
Russian				1	3	7	2	1		1			15
Scotch				22	37	16	4						79
Slovak							2						2
Spanish-American				2	1	1							4
Swedish				2	7		1						10
Syrian					1								1
Welsh				1	3	1	1						6
Other races a				8	6	7	4			1			26
Total foreign-born	1	2	32	845	1,100	494	254	94	37	18	4	1	2,882
Grand total	1	2	68	1,691	1,989	869	385	128	44	20	5	2	5,204

a "Other races" includes races having less than 10 representatives in this city and pupils whose race is not reported.

TABLE 3.—*Race, sex, and age, by grade—Number of pupils of each age in each grade, by sex and by general nativity and race of father of pupil*—Continued.

THIRD GRADE.

BOYS.

General nativity and race of father of pupil.	Number of pupils of each age.										Total.
	6.	7.	8.	9.	10.	11.	12.	13.	14.	15.	
Native-born:											
White		27	332	452	230	104	42	12	4	2	1,205
Negro		1	2	3	11	3	7	3			30
Total native-born		28	334	455	241	107	49	15	4	2	1,235
Foreign-born:											
Bohemian and Moravian			2	4	1	3	1		2		13
Canadian, French			7	13	8	6	3	3	2		42
Canadian, Other		5	64	110	66	28	13	5	1		292
Danish			4	4	4		2				14
Dutch		1	4	3	6						14
English		2	33	42	23	19	5	3	1		128
Flemish			1	3	2	1	1				8
French			5	3	7	3	2	2			22
German		14	135	180	135	61	29	11	7	3	575
Hebrew, German		1	7	7	3	1					19
Hebrew, Polish			1	2	1		1				5
Hebrew, Roumanian		2	1	2	1						6
Hebrew, Russian		3	30	31	23	26	10	9	4		136
Hebrew, Other			6	1	4	1					12
Irish			11	16	17	8		1			53
Italian, North			3	11	9	9	4	1		2	39
Italian, South			1	2	1	4	1		1		10
Lithuanian			1			1					2
Magyar			2	3	1	3			1		10
Norwegian			1	2	1		1				5
Polish		1	9	8	13	8	8	4	9	1	61
Roumanian			1			2		1			4
Russian			1	2	1					1	5
Scotch		1	19	16	17	3	4	1	1		62
Slovak					1						1
Spanish-American				1							1
Swedish			1	1	3				1		6
Syrian				1		3	1				5
Welsh				1	3						4
Other races a				1	1						2
Total foreign-born		30	350	470	352	190	86	41	30	7	1,556
Grand total		58	684	925	593	297	135	56	34	9	2,791

a "Other races" includes races having less than 10 representatives in this city and pupils whose race is not reported.

TABLE 3.—*Race, sex, and age, by grade—Number of pupils of each age in each grade, by sex and by general nativity and race of father of pupil*—Continued.

THIRD GRADE—Continued.

GIRLS.

General nativity and race of father of pupil.	Number of pupils of each age.										Total.
	6.	7.	8.	9.	10.	11.	12.	13.	14.	15.	
Native-born:											
White	1	40	383	408	210	85	21	9	3	....	1,160
Negro	....	....	2	14	11	5	5	2	....	....	39
Total native-born	1	40	385	422	221	90	26	11	3	....	1,199
Foreign-born:											
Bohemian and Moravian	....	....	5	8	5	2	....	....	....	....	20
Canadian, French	....	....	10	20	19	3	5	1	....	....	58
Canadian, Other	....	11	88	105	49	23	8	8	3	....	295
Danish	....	....	....	....	2	....	....	....	....	....	2
Dutch	....	....	5	3	2	1	1	....	1	....	13
English	....	1	36	39	24	8	5	1	....	....	114
Flemish	....	....	1	4	1	2	....	....	....	....	8
French	....	....	1	10	5	3	3	....	....	....	22
German	....	7	106	197	106	39	24	7	....	....	486
Hebrew, German	....	4	6	5	1	3	....	....	....	....	19
Hebrew, Polish	....	....	2	3	3	1	1	....	....	....	10
Hebrew, Roumanian	....	1	....	2	1	....	....	....	....	....	4
Hebrew, Russian	....	4	24	28	35	10	17	6	2	1	127
Hebrew, Other	....	3	7	3	....	....	....	....	....	....	13
Irish	....	2	13	14	6	7	1	....	....	....	43
Italian, North	....	1	6.	7	3	3	4	2	1	....	27
Italian, South	....	1	....	5	1	3	....	....	....	....	10
Lithuanian	....	....	....	....	1	....	....	....	....	....	1
Magyar	....	....	1	3	3	2	2	....	....	....	11
Norwegian	....	....	1	1	....	1	....	....	....	....	3
Polish	....	....	8	15	10	4	3	1	1	....	42
Roumanian	....	....	1	....	....	....	....	....	....	....	1
Russian	....	....	2	....	1	2	1	....	....	....	6
Scotch	....	2	16	19	12	5	1	....	....	....	55
Slovak	....	....	....	1	2	....	....	1	....	....	4
Spanish-American	....	....	....	1	....	....	....	....	....	....	1
Swedish	....	....	3	2	1	....	....	....	....	....	6
Syrian	....	....	....	2	....	....	....	....	....	....	2
Welsh	....	....	1	4	1	2	....	....	....	....	8
Other races a	....	....	2	3	2	....	....	....	1	....	8
Total foreign-born	....	37	345	504	296	124	76	27	9	1	1,419
Grand total	1	77	730	926	517	214	102	38	12	1	2,618

a "Other races" includes races having less than 10 representatives in this city and pupils whose race is not reported.

TABLE 3.—*Race, sex, and age, by grade—Number of pupils of each age in each grade, by sex and by general nativity and race of father of pupil*—Continued.

FIRST GRADE—Continued.

TOTAL.

General nativity and race of father of pupil.	Number of pupils of each age.										Total.
	6.	7.	8.	9.	10.	11.	12.	13.	14.	15.	
Native-born:											
White	1	67	715	860	440	189	63	21	7	2	2,365
Negro		1	4	17	22	8	12	5			69
Total native-born	1	68	719	877	462	197	75	26	7	2	2,434
Foreign-born:											
Bohemian and Moravian			7	12	6	5	1		2		33
Canadian, French			17	33	27	9	8	4	2		100
Canadian, Other		16	152	215	115	51	21	13	4		587
Danish			4	4	6		2				16
Dutch		1	9	6	8	1	1		1		27
English		3	69	81	47	27	10	4	1		242
Flemish			2	7	3	3	1				16
French			6	13	12	6	5	2			44
German		21	241	377	241	100	53	18	7	3	1,061
Hebrew, German		5	13	12	4	4					38
Hebrew, Polish			3	5	4	1	2				15
Hebrew, Roumanian		3	1	4	2						10
Hebrew, Russian		7	54	59	58	36	27	15	6	1	263
Hebrew, Other		3	13	4	4	1					25
Irish		2	24	30	23	15	1	1			96
Italian, North		1	9	18	12	12	8	3	1	2	66
Italian, South		1	1	7	2	7	1		1		20
Lithuanian			1		1	1					3
Magyar			3	6	4	5	2		1		21
Norwegian			2	3	1	1	1				8
Polish		1	17	23	23	12	11	5	10	1	103
Roumanian			2			2		1			5
Russian			3	2	2	2	1			1	11
Scotch		3	35	35	29	8	5	1	1		117
Slovak				1	3			1			5
Spanish-American				2							2
Swedish			4	3	4				1		12
Syrian				3		3	1				7
Welsh			1	5	4	2					12
Other races a			2	4	3				1		10
Total foreign-born		67	695	974	648	314	162	68	39	8	2,975
Grand total	1	135	1,414	1,851	1,110	511	237	94	46	10	5,409

a "Other races" includes races having less than 10 representatives in this city and pupils whose race is not reported.

TABLE **3.**—*Race, sex, and age, by grade—Number of pupils of each age in each grade, by sex and by general nativity and race of father of pupil*—Continued.

FOURTH GRADE.

BOYS.

General nativity and race of father of pupil.	Number of pupils of each age.														Total.
	7.	8.	9.	10.	11.	12.	13.	14.	15.	16.	17.	18.	19.	20.	
Native-born:															
White		35	247	331	235	133	56	25	5	2					1,069
Negro	1		2	12	9	4	3	2	1						34
Total native-born	1	35	249	343	244	137	59	27	6	2					1,103
Foreign-born:															
Bohemian and Moravian		1	2	5	5	4	1								18
Bulgarian				1											1
Canadian, French			5	9	7	5	8		2						36
Canadian, Other	1	9	52	87	97	40	20	10					1		317
Danish			2		3	1									6
Dutch		3	5	3	2	3									16
English	1	7	15	40	28	18	13	6	1						129
Flemish			5	4	2	3	1	1	1						17
French			4	3	4	2	1								14
German		4	89	154	121	92	38	20	2						520
Hebrew, German		1	6	9	4	2	1		1						24
Hebrew, Polish			1	3	2	3	1								10
Hebrew, Roumanian			1	3		1									5
Hebrew, Russian		1	26	20	17	12	5	4	4						89
Hebrew, Other		2	2	6		2	1								13
Irish		1	7	13	5	2	2	1							31
Italian, North		2	3	3	7	3	7		1	1					24
Italian, South			1		2	2	1								6
Lithuanian				1	1			3							5
Magyar						1									1
Norwegian				3	2			1							6
Polish			6	9	8	6	12	11	3						55
Russian			1	2	2										5
Scotch	1	1	8	18	15	7	2	1					1		54
Swedish		1	4	4	7	1									17
Syrian					1			1							2
Welsh				2			1								3
Other races a			3		2	2									7
Total foreign-born	3	31	246	403	344	212	115	59	15	1			2		1,431
Grand total	4	66	495	746	588	349	174	86	21	3			2		2,534

a "Other races" includes races having less than 10 representatives in this city and pupils whose race is not reported.

TABLE 3.—*Race, sex, and age, by grade—Number of pupils of each age in each grade, by sex and by general nativity and race of father of pupil*—Continued.

FOURTH GRADE—Continued.

GIRLS.

General nativity and race of father of pupil.	Number of pupils of each age.														Total.
	7.	8.	9.	10.	11.	12.	13.	14.	15.	16.	17.	18.	19.	20.	
Native-born:															
White		32	276	386	215	110	47	11	4						1,081
Negro			3	19	11	9	2	1							45
Total native-born		32	279	405	226	119	49	12	4						1,126
Foreign-born:															
Bohemian and Moravian			1	8	9	4	2								24
Bulgarian				1											1
Canadian, French		2	7	14	8	12	3	1	1						48
Canadian, Other		6	58	95	73	33	12	1							278
Danish			3	3	3		1								10
Dutch			4	8	3	4									19
English		4	25	28	19	15	8	3							102
Flemish			4	4	4	3	1	1							17
French			4	6	3	6			1						20
German		4	100	164	116	56	34	3							477
Hebrew, German		2	4	6	2	4									18
Hebrew, Polish		1	4	7	2	3	5	1							23
Hebrew, Roumanian					1	2									3
Hebrew, Russian		3	18	17	25	16	10	4							93
Hebrew, Other		1	5	2	1	1									10
Irish			5	15	7	5	3								35
Italian, North			5	2	3	6	1								17
Italian, South				1		3	2		1						7
Magyar						1									1
Norwegian			2		1										3
Polish			2	5	6	4	4								21
Russian			1		2										3
Scotch		3	12	16	8	3	1	1	2						46
Swedish		1	3	1	1	1									7
Welsh						1									1
Other races a					1										1
Total foreign-born		27	267	403	298	183	87	15	5						1,285
Grand total		59	546	808	524	302	136	27	9						2,411

a "Other races" includes races having less than 10 representatives in this city and pupils whose race is not reported.

TABLE 3.—*Race, sex, and age, by grade—Number of pupils of each age in each grade, by sex and by general nativity and race of father of pupil—Continued.*

FOURTH GRADE—Continued.

TOTAL.

General nativity and race of father of pupil.	Number of pupils of each age.														Total.
	7.	8.	9.	10.	11.	12.	13.	14.	15.	16.	17.	18.	19.	20.	
Native-born:															
White	..	67	523	717	450	243	103	36	9	2					2,150
Negro	1	....	5	31	20	13	5	3	1						79
Total native-born	1	67	528	748	470	256	108	39	10	2					2,229
Foreign-born:															
Bohemian and Moravian	...	1	3	13	14	8	3								42
Bulgarian			2												2
Canadian, French	...	2	12	23	15	17	11	1	3						84
Canadian, Other	1	15	110	182	170	73	32	11					1		595
Danish	...	....	5	3	6	1	1								16
Dutch	...	3	9	11	5	7									35
English	1	11	40	68	47	33	21	9	1						231
Flemish	...	....	9	8	6	6	2	2	1						34
French	...	....	8	9	7	8	1		1						34
German	...	8	189	318	237	148	72	23	2						997
Hebrew, German	...	3	10	15	6	6	1		1						42
Hebrew, Polish	...	1	5	10	4	6	6	1							33
Hebrew, Roumanian	...	....	1	3	1	3									8
Hebrew, Russian	...	4	44	37	42	28	15	8	4						182
Hebrew, Other	...	3	7	8	1	3	1								23
Irish	...	1	12	28	12	7	5	1							66
Italian, North	...	....	7	5	10	9	8		1	1					41
Italian, South	...	....	....	2	2	5	3		1						13
Lithuanian	...	....	....	1	1			3							5
Magyar	...	....	....	....		2									2
Norwegian	...	....	2	3	3		1								9
Polish	...	....	8	14	14	10	16	11	3						76
Russian	...	....	2	2	4										8
Scotch	1	4	20	34	23	10	3	2	2				1		100
Swedish	...	2	7	5	8	2									24
Syrian	...	....	....	....	1		1								2
Welsh	...	....	....	2		1	1								4
Other races a	...	....	3		3	2									8
Total foreign-born	3	58	513	806	642	395	202	74	20	1				2	2,716
Grand total	4	125	1,041	1,554	1,112	651	310	113	30	3				2	4,945

a "Other races" includes races having less than 10 representatives in this city and pupils whose race is not reported.

TABLE 3.—*Race, sex, and age, by grade—Number of pupils of each age in each grade, by sex and by general nativity and race of father of pupil*—Continued.

FIFTH GRADE.

BOYS.

General nativity and race of father of pupil.	Number of pupils of each age.									Total.
	8.	9.	10.	11.	12.	13.	14.	15.	16.	
Native-born:										
White	......	22	204	318	241	157	57	15	1	1,015
Negro	......	1	......	4	5	11	4	2	......	27
Total native-born	......	23	204	322	246	168	61	17	1	1,042
Foreign-born:										
Bohemian and Moravian	......		5	5	3	7	2	......	......	22
Bulgarian	......					1	1	1	......	3
Canadian, French	......	1	1	10	9	9	3	1	1	35
Canadian, Other	......	2	56	80	84	31	19	2		274
Danish	......			2						2
Dutch	......		1	1	3	3				8
English	......		21	36	31	22	10	1	......	121
French	......	1	3	2	4	3	2	1	......	16
Flemish	......			1	1	1				3
German	......	5	72	160	103	107	45	10	1	503
Hebrew, German	......	1	4	8	6	6	1			26
Hebrew, Polish	......	2	1	4	......	3	1			11
Hebrew, Roumanian	......		2	1		1				4
Hebrew, Russian	......	3	16	17	9	11	11	1	......	68
Hebrew, Other	......	2	3	7	2					14
Irish	......	1	6	11	16	12	4	1		51
Italian, North	......	1	2	1	3	1	1			9
Italian, South	......		......	1	3	1				5
Lithuanian	......			1						1
Magyar	......	1	1		2	1				5
Norwegian	......		1	......	1	1				3
Polish	......	1	4	4	7	12	5	1		34
Roumanian	......		1			1				2
Russian	......				1		2			3
Scotch	......	1	8	10	14	10	4	1	......	48
Swedish	......		1	6	......					7
Syrian	......		......	1		1				3
Welsh	......	1			1	......	2			4
Other races *a*	......			2	1	2	1			6
Total foreign-born	......	23	209	371	305	247	114	20	2	1,291
Grand total	......	46	413	693	551	415	175	37	3	2,333

a "Other races" includes races having less than 10 representatives in this city and pupils whose race is not reported.

TABLE 3.—*Race, sex, and age, by grade—Number of pupils of each age in each grade, by sex and by general nativity and race of father of pupil*—Continued.

FIFTH GRADE—Continued.

GIRLS.

General nativity and race of father of pupil.	Number of pupils of each age.									Total.
	8.	9.	10.	11.	12.	13.	14.	15.	16.	
Native-born:										
White		30	250	344	235	117	40	10	1	1,027
Negro		1	4	4	8	6	4		1	28
Total native-born		31	254	348	243	123	44	10	2	1,055
Foreign-born:										
Bohemian and Moravian			4	7	9					20
Canadian, French		1	6	8	5	8	6			34
Canadian, Other		2	44	92	66	71	19	5	6	305
Danish			5	5	2	1	1	1		15
Dutch		1	1	2	1		1		1	7
English		4	27	35	25	17	9	3	1	121
French		1	2	8	9					20
Flemish				2	4	2				8
German	1	13	80	135	115	59	15	1		419
Hebrew, German		3	4	4	3	3				17
Hebrew, Polish	1		4	6	3			1		15
Hebrew, Roumanian		1		1		1				3
Hebrew, Russian		1	17	24	20	14	4	2	2	84
Hebrew, Other		1	4		3	3	1			12
Irish			6	19	12	5	2	1		45
Italian, North		1	3	1	2	2	1			10
Italian, South				2	3		1			6
Magyar			2		2					4
Norwegian				1						1
Polish			2	5	2	4	3			16
Russian			1		1	1	1			3
Scotch			11	13	9	7	3			43
Swedish			2	2	1	3		1		9
Syrian					1					1
Welsh					1	1				2
Other races *a*				6	2					8
Total foreign-born	2	29	225	378	301	201	67	15	10	1,228
Grand total	2	60	479	726	544	324	111	25	12	2,283

a "Other races" includes races having less than 10 representatives in this city and pupils whose race is not reported.

TABLE 3.—*Race, sex, and age, by grade—Number of pupils of each age in each grade, by sex and by general nativity and race of father of pupil—Continued.*

FIFTH GRADE—Continued.

TOTAL.

General nativity and race of father of pupil.	Number of pupils of each age.									Total.
	8.	9.	10.	11.	12.	13.	14.	15.	16.	
Native-born:										
White		52	454	662	476	274	97	25	2	2,042
Negro		2	4	8	13	17	8	2	1	55
Total native-born		54	458	670	489	291	105	27	3	2,097
Foreign-born:										
Bohemian and Moravian			9	12	12	7	2			42
Bulgarian						1	1	1		3
Canadian, French		2	7	18	14	17	9	1	1	69
Canadian, Other		4	100	172	150	102	38	7	6	579
Danish			5	7	2	1	1	1		17
Dutch		1	2	3	4	3	1		1	15
English		4	48	71	56	39	19	4	1	242
French		2	5	10	13	3	2	1		36
Flemish				3	5	3				11
German	1	18	152	295	218	166	60	11	1	922
Hebrew, German		4	8	12	9	9	1			43
Hebrew, Polish	1	2	5	10	3	3	1	1		26
Hebrew, Roumanian		1	2	2		2				7
Hebrew, Russian		4	33	41	29	25	15	3	2	152
Hebrew, Other		3	7	7	5	3	1			26
Irish		1	12	30	28	17	6	2		96
Italian, North		2	5	2	5	3	2			19
Italian, South				3	6	1	1			11
Lithuanian				1						1
Magyar		1	3		4	1				9
Norwegian			1	1	1	1				4
Polish		1	6	9	9	16	8	1		50
Roumanian			1			1				2
Russian			1		2		3			6
Scotch		1	19	23	23	17	7	1		91
Swedish			3	8	1	3		1		16
Syrian					1	2	1			4
Welsh		1			2	1	2			6
Other races [a]				8	3	2	1			14
Total foreign-born	2	52	434	749	606	448	181	35	12	2,519
Grand total	2	106	892	1,419	1,095	739	286	62	15	4,616

[a] "Other races" includes races having less than 10 representatives in this city and pupils whose race is not reported.

TABLE 3.—*Race, sex, and age, by grade—Number of pupils of each age in each grade, by sex and by general nativity and race of father of pupil*—Continued.

SIXTH GRADE.

BOYS.

General nativity and race of father of pupil.	Number of pupils of each age.									Total.
	9.	10.	11.	12.	13.	14.	15.	16.	17.	
Native-born:										
White	3	32	171	261	225	134	43	6		875
Negro		1	3	7	10	4	1	1		27
Total native-born	3	33	174	268	235	138	44	7		902
Foreign-born:										
Bohemian and Moravian				5	4	5				14
Canadian, French			3	6	9	4	7	1		30
Canadian, Other		11	37	69	66	31	14	3		231
Danish			1	2	3		1			7
Dutch			1	3	1	1				6
English		2	14	29	21	14	3			83
Flemish			1	2	1					5
French			1	2	7	1	1			12
German		9	52	121	87	56	10	2		337
Hebrew, German		1	10	4	5	1				21
Hebrew, Polish		1	1	3	2					7
Hebrew, Roumanian			1	1						2
Hebrew, Russian		2	8	23	27	11				71
Hebrew, Other			5	2	2	2				11
Irish			6	4	5	4	1	1		21
Italian, North				2		2				4
Italian, South				3	1	1				5
Norwegian			3	1	2	1			1	7
Polish			2	1	6	9	2	1		21
Roumanian										1
Russian				2	1	1				4
Scotch		1			1	1				4
Swedish		1	13	17	10	6	1			48
Syrian				4	1					6
Other races *a*				1						1
Total foreign-born		27	161	307	262	149	41	8	1	956
Grand total	3	60	335	575	497	287	85	15	1	1,858

a "Other races" includes races having less than 10 representatives in this city and pupils whose race is not reported.

TABLE 3.—*Race, sex, and age, by grade—Number of pupils of each age in each grade, by sex and by general nativity and race of father of pupil*—Continued.

SIXTH GRADE—Continued.

GIRLS.

General nativity and race of father of pupil.	Number of pupils of each age.									Total.
	9.	10.	11.	12.	13.	14.	15.	16.	17.	
Native-born:										
White....................		23	202	275	222	110	22	3	1	858
Negro....................			4	5	5	7	2	1		24
Total native-born..........		23	206	280	227	117	24	4	1	882
Foreign-born:										
Bohemian and Moravian.........			2	6	2	2					12
Canadian, French...........		1	4	8	3	8	1			25
Canadian, Other...........		7	37	66	57	37	9	1		214
Danish..................		1		3	2	2				8
Dutch..................			1	1	1					3
English..................		1	26	39	35	9	3	1		114
Flemish.................			1	1	1					3
French.................			2	3	8	1				14
German.................		9	62	132	93	32	7	1		336
Hebrew, German...........		2	6	7	2	3	1			21
Hebrew, Polish...........		2		1	1	2				6
Hebrew, Roumanian.........				1	1					2
Hebrew, Russian...........			6	13	12	5			1	37
Hebrew, Other............			2	1	1					4
Irish....................			8	12	9	4	4	1		38
Italian, North...........					1					1
Italian, South...........			1	4		2				7
Norwegian...............			1	1						2
Polish..................			1	4	3	3	2			13
Russian.................				2	1					3
Scotch..................		3	12	17	11	5	1			49
Swedish.................			2		1	1				4
Other races *a*...........				2	1		1			4
Total foreign-born............		26	174	324	246	116	29	4	1	920
Grand total.............		49	380	604	473	233	53	8	2	1,802

a " Other races " includes races having less than 10 representatives in this city and pupils whose race is not reported.

TABLE 3.—*Race, sex, and age, by grade—Number of pupils of each age in each grade, by sex and by general nativity and race of father of pupil*—Continued.

SIXTH GRADE—Continued.

TOTAL.

General nativity and race of father of pupil.	Number of pupils of each age.									Total.
	9.	10.	11.	12.	13.	14.	15.	16.	17.	
Native-born:										
White...........................	3	55	373	536	447	244	65	9	1	1,733
Negro............................		1	7	12	15	11	3	2	......	51
Total native-born.............	3	56	380	548	462	255	68	11	1	1,784
Foreign-born:										
Bohemian and Moravian.........			2	11	6	7	......	......	......	26
Canadian, French................		1	7	14	12	12	8	1	......	55
Canadian, Other................		18	74	135	123	68	23	4	......	445
Danish..........................		1	1	5	5	2	1	......	......	15
Dutch...........................			2	4	2	1	......	......	......	9
English.........................		3	40	68	56	23	6	1	......	197
Flemish.........................			2	3	2	......	1	......	......	8
French..........................			3	5	15	2	1	......	......	26
German..........................		18	114	253	180	88	17	3	......	673
Hebrew, German..................		3	16	11	7	4	1	:	......	42
Hebrew, Polish..................		3	1	4	3	2	......	......	......	13
Hebrew, Roumanian...............			1	2	1	......	......	......	......	4
Hebrew, Russian.................		2	14	36	39	16	......	......	1	108
Hebrew, Other...................			7	3	3	2	......	......	......	15
Irish...........................			14	16	14	8	5	2	......	59
Italian, North..................				2	1	2	......	......	......	5
Italian, South..................			1	7	1	2	......	......	1	12
Norwegian.......................			4	2	2	1	......	......	......	9
Polish..........................			3	5	9	12	4	1	......	34
Roumanian.......................					1	......	......	......	......	1
Russian.........................				4	2	1	......	......	......	7
Scotch..........................		4	25	34	21	11	2	......	......	97
Swedish.........................			4	4	1	1	......	......	......	10
Syrian..........................					1	......	......	......	......	1
Other races *a*.................				3	1	......	1	......	......	5
Total foreign-born.............		53	335	631	508	265	70	12	2	1,876
Grand total.................	3	109	715	1,179	970	520	138	23	3	3,660

a "Other races" includes races having less than 10 representatives in this city and pupils whose race is not reported.

TABLE 3.—*Race, sex, and age, by grade—Number of pupils of each age in each grade, by sex and by general nativity and race of father of pupil—Continued.*

SEVENTH GRADE.

BOYS.

General nativity and race of father of pupil.	Number of pupils of each age.											Total.
	10.	11.	12.	13.	14.	15.	16.	17.	18.	19.	20.	
Native-born:												
White	1	37	159	240	206	72	22	2				739
Negro			1	4	5	2	3					15
Total native-born	1	37	160	244	211	74	25	2				754
Foreign-born:												
Bohemian and Moravian		1		4	5							10
Canadian, French		2	2	5	5	6	1					21
Canadian, Other		5	39	73	35	23	7	1				183
Danish			1	2		1						4
Dutch			4	3	1							8
English		2	16	22	29	12	2					83
Flemish			1	2								4
French			4	1	2	3		1				11
German		6	51	108	90	24	1					280
Hebrew, German		1	1	8	4	3						17
Hebrew, Polish		1	2	3	1	1						8
Hebrew, Roumanian		1	2	2	1							6
Hebrew, Russian		6	11	11	5	4						37
Hebrew, Other			1	3	2	1		1				8
Irish		1	8	10	4	4						27
Italian, North				3	1							4
Italian, South					1	1					1	3
Magyar			1		1							2
Norwegian				1	1	2						4
Polish				2	3	2						7
Scotch		1	4	15	13	5	1					39
Slovak												
Swedish		1	2	1	1	2				1		8
Welsh					1							1
Other races *a*		1	2				1					4
Total foreign-born		29	152	279	205	96	13	3		1	1	779
Grand total	1	66	312	523	416	170	38	5		1	1	1,533

a " Other races " includes races having less than 10 representatives in this city and pupils whose race is not reported.

TABLE 3.—*Race, sex, and age, by grade—Number of pupils of each age in each grade, by sex and by general nativity and race of father of pupil—Continued.*

SEVENTH GRADE—Continued.

GIRLS.

General nativity and race of father of pupil.	10.	11.	12.	13.	14.	15.	16.	17.	18.	19.	20.	Total.
Native-born:												
White		31	191	278	183	70	25	4				782
Negro	1		2	7	5	4	1					20
Total native-born	1	31	193	285	188	74	26	4				802
Foreign-born:												
Bohemian and Moravian			2	8	4							14
Canadian, French			3	5	11	3	1					23
Canadian, Other		5	48	55	36	30	4	1				179
Danish			2	2	2	1						7
Dutch			1	1	1							3
English		2	15	33	22	7	2					81
Flemish				2								2
French			2	3	2	1						8
German		10	68	92	50	13	2					235
Hebrew, German		1	3	9	6							19
Hebrew, Polish			1									1
Hebrew, Roumanian				2	1							3
Hebrew, Russian		2	11	5	11	3						32
Hebrew, Other			4	1	1							6
Irish		2	1	9	5	3	2					22
Italian, North				2	1	1						4
Italian, South			1		1							2
Magyar					1							1
Norwegian			1									1
Polish	1			2	2	2						7
Russian			1									1
Scotch		1	14	16	4	6						41
Slovak			1									1
Spanish-American					1							1
Swedish			2	1		1						4
Welsh					1							1
Other races a			1			1						2
Total foreign-born	1	23	182	248	163	72	11	1				701
Grand total	2	54	375	533	351	146	37	5				1,503

a "Other races" includes races having less than 10 representatives in this city and pupils whose race is not reported.

TABLE 3.—*Race, sex, and age, by grade—Number of pupils of each age in each grade, by sex and by general nativity and race of father of pupil*—Continued.

SEVENTH GRADE—Continued.

TOTAL.

General nativity and race of father of pupil.	Number of pupils of each age.											Total.
	10.	11.	12.	13.	14.	15.	16.	17.	18.	19.	20.	
Native-born:												
White	1	68	350	518	389	142	47	6				1,521
Negro	1		3	11	10	6	4					35
Total native-born	2	68	353	529	399	148	51	6				1,556
Foreign-born:												
Bohemian and Moravian		1	2	12	9							24
Canadian, French		2	5	10	16	9	2					44
Canadian, Other		10	87	128	71	53	11	2				362
Danish			3	4	2	2						11
Dutch			5	4	2							11
English		4	31	55	51	19	4					164
Flemish			1	4		1						6
French			6	4	4	4		1				19
German		16	119	200	140	37	3					515
Hebrew, German		2	4	17	10	3						36
Hebrew, Polish		1	3	3	1	1						9
Hebrew, Roumanian		1	2	4	2							9
Hebrew, Russian		8	22	16	16	7						69
Hebrew, Other			5	4	3	1		1				14
Irish		3	9	19	9	7	2					49
Italian, North			5		2	1						8
Italian, South			1		2	1					1	5
Magyar			1		2							3
Norwegian			1	1	1	2						5
Polish	1			4	5	4						14
Russian			1									1
Scotch		2	18	31	17	11	1					80
Slovak			1									1
Spanish-American					1							1
Swedish		1	4	2	1	3			1			12
Welsh					1	1						2
Other races a		1	3		1	1	1					6
Total foreign-born	1	52	334	527	368	168	24	4		1	1	1,480
Grand total	3	120	687	1,056	767	316	75	10		1	1	3,036

a "Other races" includes races having less than 10 representatives in this city and pupils whose race is not reported.

TABLE 3.—*Race, sex, and age, by grade—Number of pupils of each age in each grade, by sex and by general nativity and race of father of pupil*—Continued.

EIGHTH GRADE.

BOYS.

General nativity and race of father of pupil.	Number of pupils of each age.								Total.
	11.	12.	13.	14.	15.	16.	17.	18.	
Native-born:									
White	.....	26	131	173	121	41	7	......	499
Negro	1	1	3	3	2				10
Total native-born	1	27	134	176	123	41	7	.....	509
Foreign-born:									
Bohemian and Moravian			3	.....	3				6
Bulgarian			1	1	1	1			4
Canadian, French			2	5	4				11
Canadian, Other		5	18	46	33	13	1		116
Danish			1	1	1				3
Dutch			2	2	1				5
English		2	12	17	14	7			52
French			2	1	1	1			5
German		15	31	82	55	12	1		196
Hebrew, German			1	8	4			1	14
Hebrew, Polish	1	1	4	6	1				13
Hebrew, Roumanian		1			1	1			3
Hebrew, Russian			3	5	3	2	1		14
Hebrew, Other		1	3	2					6
Irish		2	5	7	5	1			20
Italian, North				1					1
Italian, South			2			1			3
Magyar			1		1				2
Polish					2				2
Russian				2					2
Scotch		1	6	6	7	4	1		25
Swedish			1	1					2
Welsh		1	2						3
Other races *a*			3		1				4
Total foreign-born	1	29	103	193	138	41	6	1	512
Grand total	2	56	237	369	261	82	13	1	1,021

a "Other races" includes races having less than 10 representatives in this city and pupils whose race is not reported.

TABLE 3.—*Race, sex, and age, by grade—Number of pupils of each age in each grade, by sex and by general nativity and race of father of pupil—Continued.*

EIGHTH GRADE—Continued.

GIRLS.

General nativity and race of father of pupil.	Number of pupils of each age.								Total.
	11.	12.	13.	14.	15.	16.	17.	18.	
Native-born:									
White	2	34	145	230	130	39	5	1	586
Negro			1	2	5		1		9
Total native-born	2	34	146	232	135	39	6	1	595
Foreign-born:									
Bohemian and Moravian		1	2						3
Canadian, French		1	2	5	5	1			14
Canadian, Other		4	29	49	43	18	1	1	145
Danish				1		1	1		3
Dutch			2	2	1				5
English		2	13	24	16	5			60
Flemish			1	1					2
French				1	2	1			4
German	2	7	51	77	41	6	2		186
Hebrew, German		1	3	5	5	1			15
Hebrew, Polish		1	4	2	4				11
Hebrew, Russian		2	4	7	3	1			17
Hebrew, other		1		1	1				3
Irish		1	6	7	3		1		18
Italian, North				2					2
Italian, South			1		1				2
Roumanian				1					1
Scotch		1	9	10	9	2	1		32
Swedish			1	1					2
Welsh				1					1
Othe rraces *a*				1					1
Total foreign-born	2	22	128	198	134	36	6	1	527
Grand total	4	56	274	430	269	75	12	2	1,122

a " Other races " includes races having less than 10 representatives in this city and pupils whose race is not reported.

TABLE 3.—*Race, sex, and age, by grade—Number of pupils of each age in each grade, by sex and by general nativity and race of father of pupil*—Continued

EIGHTH GRADE—Continued.

TOTAL.

General nativity and race of father of pupil.	Number of pupils of each age.								Total.
	11.	12.	13.	14.	15.	16.	17.	18.	
Native-born:									
White	2	60	276	403	251	80	12	1	1,085
Negro	1	1	4	5	7		1		19
Total native-born	3	61	280	408	258	80	13	1	1,104
Foreign-born:									
Bohemian and Moravian		1	5		3				9
Bulgarian			1	1	1		1		4
Canadian, French		1	4	10	9	1			25
Canadian, Other		9	47	95	76	31	2	1	261
Danish			1	2	1	1	1		6
Dutch			4	4	2				10
English		4	25	41	30	12			112
Flemish			1	1					2
French			2	2	3	2			9
German	2	22	82	159	96	18	3		382
Hebrew, German		1	4	13	9	1		1	29
Hebrew, Polish	1	2	8	8	5				24
Hebrew, Roumanian		1			1	1			3
Hebrew, Russian		2	7	12	6	3	1		31
Hebrew, Other		2	3	3	1				9
Irish		3	11	14	8	1	1		38
Italian, North				3					3
Italian, South			3		1		1		5
Magyar			1		1				2
Polish					2				2
Roumanian				1					1
Russian				2					2
Scotch		2	15	16	16	6	2		57
Swedish			2	2					4
Welsh		1	2	1					4
Other races a			3	1	1				5
Total foreign-born	3	51	231	391	272	77	12	2	1,039
Grand total	6	112	511	799	530	157	25	3	2,143

a "Other races" includes races having less than 10 representatives in this city and pupils whose race is not reported.

TABLE 3.—*Race, sex, and age, by grade—Number of pupils of each age in each grade, by sex and by general nativity and race of father of pupil*—Continued.

FIRST YEAR HIGH SCHOOL.

BOYS.

General nativity and race of father of pupil.	Number of pupils of each age.									Total.
	12.	13.	14.	15.	16.	17.	18.	19.	20 or over.	
Native-born:										
White........................	3	27	92	140	78	26	6	1	1	374
Negro........................					1				1	2
Total native-born..........	3	27	92	140	79	26	6	1	2	376
Foreign-born:										
Bohemian and Moravian.......		1	1	1						3
Canadian, French............			2	1	2					5
Canadian, Other.............		5	15	42	13	8	1			84
Danish......................			1	4						5
Dutch.......................			2	1						3
English.....................		1	7	8	3	2	1			22
French......................		1	2	3						6
German......................	1	13	25	36	18	4				97
Hebrew, German..............		2	6	3	2					13
Hebrew, Polish..............	1	1	4		1					7
Hebrew, Russian.............		3	6	5	3		1			18
Hebrew, Other...............			1							1
Irish.......................			3	6	3	2				14
Italian, North.............					2					2
Norwegian...................							1			1
Polish......................			3	3	2					8
Scotch......................	1	1	1	8	3		1			15
Slovak......................		1	1							2
Spanish-American............						1				1
Swedish.....................			1							1
Welsh.......................				2	2					4
Other races *a*.............				1						1
Total foreign-born.........	3	29	81	124	54	17	5			313
Grand total................	6	56	173	264	133	43	11	1	2	689

a "Other races" includes races having less than 10 representatives in this city and pupils whose race is not reported.

TABLE **3.**—*Race, sex, and age, by grade—Number of pupils of each age in each grade, by sex and by general nativity and race of father of pupil*—Continued.

FIRST YEAR HIGH SCHOOL—Continued.

GIRLS.

General nativity and race of father of pupil.	Number of pupils of each age.									Total.
	12.	13.	14.	15.	16.	17.	18.	19.	20 or over.	
Native-born:										
White	2	27	105	145	90	31	8	2	......	410
Negro				3	1	2				6
Indian			1	1						2
Total native-born	2	27	106	149	91	33	8	2	......	418
Foreign-born:										
Bohemian and Moravian			1							1
Canadian, French			2	3	4				1	10
Canadian, Other	2	6	24	35	18	8	1			94
Danish		1								1
Dutch			1	1						2
English	1		13	14	10	4			1	43
French				3	1					4
German		4	15	36	16			1		72
Hebrew, German			3	4	1					8
Hebrew, Polish				1	1					2
Hebrew, Russian	2	2	4	4	3					15
Irish		2	5	4	4	2				17
Italian, North			1							1
Magyar						1				1
Norwegian					1					1
Polish		1	3		2					6
Scotch		4	6	8	8	2				28
Swedish			1		1					2
Welsh			1							1
Other races *a*			1		1					2
Total foreign-born	5	20	81	113	71	17	1	1	2	311
Grand total	7	47	187	262	162	50	9	3	2	729

a "Other races" includes races having less than 10 representatives in this city and pupils whose race is not reported.

TABLE 3.—*Race, sex, and age, by grade—Number of pupils of each age in each grade, by sex and by general nativity and race of father of pupil—Continued.*

FIRST YEAR HIGH SCHOOL—Continued.

TOTAL.

General nativity and race of father of pupil.	Number of pupils of each age.									Total.
	12.	13.	14.	15.	16.	17.	18.	19.	20 or over.	
Native-born:										
White	5	54	197	285	168	57	14	3	1	784
Negro				3	2	2			1	8
Indian			1	1						2
Total native-born	5	54	198	289	170	59	14	3	2	794
Foreign-born:										
Bohemian and Moravian		1	2	1						4
Canadian, French			4	4	6				1	15
Canadian, Other	2	11	39	77	31	16	2			178
Danish		1	1	4						6
Dutch			3	2						5
English	1	1	20	22	13	6	1		1	65
French		1	2	6	1					10
German	1	17	40	72	34	4		1		169
Hebrew, German		2	9	7	3					21
Hebrew, Polish	1	1	4	1	2					9
Hebrew, Russian	2	5	10	9	6		1			33
Hebrew, Other			1							1
Irish		2	8	10	7	4				31
Italian, North			1		2					3
Magyar						1				1
Norwegian					1		1			2
Polish		1	6	3	4					14
Scotch	1	5	7	16	11	2	1			43
Slovak		1	1							2
Spanish-American						1				1
Swedish			2		1					3
Welsh			1	2	2					5
Other races a			1	1	1					3
Total foreign-born	8	49	162	237	125	34	6	1	2	624
Grand total	13	103	360	526	295	93	20	4	4	1,418

a "Other races" includes races having less than 10 representatives in this city and pupils whose race is not reported.

TABLE **3.**—*Race, sex, and age, by grade—Number of pupils of each age in each grade, by sex and by general nativity and race of father of pupil*—Continued.

SECOND YEAR HIGH SCHOOL.

BOYS.

General nativity and race of father of pupil.	Number of pupils of each age.								Total.
	13.	14.	15.	16.	17.	18.	19.	20.	
Native-born:									
White	4	17	63	73	52	21	4	2	236
Negro				1			1		2
Total native-born	4	17	63	74	52	21	5	2	238
Foreign-born:									
Canadian, French				1	1				2
Canadian, Other		6	12	18	9	7	3		55
Danish			1						1
English		1	10	10	5	2	1		29
French					1				1
Flemish	1			1					2
German		3	14	12	6	4			39
Hebrew, German	1	2	3	7	1				14
Hebrew, Polish			3						3
Hebrew, Russian			7	1	2				10
Irish			3	3	2				8
Magyar					1				1
Russian					1				1
Scotch			2	5	2	1			10
Swedish				2					2
Welsh					1				1
Other races a			1						1
Total foreign-born	2	12	56	60	32	14	4		180
Grand total	6	29	119	134	84	35	9	2	418

a "Other races" includes races having less than 10 representatives in this city and pupils whose race is not reported.

TABLE 3.—*Race, sex, and age, by grade—Number of pupils of each age in each grade, by sex and by general nativity and race of father of pupil*—Continued.

SECOND YEAR HIGH SCHOOL—Continued.

GIRLS.

General nativity and race of father of pupil.	Number of pupils of each age.								Total.
	13.	14.	15.	16.	17.	18.	19.	20.	
Native-born:									
White....................	1	22	88	86	55	23	4	......	279
Negro....................	......	......	2	2	6	......	......	......	10
Total native-born............	1	22	90	88	61	23	4	......	289
Foreign-born:									
Bohemian and Moravian............	......	1	......	......	......	......	......	......	1
Canadian, French............	......	1	2	3	......	......	......	......	6
Canadian, Other............	......	10	20	24	15	5	2	1	77
Danish............	......	......	......	......	1	......	......	......	1
English............	1	1	9	6	5	4	......	......	26
French............	......	......	......	2	......	......	......	......	2
Flemish............	......	......	1	......	......	......	......	......	1
German............	......	7	16	19	3	4	1	......	50
Hebrew, German............	......	2	......	1	1	......	......	......	4
Hebrew, Polish............	......	......	4	......	......	......	......	......	4
Hebrew, Russian............	......	2	2	2	......	1	......	......	7
Hebrew, Other............	......	......	......	......	1	......	......	......	1
Irish............	......	1	6	4	......	......	......	......	11
Norwegian............	......	......	......	1	......	......	......	......	1
Polish............	......	......	1	......	......	......	......	......	1
Russian............	......	......	1	......	......	......	......	......	1
Scotch............	......	3	7	7	3	1	1	......	22
Welsh............	......	......	......	1	......	......	......	......	1
Other races *a*............	......	......	2	......	......	......	......	......	2
Total foreign-born............	1	28	71	70	29	15	4	1	219
Grand total............	2	50	161	158	90	38	8	1	508

a "Other races" includes races having less than 10 representatives in this city and pupils whose race is not reported.

TABLE 3.—*Race, sex, and age, by grade—Number of pupils of each age in each grade, by sex and by general nativity and race of father of pupil*—Continued.

SECOND YEAR HIGH SCHOOL—Continued.

TOTAL.

General nativity and race of father of pupil.	Number of pupils of each age.								Total.
	13.	14.	15.	16.	17.	18.	19.	20.	
Native-born:									
White	5	39	151	159	107	44	8	2	515
Negro			2	3	6		1		12
Total native-born	5	39	153	162	113	44	9	2	527
Foreign-born:									
Bohemian and Moravian		1							1
Canadian, French		1	2	4	1				8
Canadian, Other		16	32	42	24	12	5	1	132
Danish			1		1				2
English	1	2	19	16	10	6	1		55
French				2	1				3
Flemish	1		1	1					3
German		10	30	31	9	8	1		89
Hebrew, German	1	4	3	8	2				18
Hebrew, Polish			7						7
Hebrew, Russian		2	9	3	2	1			17
Hebrew, Other					1				1
Irish		1	9	7	2				19
Magyar					1				1
Norwegian				1					1
Polish			1						1
Russian			1		1				2
Scotch		3	9	12	5	2	1		32
Swedish				2					2
Welsh				1	1				2
Other races a			3						3
Total foreign-born	3	40	127	130	61	29	8	1	399
Grand total	8	79	280	292	174	73	17	3	926

a "Other races" includes races having less than 10 representatives in this city and pupils whose race is not reported.

TABLE 3.—*Race, sex, and age, by grade—Number of pupils of each age in each grade, by sex and by general nativity and race of father of pupil—Continued.*

THIRD YEAR HIGH SCHOOL.

BOYS.

General nativity and race of father of pupil.	Number of pupils of each age.								Total.
	13.	14.	15.	16.	17.	18.	19.	20.	
Native-born, White	1	6	28	54	59	34	15	3	200
Foreign-born:									
Bohemian and Moravian				1	2				3
Canadian, French				1		2	1	1	5
Canadian, Other			5	16	17	6	4	2	50
Danish			1						1
Dutch					1				1
English		1	4	7	5	3	1		21
French				1	1		2		4
German			5	8	9	5	2		29
Hebrew, German			1	5	4				10
Hebrew, Polish				1					1
Hebrew, Russian		1	1		2	2			6
Hebrew, Other					1		1		2
Irish				1	2	2			5
Lithuanian					1				1
Polish						1			1
Scotch			2	1	2	1		1	7
Total foreign-born		2	19	41	48	22	11	4	147
Grand total	1	8	47	95	107	56	26	7	347

GIRLS.

General nativity and race of father of pupil.	Number of pupils of each age.								Total.
	13.	14.	15.	16.	17.	18.	19.	20.	
Native-born:									
White		2	16	56	81	49	7	3	214
Negro				3	2	1			6
Total native-born		2	16	59	83	50	7	3	220
Foreign-born:									
Canadian, French				1			1		2
Canadian, Other			1	12	18	15	3		49
Danish				2					2
English			2	5	3	1	1		12
French					1				1
German		1	7	13	14	4			39
Hebrew, German			3	2	1	2			8
Hebrew, Polish			1	1					2
Hebrew, Russian			1		2				3
Irish				6	4	3	1		14
Scotch				2	5		2		9
Welsh					1				1
Total foreign-born		1	15	44	49	25	8		142
Grand total		3	31	103	132	75	15	3	362

TABLE 3.—*Race, sex, and age, by grade—Number of pupils of each age in each grade, by sex and by general nativity and race of father of pupil*—Continued.

THIRD YEAR HIGH SCHOOL—Continued.
TOTAL.

General nativity and race of father of pupil.	13.	14.	15.	16.	17.	18.	19.	20.	Total.
Native-born:									
White	1	8	44	110	140	83	22	6	414
Negro				3	2	1			6
Total native-born	1	8	44	113	142	84	22	6	420
Foreign-born:									
Bohemian and Moravian				1	2				3
Canadian, French				1	1	2	2	1	7
Canadian, Other			6	28	35	21	7	2	99
Danish			1	2					3
Dutch					1				1
English		1	6	12	8	4	2		33
French				1	2		2		5
German		1	12	21	23	9	2		68
Hebrew, German			4	7	5	2			18
Hebrew, Polish			1	2					3
Hebrew, Russian		1	2		4	2			9
Hebrew, Other					1		1		2
Irish				7	6	5	1		19
Lithuanian					1				1
Polish						1			1
Scotch			2	3	7	1	2	1	16
Welsh					1				1
Total foreign-born		3	34	85	97	47	19	4	289
Grand total	1	11	78	198	239	131	41	10	709

FOURTH YEAR HIGH SCHOOL.
BOYS.

General nativity and race of father of pupil.	14.	15.	16.	17.	18.	19.	20.	Total.
Native-born, White	1	2	12	42	43	20	7	127
Foreign-born:								
Bohemian and Moravian						1	1	2
Canadian, French			1					1
Canadian, Other		1	4	10	12	8		35
English			1	4	2	3	2	12
German		1	3	6	18	7		35
Hebrew, German		1	1	3	1			6
Hebrew, Polish				1				1
Hebrew, Russian			1	2	2	1		6
Hebrew, Other					1			1
Irish				3				3
Polish			1	1				2
Scotch			1	2	1			4
Swedish							1	1
Welsh				1				1
Total foreign-born		3	13	33	37	20	4	110
Grand total	1	5	25	75	80	40	11	237

TABLE 3.—*Race, sex, and age, by grade—Number of pupils of each age in each grade, by sex and by general nativity and race of father of pupil*—Continued.

FOURTH YEAR HIGH SCHOOL—Continued.

GIRLS.

General nativity and race of father of pupil.	Number of pupils of each age.							Total.
	14.	15.	16.	17.	18.	19.	20.	
Native-born:								
White		3	16	48	64	31	8	170
Negro						1	1	2
Total native-born		3	16	48	64	32	9	172
Foreign-born:								
Bohemian and Moravian						1		1
Bulgarian						1		1
Canadian, French		1			1			2
Canadian, Other		3	10	14		13	4	44
English	1	3	9	5		4	2	24
French			1	1				2
German		2	6	7	2		2	19
Hebrew, German		1		2				3
Hebrew, Polish			3					3
Hebrew, Russian	1		5					6
Irish			4			2	1	7
Russian				1				1
Scotch		1	2	1			1	5
Spanish-American					1			1
Welsh				1				1
Other races a			1					1
Total foreign-born		2	11	41	33	24	10	121
Grand total		5	27	89	97	56	19	293

TOTAL.

General nativity and race of father of pupil.	14.	15.	16.	17.	18.	19.	20.	Total.
Native-born:								
White	1	5	28	90	107	51	15	297
Negro						1	1	2
Total native-born	1	5	28	90	107	52	16	299
Foreign-born:								
Bohemian and Moravian						2	1	3
Bulgarian						1		1
Canadian, French		2			1			3
Canadian, Other		1	7	20	26	21	4	79
English		1	4	13	7	7	4	36
French				1	1			2
German		1	5	12	25	9	2	54
Hebrew, German		1	2	3	3			9
Hebrew, Polish				4				4
Hebrew, Russian		1	1	7	2	1		12
Hebrew, Other					1			1
Irish				7		2	1	10
Polish			1	1				2
Russian					1			1
Scotch			2	4	2		1	9
Spanish-American						1		1
Swedish							1	1
Welsh				1	1			2
Other races a				1				1
Total foreign-born		5	24	74	70	44	14	231
Grand total	1	10	52	164	177	96	30	530

a "Other races" includes races having less than 10 representatives in this city and pupils whose race is not reported.

TABLE 3.—*Race, sex, and age, by grade—Number of pupils of each age in each grade, by sex and by general nativity and race of father of pupil—Continued.*

SPECIAL SCHOOL.

BOYS.

General nativity and race of father of pupil.	Number of pupils of each age.														Total.
	4.	5.	6.	7.	8.	9.	10.	11.	12.	13.	14.	15.	16.	17.	
Native-born, White		1		4		5	4	2	2	1	2	1			22
Foreign-born:															
Canadian, French						1		1							2
Canadian, Other				1		1	1								3
English					1		1								2
French									1						1
German				1	3	1				4	2		1		12
Hebrew, Russian				1											1
Hebrew, Other		1													1
Irish				1	1		1								3
Italian, South				1											1
Polish		1				2	1								4
Scotch						1									1
Swedish												1			1
Other races *a*			1												1
Total foreign-born		2	1	4	6	5	4	2	5	2		2			33
Grand total		3	1	8	6	10	8	4	7	3	2	3			55

GIRLS.

General nativity and race of father of pupil.	4.	5.	6.	7.	8.	9.	10.	11.	12.	13.	14.	15.	16.	17.	Total.
Native-born, White			2	1	2	1	2		1	2	2	1	3	1	18
Foreign-born:															
Canadian, Other						1				1					2
English										1			1		2
Flemish								1							1
German				1	1	1	3	2	1	2	1				12
Hebrew, Russian							1								1
Hebrew, Other				1	2										3
Irish									1						1
Italian, South	1			1	1		1								4
Polish							1					1			3
Russian											1				1
Total foreign-born	1		1	3	4	3	4	4	2	5	1	1	1		30
Grand total	1		3	4	6	4	6	4	3	7	3	2	4	1	48

a "Other races" includes races having less than 10 representatives in this city and pupils whose race is not reported.

TABLE 3.—*Race, sex, and age, by grade—Number of pupils of each age in each grade, by sex and by general nativity and race of father of pupil*—Continued.

SPECIAL SCHOOL—Continued.
TOTAL.

General nativity and race of father of pupil.	4.	5.	6.	7.	8.	9.	10.	11.	12.	13.	14.	15.	16.	17.	Total.
Native-born, White		1	2	5	2	6	6	2	3	3	4	2	3	1	40
Foreign-born:															
Canadian, French						1			1						2
Canadian, Other					2		1	1	1						5
English					1		1			1			1		4
Flemish								1							1
French								1							1
German				2	4	2	3	2	5	4	1	1			24
Hebrew, Russian				1		1									2
Hebrew, Other		1		1	2										4
Irish				1	1		1	1							4
Italian, South	1		1	2		1									5
Polish		1				2	2			1		1			7
Russian										1					1
Scotch						1									1
Swedish												1			1
Other races *a*			1												1
Total foreign-born	1	2	2	7	10	8	8	6	7	7	1	3	1		63
Grand total	1	3	4	12	12	14	14	8	10	10	5	5	4	1	103

a "Other races" includes races having less than 10 representatives in this city and pupils whose race is not reported.

UNGRADED SCHOOL.
BOYS.

General nativity and race of father of pupil.	7.	8.	9.	10.	11.	12.	13.	14.	15.	Total.
Native-born:										
White	1			1	3	5	5	10	5	30
Negro					3	2	3	1		9
Total native-born	1			1	6	7	8	11	5	39
Foreign-born:										
Canadian, French							1	3	2	6
Canadian, Other						2	2	3	3	10
English							2	2	1	5
German			1	4	6	8	15	7	8	49
Hebrew, German							1		1	2
Hebrew, Polish								1		1
Hebrew, Roumanian				1		1			2	4
Hebrew, Russian		1				1	1			3
Hebrew, Other				1		1	2		2	6
Italian, South		1	2	4	3	7	24	22	4	67
Polish					1			1		2
Scotch				1						1
Total foreign-born		2	3	11	10	20	48	39	23	156
Grand total	1	2	3	12	16	27	56	50	28	195

TABLE **3.**—*Race, sex, and age, by grade—Number of pupils of each age in each grade, by sex and by general nativity and race of father of pupil*—Continued.

UNGRADED SCHOOL—Continued.

TOTAL.

General nativity and race of father of pupil.	Number of pupils of each age.									Total.
	7.	8.	9.	10.	11.	12.	13.	14.	15.	
Native-born:										
White	1			1	3	5	5	10	5	30
Negro					3	2	3	1		9
Total native-born	1			1	6	7	8	11	5	39
Foreign-born:										
Canadian, French							1	3	2	6
Canadian, Other						2	2	3	3	10
English							2	2	1	5
German			1	4	6	8	15	7	8	49
Hebrew, German							1		1	2
Hebrew, Polish									1	1
Hebrew, Roumanian								1		1
Hebrew, Russian		1		1		1			1	4
Hebrew, Other						2	1			3
Italian, South				1	1		2		2	6
Polish		1	2	4	3	7	24	22	4	67
Scotch				1				1		2
Total foreign-born		2	3	11	10	20	48	39	23	156
Grand total	1	2	3	12	16	27	56	50	28	195

TABLE **4.**—*Race and grade, by age—Number of pupils of each specified age in each grade, by sex and by general nativity and race of father of pupil.*

BOYS: AGE 4 YEARS.

General nativity and race of father of pupil.	Kindergarten.
Native-born, Negro	6
Foreign-born, other races a	5
Grand total	11

a "Other races" includes races having less than 10 representatives of this sex and age and pupils whose race is not reported.

TABLE 4.—*Race and grade, by age—Number of pupils of each specified age in each grade, by sex and by general nativity and race of father of pupil*—Continued.

BOYS: AGE 5 YEARS.

General nativity and race of father of pupil.	Kinder-garten.	Elementary grades.		Ungraded and special schools.	Total.
		1.	2.		
Native-born:					
White	514	24		1	539
Negro	9				9
Total native-born	523	24		1	548
Foreign-born:					
Canadian, French	17				17
Canadian, Other	103	7			110
English	42				42
German	220	4			224
Hebrew, Other	8	1		1	10
Hebrew, Russian	17				17
Irish	20	1	1		22
Italian, North	34	1			35
Italian, South	12				12
Polish	52	2		1	55
Scotch	18	1			19
Other races a	43	1			44
Total foreign-born	586	18	1	2	607
Grand total	1,109	42	1	3	1,155

BOYS: AGE 6 YEARS.

General nativity and race of father of pupil.	Kinder-garten.	Elementary grades.		Ungraded and special schools.	Total.
		1.	2.		
Native-born:					
White	184	729	15		928
Negro	5	10			15
Total native-born	189	739	15		943
Foreign-born:					
Bohemian and Moravian	3	8			11
Canadian, French	1	24			25
Canadian, Other	45	172	7		224
English	12	46	1		59
French	3	15	1		19
German	104	275	7		386
Hebrew, German	1	15	2		18
Hebrew, Polish		9	1		10
Hebrew, Russian	7	78	2		87
Hebrew, Other	2	8			10
Irish	5	23	1		29
Italian, North	20	26			46
Italian, South	3	10			13
Polish	43	88	1		132
Scotch	6	17			23
Other races a	24	35		1	60
Total foreign-born	279	849	23	1	1,152
Grand total	468	1,588	38	1	2,095

a "Other races" includes races having less than 10 representatives of this sex and age and pupils whose race is not reported.

TABLE 4.—*Race and grade, by age—Number of pupils of each specified age in each grade, by sex and by general nativity and race of father of pupil—Continued.*

BOYS: AGE 7 YEARS.

General nativity and race of father of pupil.	Kindergarten.	Elementary grades.				Ungraded and special schools.	Total.
		1.	2.	3.	4.		
Native-born:							
White	4	501	413	27	.....	5	950
Negro	.....	12	3	1	1	.....	17
Total native-born	4	513	416	28	1	5	967
Foreign-born:							
Bohemian and Moravian	.....	4	9	.....	.....	.....	13
Canadian, French	.....	18	9	.....	.....	.....	27
Canadian, Other	.....	124	97	5	1	.....	227
English	2	39	29	2	1	.....	73
French	.....	10	3	.....	.....	.....	13
German	1	263	161	14	.....	1	440
Hebrew, German	.....	11	16	1	.....	.....	28
Hebrew, Polish	.....	.....	10	.....	.....	.....	10
Hebrew, Russian	.....	46	38	3	.....	1	88
Hebrew, Other	.....	4	4	2	.....	.....	10
Irish	.....	23	9	.....	.....	1	33
Italian, North	2	17	6	.....	.....	.....	25
Italian, South	.....	11	3	.....	.....	1	15
Magyar	.....	7	3	.....	.....	.....	10
Polish	4	89	15	1	.....	.....	109
Scotch	1	17	10	1	1	.....	30
Other races *a*	.....	27	20	1	.....	.....	48
Total foreign-born	10	710	442	30	3	4	1,199
Grand total	14	1,223	858	58	4	9	2,166

a "Other races" includes races having less than 10 representatives of this sex and age and pupils whose race is not reported.

BOYS: AGE 8 YEARS.

General nativity and race of father of pupil.	Kindergarten.	Elementary grades.				Ungraded and special schools.	Total.
		1.	2.	3.	4.		
Native-born:							
White	.....	146	469	332	35	.....	982
Negro	.....	5	10	2	.....	.....	17
Total native-born	.....	151	479	334	35	.....	999
Foreign-born:							
Bohemian and Moravian	.....	4	14	2	1	.....	21
Canadian, French	.....	12	16	7	.....	.....	35
Canadian, Other	.....	46	117	64	9	1	237
Dutch (Hollanders)	.....	1	5	4	3	.....	13
English	.....	14	48	33	7	1	103
French	.....	7	7	5	.....	.....	19
German	2	102	193	135	4	3	439
Hebrew, German	.....	4	11	7	1	.....	23
Hebrew, Russian	.....	17	44	30	.....	.....	91
Hebrew, Other	.....	.....	3	6	2	.....	11
Irish	.....	4	11	11	1	1	28
Italian, North	.....	5	11	3	.....	.....	19
Italian, South	.....	9	9	1	.....	.....	19
Polish	.....	68	36	9	.....	1	114
Scotch	.....	4	23	19	1	.....	47
Other races *a*	.....	17	25	14	2	1	59
Total foreign-born	2	314	573	350	31	8	1,278
Grand total	2	465	1,052	684	66	8	2,277

a "Other races" includes races having less than 10 representatives of this sex and age and pupils whose race is not reported.

TABLE 4.—*Race and grade, by age—Number of pupils of each specified age in each grade, by sex and by general nativity and race of father of pupil—Continued.*

BOYS: AGE 9 YEARS.

General nativity and race of father of pupil.	Kinder-garten.	Elementary grades.						Ungraded and special schools.	Total.
		1.	2.	3.	4.	5.	6.		
Native-born:									
White		33	206	452	247	22	3	5	968
Negro		3	7	3	2	1			16
Total native-born		36	213	455	249	23	3	5	984
Foreign-born:									
Bohemian and Moravian		1	6	4	2				13
Canadian, French		3	7	13	5	1		1	30
Canadian, Other		6	47	110	52	2			217
Dutch			2	3	5				10
English		4	18	42	15				79
Flemish		1	4	3	5				13
French		2	4	3	4	1			14
German		33	93	180	89	5		2	402
Hebrew, German				7	6	1			14
Hebrew, Other			3	5	4	4			16
Hebrew, Russian		2	22	31	26	3			84
Irish			10	16	7	1			34
Italian, North		6	8	11	2	1			28
Polish		31	29	8	6	1		4	79
Scotch				16	8	1		1	26
Other races *a*		7	25	18	10	2			62
Total foreign-born		96	278	470	245	23		8	1,120
Grand total		132	491	925	495	46	3	13	2,105

a "Other races" includes races having less than 10 representatives of this sex and age and pupils whose race is not reported.

BOYS: AGE 10 YEARS.

General nativity and race of father of pupil.	Kinder-garten.	Elementary grades.							Ungraded and special schools.	Total.
		1.	2.	3.	4.	5.	6.	7.		
Native-born:										
White		11	77	230	331	204	32	1	5	891
Negro		2	5	11	12		1			31
Total native-born		13	82	241	343	204	33	1	5	922
Foreign-born:										
Bohemian and Moravian		1	1	1	5	5				13
Canadian, French		1	4	8	9	1				23
Canadian, Other		5	20	66	87	56	11		1	246
English		1	9	23	40	21	2		1	97
Flemish		4			2	4				10
French			2	7	3	3				15
German		13	53	135	154	72	9		4	440
Hebrew, German			3	3	9	4	1			20
Hebrew, Russian		1	11	23	20	16	2		1	74
Hebrew, Other			1	6	12	6	1			26
Irish			3	17	13	6			1	40
Italian, North			5	9	3	2				19
Polish		1	9	19	13	9	4		5	60
Scotch			1	2	17	18	8	1	1	48
Other races *a*			3	10	22	17	5		1	53
Total foreign-born	1	39	143	352	403	209	27		15	1,189
Grand total	1	52	225	593	746	413	60	1	20	2,111

a "Other races" includes races having less than 10 representatives of this sex and age and pupils whose race is not reported.

TABLE **4.**—*Race and grade, by age—Number of pupils of each specified age in each grade, by sex and by general nativity and race of father of pupil*—Continued.

BOYS: AGE 11 YEARS.

General nativity and race of father of pupil.	Elementary grades.								Ungraded and special schools.	Total.
	1.	2.	3.	4.	5.	6.	7.	8.		
Native-born:										
White	3	17	104	235	318	171	37	.....	5	890
Negro	3	2	3	9	4	3	.....	1	3	28
Indian		1								1
Total native-born	6	20	107	244	322	174	37	1	8	919
Foreign-born:										
Bohemian and Moravian			3	5	5		1			14
Canadian, French		2	6	7	10	3	2			30
Canadian, Other		4	28	97	80	37	5		1	252
English	2	2	19	28	36	14	2		1	103
French		1	3	4	2	1			1	12
German	2	14	61	121	160	52	6		6	422
Hebrew, German			1	4	8	10	1			24
Hebrew, Russian		4	26	17	17	8	6			78
Hebrew, Other			1	2	12	7	2	1		25
Irish		1	8	5	11	6	1			32
Italian, North	2	3	9	7	1					22
Italian, South	1	2	4	2	1				1	11
Polish	3	12	8	8	4	2			3	40
Scotch			3	15	10	13	1			42
Swedish				7	6	2	1			16
Other races[a]	2	5	10	15	8	6	1			47
Total foreign-born	12	50	190	344	371	161	29	1	12	1,170
Grand total	18	70	297	588	693	335	66	2	20	2,089

[a] "Other races" includes races having less than 10 representatives of this sex and age and pupils whose race is not reported.

BOYS: AGE 12 YEARS.

General nativity and race of father of pupil.	Elementary grades.								High school, first year.	Ungraded and special schools.	Total.
	1.	2.	3.	4.	5.	6.	7.	8.			
Native-born:											
White	1	4	42	133	241	261	159	26	3	7	877
Negro			7	4	5	7	1	1		2	27
Total native-born	1	4	49	137	246	268	160	27	3	9	904
Foreign-born:											
Bohemian and Moravian		1	1	4	3	5					14
Canadian, French		2	3	5	9	6	2			1	28
Canadian, Other		2	13	40	84	69	39	5		2	254
Dutch				3	3	3	4				13
English		2	5	18	31	29	16	2			103
French			2	2	4	2	4				14
German		5	29	92	103	121	51	15	1	12	429
Hebrew, German	1			2	6	4	1				14
Hebrew, Polish			1	3		3	2	1	1		11
Hebrew, Russian	1	7	10	12	9	23	11			1	74
Hebrew, Other				3	2	3	3	2		2	15
Irish				2	16	4	8	2			32
Italian, North		1	4	3	3	2					13
Italian, South	1	2	1	2	3	3					12
Polish	1	4	8	6	7	1				7	24
Scotch			4	7	14	17	4	1	1		48
Other races[a]	1		5	9	8	12	7	1			42
Total foreign-born	5	26	86	212	305	307	152	29	3	25	1,150
Grand total	6	30	135	349	551	575	312	56	6	34	2,054

[a] "Other races" includes races having less than 10 representatives of this sex and age and pupils whose race is not reported.

Table 4.—*Race and grade, by age—Number of pupils of each specified age in each grade, by sex and by general nativity and race of father of pupil*—Continued.

BOYS: AGE 13 YEARS.

General nativity and race of father of pupil.	Elementary grades.								High school.			Ungraded and special schools.	Total.
	1.	2.	3.	4.	5.	6.	7.	8.	First year.	Second year.	Third year.		
Native-born:													
White	1	1	12	56	157	225	240	131	27	4	1	6	861
Negro			3	3	11	10	4	3				3	37
Total native-born	1	1	15	59	168	235	244	134	27	4	1	9	898
Foreign-born:													
Bohemian and Moravian				1	7	4	4	3	1				20
Canadian, French			3	8	9	9	5	2				1	37
Canadian, Other			5	20	31	66	73	18	5			2	220
English			3	13	22	21	22	12	1			2	96
French			2	1	3	7	1	2	1				17
German	1	4	11	38	107	87	108	31	13			17	417
Hebrew, German				1	6	5	8	1	2	1		1	25
Hebrew, Polish			1	3	2	3	4	1					14
Hebrew, Russian	1	1	9	5	11	27	11	3	3				71
Hebrew, Other			1	1	2	5	3					1	13
Irish			1	2	12	5	10	5					35
Italian, North	1	2	1	7	1		3						15
Polish		1	4	12	12	6	2					24	61
Scotch			1	2	10	10	15	6	1				45
Other races[a]	1	4	1	3	12	11	9	13	1	1		2	58
Total foreign-born	4	12	41	115	247	262	279	103	29	2		50	1,144
Grand total	5	13	56	174	415	497	523	237	56	6	1	59	2,042

[a] "Other races" includes races having less than 10 representatives of this sex and age and pupils whose race is not reported.

BOYS: AGE 14 YEARS.

General nativity and race of father of pupil.	Elementary grades.								High school.				Ungraded and special schools.	Total.
	1.	2.	3.	4.	5.	6.	7.	8.	First year.	Second year.	Third year.	Fourth year.		
Native-born:														
White			4	25	57	134	206	173	92	17	6	1	12	727
Negro				2	4	4	5	3					1	19
Total native-born			4	27	61	138	211	176	92	17	6	1	13	746
Foreign-born:														
Bohemian and Moravian			2		2	5	5		1				3	15
Canadian, French			2		3	4	5	5	2				3	24
Canadian, Other			1	10	19	31	35	46	15	6			3	166
English			1	6	10	14	29	17	7	1	1		2	83
German	1		7	20	45	56	90	82	25	3			7	335
Hebrew, German	1			1	1	4	8	6	2					23
Hebrew, Polish			1		1	6	4							12
Hebrew, Russian	1	2	4	4	12	11	5	5	6		1			50
Irish				1	4	4	4	7	3					23
Polish			9	11	5	9	3	3	3				22	62
Scotch			1	1	4	6	13	6	1				1	33
Other races[a]	2		3	6	9	8	11	11	8				1	59
Total foreign-born	4	2	30	59	114	149	205	193	81	12	2		39	890
Grand total	4	2	34	86	175	287	416	369	173	29	8	1	52	1,636

[a] "Other races" includes races having less than 10 representatives of this sex and age and pupils whose race is not reported.

TABLE 4.—*Race and grade, by age—Number of pupils of each specified age in each grade, by sex and by general nativity and race of father of pupil*—Continued.

BOYS: AGE 15 YEARS

General nativity and race of father of pupil.	Elementary grades.							High school.				Ungraded and special schools.	Total.
	2.	3.	4.	5.	6.	7.	8.	First year.	Second year.	Third year.	Fourth year.		
Native-born:													
White		2	5	15	43	72	121	140	63	28	2	6	497
Negro			1	2	1	2	2						8
Total native-born		2	6	17	44	74	123	140	63	28	2	6	505
Foreign-born:													
Canadian, French			2	1	7	6	4	1				2	23
Canadian, Other				2	14	23	33	42	12	5	1	3	135
English			1	1	3	12	14	8	10	4		1	54
German		3	2	10	10	24	55	36	14	5	1	9	169
Hebrew, German			1			3	4	3	3	1	1	1	17
Hebrew, Russian			4	1		4	3	5	7	1		1	26
Irish				1	1	4	5	6	3				20
Polish		1	3	1	2	2	2	3				4	18
Scotch				1	1	5	7	8	2	2			26
Other races *a*	1	3	2	2	3	13	11	12	5	1		4	57
Total foreign-born	1	7	15	20	41	96	138	124	56	19	3	25	545
Grand total	1	9	21	37	85	170	261	264	119	47	5	31	1,050

a "Other races" includes races having less than 10 representatives of this sex and age and pupils whose race is not reported.

BOYS: AGE 16 YEARS.

General nativity and race of father of pupil.	Elementary grades.					High school.				Total.
	4.	5.	6.	7.	8.	First year.	Second year.	Third year.	Fourth year.	
Native-born:										
White	2	1	6	22	41	78	73	54	12	289
Negro			1	3		1	1			6
Total native-born	2	1	7	25	41	79	74	54	12	295
Foreign-born:										
Canadian (other than French)			3	7	13	13	18	16	4	74
English				2	7	3	10	7	1	30
German		1	2	1	12	18	12	8	3	57
Scotch				1	4	3	5	1	1	15
Hebrew, German						2	7	5	1	15
Hebrew, Other					3	4	1	1	1	10
Other races *a*	1	1	3	2	2	11	7	3	2	32
Total foreign-born	1	2	8	13	41	54	60	41	13	233
Grand total	3	3	15	38	82	133	134	95	25	528

a "Other races" includes races having less than 10 representatives of this sex and age and pupils whose race is not reported.

TABLE 4.—*Race and grade, by age—Number of pupils of each specified age in each grade, by sex and by general nativity and race of father of pupil*—Continued.

BOYS: AGE 17 YEARS.

General nativity and race of father of pupil.	Elementary grades.			High school.				Total.
	6.	7.	8.	First year.	Second year.	Third year.	Fourth year.	
Native-born, White....................	......	2	7	26	52	59	42	188
Foreign-born:								
Canadian (other than French).........	......	1	1	8	9	17	10	46
English...............................				2	5	5	4	16
German...............................			1	4	6	9	6	26
Hebrew (other foreign)...............		1	1	....	3	7	6	18
Other races *a*.......................	1	1	3	3	9	10	7	34
Total foreign-born....................	1	3	6	17	32	48	33	140
Grand total.........................	1	5	13	43	84	107	75	328

a "Other races" includes races having less than 10 representatives of this sex and age and pupils whose race is not reported.

BOYS: AGE 18 YEARS.

General nativity and race of father of pupil.	Elementary grade 8.	High school.				Total.
		First year.	Second year.	Third year.	Fourth year.	
Native-born, White.................................	....	6	21	34	43	104
Foreign-born:						
Canadian (other than French).....................	....	1	7	6	12	26
German...			4	5	18	27
Other races *a*...................................	1	4	3	11	7	26
Total foreign-born.............................	1	5	14	22	37	79
Grand total...................................	1	11	35	56	80	183

a "Other races" includes races having less than 10 representatives of this sex and age and pupils whose race is not reported.

BOYS: AGE 19 YEARS.

General nativity and race of father of pupil.	Elementary grade 7.	High school.				Total.
		First year.	Second year.	Third year.	Fourth year.	
Native-born:						
White...................................	....	1	4	15	20	40
Negro...................................	....		1	....	....	1
Total native-born.....................	....	1	5	15	20	41
Foreign-born:						
Canadian (other than French)...........			3	4	8	15
Other races *a*........................	1	....	1	7	12	21
Total foreign-born.....................	1	....	4	11	20	36
Grand total............................	1	1	9	26	40	77

a "Other races" includes races having less than 10 representatives of this sex and age and pupils whose race is not reported.

TABLE **4.**—*Race and grade, by age—Number of pupils of each specified age in each grade, by sex and by general nativity and race of father of pupil*—Continued.

BOYS: AGE 20 YEARS.

General nativity and race of father of pupil.	Elementary grades.		High school.				Total.
	4.	7.	First year.	Second year.	Third year.	Fourth year.	
Native-born:							
White			1	2	3	7	13
Negro			1				1
Total native-born			2	2	3	7	14
Foreign-born, other races a	2	1			4	4	11
Grand total	2	1	2	2	7	11	25

a "Other races" includes races having less than 10 representatives of this sex and age and pupils whose race is not reported.

GIRLS: AGE 4 YEARS.

General nativity and race of father of pupil.	Kindergarten.	Elementary, 2.	Ungraded and special schools.	Total.
Native-born, White	11			11
Foreign-born, other races a	9	1	1	11
Grand total	20	1	1	22

a "Other races" includes races having less than 10 representatives of this sex and age and pupils whose race is not reported.

GIRLS: AGE 5 YEARS.

General nativity and race of father of pupil.	Kindergarten.	Elementary grades.		Total.
		1.	2.	
Native-born:				
White	474	17		491
Negro	6			6
Total native-born	480	17		497
Foreign-born:				
Canadian, French	23	1		24
Canadian, Other	101	1		102
Dutch	13	1		14
English	48	2		50
German	193	5		198
Hebrew, Russian	15	3		18
Irish	22	1		23
Italian, North	28			28
Polish	27	2	1	30
Scotch	21			21
Other races a	63	3		66
Total foreign-born	552	19	1	572
Grand total	1,034	36	1	1,071

a "Other races" includes races having less than 10 representatives of this sex and age and pupils whose race is not reported.

TABLE 4.—*Race and grade, by age—Number of pupils of each specified age in each grade, by sex and by general nativity and race of father of pupil*—Continued.

GIRLS: AGE 6 YEARS.

General nativity and race of father of pupil.	Kindergarten.	Elementary grades.			Ungraded and special schools.	Total.
		1.	2.	3.		
Native-born:						
White..	170	707	20	1	2	900
Negro..	6	18	1	....	....	25
Total native-born......................	176	725	21	1	2	925
Foreign-born:						
Bohemian and Moravian..................	5	12	....	....	....	17
Canadian, French...........................	5	28	....	....	....	33
Canadian, Other.............................	39	155	1	....	....	195
English..	7	58	1	....	....	66
French...	2	9	....	....	....	11
German..	83	258	3	....	....	344
Hebrew, German..............................	2	11	....	....	....	13
Hebrew, Russian..............................	10	72	3	....	....	85
Hebrew, Other.................................	....	17	....	....	....	17
Irish...	13	16	....	....	....	29
Italian, North..................................	14	17	1	....	....	32
Italian, South..................................	2	10	....	....	1	13
Magyar...	5	5	....	....	....	10
Polish...	36	56	....	....	....	92
Scotch..	9	25	....	....	....	34
Other races[a]..................................	12	19	....	....	....	36
Total foreign-born.....................	244	768	9	....	1	1,022
Grand total..................................	420	1,493	30	1	3	1,947

[a] "Other races" includes races having less than 10 representatives of this sex and age and pupils whose race is not reported.

GIRLS: AGE 7 YEARS.

General nativity and race of father of pupil.	Kindergarten.	Elementary grades.			Ungraded and special schools.	Total.
		1.	2.	3.		
Native-born:						
White..	2	492	422	40	1	957
Negro..	....	18	8	....	....	26
Total native-born......................	2	510	430	40	1	983
Foreign-born:						
Bohemian and Moravian..................	....	8	4	c	....	12
Canadian, French...........................	....	16	12	....	....	28
Canadian, Other.............................	....	115	83	11	....	209
English..	2	37	29	1	....	69
Flemish..	....	9	4	....	....	13
French...	....	8	5	....	....	13
German..	4	236	158	7	1	406
Hebrew, German..............................	....	8	11	4	....	23
Hebrew, Russian..............................	....	54	33	4	....	91
Hebrew, Other.................................	1	8	4	4	1	18
Irish...	....	12	9	2	....	23
Italian, North..................................	....	14	8	1	....	23
Italian, South..................................	....	10	4	1	1	16
Polish...	7	71	15	....	....	93
Scotch..	1	10	12	2	....	25
Other races[a]..................................	2	18	12	....	....	32
Total foreign-born.....................	17	632	402	37	3	1,091
Grand total..................................	19	1,144	833	77	4	2,077

[a] "Other races" includes races having less than 10 representatives of this sex and age and pupils whose race is not reported.

TABLE 4.—*Race and grade, by age—Number of pupils of each specified age in each grade, by sex and by general nativity and race of father of pupil*—Continued.

GIRLS: AGE 8 YEARS.

General nativity and race of father of pupil.	Kin-der-gar-ten.	Elementary grades.					Un-graded and special schools.	Total.
		1.	2.	3.	4.	5.		
Native-born:								
White		108	398	383	32		2	923
Negro		12	12	2				26
Total native-born		120	410	385	32		2	949
Foreign-born:								
Bohemian and Moravian			5	5				10
Canadian, French		7	13	10	2			32
Canadian, Other		37	94	88	6		1	226
Dutch		2	8	5				15
English		12	45	36	4			97
German		91	187	106	4	1	1	390
Hebrew, German		3	6	6	2			17
Hebrew, Russian		19	46	24	3			92
Hebrew, Other		1	7	9	2	1	2	22
Irish		2	12	13				27
Italian, North		8	17	6				31
Italian, South		6	4					10
Polish	1	55	45	8				109
Scotch		7	14	16	3			40
Other races a		12	24	13	1			50
Total foreign-born	1	262	527	345	27	2	4	1,168
Grand total	1	382	937	730	59	2	6	2,117

a "Other races" includes races having less than 10 representatives of this sex and age and pupils whose race is not reported.

GIRLS: AGE 9 YEARS.

General nativity and race of father of pupil.	Elementary grades.					Un-graded and special schools.	Total.
	1.	2.	3.	4.	5.		
Native-born:							
White	25	158	408	276	30	1	898
Negro	2	4	14	3	1		24
Total native-born	27	162	422	279	31	1	922
Foreign-born:							
Bohemian and Moravian		4	8	1			13
Canadian, French	4	6	20	7	1		38
Canadian, Other	7	24	105	58	2		196
Dutch		2	3	4	1		10
English		12	39	25	4		80
Flemish	1	1	4	4			10
French	2	1	10	4	1		18
German	21	81	197	100	13	1	413
Hebrew, German		1	5	4	3		13
Hebrew, Russian	5	23	28	18	1	1	76
Hebrew, Other	1	2	8	9	2		22
Irish		5	14	5			24
Italian, North	2	3	7	5	1		18
Italian, South	2	5	5			1	13
Polish	27	26	15	2			70
Scotch	1	8	19	12			40
Other races a	3	12	17	9			41
Total foreign-born	76	213	504	267	29	3	1,092
Grand total	103	378	926	546	60	4	2,017

a "Other races" includes races having less than 10 representatives of this sex and age and pupils whose race is not reported.

TABLE 4.—*Race and grade, by age—Number of pupils of each specified age in each grade, by sex and by general nativity and race of father of pupil*—Continued.

GIRLS: AGE 10 YEARS.

General nativity and race of father of pupil.	Kindergarten.	Elementary grades.							Ungraded and special schools.	Total.
		1.	2.	3.	4.	5.	6.	7.		
Native-born:										
White		7	46	210	386	250	23		2	924
Negro		1	3	11	19	4		1		39
Total native-born		8	49	221	405	254	23	1	2	963
Foreign-born:										
Bohemian and Moravian			1	5	8	4				18
Canadian, French		2	4	19	14	6	1			46
Canadian, Other		1	13	49	95	44	7			209
Danish			1	2	3	5	1			12
Dutch		1	1	2	8	1				13
English	2	1	6	24	28	27	1			89
French				5	6	2				13
German		6	38	106	164	80	9		3	406
Hebrew, German		1		1	6	4	2			14
Hebrew, Polish				3	7	4	2			16
Hebrew, Russian		3	14	35	17	17				86
Hebrew, Other		1		1	2	4				8
Irish		1	1	6	15	6				29
Italian, North		4	2	3		3				14
Magyar		4	2	3		2				11
Polish		3	17	10	5	2		1	1	39
Scotch		1	2	12	16	11	3			45
Other races *a*		6	9	10	7	3				35
Total foreign-born	2	35	111	296	403	225	26	1	4	1,103
Grand total	2	43	160	517	808	479	49	2	6	2,066

a "Other races" includes races having less than 10 representatives of this sex and age and pupils whose race is not reported.

GIRLS: AGE 11 YEARS.

General nativity and race of father of pupil.	Elementary grades.								Ungraded and special schools.	Total.
	1.	2.	3.	4.	5.	6.	7.	8.		
Native-born:										
White		11	85	215	344	202	31	2		890
Negro	2	3	5	11	4	4				29
Total native-born	2	14	90	226	348	206	31	2		919
Foreign-born:										
Bohemian and Moravian			2	9	7	2				20
Canadian, French		1	3	8	8	4				24
Canadian, Other	1	6	23	73	92	37	5			237
English			8	19	35	26	2			90
Flemish		1	2	4	2	1			1	11
French		1	3	3	8	2				17
German	2	10	39	116	135	62	10	2	2	378
Hebrew, German	2		3	2	4	6	1			18
Hebrew, Russian	1	9	10	25	24	6	2			77
Hebrew, Other			1	4	7	2				14
Irish			7	7	19	8	2		1	44
Italian, South	3	1	3		2	1				10
Polish	4	10	4	6	5	1				30
Scotch			5	8	13	12	1			39
Other races *a*	1	5	11	13	16	4				50
Total foreign-born	14	44	124	297	377	174	23	2	4	1,059
Grand total	16	58	214	524	726	380	54	4	4	1,978

a "Other races" includes races having less than 10 representatives of his sex and age and pupils whose race is not reported.

TABLE **4.**—*Race and grade, by age—Number of pupils of each specified age in each grade, by sex and by general nativity and race of father of pupil*—Continued.

GIRLS: AGE 12 YEARS.

General nativity and race of father of pupil.	Elementary grades.								Ungraded and special schools.	Total.
	1.	2.	3.	4.	5.	6.	7.	8.		
Native-born:										
White		3	21	110	235	275	191	34	1	872
Negro			5	9	8	5	2			29
Total native-born		3	26	119	243	280	193	34	1	901
Foreign-born:										
Bohemian and Moravian		1		4	9	6	2	1		23
Canadian, French			5	12	5	8	3	1		34
Canadian, Other			8	33	66	66	48	4	1	228
English			5	15	25	39	15	2		102
French		2	3	6	9	3	2			25
German		3	24	56	115	132	68	7	1	406
Hebrew, German				4	3	7	3	1		18
Hebrew, Polish			1	3	3	1	1	1		10
Hebrew, Russian	4	1	17	16	20	13	11	2		86
Hebrew, Other				3	3	2	4	1		13
Irish			1	5	12	12	1	1		32
Italian, North	1	1	4	6	2					14
Italian, South	2	1		3	3	4	1			14
Polish		1	3	4	2	4				14
Scotch			1	3	9	17	14	1		45
Other races *a*	1	1	4	10	15	10	9			50
Total foreign-born	8	11	76	183	301	324	182	22	2	1,114
Grand total	8	14	102	302	544	604	375	56	3	2,015

a "Other races" includes races having less than 10 representatives of this sex and age and pupils whose race is not reported.

GIRLS: AGE 13 YEARS.

General nativity and race of father of pupil.	Elementary grades.								High school.		Ungraded and special schools.	Total.
	1.	2.	3.	4.	5.	6.	7.	8.	First. year.	Second year.		
Native-born:												
White		1	9	47	117	222	278	145	27	1	2	849
Negro			2	2	6	5	7	1				23
Total native-born		1	11	49	123	227	285	146	27	1	2	872
Foreign-born:												
Bohemian and Moravian				2		2	8	2				14
Canadian, French			1	3	8	3	5	2				22
Canadian, Other			8	12	71	57	55	29	6			238
English			1	8	17	35	33	13		1	1	109
French	1					8	3					12
German		2	7	34	59	93	92	51	4		2	344
Hebrew, German					3	2	9	3				17
Hebrew, Polish				5		1		4				10
Hebrew, Russian	1	2	6	10	14	12	5	4	2			56
Hebrew, Other					4	2	3					9
Irish				3	5	9	9	6	2			34
Italian, North		2	2	1	2	1	2					10
Polish			1	4	4	3	2		1		1	16
Scotch				1	7	11	16	9	4			48
Other races *a*			1	4	7	6	6	6	1		1	32
Total foreign-born	2	6	27	87	201	245	248	129	20	1	5	971
Grand total	2	7	38	136	324	472	533	275	47	2	7	1,843

a "Other races" includes races having less than 10 representatives of this sex and age and pupils whose race is not reported.

Table 1.—*Race and grade, by age—Number of pupils of each specified age in each grade, by sex and by general nativity and race of father of pupil*—Continued.

GIRLS: AGE 14 YEARS.

General nativity and race of father of pupil.	1.	2.	3.	4.	5.	6.	7.	8.	First year.	Second year.	Third year.	Ungraded and special schools.	Total.
Native-born:													
White		1	3	11	40	110	183	230	105	22	2	2	709
Negro				1	4	7	5	2					19
Indian									1				1
Total native-born		1	3	12	44	117	188	232	106	22	2	2	729
Foreign-born:													
Canadian, French				1	6	8	11	5	2	1			34
Canadian, Other			3	1	19	37	36	49	24	10			179
English				3	9	9	22	24	13	1			81
German	1			3	15	32	50	77	15	7	1	1	202
Hebrew, German						3	6	5	3	2			19
Hebrew, Russian	1	2	2	4	4	5	11	7	4	2			42
Irish					2	4	5	7	5	1			24
Polish			1		3	3	2		3				12
Scotch				1	3	5	4	10	6	3			32
Other races a	1		3	2	6	10	16	14	6	1	1		59
Total foreign-born	3	2	9	15	67	116	163	198	81	28	2	1	684
Grand total	3	3	12	27	111	233	351	430	187	50	3	3	1,413

a "Other races" includes races having less than 10 representatives of this sex and age and pupils whose race is not reported.

GIRLS: AGE 15 YEARS.

General nativity and race of father of pupil.	2.	3.	4.	5.	6.	7.	8.	First year.	Second year.	Third year.	Fourth year.	Ungraded and special schools.	Total.
Native-born:													
White	1		4	10	22	70	130	145	88	16	3	1	490
Negro					2	4	5	3	2			1	17
Indian								1					1
Total native-born	1		4	10	24	74	135	149	90	16	3	2	508
Foreign-born:													
Canadian, French			1	1	1	3	5	3	2				16
Canadian, Other				5	9	30	43	35	20	1			143
English				3	3	7	16	14	9	2	1		55
German				1	7	13	41	36	16	7			121
Hebrew, German					1		5	4		3			13
Hebrew, Polish			1				4	1	4	1			11
Hebrew, Russian		1		2		3	3	4	2		1		16
Irish				1	4	3	3	4	6				21
Scotch			2		1	6	9	8	7				33
Other races a			2	1	3	7	5	4	5	1		1	29
Total foreign-born		1	5	15	29	72	134	113	71	15	2	1	458
Grand total	1	1	9	25	53	146	269	262	161	31	5	3	966

a "Other races" includes races having less than 10 representatives of this sex and age and pupils whose race is not reported.

TABLE 4.—*Race and grade, by age—Number of pupils of each specified age in each grade, by sex and by general nativity and race of father of pupil—Continued.*

GIRLS: AGE 16 YEARS.

General nativity and race of father of pupil.	Elementary grades.				High school.				Un-graded and special schools.	Total.
	5.	6.	7.	8.	First year.	Second year.	Third year.	Fourth year.		
Native-born:										
White	1	3	25	39	90	86	56	16	3	319
Negro	1	1	1	....	1	2	3	......	......	9
Total native-born	2	4	26	39	91	88	59	16	3	328
Foreign-born:										
Canadian, French	....	....	1	1	4	3	1	1	....	11
Canadian, Other	6	1	4	18	18	24	12	3	....	86
English	1	1	2	5	10	6	5	3	1	34
German	....	1	2	6	16	19	13	2	....	59
Hebrew (not specified)	2	....	....	2	5	3	3	1	....	16
Irish	....	1	2	....	4	4	6	......	....	17
Scotch	....	....	....	2	8	7	2	1	....	20
Other races [a]	1	....	....	2	6	5	2	......	....	16
Total foreign-born	10	4	11	36	71	71	44	11	1	259
Grand total	12	8	37	75	162	159	103	27	4	587

[a] "Other races" includes races having less than 10 representatives of this sex and age and pupils whose race is not reported.

GIRLS: AGE 17 YEARS.

General nativity and race of father of pupil.	Elementary grades.			High school.				Un-graded and special schools.	Total.
	6.	7.	8.	First year.	Second year.	Third year.	Fourth year.		
Native-born:									
White	1	4	5	31	55	81	48	1	226
Negro	....	....	1	2	6	2	......	....	11
Total native-born	1	4	6	33	61	83	48	1	237
Foreign-born:									
Canadian (other than French)	....	1	1	8	15	18	10	....	53
English	....	....	....	4	5	3	9	....	21
German	....	....	2	....	3	14	6	....	25
Hebrew (other foreign)	1	....	....	....	2	3	8	....	14
Irish	....	....	1	2	....	4	4	....	11
Scotch	....	....	1·	2	3	5	2	....	13
Other races [a]	....	....	1	1	1	2	2	....	7
Total foreign-born	1	1	6	17	29	49	41	....	144
Grand total	2	5	12	50	90	132	89	1	381

[a] "Other races" includes races having less than 10 representatives of this sex and age and pupils whose race is not reported.

TABLE 4.—*Race and grade, by age—Number of pupils of each specified age in each grade, by sex and by general nativity and race of father of pupil—Continued.*

GIRLS: AGE 18 YEARS.

General nativity and race of father of pupil.	Elementary grade 8.	High school.				Total.
		First year.	Second year.	Third year.	Fourth year.	
Native-born:						
White	1	8	23	49	64	145
Negro				1		1
Total native-born	1	8	23	50	64	146
Foreign-born:						
Canadian (other than French)	1	1	5	15	14	36
English			4	1	5	10
German			4	4	7	15
Other races a			2	5	7	14
Total foreign-born	1	1	15	25	33	75
Grand total	2	9	38	75	97	221

a "Other races" includes races having less than 10 representatives of this sex and age and pupils whose race is not reported.

GIRLS: AGE 19 YEARS.

General nativity and race of father of pupil.	High school.				Total.
	First year.	Second year.	Third year.	Fourth year.	
Native-born:					
White	2	4	15	31	52
Negro		1		1	2
Total native-born	2	5	15	32	54
Foreign-born:					
Canadian (other than French)		3	4	13	20
Other races a	1	1	7	11	20
Total foreign-born	1	4	11	24	40
Grand total	3	9	26	56	94

GIRLS: AGE 20 YEARS.

Native-born:					
White			3	8	11
Negro				1	1
Total native-born			3	9	12
Foreign-born, Other races a	2	1		10	13
Grand total	2	1	3	19	25

a "Other races" includes races having less than 10 representatives of this sex and age and pupils whose race is not reported.

TABLE 5.—*Race distribution in each grade—Percentages.*

[This table shows in detail only races with 100 or more pupils reporting. The totals, however, are for all races.]

General nativity and race of father of pupil	Kinder-garten	Elementary grades.									High school.					Un-graded and special schools.	Grand total.
		1.	2.	3.	4.	5.	6.	7.	8.	Total.	First year.	Second year.	Third year.	Fourth year.	Total.		
Native born:																	
White	44.0	41.5	43.5	43.7	43.5	44.2	47.3	50.1	50.6	44.6	55.3	55.6	58.4	56.0	56.1	23.5	45.4
Negro	.8	1.3	1.1	1.3	1.6	1.2	1.4	1.2	.9	1.3	.6	1.3	.8	.4	.8	3.0	1.2
Indian	.0	.0	(a)	.0	.0	.0	.0	.0	.0	(a)	(a)	.0	.0	.0	(a)	.0	(a)
Total native-born	44.9	42.8	44.6	45.0	45.1	45.4	48.7	51.3	51.5	45.9	55.9	56.9	59.2	56.4	56.9	26.5	46.6
Foreign-born:																	
Bohemian and Moravian	.7	.6	.9	.6	.8	.9	.7	.8	.4	.7	.3	.1	.4	.6	.3	.0	.7
Canadian, French	1.5	1.7	1.5	1.8	1.7	1.5	1.5	1.4	1.2	1.6	1.1	.9	1.0	.6	.9	2.7	1.5
Canadian, Other	9.4	10.0	9.9	10.9	12.0	12.5	12.2	11.9	12.2	11.2	12.6	14.3	14.0	14.9	13.6	5.0	11.3
Danish	.3	.2	.2	.3	.3	.3	.4	.4	.3	.3	.4	.2	.4		.3	.0	.3
Dutch	.7	.3	.5	.5	.7	.3	.2	.3	.5	.4	.4		.1		.2	.0	.4
English	3.7	3.2	3.9	4.5	4.7	5.2	5.4	5.4	5.2	4.5	4.6	5.9	4.7	6.8	5.3	3.0	4.5
French	.6	.5	.7	.8	.7	.8	.7	.6	.4	.7	.7	.3	.0	.4	.6	.3	.7
Flemish	.3	.5	.5	.3	.7	.8	.2	.2	.1	.4	.0	.3	.0	.0	.1	.3	.4
German	19.7	19.4	19.4	19.6	20.2	20.0	18.4	17.0	17.8	19.2	11.9	9.6	9.6	10.2	10.6	24.5	18.6
Hebrew, German	.4	.8	1.0	.7	.8	.9	1.1	1.2	1.4	.9	1.5	1.9	2.5	1.7	1.8	.7	1.0
Hebrew, Polish	.1	.8	.9	.3	.8	.3	.4	.3	1.1	.5	.6	1.8	1.3	2.3	2.0	2.0	.8
Hebrew, Russian	1.6	4.6	5.1	4.9	3.7	3.3	3.0	2.3	1.4	3.9	2.3	1.8	1.3	2.3	2.1	2.3	3.5
Hebrew, Other	.3	.3	.3	.4	.3	.6	.4	.5	.2	.4	.2	.1		.2	.1	.1	.2
Irish	2.0	1.2	1.2	1.8	1.3	2.1	1.6	1.6	1.8	1.5	2.2	2.1	2.7	1.9	2.2	1.3	1.6
Italian, North	3.2	1.6	1.4	1.2	1.8	.4	.3	.3	.2	.9	.2	.0	.0	.0	.1	3.7	1.0
Italian, South	.8	1.1	.8	.4	.3	.2		.2	.1	.5	.1	.1	.0	.0	.1	3.0	.5
Magyar	.5	.5	.3	.4	.3	.2		.1	.1	.2	.1	.1	.3		.1		.2
Polish	5.5	7.5	4.5	1.9	1.5	1.1	.9	.5	.1	2.9	1.0	1.5	.1	.4	.5	24.8	3.0
Scotch	1.8	1.2	1.5	2.1	2.0	2.0	2.7	2.6	2.7	2.0	3.0	3.5	2.3	1.7	2.8	1.0	2.0
Swedish	1.2	1.2	1.2	1.4	.5	.3	.3	.4	.9	.3	.2	.2	.0	.2	.8	.3	.3
Other races	2.1	1.3	1.4	1.4	.9	1.0	.7	.9	.9	1.1	.9	.9	.3	1.1	.8	1.0	1.2
Total foreign-born	55.1	57.2	55.4	55.0	54.9	54.6	51.3	48.7	48.5	54.1	44.0	43.1	40.8	43.6	43.1	73.5	53.4
Grand total	100.0	100.0	100.0	100.0	100.0	100.0	100.0	100.0	100.0	100.0	100.0	100.0	100.0	100.0	100.0	100.0	100.0

a Less than 0.05 per cent.

Table 6.—*Grade distribution of each race—Percentages.*

[This table shows in detail only races with 100 or more pupils reporting. The totals, however, are for all races.]

General nativity and race of father of pupil.	Kinder-garten.	Elementary grades.									High school.					Ungraded and special schools.	Grand total.
		1.	2.	3.	4.	5.	6.	7.	8.	Total.	First year.	Second year.	Third year.	Fourth year.	Total.		
Native-born:																	
White	7.0	14.5	11.7	12.2	11.1	10.5	8.9	7.8	5.6	82.3	4.0	2.7	2.1	1.5	10.4	0.4	100
Negro	5.0	17.0	11.2	13.3	15.3	10.6	9.9	6.8	3.7	87.8	1.5	2.3	1.2	.4	5.4	1.8	100
Indian	(a)	(a)	(a)	(a)	(a)	(a)	(a)	(a)	(a)	(a)	(a)	(a)	(a)	(a)	(a)	(a)	(a)
Total native-born	7.0	14.5	11.7	12.2	11.2	10.5	9.0	7.8	5.5	82.4	4.0	2.6	2.1	1.5	10.2	.4	100
Foreign-born:																	
Bohemian and Moravian	7.2	13.0	15.8	11.3	14.4	14.4	8.9	8.2	3.1	89.0	1.4	.3	1.0	1.0	3.8		100
Canadian, French	7.2	17.7	11.6	15.2	12.8	10.5	8.4	6.7	3.8	86.6	2.3	1.2	1.1	.5	5.0	1.2	100
Canadian, Other	6.1	14.1	10.7	12.2	11.5	12.0	9.2	7.5	5.4	83.5	3.7	2.7	2.1	1.6	10.1	.3	100
Danish	6.4	10.4	9.6	12.8	12.8	13.6	12.0	8.8	4.8	84.8	4.8	1.6	2.4	.0	8.8		100
Dutch	12.4	9.6	15.6	14.1	19.8	8.5	5.1	5.6	5.6	84.2	2.8	.9	.6	.0	3.4	.5	100
English	6.0	11.3	11.5	12.6	12.0	12.6	10.3	8.5	5.8	88.6	3.4	2.9	1.7	.9	9.8	.5	100
French	6.4	18.2	15.9	14.9	11.5	12.2	8.8	6.4	3.0	86.5	3.4	1.0	1.7	.7	6.8	.3	100
Flemish	6.6	23.8	12.7	10.6	22.5	7.3	5.3	4.0	1.3	90.7	.0	2.0	.0	.7	2.0	.7	100
German	7.7	16.5	12.7	13.4	12.6	11.6	8.5	6.5	4.8	86.6	2.1	1.1	.9	.7	4.8	.9	100
Hebrew, German	2.6	13.7	12.0	9.1	10.1	10.3	10.1	8.7	7.0	81.0	5.0	4.3	4.3	2.2	15.9	.5	100
Hebrew, Polish	1.1	11.2	11.2	8.1	17.6	13.8	6.9	4.8	12.8	86.2	4.8	3.7	1.6	2.1	12.2	.5	100
Hebrew, Russian	3.3	20.6	17.5	17.5	12.1	10.1	7.2	4.6	2.1	91.6	2.2	1.6	1.3	.8	4.7	.4	100
Hebrew, Other	2.5	8.9	9.6	15.9	14.6	16.6	6.6	8.9	5.7	89.8	2.6	.6	.6	.6	3.2	4.5	100
Irish	8.8	12.0	9.1	13.8	9.5	13.8	8.5	7.1	5.5	79.3	4.5	2.7	2.7	1.4	11.4	.6	100
Italian, North	23.3	25.2	16.9	15.7	9.8	4.5	1.2	1.9	.7	76.0	.7	.0	.0	.0	.7		100
Italian, South	11.2	34.0	19.1	9.3	6.0	5.1	5.6	2.3	2.3	83.7	.0	.0	.0	.0		5.1	100
Magyar	14.7	32.4	14.7	20.6	2.0	8.8		2.9	2.0	83.3	1.0	1.0	.0	.0	2.0		100
Polish	13.4	39.6	18.1	8.0	5.9	3.9	2.6	1.1	.2	79.4	1.1	.1	.1	.2	1.4	5.8	100
Scotch	6.5	9.7	9.1	13.5	11.6	10.5	11.2	9.3	6.6	81.6	4.9	3.7	1.9	1.0	11.6	.3	100
Swedish	4.4	12.3	8.8	10.5	21.1	14.0	8.8	10.5	3.5	89.5	2.6	1.8		.9	5.3	.9	100
Other races	13.3	17.7	14.3	15.1	9.3	9.5	5.4	5.2	3.8	80.3	2.6	1.6	.4	1.2	5.8	.6	100
Total foreign-born	7.5	17.0	12.6	13.0	11.9	11.0	8.2	6.5	4.6	84.8	2.7	1.7	1.3	1.0	6.8	1.0	100
Grand total	7.3	15.8	12.2	12.6	11.6	10.8	8.6	7.1	5.0	83.7	3.3	2.2	1.7	1.2	8.4	.7	100

a Not computed, owing to small number involved.

PUBLIC SCHOOL TEACHERS IN ELEMENTARY GRADES AND KINDERGARTENS.

TABLE 1.—*Number of teachers in each grade, by sex and general nativity and race.*

MALE.

[This table does not include 8 teachers not reporting complete data.]

General nativity and race.	Kindergarten.	Elementary grades.										Total kindergarten and elementary.
		1.	2.	3.	4.	5.	6.	7.	8.	Ungraded and special.	Total.	
Native-born of native father, White										3	3	3
Native-born of foreign father, by race of father:												
Canadian, French							1			1	2	2
German										1	1	1
Total							1			2	3	3
Grand total							1			5	6	6

FEMALE.

General nativity and race.	Kindergarten.	Elementary grades.										Total kindergarten and elementary.
		1.	2.	3.	4.	5.	6.	7.	8.	Ungraded and special.	Total.	
Native-born of native father:												
White	48	101	77	95	77	72	66	49	45	10	592	640
Negro				1	1						2	2
Total	48	101	77	96	78	72	66	49	45	10	594	642
Native-born of foreign father, by race of father:												
Bohemian and Moravian				2							2	2
Canadian, French							1				1	1
Canadian, Other	3	20	16	6	13	4	8	6	4		77	80
Danish								2			2	2
Dutch							1				1	1
English	4	10	20	14	21	21	14	12	6		118	122
French		1	2		1	1	1	2	2		10	10
German	6	19	23	22	13	10	11	7	14	2	121	127
Hebrew, German			1	2	4	2		1	2		12	12
Hebrew, Russian		1	2			2					5	5
Irish	1	35	28	30	28	22	15	24	19	2	203	204
Mexican	1										1	1
Scotch	5	6	8	12	13	10	10	5	3	2	69	74
Scotch-Irish				1				2		2	5	5
Swedish								2			2	2
Welsh		1				2	1				4	4
Total	20	93	100	87	95	74	62	63	50	8	632	652
Total native-born	68	194	177	183	173	146	128	112	95	18	1,226	1,294
Foreign-born:												
Canadian, French										1	1	1
Canadian, Other	1	11	6	5	4	6	5	3	2		42	43
English	3	3	2	5	1	4	1	3	5		24	27
French				2							2	2
German		2		1	2						5	5
Hebrew, German							1				1	1
Hebrew, Russian	1										1	1
Irish	1	1	4	2		3	2	3	2		17	18
Scotch	3	4	6	3	4	3	3	7	2		32	35
Scotch-Irish			1								1	1
Welsh							2				2	2
Total foreign-born	9	21	19	18	11	16	14	16	11	1	127	136
Grand total	77	215	196	201	184	162	142	128	106	19	1,353	1,430

Table 1.—*Number of teachers in each grade, by sex and general nativity and race*—Contd.

TOTAL.

General nativity and race.	Kindergarten.	Elementary grades. 1.	2.	3.	4.	5.	6.	7.	8.	Ungraded and special.	Total.	Total kindergarten and elementary.	Race distribution. Percentages. Elementary.	Elementary and kindergarten.
Native-born of native father:														
White	48	101	77	95	77	72	66	49	45	13	595	643	43.8	44.8
Negro				1	1						2	2	.1	.1
Total	48	101	77	96	78	72	66	49	45	13	597	645	43.9	44.9
Native-born of foreign father, by race of father:														
Bohemian and Moravian					2						2	2	.1	.1
Canadian, French							1	1		1	3	3	.2	.2
Canadian, Other	3	20	16	6	13	4	8	6	4		77	80	5.7	5.6
Danish						2					2	2	.1	.1
Dutch							1				1	1	.1	.1
English	4	10	20	14	21	21	14	12	6		118	122	8.7	8.5
French		1	2		1	1	1	2	2		10	10	.7	.7
German	6	19	23	22	13	10	11	7	14	3	122	128	9.0	8.9
Hebrew, German			1	2	4	2		1	2		12	12	.9	.8
Hebrew, Russian		1	2			2					5	5	.4	.3
Irish	1	35	28	30	28	22	15	24	19	2	203	204	14.9	14.2
Mexican	1											1		.1
Scotch	5	6	8	12	13	10	10	5	3	2	69	74	5.1	5.2
Scotch-Irish				1				2		2	5	5	.4	.3
Swedish								2			2	2	.1	.1
Welsh		1					2	1			4	4	.3	.3
Total	20	93	100	87	95	74	63	63	50	10	635	655	46.7	45.6
Total native-born	68	194	177	183	173	146	129	112	95	23	1,232	1,300	90.7	90.5
Foreign-born:														
Canadian, French										1	1	1	.1	.1
Canadian, Other	1	11	6	5	4	6	5	3	2		42	43	3.1	3.0
English	3	3	2	5	1	4	1	3	5		24	27	1.8	1.9
French				2							2	2	.1	.1
German		2		1	2						5	5	.4	.3
Hebrew, German							1				1	1	.1	.1
Hebrew, Russian	1											1		.1
Irish	1	1	4	2		3	2	3	2		17	18	1.3	1.3
Scotch	3	4	6	3	4	3	3	7	2		32	35	2.4	2.4
Scotch-Irish				1							1	1	.1	.1
Welsh							2				2	2	.1	.1
Total foreign-born	9	21	19	18	11	16	14	16	11	1	127	136	9.3	9.5
Grand total	77	215	196	201	184	162	143	128	106	24	1,359	1,436	100.0	100.0

TABLE 2.—*Number of teachers engaged in teaching each specified number of years, by sex and general nativity and race.*

MALE.

[This table does not include 14 teachers not reporting complete data.]

General nativity and race.	Under 5 years.	5 to 9 years.	10 to 14 years.	15 to 19 years.	20 to 24 years.	25 to 29 years.	30 years or over.	Total.
Native-born of native father, White...	....	....	2	....	1	....	....	3
Native-born of foreign father, by race of father:								
Canadian, French..............	....	....	1	....	1	....	....	2
German.....................	....	....	1	....	....	....	....	1
Total...............	....	....	2	....	1	....	....	3
Grand total..........	....	....	4	....	2	....	....	6

FEMALE.

General nativity and race.	Under 5 years.	5 to 9 years.	10 to 14 years.	15 to 19 years.	20 to 24 years.	25 to 29 years.	30 years or over.	Total.
Native-born of native father:								
White............................	133	189	109	91	52	36	29	639
Negro............................	1	....	....	1	....	....	....	2
Total......................	134	189	109	92	52	36	29	641
Native-born of foreign father, by race of father:								
Bohemian and Moravian.........	2	....	....	....	....	....	....	2
Canadian, French...............	....	....	....	....	1	....	....	1
Canadian, Other................	26	26	19	6	3	....	....	80
Danish.........................	....	....	2	....	....	....	....	2
Dutch..........................	....	....	....	1	....	....	....	1
English........................	23	19	29	16	13	9	9	118
French.........................	2	....	....	1	3	....	2	10
German.........................	28	41	16	26	12	2	2	127
Hebrew, German.................	5	2	3	2	....	....	....	12
Hebrew, Russian................	1	2	....	....	2	....	....	5
Irish..........................	39	59	35	34	8	16	12	203
Mexican........................	1	....	....	....	....	....	....	1
Scotch.........................	19	21	9	10	9	....	6	74
Scotch-Irish...................	....	2	2	....	1	....	....	5
Swedish........................	....	2	....	....	....	....	....	2
Welsh..........................	1	....	1	....	....	....	2	4
Total......................	147	174	118	96	52	27	33	647
Total native-born..............	281	363	227	188	104	63	62	1,288
Foreign-born:								
Canadian. French...............	1	....	....	....	....	....	....	1
Canadian, Other................	13	17	2	1	8	2	....	43
English........................	1	7	6	4	4	1	4	27
French.........................	....	2	....	....	....	....	....	2
German.........................	2	1	....	2	....	....	....	5
Hebrew, German.................	....	....	1	....	....	....	....	1
Hebrew, Russian................	....	....	1	....	....	....	....	1
Irish..........................	2	1	2	2	4	5	2	18
Scotch.........................	3	8	6	12	4	1	1	35
Scotch-Irish...................	....	....	....	....	1	....	....	1
Welsh..........................	....	....	....	....	....	2	....	2
Total foreign-born..............	22	36	18	21	21	11	7	136
Grand total.................	303	399	245	209	125	74	69	1,424

TABLE 2.—*Number of teachers engaged in teaching each specified number of years, by sex and general nativity and race*—Continued.

TOTAL.

General nativity and race.	Under 5 years.	5 to 9 years.	10 to 14 years.	15 to 19 years.	20 to 24 years.	25 to 29 years.	30 years or over.	Total.
Native-born of native father:								
White	133	189	111	91	53	36	29	642
Negro	1			1				2
Total	134	189	111	92	53	36	29	644
Native-born of foreign father, by race of father:								
Bohemian and Moravian	2							2
Canadian, French			1		2			3
Canadian, Other	26	26	19	6	3			80
Danish			2					2
Dutch				1				1
English	23	19	29	16	13	9	9	118
French	2		2	1	3		2	10
German	28	41	17	26	12	2	2	128
Hebrew, German	5	2	3	2				12
Hebrew, Russian	1	2			2			5
Irish	39	59	35	34	8	16	12	203
Mexican	1							1
Scotch	19	21	9	10	9		6	74
Scotch-Irish		2	2		1			5
Swedish		2						2
Welsh	1		1				2	4
Total	147	174	120	96	53	27	33	650
Total native-born	281	363	231	188	106	63	62	1,294
Foreign-born:								
Canadian, French	1							1
Canadian, Other	13	17	2	1	8	2		43
English	1	7	6	4	4	1	4	27
French		2						2
German	2	1		2				5
Hebrew, German			1					1
Hebrew, Russian			1					1
Irish	2	1	2	2	4	5	2	18
Scotch	3	8	6	12	4	1	1	35
Scotch-Irish					1			1
Welsh						2		2
Total foreign-born	22	36	18	21	21	11	7	136
Grand total	303	399	249	209	127	74	69	1,430

PAROCHIAL SCHOOL PUPILS: GENERAL INVESTIGATION.

TABLE 1.—*Grade and age—Number of pupils of each age in each grade, by sex.*

BOYS.

Age in years.	Elementary grades.								
	1.	2.	3.	4.	5.	6.	7.	8.	Total.
4	8								8
5	58		5						63
6	227	11							238
7	420	78	9						507
8	348	307	75	7	1				738
9	170	298	250	68	6				792
10	121	202	332	221	69	12			957
11	52	126	203	303	217	73	2		976
12	28	74	140	258	297	213	78	3	1,091
13	8	49	79	157	221	195	153	44	906
14	1	8	13	29	45	56	72	59	283
15		1	4	3	4	7	33	41	93
16				1		2	5	11	19
17					1			1	2
18									
19									
20 or over									
Total	1,441	1,154	1,110	1,047	861	558	343	159	6,673

Age in years.	High school.					Commercial school.	Grand total.
	First year.	Second year.	Third year.	Fourth year.	Total.		
4							8
5							63
6							238
7							507
8							738
9							792
10							957
11							976
12							1,091
13	1				1	4	911
14	5	1			6	28	317
15	16	2			18	18	129
16	9	3			12	26	57
17	3	1			4	15	21
18			1	1	2		2
19							
20 or over							
Total	34	7	1	1	43	91	6,807

TABLE 1.—*Grade and age—Number of pupils of each age in each grade, by sex*—Contd.

GIRLS.

Age in years.	Elementary grades.								Total.
	1.	2.	3.	4.	5.	6.	7.	8.	
4	14								14
5	66								66
6	171	2							173
7	328	88	3						419
8	304	296	120	2	1				723
9	201	316	217	73	7				814
10	132	243	244	220	89	8	1		937
11	48	121	184	290	236	74	5	1	959
12	27	70	133	236	326	197	60	9	1,058
13	6	29	62	105	203	200	203	41	849
14		6	5	18	21	32	113	67	262
15		2			2	4	28	71	107
16							8	20	28
17								7	7
18			1				1		2
19									
20 or over									
Total	1,297	1,173	969	944	885	515	419	216	6,418

Age in years.	High school.					Grand total.
	First year.	Second year.	Third year.	Fourth year.	Total.	
4						14
5						66
6						173
7						419
8						723
9						814
10						937
11						959
12						1,058
13	2				2	851
14	20	2			22	284
15	48	12			60	167
16	22	23	8	1	54	82
17	12	16	16	6	50	57
18	4	5	5	14	28	30
19		1	1	6	8	8
20 or over						
Total	108	59	30	27	224	6,642

TABLE 1.—*Grade and age—Number of pupils of each age in each grade, by sex*—Contd.

TOTAL.

Age in years.	Elementary grades.								
	1.	2.	3.	4.	5.	6.	7.	8.	Total.
4	22								22
5	124		5						129
6	398	13							411
7	748	166	12						926
8	652	603	195	9	2				1,461
9	371	614	467	141	13				1,606
10	253	445	576	441	158	20	1		1,894
11	100	247	387	593	453	147	7	1	1,935
12	55	144	273	494	623	410	138	12	2,149
13	14	78	141	262	424	395	356	85	1,755
14	1	14	18	47	66	88	185	126	545
15		3	4	3	6	11	61	112	200
16				1		2	13	31	47
17					1			8	9
18			1				1		2
19									
20 or over									
Total	2,738	2,327	2,079	1,991	1,746	1,073	762	375	13,091

Age in years.	High school.					Commercial school.	Grand total.
	First year.	Second year.	Third year.	Fourth year.	Total.		
4							22
5							129
6							411
7							926
8							1,461
9							1,606
10							1,894
11							1,935
12							2,149
13	3				3	4	1,762
14	25	3			28	28	601
15	64	14			78	18	296
16	31	26	8	1	66	26	139
17	15	17	16	6	54	15	78
18	4	5	6	15	30		32
19		1	1	6	8		8
20 or over							
Total	142	66	31	28	267	91	13,449

TABLE 2.—Race, sex, and grade—Number of pupils by sex of each age in each grade, by general nativity and race of father of pupil.

General nativity and race of father of pupil.	Elementary grades.									High school.					Commercial school.	Grand total.
	1.	2.	3.	4.	5.	6.	7.	8.	Total.	First year.	Second year.	Third year.	Fourth year.	Total.		
Native-born:																
White:																
Male.	372	253	255	337	259	184	108	90	1,858	21	4		1	26	39	1,923
Female.	329	303	239	283	274	169	177	101	1,875	57	31	15	13	116		1,991
Total.	701	556	494	620	533	353	285	191	3,733	78	35	15	14	142	39	3,914
Negro, female.	1	2	1	1					5							5
Indian, male.		1							1							1
Total native-born—																
Male.	372	254	255	337	259	184	108	90	1,859	21	4		1	26	39	1,924
Female.	330	305	240	284	274	169	177	101	1,880	57	31	15	13	116		1,996
Total.	702	559	495	621	533	353	285	191	3,739	78	35	15	14	142	39	3,920
Foreign-born:																
Bohemian and Moravian—																
Male.	2	5	3	5	8		1	1	25						1	26
Female.	6	5	6	5	7	2	4		35							35
Total.	8	10	9	10	15	2	5	1	60						1	61
Canadian, French—																
Male.	57	17	42	27	47	12	11	1	214	1				1	1	216
Female.	59	23	40	53	29	15	13	4	236	4	4	1		9		245
Total.	116	40	82	80	76	27	24	5	450	5	4	1		10	1	461
Canadian, Other—																
Male.	26	28	22	35	24	30	19	10	194	2	2			4	5	203
Female.	27	21	21	38	33	19	16	23	198	12	5	2	4	23		221
Total.	53	49	43	73	57	49	35	33	392	14	7	2	4	27	5	424
Dutch—																
Male.	11	6	5	8	5	1	1	1	38						1	39
Female.	4	3	3	4	5	5	4	2	30							30
Total.	15	9	8	12	10	6	5	3	68						1	69
English—																
Male.	18	7	12	5	6	5	4	1	58	1				1		59
Female.	8	3	4	5	5	5	5	2	37		2			2		39
Total.	26	10	16	10	11	10	9	3	95	1	2			3		98
French—																
Male.	20	11	21	12	15	2	2		83	1				1	2	86
Female.	14	12	23	2	10	5	1	2	69	4	4			8		77
Total.	34	23	44	14	25	7	3	2	152	5	4			9	2	163
German—																
Male.	121	141	190	170	141	95	50	21	929						35	964
Female.	117	133	131	119	146	74	49	32	801	11	1	4	3	19		820
Total.	238	274	321	289	287	169	99	53	1,730	11	1	4	3	19	35	1,784

TABLE 2.—*Race, sex, and grade—Number of pupils by sex of each age in each grade, by general nativity and race of father of pupil*—Continued.

General nativity and race of father of pupil	Elementary grades.									High school.					Commercial school.	Grand total.
---	1.	2.	3.	4.	5.	6.	7.	8.	Total.	First year.	Second year.	Third year.	Fourth year.	Total.		
Foreign-born—Continued.																
Hebrew (not specified)—																
Male			9	1		2			12							12
Female			1			2			3	1				1		4
Total			10	1		4			15	1				1		16
Irish—																
Male	38	23	50	50	33	25	26	15	260	8	1	1		10	3	273
Female	35	33	42	29	45	33	35	23	275	13	10	6	7	36		311
Total	73	56	92	79	78	58	61	38	535	21	11	7	7	46	3	584
Italian, North—																
Male	11	9	15	11	5	2	1		54							54
Female	2	13	11	8	10	7			51	1	3			4		55
Total	13	22	26	19	15	9	1		105	1	3			4		109
Italian, South—																
Male	34	27	17	7		2	1		88							88
Female	36	16	5	5	6	2	1		71							71
Total	70	43	22	12	6	4	2		159							159
Magyar—																
Male	17	9	1						27							27
Female	6	6	5	2	1				20							20
Total	23	15	6	2	1				47							47
Polish—																
Male	705	612	453	373	314	197	116	19	2,789						2	2,791
Female	646	587	424	385	305	175	114	26	2,662	2				3		2,665
Total	1,351	1,199	877	758	619	372	230	45	5,451	2				3	2	5,456
Roumanian—																
Male			5						5							5
Female			6						6							6
Total			11						11							11
Scotch—																
Male		2	4	4	1	1	1	1	14						1	15
Female	2	3	2	1					8							8
Total	2	5	6	5	1	1	1	1	22						1	23
Syrian—																
Male	5								5							5
Female	3	4			2				9							9
Total	8	4			2				14							14

Other races— a																
Male	2	3	6	2	4		2		19	3				3	1	20
Female	4	6	5	4	6	2			27							30
Total	6	9	11	6	10	2	2		46	3				3	1	50
Total foreign-born—																
Male	1,069	900	855	710	602	374	235	69	4,814	13	3	1		17	52	4,883
Female	967	868	729	660	611	346	242	115	4,538	51	28	15	14	108		4,646
Total	2,036	1,768	1,584	1,370	1,213	720	477	184	9,352	64	31	16	14	125	52	9,529
Grand total—																
Male	1,441	1,154	1,110	1,047	861	558	343	159	6,673	34	7	1	1	43	91	6,807
Female	1,297	1,173	969	944	885	515	419	216	6,418	108	59	30	27	224		6,642
Total	2,738	2,327	2,079	1,991	1,746	1,073	762	375	13,091	142	66	31	28	267	91	13,449

a "Other races" includes races having less than 10 representatives in this city and pupils whose race is not reported.

TABLE 3.—*Race, sex, and age, by grade—Number of pupils of each age in each grade, by sex and by general nativity and race of father of pupil.*

FIRST GRADE.

BOYS.

General nativity and race of father of pupil.	Number of pupils of each age.														Total.
	4.	5.	6.	7.	8.	9.	10.	11.	12.	13.	14.	15.	16.	17.	
Native-born:															
White	....	23	94	156	72	18	6	2	1	....	....	....	....	....	372
Negro	....	....	....	....	....	....	....	....	....	....	....	....	....	....	....
Total native-born	....	23	94	156	72	18	6	2	1	....	....	....	....	....	372
Foreign-born:															
Bohemian and Moravian	....	2	....	....	....	....	....	....	....	....	....	....	....	....	2
Canadian, French	....	6	14	15	11	3	5	1	2	....	....	....	....	....	57
Canadian, Other	....	1	12	8	2	2	1	....	....	....	....	....	....	....	26
Dutch	....	....	2	7	1	1	....	....	....	....	....	....	....	....	11
English	....	....	4	10	3	....	....	....	1	....	....	....	....	....	18
French	....	7	2	5	3	2	1	....	....	....	....	....	....	....	20
German	....	6	27	47	30	7	3	1	....	....	....	....	....	....	121
Irish	....	2	14	14	6	2	....	....	....	....	....	....	....	....	38
Italian, North	....	1	4	3	3	....	....	....	....	....	....	....	....	....	11
Italian, South	8	6	6	9	2	2	1	....	....	....	....	....	....	....	34
Magyar	....	....	3	4	4	6	....	....	....	....	....	....	....	....	17
Polish	....	6	39	140	208	127	104	48	24	8	1	....	....	....	705
Scotch	....	....	....	....	2	....	....	....	....	....	....	....	....	....	2
Syrian	....	....	3	2	....	....	....	....	....	....	....	....	....	....	5
Other races a	....	....	1	....	1	....	....	....	....	....	....	....	....	....	2
Total foreign-born	8	35	133	264	276	152	115	50	27	8	1	....	....	....	1,069
Grand total	8	58	227	420	348	170	121	52	28	8	1	....	....	....	1,441

GIRLS.

General nativity and race of father of pupil.	4.	5.	6.	7.	8.	9.	10.	11.	12.	13.	14.	15.	16.	17.	Total.
Native-born:															
White	1	39	97	120	53	15	3	....	1	....	....	....	....	....	329
Negro	....	....	....	....	1	....	....	....	....	....	....	....	....	....	1
Total native-born	1	39	97	120	54	15	3	....	1	....	....	....	....	....	330
Foreign-born:															
Bohemian and Moravian	....	....	1	5	....	....	....	....	....	....	....	....	....	....	6
Canadian, French	....	4	8	13	24	6	4	....	....	....	....	....	....	....	59
Canadian, Other	1	2	8	12	3	1	....	....	....	....	....	....	....	....	27
Dutch	....	....	1	1	2	....	....	....	....	....	....	....	....	....	4
English	....	1	....	6	1	....	....	....	....	....	....	....	....	....	8
French	....	2	2	4	3	....	1	1	1	....	....	....	....	....	14
German	....	2	17	51	30	12	2	2	1	....	....	....	....	....	117
Irish	....	5	7	17	4	1	1	....	....	....	....	....	....	....	35
Italian, North	....	....	1	....	1	....	....	....	....	....	....	....	....	....	2
Italian, South	11	9	9	5	2	....	....	....	....	....	....	....	....	....	36
Magyar	....	....	1	3	1	1	....	....	....	....	....	....	....	....	6
Polish	1	2	17	92	174	165	120	45	24	6	....	....	....	....	646
Scotch	....	....	....	....	....	....	....	....	....	....	....	....	....	....	....
Syrian	....	....	2	....	1	....	....	....	....	....	....	....	....	....	3
Other races a	....	....	1	1	2	....	....	....	....	....	....	....	....	....	4
Total foreign-born	13	27	74	208	250	186	129	48	26	6	....	....	....	....	967
Grand total	14	66	171	328	304	201	132	48	27	6	....	....	....	....	1,297

a "Other races" includes races having less than 10 representatives in this city and pupils whose race is not reported.

TABLE 3.—*Race, sex, and age, by grade—Number of pupils of each age in each grade, by sex and by general nativity and race of father of pupil*—Continued.

FIRST GRADE—Continued.

TOTAL.

General nativity and race of father of pupil.	Number of pupils of each age.														Total.
	4.	5.	6.	7.	8.	9.	10.	11.	12.	13.	14.	15.	16.	17.	
Native-born:															
White	1	62	191	276	125	33	9	2	2						701
Negro					1										1
Total native-born	1	62	191	276	126	33	9	2	2						702
Foreign-born:															
Bohemian and Moravian			3	5											8
Canadian, French		10	22	28	35	9	9	1	2						116
Canadian, Other	1	3	20	20	5	3	1								53
Dutch			3	8	3	1									15
English		1	4	16	4			1							26
French		9	4	9	6	2	2	1	1						34
German		8	44	98	60	19	5	3	1						238
Irish		7	21	31	10	3	1								73
Italian, North		1	5	3	4										13
Italian, South	19	15	15	14	4	2	1								70
Magyar			3	5	7	7	1								23
Polish	1	8	56	232	382	292	224	93	48	14	1				1,351
Scotch					2										2
Syrian			5	2	1										8
Other races a			2	1	3										6
Total foreign-born	21	62	207	472	526	338	244	98	53	14	1				2,036
Grand total	22	124	398	748	652	371	253	100	55	14	1				2,738

a "Other races" includes races having less than 10 representatives in this city and pupils whose race is not reported.

SECOND GRADE.

BOYS.

General nativity and race of father of pupil.	Number of pupils of each age.														Total.
	6.	7.	8.	9.	10.	11.	12.	13.	14.	15.	16.	17.	18.	19.	
Native-born:															
White	1	37	120	62	19	5	6	2	1						253
Indian				1											1
Total native-born	1	37	120	63	19	5	6	2	1						254
Foreign-born:															
Bohemian and Moravian	1		3	1											5
Canadian, French		2	3	3	2	2	2	1	1	1					17
Canadian, Other		3	6	13	3	2	1								28
Dutch		2	1	2	1										6
English			4	3											7
French	1	1	2	5		2									11
German		15	51	35	25	11	3	1							141
Irish		3	8	9	3										23
Italian, North			4	3	2										9
Italian, South	6	4	5	6	5		1								27
Magyar		1	2	1	4	1									9
Polish	2	10	96	153	137	102	61	45	6						612
Scotch			1	1											2
Other races a			1		1	1									3
Total foreign-born	10	41	187	235	183	121	68	47	7	1					900
Grand total	11	78	307	298	202	126	74	49	8	1					1,154

a "Other races" includes races having less than 10 representatives in this city and pupils whose race is not reported.

TABLE 3.—*Race, sex, and age, by grade—Number of pupils of each age in each grade, by sex and by general nativity and race of father of pupil*—Continued.

SECOND GRADE—Continued.

GIRLS.

General nativity and race of father of pupil.	Number of pupils of each age.														Total.
	6.	7.	8.	9.	10.	11.	12.	13.	14.	15.	16.	17.	18.	19.	
Native-born:															
White	1	49	137	74	27	12	2	1							303
Negro		2													2
Total native-born	1	51	137	74	27	12	2	1							305
Foreign-born:															
Bohemian and Moravian		1	2	2											5
Canadian, French			9	4	5	3									23
Canadian, Other			8	7	5	1									21
Dutch		1	1				1								3
English		1		2											3
French		2	2	2	5	1									12
German		14	49	42	20	5	2			1					133
Irish		4	20	8	1										33
Italian, North			5	7	1										13
Italian, South		1	1	5	7	2									16
Magyar				2	2	1	1								6
Polish	1	8	61	156	168	96	62	28	6	1					587
Scotch			1	1											3
Syrian				3	1										4
Other races a		5		1											6
Total foreign-born	1	37	159	242	216	109	68	28	6	2					868
Grand total	2	88	296	316	243	121	70	29	6	2					1,173

TOTAL.

General nativity and race of father of pupil.	6.	7.	8.	9.	10.	11.	12.	13.	14.	15.	16.	17.	18.	19.	Total.
Native-born:															
White	2	86	257	136	46	17	8	3	1						556
Negro		2													2
Indian				1											1
Total native-born	2	88	257	137	46	17	8	3	1						559
Foreign-born:															
Bohemian and Moravian	1	1	5	3											10
Canadian, French		2	12	7	7	5	4	1	1	1					40
Canadian, Other		3	14	20	8	3	1								49
Dutch		3	2	2	1		1								9
English		1	4	5											10
French	1	3	4	7	5	3									23
German		29	100	77	45	16	5	1		1					274
Irish		7	28	17	4										56
Italian, North			9	10	3										22
Italian, South	6	5	6	11	12	2	1								43
Magyar		1	2	3	6	2	1								15
Polish	3	18	157	309	305	198	123	73	12	1					1,199
Scotch			2	2	1										5
Syrian				3	1										4
Other races a		5	1	1	1	1									9
Total foreign-born	11	78	346	477	399	230	136	75	13	3					1,786
Grand total	13	166	603	614	445	247	144	78	14	3					2,327

a "Other races" includes races having less than 10 representatives in this city and pupils whose race is not reported.

TABLE 3.—*Race, sex, and age, by grade—Number of pupils of each age in each grade, by sex and by general nativity and race of father of pupil*—Continued.

THIRD GRADE.

BOYS.

General nativity and race of father of pupil	Number of pupils of each age.														Total.
	5.	6.	7.	8.	9.	10.	11.	12.	13.	14.	15.	16.	17.	18.	
Native-born: White			1	30	84	80	40	11	6		3				255
Foreign-born:															
Bohemian					2		1								3
Canadian, French				3	13	9	10	6	1						42
Canadian, Other			2	4	8	2	6								22
Dutch			1	1	3										5
English				5	2	3	2								12
French				4	8	4	2	2	1						21
German	5		1	17	66	48	24	19	8	1	1				190
Hebrew (not specified)					8	1									9
Irish			7	11	13	12	3	2	1	1					50
Italian, North				1	3	8	3								15
Italian, South					1	8	6	2							17
Magyar									1						1
Polish				8	56	131	107	85	56	10					453
Roumanian					2	2	1								5
Scotch					2	1	1								4
Other races *a*				1	2	2	1								6
Total foreign-born	5		8	45	166	252	163	129	73	13	1				855
Grand total	5		9	75	250	332	203	140	79	13	4				1,110

GIRLS.

General nativity and race of father of pupil	Number of pupils of each age.														Total.
	5.	6.	7.	8.	9.	10.	11.	12.	13.	14.	15.	16.	17.	18.	
Native-born:															
White			2	54	97	48	28	9	1						239
Negro						1									1
Total native-born			2	54	97	49	28	9	1						240
Foreign-born:															
Bohemian					4	1	1								6
Canadian, French				1	9	5	10	13	2						40
Canadian, Other				4	6	6	2	3							21
Dutch					1		1	1							3
English				2		1				1					4
French			1	5	7	7	1	1	1						23
German				19	29	46	23	9	4					1	131
Hebrew (not specified)				1											1
Irish				11	8	17	2	3	1		1				42
Italian, North				1	2	2	4		1	1					11
Italian, South					1	1	3								5
Magyar					2	2	1								5
Polish				22	48	101	106	92	52	3					424
Roumanian						3	2	1							6
Scotch						1	1								2
Other races *a*					2	2		1							5
Total foreign-born			1	66	120	195	156	124	61	5				1	729
Grand total			3	120	217	244	184	133	62	5				1	969

a "Other races" includes races having less than 10 representatives in this city and pupils whose race is not reported.

TABLE **3.**—*Race, sex, and age, by grade—Number of pupils of each age in each grade, by sex and by general nativity and race of father of pupil*—Continued.

THIRD GRADE—Continued.

TOTAL.

General nativity and race of father of pupil.	Number of pupils of each age.														Total.
	5.	6.	7.	8.	9.	10.	11.	12.	13.	14.	15.	16.	17.	18.	
Native-born:															
White			3	84	181	128	68	20	7		3				494
Negro						1									1
Total native-born			3	84	181	129	68	20	7		3				495
Foreign-born:															
Bohemian					4	3	1	1							9
Canadian, French			1	12	18	19	23	8	1						82
Canadian, Other			6	10	14	4	9								43
Dutch			1	2	3	1	1								8
English				2	5	3	3	2		1					16
French			1	9	15	11	3	3	2						44
German	5		1	36	95	94	47	28	12	1	1			1	321
Hebrew (not specified)				1		8	1								10
Irish			7	22	21	29	5	5	2	1					92
Italian, North				2	5	10	7		1	1					26
Italian, South					2	9	9	2							22
Magyar					2	2	1		1						6
Polish				30	104	232	213	177	108	13					877
Roumanian					2	5	3	1							11
Scotch				3	2	1									6
Other races a			1	4	4	1	1								11
Total foreign-born	5		9	111	286	447	319	253	134	18	1			1	1,584
Grand total	5		12	195	467	576	387	273	141	18	4			1	2,079

a "Other races" includes races having less than 10 representatives in this city and pupils whose race is not reported.

FOURTH GRADE.

BOYS.

General nativity and race of father of pupil.	Number of pupils of each age.													Total.
	8.	9.	10.	11.	12.	13.	14.	15.	16.	17.	18.	19.	20.	
Native-born, White	4	32	101	101	63	31	4	1						337
Foreign-born:														
Bohemian and Moravian			1	2	2									5
Canadian, French		3	5	4	7	7	1							27
Canadian, Other	1	3	12	13	3	1	2							35
Dutch			2	3	3									8
English			1	1	3									5
French		1	1	6	4									12
German		11	49	51	39	18	2							170
Hebrew (not specified)				1										1
Irish	2	8	9	16	10	4	1							50
Italian, North		1		4	3	2	1							11
Italian, South				4	3									7
Polish		9	38	97	117	92	17	2	1					373
Scotch			2	1		1								4
Other races a					1		1							2
Total foreign-born	3	36	120	202	195	126	25	2						710
Grand total	7	68	221	303	258	157	29	3	1					1,047

a "Other races" includes races having less than 10 representatives in this city and pupils whose race is not reported.

TABLE 3.—*Race, sex, and age, by grade—Number of pupils of each age in each grade, by sex and by general nativity and race of father of pupil—Continued.*

FOURTH GRADE—Continued.

GIRLS.

General nativity and race of father of pupil.	Number of pupils of each age.													Total.
	8.	9.	10.	11.	12.	13.	14.	15.	16.	17.	18.	19.	20.	
Native-born:														
White		20	87	92	66	14	4							283
Negro				1										1
Total native-born		20	87	93	66	14	4							284
Foreign-born:														
Bohemian and Moravian			2	3										5
Canadian, French		2	11	19	17	1	3							53
Canadian, Other	1	10	8	13	4	2								38
Dutch				3	1									4
English			2	1		1	1							5
French	1				1									2
German		15	28	41	30	4	1							119
Irish		6	12	6	4		1							29
Italian, North		1	1	4	2									8
Italian, South				2	1	2								5
Magyar				2										1
Polish		17	68	103	109	80	8							382
Scotch						1								5
Other races *a*		2	1		1									4
Total foreign-born	2	53	133	197	170	91	14							660
Grand total	2	73	220	290	236	105	18							944

TOTAL.

General nativity and race of father of pupil.	8.	9.	10.	11.	12.	13.	14.	15.	16.	17.	18.	19.	20.	Total.
Native-born:														
White	4	52	188	193	129	45	8	1						620
Negro				1										1
Total native-born	4	52	188	194	129	45	8	1						621
Foreign-born:														
Bohemian and Moravian			3	5	2									10
Canadian, French		5	16	23	24	8	4							80
Canadian, Other	2	13	20	26	7	3	2							73
Dutch			2	6	4									12
English			3	2	3	1	1							10
French	1	1	1	6	5									14
German		26	77	92	69	22	3							289
Hebrew (not specified)						1								1
Irish	2	14	21	22	14	4	2							79
Italian, North		2	1	8	5	2	1							19
Italian, South				6	4	2								12
Magyar				2										2
Polish		26	106	200	226	172	25	2	1					758
Scotch			2	1		2								5
Other races *a*		2	1		2		1							6
Total foreign-born	5	89	253	399	365	217	39	2	1					1,370
Grand total	9	141	441	593	494	262	47	3	1					1,991

a "Other races" includes races having less than 10 representatives in this city and pupils whose race is not reported.

TABLE 3.—*Race, sex, and age, by grade—Number of pupils of each age in each grade, by sex and by general nativity and race of father of pupil*—Continued.

FIFTH GRADE.

BOYS.

General nativity and race of father of pupil.	Number of pupils of each age.													Total.
	8.	9.	10.	11.	12.	13.	14.	15.	16.	17.	18.	19.	20.	
Native-born, White		2	27	76	84	49	19	1		1				259
Foreign-born:														
Bohemian and Moravian			1		2	5								8
Canadian, French			1	7	16	17	5	1						47
Canadian, Other			3	5	13	3								24
Dutch				1	2	2								5
English					3	2		1						6
French			2	6	3	4								15
German			13	44	52	28	3	1						141
Irish			3	4	16	9	1							33
Italian, North					2	3								5
Italian, South														
Magyar														
Polish	1	4	19	72	102	99	17							314
Scotch														
Syrian														
Other races *a*				2	2									4
Total foreign-born	1	4	42	141	213	172	26	3						602
Grand total	1	6	69	217	297	221	45	4		1				861

GIRLS.

General nativity and race of father of pupil.	8.	9.	10.	11.	12.	13.	14.	15.	16.	17.	18.	19.	20.	Total.
Native-born, White		2	37	88	102	33	11	1						274
Foreign-born:														
Bohemian and Moravian				2	2	3								7
Canadian, French			2	8	12	5	1	1						29
Canadian, Other			1	13	10	9								33
Dutch			1	1	3									5
English			1	2	2									5
French			2	4	2	1	1							10
German		2	15	45	53	29	2							146
Irish			4	7	18	13	3							45
Italian, North			3	2	4	1								10
Italian, South				2	4									6
Magyar							1							1
Polish	1	3	23	60	111	105	2							305
Scotch						1								1
Syrian						2								2
Other races *a*				2	3		1							6
Total foreign-born	1	5	52	148	224	170	10	1						611
Grand total	1	7	89	236	326	203	21	2						885

a "Other races" includes races having less than 10 representatives in this city and pupils whose race is not reported.

TABLE 3.—*Race, sex, and age, by grade—Number of pupils of each age in each grade, by sex and by general nativity and race of father of pupil*—Continued.

FIFTH GRADE—Continued.

TOTAL.

General nativity and race of father of pupil.	Number of pupils of each age.													Total.
	8.	9.	10.	11.	12.	13.	14.	15.	16.	17.	18.	19.	20.	
Native-born, White	....	4	64	164	186	82	30	2	....	1				533
Foreign-born:														
Bohemian and Moravian			1	2	4	8								15
Canadian, French			3	15	28	22	6	2						76
Canadian, Other			4	18	23	12								57
Dutch			1	2	5	2								10
English			1	2	5	2		1						11
French		4	10	5	5	1								25
German		2	28	89	105	57	5	1						287
Irish			7	11	34	22	4							78
Italian, North			3	2	6	4								15
Italian, South				2	4									6
Magyar						1								1
Polish	2	7	42	132	213	204	19							619
Scotch					1									1
Syrian						2								2
Other races *a*				4	5	1								10
Total foreign-born	2	9	94	289	437	342	36	4						1,213
Grand total	2	13	158	453	623	424	66	6	....	1				1,746

a "Other races" includes races having less than 10 representatives in this city and pupils whose race is not reported.

SIXTH GRADE.

BOYS.

General nativity and race of father of pupil.	Number of pupils of each age.							Total.
	10.	11.	12.	13.	14.	15.	16.	
Native-born, White	5	24	67	56	26	4	2	184
Foreign-born:								
Canadian, French			5	2	5			12
Canadian, Other		5	11	10	4			30
Dutch			1					1
English		1	1	2		1		5
French				1	1			2
German		7	47	33	7	1		95
Hebrew (not specified)					1	1		2
Irish	2	4	11	6	2			25
Italian, North			2					2
Italian, South				1	1			2
Polish	5	32	67	84	9			197
Scotch			1					1
Total	7	49	146	139	30	3		374
Grand total	12	73	213	195	56	7	2	558

a "Other races" includes races having less than 10 representatives in this city and pupils whose race is not reported.

TABLE 3.—*Race, sex, and age, by grade—Number of pupils of each age in each grade, by sex and by general nativity and race of father of pupil—Continued.*

SIXTH GRADE—Continued.

GIRLS.

General nativity and race of father of pupil.	Number of pupils of each age.							Total.
	10.	11.	12.	13.	14.	15.	16.	
Native-born, White	2	26	78	48	12	3		169
Foreign-born:								
Bohemian and Moravian			2					2
Canadian, French			8	6	1			15
Canadian, Other		3	7	7	2			19
Dutch		2	3					5
English			1	3	1			5
French		1	1	1	2			5
German	2	10	37	21	4			74
Hebrew, other foreign			1	1				2
Irish		5	4	22	2			33
Italian, North			5	1	1			7
Italian, South			1		1			2
Polish	4	26	49	89	6	1		175
Other races *a*		1		1				2
Total	6	48	119	152	20	1		346
Grand total	8	74	197	200	32	4		515

TOTAL.

	10.	11.	12.	13.	14.	15.	16.	Total.
Native-born, White	7	50	145	104	38	7	2	353
Foreign-born:								
Bohemian and Moravian			2					2
Canadian, French			13	8	6			27
Canadian, Other		8	18	17	6			49
Dutch		2	4					6
English		1	2	5	1	1		10
French		1	1	2	3			7
German	2	17	84	54	11	1		169
Hebrew (not specified)			1	1	1	1		4
Irish	2	9	15	28	4			58
Italian, North			7	1	1			9
Italian, South			1	1	2			4
Polish	9	58	116	173	15	1		372
Scotch			1					1
Other races *a*		1		1				2
Total	13	97	265	291	50	4		720
Grand total	20	147	410	395	88	11	2	1,073

a "Other races" includes races having less than 10 representatives in this city and pupils whose race is not reported.

TABLE 3.—*Race, sex, and age, by grade—Number of pupils of each age in each grade, by sex and by general nativity and race of father of pupil*—Continued.

SEVENTH GRADE.

BOYS.

General nativity and race of father of pupil.	Number of pupils of each age.											Total.
	10.	11.	12.	13.	14.	15.	16.	17.	18.	19.	20.	
Native-born, White			21	38	31	13	5					108
Foreign-born:												
Bohemian and Moravian						1						1
Canadian, French			2	3	3	3						11
Canadian, Other			1	7	8	3						19
Dutch			1									1
English			1		2	1						4
French				1		1						2
German			8	23	15	4						50
Irish			2	8	10	6						26
Polish		2	42	69	2	1						116
Italian, North				1								1
Italian, South					1							1
Scotch				1								1
Other races *a*				2								2
Total		2	57	†115	41	20						235
Grand total		2	78	153	72	33	5					343

GIRLS.

General nativity and race of father of pupil.	10.	11.	12.	13.	14.	15.	16.	17.	18.	19.	20.	Total.
Native-born, White	1	3	16	72	59	20	6					177
Foreign-born:												
Bohemian and Moravian			1	2	1							4
Canadian, French			1	7	4	1						13
Canadian, Other				8	5	2			1			16
Dutch				3			1					4
English		1		1	3							5
French				1								1
German			4	25	17	3						49
Irish			5	11	16	2	1					35
Polish		1	33	73	7							114
Italian, South					1							1
Total		2	44	131	54	8	2		1			242
Grand total	1	5	60	203	113	28	8		1			419

a "Other races" includes races having less than 10 representatives in this city and pupils whose race is not reported.

TABLE 3.—*Race, sex, and age, by grade—Number of pupils of each age in each grade, by sex and by general nativity and race of father of pupil—Continued.*

SEVENTH GRADE—Continued.

TOTAL.

General nativity and race of father of pupil.	Number of pupils of each age.											Total.
	10.	11.	12.	13.	14.	15.	16.	17.	18.	19.	20.	
Native-born, White	1	3	37	110	90	33	11	....	....	....	....	285
Foreign-born:												
Bohemian and Moravian	....	....	1	2	1	1						5
Canadian, French	....	....	3	10	7	4						24
Canadian, Other	....	....	1	15	13	5	....	....	1			35
Dutch	....	....	1	3	....		1					5
English	....	1	1	1	5	1						9
French	....	....	....	2	....	1						3
German	....	....	12	48	32	7						99
Irish	....	....	7	19	26	8	1					61
Polish	....	3	75	142	9	1						230
Italian, North	....	....	....	1	....							1
Italian, South	....	....	....	....	2							2
Scotch	....	....	....	1	....							1
Other races a	....	....	....	2	....							2
Total	....	4	101	246	95	28	2	....	1	....	....	477
Grand total	1	7	138	356	185	61	13	....	1	....	....	762

a "Other races" includes races having less than 10 representatives in this city and pupils whose race is not reported.

EIGHTH GRADE.

BOYS.

General nativity and race of father of pupil.	Number of pupils of each age.										Total.
	11.	12.	13.	14.	15.	16.	17.	18.	19.	20.	
Native-born, White	....	....	24	35	24	6	1	....	....	....	90
Foreign-born:											
Bohemian and Moravian	....	....	....	....	....	1					1
Canadian, French	....	....	....	....	1						1
Canadian, Other	....	....	1	3	5	1					10
Dutch	....	1	....	....	....						1
English	....	....	....	....	1						1
German	....	....	5	11	3	2					21
Irish	....	....	2	5	7	1					15
Polish	....	2	12	5	....						19
Total	....	3	20	24	17	5	....	....	....	....	69
Grand total	....	3	44	59	41	11	1	....	....	....	159

TABLE 3.—*Race, sex, and age, by grade—Number of pupils of each age in each grade, by sex and by general nativity and race of father of pupil*—Continued.

EIGHTH GRADE—Continued.

GIRLS.

General nativity and race of father of pupil.	Number of pupils of each age.										Total.
	11.	12.	13.	14.	15.	16.	17.	18.	19.	20.	
Native-born, White		2	13	43	33	8	2				101
Foreign-born:											
Canadian, French				1	2	1					4
Canadian, Other	1		1	4	9	4	4				23
Dutch					2						2
English			1			1	1				2
French					1	1					2
German			5	13	13	1					32
Irish		1	4	3	10	4	1				23
Polish		6	17	2	1						26
Scotch				1							1
Total	1	7	28	24	38	12	5				115
Grand total	1	9	41	67	71	20	7				216

TOTAL.

General nativity and race of father of pupil.	11.	12.	13.	14.	15.	16.	17.	18.	19.	20.	Total.
Native-born, White		2	37	78	57	14	3				191
Foreign-born:											
Bohemian and Moravian						1					1
Canadian, French				1	3	1					5
Canadian, Other	1		2	7	14	5	4				33
Dutch		1			2						3
English			1		1	1					3
French					1	1					2
German			10	24	16	3					53
Irish		1	6	8	17	5	1				38
Polish		8	29	7	1						45
Scotch				1							1
Total	1	10	48	48	55	17	5				184
Grand total	1	12	85	126	112	31	8				375

TABLE 3.—*Race, sex, and age, by grade—Number of pupils of each age in each grade, by sex and by general nativity and race of father of pupil*—Continued.

FIRST YEAR HIGH SCHOOL.

BOYS.

General nativity and race of father of pupil.	Number of pupils of each age.					Total.
	13.	14.	15.	16.	17.	
Native-born, White	1	4	11	3	2	21
Foreign-born:						
Canadian, French			1			1
Canadian, Other			1	1		2
English			1			1
French				1		1
Irish		1	2	4	1	8
Total		1	5	6	1	13
Grand total	1	5	16	9	3	34

GIRLS.

General nativity and race of father of pupil.	Number of pupils of each age.						Total.
	13.	14.	15.	16.	17.	18.	
Native-born, White	1	8	30	8	7	3	57
Foreign-born:							
Canadian, French		2	1	1			4
Canadian, Other			6	3	3		12
French		1	1	1	1		4
German		4	3	3	1		11
Hebrew (not specified)		1					1
Italian, North				1			1
Irish		4	7	1		1	13
Polish				2			2
Other races a	1			2			3
Total	1	12	18	14	5	1	51
Grand total	2	20	48	22	12	4	108

TOTAL.

General nativity and race of father of pupil.	Number of pupils of each age.						Total.
	13.	14.	15.	16.	17.	18.	
Native-born, White	2	12	41	11	9	3	78
Foreign-born:							
Canadian, French		2	2	1			5
Canadian, Other			7	4	3		14
English			1				1
French		1	1	2	1		5
German		4	3	3	1		11
Hebrew (not specified)		1					1
Italian, North				1			1
Irish		5	9	5	1	1	21
Polish				2			2
Other races a	1			2			3
Total	1	13	23	20	6	1	64
Grand total	3	25	64	31	15	4	142

a "Other races" includes races having less than 10 representatives in this city and pupils whose race is not reported.

TABLE 3.—*Race, sex, and age, by grade—Number of pupils of each age in each grade, by sex and by general nativity and race of father of pupil*—Continued.

SECOND YEAR HIGH SCHOOL.

BOYS.

General nativity and race of father of pupil.	Number of pupils of each age.						Total.
	14.	15.	16.	17.	18.	19.	
Native-born, White		2	2				4
Foreign-born:							
Canadian (other than French)	1			1			2
Irish			1				1
Total	1		1	1			3
Grand total	1	2	3	1			7

GIRLS.

General nativity and race of father of pupil.	14.	15.	16.	17.	18.	19.	Total.
Native-born, White	1	6	11	10	3		31
Foreign-born:							
Canadian, French		2		2			4
Canadian, Other		1	2	1	1		5
French	1	2	1				4
German				1			1
Irish			8	1	1		10
Italian, North		1		1		1	3
Polish			1				1
Total	1	6	12	6	2	1	28
Grand total	2	12	23	16	5	1	56

TOTAL.

General nativity and race of father of pupil.	14.	15.	16.	17.	18.	19.	Total.
Native-born, White	1	8	13	10	3		35
Foreign-born:							
Canadian, French		2		2			4
Canadian, Other	1	1	2	2	1		7
French	1	2	1				4
German				1			1
Irish			9	1	1		11
Italian, North		1		1		1	3
Polish			1				1
Total	2	6	13	7	2	1	31
Grand total	3	14	26	17	5	1	66

TABLE 3.—*Race, sex, and age, by grade—Number of pupils of each age in each grade, by sex and by general nativity and race of father of pupil*—Continued.

THIRD YEAR HIGH SCHOOL.

BOYS.

General nativity and race of father of pupil.	Number of pupils of each age.				Total.
	16.	17.	18.	19.	
Foreign-born, Irish			1		1
Grand total			1		1

GIRLS.

General nativity and race of father of pupil.	16.	17.	18.	19.	Total.
Native-born, White	4	8	2	1	15
Foreign-born:					
Canadian, French		1			1
Canadian, Other		2			2
English	1		1		2
German	2	2			4
Irish	1	3	2		6
Total	4	8	3		15
Grand total	8	16	5	1	30

TOTAL.

General nativity and race of father of pupil.	16.	17.	18.	19.	Total.
Native-born, White	4	8	2	1	15
Foreign-born:					
Canadian, French		1			1
Canadian, Other		2			2
English	1		1		2
German	2	2			4
Irish	1	3	3		7
Total	4	8	4		16
Grand total	8	16	6	1	31

FOURTH YEAR HIGH SCHOOL.

BOYS.

General nativity and race of father of pupil.	Number of pupils of each age.				Total.
	16.	17.	18.	19.	
Native-born, White			1		1
Grand total			1		1

GIRLS.

General nativity and race of father of pupil.	16.	17.	18.	19.	Total.
Native-born, White	1	4	6	2	13
Foreign-born:					
Canadian (other than French)			4		4
German		2	1		3
Irish			3	4	7
Total		2	8	4	14
Grand total	1	6	14	6	27

TABLE **3.**—*Race, sex, and age, by grade—Number of pupils of each age in each grade, by sex and by general nativity and race of father of pupil*—Continued.

FOURTH YEAR HIGH SCHOOL—Continued.

TOTAL.

General nativity and race of father of pupil.	Number of pupils of each age.				Total.
	16.	17.	18.	19.	
Native-born, White............	1	4	7	2	14
Foreign-born:					
Canadian (other than French)............	....	....	4	....	4
German............	....	2	1	....	3
Irish............	....	....	3	4	7
Total............	....	2	8	4	14
Grand total............	1	6	15	6	28

COMMERCIAL SCHOOL.

BOYS.

General nativity and race of father of pupil.	Number of pupils of each age.					Total.
	13.	14.	15.	16.	17.	
Native-born, White..................	1	10	6	11	11	39
Foreign-born:						
Bohemian and Moravian...............	....	1	....	....	....	1
Canadian, French............	....	1	....	....	....	1
Canadian, Other............	....	1	1	2	1	5
Dutch............	....	....	....	1	....	1
French............	....	....	1	1	....	2
German............	3	14	9	8	1	35
Irish............	....	1	....	1	1	3
Polish............	....	....	1	1	....	2
Scotch............	....	....	....	....	1	1
Other races *a*	....	....	....	1	....	1
Total foreign-born..................	3	18	12	15	4	52
Grand total..................	4	28	18	26	15	91

a "Other races" includes races having less than 10 representatives in this city and pupils whose race is not reported.

TABLE 4.—*Race distribution in each grade—Percentages.*

[This table shows in detail only races with 100 or more pupils reporting. The totals, however, are for all races.]

General nativity and race of father of pupil.	Elementary grades.									High school.						Grand total.
	1.	2.	3.	4.	5.	6.	7.	8.	Total.	First year.	Second year.	Third year.	Fourth year.	Total.	Commercial school.	
Native-born:																
White	25.6	23.9	23.8	31.1	30.5	32.9	37.4	50.9	28.5	54.9	53.0	48.4	50.0	53.2	42.9	29.1
Negro	(a)	.1	(a)	.1	.0	.0	.0	.0	(a)	.0	.0	.0	.0	.0	.0	(a)
Indian	.0	(a)	.0	.0	.0	.0	.0	.0	(a)	.0	.0	.0	.0	.0	.0	(a)
Total native-born	25.6	24.0	23.8	31.2	30.5	32.9	37.4	50.9	28.6	54.9	53.0	48.4	50.0	53.2	42.9	29.1
Foreign-born:																
Canadian, French	4.2	1.7	3.9	4.0	4.4	2.5	3.1	1.3	3.4	3.5	6.1	3.2		3.7	1.1	3.4
Canadian, Other	1.9	2.1	2.1	3.7	3.3	4.6	4.6	8.8	3.0	9.9	10.6	6.5	14.3	10.1	5.5	3.2
French	1.2	1.0	2.1	.7	1.4	.7	.4	.5	1.2	3.5	6.1			3.4	2.2	1.2
German	8.7	11.8	15.4	14.5	16.4	15.8	13.0	14.1	13.2	7.7	1.5	12.9	10.7	7.1	38.5	13.5
Irish	2.7	2.4	4.4	4.0	5.4	5.4	8.0	10.1	4.1	14.8	16.7	22.6	25.0	17.2	3.3	4.3
Italian, North	.5	.9	1.3	1.0	.9	.8	.1	.1	.8	.7	4.5			1.5		.8
Italian, South	2.6	1.8	1.1	.6	.3	4.7	.3		1.2							1.2
Polish	49.3	51.5	42.2	38.1	35.5	34.7	30.2	12.0	41.6	1.4	1.5	6.5		1.1	2.2	40.6
Other races[a]	3.2	2.7	3.2	2.3	2.9	2.3	2.9	2.1	2.8	3.5				2.6	4.4	2.8
Total foreign-born	74.4	76.0	76.2	68.8	69.5	67.1	62.6	49.1	71.4	45.1	47.0	51.6	50.0	46.8	57.1	70.9
Grand total	100.0	100.0	100.0	100.0	100.0	100.0	100.0	100.0	100.0	100.0	100.0	100.0	100.0	100.0	100.0	100.0

a Less than 0.05 per cent.

TABLE 5.—*Grade distribution of each race—Percentages.*

[This table shows in detail only races with 100 or more pupils reporting. The totals, however, are for all races.]

General nativity and race of father of pupil.	Elementary grades.									High school.					Commercial school.	Grand total.
	1.	2.	3.	4.	5.	6.	7.	8.	Total.	First year.	Second year.	Third year.	Fourth year.	Total.		
Native-born:																
White	17.9	14.2	12.6	15.8	13.6	9.0	7.3	4.9	95.4	2.0	0.9	0.4	0.4	3.6	1.0	100.0
Negro	(a)	(a)	(a)	(a)	(a)	(a)	(a)	(a)	(a)	(a)	(a)	(a)	(a)	(a)	(a)	(a)
American Indian	(a)	(a)	(a)	(a)	(a)	(a)	(a)	(a)	(a)	(a)	(a)	(a)	(a)	(a)	(a)	(a)
Total native-born	17.9	14.3	12.6	15.8	13.6	9.0	7.3	4.9	95.4	2.0	.9	.4	.4	3.6	1.0	100.0
Foreign-born:																
Canadian, French	25.2	8.7	17.8	17.4	16.5	5.9	5.2	1.1	97.6	1.1	.9	.2	.0	2.2	.2	100.0
Canadian, Other	12.5	11.6	10.1	17.2	13.4	11.6	8.3	7.8	92.5	3.3	1.7	.5	.9	6.4	1.2	100.0
French	20.9	14.1	27.0	8.6	15.3	4.3	1.8	1.2	93.3	3.1	2.5	.0	.0	5.5	1.2	100.0
German	13.3	15.4	18.0	16.2	16.1	9.5	5.5	3.0	97.0	.6	1.1	.2	.2	1.1	2.0	100.0
Irish	12.5	9.6	15.8	13.5	13.4	9.9	10.4	6.5	91.6	3.6	1.9	1.2	1.2	7.9	.5	100.0
Italian, North	11.9	20.2	23.9	17.4	13.8	8.3	.9	.0	96.3	.9	2.8	.0	.0	3.7	.0	100.0
Italian, South	44.0	27.0	13.8	7.5	3.8	2.5	1.3	.0	100.0	.0	(a)	.0	.0	.1	.0	100.0
Polish	24.8	22.0	16.1	13.9	11.3	6.8	4.2	.8	99.9	(a)	.0	.5	.0	1.9	(a)	100.0
Other races	23.3	16.4	17.5	12.2	13.2	6.6	5.8	2.1	97.1	1.3	.0	.5	.0	1.9	1.1	100.0
Total foreign-born	21.4	18.6	16.6	14.4	12.7	7.6	5.0	1.9	98.1	.7	.3	.2	.1	1.3	.5	100.0
Grand total	20.4	17.3	15.5	14.8	13.0	8.0	5.7	2.8	97.3	1.1	.5	.2	.2	2.0	.7	100.0

a Not computed, owing to small number involved.

DULUTH, MINNESOTA.

INTRODUCTORY NOTE.

PUBLIC SCHOOL PUPILS—GENERAL INVESTIGATION.

PUBLIC SCHOOL TEACHERS IN ELEMENTARY GRADES AND KINDERGARTEN.

PAROCHIAL SCHOOL PUPILS—GENERAL INVESTIGATION.

LIST OF TABLES.

DULUTH.

The investigations of the Immigration Commission in regard to the schools of Duluth embraced the pupils in both public and parochial schools. In connection with the inquiry concerning public school children certain information was gathered relating to the teachers in public schools. The results of these several inquiries are presented in detail in the general tables which follow. An account of these general tables and their contents, with an explanation of how they were constructed and the purposes which they are intended to serve, will be found in the Introduction to this volume.[a]

PUPILS OF THE PUBLIC SCHOOLS.

The number of pupils enumerated as being in actual attendance in the public schools of the city of Duluth on a day early in December, 1908, was 10,895. In the school year 1908–9 the annual average, attendance in the public schools was 10,523, or somewhat less than the number enumerated by the Commission in the middle of the school year. The close correspondence of the two figures is gratifying evidence that the work done on behalf of the Commission was comprehensive and complete, and that the figures reported may be taken as a truthful representation of average conditions in the schools of the city.

The pupils enumerated were distributed among tbe several grades as follows:

Kindergarten	519	Eighth grade	678
First grade	1,804	First year high school	354
Second grade	1,235	Second year high school	222
Third grade	1,371	Third year high school	159
Fourth grade	1,272	Fourth year high school	124
Fifth grade	1,269		
Sixth grade	1,092	Total	10,895
Seventh grade	796		

The kindergarten is relatively small, having scarcely one-third as many pupils as the first grade. The first grade is, as usual, the largest in number of all the grades. In the second to the sixth grades there is greater uniformity in the number of pupils. Differences of course occur from grade to grade, but this group presents a comparative uniformity of numbers in comparison with that which precedes and those which follow it. With the seventh grade the usual diminution in numbers begins. In the eighth or final elementary grade the numbers are about one-half those observed in the earlier grades, while the first year of the high school has barely more than one-half as many pupils as the eighth grade.

---

[a] See pp. vii to xvii.

The greater number of the pupils in the lower grades is more clearly seen by a statement which puts the several grades into large groups. Kindergarten and high school are natural groupings. Elementary grades may be grouped by designating grades 1 to 4 as primary, and 5 to 8 as grammar grades. Such a condensed statement follows.

Class of school.	Number.	Per cent.
Kindgergarten	519	4.8
Primary grades 1 to 4	5,682	52.2
Grammar grades 5 to 8	3,835	35.2
High school	859	7.9
Total	10,895	100.0

Somewhat more than one-half of all the pupils (52.2 per cent) are found in the primary grades. The high school, representing the final four years' schooling of the twelve-year course of study, embraces only 7.9 per cent of all the pupils in the schools.

Table 1 affords an opportunity of studying the distribution of pupils by ages as well as by grades. It appears that there are 527 children of 5 years of age or less in the Duluth schools but 932 of the age of 6 years. The maximum number of children is found at the age of 8 years, when there are 1,148. The number undergoes little change till after the age of 13, when there are 988 children. At 14 the number drops by a little more than 100 and at 15 reaches 598, or about half the maximum already noted.

The same table also shows the number of pupils of each age and in each grade. While from grade to grade the age most numerously represented rises in regular sequence, there is within each grade a considerable variety of ages and for each age a considerable variety of grades. The most convenient form of expressing this diversity is by resort to the idea that for each grade there is an appropriate or normal age. Thus if the appropriate ages in the first grade are 6 and 7 years, any child of 8 years or over in the first grade may be deemed to be overage, and can be designated as backward or retarded. In like manner a child of 9 years of age in the second grade is overage. Conversely a child of 9 years of age who is below the third grade may be designated as undergrade. While these forms of comparison are equally admissible, that which states the children of a given grade as being of normal age or in excess of normal age is the most familiar.

The following table applies this method to the children of Duluth public schools. It shows in each grade the whole number of children, together with the number and percentage of those who are retarded or overage. The sum of all such children compared with the total number of children in all elementary grades permits the calculation of an average for the school system.

Grade.	Number in grade.	Retarded pupils.		
		Age.	Number.	Per cent of all pupils.
First..............	1,804	8 years and over..	330	18.3
Second.............	1,235	9 years and over..	324	26.2
Third.............	1,371	10 years and over...	445	32.5
Fourth............	1,272	11 years and over...	526	41.4
Fifth.............	1,269	12 years and over...	616	48.5
Sixth.............	1,092	13 years and over...	525	48.1
Seventh..........	796	14 years and over...	353	44.3
Eighth.............	678	15 years and over...	252	37.2
Total........	9,517	....	3,371	35.4

In the public schools of Duluth something over one-third of all the children (35.4 per cent) must be regarded as retarded or backward because they are older than they should be for the grades in which they are found. Beginning with the first grade we find 18.3 per cent retarded. The number of retarded children increases, while the number in the grades is practically stationary till the fifth grade. At this point the maximum number of retarded children (616) is observed and the maximum percentage of retardation (48.5). After this the number of retarded pupils declines with the total number of pupils. But as the retarded pupils have a more rapid rate diminution, they form in each successive grade a smaller proportion of the whole. In these figures we find reflected the elimination of pupils from school which falls more heavily upon those who are relatively unsuccessful in their school work than upon those who are making regular progress.

A further method of stating the misrelation between age and grade is, as already noted, to ascertain the pupils of a given age who are in grades lower than that appropriate to their age. This is shown in the following statement for the children of 10, 11, and 12 years of age in the public schools of Duluth.

Age.	Number of pupils of this this age.	Normal grade.	Retarded, or below normal grade.	
			Number.	Per cent.
10 years..	1,060	4	373	35.2
11 years...	1,040	5	422	40.6
12 years..	1,054	6	531	50.4
Total..	3,154	....	1,326	42.0

At the age of 10 years 373 pupils among 1,060, or 35.2 per cent, are below grade or retarded. At 11 and 12 years the number grows as the result of recent failure, and at the age of 12 one-half of the children are retarded. The calculation can not be conveniently carried beyond the age of 12, as pupils begin to leave school when 13 years of age and the records become incomplete. The average of the three years is calculated in order to serve as a measure of comparison between the schools as a whole and some of the racial groups of which the pupils are composed.

An examination of Table 1 will show that it is derived from the more detailed tables which follow. These tables distinguish the pupils in the several grades not only by sex and age but by race. The investigation into race is the specific contribution of the Immigration Commission to the statistics of schools. By its means not only can the general distribution of races in the schools be studied, but also the same characteristics for each race as for the schools as a whole.

The children enumerated in the Duluth public schools, distinguished by race according to the race of the father, were distributed as in the table following, which notes specifically those foreign races which had at least 200 representatives in the schools:

General nativity and race of father of pupil.	Pupils.		General nativity and race of father of pupil.	Pupils.	
	Number.	Per cent.		Number.	Per cent.
Native-born:			Foreign-born—Continued.		
White	2,773	25.5	Hebrew, Russian	400	3.7
Negro and Indian	53	.5	Irish	211	1.9
			Norwegian	1,366	12.5
Total native-born	2,826	25.9	Polish	260	2.4
			Scotch	285	2.6
Foreign-born:			Swedish	2,383	21.9
Canadian, French	407	3.7	All others	665	6.1
Canadian, Other	957	8.8			
English	281	2.6	Total foreign-born	8,069	74.1
Finnish	284	2.6			
German	570	5.2	Grand total	10,895	100.0

In round numbers only one-fourth of the school children of Duluth had native fathers, while three-fourths had fathers of foreign birth. The predominant element among the latter is the Scandinavian, Swedish, and Norwegian fathers combined, representing about one-third of the total number. The Canadian element, especially that not of French extraction, is also prominent. The Germans, with 570, constitute 5.2 per cent. Apart from the Russian Hebrews, represented by 400 children, the races of the more recent Slavic and Italian immigration are not numerously represented.

The group "Other races" offers considerable diversity. Though the numbers are in many cases small, mention of them is useful in completing the picture of the foreign element in Duluth. They are: Bohemian and Moravian (31), Bulgarian (3), Chinese (3), Croatian (7), Dalmatian (3), Danish (111), Dutch (12), Flemish (4), French (47), Hebrew, German (57), Hebrew, Polish (25), Hebrew, Roumanian (14), Hebrew, Other (6), Italian, North (103), Italian, South (96), Japanese (1), Lithuanian (1), Magyar (11), Roumanian (4), Russian (46), Ruthenian (1), Scotch-Irish (3), Servian (1), Slovak (2), Spanish (2), Spanish-American (16), Syrian (14), and Welsh (22).

By the aid of the detailed tables it is practicable to make for the native and foreign element and for each of the prominent races such a study of grade and age distribution and of retardation as has already been given in general outlines for the schools as a whole. Some of the facts concerning the different races may be noted.

The table following shows the distribution of the pupils of different races among the several classes of schools.

General nativity and race of father of pupil.	Number of pupils.					Per cent.			
	Kinder-garten.	Pri-mary.	Gram-mar.	High.	Total.	Kinder-garten.	Pri-mary.	Gram-mar.	High.
Native-born:									
White..................	148	1,254	1,018	353	2,773	5.3	45.2	36.7	12.7
Negro and Indian.......	2	27	23	1	53	3.8	51.0	43.4	1.9
Total native-born......	150	1,281	1,041	354	2,826	5.3	45.3	36.8	12.5
Foreign-born:									
Canadian, French.......	10	264	112	21	407	2.5	64.9	27.5	5.2
Canadian, Other.........	39	448	356	114	957	4.1	46.8	37.2	11.9
English..................	12	140	100	29	281	4.3	49.8	35.6	10.3
Finnish.................	17	174	84	9	284	6.0	61.3	29.6	3.2
German.................	26	273	226	45	570	4.6	47.9	39.6	7.9
Hebrew, Russian........	50	208	127	15	400	12.5	52.0	31.8	3.8
Irish...................	11	106	72	22	211	5.2	50.2	34.1	10.4
Norwegian..............	61	733	482	90	1,366	4.5	53.7	35.3	6.6
Polish.................	6	203	47	4	260	2.3	78.1	18.1	1.5
Scotch.................	8	131	110	36	285	2.8	46.0	38.6	12.6
Swedish................	95	1,334	868	86	2,383	4.0	56.0	36.4	3.6
All others.............	34	387	210	34	665	5.1	58.2	31.6	5.1
Total foreign-born.....	369	4,401	2,794	505	8,069	4.6	54.5	34.6	6.3
Grand total.....,.....	519	5,682	3,835	859	10,895	4.8	52.2	35.2	7.9

In the kindergarten there is a somewhat larger percentage of children of native than of foreign parents. There is, however, a very large proportion of Russian Hebrew children in the kindergarten. This may be the result of exceptional facilities in neighborhoods tenanted by this race, or may be due in part to a relatively large number of young children among them.

In the primary grades there is a distinctly larger proportion of children of foreign fathers than of native fathers. Among the children of foreign fathers the races differ considerably, though not one of them reaches the relatively low proportion found among children of native parents. Those races with the largest proportion of their children in the primary grades are the Polish, French Canadian, and Finnish.

In the high schools the racial distribution is the converse of that found in the primary schools. Here the largest proportion of the pupils is found among those of native fathers, of whom 12.7 per cent are in the high school. The proportion for children of foreign fathers (6.3 per cent) is only one-half as great. A few of the foreign races approach the native white in having considerable proportions of their pupils in the high school. These are the English-speaking races—Canadians, English, Irish, and Scotch. The participation of Norwegians in the high school is practically identical with that of foreign-born children as a whole, but the Swedes have a notably small proportion of their children in this grade of school.

The degree of retardation among the several races is shown in the following table:

General nativity and race of father of pupil.	All elementary pupils.			Pupils 10, 11, and 12 years of age.		
	Number.	Retarded, over age.	Per cent retarded.	Number.	Retarded, under grade.	Per cent retarded.
Native-born:						
White	2,272	715	31.5	767	255	33.2
Negro and Indian	50	24	48.0	10	5	50.0
Total native-born	2,322	739	31.8	777	260	33.5
Foreign-born:						
Canadian, French	376	167	44.4	121	71	58.7
Canadian, Other	804	286	35.6	276	114	41.3
English	240	79	32.9	73	27	37.0
Finnish	258	78	30.2	71	37	52.1
German	499	200	40.1	160	68	42.5
Hebrew, Russian	335	111	33.1	124	48	38.7
Irish	178	69	38.8	54	24	44.4
Norwegian	1,215	447	36.8	420	187	44.5
Polish	250	151	60.4	69	54	78.3
Scotch	241	78	32.4	74	29	39.2
Swedish	2,202	739	33.6	743	312	42.0
All others	597	227	38.0	192	95	49.5
Total foreign-born	7,195	2,632	36.6	2,377	1,066	44.8
Grand total	9,517	3,371	35.4	3,154	1,326	42.0

This table is in two parts, the first three columns relating to the total number of elementary pupils, the last three only to the children of 10, 11, and 12 years of age. In the first part is contained the common measure of general retardation.

As between the children of native fathers and those of foreign fathers there is no great degree of difference in the proportion of retarded children, though it is slightly larger among those having foreign fathers. Nor do the individual races present many marked contrasts with the average for the children of foreign fathers. A high rate of retardation is observed only among the French Canadians and especially among the Polish. It is striking that the lowest rate of retardation appears to be found among the Finnish. But this race also showed a relatively large number of children in the kindergarten and in the primary grades.

Unless these children are retarded in a high degree, and the table seems to show the contrary, the only inference is that there is among the Finnish a relatively large number of very young children, a fact which if true would vitiate the comparisons between the races based upon the general retardation.

The last three columns of the table give the retardation, for each race, of the children 10, 11, and 12 years of age, and by thus assuring uniformity of age conditions eliminate any unequal elements which might disturb comparisons based on the whole number of pupils. Among children of this age those of native parentage show 33.2 per cent retarded, while those of foreign parentage show much larger proportions, namely, 44.8 per cent. Here, too, the separate races show marked variation. Among children of foreign parents the minimum retardation (37 per cent) is found among the English, the maximum

(78.3 per cent) among the Polish. In addition to the Polish, two other races show a proportion of more than one-half of the children retarded. These are the French Canadian, with a proportion of 58.7 per cent retarded and the Finnish with 52.1 per cent retarded. It should be remarked that under this rather more accurate comparison of the races the Finnish occupy quite a different place with reference to other races than in the comparison given in the first three columns of the table.

PUBLIC SCHOOL TEACHERS.

The kindergarten and elementary grades of the Duluth public schools employed 460 teachers. Of these 9 were men, of whom 4 were employed in primary and 5 in grammar grades.

Divided by nativity and parentage, these teachers were distributed as follows:

	Number.	Per cent.
Native white of native fathers.	219	47.6
Native white of foreign fathers.	193	42.0
Foreign white.	48	10.4
Total.	460	100.0

Teachers of foreign parentage outnumber those of native parentage. Among the teachers of native birth but of foreign parentage the most numerous are the German with 10.2 per cent of all teachers, the Irish with 8.5 per cent, and the Swedes with 6.3 per cent. The English-speaking races comprise among teachers of native birth but foreign parentage a considerable number, being 18.5 per cent of the whole number of teachers.

Classifying the teachers with relation to their employment in the lower or upper grades, the following statement results:

	Kindergarten and primary.	Grammar.	Total.	Per cent in grammar grades.
Native white, native fathers.	124	95	219	43.4
Native white, foreign fathers.	118	75	193	38.8
Foreign fathers.	33	15	48	31.3
Total.	275	185	460	40.2

Of the teachers of native antecedents 43.4 per cent are employed in the upper grades. Those of foreign antecedents and of foreign birth have a smaller representation in the upper classes.

Of these teachers are reported the length of service, as follows:

Under 5 years.......................... 133	From 25 to 29 years................. 6
From 5 to 9 years..................... 119	30 years and over.................... 1
From 10 to 14 years................. 116	
From 15 to 19 years................. 65	Total.......................... 460
From 20 to 24 years................. 20	

Somewhat more than one-half of the teachers had served less than ten years. Hardly more than 5 per cent of all teachers had a service of twenty years or more. The scarcity of older teachers and the frequency of younger ones is explained in part by the rapid growth of the city in recent years, involving a continuous expansion of the school system.

Length of service and race may be summarized as follows:

Race and nativity of teachers.	Length of service, in years.			
	Under 10.	10 to 19.	20 and over.	Total.
Native white, native fathers....................................	115	95	9	219
Native white, foreign fathers...................................	116	62	15	193
Foreign white..	21	24	3	48
Total..	252	181	27	460
Percentages: All teachers...	54.8	39.3	5.9	100.0

Among the teachers of ten years or more there are 104 of native parentage and an exactly equal number of foreign parentage. But among the younger teachers of less experience those of foreign parentage outnumber those of native parentage.

PUPILS OF THE PAROCHIAL SCHOOLS.

Through the courtesy of the church authorities, figures were collected in the parochial schools in exactly the same manner as in the public schools. The number of pupils enumerated as being in attendance on the day the count was made was 1,008. According to the figures published in the official directory of the Roman Catholic Church, the enrollment in the Duluth schools was 1,105 in the same year. The divergence between the enrollment figures and the attendance figures for a school system is commonly greater than that here noted. There is no reason to suppose that either pupils or schools have been omitted, and our figures can be accepted as a correct picture of conditions in the parochial schools at the time of the enumeration.

The division of the pupils by grades was as follows:

Kindergarten......................	37	Sixth grade......................	86
First grade........................	178	Seventh grade....................	78
Second grade.....................	139	Eighth grade.....................	89
Third grade.......................	132		
Fourth grade......................	120	Total......................	1,008
Fifth grade........................	149		

The figures here presented show a very regular attendance in the grades. While the first grade is more numerous than the second, from that point to the fifth grade the numbers are well maintained. The figures fall naturally into three groups, grade 1, grades 2 to 5, and grades 6 to 8, the last named being about the same in number in each grade and a little more than one-half as numerous as the preceding group.

If the grades 1 to 4 and 5 to 8 be grouped, we have a more compact statement of the relative numbers of the lower and upper grades, as follows:

	Number.	Per cent.
Kindergarten	37	3.7
Grades 1 to 4	569	56.4
Grades 5 to 8	402	39.9
Total	1,008	100.0

In round numbers four-tenths of the pupils are found in the upper grades and the remainder in the lower grades, including the kindergarten.

The ages of the pupils, as shown in Table 1, indicate that there are only 50 of the age of 6 years but 103 of the age of 8 years. This number increases slightly until at the age of 13 years there are 127 pupils. It is not until the age of 15 years that numbers fall off conspicuously, though this is noted in most other communities at the age of 14 years.

In Table 1 will be found, moreover, a statement of the ages of the children in the several grades. In the discussion of public school children it has already been pointed out how these facts can be stated in condensed form for the purpose of estimating the progress of children, so far as that is revealed by the relation which exists between their ages and the grades in which they are found.

The following table shows for each grade the whole number of pupils as well as the number and per cent of those who are older than the appropriate age for the grade in which they are:

Grade.	Number in grade.	Retarded pupils.		
		Age.	Number.	Per cent of all pupils.
First	178	8 years and over	75	42.1
Second	139	9 years and over	71	51.1
Third	132	10 years and over	81	61.4
Fourth	120	11 years and over	77	64.2
Fifth	149	12 years and over	99	66.4
Sixth	86	13 years and over	61	70.9
Seventh	78	14 years and over	31	39.7
Eighth	89	15 years and over	44	49.4
Total	971		539	55.5

In general it appears that more than one-half the children in these schools are retarded. The proportion of retarded children rises steadily from 42.1 per cent in the first grade to 70.9 in the sixth grade, after which there is a decline in the ratio.

Eliminating from consideration the very young scholars and taking up those of 10, 11, and 12 years of age, the table following presents a statement of the number of pupils of these ages who are below the grades appropriate to their respective ages.

Age.	Number of pupils of this age.	Normal grade.	Retarded, or below normal grade.	
			Number.	Per cent.
10 years	102	4	61	59.8
11 years	108	5	60	55.6
12 years	122	6	86	70.5
Total	332		207	62.3

At the ages of 10 and 11 years the retardation is about the same, but it is much higher at the age of 12 years. The general average for these pupils (62.3 per cent) is only a little less than two-thirds of the whole number.

The numbers of the more important races represented in the parochial schools of Duluth are shown in the following table:

General nativity and race of father of pupil.	Pupils.	
	Number.	Per cent.
Native-born, White	226	22.4
Foreign-born:		
Canadian, French	222	22.0
Canadian, Other	140	13.9
Irish	142	14.1
Polish	143	14.2
All others	135	13.4
Total foreign-born	782	77.6
Grand total	1,008	100.0

Less than one-fourth of all the pupils here recorded had native fathers, more than three-fourths having foreign fathers. The largest single race among the foreign element is that of the French Canadian, which makes up more than one-fifth of the whole number of pupils. Irish, Poles, and English Canadians are nearly equal in number. The group "All other" contains the following representatives: Bohemian and Moravian (2), Bulgarian (2), Chinese (1), English (6), Flemish (10), French (5), German (66), Italian, North (13), Italian, South (4), Norwegian (5), Russian (2), Scotch (4), Slovenian (7), Swedish (2), and Syrian (6).

It would carry this introductory analysis too far into detail to study the characteristics of these different races as respects grade and age distribution and retardation. The materials for such a study are contained in the general tables.

PUBLIC AND PAROCHIAL SCHOOL PUPILS COMBINED.

A combination of the figures for both systems of schools gives a more accurate picture of the racial composition of the school population and at the same time suggests some interesting contrasts. Such a combination of the figures is given in the following table:

General nativity and race of father of pupil.	Pupils by schools.			Per cent of all pupils.
	Public schools.	Parochial schools.	Total.	
Native-born:				
White	2,773	226	2,999	25.2
Negro and Indian	53		53	.4
Total native-born	2,826	226	3,052	25.6
Foreign-born:				
Canadian, French	407	222	629	5.3
Canadian, Other	957	140	1,097	9.2
English	281	6	287	2.4
Finnish	284		284	2.4
German	570	66	636	5.3
Hebrew, Russian	400		400	3.4
Irish	211	142	353	3.0
Norwegian	1,366	5	1,371	11.5
Polish	260	143	403	3.4
Scotch	285	4	289	2.4
Swedish	2,383	2	2,385	20.0
All others	665	52	717	6.0
Total foreign-born	8,069	782	8,851	74.4
Grand total	10,895	1,008	11,903	100.0

Almost precisely one-fourth of the school children have native fathers and three-fourths have foreign fathers. Precisely one-fifth of the children have Swedish parents. If to these the Norwegians be added it will be seen that the children of Scandinavian origin outnumber those of native origin. Children with fathers born in Canada constitute nearly 15 per cent of all the children. The parochial-school system is much smaller than the public-school system, yet of three races—the French Canadian, the Irish, and the Polish—it contains a goodly proportion of the whole number of children.

GENERAL TABLES.

PUBLIC SCHOOL PUPILS: GENERAL INVESTIGATION.

TABLE 1.—*Grade and age—Number of pupils of each age in each grade, by sex.*

BOYS

Age.	Kindergarten.	Elementary grades.								Total.
		1.	2.	3.	4.	5.	6.	7.	8.	
4 years	17									
5 years	199	54								54
6 years	45	447	15							462
7 years	4	286	198	12						496
8 years		117	259	186	8					570
9 years		33	107	239	124	11				514
10 years		12	58	141	215	102	9	1		538
11 years		2	14	61	162	205	157	65	12	549
12 years		1	9	25	66	188	155	117	53	523
13 years		1	3	12	36	112	155	117	53	489
14 years		1	2	4	18	42	94	118	107	386
15 years				4	9	16	34	63	86	212
16 years		1			2	5	6	6	24	44
17 years		1						1	9	11
18 years										
19 years		1								1
20 years or over				2						2
Total	265	957	665	686	640	681	554	377	291	4,851

Age.	High school.					Grand total.
	First year.	Second year.	Third year.	Fourth year.	Total.	
4 years						17
5 years						253
6 years						507
7 years						500
8 years						570
9 years						514
10 years						538
11 years						549
12 years						523
13 years	11				11	500
14 years	41	7			48	434
15 years	54	27	6		87	299
16 years	33	24	13	2	72	116
17 years	9	26	21	17	73	84
18 years	3	11	14	20	48	48
19 years	1	4	4	9	18	19
20 years or over		2	1	5	8	10
Total	152	101	59	53	365	5,481

TABLE 1.—*Grade and age—Number of pupils of each age in each grade, by sex*—Contd.

GIRLS.

Age.	Kinder- garten.	Elementary grades.								
		1.	2.	3.	4.	5.	6.	7.	8.	Total.
4 years	13									
5 years	197	47								47
6 years	43	365	17							382
7 years		275	191	16						482
8 years		113	231	218	15	1				578
9 years		27	81	255	156	20				539
10 years		7	24	131	228	120	10	2		522
11 years		5	16	32	130	194	101	13		491
12 years		2	5	15	67	153	191	78	19	530
13 years			2	14	21	67	137	161	81	483
14 years	1	1	3	2	11	25	76	122	154	394
15 years		3			3	6	22	36	96	166
16 years		2				2	1	7	31	43
17 years				2	1				6	9
18 years										
19 years										
20 years or over										
Total	254	847	570	685	632	588	538	419	387	4,666

Age.	High school.					Grand total.
	First year.	Second year.	Third year.	Fourth year.	Total.	
4 years						13
5 years						244
6 years						425
7 years						482
8 years						578
9 years						539
10 years						522
11 years						491
12 years	1				1	531
13 years	5				5	488
14 years	42	7			49	444
15 years	89	35	8	1	133	299
16 years	52	41	35	8	136	179
17 years	11	26	38	33	108	117
18 years	2	8	19	22	51	51
19 years		3		6	9	9
20 years or over			1	1	2	2
Total	202	121	100	71	494	5,414

TABLE 1.—*Grade and age—Number of pupils of each age in each grade, by sex*—Contd.

TOTAL.

Age.	Kinder-garten.	Elementary grade.								
		1.	2.	3.	4.	5.	6.	7.	8.	Total.
4 years	30									
5 years	396	101								101
6 years	88	812	32							844
7 years	4	561	389	28						978
8 years		230	490	404	23	1				1,148
9 years		60	188	494	280	31				1,053
10 years		19	82	272	443	222	19	3		1,060
11 years		7	30	93	292	399	200	19		1,040
12 years		3	14	40	133	341	348	143	31	1,053
13 years		1	5	26	57	179	292	278	134	972
14 years	1	2	5	6	29	67	170	240	261	780
15 years		3		4	12	22	56	99	182	378
16 years		3			2	7	7	13	55	87
17 years		1		2	1			1	15	20
18 years										
19 years		1								1
20 years or over				2						2
Total	519	1,804	1,235	1,371	1,272	1,269	1,092	796	678	9,517

Age.	High school.					Grand total.
	First year.	Second year.	Third year.	Fourth year.	Total.	
4 years						30
5 years						497
6 years						932
7 years						982
8 years						1,148
9 years						1,053
10 years						1,060
11 years						1,040
12 years	1				1	1,054
13 years	16				16	988
14 years	83	14			97	878
15 years	143	62	14	1	220	598
16 years	85	65	48	10	208	295
17 years	20	52	59	50	181	201
18 years	5	19	33	42	99	99
19 years	1	7	4	15	27	28
20 years or over		3	1	6	10	12
Total	354	222	159	124	859	10,895

TABLE 2.—Race, sex, and grade—Number of pupils of each sex in each grade, by general nativity and race of father of pupil.

General nativity and race of father of pupil	Kindergarten	Elementary grades										High school					Grand total.
		1.	2.	3.	4.	5.	6.	7.	8.	Total.	First year.	Second year.	Third year.	Fourth year.	Total.	
Native-born:																	
White—																	
Male	71	203	145	173	151	169	137	97	95	1,170	53	42	22	24	141	1,382
Female	77	173	119	154	136	156	131	115	118	1,102	85	49	47	31	212	1,391
Total	148	376	264	327	287	325	268	212	213	2,272	138	91	69	55	353	2,773
Negro—																	
Male	1	5	2	4	3	2	5	1		22		1			1	24
Female	1	4		2	2	7	2	2	3	22						23
Total	2	9	2	6	5	9	7	3	3	44		1			1	47
Indian—																	
Male		2		1				1		4						4
Female		1	1							2						2
Total		3	1	1				1		6						6
Total native-born—																	
Male	72	210	147	178	154	171	142	99	95	1,196	53	43	22	24	142	1,410
Female	78	178	120	156	138	163	133	117	121	1,126	85	49	47	31	212	1,416
Total	150	388	267	334	292	334	275	216	216	2,322	138	92	69	55	354	2,826
Foreign-born:																	
Bohemian and Moravian—																	
Male		2	3	4	2	3	2		1	17						17
Female	1	2	2		1	2	1	4	1	13						14
Total	1	4	5	4	3	5	3	4	2	30						31
Canadian, French—																	
Male	6	48	28	34	34	19	19	10	3	195	7	2	1	1	11	212
Female	4	42	28	20	30	20	17	15	9	181	3	3	1	3	10	195
Total	10	90	56	54	64	39	36	25	12	376	10	5	2	4	21	407
Canadian, Other—																	
Male	19	64	53	49	59	64	49	33	24	395	23	17	11	7	58	472
Female	20	68	37	66	52	51	51	49	35	409	23	12	11	10	56	485
Total	39	132	90	115	111	115	100	82	59	804	46	29	22	17	114	957
Danish—																	
Male		13	3	4	5	5	5	6	4	45	1				1	46
Female		13	7	5	9	7	4	11	5	61		3		1	4	65
Total		26	10	9	14	12	9	17	9	106	1	3		1	5	111
Dutch—																	
Male		2	1	2	2		1	1		9						9
Female				1		2				3						3
Total		2	1	3	2	2	1	1		12						12
English—																	
Male	7	25	23	22	16	15	15	13	9	138	3	2	1	3	9	154
Female	5	13	19	9	13	12	11	12	13	102	4	7	5	4	20	127
Total	12	38	42	31	29	27	26	25	22	240	7	9	6	7	29	281

Race and sex	Total						Total									
Finnish—																
Male	143	5			2	3	127	7	9	7	15	16	17	20	36	11
Female	141	4			3	1	131	7	11	10	18	14	26	13	32	6
Total	284	9			5	4	258	14	20	17	33	30	43	33	68	17
French—																
Male	22	1				1	12	1			4		1	3	4	9
Female	25						23		2	2	3		3	8	4	2
Total	47	1				1	35	1	2	2	7		4	11	8	11
German—																
Male	304	15	1	3	3	8	274	23	25	42	41	29	39	43	32	15
Female	266	30	3	6	4	17	225	19	19	34	23	34	36	29	31	11
Total	570	45	4	9	7	25	499	42	44	76	64	63	75	72	63	26
Hebrew, German—																
Male	27	5				4	21			4	6	3	5	1	2	1
Female	30	3			2		27	4	2	4	4	3	2	6	2	
Total	57	8			2	4	48	4	2	8	10	6	7	7	4	1
Hebrew, Polish—																
Male	15	3			1	4	12	1	3		2	2	1	2	2	1
Female	10						10		1	2	3	3		1		
Total	25	3			1	4	22	1	4	2	5	5	1	3	2	1
Hebrew, Roumanian—																
Male	8		1		1	2	6	1		1	1	2		2	1	
Female	6		1				5			1					1	
Total	14		2		1	2	11	1		2	1	2		2	2	
Hebrew, Russian—																
Male	198	2	1	1	1	2	163	1	10	17	19	24	26	25	35	28
Female	202	1		1			172		11	26	25	19	23	25	31	22
Total	400	3	1	2	1	2	335	1	21	43	44	43	49	50	66	50
Irish—																
Male	112	7	1	1	3	5	95	7	8	12	10	15	5	16	21	3
Female	99	8		1		4	83	12	5	8	13	15	6	16	12	8
Total	211	15	1	2	3	9	178	19	13	20	23	30	11	32	33	11
Italian, North—																
Male	61	14	4	1		2	61	8		4	6	8	10	8	21	1
Female	42	8		1		3	39	8	2	6	5	7	8	4	8	
Total	103	22	4	2		5	100	16	2	10	11	15	18	12	29	1
Italian, South—																
Male	50		4	1		1	43	2		4	1	8	3	9	16	7
Female	46	2		1			36	1		4	4	5	5	6	10	9
Total	96	2	4			1	79	3		8	5	13	8	15	26	16
Magyar—																
Male	3	1					3	1		1		2		1		
Female	8						8	1								
Total	11	1					11	2		1		2		1		
Norwegian—																
Male	663	35		7	7	12	600	40	41	72	81	81	80	87	118	28
Female	703	55		7	4	25	615	49	43	75	81	89	95	67	116	33
Total	1,366	90		14	11	37	1,215	89	84	147	162	170	175	154	234	61
Polish—																
Male	145	2	7	2	9	2	139	1	6	15	10	10	15	24	58	4
Female	115	2	10	2	13		111		5	6	4	17	19	17	43	2
Total	260	4	17	4	22	2	250	1	11	21	14	27	34	41	101	6

TABLE 2.—Race, sex, and grade—Number of pupils of each sex in each grade, by general nativity and race of father of pupil—Continued.

General nativity and race of father of pupil.	Kindergarten.	Elementary grades.									High school.					Grand total.
		1.	2.	3.	4.	5.	6.	7.	8.	Total.	First year.	Second year.	Third year.	Fourth year.	Total.	
Foreign-born—Continued.																
Russian—																
Male		4	5	5	1	5				20	1				1	21
Female	1	9	4	2	4	3	1	1		24						25
Total	1	13	9	7	5	8	1	1		44	1				1	46
Scotch—																
Male	7	16	17	16	14	19	11	14	7	114	4	2	5	1	12	133
Female	1	20	21	12	15	14	13	15	17	127	12	6	2	4	24	152
Total	8	36	38	28	29	33	24	29	24	241	16	8	7	5	36	285
Spanish-American—																
Male		1		4		2	4			11	1				1	12
Female				1			3			4						4
Total		1		5		2	7			15	1				1	16
Swedish—																
Male	45	218	143	160	148	181	121	93	57	1,121	20	8	5	3	36	1,202
Female	50	191	133	184	157	125	122	90	79	1,081	22	11	13	4	50	1,181
Total	95	409	276	344	305	306	243	183	136	2,202	42	19	18	7	86	2,383
Syrian—																
Male	3	2	1		2					5						8
Female		2	1	1	2					6						6
Total	3	4	2	1	4					11						14
Welsh—																
Male					1				1	2					1	3
Female					2			4	4		1	1	1		3	19
Total					3			4	5		1	1	1		3	22
Other races a—																
Male		7	2	6	3	3	4	2		27	1	2		1	4	31
Female		8	4	4	3	3		1		23	1	1	1	3	6	29
Total		15	6	10	6	6	4	3		50	2	3	1	4	10	60
Total foreign-born—																
Male	193	747	518	508	486	510	412	278	196	3,655	99	58	37	29	223	4,071
Female	176	669	450	529	494	425	405	302	266	3,540	117	72	53	40	282	3,998
Total	369	1,416	968	1,037	980	935	817	580	462	7,195	216	130	90	69	505	8,069
Grand total—																
Male	265	957	665	686	640	681	554	377	291	4,851	152	101	59	53	365	5,481
Female	254	847	570	685	632	588	538	419	387	4,666	202	121	100	71	494	5,414
Total	519	1,804	1,235	1,371	1,272	1,269	1,092	796	678	9,517	354	222	159	124	859	10,895

a "Other races" includes: Bulgarian, 3; Chinese, 3; Croatian, 7; Dalmatian, 3; Flemish, 4; Hebrew, (not specified), 6; Japanese, 1; Lithuanian, 1; Roumanian, 4; Ruthenian, 1; Scotch-Irish, 3; Slovak, 3; Slovak, 2; Spanish, 2; Servian, 2; Servian, 1; Race not specified, 19.

TABLE 3.—*Race, sex, and age, by grade—Number of pupils of each age in each grade, by sex and by general nativity and race of father of pupil.*

KINDERGARTEN.

BOYS.

General nativity and race of father of pupil.	Number of pupils of each age.					Total.
	4.	5.	6.	7.	14.	
Native-born:						
White	7	51	13			71
Negro		1				1
Total native-born	7	52	13			72
Foreign-born:						
Canadian, French		4	2			6
Canadian, Other		16	3			19
English		6	1			7
Finnish		10	1			11
French	3	5	1			9
German	1	11	3			15
Hebrew, German	1					1
Hebrew, Russian	1	19	6	2		28
Irish		2	1			3
Italian, South		5	2			7
Norwegian	1	20	7			28
Polish	1	2	1			4
Scotch	1	5	1			7
Swedish	1	39	3	2		45
Syrian		3				3
Total foreign-born	10	147	32	4		193
Grand total	17	199	45	4		265

GIRLS.

General nativity and race of father of pupil.	Number of pupils of each age.					Total.
	4.	5.	6.	7.	14.	
Native-born:						
White	5	62	10			77
Negro		1				1
Total native-born	5	63	10			78
Foreign-born:						
Bohemian and Moravian		1				1
Canadian, French	1	3				4
Canadian, Other	1	16	3			20
English		3	2			5
Finnish		6				6
French	1		1			2
German		6	4		1	10
Hebrew, Russian	1	16	5			22
Irish		7	1			8
Italian, North	1					1
Italian, South		9				9
Norwegian	1	24	8			33
Polish		1	1			2
Russian		1				1
Scotch		1				1
Swedish	2	40	8			50
Total foreign-born	8	134	33		1	176
Grand total	13	197	43		1	254

TABLE **3.**—*Race, sex, and age, by grade—Number of pupils of each age in each grade, by sex and by general nativity and race of father of pupil*—Continued.

KINDERGARTEN—Continued.

TOTAL.

General nativity and race of father of pupil.	Number of pupils of each age.					Total.
	4.	5.	6.	7.	14.	
Native-born:						
White...	12	113	23	....	....	148
Negro...	....	2	....	....	....	2
Total native-born...................	12	115	23	....	....	150
Foreign-born:						
Bohemian and Moravian.................	....	1	....	....	....	1
Canadian, French.....................	1	7	2	....	....	10
Canadian, Other......................	1	32	6	....	....	39
English...............................	....	9	3	....	....	12
Finnish...............................	....	16	1	....	....	17
French................................	4	5	2	....	....	11
German................................	1	17	7	....	1	26
Hebrew, German........................	1	....	....	....	....	1
Hebrew, Russian.......................	2	35	11	2	....	50
Irish.................................	....	9	2	....	....	11
Italian, North.........................	1	....	....	....	....	1
Italian, South.........................	....	14	2	....	....	16
Norwegian..............................	2	44	15	....	....	61
Polish.................................	1	3	2	....	....	6
Russian................................	....	1	....	....	....	1
Scotch.................................	1	6	1	....	....	8
Swedish................................	3	79	11	2	....	95
Syrian.................................	....	3	....	....	....	3
Total foreign-born..................	18	281	65	4	1	369
Grand total........................	30	396	88	4	1	519

TABLE 3.—*Race, sex, and age, by grade—Number of pupils of each age in each grade, by sex and by general nativity and race of father of pupil*—Continued.

FIRST GRADE.

BOYS.

General nativity and race of father of pupil.	Number of pupils of each age.															Total.
	5.	6.	7.	8.	9.	10.	11.	12.	13.	14.	15.	16.	17.	18.	19.	
Native-born:																
White	15	93	67	24	3	1										203
Negro		2	1	1	1											5
Indian		2														2
Total native-born	15	97	68	25	4	1										210
Foreign-born:																
Bohemian and Moravian		2														2
Canadian, French	2	26	15	3	1	1										48
Canadian, Other	6	36	14	6		2										64
Danish		7	4	1	1											13
Dutch					2											2
English	2	13	6	4												25
Finnish	8	13	10	4			1									36
French		1	3													4
German	1	20	9	2												32
Hebrew, German		1	1													2
Hebrew, Polish			2													2
Hebrew, Roumanian		1														1
Hebrew, Russian	1	14	11	4	1	2				1		1				35
Irish	1	6	10	3	1											21
Italian, North	3	8	5	3	1		1									21
Italian, South		5	7	3									1			16
Norwegian	3	63	32	13	6	1										118
Polish		13	18	14	7	5				1						58
Russian			1	1	2											4
Scotch	2	7	5	2												16
Swedish	10	111	62	27	7					1						218
Syrian		2														2
Other races a		1	3	2										1		7
Total foreign-born	39	350	218	92	29	11	2	1	1	1		1	1		1	747
Grand total	54	447	286	117	33	12	2	1	1	1		1	1		1	957

a "Other races" includes races having less than 10 representatives in this city and pupils whose race is not reported.

TABLE 3.—*Race, sex, and age, by grade—Number of pupils of each age in each grade, by sex and by general nativity and race of father of pupil—Continued.*

FIRST GRADE—Continued.

GIRLS.

General nativity and race of father of pupil.	Number of pupils of each age.															Total.
	5.	6.	7.	8.	9.	10.	11.	12.	13.	14.	15.	16.	17.	18.	19.	
Native-born:																
White	12	66	60	33	1	1										173
Negro		4														4
Indian					1											1
Total	12	70	60	33	2	1										178
Foreign-born:																
Bohemian and Moravian			2													2
Canadian, French		22	10	4	5		1									42
Canadian, Other	4	29	28	5	2											68
Danish	2	3	5	1	2											13
English		8	2	1	2											13
Finnish	4	18	5	4		1										32
French	1		3													4
German		15	9	4	2		1									31
Hebrew, German			1							1						2
Hebrew, Roumanian		1														1
Hebrew, Russian		20	6	2			1				1	1				31
Irish		7	2	3												12
Italian, North	3	3			2											8
Italian, South	1	5	2	1				1								10
Magyar		5	2													7
Norwegian	7	50	45	12	2											116
Polish		12	12	8	5	4		1			1					43
Russian		4	2	2			1									9
Scotch	3	5	9	2	1											20
Spanish-American		1														1
Swedish	10	82	69	27	2	1										191
Syrian		2														2
Welsh			3													3
Other races *a*		3	1	1			1				1	1				8
Total foreign-born	35	295	215	80	25	6	5	2		1	3	2				669
Grand total	47	365	275	113	27	7	5	2		1	3	2				847

a "Other races" includes races having less than 10 representatives in this city and pupils whose race is not reported.

TABLE 3.—*Race, sex, and age, by grade—Number of pupils of each age in each grade, by sex and by general nativity and race of father of pupil*—Continued.

FIRST GRADE—Continued.

TOTAL.

General nativity and race of father of pupil.	Number of pupils of each age.															Total.
	5.	6.	7.	8.	9.	10.	11.	12.	13.	14.	15.	16.	17.	18.	19.	
Native-born:																
White	27	159	127	57	4	2										376
Negro		6	1	1	1											9
Indian		2			1											3
Total native-born	27	167	128	58	6	2										388
Foreign-born:																
Bohemian and Moravian		2		2												4
Canadian, French	2	48	25	7	6	1	1									90
Canadian, Other	10	65	42	11	2	2										132
Danish	2	10	9	2	3											26
Dutch					2											2
English	2	21	8	5	2											38
Finnish	12	31	15	8			1	1								68
French	1	1	6													8
German	1	35	18	6	2			1								63
Hebrew, German		1	1	1								1				4
Hebrew, Polish			2													2
Hebrew, Roumanian		2														2
Hebrew, Russian	1	34	17	6	1	2	1			1	1	2				66
Irish	1	13	12	6	1											33
Italian, North	6	11	5	3	3		1									29
Italian, South	1	10	9	4				1					1			26
Magyar		5	2													7
Norwegian	10	113	77	25	8	1										234
Polish		25	30	22	12	9		1	1	1						101
Russian		4	3	3	2		1									13
Scotch	5	12	14	4	1											36
Spanish-American			1													1
Swedish	20	193	131	54	9		1	1								409
Syrian		4														4
Welsh			3													3
Other races *a*		4	4	3		1					1	1			1	15
Total foreign-born	74	645	433	172	54	17	7	3	1	2	3	3	1		1	1,416
Grand total	101	812	561	230	60	19	7	3	1	2	3	3	1		1	1,804

a "Other races" includes races having less than 10 representatives in this city and pupils whose race is not reported.

TABLE 3.—*Race, sex, and age, by grade—Number of pupils of each age in each grade, by sex and by general nativity and race of father of pupil*—Continued.

SECOND GRADE.

BOYS.

General nativity and race of father of pupil.	Number of pupils of each age.									Total.
	6.	7.	8.	9.	10.	11.	12.	13.	14.	
Native-born:										
White	6	49	51	23	12	3	1			145
Negro			1	1						2
Total native-born	6	49	52	24	12	3	1			147
Foreign-born:										
Bohemian and Moravian			1	1		1				3
Canadian, French		10	9	4	5					28
Canadian, Other		16	19	12	3		2	1		53
Danish			1	1	1					3
Dutch		1								1
English		12	5	2	3	1				23
Finnish	2	7	7	1	2	1				20
French		2		1						3
German	2	13	14	11	2	1				43
Hebrew, German			1							1
Hebrew, Polish		2								2
Hebrew, Russian	1	5	9	4	4	1	1			25
Irish		5	9	1	1					16
Italian, North		2	5					1		8
Italian, South			4	2	1		2			9
Magyar		1								1
Norwegian	1	22	37	13	8	2	3		1	87
Polish		2	9	7	3	3				24
Russian		2	1	1	1					5
Scotch		8	6	1	2					17
Swedish	3	39	67	21	10	1		1	1	143
Syrian			1							1
Other races a			2							2
Total foreign-born	9	149	207	83	46	11	8	3	2	518
Grand total	15	198	259	107	58	14	9	3	2	665

a "Other races" includes races having less than 10 representatives in this city and pupils whose race is not reported.

TABLE 3.—*Race, sex, and age, by grade—Number of pupils of each age in each grade, by sex and by general nativity and race of father of pupil*—Continued.

SECOND GRADE—Continued.

GIRLS.

General nativity and race of father of pupil.	Number of pupils of each age.									Total.
	6.	7.	8.	9.	10.	11.	12.	13.	14.	
Native-born:										
White	3	37	56	15	4	4				119
Indian			1							1
Total native-born	3	37	57	15	4	4				120
Foreign-born:										
Bohemian and Moravian			2							2
Canadian, French		5	14	2	6		1			28
Canadian, Other		12	17	4	2	2				37
Danish			3	3	1					7
English		9	6	4						19
Finnish		5	5	2			1			13
French		2	4	1	1					8
German	1	11	13	4						29
Hebrew, German		3	3							6
Hebrew, Polish			1							1
Hebrew, Roumanian			1			1				2
Hebrew, Russian		10	7	2	2	2		1	1	25
Irish	2	5	7	1				1		16
Italian, North	1	2		1						4
Italian, South	1	1	1	1	1		1			6
Norwegian	3	21	31	9	2		1			67
Polish		3	5	4	1	3	1			17
Russian		1			1				2	4
Scotch		6	9	3	2	1				21
Swedish	6	55	44	24	1	3				133
Syrian		1								1
Other races a		2	1	1						4
Total foreign-born	14	154	174	66	20	12	5	2	3	450
Grand total	17	191	231	81	24	16	5	2	3	570

a "Other races" includes races having less than 10 representatives in this city and pupils whose race is not reported.

TABLE **3.**—*Race, sex, and age, by grade—Number of pupils of each age in each grade, by sex and by general nativity and race of father of pupil—Continued.*

SECOND GRADE—Continued.

TOTAL.

General nativity and race of father of pupil.	Number of pupils of each age.									Total.
	6.	7.	8.	9.	10.	11.	12.	13.	14.	
Native-born:										
White	9	86	107	38	16	7	1			264
Negro			1	1						2
Indian			1							1
Total native-born	9	86	109	39	16	7	1			267
Foreign-born:										
Bohemian and Moravian			3	1		1				5
Canadian, French		15	23	6	11		1			56
Canadian, Other		27	36	16	6	2	2	1		90
Danish		1	4	4	1					10
Dutch		1								1
English		21	11	6	3	1				42
Finnish	2	12	12	3	2	1	1			33
French		4	4	2	1					11
German	3	24	27	15	2	1				72
Hebrew, German		3	4							7
Hebrew, Polish		2	1							3
Hebrew, Roumanian			1							2
Hebrew, Russian	1	15	16	6	6	3	1	1	1	50
Irish	2	10	16	2	1			1		32
Italian, North	1	4	5	1				1		12
Italian, South	1	1	5	3	2		3			15
Magyar		1								1
Norwegian	4	43	68	22	10	2	4		1	154
Polish		5	14	11	4	6	1			41
Russian		3	1	1	2				2	9
Scotch		14	15	4	4	1				38
Swedish	9	94	111	45	11	4		1	1	276
Syrian		1	1							2
Other races *a*		2	3	1						6
Total foreign-born	233	303	381	149	66	23	13	5	5	968
Grand total	32	389	490	188	82	30	14	5	5	1,235

a "Other races" includes races having less than 10 representatives in this city and pupils whose race is not reported.

TABLE 3.—*Race, sex, and age, by grade—Number of pupils of each age in each grade, by sex and by general nativity and race of father of pupil—Continued.*

THIRD GRADE.

BOYS.

General nativity and race of father of pupil.	Number of pupils of each age.														Total.
	7.	8.	9.	10.	11.	12.	13.	14.	15.	16.	17.	18.	19.	20 or over.	
Native-born:															
White	6	57	68	31	7	2	2								173
Negro		1		1	1		1								4
Indian			1												1
Total native-born	6	58	69	32	8	2	3								178
Foreign-born:															
Bohemian and Moravian		1	1			2									4
Canadian, French		2	11	9	6	3	1	2							34
Canadian, Other	2	9	21	7	6	3	1								49
Danish		1	2		1										4
Dutch		1		1											2
English		6	9	5	2										22
Finnish		6	6	4	1										17
French					1										1
German		8	14	10	4	3									39
Hebrew, German		3	2												5
Hebrew, Roumanian		1													1
Hebrew, Russian	2	7	5	5	3	3	1								26
Irish			1	2	1	1									5
Italian, North		1	3	4	1	1									10
Italian, South			1				1	1							3
Norwegian	2	19	29	13	13	3	1								80
Polish		1	3	2	4		2	1	2						15
Russian		3	2												5
Scotch		4	6	4	1		1								16
Spanish-American		2	2												4
Swedish		53	51	40	9	4	1		2						160
Other races a			1	1										2	6
Total foreign-born	6	128	170	109	53	23	9	4	4					2	508
Grand total	12	186	239	141	61	25	12	4	4					2	686

a "Other races" includes races having less than 10 representatives in this city and pupils whose race is not reported.

TABLE 3.—*Race, sex, and age, by grade—Number of pupils of each age in each grade, by sex and by general nativity and race of father of pupil—Continued.*

THIRD GRADE—Continued.

GIRLS.

General nativity and race of father of pupil.	Number of pupils of each age.														Total.
	7.	8.	9.	10.	11.	12.	13.	14.	15.	16.	17.	18.	19.	20 or over.	
Native-born:															
White	2	65	55	22	7	2	1								154
Negro			2												2
Total native-born	2	65	57	22	7	2	1								156
Foreign-born:															
Canadian, French		4	6	7	2		1								20
Canadian, Other	2	21	31	9	2	1									66
Danish		4	1												5
Dutch		1													1
English		7	1	1											9
Finnish		10	11	5											26
French		1	2												3
German		8	22	5			1								36
Hebrew, German			1	1											2
Hebrew, Russian	1	3	10	5	1	2	1								23
Irish			5	1											6
Italian, North			4	1	3										8
Italian, South		1		3	1										5
Norwegian	4	24	33	23	3	2	4	2							95
Polish		2	3	2	6	3	3								19
Russian		1		1											2
Scotch		4	4	3		1									12
Spanish-American		1													1
Swedish	7	61	61	42	7	3	3								184
Syrian							1								1
Welsh			1												1
Other races a			2									2			4
Total foreign-born	14	153	198	109	25	13	13	2			2				529
Grand total	16	218	255	131	32	15	14	2			2				685

a "Other races" includes races having less than 10 representatives in this city and pupils whose race is not reported.

TABLE **3.**—*Race, sex, and age, by grade—Number of pupils of each age in each grade, by sex and by general nativity and race of father of pupil—Continued.*

THIRD GRADE—Continued.

TOTAL.

General nativity and race of father of pupil.	Number of pupils of each age.														Total.
	7.	8.	9.	10.	11.	12.	13	14.	15.	16.	17.	18.	19.	20 or over.	
Native-born:															
White	8	122	123	53	14	4	3								327
Negro		1	2	1	1		1								6
Indian			1												1
Total native-born	8	123	126	54	15	4	4								334
Foreign-born:															
Bohemian and Moravian		1	1			2									4
Canadian, French		6	17	16	8	3	2	2							54
Canadian, Other	4	30	52	16	8	4	1								115
Danish		5	3		1										9
Dutch		2		1											3
English		13	10	6	2										31
Finnish		16	17	9	1										43
French		1	2		1										4
German		16	36	15	4	3	1								75
Hebrew, German		3	3	1											7
Hebrew, Roumanian		1													1
Hebrew, Russian	3	10	15	10	4	5	2								49
Irish			6	3	1	1									11
Italian, North		1	7	5	4	1									18
Italian, South		1	1	3	1		1	1							8
Norwegian	6	43	62	36	16	5	5	2							175
Polish		3	6	4	10	3	5	1	2						34
Russian		4	2	1											7
Scotch		8	10	7	1	1	1								28
Spanish-American		1	2	2											5
Swedish	7	114	112	82	16	7	4		2						344
Syrian						1									1
Welsh			1												1
Other races a		2	3	1							2			2	10
Total foreign-born	20	281	368	218	78	36	22	6	4		2			2	1,037
Grand total	28	404	494	272	93	40	26	6	4		2			2	1,371

a "Other races" includes races having less than 10 representatives in this city and pupils whose race is not reported.

TABLE 3.—*Race, sex, and age, by grade—Number of pupils of each age in each grade, by sex and by general nativity and race of father of pupil*—Continued.

FOURTH GRADE.

BOYS.

General nativity and race of father of pupil.	Number of pupils of each age.										Total.
	8.	9.	10.	11.	12.	13.	14.	15.	16.	17.	
Native-born:											
White....................	3	34	59	40	3	8	3	......	1	......	151
Negro....................	......	1	......	1	......	......	1	......	......	......	3
Total native-born........	3	35	59	41	3	8	4	......	1	......	154
Foreign-born:											
Bohemian.................	......	......	......	......	1	1	......	......	......	......	2
Canadian, French.........	......	5	12	6	4	3	4	......	......	......	34
Canadian, Other.........	......	13	19	14	9	......	2	2	......	......	59
Danish..................	......	......	2	1	1	1	......	......	......	......	5
Dutch...................	......	......	1	1	......	......	......	......	......	......	2
English.................	1	3	6	4	1	1	......	......	......	......	16
Finnish.................	......	3	4	4	5	......	......	......	......	......	16
German..................	......	2	6	12	2	5	1	1	......	......	29
Hebrew, German..........	......	1	2	......	......	......	......	......	......	......	3
Hebrew, Polish..........	......	1	......	1	......	......	......	......	......	......	2
Hebrew, Roumanian.......	......	......	......	1	......	......	1	......	......	......	2
Hebrew, Russian.........	......	6	9	4	2	1	1	......	1	......	24
Irish...................	......	2	1	6	4	2	......	......	......	......	15
Italian, North..........	......	1	4	2	1	......	......	......	......	......	8
Italian, South..........	......	1	2	3	1	......	......	1	......	......	8
Magyar..................	......	......	1	1	......	......	......	......	......	......	2
Norwegian...............	1	11	30	24	9	4	2	......	......	......	81
Polish..................	......	......	2	1	3	2	......	2	......	......	10
Russian.................	......	......	1	......	......	......	......	......	......	......	1
Scotch..................	1	5	3	4	1	......	......	......	......	......	14
Swedish.................	2	34	49	31	18	8	3	3	......	......	148
Syrian..................	......	......	1	......	1	......	......	......	......	......	2
Welsh...................	......	......	1	......	......	......	......	......	......	......	1
Other races *a*.........	......	1	......	1	......	......	......	......	......	......	2
Total foreign-born.......	5	89	156	121	63	28	14	9	1	......	486
Grand total.............	8	124	215	162	66	36	18	9	2	......	640

a "Other races" includes races having less than 10 representatives in this city and pupils whose race is not reported.

TABLE 3.—*Race, sex, and age, by grade—Number of pupils of each age in each grade, by sex and by general nativity and race of father of pupil—Continued.*

FOURTH GRADE—Continued.

GIRLS.

General nativity and race of father of pupil.	Number of pupils of each age.										Total.
	8.	9.	10.	11.	12.	13.	14.	15.	16.	17.	
Native-born:											
White	3	37	52	25	14	3	2				136
Negro		1		1							2
Total native-born	3	38	52	26	14	3	2				138
Foreign-born:											
Bohemian			1								1
Canadian, French		3	9	4	11	2	1				30
Canadian, Other	3	14	16	11	6	1	1				52
Danish		3	5		1						9
English		5	5	2	1						13
Finnish	2	5	4	1	2						14
German	1	3	12	10	6	2					34
Hebrew, German		1		1	1						3
Hebrew, Polish	1	1		1							3
Hebrew, Russian		8	5	2		2		2			19
Irish		7	4	1	1	1	1				15
Italian, North			3	2	2						7
Italian, South	1			3		1					5
Norwegian	1	15	44	16	7	4	2				89
Polish		1	2	5	4	4				1	17
Russian		4									4
Scotch	1	5	6	2	1						15
Swedish	2	41	60	40	10	1	2	1			157
Syrian				1			1				2
Welsh		2									2
Other races a				2			1				3
Total foreign-born	12	118	176	104	53	18	9	3		1	494
Grand total	15	156	228	130	67	21	11	3		1	632

a "Other races" includes races having less than 10 representatives in this city and pupils whose race is not reported.

66083°—VOL 31—12——11

TABLE 3.—*Race, sex, and age, by grade—Number of pupils of each age in each grade, by sex and by general nativity and race of father of pupil*—Continued.

FOURTH GRADE—Continued.

TOTAL.

General nativity and race of father of pupil.	Number of pupils of each age.										Total.
	8.	9.	10.	11.	12.	13.	14.	15.	16.	17.	
Native-born:											
White	6	71	111	65	17	11	5	......	1	......	287
Negro		2	......	2	......	......	1	......	......	......	5
Total native-born	6	73	111	67	17	11	6	......	1	......	292
Foreign-born:											
Bohemian	......	......	1	......	1	1	......	......	......	......	3
Canadian, French		8	21	10	15	5	5	......	......	......	64
Canadian, Other	3	27	35	25	15	1	3	2	......	......	111
Danish		3	7	1	2	1	......	......	......	......	14
Dutch			1		1		......	......	......	......	2
English	1	8	11	6	2	1	......	......	......	......	29
Finnish	2	8	8	5	7	......	......	......	......	......	30
German	1	5	18	22	8	7	1	1	......	......	63
Hebrew, German		2	2	1	1	......	......	......	......	......	6
Hebrew, Polish	1	2	......	2	......	......	......	......	......	......	5
Hebrew, Roumanian	......	......	1	......	1	......	......	......	......	......	2
Hebrew, Russian		14	14	6	2	3	1	2	1	......	43
Irish		9	5	7	5	3	1	......	......	......	30
Italian, North		1	7	4	3	......	......	......	......	......	15
Italian, South	1	1	2	6	1	1	......	1	......	......	13
Magyar		......	1	1	......	......	......	......	......	......	2
Norwegian	2	26	74	40	16	8	4	......	......	......	170
Polish		1	4	6	7	6	......	2	......	1	27
Russian		4	1	......	......	......	......	......	......	......	5
Scotch	2	10	9	6	2	......	......	......	......	......	29
Swedish	4	75	109	71	28	9	5	4	......	......	305
Syrian		......	1	1	1	......	1	......	......	......	4
Welsh		2	1	......	......	......	......	......	......	......	3
Other races *a*		1	......	......	3	......	1	......	......	......	5
Total foreign-born	17	207	332	225	116	46	23	12	1	1	980
Grand total	23	280	443	292	133	57	29	12	2	1	1,272

a "Other races" includes races having less than 10 representatives in this city and pupils whose race is not reported.

TABLE 3.—*Race, sex, and age, by grade—Number of pupils of each age in each grade, by sex and by general nativity and race of father of pupil*—Continued

FIFTH GRADE.

BOYS.

General nativity and race of father of pupil.	Number of pupils of each age.										Total.
	8.	9.	10.	11.	12.	13.	14.	15.	16.	17.	
Native-born:											
White		4	34	64	38	20	4	4	1		169
Negro								2			2
Total native-born		4	34	64	38	20	4	6	1		171
Foreign-born:											
Bohemian and Moravian				1	2						3
Canadian, French			2	2	2	4	6	2	1		19
Canadian, Other		1	9	22	19	8	4	1			64
Danish				2	3						5
Dutch											
English		1	2	5	4	2			1		15
Finnish		1	1	4	6	1	1	1			15
French			2	1		1					4
German		1	5	12	7	12	2	2			41
Hebrew, German				1	1	3	1				6
Hebrew, Polish				1	1						2
Hebrew, Roumanian			1								1
Hebrew, Russian		1	5	6	2	1	3	1			19
Irish			2	2	3	3					10
Italian, North					4	2					6
Italian, South				1							1
Norwegian		1	8	23	26	16	6		1		81
Polish				2	2	3	2		1		10
Russian				1	1	1	1	1			5
Scotch		1	4	5	3	5	1				19
Swedish			27	48	63	30	11	2			181
Other races *a*				2	1						3
Total foreign-born		7	68	141	150	92	38	10	4		510
Grand total		11	102	205	188	112	42	16	5		681

a "Other races" includes races having less than 10 representatives in this city and pupils whose race is not reported.

The Immigration Commission.

TABLE **3.**—*Race, sex, and age, by grade—Number of pupils of each age in each grade, by sex and by general nativity and race of father of pupil*—Continued.

FIFTH GRADE—Continued.

GIRLS.

General nativity and race of father of pupil.	Number of pupils of each age.										Total.
	8.	9.	10.	11.	12.	13.	14.	15.	16.	17.	
Native-born:											
White		11	40	42	38	17	6	1	1		156
Negro		1	1	2	1			1	1		7
Total native-born		12	41	44	39	17	6	2	2		163
Foreign-born:											
Bohemian and Moravian			1		1						2
Canadian, French		1	1	4	3	6	3	2			20
Canadian, Other		3	13	12	15	8					51
Danish				5	1	1					7
Dutch				1	1						2
English			2	4	3	2	1				12
Finnish		1	3	7	3	2	1	1			18
French				1	1		1				3
German			3	11	5	3	1				23
Hebrew, German		1	1	1	1						4
Hebrew, Polish				2	1						3
Hebrew, Russian			8	9	6	1	1				25
Irish			5	3	3	1	1				13
Italian, North		1	1	1	2						5
Italian, South					3	1					4
Norwegian			9	23	31	11	6	1			81
Polish			1	1	1	1					4
Russian			1	1	1						3
Scotch			6	3	4		1				14
Spanish-American				1		1					2
Swedish	1	1	21	59	28	12	3				125
Welsh			1								1
Other races a			2	1							3
Total foreign-born	1	8	79	150	114	50	19	4			425
Grand total	1	20	120	194	153	67	25	6	2		588

a "Other races" includes races having less than 10 representatives in this city and pupils whose race is not reported.

TABLE 3.—*Race, sex, and age, by grade—Number of pupils of each age in each grade, by sex and by general nativity and race of father of pupil*—Continued.

FIFTH GRADE—Continued.

TOTAL.

General nativity and race of father of pupil.	Number of pupils of each age.										Total.
	8.	9.	10.	11.	12.	13.	14.	15.	16.	17.	
Native-born:											
White		15	74	106	76	37	10	5	2		325
Negro		1	1	2	1			3	1		9
Total native-born		16	75	108	77	37	10	8	3		334
Foreign-born:											
Bohemian and Moravian			1	1	3						5
Canadian, French		1	3	6	5	10	9	4	1		39
Canadian, Other		4	22	34	34	16	4	1			115
Danish				7	4	1					12
Dutch				1	1						2
English		1	4	9	7	4	1		1		27
Finnish		2	4	11	9	3	2	2			33
French			2	2	1	1	1				7
German		1	8	23	12	15	3	2			64
Hebrew, German		1	1	2	2	3	1				10
Hebrew, Polish				3	2						5
Hebrew, Roumanian			1								1
Hebrew, Russian		1	13	15	8	2	4	1			44
Irish			7	5	6	4	1				23
Italian, North		1	1	1	6	2					11
Italian, South				1	3	1					5
Norwegian		1	17	46	57	27	12	1	1		162
Polish			1	3	3	4	2		1		14
Russian			1	2	2	1	1	1			8
Scotch		1	10	8	7	5	2				33
Spanish-American				1		1					2
Swedish	1	1	48	107	91	42	14	2			306
Welsh			1								1
Other races a			2	3	1						6
Total foreign-born	1	15	147	291	264	142	57	14	4		969
Grand total	1	31	222	399	341	179	67	22	7		1,235

a "Other races" includes races having less than 10 representatives in this city and pupils whose race is not reported.

TABLE 3.—*Race, sex, and age, by grade—Number of pupils of each age in each grade, by sex and by general nativity and race of father of pupil*—Continued.

SIXTH GRADE.

BOYS.

General nativity and race of father of pupil.	Number of pupils of each age.							Total.
	10.	11.	12.	13.	14.	15.	16.	
Native-born:								
White.........................	3	35	42	26	20	8	3	137
Negro..........................			1	3	....	1	....	5
Total native-born.............	3	35	43	29	20	9	3	142
Foreign-born:								
Bohemian and Moravian........			1		1			2
Canadian, French.............		2	7	3	5	1	1	19
Canadian, Other..............	2	8	15	13	6	4	1	49
Danish.......................			3	1	1			5
Dutch........................				1				1
English......................		3	8	4				15
Finnish......................		2		4		1		7
German.......................	1	5	7	14	9	6		42
Hebrew, German...............				4				4
Hebrew, Roumanian............		1						1
Hebrew, Russian..............	1	3	8	2	3			17
Irish........................		3	1	5	3			12
Italian, North...............		1	2			1		4
Italian, South...............			1	1		2		4
Norwegian....................	1	11	19	21	14	6		72
Polish.......................		4	1	5	3	2		15
Scotch.......................		1	3	5	2			11
Spanish-American.............			1	2	4			7
Swedish......................	1	20	36	39	22	2	1	121
Other races *a*...............			1	2	1			4
Total foreign-born...........	6	64	114	126	74	25	3	412
Grand total..................	9	99	157	155	94	34	6	554

a "Other races" includes races having less than 10 representatives in this city and pupils whose race is not reported.

TABLE 3.—*Race, sex, and age, by grade—Number of pupils of each age in each grade, by sex and by general nativity and race of father of pupil*—Continued.

SIXTH GRADE—Continued.

GIRLS.

General nativity and race of father of pupil.	Number of pupils of each age.							Total.
	10.	11.	12.	13.	14.	15.	16.	
Native-born:								
White................................	2	24	49	35	16	5	....	131
Negro...............................	....	....	1	1	....	....	....	2
Total native-born...............	2	24	50	36	16	5	....	133
Foreign-born:								
Bohemian and Moravian..........	....	....	....	....	1	....	....	1
Canadian, French...............	....	1	4	8	2	2	....	17
Canadian, Other.................	2	2	20	12	15	....	....	51
Danish..........................	1	1	2	....	....	....	....	4
English.........................	....	2	4	4	....	1	....	11
Finnish.........................	....	5	2	3	....	....	....	10
French..........................	....	....	....	....	2	....	....	2
German..........................	....	5	13	9	4	3	....	34
Hebrew, German..................	....	2	....	1	1	....	....	4
Hebrew, Polish..................	....	....	2	....	....	....	....	2
Hebrew, Roumanian...............	....	....	....	1	....	....	....	1
Hebrew, Russian.................	2	6	7	5	3	3	....	26
Irish...........................	....	3	1	3	....	1	....	8
Italian, North..................	....	....	1	1	3	....	1	6
Italian, South..................	....	....	2	1	1	....	....	4
Magyar..........................	....	....	1	....	....	....	....	1
Norwegian.......................	1	20	28	14	11	1	....	75
Polish..........................	....	....	1	3	1	1	....	6
Russian.........................	....	....	....	1	....	....	....	1
Scotch..........................	....	5	4	1	2	1	....	13
Swedish.........................	2	24	47	33	13	3	....	122
Welsh...........................	....	1	2	1	1	1	....	6
Total foreign-born.............	8	77	141	101	60	17	1	405
Grand total....................	10	101	191	137	76	22	1	538

TABLE 3.—*Race, sex, and age, by grade—Number of pupils of each age in each grade, by sex and by general nativity and race of father of pupil*—Continued.

SIXTH GRADE—Continued.

TOTAL.

General nativity and race of father of pupil.	Number of pupils of each age.							Total.
	10.	11.	12.	13.	14.	15.	16.	
Native-born:								
White	5	59	91	61	36	13	3	268
Negro			2	4		1		7
Total native-born	5	59	93	65	36	14	3	275
Foreign-born:								
Bohemian and Moravian			1		2			3
Canadian, French		3	11	11	7	3	1	36
Canadian, Other	4	10	35	25	21	4	1	100
Danish	1	1	5	1	1			9
Dutch				1				1
English		5	12	8		1		26
Finnish		7	2	7		1		17
French					2			2
German	1	10	20	23	13	9		76
Hebrew, German		2		5	1			8
Hebrew, Polish			2					2
Hebrew, Roumanian		1		1				2
Hebrew, Russian	3	9	15	7	6	3		43
Irish		6	2	8	3	1		20
Italian, North		1	3	1	3	1	1	10
Italian, South			3	2	1	2		8
Magyar			1					1
Norwegian	2	31	47	35	25	7		147
Polish		4	2	8	4	3		21
Russian				1				1
Scotch		6	7	6	4	1		24
Spanish-American			1	2	4			7
Swedish	3	44	83	72	35	5	1	243
Welsh		1	2	1	1	1		6
Other races a			1	2	1			4
Total foreign-born	14	141	255	227	134	42	4	817
Grand total	19	200	348	292	170	56	7	1,092

a "Other races" includes races having less than 10 representatives in this city and pupils whose race is not reported.

TABLE 3.—*Race, sex, and age, by grade—Number of pupils of each age in each grade, by sex and by general nativity and race of father of pupil*—Continued.

SEVENTH GRADE.

BOYS.

General nativity and race of father of pupil.	Number of pupils of each age.								Total.
	10.	11.	12.	13.	14.	15.	16.	17.	
Native-born:									
White		1	22	25	34	13	1	1	97
Negro						1			1
Indian				1					1
Total native-born		1	22	26	34	14	1	1	99
Foreign-born:									
Canadian, French			3	3	2	2			10
Canadian, Other			4	10	14	4	1		33
Danish				4	2				6
Dutch				1					1
English			4	3	3	3			13
Finnish			1	3	4	1			9
German		1	4	10	6	4			25
Hebrew, Polish			1		2				3
Hebrew, Russian			2	1	4	2	1		10
Irish			2		3	2	1		8
Italian, North		1		1					2
Italian, South				1					1
Norwegian		1	5	13	15	5	2		41
Polish			1		2	3			6
Scotch	1		2	5	2	4			14
Swedish		2	14	35	23	19			93
Welsh					1				1
Other races *a*				1	1				2
Total foreign-born	1	5	43	91	84	49	5		278
Grand total	1	6	65	117	118	63	6	1	377

a "Other races" includes races having less than 10 representatives in this city and pupils whose race is not reported.

TABLE 3.—*Race, sex, and age, by grade—Number of pupils of each age in each grade, by sex and by general nativity and race of father of pupil*—Continued.

SEVENTH GRADE—Continued.

GIRLS.

General nativity and race of father of pupil.	Number of pupils of each age.								Total.
	10.	11.	12.	13.	14.	15.	16.	17.	
Native-born:									
White	1	4	28	40	34	7	1		115
Negro				1		1			2
Total native-born	1	4	28	41	34	8	1	1	117
Foreign-born:									
Bohemian and Moravian			2	1	1				4
Canadian, French		1	1	7	3	3			15
Canadian, Other		2	12	16	13	5	1		49
Danish			4	6	1				11
English			1	4	4	2	1		12
Finnish				7	4				11
French				1	1				2
German			5	5	4	5			19
Hebrew, German		1					1		2
Hebrew, Polish					1				1
Hebrew, Russian			4	6	1				11
Irish			1	3	1				5
Italian, South				1					1
Norwegian		1	8	14	14	4	2		43
Polish					5				5
Russian	1								1
Scotch		1		8	2	4			15
Swedish		3	10	40	32	4	1		90
Welsh			2	1	1				4
Other races a						1			1
Total foreign-born	1	9	50	120	88	28	6		302
Grand total	2	13	78	161	122	36	7		419

a "Other races" includes races having less than 10 representatives in this city and pupils whose race is not reported.

TABLE 3.—*Race, sex, and age, by grade—Number of pupils of each age in each grade, by sex and by general nativity and race of father of pupil*—Continued.

SEVENTH GRADE—Continued.

TOTAL.

General nativity and race of father of pupil.	Number of pupils of each age.								Total.
	10.	11.	12.	13.	14.	15.	16.	17.	
Native-born:									
White	1	5	50	65	68	20	2	1	212
Negro				1		2			3
Indian				1					1
Total native-born	1	5	50	67	68	22	2	1	216
Foreign-born:									
Bohemian and Moravian			2	1	1				4
Canadian, French		1	4	10	5	5			25
Canadian, Other		2	16	26	27	9	2		82
Danish			4	10	3				17
Dutch				1					1
English			5	7	7	5	1		25
Finnish			1	10	8	1			20
French				1	1				2
German		1	9	15	10	9			44
Hebrew, German		1					1		2
Hebrew, Polish			1		3				4
Hebrew, Russian			6	7	5	2	1		21
Irish			3	3	4	2	1		13
Italian, North		1		1					2
Italian, South				2					2
Norwegian		2	13	27	29	9	4		84
Polish			1		7	3			11
Russian	1								1
Scotch	1	1	2	13	4	8			29
Swedish		5	24	75	55	23	1		183
Welsh			2	1	2				5
Other races *a*				1	1	1			3
Total foreign-born	2	14	93	211	172	77	11		580
Grand total	3	19	143	278	240	99	13	1	796

a "Other races" includes races having less than 10 representatives in this city and pupils whose race is not reported.

TABLE **3.**—*Race, sex, and age, by grade—Number of pupils of each age in each grade, by sex and by general nativity and race of father of pupil*—Continued.

EIGHTH GRADE.

BOYS.

General nativity and race of father of pupil.	Number of pupils of each age.						Total.
	12.	13.	14.	15.	16.	17.	
Native-born, White	5	13	36	28	8	5	95
Foreign-born:							
Bohemian and Moravian			1				1
Canadian, French		1		2			3
Canadian, Other	1	6	6	8	3		24
Danish			1	1	2		4
English		4	3	2			9
Finnish	1		2	3	1		7
German	1	5	8	6	2	1	23
Hebrew, Polish			1				1
Hebrew, Russian	1	2	2	1	1		7
Irish	2		3	2	1		8
Italian, North			2				2
Italian, South			1				1
Norwegian		7	16	15	1	1	40
Polish					1		1
Scotch		5		1		1	7
Swedish	1	10	25	16	4	1	57
Other races a				1			1
Total foreign-born	7	40	71	58	16	4	196
Grand total	12	53	107	86	24	9	291

GIRLS.

General nativity and race of father of pupil.	12.	13.	14.	15.	16.	17.	Total.
Native-born:							
White	5	20	51	36	3	3	118
Negro		1			1	1	3
Total native-born	5	21	51	36	4	4	121
Foreign-born:							
Bohemian and Moravian		1					1
Canadian, French		1	3	3	2		9
Canadian, Other	3	5	13	7	7		35
Danish	1	1	2	1			5
English		5		5	3		13
Finnish		1	4		2		7
German	1	2	10	5	1		19
Hebrew, German		1	3				4
Hebrew, Roumanian			1				1
Hebrew, Russian		5	5	1		1	12
Irish			4	2	2		8
Italian, North			1				1
Italian, South		1					1
Norwegian	1	14	16	12	5	1	49
Scotch	1	3	6	5	2		17
Swedish	7	18	32	19	3		79
Other races a			2	3			5
Total foreign-born	14	60	103	60	27	2	266
Grand total	19	81	154	96	31	6	387

a "Other races" includes races having less than 10 representatives in this city and pupils whose race is not reported.

TABLE **3.**—*Race, sex, and age, by grade—Number of pupils of each age in each grade, by sex and by general nativity and race of father of pupil*—Continued.

EIGHTH GRADE—Continued.

TOTAL.

General nativity and race of father of pupil.	Number of pupils of each age.						Total.
	12.	13.	14.	15.	16.	17.	
Native-born:							
White.................................	10	33	87	64	11	8	213
Negro.................................	....	1	....	....	1	1	3
Total native-born.....................	10	34	87	64	12	9	216
Foreign-born:							
Bohemian and Moravian.............	....	1	1	....	....	....	2
Canadian, French....................	....	2	3	5	2	....	12
Canadian, Other.....................	4	11	19	15	10	....	59
Danish...............................	1	1	3	2	2	....	9
English..............................	....	9	3	7	3	....	22
Finnish..............................	1	1	6	3	3	....	14
German..............................	2	7	18	11	3	1	42
Hebrew, German.....................	....	1	3	....	....	....	4
Hebrew, Polish......................	....	....	1	....	....	....	1
Hebrew, Roumanian..................	....	....	1	....	....	....	1
Hebrew, Russian.....................	1	7	7	2	1	1	19
Irish.................................	2	....	7	4	3	....	16
Italian, North.......................	....	....	3	....	....	....	3
Italian, South.......................	....	1	1	....	....	....	2
Norwegian...........................	1	21	32	27	6	2	89
Polish................................	....	....	....	....	1	....	1
Scotch...............................	1	8	6	6	2	1	24
Swedish..............................	8	28	57	35	7	1	136
Other races *a*......................	....	2	3	1	....	....	6
Total foreign-born...................	21	100	174	118	43	6	462
Grand total..........................	31	134	261	182	55	15	678

a "Other races" includes races having less than 10 representatives in this city and pupils whose race is not reported.

TABLE 3.—*Race, sex, and age, by grade—Number of pupils of each age in each grade, by sex and by general nativity and race of father of pupil*—Continued.

FIRST YEAR HIGH SCHOOL.

BOYS.

General nativity and race of father of pupil.	Number of pupils of each age.								Total.
	12.	13.	14.	15.	16.	17.	18.	19.	
Native-born, White		6	14	18	12	3			53
Foreign-born:									
Canadian, French			3	1	1	1	1		7
Canadian, Other		1	6	12	3	1			23
Danish					1				1
English			1	2					3
Finnish			1	1	1				3
French						1			1
German			2	2	4				8
Hebrew, German			2	1			1		4
Hebrew, Polish				2					2
Hebrew, Russian		1		1	3				5
Irish				1	1				2
Norwegian			5	3	1	2	1		12
Polish					2				2
Russian				1					1
Scotch			1		2			1	4
Swedish		3	6	8	2	1			20
Other races *a*				1					1
Total foreign-born		5	27	36	21	6	3	1	99
Grand total		11	41	54	33	9	3	1	152

GIRLS.

General nativity and race of father of pupil.	12.	13.	14.	15.	16.	17.	18.	19.	Total.
Native-born, White		1	18	37	22	7			85
Foreign-born:									
Canadian, French	1			1	1				3
Canadian, Other		1	2	9	9	2			23
English			1	3					4
Finnish		1							1
German			6	6	5				17
Hebrew, Russian			1	1	2				4
Irish			1	1	1				3
Italian, South				1					1
Norwegian			6	10	7	1	1		25
Scotch			1	8	2	1			12
Swedish		1	6	12	3				22
Welsh							1		1
Other races *a*		1							1
Total foreign-born	1	4	24	52	30	4	2		117
Grand total	1	5	42	89	52	11	2		202

a "Other races" includes races having less than 10 representatives in this city and pupils whose race is not reported.

TABLE 3.—*Race, sex, and age, by grade—Number of pupils of each age in each grade, by sex and by general nativity and race of father of pupil*—Continued.

FIRST YEAR HIGH SCHOOL—Continued.

TOTAL.

General nativity and race of father of pupil.	Number of pupils of each age.								Total.
	12.	13.	14.	15.	16.	17.	18.	19.	
Native-born, White		7	32	55	34	10			138
Foreign-born:									
Canadian, French	1		3	2	2	1	1		10
Canadian, Other		2	8	21	12	3			46
Danish					1				1
English			2	5					7
Finnish		1	1	1	1				4
French						1			1
German			8	8	9				25
Hebrew, German			2	1			1		4
Hebrew, Polish				2					2
Hebrew, Russian		1	1	2	5				9
Irish			1	2	2				5
Italian, South				1					1
Norwegian			11	13	8	3	2		37
Polish					2				2
Russian				1					1
Scotch			2	8	4	1		1	16
Swedish		4	12	20	5	1			42
Welsh							1		1
Other races *a*		1		1					2
Total foreign-born	1	9	51	88	51	10	5	1	216
Grand total	1	16	83	143	85	20	5	1	354

a "Other races" includes races having less than 10 representatives in this city and pupils whose race is not reported.

SECOND YEAR HIGH SCHOOL.

BOYS.

General nativity and race of father of pupil.	Number of pupils of each age.							Total.
	14.	15.	16.	17.	18.	19.	20 or over.	
Native-born:								
White	2	10	14	10	4	2		42
Negro				1				1
Total native-born	2	10	14	11	4	2		43
Foreign-born:								
Canadian, French				1	1			2
Canadian, Other	1	4	4	6	2			17
English		1			1			2
Finnish		1	1					2
German					1	2		3
Hebrew, Polish				1				1
Hebrew, Roumanian				1				1
Irish	2	2	2	1				7
Norwegian		4	1	3	1			9
Scotch		1		1				2
Spanish-American	1							1
Swedish	1	4	2		1			8
Welsh						1		1
Other races *a*				1			1	2
Total foreign-born	5	17	10	15	7	2	2	58
Grand total	7	27	24	26	11	4	2	101

a "Other races" includes races having less than 10 representatives in this city and pupils whose race is not reported.

TABLE 3.—*Race, sex, and age, by grade—Number of pupils of each age in each grade, by sex and by general nativity and race of father of pupil*—Continued.

SECOND YEAR HIGH SCHOOL—Continued.

GIRLS.

General nativity and race of father of pupil.	Number of pupils of each age.							Total.
	14.	15.	16.	17.	18.	19.	20 or over.	
Native-born, White	2	10	22	7	4	3	1	49
Foreign-born:								
Canadian, French		1	1	1				3
Canadian, Other		5	2	4	1			12
Danish		3						3
English			4	3				7
Finnish	2	1						3
German	1			3				4
Hebrew, German			1		1			2
Hebrew, Polish								
Hebrew, Roumanian								
Hebrew, Russian		1	2					3
Irish		2	2					4
Norwegian	1	4	3	5				13
Scotch		2	1	2	1			6
Spanish-American								
Swedish	1	6	2	1	1			11
Welsh								
Other races *a*			1					1
Total foreign-born	5	25	19	19	4			72
Grand total	7	35	41	26	8	3	1	121

a "Other races" includes races having less than 10 representatives in this city and pupils whose race is not reported.

TOTAL.

General nativity and race of father of pupil.	14.	15.	16.	17.	18.	19.	20 or over.	Total.
Native-born:								
White	4	20	36	17	8	5	1	91
Negro				1				1
Total native-born	4	20	36	18	8	5	1	92
Foreign-born:								
Canadian, French		1	1	2	1			5
Canadian, Other	1	9	6	10	3			29
Danish		3						3
English		1	4	3	1			9
Finnish	2	2	1					5
German	1			3	1	2		7
Hebrew, German			1		1			2
Hebrew, Polish				1				1
Hebrew, Roumanian				1				1
Hebrew, Russian		1	2					3
Irish	2	4	4	1				11
Norwegian	1	8	4	8	1			22
Scotch		3	1	3	1			8
Spanish-American	1							1
Swedish	2	10	4	1	2			19
Welsh							1	1
Other races *a*			1	1			1	3
Total foreign-born	10	42	29	34	11	2	2	130
Grand total	14	62	65	52	19	7	3	222

a "Other races" includes races having less than 10 representatives in this city and pupils whose race is not reported.

TABLE 3.—*Race, sex, and age, by grade—Number of pupils of each age in each grade, by sex and by general nativity and race of father of pupil*—Continued.

THIRD YEAR HIGH SCHOOL.

BOYS.

General nativity and race of father of pupil.	Number of pupils of each age.						Total.
	15.	16.	17.	18.	19.	20 or over.	
Native-born, White	2	3	11	4	1	1	22
Foreign-born:							
Canadian, French			1				1
Canadian, Other	3	1	2	3	2		11
English		1					1
German		1		2			3
Hebrew, German			1				1
Hebrew, Russian			1				1
Irish				1			1
Norwegian		2	4	1			7
Scotch		2	1	1	1		5
Swedish	1	2		2			5
Other races a		1					1
Total foreign-born	4	10	10	10	3		37
Grand total	6	13	21	14	4	1	59

GIRLS.

General nativity and race of father of pupil.	15.	16.	17.	18.	19.	20 or over.	Total.
Native-born, White	2	15	25	5			47
Foreign-born:							
Canadian, French		1					1
Canadian, Other	1	2	4	4			11
Danish	1						1
English		4		1			5
German	1	1	2	2			6
Hebrew, German			1				1
Hebrew, Russian				1			1
Irish		1					1
Italian, North	1						1
Norwegian		1	1	5			7
Polish		1	1				2
Scotch	1		1				2
Swedish	1	9	3				13
Welsh				1			1
Total foreign-born	6	20	13	14			53
Grand total	8	35	38	19			100

a "Other races" includes races having less than 10 representatives in this city and pupils whose race is not reported.

TABLE 3.—*Race, sex, and age, by grade—Number of pupils of each age in each grade, by sex and by general nativity and race of father of pupil*—Continued.

THIRD YEAR HIGH SCHOOL—Continued.

TOTAL.

General nativity and race of father of pupil.	Number of pupils of each age.						Total.
	15.	16.	17.	18.	19.	20 or over.	
Native-born, White	4	18	36	9	1	1	69
Foreign-born:							
Canadian, French		1	1				2
Canadian, Other	4	3	6	7	2		22
Danish	1						1
English		5		1			6
German	1	2	2	4			9
Hebrew, German			2				2
Hebrew, Russian				1			2
Irish		1		1			2
Italian, North	1						1
Norwegian		3	5	6			14
Polish			1	1			2
Scotch	1	2	2	1	1		7
Swedish	2	11	3	2			18
Welsh				1			1
Other races a		1					1
Total foreign-born	10	30	23	24	3		90
Grand total	14	48	59	33	4	1	159

FOURTH YEAR HIGH SCHOOL.

BOYS.

General nativity and race of father of pupil.	Number of pupils of each age.						Total.
	15.	16.	17.	18.	19.	20 or over.	
Native-born, White		1	3	14	3	3	24
Foreign-born:							
Canadian, French			1				1
Canadian, Other			2	3	1	1	7
English			2			1	3
German					1		1
Hebrew, Roumanian			1				1
Hebrew, Russian			1				1
Irish			1		3		4
Norwegian			4	3			7
Scotch					1		1
Swedish		1	2				3
Total foreign-born		1	14	6	6	2	29
Grand total		2	17	20	9	5	53

a "Other races" includes races having less than 10 representatives in this city and pupils whose race is not reported.

TABLE 3.—*Race, sex, and age, by grade—Number of pupils of each age in each grade, by sex and by general nativity and race of father of pupil*—Continued.

FOURTH YEAR HIGH SCHOOL—Continued.

GIRLS.

General nativity and race of father of pupil.	Number of pupils of each age.						Total.
	15.	16.	17.	18.	19.	20 or over.	
Native-born, White		3	13	14	1		31
Foreign-born:							
Canadian, French			2			1	3
Canadian, Other		1	3	4	2		10
English		1	2	1			4
German		1	2				3
Hebrew, Roumanian	1						1
Italian, North		1					1
Norwegian		1	6	2	1		10
Scotch			2	1	1		4
Swedish			3		1		4
Total foreign-born	1	5	20	8	5	1	40
Grand total	1	8	33	22	6	1	71

TOTAL.

General nativity and race of father of pupil.	15.	16.	17.	18.	19.	20 or over.	Total.
Native-born, White		4	16	28	4	3	55
Foreign-born:							
Canadian, French			3			1	4
Canadian, Other		1	5	7	3	1	17
English		1	4	1		1	7
German		1	2		1		4
Hebrew, Roumanian	1		1				2
Hebrew, Russian			1				1
Irish			1		3		4
Italian, North		1					1
Norwegian		1	10	5	1		17
Scotch			2	1	2		5
Swedish		1	5		1		7
Total foreign-born	1	6	34	14	11	3	69
Grand total	1	10	50	42	15	6	124

TABLE 4.—*Race and grade, by age—Number of. pupils of each specified age in each grade, by general nativity and race of father of pupil.*

BOYS: AGE 4 YEARS.

General nativity and race of father of pupil.	Kindergarten.
Native-born, White	7
Foreign-born, other races *a*	10
Grand total	17

a "Other races" includes races having less than 10 representatives of this sex and age and pupils whose race is not reported.

TABLE 4.—*Race and grade, by age—Number of pupils of each specified age in each grade, by general nativity and race of father of pupil—*Continued.

BOYS: AGE 5 YEARS.

General nativity and race of father of pupil.	Kinder-garten.	Elementary grade 1.	Total.
Native-born:			
White	51	15	66
Negro	1		1
Total native-born	52	15	67
Foreign-born:			
Canadian (other than French)	16	6	22
Finnish	10	8	18
German	11	1	12
Hebrew, Russian	19	1	20
Norwegian	20	3	23
Swedish	39	10	49
Other races a	32	10	42
Total foreign-born	147	39	186
Grand total	199	54	253

a "Other races" includes races having less than 10 representatives of this sex and age and pupils whose race is not reported.

BOYS: AGE 6 YEARS.

General nativity and race of father of pupil.	Kinder-garten.	Elementary grades.		Total.
		1.	2.	
Native-born:				
White	13	93	6	112
Negro		2		2
Indian		2		2
Total native-born	13	97	6	116
Foreign-born:				
Canadian, French	2	26		28
Canadian, Other	3	36		39
English	1	13		14
Finnish	1	13	2	16
German	3	20	2	25
Hebrew, Russian	6	14	1	21
Norwegian	7	63	1	71
Polish	1	13		14
Swedish	3	111	3	117
Other races a	5	41		46
Total foreign-born	32	350	9	391
Grand total	45	447	15	507

a "Other races" includes races having less than 10 representatives of this sex and age and pupils whose race is not reported.

TABLE 4.—*Race and grade, by age—Number of pupils of each specified age in each grade, by general nativity and race of father of pupil*—Continued.

BOYS: AGE 7 YEARS.

General nativity and race of father of pupil.	Kinder-garten.	Elementary grades.			Total.
		1.	2.	3.	
Native-born:					
White.........	....	67	49	6	122
Negro.........	....	1	....	....	1
Total native-born.........	....	68	49	6	123
Foreign-born:					
Canadian, French.........	....	15	10	....	25
Canadian, Other.........	....	14	15	2	31
English.........	....	6	12	....	18
Finnish.........	....	10	7	....	17
German.........	....	9	13	....	22
Hebrew, Russian.........	2	11	5	2	20
Irish.........	....	10	5	....	15
Norwegian.........	....	32	22	2	56
Polish.........	....	18	2	....	20
Scotch.........	....	5	8	....	13
Swedish.........	2	62	39	....	103
Other races a.........	....	26	11	....	37
Total foreign-born.........	4	218	149	6	377
Grand total.........	4	286	198	12	500

a "Other races" includes races having less than 10 representatives of this sex and age and pupils whose race is not reported.

BOYS: AGE 8 YEARS.

General nativity and race of father of pupil.	Elementary grades.				Total.
	1.	2.	3.	4.	
Native-born:					
White.........	24	51	57	3	135
Negro.........	1	1	1	....	3
Total native-born.........	25	52	58	3	138
Foreign-born:					
Canadian, French.........	3	9	2	....	14
Canadian Other.........	6	19	9	....	34
English.........	4	5	6	1	16
Finnish.........	4	7	6	....	17
German.........	2	14	8	....	24
Hebrew, Russian.........	4	9	7	....	20
Irish.........	3	9	....	....	12
Norwegian.........	13	37	19	1	70
Polish.........	14	9	1	....	24
Scotch.........	2	6	4	1	13
Swedish.........	27	67	53	2	149
Other races a.........	10	16	13	....	39
Total foreign-born.........	92	207	128	5	432
Grand total.........	117	259	186	8	570

a "Other races" includes races having less than 10 representatives of this sex and age and pupils whose race is not reported.

TABLE 4.—*Race and grade, by age—Number of pupils of each specified age in each grade, by general nativity and race of father of pupil*—Continued.

BOYS: AGE 9 YEARS.

General nativity and race of father of pupil.	Elementary grades.					Total.
	1.	2.	3.	4.	5.	
Native-born:						
White	3	23	68	34	4	132
Negro	1	1		1		3
Indian			1			1
Total native-born	4	24	69	35	4	136
Foreign-born:						
Canadian, French	1	4	11	5		21
Canadian, Other		12	21	13	1	47
English		2	9	3	1	15
Finnish		1	6	3	1	11
German		11	14	2	1	28
Hebrew, Russian	1	4	5	6	1	17
Norwegian	6	13	29	11	1	60
Polish	7	7	3			17
Scotch		1	6	5	1	13
Swedish	7	21	51	34		113
Other races a	7	7	15	7		36
Total foreign-born	29	83	170	89	7	378
Grand total	33	107	239	124	11	514

a "Other races" includes races having less than 10 representatives of this sex and age and pupils whose race is not reported.

BOYS: AGE 10 YEARS.

General nativity and race of father of pupil.	Elementary grades.							Total.
	1.	2.	3.	4.	5.	6.	7.	
Native-born:								
White	1	12	31	59	34	3		140
Negro			1					1
Total native-born	1	12	32	59	34	3		141
Foreign-born:								
Canadian, French	1	5	9	12	2			29
Canadian, Other	2	4	7	19	9	2		43
English		3	5	6	2			16
Finnish		2	4	4	1			11
German		2	10	6	5	1		24
Hebrew, Russian	2	4	5	9	5	1		26
Norwegian	1	8	13	30	8	1		61
Polish	5	3	2	2				12
Scotch		2	4	3	4		1	14
Swedish		10	40	49	27	1		127
Other races a		3	10	16	5			34
Total foreign-born	11	46	109	146	68	6	1	397
Grand total	12	58	141	215	102	9	1	538

a "Other races" includes races having less than 10 representatives of this sex and age and pupils whose race is not reported.

TABLE 4.—*Race and grade, by age—Number of pupils of each specified age in each grade, by general nativity and race of father of pupil*—Continued.

BOYS: AGE 11 YEARS.

General nativity and race of father of pupil.	Elementary grades.							Total.
	1.	2.	3.	4.	5.	6.	7.	
Native-born:								
White		3	7	40	64	35	1	150
Negro			1	1				2
Total native-born		3	8	41	64	35	1	152
Foreign-born:								
Canadian, French			6	6	2	2		16
Canadian, Other			6	14	22	8		50
English		1	2	4	5	3		15
Finnish	1	1	1	4	4	2		13
German		1	3	12	12	5	1	34
Hebrew, Russian		1	3	4	6	3		17
Irish			1	6	2	3		12
Norwegian		2	13	24	23	11	1	74
Polish		3	4	1	2	4		14
Scotch			1	4	5	1		11
Swedish		1	9	31	48	20	2	111
Other races *a*	1	1	4	11	10	2	1	30
Total foreign-born	2	11	53	121	141	64	5	397
Grand total	2	14	61	162	205	99	6	549

a "Other races" includes races having less than 10 representatives of this sex and age and pupils whose race is not reported.

BOYS: AGE 12 YEARS.

General nativity and race of father of pupil.	Elementary grades.								Total.
	1.	2.	3.	4.	5.	6.	7.	8.	
Native-born:									
White		1	2	3	38	42	22	5	113
Negro						1			1
Total native-born		1	2	3	38	43	22	5	114
Foreign-born:									
Canadian, French			3	4	2	7	3		19
Canadian, Other		2	3	9	19	15	4	1	53
English				1	4	7	4	1	17
Finnish					5	6	1	1	13
German			3	2	7	7	4	1	24
Hebrew, German		1	3	2	2	8	2	1	19
Irish			1	4	3	1	2	2	13
Norwegian	1	2	3	9	26	19	5		65
Swedish		3	3	18	63	36	14		137
Other races *a*			4	14	19	8	4		49
Total foreign-born	1	8	23	63	150	114	43	7	409
Grand total	1	9	25	66	188	157	65	12	523

a "Other races" includes races having less than 10 representatives of this sex and age and pupils whose race is not reported.

TABLE 4.—*Race and grade, by age—Number of pupils of each specified age in each grade, by general nativity and race of father of pupil*—Continued.

BOYS: AGE 13 YEARS.

General nativity and race of father of pupil.	Elementary grades.								High school, first year.	Total.
	1.	2.	3.	4.	5.	6.	7.	8.		
Native-born:										
White			2	8	20	26	25	13	6	100
Negro			1			3				4
Indian							1			1
Total native-born			3	8	20	29	26	13	6	105
Foreign-born:										
Canadian, French			1	3	4	3	3	1		15
Canadian, Other		1	1		8	13	10	6	1	40
English				1	2	4	3	4		14
German				5	12	14	10	5		46
Hebrew (not specified)			1	1	4	6	1	2	1	16
Irish				2	3	5				10
Norwegian			1	4	16	21	13	7		62
Polish	1		2	2	3	5				13
Scotch			1		5	5	5	5		21
Swedish		1	1	8	30	39	35	10	3	127
Other races [a]		1	1	2	5	11	11			31
Total foreign-born	1	3	9	28	92	126	91	40	5	395
Grand total	1	3	12	36	112	155	117	53	11	500

[a] "Other races" includes races having less than 10 representatives of this sex and age and pupils whose race is not reported.

BOYS: AGE 14 YEARS.

General nativity and race of father of pupil.	Elementary grades.								High school.		Total.
	1.	2.	3.	4.	5.	6.	7.	8.	First year.	Second year.	
Native-born:											
White				3	4	20	34	36	14	2	113
Negro				1							1
Total native-born				4	4	20	34	36	14	2	114
Foreign-born:											
Canadian, French			2	4	6	5	2		3		22
Canadian, Other				2	4	6	14	6	6	1	39
German				1	2	9	6	8	2		28
Hebrew, Russian	1			1	3	3	4	2			14
Irish						3	3	3		2	11
Norwegian		1		2	2	14	15	16	5		55
Swedish		1		3	11	22	23	25	6	1	92
Other races [a]			2	1	10	12	17	11	5	1	59
Total foreign-born	1	2	4	14	38	74	84	71	27	5	320
Grand total	1	2	4	18	42	94	118	107	41	7	434

[a] "Other races" includes races having less than 10 representatives of this sex and age and pupils whose race is not reported.

TABLE 4.—*Race and grade, by age—Number of pupils of each specified age in each grade, by general nativity and race of father of pupil*—Continued.

BOYS: AGE 15 YEARS.

General nativity and race of father of pupil.	Elementary grades.						High school.			Total.
	3.	4.	5.	6.	7.	8.	First year.	Second year.	Third year.	
Native-born:										
White			4	8	13	28	18	10	2	83
Negro		2	1	1						4
Total native-born			6	9	14	28	18	10	2	87
Foreign-born:										
Canadian (other than French)		2	1	4	4	8	12	4	3	38
German		1	2	6	4	6	2			21
Norwegian				6	5	15	3	4		33
Swedish	2	3	2	2	19	16	8	4	1	57
Other races *a*	2	3	5	7	17	13	11	5		63
Total foreign-born	4	9	10	25	49	58	36	17	4	212
Grand total	4	9	16	34	63	86	54	27	6	299

a "Other races" includes races having less than 10 representatives of this sex and age and pupils whose race is not reported.

BOYS: AGE 16 YEARS.

General nativity and race of father of pupil.	Elementary grades.								High school.				Total.
	1.	2.	3.	4.	5.	6.	7.	8.	First year.	Second year.	Third year.	Fourth year.	
Native-born, White				1	1	3	1	8	12	14	3	1	44
Foreign-born:													
Canadian (other than French)						1	1	3	3	4	1		13
Swedish						1		4	2	2	2	1	12
Other races *a*	1			1	4	1	4	9	16	4	7		47
Total foreign-born	1			1	4	3	5	16	21	10	10	1	72
Grand total	1			2	5	6	6	24	33	24	13	2	116

BOYS: AGE 17 YEARS.

General nativity and race of father of pupil.	Elementary grades.								High school.				Total.
	1.	2.	3.	4.	5.	6.	7.	8.	First year.	Second year.	Third year.	Fourth year.	
Native-born:													
White							1	5	3	10	11	3	33
Negro										1			1
Total native-born							1	5	3	11	11	3	34
Foreign-born:													
Canadian (other than French)									1	6	2	2	11
Norwegian								1	2	3	4	4	14
Other races *a*	1							3	3	6	4	8	25
Total foreign-born	1							4	6	15	10	14	50
Grand total	1						1	9	9	26	21	17	84

a "Other races" includes races having less than 10 representatives of this sex and age and pupils whose race is not reported.

TABLE 4.—*Race and grade, by age—Number of pupils of each specified age in each grade, by general nativity and race of father of pupil*—Continued.

BOYS: AGE 18 YEARS.

General nativity and race of father of pupil.	High school.				Total.
	First year.	Second year.	Third year.	Fourth year.	
Native-born, White		4	4	14	22
Foreign-born, other races a	3	7	10	6	26
Grand total	3	11	14	20	48

a "Other races" includes races having less than 10 representatives of this sex and age and pupils whose race is not reported.

BOYS: AGE 19 YEARS.

General nativity and race of father of pupil.	Elementary grade 1.	High school.				Total.
		First year.	Second year.	Third year.	Fourth year.	
Native-born, White			2	1	3	6
Foreign-born, other races a	1	1	2	3	6	13
Grand total	1	1	4	4	9	19

a "Other races" includes races having less than 10 representatives of this sex and age and pupils whose race is not reported.

BOYS: AGE 20 YEARS.

General nativity and race of father of pupil.	Elementary grade 3.	High school.			Total.
		Second year.	Third year.	Fourth year.	
Native-born, White			1	3	4
Foreign-born, other races a	2	2		2	6
Grand total	2	2	1	5	10

a "Other races" includes races having less than 10 representatives of this sex and age and pupils whose race is not reported.

GIRLS: AGE 4 YEARS.

General nativity and race of father of pupil.	Kindergarten.
Native-born, White	5
Foreign-born, other races a	8
Grand total	13

a "Other races" includes races having less than 10 representatives of this sex and age and pupils whose race is not reported.

TABLE 4.—*Race and grade, by age—Number of pupils of each specified age in each grade, by general nativity and race of father of pupil—Continued.*

GIRLS; AGE 5 YEARS.

General nativity and race of father of pupil.	Kinder-garten.	Elemen-tary grade 1.	Total.
Native-born:			
White	62	12	74
Negro	1		1
Total native-born	63	12	75
Foreign-born:			
Canadian (other than French)	16	4	20
Finnish	6	4	10
Hebrew, Russian	16		16
Italian, South	9	1	10
Norwegian	24	7	31
Swedish	40	10	50
Other races a	23	9	32
Total foreign-born	134	35	169
Grand total	197	47	244

a "Other races" includes races having less than 10 representatives of this sex and age and pupils whose race is not reported.

GIRLS: AGE 6 YEARS.

General nativity and race of father of pupil.	Kinder-garten.	Elementary grades.		Total.
		1.	2.	
Native-born:				
White	10	66	3	79
Negro		4		4
Total native-born	10	70	3	83
Foreign-born:				
Canadian, French		22		22
Canadian, Other	3	28		31
English	2	8		10
Finnish		18		18
Germany	4	15	1	20
Hebrew, Russian	5	20		25
Irish	1	7	2	10
Norwegian	8	50	3	61
Polish	1	12		13
Swedish	8	82	6	96
Other races a	1	33	2	36
Total foreign-born	33	295	14	342
Grand total	43	365	17	425

a "Other races" includes races having less than 10 representatives of this sex and age and pupils whose race is not reported.

TABLE 4.—*Race and grade, by age—Number of pupils of each specified age in each grade, by general nativity and race of father of pupil*—Continued.

GIRLS: AGE 7 YEARS.

General nativity and race of father of pupil.	Elementary grades.			Total.
	1.	2.	3.	
Native-born, White	60	37	2	99
Foreign-born:				
Canadian, French	10	5		15
Canadian, Other	28	12	2	42
English	2	9		11
Finnish	5	5		10
German	9	11		20
Hebrew, Russian	6	10	1	17
Norwegian	45	21	4	70
Polish	12	3		15
Scotch	9	6		15
Swedish	69	55	7	131
Other races a	20	17		37
Total foreign-born	215	154	14	383
Grand total	275	191	16	482

a "Other races" includes races having less than 10 representatives of this sex and age and pupils whose race is not reported.

GIRLS: AGE 8 YEARS.

General nativity and race of father of pupil.	Elementary grades.					Total.
	1.	2.	3.	4.	5.	
Native-born:						
White	33	56	65	3		157
Indian		1				1
Total native-born	33	57	65	3		158
Foreign-born:						
Canadian, French	4	14	4			22
Canadian, Other	5	17	21	3		46
English	1	6	7			14
Finnish	4	5	10	2		21
German	4	13	8	1		26
Hebrew, Russian	2	7	3			12
Irish	3	7				10
Norwegian	12	31	24	1		68
Polish	8	5	2			15
Scotch	2	9	4	1		16
Swedish	27	44	61	2	1	135
Other races a	8	16	9	2		35
Total foreign-born	80	174	153	12	1	420
Grand total	113	231	218	15	1	578

a "Other races" includes races having less than 10 representatives of this sex and age and pupils whose race is not reported.

TABLE 4.—*Race and grade, by age—Number of pupils of each specified age in each grade, by general nativity and race of father of pupil—Continued.*

GIRLS: AGE 9 YEARS.

General nativity and race of father of pupil.	Elementary grades.					Total.
	1.	2.	3.	4.	5.	
Native-born:						
White	1	15	55	37	11	119
Negro			2	1	1	4
Indian	1					1
Total native-born	2	15	57	38	12	124
Foreign-born:						
Canadian, French	5	2	6	3	1	17
Canadian, Other	2	4	31	14	3	54
English	2	4	1	5		12
Finnish		2	11	5	1	19
German	2	4	22	3		31
Hebrew, Russian		2	10	8		20
Irish		1	5	7		13
Norwegian	2	9	33	15		59
Polish	5	4	3	1		13
Scotch	1	3	4	5		13
Swedish	2	24	61	41	1	129
Other races *a*	4	7	11	11	2	35
Total foreign-born	25	66	198	118	8	415
Grand total	27	81	255	156	20	539

a "Other races" includes races having less than 10 representatives of this sex and age and pupils whose race is not reported.

GIRLS: AGE 10 YEARS.

General nativity and race of father of pupil.	Elementary grades.							Total.
	1.	2.	3.	4.	5.	6.	7.	
Native-born:								
White	1	4	22	52	40	2	1	122
Negro					1			1
Total native-born	1	4	22	52	41	2	1	123
Foreign-born:								
Canadian, French		6	7	9	1			23
Canadian, Other		2	9	16	13	2		42
Finnish	1		5	4	3			13
German			5	12	3			20
Hebrew, Russian		2	5	5	8	2		22
Irish			1	4	5			10
Norwegian		2	23	44	9	1		79
Polish	4	1	2	2	1			10
Scotch		2	3	6	6			17
Swedish	1		42	60	21	2		126
Other races *a*	1	4	7	14	9	1	1	37
Total foreign-born	6	20	109	176	79	8	1	399
Grand total	7	24	131	228	120	10	2	522

a "Other races" includes races having less than 10 representatives of this sex and age and pupils whose race is not reported.

TABLE 4.—*Race and grade, by age—Number of pupils of each specified age in each grade, by general nativity and race of father of pupil*—Continued.

GIRLS: AGE 11 YEARS.

General nativity and race of father of pupil.	Elementary grades.							Total.
	1.	2.	3.	4.	5.	6.	7.	
Native-born:								
White		4	7	25	42	24	4	106
Negro				1	2			3
Total native-born		4	7	26	44	24	4	109
Foreign-born:								
Canadian, French	1		2	4	4	1	1	13
Canadian, Other		2	2	11	12	2	2	31
Finnish				1	7	5		13
German	1			10	11	5		27
Hebrew, Russian	1	2	1	2	9	6		21
Norwegian			3	16	23	20	1	63
Polish		3	6	5	1			15
Scotch		1		2	3	5	1	12
Swedish	1	3	7	40	59	24	3	137
Other races a	1	1	4	13	21	9	1	50
Total foreign-born	5	12	25	104	150	77	9	382
Grand total	5	16	32	130	194	101	13	491

a "Other races" includes races having less than 10 representatives of this sex and age and pupils whose race is not reported.

GIRLS: AGE 12 YEARS.

General nativity and race of father of pupil.	Elementary grades.								High school, first year.	Total.
	1.	2.	3.	4.	5.	6.	7.	8.		
Native-born:										
White			2	14	38	49	28	5		136
Negro					1	1				2
Total native-born			2	14	39	50	28	5		138
Foreign-born:										
Canadian, French		1		11	3	4	1		1	21
Canadian, Other			1	6	15	20	12	3		57
German				6	5	13	5	1		30
Hebrew, Russian			2		6	7	4			19
Norwegian		1	2	7	31	28	8	1		78
Polish	1	1	3	4	1	1				11
Scotch			1	1	4	4		1		11
Swedish			3	10	28	47	10	7		105
Other races a	1	2	1	8	21	17	10	1		61
Total foreign-born	2	5	13	53	114	141	50	14	1	393
Grand total	2	5	15	67	153	191	78	19	1	531

a "Other races" includes races having less than 10 representatives of this sex and age and pupils whose race is not reported.

TABLE 4.—*Race and grade, by age—Number of pupils of each specified age in each grade, by general nativity and race of father of pupil*—Continued.

GIRLS: AGE 13 YEARS.

General nativity and race of father of pupil.	Elementary grades.							High school, first year.	Grand total.
	2.	3.	4.	5.	6.	7.	8.		
Native-born:									
White		1	3	17	35	40	20	1	117
Negro					1	1	1		3
Total native-born		1	3	17	36	41	21	1	120
Foreign-born:									
Canadian, French		1	2	6	8	7	1		25
Canadian, Other			1	8	12	16	5	1	43
English				2	4	4	5		15
Finnish				2	3	7	1	1	14
German		1	2	3	9	5	2		22
Hebrew, Russian	1	1	2	1	5	6	5		21
Norwegian		4	4	11	14	14	14		61
Polish		3	4	1	3				11
Scotch					1	8	3		12
Swedish		3	1	12	33	40	18	1	108
Other races a	1		2	4	9	13	6	1	36
Total foreign-born	2	13	18	50	101	120	60	4	368
Grand total	2	14	21	67	137	161	81	5	488

a "Other races" includes races having less than 10 representatives of this sex and age and pupils whose race is not reported.

GIRLS: AGE 14 YEARS.

General nativity and race of father of pupil.	Kindergarten.	Elementary grades.								High school.		Grand total.
		1.	2.	3.	4.	5.	6.	7.	8.	First year.	Second year.	
Native-born, White					2	6	16	34	51	18	2	129
Foreign-born:												
Canadian, French					1	3	2	3	3			12
Canadian, Other					1		15	13	13	2		44
Finnish						1		4	4		2	11
German	1					1	4	4	9	6	1	26
Hebrew, Russian			1			1	3	1	5	1		12
Norwegian				2	2	6	11	14	16	6	1	58
Scotch							1	4	6	1		12
Swedish					2	3	13	32	32	6	1	89
Other races a		1	2		3	4	11	13	15	2		51
Total foreign-born	1	1	3	2	9	19	60	88	103	24	5	315
Grand total	1	1	3	2	11	25	76	122	154	42	7	444

a "Other races" includes races having less than 10 representatives of this sex and age and pupils whose race is not reported.

TABLE 4.—*Race and grade, by age—Number of pupils of each specified age in each grade, by general nativity and race of father of pupil*—Continued.

GIRLS: AGE 15 YEARS.

General nativity and race of father of pupil.	Elementary grades.								High school.				Grand total.
	1.	2.	3.	4.	5.	6.	7.	8.	First year.	Second year.	Third year.	Fourth year.	
Native-born:													
White					1	5	7	36	37	10	2		98
Negro					1		1						2
Total native-born					2	5	8	36	37	10	2		100
Foreign-born:													
Canadian, French					2	2	3	3	1	1			12
Canadian, Other							5	7	9	5	1		27
English						1	2	5	3				11
German						3	5	5	6		1		20
Hebrew, Russian	1		2			3		1	1	1		1	10
Norwegian					1	1	4	12	10	4			32
Scotch						1	4	5	8	2	1		21
Swedish			1			3	4	19	12	6	1		46
Other races *a*	2				1	3	1	3	2	6	2		20
Total foreign-born	3		3		4	17	28	60	52	25	6	1	199
Grand total	3		3		6	22	36	96	89	35	8	1	299

GIRLS: AGE 16 YEARS.

General nativity and race of father of pupil.	Elementary grades.								High school.				Grand total.
	1.	2.	3.	4.	5.	6.	7.	8.	First year.	Second year.	Third year.	Fourth year.	
Native-born:													
White					1		1	3	22	22	15	3	67
Negro					1			1					2
Total native-born					2		1	4	22	22	15	3	69
Foreign-born:													
Canadian (other than French)							1	7	9	2	2	1	22
English							1	3		4	4	1	13
Norwegian							2	5	7	3	1	1	19
Swedish							1	3	3	2	9		18
Other races *a*	2					1	1	9	11	8	4	2	38
Total foreign-born	2					1	6	27	30	19	20	5	110
Grand total	2				2	1	7	31	52	41	35	8	179

a "Other races" includes races having less than 10 representatives of this sex and age and pupils whose race is not reported

GIRLS: AGE 17 YEARS.

General nativity and race of father of pupil.	Elementary grades.						High school.				Grand total.
	3.	4.	5.	6.	7.	8.	First year.	Second year.	Third year.	Fourth year.	
Native-born:											
White						3	7	7	25	13	55
Negro						1					1
Total native-born						4	7	7	25	13	56
Foreign-born:											
Canadian (other than French)							1	4	4	3	12
Norwegian					1		1	5	1	6	14
Other races *a*	2	1				1	2	10	8	11	35
Total foreign-born	2	1				2	4	19	13	20	61
Grand total	2	1				6	11	26	38	33	117

a "Other races" includes races having less than 10 representatives of this sex and age and pupils whose race is not reported.

TABLE 4.—*Race and grade, by age—Number of pupils of each specified age in each grade, by general nativity and race of father of pupil—*Continued.

GIRLS: AGE 18 YEARS.

General nativity and race of father of pupil.	High school.				Total.
	First year.	Second year.	Third year.	Fourth year.	
Native-born:					
White..		4	5	14	23
Negro..					
Foreign-born, Other races *a*............................	2	4	14	8	28
Grand total.....................................	2	8	19	22	51

a "Other races" includes races having less than 10 representatives of this sex and age and pupils whose race is not reported.

GIRLS: AGE 19 YEARS.

General nativity and race of father of pupil.	High school.		Total.
	First year.	Second year.	
Native-born:			
White..	3	1	4
Negro..			
Foreign-born, Other races *a*............................		5	5
Grand total.....................................	3	6	9

a "Other races" includes races having less than 10 representatives of this sex and age and pupils whose race is not reported.

GIRLS: AGE 20 YEARS.

General nativity and race of father of pupil.	High school.			Total.
	Second year.	Third year.	Fourth year.	
Native-born, White.................................	1			1
Foreign-born, Other races *a*........................			1	1
Grand total.....................................	1		1	2

a "Other races" includes races having less than 10 representatives of this sex and age and pupils whose race is not reported.

TABLE 5.—*Race distribution in each grade—Percentages.*

[This table shows in detail only races with 100 or more pupils reporting. The totals, however, are for all races.]

General nativity and race of father of pupil.	Kindergarten.	Elementary grades.									High school.					Grand total.
		1.	2.	3.	4.	5.	6.	7.	8.	Total.	First year.	Second year.	Third year.	Fourth year.	Total.	
Native-born:																
White	28.5	20.8	21.4	23.8	22.6	25.6	24.5	26.6	31.4	23.9	37.0	41.0	43.4	44.4	41.1	25.5
Negro and Indian	.4	.7	.2	.5	.4	.7	.6	.5	.4	.5	.0	.5	.0	.0	.5	.5
Total native-born	28.9	21.5	21.6	24.4	23.0	26.3	25.2	27.1	31.9	24.4	39.0	41.4	43.4	44.4	41.2	25.9
Foreign-born:																
Canadian, French	1.9	5.0	4.5	3.9	5.0	3.1	3.3	3.1	1.8	4.0	2.8	2.3	1.3	3.2	2.4	3.7
Canadian, Other	7.5	7.3	7.3	8.7	8.7	9.1	9.2	10.3	8.7	8.4	13.0	13.1	13.8	13.7	13.3	8.8
Danish	7.0	1.1	.8	.7	1.1	.9	.8	2.1	1.3	1.1	.8	1.4	.8	.8	.6	1.0
English	2.3	2.1	3.4	2.3	2.3	2.1	2.4	1.3	3.2	2.5	2.0	4.1	3.6	5.6	3.4	2.6
Finnish	3.3	3.8	2.7	3.1	2.4	2.6	1.6	2.5	2.1	2.7	1.1	2.3	.8	.0	1.0	2.6
German	5.0	3.5	5.8	5.5	5.0	5.0	7.0	5.5	6.2	5.2	7.1	3.2	5.7	3.2	5.2	5.2
Hebrew, Russian	9.6	3.7	4.0	3.6	3.4	3.5	3.9	2.6	2.8	3.5	2.5	1.4	1.3	.8	1.7	3.7
Irish	2.1	1.6	2.6	.8	2.4	1.8	1.8	1.3	2.4	1.9	1.4	5.0	1.3	3.2	2.6	1.9
Italian, North	1.2	1.3	1.0	1.3	1.2	.9	.9	.3	.4	1.1	.0	.0	.6	1.1	.2	1.9
Norwegian	11.8	13.0	12.5	12.8	13.4	12.8	13.5	10.6	13.1	12.8	10.5	9.9	8.8	13.7	10.5	12.5
Polish	1.2	5.6	3.3	2.5	2.1	1.1	1.9	1.4	.1	2.6	.6	.0	1.3	.0	.5	2.4
Scotch	1.5	2.0	3.1	2.0	2.3	2.6	2.2	3.6	3.5	2.5	4.5	3.6	4.4	4.0	4.2	2.6
Swedish	18.3	22.7	22.3	25.1	24.0	24.1	22.3	23.0	20.1	23.1	11.9	8.6	11.3	5.6	10.0	21.9
Other races	6.4	5.0	5.0	3.7	3.9	4.1	4.1	3.0	2.2	4.1	3.4	4.1	2.5	1.6	3.1	4.1
Total foreign-born	71.1	78.5	78.4	75.6	77.0	73.7	74.8	72.9	68.1	75.6	61.0	58.6	56.6	55.6	58.8	74.1
Grand total	100.0	100.0	100.0	100.0	100.0	100.0	100.0	100.0	100.0	100.0	100.0	100.0	100.0	100.0	100.0	100.0

TABLE 6.—*Grade distribution of each race—Percentages.*

[This table shows in detail only races with 100 or more pupils reporting. The totals, however, are for all races.]

General nativity and race of father of pupil.	Kindergarten.	Elementary grades.									High school.					Grand total.
		1.	2.	3.	4.	5.	6.	7.	8.	Total.	First year.	Second year.	Third year.	Fourth year.	Total.	
Native-born:																
White	5.3	13.5	9.5	11.8	10.3	11.7	9.7	7.6	7.7	81.9	5.0	3.3	2.5	2.0	12.7	100.0
Negro	4.3	19.1	4.3	12.7	10.6	19.1	14.9	6.4	6.4	93.6	.0	2.1	.0	.0	2.1	100.0
Indian	(a)	(a)	(a)	(a)	(a)	(a)	(a)	(a)	(a)	(a)	(a)	(a)	(a)	(a)	(a)	(a)
Total native-born	5.3	13.7	9.4	11.8	10.3	11.8	9.7	7.6	7.6	82.2	4.9	3.3	2.4	1.9	12.5	100.0
Foreign-born:																
Canadian, French	2.5	22.1	13.8	13.3	15.7	9.6	8.8	6.1	2.9	92.4	2.5	1.2	.5	1.0	5.2	100.0
Canadian, Other	4.1	13.8	9.4	12.0	11.6	12.0	10.4	8.6	6.2	84.0	4.8	3.0	2.3	1.8	11.9	100.0
Danish	.0	23.4	9.0	8.1	12.6	10.8	8.1	15.3	8.1	95.5	.9	2.7	.9	.0	4.5	100.0
English	4.3	13.5	14.9	11.0	10.3	9.6	9.3	8.9	7.8	85.4	2.5	3.2	2.1	2.5	10.3	100.0
Finnish	6.0	23.9	11.6	15.1	10.6	11.6	6.0	7.0	4.9	90.8	1.4	1.8	.0	.0	3.2	100.0
German	4.6	11.1	12.6	13.2	11.1	11.2	13.3	7.7	7.4	87.5	4.4	1.2	1.6	.3	7.9	100.0
Hebrew, Russian	12.5	16.5	12.5	12.3	10.8	11.0	10.8	5.3	4.8	83.8	2.3	.8	.5	.3	3.8	100.0
Irish	5.2	15.6	15.2	5.2	14.2	10.9	9.5	6.2	7.6	84.4	2.4	5.2	.9	1.9	10.4	100.0
Italian, North	1.0	28.2	11.7	17.5	14.6	10.7	9.7	1.9	2.9	97.1			1.0	1.0	1.9	100.0
Norwegian	4.5	17.1	11.3	12.8	12.4	11.9	10.8	6.1	6.5	88.9	2.7	1.6	1.0	1.2	6.6	100.0
Polish	2.3	38.8	15.8	13.1	10.4	5.4	8.1	4.2	.4	96.2	.8	.0	.8	.0	1.5	100.0
Scotch	2.8	12.6	13.3	9.8	10.2	11.6	8.4	10.2	8.4	84.6	5.6	2.8	2.5	1.8	12.6	100.0
Swedish	4.0	17.1	11.6	14.4	12.8	12.8	10.2	7.7	5.7	92.4	1.8	.0	.8	.3	3.6	100.0
Other races	7.3	20.2	13.7	11.3	11.1	11.5	10.0	5.3	3.5	86.7	2.7	2.0	.9	.4	6.0	100.0
Total foreign-born	4.6	17.6	12.1	12.8	12.2	11.6	10.1	7.2	5.7	89.2	2.7	1.6	1.1	.9	6.2	100.0
Grand total	4.8	16.6	11.3	12.6	11.7	11.6	10.0	7.3	6.2	87.4	3.2	2.0	1.5	1.1	7.9	100.0

a Not computed, owing to small number involved.

PUBLIC SCHOOL TEACHERS IN ELEMENTARY GRADES AND KINDERGARTEN.

TABLE 1.—*Number of teachers in each grade, by sex and general nativity and race.*

MALE.

[This table does not include 4 teachers not reporting complete data.]

General nativity and race.	Kinder-garten.	Elementary grades.									Total kinder-garten and ele-mentary.
		1.	2.	3.	4.	5.	6.	7.	8.	Total.	
Native-born of native father, White								2		2	2
Native-born of foreign father, by race of father:											
German		1	1	1	1	1				5	5
Norwegian								1	1	2	2
Total		1	1	1	1	1		1	1	7	7
Total native-born		1	1	1	1	1		3	1	9	9
Grand total		1	1	1	1	1		3	1	9	9

FEMALE.

General nativity and race.	Kinder-garten.	Elementary grades.									Total kinder-garten and ele-mentary.
		1.	2.	3.	4.	5.	6.	7.	8.	Total.	
Native-born of native father, White	7	38	27	27	25	27	20	26	20	210	217
Native-born of foreign father, by race of father:											
Canadian, French				1						1	1
Canadian, Other	1	3	1	4	2	2	2			14	15
Danish	1			2			1			3	4
Dutch						1				1	1
English			2	5	3		1	1	1	13	13
French		1	1	1	1	3				7	7
German	1	8	12	3	7	5	4	2		41	42
Hebrew, German				1						1	1
Irish		4	4	6	8	8	8	3		39	39
Norwegian		2	3	1	3	4	2	1		16	16
Scotch			1	4	1	1		2	2	11	11
Scotch-Irish							1			1	1
Swedish	1	5	3	1	1	5	6	3	3	28	29
Welsh	2	3	1							4	6
Total	6	26	28	29	25	28	21	12	6	180	186
Total native-born	13	64	55	56	50	55	46	38	26	390	403
Canadian, French				1						1	1
Canadian, Other			1	2		2				5	5
Danish								1		1	1
English				2	3	4	3			12	12
German					1				3	4	4
Hebrew, Roumanian		1								1	1
Irish	1	1		1	1				1	4	5
Norwegian					1				1	2	2
Scotch	1	3	1							4	5
Swedish		3	2	2	4					11	11
Welsh	1									1	1
Total foreign-born	2	9	4	8	10	6	3	1	5	46	48
Grand total	15	73	59	64	60	61	49	39	31	436	451

TABLE 1.—*Number of teachers in each grade, by sex and general nativity and race*—Contd.

TOTAL.

General nativity and race.	Kindergarten.	Elementary grades.									Total kindergarten and elementary.	Race distribution. Percentages.	
		1.	2.	3.	4.	5.	6.	7.	8.	Total.		Elementary	Elementary and kindergarten.
Native-born of native father, White	7	38	27	27	25	27	20	28	20	212	219	47.6	47.6
Native-born of foreign father, by race of father:													
Canadian, French				1						1	1	.2	.2
Canadian, Other	1	3	1	4	2	2	2			14	15	3.1	3.3
Danish	1		2				1			3	4	.7	.9
Dutch						1				1	1	.2	.2
English			2	5	3		1	1	1	13	13	2.9	2.8
French		1	1	1	1	3				7	7	1.6	1.5
German	1	9	13	4	8	6	4	2		46	47	10.3	10.2
Hebrew, German				1						1	1	.2	.2
Irish		4	4	6	6	8	8	3		39	39	8.8	8.5
Norwegian		2	3	1	3	4	2	2	1	18	18	4.0	3.9
Scotch			1	4	1	1		2	2	11	11	2.5	2.4
Scotch-Irish							1			1	1	.2	.2
Swedish	1	5	3	1	1	5	6	3	3	28	29	6.3	6.3
Welsh	2	3	1							4	6	.9	1.3
Total	6	27	29	30	26	29	26	13	7	187	193	42.0	42.0
Total native-born	13	65	56	57	51	56	46	41	27	399	412	89.7	89.6
Foreign-born:													
Canadian, French				1						1	1	.2	.2
Canadian, Other			1	2		2				5	5	1.1	1.1
Danish								1		1	1	.2	.2
English			2	3	4	3				12	12	2.7	2.6
German					1				3	4	4	.9	.9
Hebrew, Roumanian		1								1	1	.2	.2
Irish	1	1		1	1				1	4	5	.9	1.1
Norwegian					1				1	2	2	.4	.4
Scotch	1	3	1							4	5	.9	1.1
Swedish		3	2	2	4					11	11	2.5	2.4
Welsh		1								1	1	.2	.2
Total foreign-born	2	9	4	8	10	6	3	1	5	46	48	10.3	10.4
Grand total	15	74	60	65	61	62	49	42	32	445	460	100.0	100.0

TABLE 2.—*Number of teachers engaged in teaching each specified number of years, by sex and general nativity and race.*

MALE.

[This table does not include 4 teachers not reporting complete data.]

General nativity and race.	Under 5 years.	5 to 9 years.	10 to 14 years.	15 to 19 years.	20 to 24 years.	25 to 29 years.	30 years or over.	Total.
Native-born of native father, White..		2						2
Native-born of foreign father, by race of father:								
German			5					5
Norwegian		2						2
Total		2	5					7
Total native-born		4	5					9
Grand total		4	5					9

FEMALE.

General nativity and race.	Under 5 years.	5 to 9 years.	10 to 14 years.	15 to 19 years.	20 to 24 years.	25 to 29 years.	30 years or over.	Total.
Native-born of native father, White..	65	48	55	40	7	2		217
Native-born of foreign father, by race of father:								
Canadian, French	1							1
Canadian, Other	8	6	1					15
Danish	2	2						4
Dutch			1					1
English	2	1	5	2		3		13
French	5		2					7
German	13	12	8	6	2	1		42
Hebrew, German	1							1
Irish	7	18	10	3	1			39
Norwegian	6	7	2				1	16
Scotch	3	1	2	2	3			11
Scotch-Irish	1							1
Swedish	9	5	8	5	2			29
Welsh	4				2			6
Total	62	52	39	18	10	4	1	186
Total native-born	127	100	94	58	17	6	1	403
Foreign-born:								
Canadian, French				1				1
Canadian, Other		3	2					5
Danish		1						1
English	5	2	3		2			12
German		3			1			4
Hebrew, Roumanian	1							1
Irish		1	1	3				5
Norwegian		1	1					2
Scotch			3	2				5
Swedish		4	6	1				11
Welsh			1					1
Total foreign-born	6	15	17	7	3			48
Grand total	133	115	111	65	20	6	1	451

TABLE 2.—*Number of teachers engaged in teaching each specified number of years, by sex and general nativity and race*—Continued.

TOTAL.

General nativity and race.	Under 5 years.	5 to 9 years.	10 to 14 years.	15 to 19 years.	20 to 24 years.	25 to 29 years.	30 years or over.	Total.
Native-born of native father, White..	65	50	55	40	7	2	....	219
Native-born of foreign father, by race of father:								
Canadian, French.............	1	....	....	....	....	....	....	1
Canadian, Other.............	8	6	1	....	....	....	....	15
Danish......................	2	2	....	....	....	....	....	4
Dutch.......................	....	....	1	....	....	....	....	1
English.....................	2	1	5	2	....	3	....	13
French......................	5	....	2	....	....	....	....	7
German.....................	13	12	13	6	2	1	....	47
Hebrew, German.............	1	....	....	....	....	....	....	1
Irish.......................	7	18	10	3	1	....	....	39
Norwegian..................	6	9	2	....	....	....	1	18
Scotch.....................	3	1	2	2	3	....	....	11
Scotch-Irish................	1	....	....	....	....	....	....	1
Swedish....................	9	5	8	5	2	....	....	29
Welsh......................	4	....	....	....	2	....	....	6
Total...................	62	54	44	18	10	4	1	193
Total native-born..........	127	104	99	58	17	6	1	412
Foreign-born:								
Canadian, French...........	....	....	....	1	....	....	....	1
Canadian, Other...........	....	3	2	....	....	....	....	5
Danish.....................	....	1	....	....	....	....	....	1
English....................	5	2	3	....	2	....	....	12
German....................	....	3	....	....	1	....	....	4
Hebrew, Roumanian.........	1	....	....	....	....	....	....	1
Irish.......................	....	1	1	3	....	....	....	5
Norwegian..................	....	1	1	....	....	....	....	2
Scotch.....................	....	....	3	2	....	....	....	5
Swedish....................	....	4	6	1	....	....	....	11
Welsh......................	....	....	1	....	....	....	....	1
Total foreign-born..........	6	15	17	7	3	....	....	48
Grand total.................	133	119	116	65	20	6	1	460

PAROCHIAL SCHOOL PUPILS: GENERAL INVESTIGATION.

TABLE 1.—*Grade and age—Number of pupils of each age in each grade, by sex.*

BOYS.

Age.	Kindergarten.	Elementary grades.									Grand total.
		1.	2.	3.	4.	5.	6.	7.	8.	Total.	
4 years		1								1	1
5 years	6	8								8	14
6 years	9	16	1							17	26
7 years	1	30	9	1						40	41
8 years	3	18	24	3	1					46	49
9 years		7	13	26	7	1				54	54
10 years		1	10	20	11	8				50	50
11 years		1	4	7	17	14	3	1		47	47
12 years			5	7	12	24	4	13	1	66	66
13 years			2	3	5	16	17	17	4	64	64
14 years		5		4	6	9	6	14	20	64	64
15 years		10		1		3	2	1	14	31	31
16 years		6	5		1		1		2	15	15
17 years			5					1	1	7	7
18 years			2						1	3	3
19 years			1							1	1
20 years or over						1					
Total	19	103	81	72	60	75	34	46	43	514	533

GIRLS.

Age.	Kindergarten.	Elementary grades.									Grand total.
		1.	2.	3.	4.	5.	6.	7.	8.	Total.	
4 years											
5 years	2	4								4	6
6 years	7	16	1							17	24
7 years	4	28	11							39	43
8 years	4	19	22	6	3					50	54
9 years	1	5	8	15	2					30	31
10 years		2	8	20	19	3				52	52
11 years			6	9	16	24	6			61	61
12 years			2	4	13	19	12	6		56	56
13 years		1		5	5	17	20	10	5	63	63
14 years				1	2	10	8	11	15	47	47
15 years						1	5	5	17	28	28
16 years							1		5	6	6
17 years									3	3	3
18 years									1	1	1
19 years											
20 years or over											
Total	18	75	58	60	60	74	52	32	46	457	475

TABLE 1.—*Grade and age—Number of pupils of each age in each grade, by sex*—Contd.

TOTAL.

Age.	Kinder-garten.	Elementary grades.									Grand total.
		1.	2.	3.	4.	5.	6.	7.	8.	Total.	
4 years		1								1	1
5 years	8	12								12	20
6 years	16	32	2							34	50
7 years	5	58	20	1						79	84
8 years	7	37	46	9	4					96	103
9 years	1	12	21	41	9	1				84	85
10 years		3	18	40	30	11				102	102
11 years		1	10	16	33	38	9	1		108	108
12 years			7	11	25	43	16	19	1	122	122
13 years		1	2	8	10	33	37	27	9	127	127
14 years		5		5	8	19	14	25	35	111	111
15 years		10		1		4	7	6	31	59	59
16 years		6	5		1		2		7	21	21
17 years			5				1		4	10	10
18 years			2						2	4	4
19 years			1							1	1
20 years or over											
Total	37	178	139	132	120	149	86	78	89	971	1,008

TABLE 2.—*Race, sex, and grade—Number of pupils of each sex in each grade, by general nativity and race of father of pupil.*

General nativity and race of father of pupil.	Kindergarten	Elementary grades.									Grand total.
		1.	2.	3.	4.	5.	6.	7.	8.	Total.	
Native-born:											
White—											
Male	2	30	14	12	8	16	12	17	15	124	126
Female	1	21	11	6	11	13	11	6	20	99	100
Total	3	51	25	18	19	29	23	23	35	223	226
Foreign-born:											
Bulgarian—											
Male											
Female								1		1	1
Total								1		1	1
Canadian, French—											
Male	17	12	14	20	20	16	7	7	5	101	118
Female	16	11	8	12	11	18	18	9	1	88	104
Total	33	23	22	32	31	34	25	16	6	189	222
Canadian, Other—											
Male		13	10	15	5	7	9	5	13	77	77
Female	1	10	5	6	3	9	10	6	13	62	63
Total	1	23	15	21	8	16	19	11	26	139	140
Flemish—											
Male		2	2	1		1				6	6
Female		2	1	1						4	4
Total		4	3	2		1				10	10
German—											
Male		8	3	3	8	3	2	2	2	31	31
Female		1	7	6	5	8	5	1	2	35	35
Total		9	10	9	13	11	7	3	4	66	66
Irish—											
Male		9	18	12	13	23		9	3	87	87
Female		7	7	8	12	9	5	3	4	55	55
Total		16	25	20	25	32	5	12	7	142	142
Italian, North—											
Male		2		1					1	4	4
Female		2		2	2	2			1	9	9
Total		4		3	2	2			2	13	13
Polish—											
Male		24	16	6	6	3	1	4	1	61	61
Female		20	17	14	12	8	2	6	3	82	82
Total		44	33	20	18	11	3	10	4	143	143
Other races—*a*											
Male		3	4	2		6	3	2	3	23	23
Female		1	2	5	4	7	1		2	22	22
Total		4	6	7	4	13	4	2	5	45	45
Total—											
Male	17	73	67	60	52	59	22	29	28	390	407
Female	17	54	47	54	49	61	41	26	26	358	375
Total	34	127	114	114	101	120	63	55	54	748	782
Grand total—											
Male	19	103	81	72	60	75	34	46	43	514	533
Female	18	75	58	60	60	74	52	32	46	457	475
Total	37	178	139	132	120	149	86	78	89	971	1,008

a "Other races" include Bohemian, 2; Bulgarian, 1; Chinese, 1; English, 6; French, 5; Italian, South, 4; Norwegian, 5; Russian, 2; Scotch, 4; Syrian, 6; Slovenian, 7; Swedish, 2; total, 45.

TABLE 3.—*Race, sex, and age, by grade—Number of pupils of each age in each grade, by sex and by general nativity and race of father of pupil.*

KINDERGARTEN.

BOYS.

General nativity and race of father of pupil.	Number of pupils of each age.						Total.
	5.	6.	7.	8.	9.	10.	
Native-born, White		2					2
Foreign-born, Canadian, French	6	7	1	3			17
Total	6	9	1	3			19

GIRLS.

	5.	6.	7.	8.	9.	10.	Total.
Native-born, White		1					1
Foreign-born:							
Canadian, French	2	6	4	3	1		16
Canadian, Other				1			1
Total	2	6	4	4	1		17
Grand total	2	7	4	4	1		18

TOTAL.

	5.	6.	7.	8.	9.	10.	Total.
Native-born, White		3					3
Foreign-born:							
Canadian, French	8	13	5	6	1		33
Canadian, Other				1			1
Total	8	13	5	7	1		34
Grand total	8	16	5	7	1		37

TABLE 3.—*Race, sex, and age, by grade—Number of pupils of each age in each grade, by sex and by general nativity and race of father of pupil*—Continued.

FIRST GRADE.

BOYS.

General nativity and race of father of pupil.	Number of pupils of each age.															Total.
	4.	5.	6.	7.	8.	9.	10.	11.	12.	13.	14.	15.	16.	17.	18.	
Native-born White		5	4	11	1	1						2	6				30
Foreign-born:																
Canadian, French		1	1	2	3	2						1	1	1			12
Canadian, Other	1		3	7	2												13
Flemish					1	1											2
German		1	1	1	1							1	1	2			8
Irish		1	1		1	1							2	3			9
Italian, North			1		1												2
Polish			4	8	8	2	1	1									24
Other races *a*			1	1								1					3
Total	1	3	12	19	17	6	1	1				3	4	6			73
Grand total	1	8	16	30	18	7	1	1				5	10	6			103

GIRLS.

General nativity and race of father of pupil.	4.	5.	6.	7.	8.	9.	10.	11.	12.	13.	14.	15.	16.	17.	18.	Total.
Native-born, White			3	11	6	1										21
Foreign-born:																
Canadian, French		2	1	2	4	2										11
Canadian, Other			2	7	1											10
Flemish					1	1										2
German					1											1
Irish		1	2	2	1	1										7
Italian, North			2													2
Polish		1	6	6	4		2			1						20
Other races *a*					1											1
Total		4	13	17	13	4	2			1						54
Grand total		4	16	28	19	5	2			1						75

TOTAL.

General nativity and race of father of pupil.	4.	5.	6.	7.	8.	9.	10.	11.	12.	13.	14.	15.	16.	17.	18.	Total.
Native-born, White		5	7	22	7	2					2	6				51
Foreign-born:																
Canadian, French		3	2	4	7	4					1	1	1			23
Canadian, Other	1		5	14	3											23
Flemish					2	2										4
German		1	1	1	2						1	1	2			9
Irish		2	3	2	2	2						2	3			16
Italian, North			3		1											4
Polish		1	10	14	12	2	3	1		1						44
Other races *a*			1	1	1						1					4
Total	1	7	25	36	30	10	3	1		1	3	4	6			127
Grand total	1	12	32	58	37	12	3	1		1	5	10	6			178

a "Other races" includes races having less than 10 representatives in this city and pupils whose race is not reported.

TABLE **3.**—*Race, sex, and age, by grade—Number of pupils of each age in each grade, by sex and by general nativity and race of father of pupil*—Continued.

SECOND GRADE.

BOYS.

General nativity and race of father of pupil.	Number of pupils of each age.															Total.
	6.	7.	8.	9.	10.	11.	12.	13.	14.	15.	16.	17.	18.	19.	20.	
Native-born, White		3	6	3							2					14
Foreign-born:																
Canadian, French		2	3	3	2	1	1	1			1					14
Canadian, Other	1	2	1		1						1	3	1			10
Flemish							2									2
German		1	2													3
Irish		1	6	5	2						1	2	1	1		18
Polish			4	2	3	3	2	1								16
Other races *a*			2		2											4
Total	1	6	18	10	10	4	5	2			3	5	2	1		67
Grand total	1	9	24	13	10	4	5	2			5	5	2	1		81

GIRLS.

General nativity and race of father of pupil.	6.	7.	8.	9.	10.	11.	12.	13.	14.	15.	16.	17.	18.	19.	20.	Total.
Native-born, White		2	7	1	1											11
Foreign-born:																
Canadian, French		2	4	2												8
Canadian, Other		2	3													5
Flemish			1													1
German		2	3		2											7
Irish	1	1	3	1	1											7
Polish		2	1	3	4	5	2									17
Other races *a*				1		1										2
Total	1	9	15	7	7	6	2									47
Grand total	1	11	22	8	8	6	2									58

TOTAL.

General nativity and race of father of pupil.	6.	7.	8.	9.	10.	11.	12.	13.	14.	15.	16.	17.	18.	19.	20.	Total.
Native-born, White		5	13	4	1						2					25
Foreign-born:																
Canadian, French		4	7	5	2	1	1	1			1					22
Canadian, Other	1	4	4		1						1	3	1			15
Flemish			1				2									3
German		3	5		2											10
Irish	1	2	9	6	3						1	2	1	1		25
Polish		2	5	5	7	8	4	1								33
Other races *a*			2	1	2	1										6
Total	2	15	33	17	17	10	7	2			3	5	2	1		114
Grand total	2	20	46	21	18	10	7	2			5	5	2	1		139

a "Other races" includes races having less than 10 representatives in this city and pupils whose race is not reported.

TABLE **3**.—*Race, sex, and age, by grade—Number of pupils of each age in each grade' by sex and by general nativity and race of father of pupil*—Continued.

THIRD GRADE.

BOYS.

General nativity and race of father of pupil.	Number of pupils of each age.											Total.
	7.	8.	9.	10.	11.	12.	13.	14.	15.	16.	17.	
Native-born, White	....	....	6	4	1	1	....	....	....	....	....	12
Foreign-born:												
Canadian, French		1	5	4	2	3	1	3	1	....	....	20
Canadian, Other		1	6	7	1	....	....	....	....	....	....	15
German		....	2	....	1	....	....	....	....	....	....	3
Irish	1	....	5	4	1	1	....	....	....	....	....	12
Italian, North		1	....	....	....	....	....	....	....	....	....	1
Polish		....	1	....	1	1	2	1	....	....	....	6
Flemish		....	....	....	....	....	1	....	....	....	....	1
Other races *a*		....	1	1	....	....	....	....	....	....	....	2
Total	1	3	20	16	6	6	3	4	1	....	....	60
Grand total	1	3	26	20	7	7	3	4	1	....	....	72

GIRLS.

General nativity and race of father of pupil.	Number of pupils of each age.											Total.
	7.	8.	9.	10.	11.	12.	13.	14.	15.	16.	17.	
Native-born, White	....	1	2	2	....	....	1	....	....	....	....	6
Foreign-born:												
Canadian, French		3	4	2	3	....	....	....	....	....	....	12
Canadian, Other		1	3	2	....	....	....	....	....	....	....	6
German		....	2	1	2	1	....	....	....	....	....	6
Irish		....	....	8	....	....	....	....	....	....	....	8
Italian, North		1	1	....	....	....	....	....	....	....	....	2
Polish		....	1	3	3	3	3	1	....	....	....	14
Flemish		....	....	....	....	....	1	....	....	....	....	1
Other races *a*		....	2	2	1	....	....	....	....	....	....	5
Total		5	13	18	9	4	4	1	....	....	....	54
Grand total		6	15	20	9	4	5	1	....	....	....	60

TOTAL.

General nativity and race of father of pupil.	Number of pupils of each age.											Total.
	7.	8.	9.	10.	11.	12.	13.	14.	15.	16.	17.	
Native-born, White	....	1	8	6	1	1	1	....	....	....	....	18
Foreign-born:												
Canadian, French		4	9	6	5	3	1	3	1	....	....	32
Canadian, Other		2	9	9	1	....	....	....	....	....	....	21
German		....	4	1	3	1	....	....	....	....	....	9
Irish	1	....	5	12	1	1	....	....	....	....	....	20
Italian, North		2	1	....	....	....	....	....	....	....	....	3
Polish		....	2	3	4	4	5	2	....	....	....	20
Flemish		....	....	....	....	....	1	1	....	....	....	2
Other races *a*		....	3	3	1	....	....	....	....	....	....	7
Total	1	8	33	34	15	10	7	5	1	....	....	114
Grand total	1	9	41	40	16	11	8	5	1	....	....	132

a "Other races" includes races having less than 10 representatives in this city and pupils whose race is not reported.

TABLE **3.**—*Race, sex, and age, by grade—Number of pupils of each age in each grade, by sex and by general nativity and race of father of pupil*—Continued.

FOURTH GRADE.

BOYS.

General nativity and race of father of pupil.	Number of pupils of each age.									Total.
	9.	10.	11.	12.	13.	14.	15.	16.	17.	
Native-born, White		1	1	3	2		1			8
Foreign-born:										
Canadian, French	1	1	3	6	4	2	2		1	20
Canadian, Other		3		1			1			5
German			3	3	2					8
Irish		2	4	4	1	1	1			13
Italian, North										
Polish					3	2	1			6
Other races a										
Total	1	6	10	14	10	5	5		1	52
Grand total	1	7	11	17	12	5	6		1	60

GIRLS.

General nativity and race of father of pupil.	9.	10.	11.	12.	13.	14.	15.	16.	17.	Total.
Native-born, White	2	1	4	3	1					11
Foreign-born:										
Canadian, French	1	1	3	3	3					11
Canadian, Other			2		1					3
German			2	2			1			5
Irish			5	3	3	1				12
Italian, North			2							2
Polish			1		3	4	1			12
Other races a				2	2					4
Total	1	1	15	13	12	5	2			49
Grand total	3	2	19	16	13	5	2			60

TOTAL.

General nativity and race of father of pupil.	9.	10.	11.	12.	13.	14.	15.	16.	17.	Total.
Native-born, White	2	2	5	6	3		1			19
Foreign-born:										
Canadian, French	2	2	6	9	7	2	2		1	31
Canadian, Other		3	2	1	1		1			8
German			5	5	2		1			13
Irish		2	9	7	4	2	1			25
Italian, North			2							2
Polish			1		3	6	2			18
Other races a				2	2					4
Total	2	7	25	27	22	10	7		1	101
Grand total	4	9	30	33	25	10	8		1	120

a "Other races" includes races having less than 10 representatives in this city and pupils whose race is not reported.

TABLE 3.—*Race, sex, and age, by grade—Number of pupils of each age in each grade, by sex and by general nativity and race of father of pupil*—Continued.

FIFTH GRADE.

BOYS.

General nativity and race of father of pupil.	Number of pupils of each age.									Total.
	8.	9.	10.	11.	12.	13.	14.	15.	16.	
Native-born, White		3	2	6	3	1	1			16
Foreign-born:										
Canadian, French	1	3	3	5	3	1				16
Canadian, Other			2	2	2	1				7
Flemish				1						1
German			1				2			3
Irish										
Italian, North		2	2	10	5	4				23
Polish					1	2				3
Other races a			4		2					6
Total	1	5	12	18	13	8	2			59
Grand total	1	8	14	24	16	9	3			75

GIRLS.

General nativity and race of father of pupil.	8.	9.	10.	11.	12.	13.	14.	15.	16.	Total.
Native-born, White		1	5	4	2	1				13
Foreign-born:										
Canadian, French		2	5	5	4	2				18
Canadian, Other			3	2	2	2				9
Flemish										
German			3	3	1	1				8
Irish				1	1					2
Italian, North			5	2		2				9
Polish			2	2	2	1	1			8
Other races a			1		5	1				7
Total		2	19	15	15	9	1			61
Grand total		3	24	19	17	10	1			74

TOTAL.

General nativity and race of father of pupil.	8.	9.	10.	11.	12.	13.	14.	15.	16.	Total.
Native-born, White		4	7	10	5	2	1			29
Foreign-born:										
Canadian, French	1	5	8	10	7	3				34
Canadian, Other			5	4	4	3				16
Flemish				1						1
German			4	3	1	1	2			11
Irish				1	1					2
Italian, North		2	7	12	5	6				32
Polish			2	2	3	3	1			11
Other races a			5		7	1				13
Total	1	7	31	33	28	17	3			120
Grand total	1	11	38	43	33	19	4			149

a "Other races" includes races having less than 10 representatives in this city and pupils whose race is not reported.

TABLE 3.—*Race, sex, and age, by grade—Number of pupils of each age in each grade, by sex and by general nativity and race of father of pupil*—Continued.

SIXTH GRADE.

BOYS.

General nativity and race of father of pupil.	Number of pupils of each age.							Total.
	11.	12.	13.	14.	15.	16.	17.	
Native-born, White	1	3	4	4				12
Foreign-born:								
Canadian, French	1	1	2	2			1	7
Canadian, Other			6		2	1		9
German	1		1					2
Irish								
Polish			1					1
Other races a			3					3
Total	2	1	13	2	2	1	1	22
Grand total	3	4	17	6	2	1	1	34

GIRLS.

General nativity and race of father of pupil.	11.	12.	13.	14.	15.	16.	17.	Total.
Native-born, White	2	2	5	2				11
Foreign-born:								
Canadian, French	3	4	7	2	2			18
Canadian, Other		5	3		2			10
German		1	1	2	1			5
Irish	1		2	1		1		5
Polish			2					2
Other races a				1				1
Total	4	10	15	6	5	1		41
Grand total	6	12	20	8	5	1		52

TOTAL.

General nativity and race of father of pupil.	11.	12.	13.	14.	15.	16.	17.	Total.
Native-born, White	3	5	9	6				23
Foreign-born:								
Canadian, French	4	5	9	4	2		1	25
Canadian, Other		5	9		4	1		19
German	1	1	2	2	1			7
Irish	1		2	1		1		5
Polish			3					3
Other races a			3	1				4
Total	6	11	28	8	7	2	1	63
Grand total	9	16	37	14	- 7	2	1	86

a "Other races" includes races having less than 10 representatives in this city and pupils whose race is not reported.

TABLE 3.—*Race, sex, and age, by grade—Number of pupils of each age in each grade, by sex and by general nativity and race of father of pupil*—Continued.

SEVENTH GRADE.

BOYS.

General nativity and race of father of pupil	Number of pupils of each age.						Total.
	10.	11.	12.	13.	14.	15	
Native-born, White			6	9	2		17
Foreign-born:							
Bulgarian							
Canadian, French			1		5	1	7
Canadian, Other			2	2	1		5
German			1	1			2
Irish		1	2	2	4		9
Polish			1	1	2		4
Other races a				2			2
Total		1	7	8	12	1	29
Grand total		1	13	17	14	1	46

GIRLS.

General nativity and race of father of pupil	10.	11.	12.	13.	14.	15	Total.
Native-born, White				3	1	2	6
Foreign-born:							
Bulgarian				1			1
Canadian, French			2	1	4	2	9
Canadian, Other			1	1	4		6
German				1			1
Irish							
Polish			1	1		1	3
Other races a			2	2	2		6
Total			6	7	10	3	26
Grand total			6	10	11	5	32

TOTAL.

General nativity and race of father of pupil	10.	11.	12.	13.	14.	15	Total.
Native-born, White			6	12	3	2	23
Foreign-born:							
Bulgarian				1			1
Canadian, French			3	1	9	3	16
Canadian, Other			3	3	5		11
German			1	2			3
Irish		1	3	3	4	1	12
Polish			3	3	4		10
Other races a				2			2
Total		1	13	15	22	4	55
Grand total		1	19	27	25	6	78

a "Other races" includes races having less than 10 representatives in this city and pupils whose race is not reported.

TABLE 3.—*Race, sex, and age, by grade—Number of pupils of each age in each grade, by sex and by general nativity and race of father of pupil*—Continued.

EIGHTH GRADE.

BOYS.

General nativity and race of father of pupil	Number of pupils of each age.							Total.
	12.	13.	14.	15.	16.	17.	18.	
Native-born, White	1	1	8	4	1			15
Foreign-born:								
Canadian, French			3	1	1			5
Canadian, Other		2	5	4		1	1	13
German			1	1				2
Irish		1		2				3
Italian, North			1					1
Polish			1					1
Other races *a*			1	2				3
Total		3	12	10	1	1	1	28
Grand total	1	4	20	14	2	1	1	43

GIRLS.

General nativity and race of father of pupil	12.	13.	14.	15.	16.	17.	18.	Total.
Native-born, White		4	4	7	2	2	1	20
Foreign-born:								
Canadian, French			1					1
Canadian, Other			6	3	3	1		13
German				2				2
Irish		1	1	2				4
Italian, North			1					1
Polish			2	1				3
Other races *a*				2				2
Total		1	11	10	3	1		26
Grand total		5	15	17	5	3	1	46

TOTAL.

General nativity and race of father of pupil	12.	13.	14.	15.	16.	17.	18.	Total.
Native-born, White	1	5	12	11	3	2	1	35
Foreign-born:								
Canadian, French			4	1	1			6
Canadian, Other		2	11	7	3	2	1	26
German			1	3				4
Irish		2	1	4				7
Italian, North			2					2
Polish			3	1				4
Other races *a*			1	4				5
Total		4	23	20	4	2	1	54
Grand total	1	9	35	31	7	4	2	89

a "Other races" includes races having less than 10 representatives in this city and pupils whose race is not reported.

TABLE 4.—*Race distribution in each grade—Percentages.*

[This table shows in detail only races with 100 or more pupils reporting. The totals, however, are for all races.]

General nativity and race of father of pupil.	Kinder-garten.	Elementary grades.									Grand total.
		1.	2.	3.	4.	5.	6.	7.	8.	Total.	
Native-born, White..........	8.1	28.7	18.0	13.6	15.8	19.5	26.7	29.5	39.3	23.0	22.4
Foreign-born:											
Canadian, French........	89.2	12.9	15.8	24.2	25.8	22.8	29.1	20.5	6.7	19.5	22.0
Canadian, Other..........	2.7	12.9	10.8	15.9	6.7	10.7	22.1	14.1	29.2	14.3	13.9
Irish.....................	.0	9.0	18.0	15.2	20.8	21.5	5.8	15.4	7.9	14.6	14.1
Polish....................	.0	24.7	23.7	15.2	15.0	7.4	3.5	12.8	4.5	14.7	14.2
Other races..............	.0	11.8	13.7	15.9	15.8	18.1	12.8	7.7	12.4	13.9	13.4
Total..............	91.9	71.3	82.0	86.4	84.2	80.5	73.3	70.5	60.7	77.0	77.6
Grand total.............	100.0	100.0	100.0	100.0	100.0	100.0	100.0	100.0	100.0	100.0	100.0

TABLE 5.—*Grade distribution of each race—Percentages.*

[This table shows in detail only races with 100 or more pupils reporting. The totals, however, are for all races.]

General nativity and race of father of pupil.	Kinder-garten.	Elementary grades.									Grand total.
		1.	2.	3.	4.	5.	6.	7.	8.	Total.	
Native-born, White..........	1.3	22.6	11.1	8.0	8.4	12.8	10.2	10.2	15.5	98.7	100.0
Foreign-born:											
Canadian, French........	14.9	10.4	9.9	14.4	14.0	15.3	11.3	7.2	2.7	85.1	100.0
Canadian, Other..........	.7	16.4	10.7	15.0	5.7	11.4	13.6	7.9	18.6	99.3	100.0
Irish.....................		11.3	17.6	14.1	17.6	22.5	3.5	8.5	4.9	100.0	100.0
Polish....................		30.8	23.1	14.0	12.6	7.7	2.1	7.0	2.8	100.0	100.0
Other races..............		15.6	14.1	15.6	14.1	20.0	8.1	4.4	8.1	100.0	100.0
Total..............	4.3	16.2	14.6	14.6	12.9	15.3	8.1	7.0	6.9	95.7	100.0
Grand total.............	3.7	17.7	13.8	13.1	11.9	14.8	8.5	7.7	8.8	96.3	100.0

FALL RIVER, MASSACHUSETTS.

195

LIST OF TABLES.

197

FALL RIVER.

In the following, tables are presented relating to the public school children of the city of Fall River, and to the teachers in the public schools, as well as to the children in the parochial schools of the city. The information for the two groups of schools is on parallel lines. In each it was obtained by a system of records showing in each grade the number of pupils of each age and of each race. The methods of this general investigation and the subsidiary inquiry in regard to teachers are fully described in the introduction to this volume.[a] An account will also be found there of the characteristics of the general tasks resulting from these investigations and some indication of the purposes which they serve.

PUBLIC SCHOOL PUPILS.

The public schools of Fall River on the day of the enumeration in the early part of December, 1908, are reported to have had 13,926 pupils in actual attendance. During the school year 1908–9 the average annual attendance of the public schools of the city was 13,193, a figure slightly less than the number enumerated for the Immigration Commission. These figures evidence the fact that the enumeration was well done and that omissions did not occur, and warrant us in considering the pupils reported as representative of conditions usually prevailing in the city schools.

The distribution of these 13,926 pupils among the grades was as follows:

Kindergarten	123	Ninth grade	394
First grade	2,966	First year high school	296
Second grade	1,968	Second year high school	209
Third grade	1,940	Third year high school	164
Fourth grade	1,811	Fourth year high school	120
Fifth grade	1,424	Mixed and illiterate	132
Sixth grade	1,066		
Seventh grade	781	Total	13,926
Eighth grade	532		

In the Fall River system the kindergarten has a wholly insignificant part. Beginning with the first grade we find 2,966 pupils, a number much in excess of that for the second grade, 1,968. This disproportion between first and second grades is not unusual, but is not commonly so marked. The next three grades form a group of about equal number. With the fifth grade there is a falling off in numbers, and in the sixth grade this is quite pronounced. The seventh is little more than half as numerous as the third, while the eighth grade falls to a little more than one-half as many as the sixth. Fall River has a ninth grade as the completion of the elementary schools. It has 394 pupils, or about one-fifth as many as the second grade.

---

[a] See pp. VII to XVII.

The relation of upper and lower grades is brought out more clearly by a system of grouping, which contrasts the grades 1 to 4, designated for convenience as primary, with grades 5 to 9, designated as grammar grades. The results of such grouping appear in the next table.

Class of school.	Number.	Per cent.
Kindergarten	123	0.9
Primary, grades 1 to 4	8,685	63.0
Grammar, grades 5 to 9	4,197	30.4
High school	789	5.7
Total	13,794	100.0

Nearly two-thirds of the Fall River children are in the primary grades. Only a little more than 5 per cent of all the school pupils are in the high school.

The small numbers in the high school and the grammer grades find an explanation in a consideration of the ages of the school children, as shown in Table 1. As early as at 5 years of age there are 1,024 children in the schools. This number increases slowly until the age of compulsory education is reached. At 7 there are 1,399 children, and at 8, 1,474. The numbers do not greatly vary for the different ages until 14 is reached, though the largest number of pupils (1,584) is found at the age of 13 years. It may be surmised that this figure is swollen by some who desire to appear older than they really are in order the sooner to get to work. The significant point in these figures is that from 1,584 pupils at 13 years of age the number drops to 671 at 14 and 363 at 15. So early a desertion of the schools in such large measure is not usual and can only be explained by the character of Fall River industries and the more than usually large demand for the service of young persons.

In Table 1 can be found also a statement of the ages of the children in each grade, which shows for each grade a considerable variety of ages, and for each age a considerable variety of grades. The very numerous figures of this table can, however, be reduced to a much simpler expression by classing the pupils of each grade as of ages appropriate to the grade or in excess of such ages. This gives us in each grade the number and proportion of pupils who are too old for the grade, who are overage for the grade, and who, in current educational discussion, are designated as retarded or backward children, retardation expressing simply a misrelation between the age of the pupil and the grade in which he is found. This misrelation can also be stated by ascertaining how many pupils of a given age are in grades below that which is appropriate to the age. The form of expression which determines the number of overage pupils in the grades is the most common.

The following table, derived from Table 1, shows for Fall River and for each grade of the elementary schools the number of pupils and number and per cent of such pupils as are overage or retarded. It also compares the sum of all overage children with the total number of children, and thus establishes a rate of retardation for the entire school system.

Grade.	Number in grade.	Retarded pupils.		
		Age.	Number.	Per cent of all pupils.
First	2,966	8 years and over	609	20.5
Second	1,968	9 years and over	568	28.9
Third	1,940	10 years and over	745	38.4
Fourth	1,811	11 years and over	847	46.8
Fifth	1,424	12 years and over	522	36.7
Sixth	1,066	13 years and over	264	24.8
Seventh	781	14 years and over	79	10.1
Eighth	532	15 years and over	29	5.5
Ninth	394	16 years and over	21	5.3
Total	12,882		3,684	28.6

In the entire school system 28.6 per cent of the children must be regarded as retarded, but the different grades show a very wide variety. At the outset in the first grade as many as 20.5 per cent of the pupils are retarded, a proportion which must be regarded as rather larger, considering the early age at which so many children begin their school attendance. From the second to the fourth grade the number of retarded children grows, but as the whole number of children is fairly constant the proportion rises rapidly till it reaches, in the fourth grade, a maximum of 46.8 per cent of all the pupils. But after this point the percentage of retarded children diminishes rapidly. In the seventh grade children of normal age are still under the compulsory school law, but all of those who are backward are relieved from such restraint. The proportion of average pupils drops to 10.1 per cent. In the eighth and ninth grades the elimination of the backward has so progressed that only 5 per cent of those remaining in school are backward. Instructive in this connection is a comparison of the fourth and ninth grades. Of normal pupils there are in the fourth grade 964, and in the ninth 394, while of backward pupils the fourth grade contains 847 and the ninth grade only 21.

One reason why retardation in Fall River is lower than in some other places is that, as already stated, there are very many young children in the schools. As by the term of the definition only children of 8 years of age can be retarded, the presence of so many younger children tends to reduce the average. A comparison of older pupils avoids this difficulty. The following table is confined to pupils of 10, 11, and 12 years of age, and shows for each of these ages the number and per cent of undergrade or retarded pupils.

Age.	Number of pupils of this age.	Normal grade.	Retarded, or below normal grade.	
			Number.	Per cent.
10 years	1,345	4	436	32.4
11 years	1,296	5	549	42.4
12 years	1,562	6	786	50.3
Total	4,203		1,771	42.1

Dealing as it does with older children, higher percentages of retardation are here observed than in the schools as a whole. From very nearly one-third the children retarded at the age of 10 the proportion rises to a little more than one-half at the age of 12 years. The average for the three years is computed in order that it may be compared subsequently with like averages for different groups and races. Some of the latter are not numerous, which makes it questionable to calculate percentages upon the figures for a single year of age. In such cases accidental variation is assumed to be eliminated in an average covering three years.

The method of computing retardation upon the age basis has its limitations. While the table just given could be carried to the age of 13 years, it could hardly be extended to 14 years, as so many of the retarded children would then have passed beyond the ken of the school authorities.

These considerations have been drawn wholly from Table 1. The most significant feature of the statistics here presented, and that which in this form is quite new, is the information given concerning the race of pupils. By the aid of Tables 2 and 3, which give the facts of sex, age, and grade separately for each race, it is possible to construct for each race separately the counterpart of Table 1 and to draw from it conclusions as to the same matters which have been thus far discussed.

The first matter of interest is to know what races are represented among the school children of Fall River. The race indicated is that of the father of the children. The following table includes the groups of children of native-born and foreign-born fathers, and those of each race which are represented by as many as 200 pupils:

General nativity and race of father of pupil.	Pupils.		General nativity and race of father of pupil.	Pupils.	
	Number.	Per cent.		Number.	Per cent.
Native-born:			Foreign-born—Continued.		
White	4,518	32.4	Hebrew, Russian	783	5.6
Negro and Indian	50	.4	Irish	1,032	7.4
			Portuguese	1,811	13.0
Total native-born	4,568	32.8	Scotch	281	2.0
			All other	898	6.4
Foreign-born:					
Canadian, French	1,694	12.2	Total foreign-born	9,358	67.2
Canadian, Other	229	1.6			
English	2,630	18.9	Grand total	13,926	100.0

Of the pupils in the public schools of Fall River practically one-third had native fathers and two-thirds foreign fathers. Among the latter three races are especially prominent. They are the English, with 18.9 per cent, or one-sixth of the whole number of children, and the French Canadian and the Portuguese, each of which has about one-eighth of the whole number of children. The English-speaking groups comprise in all 4,213 children, or 30 per cent of the whole number, the dominant element being the English.

The group "All other," with 898, contains a considerable number of races, to name which adds to the detail of the picture of the racial density of the Fall River school children. They are: Armenian (2), Bohemian and Moravian (3), Bulgarian (9), Chinese (5), Danish

(18), Finnish (13), French (94), German (81), Greek (7), Hebrew, German (32), Hebrew, Polish (47), Hebrew, Roumanian (16), Hebrew, Other (37), Italian, North (136), Italian, South (146), Magyar (1), Negro (1), Norwegian (8), Polish (119), Roumanian (6), Russian (14), Scotch-Irish (5), Spanish (3), Spanish-American (2), Swedish (27), Syrian (29), and Welsh (36).

The characteristics of the native as contrasted with the foreign and those of the more important races represented in Fall River schools may be briefly considered. The grade distribution combining so many elements as well as grades can best be studied by grouping the elementary grades as in the following table:

General nativity and race of father of pupil.	Number of pupils.					Per cent.			
	Kinder-garten.	Pri-mary.	Gram-mar.	High.	Total.	Kinder-garten.	Pri-mary.	Gram-mar.	High.
Native-born:									
White	28	2,276	1,659	511	4,474	0.6	50.9	37.1	11.4
Negro and Indian	1	28	16	3	48	2.1	58.3	33.3	6.3
Total native-born	29	2,304	1,675	514	4,522	.6	51.0	37.0	11.4
Foreign-born:									
Canadian, French	21	1,380	251	12	1,664	1.3	82.9	15.1	.7
Canadian, Other	6	98	103	7	214	2.8	45.8	48.1	3.3
English	24	1,456	1,062	87	2,629	.9	55.4	40.4	3.3
Hebrew, Russian	30	481	230	40	781	3.8	61.6	29.4	5.1
Irish	7	548	394	83	1,032	.7	53.1	38.2	8.0
Portuguese	2	1,617	157	3	1,779	.1	90.9	8.8	.2
Scotch	1	144	119	16	280	.4	51.4	42.5	5.7
All other	3	657	206	27	893	.3	73.6	23.1	3.0
Total foreign-born	94	6,381	2,522	275	9,272	1.0	68.8	27.2	3.0
Grand total	123	8,685	4,197	789	13,794	.9	63.0	30.4	5.7

The contrast between the children of native and those of foreign fathers is very marked. Of the former 50.9 per cent and of the latter 68.8 per cent are in the primary grades. Of the specified races the Portuguese occupies a unique place. No less than 90.9 per cent of all the pupils of this race are in the primary grades. Among 1,779 pupils only 3 are in the high school. The French Canadians have more than four-fifths of their number, 82.9 per cent, in the primary grades. On the other hand, English and Scotch approach the same position as that of the children of native-born parents. There are fewer children of English Canadian fathers in the primary grades in proportion to their total number than there are of children of native fathers.

In the grammar grades there are 37.1 per cent of the children of native fathers, against 27.2 per cent of the children of foreign fathers. None the less, among the latter the English Canadians, the English, the Irish, and the Scotch have a somewhat larger proportion in these grades than have the children of native fathers. On the other hand, these races have smaller proportions in the high schools.

It is in the high schools that the greatest contrast is noticed. In these schools are found 11.4 per cent of the children of native fathers, but only 3 per cent of those whose fathers were foreign-born. With the exception of the Irish, which have 8 per cent of their number in the high school, no race rises in any marked degree above the general average for the group.

The number and percentage of retarded children among those of different races are shown in the next table.

General nativity and race of father of pupil.	All elementary pupils.			Pupils 10, 11, and 12 years of age.		
	Number.	Retarded, overage.	Per cent retarded.	Number.	Retarded, under-grade.	Per cent retarded.
Native-born:						
White	3,935	572	14.5	1,258	276	21.9
Negro and Indian	44	14	31.8	18	9	50.0
Total native-born	3,979	586	14.7	1,276	285	22.3
Foreign-born:						
Canadian, French	1,631	784	48.1	380	301	79.2
Canadian, Other	201	85	42.3	62	33	53.2
English	2,518	465	18.5	937	259	27.6
Hebrew, Russian	711	158	22.2	235	90	38.3
Irish	942	194	20.6	347	104	30.0
Portuguese	1,774	1,075	60.6	623	538	86.4
Scotch	263	41	15.6	98	22	22.4
All others	863	296	34.3	245	139	56.7
Total foreign-born	8,903	3,098	34.8	2,927	1,486	50.8
Grand total	12,882	3,684	28.6	4,203	1,771	42.1

This table is in two distinct sections. The first section, of three columns, refers to all elementary pupils; the second, in three further columns, concerns children of 10, 11, and 12 years of age. The first measures general retardation, the second that of a particular group, which is, however, more compact and less variable as between different races.

Again marked contrasts are observed. The general retardation of the children of native parents, 14.5 per cent, is less than one-half as great as that of children with foreign parents, 34.8 per cent There is, moreover, the greatest diversity among the races which make up the foreign-born. Scotch and English, with percentages of retardation of 15.6 and 18.5 per cent, respectively, are not far removed from the condition prevailing among the children of native parents. The Canadians, both French and English, have high rates of retardation, and among the very numerous Portuguese as many as 60.6 per cent are retarded.

Attention has already been called to the fact that in Fall River children go to school very early, and the presence of these younger children has some effect in lowering general percentages of retardation. In the second part of this table, where the rates refer to the older children, we find, therefore, a considerably higher range of retardation. Among the children of native parentage in these ages those who are retarded form 21.9 per cent of the whole, while among those of foreign parents the retarded children form 50.8 per cent of all. Scotch and English again approximate the same conditions as are seen among children with native fathers. Noteworthy are the percentages of retardation among the French Canadian and the Portuguese, which indicate that four out of every five children are behind in their studies at the average age of 11 years.

PUBLIC SCHOOL TEACHERS.

There were employed in the public schools of Fall River 413 teachers. Of these, 6 were men, employed in the eighth and ninth grades and in special work.

The table following gives the distribution of these teachers by nativity and parentage.

	Number.	Per cent.
Native white of native fathers	222	53. 8
Native white of foreign fathers	173	41. 9
Foreign white	18	4. 4
Total	413	100. 0

Rather more than one-half of the teachers are both of native birth and of native parentage. The remainder are of foreign parentage, but less than 5 per cent are of foreign birth. Among the 173 teachers of native birth and foreign parentage the Irish, who furnish 103, are by far the most numerous. With the exception of one teacher who had French Canadian parentage and four who had Portuguese or German fathers, all the teachers in this group came of English-speaking races.

The following table shows the division of the teachers between grammar and primary grades, distinguishing also nativity and parentage:

	Kindergarten and primary.	Grammar and special.	Total.	Per cent in grammar grades.
Native white, native fathers	150	72	222	32. 4
Native white, foreign fathers	122	51	173	29. 5
Foreign fathers	7	11	18	61. 1
Total	279	134	413	32. 4

The teachers of native and of foreign parentage have the same proportions employed in the lower and upper schools.

Length of service was reported for 407 teachers, as follows:

Under 5 years	34	From 25 to 29 years	33
From 5 to 9 years	137	30 years and over	29
From 10 to 14 years	73		
From 15 to 19 years	64	Total	407
From 20 to 24 years	37		

As in every school system there is a considerable percentage of young teachers, but about two-fifths of the teachers had had at least fifteen years' experience in their work, while nearly one-fourth had seen a service of twenty years or more.

The length of service for each of the main groups, according to parentage and nativity, is shown in the following table:

Race and nativity of teachers.	Length of service, in years.			
	Under 10.	10 to 19.	20 and over.	Total.
Native white, native fathers	76	71	70	217
Native white, foreign fathers	86	59	27	172
Foreign white	9	7	2	18
Total	171	137	99	407
Percentages: All teachers	42.0	33.7	24.3	100.0

Among the teachers of native birth and parentage, two-thirds had been in service ten years or more. Among those of native birth and foreign parentage, and those of foreign birth, exactly one-half had been in service for ten years or more. Among the younger teachers those of foreign parentage are most numerous, but among the older teachers those of native birth and parentage outnumber those of foreign parentage more than two to one.

PUPILS OF THE PAROCHIAL SCHOOLS.

In the parochial schools of Fall River there were enumerated as in actual attendance on a day in December, 1908, as many as 5,722 pupils, more than one-third as many as in the public schools. The official directory of the Roman Catholic Church informs us that the enrollment of parochial schools in Fall River was 6,295. The figures collected for the Commission are 90.2 per cent of the total enrollment. As such a divergence frequently occurs between the total enrollment of a school system and its average annual attendance, there is every reason to believe that the enumeration of these schools was as full and complete as that of the public schools, and that the resulting figures give a correct picture of the conditions generally prevailing in these schools.

The distribution of these pupils among the grades was as follows:

Kindergarten	88	Eighth grade	121
First grade	1,496	Ninth grade	60
Second grade	994	First year high school	4
Third grade	1,027	Third year high school	11
Fourth grade	763	Special schools	60
Fifth grade	455		
Sixth grade	394	Total	5,722
Seventh grade	249		

In these figures there is an apparent irregularity in the fact that the third grade has 34 more pupils than the second, but this is not considerable. It is usual for the first grade to outnumber considerably any of the others. There is a marked falling off in numbers after the third grade; the fifth grade being less than one-half and the eighth but little more than one-tenth as numerous as the third grade.

In the table following the early and late grades are grouped for the purpose of showing more concisely their numerical relations:

Class of school.	Number.	Per cent.
Kindergarten	88	1.6
Grades 1 to 4	4,280	75.6
Grades 5 to 9	1,279	22.6
High school	15	.3
Total	5,662	100.0

Three-fourths of the pupils of the parochial schools are in the first four or primary grades. The remainder are almost exclusively in the grammar grades, as the high school, with 15 pupils, is, so far as numbers are concerned, only rudimentary.

With respect to the ages of the pupils it may be noted in Table 1 that only 296 are of 5 years of age, while about double that number are 7 years old. The number of pupils reaches a maximum of 857 at the age of 11 years, after which it declines rapidly. At 13 years of age there are only 386 pupils, and a year later the number sinks to 126. Of pupils 15 years of age and upward there are only 65.

The relation of the ages of the pupils to the grades in which they are found can be expressed, as explained in the discussion of public school children, by ascertaining the number of overage or retarded children in each grade. This is given in the following table:

Grade.	Number in grade.	Retarded pupils.		
		Age.	Number.	Per cent of all pupils.
First	1,496	8 years and over	535	35.8
Second	994	9 years and over	529	53.2
Third	1,027	10 years and over	591	57.5
Fourth	763	11 years and over	381	49.9
Fifth	455	12 years and over	191	42.0
Sixth	394	13 years and over	100	25.4
Seventh	249	14 years and over	28	11.2
Eighth	121	15 years and over	17	14.0
Ninth	60	16 years and over	11	18.3
Total	5,559		2,383	42.9

It thus appears that of the children in the parochial schools 42.9 per cent are to be regarded as retarded. This proportion is almost attained in the first grade. In the third grade it rises to 57.5 per cent. It is somewhat less, but still considerable, in the fourth and fifth grades. But with the sixth grade a rapid decline takes place in the proportion, falling below 20 per cent in the three upper grades.

It was also pointed out that this relationship of ages and grades could also be expressed by calculating the percentage of children of a given age who were below the proper grade for their age. This is done for the parochial schools of Fall River and for children of 10, 11, and 12 years of age, in the following table:

Age.	Number of pupils of this age.	Normal grade.	Retarded, or below normal grade.	
			Number.	Per cent.
10 years.............................	758	4	417	55.0
11 years.............................	848	5	554	65.3
12 years.............................	695	6	461	66.3
Total........................	2,301	....	1,432	66.2

This statement shows that in the ages of 10 to 12 years about two-thirds of all the pupils are retarded.

As in the public so in the parochial schools particular attention was given to the race of the pupils. The distribution of the races in the parochial schools was as follows:

General nativity and race of father of pupil.	Pupils.		General nativity and race of father of pupil.	Pupils.	
	Number.	Per cent.		Number.	Per cent.
Native-born, White............	1,048	18.3	Foreign-born—Continued.		
			All other..................	174	3.0
Foreign-born:					
Canadian, French.........	3,322	58.1	Total foreign-born......	4,674	81.7
English...................	386	6.7			
Irish.....................	577	10.1	Grand total.............	5,722	100.0
Polish....................	215	3.8			

In these schools the children of native parentage play a small rôle. They constitute less than one-fifth of the whole number of pupils, four-fifths having foreign parents. It stands out clearly that these schools are mainly for children of French Canadian extraction, as such children form 58.1 per cent of the whole number recorded. The Irish form 10 per cent of the whole number. The small group classed as "All other" contains representations of various races, as follows: Canadian, other than French (43), Chinese (3), Dutch (9), Finnish (3), French (21), German (3), Hebrew, Russian (2), Hebrew, other (17), Italian, North (6), Italian, South (2), Portuguese (37), Scotch (16), Syrian (1), and Welsh (11).

The general tables which follow are so arranged that these prominent races can be studied, as respects age and grade distribution and as respects retardation, in the same way of the school system as a whole. It would lead too far into detail to attempt to present the figures here.

PUBLIC AND PAROCHIAL SCHOOL PUPILS COMBINED.

A combination of the figures for the public and parochial schools offers a more complete picture of the general racial distribution of the children in the community than do the figures for either one separately. It may be assumed that the children attending private school are few in number and that these combined figures cover practically all the children in the city. Such a combination of the ten sets of figures appears in the following table:

General nativity and race of father of pupil.	Pupils by schools.			Per cent of all pupils.
	Public schools.	Parochial schools.	Total.	
Native-born:				
White........	4,518	1,048	5,566	28.3
Negro and Indian........	50	....	50	.3
Total native-born........	4,568	1,048	5,616	28.6
Foreign-born:				
Canadian, French........	1,694	3,322	5,016	25.5
Canadian, Other........	229	43	272	1.4
English........	2,630	386	3,016	15.4
Hebrew, Russian........	783	2	785	4.0
Irish........	1,032	577	1,609	8.2
Portuguese........	1,811	37	1,848	9.4
Scotch........	281	16	297	1.5
All others........	898	291	1,189	6.1
Total foreign-born........	9,358	4,674	14,032	71.4
Grand total........	13,926	5,722	19,648	100.0

Somewhat more than one-fourth of the children (28.6 per cent) have native fathers, while as many as 71.4 per cent have foreign fathers. In the city as a whole the most numerous race is the French Canadian, which has one-fourth (25.5 per cent) of all the children. This is followed by the English with 15.4 per cent, the Portuguese with 9.4 per cent, and the Irish with 8.2 per cent. It can not fail to be noted that the smaller parochial school system has a very considerable proportion of all the Irish children, and twice as many French Canadian children as are in the public schools.

GENERAL TABLES.

PUBLIC SCHOOL PUPILS: GENERAL INVESTIGATION.

Table **1.**—*Grade and age—Number of pupils of each age in each grade, by sex.*

BOYS.

Age.	Kindergarten.	Elementary grades.									
		1.	2.	3.	4.	5.	6.	7.	8.	9.	Total.
3 years	8										
4 years	40	1									1
5 years	4	532	2								534
6 years	2	459	177	3							639
7 years		226	303	139	5						673
8 years		142	212	256	121	7	1				739
9 years		66	142	192	201	112	11				724
10 years ...		39	71	133	181	163	101	11	1		700
11 years ...		22	43	65	156	167	142	72	10		677
12 years ...		25	30	96	142	107	161	131	78	10	780
13 years ...		18	34	74	126	139	122	117	137	72	839
14 years ...		3	7	26	47	15	25	38	48	58	267
15 years ...		2	5	11	6	4	5	6	14	35	88
16 years ...			1		1		1		1	8	12
17 years ...								1			1
18 years ...											
19 years ...											
20 years or over....											
Total.	54	1,535	1,027	995	986	714	569	376	289	183	6,674

Age.	High school.					Mixed and illiterate.	Grand total.
	First year.	Second year.	Third year.	Fourth year.	Total.		
3 years							8
4 years							41
5 years						3	541
6 years						4	645
7 years						2	675
8 years						2	741
9 years						2	726
10 years						3	703
11 years						3	680
12 years						3	783
13 years	9				9	17	865
14 years	58	9	1		68	18	353
15 years	51	29	10	1	91	9	188
16 years	25	36	23	4	88	1	101
17 years	6	17	29	18	70		71
18 years	1	4	17	17	39		39
19 years		1	2	6	9		9
20 years or over	1		1	1	3		3
Total	151	96	83	47	377	67	7,172

TABLE 1.—*Grade and age—Number of pupils of each age in each grade, by sex*—Contd.

GIRLS.

Age.	Kindergarten.	Elementary grades.										
		1.	2.	3.	4.	5.	6.	7.	8.	9.	Total.
3 years	11										
4 years	47	1									1
5 years	10	470	3								473
6 years	1	419	207	3							629
7 years		249	292	177	4						722
8 years		117	204	251	149	6	1				728
9 years		50	76	174	157	127	8				592
10 years		41	52	100	146	188	100	17	1		645
11 years		31	34	70	128	132	132	81	11		619
12 years		25	31	75	120	135	145	157	85	9	782
13 years		20	25	66	96	111	98	116	83	77	692
14 years		5	13	24	22	10	11	29	49	70	233
15 years		3	4	4	3	1	2	5	11	42	75
16 years				1					1	12	14
17 years									2	1	3
18 years											
19 years											
20 years or over											
Total.	69	1,431	941	945	825	710	497	405	243	211	6,208

Age.	High school.					Mixed and illiterate.	Grand total.
	First year.	Second year.	Third year.	Fourth year.	Total.		
3 years							11
4 years						2	50
5 years							483
6 years						5	635
7 years						2	724
8 years						5	733
9 years						6	598
10 years						3	648
11 years						3	622
12 years						1	783
13 years	11				11	16	719
14 years	59	11	2		72	13	318
15 years	51	34	8		93	7	175
16 years	18	45	35	11	109	1	124
17 years	6	16	24	25	71		74
18 years		5	9	30	44	1	45
19 years		2	2	5	9		9
20 years or over			1	2	3		3
Total	145	113	81	73	412	65	6,754

TABLE 1.—*Grade and age—Number of pupils of each age in each grade, by sex*—Contd.

TOTAL.

Age.	Kinder-garten.	Elementary grades.									
		1.	2.	3.	4.	5.	6.	7.	8.	9.	Total.
3 years	19										
4 years	87	2									2
5 years	14	1,002	5								1,007
6 years	3	878	384	6							1,268
7 years		475	595	316	9						1,395
8 years		259	416	507	270	13	2				1,467
9 years		116	218	366	358	239	19				1,316
10 years		80	123	233	327	351	201	28	2		1,345
11 years		53	77	135	284	299	274	153	21		1,296
12 years		50	61	171	262	242	306	288	163	19	1,562
13 years		38	59	140	222	250	220	233	220	149	1,531
14 years		8	20	50	69	25	36	67	97	128	500
15 years		5	9	15	9	5	7	11	25	77	163
16 years			1	1	1		1		2	20	26
17 years								1	2	1	4
18 years											
19 years											
20 years or over....											
Total.	123	2,966	1,968	1,940	1,811	1,424	1,066	781	532	394	12,882

Age.	High school.					Mixed and il-literate	Grand total.
	First year.	Second year.	Third year.	Fourth year.	Total.		
3 years							19
4 years						2	91
5 years						3	1,024
6 years						9	1,280
7 years						4	1,399
8 years						7	1,474
9 years						8	1,324
10 years						6	1,351
11 years						6	1,302
12 years						4	1,566
13 years	20		3		20	33	1,584
14 years	117	20	3		140	31	671
15 years	102	63	18	1	184	16	363
16 years	43	81	58	15	197	2	225
17 years	12	33	53	43	141		145
18 years	1	9	26	47	83	1	84
19 years		3	4	11	18		18
20 years or over	1		2	3	6		6
Total	296	209	164	120	789	132	13,926

TABLE 2.—Race, sex, and grade—Number of pupils of each sex in each grade, by general nativity and race of father of pupil.

General nativity and race of father of pupil	Kinder-garten	Elementary grades										High school					Illiter-ate and un-graded	Grand total
		1	2	3	4	5	6	7	8	9	Total	First year	Second year	Third year	Fourth year	Total		
Native-born:																		
White—																		
Male	13	359	257	275	268	246	217	150	142	101	2,015	99	69	47	31	246	19	2,293
Female	15	345	260	281	231	216	180	183	107	117	1,920	89	74	50	52	265	25	2,225
Total	28	704	517	556	499	462	397	333	249	218	3,935	188	143	97	83	511	44	4,518
Negro—																		
Male		3	4	3			6	1			17						1	18
Female	1	5	1	7	5	1	4	1	2	1	27						1	29
Total	1	8	5	10	5	1	10	2	2	1	44						2	47
Indian—																		
Male																	1	1
Female																	2	2
Total																	3	3
Total native-born—																		
Male	13	362	261	278	268	246	223	151	142	101	2,032	99	69	47	31	246	21	2,312
Female	16	350	261	288	236	217	184	184	109	118	1,947	89	74	50	52	265	28	2,256
Total	29	712	522	566	504	463	407	335	251	219	3,979	188	143	97	83	511	49	4,568
Foreign-born:																		
Canadian, French—																		
Male	13	290	170	135	172	44	55	16	14	3	899	3		2		5	14	931
Female	8	241	124	135	113	55	39	15	5	5	732	3	3		1	7	16	763
Total	21	531	294	270	285	99	94	31	19	8	1,631	6	3	2	1	12	30	1,694
Canadian, Other—																		
Male	2	7	15	20	11	39	4	4	7	4	111	2				2	11	126
Female	4	13	6	13	13	36	3	3	3		90	1	1	3		5	4	103
Total	6	20	21	33	24	75	7	7	10	4	201	3	1	3		7	15	229
Danish—																		
Male		2	2	1	1		2				8	1				1		9
Female			2	1		5			1		9							9
Total		2	4	2	1	5	2		1		17	1				1		18
English—																		
Male	11	211	171	159	216	176	151	101	71	34	1,290	11	4	13	7	35		1,336
Female	13	196	157	177	169	180	138	110	65	36	1,228	17	16	15	4	52	1	1,294
Total	24	407	328	336	385	356	289	211	136	70	2,518	28	20	28	11	87	1	2,630
Finnish—																		
Male		6	1	1		2					10							10
Female			1			1		1			3							3
Total		6	2	1		3		1			13							13

French—																		
Male		2	14	2	9	6		4			37				1	1		38
Female		7	7	3	23	8		4	2		54	1	1			2		56
Total		9	21	5	32	14		8	2		91	1	1		1	3		94
German—																		
Male		8	10	5	6	4	3		1	1	38	1		2		3		41
Female		6	8	1	8	4	5	4	3	1	40							40
Total		14	18	6	14	8	8	4	4	2	78	1		2		3		81
Hebrew, German—																		
Male		2	3	1	3			2			11	1	1			2		13
Female		2	4	4	2	3		2			17	2				2		19
Total		4	7	5	5	3		4			28	3	1			4		32
Hebrew, Polish—																		
Male		7			3		2	3	3		18		2		1	3		21
Female		5	4	1	6	1	4		2	1	24		1		1	2		26
Total		12	4	1	9	1	6	3	5	1	42		3		2	5		47
Hebrew, Roumanian—																		
Male		2	1	1			2	1			7			1		1		8
Female			1	3	1						5		1			1	2	8
Total		2	2	4	1		2	1			12		1	1		2	2	16
Hebrew, Russian—																		
Male	14	89	58	55	49	38	25	20	12	11	357	11	6	4	1	22	1	394
Female	16	77	50	56	47	40	33	21	14	16	354	10	1	3	4	18	1	389
Total	30	166	108	111	96	78	58	41	26	27	711	21	7	7	5	40	2	783
Hebrew, Other—																		
Male		6	2	6	3		5			1	23							23
Female		4	3	1	2	3			1		14							14
Total		10	5	7	5	3	5		1	1	37							37
Irish—																		
Male		80	70	66	82	66	45	44	29	22	504	18	6	13	6	43		547
Female	7	73	59	52	66	63	53	40	23	9	438	16	8	7	9	40		485
Total	7	153	129	118	148	129	98	84	52	31	942	24	14	20	15	83		1,032
Italian, North—																		
Male		14	15	19	6	7	1				62		1			1		63
Female		26	8	6	8	6	3		3	12	72		1			1		73
Total		40	23	25	14	13	4		3	12	134		2			2		136
Italian, South—																		
Male		29	13	15	7	4	3	2	2		75	1				1		76
Female		20	26	6	9	5	2	1			69		1			1		70
Total		49	39	21	16	9	5	3	2		144	1	1			2		146
Polish—																		
Male		23	7	19	11	4	3	1			68							68
Female		27	7	8	5		3				50						1	51
Total		50	14	27	16	4	6	1			118						1	119
Portuguese—																		
Male		360	191	184	101	51	22	11	1	1	922	2	1			3	20	945
Female	2	347	178	163	93	53	10	5	3		852						12	866
Total	2	707	369	347	194	104	32	16	4	1	1,774	2	1			3	32	1,811
Russian—																		
Male		2		2	2	1					7							7
Female		1		1	3	1				1	7							7
Total		3		3	5	2				1	14							14

TABLE **2.**—*Race, sex, and grade—Number of pupils of each sex in each grade, by general nativity and race of father of pupil*—Continued.

General nativity and race of father of pupil	Kindergarten	Elementary grades 1.	2.	3.	4.	5.	6.	7.	8.	9.	Total.	High school First year.	Second year.	Third year.	Fourth year.	Total.	Illiterate and ungraded.	Grand total.
Foreign-born—Continued.																		
Scotch—																		
Male	1	18	15	17	27	16	19	13	7	4	136	1	3	1		5	1	143
Female		16	23	15	13	18	15	12	6	9	127	4	4	2	1	11		138
Total	1	34	38	32	40	34	34	25	13	13	263	5	7	3	1	16	1	281
Swedish—																		
Male		3	4			2	2	1			10							10
Female		5	2	2	1	2		2			16	1				1		17
Total		8	6	2	1	4	2	3			26	1				1		27
Syrian—																		
Male		4	4	3	4	1					16							16
Female		4	1	1	2	1	2	1			11						2	13
Total		8	5	4	6	2	2	1			27						2	29
Welsh—																		
Male		2	1	1	3	1	1		1	1	11	1	1			2		13
Female		6	3	2	3	2	2	1		1	20	1	1	1		3		23
Total		8	4	3	6	3	3	1	1	2	31	2	2	1		5		36
Other races—*a*																		
Male	2	6	1	6	2	5	1	1			22							22
Female		4	6	5	1	7		2	2	3	29					2		31
Total	2	10	7	11	3	12	1	3	2	3	51					2		53
Total foreign-born—																		
Male	41	1,173	766	717	718	468	346	225	147	82	4,642	52	26	36	16	130	47	4,860
Female	52	1,081	680	657	589	493	313	221	134	93	4,261	55	39	31	20	145	39	4,498
Total	94	2,254	1,446	1,374	1,307	961	659	446	281	175	8,903	107	65	67	36	275	86	9,358
Grand total—																		
Male	54	1,535	1,027	995	986	714	569	376	289	183	6,674	151	96	83	47	377	67	7,172
Female	69	1,431	941	945	825	710	497	405	243	211	6,208	145	113	81	73	412	65	6,754
Total	123	2,966	1,968	1,940	1,811	1,424	1,066	781	532	394	12,882	296	209	164	120	789	132	13,926

a "Other races" includes 2 Armenians, 3 Bohemians, 9 Bulgarians, 5 Chinese, 7 Greeks, 1 Magyar, 1 Negro, 8 Norwegians, 6 Roumanians, 5 Scotch-Irish, 3 Spanish, 2 Spanish-Americans, 1 race not specified.

TABLE 3.—*Race, sex, and age, by grade—Number of pupils of each age in each grade, by sex and by general nativity and race of father of pupil.*

KINDERGARTEN.

BOYS.

General nativity and race of father of pupil.	Number of pupils of each age.				Total.
	3.	4.	5.	6.	
Native-born, White	1	9	2	1	13
Foreign-born:					
Canadian, French	1	12			13
Canadian, Other		2			2
English		9	1	1	11
Hebrew, Russian	6	7	1		14
Scotch		1			1
Total foreign-born	7	31	2	1	41
Grand total	8	40	4	2	54

GIRLS.

	3.	4.	5.	6.	Total.
Native-born:					
White	4	10	1		15
Negro		1			1
Total native-born	4	11	1		16
Foreign-born:					
Canadian, French	1	5	2		8
Canadian, Other		3	1		4
English	2	8	3		13
Hebrew, Russian	4	11	1		16
Irish		5	2		7
Portuguese		2			2
Swedish		1			1
Other races a		1		1	2
Total foreign-born	7	36	9	1	53
Grand total	11	47	10	1	69

TOTAL.

	3.	4.	5.	6.	Total.
Native-born:					
White	5	19	3	1	28
Negro		1			1
Total native-born	5	20	3	1	29
Foreign-born:					
Canadian, French	2	17	2		21
Canadian, Other		5	1		6
English	2	17	4	1	24
Hebrew, Russian	10	18	2		30
Irish		5	2		7
Portuguese		2			2
Scotch		1			1
Swedish		1			1
Other races a		1		1	2
Total foreign-born	14	67	11	2	94
Grand total	19	87	14	3	123

a "Other races" includes races having less than 10 representatives in this city and pupils whose race is not reported.

TABLE 3.—*Race, sex, and age, by grade—Number of pupils of each age in each grade, by sex and by general nativity and race of father of pupil*—Continued.

FIRST GRADE.

BOYS.

General nativity and race of father of pupil.	Number of pupils of each age.												Total.
	4.	5.	6.	7.	8.	9.	10.	11.	12.	13.	14.	15.	
Native-born:													
White	....	177	109	41	24	4	3	....	1	....	....	....	359
Negro	....	1	1	1	....	....	....	....	....	....	....	....	3
Total native-born	....	178	110	42	24	4	3	....	1	....	....	....	362
Foreign-born:													
Canadian, French	....	82	88	55	29	17	6	3	7	3	....	....	290
Canadian, Other	....	4	3	....	....	....	....	....	....	....	....	....	7
Danish	....	1	....	1	....	....	....	....	....	....	....	....	2
English	....	96	83	20	8	2	1	....	....	1	....	....	211
French	....	1	....	....	....	1	....	....	....	....	....	....	2
Finnish	....	....	2	2	1	1	....	....	....	....	....	....	6
German	....	4	4	....	....	....	....	....	....	....	....	....	8
Hebrew, German	....	1	1	....	....	....	....	....	....	....	....	....	2
Hebrew, Polish	....	2	1	2	....	1	....	....	1	....	....	....	7
Hebrew, Russian	....	35	28	14	7	....	1	3	....	1	....	....	89
Hebrew, Roumanian	....	1	1	....	....	....	....	....	....	....	....	....	2
Hebrew, Other	....	3	2	....	1	....	....	....	....	....	....	....	6
Irish	....	40	27	8	3	1	1	....	....	....	....	....	80
Italian, North	....	9	4	1	....	....	....	....	....	....	....	....	14
Italian, South	....	9	10	3	4	1	....	....	2	....	....	....	29
Polish	....	6	8	4	1	2	1	1	....	....	....	....	23
Portuguese	1	41	79	71	61	35	26	15	14	12	3	2	360
Russian	....	1	....	....	....	1	....	....	....	....	....	....	2
Scotch	....	12	4	2	....	....	....	....	....	....	....	....	18
Swedish	....	2	1	....	....	....	....	....	....	....	....	....	3
Syrian	....	1	....	1	2	....	....	....	....	....	....	....	4
Welsh	....	1	1	....	....	....	....	....	....	....	....	....	2
Other races a	....	2	2	....	1	....	....	....	....	1	....	....	6
Total foreign-born	1	354	349	184	118	62	36	22	24	18	3	2	1,173
Grand total	1	532	459	226	142	66	39	22	25	18	3	2	1,535

a "Other races" includes races having less than 10 representatives in this city and pupils whose race is not reported.

TABLE 3.—*Race, sex, and age, by grade—Number of pupils of each age in each grade by sex and by general nativity and race of father of pupil*—Continued.

FIRST GRADE—Continued.

GIRLS.

General nativity and race of father of pupil.	Number of pupils of each age.												Total.
	4.	5.	6.	7.	8.	9.	10.	11.	12.	13.	14.	15.	
Native-born:													
White	1	174	104	36	18	4	1	3	1	2	1	....	345
Negro	....	1	2	2									5
Total native-born	1	175	106	38	18	4	1	3	1	2	1	....	350
Foreign-born:													
Canadian, French	....	69	75	54	26	8	3	....	2	4	....	....	241
Canadian, Other	....	4	6	2			1						13
Danish	....		1										1
English	....	79	81	27	7	2							196
French	....	2	1	3	1								7
German	....		5	1									6
Hebrew, German		1	1										2
Hebrew, Polish		1	1	2	1								5
Hebrew, Russian		27	24	13	2	1	3	3	1	2	....	1	77
Hebrew, Other		1	1			1							4
Irish		32	21	15	4			1					73
Italian, North		9	13	1	2	1							26
Italian, South		9	6	4			1						20
Polish		8	6	7	2	1	3						27
Portuguese		38	65	77	48	31	28	22	20	12	4	2	347
Russian					1								1
Scotch		9		2	3	2							16
Swedish		4		1									5
Syrian		1	2				1						4
Welsh			1	1	2	2							6
Other races *a*		1	1					1	1				4
Total foreign-born	....	295	313	211	99	46	40	28	24	18	4	3	1,081
Grand total	1	470	419	249	117	50	41	31	25	20	5	3	1,431

a "Other races" includes races having less than 10 representatives in this city and pupils whose race is not reported.

TABLE 3.—*Race, sex, and age, by grade—Number of pupils of each age in each grade, by sex and by general nativity and race of father of pupil—Continued.*

FIRST GRADE—Continued.

TOTAL.

General nativity and race of father of pupil.	Number of pupils of each age.												Total.
	4.	5.	6.	7.	8.	9.	10.	11.	12.	13.	14.	15.	
Native-born:													
White	1	351	213	77	42	8	4	3	2	2	1	....	704
Negro	....	2	3	3	....	....	....	....	....	....	....	....	8
Total native-born	1	353	216	80	42	8	4	3	2	2	1	....	712
Foreign-born:													
Canadian, French	....	151	163	109	55	25	9	3	9	7	....	....	531
Canadian, Other	....	8	9	2	....	....	....	1	....	....	....	....	20
Danish	....	1	1	1	....	....	....	....	....	....	....	....	3
English	....	175	164	47	15	4	1	....	....	1	....	....	407
French	....	3	1	3	1	1	....	....	....	....	....	....	9
Finnish	....	....	2	2	1	1	....	....	....	....	....	....	6
German	....	4	9	1	....	....	....	....	....	....	....	....	14
Hebrew, German	....	2	2	....	....	....	....	....	....	....	....	....	4
Hebrew, Polish	....	3	2	4	1	1	....	....	1	....	....	....	12
Hebrew, Russian	....	62	52	27	9	1	4	6	1	3	....	1	166
Hebrew, Roumanian	....	1	1	....	....	....	....	....	....	....	....	....	2
Hebrew, Other	....	4	3	....	2	....	1	....	....	....	....	....	10
Irish	....	72	48	23	7	1	1	1	....	....	....	....	153
Italian, North	....	18	17	2	2	1	....	....	....	....	....	....	40
Italian, South	....	18	16	7	4	1	1	....	2	....	....	....	49
Polish	....	14	14	11	3	3	4	1	....	....	....	....	50
Portuguese	1	79	144	148	109	66	54	37	34	24	7	4	707
Russian	....	1	....	....	1	1	....	....	....	....	....	....	3
Scotch	....	21	6	5	2	....	....	....	....	....	....	....	34
Swedish	....	6	1	1	....	....	....	....	....	....	....	....	8
Syrian	....	2	2	1	2	....	1	....	....	....	....	....	8
Welsh	....	1	2	1	2	2	....	....	....	....	....	....	8
Other races *a*	....	3	3	....	1	....	....	1	1	1	....	....	10
Total foreign-born	1	649	662	395	217	108	76	50	48	36	7	5	2,254
Grand total	2	1,002	878	475	259	116	80	53	50	38	8	5	2,966

a "Other races" includes races having less than 10 representatives in this city and pupils whose race is not reported.

TABLE 3.—*Race, sex, and age, by grade—Number of pupils of each age in each grade, by sex and by general nativity and race of father of pupil*—Continued.

SECOND GRADE.

BOYS.

General nativity and race of father of pupil.	Number of pupils of each age.												Total.
	5.	6.	7.	8.	9.	10.	11.	12.	13.	14.	15.	16.	
Native-born:													
White		69	91	56	19	10	4	6	1	1			257
Negro			1	2	1								4
Total native-born		69	92	58	20	10	4	6	1	1			261
Foreign-born:													
Canadian, French	1	16	45	37	25	13	10	9	9	2	3		170
Canadian, Other		6	5	2	1				1				15
Danish		1	1										2
English		38	70	32	21	7	3						171
Finnish				1									1
French		3	5	2	2	1		1					14
German		1	7	2									10
Hebrew, German		1	1	1									3
Hebrew, Roumanian			1										1
Hebrew, Russian		14	18	13	6	4	2		1				58
Hebrew, Other		1	1										2
Irish		16	22	13	12	5	1		1				70
Italian, North		2	3	3	3	2	2						15
Italian, South			4	5	2	2							13
Polish			2	3	1					1			7
Portuguese	1	5	16	33	47	27	21	14	21	4	1	1	191
Scotch		4	6	4	1								15
Swedish			1		1								2
Syrian			2	2									4
Welsh			1										1
Other races *a*				1									1
Total foreign-born	2	108	211	154	122	61	39	24	33	6	5	1	766
Grand total	2	177	303	212	142	71	43	30	34	7	5	1	1,027

a "Other races" includes races having less than 10 representatives in this city and pupils whose race is not reported.

TABLE **3.**—*Race, sex, and age, by grade*—*Number of pupils of each age in each grade, by sex and by general nativity and race of father of pupil*—Continued.

SECOND GRADE—Continued.

GIRLS.

General nativity and race of father of pupil.	Number of pupils of each age.												Total.
	5.	6.	7.	8.	9.	10.	11.	12.	13.	14.	15.	16.	
Native-born:													
White	....	99	90	51	11	5	3	1	....	....	....	....	260
Negro	....	....	1	....	....	....	....	....	....	....	....	....	1
Total native-born	....	99	91	51	11	5	3	1	....	....	....	....	261
Foreign-born:													
Canadian, French	....	8	41	38	7	8	5	6	5	4	2	....	124
Canadian, Other	....	2	1	2	1	....	....	....	....	....	....	....	6
English	1	44	58	36	7	5	2	2	2	....	....	....	157
Finnish	....	....	1	....	....	....	....	....	....	....	....	....	1
French	....	....	2	4	....	1	....	....	....	....	....	....	7
German	....	3	3	1	....	....	....	....	1	....	....	....	8
Hebrew, German	....	2	1	1	....	....	....	....	....	....	....	....	4
Hebrew, Roumanian	....	....	1	....	....	....	....	....	....	....	....	....	1
Hebrew, Russian	....	11	20	10	3	2	3	1	....	....	....	....	50
Hebrew, Polish	....	....	2	2	....	....	....	....	....	....	....	....	4
Hebrew, Other	....	....	1	1	....	1	....	....	....	....	....	....	3
Irish	....	19	22	9	6	....	1	....	1	....	....	....	59
Italian, North	....	1	5	....	1	1	....	....	....	....	....	....	8
Italian, South	....	2	5	5	5	2	2	1	2	1	1	....	26
Polish	1	1	2	2	1	....	....	....	....	....	....	....	7
Portuguese	....	4	22	35	33	25	17	19	15	7	1	....	178
Scotch	1	9	8	3	1	1	....	....	....	....	....	....	23
Swedish	....	....	2	2	....	....	....	....	....	....	....	....	4
Syrian	....	1	....	....	....	....	....	....	....	....	....	....	1
Welsh	....	....	3	....	....	....	....	....	....	....	....	....	3
Other races a	....	1	1	2	....	1	1	....	....	....	....	....	6
Total foreign-born	3	108	201	153	65	47	31	30	25	13	4	....	680
Grand total	3	207	292	204	76	52	34	31	25	13	4	....	941

a "Other races" includes races having less than 10 representatives in this city and pupils whose race is not reported.

TABLE 3.—*Race, sex, and age, by grade—Number of pupils of each age in each grade, by sex and by general nativity and race of father of pupil*—Continued.

SECOND GRADE—Continued.

TOTAL.

General nativity and race of father of pupil.	Number of pupils of each age.												Total.
	5.	6.	7.	8.	9.	10.	11.	12.	13.	14.	15.	16.	
Native-born:													
White	....	168	181	107	30	15	7	7	1	1	....	....	517
Negro	....	....	2	2	1	....	....	....	....	....	....	....	5
Total native-born	....	168	183	109	31	15	7	7	1	1	....	....	522
Foreign-born:													
Canadian, French	1	24	86	75	32	21	15	15	14	6	5	....	294
Canadian, Other	....	8	6	4	2	....	....	....	1	....	....	....	21
Danish	....	1	1	....	....	....	....	....	....	....	....	....	2
English	1	82	128	68	28	12	5	2	2	....	....	....	328
Finnish	....	....	1	1	....	....	....	....	....	....	....	....	2
French	....	3	7	6	2	1	1	1	....	....	....	....	21
German	....	4	10	3	....	....	....	....	1	....	....	....	18
Hebrew, German	....	3	2	2	....	....	....	....	....	....	....	....	7
Hebrew, Roumanian	....	....	2	....	....	....	....	....	....	....	....	....	2
Hebrew, Russian	....	25	38	23	9	6	5	1	1	....	....	....	108
Hebrew, Polish	....	....	2	2	....	....	....	....	....	....	....	....	4
Hebrew, Other	....	1	2	1	....	1	....	....	....	....	....	....	5
..ish	....	35	44	22	18	6	1	1	1	1	....	....	129
Italian, North	....	3	8	3	4	3	2	....	....	....	....	....	23
Italian, South	....	2	9	10	7	4	2	1	2	1	1	....	39
Polish	1	1	4	5	2	....	....	....	....	....	1	....	14
Portuguese	1	9	38	68	80	52	38	33	36	11	2	1	369
Scotch	1	13	14	7	2	1	....	....	....	....	....	....	38
Swedish	....	....	3	2	1	....	....	....	....	....	....	....	6
Syrian	....	1	2	2	....	....	....	....	....	....	....	....	5
Welsh	....	....	4	....	....	....	....	....	....	....	....	....	4
Other races a	....	1	1	3	....	1	1	....	....	....	....	....	7
Total foreign-born	5	216	412	307	187	108	70	54	58	19	9	1	1,446
Grand total	5	384	595	416	218	123	77	61	59	20	9	1	1,968

a "Other races" includes races having less than 10 representatives in this city and pupils whose races not reported.

66083°—VOL 31—12——16

TABLE **3.**—*Race, sex, and age, by grade—Number of pupils of each age in each grade, by sex and by general nativity and race of father of pupil*—Continued.

THIRD GRADE.

BOYS.

General nativity and race of father of pupil.	Number of pupils of each age.											Total.
	6.	7.	8.	9.	10.	11.	12.	13.	14.	15.	16.	
Native-born:												
White	1	68	97	46	30	10	17	5	1			275
Negro					1	2						3
Total native-born	1	68	97	46	31	12	17	5	1			278
Foreign-born:												
Canadian, French		3	27	17	11	12	22	30	9	4		135
Canadian, Other	1	2	5	6	1							20
English		30	53	42	22	8	1	3	1			159
Danish			1									1
French			1		1							2
German			1	2	1		1					5
Hebrew, German				1								1
Hebrew, Roumanian		1										1
Hebrew, Russian	1	8	18	9	9	3	3	1	2	1		55
Hebrew, Other		1		3	2							6
Irish		16	21	14	7	2	4	2				66
Italian, North		1	3	6	4	1	3	1				19
Italian, South			2	5	6		2					15
Portuguese		5	14	29	32	23	40	24	12	5		184
Polish			5	5	1	3	3	2				19
Russian			1		1							2
Scotch		3	6	5	2			1				17
Syrian				1	1					1		3
Welsh						1						1
Other races [a]		1	1	1	1			1	1			6
Total foreign-born	2	71	159	146	102	53	79	69	25	11		717
Grand total	3	139	256	192	133	65	96	74	26	11		995

[a] "Other races" includes races having less than 10 representatives in this city and pupils whose race is not reported.

TABLE 3.—*Race, sex, and age, by grade—Number of pupils of each age in each grade, by sex and by general nativity and race of father of pupil*—Continued.

THIRD GRADE—Continued.

GIRLS.

General nativity and race of father of pupil.	Number of pupils of each age.											Total.
	6.	7.	8.	9.	10.	11.	12.	13.	14.	15.	16.	
Native-born:												
White	2	79	95	61	17	9	10	6	1	1	....	281
Negro	....	.....	.....	5	1	.....	1	.....	.....	.....	....	7
Total native-born	2	79	95	66	18	9	11	6	1	1	....	288
Foreign-born:												
Canadian, French	....	10	24	14	12	11	22	32	9	1	....	135
Canadian, Other	....	2	2	4	1	2	2	.....	.....	.....	....	13
English	....	46	60	38	13	14	4	2	.....	.....	....	177
Danish	....	.....	1	.....	.....	.....	.....	.....	.....	.....	....	1
Finnish	....	.....	.....	.....	1	.....	.....	.....	.....	.....	....	1
French	....	1	1	.....	1	.....	.....	.....	.....	.....	....	3
German	....	.....	1	.....	.....	.....	.....	.....	.....	.....	....	1
Hebrew, German	....	.....	1	.....	1	.....	1	.....	1	.....	....	4
Hebrew, Polish	....	1	.....	.....	.....	.....	.....	.....	.....	.....	....	1
Hebrew, Roumanian	....	.....	1	.....	.....	1	1	.....	.....	.....	....	3
Hebrew, Russian	....	14	17	11	4	2	4	1	1	1	1	56
Hebrew, Other	....	.....	1	.....	.....	.....	.....	.....	.....	.....	....	1
Irish	....	13	18	7	7	2	5	.....	.....	.....	....	52
Italian, North	....	1	2	1	.....	2	2	.....	.....	.....	....	6
Italian, South	....	.....	1	.....	.....	2	2	1	.....	.....	....	6
Portuguese	....	4	16	26	37	22	25	21	12	.....	....	163
Polish	....	1	3	1	1	1	.....	1	.....	.....	....	8
Russian	....	.....	.....	1	.....	.....	.....	.....	.....	.....	....	1
Scotch	1	4	5	3	1	1	.....	.....	.....	.....	....	15
Swedish	....	1	1	.....	.....	.....	.....	.....	.....	.....	....	2
Syrian	....	.....	.....	1	.....	.....	.....	.....	.....	.....	....	1
Welsh	....	.....	.....	1	1	.....	.....	.....	.....	.....	....	2
Other races a	....	.....	1	.....	.....	1	.....	2	.....	1	....	5
Total foreign-born	1	98	156	108	82	61	64	60	23	3	1	657
Grand total	3	177	251	174	100	70	75	66	24	4	1	945

a "Other races" includes races having less than 10 representatives in this city and pupils whose race is not reported.

TABLE 3.—*Race, sex, and age, by grade—Number of pupils of each age in each grade, by sex and by general nativity and race of father of pupil*—Continued.

THIRD GRADE—Continued.

TOTAL.

General nativity and race of father of pupil.	Number of pupils of each age.											Total.
	6.	7.	8.	9.	10.	11.	12.	13.	14.	15.	16.	
Native-born:												
White	3	147	192	107	47	19	27	11	2	1	....	556
Negro				5	2	2	1					10
Total native-born	3	147	192	112	49	21	28	11	2	1	....	566
Foreign-born:												
Canadian, French		13	51	31	23	23	44	62	18	5	....	270
Canadian, Other	1	4	7	10	2	2	3	3	1			33
English		76	113	80	35	22	5	5				336
Danish			2									2
Finnish					1							1
French		1	2		2							5
German			2	2	1		1					6
Hebrew, German			1	1	1		1					5
Hebrew, Polish		1						1				1
Hebrew, Roumanian		1	1			1	1					4
Hebrew, Russian	1	22	35	20	13	5	7	2	3	2	1	111
Hebrew, Other		1	1	3	2							7
Irish		29	39	21	14	4	9	2				118
Italian, North		2	5	7	4	3	3	1				25
Italian, South			3	5	8	2	1	2				21
Portuguese		9	30	55	69	45	65	45	24	5		347
Polish		1	8	6	2	4	3	3				27
Russian			1	1	1							3
Scotch	1	7	11	8	3	1		1				32
Swedish		1	1			1						2
Syrian				2		1				1		4
Welsh				1	2							3
Other races *a*		1	2	1	1	1		3	1	1		11
Total foreign-born	3	169	315	254	184	114	143	129	48	14	1	1,374
Grand total	6	316	507	366	233	135	171	140	50	15	1	1,940

a "Other races" includes races having less than 10 representatives in this city and pupils whose race is not reported.

TABLE 3.—*Race, sex, and age, by grade—Number of pupils of each age in each grade, by sex and by general nativity and race of father of pupil*—Continued.

FOURTH GRADE.

BOYS.

General nativity and race of father of pupil.	Number of pupils of each age.										Total.
	7.	8.	9.	10.	11.	12.	13.	14.	15.	16.	
Native-born, White............	2	59	82	48	36	21	14	4	1	1	268
Foreign-born:											
Canadian, French...........	......	6	11	8	10	52	63	18	4	....	172
Canadian, Other............	......	2	1	4	2	......	1	1	.....	....	11
Danish.....................	......	......	......	1	......	......	......	.....	.....	....	1
English....................	......	30	56	57	45	21	6	1	.....	....	216
French.....................	......	......	......	......	......	1	5	3	.....	....	9
German....................	......	......	2	2	2	......	......	.....	.....	....	6
Hebrew, German...........	......	......	1	1	1	......	......	.....	.....	....	3
Hebrew, Polish............	......	......	......	2	......	1	......	.....	.....	....	3
Hebrew, Russian...........	......	5	12	12	9	5	5	1	.....	....	49
Hebrew, Other.............	......	1	......	......	......	2	......	.....	.....	....	3
Irish......................	1	10	18	22	14	7	9	1	.....	....	82
Italian, North.............	......	......	3	1	1	......	......	1	.....	....	6
Italian, South.............	......	......	......	1	3	2	......	1	.....	....	7
Polish.....................	......	......	......	......	3	4	1	3	.....	....	11
Portuguese................	......	2	7	12	24	21	22	12	1	....	101
Russian...................	1	1	......	......	......	......	......	.....	.....	....	2
Scotch....................	......	5	5	9	4	3	......	1	.....	....	27
Syrian....................	......	......	1	1	2	......	......	.....	.....	....	4
Welsh....................	......	......	2	......	......	1	......	.....	.....	....	3
Other races *a*...........	1	......	......	......	......	1	......	.....	.....	....	2
Total foreign-born........	3	62	119	133	120	121	112	43	5	....	718
Grand total..............	5	121	201	181	156	142	126	47	6	1	986

a "Other races" includes races having less than 10 representatives in this city and pupils whose race is not reported.

TABLE 3.—*Race, sex, and age, by grade—Number of pupils of each age in each grade, by sex and by general nativity and race of father of pupil*—Continued.

FOURTH GRADE—Continued.

GIRLS.

General nativity and race of father of pupil.	Number of pupils of each age.										Total.
	7.	8.	9.	10.	11.	12.	13.	14.	15.	16.	
Native-born:											
White	3	78	56	49	23	11	8	3	....	....	231
Negro	....	....	2	....	3	....	....	....	....	....	5
Total native-born	3	78	58	49	26	11	8	3	....	....	236
Foreign-born:											
Canadian, French	....	3	5	5	14	32	47	6	1	....	113
Canadian, Other	....	5	2	3	....	1	2	....	....	....	13
English	....	32	38	36	33	21	9	....	....	....	169
French	....	1	1	1	1	8	4	6	1	....	23
Finnish	....	....	1	....	....	....	....	....	....	....	1
German	....	4	2	1	....	....	1	....	....	....	8
Hebrew, German	....	....	1	....	1	....	....	....	....	....	2
Hebrew, Polish	....	1	4	1	....	....	....	....	....	....	6
Hebrew, Roumanian	....	....	1	....	....	....	....	....	....	....	1
Hebrew, Russian	....	5	12	13	10	5	1	....	1	....	47
Hebrew, Other	....	....	2	....	....	....	....	....	....	....	2
Irish	1	13	14	13	11	12	2	....	....	....	66
Italian, North	....	1	1	1	2	2	1	....	....	....	8
Italian, South	....	....	2	2	3	....	1	1	....	....	9
Polish	....	....	1	1	....	1	1	1	....	....	5
Portuguese	....	3	6	16	20	26	18	4	....	....	93
Russian	....	....	2	....	1	....	....	....	....	....	3
Scotch	....	2	4	2	5	....	....	....	....	....	13
Swedish	....	1	....	....	....	....	....	....	....	....	1
Syrian	....	....	....	1	....	....	....	1	....	....	2
Welsh	....	....	....	1	1	....	1	....	....	....	3
Other races a	....	....	....	....	....	1	....	....	....	....	1
Total foreign-born	1	71	99	97	102	109	88	19	3	....	589
Grand total	4	149	157	146	128	120	96	22	3	....	825

a "Other races" includes races having less than 10 representatives in this city and pupils whose race is not reported.

TABLE 3.—*Race, sex, and age, by grade—Number of pupils of each age in each grade, by sex and by general nativity and race of father of pupil*—Continued.

FOURTH GRADE—Continued.

TOTAL.

General nativity and race of father of pupil.	Number of pupils of each age.										Total.
	7.	8.	9.	10.	11.	12.	13.	14.	15.	16.	
Native-born:											
White	5	137	138	97	59	32	22	7	1	1	499
Negro			2		3						5
Total native-born	5	137	140	97	62	32	22	7	1	1	504
Foreign-born:											
Canadian, French		9	16	13	24	84	110	24	5		285
Canadian, Other		7	3	7	2	1	3	1			24
Danish				1							1
English		62	94	93	78	42	15	1			385
French		1	1	1	1	9	9	9	1		32
Finnish			1								1
German		4	4	3	2		1				14
Hebrew, German			2	1	2						5
Hebrew, Polish		1	4	3		1					9
Hebrew, Roumanian			1								1
Hebrew, Russian		10	24	25	19	10	6	1	1		96
Hebrew, Other		1	2			2					5
Irish	2	23	32	35	25	19	11	1			148
Italian, North		1	4	2	3	2	1	1			14
Italian, South			2	3	6	2	1	2			16
Polish			1	1	3	5	2	4			16
Portuguese		5	13	28	44	47	40	16	1		194
Russian	1	1	2		1						5
Scotch		7	9	11	9	3		1			40
Swedish		1									1
Syrian			1	2	2			1			6
Welsh			2	1	1	1	1				6
Other races *a*	1					2					3
Total foreign-born	4	133	218	230	222	230	200	62	8		1,307
Grand total	9	270	358	327	284	262	222	69	9	1	1,811

a "Other races" includes races having less than 10 representatives in this city and pupils whose race is **not** reported.

TABLE 3.—*Race, sex, and age, by grade—Number of pupils of each age in each grade, by sex and by general nativity and race of father of pupil—Continued.*

FIFTH GRADE.

BOYS.

General nativity and race of father of pupil.	Number of pupils of each age.								Total.
	8.	9.	10.	11.	12.	13.	14.	15.	
Native-born, White	5	56	70	58	30	25	2	......	246
Foreign-born:									
Canadian, French	......	2	6	1	9	19	5	2	44
Canadian, Other	......	......	3	5	7	23	1	......	39
English	......	28	46	49	25	27	1	......	176
French	......	......	1	......	......	4	1	......	6
Finnish	......	......	......	2	......	......	1	......	3
German	......	......	......	......	2	2	......	......	4
Hebrew, Russian	......	9	15	6	5	3	......	......	38
Irish	1	8	16	22	10	7	1	1	66
Italian, North	......	......	1	2	3	1	......	......	7
Italian, South	......	1	......	......	1	2	......	......	4
Polish	......	......	......	3	......	1	......	......	4
Portuguese	......	1	3	11	11	22	3	......	51
Russian	......	......	......	......	1	......	......	......	1
Scotch	1	5	2	5	2	1	......	......	16
Swedish	......	1	......	1	......	......	......	......	2
Syrian	......	......	......	......	......	......	......	1	1
Welsh	......	1	......	......	......	......	......	......	1
Other races a	......	......	......	2	1	2	......	......	5
Total foreign-born	2	56	93	109	77	114	13	4	468
Grand total	7	112	163	167	107	139	15	4	714

a "Other races" includes races having less than 10 representatives in this city and pupils whose race is not reported.

TABLE 3.—*Race, sex, and age, by grade—Number of pupils of each age in each grade, by sex and by general nativity and race of father of pupil*—Continued.

FIFTH GRADE—Continued.

GIRLS.

General nativity and race of father of pupil.	Number of pupils of each age.								Total.
	8.	9.	10.	11.	12.	13.	14.	15.	
Native-born:									
White	4	71	65	37	24	14	......	1	216
Negro	......	......	......	......	1	......	......	......	1
Total native-born	4	71	65	37	25	14	......	1	217
Foreign-born:									
Canadian, French	1	2	5	4	22	20	1	......	55
Canadian, Other	......	3	3	1	15	11	3	......	36
Danish	......	......	2	1	1	1	......	......	5
English	......	26	59	40	32	21	2	......	180
French	......	......	1	1	4	2	......	......	8
German	1	......	......	3	......	......	......	......	4
Hebrew, German	......	......	......	2	......	1	......	......	3
Hebrew, Polish	......	......	......	......	......	1	......	......	1
Hebrew, Russian	......	9	10	9	8	4	......	......	40
Hebrew, Other	......	......	2	......	......	1	......	......	3
Irish	......	9	20	12	13	8	1	......	63
Italian, North	......	1	3	1	......	1	......	......	6
Italian, South	......	......	......	1	......	4	......	......	5
Portuguese	......	1	6	16	9	19	2	......	53
Russian	......	......	1	......	......	......	......	......	1
Scotch	......	4	8	1	3	1	1	......	18
Swedish	......	1	......	1	......	......	......	......	2
Syrian	......	......	......	......	1	......	......	......	1
Welsh	......	......	1	......	1	......	......	......	2
Other races *a*	......	......	2	2	1	2	......	......	7
Total foreign-born	2	56	123	95	110	97	10	......	493
Grand total	6	127	188	132	135	111	10	1	710

a "Other races" includes races having less than 10 representatives in this city and pupils whose race is not reported.

TABLE **3.**—*Race, sex, and age, by grade—Number of pupils of each age in each grade, by sex and by general nativity and race of father of pupil—*Continued.

FIFTH GRADE—Continued.

TOTAL.

General nativity and race of father of pupil.	Number of pupils of each age.								Total.
	8.	9.	10.	11.	12.	13.	14.	15.	
Native-born:									
White	9	127	135	95	54	39	2	1	462
Negro					1				1
Total native-born	9	127	135	95	55	39	2	1	463
Foreign-born:									
Canadian, French	1	4	11	5	31	39	6	2	99
Canadian, Other		3	6	6	22	34	4		75
Danish			2	1	1	1			5
English		54	105	89	57	48	3		356
French			2	1	4	6	1		14
Finnish				2			1		3
German	1			3	2	2			8
Hebrew, German				2		1			3
Hebrew, Polish						1			1
Hebrew Russian		18	25	15	13	7			78
Hebrew, Other			2			1			3
Irish	1	17	36	34	23	15	2	1	129
Italian, North		1	4	3	3	2			13
Italian, South		1		1	1	6			9
Polish				3		1			4
Portuguese		2	9	27	20	41	5		104
Russian			1		1				2
Scotch	1	9	10	6	5	2	1		34
Swedish		2		2					4
Syrian					1			1	2
Welsh		1		1	1				3
Other races a			2	4	2	4			12
Total foreign-born	4	112	216	204	187	211	23	4	961
Grand total	13	239	351	299	242	250	25	5	1,424

TABLE 3.—*Race, sex, and age, by grade—Number of pupils of each age in each grade, by sex and by general nativity and race of father of pupil—Continued.*

SIXTH GRADE.

BOYS.

General nativity and race of father of pupil.	Number of pupils of each age.									Total.
	8.	9.	10.	11.	12.	13.	14.	15.	16.	
Native-born:										
White.................	1	6	48	71	54	29	6	1	1	217
Negro.................					3		3			6
Total native-born..............	1	6	48	71	57	29	9	1	1	223
Foreign-born:										
Canadian, French........			4	5	9	24	11	2		55
Canadian, Other........				1	3					4
Danish................			1			1				2
English...............		4	28	30	54	34	1			151
German...............					1	2				3
Hebrew, Polish........			1					1		2
Hebrew, Roumanian....				1	1					2
Hebrew, Russian......		1	3	7	8	4	2			25
Hebrew, Other........				1	2	2				5
Irish.................			6	16	14	7	2			45
Italian, North........						1				1
Italian, South........				1		2				3
Portuguese...........				3	7	11		1		22
Polish................			1	1		1				3
Scotch................			8	4	4	3				19
Swedish...............					1	1				2
Welsh................				1						1
Other races *a*........			1							1
Total foreign-born........		5	53	71	104	93	16	4		346
Grand total............	1	11	101	142	161	122	25	5	1	569

a "Other races" includes races having less than 10 representatives in this city and pupils whose race is not reported.

TABLE 3.—*Race, sex, and age, by grade—Number of pupils of each age in each grade, by sex and by general nativity and race of father of pupil*—Continued.

SIXTH GRADE—Continued.

GIRLS.

General nativity and race of father of pupil.	Number of pupils of each age.									Total.
	8.	9.	10.	11.	12.	13.	14.	15.	16.	
Native-born:										
White	1	4	54	50	40	29	2			180
Negro				1	2		1			4
Total native-born	1	4	54	51	42	29	3			184
Foreign-born:										
Canadian, French			2	1	15	15	4	2		39
Canadian, Other		1				2				3
Danish				1						1
English			25	46	39	27	1			138
German				2	3					5
Hebrew, Polish				2	2					4
Hebrew, Russian		2	2	10	14	3	2			33
Irish		1	13	12	17	10				53
Italian, North					1	2				3
Italian, South					1	1				2
Portuguese			1	1	2	5	1			10
Polish					3					3
Scotch			3	5	4	3				15
Syrian					2					2
Welsh				1		1				2
Total foreign-born		4	46	81	103	69	8	2		313
Grand total	1	8	100	132	145	98	11	2		497

TOTAL.

General nativity and race of father of pupil.	8.	9.	10.	11.	12.	13.	14.	15.	16.	Total.
Native-born:										
White	2	10	102	121	94	58	8	1	1	397
Negro				1	5		4			10
Total native-born	2	10	102	122	99	58	12	1	1	407
Foreign-born:										
Canadian, French			6	6	24	39	15	4		94
Canadian, Other		1		1	3	2				7
Danish			1	1		1				3
English		4	53	76	93	61	2			289
German				2	4	2				8
Hebrew, Polish			1	2	2			1		6
Hebrew, Roumanian				1	1					2
Hebrew, Russian		3	5	17	22	7	4			58
Hebrew, Other				1	2	2				5
Irish		1	19	28	31	17	2			98
Italian, North					1	3				4
Italian, South				1	1	3				5
Portuguese			1	4	9	16	1	1		32
Polish			1	1	3	1				6
Scotch			11	9	8	6				34
Syrian					2					2
Swedish						1	1			2
Welsh				2		1				3
Other races a			1							1
Total foreign-born		9	99	152	207	162	24	6		659
Grand total	2	19	201	274	306	220	36	7	1	1,066

a "Other races" includes races having less than 10 representatives in this city and pupils whose **race is** not reported.

TABLE 3.—*Race, sex, and age, by grade—Number of pupils of each age in each grade, by sex and by general nativity and race of father of pupil*—Continued.

SEVENTH GRADE.

BOYS.

General nativity and race of father of pupil.	Number of pupils of each age.							Total.
	10.	11.	12.	13.	14.	15.	17.	
Native-born:								
White	5	41	53	35	12	3	1	150
Negro			1					1
Total native-born	5	41	54	35	12	3	1	151
Foreign-born:								
Canadian, French		2	2	10	1	1		16
Canadian, Other	1	1	1	1				4
English	3	8	40	40	10			101
French				2	2			4
Hebrew, German				1	1			2
Hebrew, Polish		2			1			3
Hebrew, Roumanian				1				1
Hebrew, Russian		2	8	7	3			20
Irish	2	9	16	13	3	1		44
Italian, South			1		1			2
Polish				1				1
Portuguese		1	4	4	2			11
Scotch		5	4	2	1	1		13
Swedish			1					1
Welsh		1						1
Other races a					1			1
Total foreign-born	6	31	77	82	26	3		225
Grand total	11	72	131	117	38	6	1	376

GIRLS.

General nativity and race of father of pupil.	10.	11.	12.	13.	14.	15.	17.	Total.
Native-born:								
White	10	40	77	43	10	3		183
Negro	1							1
Total native-born	11	40	77	43	10	3		184
Foreign-born:								
Canadian, French		3	5	3	3	1		15
Canadian, Other	1			2				3
English	1	25	42	36	6			110
French			2	2				4
German			2	2				4
Hebrew, German	1				1			2
Hebrew, Russian	1	2	11	3	4			21
Irish	2	7	12	15	3	1		40
Italian, South					1			1
Portuguese			2	3				5
Scotch		2	3	6	1			12
Swedish		1		1				2
Other races a		1	1					2
Total foreign-born	6	41	80	73	19	2		221
Grand total	17	81	157	116	29	5		405

a "Other races" includes races having less than 10 representatives in this city and pupils whose race is not reported.

TABLE 3.—*Race, sex, and age, by grade—Number of pupils of each age in each grade, by sex and by general nativity and race of father of pupil*—Continued.

SEVENTH GRADE—Continued.

TOTAL.

General nativity and race of father of pupil.	Number of pupils of each age.							Total.
	10.	11.	12.	13.	14.	15.	17.	
Native-born:								
White....................	15	81	130	78	22	6	1	333
Negro....................	1	....	1	....	....	....	....	2
Total native-born..............	16	81	131	78	22	6	1	335
Foreign-born:								
Canadian, French........	....	5	7	13	4	2	....	31
Canadian, Other........	2	1	1	3	....	....	....	7
English................	4	33	82	76	16	....	....	211
French................	....	....	2	4	2	....	....	8
German................	....	....	2	2	....	....	....	4
Hebrew, German........	1	....	....	1	2	....	....	4
Hebrew, Polish........	....	2	....	....	1	....	....	3
Hebrew, Roumanian........	....	....	....	1	....	....	....	1
Hebrew, Russian........	1	4	19	10	7	....	....	41
Irish................	4	16	28	28	6	2	....	84
Italian, South........	....	....	1	....	2	....	....	3
Polish................	....	....	....	1	....	....	....	1
Portuguese........	....	1	6	7	2	....	....	16
Scotch................	....	7	7	8	2	1	....	25
Swedish................	....	1	1	1	....	....	....	3
Welsh................	....	1	....	....	....	....	....	1
Other races *a*........	....	1	1	....	1	....	....	3
Total foreign-born..............	12	72	157	155	45	5	....	446
Grand total..................	28	153	288	233	67	11	1	781

a "Other races" includes races having less than 10 representatives in this city and pupils whose race is not reported.

EIGHTH GRADE.

BOYS.

General nativity and race of father of pupil.	Number of pupils of each age.								Total.
	10.	11.	12.	13.	14.	15.	16.	17.	
Native-born, White....................	1	6	46	61	20	8	....	....	142
Foreign-born:									
Canadian, French........	....	....	2	8	2	2	....	....	14
Canadian, Other........	....	....	....	4	3	....	....	....	7
English................	....	2	16	41	11	....	1	....	71
German................	....	....	....	1	....	....	....	....	1
Hebrew, Polish........	....	....	1	1	....	1	....	....	3
Hebrew, Russian........	....	....	5	2	5	....	....	....	12
Irish................	....	1	5	14	7	2	....	....	29
Italian, South........	....	....	....	1	....	1	....	....	2
Portuguese........	....	....	....	1	....	....	....	....	1
Scotch................	....	1	3	3	....	....	....	....	7
Total foreign-born..................	....	4	32	76	28	6	1	....	147
Grand total..................	1	10	78	137	48	14	1	....	289

TABLE 3.—*Race, sex, and age, by grade—Number of pupils of each age in each grade, by sex and by general nativity and race of father of pupil*—Continued.

EIGHTH GRADE—Continued.

GIRLS.

General nativity and race of father of pupil.	Number of pupils of each age.								Total.
	10.	11.	12.	13.	14.	15.	16.	17.	
Native-born:									
White	1	6	40	35	18	6	......	1	107
Negro			1	1					2
Total native-born	1	6	41	36	18	6	......	1	109
oreign-born:									
Canadian, French				4	1				5
Canadian, Other			2				1		3
Danish			1						
English		3	28	24	8	2			65
French			1		1				2
German			1	1		1			3
Hebrew, Polish			1	1					2
Hebrew, Russian		2	3	3	4	1		1	14
Hebrew, Other				1					1
Irish			5	5	13				23
Italian, North				1	1	1			3
Portuguese				2	1				3
Scotch			2	2	2				6
Welsh				2					2
Other races *a*				1					1
Total foreign-born		5	44	47	31	5	1	1	134
Grand total	1	11	85	83	49	11	1	2	243

TOTAL.

General nativity and race of father of pupil.	Number of pupils of each age.								Total.
	10.	11.	12.	13.	14.	15.	16.	17.	
Native-born:									
White	2	12	86	96	38	14	......	1	249
Negro			1	1					2
Total native-born	2	12	87	97	38	14		1	251
Foreign-born:									
Canadian, French			2	12	3	2			19
Canadian, Other			2	4	3		1		10
Danish			1						1
English		5	44	65	19	2	1		136
French			1		1				2
German			1	2		1			4
Hebrew, Polish			2	2		1			5
Hebrew, Russian		2	8	5	9	1		1	26
Hebrew, Other				1					1
Irish		1	10	19	20	2			52
Italian, North				1	1	1			3
Italian, South				1		1			2
Portuguese				3	1				4
Scotch		1	5	5	2				13
Welsh				2					2
Other races *a*				1					1
Total foreign-born		9	76	123	59	11	2	1	281
Grand total	2	21	163	220	97	25	2	2	532

a "Other races" includes races having less than 10 representatives in this city and pupils whose race is not reported.

TABLE 3.—*Race, sex, and age, by grade—Number of pupils of each age in each grade, by sex and by general nativity and race of father of pupil—Continued.*

NINTH GRADE.

BOYS.

General nativity and race of father of pupil.	Number of pupils of each age.						Total.
	12.	13.	14.	15.	16.	17.	
Native-born, White	8	35	32	21	5	....	101
Foreign-born:							
Canadian, French			2	1			3
Canadian, Other		2	2				4
English	1	14	12	5	2		34
German				1			1
Hebrew, Russian	1	5	4	1			11
Hebrew, Other			1				1
Irish		13	3	6			22
Portuguese			1				1
Scotch		2	1		1		4
Welsh		1					1
Total foreign-born	2	37	26	14	3	....	82
Grand total	10	72	58	35	8	....	183

GIRLS.

General nativity and race of father of pupil.	12.	13.	14.	15.	16.	17.	Total.
Native-born:							
White	4	48	34	24	6	1	117
Negro				1			1
Total native-born	4	48	34	25	6	1	118
Foreign-born:							
Canadian, French			3		2		5
English		13	16	7			36
German					1		1
Hebrew, Polish			1				1
Hebrew, Russian	1	3	7	4	1		16
Irish	1	4		3	1		9
Italian, North	2	4	5		1		12
Russian			1				1
Scotch	1	3	3	2			9
Other races a		1	1	1			3
Total foreign-born	5	29	36	17	6	....	93
Grand total	9	77	70	42	12	1	211

a "Other races" includes races having less than 10 representatives in this city and pupils whose race is not reported.

TABLE 3.—*Race, sex, and age, by grade—Number of pupils of each age in each grade, by sex and by general nativity and race of father of pupil*—Continued.

NINTH GRADE—Continued.
TOTAL.

General nativity and race of father of pupil.	Number of pupils of each age.						Total.
	12.	13.	14.	15.	16.	17.	
Native-born:							
White....................	12	83	66	45	11	1	218
Negro....................				1			1
Total native-born................	12	83	66	46	11	1	219
Foreign-born:							
Canadian, French...........			5	1	2		8
Canadian, Other...........		2	2				4
English....................	1	27	28	12	2		70
German....................				1	1		2
Hebrew, Polish............			1				1
Hebrew, Russian...........	2	8	11	5	1		27
Hebrew, Other............			1				1
Irish......................	1	17	3	9	1		31
Italian, North............	2	4	5		1		12
Portuguese................			1				1
Russian...................		1					1
Scotch....................	1	5	4	2	1		13
Welsh.....................		1					1
Other races a.............		1	1	1			3
Total foreign-born................	7	66	62	31	9		175
Grand total................	19	149	128	77	20	1	394

a "Other races" includes races having less than 10 representatives in this city and pupils whose race is not reported.

FIRST YEAR HIGH SCHOOL.
BOYS.

General nativity and race of father of pupil.	Number of pupils of each age.								Total.
	13.	14.	15.	16.	17.	18.	19.	20.	
Native-born, White.....................	5	43	32	15	2	1			99
Foreign-born:									
Canadian, French..........		2	1						3
Canadian, Other...........			1	1					2
English....................	2	2	4	2	1				11
German....................				1					1
Hebrew, German...........			1						1
Hebrew, Russian...........		2	5	3				1	11
Irish......................		7	6	1	2				18
Italian, South............	2		1						1
Portuguese................		1			1				2
Scotch....................		1							1
Welsh.....................				1					1
Total foreign-born................	4	15	19	9	4			1	52
Grand total................	9	58	51	25	6	1		1	151

TABLE 3.—*Race, sex, and age, by grade—Number of pupils of each age in each grade, by sex and by general nativity and race of father of pupil*—Continued.

FIRST YEAR HIGH SCHOOL—Continued.

GIRLS.

General nativity and race of father of pupil.	Number of pupils of each age.								Total.
	13.	14.	15.	16.	17.	18.	19.	20.	
Native-born:									
White	7	32	35	11	4				89
Negro					1				1
Total native-born	7	32	35	11	5				90
Foreign-born:									
Canadian, French		3							3
Canadian, Other	1								1
English		11	4	2					17
French		1							1
Hebrew, German		1	1						2
Hebrew, Russian		2	6	2					10
Irish	3	6	4	2	1				16
Scotch		2	1	1					4
Welsh		1							1
Total foreign-born	4	27	16	7	1				55
Grand total	11	59	51	18	6				145

TOTAL.

General nativity and race of father of pupil.	Number of pupils of each age.								Total.
	13.	14.	15.	16.	17.	18.	19.	20.	
Native-born:									
White	12	75	67	27	6	1			188
Negro					1				1
Total native-born	12	75	67	27	7	1			189
Foreign-born:									
Canadian, French		5	1						6
Canadian, Other	1		1	1					3
English	2	13	8	4	1				28
French		1							1
German				1					1
Hebrew, German		1	2						3
Hebrew, Russian		4	11	5				1	21
Irish	5	13	10	3	3				34
Italian, South			1						1
Portuguese		1			1				2
Scotch		3	1	1					5
Welsh		1		1					2
Total foreign-born	8	42	35	16	5			1	107
Grand total	20	117	102	43	12	1		1	296

TABLE 3.—*Race, sex, and age, by grade—Number of pupils of each age in each grade, by sex and by general nativity and race of father of pupil*—Continued.

SECOND YEAR HIGH SCHOOL.

BOYS.

General nativity and race of father of pupil.	Number of pupils of each age.						Total.
	14.	15.	16.	17.	18.	19.	
Native-born:							
White..................................	6	20	27	13	3	....	69
Negro..................................	....	1	....	....	....	....	1
Total native-born......................	6	21	27	13	3	....	70
Foreign-born:							
Danish.................................	....	....	1	....	....	....	1
English................................	1	2	....	1	....	....	4
Hebrew, German.......................	....	....	1	....	....	....	1
Hebrew, Polish........................	1	....	1	....	....	....	2
Hebrew, Russian.......................	1	3	1	1	....	....	6
Irish..................................	....	2	2	1	1	....	6
Italian, North.........................	....	....	....	1	....	....	1
Portuguese............................	....	....	....	....	....	1	1
Scotch................................	....	....	3	....	....	....	3
Welsh.................................	....	1	....	....	....	....	1
Total foreign-born.....................	3	8	9	4	1	1	26
Grand total...........................	9	29	36	17	4	1	96

GIRLS.

General nativity and race of father of pupil.	14.	15.	16.	17.	18.	19.	Total.
Native-born, White......................	8	20	27	12	5	2	74
Foreign-born:							
Canadian, French......................	....	1	2	....	....	....	3
Canadian, Other.......................	....	....	....	1	....	....	1
English................................	1	8	7	....	....	....	16
French................................	....	....	1	....	....	....	1
Hebrew, Polish........................	....	....	1	....	....	....	1
Hebrew, Roumanian...................	....	1	....	....	....	....	1
Hebrew, Russian.......................	....	....	1	....	....	....	1
Irish..................................	1	2	3	2	....	....	8
Italian, North.........................	....	....	1	....	....	....	1
Italian, South.........................	....	....	1	....	....	....	1
Scotch................................	1	2	....	1	....	....	4
Welsh.................................	....	....	1	....	....	....	1
Total foreign-born.....................	3	14	18	4	....	....	39
Grand total...........................	11	34	45	16	5	2	113

TABLE 3.—*Race, sex, and age, by grade—Number of pupils of each age in each grade, by sex and by general nativity and race of father of pupil*—Continued.

SECOND YEAR HIGH SCHOOL—Continued.

TOTAL.

General nativity and race of father of pupil.	Number of pupils of each age.						Total.
	14.	15.	16.	17.	18.	19.	
Native-born:							
White	14	40	54	25	8	2	143
Negro		1					1
Total native-born	14	41	54	25	8	2	144
Foreign-born:							
Canadian, French		1	2				3
Canadian, Other				1			1
Danish			1				1
English	2	10	7	1			20
French			1				1
Hebrew, German			1				1
Hebrew, Polish	1		2				3
Hebrew, Roumanian		1					1
Hebrew, Russian	1	3	2	1			7
Irish	1	4	5	3	1		14
Italian, North			1	1			2
Italian, South			1				1
Portuguese						1	1
Scotch	1	2	3	1			7
Welsh		1	1				2
Total foreign-born	6	22	27	8	1	1	65
Grand total	20	63	81	33	9	3	209

THIRD YEAR HIGH SCHOOL.

BOYS.

General nativity and race of father of pupil.	Number of pupils of each age.							Total.
	14.	15.	16.	1ʋ	18.	19.	20.	
Native-born, White	1	5	13	14	12	1	1	47
Foreign-born:								
Canadian, French			1		1			2
English		3	5	2	2	1		13
German			2					2
Hebrew, Roumanian			1					1
Hebrew, Russian			1	3				4
Irish		2	2	7	2			13
Scotch			1					1
Total foreign-born		5	10	15	5	1		36
Grand total	1	10	23	29	17	2	1	83

TABLE **3.**—*Race, sex, and age, by grade—Number of pupils of each age in each grade, by sex and by general nativity and race of father of pupil—Continued.*

THIRD YEAR HIGH SCHOOL—Continued.

GIRLS.

General nativity and race of father of pupil.	Number of pupils of each age.							Total.
	14.	15.	16.	17.	18.	19.	20.	
Native-born, White	1	4	23	17	4	....	1	50
Foreign-born:								
Canadian, Other..............				1	2	....		3
English......................	1	3	5	3	2	1		15
Hebrew, Russian..............		1	1		1			3
Irish........................			6	1				7
Scotch......................				1		1		2
Welsh......................				1				1
Total foreign-born..............	1	4	12	7	5	2	....	31
Grand total...................	2	8	35	24	9	2	1	81

TOTAL.

General nativity and race of father of pupil.	Number of pupils of each age.							Total.
	14.	15.	16.	17.	18.	19.	20.	
Native-born, White	2	9	36	31	16	1	2	97
Foreign-born:								
Canadian, French..............			1		1			2
Canadian, Other..............				1	2			3
English......................	1	6	10	5	4	2		28
German......................				2				2
Hebrew, Roumanian..............			1					1
Hebrew, Russian..............		1	2	3	1			7
Irish........................		2	8	8	2			20
Scotch......................				2		1		3
Welsh......................				1				1
Total foreign-born..............	1	9	22	22	10	3	....	67
Grand total...................	3	18	58	53	26	4	2	164

FOURTH YEAR HIGH SCHOOL.

BOYS.

General nativity and race of father of pupil.	Number of pupils of each age.						Total.
	15.	16.	17.	18.	19.	20.	
Native-born, White	1	3	11	10	5	1	31
Foreign-born:							
English...........................	....	1	1	4	1	....	7
French...........................				1			1
Hebrew, Polish...................				1			1
Hebrew, Russian..................			1				1
Irish.............................			5	1			6
Total foreign-born.................	....	1	7	7	1	....	16
Grand total.....................	1	4	18	17	6	1	47

TABLE 3.—*Race, sex, and age, by grade—Number of pupils of each age in each grade, by sex and by general nativity and race of father of pupil*—Continued.

FOURTH YEAR HIGH SCHOOL—Continued.

GIRLS.

General nativity and race of father of pupil.	Number of pupils of each age.						Total.
	15.	16.	17.	18.	19.	20.	
Native-born:							
White		8	19	20	4	1	52
Indian				1			1
Total native-born		8	19	21	4	1	53
Foreign-born:							
Canadian, French			1				1
English		2		1		1	4
Hebrew, Polish				1			1
Hebrew, Russian			1	3			4
Irish		1	3	4	1		9
Scotch			1				1
Total foreign-born		3	6	9	1	1	20
Grand total		11	25	30	5	2	73

TOTAL.

General nativity and race of father of pupil.	15.	16.	17.	18.	19.	20.	Total.
Native-born:							
White	1	11	30	30	9	2	83
Indian				1			1
Total native-born	1	11	30	31	9	2	84
Foreign-born:							
Canadian, French			1				1
English		3	1	5	1	1	11
French				1			1
Hebrew, Polish				2			2
Hebrew, Russian			2	3			5
Irish		1	8	5	1		15
Scotch			1				1
Total foreign-born		4	13	16	2	1	36
Grand total	1	15	43	47	11	3	120

MIXED GRADE.

BOYS.

General nativity and race of father of pupil.	Number of pupils of each age.													Total.
	4.	5.	6.	7.	8.	9.	10.	11.	12.	13.	14.	15.	16.	
Native-born:														
White		3	2	2	1	2	2	2	2	2			1	19
Indian											1			1
Total native-born		3	2	2	1	2	2	2	2	2	1		1	20
Foreign-born:														
Canadian, French			1		1									2
Canadian, Other			1								1			2
Portuguese							1	1						2
Scotch									1					1
Total foreign-born			2		1		1	1	1		1			7
Grand total		3	4	2	2	2	3	3	3	2	2		1	27

TABLE 3.—*Race, sex, and age, by grade—Number of pupils of each age in each grade, by sex and by general nativity and race of father of pupil—Continued.*

MIXED GRADE—Continued.

GIRLS.

General nativity and race of father of pupil.	Number of pupils of each age.													Total.
	4.	5.	6.	7.	8.	9.	10.	11.	12.	13.	14.	15.	16.	
Native-born:														
White	2	....	4	2	4	6	3	2	....	....	2	....	....	25
Indian	....	....	....	....	....	....	....	....	....	....	....	....	1	1
Total native-born	2	....	4	2	4	6	3	2	....	....	2	....	1	26
Foreign-born:														
Canadian, French	....	....	1	....	1	....	....	....	....	....	....	....	....	2
Canadian, Other	....	....	....	....	....	....	....	....	1	....	....	....	....	1
English	....	....	....	....	....	....	....	1	....	....	....	....	....	1
Total foreign-born	....	....	1	....	1	....	....	1	1	....	....	....	....	4
Grand total	2	....	5	2	5	6	3	3	1	....	2	....	1	30

TOTAL.

General nativity and race of father of pupil.	Number of pupils of each age.													Total.
	4.	5.	6.	7.	8.	9.	10.	11.	12.	13.	14.	15.	16.	
Native-born:														
White	2	3	6	4	5	8	5	4	2	2	2	....	1	44
Indian	....	....	....	....	....	....	....	....	....	....	1	....	1	2
Total native-born	2	3	6	4	5	8	5	4	2	2	3	....	2	46
Foreign-born:														
Canadian, French	....	....	2	....	2	....	....	....	....	....	....	....	....	4
Canadian, Other	....	....	1	....	....	....	....	....	1	....	1	....	....	3
English	....	....	....	....	....	....	....	1	....	....	....	....	....	1
Portuguese	....	....	....	....	....	....	1	1	....	....	....	....	....	2
Scotch	....	....	....	....	....	....	....	....	1	....	....	....	....	1
Total foreign-born	....	....	3	....	2	....	1	2	2	....	1	....	....	11
Grand total	2	3	9	4	7	8	6	6	4	2	4	....	2	57

ILLITERATE GRADE.

BOYS.

General nativity and race of father of pupil.	Number of pupils at each age.						Total.
	13.	14.	15.	16.	17.	18.	
Foreign-born:							
Canadian, French	7	4	1	....	....	....	12
Canadian, Other	6	2	1	....	....	....	9
Hebrew, Russian	....	....	1	....	....	....	1
Polish	....	....	2	....	....	....	2
Portuguese	2	10	6	....	....	....	18
Syrian	....	....	....	....	....	....	
Total foreign-born	15	16	9	....	....	....	40

TABLE **3.**—*Race, sex, and age, by grade—Number of pupils of each age in each grade, by sex and by general nativity and race of father of pupil*—Continued.

ILLITERATE GRADE—Continued.

GIRLS.

General nativity and race of father of pupil.	Number of pupils at each age.						Total.
	13.	14.	15.	16.	17.	18.	
Foreign-born:							
Canadian, French	10	2	1			1	14
Canadian, Other	3						3
Hebrew, Roumanian		1	1				2
Hebrew, Russian	1						1
Polish			1				1
Portuguese	2	6	4				12
Syrian		2					2
Total foreign-born	16	11	7			1	35

TOTAL.

General nativity and race of father of pupil.	13.	14.	15.	16.	17.	18.	Total.
Foreign-born:							
Canadian, French	17	6	2			1	26
Canadian, Other	9	2	1				12
Hebrew, Roumanian		1	1				2
Hebrew, Russian	1		1				2
Polish			1				1
Portuguese	4	16	10				30
Syrian		2					2
Total foreign-born	31	27	16			1	75

TABLE **4.**—*Race and grade, by age—Number of pupils of each specified age in each grade, by general nativity and race of father of pupil.*

BOYS: AGE 3 YEARS.

General nativity and race of father of pupil.	Kinder-garten.
Native-born, White	1
Foreign-born other races a	7
Total	8

a "Other races" includes races having less than 10 representatives of this sex and age and pupils whose race is not reported.

BOYS: AGE 4 YEARS.

General nativity and race of father of pupil.	Kinder-garten.	Elemen-tary, first grade.	Total.
Native-born, White	9		9
Foreign-born:			
Canadian, French	12		12
Other races a	19	1	20
Total foreign-born	31	1	32
Grand total	40	1	41

a "Other races" includes races having less than 10 representatives of this sex and age and pupils whose race is not reported.

TABLE 4.—*Race and grade, by age—Number of pupils of each specified age in each grade, by general nativity and race of father of pupil—Continued.*

BOYS: AGE 5 YEARS.

General nativity and race of father of pupil.	Kinder-garten.	Elementary grades.		Un-graded.	Grand total.
		1.	2.		
Native-born:					
White	2	177	....	3	182
Negro	....	1	....	....	1
Total native-born	2	178	....	3	183
Foreign-born:					
Canadian, French	....	82	1	....	83
English	1	96	....	....	97
Hebrew, Russian	1	35	....	....	36
Irish	....	40	....	....	40
Portuguese	....	41	1	....	42
Scotch	....	13	....	....	13
Other races a	....	47	....	....	47
Total foreign-born	2	354	2	....	358
Grand total	4	532	2	3	541

a "Other races" includes races having less than 10 representatives of this sex and age and pupils whose race is not reported.

BOYS: AGE 6 YEARS.

General nativity and race of father of pupil.	Kinder-garten.	Elementary grades.			Mixed grade.	Grand total.
		1.	2.	3.		
Native-born:						
White	1	109	69	1	2	182
Negro	....	1	....	....	....	1
Total native-born	1	110	69	1	2	183
Foreign-born:						
Canadian, French	....	88	16	....	1	105
Canadian, Other	....	3	6	1	1	11
English	1	83	38	....	....	122
Hebrew, Russian	....	28	14	1	....	43
Irish	....	27	16	....	....	43
Italian, South	....	10	....	....	....	10
Portuguese	....	79	5	....	....	84
Other races a	....	31	13	....	....	44
Total foreign-born	1	349	108	2	2	462
Grand total	2	459	177	3	4	645

a "Other races" includes races having less than 10 representatives of this sex and age and pupils whose race is not reported.

TABLE 4.—*Race and grade, by age—Number of pupils of each specified age in each grade, by general nativity and race of father of pupil*—Continued.

BOYS: AGE 7 YEARS.

General nativity and race of father of pupil.	Elementary grades.				Mixed grade.	Total.
	1.	2.	3.	4.		
Native-born:						
White	41	91	68	2	2	204
Negro	1	1				2
Total native-born	42	92	68	2	2	206
Foreign-born:						
Canadian, French	55	45	3			103
English	20	70	30			120
Hebrew, Russian	14	18	8			40
Irish	8	22	16	1		47
Portuguese	71	16	5			92
Scotch	2	6	3			11
Other races a	14	34	6	2		56
Total foreign-born	184	211	71	3		469
Grand total	226	303	139	5	2	675

a "Other races" includes races having less than 10 representatives of this sex and age and pupils whose race is not reported.

BOYS: AGE 8 YEARS.

General nativity and race of father of pupil.	Elementary grades.						Mixed grade.	Total.
	1.	2.	3.	4.	5.	6.		
Native-born:								
White	24	56	97	59	5	1	1	243
Negro		2						2
Total native-born	24	58	97	59	5	1	1	245
Foreign-born:								
Canadian, French	29	37	27	6			1	100
English	8	32	53	30				123
Hebrew, Russian	7	13	18	5				43
Irish	3	13	21	10	1			48
Italian, South	4	5	2					11
Portuguese	61	33	14	2				110
Scotch		4	6	5	1			16
Other races a	6	17	18	4				45
Total foreign-born	118	154	159	62	2		1	496
Grand total	142	212	256	121	7	1	2	741

a "Other races" includes races having less than 10 representatives of this sex and age and pupils whose race is not reported.

TABLE 4.—*Race and grade, by age—Number of pupils of each specified age in each grade, by general nativity and race of father of pupil—Continued.*

BOYS: AGE 9 YEARS.

General nativity and race of father of pupil.	Elementary grades.						Mixed grade.	Total.
	1.	2.	3.	4.	5.	6.		
Native-born:								
White.........................	4	19	46	82	56	6	2	215
Indian........................			1					1
Negro.........................		1						1
Total native-born..............	4	20	47	82	56	6	2	217
Foreign-born:								
Canadian, French...............	17	25	17	11	2			72
English.......................	2	21	42	56	28	4		153
Hebrew, Russian...............		6	9	12	9	1		37
Irish.........................	1	12	14	18	8			53
Italian, North.................		3	6	3				12
Portuguese....................	35	47	29	7	1			119
Scotch.......................		1	5	5	5			16
Other races a.................	7	7	23	7	3			47
Total foreign-born.............	62	122	145	119	56	5		509
Grand total...................	66	142	192	201	112	11	2	726

a "Other races" includes races having less than 10 representatives of this sex and age and pupils whose race is not reported.

BOYS: AGE 10 YEARS.

General nativity and race of father of pupil.	Elementary grades.								Mixed grade.	Total.
	1.	2.	3.	4.	5.	6.	7.	8.		
Native-born:										
White.........................	3	10	30	48	70	48	5	1	2	217
Negro.........................			1							1
Total native-born..............	3	10	31	48	70	48	5	1	2	218
Foreign-born:										
Canadian, French...............	6	13	11	8	6	4				48
English.......................	1	7	22	57	46	28	3			164
Hebrew, Russian...............	1	4	9	12	15	3				44
Irish.........................	1	5	7	22	16	6	2			59
Portuguese....................	26	27	32	12	3				1	101
Scotch.......................			2	9	2	8				21
Other races a.................	1	5	19	13	5	4	1			48
Total foreign-born.............	36	61	102	133	93	53	6		1	485
Grand total...................	39	71	133	181	163	101	11	1	3	703

a "Other races" includes races having less than 10 representatives of this sex and age and pupils whose race is not reported.

TABLE 4.—*Race and grade, by age—Number of pupils of each specified age in each grade, by general nativity and race of father of pupil—Continued.*

BOYS: AGE 11 YEARS.

General nativity and race of father of pupil.	Elementary grades.								Special and un-graded schools.	Total.
	1.	2.	3.	4.	5.	6.	7.	8.		
Native-born:										
White		4	10	36	58	71	41	6	2	228
Negro			2							2
Total native-born		4	12	36	58	71	41	6	2	230
Foreign-born:										
Canadian, French	3	10	12	10	1	5	2			43
English		3	8	45	49	30	8	2		145
Hebrew, Russian	3	2	3	9	6	7	2			32
Irish				14	22	16	9	1		62
Polish	1		3	3	3	1				11
Portuguese	15	21	23	24	11	3	1		1	99
Scotch				4	5	4	5	1		19
Other races a		3	4	11	12	5	4			39
Total foreign-born	22	39	53	120	109	71	31	4	1	450
Grand total	22	43	65	156	167	142	72	10	3	680

a "Other races" includes races having less than 10 representatives of this sex and age and pupils whose race is not reported.

BOYS: AGE 12 YEARS.

General nativity and race of father of pupil.	Elementary grades.									Special and un-graded schools.	Total.
	1.	2.	3.	4.	5.	6.	7.	8.	9.		
Native-born:											
White	1	6	17	21	30	54	53	46	8	2	238
Negro						3	1				4
Total native-born	1	6	17	21	30	57	54	46	8	2	242
Foreign-born:											
Canadian, French	7	9	22	52	9	9	2	2			112
Canadian, Other			1		7	3	1				12
English			1	21	25	54	40	16	1		158
Hebrew, Russian			3	5	5	8	8	5	1		35
Irish			4	7	10	14	16	5			56
Scotch				3	2	4	4	3		1	17
Portuguese	14	14	40	21	11	7	4				111
Other races a	3	1	8	12	8	5	2	1	1		40
Total foreign-born	24	24	79	121	77	104	77	32	2	1	541
Grand total	25	30	96	142	107	161	131	78	10	3	783

a "Other races" includes races having less than 10 representatives of this sex and age and pupils whose race is not reported.

TABLE 4.—*Race and grade, by age—Number of pupils of each specified age in each grade, by general nativity and race of father of pupil*—Continued.

BOYS: AGE 13 YEARS.

General nativity and race of father of pupil.	Elementary grades.									Mixed and illiterate grades.	High school, first year.	Grand total.
	1.	2.	3.	4.	5.	6.	7.	8.	9.			
Native-born, White		1	5	14	25	29	35	61	35	2	5	212
Foreign-born:												
Canadian, French	3	9	30	63	19	24	10	8		7		173
Canadian, Other		1	3	1	23		1	4	2	6		41
English	1		3	6	27	34	40	41	14		2	168
French				5	4		2					11
Hebrew, Russian	1	1	1	5	3	4	7	2	5			29
Irish		1	2	9	7	7	13	14	13		2	68
Portuguese	12	21	24	22	22	11	4	1		2		119
Scotch			1		1	3	2	3	2			12
Other races a	1		5	1	8	10	3	3	1			32
Total foreign-born	18	33	69	112	114	93	82	76	37	15	4	653
Grand total	18	34	74	126	139	122	117	137	72	17	9	865

a "Other races" includes races having less than 10 representatives of this sex and age and pupils whose race is not reported.

BOYS: AGE 14 YEARS.

General nativity and race of father of pupil.	Elementary grades.									High school.				Special and ungraded schools.	Grand total.
	1.	2.	3.	4.	5.	6.	7.	8.	9.	First year.	Second year.	Third year.	Fourth year.		
Native-born:															
White		1	1	4	2	6	12	20	32	43	6	1			128
Negro						3									3
Indian														1	1
Total native-born		1	1	4	2	9	12	20	32	43	6	1		1	132
Foreign-born:															
Canadian, French		2	9	18	5	11	1	2	2	2				4	56
Canadian, Other			1	1	1		3	2						3	11
English				1	1	1	10	11	12	2	1				39
Hebrew, Russian			2	1		2	3	5	4	2	1				20
Hebrew, Other			1						2	7	1				11
Irish				1	1	2	3	7	3						17
Portuguese	3	4	12	12	3		2		1	1				10	48
Other races a				9	2		4	1	2	1					19
Total foreign-born	3	6	25	43	13	16	26	28	26	15	3			17	221
Grand total	3	7	26	47	15	25	38	48	58	58	9	1		18	353

a "Other races" includes races having less than 10 representatives of this sex and age and pupils whose race is not reported.

TABLE 4.—*Race and grade, by age—Number of pupils of each specified age in each grade, by general nativity and race of father of pupil*—Continued.

BOYS: AGE 15 YEARS.

General nativity and race of father of pupil.	Elementary grades.									Illiterate grade.	High school.				Grand total.
	1.	2.	3.	4.	5.	6.	7.	8.	9.		First year.	Second year.	Third year.	Fourth year.	
Native-born:															
White				1		1	3	8	21		32	20	5	1	92
Negro												1			1
Total native-born				1		1	3	8	21		32	21	5	1	93
Foreign-born:															
Canadian, French		3	4	4	2	2	1	2	1	1	1				21
English									5		4	2	3		14
Hebrew, Russian					1				1	1	5	3			11
Irish			1				1	2	6		6	2	2		20
Portuguese	2	1	5	1		1				6					16
Other races *a*		1	1		1	1	1	2	1	1	3	1			13
Total foreign-born	2	5	11	5	4	4	3	6	14	9	19	8	5		95
Grand total	2	5	11	6	4	5	6	14	35	9	51	29	10	1	188

a "Other races" includes races having less than 10 representatives of this sex and age and pupils whose race is not reported.

BOYS: AGE 16 YEARS.

General nativity and race of father of pupil.	Elementary grades.								High school.				Special and ungraded schools.	Grand total.
	2.	3.	4.	5.	6.	7.	8.	9.	First year.	Second year.	Third year.	Fourth year.		
Native-born, White				1				5	16	27	13	3	1	66
Total native-born				1				5	16	27	13	3	1	66
Foreign-born:														
English							1	2	2		5	1		11
Other races *a*	1							1	7	9	5			23
Total foreign-born	1						1	3	9	9	10	1		34
Grand total	1			1			1	8	25	36	23	4	1	100

a "Other races" includes races having less than 10 representatives of this sex and age and pupils whose race is not reported.

BOYS: AGE 17 YEARS.

General nativity and race of father of pupil.	Elementary grade 7.	High school.				Grand total.
		First year.	Second year.	Third year.	Fourth year.	
Native-born, White	1	2	13	14	11	41
Foreign-born:						
Irish		2	1	7	5	15
Other races *a*		2	3	8	2	15
Total foreign-born		4	4	15	7	30
Grand total	1	6	17	29	18	71

a "Other races" includes races having less than 10 representatives of this sex and age and pupils whose race is not reported.

TABLE 4.—*Race and grade, by age—Number of pupils of each specified age in each grade, by general nativity and race of father of pupil*—Continued.

BOYS: AGE 18 YEARS.

General nativity and race of father of pupil.	Elementary grade 4.	High school.				Grand total.
		First year.	Second year.	Third year.	Fourth year.	
Native-born, White....................	1	1	3	12	10	27
Foreign-born, other races *a*..............	....	....	1	5	7	13
Total.................	1	1	4	17	17	40

a "Other races" includes races having less than 10 representatives of this sex and age and pupils whose race is not reported.

BOYS: AGE 19 YEARS.

General nativity and race of father of pupil.	High school.				Total.
	First year.	Second year.	Third year.	Fourth year.	
Native-born, White.....................	....	....	1	5	6
Foreign-born, other races *a*	....	1	1	1	3
Total.....................	....	1	2	6	9

BOYS: AGE 20 YEARS.

	First year.	Second year.	Third year.	Fourth year.	
Native-born, White.....................	....	....	1	1	2
Foreign-born, other races *a*	1	....	....	....	1
Total.........................	1	....	1	1	3

a "Other races" includes races having less than 10 representatives of this sex and age and pupils whose race is not reported.

GIRLS: AGE 3 YEARS.

General nativity and race of father of pupil.	Kindergarten.
Native-born, White......	4
Foreign-born, other races *a*	7
Total......	11

a "Other races" includes races having less than 10 representatives of this sex and age and pupils whose race is not reported.

TABLE 4.—*Race and grade, by age—Number of pupils of each specified age in each grade, by general nativity and race of father of pupil—Continued.*

GIRLS: AGE 4 YEARS.

General nativity and race of father of pupil.	Kindergarten.	Elementary grade 1.	Mixed grade.	Grand total.
Native-born:				
White......	10	1	2	13
Negro......	1			1
Total native-born......	11	1	2	14
Foreign-born:				
Hebrew, Russian......	11			11
Other races a......	25			25
Total foreign-born......	36			36
Grand total......	47	1	2	50

a "Other races" includes races having less than 10 representatives of this sex and age and pupils whose race is not reported.

GIRLS: AGE 5 YEARS.

General nativity and race of father of pupil.	Kindergarten.	Elementary grades.		Grand total.
		1.	2.	
Native-born:				
White......	1	174		175
Negro......		1		1
Total native-born......	1	175		176
Foreign-born:				
Canadian, French......	2	69		71
English......	3	79	1	83
Hebrew, Russian......	1	27		28
Irish......	2	32		34
Scotch......		9	1	10
Portuguese......		38		38
Other races a......	1	41	1	43
Total foreign-born......	9	295	3	307
Grand total......	10	470		483

a "Other races" includes races having less than 10 representatives of this sex and age and pupils whose race is not reported.

TABLE 4.—*Race and grade, by age—Number of pupils of each specified age in each grade, by general nativity and race of father of pupil*—Continued.

GIRLS: AGE 6 YEARS.

General nativity and race of father of pupil.	Kinder-garten.	Elementary grades.			Mixed grade.	Grand total.
		1.	2.	3.		
Native-born:						
White....	....	104	99	2	4	209
Negro....	....	2	....	....	....	2
Total native-born....	....	106	99	2	4	211
Foreign-born:						
Canadian, French....	....	75	8	....	1	84
English....	....	81	44	....	....	125
Hebrew, Russian....	....	24	11	....	....	35
Irish....	....	21	19	....	....	40
Italian, North....	....	13	1	....	....	14
Scotch....	....	2	9	1	....	12
Portuguese....	....	65	4	....	....	69
Other races *a*....	1	32	12	....	....	45
Total foreign-born....	1	313	108	1	1	424
Grand total....	1	419	207	3	5	635

a "Other races" includes races having less than 10 representatives of this sex and age and pupils whose race is not reported.

GIRLS: AGE 7 YEARS.

General nativity and race of father of pupil.	Elementary grades.				Mixed grade.	Grand total.
	1.	2.	3.	4.		
Native-born:						
White....	36	90	79	3	2	210
Negro....	2	1	....	....	....	3
Total native-born....	38	91	79	3	2	213
Foreign-born:						
Canadian, French....	54	41	10	....	....	105
English....	27	58	46	....	....	131
Hebrew, Russian....	13	20	14	....	....	47
Irish....	15	22	13	1	....	51
Polish....	7	2	1	....	....	10
Scotch....	3	8	4	....	....	15
Portuguese....	77	22	4	....	....	103
Other races *a*....	15	28	6	....	....	49
Total foreign-born....	211	201	98	....	....	511
Grand total....	249	292	177	4	2	724

a "Other races" includes races having less than 10 representatives of this sex and age and pupils whose race is not reported.

TABLE 4.—*Race and grade, by age—Number of pupils of each specified age in each grade, by general nativity and race of father of pupil*—Continued.

GIRLS: AGE 8 YEARS.

General nativity and race of father of pupil.	Elementary grades.						Mixed grade.	Grand total.
	1.	2.	3.	4.	5.	6.		
Native-born, White	18	51	95	78	4	1	4	251
Foreign-born:								
Canadian, French	26	38	24	3	1	....	1	93
English	8	36	60	32	....	....	....	136
Hebrew, Russian	2	10	17	5	....	....	....	34
Hebrew, Other	2	4	3	1	....	....	....	10
Irish	3	9	18	13	....	....	....	43
Scotch	2	3	5	2	....	....	....	12
Portuguese	48	35	16	3	....	....	....	102
Other races a	8	18	13	12	1	....	....	52
Total foreign-born	99	153	156	71	2	....		482
Grand total	117	204	251	149	6	1	5	733

GIRLS: AGE 9 YEARS.

General nativity and race of father of pupil.	Elementary grades.						Mixed grade.	Grand total.
	1.	2.	3.	4.	5.	6.		
Native-born:								
White	4	11	61	56	71	4	6	213
Negro	....	....	5	2	....	....	....	7
Total native-born	4	11	66	58	71	4	6	220
Foreign-born:								
Canadian, French	8	7	14	5	2	1	....	37
Canadian, Other	....	1	4	2	3	....	....	10
English	2	7	38	38	26	....	....	111
Hebrew, Russian	1	3	11	12	9	2	....	38
Irish	....	6	7	14	9	1	....	37
Scotch	....	1	3	4	4	....	....	12
Portuguese	31	33	26	6	1	....	....	97
Other races a	4	7	5	18	2	....	....	36
Total foreign-born	46	65	108	99	56	4	....	378
Grand total	50	76	174	157	127	8	6	598

a "Other races" includes races having less than 10 representatives of this sex and age and pupils whose race is not reported.

TABLE 4.—*Race and grade, by age—Number of pupils of each specified age in each grade, by general nativity and race of father of pupil—Continued.*

GIRLS: AGE 10 YEARS.

General nativity and race of father of pupil.	Elementary grades.								Mixed grade.	Grand total.
	1.	2.	3.	4.	5.	6.	7.	8.		
Native-born:										
White	1	5	17	49	65	54	10	1	3	205
Negro			1				1			2
Total native-born	1	5	18	49	65	54	11	1	3	207
Foreign-born:										
Canadian, French	3	8	12	5	5	2				35
English		5	13	36	59	25	1			139
Hebrew, Russian	3	2	4	13	10	2	1			35
Irish		1	7	13	20	13	2			56
Scotch		1	1	2	8	3				15
Portuguese	28	25	37	16	6	1				113
Other races *a*	6	5	8	12	15		2			48
Total foreign-born	40	47	82	97	123	46	6			441
Grand total	41	52	100	146	188	100	17	1	3	648

GIRLS: AGE 11 YEARS.

General nativity and race of father of pupil.	Elementary grades.								Mixed grade.	Grand total.
	1.	2.	3.	4.	5.	6.	7.	8.		
Native-born:										
White	3	3	9	23	37	50	40	6	2	173
Negro				3		1				4
Total native-born	3	3	9	26	37	51	40	6	2	177
Foreign-born:										
Canadian, French		5	11	14	4	1	3			38
English	1	2	14	33	40	46	25	2	1	164
Hebrew, Russian	2	3	2	10	9	10	2	3		41
Irish	1		2	11	12	12	7			45
Portuguese	18	17	22	20	16	1	1			95
Scotch			1	5	1	5	2			14
Other races *a*	2	4	9	9	13	6	1			44
Total foreign-born	24	31	61	102	95	81	41	5	1	441
Grand total	27	34	70	128	132	132	81	11	3	618

a "Other races" includes races having less than 10 representatives of this sex and age and pupils whose race is not reported.

TABLE 4.—*Race and grade, by age—Number of pupils of each specified age in each grade, by general nativity and race of father of pupil—Continued.*

GIRLS: AGE 12 YEARS.

General nativity and race of father of pupil.	Elementary grades.									Mixed grade.	Grand total.
	1.	2.	3.	4.	5.	6.	7.	8.	9.		
Native-born:											
White	1	1	10	11	24	40	77	40	4	....	208
Negro	......	......	1	......	1	2	......	1	......	....	5
Total native-born	1	1	11	11	25	42	77	41	4	....	213
Foreign-born:											
Canadian, French	2	6	22	32	30	15	5	......	......	......	112
Canadian, Other	......	......	2	1	7	......	......	2	......	1	13
English	......	2	4	21	32	39	42	28	......	......	168
French	......	......	......	8	4	......	2	1	......	......	15
Hebrew, Russian	1	1	4	5	8	14	11	3	1	......	48
Irish	......	1	5	12	13	17	12	5	1	......	66
Portuguese	20	19	25	26	9	2	2	......	......	......	103
Scotch	......	......	......	......	3	4	3	2	......	......	13
Other races a	1	1	2	4	4	12	3	3	2	......	32
Total foreign-born	24	30	64	109	110	103	80	44	5	1	570
Grand total	25	31	75	120	135	145	157	85	9	1	783

a "Other races" includes races having less than 10 representatives of this sex and age and pupils whose race is not reported.

GIRLS: AGE 13 YEARS.

General nativity and race of father of pupil.	Elementary grades.									Illiterate grade.	High school.	Grand total.
	1.	2.	3.	4.	5.	6.	7.	8.	9.			
Native born:												
White	2	....	6	8	14	29	43	35	48	....	7	192
Negro	......	....	......	......	......	......	......	1	......	....	......	1
Total native-born	2	....	6	8	14	29	43	36	48	....	7	193
Foreign-born:												
Canadian, French	4	5	32	47	20	15	3	4	......	10	......	140
Canadian, Other	......	......	......	2	11	2	2	......	......	3	1	21
English	......	2	2	9	21	27	36	24	13	......	......	134
Hebrew, Russian	2	......	1	1	4	3	3	3	3	1	......	21
Irish	......	......	......	2	8	10	15	5	4	......	3	47
Scotch	......	......	......	......	1	3	6	2	3	......	......	15
Portuguese	12	15	21	18	19	5	3	2	......	2	......	97
Other races a	......	3	4	9	13	4	5	7	6	......	......	51
Total foreign-born	18	25	60	88	97	69	73	47	29	16	4	526
Grand total	20	25	66	96	111	98	116	83	77	16	11	719

a "Other races" includes races having less than 10 representatives of this sex and age and pupils whose race is not reported.

TABLE 4.—*Race and grade, by age—Number of pupils of each specified age in each grade, by general nativity and race of father of pupil*—Continued.

GIRLS: AGE 14 YEARS.

General nativity and race of father of pupil.	Elementary grades.									Illiterate and mixed grades.	High schools.			Grand total.
	1.	2.	3.	4.	5.	6.	7.	8.	9.		First year.	Second year.	Third year.	
Native-born:														
White	1	....	1	3	....	2	10	18	34	2	32	8	1	112
Negro						1								1
Total native-born	1	....	1	3	....	3	10	18	34	2	32	8	1	113
Foreign-born:														
Canadian, French		4	9	6	1	4	3	1	3	2	3			36
English					2	1	6	8	16		11	1	1	46
Hebrew, Russian			1			2	4	4	7		2			20
Irish		1			1		3	13			6	1		25
Scotch					1		1	2	3		2	1		10
Portuguese	4	7	12	4	2	1		1		6				37
Other races a		1	1	9	3		2	2	7	3	3			31
Total foreign-born	4	13	23	19	10	8	19	31	36	11	27	3	1	205
Grand total	5	13	24	22	10	11	29	49	70	13	59	11	2	318

GIRLS: AGE 15 YEARS.

General nativity and race of father of pupil.	Elementary grades.									Illiterate and mixed grades.	High schools.			Grand total.
	1.	2.	3.	4.	5.	6.	7.	8.	9.		First year.	Second year.	Third year.	
Native-born:														
White			1		2		3	6	24		35	20	4	95
Negro									1					1
Total native-born			1		2		3	6	25		35	20	4	96
Foreign-born:														
English								2	7		4	8	3	24
Hebrew, Russian	1		1	1				1	4		6		1	15
Irish							1		3		4	2		10
Other races a	2	4	2	2		2	1	2	3	7	2	4		31
Total foreign-born	3	4	3	3		2	2	5	17	7	16	14	4	80
Grand total	3	4	4	3	2	2	5	11	42	7	51	34	8	176

a "Other races" includes races having less than 10 representatives of this sex and age and pupils whose race is not reported.

GIRLS: AGE 16 YEARS.

General nativity and race of father of pupil.	Elementary grades.			Mixed grade.	High school.				Grand total.
	3.	8.	9.		First year.	Second year.	Third year.	Fourth year.	
Native-born:									
White			6		11	27	23	8	75
Indian				1					1
Total native-born			6	1	11	27	23	8	76
Foreign-born:									
English					2	7	5	2	16
Irish			1		2	3	6	1	13
Other races a	1	1	5		3	8	2		20
Total foreign-born	1	1	6		7	18	13	3	49
Grand total	1	1	12	1	18	45	36	11	125

a "Other races" includes races having less than 10 representatives of this sex and age and pupils whose race is not reported.

TABLE 4.—*Race and grade, by age—Number of pupils of each specified age in each grade, by general nativity and race of father of pupil—Continued.*

GIRLS: AGE 17 YEARS.

General nativity and race of father of pupil.	Elementary grades.		High school.				Grand total.
	8	9.	First year.	Second year.	Third year.	Fourth year.	
Native-born:							
White	1	1	4	12	17	19	54
Negro			1				1
Total native-born	1	1	5	12	17	19	55
Foreign-born, other races a	1		1	4	8	6	20
Grand total	2	1	6	16	25	25	75

a "Other races" includes races having less than 10 representatives of this sex and age and pupils whose race is not reported.

GIRLS: AGE 18 YEARS.

General nativity and race of father of pupil.	Illiterate grade.	High school.			Grand total.
		Second year.	Third year.	Fourth year.	
Native-born:					
White		5	4	20	29
Indian				1	1
Total native-born		5	4	21	30
Foreign-born, other races a	1		3	9	13
Grand total	1	5	7	30	43

a "Other races" includes races having less than 10 representatives of this sex and age and pupils whose race is not reported.

GIRLS: AGE 19 YEARS.

General nativity and race of father of pupil.	High school.			Grand total.
	Second year.	Third year.	Fourth year.	
Native-born, White	2		4	6
Foreign-born, other races a	1	2	1	4
Total	3	2	5	10

a "Other races" includes races having less than 10 representatives of this sex and age and pupils whose race is not reported.

GIRLS: AGE 20 YEARS.

General nativity and race of father of pupil.	High school.		Grand total.
	Third year.	Fourth year.	
Native-born, White	1	1	2
Foreign-born, other races a		1	1
Total	1	2	3

a "Other races" includes races having less than 10 representatives of this sex and age and pupils whose race is not reported.

TABLE 5.—*Race distribution in each grade—Percentages.*

[This table shows in detail only races with 100 or more pupils reporting. The totals, however, are for all races.]

General nativity and race of father of pupil.	Kinder-garten.	Elementary grades.										High school.					Special and un-graded schools.	Grand total.
		1.	2.	3.	4.	5.	6.	7.	8.	9.	Total.	First year.	Second year.	Third year.	Fourth year.	Total.		
Native-born:																		
White	22.8	23.7	26.2	28.7	27.6	32.4	37.2	42.6	46.8	55.3	30.5	63.5	68.4	59.1	69.2	64.8	33.3	32.4
Negro	.8	.3	.3	.5	.3	.1	.9	.3	.4	.3	.3	.3	.5		.8	.4	1.5	.4
Indian																		(a)
Total native-born	23.6	24.0	26.5	29.2	27.8	32.5	38.2	42.9	47.2	55.6	30.9	63.9	68.9	59.1	70.0	65.1	34.8	32.8
Foreign-born:																		
Canadian, French	17.1	17.9	14.9	13.9	15.7	7.0	8.8	4.0	3.6	2.0	12.7	2.0	1.4	1.2	.8	1.5	22.7	12.2
Canadian, Other	4.9	.7	1.1	1.7	1.3	5.3	.7	.9	1.9	1.0	1.6	1.0	.5	1.8		.9	11.4	1.6
English	19.5	13.7	16.7	17.3	21.3	25.0	27.1	27.0	25.6	17.8	19.5	9.5	9.6	17.1	9.2	11.0	.8	18.9
Hebrew, Russian	24.4	5.6	5.5	5.7	5.3	6.5	5.4	5.2	4.9	6.9	5.5	7.1	3.3	4.3	4.2	5.1		5.6
Irish	5.7	5.2	6.6	6.1	8.2	9.1	9.2	10.8	9.8	7.9	7.3	11.5	6.7	12.2	12.5	10.5	1.5	7.4
Italian, North		1.3	1.2	1.3	.9	.6	.5	.1	.6	3.0	1.0		1.0			.3		1.0
Italian, South		1.7	2.0	1.1	.9	.6	.6	.4	.4		1.1	.3	.5			.3		1.0
Polish	1.6	23.8	18.8	17.9	10.7	7.3	3.0	2.0	2.4	3.3	13.8		.5				.8	13.0
Portuguese	.8	1.1	1.9	1.6	2.2	2.4	3.0	3.3	3.0	2.3	2.0	.7			.8		24.2	2.0
Scotch											1.0	1.7	3.3	1.8		2.0	3.0	.9
Other races	2.4	3.3	4.2	2.8	4.9	4.2	3.0	3.5			3.6	2.4	4.3	2.4	2.5	2.9		3.6
Total foreign-born	76.4	76.0	73.5	70.8	72.2	67.5	61.8	57.1	52.8	44.4	69.1	36.1	31.1	40.9	30.0	34.9	65.2	67.2
Grand total	100.0	100.0	100.0	100.0	100.0	100.0	100.0	100.0	100.0	100.0	100.0	100.0	100.0	100.0	100.0	100.0	100.0	100.0

a Less than 0.05 per cent.

TABLE 6.—*Grade distribution of each race—Percentages.*

[This table shows in detail only races with 100 or more pupils reporting. The totals, however, are for all races.]

General nativity and race of father of pupil.	Kindergarten.	Elementary grades.										High school.					Special and ungraded schools.	Grand total.
		1.	2.	3.	4.	5.	6.	7.	8.	9.	Total.	First year.	Second year.	Third year.	Fourth year.	Total.		
Native-born:																		
White	0.6	15.6	11.4	12.3	11.0	10.2	8.8	7.4	5.5	4.8	87.1	4.2	3.2	2.1	1.8	11.3	1.0	100.0
Negro	(a)	(a)	(a)	(a)	(a)	(a)	(a)	(a)	(a)	(a)	(a)	(a)	(a)	(a)	(a)	(a)	(a)	100.0
Indian	(a)	(a)	(a)	(a)	(a)	(a)	(a)	(a)	(a)	(a)	(a)	(a)	(a)	(a)	(a)	(a)	(a)	100.0
Total native-born	.6	15.6	11.4	12.4	11.0	10.1	8.9	7.3	5.5	4.8	87.1	4.1	3.2	2.1	1.8	11.3	1.0	100.0
Foreign-born:																		
Canadian, French	1.2	31.3	17.4	15.9	16.8	5.8	5.5	1.8	1.1	.5	96.3	.4	.2	.1	.1	.7	1.8	100.0
Canadian, Other	2.6	8.7	9.2	14.4	10.5	32.8	3.1	3.1	4.4	1.7	87.8	1.3	.4	1.3		3.1	6.6	100.0
English	.9	15.5	12.5	14.6	14.6	13.5	11.0	8.0	4.5	2.7	95.7	1.1	.8	1.1		1.1	.1	100.0
Hebrew, Russian	3.8	21.2	13.8	14.2	12.3	10.0	7.4	5.2	3.3	3.4	90.8	2.7	.9	.9	.6	5.1	.3	100.0
Irish	.7	14.8	12.5	11.4	14.3	12.5	9.5	8.1	5.0	3.0	91.3	3.3	1.4	1.9	1.5	8.0	.3	100.0
Italian, North		29.4	16.9	18.4	10.3	9.6	2.9	2.1	2.2	8.8	98.5	.7	1.5			1.5		100.0
Italian, South		33.6	26.7	22.7	11.0	6.2	3.4		1.4	1.4	98.6		.7			1.4		100.0
Polish	.1	42.0	11.8	19.2	13.4	3.4	5.0	.8		.1	99.2						.8	100.0
Portuguese		39.0	20.4	11.4	10.7	5.7	1.8	.9		4.6	98.0						1.8	100.0
Scotch	.4	12.1	13.5	10.9	14.2	12.1	12.1	8.9	4.6	1.8	93.6	1.8	2.5	1.1	.4	5.7	.4	100.0
Other races	.6	19.5	16.7		17.9	12.1	6.4	5.4	3.2		94.0	1.4	1.8	.8	.6	4.6	.8	100.0
Total foreign-born	1.0	24.1	15.5	14.7	14.0	10.3	7.0	4.8	3.0	1.9	95.1	1.1	.7	.7	.4	2.9	.9	100.0
Grand total	.9	21.3	14.1	13.9	13.0	10.2	7.7	5.6	3.8	2.8	92.5	2.1	1.5	1.2	.9	5.7	.9	100.0

a Not computed, owing to small number involved.

PUBLIC SCHOOL TEACHERS IN ELEMENTARY GRADES AND KINDERGARTEN.

TABLE 1.—*Number of teachers in each grade, by sex and general nativity and race.*

MALE.

[This table does not include 5 teachers not reporting complete data.]

General nativity and race.	Kindergarten.	Elementary grades.											Total kindergarten and elementary.
		1.	2.	3.	4.	5.	6.	7.	8.	9.	Ungraded and special.	Total.	
Native-born of native father, White										1	1	2	2
Native-born of foreign father, by race of father, Scotch										2		2	2
Total native-born										3	1	4	4
Foreign-born, English									1	1		2	2
Grand total									1	4	1	6	6

FEMALE.

General nativity and race.	Kindergarten.	1.	2.	3.	4.	5.	6.	7.	8.	9.	Ungraded and special.	Total.	Total kindergarten and elementary.
Native-born of native father, White	2	44	40	32	32	20	16	15	8	8	3	218	220
Native-born of foreign father, by race of father:													
Canadian, French							1					1	1
English	1	10	3	4	5	5	2		3	1		33	34
German		2	1		1							4	4
Irish		25	26	14	12	9	8	4	2	1	3	104	104
Portuguese			1	1	1	1						4	4
Scotch		4	3	3	2	3	1	1	1		1	19	19
Scotch-Irish			2	1			2					5	5
Total	1	41	36	23	21	18	14	5	6	2	4	170	171
Total native-born	3	85	76	55	53	38	30	20	14	10	7	388	391
Foreign-born:													
Canadian (other than French)		1			1							2	2
English				2	1	1	1		1			6	6
Hebrew, German									1	1		2	2
Irish				1		3	1					5	5
Scotch		1										1	1
Total foreign-born		2		3	2	4	2		2	1		16	16
Grand total	3	87	76	58	55	42	32	20	16	11	7	404	407

TABLE 1.—*Number of teachers in each grade, by sex and general nativity and race*—Con.

TOTAL.

General nativity and race.	Kindergarten.	Elementary grades.									Ungraded and special.	Total.	Total kindergarten and elementary.	Race distribution (percentages).	
		1.	2.	3.	4.	5.	6.	7.	8.	9.				Elementary.	Elementary and kindergarten.
Native-born of native father, White...................	2	44	40	32	32	20	16	15	8	9	4	220	222	53.7	53.8
Native-born of foreign father, by race of father:															
Canadian, French........							1					1	1	.2	.2
English..................	1	10	3	4	5	5	2	....	3	1	......	33	34	8.2	8.2
German..................		2	1	....	1	....	....	....	....	....	......	4	4	1.0	1.0
Irish...................		25	26	14	12	9	8	4	2	1	3	104	104	25.1	25.2
Portuguese..............			1	1	1	1	....	....	....	....	......	4	4	1.0	1.0
Scotch..................		4	3	3	2	3	1	1	1	2	1	21	21	5.0	5.1
Scotch-Irish............			2	1	....	....	2	....	....	....	......	5	5	1.2	1.2
Total..................	1	41	36	23	21	18	14	5	6	4	4	172	173	41.8	41.9
Total native-born.....	3	85	76	55	53	38	30	20	14	13	8	392	395	95.5	95.6
Foreign-born:															
Canadian (other than French)................		1		1								2	2	.5	.5
English.................				2	1	1	1	....	2	1	......	8	8	2.0	1.9
Hebrew, German.........								1	1	....	......	2	2	.5	.5
Irish...................			1		3	1						5	5	1.2	1.2
Scotch.................	1											1	1	.2	.2
Total foreign-born.....		2	....	3	2	4	2	....	3	2	......	18	18	4.5	4.4
Grand total..........	3	87	76	58	55	42	32	20	17	15	8	410	413	100.0	100.0

TABLE 2.—*Number of teachers engaged in teaching each specified number of years, by sex, general nativity, and race.*

MALE.

[This table does not include 11 teachers not reporting complete data.]

General nativity and race.	Under 5 years.	5 to 9 years.	10 to 14 years.	15 to 19 years.	20 to 24 years.	25 to 29 years.	30 years or over.	Total.
Native-born of native father, White..	1	....	....	1	....	....	....	2
Native-born of foreign father, by race of father, Scotch....................		1	....	1	....	....	....	2
Total native-born..............	1	1	....	2	....	....	....	4
Foreign-born, English.............	....	1	....	1	....	....	....	2
Grand total..................	1	2	....	3	....	....	....	6

TABLE 2.—*Number of teachers engaged in teaching each specified number of years, by sex, general nativity, and race*—Continued.

FEMALE.

General nativity and race.	Under 5 years.	5 to 9 years.	10 to 14 years.	15 to 19 years.	20 to 24 years.	25 to 29 years.	30 years or over.	Total.
Native-born of native father, White..	16	59	34	36	23	26	21	215
Native-born of foreign father, by race of father:								
Canadian, French		1						1
English	7	12	6	5	2	2		34
German				3	1			4
Irish	5	47	22	14	10	2	3	103
Portuguese		2	2					4
Scotch	1	9	3	1		3	2	19
Scotch-Irish		1		2	1		1	5
Total	13	72	33	25	14	7	6	170
Total native-born	29	131	67	61	37	33	27	385
Foreign-born:								
Canadian (other than French)		1	1					2
English			4				2	6
Hebrew, German	2							2
Irish	1	3	1					5
Scotch	1							1
Total foreign-born	4	4	6				2	16
Grand total	33	135	73	61	37	33	29	401

TOTAL.

General nativity and race.	Under 5 years.	5 to 9 years.	10 to 14 years.	15 to 19 years.	20 to 24 years.	25 to 29 years.	30 years or over.	Total.
Native-born of native father, White..	17	59	34	37	23	26	21	217
Native-born of foreign father, by race of father:								
Canadian, French		1						1
English	7	12	6	5	2	2		34
German				3	1			4
Irish	5	47	22	14	10	2	3	103
Portuguese		2	2					4
Scotch	1	10	3	2		3	2	21
Scotch-Irish		1		2	1		1	5
Total	13	73	33	26	14	7	6	172
Total native-born	30	132	67	63	37	33	27	389
Foreign-born:								
Canadian (other than French)		1	1					2
English		1	4	1			2	8
Hebrew, German	2							2
Irish	1	3	1					5
Scotch	1							1
Total foreign-born	4	5	6	1			2	18
Grand total	34	137	73	64	37	33	29	407

PAROCHIAL SCHOOL PUPILS: GENERAL INVESTIGATION.

TABLE 1.—*Grade and age—Number of pupils of each age in each grade, by sex.*

BOYS.

Age.	Kinder-garten.	Elementary grades.									Total.	Grand total.
		1.	2.	3.	4.	5.	6.	7.	8.	9.		
4 years	6	13									13	19
5 years	22	138									138	160
6 years	17	179	41	3							223	240
7 years	5	187	76	20	1						284	289
8 years	2	139	91	66	26	2					324	326
9 years		87	78	113	51	13	2				344	344
10 years		52	47	105	43	29	5				398	398
11 years		37	33	75	107	79	40	17			388	388
12 years			51	57	67	72	60	39	10		356	356
13 years		1	15	26	32	30	46	26	22	3	201	201
14 years		1	8	3	2	4	9	14	15	14	70	70
15 years			1	1			2	3	5	6	18	18
16 years									1	6	7	7
17 years									1	3	4	4
18 years												
19 years												
20 years or over												
Total	52	834	441	481	391	243	188	104	54	32	2,768	2,820

GIRLS.

Age.	Kinder-garten.	Elementary grades.										High school.				Special schools.	Grand total.
		1.	2.	3.	4.	5.	6.	7.	8.	9.	Total.	First year.	Second year.	Third year.	Total.		
4 years	2	14									14						16
5 years	8	128									128						136
6 years	18	150	45	1							196						214
7 years	8	152	88	23	1						264					3	275
8 years		102	125	100	28						355					21	376
9 years		70	123	110	75	25	11				414					10	424
10 years		25	66	110	95	42	21	1			360					16	376
11 years		8	79	120	95	60	69	26	3		460					9	469
12 years		12	25	55	60	61	62	52	11		338					1	399
13 years		1	2	25	14	21	35	55	25	6	184	1			1		185
14 years				2	4	2	6	8	18	16	56						56
15 years						1	2	3	9	4	19						19
16 years										2	2			6	6		8
17 years								1			1	1		2	3		4
18 years												1		2	3		3
19 years																	
20 years or over														1	1	2	2
Total	36	662	553	546	372	212	206	145	67	28	2,791	4		11	15	60	2,902

TABLE 1.—*Grade and age—Number of pupils of each age in each grade, by sex*—Contd.

TOTAL.

Age.	Kin-der-garten.	Elementary grades.										High school				Special schools.	Grand total.
		1.	2.	3.	4.	5.	6.	7.	8.	9.	Total.	First year.	Second year.	Third year.	Total.		
4 years	8	27										27						35
5 years	30	266										266						296
6 years	35	329	86	4								419						454
7 years	13	339	164	43	2							548					3	564
8 years	2	241	215	166	54	2						678					21	701
9 years		157	201	223	126	38	13					758					10	768
10 years		77	113	227	200	85	50	6				758					16	774
11 years		45	112	195	202	139	109	43	3			848					9	857
12 years		12	77	112	127	133	122	91	21			695					1	696
13 years		2	17	51	46	51	81	81	47	9		385	1			1		386
14 years		1	8	5	6	6	15	22	33	30		126						126
15 years			1	1		1	4	6	14	10		37						37
16 years								1	8			9			6	6		15
17 years									2	3		5	1		2	3		8
18 years													1		2	3		3
19 years																		
20 years or over													1		1	2		2
Total	88	1,496	994	1,027	763	455	394	249	121	60		5,559	4		11	15	60	5,722

TABLE 2.—*Race, sex, and grade—Number of pupils of each sex in each grade, by general nativity and race of father of pupil.*

General nativity and race of father of pupil	Kindergarten	Elementary grades										High school				Special school	Grand total
		1.	2.	3.	4.	5.	6.	7.	8.	9.	Total.	First year.	Second year.	Third year.	Total.		
Native-born, White:																	
Male	4	146	85	70	64	26	40	27	14	11	483						487
Female	3	145	80	82	77	31	47	37	11	7	517					41	561
Total	7	291	165	152	141	57	87	64	25	18	1,000					41	1,048
Foreign-born:																	
Canadian, French—																	
Male	48	528	242	305	242	154	102	45	18	11	1,647						1,695
Female	33	371	354	333	189	141	96	64	21	4	1,573			2	2	19	1,627
Total	81	899	596	638	431	295	198	109	39	15	3,220			2	2	19	3,322
Canadian, Other—																	
Male		2	17	3	2	1	5	1	2		32						32
Female		1	2	1	2		1		2	1	10	1			1		11
Total		3	19	4	4	1	6	1	4	1	42	1			1		43
English—																	
Male		50	31	40	29	24	13	13	8	2	210						210
Female		29	37	31	27	13	17	13	5	4	176						176
Total		79	68	71	56	37	30	26	13	6	386						386
French—																	
Male		2	3	1	3						9						9
Female			2	5	2	1	1		1		12						12
Total		2	5	6	5	1	2		1		21						21
Hebrew (not specified)—																	
Male					4						4						4
Female					13				1		13						13
Total					17				1		17						17
Irish—																	
Male		53	34	38	19	35	24	19	8	8	238						238
Female		59	41	61	40	23	40	28	26	11	329	2		8	10		339
Total		112	75	99	59	58	64	47	34	19	567	2		8	10		577
Polish—																	
Male		39	25	20	22						106						106
Female		41	23	27	18						109						109
Total		80	48	47	40						215						215
Portuguese—																	
Male		9	1	2	2		2	2	2		20						20
Female		2	6	2	2	1					15	1		1	2		17
Total		11	7	4	4	1	2	2	2		35	1		1	2		37
Scotch—																	
Male		2			3		1		1	2	8						8
Female			2	2	1	1	1		1		8						8
Total		2	2	2	4	1	2		2	2	16						16

Welsh—																
Male	...	...	2	2	...	1	1	...	...	2	...	...	...	...	...	2
Female	...	2	2	...	...	1	2	...	2	2	...	...	...	...	...	9
Total	1	2	4	...	1	2	2	...	2	2	...	...	...	...	...	11
Other races—a																
Male	5	2	2	...	1	...	...	1	...	9	...	11	...	...	...	9
Female	11	4	...	...	1	...	...	1	...	20	...	...	15	19	...	20
Total	16	6	2	...	2	...	...	1	...	29	...	11	15	19	...	29
Total—																
Male	688	356	411	327	217	148	77	40	21	2,285	4	11	15	...	...	2,333
Female	517	473	464	295	181	159	108	56	21	2,274	...	11	15	19	...	2,341
Total	1,205	829	875	622	398	307	185	96	42	4,559	4	...	...	19	...	4,674
Grand total—																
Male	834	441	481	391	243	188	104	54	32	2,768	4	11	15	...	60	2,820
Female	662	553	546	372	212	206	145	67	28	2,791	...	11	15	...	60	2,902
Total	1,496	994	1,027	763	455	394	249	121	60	5,559	4	...	...	...	60	5,722

a "Other races" include Chinese, 3; Dutch, Finnish, 3; German, 3; Hebrew, Russian, 2; Italian, North, 6; Italian, South, 2; Syrian, 1.

TABLE 3.—*Race, sex, and age, by grade—Number of pupils of each age in each grade, by sex and by general nativity and race of father of pupil.*

KINDERGARTEN.

BOYS.

General nativity and race of father of pupil.	Number of pupils of each age.					Total.
	4.	5.	6.	7.	8.	
Native-born, White..................................		1	2	1	.....	4
Foreign-born, Canadian, French	6	21	15	4	2	48
Grand total..	6	22	17	5	2	52

GIRLS.

	4.	5.	6.	7.	8.	Total.
Native-born, White..................................		.....	3	.....	.....	3
Foreign-born, Canadian, French.................	2	8	15	8	.....	33
Grand total..	2	8	18	8	.....	36

TOTAL.

	4.	5.	6.	7.	8.	Total.
Native-born, White..................................	.....	1	5	1	.....	7
Foreign-born, Canadian, French	8	29	30	12	2	81
Grand total..	8	30	35	13	2	88

PRIMARY AND FIRST GRADE.

BOYS.

General nativity and race of father of pupil.	Number of pupils of each age.											Total.
	4.	5.	6.	7.	8.	9.	10.	11.	12.	13.	14.	
Native-born, White................	2	59	34	30	10	4	2	5	....	....	....	146
Foreign-born:												
Canadian, French..............	5	35	90	125	113	80	47	31	....	1	1	528
Canadian, Other...............	....	2	....	....	....	....	....	....	....	....	....	2
English.......................	....	17	21	5	5	....	2	....	....	....	....	50
Irish.........................	5	17	18	10	2	1	....	....	....	....	....	53
Polish	....	4	11	15	8	....	....	1	....	....	....	39
Portuguese.....................	....	2	4	....	....	2	1	....	....	....	....	9
Scotch........................	....	1	....	1	....	....	....	....	....	....	....	2
Welsh.........................	....	....	....	....	....	....	....	....	....	....	....	
Other races a.................	1	1	1	1	1	....	....	....	....	....	....	5
Total......................	11	79	145	157	129	83	50	32	....	1	1	688
Grand total................	13	138	179	187	139	87	52	37	....	1	1	834

a "Other races" includes races having less than 10 representatives in this city and pupils whose race is not reported.

TABLE 3.—*Race, sex, and age, by grade—Number of pupils of each age in each grade, by sex and by general nativity and race of father of pupil—Continued.*

PRIMARY AND FIRST GRADE—Continued.

GIRLS.

General nativity and race of father of pupil.	Number of pupils of each age.											Total.
	4.	5.	6.	7.	8.	9.	10.	11.	12.	13.	14.	
Native-born, White	6	53	36	28	12	8	2					145
Foreign-born:												
Canadian, French	8	32	71	92	75	55	19	6	12	1		371
Canadian, Other			1									1
English		6	9	6	3	4	1					29
French			1	1								2
Irish		26	17	8	5	1	1	1				59
Polish		5	12	13	7	1	2	1				41
Portuguese				1		1						2
Welsh				1								1
Other races a		6	3	2								11
Total	8	75	114	124	90	62	23	8	12	1		517
Grand total	14	128	150	152	102	70	25	8	12	1		662

TOTAL.

General nativity and race of father of pupil.	Number of pupils of each age.											Total.
	4.	5.	6.	7.	8.	9.	10.	11.	12.	13.	14.	
Native-born, White	8	112	70	58	22	12	4	5				291
Foreign-born:												
Canadian, French	13	67	161	217	188	135	66	37	12	2	1	899
Canadian, Other		2	1									3
English		23	30	11	8	4	3					79
French			1	1								2
Irish	5	43	35	18	7	2	1	1				112
Polish		9	23	28	15	1	2	2				80
Portuguese		2	4	1		3	1					11
Scotch		1		1								2
Welsh				1								1
Other races a	1	7	4	3	1							16
Total	19	154	259	281	219	145	73	40	12	2	1	1,205
Grand total	27	266	329	339	241	157	77	45	12	2	1	1,496

a "Other races" includes races having less than 10 representatives in this city and pupils whose race is not reported.

66083°—VOL 31—12——19

TABLE 3.—*Race, sex, and age, by grade—Number of pupils of each age in each grade, by sex and by general nativity and race of father of pupil*—Continued.

SECOND GRADE.

BOYS.

General nativity and race of father of pupil.	Number of pupils of each age.										Total.
	6.	7.	8.	9.	10.	11.	12.	13.	14.	15.	
Native-born, White	15	28	20	6	2	2	9	2	1	......	85
Foreign-born:											
Scotch					1						1
Canadian, French		27	48	55	40	24	35	9	4		242
Canadian, Other	15	1				1					17
English	6	12	8	2	1	2					31
French			1	1				1			3
Irish	4	7	7	3	1	2	4	2	3	1	34
Polish		1	5	11	2	2	3	1			25
Portuguese	1										1
Other races a			2								2
Total	26	48	71	72	45	31	42	13	7	1	356
Grand total	41	76	91	78	47	33	51	15	8	1	441

GIRLS.

General nativity and race of father of pupil.	6.	7.	8.	9.	10.	11.	12.	13.	14.	15.	Total.
Native-born, White	22	15	21	9	3	4	4	2			80
Foreign-born:											
Scotch			1		1						2
Canadian, French	17	42	81	90	44	66	14				354
Canadian, Other	2										2
English	1	12	7	3	7	4	3				37
French			1	1							2
Irish	1	10	7	10	5	4	4				41
Polish		6	4	8	4	1					23
Portuguese		3	2	1							6
Welsh	1		1								2
Other races a	1			1	2						4
Total	23	73	104	114	63	75	21				473
Grand total	45	88	125	123	66	79	25	2			553

TOTAL.

General nativity and race of father of pupil.	6.	7.	8.	9.	10.	11.	12.	13.	14.	15.	Total.
Native-born, White	37	43	41	15	5	6	13	4	1		165
Foreign-born:											
Scotch			1		2						3
Canadian, French	17	69	129	145	84	90	49	9	4		596
Canadian, Other	17	1				1					19
English	7	24	15	5	8	6	3				68
French			2	2			1				5
Irish	5	17	14	13	6	6	8	2	3	1	75
Polish		7	9	19	6	3	3	1			48
Portuguese	1	3	2	1							7
Welsh	1		1								2
Other races a	1		2	1	2						6
Total	49	121	174	186	106	106	64	12	7	1	829
Grand total	86	164	215	201	113	112	77	17	8	1	994

a "Other races" includes races having less than 10 representatives in this city and pupils whose race is not reported.

TABLE 3.—*Race, sex, and age, by grade—Number of pupils of each age in each grade, by sex and by general nativity and race of father of pupil—Continued.*

THIRD GRADE.

BOYS.

General nativity and race of father of pupil.	Number of pupils of each age.										Total.
	6.	7.	8.	9.	10.	11.	12.	13.	14.	15.	
Native-born, White	1	7	12	18	12	16	4				70
Foreign-born:											
Canadian, French	1	1	34	61	84	48	48	24	3	1	305
Canadian, Other				2		1					3
English		6	9	11	9	4	1				40
French				1							1
Irish	1	5	11	11	5	4	1				38
Polish				7	7	2	3	1			20
Portuguese				1				1			2
Welsh		1		1							2
Total	2	13	54	95	105	59	53	26	3	1	411
Grand total	3	20	66	113	117	75	57	26	3	1	481

GIRLS.

General nativity and race of father of pupil.	6.	7.	8.	9.	10.	11.	12.	13.	14.	15.	Total.
Native-born, White	1	9	22	20	12	12	3	3			82
Foreign-born:											
Canadian, French		2	36	56	75	96	47	19	2		333
Canadian, Other							1				1
English		6	11	5	6		1	2			31
French			1	2	1	1					5
Irish		5	21	18	11	6					61
Polish			1	6	9	5	4	2			27
Portuguese			2								2
Welsh			1				1				2
Other races a							1	1			2
Total		14	78	90	98	108	52	22	2		464
Grand total	1	23	100	110	110	120	55	25	2		546

TOTAL.

General nativity and race of father of pupil.	6.	7.	8.	9.	10.	11.	12.	13.	14.	15.	Total.
Native-born, White	2	16	34	38	24	28	7	3			152
Foreign-born:											
Canadian, French	1	3	70	117	159	144	95	43	5	1	638
Canadian, Other				2		1	1				4
English		12	20	16	15	4	2	2			71
French			1	3	1	1					6
Irish	1	10	32	29	16	10	1				99
Polish		1	6	16	12	6	5	1			47
Portuguese			2	1				1			4
Welsh		1	1	1		1					4
Other races a							1	1			2
Total	2	27	132	185	203	167	105	48	5	1	875
Grand total	4	43	166	223	227	195	112	51	5	1	1,027

a "Other races" includes races having less than 10 representatives in this city and pupils whose race is not reported.

TABLE 3.—*Race, sex, and age, by grade—Number of pupils of each age in each grade, by sex and by general nativity and race of father of pupil*—Continued.

FOURTH GRADE.

BOYS.

General nativity and race of father of pupil.	Number of pupils of each age.								Total.
	7.	8.	9.	10.	11.	12.	13.	14.	
Native-born, White		10	15	12	12	7	7	1	64
Foreign-born:									
Canadian, French	1	13	26	58	77	47	19	1	242
Canadian, Other					2				2
English		1	2	17	6	3			29
French				1	1		1		3
Hebrew (not specified)			1	3					4
Irish		2	2	8	1	4	2		19
Polish			3	5	6	5	3		22
Scotch			1		1	1			3
Portuguese				1	1				2
Other races *a*					1				1
Total	1	16	36	93	95	60	25	1	327
Grand total	1	26	51	105	107	67	32	2	391

GIRLS.

General nativity and race of father of pupil.	7.	8.	9.	10.	11.	12.	13.	14.	Total.
Native-born, White		16	17	22	12	9		1	77
Foreign-born:									
Canadian, French	1	5	33	48	63	30	8	1	189
Canadian, Other		1	1						2
English			7	8	7	4	1		27
French				1		1			2
Hebrew (not specified)		4	6	3					13
Irish		2	8	9	10	7	2	2	40
Polish			2	3	3	7	3		18
Scotch				1					1
Portuguese			1			1			2
Other races *a*						1			1
Total	1	12	58	73	83	5	14	3	295
Grand total	1	28	75	95	95	60	14	4	372

TOTAL.

General nativity and race of father of pupil.	7.	8.	9.	10.	11.	12.	13.	14.	Total.
Native-born, White		26	32	34	24	16	7	2	141
Foreign-born:									
Canadian, French	2	18	59	106	140	77	27	2	431
Canadian, Other		1	1		2				4
English		1	9	25	13	7	1		56
French				1	2	1	1		5
Hebrew (not specified)		4	7	6					17
Irish		4	10	17	11	11	4	2	59
Polish			5	8	9	12	6		40
Scotch			1	1	1	1			4
Portuguese			1	1	1	1			4
Other races *a*					1	1			2
Total	2	28	94	166	178	111	39	4	622
Grand total	2	54	126	200	202	127	46	6	763

a "Other races" includes races having less than 10 representatives in this city and pupils whose race is not reported.

TABLE **3.**—*Race, sex, and age, by grade—Number of pupils of each age in each grade, by sex and by general nativity and race of father of pupil*—Continued.

FIFTH GRADE.

BOYS.

General nativity and race of father of pupil.	Number of pupils of each age.								Total.
	8.	9.	10.	11.	12.	13.	14.	15.	
Native-born, White..........................	1	3	3	8	8	3	......	......	**26**
Foreign-born:									
Canadian, French.....................	1	6	22	53	46	23	3	......	154
Canadian, Other......................			1						1
English................................		1	2	12	6	2	1		24
Irish..................................		3	15	6	10	1			35
Portuguese.............................					1	1			2
Other races *a*					1				1
Total...........................	1	10	40	71	64	27	4	......	217
Grand total.....................	2	13	43	79	72	30	4	......	243

GIRLS.

General nativity and race of father of pupil.	8.	9.	10.	11.	12.	13.	14.	15.	Total.
Native-born, White..........................	......	3	8	9	9	1	......	1	31
Foreign-born:									
Canadian, French.....................		16	27	42	37	17	2	......	141
English................................		......	2	3	7	1			13
Irish..................................		6	5	4	6	2			23
Scotch................................				1					1
Welsh.................................					2				2
Other races *a*				1					1
Total...........................		22	34	51	52	20	2	......	181
Grand total.....................		25	42	60	61	21	2	1	212

TOTAL.

General nativity and race of father of pupil.	8.	9.	10.	11.	12.	13.	14.	15.	Total.
Native-born, White..........................	1	6	11	17	17	4	......	1	57
Foreign-born:									
Canadian, French.....................	1	22	49	95	83	40	5	......	295
Canadian, Other......................			1						1
English................................		1	4	15	13	3	1		37
Irish..................................		9	20	10	16	3			58
Scotch................................				1					1
Welsh.................................					2				2
Portuguese.............................					1	1			2
Other races *a*				1	1				2
Total...........................	1	32	74	122	116	47	6	......	398
Grand total.....................	2	38	85	139	133	51	6	1	455

a "Other races" includes races having less than 10 representatives in this city and pupils whose race is not reported.

TABLE 3.—*Race, sex, and age, by grade—Number of pupils of each age in each grade, by sex and by general nativity and race of father of pupil*—Continued.

SIXTH GRADE.

BOYS.

General nativity and race of father of pupil.	Number of pupils of each age.							Total.
	9.	10.	11.	12.	13.	14.	15.	
Native-born, White	....	9	9	8	14	....	....	40
Foreign-born:								
Canadian, French	1	9	23	38	22	8	1	102
Canadian. Other	....	2	....	2	1	....	....	5
English	....	3	2	5	3	....	....	13
French	....	1	....	....	....	....	....	1
Irish	1	5	5	7	4	1	1	24
Portuguese	....	....	1	....	1	....	....	2
Scotch	....	....	....	....	1	....	....	1
Total	2	20	31	52	32	9	2	148
Grand total	2	29	40	60	46	9	2	188

GIRLS.

General nativity and race of father of pupil.	9.	10.	11.	12.	13.	14.	15.	Total.
Native-born, White	6	2	19	12	7	1	....	47
Foreign-born:								
Canadian, French	1	15	27	36	13	3	1	96
Canadian, Other	....	....	....	1	....	....	....	1
English	....	2	4	7	4	....	....	17
French	....	....	....	1	....	....	....	1
Irish	4	2	19	5	8	1	1	40
Portuguese	....	....	....	....	....	1	....	1
Scotch	....	....	....	....	1	....	....	1
Welsh	....	....	....	....	2	....	....	2
Total	5	19	50	50	28	5	2	159
Grand total	11	21	69	62	35	6	2	206

TOTAL.

General nativity and race of father of pupil.	9.	10.	11.	12.	13.	14.	15.	Total.
Native-born, White	6	11	28	20	21	1	....	87
Foreign-born:								
Canadian, French	2	24	50	74	35	11	2	198
Canadian, Other	....	2	....	3	1	....	....	6
English	....	5	6	12	7	....	....	30
French	....	1	....	1	....	....	....	2
Irish	5	7	24	12	12	2	2	64
Portuguese	....	....	1	....	1	1	....	3
Scotch	....	....	....	....	2	....	....	2
Welsh	....	....	....	....	2	....	....	2
Total	7	39	81	102	60	14	4	307
Grand total	13	50	109	122	81	15	4	394

TABLE 3.—*Race, sex, and age, by grade—Number of pupils of each age in each grade, by sex and by general nativity and race of father of pupil*—Continued.

SEVENTH GRADE.

BOYS.

General nativity and race of father of pupil.	Number of pupils of each age.						Total.
	10.	11.	12.	13.	14.	15.	
Native-born, White..........................	....	4	8	8	7	....	27
Foreign-born:							
Canadian, French.........................	5	10	12	11	4	3	45
Canadian, Other..........................	....	....	....	....	....	....	....
English..................................	....	1	8	3	1	....	13
Irish....................................	....	2	11	4	2	....	19
Portuguese...............................	....	....	....	....	....	....	....
Total................................	5	13	31	18	7	3	77
Grand total..........................	5	17	39	26	14	3	104

GIRLS.

General nativity and race of father of pupil.	10.	11.	12.	13.	14.	15.	Total.
Native-born, White..........................	....	5	12	19	1	....	37
Foreign-born:							
Canadian, French.........................	1	15	23	18	5	2	64
Canadian, Other..........................	....	1	....	....	....	....	1
English..................................	....	2	4	7	....	....	13
Irish....................................	....	3	12	10	2	1	28
Portuguese...............................	....	....	1	1	....	....	2
Total................................	1	21	40	36	7	3	108
Grand total..........................	1	26	52	55	8	3	145

TOTAL.

General nativity and race of father of pupil.	10.	11.	12.	13.	14.	15.	Total.
Native-born, White..........................	....	9	20	27	8	....	64
Foreign-born:							
Canadian, French.........................	6	25	35	29	9	5	109
Canadian, Other..........................	....	1	....	....	....	....	1
English..................................	....	3	12	10	1	....	26
Irish....................................	....	5	23	14	4	1	47
Portuguese...............................	....	....	1	1	....	....	2
Total................................	6	34	71	54	14	6	185
Grand total..........................	6	43	91	81	22	6	249

TABLE 3.—*Race, sex, and age, by grade—Number of pupils of each age in each grade, by sex and by general nativity and race of father of pupil*—Continued.

EIGHTH GRADE.

BOYS.

General nativity and race of father of pupil.	Number of pupils of each age.							Total.
	11.	12.	13.	14.	15.	16.	17.	
Native-born, White		3	6	4	1			14
Foreign-born:								
Canadian, French		3	6	7	2			18
Canadian, Other						1	1	2
English		3	4	1				8
French			1					1
Irish		1	4	1	2			8
Portuguese			1	1				2
Scotch				1				1
Total foreign-born		7	16	11	4	1	1	40
Grand total		10	22	15	5	1	1	54

GIRLS.

General nativity and race of father of pupil.	11.	12.	13.	14.	15.	16.	17.	Total.
Native-born, White		3	4	3	1			11
Foreign-born:								
Canadian, French	1	3	8	3	5		1	21
Canadian, Other			1	1				2
English		1	2	2				5
Irish	2	4	9	8	3			26
Scotch			1					1
Other races a				1				1
Total foreign-born	3	8	21	15	8		1	56
Grand total	3	11	25	18	9		1	67

TOTAL.

General nativity and race of father of pupil.	11.	12.	13.	14.	15.	16.	17.	Total.
Native-born, White		6	10	7	2			25
Foreign-born:								
Canadian, French	1	6	14	10	7		1	39
Canadian, Other			1	1		1	1	4
English		4	6	3				13
French			1					1
Irish	2	5	13	9	5			34
Portuguese			1	1				2
Scotch			1	1				2
Other races a				1				1
Total foreign-born	3	15	37	26	12	1	2	96
Grand total	3	21	47	33	14	1	2	121

a "Other races" includes races having less than 10 representatives in this city and pupils whose race is not reported.

TABLE **3.**—*Race, sex, and age, by grade—Number of pupils of each age in each grade, by sex and by general nativity and race of father of pupil*—Continued.

NINTH GRADE.

BOYS.

General nativity and race of father of pupil.	Number of pupils of each age.					Total.
	13.	14.	15.	16.	17.	
Native-born, White	1	7	2		1	11
Foreign-born:						
Canadian, French		2	4	5		11
English	1	1				2
Irish	1	4		1	2	8
Total foreign-born	2	7	4	6	2	21
Grand total	3	14	6	6	3	32

GIRLS.

	13.	14.	15.	16.	17.	Total.
Native-born, White	3	2	2			7
Foreign-born:						
Canadian, French		2	1	1		4
English	1	3				4
Irish	1	9		1		11
Scotch	1		1			2
Total foreign-born	3	14	2	2		21
Grand total	6	16	4	2		28

TOTAL.

	13.	14.	15.	16.	17.	Total.
Native-born, White	4	9	4		1	18
Foreign-born:						
Canadian, French		4	5	6		15
English	2	4				6
Irish	2	13		2	2	19
Scotch	1		1			2
Total foreign-born	5	21	6	8	2	42
Grand total	9	30	10	8	3	60

TABLE 3.—*Race, sex, and age, by grade—Number of pupils of each age in each grade, by sex and by general nativity and race of father of pupil*—Continued.

FIRST YEAR HIGH SCHOOL.

GIRLS.

General nativity and race of father of pupil.	Number of pupils of each age.													Total.
	8.	9.	10.	11.	12.	13.	14.	15.	16.	17.	18.	19.	20.	
Foreign-born:														
Irish.............................						1							1	2
Portuguese........................											1			1
Other races a.....................									1					1
Total........................						1				1	1		1	4

a "Other races" includes races having less than 10 representatives in this city and pupils whose race is not reported.

THIRD YEAR HIGH SCHOOL.

GIRLS.

General nativity and race of father of pupil.	Number of pupils of each age.					Total.
	16.	17.	18.	18.	20.	
Foreign-born:						
Canadian, French.................		1	1			2
Irish.............................	6	1			1	8
Portuguese........................			1			1
Total........................	6	2	2		1	11

SPECIAL SCHOOLS.

GIRLS.

General nativity and race of father of pupil.	Number of pupils of each age.						Total.
	7.	8.	9.	10.	11.	12.	
Native-born, White......................	3	15	8	12	2	1	41
Foreign-born, Canadian, French............		6	2	4	7		19
Total................................	3	21	10	16	9	1	60

TABLE 4.—Race distribution in each grade—Percentages.

[This table shows in detail only races with 100 or more pupils reporting. The totals, however, are for all races.]

General nativity and race of father of pupil.	Kindergarten.	Elementary grades.										High school.				Special schools.	Grand total.
		1.	2.	3.	4.	5.	6.	7.	8.	9.	Total.	First year.	Second year.	Third year.	Total.		
Native-born, White	8.0	19.5	16.6	14.8	18.5	12.5	22.1	25.7	20.7	30.0	18.0	0.0		0.0	0.0	68.3	18.3
Foreign-born:																	
Canadian, French	92.0	60.1	60.0	62.1	56.5	64.8	50.3	43.8	32.2	25.0	57.9	.0		18.2	13.3	31.7	58.1
English	.0	5.5	6.8	6.9	7.3	8.1	7.6	10.4	10.7	10.0	6.9			22.7	66.7	.0	6.7
Irish	.0	7.5	7.5	9.6	7.7	12.7	16.2	18.9	28.1	31.7	10.2	50.0		72.7	66.7	.0	10.1
Polish	.0	5.3	4.6	4.6	5.2	.0	.0	.0	.0	3.3	3.9	50.0		9.1	20.0	.0	3.8
Other races	.0	2.3	4.2	1.9	4.7	1.8	3.8	1.2	8.3	3.1	3.1					.0	3.0
Total	92.0	80.5	83.4	85.2	81.5	87.5	77.9	74.3	79.3	70.0	82.0	100.0		100.0	100.0	31.7	81.7
Grand total	100.0	100.0	100.0	100.0	100.0	100.0	100.0	100.0	100.0	100.0	100.0	100.0		100.0	100.0	100.0	100.0

TABLE 5.—Grade distribution of each race—Percentages.

[This table shows in detail only races with 100 or more pupils reporting. The totals, however, are for all races.]

General nativity and race of father of pupil.	Kindergarten.	Elementary grades.										High school.				Special schools.	Grand total.
		1.	2.	3.	4.	5.	6.	7.	8.	9.	Total.	First year.	Second year.	Third year.	Total.		
Native-born, White	0.7	27.8	15.7	14.5	13.5	5.4	8.3	6.1	2.4	1.7	95.4	0.0		0.0	0.0	3.9	100.0
Foreign-born:																	
Canadian, French	2.4	27.1	17.9	19.2	13.0	8.9	6.0	3.3	1.2	.5	96.9	.0		.1	.1	.6	100.0
English	.0	20.5	17.6	18.4	14.2	9.6	7.8	6.7	3.4	1.6	98.3	.0		1.4	1.7	.0	100.0
Irish	.0	19.4	13.0	21.9	10.2	10.1	11.0	8.1	5.9	3.3	98.3	.3		.6	.9	.0	100.0
Polish	.0	37.2	22.3	11.5	18.6	4.6	.0	1.7	.0	1.1	98.3	1.1		.0	1.7	.0	100.0
Other races	.0	20.1	24.1	11.5	20.7	4.6	8.6	1.7	5.7	1.1	98.3	.0		.6	.6	.0	100.0
Total	1.7	25.8	17.7	18.7	13.3	8.5	6.6	4.0	2.1	.9	97.5	.1		.2	.2	.4	100.0
Grand total	1.5	26.1	17.4	17.9	13.3	8.0	6.9	4.4	2.1	1.0	97.2	.1		.2	.3	1.0	100.0

HAVERHILL, MASSACHUSETTS.

INTRODUCTORY NOTE.
PUBLIC SCHOOL PUPILS—GENERAL INVESTIGATION.
PUBLIC SCHOOL PUPILS—INTENSIVE INVESTIGATION.
PAROCHIAL SCHOOL PUPILS—GENERAL INVESTIGATION.

LIST OF TABLES.

285

HAVERHILL.

In Haverhill, Mass., the investigations of the Immigration Commission relate to pupils in the public and the parochial schools. But here what is described in the introduction as the "intensive investigation" was conducted in the public schools. A distinct record slip was prepared for each pupil, containing not only the usual questions as to grade, sex, race, and age, but a wide variety of other inquiries designed to throw light upon the school history and social environment of the pupil. By means of various sortings these cards were grouped according to various characteristics, and the statistical tables here presented were obtained. The general tables, though obtained by other methods, are parallel in their contents to those given for other cities. An account of the results of these tables may conveniently precede the discussion of the special tables of the intensive investigation. The general character of both sets of tables is set forth in the introduction,[a] where there will be found also an account of the methods of the investigation and some discussion of the value and significance of the tables as an aid to the comprehension of school conditions.

PUBLIC SCHOOL PUPILS—GENERAL TABLES.

The whole number of pupils reported in attendance in the elementary schools of Haverhill was 4,380. No cards were collected in the high school. This number falls short of the average annual attendance for the year 1908–9, which was 4,969. Before proceeding to an analysis of the figures reported, it is important to consider the nature of this shortage. It is somewhat too large to be wholly explained by the variations of attendance in a single month or on a single day from the annual average. Such variations would hardly be so considerable, the figures reported being 11.9 per cent lower than the annual average. To some extent therefore this difference must be due to omissions. Under the method of investigation by individual cards such omissions might extend to a whole school, or they might be spread uniformly over all the grades, or they might be most frequent in certain grades, especially, for example, in the lower grades, where the collection of the information encounters the greatest difficulty. Fortunately we have means of testing this, as the Haverhill reports give us information by grades, which relate, it is true, not to the attendance of the pupils but to the enrollment for the grade.

---

[a] See pp. VII to XVII.

A comparison of these figures follows:

Public school pupils in Haverhill.

Grade.	Total enrollment 1908–9.	Cards supplied to Immigration Commission.	
		Number.	Per cent of total enrollment.
First........	773	594	76.8
Second........	601	486	80.8
Third........	617	487	78.9
Fourth........	616	530	86.0
Fifth........	584	450	77.1
Sixth........	577	520	87.0
Seventh........	513	467	91.0
Eighth........	462	401	86.8
Ninth........	385	347	90.0
Total........	5,123	4,264	83.2

The total enrollment here reported was 5,123. It has been previously noted that the average annual attendance was 4,969, or 97 per cent of the enrollment. If there were available any figures for the attendance by grades it would not be found that the latter was in each grade exactly 97 per cent of the enrollment. In the earlier grades, especially in grades 1 and 2, it would be less than this proportion, and in the upper grades somewhat more. In other words, the distribution of pupils by grades is not identical by enrollment and by attendance, and this must be borne in mind in studying the foregoing table. In that table the number of cards reported is, in the different grades, a somewhat different percentage of the enrollment, per cents being on the whole somewhat larger in the upper than in the lower grades. This demonstrates that the omissions have been fairly equally distributed, and that the resulting figures, which undoubtedly represent from 90 to 95 per cent of all the children in the Haverhill schools, shows a normal and regular distribution among the grades. This dispels any misgivings that the figures given might not present a fairly complete and comprehensive picture of conditions in the Haverhill schools.

Divided by the several grades of the elementary schools, the children in Haverhill are distributed as follows:

First grade....................	594	Seventh grade....................	467
Second grade....................	486	Eighth grade....................	401
Third grade....................	487	Ninth grade....................	347
Fourth grade....................	530		
Fifth grade.,....................	450	Total....................	4,264
Sixth grade....................	502		

Despite variations, the striking fact of this table is the comparative equality of numbers of the second to the seventh grades. The eighth and ninth grades show some falling off, but even in the latter the number of pupils is relatively high. If we call the grades 1 to 4 the primary grades we find in them 2,097 children, or 49.2 per cent of all, while in grades 5 to 9, the grammar grades, there are 2,167 children, or 50.8 per cent of the total, an almost equal division between primary and grammar grades.

Table 1 indicates also a very uniform distribution of ages, as follows:

Age.	Number.	Age.	Number.	Age.	Number.
5 years and under......	309	10 years..............	449	15 years..............	110
6 years...............	455	11 years..............	441	16 years..............	24
7 years...............	421	12 years..............	479	17 years and over......	7
8 years...............	451	13 years..............	414		
9 years...............	409	14 years..............	295		

At 14 years of age there is a considerable falling off in the number, many of the pupils having left school, and some of them having passed on to the high school. The absence of figures for the high schools makes the figures for the upper ages of no value for estimating the amount of elimination.

The same table (1) shows the number of pupils of each age in each grade, and thus presents a somewhat elaborate scheme of figures. To reduce this to a more simple expression the pupils in each grade may be divided into two groups, one containing those who are of normal age or under, the other containing those of over normal age. Comparing the number of overage pupils with the whole number, we find a proportion frequently designated as the percentage of retardation. The idea of a normal age for each grade carries with it that of a normal grade for each age. The pupils of a given age would be deemed undergrade or retarded who had not attained the grade suitable for the age. Either of these methods gives in a negative way some notion of the general progress of pupils in the schools by indicating the proportion who are below a certain fixed standard of advancement or who are retarded. The most usual form is that which determines in each grade the proportion of overage pupils.

The following table gives for the Haverhill schools a statement for each grade of the number of retarded pupils and the proportion which such number bears to the total number of pupils in the grade:

Grade.	Number in grade.	Retarded pupils.		
		Age.	Number.	Per cent of all pupils.
First..............	594	8 years and over....................................	22	3.7
Second.............	486	9 years and over....................................	30	6.2
Third.............	487	10 years and over...................................	47	9.7
Fourth............	530	11 years and over...................................	69	13.0
Fifth.............	450	12 years and over...................................	72	16.0
Sixth.............	502	13 years and over...................................	70	13.9
Seventh...........	467	14 years and over...................................	52	11.1
Eighth............	401	15 years and over...................................	29	7.2
Ninth.............	347	16 years and over...................................	19	5.5
Total........	4,264		410	9.6

By comparing the aggregate number of retarded pupils with the whole number of pupils, it is found that only 9.6 per cent of the pupils of the city belong in the retarded class. In the first grade less than 5 per cent are retarded. As the grades advance the proportion of such pupils slowly increases, and in grade 5 reaches a maximum of 16 per cent. After this point the proportion slowly declines, as the number of pupils generally becomes less, indicating a more frequent elimination of the retarded than of the normal pupils.

A consideration of retardation by age is given in the statement following, which shows for pupils of the ages 10, 11, and 12 years the number who are under the proper grade for those years and the proportion which this number bears to all the pupils of these ages:

Age.	Number of pupils of this age.	Normal grade.	Retarded, or below normal grade.	
			Number.	Per cent.
10 years	449	4	34	7.6
11 years	441	5	51	11.6
12 years	479	6	72	15.0
Total	1,369		157	11.5

While at the age of 10 years only 7.6 per cent of the children are undergrade, at the age of 12 this proportion has increased to 15 per cent. The average for the group (11.5 per cent) is somewhat higher than for all the school children, as shown in an earlier table, because this group has a somewhat higher average age. The group average is calculated for the purpose of comparing it later with similar averages for individual races.

The examination into the race of the pupils constitutes the characteristic feature of the researches of the Immigration Commission. By means of the material printed in Tables 2, 3, and 4, special studies can be made for each race parallel to those which have been indicated for the schools as a whole. The composition of the school population of Haverhill as regards race is exhibited in the table following. This gives children of native and of foreign fathers, and among the latter various races individually, which have as many as 200 representatives in the schools.

General nativity and race of father of pupil.	Pupils.		General nativity and race of father of pupil.	Pupils.	
	Number.	Per cent.		Number.	Per cent.
Native-born:			Foreign-born—Continued.		
White	2,539	59.5	Hebrew, Russian	323	7.6
Negro	57	1.3	Irish	238	5.6
Total native-born	2,596	60.9	All other	550	12.9
Foreign-born:			Total foreign-born	1,668	39.1
Canadian, French	245	5.7	Grand total	4,264	100.0
Canadian, Other	312	7.3			

In round numbers six-tenths of the pupils in Haverhill schools have native white fathers and four-tenths have foreign fathers. Among the latter group the Canadians, both of French and English extraction, are most numerous, constituting 13 per cent of all the school children. Rather more than one-half of the Canadians are of English origin. Another important group of 323 children, or 7.6 per cent of the whole number reported, is that of children having Russian Hebrew fathers. The Irish also are relatively numerous.

The group, "All other," comprising about one-eighth of all the school children, is made up of many different races, as follows:

Armenian (20), Danish (5), Dutch (3), English (131), French (13), German (24), Greek (3), Hebrew, German (2), Hebrew, Polish (2), Hebrew, Roumanian (5), Hebrew, Other, (38), Italian, North (69), Italian, South (74), Italian, not specified (65), Lithuanian (4), Macedonian (2), Norwegian (6), Polish (5), Roumanian (1), Russian (2), Scotch (53), Scotch-Irish, (4), Swedish (14), and Welsh (5).

The distribution of the various classes among the grades can be most conveniently studied by a grouping of the grades into the primary, including grades 1 to 4, and the grammar grades 5 to 9. This is shown in the following table:

General nativity and race of father of pupil.	Number of pupils.			Per cent.	
	Primary.	Grammar.	Total.	Primary.	Grammar.
Native-born:					
White	1,176	1,363	2.539	46.3	53.7
Negro	25	32	57	44.0	56.0
Total native-born	1,201	1,395	2,596	46.2	53.8
Foreign-born:					
Canadian, French	141	104	245	57.6	42.4
Canadian, Other	150	162	312	48.1	51.9
Hebrew, Russian	186	137	323	57.6	42.4
Irish	103	135	238	43.3	56.7
All others	316	234	550	57.5	42.5
Total foreign-born	896	772	1,668	53.7	46.3
Grand total	2,097	2,167	4.264	49.2	50.8

The proportion of children of foreign fathers who are in the primary grades is somewhat larger than that of children having native fathers. The Irish children have, however, a smaller proportion in the primary grades than have those of native fathers. For the French Canadians and Russian Hebrews the proportion of the children in the primary grades somewhat exceeds the average for the group of those with foreign parents.

Retardation by races in the Haverhill schools is shown in the table next presented:

General nativity and race of father of pupil.	All elementary pupils.			Pupils 10, 11, and 12 years of age.		
	Number.	Retarded, overage.	Per cent retarded.	Number.	Retarded, under-grade.	Per cent retarded.
Native-born:						
White	2,539	205	8.1	641	84	13.1
Negro	57	10	17.5			
Total native-born	2,596	215	8.3	845	74	
Foreign-born:						
Canadian, French	245	39	15.9	69	13	18.8
Canadian, Other	312	21	6.7	103	5	4.9
Hebrew, Russian	323	43	13.3	95	22	23.2
Irish	238	16	6.7	81	4	4.9
All others	550	76	13.8	176	39	22.2
Total foreign-born	1,668	195	11.7	524	83	15.8
Grand total	4.264	410	9.6	1,369	157	11.5

This table gives in the first three columns general retardation relating to all elementary pupils, and in the last three columns the retardation of a special class—those of 10, 11, and 12 years of age.

The first section of the table shows that children of native parents have somewhat less retardation than those of foreign parents. Among the special races retardation is low among the Irish and the English Canadians, lower, in fact, than among children of native parentage. It is high among the French Canadians.

The second section indicates that the selected group of children of 10, 11, and 12 years of age has essentially the same relative retardation. It may, however, be remarked that in these ages the Russian Hebrews show a high degree of retardation, this being due in part to the larger number of recent arrivals among children of this race as compared with those of other races.

PUBLIC SCHOOL PUPILS—INTENSIVE TABLES.

The considerations thus far given are only the most general results of the school investigation in Haverhill, and form a necessary introduction to the more detailed tables which deal with the school history of the pupils and certain facts of their social environment. In these general tables there is presented a mass of detail, with divisions of the pupils by racial groups and with specific mention of the more important races. In the tables which follow space does not permit of a consideration of the individual races, but only of broad general groups.

PUPILS BY RACE.

Pupils of native parentage are in the following contrasted with those of foreign parentage, and the latter are divided into English-speaking and non-English-speaking races. The small number of negro children is disregarded, and the tables relate exclusively to whites. But by reason of this omission the total of native and foreign falls somewhat short of the aggregate for all pupils. As a preliminary to this discussion, it may be noted that a few of the cards furnished had for some questions ambiguous answers or omitted any response. These had to be disregarded in tabulations. Hence, the totals for the various tables here presented are those reporting complete information on the particular point under consideration, and these totals vary slightly from table to table.

The general object of the investigation was to determine, by race, the relation to school progress and advancement of various facts in the individual experience of the children and in the conditions in their home surroundings which might be supposed to have an influence upon their school standings.

One of these is the mobility of the population as exemplified in changes of residence. Our first table, therefore, concerns the birthplace of the pupils, and shows the number born in Haverhill in comparison with those born elsewhere.

Racial group.	Birthplace of pupil.			
	Haver-hill.	Else-where.	Total.	Per cent born else-where.
All pupils...........	2,897	1,231	4,128	29.8
Native-born white fathers	1,797	671	2,468	23.1
Foreign-born fathers............	1,063	545	1,608	33.9
English-speaking.............	501	218	719	30.3
Non-English-speaking............	562	327	889	36.8

Of all the pupils in the Haverhill schools 70.2 per cent were natives of the city and 29.8 per cent were born elsewhere. The percentage of those born elsewhere is naturally greater among those children who had foreign parents than among those of native parents. None the less, the fact that among the latter more than one-fifth were born out of Haverhill reflects the growth of city population by accessions from the outside. Of the children of foreign parents, one-third were not born in Haverhill, the proportion being below this average for the English-speaking races and above it for those who do not speak English.

From an educational standpoint the significance of these figures lies in the fact that the children born in the city and living there continuously, as may be inferred, have not been obliged to suffer any interruption of their schooling. On the other hand, those who were not born in Haverhill may, unless they were brought to the city by their parents before they reached the school age, have suffered an interruption in their schooling, with the attendant disadvantages of a shifting from one school to another. How far these considerations are applicable to the Haverhill children can be seen by distinguishing the number who had attended school elsewhere from those who had not done so. The following table refers only to pupils born in the United States but not in Haverhill, the city of their present residence.

Racial group.	Children born in United States but not in Haverhill.		
	Total.	Having attended school elsewhere.	
		Number.	Per cent.
All pupils.........	969	460	47.5
Native-born white fathers.............	657	328	49.9
Foreign-born fathers...........	297	126	42.4
English-speaking.............	149	73	48.7
Non-English-speaking..........	148	53	35.8

In the aggregate about one-half of the children had attended school elsewhere. Those who had not attended school in other cities are for the most part the children who left the places of their birth before they reached the age for attending school. It will be noted that for the native white and for the children of English-speaking foreign fathers these proportions are about the same. For the group of children of foreign fathers of non-English-speaking races the proportion of children who had not been to school is somewhat larger—an indication of a larger number of young children at the time of their settling down in Haverhill.

Other things being equal, the progress made by a child in school depends upon the length of time he remains therein, and this in turn depends not only upon the age when he leaves school but also in some degree upon the age when he enters. In the general tables the presence of a large number of 5-year-old children in school was noted, and by inference the conclusion was reached that a large proportion of children began their school life at this early age. The intensive investigation does not leave this to inference. It asked directly of each pupil the age at which he entered the public schools of the United States. The replies to the question are summarized for all pupils in the following table:

Pupils entering school at different ages.

Age.	Number.	Per cent.
5 years and under	2,737	66.8
6 years	959	23.4
7 years	215	5.2
8 years and over	186	4.5
Total	4,097	100.0

Two-thirds of the children in Haverhill began to go to school when they were 5 years of age, and nearly one-fourth began school at the age of 6. Over nine-tenths of all the pupils now in the schools began their schooling before reaching the seventh year of age—conditions highly favorable to school progress. Of the belated pupils, it is probable that not all were wholly without previous schooling, as some had probably had experience in private or parochial schools in this country or in schools abroad. Concerning the former we have no record, but there is a record of 66 children who attended foreign schools, and these are without doubt numbered among those who entered the public schools of the United States after the age of 6 years.

There is a peculiar interest attaching to the belated pupils. Pupils who do not enter school till they reach 8 years of age are kept out of school by their parents until the compulsory law goes into effect, either through indifference of parents or, more particularly, because many parents believe this to be advantageous for the children. In the following a separate statement is made of the number and percentage of children entering the public schools of the United States at the age of 8 years and upward:

Racial group.	Total number of pupils.	Pupils entering at the age of 8 years and upward.	
		Number	Per cent.
All pupils	4,097	186	4.5
Native-born white fathers	2,466	48	1.9
Foreign-born fathers	1,578	138	8.7
English speaking	713	42	5.9
Non-English-speaking	865	96	11.1

Less than 5 per cent of all the children were 8 years of age and over when they first went to public school. Among the children of native parents the proportion was less than 2 per cent. Even of this small number a few may have been previously in parochial or private schools. Of the children of foreign-born fathers 138, or 8.7 per cent, did not go to public school in the United States till they were 8 years of age. But quite a number of these children, 224 in fact, were born abroad. If these be deducted we have 1,354 children born in this country of foreign parents. Of this group 45, or 3.3 per cent, were 8 years of age or over before they attended the public schools. It appears, therefore, that the number of children whose attendance at school began after they reached the age of 8 years is very small for all groups of the population.

As the figures show that the great bulk of the children are in school before the age of 8 years, it is to anticipated that most begin their school life in the first grade. This is indicated directly by the following table:

	Pupils entering public schools.		
		Entering first grade.	
Racial group.	Total.		
		Number.	Per cent.
All pupils	4,061	3,865	95.2
Native-born white fathers	2,427	2,333	96.1
Foreign-born fathers	1,585	1,485	93.7
English-speaking	710	658	92.7
Non-English-speaking	875	827	94.5

More than 95 per cent of all the pupils began in the first grades of the public schools. The small remainder who began at a higher point represent a few children who had, before entering public school, enjoyed the benefits of home instruction or been to a private, parochial, or foreign school, where they had gained sufficient knowledge to permit their being placed in the second or a higher grade. Of 84 children of native parents who entered school at a point above the first grade 54 began in the second grade.

It has sometimes been contended among educators that pupils who do not go to school till they are 8 years of age frequently enter higher grades than the first. On this point our figures offer no conclusive evidence, as they do not refer to schools generally but to public schools in the United States. However, the facts contained in the general tables are summarized here as follows:

	Pupils entering school at the age of 8 years and over.		
		Entering first grade.	
Racial group.	Total.		
		Number.	Per cent.
All pupils	182	76	41.8
Native-born white fathers	47	13	27.7
Foreign-born fathers	135	63	46.7
English-speaking	42	3	7.1
Non-English-speaking	93	60	64.5

Of all the pupils who were 8 years of age or older when they first went to the public schools a goodly proportion (41.8 per cent) had to begin with the first grade. The percentage is somewhat less among children of native fathers and is very small among those of English-speaking foreign fathers. The inference seems more probable that the children entering a higher grade received instruction in some other kind of school than that they received home instruction. Children of non-English-speaking foreign parents, especially those born abroad, are often forced by reason of their unfamiliarity with the English language to enter the first grade, even though they may previously have had some instruction in their native language.

A further series of tables relates exclusively to the children of foreign parents, and notes contain facts as to home conditions, which may be supposed to have a bearing upon the schooling of the children.

The question of citizenship is in part connected with that of length of residence, since five years' residence is necessary for naturalization. How far the parents who may become naturalized have thus far failed to take any steps in this direction is indicated by the following table:

Racial group.	Foreign fathers of five or more years' residence.		
	Total.	Aliens.	
		Number.	Per cent.
English-speaking	649	166	25.6
Non-English-speaking	799	194	24.3
Total	1,448	360	24.9

It will be noted that in round numbers one-fourth of the children have alien fathers. Other things being equal, it can be generally assumed that foreign residents who remain aliens are less closely identified with the general life of the community than those who become naturalized, and that this aloofness is a condition rather unfavorable to the schooling of their children.

Quite as important in this connection is the length of residence of the fathers of pupils, which is shown in the following statement:

Length of residence of foreign-born fathers.

Period.	Number.	Per cent.
Under 5 years	82	5.3
5 to 9 years	109	7.0
10 to 19 years	536	34.4
20 years and over	831	53.3
Total	1,558	100.0

Of the Haverhill school children only 12.3 per cent have fathers who have been less than ten years in this country. Most of the children in this group are probably themselves of foreign birth as well. A much larger number of children, over one-third of the whole number, had fathers who had been in this country from ten to nineteen years, while more than one-half of the children had fathers of more than twenty years' residence.

Another factor of importance in this connection is the matter of language. There are about 900 children whose fathers did not speak English as their native tongue. Of them, however, only 65 had fathers who had failed to acquire a knowledge of English, but as many as 391 of them came from homes in which it was reported that no English was used.

Turning again to facts concerning all the pupils, an effort was made to gather some information concerning the regularity of the attendance of pupils. The number of days attended by each pupil was reported. For the purpose of tabulation these figures were arranged in groups according to the proportions they bore to the whole number of school days. A very defective attendance was indicated by pupils present less than half the school term. The number of such pupils is given below:

Racial group.	Pupils reporting duration of attendance.		
	Total.	Less than one-half of term.	
		Number.	Per cent.
All pupils	3,903	134	3.4
Native-born white fathers	2,354	84	3.6
Foreign-born fathers	1,495	50	3.3
English-speaking	660	24	3.6
Non-English-speaking	835	26	3.1

Only a small percentage of the pupils had a very defective attendance and the proportion was substantially the same for each of the groups noted.

The first table of this series gave a view of the mobility of the population by its figures on birthplace. This is also reflected in the table following, which shows the method of gaining access to the grade. It also reflects, however, by its statement of transfers, the mobility of the population within the city.

Pupils reporting method of access to present grade.

Method.	Number.	Per cent.
By regular course	3,211	81.4
By transfer from another public school of the city	254	6.4
By transfer from a public school elsewhere	165	4.2
By transfer from a private school	35	.9
Not promoted	279	7.1
Total	3,944	100.0

Over four-fifths of the pupils reached their present grade in the regular course, in the upper grades by promotion, and in grade 1 as newcomers entering school for the first time. Over 10 per cent were transferred from other schools, and 7 per cent failed of promotion.

The following table divides those who followed a regular course, by racial groups:

Racial group.	Pupils reporting method of access to present grade.		
	Total.	By regular course.	
		Number.	Per cent.
All pupils	3,944	3,211	81.4
Native-born white fathers	2,358	1,932	81.9
Foreign-born fathers	1,536	1,239	80.7
English-speaking	669	540	80.7
Non-English-speaking	867	699	80.7

There is no appreciable difference among the various groups in regard to the number reaching grades by regular course, and hence in regard to the number of transfers and nonpromotions considered together.

PUPILS BY NATIVITY.

The intensive investigation enables us to distinguish not only, as in the foregoing tables, the pupils of foreign parentage, but among them also the pupils who were of foreign birth. The 1,608 pupils of foreign parentage included 245 who were born abroad. The proportions vary greatly for the different races. Among 719 pupils of foreign English-speaking races, only 66, or less than 10 per cent, were born in foreign countries. Among those of non-English-speaking races, 179 out of 889, or 20.1 per cent, were born abroad. The proportion is largest among the Russian Hebrews; nearly 30 per cent were born in Russia.

Of 239 pupils born abroad, 129, or about one-half, were less than 6 years old when they arrived in this country. A considerable number of them were therefore of an age to attend school before coming here. Of 108 who were over 6 years of age on arrival, 66 had previously attended school in the country of their birth. Of 224 pupils of foreign birth for whom the information is given, as many as 95 were 8 years of age or over when they first attended school in the United States. But in spite of their superior age, the greater part of them began work in the American public schools in the first grade—as many as 196 out of 238. Of these, 92 were at least 8 years of age when they entered school, and among them 54 entered the first grade.

As might be anticipated, the home conditions among children of this class are not very favorable for the school progress of the children. The parents are of very recent arrival. Out of 226 pupils, 170 belong to families which had been less than ten years in the United States. Only 146 children came from families of sufficient residence to permit the naturalization of the father, and in only 99 cases had steps been taken toward naturalization. While fathers of 139 children spoke English, 36 did not, but in 127 homes the children heard no English, in comparison with 52 homes where English is used to some extent.

That these conditions are unfavorable to the school progress is obvious. How far they affect the degree of retardation among the group of children of foreign parents is seen in the following:

Nativity and parentage.	Number of pupils.		
	Total.	Retarded.	
		Number.	Per cent.
Native white native parents	2,539	205	8.1
White foreign parents	1,668	195	11.7
Native white foreign parents	1,423	115	8.8
Foreign white	245	80	32.6

The significant fact here indicated is that there is practically no difference among native whites, whether of native or of foreign parentage.

SCHOOL PROGRESS AND RETARDATION.

The tables of the intensive investigation are so arranged that in connection with the various racial groups the influence of the various factors under discussion in promoting or impeding school progress may be noted. This is done by indicating in each group of facts the number of retarded children, as well as the whole number of children. One of the tables, however, is designed to throw light directly upon the subject of school progress, without resort to the notation of retardation. This table is obtained by a comparison of the number of years a child has been in school and the grade. Thus if a child in the fifth grade is in his fourth year of schooling, he has been at school less years than the grade implies, but if he is in his sixth year of schooling, he has taken more years than are normally required to reach his grade. The facts observed in this comparison are given in the following statement for the pupils who have been at school longer than the grade implies:

Racial group.	Pupils reporting the number of years in school.		
	Total.	More than grade.	
		Number.	Per cent.
All pupils	3,953	1,136	28.7
Native-born white fathers	2,374	689	29.0
Foreign-born fathers	1,528	429	28.1
English-speaking	686	192	28.0
Non-English-speaking	842	237	28.1

Over one-fourth of the pupils have at some time in their school career failed of promotion and have been in school longer than their grades imply. For the various racial groups the ratio is practically the same. These percentages of failure are considerably higher than the percentages of retardation hitherto discussed. The reason for this difference is that the table immediately preceding measures all failures, but the common measure of retardation contains only those failures which result in bringing about a misrelation between the age and the grade. The standard for the first grade is so fixed that pupils entering early at 5 and 6 years of age may have one or two failures and repeat one or two years without coming into the retarded class, but they would take longer to complete the school course than the plan provides.

In the general discussion of retardation note was made of the fact that the ages of the pupils had a great deal of influence upon the resulting ratios. The whole number of pupils of the school system or of any racial group within it is made up of three elements, (a) young children less than 8 years of age, (b) children of 8 years of age and over, who are of normal age for their grades, and (c) children in the same ages who are average for their respective grades. The percentage of retardation is commonly expressed as the relation of the last element to the aggregate. Such a comparison assumes that the first element (a), the number of children under 8 years, is a constant. Whether this assumption is correct as between racial groups in the schools of Haverhill can be tested by the following table:

Racial group.	Number of pupils.		
	Total.	Under 8 years of age.	
		Number.	Per cent.
All pupils.			
Native-born white fathers.	4,264	1,186	27.8
Foreign-born fathers.	2,539	657	25.9
English-speaking.	1,668	510	30.6
Non-English-speaking.	743	196	26.4
	925	314	33.9

It appears that among children of native fathers there are fewer children under 8 than among those of foreign fathers. To these children the criterion of retardation does not apply, and all become nonretarded children. The inclusion of these children lessens the resulting percentage of retardation to a greater degree among children of foreign than among those of native parentage.

A more correct picture, therefore, of the relative retardation of different racial groups can be had by confining the computation of the retarded children to those of 8 years of age and over, as in the following statement:

Racial group.	Pupils of 8 years of age and over.		
	Total.	Retarded.	
		Number.	Per cent.
All pupils.			
Native-born white fathers.	3,079	410	13.3
Foreign-born fathers.	1,882	205	10.9
English-speaking.	1,158	195	16.8
Non-English-speaking.	547	52	9.5
	611	143	23.4

On this basis it appears that of all the pupils of Haverhill 13.3 per cent are retarded. Those having native parents have a retardation of 10.9 per cent, against a ratio of 16.8 per cent for those of foreign parents. It will, moreover, be noted that the greater retardation among children of foreign-born fathers is found entirely among those whose fathers are of the non-English-speaking races. Children of English-speaking foreign races have in Haverhill even less retardation than those of native parentage.

By means of the tables here printed in great detail the concept of retardation thus defined can be conveniently applied to each of the racial groups, with reference to the various matters which form the subjects of the intensive tables. To carry such an analysis for each racial group would unduly expand this introductory note. It must suffice here to show the relation of the various topics treated to retardation, exhibiting how certain conditions seem to enhance, others to lessen its proportion of the whole number. The application of these general tendencies to the particular racial groups must be left to the interested reader.

For all the pupils to which each table refers, irrespective of racial divisions, the salient facts in regard to retardation are brought out in the following summary:

Characteristics and pupils to whom they refer.	Pupils of 8 years of age and more reported.		
	Total.	Retarded.	
		Number.	Per cent.
Birthplace, all pupils:			
Born in Haverhill	2,074	204	9.8
Born elsewhere in United States	749	114	15.2
Born abroad	184	80	43.5
School attendance, pupils born in United States outside of city:			
Having attended school elsewhere	411	78	19.0
Not having attended school elsewhere	323	35	10.8
Age at entering school, all pupils:			
5 years and under	1,857	125	6.7
6 years	754	9	13.1
7 years	193	64	33.2
8 years	64	30	46.9
9 years	34	15	44.1
10 years and over	88	45	51.1
Grade entered, all pupils:			
First	2,771	343	12.4
Second	81	19	23.5
Third	29	7	24.1
Fourth	38	10	26.3
Fifth and higher	39	3	7.7
Years in school, all pupils:			
In school less years than grade	316	38	12.0
In school same years as grade	1,599	64	4.0
In school more years than grade	972	250	25.7
Ability to speak English, pupils of fathers of non-English-speaking foreign races:			
Fathers speak English	546	111	20.3
Fathers do not speak English	51	27	52.9
Citizenship, pupils with foreign-born fathers:			
Fathers have first or second naturalization papers	766	98	12.9
Fathers are aliens	297	79	26.6
Residence of fathers, pupils with foreign-born fathers:			
Under 5 years	53	33	62.3
5 to 9 years	74	28	37.8
10 to 19 years	334	33	9.9
20 years or more	608	81	13.3
Home language, pupils with fathers of non-English-speaking foreign races:			
English used in the home	369	61	16.5
English not used in the home	240	82	34.2
Proportion of term attended, all pupils:			
Nine-tenths or more	2,389	270	11.3
Three-fourths, but less than nine-tenths	342	56	16.4
One-half, but less than three-fourths	93	20	21.5
Less than one-half	73	26	35.6
Access to present grade, all pupils:			
Regular course	2,340	231	9.9
By transfer from another public school in city	201	32	15.9
By transfer from public schools elsewhere	124	24	19.4
By transfer from private school	33	11	33.3
Not promoted	174	71	40.8

In estimating the general significance of the figures here given, it is to be remembered that the average retardation for pupils of 8 years and over is 13.3 per cent. Whenever, therefore, a proportion of less than 13.3 per cent is found for any group, it denotes conditions favorable to school progress. When, on the contrary, this rate is exceeded, it is plain that the conditions indicated are unfavorable to the school progress of the children.

Children born in Haverhill have less retardation than the average; those born in other parts of the United States somewhat more retardation than the average. The children born abroad have a very high percentage of retardation. Furthermore, among children born in the United States but not in Haverhill, those who attended school elsewhere have a high rate of retardation. These are the pupils whose schooling has been interrupted by the change of residence. On the other hand, those children born outside of Haverhill but who never attended school elsewhere have a low percentage of retardation, but little in excess of that for the pupils born in Haverhill. These are for the most part children who were too young to go to school when the change of residence took place.

The relation which exists between the age of the child when he enters school and the amount of retardation is clearly shown in the following figures. Among the children who entered at the age of 5 years very few (6.7 per cent) are retarded. Those who entered at the age of 6 years have nearly doubled as large a proportion of retarded ones, but the ratio is still somewhat below the average. On the other hand the children who entered at 7 years have one-third retarded, and the proportion is even larger for those who were still older when they first entered school. The normal course of schooling is for children to enter the schools young and begin at the first grade. Hence we find among those who began at the first grade somewhat less retardation than the average. Those who entered at a higher point in the school system have generally a very much higher proportion of retarded children. As has already been indicated, these are not the peculiarly gifted ones, but more frequently children who, having commenced in private, parochial, or foreign schools, enter the public schools of the United States comparatively late, and are not at the time of entering as far advanced as children of the same ages who began their school work at the beginning of the public school course.

A series of figures gives the relation between the number of years passed in the school and retardation. It might be expected that none of the children who had been in school a shorter time than their grades indicate would be retarded. This would be the case if this number represented wholly the brighter pupils who, entering at the usual time, had traversed the grades more rapidly than the school plan contemplated. But this is not the case, as the group contains other elements. The foreign child of 10 years of age who is entered for the first time in the second grade is retarded, though he is in his first year in the public schools. The same would be true of a sickly or invalid child of the same age, who had received some training at home, and who upon entering his first year at school was placed in the second grade. Among those who had been in school the same number of years as the school plan contemplated, the percentage of retardation is very small. Here we have a few cases of where the children are, by the terms of the definition, retarded from the start. Much larger is the percentage of retardation among those who have been in school more years than the grades indicate. All of them have failed at some time, and were it not for the strictly technical definition given to retardation 100 per cent might be regarded as backward. But this technical definition has an element as it were of generosity, since it does not reckon a child as retarded, even though he fails, unless such failure makes his age distinctly inappropriate to the grade in which he is found. If, as the table indicates, as many as 972 have failed, the failure is condoned, as it were, in nearly three-fourths of the cases.

Another series of figures relates to the pupils having foreign fathers. They show that children of fathers who have been less than five years in the United States are for the most part retarded. Where the fathers have been from five to nine years in this country the proportion, still large, is only half as great as for those of shorter residence. When the fathers have been here more than ten years the children show only average retardation. Similarly the children of naturalized fathers have average retardation, those of alien fathers a considerably higher retardation. Among the pupils of fathers speaking foreign languages as their native tongue, the per cent of retardation is less than the average where English is used in the home, and much above the average where no English is used. For the much smaller group whose fathers have not learned to speak English over one-half of the children are retarded.

Regular attendance at school promotes regular progress, while irregular attendance breeds retardation. It was not possible in the inquiry to cover the entire school life of each child, but only a small portion of it, that of the term in which the inquiry was made. The results, however, have no significance unless the record of the term was, generally speaking, the counterpart of the longer school history of each child. That it was so representative seems to be indicated by the fact that the percentage of retardation, below the average for the children of excellent attendance records, rises rapidly as groups are reached whose attendance deteriorates. Along the same line are the figures relating to the method of securing access to the present grade. When this was attained by regular advancement the percentage of retardation is less than the average. It rises above the average for the transferred children and forms 40.8 per cent of those who were not promoted.

PUPILS OF THE PAROCHIAL SCHOOLS.

Information was furnished to the Immigration Commission along the lines of the general inquiry concerning 1,737 pupils in the parochial schools of Haverhill. The official directory of the Roman Catholic Church gives as the total enrollment of these schools 1,834. The difference between the figures is not greater than that frequently observed between the total enrollment and the average attendance. Hence these figures can be deemed comprehensive and complete and a satisfactory picture of conditions generally prevailing in the parochial schools of the city.

Divided by grades, these pupils were distributed as follows:

Kindergarten	82	Seventh grade	141
First grade	313	Eighth grade	98
Second grade	241	Ninth grade	56
Third grade	236	First year high school	37
Fourth grade	178		
Fifth grade	193	Total	1,737
Sixth grade	162		

From the first to the second grade there is the customary falling off in numbers. From the second to the seventh grade the diminution in numbers, not always quite regular, is at a lessened rate. But with the eighth grade there is a more marked diminution.

Of all the pupils 1,050, or 60.4 per cent, are in the kindergarten and primary grades.

There are fewer 5-year-old children in the parochial than in the public schools. At 6 years of age there are 155 pupils, and this number increases till it reaches a maximum of 204 at the age of 10 years. It then declines, and at the age of 13 years there are 153 pupils, or almost exactly as many as at the age of 6. There is a falling off to 93 at the age of 14 years and to 51 at the age of 15.

The relation of grades and ages expressed in the now familiar notation of retardation is stated in the following table, which gives for each grade the number of retarded pupils and the percentage which this number is of the total number of pupils:

Grade.	Number in grade.	Retarded pupils.		
		Age.	Number.	Per cent of all pupils.
First	313	8 years and over	46	14.7
Second	241	9 years and over	85	35.3
Third	236	10 years and over	101	42.4
Fourth	178	11 years and over	63	35.4
Fifth	193	12 years and over	60	31.1
Sixth	162	13 years and over	35	21.6
Seventh	141	14 years and over	24	17.0
Eighth	98	15 years and over	15	15.3
Ninth	56	16 years and over	5	8.9
Total	1,618		434	26.8

The comparison of the retarded pupils in all the grades with the whole number of pupils in the schools shows an average retardation of 26.8 per cent. The first grade shows 14.7 per cent of retarded pupils, but the third grade as large a proportion as 42.4 per cent. The ratio then declines, and in the sixth to ninth grades is below the average. It first drops below the average in the sixth grade. A consideration of the figures shows the cause. In the fifth grade there are 133 normal and 60 retarded children, while in the sixth there are 127 normal children, but only 35 who are retarded. In other words, the retarded children leave school, the normal children stay.

Supplementing the last table, the one following gives the retardation among the special class of pupils 10, 11, and 12 years of age:

Age.	Number of pupils of this age.	Normal grade.	Retarded, or below normal grade.	
			Number.	Per cent.
10 years	204	4	64	31.4
11 years	174	5	53	30.5
12 years	195	6	69	35.4
Total	573		186	32.5

The average here noted is very nearly one-third of all the pupils who are undergrade or retarded.

The distribution of pupils in the parochial schools by racial groups and by certain individual races is noted in the following table:

General nativity and race of father of pupil.	Pupils.		General nativity and race of father of pupil.	Pupils.	
	Number.	Per cent.		Number.	Per cent.
Native-born:			Foreign-born—continued:		
White	331	19.1	Irish	540	31.1
Negro	2	0.1	All others	168	9.7
Total native-born	333	19.2	Total foreign-born	1,404	80.8
Foreign-born:			Grand total	1,737	100.0
Canadian, French	696	40.1			

Of all the pupils one-fifth are of native and four-fifths are of foreign origin. Among the latter the French Canadians are most numerous, constituting 40.1 per cent of all the pupils. Most of the remainder in the foreign group are Irish, who form 31.1 per cent of all the pupils. The small group of "all others" is composed of the following: Canadian, other than French (35), Cuban (1), Dutch (1), English (19), German (1), Italian, north (19), Italian, South (5), Japanese (4), Lithuanian (29), Magyar (1), Polish (41), Russian (9), Scotch (2), and Welsh (1).

PUBLIC AND PAROCHIAL SCHOOL PUPILS COMBINED.

A combination of the figures heretofore considered for the public and the parochial schools separately gives a complete junction of the distribution of races among the children of the population at large. A combined table follows:

General nativity and race of father of pupil.	Pupils by schools.			Per cent of all pupils.
	Public schools.	Parochial schools.	Total.	
Native-born:				
White	2,539	331	2,870	47.8
Negro	57	2	59	1.0
Total native-born	2,596	333	2,929	48.8
Foreign-born:				
Canadian, French	245	696	941	15.7
Canadian, Other	312	35	347	5.8
Hebrew, Russian	323		323	5.4
Irish	238	540	778	13.0
All others	550	133	683	11.4
Total foreign-born	1,668	1,404	3,072	51.2
Grand total	4,264	1,737	6,001	100.0

Rather more than one-half of the school children here recorded have foreign fathers and rather less than one-half have native fathers. Over 20 per cent of the children are of Canadian origin, three-fourths of them French and the remainder English. Another large element is the Irish, who form 13 per cent of all the pupils here recorded. It may be noted further that considerably more than one-half the children of French Canadian and of Irish parentage attend the parochial schools.

GENERAL TABLES.

PUBLIC SCHOOL PUPILS: GENERAL INVESTIGATION.

TABLE 1.—*Grade and age—Number of pupils of each age in each grade, by sex.*

BOYS.

Age.	Elementary grades.									Total.
	1.	2.	3.	4.	5.	6.	7.	8	9.	
4 years	5									5
5 years	155	4								159
6 years	133	106	7							246
7 years	18	90	85	7						200
8 years	6	38	100	71	6					221
9 years	2	9	33	91	69	13	2			219
10 years	3	1	14	46	60	67	13			204
11 years		2	5	11	48	73	48	7		194
12 years				15	33	52	75	57	11	243
13 years			1	2	11	24	58	60	43	199
14 years			2	2	4	8	22	49	75	162
15 years				1		3	9	14	26	53
16 years	1				1	1	2	1	11	17
17 years								1	2	3
18 years										
19 years										
20 years or over										
Total	323	250	247	246	232	241	229	189	168	2,125

GIRLS.

Age.	1.	2.	3.	4.	5.	6.	7.	8	9.	Total.
4 years	7									7
5 years	130	8								138
6 years	99	103	7							209
7 years	25	81	103	11	1					221
8 years	3	26	84	114	3					230
9 years	4	6	21	81	66	11	1			190
10 years	1	5	10	40	88	82	19			245
11 years	1	4	5	23	37	83	84	10		247
12 years	1		4	6	13	51	81	75	5	236
13 years		1	1	6	7	24	34	79	63	215
14 years		2	3	2	1	8	16	35	66	133
15 years			1	1	1	2	2	11	39	57
16 years					1		1		5	7
17 years								2	1	3
18 years			1							1
19 years										
20 years or over										
Total	271	236	240	284	218	261	238	212	179	2,139

307

TABLE 1.—*Grade and age—Number of pupils of each age in each grade, by sex*—Contd.

TOTAL.

Age.	Elementary grades.									Total.
	1.	2.	3.	4.	5.	6.	7.	8.	9.	
4 years	12									12
5 years	285	12								297
6 years	232	209	14							455
7 years	43	171	188	18	1					421
8 years	9	64	184	185	9					451
9 years	6	15	54	172	135	24	3			409
10 years	4	6	24	86	148	149	32			449
11 years	1	6	10	34	85	156	132	17		441
12 years	1		4	21	46	103	156	132	16	479
13 years		1	2	8	18	48	92	139	106	414
14 years		2	5	4	5	16	38	84	141	295
15 years			1	2	1	5	11	25	65	110
16 years	1				2	1	3	1	16	24
17 years								3	3	6
18 years				1						1
19 years										
20 years or over										
Total	594	486	487	530	450	502	467	401	347	4,264

TABLE 2.—*Race, sex, and grade—Number of pupils of each sex in each grade, by general nativity and race of father of pupil.*

General nativity and race of father of pupil.	Elementary grades.									Total.
	1.	2.	3.	4.	5.	6.	7.	8.	9.	
Native-born:										
White—										
Male	184	136	147	155	142	147	152	127	106	1,296
Female	123	127	140	164	139	160	133	133	124	1,243
Total	307	263	287	319	281	307	285	260	230	2,539
Negro—										
Male	8	3	2		4	3	4	3	3	30
Female	3	4	3	2	5	3	4	2	1	27
Total	11	7	5	2	9	6	8	5	4	57
Total native-born—										
Male	192	139	149	155	146	150	156	130	109	1.326
Female	126	131	143	166	144	163	137	135	125	1,270
Total	318	270	292	321	290	313	293	265	234	2,596
Foreign-born:										
Armenian—										
Male	2	3	1	2	1			1	1	9
Female	4		1		4		1	1		11
Total	6	3	2	2	5		1	1		20
Canadian, French—										
Male	15	19	21	13	11	10	12	9	6	116
Female	29	17	12	15	14	19	8	8	7	129
Total	44	36	33	28	25	29	20	17	13	245
Canadian, Other—										
Male	22	15	15	19	18	20	12	11	11	143
Female	21	20	17	21	11	22	19	25	13	169
Total	43	35	32	40	29	42	31	36	24	312
English—										
Male	11	9	7	7	6	9	6	4	8	67
Female	5	6	2	13	4	12	10	7	5	64
Total	16	15	9	20	10	21	16	11	13	131
French—										
Male	1		1	2	4			1	1	10
Female	1						2			3
Total	2		1	2	4		2	1	1	13
German—										
Male	1	1	2		1	1	1	1	2	10
Female	4	1	3	1	1	1	2	1	1	14
Total	5	2	5	1	1	2	3	2	3	24

TABLE 2.—*Race, sex, and grade—Number of pupils of each sex in each grade, by general nativity and race of father of pupil—Continued.*

General nativity and race of father of pupil.	Elementary grades.									Total.
	1.	2.	3.	4.	5.	6.	7.	8.	9.	
Foreign-born—Continued.										
Hebrew, Russian—										
Male	30	25	22	16	15	15	14	7	14	158
Female	23	29	19	22	14	17	15	13	13	165
Total	53	54	41	38	29	32	29	20	27	323
Hebrew, Other—										
Male	5	2	1	3	1	3	2	2	1	20
Female	3	1	1	3	1	4	2	2	1	18
Total	8	3	2	6	2	7	4	4	2	38
Irish—										
Male	10	17	10	11	13	16	17	12	9	115
Female	19	10	9	17	12	11	26	9	10	123
Total	29	27	19	28	25	27	43	21	19	238
Italian, North—										
Male	9	4	4	4	7			5	1	34
Female	7		8	7	4	4	3	1	1	35
Total	16	4	12	11	11	4	3	6	2	69
Italian, South—										
Male	17	7	4	5	2	3	4		1	37
Female	11	10	8	3	1	2	2			37
Total	22	17	12	8	3	5	6		1	74
Italian (not specified)—										
Male	7	5	5	3		3				23
Female	8	7	9	11	3	1	3			42
Total	15	12	14	14	3	4	3			65
Scotch—										
Male	2		4	4	2	8	3	2	3	28
Female	3	2	1	2	2	4	5	6		25
Total	5	2	5	6	4	12	8	8	3	53
Swedish—										
Male	2	2			1		1	2		8
Female	1			1		1	1		2	6
Total	3	2		1	1	1	2	2	2	14
Other *a*—										
Male	3	2	1	2	4	3	1	3	2	21
Female	6	2	7	2	4		2	4	1	28
Total	9	4	8	4	8	3	3	7	3	49
Total foreign-born—										
Male	131	111	98	91	86	91	73	59	59	799
Female	145	105	97	118	74	98	101	77	54	869
Total	276	216	195	209	160	189	174	136	113	1,668
Grand total—										
Male	323	250	247	246	232	241	229	189	168	2,125
Female	271	236	240	284	218	261	238	212	179	2,139
Total	594	486	487	530	450	502	467	401	347	4,264

a "Other races" include 5 Danish, 3 Dutch, 3 Greek, 2 Hebrew (German), 2 Hebrew (Polish), 5 Hebrew (Roumanian), 4 Lithuanian, 2 Macedonian, 6 Norwegian, 5 Polish, 1 Roumanian, 2 Russian, 4 Scotch-Irish, 5 Welsh.

The Immigration Commission.

TABLE 3.—*Race, sex, and age, by grade—Number of pupils of each age in each grade, by sex and by general nativity and race of father of pupil.*

KINDERGARTEN.

BOYS.

General nativity and race of father of pupil.	Number of pupils of each age.						Total.
	4.	5.	6.	7.	8.	9.	
Native-born:							
White	202	463	107	17			789
Negro	10	32	20				62
Total native-born	212	495	127	17			851
Foreign-born:							
Bohemian and Moravian		3					3
Canadian, Other	2	1	1				4
Danish	1	3	2				6
English	20	33	10	1			64
Finnish	1		1				2
French	1	3					4
German	56	133	48	5			242
Hebrew, German	17	38	12				67
Hebrew, Polish	3	15	3				21
Hebrew, Roumanian	13	10	8				31
Hebrew, Russian	102	187	93	10		1	393
Hebrew, Other	32	72	18	1			123
Irish	13	19	7	1			40
Italian, North	12	20	9	2			43
Italian, South	127	229	103	6	1		466
Lithuanian		2					2
Magyar	10	18	9				37
Norwegian		2					2
Polish	1	15	8				24
Roumanian	4	5	1				10
Russian	4	17	7	2			30
Scotch	7	9	2	1			19
Slovak	2	3	1				6
Slovenian	2						2
Spanish-American		1					1
Swedish	5	5	1				11
Welsh		1	2				3
Other races *a*		4		1			5
Total foreign-born	435	847	346	30	1	1	1,660
Grand total	647	1,342	473	47	1	1	2,511

a "Other races" includes races having less than 10 representatives in this city and pupils whose race is not reported.

TABLE **3.**—*Race, sex, and age, by grade—Number of pupils of each age in each grade, by sex and by general nativity and race of father of pupil*—Continued.

KINDERGARTEN—Continued.

GIRLS.

General nativity and race of father of pupil.	Number of pupils of each age.						Total.
	4.	5.	6.	7.	8.	9.	
Native-born:							
White.........	188	402	143	12			745
Negro.........	11	33	9				53
Total native-born.........	199	435	152	12			798
Foreign-born:							
Bohemian and Moravian.........	3	2	3				8
Canadian, French.........		1	1				2
Canadian, Other.........		7	1				8
Danish.........	2		1				3
Dutch.........		1	1				2
English.........	17	21	14	1			53
French.........		2					2
German.........	49	137	43	5			234
Hebrew, German.........	21	45	14	2			82
Hebrew, Polish.........	8	17	3				28
Hebrew, Roumanian.........	9	22	10				41
Hebrew, Russian.........	95	182	110	6			393
Hebrew, Other.........	24	54	14	1			93
Irish.........	5	23	7				35
Italian, North.........	22	23	8				53
Italian, South.........	109	210	100	5			424
Lithuanian.........			1				1
Magyar.........	9	33	11				53
Norwegian.........		1					1
Polish.........	2	15	5				22
Roumanian.........			2				2
Russian.........	12	5	5				22
Scotch.........	6	11	6				23
Slovak.........	3	4					7
Swedish.........	1	6	1				8
Welsh.........		1					1
Other races a.........	3	6	1				10
Total foreign-born.........	400	829	362	20			1,611
Grand total.........	599	1,264	514	32			2,401

a "Other races" includes races having less than 10 representatives in this city and pupils whose race is not reported.

TABLE 3.—*Race, sex, and age, by grade—Number of pupils of each age in each grade, by sex and by general nativity and race of father of pupil—Continued.*

KINDERGARTEN—Continued.

TOTAL.

General nativity and race of father of pupil.	Number of pupils of each age.						Total.
	4.	5.	6.	7.	8.	9.	
Native-born:							
White........................	390	865	250	29			1,534
Negro........................	21	65	29				115
Total native-born...........	411	930	279	29			1,649
Foreign-born:							
Bohemian and Moravian........	3	5	3				11
Canadian, French.............		1	1				2
Canadian, Other..............	2	8	2				12
Danish.......................	3	3	3				9
Dutch........................		1	1				2
English......................	37	54	24	2			117
Finnish......................	1		1				2
French.......................	1	5					6
German.......................	105	270	91	10			476
Hebrew, German...............	38	83	26	2			149
Hebrew, Polish...............	11	32	6				49
Hebrew, Roumanian............	22	32	18				72
Hebrew, Russian..............	197	369	203	16		1	786
Hebrew, Other................	56	126	32	2			216
Irish........................	18	42	14	1			75
Italian, North...............	34	43	17	2			96
Italian, South...............	236	439	203	11	1		890
Lithuanian...................		2	1				3
Magyar.......................	19	51	20				90
Norwegian....................		3					3
Polish.......................	3	30	13				46
Roumanian....................	4	5	3				12
Russian......................	16	22	12	2			52
Scotch.......................	13	20	8	1			42
Slovak.......................	5	7	1				13
Slovenian....................	2						2
Spanish-American.............		1					1
Swedish......................	6	11	2				19
Welsh........................		2	2				4
Other races *a*..............	3	10	1	1			15
Total foreign-born..........	835	1,676	708	50	1	1	3,271
Grand total.................	1,246	2,606	987	79	1	1	4,920

a "Other races" includes races having less than 10 representatives in this city and pupils whose race is not reported.

TABLE 3.—*Race, sex, and age, by grade—Number of pupils of each age in each grade, by sex and by general nativity and race of father of pupil—Continued*

FIRST GRADE.

BOYS.

General nativity and race of father of pupil.	Number of pupils of each age.													Total.
	4.	5.	6.	7.	8.	9.	10.	11.	12.	13.	14.	15.	16.	
Native-born:														
White	1	93	76	10	3	1								184
Negro		3	5											8
Total native-born	1	96	81	10	3	1								192
Foreign-born:														
Armenian		2												2
Canadian, French		8	7											15
Canadian, Other		10	11	1										22
English		6	5											11
French		1												1
German				1										1
Hebrew, Russian	3	12	11		1		3							30
Hebrew, Other	1	3				1								5
Irish		6	3	1										10
Italian, North		4	3	1	1									9
Italian, South		2	5	2	1								1	11
Italian (not specified)		3	3	1										7
Scotch		1	1											2
Swedish			1	1										2
Other races a		1	2											3
Total foreign-born	4	59	52	8	3	1	3						1	131
Grand total	5	155	133	18	6	2	3						1	323

GIRLS.

General nativity and race of father of pupil.	Number of pupils of each age.													Total.
	4.	5.	6.	7.	8.	9.	10.	11.	12.	13.	14.	15.	16.	
Native-born:														
White	1	63	45	9	3	1	1							123
Negro		2	1											3
Total native-born	1	65	46	9	3	1	1							126
Foreign-born:														
Armenian			1	3										4
Canadian, French	2	10	13	4										29
Canadian, Other		10	8	3										21
English		3	2											5
French			1											1
German		2	2											4
Hebrew, Russian	2	11	5	3		1			1					23
Hebrew, Other		2	1											3
Irish	2	11	6											19
Italian, North		3	3	1										7
Italian, South		5	4	1		1								11
Italian (not specified)		2	4	1				1						8
Scotch		1	2											3
Swedish		1												1
Other races a		4	1			1								6
Total foreign-born	6	65	53	16		3		1	1					145
Grand total	7	130	99	25	3	4	1	1	1					271

a "Other races" includes races having less than 10 representatives in this city and pupils whose race is not reported.

TABLE 3.—*Race, sex, and age, by grade—Number of pupils of each age in each grade, by sex and by general nativity and race of father of pupil*—Continued.

FIRST GRADE—Continued.

TOTAL.

General nativity and race of father of pupil.	Number of pupils of each age.													Total.
	4.	5.	6.	7.	8.	9.	10.	11.	12.	13.	14.	15.	16.	
Native-born:														
White	2	156	121	19	6	2	1							307
Negro		5	6											11
Total native-born	2	161	127	19	6	2	1							318
Foreign-born:														
Armenian		2	1	3										6
Canadian, French	2	18	20	4										44
Canadian, Other		20	19	4										43
English		9	7											16
French		1	1											2
German		2	2	1										5
Hebrew, Russian	5	23	16	3	1	1	3		1					53
Hebrew, Other	1	5	1			1								8
Irish	2	17	9	1										29
Italian, North		7	6	2	1									16
Italian, South		7	9	3	1	1						1		22
Italian (not specified)		5	7	2				1						15
Scotch		2	3											5
Swedish		1	1	1										3
Other races *a*		5	3	1										9
Total foreign-born	10	124	105	24	3	4	3	1	1			1		276
Grand total	12	285	232	43	9	6	4	1	1			1		594

a "Other races" includes races having less than 10 representatives in this city and pupils whose race is not reported.

SECOND GRADE.

BOYS.

General nativity and race of father of pupil.	Number of pupils of each age.										Total.
	5.	6.	7.	8.	9.	10.	11.	12.	13.	14.	
Native-born:											
White	2	61	50	18	4		1				136
Negro		1	1	1							3
Total native-born	2	62	51	19	4		1				139
Foreign-born:											
Armenian			2	1							3
Canadian, French		9	5	3	1	1					19
Canadian, Other		5	7	2	1						15
English		6		1	2						9
German			1								1
Hebrew, Russian	2	10	7	5			1				25
Hebrew, Other			2								2
Irish		8	7	1	1						17
Italian, North		2	2								4
Italian, South		2	3	2							7
Italian (not specified)		2	1	2							5
Swedish			1	1							2
Other races *a*			1	1							2
Total foreign-born	2	44	39	19	5	1	1				111
Grand total	4	106	90	38	9	1	2				250

a "Other races" includes races having less than 10 representatives in this city and pupils whose race is not reported.

TABLE **3.**—*Race, sex, and age, by grade—Number of pupils of each age in each grade, by sex and by general nativity and race of father of pupil*—Continued.

SECOND GRADE—Continued.

GIRLS.

General nativity and race of father of pupil.	Number of pupils of each age.										Total.
	5.	6.	7.	8.	9.	10.	11.	12.	13.	14.	
Native-born:											
White	3	54	50	12	4	3	1				127
Negro			3	1							4
Total native-born	3	54	53	13	4	3	1				131
Foreign-born:											
Canadian, French		7	4	3	1	1	1				17
Canadian, Other		13	6	1							20
English	1	3	2								6
German		1									1
Hebrew, Russian	4	10	8	3			2		1	1	29
Hebrew, Other			1								1
Irish		5	3	2							10
Italian, South		4	1	4						1	10
Italian (not specified)		3	2		1	1					7
Scotch		1	1								2
Other races *a*		2									2
Total foreign-born	5	49	28	13	2	2	3		1	2	105
Grand total	8	103	81	26	6	5	4		1	2	236

TOTAL.

General nativity and race of father of pupil.	5.	6.	7.	8.	9.	10.	11.	12.	13.	14.	Total.
Native-born:											
White	5	115	100	30	8	3	2				263
Negro		1	4	2							7
Total native-born	5	116	104	32	8	3	2				270
Foreign-born:											
Armenian			2	1							3
Canadian, French		16	9	6	2	2	1				36
Canadian, Other		18	13	3	1						35
English	1	9	2	1	2						15
German		1	1								2
Hebrew, Russian	6	20	15	8			3		1	1	54
Hebrew, Other			3								3
Irish		13	10	3	1						27
Italian, North		2	2								4
Italian, South		6	4	6						1	17
Italian (not specified)		5	3	2	1	1					12
Scotch		1	1								2
Swedish			1	1							2
Other races *a*		2	1	1							4
Total foreign-born	7	93	67	32	7	3	4		1	2	216
Grand total	12	209	171	64	15	6	6		1	2	486

a "Other races" includes races having less than 10 representatives in this city and pupils whose race is not reported.

TABLE **3.**—*Race, sex, and age, by grade—Number of pupils of each age in each grade, by sex and by general nativity and race of father of pupil*—Continued.

THIRD GRADE.

BOYS.

General nativity and race of father of pupil.	Number of pupils of each age.													Total.
	6.	7.	8.	9.	10.	11.	12.	13.	14.	15.	16.	17.	18.	
Native-born:														
White	2	51	64	20	8	2								147
Negro			1	1										2
Total native-born	2	51	65	21	8	2								149
Foreign-born:														
Armenian	1													1
Canadian, French		8	8	3	1		1							21
Canadian, Other	2	8	2	3										15
English		1	5		1									7
French	1													1
German			1	1										2
Hebrew, Russian		8	4	4	1	3		2						22
Hebrew, Other			1											1
Irish	1	3	4	1	1									10
Italian, North		1	3											4
Italian, South			3		1									4
Italian (not specified)		2	2		1									5
Scotch		1	3											4
Other races *a*		1												1
Total foreign-born	5	34	35	12	6	3		1	2					98
Grand total	7	85	100	33	14	5		1	2					247

GIRLS.

General nativity and race of father of pupil.	Number of pupils of each age.													Total.
	6.	7.	8.	9.	10.	11.	12.	13.	14.	15.	16.	17.	18.	
Native-born:														
White	6	68	50	10	2	3	1							140
Negro		2	1											3
Total native-born	6	70	51	10	2	3	1							143
Foreign-born:														
Armenian			1											1
Canadian, French		3	3	2	1			1	1	1				12
Canadian, Other		8	6	2		1								17
English		1					1							2
German		3												3
Hebrew, Russian	1	7	6	1	2		1		1					19
Hebrew, Other		1												1
Irish		4	5											9
Italian, North			4	1	2	1								8
Italian, South		2	2	1	2				1					8
Italian (not specified)			4	3	1			1						9
Scotch			1											1
Other races *a*		3	2	1			1							7
Total foreign-born	1	33	33	11	8	2	3	1	3	1	1			97
Grand total	7	103	84	21	10	5	4	1	3	1	1			240

a "Other races" includes races having less than 10 representatives in this city and pupils whose race is not reported.

TABLE **3.**—*Race, sex, and age, by grade—Number of pupils of each age in each grade, by sex and by general nativity and race of father of pupil*—Continued.

THIRD GRADE—Continued.

TOTAL.

General nativity and race of father of pupil.	Number of pupils of each age.													Total.
	6.	7.	8.	9.	10.	11.	12.	13.	14.	15.	16.	17.	18.	
Native-born:														
White	8	119	114	30	10	5	1							287
Negro		2	2	1										5
Total native-born	8	121	116	31	10	5	1							292
Foreign-born:														
Armenian	1		1											2
Canadian, French		11	11	5	2			1	1	1	1			33
Canadian, Other	2	16	8	5		1								32
English		2	5		1		1							9
French	1													1
German		3	1	1										5
Hebrew, Russian	1	15	10	5	3	3	1		3					41
Hebrew, Other		2												2
Irish	1	7	9	1	1									19
Italian, North		1	7	1	2	1								12
Italian, South		2	5	1	3			1						12
Italian (not specified)		2	6	3	2		1							14
Scotch		2	3											5
Other races *a*		4	2	1			1							8
Total foreign-born	6	67	68	23	14	5	3	2	5	1	1			195
Grand total	14	188	184	54	24	10	4	2	5	1	1			487

a "Other races" includes races having less than 10 representatives in this city and pupils whose race is not reported.

FOURTH GRADE.

BOYS.

General nativity and race of father of pupil.	Number of pupils of each age.									Total.
	7.	8.	9.	10.	11.	12.	13.	14.	15.	
Native-born:										
White	3	52	57	32	7	4				155
Negro										
Total native-born	3	52	57	32	7	4				155
Foreign-born:										
Armenian			1			1				2
Canadian, French	1	2	6	1	1	2				13
Canadian, Other	1	5	5	5	1	1		1		19
English		1	3	2		1				7
French			2							2
Hebrew, Russian	1	5	4	1	1	3			1	16
Hebrew, Other			3							3
Irish	1	4	3	2		1				11
Italian, North			2			1	1			4
Italian, South		1	2		1		1			5
Italian (not specified)			2	1						3
Scotch		1	1	1		1				4
Other races *a*				1				1		2
Total foreign-born	4	19	34	14	4	11	2	2	1	91
Grand total	7	71	91	46	11	15	2	2	1	246

a "Other races" includes races having less than 10 representatives in this city and pupils whose race is not reported.

TABLE 3.—*Race, sex, and age, by grade—Number of pupils of each age in each grade, by sex and by general nativity and race of father of pupil—Continued.*

FOURTH GRADE—Continued.

GIRLS.

General nativity and race of father of pupil.	Number of pupils of each age.									Total.
	7.	8.	9.	10.	11.	12.	13.	14.	15.	
Native-born:										
White	9	66	48	25	10	3	2	1	......	164
Negro	......	1	1	......	......	......	......	......	......	2
Total native-born	9	67	49	25	10	3	2	1	......	166
Foreign-born:										
Canadian, French	......	7	3	2	2	......	1	......	......	15
Canadian, Other	......	8	7	4	1	......	1	......	......	21
English	......	7	3	2	1	......	......	......	......	13
German	......	1	......	......	......	......	......	......	......	1
Hebrew, Russian	......	12	5	3	......	......	1	1	......	22
Hebrew, Other	1	......	......	......	1	1	......	......	......	3
Irish	1	11	3	1	......	1	......	......	......	17
Italian, North	......	......	3	1	1	1	1	......	......	7
Italian, South	......	......	......	......	2	......	......	......	1	3
Italian (not specified)	......	1	6	2	2	......	......	......	......	11
Scotch	......	......	1	......	1	......	......	......	......	2
Swedish	......	......	......	......	1	......	......	......	......	1
Other races *a*	......	......	1	......	1	......	......	......	......	2
Total foreign-born	2	47	32	15	13	3	4	1	1	118
Grand total	11	114	81	40	23	6	6	2	1	284

TOTAL.

General nativity and race of father of pupil.	Number of pupils of each age.									Total.
	7.	8.	9.	10.	11.	12.	13.	14.	15.	
Native-born:										
White	12	118	105	57	17	7	2	1	......	319
Negro	......	1	1	......	......	......	......	......	......	2
Total native-born	12	119	106	57	17	7	2	1	......	321
Foreign-born:										
Armenian	......	......	1	......	......	1	......	......	......	2
Canadian, French	1	9	9	3	3	2	1	......	......	28
Canadian, Other	1	13	12	9	2	1	1	1	......	40
English	......	8	6	4	1	1	......	......	......	20
French	......	......	2	......	......	......	......	......	......	2
German	......	1	......	......	......	......	......	......	......	1
Hebrew, Russian	1	17	9	4	1	3	1	1	1	38
Hebrew, Other	1	......	3	......	1	1	......	......	......	6
Irish	2	15	6	3	......	2	......	......	......	28
Italian, North	......	......	5	1	1	2	2	......	......	11
Italian, South	......	1	2	......	3	......	1	......	1	8
Italian (not specified)	......	1	8	3	2	......	......	......	......	14
Scotch	......	1	2	1	......	1	......	......	......	6
Swedish	......	......	......	......	1	......	......	......	......	1
Other races *a*	......	......	1	1	1	......	......	1	......	4
Total foreign-born	6	66	66	29	17	14	6	3	2	209
Grand total	18	185	172	86	34	21	8	4	2	530

a "Other races" includes races having less than 10 representatives in this city and pupils whose race is not reported.

TABLE **3.**—*Race, sex, and age, by grade—Number of pupils of each age in each grade, by sex and by general nativity and race of father of pupil*—Continued.

FIFTH GRADE.

BOYS.

General nativity and race of father of pupil.	Number of pupils of each age.									Total.
	8.	9.	10.	11.	12.	13.	14.	15.	16.	
Native-born:										
White	4	42	38	32	21	3	2			142
Negro		1	1	1	1					4
Total native-born	4	43	39	33	22	3	2			146
Foreign-born:										
Armenian					1					1
Canadian, French		1	2	3	1	4				11
Canadian, Other		6	4	4	1	2	1			18
English	1	1	3	1						6
French		2			2					4
German				1						1
Hebrew, Russian		5	4	1	3		1		1	15
Hebrew, Other				1						1
Irish	1	7	4			1				13
Italian, North		2	1	2	2					7
Italian, South				1	1					2
Scotch			1	1						2
Swedish			1							1
Other races a		2	1				1			4
Total	2	26	21	15	11	8	2		1	86
Grand total	6	69	60	48	33	11	4		1	232

a "Other races" includes races having less than 10 representatives in this city and pupils whose race is not reported.

GIRLS.

General nativity and race of father of pupil.	Number of pupils of each age.										Total.
	7.	8.	9.	10.	11.	12.	13.	14.	15.	16.	
Native-born:											
White		2	48	54	24	4	5	1	1		139
Negro			1		1	2	1				5
Total native-born		2	49	54	25	6	6	1	1		144
Foreign-born:											
Armenian				3	1						4
Canadian, French			4	4	3	2	1				14
Canadian, Other			3	7	1						11
English			1	2		1					4
Hebrew, Russian	1		4	7		1				1	14
Hebrew, Other					1						1
Irish		1	2	5	3	1					12
Italian, North			1	1	1	1					4
Italian, South				1							1
Italian (not specified)				1	1	1					3
Scotch			1		1						2
Other races a			1	3							4
Total foreign-born	1	1	17	34	12	7	1			1	74
Grand total	1	3	66	88	37	13	7	1	1	1	218

a "Other races" includes races having less than 10 representatives in this city and pupils whose race is not reported.

TABLE **3.**—*Race, sex, and age, by grade—Number of pupils of each age in each grade, by sex and by general nativity and race of father of pupil*—Continued.

FIFTH GRADE—Continued.

TOTAL.

General nativity and race of father of pupil.	Number of pupils of each age.										Total.
	7.	8.	9.	10.	11.	12.	13.	14.	15.	16.	
Native-born:											
White		6	90	92	56	25	8	3	1		281
Negro			2	1	2	3	1				9
Total native-born		6	92	93	58	28	9	3	1		290
Foreign-born:											
Armenian				3	1	1					5
Canadian, French			5	6	6	3	5				25
Canadian, Other			9	11	5	1	2	1			29
English		1	2	5	1	1					10
French			2			2					4
German					1						1
Hebrew, Russian	1		9	11	1	4		1		2	29
Hebrew, Other					2						2
Irish		2	9	9	3	1	1				25
Italian, North			3	2	3	3					11
Italian, South				1	1	1					3
Italian (not specified)				1	1	1					3
Scotch			1	1	2						4
Swedish				1							1
Other races *a*			3	4				1			8
Total foreign-born	1	3	43	55	27	18	9	2		2	160
Grand total	1	9	135	148	85	46	18	5	1	2	450

a "Other races" includes races having less than 10 representatives in this city and pupils whose race is not reported.

SIXTH GRADE.

BOYS.

General nativity and race of father of pupil.	Number of pupils of each age.								Total.
	9.	10.	11.	12.	13.	14.	15.	16.	
Native-born:									
White	7	45	37	33	17	4	3	1	147
Negro	1			1		1			3
Total native-born	8	45	37	34	17	5	3	1	150
Foreign-born:									
Canadian, French		2	5	2	1				10
Canadian, Other	1	6	7	5		1			20
English		2	4	3					9
German		1							1
Hebrew, Russian	2	3	7	2		1			15
Hebrew, Other	1	1	1						3
Irish	1	6	6	1	2				16
Italian, North									
Italian, South			1	1		1			3
Italian (not specified)			1		2				3
Scotch			3	3	2				8
Swedish									
Other races *a*	1	1	1	1					3
Total foreign-born	5	22	36	18	7	3			91
Grand total	13	67	73	52	24	8	3	1	241

a "Other races" includes races having less than 10 representatives in this city and pupils whose race is not reported.

TABLE 3.—*Race, sex, and age, by grade—Number of pupils of each age in each grade, by sex and by general nativity and race of father of pupil—Continued.*

SIXTH GRADE—Continued.

GIRLS.

General nativity and race of father of pupil.	Number of pupils of each age.								Total.
	9.	10.	11.	12.	13.	14.	15.	16.	
Native-born:									
White	6	49	53	33	13	5	1	......	160
Negro	......	2	1	......	......	......	......	......	3
Total native-born	6	51	54	33	13	5	1	......	163
Foreign-born:									
Canadian, French	......	3	5	7	2	2	......	......	19
Canadian, Other	2	8	8	2	1	......	1	......	22
English	1	4	2	3	2	......	......	......	12
German	......	1	......	......	......	......	......	......	1
Hebrew, Russian	......	8	5	3	1	......	......	......	17
Hebrew, Other	......	2	1	......	1	......	......	......	4
Irish	2	2	4	1	1	1	......	......	11
Italian, North	......	2	1	......	1	......	......	......	4
Italian, South	......	......	1	1	......	......	......	......	2
Italian (not specified)	......	......	......	......	1	......	......	......	1
Scotch	......	......	2	1	1	......	......	......	4
Swedish	......	1	......	......	......	......	......	......	1
Other races [a]	......	......	......	......	......	......	......	......	......
Total foreign-born	5	31	29	18	11	3	1	......	98
Grand total	11	82	83	51	24	8	2	......	261

TOTAL.

	9.	10.	11.	12.	13.	14.	15.	16.	Total.
Native-born:									
White	13	94	90	66	30	9	4	1	307
Negro	1	2	1	1	......	1	......	......	6
Total native-born	14	96	91	67	30	10	4	1	313
Foreign-born:									
Canadian, French	......	5	10	9	3	2	......	......	29
Canadian, Other	3	14	15	7	1	1	1	......	42
English	1	6	6	6	2	......	......	......	21
German	......	2	......	......	......	......	......	......	2
Hebrew, Russian	2	11	12	5	1	1	......	......	32
Hebrew, Other	1	3	2	......	1	......	......	......	7
Irish	3	8	10	2	3	1	......	......	27
Italian, North	......	2	1	......	1	......	......	......	4
Italian, South	......	......	2	2	......	1	......	......	5
Italian (not specified)	......	......	1	......	3	......	......	......	4
Scotch	......	......	5	4	3	......	......	......	12
Swedish	......	1	......	......	......	......	......	......	1
Other races [a]	......	1	1	1	......	......	......	......	3
Total foreign-born	10	53	65	36	18	6	1	......	189
Grand total	24	149	156	103	48	16	5	1	502

a "Other races" includes races having less than 10 representatives in this city and pupils whose race is not reported.

TABLE 3.—*Race, sex, and age, by grade—Number of pupils of each age in each grade, by sex and by general nativity and race of father of pupil—*Continued.

SEVENTH GRADE.

BOYS.

General nativity and race of father of pupil.	Number of pupils of each age.								Total.
	9.	10.	11.	12.	13.	14.	15.	16.	
Native-born:									
White........	2	7	37	51	32	18	4	1	152
Negro........				1	1	1	1		4
Total native-born........	2	7	37	52	33	19	5	1	156
Foreign-born:									
Canadian, French........			3	2	4	2		1	12
Canadian, Other........			3	6	3				12
English........			1	1	4				6
German........				1					1
Hebrew, Russian........		2	2	4	4		2		14
Hebrew, Other........					2				2
Irish........		4	2	4	5	1	1		17
Italian, South........					3		1		4
Scotch........				1	2				3
Swedish........					1				1
Other races *a*........				1					1
Total foreign-born........		6	11	23	25	3	4	1	73
Grand total........	2	13	48	75	58	22	9	2	229

GIRLS.

General nativity and race of father of pupil.	Number of pupils of each age.								Total.
	9.	10.	11.	12.	13.	14.	15.	16.	
Native-born:									
White........		6	51	48	20	6	1	1	133
Negro........		1	1	1		1			4
Total native-born........		7	52	49	20	7	1	1	137
Foreign-born:									
Armenian........				1					1
Canadian, French........			2	3	2	1			8
Canadian, Other........		3	6	5	3	1	1		19
English........			5	2	3				10
French........			2						2
German........			1		1				2
Hebrew, Russian........		4	1	6	1	3			15
Hebrew, Other........		1		1					2
Irish........	1	4	10	7	2	2			26
Italian, North........			1	1	1				3
Italian, South........				1		1			2
Italian (not specified)........			1	1	1				3
Scotch........			1	3		1			5
Swedish........				1					1
Other races *a*........			2						2
Total foreign-born........	1	12	32	32	14	9	1		101
Grand total........	1	19	84	81	34	16	2	1	238

a "Other races" includes races having less than 10 representatives in this city and pupils whose race in not reported.

TABLE 3.—*Race, sex, and age, by grade—Number of pupils of each age in each grade, by sex and by general nativity and race of father of pupil*—Continued.

SEVENTH GRADE—Continued.

TOTAL.

General nativity and race of father of pupil.	Number of pupils of each age.								Total.
	9.	10.	11.	12.	13.	14.	15.	16.	
Native-born:									
White	2	13	88	99	52	24	5	2	285
Negro		1	1	2	1	2	1		8
Total native-born	2	14	89	101	53	26	6	2	293
Foreign-born:									
Armenian				1					1
Canadian, French			5	5	6	3		1	20
Canadian, Other		3	9	11	6	1	1		31
English			6	3	7				16
French			2						2
German			1	1	1				3
Hebrew, Russian		6	3	10	5	3	2		29
Hebrew, Other		1		1	2				4
Irish	1	8	12	11	7	3	1		43
Italian, North			1	1	1				3
Italian, South				4		1	1		6
Italian (not specified)			1	1	1				3
Scotch			1	4	2	1			8
Swedish				1	1				2
Other races a			2	1					3
Total foreign-born	1	18	43	55	39	12	5	1	174
Grand total	3	32	132	156	92	38	11	3	467

a "Other races" includes races having less than 10 representatives in this city and pupils whose race is not reported.

EIGHTH GRADE.

BOYS.

General nativity and race of father of pupil.	Number of pupils of each age.							Total.
	11.	12.	13.	14.	15.	16.	17.	
Native-born:								
White	2	40	41	35	7	1	1	127
Negro			2	1				3
Total native-born	2	40	43	36	7	1	1	130
Foreign-born:								
Canadian, French		3	2	1	3			9
Canadian, Other	1	2	3	5				11
English	1	1	2					4
French			1					1
German		1						1
Hebrew, Russian		3	2	1	1			7
Hebrew, Other		1		1				2
Irish	2	4	5	1				12
Italian, North			1	2	2			5
Scotch			1	1				2
Swedish				1	1			2
Other races a	1	2						3
Total foreign-born	5	17	17	13	7			59
Grand total	7	57	60	49	14	1	1	189

a "Other races" includes races having less than 10 representatives in this city and pupils whose race is not reported.

TABLE 3.—*Race, sex, and age, by grade—Number of pupils of each age in each grade, by sex and by general nativity and race of father of pupil—Continued.*

EIGHTH GRADE—Continued.

GIRLS.

General nativity and race of father of pupil.	Number of pupils of each age.							Total.
	11.	12.	13.	14.	15.	16.	17.	
Native-born:								
White	4	46	53	22	8			133
Negro			1				1	2
Total native-born	4	46	54	22	8		1	135
Foreign-born:								
Armenian			1					1
Canadian, French		2	1	3	2			8
Canadian, Other	1	10	8	4	1		1	25
English	1	3	2	1				7
German		1						1
Hebrew, Russian	3	3	4	3				13
Hebrew, Other	1	1						2
Irish		5	4					9
Italian, North				1				1
Scotch		2	3	1				6
Other races a		2	2					4
Total foreign-born	6	29	25	13	3		1	77
Grand total	10	75	79	35	11		2	212

TOTAL.

General nativity and race of father of pupil.	Number of pupils of each age.							Total.
	11.	12.	13.	14.	15.	16.	17.	
Native-born:								
White	6	86	94	57	15	1	1	260
Negro			3	1			1	5
Total native-born	6	86	97	58	15	1	2	265
Foreign-born:								
Armenian			1					1
Canadian, French		5	3	4	5			17
Canadian, Other	2	12	11	9	1		1	36
English	2	4	4	1				11
French			1					1
German		2						2
Hebrew, Russian	3	6	6	4	1			20
Hebrew, Other	1	2		1				4
Irish	2	9	9	1				21
Italian, North			1	3	2			6
Scotch		2	4	2				8
Swedish				1	1			2
Other races a	1	4	2					7
Total foreign-born	11	46	42	26	10		1	136
Grand total	17	132	139	84	25	1	3	401

a "Other races" includes races having less than 10 representatives in this city and pupils whose race is not reported.

TABLE 3.—*Race, sex, and age, by grade—Number of pupils of each age in each grade, by sex and by general nativity and race of father of pupil*—Continued.

NINTH GRADE.

BOYS.

General nativity and race of father of pupil.	Number of pupils of each age.						Total
	12.	13.	14.	15.	16.	17.	
Native-born:							
White	8	27	48	15	8	......	106
Negro			2			1	3
Total native-born	8	27	50	15	8	1	109
Foreign-born:							
Canadian, French	2	3	1				6
Canadian, Other		2	4	3	1	1	11
English			7	1			8
French				1			1
German		2					2
Hebrew, Russian	1	4	6	3			14
Hebrew, Other		1					1
Irish		2	4	2	1		9
Italian, North			1				1
Italian, South					1		1
Scotch		2		1			3
Other races *a*			2				2
Total foreign-born	3	16	25	11	3	1	59
Grand total	11	43	75	26	11	2	168

GIRLS.

General nativity and race of father of pupil.	12.	13.	14.	15.	16.	17.	Total
Native-born:							
White	5	42	42	32	2	1	124
Negro		1					1
Total native-born	5	43	42	32	2	1	125
Foreign born:							
Canadian, French		1	4	2			7
Canadian, Other		6	5	1	1		13
English		1	3	1			5
German			1				1
Hebrew, Russian		4	6	3			13
Hebrew, Other		1					1
Irish		5	4		1		10
Italian, North					1		1
Swedish		1	1				2
Other races *a*		1					1
Total foreign-born		20	24	7	3		54
Grand total	5	63	66	39	5	1	179

a "Other races" includes races having less than 10 representatives in this city and pupils whose race is not reported.

TABLE 3.—*Race, sex, and age, by grade—Number of pupils of each age in each grade, by sex and by general nativity and race of father of pupil*—Continued.

NINTH GRADE—Continued.

TOTAL.

General nativity and race of father of pupil.	Number of pupils of each age.						Total.
	12.	13.	14.	15.	16.	17.	
Native-born:							
White	13	69	90	47	10	1	230
Negro		1	2			1	4
Total native-born	13	70	92	47	10	2	234
Foreign-born:							
Canadian, French	2	4	5	2			13
Canadian, Other		8	9	4	2	1	24
English		1	10	2			13
French				1			1
German		2	1				3
Hebrew, Russian	1	8	12	6			27
Hebrew, Other		2					2
Irish		7	8	2	2		19
Italian, North			1		1		2
Italian, South					1		1
Scotch		2		1			3
Swedish		1	1				2
Other races *a*		1	2				3
Total foreign-born	3	36	49	18	6	1	113
Grand total	16	106	141	65	16	3	347

a "Other races" includes races having less than 10 representatives in this city and pupils whose race is not reported.

TABLE 4.—*Race and grade, by age—Number of pupils of each specified age in each grade, by general nativity and race of father of pupil.*

BOYS: AGE 4 YEARS.

General nativity and race of father of pupil.	Elementary grades.		Total.
	1.	2.	
Native-born, White	1		1
Foreign-born, other races *a*	4		4
Grand total	5		5

a "Other races" includes races having less than 10 representatives of this sex and age and pupils whose race is not reported.

TABLE 4.—*Race and grade, by age—Number of pupils of each specified age in each grade, by general nativity and race of father of pupil*—Continued.

BOYS: AGE 5 YEARS.

General nativity and race of father of pupil.	Elementary grades.		Total.
	1.	2.	
Native-born:			
White	93	2	95
Negro	3		3
Total native-born	96	2	98
Foreign-born:			
Canadian (other than French)	10		10
Hebrew, Russian	12	2	14
Other races *a*	37		37
Total foreign-born	59	2	61
Grand total	155	4	159

a "Other races" includes races having less than 10 representatives of this sex and age and pupils whose race is not reported.

BOYS: AGE 6 YEARS.

General nativity and race of father of pupil.	Elementary grades.			Total.
	1.	2.	3.	
Native-born:				
White	76	61	2	139
Negro	5	1		6
Total native-born	81	62	2	145
Foreign-born:				
Canadian, French	7	9		16
Canadian, Other	11	5	2	18
English	5	6		11
Hebrew, Russian	11	10		21
Irish	3	8	1	12
Other races *a*	15	6	2	23
Total foreign-born	52	44	5	101
Grand total	133	106	7	246

a "Other races" includes races having less than 10 representatives of this sex and age and pupils whose race is not reported.

TABLE 4.—*Race and grade, by age—Number of pupils of each specified age in each grade, by general nativity and race of father of pupil*—Continued.

BOYS: AGE 7 YEARS.

General nativity and race of father of pupil.	Elementary grades.				Total.
	1.	2.	3.	4.	
Native-born:					
White	10	50	51	3	114
Negro		1			1
Total native-born	10	51	51	3	115
Foreign-born:					
Canadian, French		5	8	1	14
Canadian, Other	1	7	8	1	17
Hebrew, Russian		7	8	1	16
Irish	1	7	3	1	12
Other races a	6	13	7		26
Total foreign-born	8	39	34	4	85
Grand total	18	90	85	7	200

a "Other races" includes races having less than 10 representatives of this sex and age and pupils whose race is not reported

BOYS: AGE 8 YEARS.

General nativity and race of father of pupil.	Elementary grades.					Total.
	1.	2.	3.	4.	5.	
Native-born:						
White	3	18	64	52	4	141
Negro		1	1			2
Total native-born	3	19	65	52	4	143
Foreign-born:						
Canadian, French		3	8	2		13
Hebrew, Russian	1	5	4	5		15
Irish		1	4	4	1	10
Other races a	2	10	19	8	1	40
Total foreign-born	3	19	35	19	2	78
Grand total	6	38	100	71	6	221

a "Other races" includes races having less than 10 representatives of this sex and age and pupils whose race is not reported.

BOYS: AGE 9 YEARS.

General nativity and race of father of pupil.	Elementary grades.							Total.
	1.	2.	3.	4.	5.	6.	7.	
Native-born:								
White	1	4	20	57	42	7	2	133
Negro			1		1	1		3
Total native-born	1	4	21	57	43	8	2	136
Foreign-born:								
Canadian, French		1	3	6	1			11
Canadian, Other		1	3	5	6	1		16
Hebrew, Russian			4	4	5	2		15
Irish		1	1	3	7	1		13
Other races a	1	2	1	16	7	1		28
Total foreign-born	1	5	12	34	26	5		83
Grand total	2	9	33	91	69	13	2	219

a "Other races" includes races having less than 10 representatives of this sex and age and pupils whose race is not reported.

TABLE 4.—*Race and grade, by age—Number of pupils of each specified age in each grade, by general nativity and race of father of pupil*—Continued.

BOYS: AGE 10 YEARS.

General nativity and race of father of pupil	Elementary grades.							Total.
	1.	2.	3.	4.	5.	6.	7.	
Native-born:								
White			8	32	38	45	7	130
Negro					1			1
Total native-born			8	32	39	45	7	131
Foreign-born:								
Canadian (other than French)				5	4	6		15
Hebrew, Russian	3		1	1	4	3	2	14
Irish			1	2	4	6	4	17
Other races a		1	4	6	9	7		27
Total foreign-born	3	1	6	14	21	22	6	73
Grand total	3	1	14	46	60	67	13	204

a "Other races" includes races having less than 10 representatives of this sex and age and pupils whose race is not reported.

BOYS: AGE 11 YEARS.

General nativity and race of father of pupil	Elementary grades.							Total.
	2.	3.	4.	5.	6.	7.	8.	
Native-born:								
White	1	2	7	32	37	37	2	118
Negro				1				1
Total native-born	1	2	7	33	37	37	2	119
Foreign-born:								
Canadian, French			1	3	5	3		12
Canadian, Other			1	4	7	3	1	16
Hebrew, Russian	1	3	1	1	7	2		15
Irish					6	2	2	10
Other races a			1	7	11	1	2	22
Total foreign-born	1	3	4	15	36	11	5	75
Grand total	2	5	11	48	73	48	7	194

a "Other races" includes races having less than 10 representatives of this sex and age and pupils whose race is not reported.

BOYS: AGE 12 YEARS.

General nativity and race of father of pupil	Elementary grades.						Total.
	4.	5.	6.	7.	8.	9.	
Native-born:							
White	4	21	33	51	40	8	157
Negro		1	1	1			3
Total native-born	4	22	34	52	40	8	160
Foreign-born:							
Canadian, French	2	1	2	2	3	2	12
Canadian, Other	1	1	5	6	2		15
Hebrew, Russian	3	3	2	4	3	1	16
Irish	1		1	4	4		10
Other races a	4	6	8	7	5		30
Total foreign-born	11	11	18	23	17	3	83
Grand total	15	33	52	75	57	11	243

a "Other races" includes races having less than 10 representatives of this sex and age and pupils whose race is not reported.

TABLE **4.**—*Race and grade, by age*—*Number of pupils of each specified age in each grade, by general nativity and race of father of pupil*—Continued.

BOYS: AGE 13 YEARS.

General nativity and race of father of pupil.	Elementary grades.							Total.
	3.	4.	5.	6.	7.	8.	9.	
Native-born:								
White....			3	17	32	41	27	120
Negro....					1	2		3
Total native-born....			3	17	33	43	27	123
Foreign-born:								
Canadian, French....	1		4	1	4	2	3	15
Canadian, Other....			2		3	3	2	10
Hebrew, Russian....					4	2	4	10
Irish....			1	2	5	5	2	15
Other races *a*		2	1	4	9	5	5	26
Total foreign-born....	1	2	8	7	25	17	16	76
Grand total....	1	2	11	24	58	60	43	199

a "Other races" includes races having less than 10 representatives of this sex and age and pupils whose race is not reported.

BOYS: AGE 14 YEARS.

	3.	4.	5.	6.	7.	8.	9.	Total.
Native-born:								
White			2	4	18	35	48	107
Negro....				1	1	1	.2	5
Total native-born....			2	5	19	36	50	112
Foreign-born:								
Canadian (other than French)....		1	1	1		5	4	12
Hebrew, Russian....	2		1	1		1	6	11
Other races *a*		1		1	3	7	15	27
Total foreign-born....	2	2	2	3	3	13	25	50
Grand total....	2	2	4	8	22	49	75	162

a "Other races" includes races having less than 10 representatives of this sex and age and pupils whose race is not reported.

BOYS: AGE 15 YEARS.

General nativity and race of father of pupil.	Elementary grades.						Total.
	4.	5.	6.	7.	8.	9.	
Native-born:							
White....			3	4	7	15	29
Negro....				1			1
Total native-born....			3	5	7	15	30
Foreign-born, other races *a*	1			4	7	11	23
Grand total....	1		3	9	14	26	53

a "Other races" includes races having less than 10 representatives of this sex and age and pupils whose race is not reported.

TABLE 4.—*Race and grade, by age—Number of pupils of each specified age in each grade, by general nativity and race of father of pupil—Continued.*

BOYS: AGE 16 YEARS.

General nativity and race of father of pupil.	Elementary grades.									Total.
	1.	2.	3.	4.	5.	6.	7.	8.	9.	
Native-born, White						1	1	1	8	11
Foreign-born, other races a	1				1		1		3	6
Total	1				1	1	2	1	11	17

a "Other races" includes races having less than 10 representatives of this sex and age and pupils whose race is not reported.

BOYS: AGE 17 YEARS.

General nativity and race of father of pupil.	Elementary grades.		Total.
	8.	9.	
Native-born:			
White	1		1
Negro		1	1
Total native-born	1	1	2
Foreign-born, other races a		1	1
Grand total	1	2	3

a "Other races" includes races having less than 10 representatives of this sex and age and pupils whose race is not reported.

GIRLS: AGE 4 YEARS.

General nativity and race of father of pupil.	Elementary grade 1.
Native-born, White	1
Foreign-born, other races a	6
Total	7

a "Other races" includes races having less than 10 representatives of this sex and age and pupils whose race is not reported.

GIRLS: AGE 5 YEARS.

General nativity and race of father of pupil.	Elementary grade.		Total.
	1.	2.	
Native-born:			
White	63	3	66
Negro	2		2
Total native-born	65	3	68
Foreign-born:			
Canadian, French	10		10
Canadian, Other	10		10
Hebrew, Russian	11	4	15
Irish	11		11
Other races a	23	1	24
Total foreign-born	65	5	70
Grand total	130	8	138

a "Other races" includes races having less than 10 representatives of this sex and age and pupils whose race is not reported.

TABLE 4.—*Race and grade, by age—Number of pupils of each specified age in each grade, by general nativity and race of father of pupil*—Continued.

GIRLS: AGE 6 YEARS.

General nativity and race of father of pupil.	Elementary grades.			Total.
	1.	2.	3.	
Native-born:				
White	45	54	6	105
Negro	1			1
Total native-born	46	54	6	106
Foreign-born:				
Canadian, French	13	7		20
Canadian, Other	8	13		21
Hebrew, Russian	5	10	1	16
Irish	6	5		11
Other races a	21	14		35
Total foreign-born	53	49	1	103
Grand total	99	103	7	209

a "Other races" includes races having less than 10 representatives of this sex and age and pupils whose race is not reported.

GIRLS: AGE 7 YEARS.

General nativity and race of father of pupil.	Elementary grades.					Total.
	1.	2.	3.	4.	5.	
Native-born:						
White	9	50	68	9		136
Negro		3	2			5
Total native-born	9	53	70	9		141
Foreign-born:						
Canadian, French	4	4	3			11
Canadian, Other	3	6	8			17
Hebrew, Russian	3	8	7		1	19
Other races a	6	10	15	2		33
Total foreign-born	16	28	33	2	1	80
Grand total	25	81	103	11	1	221

a "Other races" includes races having less than 10 representatives of this sex and age and pupils whose race is not reported.

TABLE **4.**—*Race and grade, by age—Number of pupils of each specified age in each grade, by general nativity and race of father of pupil*—Continued.

GIRLS: AGE 8 YEARS.

| General nativity and race of father of pupil. | Elementary grades. | | | | | Total. |
	1.	2.	3.	4.	5.	
Native-born:						
White.................................	3	12	50	66	2	133
Negro.................................	....	1	1	1	....	3
Total native-born...................	3	13	51	67	2	136
Foreign-born:						
Canadian, French...................	....	3	3	7	....	13
Canadian, Other....................	....	1	6	8	....	15
Hebrew, Russian....................	....	3	6	12	....	21
Irish.................................	....	2	5	11	1	19
Other races a.......................	....	4	13	9	....	26
Total foreign-born..................	....	13	33	47	1	94
Grand total........................	3	26	84	114	3	230

a "Other races" includes races having less than 10 representatives of this sex and age and pupils whose race is not reported.

GIRLS: AGE 9 YEARS.

| General nativity and race of father of pupil. | Elementary grades. | | | | | | | Total. |
	1.	2.	3.	4.	5.	6.	7.	
Native-born:								
White.................................	1	4	10	48	48	6	....	117
Negro.................................	....	....	....	1	1	....	....	2
Total native-born...................	1	4	10	49	49	6	....	119
Foreign-born:								
Canadian, French...................	....	1	2	3	4	....	....	10
Canadian, Other....................	....	....	2	7	3	2	....	14
Hebrew, Russian....................	1	....	1	5	4	....	....	11
Italian (not specified).............	....	1	3	6	....	....	....	10
Other races a.......................	2	....	3	11	6	3	1	26
Total foreign-born..................	3	2	11	32	17	5	1	71
Grand total........................	4	6	21	81	66	11	1	190

a "Other races" includes races having less than 10 representatives of this sex and age and pupils whose race is not reported.

TABLE **4.**—*Race and grade, by age—Number of pupils of each specified age in each grade, by general nativity and race of father of pupil*—Continued.

GIRLS: AGE 10 YEARS.

General nativity and race of father of pupil.	Elementary grades.							Total.
	1.	2.	3.	4.	5.	6.	7.	
Native-born:								
White.................	1	3	2	25	54	49	6	140
Negro.................						2	1	3
Total native-born..............	1	3	2	25	54	51	7	143
Foreign-born:								
Canadian, French..............		1	1	2	4	3	....	11
Canadian, Other..............			....	4	7	8	3	22
Hebrew, Russian..............			2	3	7	8	4	24
Irish..........................		....	....	1	5	2	4	12
Other races *a*..............		1	5	5	11	10	1	33
Total foreign-born..............	....	2	8	15	34	31	12	102
Grand total...................	1	5	10	40	88	82	19	245

a "Other races" includes races having less than 10 representatives of this sex and age and pupils whose race is not reported.

GIRLS: AGE 11 YEARS.

General nativity and race of father of pupil.	Elementary grades.								Total.
	1.	2.	3.	4.	5.	6.	7.	8.	
Native-born:									
White...........	......	1	3	10	24	53	51	4	146
Negro..........	......	......	......	......	1	1	1	......	3
Total native-born...............	......	1	3	10	25	54	52	4	149
Foreign-born:									
Canadian, French..............	......	1	......	2	3	5	2	......	13
Canadian, Other..............	......	......	1	1	1	8	6	1	18
Hebrew, Russian..............	......	2	......	......	......	5	1	3	11
Irish..........................	......	......	......	......	3	4	10	......	17
Other races *a*..............	1	......	1	10	5	7	13	2	39
Total foreign-born...................	1	3	2	13	12	29	32	6	98
Grand total.....	1	4	5	23	37	83	84	10	247

a "Other races" includes races having less than 10 representatives of this sex and age and pupils whose race is not reported.

TABLE **4.**—*Race and grade, by age—Number of pupils of each specified age in each grade, by general nativity and race of father of pupil*—Continued.

GIRLS: AGE 12 YEARS.

General nativity and race of father of pupil.	Elementary grades.									Total.
	1.	2.	3.	4.	5.	6.	7.	8.	9.	
Native-born:										
White......	......	......	1	3	4	33	48	46	5	140
Negro......	......	......	......	......	2	......	1	......	......	3
Total native-born......	......	......	1	3	6	33	49	46	5	143
Foreign-born:										
Canadian, French......	......	......	......	......	2	7	3	2	......	14
Canadian, Other......	......	......	......	......	......	2	5	10	......	17
English......	......	......	1	......	1	3	2	3	......	10
Hebrew, Russian......	1	......	1	......	1	3	6	3	......	15
Irish......	......	......	......	1	1	1	7	5	......	15
Other races *a*......	......	......	1	2	2	2	9	6	......	22
Total foreign-born......	1	......	3	3	7	18	32	29	......	93
Grand total......	1	......	4	6	13	51	81	75	5	236

a"Other races" includes races having less than 10 representatives of this sex and age and pupils whose race is not reported.

GIRLS: AGE 13 YEARS.

General nativity and race of father of pupil.	Elementary grades.								Total.
	2.	3.	4.	5.	6.	7.	8.	9.	
Native-born:									
White......	......	......	2	5	13	20	53	42	135
Negro......	......	......	......	1	......	......	1	1	3
Total native-born......	......	......	2	6	13	20	54	43	138
Foreign-born:									
Canadian (other than French)......	......	......	1	......	1	3	8	6	19
Hebrew, Russian......	1	......	1	......	1	1	4	4	12
Irish......	......	......	......	......	1	2	4	5	12
Other races *a*......	......	1	2	1	8	8	9	5	34
Total foreign-born......	1	1	4	1	11	14	25	20	77
Grand total......	1	1	6	7	24	34	79	63	215

a"Other races" includes races having less than 10 representatives of this sex and age and pupils whose race is not reported.

TABLE **4.**—*Race and grade, by age—Number of pupils of each specified age in each grade, by general nativity and race of father of pupil*—Continued.

GIRLS: AGE 14 YEARS.

General nativity and race of father of pupil.	Elementary grades.								Total.
	2.	3.	4.	5.	6.	7.	8.	9.	
Native-born:									
White			1	1	5	6	22	42	77
Negro						1			1
Total native-born			1	1	5	7	22	42	78
Foreign-born:									
Canadian, French		1			2	1	3	4	11
Canadian, Other						1	4	5	10
Hebrew, Russian	1	1	1			3	3	6	15
Other races *a*	1	1			1	4	3	9	19
Total foreign-born	2	3	1		3	9	13	24	55
Grand total	2	3	2	1	8	16	35	66	133

a "Other races" includes races having less than 10 representatives of this sex and age and pupils whose race is not reported.

GIRLS: AGE 15 YEARS.

General nativity and race of father of pupil.	Elementary grades.							Total.
	3.	4.	5.	6.	7.	8.	9.	
Native-born, White			1	1	1	8	32	43
Foreign-born, other races *a*	1	1		1	1	3	7	14
Total	1	1	1	2	2	11	39	57

a "Other races" includes races having less than 10 representatives of this sex and age and pupils whose race is not reported.

GIRLS: AGE 16 YEARS.

General nativity and race of father of pupil.	Elementary grades.					Total.
	5.	6.	7.	8.	9.	
Native-born, White			1		2	3
Foreign-born, other races *a*	1				3	4
Total	1		1		5	7

a "Other races" includes races having less than 10 representatives of this sex and age and pupils whose race is not reported.

GIRLS: AGE 17 YEARS.

General nativity and race of father of pupil.	Elementary grades.		Total.
	8.	9.	
Native-born:			
White		1	1
Negro	1		1
Total native-born	1	1	2
Foreign-born, other races *a*	1		1
Grand total	2	1	3

a "Other races" includes races having less than 10 representatives of this sex and age and pupils whose race is not reported.

TABLE 4.—*Race and grade, by age—Number of pupils of each specified age in each grade, by general nativity and race of father of pupil*—Continued.

GIRLS: AGE 18 YEARS.

General nativity and race of father of pupil.	Elementary grade.
Foreign-born, other races *a*	1

a "Other races" includes races having less than 10 representatives of this sex and age and pupils whose race is not reported.

TABLE 5.—*Race distribution in each grade—Percentages.*

[This table shows in detail only races with 100 or more pupils reporting. The totals, however, are for all races.]

General nativity and race of father of pupil.	Elementary grades.									Total.
	1.	2.	3.	4.	5.	6.	7.	8.	9.	
Native-born:										
White....................	51.7	54.1	58.9	60.2	62.4	61.2	61.0	64.8	66.3	59.5
Negro....................	1.9	1.4	1.0	.4	2.0	1.2	1.7	1.2	1.2	1.3
Total native-born.......	53.5	55.6	60.0	60.6	64.4	62.4	62.7	66.1	67.4	60.9
Foreign-born:										
Canadian, French.........	7.4	7.4	6.8	5.3	5.6	5.8	4.3	4.2	3.7	5.7
Canadian, Other..........	7.2	7.2	6.6	7.5	6.4	8.4	6.6	9.0	6.9	7.3
English.................	2.7	3.1	1.8	3.8	2.2	4.2	3.4	2.7	3.7	3.1
Hebrew, Russian.........	8.9	11.1	8.4	7.2	6.4	6.4	6.2	5.0	7.8	7.6
Irish...................	4.9	5.6	3.9	5.3	5.6	5.4	9.2	5.2	5.5	5.6
Other races.............	15.3	10.1	12.5	10.4	9.3	7.6	7.5	7.7	4.9	9.8
Total foreign-born.......	46.5	44.4	40.0	39.4	35.6	37.6	37.3	33.9	32.6	39.1
Grand total.............	100.0	100.0	100.0	100.0	100.0	100.0	100.0	100.0	100.0	100.0

TABLE 6.—*Grade distribution of each race—Percentages.*

[This table shows in detail only races with 100 or more pupils reporting. The totals, however, are for all races.]

General nativity and race of father of pupil.	Elementary grades.									Total.
	1.	2.	3.	4.	5.	6.	7.	8.	9.	
Native-born:										
White...................	12.1	10.4	11.3	12.6	11.1	12.1	11.2	10.2	9.1	100.0
Negro...................	19.3	12.3	8.8	3.5	15.8	10.5	14.0	8.8	7.0	100.0
Total native-born.......	12.2	10.4	11.2	12.4	11.2	12.1	11.3	10.2	9.0	100.0
Foreign-born:										
Canadian, French........	18.0	14.7	13.5	11.4	10.2	11.8	8.2	6.9	5.3	100.0
Canadian, Other.........	13.8	11.2	10.3	12.8	9.3	13.5	9.9	11.5	7.7	100.0
English.................	12.2	11.5	6.9	15.3	7.6	16.0	12.2	8.4	9.9	100.0
Hebrew, Russian.........	16.4	16.7	12.7	11.8	9.0	9.9	9.0	6.2	8.4	100.0
Irish...................	12.2	11.3	8.0	11.8	10.5	11.3	18.1	8.8	8.0	100.0
Other races.............	21.7	11.7	14.6	13.1	10.0	9.1	8.4	7.4	4.1	100.0
Total foreign-born......	16.5	12.9	11.7	12.5	9.6	11.3	10.4	8.2	6.8	100.0
Grand total.............	13.9	11.4	11.4	12.4	10.6	11.8	11.0	9.4	8.1	100.0

PUBLIC SCHOOL PUPILS: INTENSIVE INVESTIGATION.

TABLE 1.—*Birthplace of pupils, by general nativity and race of father.*

General nativity and race of father of pupil.	Born in Haverhill. Number.	Pupils 8 years of age or over. Number.	Number retarded.	Born elsewhere in United States. Number.	Pupils 8 years of age or over. Number.	Number retarded.	Born abroad. Number.	Pupils 8 years of age or over. Number.	Number retarded.	Total reporting complete data. Number.	Pupils 8 years of age or over. Number.	Number retarded.	Not reporting complete data. Number.	Pupils 8 years of age or over. Number.	Number retarded.
Native-born:															
White	1,797	1,319	126	671	524	74				2,468	1,843	200	71	39	5
Negro	37	26	6	15	11	3				52	37	9	5	2	1
Total native-born	1,834	1,345	132	686	535	77				2,520	1,880	209	76	41	6
Foreign-born:															
English speaking races—															
Canadian (other than French)	201	138	9	66	33	7	37	31	5	304	215	21	8	4	
English	72	55	2	39	26	7	16	10		127	98	9	4	3	
Irish	193	144	13	31	14	1	3	1	1	227	171	15	11	5	1
Scotch	29	25	1	15	1	3	8	5	2	52	44	6	1		
Other races	6	4		1			2	2		9	7				
Total	501	366	25	152	120	18	66	49	8	719	535	51	24	12	1
Non-English-speaking races—															
Canadian, French	195	133	25	30	18	7	12	8	4	237	159	36	8	5	3
Hebrew, Russian	172	114	3	49	29	2	94	70	37	315	213	42	8	4	1
Italian, North	41	27	6	12	9	4	12	10	6	65	46	16	4	3	
Italian, South	39	17	5	11	7	2	18	17	11	68	41	18	6	2	
Italian (not specified)	45	26	6	8	6	1	12	9	5	65	41	12			
Other races	70	46	2	38	25	3	31	21	9	139	92	14	10	5	1
Total	562	363	47	148	94	19	179	135	72	889	592	138	36	19	5
Total foreign-born	1,063	729	72	300	214	37	245	184	80	1,608	1,127	189	60	31	6
Grand total	2,897	2,074	204	986	749	114	245	184	80	4,128	3,007	398	136	72	12

TABLE 2.—*School attendance of pupils born in the United States but elsewhere than in Haverhill, by general nativity and race of father.*

General nativity and race of father of pupil.	Having attended school elsewhere.			Not having attended school elsewhere.			Total reporting complete data.			Not reporting complete data.		
	Number.	Pupils 8 years of age or over — Number.	Number retarded.	Number.	Pupils 8 years of age or over — Number.	Number retarded.	Number.	Pupils 8 years of age or over — Number.	Number retarded.	Number.	Pupils 8 years of age or over — Number.	Number retarded.
Native-born:												
White.	328	295	55	329	217	18	657	512	73	14	12	1
Negro.	6	6	1	9	5	2	15	11	3			
Total native-born.	334	301	56	338	222	20	672	523	76	14	12	1
Foreign-born:												
English-speaking races—												
Canadian (other than French).	28	23	3	36	21	4	64	44	7	2	2	
English.	22	20	5	16	12	2	38	32	7	1	1	
Irish.	14	13		17	13	1	31	26	1			
Scotch.	8	8	1	7	6	2	15	14	3			
Other, races.	1	1					1	1				
Total.	73	65	9	76	52	9	149	117	18	3	3	
Non-English speaking races:												
Canadian, French.	13	11	5	17	7	2	30	18	7			
Hebrew, Russian.	18	13	1	31	16	1	49	29	2			
Italian, North.	9	8	4	3	1		12	9	4			
Italian, South.	1	1		10	6	2	11	7	2			
Italian (not specified).	1	1	1	7	5		8	6	1			
Other races.	11	11	2	27	14	1	38	25	3			
Total.	53	45	13	95	49	6	148	94	19			
Total foreign-born.	126	110	22	171	101	15	297	211	37	3	3	
Grand total.	460	411	78	509	323	35	969	734	113	17	15	1

TABLE 3.—*Age of foreign-born pupils at time of arrival in the United States, by race of father.*

Race of father of pupil.	Under 6 years.			6 or 7 years.			8 or 9 years.			10 years or over.			Total reporting complete data.			Not reporting complete data.		
	Number.	Pupils 8 years of age or over.		Number.	Pupils 8 years of age or over.		Number.	Pupils 8 years of age or over.		Number.	Pupils 8 years of age or over.		Number.	Pupils 8 years of age or over.		Number.	Pupils 8 years of age or over.	
		Number.	Number retarded.		Number.	Number retarded.		Number.	Number retarded.		Number.	Number retarded.		Number.	Number retarded.		Number.	Number retarded.
Hebrew, Russian	42	20	....	16	15	5	19	19	16	16	16	16	93	70	37	1	....	....
Other races	87	53	10	19	18	10	16	16	7	24	24	16	146	111	43	5	....	3
Total	129	73	10	35	33	15	35	35	23	40	40	32	239	181	80	6	....	3

TABLE 4.—*School attendance abroad of foreign-born pupils who were 6 years of age or over at time of arrival in the United States, by race of father.*

Race of father of pupil.	Having attended school abroad.			Not having attended school abroad.			Total reporting complete data.			Not reporting complete data.		
	Number.	Pupils 8 years of age or over.		Number.	Pupils 8 years of age or over.		Number.	Pupils 8 years of age or over.		Number.	Pupils 8 years of age or over.	
		Number.	Number retarded.		Number.	Number retarded.		Number.	Number retarded.		Number.	Number retarded.
Hebrew, Russian	22	22	16	29	28	21	51	50	37	....	....	....
Other races	44	43	23	13	13	9	57	56	32	2	2	1
Total	66	65	39	42	41	30	108	106	69	2	2	1

TABLE 5.—*Age of pupils at time of entering public school in the United States, by general nativity and race of father.*

[The data refer to age at entering grades and not kindergarten.]

General nativity and race of father of pupil.	5 years or under.			6 years.			7 years.			8 years.		
	Number.	Pupils 8 years of age or over.		Number.	Pupils 8 years of age or over.		Number.	Pupils 8 years of age or over.		Number.	Pupils 8 years of age or over.	
		Number.	Number retarded.		Number.	Number retarded.		Number.	Number retarded.		Number.	Number retarded.
Native-born:												
White	1,682	1,179	77	612	498	63	124	112	36	23	23	10
Negro	30	18	3	18	14	3	5	5	4			
Total native-born	1,712	1,197	80	630	512	66	129	117	40	23	23	10
Foreign-born:												
English-speaking races—												
Canadian (other than French)	189	120	6	75	58	5	22	21	5	2	2	1
English	88	68		22	16	3	10	9	5	2	2	
Irish	169	121	7	30	23	5	10	7	1	5	5	
Scotch	32	27	3	11	8		5	5	2	1	1	
Other races	7	5		1	1					1	1	1
Total	485	341	16	139	106	13	47	42	13	11	11	2
Non-English-speaking races—												
Canadian, French	154	99	13	46	29	7	14	13	6	8	8	3
Hebrew, Russian	191	110	2	66	49	3	9	7	1	10	10	5
Italian, North	32	19	3	20	18	5				4	4	4
Italian, South	39	18	6	12	8		4	3	3	3	3	2
Italian (not specified)	26	12	1	21	14	3	5	5	1	1	1	1
Other races	98	61	4	25	18	2	7	6		4	4	3
Total	540	319	29	190	136	20	39	34	11	30	30	18
Total foreign-born	1,025	660	45	329	242	33	86	76	24	41	41	20
Grand total	2,737	1,857	125	959	754	99	215	193	64	64	64	30

TABLE 5.—*Age of pupils at time of entering public school in the United States, by general nativity and race of father*—Continued.

General nativity and race of father of pupil	9 years.			10 years or over.			Total reporting complete data.			Not reporting complete data.		
	Number.	Pupils 8 years of age or over.		Number.	Pupils 8 years of age or over.		Number.	Pupils 8 years of age or over.		Number.	Pupils 8 years of age or over.	
		Number.	Number retarded.		Number.	Number retarded.		Number.	Number retarded.		Number.	Number retarded.
Native-born:												
White	10	10	3	15	15	1	2,466	1,837	190	73	45	15
Negro							53	37	10	4	2	
Total native-born	10	10	3	15	15	1	2,519	1,874	200	77	47	15
Foreign-born:												
English-speaking races—												
Canadian (other than French)	1	1		7	7		296	209	19	16	10	2
English	1	1		4	4	2	127	100	8	4	1	1
Irish	4	4		11	11		229	171	14	9	5	2
Scotch	1	1		2	2	1	52	44	6	1		
Other races							9	7				
Total	7	7		24	24	3	713	531	47	30	16	5
Non-English-speaking races—												
Canadian, French	2	2	2	8	8	4	232	159	35	13	5	4
Hebrew, Russian	7	7	4	25	25	24	308	208	39	15	9	4
Italian, North	1	1	1	1	1	1	58	43	14	11	6	2
Italian, South	2	2	1	6	6	6	66	40	18	8	3	
Italian (not specified)	3	3	2	3	3	2	59	38	10	6	3	2
Other races	2	2	2	6	6	4	142	97	15	7		
Total	17	17	12	49	49	41	865	585	131	60	26	12
Total foreign-born	24	24	12	73	73	44	1,578	1,116	178	90	42	17
Grand total	34	34	15	88	88	45	4,097	2,990	378	167	89	32

TABLE 6.—*Age of pupils at time of entering public school in the United States, by race of father (foreign-born pupils only).*

Race of father of pupil.	5 years or under.			6 years.			7 years.			8 years.		
	Number.	Pupils 8 years of age or over.		Number.	Pupils 8 years of age or over.		Number.	Pupils 8 years of age or over.		Number.	Pupils 8 years of age or over.	
		Number.	Number retarded.		Number.	Number retarded.		Number.	Number retarded.		Number.	Number retarded.
Hebrew, Russian	27	12	......	11	7	......	6	4	1	10	10	5
Other races	43	26	4	32	18	......	12	11	4	13	13	10
Total	70	38	4	43	25	......	18	15	5	23	23	15

Race of father of pupil.	9 years.			10 years or over.			Total reporting complete data.			Not reporting complete data.		
	Number.	Pupils 8 years of age or over.		Number.	Pupils 8 years of age or over.		Number.	Pupils 8 years of age or over.		Number.	Pupils 8 years of age or over.	
		Number.	Number retarded.		Number.	Number retarded.		Number.	Number retarded.		Number.	Number retarded.
Hebrew, Russian	7	7	4	25	25	24	86	65	34	8	5	3
Other races	9	9	5	29	29	16	138	106	39	13	8	4
Total	16	16	9	54	54	40	224	171	73	21	13	7

TABLE 7.—*Grade entered by pupils, by general nativity and race of father.*

[The data refer to grade entered in public school. No account is taken of entrance into kindergarten.]

General nativity and race of father of pupil.	First grade.			Second grade.			Third grade.			Fourth grade.		
	Number.	Pupils 8 years of age or over.		Number.	Pupils 8 years of age or over.		Number.	Pupils 8 years of age or over.		Number.	Pupils 8 years of age or over.	
		Number.	Number retarded.		Number.	Number retarded.		Number.	Number retarded.		Number.	Number retarded.
Native-born:												
White	2,333	1,718	178	53	49	8	10	9	1	16	16	1
Negro	47	32	10	2	2							
Total native-born	2,380	1,750	188	55	51	8	10	9	1	16	16	1
Foreign-born:												
English-speaking races—												
Canadian (other than French)	281	196	17	5	5	1	2	2		5	5	2
English	119	91	8	1	1		1	1		2	2	
Irish	206	147	15	2	2		6	6		4	4	
Scotch	44	36	5	3	3					1	1	
Other races	8	6		1	1							
Total	658	476	45	12	12	1	9	9		12	12	2
Non-English-speaking races—												
Canadian, French	216	142	29	6	6	2	5	5	4	1	1	
Hebrew, Russian	296	199	33	8	6	4	2	2	1	3	3	3
Italian, North	58	43	14				1	1		1	1	1
Italian, South	65	39	16	2	2	1				1	1	1
Italian (not specified)	57	35	9	2	2	1				1	1	1
Other races	135	87	9	4	3	2	3	3	1	3	3	2
Total	827	545	110	22	18	10	11	11	6	10	10	7
Total foreign-born	1,485	1,021	155	34	30	11	20	20	6	22	22	9
Grand total	3,865	2,771	343	89	81	19	30	29	7	38	38	10

General nativity and race of father of pupil	Fifth grade or above.			Total reporting complete data.			Not reporting complete data.		
	Number.	Pupils 8 years of age or over. Number.	Number retarded.	Number.	Pupils 8 years of age or over. Number.	Number retarded.	Number.	Pupils 8 years of age or over. Number.	Number retarded.
Native-born:									
White	15	15	1	2,427	1,807	189	112	75	16
Negro				49	34	10	8	5	5
Total native-born	15	15	1	2,476	1,841	199	120	80	16
Foreign-born:									
English-speaking races—									
Canadian (other than French)	2	2		295	210	20	17	9	1
English	3	3		126	98	8	5	3	1
Irish	13	13	1	231	172	16	7	4	
Scotch	1	1		49	41	5	4	3	1
Other races				9	7				
Total	19	19	1	710	528	49	33	19	3
Non-English-speaking races—									
Canadian, French	4	4	1	232	158	36	13	6	3
Hebrew, Russian	1	1		310	211	40	13	4	3
Italian, North				60	45	15	9	2	1
Italian, South				68	41	18	6	3	
Italian (not specified)				60	38	11	5	1	1
Other races				145	96	14	4	1	1
Total	5	5	1	875	589	134	50	22	9
Total foreign-born	24	24	2	1,585	1,117	183	83	41	12
Grand total	39	39	3	4,061	2,958	382	203	121	28

TABLE 8.—*Grade entered by pupils, by race of father (foreign-born pupils only).*

[The data refer to grade entered in public school. No account is taken of entrance into kindergarten.]

Race of father of pupil.	First grade.			Second grade.			Third grade.			Fourth grade.			Not reporting complete data.		
		Pupils 8 years of age or over.			Pupils 8 years of age or over.			Pupils 8 years of age or over.			Pupils 8 years of age or over.			Pupils 8 years of age or over.	
	Number.	Number.	Number retarded.	Number.	Number.	Number retarded.	Number.	Number.	Number retarded.	Number.	Number.	Number retarded.	Number.	Number.	Number retarded.
Hebrew, Russian	80	60	30	6	4	3	1	1	......	3	3	3	3	1	1
Other races	116	80	28	8	8	5	6	6	3	12	12	6	4	3	1
Total	196	140	58	14	12	8	7	7	3	15	15	9	7	4	2

Race of father of pupil.	Fifth grade or above.			Total reporting complete data.		
		Pupils 8 years of age or over.			Pupils 8 years of age or over.	
	Number.	Number.	Number retarded.	Number.	Number.	Number retarded.
Hebrew, Russian	......	1	1	91	69	36
Other races	......	5	5	147	111	42
Total	......	6	6	238	180	78

TABLE 9.—*Grade entered by pupils 8 years of age or over at time of entering, by general nativity and race of father.*

[The data refer to grade entered in public school.   No account is taken of entrance into kindergarten.]

General nativity and race of father of pupil.	First grade.	Second grade.	Third grade.	Fourth grade.	Fifth grade.	Sixth grade.	Seventh grade.	Eighth grade.	Total reporting complete data.	Not reporting complete data.
Native-born, White...............	13	9	6	9	2	4	2	2	47	1
Foreign-born:										
English-speaking races—										
Canadian (other than French)...	1	1	1	5	.....	.....	1	1	10	.....
English.....................	1	.....	1	2	.....	2	1	.....	7	.....
Irish......................	.....	.....	4	3	4	2	5	2	20	.....
Scotch....................	1	1	.....	1	1	.....	.....	.....	4	.....
Other races..............	.....	1	.....	.....	.....	.....	.....	.....	1	.....
Total.................	3	3	6	11	5	4	7	3	42	.....
Non-English-speaking races—										
Canadian, French...........	4	4	4	1	1	1	.....	1	16	2
Hebrew, Russian...........	32	4	1	3	1	.....	.....	.....	41	1
Italian, North............	5	.....	1	.....	.....	.....	.....	.....	6	.....
Italian, South............	9	1	.....	1	.....	.....	.....	.....	11	.....
Italian (not specified)........	4	2	.....	1	.....	.....	.....	.....	7	.....
Other races..............	6	2	2	2	.....	.....	.....	.....	12	.....
Total.................	60	13	8	8	2	1	.....	1	93	3
Total foreign-born...........	63	16	14	19	7	5	7	4	135	3
Grand total...............	76	25	20	28	9	9	9	6	182	4

TABLE 10.—*Grade entered by pupils 8 years of age or over at time of entering, by race of father (foreign-born pupils only).*

[The data refer to grade entered in public school.   No account is taken of entrance into kindergarten.]

Race of father of pupil.	First grade.	Second grade.	Third grade.	Fourth grade.	Fifth grade.	Sixth grade.	Seventh grade.	Eighth grade or above.	Total reporting complete data.	Not reporting complete data.
Hebrew, Russian................	32	4	1	3	1	.....	.....	.....	41	1
Other races..................	22	6	6	12	1	2	1	1	51	.....
Total.................	54	10	7	15	2	2	1	1	92	1

TABLE 11.—Rate of progress of pupils and time in school in the United States, by general nativity and race of father.

General nativity and race of father of pupil	Less years than grade — Number	Less — 8 yrs+ Number	Less — 8 yrs+ Retarded	Same years — Number	Same — 8 yrs+ Number	Same — 8 yrs+ Retarded	More years — Number	More — 8 yrs+ Number	More — 8 yrs+ Retarded	Total reporting — Number	Total — 8 yrs+ Number	Total — 8 yrs+ Retarded	Not reporting — Number	Not rep — 8 yrs+ Number	Not rep — 8 yrs+ Retarded
Native-born:															
White	188	154	....	1,497	1,008	24	689	609	151	2,374	1,771	175	165	111	30
Negro	4	4	....	29	18	3	18	15	7	51	37	10	6	2	....
Total native-born	192	158	....	1,526	1,026	27	707	624	158	2,425	1,808	185	171	113	30
Foreign-born:															
English-speaking races—															
Canadian (other than French)	33	31	2	185	114	1	70	62	15	288	207	18	24	12	3
English	12	10	....	73	53	2	37	34	6	122	97	8	9	4	1
Irish	11	11	....	148	102	1	61	52	12	220	165	13	18	11	3
Scotch	4	4	....	24	17	2	20	19	4	48	40	6	5	4	....
Other races	2	2	....	2	2	....	4	3	....	8	7	....	1	....	....
Total	62	58	2	432	288	6	192	170	37	686	516	45	57	31	7
Non-English-speaking races:															
Canadian, French	21	19	6	126	68	2	77	68	27	224	155	35	21	9	4
Hebrew, Russian	49	46	16	190	111	14	62	46	7	301	203	37	22	14	6
Italian, North	3	3	2	39	27	4	18	12	5	60	42	11	9	7	5
Italian, South	6	6	4	32	16	6	28	16	7	66	38	17	8	5	1
Italian (not specified)	5	5	2	28	14	2	17	12	4	51	31	8	14	10	4
Other races	22	21	6	83	49	3	35	24	5	140	94	14	9	3	1
Total	106	100	36	499	285	31	237	178	55	842	563	122	83	48	21
Total foreign-born	168	158	38	931	573	37	429	348	92	1,528	1,079	167	140	79	28
Grand total	360	316	38	2,457	1,599	64	1,136	972	250	3,953	2,887	352	311	192	58

TABLE **12.**—*Rate of progress of pupils and time in school in the United States, by race of father (foreign-born pupils only).*

Race of father of pupil.	Pupils in school less years than grade.			Pupils in school same years as grade.			Pupils in school more years than grade.			Total reporting complete data.			Not reporting complete data.		
	Number.	Pupils 8 years of age or over.		Number.	Pupils 8 years of age or over.		Number.	Pupils 8 years of age or over.		Number.	Pupils 8 years of age or over.		Number.	Pupils 8 years of age or over.	
		Number.	Number retarded.		Number.	Number retarded.		Number.	Number retarded.		Number.	Number retarded.		Number.	Number retarded.
Hebrew, Russian	27	27	16	46	28	13	10	6	2	83	61	31	11	9	6
Other races	42	40	15	68	38	13	32	30	12	142	108	40	9	6	3
Total	69	67	31	114	66	26	42	36	14	225	169	71	20	15	9

TABLE **13.**—*Ability to speak English of foreign-born fathers of pupils, by race of father.*

[This table includes only non-English-speaking races.]

Race of father of pupil.	Pupils whose fathers speak English.			Pupils whose fathers do not speak English.			Total reporting complete data.			Not reporting complete data.		
	Number.	Pupils 8 years of age or over.		Number.	Pupils 8 years of age or over.		Number.	Pupils 8 years of age or over.		Number.	Pupils 8 years of age or over.	
		Number.	Number retarded.		Number.	Number retarded.		Number.	Number retarded.		Number.	Number retarded.
Canadian, French	226	150	33	9	8	3	235	158	36	10	6	3
Hebrew, Russian	300	198	31	18	16	11	318	214	42	5	3	1
Italian, North	60	43	11	8	5	5	68	48	16	1	1	
Italian, South	64	36	14	8	6	3	72	42	17	2	1	1
Italian (not specified)	55	35	11	8	5	1	63	40	12	2	1	
Other races	131	84	11	14	11	4	145	95	15	4	2	
Total	836	546	111	65	51	27	901	597	138	24	14	5

TABLE 14.—*Ability to speak English of foreign-born fathers of pupils, by race of father (foreign-born pupils only).*

[This table includes only non-English-speaking races.]

Race of father of pupil.	Pupils whose fathers speak English.			Pupils whose fathers do not speak English.			Total reporting complete data.			Not reporting complete data.		
	Number.	Pupils 8 years of age or over.		Number.	Pupils 8 years of age or over.		Number.	Pupils 8 years of age or over.		Number.	Pupils 8 years of age or over.	
		Number.	Number retarded.		Number.	Number retarded.		Number.	Number retarded.		Number.	Number retarded.
Hebrew, Russian	76	54	26	17	15	10	93	69	36	1	1	1
Other races	63	47	23	19	17	11	82	64	34	3	1	1
Total	139	101	49	36	32	21	175	133	70	4	2	2

TABLE **15.**—*Citizenship of foreign-born fathers of pupils, by race of father.*

Race of father of pupil.	Pupils whose fathers have either first or second naturalization papers.			Pupils whose fathers have neither first nor second naturalization papers.			Total reporting complete data.			Not reporting complete data.		
	Number.	Pupils 8 years of age or over.		Number.	Pupils 8 years of age or over.		Number.	Pupils 8 years of age or over.		Number.	Pupils 8 years of age or over.	
		Number.	Number retarded.		Number.	Number retarded.		Number.	Number retarded.		Number.	Number retarded.
English-speaking races:												
Canadian (other than French)	164	114	9	109	78	9	273	192	18	39	27	3
English	76	61	4	40	28	2	116	89	6	15	12	3
Irish	196	144	10	23	18	3	219	162	13	19	14	3
Scotch	41	34	3	10	9	3	51	43	6	2	1	
Other races	6	4		3	3		9	7				
Total	483	357	26	185	136	17	668	493	43	75	54	9
Non-English-speaking races:												
Canadian, French	143	96	19	76	51	16	219	147	35	26	17	4
Hebrew, Russian	246	172	28	66	39	14	312	211	42	11	6	1
Italian, North	41	30	7	23	15	8	64	45	15	5	4	1
Italian, South	31	19	8	40	22	9	71	41	17	3	2	1
Italian (not specified)	32	20	4	30	21	8	62	41	12	3		
Other races	112	72	6	22	13	7	134	85	13	15	12	2
Total	605	409	72	257	161	62	862	570	134	63	41	9
Total foreign-born	1,088	766	98	442	297	79	1,530	1,063	177	138	95	18

TABLE **16.**—*Citizenship of foreign-born fathers of pupils, by race of father (foreign-born pupils only).*

Race of father of pupil.	Pupils whose fathers have either first or second naturalization papers.			Pupils whose fathers have neither first nor second naturalization papers.			Total reporting complete data.			Not reporting complete data.		
	Number.	Pupils 8 years of age or over.		Number.	Pupils 8 years of age or over.		Number.	Pupils 8 years of age or over.		Number.	Pupils 8 years of age or over.	
		Number.	Number retarded.		Number.	Number retarded.		Number.	Number retarded.		Number.	Number retarded.
Hebrew, Russian	57	46	23	35	22	13	92	68	36	2	2	1
Other races	42	27	8	94	77	31	136	104	39	15	10	4
Total	99	73	31	129	99	44	228	172	75	17	12	5

TABLE 17.—*Length of residence in the United States of foreign-born fathers of pupils, by race of father.*

[By years in the United States is meant years since first arrival in the United States. No deduction is made for time spent abroad.]

Race of father of pupil.	Pupils whose fathers have been in the United States under 5 years.			Pupils whose fathers have been in the United States 5 to 9 years.			Pupils whose fathers have been in the United States 10 to 19 years.			Pupils whose fathers have been in the United States 20 years or over.			Total reporting complete data.			Not reporting complete data.		
	Number.	Pupils 8 yrs or over Number.	Number retarded.	Number.	Pupils 8 yrs or over Number.	Number retarded.	Number.	Pupils 8 yrs or over Number.	Number retarded.	Number.	Pupils 8 yrs or over Number.	Number retarded.	Number.	Pupils 8 yrs or over Number.	Number retarded.	Number.	Pupils 8 yrs or over Number.	Number retarded.
English-speaking races:																		
Canadian (other than French)	7	4	1	13	10	2	87	58	2	175	124	14	282	196	19	30	23	2
English	7	4		8	6		29	24	1	73	56	5	117	90	6	14	11	3
Irish				1	1	1	28	18	1	193	144	12	222	163	14	16	13	2
Scotch	5	3		3	2		8	6		30	26	2	46	37	4	7	7	2
Other races				2	2	2	3	3		4	2		9	7				
Total	19	11	1	27	21	5	155	109	4	475	352	33	676	493	43	67	54	9
Non-English-speaking races:																		
Canadian, French	1	1	1	5	2	1	51	32	4	170	115	30	227	150	36	18	14	3
Hebrew, Russian	38	25	20	49	32	13	140	87	6	87	66	1	314	210	40	9	7	3
Italian, North	7	5	3	4	4	3	40	24	3	17	15	6	68	48	15	1	1	1
Italian, South	2	2	2	7	6	2	48	23	9	10	6	2	67	37	15	7	6	3
Italian (not specified)	1	1	1	2	1	1	44	25	4	18	14	6	65	41	12			
Other races	14	8	5	15	8	3	58	34	3	54	40	3	141	90	14	8	7	1
Total	63	42	32	82	53	23	381	225	29	356	256	48	882	576	132	43	35	11
Total foreign-born	82	53	33	109	74	28	536	334	33	831	608	81	1,558	1,069	175	110	89	20

TABLE 18.—*Length of residence in the United States of foreign-born fathers, by race of father (foreign-born pupils only).*

[By years in the United States is meant years since first arrival in the United States. No deduction is made for time spent abroad.]

Race of father of pupil.	Pupils whose fathers have been in the United States under 5 years.			Pupils whose fathers have been in the United States 5 to 9 years.			Pupils whose fathers have been in the United States 10 to 19 years.			Pupils whose fathers have been in the United States 20 years or over.			Total reporting complete data.			Not reporting complete data.		
	Number.	Pupils 8 years of age or over.		Number.	Pupils 8 years of age or over.		Number.	Pupils 8 years of age or over.		Number.	Pupils 8 years of age or over.		Number.	Pupils 8 years of age or over.		Number.	Pupils 8 years of age or over.	
		Number.	Number retarded.		Number.	Number retarded.		Number.	Number retarded.		Number.	Number retarded.		Number.	Number retarded.		Number.	Number retarded.
Hebrew, Russian	38	25	20	42	31	13	11	11	2				91	67	35	3	3	2
Other races	42	26	13	48	37	14	35	30	10	10	8	3	135	101	40	16	13	3
Total	80	51	33	90	68	27	46	41	12	10	8	3	226	168	75	19	16	5

TABLE 19.—*Home language—Pupils of foreign-born fathers of non-English-speaking races, by race of father.*

Race of father of pupil.	Pupils in homes where English is used.			Pupils in homes where English is not used.			Total reporting complete data.			Not reporting complete data.		
	Number.	Pupils 8 years of age or over.		Number.	Pupils 8 years of age or over.		Number.	Pupils 8 years of age or over.		Number.	Pupils 8 years of age or over.	
		Number.	Number retarded.		Number.	Number retarded.		Number.	Number retarded.		Number.	Number retarded.
Canadian, French	183	126	28	62	38	11	245	164	39			
Hebrew, Russian	180	129	11	142	87	32	322	216	43	1	1	1
Italian, North	24	20	4	45	29	12	69	49	16			
Italian, South	26	14	4	48	29	14	74	43	18			
Italian, (not specified)	22	15	5	42	26	7	64	41	12	1	1	
Other races	95	65	9	52	31	6	147	96	15	2		1
Total	530	369	61	391	240	82	921	609	143	4	2	2

TABLE **20.**—*Home language—Pupils of foreign-born fathers of non-English-speaking races, by race of father (foreign-born pupils only).*

Race of father of pupil.	Pupils in homes where English is used.			Pupils in homes where English is not used.			Total reporting complete data.			Not reporting complete data.		
	Number.	Pupils 8 years of age or over.		Number.	Pupils 8 years of age or over.		Number.	Pupils 8 years of age or over.		Number.	Pupils 8 years of age or over.	
		Number.	Number retarded.		Number.	Number retarded.		Number.	Number retarded.		Number.	Number retarded.
Hebrew, Russian	26	23	8	68	47	29	94	70	37			
Other races	26	19	8	59	46	27	85	65	35			
Total	52	42	16	127	93	56	179	135	72			

TABLE **21.**—*Proportion of term attended, by general nativity and race of father.*

PRIMARY GRADES.

[By term is meant the period from the beginning of the school year to December 31, 1908.]

General nativity and race of father of pupil.	Pupils who attended nine-tenths or over.			Pupils who attended three-fourths and less than nine-tenths.			Pupils who attended one-half and less than three-fourths.			Pupils who attended less than one-half.			Total reporting complete data.			Not reporting complete data.		
	Number.	8 yrs. Number.	8 yrs. No. retarded.	Number.	8 yrs. Number.	8 yrs. No. retarded.	Number.	8 yrs. Number.	8 yrs. No. retarded.	Number.	8 yrs. Number.	8 yrs. No. retarded.	Number.	8 yrs. Number.	8 yrs. No. retarded.	Number.	8 yrs. Number.	8 yrs. No. retarded.
Native-born:																		
White	736	355	35	161	57	6	57	18	5	58	17	7	1,012	447	53	164	72	12
Negro	15	4		6	1		1	1					22	6		3	1	
Total native-born	751	359	35	167	58	6	58	19	5	58	17	7	1,034	453	53	167	73	12
Foreign-born:																		
English-speaking races—																		
Canadian (other than French)	88	33	2	36	12	1	3	1		4	2	1	131	48	4	19	9	3
English	31	15		3	1	1	3	2		3	1	1	40	19	3	20	11	3
Irish	58	24	4	8	4	1	6	1	1	6	1		78	30	4	25	11	1
Scotch	9	4	4	2	1								11	5	1	7	4	1
Other races	2	1	1										2	1		1		
Total	188	77	7	49	18	2	12	4	1	13	4	2	262	103	12	72	35	7
Non-English-speaking races—																		
Canadian, French	87	35	7	18	7	4	6	2	1	7	3	1	118	47	14	23	13	3
Hebrew, Russian	113	55	21	33	14	3	13	1		4	1	1	163	71	25	24	10	3
Italian, North	28	15	6	3	2	1	3	3	1	2	1		36	21	8	7	7	1
Italian, South	37	19	7	9	4	1	3	3		3	2	2	52	25	10	6	2	2
Italian (not specified)	33	20	4	10	5	2	2			1			46	25	6	7	4	2
Other races	43	15	3	10	2	2	3			3	2	2	59	19	7	19	7	2
Total	341	159	48	83	34	13	30	6	2	20	9	7	474	208	70	86	38	13
Total foreign-born	529	236	55	132	52	15	42	10	3	33	13	9	736	311	82	158	73	20
Grand total	1,280	595	90	299	110	21	100	29	8	91	30	16	1,770	764	135	325	146	32

GRAMMAR GRADES.

Native-born:																		
White	1,133	1,133	104	139	139	19	44	44	8	26	26	6	1,342	1,342	137	21	21	3
Negro	29	29	9	3	3	1							32	32	10			
Total native-born	1,162	1,162	113	142	142	20	44	44	8	26	26	6	1,374	1,374	147	21	21	3
Foreign-born:																		
English-speaking races—																		
Canadian (other than French)	131	131	6	12	12	4	9	9	2	5	5	1	157	157	13	5	5	1
English	56	56	2	7	7		2	2	2	5	5	1	70	70	3	1	1	
Irish	106	106	10	19	19	1	5	5		1	1		131	131	12	4	4	
Scotch	27	27	3	6	6		1	1					34	34	4	1	1	
Other races	5	5		1	1	1	1	1					6	6				
Total	325	325	21	45	45	5	17	17	4	11	11	2	398	398	32	11	11	1
Non-English-speaking races—																		
Canadian, French	85	85	16	11	11	2	2	2		4	4	2	102	102	20	2	2	2
Hebrew, Russian	118	118	13	16	16	2				1	1		135	135	15	1	1	
Italian, North	23	23	1	3	3	1							26	26	7			
Italian, South	12	12	4	4	4	2	1	1		1	1	1	16	16	6	1	1	
Italian (not specified)	9	9		2	2	1							11	11	4			
Other races	60	60	4	9	9	2	1	1		1	1		71	71	6	1	1	
Total	307	307	46	45	45	10	3	3	4	6	6	2	361	361	58	4	4	2
Total foreign-born	632	632	67	90	90	15	20	20	12	17	17	4	759	759	90	15	15	3
Grand total	1,794	1,794	180	232	232	35	64	64	12	43	43	10	2,133	2,133	237	36	36	6

TABLE **21.**—*Proportion of term attended, by general nativity and race of father*—Continued.

ALL ELEMENTARY GRADES.

General nativity and race of father of pupil.	Pupils who attended nine-tenths or over.			Pupils who attended three-fourths and less than nine-tenths.			Pupils who attended one-half and less than three-fourths.			Pupils who attended less than one-half.			Total reporting complete data.			Not reporting complete data.		
	Number.	Pupils 8 years of age or over: Number.	Number retarded.	Number.	Pupils 8 years of age or over: Number.	Number retarded.	Number.	Pupils 8 years of age or over: Number.	Number retarded.	Number.	Pupils 8 years of age or over: Number.	Number retarded.	Number.	Pupils 8 years of age or over: Number.	Number retarded.	Number.	Pupils 8 years of age or over: Number.	Number retarded.
Native-born:																		
White	1,869	1,488	139	300	196	25	101	62	13	84	43	13	2,354	1,789	190	185	93	15
Negro	44	33	9	9	4	1	1	1					54	38	10	3	1	
Total native-born	1,913	1,521	148	309	200	26	102	63	13	84	43	13	2,408	1,827	200	188	94	15
Foreign-born:																		
English-speaking races—																		
Canadian (other than French)	219	164	8	48	24	5	12	10	2	9	7	2	288	205	17	24	14	4
English	87	71	2	10	8	1	5	4	1	8	6	2	110	89	6	21	12	3
Irish	164	130	14	27	23		11	6	2	7	2		209	161	16	29	15	
Scotch	36	31	4	8	7	1	1	1					45	39	5	8	5	1
Other races	7	6		1	1								8	7		1		
Total	513	402	28	94	63	7	29	21	5	24	15	4	660	501	44	83	46	8
Non-English-speaking races:																		
Canadian, French	172	120	23	29	18	6	8	4	1	11	7	4	220	149	34	25	15	5
Hebrew, Russian	231	173	34	49	30	5	13			5	2	1	298	206	40	25	11	3
Italian, North	51	38	12	6	5	2	3	1	1	2	1		62	47	15	7	2	1
Italian, South	49	31	11	13	8	3	3	3		3	2	2	68	41	16	6	2	2
Italian (not specified)	42	29	7	12	7	3	2			1			57	36	10	8	5	2
Other races	103	75	7	19	11	4	4	1		4	3	2	130	90	13	19	7	2
Total	648	466	94	128	79	23	33	9	2	26	15	9	835	569	128	90	42	15
Total foreign-born	1,161	868	122	222	142	30	62	30	7	50	30	13	1,495	1,070	172	173	88	23
Grand total	3,074	2,389	270	531	342	56	164	93	20	134	73	26	3,903	2,897	372	361	182	38

TABLE 22.—*Proportion of term attended, by race of father (foreign-born pupils only).*

PRIMARY GRADES.

[By term is meant the period from the beginning of the school year to December 31, 1908.]

Race of father of pupil.	Pupils who attended nine-tenths or over.			Pupils who attended three-fourths and less than nine-tenths.			Pupils who attended one-half and less than three-fourths.			Pupils who attended less than one-half.			Total reporting complete data.			Not reporting complete data.		
	Number.	Pupils 8 years of age or over.		Number.	Pupils 8 years of age or over.		Number.	Pupils 8 years of age or over.		Number.	Pupils 8 years of age or over.		Number.	Pupils 8 years of age or over.		Number.	Pupils 8 years of age or over.	
		Number.	Number retarded.		Number.	Number retarded.		Number.	Number retarded.		Number.	Number retarded.		Number.	Number retarded.		Number.	Number retarded.
Hebrew, Russian	44	29	20	10	7	3	4			2	1	1	60	37	24	7	6	3
Other races	48	28	13	14	9	6	7	3	2	6	4	4	75	44	25	15	9	6
Total	92	57	33	24	16	9	11	3	2	8	5	5	135	81	49	22	15	9

GRAMMAR GRADES.

Race of father of pupil.	Pupils who attended nine-tenths or over.			Pupils who attended three-fourths and less than nine-tenths.			Pupils who attended one-half and less than three-fourths.			Pupils who attended less than one-half.			Total reporting complete data.			Not reporting complete data.		
	Number.	Number.	Number retarded.	Number.	Number.	Number retarded.	Number.	Number.	Number retarded.	Number.	Number.	Number retarded.	Number.	Number.	Number retarded.	Number.	Number.	Number retarded.
Hebrew, Russian	25	25	8	2	2	2							27	27	10			
Other races	47	47	8	8	8	4	2	2		2	2		59	59	12	2	2	
Total	72	72	16	10	10	6	2	2		2	2		86	86	22	2	2	

ALL ELEMENTARY GRADES.

Race of father of pupil.	Pupils who attended nine-tenths or over.			Pupils who attended three-fourths and less than nine-tenths.			Pupils who attended one-half and less than three-fourths.			Pupils who attended less than one-half.			Total reporting complete data.			Not reporting complete data.		
	Number.	Number.	Number retarded.	Number.	Number.	Number retarded.	Number.	Number.	Number retarded.	Number.	Number.	Number retarded.	Number.	Number.	Number retarded.	Number.	Number.	Number retarded.
Hebrew, Russian	69	54	28	12	9	5	4			2	1	1	87	64	34	7	6	3
Other races	95	75	21	22	17	10	9	5	2	8	6	4	134	103	37	17	11	6
Total	164	129	49	34	26	15	13	5	2	10	7	5	221	167	71	24	17	9

TABLE 23.—*Access to present grade, by general nativity and race of father.*

General nativity and race of father of pupil.	Regular course.			Transfer from other public school in city.			Transfer from public school elsewhere.			Transfer from private school.		
	Number.	Pupils 8 years of age or over.		Number.	Pupils 8 years of age or over.		Number.	Pupils 8 years of age or over.		Number.	Pupils 8 years of age or over.	
		Number.	Number retarded.		Number.	Number retarded.		Number.	Number retarded.		Number.	Number retarded.
Native-born:												
White	1,932	1,447	107	148	115	17	109	80	13	11	9	2
Negro	40	30	7	3	2		2	2				
Total native-born	1,972	1,477	114	151	117	17	111	82	13	11	9	2
Foreign-born:												
English-speaking races—												
Canadian (other than French)	227	159	6	22	16	3	15	13	2	2	2	1
English	89	72	3	9	7	1	10	7	3	1	1	1
Irish	179	136	10	5	3		4	3		7	7	
Scotch	39	31	4	4	4		2	2				
Other races	6	5		1	1							
Total	540	403	23	41	31	4	31	25	5	10	10	2
Non-English-speaking races—												
Canadian, French	178	116	22	8	8	2	1	1		8	8	4
Hebrew, Russian	254	166	30	35	29	6	12	9	4			
Italian, North	54	41	14	4	3							
Italian, South	59	35	13	4	4	1		2		2	2	2
Italian (not specified)	48	33	8	2	2		4	5	2			
Other races	106	69	7	9	7	2	6			4	4	1
Total	699	460	94	62	53	11	23	17	6	14	14	7
Total foreign-born	1,239	863	117	103	84	15	54	42	11	24	24	9
Grand total	3,211	2,340	231	254	201	32	165	124	24	35	33	11

General nativity and race of father of pupil.	Not promoted.			Total reporting complete data.			Not reporting complete data.		
	Number.	Pupils 8 years of age or over.		Number.	Pupils 8 years of age or over.		Number.	Pupils 8 years of age or over.	
		Number.	Number retarded.		Number.	Number retarded.		Number.	Number retarded.
Native-born:									
White	158	116	45	2,358	1,767	184	181	115	21
Negro	5	3	2	50	37	9	7	2	1
Total native-born	163	119	47	2,408	1,804	193	188	117	22
Foreign-born:									
English-speaking races—									
Canadian (other than French)	20	10	4	286	200	16	26	19	5
English	7	5	2	116	92	9	15	9	
Irish	18	10	5	213	159	16	25	17	
Scotch	2	2	1	47	39	5	6	5	1
Other races				7	6		2	1	
Total	47	27	12	669	496	46	74	51	6
Non-English-speaking races—									
Canadian, French	20	10	5	215	143	33	30	21	6
Hebrew, Russian	13	6	1	314	210	41	9	7	2
Italian, North	8	4	1	66	48	15	3	1	1
Italian, South	7			72	41	16	2	2	2
Italian (not specified)	8	2	1	62	39	11	3	2	1
Other races	13	6	4	138	91	14	11	6	1
Total	69	28	12	867	572	130	58	39	13
Total foreign-born	116	55	24	1,536	1,068	176	132	90	19
Grand total	279	174	71	3,944	2,872	369	320	207	41

TABLE 24.—*Access to present grade, by race of father (foreign-born pupils only).*

Race of father of pupil	Regular course.			Transfer from other public school in city.			Transfer from public school elsewhere.			Transfer from private school.		
	Number.	Pupils 8 years of age or over. Number.	Number retarded.	Number.	Pupils 8 years of age or over. Number.	Number retarded.	Number.	Pupils 8 years of age or over. Number.	Number retarded.	Number.	Pupils 8 years of age or over. Number.	Number retarded.
Hebrew, Russian	72	52	26	12	12	6	5	4	3	......	......	......
Other races	107	84	29	9	8	2	13	8	2	2	2	2
Total	179	136	55	21	20	8	18	12	5	2	2	2

Race of father of pupil	Not promoted.			Total reporting complete data.			Not reporting complete data.		
	Number.	Pupils 8 years of age or over. Number.	Number retarded.	Number.	Pupils 8 years of age or over. Number.	Number retarded.	Number.	Pupils 8 years of age or over. Number.	Number retarded.
Hebrew, Russian	2	......	......	91	68	35	3	2	2
Other races	8	2	2	139	104	37	12	10	6
Total	10	2	2	230	172	72	15	12	8

PAROCHIAL SCHOOL PUPILS: GENERAL INVESTIGATION.

TABLE 1.—*Grade and age—Number of pupils of each age in each grade, by sex.*

BOYS.

Age.	Kinder-garten.	Elementary grades.										High school, first year.	Grand total.
		1.	2.	3.	4.	5.	6.	7.	8.	9.	Total.		
4 years	16												16
5 years	24	9										9		33
6 years		82	12									94		94
7 years		37	28	10								75		75
8 years		18	38	32	10	1						99		99
9 years		2	27	26	21	12						88		88
10 years		2	12	17	28	32	12	2				105		105
11 years		1	1	5	17	23	28	18				93		93
12 years			1	8	11	22	33	22	9			106		106
13 years			1	4	8	14	12	19	20	6		84		84
14 years				1	1	3	4	6	13	5		33	3	36
15 years			1			1	3	3	8	7		23	6	29
16 years			1	3		1			1	4	2	12	4	16
17 years			1	1							1	3	1	4
18 years			1									1		1
19 years														
20 years or over														
Total	40	151	124	107	96	109	92	71	54	21	825	14	879

GIRLS.

Age.	Kinder-garten.	Elementary grades.										High school, first year.	Grand total.
		1.	2.	3.	4.	5.	6.	7.	8.	9.	Total.		
4 years	22												22
5 years	20	44										44		64
6 years		50	11									61		61
7 years		45	40	10								95		95
8 years		10	27	31	7							75		75
9 years		9	22	26	28	7						92		92
10 years		2	6	25	21	37	8					99		99
11 years		1	3	15	10	21	27	3	1			81		81
12 years		1		5	10	11	19	36	7			89		89
13 years				1	5	6	10	17	22	8		69		69
14 years				1	1	2	5	13	14	16		52	5	57
15 years			2				1	1			9	13	9	22
16 years			5	5						2		12	8	20
17 years			1	6								7	1	8
18 years				4								4		4
19 years														
20 years or over														
Total	42	162	117	129	82	84	70	70	44	35	793	23	858

TOTAL.

Age.	Kinder-garten.	Elementary grades.										High school, first year.	Grand total.
		1.	2.	3.	4.	5.	6.	7.	8.	9.	Total.		
4 years	38												38
5 years	44	53										53		97
6 years		132	23									155		155
7 years		82	68	20								170		170
8 years		28	65	63	17	1						174		174
9 years		11	49	52	49	19						180		180
10 years		4	18	42	49	69	20	2				204		204
11 years		2	4	20	27	44	55	21	1			174		174
12 years		1	1	13	21	33	52	58	16			195		195
13 years			1	5	13	20	22	36	42	14		153		153
14 years				2	2	5	9	19	27	21		85	8	93
15 years			3			1	4	4	8	16		36	15	51
16 years			6	8		1			1	4	4	24	12	36
17 years			2	7							1	10	2	12
18 years			1	4								5		5
19 years														
20 years or over														
Total	82	313	241	236	178	193	162	141	98	56	1,618	37	1,737

TABLE 2.—Race, sex, and grade—Number of pupils of each sex in each grade, by general nativity and race of father of pupil.

General nativity and race of father of pupil	Kindergarten	1.	2.	3.	4.	5.	6.	7.	8.	9.	Total.	High school, first year.	Grand total.
Native-born:													
White—													
Male	8	19	23	12	21	19	17	14	6	8	139	6	153
Female	17	24	13	23	25	22	13	15	11	5	151	10	178
Total	25	43	36	35	46	41	30	29	17	13	290	16	331
Negro—													
Male						1				1	2		2
Total native-born:													
Male	8	19	23	12	21	20	17	14	6	9	141	6	155
Female	17	24	13	23	25	22	13	15	11	5	151	10	178
Total	25	43	36	35	46	42	30	29	17	14	292	16	333
Foreign-born:													
Canadian, French—													
Male	2	78	52	59	41	48	42	30	19		369	7	378
Female	3	90	57	69	12	21	28	14	13	11	315		318
Total	5	168	109	128	53	69	70	44	32	11	684	7	696
Canadian, Other—													
Male	1		3	1	1	2		2	1	2	12	1	13
Female	1	1	2	2	3	4	2	2	3	1	20	2	22
Total	2	1	5	3	4	6	2	4	4	3	32	3	35
Dutch—													
Male					1						1		1
English—													
Male	1	2		2			1	2	1		7		7
Female	1		3		3	2				2	11	1	12
Total	2	2	3	2	3	2	1	2	1	2	18	1	19
Irish—													
Male	15	35	34	26	31	35	31	22	26	10	250		266
Female	16	32	36	27	28	30	24	37	17	15	246	12	274
Total	31	67	70	53	59	65	55	59	43	25	496	13	543
Italian, North—													
Male	4	1		2	1	1	1				8		12
Female	4	3	4	2	2						7		7
Total	4	4	4	2	3	1	1				15		19
Lithuanian—													
Male	2	1	4	5							13		15
Female	2	3	1	5	2	2		1	1		14		14
Total		4	5	10	2	2		1	1		27		29
Polish—													
Male	6	13	4		4	1					18		24
Female	4	4	3	2				1			13		17
Total	10	17	7	2	4	1		1			31		41

Welsh— Female	2										1	1		1
Other races a— Male	2	2	2			1	2	1	48	12	6	8	8
Female		5	2	1	3	2	1	1	33	30	15	13	15
Total		7	2	1	3	3	3	2	81	42	21	21	23
Total foreign-born— Male	32	132	101	95	75	89	75	57			684		724
Female	25	138	104	106	57	62	57	55			642		680
Total	57	270	205	201	132	151	132	112			1,326		1,404
Grand total— Male	40	151	124	107	96	109	92	71	54	21	825	14	879
Female	42	162	117	129	82	84	70	70	44	35	793	23	858
Total	82	313	241	236	178	193	162	141	98	56	1,618	37	1,737

a "Other races" includes: Cuban, 1; German, 1; South Italians, 5; Japanese, 4; Magyar, 1; Russians, 9; Scotch, 2.

TABLE **3.**—*Race, sex, and age, by grade—Number of pupils of each age in each grade, by sex and by general nativity and race of father of pupil.*

KINDERGARTEN.

BOYS.

General nativity and race of father of pupil.	Number of pupils of each age.		Total.
	4.	5.	
Native-born, White	2	6	8
Foreign-born:			
Canadian, French	1	1	2
Canadian, Other		1	1
Irish	7	8	15
Italian, North	2	2	4
Lithuanian	1	1	2
Polish	2	4	6
Other races *a*	1	1	2
Total	14	18	32
Grand total	16	24	40

GIRLS.

General nativity and race of father of pupil.	4.	5.	Total.
Native-born, White	12	5	17
Foreign-born:			
Canadian, French	1	2	3
Canadian, Other		1	1
English	1		1
Irish	8	8	16
Polish		4	4
Total	10	15	25
Grand total	22	20	42

TOTAL.

General nativity and race of father of pupil.	4.	5.	Total.
Native-born, White	14	11	25
Foreign-born:			
Canadian, French	2	3	5
Canadian, Other		2	2
English	1		1
Irish	15	16	31
Italian, North	2	2	4
Lithuanian	1	1	2
Polish	2	8	10
Other races *a*	1	1	2
Total	24	33	57
Grand total	38	44	82

a "Other races" includes races having less than 10 representatives in this city and pupils whose race is not reported.

TABLE 3.—*Race, sex, and age, by grade—Number of pupils of each age in each grade, by sex and by general nativity and race of father of pupil—Continued.*

FIRST GRADE.

BOYS.

General nativity and race of father of pupil.	Number of pupils of each age.								Total.
	5.	6.	7.	8.	9.	10.	11.	12.	
Native-born, White....................	2	12	4	......	1	......	......	......	19
Foreign-born:									
Canadian, French....................	4	30	27	13	1	2	1	......	78
English............................	......	2	......	......	......	......	......	......	2
Irish..............................	3	26	3	3	......	......	......	......	35
Italian, North......................	......	......	......	1	......	......	......	......	1
Lithuanian..........................	......	1	......	......	......	......	......	......	1
Polish.............................	......	10	3	......	......	......	......	......	13
Other races a.....................	......	1	......	1	......	......	......	......	2
Total.............................	7	70	33	18	1	2	1	......	132
Grand total......................	9	82	37	18	2	2	1	......	151

GIRLS.

General nativity and race of father of pupil.	5.	6.	7.	8.	9.	10.	11.	12.	Total.
Native-born, White....................	14	6	4	......	......	......	......	......	24
Foreign-born:									
Canadian, French....................	11	29	27	9	9	2	......	1	90
Canadian, Other....................	......	......	1	......	......	......	......	......	1
Irish..............................	14	12	6	......	......	......	......	......	32
Italian, North......................	1	1	1	......	......	......	......	......	3
Lithuanian..........................	1	1	1	......	......	......	......	......	3
Polish.............................	1	......	2	......	......	......	1	......	4
Other races a.....................	2	1	1	1	......	......	......	......	5
Total.............................	30	44	41	10	9	2	1	1	138
Grand total......................	44	50	45	10	9	2	1	1	162

TOTAL.

General nativity and race of father of pupil.	5.	6.	7.	8.	9.	10.	11.	12.	Total.
Native-born, White....................	16	18	8	......	1	......	......	......	43
Foreign-born:									
Canadian, French....................	15	59	56	22	10	4	1	1	168
Canadian, Other....................	......	......	1	......	......	......	......	......	1
English............................	......	2	......	......	......	......	......	......	2
Irish..............................	17	38	9	3	......	......	......	......	67
Italian, North......................	1	1	1	1	......	......	......	......	4
Lithuanian..........................	1	2	1	......	......	......	......	......	4
Polish.............................	1	10	5	......	......	......	1	......	17
Other races a.....................	2	2	1	2	......	......	......	......	7
Total.............................	37	114	74	28	10	4	2	1	270
Grand total......................	53	132	82	28	11	4	2	1	313

a "Other races" includes races having less than 10 representatives in this city and pupils whose race is not reported.

TABLE 3.—*Race, sex, and age, by grade—Number of pupils of each age in each grade, by sex and by general nativity and race of father of pupil*—Continued.

SECOND GRADE.

BOYS.

General nativity and race of father of pupil.	Number of pupils of each age.													Total.
	6.	7.	8.	9.	10.	11.	12.	13.	14.	15.	16.	17.	18.	
Native-born, White	....	11	5	4	....	....	....	....	....	....	1	1	1	23
Foreign-born:														
Canadian, French	2	6	15	16	10	1	1	1						52
Canadian, Other			2	1										3
Irish	9	11	11	1	1					1				34
Italian, North			1	2	1									4
Lithuanian			2	2										4
Polish	1		2	1										4
Total	12	17	33	23	12	1	1	1	....	1				101
Grand total	12	28	38	27	12	1	1	1	....	1	1	1	1	124

GIRLS.

General nativity and race of father of pupil.	Number of pupils of each age.													Total.
	6.	7.	8.	9.	10.	11.	12.	13.	14.	15.	16.	17.	18.	
Native-born, White	4	6	1	1	....	....	....	....	....	....	1			13
Foreign-born:														
Canadian, French	1	12	16	18	5	3				2				57
Canadian, Other		2												2
English	1	1		1										3
Irish	5	15	9	1	1						4	1		36
Lithuanian				1										1
Polish		3												3
Other races a		1	1											2
Total	7	34	26	21	6	3				2	4	1	....	104
Grand total	11	40	27	22	6	3				2	5	1	....	117

TOTAL.

General nativity and race of father of pupil.	Number of pupils of each age.													Total.
	6.	7.	8.	9.	10.	11.	12.	13.	14.	15.	16.	17.	18.	
Native-born, White	4	17	6	5	....	....	....	....	....	....	2	1	1	36
Foreign-born:														
Canadian, French	3	18	31	34	15	4	1	1	....	2				109
Canadian, Other		2	2	1										5
English	1	1		1										3
Irish	14	26	20	2	2					1	4	1	....	70
Italian, North			1	2	1									4
Lithuanian			2	3										5
Polish	1	3	2	1										7
Other races a		1	1											2
Total	19	51	59	44	18	4	1	1	....	3	4	1	....	205
Grand total	23	68	65	49	18	4	1	1	....	3	6	2	1	241

a "Other races" includes races having less than 10 representatives in this city and pupils whose race is not reported.

TABLE 3.—*Race, sex, and age, by grade—Number of pupils of each age in each grade, by sex and by general nativity and race of father of pupil*—Continued.

THIRD GRADE.

BOYS.

General nativity and race of father of pupil.	Number of pupils of each age.												Total.
	7.	8.	9.	10.	11.	12.	13.	14.	15.	16.	17.	18.	
Native-born, White	1	7	3	1	....	....	....	....	....	....	....	....	12
Foreign-born:													
Canadian, French	6	13	15	11	4	6	3	1	....	....	....	....	59
Canadian, Other	....	1	....	....	....	....	....	....	....	....	....	....	1
English	....	1	....	....	....	....	....	....	....	....	1	....	2
Irish	3	10	7	2	1	1	....	....	....	2	....	....	26
Italian, North	....	....	1	....	....	....	1	....	....	....	....	....	2
Lithuanian	....	....	1	2	....	1	....	....	....	1	....	....	5
Total	9	25	23	16	5	8	4	1	....	3	1	....	95
Grand total	10	32	26	17	5	8	4	1	....	3	1	....	107

GIRLS.

General nativity and race of father of pupil.	7.	8.	9.	10.	11.	12.	13.	14.	15.	16.	17.	18.	Total.
Native-born, White	5	11	....	1	....	....	....	....	....	1	2	3	23
Foreign-born:													
Canadian, French	....	4	18	23	14	5	1	1	....	2	1	....	69
Canadian, Other	....	....	2	....	....	....	....	....	....	....	....	....	2
Irish	5	14	2	....	....	....	....	....	....	2	3	1	27
Lithuanian	....	....	3	1	1	....	....	....	....	....	....	....	5
Polish	....	2	....	....	....	....	....	....	....	....	....	....	2
Other races a	....	....	1	....	....	....	....	....	....	....	....	....	1
Total	5	20	26	24	15	5	1	1	....	4	4	1	106
Grand total	10	31	26	25	15	5	1	1	....	5	6	4	129

TOTAL.

General nativity and race of father of pupil.	7.	8.	9.	10.	11.	12.	13.	14.	15.	16.	17.	18.	Total.
Native-born, White	6	18	3	2	....	....	....	....	....	1	2	3	35
Foreign-born:													
Canadian, French	6	17	33	34	18	11	4	2	....	2	1	....	128
Canadian, Other	....	1	2	....	....	....	....	....	....	....	....	....	3
English	....	1	....	....	....	....	....	....	....	....	1	....	2
Irish	8	24	9	2	1	1	....	....	....	4	3	1	53
Italian, North	....	....	....	1	....	....	1	....	....	....	....	....	2
Lithuanian	....	....	4	3	1	1	....	....	....	1	....	....	10
Polish	....	2	....	....	....	....	....	....	....	....	....	....	2
Other races a	....	....	1	....	....	....	....	....	....	....	....	....	1
Total	14	45	49	40	20	13	5	2	....	7	5	1	201
Grand total	20	63	52	42	20	13	5	2	....	8	7	4	236

a "Other races" includes races having less than 10 representatives in this city and pupils whose race is not reported.

TABLE 3.—*Race, sex, and age, by grade—Number of pupils of each age in each grade, by sex and by general nativity and race of father of pupil*—Continued.

FOURTH GRADE.

BOYS.

General nativity and race of father of pupil.	Number of pupils of each age.							Total.
	8.	9.	10.	11.	12.	13.	14.	
Native-born, White	4	5	6	4	2			21
Foreign-born:								
Canadian, French	1	4	13	8	7	7	1	41
Canadian, Other					1			1
Dutch				1				1
Irish	5	12	8	4	1	1		31
Italian, North			1					1
Total	6	16	22	13	9	8	1	75
Grand total	10	21	28	17	11	8	1	96

GIRLS.

General nativity and race of father of pupil.	Number of pupils of each age.							Total.
	8.	9.	10.	11.	12.	13.	14.	
Native-born, White	2	8	8	4	2	1		25
Foreign-born:								
Canadian, French			1	3	7	1		12
Canadian, Other	1	2						3
English			1	1	1			3
Irish	4	13	8	2		1		28
Italian, North		2						2
Lithuanian		1	1					2
Polish		1	1			2		4
Other races [a]		1	1				1	3
Total	5	20	13	6	8	4	1	57
Grand total	7	28	21	10	10	5	1	82

TOTAL.

General nativity and race of father of pupil.	Number of pupils of each age.							Total.
	8.	9.	10.	11.	12.	13.	14.	
Native-born, White	6	13	14	8	4	1		46
Foreign-born:								
Canadian, French	1	4	14	11	14	8	1	53
Canadian, Other	1	2			1			4
Dutch				1				1
English			1	1	1			3
Irish	9	25	16	6	1	2		59
Italian, North		2	1					3
Lithuanian		1	1					2
Polish		1	1			2		4
Other races [a]		1	1				1	3
Total	11	36	35	19	17	12	2	132
Grand total	17	49	49	27	21	13	2	178

[a] "Other races" includes races having less than 10 representatives in this city and pupils whose race is not reported.

TABLE 3.—*Race, sex, and age, by grade—Nujber of pupils of each age in each grade, by sex and by general nativity and race of father of pupil*—Continued.

FIFTH GRADE.

BOYS.

General nativity and race of father of pupil.	Number of pupils of each age.									Total.
	8.	9.	10.	11.	12.	13.	14.	15.	16.	
Native-born:										
White		3	5	5	4	1		1		19
Negro						1				1
Total native-born		3	5	5	4	2		1		20
Foreign-born:										
Canadian, French	1	3	12	12	7	9	3		1	48
Canadian, Other			1			1				2
Irish		6	14	4	10	1				35
Lithuanian					1	1				2
Polish				1						1
Other races a				1						1
Total foreign-born	1	9	27	18	18	12	3		1	89
Grand total	1	12	32	23	22	14	3	1	1	109

GIRLS.

General nativity and race of father of pupil.	8.	9.	10.	11.	12.	13.	14.	15.	16.	Total.
Native-born:										
White			12	7	2	1				22
Negro										
Total native-born			12	7	2	1				22
Foreign-born:										
Canadian, French			5	4	8	2	2			21
Canadian, Other			2	2						4
English		1	1							2
Irish		6	14	6	1	3				30
Italian, North				1						1
Lithuanian			2							2
Other races a			1	1						2
Total foreign-born		7	25	14	9	5	2			62
Grand total		7	37	21	11	6	2			84

TOTAL.

General nativity and race of father of pupil.	8.	9.	10.	11.	12.	13.	14.	15.	16.	Total.
Native-born:										
White		3	17	12	6	2		1		41
Negro						1				1
Total native-born		3	17	12	6	3		1		42
Foreign-born:										
Canadian, French	1	3	17	16	15	11	5		1	69
Canadian, Other			3	2		1				6
English		1	1							2
Irish		12	28	10	11	4				65
Italian, North				1						1
Lithuanian			2		1	1				4
Polish				1						1
Other races a			1	2						3
Total foreign-born	1	16	52	32	27	17	5		1	151
Grand total	1	19	69	44	33	20	5	1	1	193

a "Other races" includes races having less than 10 representatives in this city and pupils whose race is not reported.

TABLE **3.**—*Race, sex, and age, by grade*—*Number of pupils of each age in each grade, by sex and by general nativity and race of father of pupil*—Continued.

SIXTH GRADE.

BOYS.

General nativity and race of father of pupil.	Number of pupils of each age.						Total.
	10.	11.	12.	13.	14.	15.	
Native-born, White...................	3	6	7	1	....	....	17
Foreign-born:							
Canadian, French...................	7	11	13	8	2	1	42
Irish................................	2	11	11	3	2	2	31
Other races *a*.....................	....	....	2	....	....	....	2
Total........................	9	22	26	11	4	3	75
Grand total.................	12	28	33	12	4	3	92

GIRLS.

General nativity and race of father of pupil.	Number of pupils of each age.						Total.
	10.	11.	12.	13.	14.	15.	
Native-born, White...................	3	6	1	2	1	....	13
Foreign-born:							
Canadian, French...................	....	11	9	4	4	....	28
Canadian, Other...................	....	1	1	....	....	....	2
English...........................	....	....	....	1	....	....	1
Irish..............................	5	9	6	3	....	1	24
Italian, North.....................	....	....	1	....	....	....	1
Other races *a*.....................	....	....	1	....	....	....	1
Total........................	5	21	18	8	4	1	57
Grand total.................	8	27	19	10	5	1	70

TOTAL.

General nativity and race of father of pupil.	Number of pupils of each age.						Total.
	10.	11.	12.	13.	14.	15.	
Native-born, White...................	6	12	8	3	1	....	30
Foreign-born:							
Canadian, French...................	7	22	22	12	6	1	70
Canadian, Other...................	....	1	1	....	....	....	2
English...........................	....	....	....	1	....	....	1
Irish..............................	7	20	17	6	2	3	55
Italian, North.....................	....	....	1	....	....	....	1
Other races *a*.....................	....	....	3	....	....	....	3
Total........................	14	43	44	19	8	4	132
Grand total.................	20	55	52	22	9	4	162

a "Other races" includes races having less than 10 representatives in this city and pupils whose race is not reported.

TABLE 3.—*Race, sex, and age, by grade—Number of pupils of each age in each grade, by sex and by general nativity and race of father of pupil*—Continued.

SEVENTH GRADE.

BOYS.

General nativity and race of father of pupil.	Number of pupils of each age.							Total.
	10.	11.	12.	13.	14.	15.	16.	
Native-born, White.................	....	2	4	7	1	....	....	14
Foreign-born:								
Canadian, French..............	....	10	12	4	1	2	1	30
Canadian, Other...............	1	....	....	1	....	....	....	2
English.......................	1	....	....	....	....	1	....	2
Irish.........................	....	6	6	6	4	....	....	22
Other races a	....	....	....	1	....	....	....	1
Total....................	2	16	18	12	5	3	1	57
Grand total.................	2	18	22	19	6	3	1	71

GIRLS.

Native-born, White.................	....	....	9	3	3	....	....	15
Foreign-born:								
Canadian, French..............	....	....	3	7	4	....	....	14
Canadian, Other...............	....	....	2	....	....	....	....	2
Irish.........................	....	3	22	7	5	....	....	37
Lithuanian....................	....	....	....	....	1	....	....	1
Other races a	....	....	....	....	....	1	....	1
Total....................	....	3	27	14	10	1	....	55
Grand total.................	....	3	36	17	13	1	....	70

TOTAL.

Native-born, White.................	....	2	13	10	4	....	....	29
Foreign-born:								
Canadian, French..............	....	10	15	11	5	2	1	44
Canadian, Other.......	1	....	2	1	....	....	....	4
English.......................	1	....	....	....	....	1	....	2
Irish.........................	....	9	28	13	9	....	....	59
Lithuanian....................	....	....	....	....	1	....	....	1
Other races a	....	....	....	1	....	1	....	2
Total....................	2	19	45	26	15	4	1	112
Grand total.................	2	21	58	36	19	4	1	141

a "Other races" includes races having less than 10 representatives in this city and pupils whose race is not reported.

TABLE 3.—*Race, sex, and age, by grade—Number of pupils of each age in each grade, by sex and by general nativity and race of father of pupil*—Continued.

EIGHTH GRADE.

BOYS.

General nativity and race of father of pupil.	Number of pupils of each age.						Total.
	11.	12.	13.	14.	15.	16.	
Native-born, White		2	2	1	1		6
Foreign-born:							
Canadian, French			7	4	4	4	19
Canadian, Other				1			1
English				1			1
Irish		7	10	6	3		26
Lithuanian			1				1
Total		7	18	12	7	4	48
Grand total		9	20	13	8	4	54

GIRLS.

General nativity and race of father of pupil.	11.	12.	13.	14.	15.	16.	Total.
Native-born, White		1	7	3			11
Foreign-born:							
Canadian, French	1	2	6	4			13
Canadian, Other		1	1	1			3
Irish		3	8	6			17
Total	1	6	15	11			33
Grand total	1	7	22	14			44

TOTAL.

General nativity and race of father of pupil.	11.	12.	13.	14.	15.	16.	Total.
Native-born, White		3	9	4	1		17
Foreign-born:							
Canadian, French	1	2	13	8	4	4	32
Canadian, Other		1	1	2			4
English				1			1
Irish		10	18	12	3		43
Lithuanian			1				1
Total	1	13	33	23	7	4	81
Grand total	1	16	42	27	8	4	98

TABLE 3.—*Race, sex, and age, by grade—Number of pupils of each age in each grade, by sex and by general nativity and race of father of pupil*—Continued.

NINTH GRADE.

BOYS.

General nativity and race of father of pupil.	Number of pupils of each age.					Total.
	13.	14.	15.	16.	17.	
Native-born:						
White	2	3	3			8
Negro			1			1
Total native-born	2	3	4			9
Foreign-born:						
Canadian, Other	1	1				2
Irish	3	1	3	2	1	10
Total foreign-born	4	2	3	2	1	12
Grand total	6	5	7	2	1	21

GIRLS.

	13.	14.	15.	16.	17.	Total.
Native-born, White	1	2	2			5
Foreign born:						
Canadian, French	4	6	1			11
Canadian, Other		1				1
English		1	1			2
Irish	3	6	5	1		15
Welsh				1		1
Total foreign-born	7	14	7	2		30
Grand total	8	16	9	2		35

TOTAL.

	13.	14.	15.	16.	17.	Total.
Native-born:						
White	3	5	5			13
Negro			1			1
Total native-born	3	5	6			14
Foreign-born:						
Canadian, French	4	6	1			11
Canadian, Other	1	2				3
English		1	1			2
Irish	6	7	8	3	1	25
Welsh				1		1
Total foreign-born	11	16	10	4	1	42
Grand total	14	21	16	4	1	56

TABLE 3.—*Race, sex, and age, by grade—Number of pupils of each age in each grade, by sex and by general nativity and race of father of pupil*—Continued.

FIRST YEAR HIGH SCHOOL.

BOYS.

General nativity and race of father of pupil.	Number of pupils of each age.				Total.
	14.	15.	16.	17.	
Native-born, White............................	1	3	1	1	6
Foreign-born:					
Canadian, French........................	1	3	3	....	7
Irish....................................	1	....	....	....	1
Total...............................	2	3	3	....	8
Grand total..........................	3	6	4	1	14

GIRLS.

General nativity and race of father of pupil.	Number of pupils of each age.				Total.
	14.	15.	16.	17.	
Native-born, White............................	3	3	3	1	10
Foreign-born:					
Canadian, Other.........................	....	....	1	....	1
Irish....................................	2	6	4	....	12
Total...............................	2	6	5	....	13
Grand total..........................	5	9	8	1	23

TOTAL.

General nativity and race of father of pupil.	Number of pupils of each age.				Total.
	14.	15.	16.	17.	
Native-born, White............................	4	6	4	2	16
Foreign-born:					
Canadian, French........................	1	3	3	....	7
Canadian, Other.........................	....	....	1	....	1
Irish....................................	3	6	4	....	13
Total...............................	4	9	8	....	21
Grand total..........................	8	15	12	2	37

TABLE 4.—*Race distribution in each grade—Percentages.*

[This table shows in detail only races with 100 or more pupils reporting. The totals, however, are for all races.]

General nativity and race of father of pupil.	Kindergarten.	Elementary grades.										High school, first year.	Grand total.
		1.	2.	3.	4.	5.	6.	7.	8.	9.	Total.		
Native-born:													
White	30.5	13.7	14.9	14.8	25.8	21.2	18.5	20.6	17.3	23.2	17.9	43.2	19.1
Negro	.0	.0	.0	.0	.0	.5	.0	.0	.0	1.8	.1	.0	.1
Total native-born	30.5	13.7	14.9	14.8	25.8	21.8	18.5	20.6	17.3	25.0	18.0	43.2	19.2
Foreign-born:													
Canadian, French	6.1	53.7	45.2	54.2	29.8	35.8	43.2	31.2	32.2	19.6	42.3	18.9	40.1
Irish	37.8	21.4	29.0	22.5	33.1	33.7	34.0	41.8	43.9	44.6	30.7	35.1	31.1
Other races	25.6	11.2	10.8	8.5	11.2	8.8	4.3	6.4	6.1	10.7	9.0	2.7	9.7
Total foreign-born	69.5	86.3	85.1	85.2	74.2	78.2	81.5	79.4	82.7	75.0	82.0	56.8	80.8
Grand total	100.0	100.0	100.0	100.0	100.0	100.0	100.0	100.0	100.0	100.0	100.0	100.0	100.0

TABLE 5.—*Grade distribution of each race—Percentages.*

[This table shows in detail only races with 100 or more pupils reporting. The totals, however, are for all races.]

General nativity and race of father of pupil.	Kindergarten.	Elementary grades.									Total.	High school, first year.	Grand total.
		1.	2.	3.	4.	5.	6.	7.	8.	9.			
Native-born:													
White............	7.6	13.0	10.9	10.6	13.9	12.4	9.1	8.8	5.1	3.9	87.6	4.8	100.0
Negro............	(a)	(a)	(a)	(a)	(a)	(a)	(a)	(a)	(a)	(a)	(a)	(a)	(a)
Total native-born....	7.5	12.9	10.8	10.5	13.8	12.6	9.0	8.7	5.1	4.2	87.7	4.8	100.0
Foreign-born:													
Canadian, French.....	.7	24.1	15.7	18.4	7.6	9.9	10.1	6.3	4.6	1.6	98.3	1.0	100.0
Irish...............	5.7	12.4	13.0	9.8	10.9	12.0	10.2	10.9	8.0	4.6	91.9	2.4	100.0
Other races.........	12.5	20.8	16.5	11.9	11.9	10.1	4.2	5.4	3.6	3.6	86.9	.6	100.0
Total foreign-born...	4.1	19.2	14.6	14.3	9.4	10.8	9.4	8.0	5.8	3.0	94.4	1.5	100.0
Grand total.........	4.7	18.0	13.9	13.6	10.2	11.1	9.3	8.1	5.6	3.2	93.1	2.1	100.0

a Not computed, owing to small number involved.

JOHNSTOWN, PENNSYLVANIA.

INTRODUCTORY NOTE.
PUBLIC SCHOOL PUPILS—GENERAL INVESTIGATION.
PUBLIC SCHOOL PUPILS—INTENSIVE INVESTIGATION.

LIST OF TABLES.

JOHNSTOWN.

In Johnstown, Pa., the investigation of the Immigration Commission concerned only the pupils in the public schools. The information was obtained by means of an individual record slip for each pupil. This slip contained information not only concerning the sex, grade, age, and race of the pupil, but also on a wide variety of other topics, which were designed to throw light on the school history of the child and the social environment in which he lived. The method of tabulation as described in the introduction to this volume [a] was by sorting the cards and counting the numbers resulting from such sorting. The first sorts were made for the purpose of constructing the general tables, which are exactly parallel to those produced from other forms and by another statistical procedure in the other cities covered by the researches of the Commission. After the tables of the general investigation were completed, there was a special sorting of the cards for the purpose of preparing the special tables in which the information peculiar to these cards is displayed. As a result, the tables fall into two main sections—(1) the general tables and (2) the special tables of the intensive investigation. A list and description of the tables forming each of these series will be found in the general introduction to this volume, where further information regarding the method of compilation and the general character of the results obtained may also be sought. The present note is concerned with as brief a statement as possible of the main results in the city of Johnstown.

PUPILS OF THE PUBLIC SCHOOLS—GENERAL TABLES.

The whole number of pupils for whom information was obtained in the public schools of Johnstown, Pa., was 5,419. As already explained, the information was obtained by means of individual cards. Some of these were incomplete even as to the main items of the inquiry, and could not therefore be included in the tabulation. They are, however, included in the total above given, because each card—though some of them could not be used—represents a pupil. Comparing the results of this investigation with the official records of the schools, we find that in the school year 1908–9 the average attendance recorded was 5,677. The difference between this figure and the number reported to the Commission is very slight, and this affords evidence that the enumeration of the pupils in Johnstown was comprehensive and complete. It may be noted in passing that the responsibility placed on the school authorities by this form of investigation was much greater than where the questions were fewer and the schedules simpler. The cordial cooperation of the school authorities, which resulted in a practically complete census of children in

---

[a] See pp. VII to XVII.

Johnstown schools, is highly appreciated by those connected with the investigation.

Divided by grades, the pupils in the Johnstown schools were distributed as follows:

First grade	855	Eighth grade	383
Second grade	819	First year high school	215
Third grade	635	Second year high school	99
Fourth grade	597	Third year high school	92
Fifth grade	683	Fourth year high school	35
Sixth grade	483		
Seventh grade	424	Total	5,320

It will be noted that as the grades advance there is a general diminution in numbers, with the result that the seventh and eighth grades are about one-half as numerous as the first.

The distribution of pupils by grades can be conveniently stated by groups. To form such groups grades 1 to 4 are classed together as primary and grades 5 to 8 as grammar grades, and the figures contrasted with the high school, as in the following table:

Class of school.	Number.	Per cent.
Primary, grades 1 to 4	2,906	54.6
Grammar, grades 5 to 8	1,973	37.1
High school	441	8.3
Total	5,320	100.0

Somewhat more than one-half the children were in the primary grades and most of the remainder were in the grammar grades, the high school being represented by less than one-tenth of the whole number of school children.

An examination of Table 1 shows that in Johnstown few children are in school before the age of 6 years. However, the number who were in school at 6 years of age (524) is almost as large as in any succeeding year of age. The maximum is 578 pupils at the age of 8 years. At the age of 13 years there are 483 pupils in school, but at the age of 14 there are only 402. Between the latter age and that of 15 there is a still higher diminution in number, as the 15-year-old children number only 278.

Table 1 shows that while there is a certain correspondence between the ages of the pupils and the grades in which they are found, this correspondence is by no means exact. In each grade there are pupils of various ages, and conversely at each age the pupils are found in several grades. In order to give a concise expression to the many details which this table presents, we can distinguish in each grade those pupils who are beyond the age which is appropriate to that grade, who may be termed overage pupils. In analogous manner we can for the pupils of each age determine the number who have not yet attained the grade which is appropriate to that age. Such pupils may be called undergrade pupils. Both overage pupils and undergrade pupils can be designated as retarded, this phrase expressing an unsatisfactory state of advancement in the school work for the age of the pupil. In current educational discussion the most usual form of expression is that which ascertains the retarded pupils in each grade.

The following table states the ages which are regarded as excessive for each grade and the number of pupils in the Johnstown schools who are in these excessive ages:

Grade.	Number in grade.	Retarded pupils.		
		Age.	Number.	Per cent of all pupils.
First...............	855	8 years and over......................................	113	13.2
Second.............	819	9 years and over......................................	196	23.9
Third..............	635	10 years and over.....................................	208	32.8
Fourth.............	597	11 years and over.....................................	222	37.2
Fifth...............	683	12 years and over.....................................	305	44.7
Sixth..............	483	13 years and over.....................................	187	38.7
Seventh...........	424	14 years and over.....................................	154	36.3
Eighth............	383	15 years and over.....................................	130	33.9
Total........	4,879		1,515	31.1

There is an aggregate of 1,515 pupils who are overage or retarded, and they form 31.1 per cent of the whole number of pupils. In the first grade the proportion of such retarded pupils is 13.2 per cent, and this proportion increases as the grades advance until both the maximum number of retarded pupils, 305, and the maximum percentage, 44.7, are found in the fifth grade. Later grades have somewhat smaller proportions of retarded children, though they remain above the average.

If we seek to measure the degree of retardation by reference to the pupils of given ages, care must be observed to consider only those ages in which all the pupils are in school. If older pupils are drawn into the calculation we are confronted with the fact that many of them who had previously been retarded have at these ages left school and so escape the record. The following statement, therefore, is confined to the pupils of 10, 11, and 12 years of age:

Age.	Number of pupils of this age.	Normal grade.	Retarded, or below normal grade.	
			Number.	Per cent.
10 years.............	499	4	160	32.1
11 years.............	537	5	196	36.5
12 years.............	536	6	251	46.8
Total.............	1,572	....	607	38.6

This table shows clearly how the increasing retardation in upper grades is to a certain point the result of the increasing age of the pupils. At 10 years of age 32.1 per cent of the pupils are retarded, but the proportion rises at 12 years of age to 46.8.

The primary object of the researches of the Immigration Commission was to determine such relationships as might exist between school attendance and school progress to the several racial components of the population. The results of the inquiry are printed in full in the general tables, and a summary of the results may be given here.

In the first instance the actual distribution of pupils by races is of importance. This is given in the following table:

General nativity and race of father of pupil.	Pupils.	
	Number.	Per cent.
Native-born:		
White	3,957	74. 4
Negro	41	.8
Total native-born	3,998	75. 2
Foreign-born:		
Germany	446	8. 4
All other	876	16. 5
Total foreign-born	1,322	24. 8
Grand total	5,320	100. 0

It appears that three-fourths of the pupils of Johnstown had native and one-fourth had foreign parents. Among the pupils of foreign parents there is only one race, the German, which is represented in the schools by as many as 200 representatives. Children of German parents numbered 446 and formed 8.4 per cent of the whole number of children. The pupils of other races were twice as numerous, but they were divided into many special groups, none of which had any considerable number. They are: Bohemian and Moravian (6), Bulgarian (2), Canadian, French (2), Canadian, other than French (15), Croatian (7), Danish (8), English (191), French (5), Greek (3), Hebrew, German (13), Hebrew, Roumanian (1), Hebrew, Russian (72), Hebrew, Other (32), Irish (81), Italian, North (18), Italian, South (25), Italian, not specified (63), Magyar (81), Mexican (1), Polish (35), Russian (2), Ruthenian (10), Scotch (21,) Scotch-Irish (1), Servian (6), Slovak (56), Slovenian (6), Swedish (14), Syrian (15), Welsh (83), and West Indian (1).

To show the distribution of the pupils by grades and races would involve considerable detail in an effort to give facts for each particular grade of the schools. A summary of the situation as concerns the different races can be found in the statement following, where the elementary grades are, as in a previous table, divided into two groups, the primary and its grammar grades.

General nativity and race of father of pupil.	Number of pupils.				Per cent.		
	Primary.	Grammar.	High.	Total.	Primary.	Grammar.	High.
Native-born:							
White	2,066	1,529	362	3,957	52. 2	38. 6	9. 1
Negro	28	13		41	68. 3	31. 7	
Total native-born	2,094	1,542	362	3,998	52. 4	38. 6	9. 1
Foreign-born:							
German	252	174	20	446	56. 5	39. 0	4. 5
All others	560	257	59	876	63. 9	29. 3	6. 7
Total foreign-born	812	431	79	1,322	61. 6	32. 7	5. 7
Grand total	2,906	1,973	441	5,320	54. 6	37. 1	8. 3

This table shows that while the primary schools contain 52.2 per cent of all pupils having native white parents, they contain 61.6 per cent of those having foreign white parents. The only race specifically named in this table, the German, approaches more closely the pupils of native parents than it does the group of pupils of foreign parents, to which it belongs. This parallelism between the children of native parentage and those of German parentage is even more marked in the grammar school, these grades having just about the same proportion of each. On the other hand, by reason of the smaller proportions of pupils of foreign races, the general average for the foreign-born is not a little lower than that for children of native parentage. The contrast between the two groups is still more marked in the high schools. These schools contain 9.1 per cent of the children of native parents and only 5.7 per cent of those of foreign parents. Nor do the Germans rise above the average in this class of school; rather, they fall below it.

The relation which exists between the ages of the pupils and the grades in which they are found is expressed in the following table relating to the retardation of elementary pupils generally and of those of the ages of 10 to 12 years in particular.

	All elementary pupils.			Pupils 10, 11, and 12 years of age.		
General nativity and race of father of pupil.	Number.	Retarded, overage.	Per cent retarded.	Number.	Retarded, under grade.	Per cent retarded.
Native-born:						
White....................	3,595	1,089	30.3	1,159	412	35.5
Negro....................	41	26	63.4	179	76	....
Total native-born..........	3,636	1,115	30.7	1,338	488	36.5
Foreign-born:						
German....................	426	133	31.2	165	65	39.4
All others....................	817	267	32.7	234	119	....
Total foreign-born..........	1,243	400	32.2	399	184	46.1
Grand total..........	4,879	1,515	31.1	1,572	607	38.6

The first three columns of this table, devoted to a general retardation, show a striking uniformity, in the percentage of retardation thus calculated, between children of native-born and those of foreign-born parents.

In the second section of the table a comparison is given which applies to a more limited group of pupils, namely, those in the ages of 10 to 12 years. When the pupils are thus selected so as to secure a uniform age distribution in comparing the different groups, it will be noted that the children of foreign-born parents have a greater retardation than those of native parents.

PUPILS OF THE PUBLIC SCHOOLS—INTENSIVE TABLES.

The tables thus far given present only the most general aspect of the school statistics of Johnstown, and form an introduction to the consideration of the more detailed tables dealing with such facts relating to the school history of the pupils and their home environment as were made the subject of study in the schedules of the Immigration Commission. The general tables relating to these subjects present a considerable body of detail with division of the pupils by race and with specific mention of some of the more important races. In the summary tables to be presented here space will permit only the consideration of general groups, and not that of special races.

PUPILS BY RACE.

In the general tables, as well as in the summaries which follow, the pupils of native parentage are contrasted with those of foreign parentage. In the general tables the latter are further divided according to races, but in the summaries which here follow the only division will be into two groups, one representing the English-speaking race and the other the non-English-speaking races. The small number of negro children, while it appears in the aggregate for all pupils, is not separately mentioned. Hence it will be noted that the total for the native white and for the foreign is somewhat short of the aggregate for all pupils.

As a preliminary to the discussion of these tables it may be noted that the cards furnished the Commission were at times defective. Questions were answered ambiguously or the answers were omitted. In some cases this ambiguity or omission concerned one item, in other cases different items. In tabulation, therefore, these cards had to be disregarded, and consequently the totals which are given in the several tables, though closely approximate to one another in number, are not identical.

The general object of the investigation was to determine, by race, the relation to school progress and advancement of various facts in the individual experience of the children and in the conditions under which they lived which might have an influence upon their school standing.

One of the most important considerations in this connection is the fact that the population in our cities is constantly shifting from place to place, and that this change in residence, where it involves changes in school for the children, means an interruption of studies which is generally not to the advantage of the child. The first table, therefore, is concerned with the birthplace of the pupils, and shows the number of pupils born in Johnstown in comparison with those born elsewhere.

Racial group.	Birthplace of pupil.			
	Johns-town.	Else-where.	Total.	Per cent born else-where.
All pupils	3,704	1,369	5,073	27.0
Native-born white fathers	2,907	857	3,764	22.8
Foreign-born fathers	776	493	1,269	38.8
English-speaking	254	119	373	31.9
Non-English-speaking	522	374	896	41.7

Of all the pupils in the schools of Johnstown 73 per cent were born in the city itself and 27 per cent were born elsewhere. As would naturally be expected, the proportion of children born elsewhere is larger among the group having foreign-born parents than among those having native parents. It is largest in the non-English-speaking group, probably because this group represents, in the main, migration of a later date than does the English-speaking group. There is, however, a very notable proportion (over one-fifth) of pupils having native fathers who were born outside of Johnstown, the city of their present residence, and the change in residence thus indicated must have had some effect upon the school standing.

From the standpoint of the schools the important question is not whether the child was born in another city, but whether he lived in another city long enough to go to school there. In such case his schooling has been interrupted probably to his disadvantage, while in the case of children born elsewhere but who were brought to Johnstown before the school age was attained no such interruption of studies has taken place. How far the children of Johnstown who were not born in that city have suffered the disadvantage of a change of schools is in part indicated by the table following, which refers to children born in the United States but not in Johnstown, and indicates the number of those who had previously attended school.

Racial group.	Children born in the United States but not in Johnstown.		
	Total.	Having attended school elsewhere.	
		Number.	Per cent.
All pupils	1,106	494	44.7
Native-born white fathers	842	368	43.7
Foreign-born fathers	245	118	48.2
English-speaking	100	59	59.0
Non-English-speaking	145	59	40.7

It appears from this table that 44.7 per cent of these pupils had attended school elsewhere. This proportion is fairly uniform for the different racial groups, though it is somewhat larger for the English-speaking group than for the non-English-speaking. It is not to be inferred, as already indicated, that the other children born outside of Johnstown but who had not attended school elsewhere were neglected by their parents, since for the most part they were probably too young to have attended school in the city of their birth before the change in the residence of their parents occurred.

Other things being equal, the progress of the child in school depends, obviously, upon the number of years which he remains in school. This in turn depends not only upon the age at which he leaves the school but also in some degree upon the age at which he enters. There is generally some option allowed to parents as to when they will send their children to school, as under ordinary circumstances they may send them to school at the age of 6 years but are not required by compulsory school laws to do so until the children reach 8 years. Hence the importance of determining the age at which pupils actually enter school. This was done by inference in the general discussion by showing the ages of the pupils actually in school. In the special investigation this information was obtained directly from all the pupils by ascertaining the age at which they first went to the public schools of the United States. The answers to the question are tabulated in the following statement:

Pupils entering school at different ages.

Age.	Number.	Per cent.
5 years and under	235	4.5
6 years	3,899	75.3
7 years	697	13.5
8 years and over	348	6.7
Total	5,179	100.0

It appears from this statement that only a small percentage of the children entered school at the age of 5 years or less. In considering this statement it must be remembered that the question as formulated takes no cognizance of the age at which the pupils may have entered the kindergarten, but refers only to the age at entering the first grade. On the other hand, three-fourths of the children entered school at the age of 6 years. Of the remainder more than one-half entered school at the age of 7 years, and only a comparatively small percentage (6.7) went to the public schools for the first time at the age of 8 years or over.

There is a peculiar interest which attaches to the belated pupils. Those who do not enter school until they are 8 years of age are not infrequently children whose parents have refrained from sending them to school because they believed it to be in the best interests of the child not to send it to school until it had reached a better physical development than could be anticipated at 6 years of age. The proportion of children who entered school at the age of 8 years and over is indicated for each of the racial groups in the table following:

Racial group.	Total number of pupils.	Pupils entering at the age of 8 years and over.	
		Number.	Per cent.
All pupils	5,179	348	6.7
Native-born white fathers	3,877	195	5.0
Foreign-born fathers	1,262	141	11.2
English-speaking	378	24	6.3
Non-English-speaking	884	117	13.2

Only 5 per cent of the children having native parents deferred their entering the public schools until they were 8 years of age or over. In formulating the question it did not seem practicable to make it apply to all schools, and it may well be that some of the children here noted had previously had some experience in private or parochial schools. This consideration applies with still greater force to the children of foreign-born fathers, of whom 11.2 per cent did not go to the public schools of the United States until they were 8 years of age or over. Some of these pupils may have attended the parochial schools and some of them may have attended schools abroad before coming to this country.   While we have no positive information of the numbers who may have been in the public and parochial schools, we know that at least 53 of the pupils here under consideration attended schools abroad before coming to this country.   If we eliminate the pupils born abroad, we find that there were 1,172 pupils of native birth and of foreign parentage, of whom 88 did not go to the public schools until they were 8 years of age or over.   This number represents a percentage of 7.5 of the whole number, only slightly greater than that noted for the children of both native birth and native parentage.

The figures just cited show that the great majority of pupils begin school work at a very early age.   It follows therefore as a matter of course, that most of them begin with the first grade of the public schools.   The table referring to the grade in which pupils enter school confirms this assumption, the facts for those entering the first grade being noted in the summary following:

Racial group.	Pupils entering the public schools.		
	Total.	Entering first grade.	
		Number.	Per cent.
All pupils	5,209	4,953	95.1
Native-born white fathers	3,882	3,713	95.6
Foreign-born fathers	1,286	1,201	93.4
English-speaking	384	369	96.1
Non-English-speaking	902	832	92.2

Of the entire number of pupils 95 per cent began school work in the first grade, though the percentage is somewhat smaller for pupils of foreign parentage than for those of native parentage.   It is smallest among the group of non-English-speaking races, which, as already noted, contains a somewhat larger proportion of children who were themselves born abroad than does the group of English-speaking races.

The effect of late entrance in the schools on the standing of pupils has often been a matter of discussion in educational circles.   The thought has been expressed that the belated pupils not infrequently enter the second or higher grades by reason of the fact that they have enjoyed some training at home.   How far this may be the case is in part indicated by the table following, which shows how many pupils entering school for the first time at 8 years of age enter the first grade:

Racial group.	Pupils entering school at the age of 8 years and over.		
	Total.	Entering the first grade.	
		Number.	Per cent.
All pupils	340	196	57.6
Native-born white fathers	191	104	54.5
Foreign-born fathers	137	81	59.1
English-speaking	22	13	59.1
Non-English-speaking	115	81	70.4

The evidence of the table is not wholly conclusive. It shows that among all the pupils 57.6 per cent had to begin at the beginning. Whether the remainder were enabled to begin somewhat higher up in the school course because they had received some instruction at home, or whether it was because they had previously attended a private or parochial school, is not disclosed by the investigation. The largest proportion of pupils entering the first grade is found among the children of non-English-speaking foreign fathers. While this seems in contradiction with the fact that some of these pupils had attended school abroad, it is of course explained by the unfamiliarity of the children with the English language, which in many cases necessitates placing them in the first grade in order to acquire English, irrespective of what their attainments may be in their native tongue.

A further series of tables relates exclusively to children of foreign parents, and is designed to bring out so far as this can be done by statistical methods some relationship between the school advancement of the pupils and the conditions under which they live.

The first of these tables relates to the citizenship of the father. Other things being equal, it can be assumed that where the father is naturalized or has taken some steps toward naturalization there is a closer contact between the home life and the conditions generally prevailing in the community than where the father is an alien. It must, however, be remembered that the matter of citizenship is intimately bound up with the length of residence. Persons can not be naturalized until they have been five years in the United States, and hence the following table relates only to the children whose fathers had been in the United States five years or more:

Racial group.	Foreign fathers of 5 or more years' residence.		
	Total.	Aliens.	
		Number.	Per cent.
English-speaking	352	38	10.8
Non-English-speaking	843	203	24.1
Total.	1,195	241	20.2

This table shows that among children of English-speaking antecedents 10.8 per cent of the fathers are aliens, but among those of non-English-speaking origin 24.1 per cent are aliens. In considering these figures it should be remembered that the two groups are not exactly comparable with respect to the length of residence. Though all have been here five years and are eligible for naturalization, the non-English-speaking fathers have had, as a rule, somewhat shorter terms of residence than those which speak English.

It is therefore of importance to note the length of residence.   For the fathers of all the pupils this is done in the following table:

Length of residence of foreign-born fathers.

Period.	Number.	Per cent.
Under 5 years	49	4.0
5 to 9 years	144	11.8
10 to 19 years	247	20.2
20 years and over	783	64.0
Total	1,223	100.0

It appears from this table that most of the children, 64 per cent, had fathers who had been twenty years or more in the United States, 20.2 per cent had fathers who had been here from ten to nineteen years, and an even smaller number had fathers whose residence had been shorter than ten years.   To ascertain how far these conditions may differ among the different racial groups, the reader is referred to the general tables.

Another series of tables is devoted to the exhibiting of certain features of the immediate school history of the children.   These refer to the character of attendance and the method by which the pupils obtained access to the grades in which they are now found.

That regular attendance is an indispensable requisite for regular advancement in the schools is so obvious that it needs little comment.   Just how far attendance is regular and how far it is irregular was sought to be ascertained by a question as to the number of days during the term which had been attended by each pupil.   The answers were very various and for the purpose of tabular presentation they were divided into groups according to definite proportions of the whole term.   The following summary derived from this table gives, by racial groups, the number of pupils whose attendance was distinctly bad in that they were absent from school at least half of the term in question.

Racial group.	Pupils reporting duration of attendance.		
	Total.	Less than one-half of the term.	
		Number.	Per cent.
All pupils	4,689	124	2.6
Native-born white fathers	3,465	86	2.5
Foreign-born fathers	1,187	37	3.1
English-speaking	334	4	1.2
Non-English-speaking	853	33	3.9

This table shows that the number of pupils with very imperfect attendance is, among the whole number of pupils, very inconsiderable.   It is, however, somewhat larger for pupils of foreign-born parents, and especially those of the non-English-speaking races, than it is for the children of native parents.

The introductory table of this series refers to the birthplace of the pupils, and endeavors to throw some light upon the mobility of the population in relation to the school attendance of children. It does not, however, include within its scope changes in residence which may have taken place within the city itself. This is in part indicated by the table which reports the method by which the pupils gained access to the grade in which they are now found. The results for all of the pupils are shown in the table following.

Pupils reporting method of access to present grade.

Method.	Number.	Per cent.
By regular course	3,521	77.0
By transfer from another public school of the city	188	4.1
By transfer from a public school elsewhere	159	3.5
By transfer from a private school	64	1.4
Not promoted	640	14.0
Total	4,572	100.0

It appears from this table that little more than three-fourths of the pupils in attendance in Johnstown schools reached the grade in which they are now found by the regular course, that is, by promotion from a lower grade or, in the case of first-grade pupils, by entering school for the first time. A considerable number represent transfer either from other schools in the city or from outside schools. As many as 14 per cent failed of promotion in the previous year.

The following table gives the number and proportion of pupils who entered their present grade by the regular course, divided by racial groups:

Racial group.	Pupils reporting method of access to present grade.		
	Total.	By regular course.	
		Number.	Per cent.
All pupils	4,572	3,521	77.0
Native-born white fathers	3,377	2,629	77.8
Foreign-born fathers	1,156	867	75.0
English-speaking	329	249	75.7
Non-English-speaking	827	618	74.5

It will be noted that as between the various racial groups there is comparatively little difference in the proportions of pupils who entered the grades by the regular course and of those who were transferred to it and failed of promotion.

PUPILS BY NATIVITY.

The intensive investigation enables us to distinguish the pupils not only by parentage but also by nativity. Hence, among the pupils of foreign parentage we can distinguish from the total group those who were themselves born abroad. These numbered 247 pupils in the Johnstown schools, most of them (228) being pupils of the non-

English-speaking races. The proportion of such pupils who were born abroad is most conspicuous among the children of Italian parentage.

Of 237 pupils born abroad, a large number—147, or more than one-half—were under 6 years of age at the time of their arrival in the United States. Of 90 pupils who at the time of their arrival in the United States were 6 years of age or over, 53 had attended school abroad. Information is contained in the tables regarding 228 pupils with respect to their age at the time of entering public schools in the United States. Of these pupils, 78 were 8 years of age and over. A large number (50) of them, however, entered the first grade.

Among this small group of pupils born abroad it would naturally be expected that the home conditions would hardly be favorable to school progress, as not only the children but most of the parents have arrived only recently in the United States. The parents are generally aliens, 160 out of 234 being so reported. Since, moreover, the greater number of these children had parents who did not speak English as their mother tongue, and as the parents had been a short time here, there is a very large proportion of these children who hear no English whatever in their homes. This is true of 198 out of 226 pupils. The number of pupils whose fathers did not speak the English language was 113 in a total of 221.

That the conditions here noted are not favorable to school progress is obvious, and it is equally evident that the presence of these children born abroad must have some effect upon the resulting percentages for retardation of the total number of children having foreign parents. How far this is the case is indicated by the following table:

	Number of pupils.		
Nativity and parentage.		Retarded.	
	Total.	Number.	Per cent.
Native white, native parents	3,595	1,089	30.3
White, foreign parents	1,243	400	32.2
Native white, foreign parents	996	286	28.6
Foreign white	247	114	46.1

The significant fact which is here indicated is that the children of foreign parents who are themselves of native birth show quite as favorable conditions as regards school progress as those children of wholly native antecedents. This analysis shows clearly that the only reason why the pupils of foreign parentage taken as a whole fall below those of native parentage as respects school progress is because of those pupils who are born abroad, inasmuch as the pupils of the second generation show equally favorable conditions with the children of native birth.

SCHOOL PROGRESS AND RETARDATION.

The general tables for the intensive investigation are so arranged that the various characteristics to which these tables refer can be studied with reference to the distribution of the pupils by races and at the same time with reference to the progress of these pupils in the schools, as indicated negatively by the degree of retardation. In each group the number of retarded children, as well as the whole number of children, is indicated. One of these tables, however, is designed to measure school progress directly. The table results from a comparison of the number of years which the pupils have been in school and the grades in which they are found. A pupil who has been two years in school is, if in the third grade, in advance of the position which would normally be expected. If that pupil is in the second grade his progress has been regular. If in the first grade his progress has been slower than the school plan contemplates. The facts of the table are here summarized by racial groups for those pupils who had been in school longer than the grades would imply.

Racial group.	Pupils reporting number of years in school.		
	Total.	More than grade.	
		Number.	Per cent.
All pupils	5,070	2,448	48.3
Native-born white fathers	3,796	1,884	49.6
Foreign-born fathers	1,236	547	44.2
English-speaking	366	169	46.2
Non-English-speaking	870	378	43.4

It appears that nearly one-half of the pupils have been in school longer than the time necessary to attain their present grades by regular advancement, this proportion being somewhat larger among the children of native parents than among those of foreign parents. These numbers are higher than those which have already been cited for the retardation of all pupils. The reason for this difference lies in the fact that the present table measures all the failures which have occurred, while previous tables measure only those failures whose result is to bring the child to an age which is inappropriate for the grade in which he is found. A child who enters the first grade at the age of 6 years and is obliged to repeat the grade will through the remainder of his school life have been in school a longer number of years than the grade, but will not, unless he has further failures, be regarded as a retarded child. This accounts for the difference between the two tables, and confirms a general experience that if retardation be measured strictly by the progress of the children rather than by the relation between their ages and their grades, the number of retarded children will always be greater in the former than in the latter case.

In the general discussion of retardation a note has been made of the fact that the ages of the pupils may have a considerable influence in determining the degree of retardation when this is measured by a comparison of all the pupils. Cautions have been expressed at various points lest false conclusions be drawn concerning certain races which may have an unusually large or unusually small proportion of young pupils. Before discussing the relation to the question of retardation of the various factors examined in the special investigation, it may be well to indicate how far these considerations apply to the groups now under discussion.

The table following, therefore, gives a statement which shows the number and proportion of children in each racial group who are under 8 years of age.

Racial group.	Number of pupils.		
	Total.	Under 8 years of age.	
		Number.	Per cent.
All pupils....	5,320	1,108	20.8
Native-born white fathers....	3,957	795	20.1
Foreign-born fathers....	1,322	305	23.1
English-speaking....	392	60	15.3
Non-English-speaking....	930	245	26.3

It will be observed that contrasting the children of native fathers with those of foreign fathers the former have a somewhat smaller percentage of these young children. If, on the other hand, the children of foreign-born fathers be divided into two groups, it will be noted that among the children of English-speaking foreign fathers the percentage of young children is considerably smaller than among the children of native fathers, while this percentage is considerably greater in the case of non-English-speaking fathers. The effect of these different proportions is to increase relatively the divisor by which the proportion of retardation is obtained in the case of the children of foreign fathers more than in the case of children of native fathers, with the consequent result that for native children the percentage of retardation is relatively heightened and for those of foreign fathers relatively depressed.

In order to eliminate the differences in ages as a factor in retardation, the following table confines the computation to children of 8 years of age and over.

Racial group.	Pupils 8 years of age and over.		
	Total.	Retarded.	
		Number.	Per cent.
All pupils....	4,212	1,659	39.4
Native-born white fathers....	3,162	1,212	38.3
Foreign-born fathers....	1,017	423	41.6
English-speaking....	332	115	34.6
Non-English-speaking....	685	308	45.0

It will be observed that the average retardation is 39.4 per cent, and that this is somewhat higher for the children of foreign fathers and somewhat less for those of native fathers.

Bearing in mind the fact that general retardation is represented by 39.4 per cent of pupils of 8 years of age and over, we may in the following table present the relationship which exists between the several factors investigated by the Commission and the degree of retardation. In interpreting this table conditions favorable to school progress will be found wherever the particular percentage of retardation falls below the average 39.4, while in those cases where the percentage of retardation rises above this average conditions unfavorable to school progress must be inferred.

Characteristics, and pupils to whom they refer.	Pupils of 8 years of age and more reported.		
	Total.	Retarded.	
		Number.	Per cent.
Birthplace, all pupils:			
Born in Johnstown	2,894	1,031	35.6
Born elsewhere in United States	954	434	45.5
Born abroad	184	114	62.0
School attendance, pupils born in United States outside of city:			
Having attended school elsewhere	460	243	52.8
Not having attended school elsewhere	479	184	38.4
Age at entering school, all pupils:			
5 years and under	160	44	27.5
6 years	2,966	968	32.6
7 years	625	333	53.3
8 years	171	126	73.7
9 years	36	31	86.1
10 years and over	141	96	68.1
Grade entered, all pupils:			
First	3,857	1,472	38.2
Second	103	56	54.4
Third	30	21	70.0
Fourth	28	22	78.6
Fifth and higher	91	43	47.3
Years in school, all pupils:			
In school less years than grade	273	66	24.2
In schools same years as grade	1,469	203	13.8
In school more years than grade	2,275	1,307	57.5
Ability to speak English, pupils of fathers of non-English-speaking foreign races:			
Fathers speak English	573	234	40.8
Fathers do not speak English	94	62	66.0
Citizenship, pupils with foreign-born fathers:			
Fathers have first or second naturalization papers	767	286	37.3
Fathers are aliens	189	115	60.8
Residence of fathers, pupils with foreign-born fathers:			
Under 5 years	29	17	58.6
5 to 9 years	87	50	57.5
10 to 19 years	172	67	39.0
20 years or more	643	242	37.6
Home language, pupils with fathers of non-English-speaking foreign races:			
English used in the home	350	145	41.4
English not used in the home	333	162	48.6
Proportion of term attended, all pupils:			
Nine-tenths or more	2,943	1,090	37.0
Three-fourths but less than nine-tenths	452	215	47.6
One-half but less than three-fourths	149	86	57.7
Less than one-half	94	58	61.7
Access to present grade, all pupils:			
Regular course	2,639	822	31.1
By transfer from another public school in city	171	83	48.5
By transfer from public school elsewhere	139	90	64.7
By transfer from private school	60	33	55.0
Not promoted	517	356	68.9

This table shows that the retardation of pupils born in Johnstown is less than the average, and of pupils born in the United States but not in Johnstown it is above the average, while it reaches a much higher point for the small group of children who were born abroad. It shows, moreover, for those pupils who were born in the United States but not in Johnstown that the percentage of retardation was much greater among those who had attended school elsewhere than among those who had not previously been to school. As already explained, the first group comprises those children whose school attendance has been interrupted by the change of residence of their parents, while the latter group comprises for the most part children who were brought to Johnstown by their parents before they had attained the school age.

The relation which exists between the age of the pupils at entering school and their progress in the schools seems clearly indicated by these figures. In the small group of children who entered the grades at the age of 5 years and under, only 27.5 per cent are retarded. For the much larger number who entered school at the age of 6 years 32.6 per cent are retarded. Both of these proportions are considerably below the general average. On the other hand, for those pupils who entered school at the age of 7 and above, considerably higher percentages of retardation are observed, the proportion growing as the age of the pupil entering school advances. The only exception to this is in the small group of those who enter school at the age of 10 years and upward. This group, as already explained, consists to a considerable extent of children who had previously been in some other type of school than the public school of the United States. In like manner it is observed that for the great bulk of the pupils who entered school in the first grade, the rate of retardation approximates the average for the entire number but is slightly below it. For the much smaller groups who entered school above the first grade much higher percentages of retardation are recorded, increasing generally as the pupils entered at a more advanced stage. These pupils, as has already been indicated, may include some particularly gifted children, but also include those who had previously been at school but not in public schools.

A comparison of retardation with the number of years of school shows that among those pupils who are now in the same grade as the years in school would indicate only 13.8 per cent are in the retarded class, but of those pupils who are in school a less number of years than their grade 24.2 per cent are retarded. In both of these cases we are probably dealing with children who have been to school somewhere before but whose experience in the public schools of the United States is only equal to or is even less than the number of years which their present grade implies. It might be anticipated that all of the children who had been in school for any greater number of years than the grade implies would be retarded, but by the technical definition which has been given to this term it is applicable to only 57.5 per cent of these pupils. The technical definition therefore allows for a certain amount of failure, and it might be said that this technical definition is therefore somewhat more generous to the pupils than the strict record of the amount of time spent in schools.

Certain groups of figures relate exclusively to the children of foreign-born fathers. If attention be directed to the length of residence it is found that the retardation of the pupil diminishes in proportion generally as the length of residence of the fathers in the United States increases. This being the case, it is not surprising that there is marked difference in the retardation among those children whose fathers are aliens as compared with those who have taken some steps toward naturalization, the aliens being for the most part persons of shorter residence than the naturalized. Among the group of children whose parents had no linguistic English antecedents, the proportion of retardation is greater where English is not used in the home than where the language is in use. It is still more conspicuous in the few cases where the fathers did not speak English.

No record could be made of the school habits of the children covering their entire school history, but certain information is contained in the tables regarding the more recent happenings. Thus the figures are available concerning the duration of attendance in the present term. If these figures be brought into conjunction with those for retardation it should be remembered that this is done with the idea that the present school habits of the children as to attendance are presumably the same as those which have characterized them in the past. That this presumption is reasonably accurate seems to be evident by the figures here printed. They show that the children with a perfect attendance have less retardation than the average, while the degree of retardation increases as the attendance diminishes in quantity. Somewhat analogous are the figures indicating the access of pupils to the present grade. Among those who reached their present grade in the regular course the percentage of retardation is considerably lower than the average, while among all of those who came into their present grades by irregular methods the percentage of retardation is much above the average. This applies, of course, in the most marked degree to those children who were not promoted, but it is also applicable to those children who were transferred from other schools.

GENERAL TABLES.

PUBLIC SCHOOL PUPILS: GENERAL INVESTIGATION.

TABLE **1.**—*Grade and age—Number of pupils of each age in each grade, by sex.*

BOYS.

Ages in years.	Elementary grades.								Total.	High school.				Total.	Grand total.
	1.	2.	3.	4.	5.	6.	7.	8.		First year.	Second year.	Third year.	Fourth year.		
4															
5	24								24						24
6	229	16							245						245
7	111	142	10						263						263
8	47	157	88	5					297						297
9	17	68	111	88	11	1			296						296
10	2	23	67	68	62	10	1		233						233
11	2	14	27	63	96	54	15	1	272	1				1	273
12		5	19	30	79	87	42	5	267	1				1	268
13	1	3	4	14	55	48	43	46	214	4				4	218
14	1	4	4	5	22	39	48	63	186	16	2			18	204
15				4	9	7	23	40	83	35	10	5		50	133
16	1		1	2	2	2	6	18	32	20	12	15		47	79
17			1					3	4	13	9	8	4	34	38
18										2	4	5	8	19	19
19											4	2	4	10	10
20 or over										1				1	1
Total	435	432	332	279	336	248	178	176	2,416	92	42	35	16	185	2,601

GIRLS.

Ages in years.	Elementary grades.								Total.	High school.				Total.	Grand total.
	1.	2.	3.	4.	5.	6.	7.	8.		First year.	Second year.	Third year.	Fourth year.		
4															
5	27	3							30						30
6	249	30							279						279
7	102	151	13	1					267						267
8	22	124	117	17	1				281						281
9	12	49	90	103	19	2			275						275
10	4	14	50	93	92	11	2		266						266
11	1	10	14	65	97	62	15		264						264
12	1	6	13	23	75	69	69	12	268						268
13	2		5	11	46	60	83	48	255	10				10	265
14				5	12	22	46	78	163	33	2			35	198
15					5	9	24	51	89	43	13			56	145
16							5	16	21	28	24	13		65	86
17			1				2	2	5	7	15	25	3	50	55
18										1	3	13	8	25	25
19												6	7	13	13
20 or over										1			1	2	2
Total	420	387	303	318	347	235	246	207	2,463	123	57	57	19	256	2,719

The Immigration Commission.

TABLE 1.—*Grade and age—Number of pupils of each age in each grade, by sex*—Contd.

TOTAL.

Ages in years.	Elementary grades.									High school.					Grand total.
	1.	2.	3.	4.	5.	6.	7.	8.	Total.	First year.	Second year.	Third year.	Fourth year.	Total.	
4															
5	51	3							54						54
6	478	46							524						524
7	213	293	23	1					530						530
8	69	281	205	22	1				578						578
9	29	117	201	191	30	3			571						571
10	6	37	117	161	154	21	3	1	499						499
11	3	24	41	128	193	116	30	1	536	1				1	537
12	1	11	32	53	154	156	111	17	535	1				1	536
13	3	3	9	25	101	108	126	94	469	14				14	483
14	1	4	4	10	34	61	94	141	349	49	4			53	402
15			4	14	16	47	91	172	78	23	5		106	278	
16	1		1	2	2	2	11	34	53	48	36	28		112	165
17			2				2	5	9	20	24	33	7	84	93
18										3	7	18	16	44	44
19											4	8	11	23	23
20 or over										1	1		1	3	3
Total	855	819	635	597	683	483	424	383	4,879	215	99	92	35	441	5,320

TABLE 2.—*Race, sex, and grade*—*Number of pupils of each sex in each grade, by general nativity and race of father of pupil.*

General nativity and race of father of pupil.	Elementary grades.									High school.					Grand total.
	1.	2.	3.	4.	5.	6.	7.	8.	Total.	First year.	Second year.	Third year.	Fourth year.	Total.	
Native-born:															
White—															
Male	293	313	229	206	264	180	142	138	1,765	76	34	28	14	152	1,917
Female	303	286	202	234	257	188	194	166	1,830	99	46	48	17	210	2,040
Total	596	599	431	440	521	368	336	304	3,595	175	80	76	31	362	3,957
Negro—															
Male	5	2	4	2	3	3	1		18						18
Female	3	7	3	2	1	2	2	1	23						23
Total	8	9	7	4	4	5	3	1	41						41
Total native-born—															
Male	298	315	233	208	265	183	143	138	1,783	76	34	28	14	152	1,935
Female	306	293	205	236	260	190	196	167	1,853	99	46	48	17	210	2,063
Total	604	608	438	444	525	373	339	305	3,636	175	80	76	31	362	3,998
Foreign-born:															
Canadian (other than French)—															
Male	1	1			1		1	1	4	1		1		1	5
Female			2		2	1	1	2	9					1	10
Total	1	1	2		3	1	2	3	13	1		1		2	15
English—															
Male	9	12	13	15	10	15	5	7	86	3	1	1	1	6	92
Female	5	10	13	13	19	8	9	8	85	9	2	2	1	14	99
Total	14	22	26	28	29	23	14	15	171	12	3	3	2	20	191
German—															
Male	31	34	34	23	35	26	10	11	204	3	3	2		8	212
Female	29	26	37	37	36	23	20	14	222	5	5	2		12	234
Total	60	60	71	60	71	49	30	25	426	8	8	4		20	446
Hebrew, German—															
Male			1		1		1		3	1				1	4
Female		1	1	1	2				5	3	1			4	9
Total		1	2	1	3		1		8	4	1			5	13
Hebrew, Russian—															
Male	6	8	5	8	3	2	2	3	39	3	1	1		5	44
Female	5	2	8	3	1		2	1	26	1	1			2	28
Total	11	10	13	11	4	2	4	4	65	4	2	1		7	72
Hebrew, Other—															
Male	3	3	2	1	1		2	2	13	1	1	1		3	16
Female	3	3		1	1	2	5	3	16						16
Total	3	6	2	2	2	2	7	5	29	1	1	1		3	32

TABLE 2.—Race, sex, and grade—Number of pupils of each sex in each grade, by general nativity and race of father of pupil—Continued.

General nativity and race of father of pupil.	Elementary grades.									High school.					Grand total.
	1.	2.	3.	4.	5.	6.	7.	8.	Total.	First year.	Second year.	Third year.	Fourth year.	Total.	
Foreign-born—Continued.															
Irish—															
Male	10		5	1	3	3	4	3	29	1	2		1	4	33
Female	5	9	6	2	7	1	4	7	41	4	1	1	1	7	48
Total	15	9	11	3	10	4	8	10	70	5	3	1	2	11	81
Italian, North—															
Male	3	7			2				12						12
Female	6								6						6
Total	9	7			2				18						18
Italian, South—															
Male	4	6	4	4					18						18
Female	4	2				1			7						7
Total	8	8	4	4		1			25						25
Italian (not specified)—															
Male	11	11	6	3	2				33						33
Female	10	7	8	4			1		30						30
Total	21	18	14	7	2		1		63						63
Magyar—															
Male	13	9	9	2	1	3	2		39						39
Female	13	8	12	5	2	1	1		42						42
Total	26	17	21	7	3	4	3		81						81
Polish—															
Male	10	6	2	1	1				20						20
Female	10	3		2					15						15
Total	20	9	2	3	1				35						35
Ruthenian—															
Male	3	3		1					7						7
Female		1	1	1					3						3
Total	3	4	1	2					10						10
Scotch—															
Male	2	2	1	1	2	1	1	1	11	1				1	12
Female	2	4	1		1		1		9						9
Total	4	6	2	1	3	1	2	1	20	1				1	21
Slovak—															
Male	13	7	4	2	2		1	3	32						32
Female	8	7	3	2	1		1	2	24						24
Total	21	14	7	4	3		2	5	56						56
Swedish—															
Male	1	1	1	1	2		1	1	8						8
Female	1	1		1	1		1		5			1		1	6
Total	2	2	1	2	3		2	1	13			1		1	14

									Total					Total	Grand total
Syrian—															
Male............	4			1					5						5
Female..........	6	1	2	1					10						10
Total............	10	1	2	2					15						15
Welsh—															
Male............	8	2	8	6	4	7	4	5	44	1		2		3	47
Female..........	2	3	2	5	11	3	4	1	31	2	2	1		5	36
Total............	10	5	10	11	15	10	8	6	75	3	2	3		8	83
Other races—*a*															
Male............	9	5	3	2	1	3	1	2	26	1				1	27
Female..........	4	6	4	4	2	3		1	24						24
Total............	13	11	7	6	3	6	1	3	50	1				1	51
Total foreign-born—															
Male............	137	117	99	71	71	65	35	38	633	16	8	7	2	33	666
Female..........	114	94	98	82	87	45	50	40	610	24	11	9	2	46	656
Total............	251	211	197	153	158	110	85	78	1,243	40	19	16	4	79	1,322
Grand total—															
Male............	435	432	332	279	336	248	178	176	2,416	92	42	35	16	185	2,601
Female..........	420	387	303	318	347	235	246	207	2,463	123	57	57	19	256	2,719
Total............	855	819	635	597	683	483	424	383	4,879	215	99	92	35	441	5,320

a "Other races" include 6 Bohemian, 2 Bulgarian, 2 Canadian, French; 7 Croatian, 8 Danish, 5 French, 3 Greek, 1 Hebrew, Roumanian; 1 Mexican, 2 Russian, 6 Servian, 6 Slovenian, 1 West Indian, 1 Scooch-Irish.

TABLE 3.—*Race, sex, and age, by grade—Number of pupils of each age in each grade, by sex and by general nativity and race of father of pupil.*

FIRST GRADE.

BOYS.

General nativity and race of father of pupil.	Number of pupils of each age.												Total.
	5.	6.	7.	8.	9.	10.	11.	12.	13.	14.	15.	16.	
Native-born:													
White	13	165	72	32	7	1	2					1	293
Negro		2		2	1								5
Total native-born	13	167	72	34	8	1	2					1	298
Foreign-born:													
English	1	6		1	1								9
German		13	13	3	2								31
Hebrew, Russian	1	3	1	1									6
Irish	1	6	2	1									10
Italian, North		2	1										3
Italian, South		2		2									4
Italian (not specified)	1	4	4	1	1								11
Magyar	3	5	5										13
Polish	1	6	1	1	1								10
Ruthenian	1		1						1				3
Scotch			1	1									2
Slovak		6	3	1	3								13
Swedish		1											1
Syrian	1	2								1			4
Welsh		4	4										8
Other races a	1	2	3	1	1	1							9
Total foreign-born	11	62	39	13	9	1			1	1			137
Grand total	24	229	111	47	17	2	2		1	1		1	435

GIRLS.

General nativity and race of father of pupil.	Number of pupils of each age.												Total.
	5.	6.	7.	8.	9.	10.	11.	12.	13.	14.	15.	16.	
Native-born:													
White	16	187	70	19	8	1			2				303
Negro		1	2										3
Total native-born	16	188	72	19	8	1			2				306
Foreign-born:													
Canadian (other than French)		1											1
English		3	2										5
German		18	9	1		1							29
Hebrew, Russian	3	2											5
Hebrew, Other		2	1										3
Irish	1	4											5
Italian, North	1	4					1						6
Italian, South	1	2	1										4
Italian (not specified)	1	4	3	1	1								10
Magyar	3	3	4	1		1	1						13
Polish		4	4		2								10
Scotch		2											2
Slovak	1	4	3										8
Swedish		1											1
Syrian		4	1			1							6
Welsh		1	1										2
Other races a		2	1		1								4
Total foreign-born	11	61	30	3	4	3	1	1					114
Grand total	27	249	102	22	12	4	1	1	2				420

a "Other races" includes races having less than 10 representatives in this city and pupils whose race is not reported.

TABLE 3.—*Race, sex, and age, by grade—Number of pupils of each age in each grade, by sex and by general nativity and race of father of pupil—Continued.*

FIRST GRADE—Continued.

TOTAL.

General nativity and race of father of pupil.	Number of pupils of each age.												Total.
	5.	6.	7.	8.	9.	10.	11.	12.	13.	14.	15.	16.	
Native-born:													
White........................	29	352	142	51	15	2	2	....	2	....	....	1	596
Negro........................	....	3	2	2	1	....	....	....	....	....	....		8
Total native-born...........	29	355	144	53	16	2	2	....	2	....	....	1	604
Foreign-born:													
Canadian (other than French).....	....	1	....	....	....	....	....	....	....	....	....		1
English........................	1	9	2	1	1	....	....	....	....	....	....		14
German........................	....	31	22	4	2	1	....	....	....	....	....		60
Hebrew, Russian...............	4	5	1	1	....	....	....	....	....	....	....		11
Hebrew, Other................	....	2	1	....	....	....	....	....	....	....	....		3
Irish.........................	2	10	2	1	....	....	....	....	....	....	....		15
Italian, North................	1	6	1	....	....	....	....	1	....	....	....		9
Italian, South................	1	4	1	2	....	....	....	....	....	....	....		8
Italian (not specified)........	2	8	7	2	2	....	....	....	....	....	....		21
Magyar........................	6	8	9	1	....	1	1	....	....	....	....		26
Polish........................	1	10	5	1	3	....	....	....	....	....	....		20
Ruthenian....................	1	....	1	....	....	....	....	....	1	....	....		3
Scotch........................	....	2	1	1	....	....	....	....	....	....	....		4
Slovak........................	1	10	6	1	3	....	....	....	....	....	....		21
Swedish.......................	....	2	....	....	....	....	....	....	....	....	....		2
Syrian........................	1	6	1	....	....	1	....	....	....	1	....		10
Welsh........................	....	5	5	....	....	....	....	....	....	....	....		10
Other races *a*...............	1	4	4	1	2	1	....	....	....	....	....		13
Total foreign-born...........	22	123	69	16	13	4	1	1	1	1	....	....	251
Grand total..................	51	478	213	69	29	6	3	1	3	1	....	1	855

a "Other races" includes races having less than 10 representatives in this city and pupils whose race is not reported.

TABLE 3.—*Race, sex, and age, by grade—Number of pupils of each age in each grade, by sex and by general nativity and race of father of pupil*—Continued.

SECOND GRADE.

BOYS.

General nativity and race of father of pupil.	Number of pupils of each age.										Total.
	5.	6.	7.	8.	9.	10.	11.	12.	13.	14.	
Native-born:											
White		11	104	115	49	17	9	3	2	3	313
Negro				1						1	2
Total native-born		11	104	116	49	17	9	3	2	4	315
Foreign-born:											
Canadian (other than French)				1							1
English			5	5	1	1					12
German		1	12	14	3	3		1			34
Hebrew, Russian		1	3	3	1						8
Hebrew, Other				1	1		1				3
Italian, North			3	3	1						7
Italian, South			3	1	1	1					6
Italian (not specified)		1	1	5	1		2	1			11
Magyar			3	5	1						9
Polish		1	1		1	1	1		1		6
Ruthenian			1		2						3
Scotch			1	1							2
Slovak		1	1	1	3		1				7
Swedish			1								1
Welsh			1		1						2
Other races *a*			2	1	2						5
Total foreign-born		5	38	41	19	6	5	2	1		117
Grand total		16	142	157	68	23	14	5		4	432

GIRLS.

General nativity and race of father of pupil.	5.	6.	7.	8.	9.	10.	11.	12.	13.	14.	Total.
Native-born:											
White	3	22	117	90	33	11	7	3			286
Negro		1	2	3		1					7
Total native-born	3	23	119	93	33	12	7	3			293
Foreign-born:											
English			5	3		1		1			10
German		2	15	6	2		1				26
Hebrew, German		1									1
Hebrew, Russian			1	1							2
Hebrew, Other		1		1	1						3
Irish			4	4	1						9
Italian, South		1		1							2
Italian (not specified)			1	5	1						7
Magyar			2	2	3			1			8
Polish		1			2						3
Ruthenian			1								1
Scotch				2	2						4
Slovak		1		2	2	1		1			7
Swedish			1								1
Syrian				1							1
Welsh			1	1	1						3
Other races *a*			1	2	1		2				6
Total foreign-born		7	32	31	16	2	3	3			94
Grand total	3	30	151	124	49	14	10	6			387

a "Other races" includes races having less than 10 representatives in this city and pupils whose race is not reported.

TABLE 3.—*Race, sex, and age, by grade—Number of pupils of each age in each grade, by sex and by general nativity and race of father of pupil*—Continued.

SECOND GRADE—Continued.

TOTAL.

General nativity and race of father of pupil.	\multicolumn{10}{c}{Number of pupils of each age.}										Total.
	5.	6.	7.	8.	9.	10.	11.	12.	13.	14.	
Native-born:											
White	3	33	221	205	82	28	16	6	2	3	599
Negro		1	2	4		1				1	9
Total native-born	3	34	223	209	82	29	16	6	2	4	608
Foreign-born:											
Canadian (other than French)				1							1
English			10	8	1	2		1			22
German		3	27	20	5	3	1	1			60
Hebrew, German		1									1
Hebrew, Russian		1	4	4	1						10
Hebrew, Other		1		2	2		1				6
Irish			4	4	1						9
Italian, North			3	3	1						7
Italian, South		1	3	2	1	1					8
Italian (not specified)		1	2	10	2		2	1			18
Magyar			5	7	4			1			17
Polish		2	1		3	1	1		1		9
Ruthenian			2		2						4
Scotch			1	3	2						6
Slovak		2	1	3	5	1	1	1			14
Swedish			2								2
Syrian				1							1
Welsh			2	1	2		2				5
Other races a			3	3	3						11
Total foreign-born		12	70	72	35	8	8	5	1		211
Grand total	3	46	293	281	117	37	24	11	3	4	819

a "Other races" includes races having less than 10 representatives in this city and pupils whose race is not reported.

TABLE **3.**—*Race, sex, and age, by grade—Number of pupils of each age in each grade, by sex and by general nativity and race of father of pupil*—Continued.

THIRD GRADE.

BOYS.

General nativity and race of father of pupil.	Number of pupils of each age.												Total.
	7.	8.	9.	10.	11.	12.	13.	14.	15.	16.	17.	18.	
Native-born:													
White	8	60	77	46	18	14	2	3	....	1	....	....	229
Negro	....	....	1	2	....	1	....	....	....	....	....	....	4
Total native-born	8	60	78	48	18	15	2	3	....	1	....	....	233
Foreign-born:													
English	....	1	8	1	2	1							13
German	....	13	9	9	1	1	....	....	....	1	....		34
Hebrew, German	....	1											1
Hebrew, Russian	1	1	2	1									5
Hebrew, Other	....	1	....	....	....	1							2
Irish	1	3	1										5
Italian, South	....	....	....	2	1	....	1						4
Italian (not specified)	....	1	2	1	....	2							6
Magyar	....	1	2	1	5								9
Polish	....	....	1										1
Scotch	....	1	1										2
Slovak	....	....	2	1	....	1							4
Swedish	....	....	2										2
Welsh	....	3	3	2									8
Other races *a*	....	2	....	1									3
Total foreign-born	2	28	33	19	9	4	2	1	....	....	1	....	99
Grand total	10	88	111	67	27	19	4	4	....	1	1	....	332

GIRLS.

General nativity and race of father of pupil.	7.	8.	9.	10.	11.	12.	13.	14.	15.	16.	17.	18.	Total.
Native-born:													
White	7	87	62	31	9	3	2	....	....	1	....		202
Negro	....	....	....	1	1	1							3
Total native-born	7	87	62	32	10	4	2	....	....	1	....		205
Foreign-born:													
Canadian (other than French)	....	1	1										2
English	2	4	4	1	....	2							13
German	2	13	11	7	....	2	2						37
Hebrew, German	....	....	....	1									1
Hebrew, Russian	....	3	3	1	....	1							8
Irish	....	4	1	....	1								6
Italian (not specified)	....	1	....	5	....	2							8
Magyar	2	1	4	1	3	1							12
Slovak	....	1	2										3
Syrian	....	....	....	1	....	1							2
Welsh	....	1	1										2
Other races *a*	....	1	1	1	....	1							4
Total foreign-born	6	30	28	18	4	9	3	....	....	....	....		98
Grand total	13	117	90	50	14	13	5	....	....	1	....		303

a "Other races" includes races having less than 10 representatives in this city and pupils whose race is not reported.

TABLE 3.—*Race, sex, and age, by grade—Number of pupils of each age in each grade, by sex and by general nativity and race of father of pupil*—Continued.

THIRD GRADE—Continued.

TOTAL.

General nativity and race of father of pupil.	Number of pupils of each age.												Total.
	7.	8.	9.	10.	11.	12.	13.	14.	15.	16.	17.	18.	
Native-born:													
White...............	15	147	139	77	27	17	4	3	....	1	1	....	431
Negro...............	....	....	1	3	1	2	....	....	....	....	....	....	7
Total native-born..............	15	147	140	80	28	19	4	3	....	1	1	....	438
Foreign-born:													
Canadian (other than French)..	...	1	1	....	....	....	....	....	....	....	....	....	2
English........................	2	5	12	2	2	3	....	....	....	....	....	....	26
German........................	2	26	20	16	1	3	2	....	....	....	1	....	71
Hebrew, German................	...	1	....	1	....	....	....	....	....	....	....	....	2
Hebrew, Russian...............	1	4	5	2	....	1	....	....	....	....	....	....	13
Hebrew, Other.................	....	1	....	....	....	1	....	....	....	....	....	....	2
Irish.........................	1	7	2	....	1	....	....	....	....	....	....	....	11
Italian, South................	....	....	....	2	1	....	....	1	....	....	....	....	4
Italian (not specified).......	...	2	2	6	....	2	2	....	....	....	....	....	14
Magyar........................	2	2	6	2	8	1	....	....	....	....	....	....	21
Polish........................	....	....	1	....	....	....	....	....	....	....	....	....	1
Scotch........................	....	1	1	....	....	....	....	....	....	....	....	....	2
Slovak........................	....	1	4	1	....	1	....	....	....	....	....	....	7
Swedish.......................	....	....	2	....	....	....	....	....	....	....	....	....	2
Syrian........................	....	....	....	1	....	....	1	....	....	....	....	....	2
Welsh.........................	....	4	4	2	....	....	....	....	....	....	....	....	10
Other races a.................	....	3	1	2	....	1	....	....	....	....	....	....	7
Total foreign-born..............	8	58	61	37	13	13	5	1	....	....	1	....	197
Grand total....................	23	205	201	117	41	32	9	4	....	1	2	....	635

a "Other races" includes races having less than 10 representatives in this city and pupils whose race is not reported.

TABLE 3.—*Race, sex, and age, by grade—Number of pupils of each age in each grade, by sex and by general nativity and race of father of pupil*—Continued.

FOURTH GRADE.

BOYS.

General nativity and race of father of pupil.	Number of pupils of each age.										Total.
	7.	8.	9.	10.	11.	12.	13.	14.	15.	16.	
Native-born:											
White		5	73	48	42	20	11	3	2	2	206
Negro				1	1						2
Total native-born		5	73	49	43	20	11	3	2	2	208
Foreign-born:											
English			2	4	6	2			1		15
German			4	8	7	4					23
Hebrew, Russian			5	1	1	1					8
Hebrew, Other					1						1
Irish				1							1
Italian, South				1	1			2			4
Italian (not specified)				1	1		1				3
Magyar			1				1				2
Polish				1							1
Ruthenian						1					1
Scotch				1							1
Slovak			1		1						2
Syrian				1							1
Welsh			2		1	1	1		1		6
Other races *a*					1	1					2
Total foreign-born			15	19	20	10	3	2	2		71
Grand total		5	88	68	63	30	14	5	4	2	279

GIRLS.

General nativity and race of father of pupil.	7.	8.	9.	10.	11.	12.	13.	14.	15.	16.	Total.
Native-born:											
White		12	80	68	46	17	6	5			234
Negro						1	1				2
Total native-born		12	80	68	46	18	7	5			236
Foreign-born:											
English			6	2	5						13
German		2	7	18	5	3	2				37
Hebrew, German	1										1
Hebrew, Russian		1	1	1							3
Hebrew, Other			1								1
Irish			1		1						2
Italian (not specified)			1		3						4
Magyar		1	1	1	1	1					5
Polish			2								2
Ruthenian					1						1
Slovak			2								2
Swedish					1						1
Syrian							1				1
Welsh		1	1	2	1						5
Other races *a*				1	1			2			4
Total foreign-born	1	5	23	25	19	5	4				82
Grand total	1	17	103	93	65	23	11	5			318

a "Other races" includes races having less than 10 representatives in this city and pupils whose race is not reported.

TABLE 3.—*Race, sex, and age, by grade—Number of pupils of each age in each grade, by sex and by general nativity and race of father of pupil*—Continued.

FOURTH GRADE—Continued.

TOTAL.

General nativity and race of father of pupil.	Number of pupils of each age.										Total.
	7.	8.	9.	10.	11.	12.	13.	14.	15.	16.	
Native-born:											
White................		17	153	116	88	37	17	8	2	2	440
Negro................				1	1	1	1				4
Total native-born........		17	153	117	89	38	18	8	2	2	444
Foreign-born:											
English................			8	6	11	2			1		28
German................		2	11	26	12	7	2				60
Hebrew, German........	1										1
Hebrew, Russian........		1	6	2		1	1				11
Hebrew, Other........			1		1						2
Irish................			1	1	1						3
Italian, South........				1	1			2			4
Italian (not specified)........			1	1	4		1				7
Magyar................		1	2	1	1	1	1				7
Polish................			2	1							3
Ruthenian................					1	1					2
Scotch................				1							1
Slovak................			3		1						4
Swedish................					1						1
Syrian................				1		1					2
Welsh................		1	3	2	2	1	1		1		11
Other races *a*........				1	2	1	2				6
Total foreign-born........	1	5	38	44	39	15	7	2	2		153
Grand total................	1	22	191	161	128	53	25	10	4	2	597

a "Other races" includes races having less than 10 representatives in this city and pupils whose race is not reported.

TABLE 3.—*Race, sex, and age, by grade—Number of pupils of each age in each grade, by sex and by general nativity and race of father of pupil*—Continued.

FIFTH GRADE.

BOYS.

General nativity and race of father of pupil.	8.	9.	10.	11.	12.	13.	14.	15.	16.	Total.
Native-born:										
White		7	48	79	62	37	21	8	2	264
Negro								1		1
Total native-born		7	48	79	62	37	21	9	2	265
Foreign-born:										
Canadian (other than French)				1						1
English			4	3		3				10
German		1	6	9	8	10	1			35
Hebrew, German			1							1
Hebrew, Russian		2	1							3
Hebrew, Other					1					1
Irish		1		1	1					3
Italian, North				1		1				2
Italian (not specified)					1	1				2
Magyar						1				1
Polish						1				1
Scotch			1		1					2
Slovak			1			1				2
Swedish					2					2
Welsh					2					2
Other races *a*				2	1	1				4
Total foreign-born		4	14	17	17	18	1			71
Grand total		11	62	96	79	55	22	9	2	336

GIRLS.

General nativity and race of father of pupil.	8.	9.	10.	11.	12.	13.	14.	15.	16.	Total.
Native-born:										
White	1	16	68	79	50	31	9	3		257
Negro					2	1				3
Total native-born	1	16	68	79	52	32	9	3		260
Foreign-born:										
Canadian (other than French)			1		1					2
English			3	4	5	4	2	1		19
German		1	10	6	12	5	1	1		36
Hebrew, German			1	1						2
Hebrew, Russian			1							1
Hebrew, Other			1							1
Irish			2	2	2	1				7
Magyar			1		1					2
Ruthenian			1			1				2
Scotch				1						1
Slovak						1				1
Swedish						1				1
Welsh				1						1
Other races *a*		2	3	3	2	1				11
Total foreign-born		3	24	18	23	14	3	2		87
Grand total	1	19	92	97	75	46	12	5		347

a "Other races" includes races having less than 10 representatives in this city and pupils whose race is not reported.

TABLE 3.—*Race, sex, and age, by grade—Number of pupils of each age in each grade, by sex and by general nativity and race of father of pupil—Continued.*

FIFTH GRADE—Continued.

TOTAL.

General nativity and race of father of pupil.	Number of pupils of each age.									Total.
	8.	9.	10.	11.	12.	13.	14.	15.	16.	
Native-born:										
White	1	23	116	158	112	68	30	11	2	521
Negro					2	1		1		4
Total native-born	1	23	116	158	114	69	30	12	2	525
Foreign-born:										
Canadian (other than French)			1	1	1					3
English			7	7	5	7	2	1		29
German		2	16	15	20	15	2	1		71
Hebrew, German			2	1						3
Hebrew, Russian		2	2							4
Hebrew, Other			1		1					2
Irish		1	2	3	3	1				10
Italian, North				1		1				2
Italian (not specified)					1	1				2
Magyar			2		1					3
Polish						1				1
Ruthenian						1				1
Scotch			1	1		1				3
Slovak					2	1				3
Swedish				1	2					3
Welsh		2	3	5	3	2				15
Other races *a*			1		1	1				3
Total foreign-born		7	38	35	40	32	4	2		158
Grand total	1	30	154	193	154	101	34	14	2	683

a "Other races" includes races having less than 10 representatives in this city and pupils whose race is not reported.

SIXTH GRADE.

BOYS.

General nativity and race of father of pupil.	Number of pupils of each age.								Total.
	9.	10.	11.	12.	13.	14.	15.	16.	
Native-born:									
White	1	7	43	59	39	26	3	2	180
Negro				1		1	1		3
Total native-born	1	7	43	60	39	27	4	2	183
Foreign-born:									
English		1	4	5	1	4			15
German		1	4	13	3	5			26
Hebrew, Russian				2	2				4
Hebrew, Other					1		1		2
Irish				3					3
Magyar				1	1	1			3
Polish							1		1
Scotch			1						1
Welsh		1	2	2	1		1		7
Other races *a*				1		2			3
Total foreign-born		3	11	27	9	12	3		65
Grand total	1	10	54	87	48	39	7	2	248

a "Other races" includes races having less than 10 representatives in this city and pupils whose race is not reported.

Table 3.—*Race, sex, and age, by grade—Number of pupils of each age in each grade, by sex and by general nativity and race of father of pupil—Continued.*

SIXTH GRADE—Continued.

GIRLS.

General nativity and race of father of pupil.	Number of pupils of each age.								Total.
	9.	10.	11.	12.	13.	14.	15.	16.	
Native-born:									
White	1	10	52	59	38	20	8	......	188
Negro	......	......	......	1	1	......	......	......	2
Total native-born	1	10	52	60	39	20	8	......	190
Foreign-born:									
Canadian (other than French)	......	......	......	1	......	......	......	......	1
English	......	......	2	3	3	......	......	......	8
German	......	1	5	5	9	2	1	......	23
Hebrew, Russian	......	......	......	......	4	......	......	......	4
Irish	1	......	......	......	......	......	......	......	1
Italian. South	......	......	1	......	......	......	......	......	1
Magyar	......	......	1	......	......	......	......	......	1
Welsh	......	......	1	......	2	......	......	......	3
Other races a	......	......	......	......	3	......	......	......	3
Total foreign-born	1	1	10	9	21	2	1	......	45
Grand total	2	11	62	69	60	22	9	......	235

TOTAL.

General nativity and race of father of pupil.	Number of pupils of each age.								Total.
	9.	10.	11.	12.	13.	14.	15.	16.	
Native-born:									
White	2	17	95	118	77	46	11	2	368
Negro	......	......	......	2	1	1	1	......	5
Total native-born	2	17	95	120	78	47	12	2	373
Foreign-born:									
Canadian (other than French)	......	......	......	1	......	......	......	......	1
English	......	1	6	8	4	4	......	......	23
German	......	2	9	18	12	7	1	......	49
Hebrew, Russian	......	......	......	2	6	......	......	......	8
Hebrew, Other	......	......	......	......	1	......	1	......	2
Irish	1	......	......	3	......	......	......	......	4
Italian, South	......	......	1	......	......	......	......	......	1
Magyar	......	......	1	1	1	1	......	......	4
Polish	......	......	......	......	......	......	1	......	1
Scotch	......	......	1	......	......	......	......	......	1
Welsh	......	1	3	2	3	......	1	......	10
Other races a	......	......	......	1	3	2	......	......	6
Total foreign-born	1	4	21	36	30	14	4	......	110
Grand total	3	21	116	156	108	61	16	2	483

a "Other races" includes races having less than 10 representatives in this city and pupils whose race is not reported.

TABLE 3.—*Race, sex, and age, by grade—Number of pupils of each age in each grade, by sex and by general nativity and race of father of pupil*—Continued.

SEVENTH GRADE.

BOYS.

General nativity and race of father of pupil.	Number of pupils of each age.								Total.
	10.	11.	12.	13.	14.	15.	16.	17.	
Native-born:									
White..........................	......	13	36	29	37	21	6	......	142
Negro...........................	......	......	......	......	1	......	......	......	1
Total native-born..............	......	13	36	29	38	21	6	......	143
Foreign-born:									
Canadian (other than French).......	......	......	......	......	1	......	......	......	1
English........................	1	......	1	2	1	......	......	......	5
German.........................	......	1	2	5	2	......	......	......	10
Hebrew, German.................	......	......	......	1	......	......	......	......	1
Hebrew, Russian................	......	1	1	......	......	......	......	......	2
Hebrew, Other..................	......	......	1	......	1	......	......	......	2
Irish..........................	......	......	......	1	2	1	......	......	4
Magyar.........................	......	......	......	1	1	......	......	......	2
Scotch.........................	......	......	......	......	1	......	......	......	1
Slovak.........................	......	......	......	......	1	......	......	......	1
Swedish........................	......	......	......	1	......	......	......	......	1
Welsh..........................	......	......	1	1	1	1	......	......	4
Other races *a*.................	......	......	......	......	1	......	......	......	1
Total foreign-born.............	1	2	6	14	10	2	......	......	35
Grand total....................	1	15	42	43	48	23	6	......	178

GIRLS.

General nativity and race of father of pupil.	10.	11.	12.	13.	14.	15.	16.	17.	Total.
Native-born:									
White..........................	1	8	55	67	34	22	5	2	194
Negro...........................	......	......	......	......	1	1	......	......	2
Total native-born..............	1	8	55	67	35	23	5	2	196
Foreign-born:									
Canadian (other than French).......	......	......	......	......	1	......	......	......	1
English........................	1	2	1	5	......	......	......	......	9
German.........................	......	2	7	4	6	1	......	......	20
Hebrew, Russian................	......	2	......	......	......	......	......	......	2
Hebrew, Other..................	......	1	1	3	......	......	......	......	5
Irish..........................	......	......	2	1	1	......	......	......	4
Italian (not specified)............	......	......	......	1	......	......	......	......	1
Magyar.........................	......	......	1	......	......	......	......	......	1
Scotch.........................	......	......	1	......	......	......	......	......	1
Slovak.........................	......	......	1	......	......	......	......	......	1
Swedish........................	......	......	......	......	1	......	......	......	1
Welsh..........................	......	......	......	2	2	......	......	......	4
Total foreign-born.............	1	7	14	16	11	1	......	......	50
Grand total....................	2	15	69	83	46	24	5	2	246

a "Other races" includes races having less than 10 representatives in this city and pupils whose race is not reported.

TABLE **3.**—*Race, sex, and age, by grade—Number of pupils of each age in each grade, by sex and by general nativity and race of father of pupil*—Continued.

SEVENTH GRADE—Continued.

TOTAL.

General nativity and race of father of pupil.	Number of pupils of each age.								Total.
	10.	11.	12.	13.	14.	15.	16.	17.	
Native-born:									
White	1	21	91	96	71	43	11	2	336
Negro					2	1			3
Total native-born	1	21	91	96	73	44	11	2	339
Foreign-born:									
Canadian (other than French)				1	1				2
English	2	2	2	7	1				14
German		3	9	9	8	1			30
Hebrew, German				1					1
Hebrew, Russian		3	1						4
Hebrew, Other		1	2	3	1				7
Irish			2	2	3	1			8
Italian (not specified)				1					1
Magyar			1	1	1				3
Scotch			1		1				2
Slovak			1		1				2
Swedish				1	1				2
Welsh			1	3	3	1			8
Other races *a*				1					1
Total foreign-born	2	9	20	30	21	3			85
Grand total	3	30	111	126	94	47	11	2	424

a "Other races" includes races having less than 10 representatives in this city and pupils whose race is not reported.

EIGHTH GRADE·

BOYS.

General nativity and race of father of pupil.	Number of pupils of each age.								Total.
	11.	12.	13.	14.	15.	16.	17.	18.	
Native-born, White		5	33	49	32	16	3		138
Foreign-born:									
Canadian (other than French)				1					1
English			4	1	2				7
German			4	4	2	1			11
Hebrew, Russian	1		2						3
ebrew, Other				1	1				2
Irish				2	1				3
Slovak			1	1	1				3
Swedish				1					1
Welsh			2	2		1			5
Other races *a*				1	1				2
Total foreign-born	1		13	14	8	2			38
Grand total	1	5	46	63	40	18	3		176

a "Other races" includes races having less than 10 representatives in this city and pupils whose race is not reported.

TABLE **3.**—*Race, sex, and age, by grade—Number of pupils of each age in each grade, by sex and by general nativity and race of father of pupil*—Continued.

EIGHTH GRADE—Continued.

GIRLS.

General nativity and race of father of pupil.	Number of pupils of each age.								Total.
	11.	12.	13.	14.	15.	16.	17.	18.	
Native-born:									
White	......	7	35	66	44	13	1	......	166
Negro	......	......	......	1	......	......	......	......	1
Total native-born	......	7	35	67	44	13	1	......	167
Foreign-born:									
Canadian (other than French)	......	1	......	4	2	1	......	......	2
English	......	1	1	4	2	......	......	......	8
German	......	2	7	2	1	2	......	......	14
Hebrew, Russian	......	......	......	......	1	......	......	......	1
Hebrew, Other	......	......	1	1	1	......	......	......	3
Irish	......	1	2	2	1	......	1	......	7
Scotch	......	......	......	......	1	......	......	......	1
Slovak	......	......	1	1	......	......	......	......	2
Welsh	......	......	......	1	......	......	......	......	1
Other races*a*	......	......	1	......	......	......	......	......	1
Total foreign-born	......	5	13	11	7	3	1	......	40
Grand total	......	12	48	78	51	16	2	......	207

TOTAL.

General nativity and race of father of pupil.	Number of pupils of each age.								Total.
	11.	12.	13.	14.	15.	16.	17.	18.	
Native-born:									
White	......	12	68	115	76	29	4	......	304
Negro	......	......	......	1	......	......	......	......	1
Total native-born	......	12	68	116	76	29	4	......	305
Foreign-born:									
Canadian (other than French)	......	1	......	1	......	1	......	......	3
English	......	1	5	5	4	......	......	......	15
German	......	2	11	6	3	3	......	......	25
Hebrew, Russian	1	......	2	......	1	......	......	......	4
Hebrew, Other	......	......	1	2	2	......	......	......	5
Irish	......	1	2	4	2	......	1	......	10
Scotch	......	......	......	......	1	......	......	......	1
Slovak	......	......	2	2	1	......	......	......	5
Swedish	......	......	......	1	......	......	......	......	1
Welsh	......	......	2	3	......	1	......	......	6
Other races*a*	......	......	1	1	1	......	......	......	3
Total foreign-born	1	5	26	25	15	5	1	......	78
Grand total	1	17	94	141	91	34	5	......	383

a " Other races " includes races having less than 10 representatives in this city and pupils whose race is not reported.

TABLE 3.—*Race, sex, and age, by grade—Number of pupils of each age in each grade, by sex and by general nativity and race of father of pupil*—Continued.

FIRST YEAR HIGH SCHOOL.

BOYS.

General nativity and race of father of pupil.	Number of pupils of each age.										Total.
	11.	12.	13.	14.	15.	16.	17.	18.	19.	20.	
Native-born, White	1	1	4	14	26	18	10	2			76
Foreign-born:											
Canadian (other than French)					1						1
English					2		1				3
German					2	1					3
Hebrew, German					1						1
Hebrew, Russian				2	1						3
Hebrew, Other							1				1
Irish							1				1
Scotch						1					1
Welsh					1						1
Other races [a]					1						1
Total				2	9	2	3				16
Grand total	1	1	4	16	35	20	13	2			92

GIRLS.

General nativity and race of father of pupil.	Number of pupils of each age.										Total.
	11.	12.	13.	14.	15.	16.	17.	18.	19.	20.	
Native-born, White			9	24	33	25	6	1		1	99
Foreign-born:											
English			1	4	4						9
German					4	1					5
Hebrew, German				1	2						3
Hebrew, Russian				1							1
Irish				2		1	1				4
Welsh				1		1					2
Total			1	9	10	3	1				24
Grand total			10	33	43	28	7	1		1	123

TOTAL.

General nativity and race of father of pupil.	Number of pupils of each age.										Total.
	11.	12.	13.	14.	15.	16.	17.	18.	19.	20.	
Native-born, White	1	1	13	38	59	43	16	3		1	175
Foreign-born:											
Canadian (other than French)					1						1
English			1	4	6		1				12
German					6	2					8
Hebrew, German				1	3						4
Hebrew, Russian				3	1						4
Hebrew, Other							1				1
Irish				2		1	2				5
Scotch						1					1
Welsh				1	1	1					3
Other races [a]					1						1
Total			1	11	19	5	4				40
Grand total	1	1	14	49	78	48	20	3		1	215

[a] "Other races" includes races having less than 10 representatives in this city and pupils whose race is not reported.

TABLE 3.—*Race, sex, and age, by grade—Number of pupils of each age in each grade, by sex and by general nativity and race of father of pupil*—Continued.

SECOND YEAR HIGH SCHOOL.

BOYS.

General nativity and race of father of pupil.	Number of pupils of each age.								Total.
	13.	14.	15.	16.	17.	18.	19.	20.	
Native-born, White		1	9	9	9	2	3	1	34
Foreign-born:									
English				1					1
German			1	1		1			3
Hebrew, Russian				1					1
Hebrew, Other						1			1
Irish		1					1		2
Total		1	1	3		2	1		8
Grand total		2	10	12	9	4	4	1	42

GIRLS.

General nativity and race of father of pupil.	13.	14.	15.	16.	17.	18.	19.	20.	Total.
Native-born, White		1	10	21	12	2			46
Foreign-born:									
English				1	1				2
German		1	1	1	2				5
Hebrew, Russian			1						1
Irish			1						1
Welsh				1		1			2
Other races a									
Total		1	3	3	3	1			11
Grand total		2	13	24	15	3			57

TOTAL.

General nativity and race of father of pupil.	13.	14.	15.	16.	17.	18.	19.	20.	Total.
Native-born, White		2	19	30	21	4	3	1	80
Foreign-born:									
English				2	1				3
German		1	2	2	2	1			8
Hebrew, Russian			1	1					2
Hebrew, Other						1			1
Irish		1	1				1		3
Welsh				1		1			2
Total		2	4	6	3	3	1		19
Grand total		4	23	36	24	7	4	1	99

a "Other races" includes races having less than 10 representatives in this city and pupils whose race is not reported.

TABLE 3.—*Race, sex, and age, by grade—Number of pupils of each age in each grade, by sex and by general nativity and race of father of pupil*—Continued.

THIRD YEAR HIGH SCHOOL

BOYS.

General nativity and race of father of pupil.	Number of pupils of each age.						Total.
	14.	15.	16.	17.	18.	19.	
Native-born, White		4	13	6	4	1	28
Foreign-born:							
English			1				1
German				1		1	2
Hebrew, Russian					1		1
Hebrew, Other			1				1
Welsh		1		1			2
Total		1	2	2	1	1	7
Grand total		5	15	8	5	2	35

GIRLS.

	14.	15.	16.	17.	18.	19.	Total.
Native-born, White			9	23	10	6	48
Foreign-born:							
Canadian (other than French)					1		1
English				1	1		2
German			2				2
Hebrew, German			1				1
Irish				1			1
Swedish					1		1
Welsh			1				1
Total			4	2	3		9
Grand total			13	25	13	6	57

TOTAL.

	14.	15.	16.	17.	18.	19.	Total.
Native-born, White		4	22	29	14	7	76
Foreign-born:							
Canadian (other than French)					1		1
English			1	1	1		3
German			2	1		1	4
Hebrew, German			1				1
Hebrew, Russian					1		1
Hebrew, Other			1				1
Irish				1			1
Swedish					1		1
Welsh		1	1	1			3
Total		1	6	4	4	1	16
Grand total		5	28	33	18	8	92

a "Other races" includes races having less than 10 representatives in this city and pupils whose race is not reported.

TABLE 3.—*Race, sex, and age, by grade—Number of pupils of each age in each grade, by sex and by general nativity and race of father of pupil*—Continued.

FOURTH YEAR HIGH SCHOOL.

BOYS.

General nativity and race of father of pupil.	Number of pupils of each age.				Total.
	17.	18.	19.	20.	
Native-born, White..........................	4	6	4	....	14
Foreign-born:					
English.........................	....	1	....	....	1
Irish...........................	....	1	....	....	1
Total...............	....	2	....	....	2
Grand total.........	4	8	4	....	16

GIRLS.

General nativity and race of father of pupil.	17.	18.	19.	20.	Total.
Native-born, White...........................	3	8	5	1	17
Foreign-born:					
English...........................	....	....	1	....	1
Irish.............................	....	....	1	....	1
Total................	....	....	2	....	2
Grand total..........	3	8	7	1	19

TOTAL.

General nativity and race of father of pupil.	17.	18.	19.	20.	Total.
Native-born, White...........................	7	14	9	1	31
Foreign-born:					
English...........................	....	1	1	....	2
Irish.............................	....	1	1	....	2
Total................	....	2	2	....	4
Grand total..........	7	16	11	1	35

TABLE 4.—*Race and grade, by age—Number of pupils of each specified age in each grade, by general nativity and race of father of pupil.*

BOYS: AGE 5 YEARS.

General nativity and race of father of pupil.	Elementary grade 1.
Native-born, White..	13
Foreign-born, Other races [a].............................	11
Grand total.......................	24

[a] "Other races" includes races having less than 10 representatives of this sex and age and pupils whose race is not reported.

TABLE 4.—*Race and grade, by age—Number of pupils of each specified age in each grade, by general nativity and race of father of pupil*—Continued.

BOYS: AGE 6 YEARS.

General nativity and race of father of pupil.	Elementary grades.		Total.
	1.	2.	
Native-born:			
White..	165	11	176
Negro..	2	....	2
Total native-born...............................	167	11	178
Foreign-born:			
German...	13	1	14
Other races *a*..	49	4	53
Total foreign-born	62	5	67
Grand total..	229	16	245

a "Other races" includes races having less than 10 representatives of this sex and age and pupils whose race is not reported.

BOYS: AGE 7 YEARS.

General nativity and race of father of pupil.	Elementary grades.			Total.
	1.	2.	3.	
Native-born, White...............................	72	104	8	184
Foreign-born:				
German...	13	12	....	25
Other races *a*..	26	26	2	54
Total foreign-born	39	38	2	79
Grand total..	111	142	10	263

a "Other races" includes races having less than 10 representatives of this sex and age and pupils whose race is not reported.

BOYS: AGE 8 YEARS.

General nativity and race of father of pupil.	Elementary grades.				Total.
	1.	2.	3.	4.	
Native-born:					
White..	32	115	60	5	212
Negro..	2	1	....	....	3
Total native-born...............................	34	116	60	5	215
Foreign-born:					
German...	3	14	13	....	30
Other races *a*..	10	27	15	....	52
Total foreign-born	13	41	28	....	82
Grand total..	47	157	88	5	297

a "Other races" includes races having less than 10 representatives of this sex and age and pupils whose race is not reported.

TABLE **4.**—*Race and grade, by age—Number of pupils of each specified age in each grade, by general nativity and race of father of pupil*—Continued.

BOYS: AGE 9 YEARS.

General nativity and race of father of pupil.	Elementary grades.						Total.
	1.	2.	3.	4.	5.	6.	
Native-born:							
White..................................	7	49	77	73	7	1	214
Negro.................................	1	....	1	....	....	....	2
Total native-born.....................	8	49	78	73	7	1	216
Foreign-born:							
English..............................	1	1	8	2	....	....	12
German.............................	2	3	9	4	1	....	19
Other races *a*.......................	6	15	16	9	3	....	49
Total foreign-born....................	9	19	33	15	4	....	80
Grand total..........................	17	68	111	88	11	1	296

a "Other races" includes races having less than 10 representatives of this sex and age and pupils whose race is not reported.

BOYS: AGE 10 YEARS.

General nativity and race of father of pupil.	Elementary grades.							Total.
	1.	2.	3.	4.	5.	6.	7.	
Native-born:								
White..............................	1	17	46	48	48	7	....	167
Negro.............................	....	....	2	1	....	....	....	3
Total native-born...............	1	17	48	49	48	7	....	170
Foreign-born:								
English...........................	....	1	1	4	4	1	1	12
German...........................	....	3	9	8	6	1	....	27
Other races *a*....................	1	2	9	7	4	1	....	24
Total foreign-born..............	1	6	19	19	14	3	1	63
Grand total....................	2	23	67	68	62	10	1	233

a "Other races" includes races having less than 10 representatives of this sex and age and pupils whose race is not reported.

BOYS: AGE 11 YEARS.

General nativity and race of father of pupil.	Elementary grades.								High school.	Total.
	1.	2.	3.	4.	5.	6.	7.	8.	First year.	
Native-born:										
White..............................	2	9	18	42	79	43	13	......	1	207
Negro.............................	....	....	....	1	....	....	....	....	....	1
Total native-born.............	2	9	18	43	79	43	13	......	1	208
Foreign-born:										
English...........................	....	....	2	6	3	4	......	....	....	15
German...........................	....	....	1	7	9	4	1	....	....	22
Other races *a*....................	....	5	6	7	5	3	1	1	....	28
Total foreign-born..............	....	5	9	20	17	11	2	1	....	65
Grand total....................	2	14	27	63	96	54	15	1	1	273

a "Other races" includes races having less than 10 representatives of this sex and age and pupils whose race is not reported.

TABLE **4.**—*Race and grade, by age—Number of pupils of each specified age in each grade, by general nativity and race of father of pupil*—Continued.

BOYS: AGE 12 YEARS.

General nativity and race of father of pupil.	Elementary grades.								High school, first year.	Total.
	1.	2.	3.	4.	5.	6.	7.	8.		
Native-born:										
White		3	14	20	62	59	36	5	1	200
Negro			1				1			2
Total native-born		3	15	20	62	60	36	5	1	202
Foreign-born:										
German		1	1	4	8	13	2			29
Other races *a*		1	3	6	9	14	4			37
Total foreign-born		2	4	10	17	27	6			66
Grand total		5	19	30	79	87	42	5	1	268

BOYS: AGE 13 YEARS.

Native-born, White		2	2	11	37	39	29	33	4	157
Foreign-born:										
English					3	1	2	4		10
German					10	3	5	4		22
Other races *a*	1	1	2	3	5	5	7	5		29
Total foreign-born	1	1	2	3	18	9	14	13		61
Grand total	1	3	4	14	55	48	43	46	4	218

a "Other races" includes races having less than 10 representatives of this sex and age and pupils whose race is not reported.

BOYS: AGE 14 YEARS.

General nativity and race of father of pupil.	Elementary grades.								High school.		Total.
	1.	2.	3.	4.	5.	6.	7.	8.	First year.	Second year.	
Native-born:											
White		3	3	3	21	26	37	49	14	1	157
Negro		1				1	1				3
Total native-born		4	3	3	21	27	38	49	14	1	160
Foreign-born:											
German					1	5	2	4			12
Other races *a*	1		1	2		7	8	10	2	1	32
Total foreign-born	1		1	2	1	12	10	14	2	1	44
Grand total	1	4	4	5	22	39	48	63	16	2	204

a "Other races" includes races having less than 10 representatives of this sex and age and pupils whose race is not reported.

TABLE 4.—*Race and grade, by age—Number of pupils of each specified age in each grade, by general nativity and race of father of pupil*—Continued.

BOYS: AGE 15 YEARS.

General nativity and race of father of pupil.	Elementary grades.								High school.			Total.
	1.	2.	3.	4.	5.	6.	7.	8.	First year.	Second year.	Third year.	
Native-born: White				2	8	3	21	32	26	9	4	105
Negro					1	1						2
Total native-born				2	9	4	21	32	26	9	4	107
Foreign-born, Other races *a*				2		3	2	8	9	1	1	26
Grand total				4	9	7	23	40	35	10	5	133

BOYS: AGE 16 YEARS.

	1.	2.	3.	4.	5.	6.	7.	8.	First year.	Second year.	Third year.	Total.
Native-born, White	1		1	2	2	2	6	16	18	9	13	70
Foreign-born, Other races *a*								2	2	3	2	9
Grand total	1		1	2	2	2	6	18	20	12	15	79

a "Other races" includes races having less than 10 representatives of this sex and age and pupils whose race is not reported.

BOYS: AGE 17 YEARS.

General nativity and race of father of pupil.	Elementary grades.								High school.				Total.
	1.	2.	3.	4.	5.	6.	7.	8.	First year.	Second year.	Third year.	Fourth year	
Native-born, White								3	10	9	6	4	32
Foreign-born, Other races *a*			1						3		2		6
Grand total			1					3	13	9	8	4	38

a "Other races" includes races having less than 10 representatives of this sex and age and pupils whose race is not reported.

BOYS: AGE 18 YEARS.

General nativity and race of father of pupil.	High school.				Total.
	First year.	Second year.	Third year.	Fourth year.	
Native-born, White	2	2	4	6	14
Foreign-born, Other races *a*		2	1	2	5
Grand total	2	4	5	8	19

a "Other races" includes races having less than 10 representatives of this sex and age and pupils whose race is not reported.

TABLE 4.—*Race and grade, by age—Number of pupils of each specified age in each grade, by general nativity and race of father of pupil*—Continued.

BOYS: AGE 19 YEARS.

General nativity and race of father of pupil.	High school.				Total.
	First year.	Second year.	Third year.	Fourth year.	
Native-born, White...............	....	3	1	4	8
Foreign-born, Other races a...............	....	1	1	....	2
Grand total...............	....	4	2	4	10

a "Other races" includes races having less than 10 representatives of this sex and age and pupils whose race is not reported.

BOYS: AGE 20 YEARS.

General nativity and race of father of pupil.	High school.	
	First year.	Second year.
Native-born, White...............	....	1

GIRLS: AGE 5 YEARS.

General nativity and race of father of pupil.	Elementary grades.		Total.
	1.	2.	
Native-born, White...............	16	3	19
Foreign-born, Other races.a...............	11	....	11
Grand total...............	27	3	30

GIRLS: AGE 6 YEARS.

Native-born:			
White...............	187	22	209
Negro...............	1	1	2
Total native-born...............	188	23	211
Foreign-born:			
German...............	18	2	20
Other races a...............	43	5	48
Total foreign-born...............	61	7	68
Grand total...............	249	30	279

a "Other races" includes races having less than 10 representatives of this sex and age and pupils whose race is not reported.

TABLE 4.—*Race and grade, by age—Number of pupils of each specified age in each grade, by general nativity and race of father of pupil*—Continued.

GIRLS: AGE 7 YEARS.

General nativity and race of father of pupil.	Elementary grades.				Total.
	1.	2.	3.	4.	
Native-born:					
White	70	117	7	....	194
Negro	2	2	....	....	4
Total native-born	72	119	7	....	198
Foreign-born:					
German	9	15	2	....	26
Other races *a*	21	17	4	1	43
Total foreign-born	30	32	6	1	69
Grand total	102	151	13	1	267

a "Other races" includes races having less than 10 representatives of this sex and age and pupils whose race is not reported.

GIRLS: AGE 8 YEARS.

General nativity and race of father of pupil.	Elementary grades.					Total.
	1.	2.	3.	4.	5.	
Native-born:						
White	19	90	87	12	1	209
Negro	....	3	....	....	....	3
Total native-born	19	93	87	12	1	212
Foreign-born:						
German	1	6	13	2	....	22
Other races *a*	2	25	17	3	....	47
Total foreign-born	3	31	30	5	....	69
Grand total	22	124	117	17	1	281

a "Other races" includes races having less than 10 representatives of this sex and age and pupils whose race is not reported.

GIRLS: AGE 9 YEARS.

General nativity and race of father of pupil.	Elementary grades.						Total.
	1.	2.	3.	4.	5.	6.	
Native-born, White	8	33	62	80	16	1	200
Foreign-born:							
English	....	....	4	6	....	....	10
German	....	2	11	7	1	....	21
Other races *a*	4	14	13	10	2	1	44
Total foreign-born	4	16	28	23	3	1	75
Grand total	12	49	90	103	19	2	275

a "Other races" includes races having less than 10 representatives of this sex and age and pupils whose race is not reported.

TABLE 4.—*Race and grade, by age—Number of pupils of each specified age in each grade, by general nativity and race of father of pupil*—Continued.

GIRLS: AGE 10 YEARS.

General nativity and race of father of pupil.	Elementary grades.							Total.
	1.	2.	3.	4.	5.	6.	7.	
Native-born:								
White........................	1	11	31	68	68	10	1	190
Negro........................		1	1	......	......	......	......	2
Total native-born...........	1	12	32	68	68	10	1	192
Foreign-born:								
German.......................	1	......	7	18	10	1	......	37
Other races *a*..............	2	2	11	7	14	......	1	37
Total foreign-born...........	3	2	18	25	24	1	1	74
Grand total.................	4	14	50	93	92	11	2	266

GIRLS: AGE 11 YEARS.

General nativity and race of father of pupil.	Elementary grades.							Total.
	1.	2.	3.	4.	5.	6.	7.	
Native-born:								
White........................	......	7	9	46	79	52	8	201
Negro........................	......	......	1	......	......	......	......	1
Total native-born...........	......	7	10	46	79	52	8	202
Foreign-born:								
English......................	......	......	......	5	4	2	2	13
German.......................	......	1	......	5	6	5	2	19
Other races *a*..............	1	2	4	9	8	3	3	30
Total foreign-born...........	1	3	4	19	18	10	7	62
Grand total.................	1	10	14	65	97	62	15	264

a "Other races" includes races having less than 10 representatives of this sex and age and pupils whose race is not reported.

GIRLS: AGE 12 YEARS.

General nativity and race of father of pupil.	Elementary grades.								Total.
	1.	2.	3.	4.	5.	6.	7.	8.	
Native-born:									
White........................	......	3	3	17	50	59	55	7	194
Negro........................	......	......	1	1	2	1	......	......	5
Total native-born........	......	3	4	18	52	60	55	7	199
Foreign-born:									
English......................	......	1	2	......	5	3	1	1	13
German.......................	......	......	2	3	12	5	7	2	31
Other races *a*..............	1	2	5	2	6	1	6	2	25
Total foreign-born........	1	3	9	5	23	9	14	5	69
Grand total.................	1	6	13	23	75	69	69	12	268

a "Other races" includes races having less than 10 representatives of this sex and age and pupils whose race is not reported.

TABLE 4.—*Race and grade, by age—Number of pupils of each specified age in each grade, by general nativity and race of father of pupil*—Continued.

GIRLS: AGE 13 YEARS.

General nativity and race of father of pupil.	Elementary grades.								High school, first year.	Total.
	1.	2.	3.	4.	5.	6.	7.	8.		
Native-born:										
White...................	2	......	2	6	31	38	67	35	9	190
Negro..................				1	1	1	......			3
Total native-born..........	2	......	2	7	32	39	67	35	9	193
Foreign-born:										
English...............					4	3	5	1	1	14
German..............			2	2	5	9	4	7		29
Other races a.........			1	2	5	9	7	5	......	29
Total foreign-born.........			3	4	14	21	16	13	1	72
Grand total..............	2	......	5	11	46	60	83	48	10	265

a "Other races" includes races having less than 10 representatives of this sex and age and pupils whose ace is not reported.

GIRLS: AGE 14 YEARS.

General nativity and race of father of pupil.	Elementary grades.					High school.		Total.
	4.	5.	6.	7.	8.	First year.	Second year.	
Native-born:								
White...................	5	9	20	34	66	24	1	159
Negro..................				1	1		1	2
Total native-born..........	5	9	20	35	67	24	1	161
Foreign-born:								
English...............		2			4	4		10
German..............		1	2	6	2		1	12
Other races a.........				5	5	5		15
Total foreign-born.........		3	2	11	11	9	1	37
Grand total..............	5	12	22	46	78	33	2	198

a "Other races" includes races having less than 10 representatives of this sex and age and pupils whose race is not reported.

GIRLS: AGE 15 YEARS.

General nativity and race of father of pupil.	Elementary grades.				High school.		Total.
	5.	6.	7.	8.	First year.	Second year.	
Native-born:							
White...................	3	8	22	44	33	10	120
Negro..................			1				1
Total native-born............	3	8	23	44	33	10	121
Foreign-born, other races a	2	1	1	7	10	3	24
Grand total.............	5	9	24	51	43	13	145

a "Other races" includes races having less than 10 representatives of this sex and age and pupils whose race is not reported.

TABLE 4.—*Race and grade, by age—Number of pupils of each specified age in each grade, by general nativity and race of father of pupil—*Continued.

GIRLS: AGE 16 YEARS.

General nativity and race of father of pupil.	Elementary grades.		High school.			Total.
	7.	8.	First year.	Second year.	Third year.	
Native-born, White	5	13	25	21	9	73
Foreign-born, other races a		3	3	3	4	13
Grand total	5	16	28	24	13	86

GIRLS: AGE 17 YEARS.

Native-born, White	2	1	6	12	23	44
Foreign-born, other races a		1	1	3	2	7
Grand total	2	2	7	15	25	51

a "Other races" includes races having less than 10 representatives of this sex and age and pupils whose race is not reported.

GIRLS: AGE 18 YEARS.

General nativity and race of father of pupil.	High school.			Total.
	First year.	Second year.	Third year.	
Native-born, White	1	2	10	13
Foreign-born, other races a		1	3	4
Grand total	1	3	13	17

a "Other races" includes races having less than 10 representatives of this sex and age and pupils whose race is not reported.

GIRLS: AGE 19 YEARS.

General nativity and race of father of pupil.	High school.
	Third year.
Native-born, White	6

GIRLS, AGE 20 YEARS.

General nativity and race of father of pupil.	High school.		Total.
	First year.	Fourth year.	
Native-born, White	1	1	2

TABLE 5.—*Race distribution in each grade—Percentages.*

[This table shows in detail only races with 100 or more pupils reporting. The totals, however, are for all races.]

General nativity and race of father of pupil.	Elementary grades.									High school.					Grand total.
	1.	2.	3.	4.	5.	6.	7.	8.	Total.	First year.	Second year.	Third year.	Fourth year.	Total.	
Native-born:															
White	69.7	73.1	67.9	73.7	76.3	76.2	79.2	79.4	73.7	81.4	80.8	82.6	88.6	82.1	74.4
Negro	.9	1.1	1.1	.7	.6	1.0	.7	.3	.8	...	...	...	...	...	.8
Total native-born	70.6	74.2	69.0	74.4	76.9	77.2	80.0	79.6	74.5	81.4	80.8	82.6	88.6	82.1	75.2
Foreign-born:															
English	1.6	2.7	4.1	4.7	4.2	4.8	3.3	3.9	3.5	5.6	3.0	3.3	5.7	4.5	3.6
German	7.0	7.3	11.2	10.1	10.4	10.1	7.1	6.5	8.7	3.7	8.1	4.3	...	4.5	8.4
Other races	20.7	15.8	15.7	10.9	8.5	7.9	9.7	9.9	13.2	9.3	8.1	9.8	5.7	8.8	12.9
Total foreign-born	29.4	25.8	31.0	25.6	23.1	22.8	20.0	20.4	25.5	18.6	19.2	17.4	11.4	17.9	24.8
Grand total	100.0	100.0	100.0	100.0	100.0	100.0	100.0	100.0	100.0	100.0	100.0	100.0	100.0	100.0	100.0

TABLE 6.—*Grade distribution of each race—Percentages.*

[This table shows in detail only races with 100 or more pupils reporting. The totals, however, are for all races.]

General nativity and race of father of pupil.	Elementary grades.									High school.					Grand total.
	1.	2.	3.	4.	5.	6.	7.	8.	Total.	First year.	Second year.	Third year.	Fourth year.	Total.	
Native-born:															
White............	15.1	15.1	10.9	11.1	13.2	9.3	8.5	7.7	90.9	4.4	2.0	1.9	0.8	9.1	100.0
Negro............	19.5	22.0	17.1	9.8	9.8	12.2	7.3	2.4	100.0						100.0
Total native-born.......	15.1	15.2	11.0	11.1	13.1	9.3	8.5	7.6	90.9	4.4	2.0	1.9	.8	9.1	100.0
Foreign-born:															
English...........	7.3	11.5	13.6	14.7	15.2	12.0	7.3	7.9	89.5	6.3	1.6	1.6	1.0	10.5	100.0
German...........	13.5	13.5	15.9	13.5	15.9	11.0	6.7	5.6	95.5	1.8	1.8	.9	.3	4.5	100.0
Other races........	25.8	18.8	14.6	9.5	8.5	5.5	6.0	5.5	94.3	2.9	1.2	1.3	.3	5.7	100.0
Total foreign-born......	19.0	16.0	14.9	11.6	12.0	8.3	6.4	5.9	94.0	3.0	1.4	1.2	.3	6.0	100.0
Grand total.........	16.1	15.4	11.9	11.2	12.8	9.1	8.0	7.2	91.7	4.0	1.9	1.7	.7	8.3	100.0

PUBLIC SCHOOL PUPILS: INTENSIVE INVESTIGATION.

TABLE 1.—*Birthplace of pupils, by general nativity and race of father.*

General nativity and race of father of pupil.	Born in Johnstown.			Born elsewhere in United States.			Born abroad.			Total reporting complete data.			Not reporting complete data.		
	Number.	Pupils 8 years of age or over.		Number.	Pupils 8 years of age or over.		Number.	Pupils 8 years of age or over.		Number.	Pupils 8 years of age or over.		Number.	Pupils 8 years of age or over.	
		Number.	Number retarded.		Number.	Number retarded.		Number.	Number retarded.		Number.	Number retarded.		Number.	Number retarded.
Native-born:															
White	2,907	2,294	803	857	725	341				3,764	3,019	1,144	193	143	68
Negro	21	15	9	19	17	15				40	32	24	1	1	
Total native-born	2,928	2,309	812	876	742	356				3,804	3,051	1,168	194	144	68
Foreign-born:															
English-speaking races—															
English	118	102	34	51	45	16	15	14	7	184	161	57	7	6	2
Irish	62	45	15	11	10	4	1	1	1	74	56	20	7	6	
Welsh	60	52	14	17	15	8	3	2	2	80	69	24	3	2	1
Other races	14	13	6	21	18	5				35	31	11	1	1	
Total	254	212	69	100	88	33	19	17	10	373	317	112	19	15	3
Non-English-speaking races—															
German	346	273	106	52	48	15	31	25	12	429	346	133	17	15	6
Hebrew, Russian	24	15	5	30	23	3	16	16	7	70	54	15	2	2	
Italian, North	10	1		3	2		5	4	3	18	7	3			
Italian, South	4			4	4	2	17	11	9	25	15	11			
Italian (not specified)	11	6	2	8	7	6	43	30	18	62	43	26	1		
Magyar	34	15	7	12	9	3	33	26	16	79	50	26	2	1	
Slovak	24	17	7	8	4	2	19	13	9	51	34	18	5	2	2
Other races	69	46	23	29	27	14	64	42	30	162	115	67	7	1	1
Total	522	373	150	146	124	45	228	167	104	896	664	299	34	21	9
Total foreign-born	776	585	219	246	212	78	247	184	114	1,269	981	411	53	36	12
Grand total	3,704	2,894	1,031	1,122	954	434	247	184	114	5,073	4,032	1,579	247	180	80

TABLE 2.—School attendance of pupils born in the United States but elsewhere than in Johnstown, by general nativity and race of father.

General nativity and race of father of pupil.	Having attended school elsewhere.			Not having attended school elsewhere.			Total reporting complete data.			Not reporting complete data.		
	Number.	Pupils 8 years of age or over.		Number.	Pupils 8 years of age or over.		Number.	Pupils 8 years of age or over.		Number.	Pupils 8 years of age or over.	
		Number.	Number retarded.		Number.	Number retarded.		Number.	Number retarded.		Number.	Number retarded.
Native-born:												
White	368	341	186	474	370	149	842	711	335	15	14	6
Negro	8	7	7	11	10	8	19	17	15			
Total native-born	376	348	193	485	380	157	861	728	350	15	14	6
Foreign-born:												
English-speaking races—												
English	30	28	13	21	17	3	51	45	16			
Irish	8	8	4	3	2		11	10	4			
Welsh	11	11	6	6	4	2	17	15	8			
Other races	10	10	3	11	8	2	21	18	5			
Total	59	57	26	41	31	7	100	88	33			
Non-English-speaking races—												
German	26	24	11	26	24	4	52	48	15			
Hebrew, Russian	9	8	1	21	15	2	30	23	3			
Italian, North				3	2		3	2				
Italian, South	2	2	1	2	2	1	4	4	2			
Italian (not specified)	3	3	2	5	4	4	8	7	6			
Magyar	3	3	1	9	6	2	12	9	3			
Slovak	5	4	2	3	3		8	4	2			
Other races	11	11	6	17	15	7	28	26	13	1	1	1
Total	59	55	24	86	68	20	145	123	44	1	1	1
Total foreign-born	118	112	50	127	99	27	245	211	77	1	1	1
Grand total	494	460	243	612	479	184	1,106	939	427	16	15	7

TABLE 3.—*Age of foreign-born pupils at time of arrival in the United States, by race of father.*

Race of father of pupil.	Under 6 years.			6 or 7 years.			8 or 9 years.			10 years or over.			Total reporting complete data.			Not reporting complete data.		
	Number.	Pupils 8 years of age or over.		Number.	Pupils 8 years of age or over.		Number.	Pupils 8 years of age or over.		Number.	Pupils 8 years of age or over.		Number.	Pupils 8 years of age or over.		Number.	Pupils 8 years of age or over.	
		Number.	Number retarded.		Number.	Number retarded.		Number.	Number retarded.		Number.	Number retarded.		Number.	Number retarded.		Number.	Number retarded.
Italian (not specified)	36	20	8	10	8	5	6	6	6	9	9	9	61	43	28	4	2	2
Other races	111	71	33	39	39	24	12	12	12	14	14	13	176	136	82	6	3	2
Total	147	91	41	49	47	29	18	18	18	23	23	22	237	179	110	10	5	4

TABLE 4.—*School attendance abroad of foreign-born pupils who were 6 years of age or over at time of arrival in the United States, by race of father.*

Race of father of pupil.	Having attended school abroad.			Not having attended school abroad.			Total reporting complete data.			Not reporting complete data.		
	Number.	Pupils 8 years of age or over.		Number.	Pupils 8 years of age or over.		Number.	Pupils 8 years of age or over.		Number.	Pupils 8 years of age or over.	
		Number.	Number retarded.		Number.	Number retarded.		Number.	Number retarded.		Number.	Number retarded.
Italian (not specified)	11	11	10	14	12	10	25	23	20			
Other races	42	42	30	23	23	19	65	65	49			
Total	53	53	40	37	35	29	90	88	69			

TABLE 5.—*Age of pupils at time of entering public school in the United States, by general nativity and race of father.*

[The data refer to age at entering grades and not kindergarten.]

General nativity and race of father of pupil.	5 years or under.			6 years.			7 years.			8 years.		
	Number.	Pupils 8 years of age or over.		Number.	Pupils 8 years of age or over.		Number.	Pupils 8 years of age or over.		Number.	Pupils 8 years of age or over.	
		Number.	Number retarded.		Number.	Number retarded.		Number.	Number retarded.		Number.	Number retarded.
Native-born:												
White	176	128	37	3,001	2,307	752	505	464	252	110	110	86
Negro	1	—	—	22	15	8	5	5	4	7	7	6
Total native-born	177	128	37	3,023	2,322	760	510	469	256	117	117	92
Foreign-born:												
English-speaking races—												
English	9	5	—	139	121	38	27	27	14	5	5	2
Irish	1	—	—	49	34	9	17	16	7	3	3	2
Welsh	—	—	—	70	58	17	8	8	4	2	2	1
Other races	1	1	—	26	21	5	7	7	4	2	2	2
Total	11	6	—	284	234	69	59	58	29	12	12	7
Non-English-speaking races—												
German	15	13	2	337	267	87	58	46	25	9	9	6
Hebrew, Russian	7	5	—	48	34	6	7	7	2	4	4	2
Italian, North	2	—	—	11	2	—	2	2	—	2	2	2
Italian, South	1	—	—	14	7	5	3	1	1	2	2	1
Italian (not specified)	2	1	1	24	13	4	17	10	4	4	4	2
Magyar	4	1	—	42	19	7	9	8	3	8	8	5
Slovak	2	—	—	24	8	2	8	7	3	2	2	2
Other races	14	6	4	92	60	28	24	17	10	11	11	7
Total	47	26	7	592	410	139	128	98	48	42	42	27
Total foreign-born	58	32	7	876	644	208	187	156	77	54	54	34
Grand total	235	160	44	3,899	2,966	968	697	625	333	171	171	126

General nativity and race of father of pupil	9 years.			10 years or over.			Total reporting complete data.			Not reporting complete data.		
	Number.	Pupils 8 years of age or over.		Number.	Pupils 8 years of age or over.		Number.	Pupils 8 years of age or over.		Number.	Pupils 8 years of age or over.	
		Number.	Number retarded.		Number.	Number retarded.		Number.	Number retarded.		Number.	Number retarded.
Native-born:												
White	14	14	12	71	71	41	3,877	3,094	1,180	80	68	32
Negro	2	2	2	3	3	3	40	32	23	1	1	1
Total native-born	16	16	14	74	74	44	3,917	3,126	1,203	81	69	33
Foreign-born:												
English-speaking races—												
English				2	2	1	182	160	55	9	7	4
Irish				7	7	2	77	60	20	4	2	
Welsh	1	1	1	2	2	2	83	71	25			
Other races							36	31	11	1	1	
Total	1	1	1	11	11	5	378	322	111	14	10	4
Non-English-speaking races—												
German	1	1	1	14	14	11	434	350	132	12	11	7
Hebrew, Russian	3	3	2	3	3	3	72	56	15			
Italian, North				1	1	1	18	7	3			
Italian, South	1	1	1	3	3	3	24	14	11	1	1	
Italian (not specified)	3	3	3	5	5	5	55	36	19	8	7	7
Magyar	5	5	3	4	4	4	72	45	22	9	6	4
Slovak	2	2	2	11	11	7	49	30	16	7	6	4
Other races	4	4	4	15	15	13	160	113	66	9	3	2
Total	19	19	16	56	56	47	884	651	284	46	34	24
Total foreign-born	20	20	17	67	67	52	1,262	973	395	60	44	28
Grand total	36	36	31	141	141	96	5,179	4,099	1,598	141	113	61

TABLE 6.—*Age of pupils at time of entering public schools in the United States, by race of father (foreign-born pupils only).*

[The data refer to age at entering grades and not kindergarten.]

Race of father of pupil.	5 years or under.			6 years.			7 years.			8 years.		
	Number.	Pupils 8 years of age or over.		Number.	Pupils 8 years of age or over.		Number.	Pupils 8 years of age or over.		Number.	Pupils 8 years of age or over.	
		Number.	Number retarded.		Number.	Number retarded.		Number.	Number retarded.		Number.	Number retarded.
Italian (not specified)	3	......	......	20	11	5	15	8	3	7	7	4
Other races	9	5	2	74	43	18	29	24	13	22	22	11
Total	12	5	2	94	54	23	44	32	16	29	29	15

Race of father of pupil.	9 years.			10 years or over.			Total reporting complete data.			Not reporting complete data.		
	Number.	Pupils 8 years of age or over.		Number.	Pupils 8 years of age or over.		Number.	Pupils 8 years of age or over.		Number.	Pupils 8 years of age or over.	
		Number.	Number retarded.		Number.	Number retarded.		Number.	Number retarded.		Number.	Number retarded.
Italian (not specified)	3	3	3	9	9	9	57	38	24	8	7	6
Other races	11	11	9	26	26	24	171	131	77	11	8	7
Total	14	14	12	35	35	33	228	169	101	19	15	13

TABLE 7.—*Grade entered by pupils, by general nativity and race of father.*

[The data refer to grade entered in public school. No account is taken of entrance into kindergarten.]

General nativity and race of father of pupil	First grade — Number	First grade — Pupils 8 years of age or over, Number	First grade — Pupils 8 years of age or over, Number retarded	Second grade — Number	Second grade — Pupils 8 years of age or over, Number	Second grade — Pupils 8 years of age or over, Number retarded	Third grade — Number	Third grade — Pupils 8 years of age or over, Number	Third grade — Pupils 8 years of age or over, Number retarded	Fourth grade — Number	Fourth grade — Pupils 8 years of age or over, Number	Fourth grade — Pupils 8 years of age or over, Number retarded
Native-born:												
White	3,713	2,923	1,100	78	76	38	15	15	8	16	16	11
Negro	39	31	22	1	1	1				1	1	1
Total native-born	3,752	2,954	1,122	79	77	39	15	15	8	17	17	12
Foreign-born:												
English-speaking races—												
English	185	161	56	1	1		1	1	1	1	1	1
Irish	69	50	16	1	1	1	1	1		2	2	2
Welsh	78	66	22	1	1							
Other races	37	32	11									
Total	309	309	105	3	3	1	2	2	1	3	3	3
Non-English-speaking races—												
German	402	318	110	10	10	10	3	3	3	5	5	4
Hebrew, Russian	68	52	13	2	2	2	1	1	1			
Italian, North	18	7	3				1	1	1			
Italian, South	21	11	8	2	2	1	1	1	1	1	1	1
Italian (not specified)	60	40	23							1	1	1
Magyar	70	45	21	3	2	2	3	3	2	1	1	1
Slovak	40	21	11	4	3	3	3	3	4	1	1	1
Other races	153	100	56	4	4	3	4	4	4			
Total	832	594	245	25	23	16	13	13	12	8	8	7
Total foreign-born	1,201	903	350	28	26	17	15	15	13	11	11	10
Grand total	4,953	3,857	1,472	107	103	56	30	30	21	28	28	22

TABLE 7.—Grade entered by pupils, by general nativity and race of father—Continued.

General nativity and race of father of pupil.	Fifth grade or above.			Total reporting complete data.			Not reporting complete data.		
	Number.	Pupils 8 years of age or over.		Number.	Pupils 8 years of age or over.		Number.	Pupils 8 years of age or over.	
		Number.	Number retarded.		Number.	Number retarded.		Number.	Number retarded.
Native-born:									
White...........	60	60	26	3,882	3,090	1,183	75	72	29
Negro...........				41	33	24			
Total native-born...	60	60	26	3,923	3,123	1,207	75	72	29
Foreign-born:									
English-speaking races—									
English...........	6	6	2	188	164	57	3	3	2
Irish.............	1	1	1	77	58	20	4	4	
Welsh............				82	70	25	1	1	
Other races.......				37	32	11			
Total...........	7	7	3	384	324	113	8	8	2
Non-English-speaking races—									
German...........	11	11	9	431	347	132	15	14	7
Hebrew, Russian...	1	1		72	56	15			
Italian, North.....				18	7	3			
Italian, South.....				24	14	10	1	1	1
Italian (not specified).				61	41	24	2	2	2
Magyar...........	3	3	2	77	51	26	4	2	1
Slovak...........	6	6	2	54	34	19	2		
Other races.......	3	3	1	165	112	65	4	4	3
Total...........	24	24	14	902	662	294	28	23	14
Total foreign-born...	31	31	17	1,286	986	407	36	31	16
Grand total.......	91	91	43	5,209	4,109	1,614	111	103	45

TABLE 8.—*Grade entered by pupils, by race of father (foreign-born pupils only).*

[The data refer to grade entered in public school. No account is taken of entrance into kindergarten.]

Race of father of pupil.	First grade.			Second grade.			Third grade.			Fourth grade.			Not reporting complete data.		
	Number.	Pupils 8 years of age or over.		Number.	Pupils 8 years of age or over.		Number.	Pupils 8 years of age or over.		Number.	Pupils 8 years of age or over.		Number.	Pupils 8 years of age or over.	
		Number.	Number retarded.		Number.	Number retarded.		Number.	Number retarded.		Number.	Number retarded.		Number.	Number retarded.
Italian (not specified)	59	39	24	1	1	1	1	1	1	1	1	1			
Other races	150	108	58	13	13	10	6	6	6	5	5	4			
Total	209	147	82	14	14	11	7	7	7	6	6	5			

Race of father of pupil.	Fifth grade or above.			Total reporting complete data.			Not reporting complete data.		
	Number.	Pupils 8 years of age or over.		Number.	Pupils 8 years of age or over.		Number.	Pupils 8 years of age or over.	
		Number.	Number retarded.		Number.	Number retarded.		Number.	Number retarded.
Italian (not specified)				62	42	27	3	3	3
Other races	3	3	2	177	135	80	5	4	4
Total	3	3	2	239	177	107	8	7	7

TABLE 9.—*Grade entered by pupils 8 years or over at time of entering, by general nativity and race of father.*

[The data refer to grade entered in public school. No account is taken of entrance into kindergarten.]

General nativity and race of father of pupil.	First grade.	Second grade.	Third grade.	Fourth grade.	Fifth grade.	Sixth grade.	Seventh grade.	Eighth grade or above.	Total reporting complete data.	Not reporting complete data.
Native-born:										
White	104	15	5	12	9	8	17	21	191	4
Negro	11			1					12	
Total native-born	115	15	5	13	9	8	17	21	203	4
Foreign-born:										
English-speaking races—										
English	6								6	1
Irish	3		1			1		4	9	1
Welsh	2	1		1	1				5	
Other races	2								2	
Total	13	1	1	1	1	1		4	22	2
Non-English-speaking races—										
German	7	4		3	5	1	3	1	24	
Hebrew, Russian	7	2	1						10	
Italian, North	3								3	
Italian, South	3	1	1						5	1
Italian (not specified)	11			1					12	
Magyar	11	2	1	1	1	1	1		17	
Slovak	5	1	2	1	1	1	1	3	15	
Other races	21	2	2	1	1	1	1		29	1
Total	68	12	7	6	8	4	6	4	115	2
Total foreign-born	81	13	8	7	9	5	6	8	137	4
Grand total	196	28	13	20	18	13	23	29	340	8

TABLE 10.—*Grade entered by pupils 8 years of age or over at time of entering, by race of father (foreign-born pupils only).*

[The data refer to grade entered in public school. No account is taken of entrance into kindergarten.]

Race of father of pupil.	First grade.	Second grade.	Third grade.	Fourth grade.	Fifth grade.	Sixth grade.	Seventh grade.	Eighth grade or above.	Total reporting complete data.	Not reporting complete data.
Italian (not specified)	15	1	1	1					18	1
Other races	35	10	6	4	1	1	1		58	1
Total	50	11	7	5	1	1	1		76	2

TABLE 11.—*Rate of progress of pupils and time in school in the United States, by general nativity and race of father.*

General nativity and race of father of pupil.	Pupils in school less years than grade.			Pupils in school same years as grade.			Pupils in school more years than grade.			Total reporting complete data.			Not reporting complete data.		
	Number.	Pupils 8 years of age or over — Number.	Number retarded.	Number.	Pupils 8 years of age or over — Number.	Number retarded.	Number.	Pupils 8 years of age or over — Number.	Number retarded.	Number.	Pupils 8 years of age or over — Number.	Number retarded.	Number.	Pupils 8 years of age or over — Number.	Number retarded.
Native-born:															
White	192	184	31	1,720	1,082	131	1,884	1,767	1,001	3,796	3,033	1,163	161	129	49
Negro	2	2	2	19	12	7	17	16	12	38	30	21	3	3	3
Total native-born	194	186	33	1,739	1,094	138	1,901	1,783	1,013	3,834	3,063	1,184	164	132	52
Foreign-born:															
English-speaking races—															
English	15	15	3	69	52	2	94	89	48	178	156	53	13	11	6
Irish	14	14	5	37	22	2	22	20	13	73	56	20	8	6	1
Welsh	4	4	2	37	31	2	38	33	20	79	68	24	4	3	
Other races	3	3	2	18	13	2	15	15	7	36	31	11	1	1	
Total	36	36	12	161	118	8	169	157	88	366	311	108	26	21	7
Non-English-speaking races—															
German	17	16	3	189	121	8	223	210	122	429	347	133	17	14	6
Hebrew, Russian	11	11	3	35	24	4	21	16	7	67	51	14	5	5	1
Italian, North	4	3	3	14	6	2	3	1	1	17	7	3	1		3
Italian, South	3	3	2	10	2		8	7	5	22	12	8	3	3	4
Italian (not specified)				35	21	10	21	15	10	59	39	22	4	4	
Magyar	5	5	3	44	23	8	25	20	14	74	48	25	7	3	1
Slovak	6	6	2	28	14	5	14	12	11	48	32	18	8	4	2
Other races	8	7	5	83	46	20	63	54	36	154	107	61	15	9	7
Total	54	51	21	438	257	57	378	335	206	870	643	284	60	42	24
Total foreign-born	90	87	33	599	375	65	547	492	294	1,236	954	392	86	63	31
Grand total	284	273	66	2,338	1,469	203	2,448	2,275	1,307	5,070	4,017	1,576	250	195	83

TABLE 12.—*Rate of progress of pupils and time in school in the United States, by race of father (foreign-born pupils only).*

Race of father of pupil.	Pupils in school less years than grade.			Pupils in school same years as grade.			Pupils in school more years than grade.			Total reporting complete data.			Not reporting complete data.		
	Number.	Pupils 8 years of age or over.		Number.	Pupils 8 years of age or over.		Number.	Pupils 8 years of age or over.		Number.	Pupils 8 years of age or over.		Number.	Pupils 8 years of age or over.	
		Number.	Number retarded.		Number.	Number retarded.		Number.	Number retarded.		Number.	Number retarded.		Number.	Number retarded.
Italian (not specified)	7	6	5	33	20	9	19	13	10	59	39	24	6	6	6
Other races	30	30	17	83	53	27	55	46	31	168	129	75	14	10	9
Total	37	36	22	116	73	36	74	59	41	227	168	99	20	16	15

TABLE 13.—*Ability to speak English of foreign-born fathers of pupils, by race of father.*

[This table includes only non-English-speaking races.]

Race of father of pupil.	Pupils whose fathers speak English.			Pupils whose fathers do not speak English.			Total reporting complete data.			Not reporting complete data.		
	Number.	Pupils 8 years of age or over.		Number.	Pupils 8 years of age or over.		Number.	Pupils 8 years of age or over.		Number.	Pupils 8 years of age or over.	
		Number.	Number retarded.		Number.	Number retarded.		Number.	Number retarded.		Number.	Number retarded.
German	404	326	122	29	24	12	433	350	134	13	11	5
Hebrew, Russian	69	53	14	3	3	1	72	56	15			
Italian, North	13	4	2	5	3	1	18	7	3			
Italian, South	21	12	8	3	2	2	24	14	10	1	1	1
Italian (not specified)	32	20	11	28	20	12	60	40	23	3	3	3
Magyar	55	33	13	21	15	10	76	48	23	5	3	3
Slovak	40	28	14	15	8	6	55	36	20	1		
Other races	128	97	50	40	19	18	168	116	68	1		
Total	762	573	234	144	94	62	906	667	296	24	18	12

TABLE 14.—*Ability to speak English of foreign-born fathers of pupils, by race of father (foreign-born pupils only).*

[This table includes only non-English-speaking races.]

Race of father of pupil.	Pupils whose fathers speak English.			Pupils whose fathers do not speak English.			Total reporting complete data.			Not reporting complete data.		
	Number.	Pupils 8 years of age or over.		Number.	Pupils 8 years of age or over.		Number.	Pupils 8 years of age or over.		Number.	Pupils 8 years of age or over.	
		Number.	Number retarded.		Number.	Number retarded.		Number.	Number retarded.		Number.	Number retarded.
Italian (not specified)	29	19	12	32	22	14	61	41	26	4	4	4
Other races	79	67	34	81	53	38	100	120	72	3	2	2
Total	108	86	46	113	75	52	221	161	98	7	6	6

TABLE 15.—*Citizenship of foreign-born fathers of pupils, by race of father.*

Race of father of pupil.	Pupils whose fathers have either first or second naturalization papers.			Pupils whose fathers have neither first nor second naturalization papers.			Total reporting complete data.			Not reporting complete data.		
	Number.	Pupils 8 years of age or over.		Number.	Pupils 8 years of age or over.		Number.	Pupils 8 years of age or over.		Number.	Pupils 8 years of age or over.	
		Number.	Number retarded.		Number.	Number retarded.		Number.	Number retarded.		Number.	Number retarded.
English-speaking races:												
English	141	124	41	33	31	15	174	155	56	17	12	3
Irish	75	57	16	2	2	2	77	59	18	4	3	2
Welsh	67	57	21	7	5	3	74	62	24	9	9	1
Other races	31	26	9	3	3	2	34	29	11	3	3	
Total	314	264	87	45	41	22	359	305	109	33	27	6
Non-English-speaking races:												
German	387	315	120	32	25	11	419	340	131	27	21	8
Hebrew, Russian	60	50	13	10	4	1	70	54	14	2	2	1
Italian, North	8	3	1	10	4	2	18	7	3			
Italian, South	5	1		18	12	9	23	13	9	2	2	2
Italian (not specified)	22	19	8	37	22	17	59	41	25	4	2	1
Magyar	29	17	9	47	31	14	76	48	23	5	3	3
Slovak	30	21	9	25	14	11	55	35	20	1	1	
Other races	99	77	39	66	36	28	165	113	67	4	3	1
Total	640	503	199	245	148	93	885	651	292	45	34	16
Total foreign-born	954	767	286	290	189	115	1,244	956	401	78	61	22

TABLE 16.—*Citizenship of foreign-born fathers of pupils, by race of father (foreign-born pupils only).*

Race of father of pupil.	Pupils whose fathers have either first or second naturalization papers.			Pupils whose fathers have neither first nor second naturalization papers.			Total reporting complete data.			Not reporting complete data.		
	Number.	Pupils 8 years of age or over.		Number.	Pupils 8 years of age or over.		Number.	Pupils 8 years of age or over.		Number.	Pupils 8 years of age or over.	
		Number.	Number retarded.		Number.	Number retarded.		Number.	Number retarded.		Number.	Number retarded.
Italian (not specified)	13	12	4	45	28	22	58	40	26	7	5	4
Other races	61	59	34	115	75	47	176	134	81	6	5	3
Total	74	71	38	160	103	69	234	174	107	13	10	7

TABLE 17.—Length of residence in the United States of foreign-born fathers of pupils, by race of father.

[By years in the United States is meant years since first arrival in the United States. No deduction is made for time spent abroad.]

Race of father of pupil.	Pupils whose fathers have been in the United States under 5 years.			Pupils whose fathers have been in the United States 5 to 9 years.			Pupils whose fathers have been in the United States 10 to 19 years.			Pupils whose fathers have been in the United States 20 years or over.			Total reporting complete data.			Not reporting complete data.		
	Number.	Pupils 8 years of age or over.		Number.	Pupils 8 years of age or over.		Number.	Pupils 8 years of age or over.		Number.	Pupils 8 years of age or over.		Number.	Pupils 8 years of age or over.		Number.	Pupils 8 years of age or over.	
		Number.	Number retarded.		Number.	Number retarded.		Number.	Number retarded.		Number.	Number retarded.		Number.	Number retarded.		Number.	Number retarded.
English-speaking races:																		
English	5	5	2	3	2	2	20	19	9	144	124	41	172	150	52	19	17	7
Irish	....	....	....	....	....	....	3	2	....	65	51	16	68	53	16	13	9	4
Welsh	2	1	1	....	....	....	9	4	....	54	49	16	65	54	17	18	17	8
Other races	....	....	....	....	....	....	5	3	....	30	27	10	35	30	10	2	2	1
Total	7	6	3	3	2	2	37	28	9	293	251	83	340	287	95	52	45	20
Non-English-speaking races:																		
German	4	3	1	20	16	7	78	57	23	323	266	97	425	342	128	21	19	11
Hebrew, Russian	2	2	....	15	10	3	24	20	3	28	21	6	69	53	12	3	3	1
Italian, North	....	....	....	4	2	1	4	1	2	9	3	1	17	6	4	1	1	1
Italian, South	1	....	....	12	7	6	10	6	3	1	1	1	24	14	10	1	1	1
Italian (not specified)	9	6	3	26	15	8	14	10	7	8	7	3	57	38	21	6	5	5
Magyar	5	5	4	18	8	4	22	12	....	29	21	14	74	46	22	7	5	4
Slovak	4	1	1	12	8	7	13	6	2	25	19	10	54	34	20	2	2	....
Other races	17	6	5	34	19	14	45	32	18	67	54	27	163	111	64	6	5	4
Total	42	23	14	141	85	50	210	144	58	490	392	159	883	644	281	47	41	27
Total foreign-born	49	29	17	144	87	52	247	172	67	783	643	242	1,223	931	376	99	86	47

TABLE 18.—*Length of residence in the United States of foreign-born fathers, by race of father (foreign-born pupils only).*

[By years in the United States is meant years since first arrival in the United States. No deduction is made for time spent abroad.]

Race of father of pupil.	Pupils whose fathers have been in the United States under 5 years.			Pupils whose fathers have been in the United States 5 to 9 years.			Pupils whose fathers have been in the United States 10 to 19 years.			Pupils whose fathers have been in the United States 20 years or over.			Total reporting complete data.			Not reporting complete data.		
	Number.	Pupils 8 years of age or over.		Number.	Pupils 8 years of age or over.		Number.	Pupils 8 years of age or over.		Number.	Pupils 8 years of age or over.		Number.	Pupils 8 years of age or over.		Number.	Pupils 8 years of age or over.	
		Number.	Number retarded.		Number.	Number retarded.		Number.	Number retarded.		Number.	Number retarded.		Number.	Number retarded.		Number.	Number retarded.
Italian (not specified)	10	6	3	39	24	15	6	6	4	2	2	1	57	38	23	8	7	7
Other races	39	23	14	84	60	33	44	42	26	8	7	5	175	132	78	7	7	6
Total	49	29	17	123	84	48	50	48	30	10	9	6	232	170	101	15	14	13

TABLE 19.—*Home language—Pupils of foreign-born fathers of non-English-speaking races, by race of father.*

Race of father of pupil.	Pupils in homes where English is used.			Pupils in homes where English is not used.			Total reporting complete data.			Not reporting complete data.		
	Number.	Pupils 8 years of age or over.		Number.	Pupils 8 years of age or over.		Number.	Pupils 8 years of age or over.		Number.	Pupils 8 years of age or over.	
		Number.	Number retarded.		Number.	Number retarded.		Number.	Number retarded.		Number.	Number retarded.
German	279	225	84	167	136	55	446	361	139			
Hebrew, Russian	41	31	10	31	25	5	72	56	15			
Italian, North	8	3	2	10	4	1	18	7	3			
Italian, South	8	4	2	17	11	9	25	15	11			
Italian (not specified)	16	13	9	46	29	17	62	42	26	1	1	1
Magyar	14	8	6	65	42	19	79	50	25	2	1	1
Slovak	11	9	4	45	27	16	56	36	20			
Other races	70	57	28	99	59	40	169	116	68			
Total	447	350	145	480	333	162	927	683	307	3	2	1

TABLE 20.—*Home language—Pupils of foreign-born fathers of non-English-speaking races, by race of father (foreign-born pupils only).*

Race of father of pupil.	Pupils in homes where English is used.			Pupils in homes where English is not used.			Total reporting complete data.			Not reporting complete data.		
	Number.	Pupils 8 years of age or over.		Number.	Pupils 8 years of age or over.		Number.	Pupils 8 years of age or over.		Number.	Pupils 8 years of age or over.	
		Number.	Number retarded.		Number.	Number retarded.		Number.	Number retarded.		Number.	Number retarded.
Italian (not specified)	8	6	5	56	38	25	64	44	30	1	1	......
All others	20	19	10	142	102	63	162	121	73	1	1	1
Total	28	25	15	198	140	88	226	165	103	2	2	1

TABLE 21.—*Proportion of term attended, by general nativity and race of father.*

[By term is meant the period from the beginning of the school year to December 31, 1908.]

PRIMARY GRADES.

General nativity and race of father of pupil.	Pupils who attended nine-tenths or over.			Pupils who attended three-fourths and less than nine-tenths.			Pupils who attended one-half and less than three-fourths.			Pupils who attended less than one-half.			Total reporting complete data.			Not reporting complete data.		
	Number.	Pupils 8 years of age or over. Number.	Number retarded.	Number.	Pupils 8 years of age or over. Number.	Number retarded.	Number.	Pupils 8 years of age or over. Number.	Number retarded.	Number.	Pupils 8 years of age or over. Number.	Number retarded.	Number.	Pupils 8 years of age or over. Number.	Number retarded.	Number.	Pupils 8 years of age or over. Number.	Number retarded.
Native-born:																		
White..........	1,538	976	340	283	166	78	114	62	38	63	39	23	1,998	1,243	479	68	28	15
Negro..........	24	18	12	1	1	1				1	1	1	26	20	14	2		
Total native-born..	1,562	994	352	284	167	79	114	62	38	64	40	24	2,024	1,263	493	70	28	15
Foreign-born:																		
English-speaking races—																		
English........	69	51	20	14	10	4	4	2	1	1	1	1	88	64	26	2	2	1
Irish.........	29	14	2	5	3	1	2	1	1				36	18	4	2	1	
Welsh.........	25	18	7	6	4	1	4	2	1				35	24	9	1		
Other races...	12	8	1	1	1		3	2	2	1	1		17	12	3			
Total......	135	91	30	26	18	6	13	7	5	2	2	1	176	118	42	5	3	1
Non-English-speaking races—																		
German........	195	126	44	30	20	10	15	12	3	6	6	3	246	164	60	6	3	3
Hebrew, Russian.	40	26	5	1	1	1	1	1		1			43	28	6	2	1	
Italian, North..	13	4	1	1	1	1	1						15	5	2	2	1	
Italian, South..	16	11	8	2	1	1	2	1	1	2			22	13	10	1	2	1
Italian (not specified)..	44	30	18	4	2	1	8	4	2	3	4	3	59	40	24	1	1	1
Magyar........	51	30	13	10	7	5	3	1	1	4	1	1	68	39	20	3	1	1
Slovak........	32	17	10	3	3	2	2	1	1	5	4	1	42	25	14	4	2	2
Other races....	83	47	31	10	4	4	12	3		7	7	6	112	61	41	5	2	2
Total......	474	291	130	61	39	24	44	23	8	28	22	15	607	375	177	24	11	9
Total foreign-born..	609	382	160	87	57	30	57	30	13	30	24	16	783	493	219	29	14	10
Grand total.....	2,171	1,376	512	371	224	109	171	92	51	94	64	40	2,807	1,756	712	99	42	25

GRAMMAR GRADES.

Race or nativity																			
Native-born:																			
White	28	62	62	567	1,467	1,467	13	23	23	26	42	42	76	168	168	452	1,234	1,234	1,234
Negro	2	2	2	8	11	11				2	2	2				6	9	9	9
Total native-born	30	64	64	575	1,478	1,478	13	23	23	28	44	44	76	168	168	458	1,243	1,243	1,243
Foreign-born:																			
English-speaking races—																			
English	4	10	10	24	71	71	1	2	2	2	3	3	4	14	14	17	52	52	52
Irish		1	1	11	32	32				1	2	2	4	5	5	7	27	27	27
Welsh				14	38	38					1	1	3	6	6	10	30	30	30
Other races				6	17	17										6	16	16	16
Total	4	11	11	55	158	158	1	2	2	3	6	6	11	25	25	40	125	125	125
Non-English-speaking races—																			
German	4	9	9	68	165	165	4	5	5	1	3	3	8	20	20	55	137	137	137
Hebrew, Russian		1	1	7	19	19							2	3	3	5	16	16	16
Italian, North		1	1	1	1	1										1	1	1	1
Italian, South																			
Italian (not specified)				2	3	3										2	3	3	3
Magyar		2	2	4	10	10				2			2	4	4	2	6	6	6
Slovak		2	2	4	8	8				1	2	2	1	1	1	1	5	5	5
Other races	1	1	1	21	40	40					2	2	6	7	7	14	31	31	31
Total	5	16	16	107	246	246	4	5	5	4	7	7	19	35	35	80	199	199	199
Total foreign-born	9	27	27	162	404	404	5	7	7	7	13	13	30	60	60	120	324	324	324
Grand total	39	91	91	737	1,882	1,882	18	30	30	35	57	57	106	228	228	578	1,567	1,567	1,567

Table **21.**—*Proportion of term attended, by general nativity and race of father*—Continued.

ALL ELEMENTARY GRADES.

General nativity and race of father of pupil.	Pupils who attended nine-tenths or over.			Pupils who attended three-fourths and less than nine-tenths.			Pupils who attended one-half and less than three-fourths.			Pupils who attended less than one-half.			Total reporting complete data.			Not reporting complete data.		
	Number.	8 yrs. Number.	8 yrs. Number retarded.	Number.	8 yrs. Number.	8 yrs. Number retarded.	Number.	8 yrs. Number.	8 yrs. Number retarded.	Number.	8 yrs. Number.	8 yrs. Number retarded.	Number.	8 yrs. Number.	8 yrs. Number retarded.	Number.	8 yrs. Number.	8 yrs. Number retarded.
Native-born:																		
White	2,772	2,210	792	451	334	154	156	104	64	86	62	36	3,465	2,710	1,046	130	90	43
Negro	33	27	18	1	1	1	2	2	2	1	1	1	37	31	22	4	2	2
Total native-born	2,805	2,237	810	452	335	155	158	106	66	87	63	37	3,502	2,741	1,068	134	92	45
Foreign-born:																		
English-speaking races—																		
English	121	103	37	28	24	8	7	5	4	3	3	1	159	135	50	12	12	5
Irish	56	41	9	10	8	5	2	1	1				68	50	15	2	1	
Welsh	55	48	17	12	10	4	6	4	2			1	73	62	23	2	1	
Other races	28	24	7	1	1		4	3	1	1	1		34	29	9			
Total	260	216	70	51	43	17	19	13	8	4	4	2	334	276	97	16	14	5
Non-English-speaking races—																		
German	332	263	99	50	40	18	18	15	4	11	11	7	411	329	128	15	12	5
Hebrew, Russian	56	42	10	4	4	2	2	1	1				62	47	13	3	2	1
Italian, North	14	5	2	1	1		1	1	1				16	6	3	2	1	
Italian, South	16	11	8	2		1	1			3	1	1	22	13	10	3	2	1
Italian (not specified)	47	33	20	4	3	2	8	4	2	3	3	1	62	43	26	1		
Magyar	57	36	15	14	11	7	3	3	2	4	2	2	78	49	24	3	2	2
Slovak	37	22	11	4	4	3	4			5	4	2	50	33	18	6	3	2
Other races	114	78	45	17	11	10	14	6	2	7	6	5	152	101	62	7	5	3
Total	673	490	210	96	74	43	51	30	12	33	27	19	853	621	284	40	27	14
Total foreign-born	933	706	280	147	117	60	70	43	20	37	31	21	1,187	897	381	56	41	19
Grand total	3,738	2,943	1,090	599	452	215	228	149	86	124	94	58	4,689	3,638	1,449	190	133	64

TABLE **22.**—*Proportion of term attended, by race of father (foreign-born pupils only).*

PRIMARY GRADES.

[By term is meant the period from the beginning of the school year to December 31, 1908.]

Race of father of pupil.	Pupils who attended nine-tenths or over.			Pupils who attended three-fourths and less than nine-tenths.			Pupils who attended one-half and less than three-fourths.			Pupils who attended less than one-half.			Total reporting complete data.			Not reporting complete data.		
	Number.	Pupils 8 years of age or over.		Number.	Pupils 8 years of age or over.		Number.	Pupils 8 years of age or over.		Number.	Pupils 8 years of age or over.		Number.	Pupils 8 years of age or over.		Number.	Pupils 8 years of age or over.	
		Number.	Number retarded.		Number.	Number retarded.		Number.	Number retarded.		Number.	Number retarded.		Number.	Number retarded.		Number.	Number retarded.
Italian (not specified)	50	36	23	5	3	3	5	3	2	3	2	1	63	44	29	2	1	1
Other races	108	73	41	12	12	9	11	5	2	7	7	5	138	97	57	7	5	4
Total	158	109	64	17	15	12	16	8	4	10	9	6	201	141	86	9	6	5

GRAMMAR GRADES.

Race of father of pupil.	Pupils who attended nine-tenths or over.			Pupils who attended three-fourths and less than nine-tenths.			Pupils who attended one-half and less than three-fourths.			Pupils who attended less than one-half.			Total reporting complete data.			Not reporting complete data.		
	Number.	Number.	Number retarded.	Number.	Number.	Number retarded.	Number.	Number.	Number retarded.	Number.	Number.	Number retarded.	Number.	Number.	Number retarded.	Number.	Number.	Number retarded.
All races	25	25	15	8	8	6	1	1	1	1	1	......	35	35	22	1	1	1

ALL ELEMENTARY GRADES.

Race of father of pupil.	Pupils who attended nine-tenths or over.			Pupils who attended three-fourths and less than nine-tenths.			Pupils who attended one-half and less than three-fourths.			Pupils who attended less than one-half.			Total reporting complete data.			Not reporting complete data.		
	Number.	Number.	Number retarded.	Number.	Number.	Number retarded.	Number.	Number.	Number retarded.	Number.	Number.	Number retarded.	Number.	Number.	Number retarded.	Number.	Number.	Number retarded.
Italian (not specified)	50	36	23	5	3	3	5	3	2	3	2	1	63	44	29	2	1	1
Other races	133	98	56	20	20	15	12	6	3	8	8	5	173	132	79	8	6	5
Total	183	134	79	25	23	18	17	9	5	11	10	6	236	176	108	10	7	6

TABLE 23.—*Access to present grade, by general nativity and race of father.*

General nativity and race of father of pupil.	Regular course.			Transfer from other public school in city.			Transfer from public school elsewhere.			Transfer from private school.		
	Number.	Pupils 8 years of age or over.		Number.	Pupils 8 years of age or over.		Number.	Pupils 8 years of age or over.		Number.	Pupils 8 years of age or over.	
		Number.	Number retarded.		Number.	Number retarded.		Number.	Number retarded.		Number.	Number retarded.
Native-born:												
White	2,629	1,984	599	133	118	58	112	97	62	35	33	17
Negro	25	19	11	1	1	1	3	3	3	3	1	1
Total native-born	2,654	2,003	610	134	119	59	115	100	65	38	34	18
Foreign-born:												
English-speaking races—												
English	116	99	25	8	8	3	9	8	5			
Irish	53	40	11	3	3		1	1	1	3	3	2
Welsh	55	49	16	4	4	2	2	2	1			
Other races	25	20	4	2	2	1	2	2	2			
Total	249	208	56	17	17	6	14	12	9	3	3	2
Non-English-speaking races—												
German	295	226	61	16	16	7	19	17	8	14	14	10
Hebrew, Russian	47	34	5	6	6	3	1	1	1			
Italian, North	10	3	1	2	2	1	1	1	1			
Italian, South	16	7	5	2	2	1	1	1	1			
Italian (not specified)	48	33	18				1	1	1			
Magyar	50	30	11	6	6	4	3	2	1	3	3	3
Slovak	35	19	11	1	1	1				5	5	
Other races	117	76	44	4	2	1	4	4	3	1	1	
Total	618	428	156	37	35	18	30	27	16	23	23	13
Total foreign-born	867	636	212	54	52	24	44	39	25	26	26	15
Grand total	3,521	2,639	822	188	171	83	159	139	90	64	60	33

General nativity and race of father of pupil.	Not promoted.			Total reporting complete data.			Not reporting complete data.		
	Number.	Pupils 8 years of age or over.		Number.	Pupils 8 years of age or over.		Number.	Pupils 8 years of age or over.	
		Number.	Number retarded.		Number.	Number retarded.		Number.	Number retarded.
Native-born:									
White	408	389	263	3,377	2,621	999	218	179	90
Negro	7	7	6	39	31	22	2	2	2
Total native-born	475	396	269	3,416	2,652	1,021	220	181	92
Foreign-born:									
English-speaking races—									
English	25	23	17	158	138	50	13	9	5
Irish	6	3	1	66	50	15	4	1	
Welsh	11	8	3	72	62	22	3	1	1
Other races	4	4	2	33	28	9	1	1	
Total	46	38	23	329	278	96	21	12	6
Non-English-speaking races—									
German	64	52	39	408	325	125	18	16	8
Hebrew, Russian	6	4	3	60	45	12	5	4	2
Italian, North	5	2	1	16	6	3	2	1	
Italian, South	4	3	2	23	13	9	2	2	2
Italian (not specified)	7	4	4	58	40	24	5	3	2
Magyar	14	6	5	73	45	23	8	6	3
Slovak	5	4	3	49	31	16	7	5	4
Other races	14	8	7	140	91	55	19	15	10
Total	119	83	64	827	596	267	66	52	31
Total foreign-born	165	121	87	1,156	874	363	87	64	37
Grand total	640	517	356	4,572	3,526	1,384	307	245	129

TABLE 24.—*Access to present grade, by race of father (foreign-born pupils only).*

Race of father of pupil.	Regular course.			Transfer from other public school in city.			Transfer from public school elsewhere.			Transfer from private school.		
	Number.	Pupils 8 years of age or over.		Number.	Pupils 8 years of age or over.		Number.	Pupils 8 years of age or over.		Number.	Pupils 8 years of age or over.	
		Number.	Number retarded.		Number.	Number retarded.		Number.	Number retarded.		Number.	Number retarded.
Italian (not specified)	47	32	18	1	1	1	2	2	2	......	......	......
Other races	126	93	49	8	7	4	7	7	6	5	5	2
Total	173	125	67	9	8	5	9	9	8	5	5	2

Race of father of pupil.	Not promoted.			Total reporting complete data.			Not reporting complete data.		
	Number.	Pupils 8 years of age or over.		Number.	Pupils 8 years of age or over.		Number.	Pupils 8 years of age or over.	
		Number.	Number retarded.		Number.	Number retarded.		Number.	Number retarded.
Italian (not specified)	11	7	6	61	42	27	4	3	3
Other races	17	12	10	163	124	71	18	14	13
Total	28	19	16	224	166	98	22	17	16

KANSAS CITY, MISSOURI.

INTRODUCTORY NOTE.
PUBLIC SCHOOL PUPILS—GENERAL INVESTIGATION.
PUBLIC SCHOOL TEACHERS IN ELEMENTARY GRADES
    AND KINDERGARTEN.
PAROCHIAL SCHOOL PUPILS—GENERAL INVESTIGATION.

461

LIST OF TABLES.

KANSAS CITY.[a]

The investigations of the Immigration Commission concerning schools in Kansas City, Mo., related to the pupils in the public schools and in the parochial schools. At the same time that information was gathered concerning pupils in the public schools certain data relating to the teachers in those schools were collected. The material relating to these three more or less distinct investigations is presented herewith in a series of general tables. The account of these general tables, with a description of the methods by which the figures were assembled and tabulated, is given in the introduction to this volume,[b] where also the significance of the tables and the general purpose which they serve are explained in some detail. The present note is concerned not so much with the methods of investigation as with the results which were obtained in Kansas City.

PUPILS OF THE PUBLIC SCHOOLS.

The number of pupils enumerated as being in actual attendance in the public schools of Kansas City, Mo., on a day early in December, 1908, was 27,159. During the school year 1908–9 the average attendance was 25,800. Inasmuch as the number reported to the Immigration Commission exceeds the average annual attendance, the inference must be that the December attendance is, on the whole, somewhat larger than that for some other parts of the school year. The excess of the figures furnished the Commission over the annual average attendance is ample evidence that the enumeration in the schools was comprehensive and complete. The figures here analyzed can therefore be accepted without hesitation as a faithful representation of the conditions generally prevailing in the public schools of the city.

The distribution among the grades of these 27,159 children was as follows:

Kindergarten	1,170	First year high school	1,404
First grade	4,522	Second year high school	937
Second grade	3,014	Third year high school	689
Third grade	3,482	Fourth year high school	588
Fourth grade	3,684	Normal	4
Fifth grade	3,051	Mixed grades	81
Sixth grade	2,530		
Seventh grade	2,003	Total	27,159

The attendance in the first grade is here, as frequently, much larger than in the succeeding grades. Grades 2 to 5 form a group having approximately the same number of pupils. Between the fifth grade and the sixth there is a falling off in number of about one-sixth of all the pupils. Between the sixth and seventh grade the diminution is about one-fourth. In the Kansas City school system the seventh grade is the final elementary grade.

---

[a] Missouri. [b] See pp. VII to XVII.

As the grades in the schools are numerous, a picture of the distribution of the pupils can be more conveniently obtained by grouping of the grades. Kindergarten and high school form natural groups. The elementary grades may be divided into primary and grammar, designating as the former the four lower grades and as the latter the three upper grades. Such a grouping of the pupils gives the following results:

Class of school.	Number.	Per cent.
Kindergarten	1,170	4.3
Primary, grades 1 to 4	14,702	54.3
Grammar, grades 5 to 7	7,584	28.0
High school	3,618	13.4
Total	27,074	100.0

These figures show that 54.3 per cent of the pupils of the Kansas City schools are in the primary grades, while as many as 13.4 per cent are in the high school. Comparing grammar grades with high school, it should not be forgotten that the former cover three years' work and the latter four, and this unusual distribution possibly accounts in part for the rather large percentage of pupils found in the high school.

Table 1 is arranged so that the distribution of pupils not only by grades but also by ages can be studied. There are only 37 pupils in the schools of Kansas City of less than 6 years of age. The laws of Missouri differ from those of most States in providing that no child shall receive instruction at the public expense until he shall have reached the age of 6 years. Consequently the kindergarten is filled with 6-year-old pupils and not with 5-year-olds, as is generally the case. We find in the schools of Kansas City 2,472 children of the age of 6 years. From 6 to 14 years of age the numbers are about the same for the different ages, ranging between 2,759 and 2,261. It is not until the age of 15 years is reached that there is any falling off in the number of pupils. At this age there are 1,524 pupils, and at 16 years of age there are 1,119, or about one-half as many as at the age of 14 years.

In Table 1 there is found also a statement of the number of pupils of each age in each grade. This table shows that many of the grades have pupils of a wide variety of ages, and conversely that the pupils of a given age are scattered through many grades. The table offers a wealth of detailed statement, which can best be summarized by a resort to the idea of an appropriate or normal age for each grade. If we assume that in each grade there is a normal age, the children of each grade can be separated into those of the normal grade and under and those which can be designated as overage or inappropriate to the grade in which they are found. These overage pupils are designated in current educational discussion as backward or retarded. Backwardness or retardation thus defined can also be measured by ascertaining for the pupils of a given age how many are in the grade appropriate to their age or above it and how many are in grades lower than the appropriate grade. Such undergrade pupils can then be classed as backward or retarded. It will be observed that in each case retardation expresses a misrelation between the age of the pupil and the grade in which he is found.   The measurement of retardation by means of the overage pupils is the most general form of expression.   The facts for the Kansas City schools are given in the table following, which shows the number of pupils in each grade and the number and percentage of those who are overage or retarded for their respective grades.   The sum of such overage pupils compared with the total number of pupils gives the general average for the city.

Grade.	Number in grade.	Retarded pupils.		
		Age.	Number.	Per cent of all pupils.
First...............	4,522	8 years and over..........................	1,311	29.0
Second.............	3,014	9 years and over..........................	1,216	40.3
Third...............	3,482	10 years and over.........................	1,724	49.5
Fourth.............	3,684	11 years and over.........................	2,134	57.9
Fifth...............	3,051	12 years and over.........................	1,972	64.6
Sixth..............	2,530	13 years and over.........................	1,612	63.7
Seventh...........	2,003	14 years and over.........................	1,209	60.4
Total.........	22,286		11,178	50.2

In round numbers one-half of the children in the Kansas City schools belong in the retarded class.   It will be observed that any pupil of the age of 8 years or over in the first grade is designated as retarded. The percentage of such retarded pupils in the first grade is 29.   Inasmuch as pupils in Kansas City can not enter kindergarten until they are 6 years of age, there are a great many children who enter the first grade at the age of 7.   For such children one failure places them in the retarded class.   For those children who enter school at the age of 6 years, two failures are possible before they reach the class designated as retarded.   The number of retarded children reaches its maximum in the fourth and fifth grades.   In the latter 64.6 per cent of the children, or nearly two-thirds, are retarded, and while this proportion diminishes somewhat in the sixth and seventh grades there are in the final or seventh grade of the elementary schools as many as 60 per cent of the children who are regarded as retarded.

Another method of indicating retardation has already been pointed out.   This takes as its basis the number of children of a given age and determines the proportion who are below the proper grade for their age.   For a selected class of pupils of the ages 10, 11, and 12 years, the figures for Kansas City are given in the table following.

Age.	Number of pupils of this age.	Normal grade.	Retarded, or below normal grade.	
			Number.	Per cent.
10 years..........	2,751	4	1,334	48.5
11 years..........	2,560	5	1,575	72.9
12 years..........	2,714	6	1,853	68.3
Total..........	8,025	....	4,762	62.5

This table shows that at 10 years of age nearly one-half of the children and at 11 and 12 years more than two-thirds of the children are retarded. The average for the three years is slightly less than two-thirds. This average is computed for the purpose of using it hereafter in comparison with smaller groups within the population of the schools.

The primary object of the investigation undertaken by the Immigration Commission was to determine, if possible, whether there were any important differences displayed by the different races which constitute the population of the public schools, the race in each case being determined by that of the father of the pupil. The general tables contain many details on this point. A few of the more salient results are here summarized.

The distribution of the pupils in the Kansas City public schools by race is given in the table following, which includes the two large groups native and foreign, and among the latter such individual races as are represented by as many as 200 children in the schools.

General nativity and race of father of pupil.	Pupils.		General nativity and race of father of pupil.	Pupils.	
	Number.	Per cent.		Number.	Per cent.
Native-born:			Foreign-born—Continued.		
White....................	19,018	70.0	Hebrew, German............	299	1.1
Negro and Indian.........	2,352	8.7	Hebrew, Russian..........	693	2.6
			Irish........................	540	2.0
Total native-born.......	21,370	78.7	Italian, South.............	591	2.2
			Swedish....................	523	1.9
Foreign-born:			All others.................	1,103	4.1
Canadian (other than French).................	267	1.0			
English...................	455	1.7	Total foreign-born.......	5,789	21.3
German....................	1,318	4.9	Grand total.............	27,159	100.0

A very large proportion of the children of Kansas City are of native origin, 70 per cent having native white fathers and 8.7 per cent negro fathers. The foreign-born are not so conspicuous as in many other cities, constituting, as the table shows, only 21.3 per cent of the whole number of pupils. Among the foreign-born the Germans, with nearly 5 per cent of the whole number of pupils, are the most conspicuous individual race. While several other races are represented by as many as 500 pupils, their proportion in the total for the city is not very great. The group "All others," comprising over 1,000 children, contains the representatives of many races, the mention of which will add to the completeness of the picture of the racial diversity among Kansas City school children. They are: Arabian (1), Assyrian (1), Bohemian and Moravian (18), Bulgarian (3), Canadian, French (29), Chinese (1), Croatian (2), Dalmatian (1), Danish (98), Dutch (50), Finnish (10), Flemish (3), French (74), Greek (5), Hebrew, Polish (197), Hebrew, Roumanian (40), Hebrew, Other (77), Italian, North (104), Japanese (3), Magyar (11), Mexican (4), Negro (1), Norwegian (40), Polish (10), Roumanian (8), Russian (55), Ruthenian (25), Scotch (165), Scotch-Irish (3), Spanish (2), Spanish-American (6), Syrian (12), and Welsh (32).

The distribution of the pupils of the different races by grades can best be studied by grouping the elementary grades as primary and grammar and contrasting these with the kindergarten and high school. This is done in the table next presented.

General nativity and race of father of pupil.	Number of pupils.					Per cent.			
	Kinder-garten.	Pri-mary.	Gram-mar.	High.	Total.	Kinder-garten.	Pri-mary.	Gram-mar.	High.
Native-born:									
White..................	782	10,074	5,400	2,758	19,014	4.1	53.0	28.4	14.5
Negro and Indian........	78	1,426	531	237	2,272	3.4	62.8	23.4	10.4
Total native-born......	860	11,500	5,931	2,995	21,286	4.0	54.0	27.9	14.1
Foreign-born:									
Canadian (other than French)...............	5	119	91	52	267	1.9	44.6	34.1	19.5
English.................	26	230	133	66	455	5.7	50.5	29.2	14.5
German.................	51	654	421	192	1,318	3.9	49.6	31.9	14.6
Hebrew, German........	12	144	102	41	299	4.0	48.2	34.1	13.7
Hebrew, Russian........	44	435	175	39	693	6.3	62.8	25.3	5.6
Irish...................	19	271	158	92	540	3.5	50.2	29.3	17.0
Italian, South...........	76	463	51	1	591	12.9	78.3	8.6	.2
Swedish.................	25	276	182	40	523	4.8	52.8	34.8	7.6
All others..............	52	610	340	100	1,102	4.7	55.4	30.9	9.1
Total foreign-born.....	310	3,202	1,653	623	5,788	5.4	55.3	28.6	10.8
Grand total..........	1,170	14,702	7,584	3,618	27,074	4.3	54.3	28.0	13.4

The proportion of children of native white fathers in the primary schools is 53 per cent, and that of children of foreign father is 55.3 per cent. While between the two groups considered as such there is not a very wide diversity, there is considerable variation among the different individual races which constitute the foreign-born. Several of these, the Canadian, the English, the German, the German Hebrew, the Irish, and the Swedish, have smaller proportions of their total in the primary grades than the native whites, while others, notably the Russian Hebrews and South Italians, have a very large proportion of their pupils in the primary grades.

A somewhat greater difference between children of native white and of foreign parents is found in the high schools. These schools contain 14.5 per cent of the children of native white parents and 10.8 per cent of those of foreign parents. The races which have in the primary grades smaller proportions than the native white have, with the exception of the Swedes, larger proportions in the high school. Russian Hebrews and Italians have very much smaller percentages in the high school. Somewhat smaller is the percentage of Swedish students; this is made up in part by a rather large proportion of pupils of this race in the grammar school.

The standing of the pupils in the schools as respects retardation is shown for the different races in the following table:

General nativity and race of father of pupil.	All elementary pupils.			Pupils 10, 11, and 12 years of age.		
	Number.	Retarded, overage.	Per cent retarded.	Number.	Retarded, under-grade.	Per cent retarded.
Native-born:						
White	15,474	7,468	48.3	5,516	3,175	57.6
Negro and Indian	1,957	1,271	64.9	687	518	75.4
Total native-born	17,431	8,739	50.1	6,203	3,693	59.5
Foreign-born:						
Canadian (other than French)	210	106	50.5	78	44	56.4
English	363	184	50.7	128	71	55.5
German	1,075	499	46.4	428	219	51.2
Hebrew, German	246	105	42.7	91	41	45.1
Hebrew, Russian	610	269	44.1	216	119	55.1
Irish	429	238	55.5	161	103	64.0
Italian, South	514	314	61.1	186	64	88.2
Swedish	458	223	48.7	180	93	58.7
All others	950	501	52.7	354	215	60.7
Total foreign-born	4,855	2,439	50.2	1,822	1,069	58.7
Grand total	22,286	11,178	50.2	8,025	4,762	59.3

This table is in two sections, the first, of three columns, referring to all elementary pupils, and the second, also of three columns, referring to the selected group of pupils 10, 11, and 12 years of age. If attention be directed to the first section, which gives general retardation, it will be noted that between the children of native white fathers as a class and those of foreign fathers as a class very little difference is observed. Many foreign races have less retardation among their children than the native white, and with the exception of the group of South Italian children it can not be said that there is any marked variation from the general standard observed throughout this city.

An examination of the second section of the table, referring to pupils 10, 11, and 12 years of age, shows that in this selected group very much the same conditions prevail as among the pupils at large. The contrast between the children of native and those of foreign parents is very slight. Apart from the negroes, the only race having a noticeably higher amount of retardation than the general average is the South Italian.

PUBLIC SCHOOL TEACHERS.

Incidental to the inquiry in regard to public school pupils, it was ascertained that in the kindergarten and elementary grades of Kansas City 672 teachers were employed. Of these only 16 were men, all having native parents and 12 of them being negroes. Of this small male contingent 12 were employed in the grammar and special grades.

Divided by race, the teachers are as follows:

	Number.	Per cent.
Native white of native fathers	478	71.1
Native negro of native fathers	55	8.2
Native white of foreign fathers	129	19.2
Foreign white	10	1.5
Total	672	100.0

The distribution of the teachers is about the same as that of the children, over 70 per cent having native white fathers. Among the small group of 129 teachers of native birth but foreign parentage, the most prominent races are the German, with 5.2 per cent, and the Irish, with 4.3 per cent, of the whole number of teachers in the schools.

If these teachers be classified by grades, and the statement condensed by considering the four lower grades as primary and uniting them with the kindergarten, and the three upper grades as grammar and uniting them with the special grades, we have the following statement:

	Kindergarten and primary.	Grammar and special.	Total.	Per cent in grammar grades.
Native white of native fathers	343	190	533	35.6
Native negro of native fathers	34	21	55	38.2
Native white of foreign fathers	83	46	129	35.7
Foreign fathers	5	5	10	50.0
Total	465	262	727	35.0

There is substantial uniformity in the distribution of the several racial groups with respect to upper and lower grades.

Of these teachers 688 reported length of service, as follows:

Under 5 years	96	From 25 to 29 years	25
From 5 to 9 years	154	30 years and over	19
From 10 to 14 years	181		
From 15 to 19 years	117	Total	668
From 20 to 24 years	76		

Only a little more than one-third of the teachers belong in the younger groups of those who have less than ten years' experience, the bulk of the teachers having had from ten to twenty years' service in the schools.

Length of service and race are summarized in the following statement:

Race and nativity of teachers.	Length of service, in years.			
	Under 10.	10 to 19.	20 and over.	Total.
Native white of native fathers	176	220	80	476
Native negro of native fathers	19	22	14	55
Native white of foreign fathers	52	54	21	127
Foreign white	3	2	5	10
Total	250	298	120	668
Percentages: All teachers	37.4	44.6	18.0	100.0

PUPILS IN THE PAROCHIAL SCHOOLS.

Figures were collected in the parochial schools of Kansas City for 983 pupils. Inasmuch as the official directory of the Roman Catholic Church gives the total enrollment of Kansas City, Mo., as 3,149, we have to do here with only a small proportion of the whole number of pupils in the parochial schools of the city. Allowing for the divergence which always exists for the figures for total enrollment and for the average attendance, the available figures refer to rather more than one-third of the parochial school pupils but probably less than one-half of the whole number. As explained in the introduction, the omissions in enumeration, when they occurred, were generally for entire schools. It follows thus that our figures, while not representing all of the schools of the city, are probably a fair sample of conditions existing in those schools.

In view of the incompleteness of the data it seems best to present a few derivative tables without attempting to draw conclusions from them. The distribution of the pupils by grades is as follows:

Kindergarten	23	Eighth grade	26
First grade	191	First year high school	9
Second grade	146	Second year high school	12
Third grade	151	Third year high school	3
Fourth grade	151	Fourth year high school	2
Fifth grade	130		
Sixth grade	90	Total	983
Seventh grade	49		

The concentration of these figures into the several groups is as follows:

Class of school.	Number.	Per cent.
Kindergarten	23	2.3
Grades 1 to 4	639	65.0
Grades 5 to 8	295	30.0
High school	26	2.6
Total	983	100.0

The progress of the pupils in these schools, as measured by general retardation, is indicated in the table following.

Grade.	Number in grade.	Retarded pupils.		
		Age.	Number.	Per cent of all pupils.
First	191	8 years and over	37	19.4
Second	146	9 years and over	74	50.7
Third	151	10 years and over	85	56.3
Fourth	151	11 years and over	73	48.3
Fifth	130	12 years and over	46	35.4
Sixth	90	13 years and over	51	56.7
Seventh	49	14 years and over	22	44.9
Eighth	26	15 years and over	2	7.7
Total	934		390	41.8

The general percentage of retardation of 41.8 is considerably exceeded in the sixth grade, where 56.7 per cent of the children are retarded. The retardation of pupils of 10, 11, and 12 years is shown in the following table:

Age.	Number of pupils of this age.	Normal grade.	Retarded, or below normal grade.	
			Number.	Per cent.
10 years	149	4	70	47.0
11 years	131	5	67	51.1
12 years	89	6	48	53.9
Total	369	....	185	50.1

The average retardation of 50 per cent is somewhat higher than in the preceding table.

The next table gives the distribution of these pupils by race.

General nativity and race of father of pupil.	Pupils.	
	Number.	Per cent.
Native-born:		
White	500	50.9
Negro	7	.7
Total native-born	507	51.6
Foreign-born:		
German	265	27.0
Irish	132	13.4
All others	79	8.0
Total foreign-born	476	48.4
Grand total	983	100.0

This table shows that about one-half of the pupils in these schools had native fathers and one-half had foreign fathers, most of the latter being Germans. There are only a few races included in the group "all others," as follows: Belgian (2), Bohemian and Moravian (1), Canadian, French (1), Canadian, Other (3), Dutch (3), English (12), Flemish (20), French (5), Hebrew, German (20), Italian, North (8), Magyar (1), Polish (1), and Swedish (2).

PUBLIC AND PAROCHIAL PUPILS COMBINED.

The following table gives the statement concerning all the pupils enumerated in Kansas City:

General nativity and race of father of pupil.	Pupils by schools.			Per cent of all pupils.
	Public schools.	Parochial schools.	Total.	
Native-born:.				
White..	19,018	500	19,518	69.4
Negro and Indian...........................	2,352	7	2,359	8.4
Total native-born.......................	21,370	507	21,877	77.7
Foreign-born:				
Canadian (other than French)...............	267	3	270	1.0
English......................................	455	12	467	1.7
German......................................	1,318	265	1,583	5.6
Hebrew, German.............................	299	20	319	1.1
Hebrew, Russian............................	693	....	693	2.5
Irish..	540	132	672	2.4
Italian, South..............................	591	....	591	2.1
Swedish.....................................	523	2	525	1.9
All others..................................	1,103	42	1,145	4.1
Total foreign-born......................	5,789	476	6,265	22.3
Grand total.............................	27,159	983	28,142	100.0

Inasmuch as the aggregate of parochial schools so far as recorded is very small in contrast with the public schools, the distribution of races here indicated varies little from that given for the public schools alone.

GENERAL TABLES.

PUBLIC SCHOOL PUPILS: GENERAL INVESTIGATION.

Table 1.—*Grade and age—Number of pupils of each age in each grade, by sex.*

BOYS.

Age.	Kindergarten.	Elementary grades.							
		1.	2.	3.	4.	5.	6.	7.	Total.
4 years	1								
5 years	17	2							2
6 years	543	698	13						711
7 years	44	927	259	23					1,209
8 years	7	453	629	269	18				1,369
9 years	1	169	344	557	206	6			1,282
10 years		72	180	450	531	160	8	1	1,402
11 years		21	76	233	484	368	84	10	1,276
12 years		9	34	123	339	444	295	78	1,322
13 years		6	16	51	186	333	383	240	1,215
14 years		5	6	36	80	144	289	285	845
15 years			1	6	26	48	110	170	361
16 years					2	12	21	60	95
17 years		2		1	1	1	3	8	16
18 years					1	1	2	1	5
19 years				1					1
20 years or over						1			1
Total	613	2,364	1,558	1,750	1,874	1,518	1,195	853	11,112

Age.	High school.					Mixed grades.	Grand total.
	First year.	Second year.	Third year.	Fourth year.	Total.		
4 years							
5 years							19
6 years						2	1,256
7 years						4	1,257
8 years						5	1,381
9 years						2	1,285
10 years						3	1,405
11 years						8	1,284
12 years	4				4	2	1,328
13 years	53	2			55	3	1,273
14 years	170	46	7	3	226	4	1,075
15 years	176	110	18	7	311	4	676
16 years	127	128	105	42	402		497
17 years	50	70	80	71	271		287
18 years	9	31	42	58	140		145
19 years	5	12	16	25	58	1	60
20 years or over	6	2	7	7	22		23
Total	600	401	275	213	1,489	38	13,252

Table 1.—*Grade and age—Number of pupils of each age in each grade, by sex*—Contd.

GIRLS.

Age.	Kindergarten.	Elementary grades.							
		1.	2.	3.	4.	5.	6.	7.	Total.
4 years									
5 years	14	2	1						3
6 years	519	688	7	1					696
7 years	21	894	305	28	1				1,228
8 years	3	371	584	318	19	1			1,293
9 years		125	320	562	238	12			1,257
10 years		57	136	439	537	169	11		1,349
11 years		14	51	209	487	361	151	11	1,284
12 years		5	35	109	298	457	369	107	1,380
13 years		2	12	39	166	351	420	348	1,338
14 years			4	19	44	152	266	393	878
15 years			1	6	13	26	95	213	354
16 years				1	5	2	20	60	88
17 years					2	1	3	15	21
18 years								3	3
19 years						1			1
20 years or over				1					1
Total	557	2,158	1,456	1,732	1,810	1,533	1,335	1,150	11,174

Age.	High school.					Normal.	Mixed.	Total.	Grand total.
	First year.	Second year.	Third year.	Fourth year.	Total.				
4 years									
5 years									17
6 years							1	1	1,216
7 years							3	3	1,252
8 years							2	2	1,298
9 years							4	4	1,261
10 years							5	5	1,354
11 years							2	2	1,286
12 years	8				8		4	4	1,392
13 years	73	5		1	79		7	7	1,424
14 years	238	48	9	6	301		7	7	1,186
15 years	279	157	45	8	489		5	5	848
16 years	147	181	138	66	532		2	2	622
17 years	37	104	145	139	425		1	1	447
18 years	16	25	57	99	197				200
19 years	4	12	14	48	78	3		3	82
20 years or over	2	4	6	8	20	1		1	22
Total	804	536	414	375	2,129	4	43	47	13,907

TABLE 1.—*Grade and age—Number of pupils of each age in each grade, by sex*—Contd.

TOTAL.

Age.	Kinder-garten.	Elementary grades.							
		1.	2.	3.	4.	5.	6.	7.	Total.
4 years	1								
5 years	31	4	1						5
6 years	1,062	1,386	20	1					1,407
7 years	65	1,821	564	51	1				2,437
8 years	10	824	1,213	587	37	1			2,662
9 years	1	294	664	1,119	444	18			2,539
10 years		129	316	889	1,068	329	19	1	2,751
11 years		35	127	442	971	729	235	21	2,560
12 years		14	69	232	637	901	664	185	2,702
13 years		8	28	90	352	684	803	588	2,553
14 years		5	10	55	124	296	555	678	1,723
15 years			2	12	39	74	205	383	715
16 years				1	7	14	41	120	183
17 years		2		1	3	2	6	23	37
18 years					1	1	2	4	8
19 years				1		1			2
20 years or over				1		1			2
Total	1,170	4,522	3,014	3,482	3,684	3,051	2,530	2,003	22,286

Age.	High school.					Nor-mal.	Mixed.	Total.	Grand total.
	First year.	Second year.	Third year.	Fourth year.	Total.				
4 years									1
5 years									36
6 years							3	3	2,472
7 years							7	7	2,509
8 years							7	7	2,679
9 years							6	6	2,546
10 years							8	8	2,759
11 years							10	10	2,570
12 years	12				12		6	6	2,720
13 years	126	7		1	134		10	10	2,697
14 years	408	94	16	9	527		11	11	2,261
15 years	455	267	63	15	800		9	9	1,524
16 years	274	309	243	108	934		2	2	1,119
17 years	87	174	225	210	696		1	1	734
18 years	25	56	99	157	337				345
19 years	9	24	30	73	136	3	1	4	142
20 years or over	8	6	13	15	42	1		1	45
Total	1,404	937	689	588	3,618	4	81	85	27,159

TABLE 2.—Race, sex, and grade—Number of pupils of each sex in each grade, by general nativity and race of father of pupil.

General nativity and race of father of pupil	Kindergarten	Elementary grades 1	2	3	4	5	6	7	Total	High school First year	Second year	Third year	Fourth year	Total	Mixed	Normal	Grand total
Native-born of native father:																	
White—																	
Male	414	1,585	1,055	1,188	1,347	1,066	861	617	7,719	471	289	219	163	1,142			9,275
Female	368	1,440	984	1,214	1,261	1,095	926	835	7,755	602	410	323	281	1,616		4	9,743
Total	782	3,025	2,039	2,402	2,608	2,161	1,787	1,452	15,474	1,073	699	542	444	2,758		4	19,018
Negro—																	
Male	28	261	145	157	147	108	73	44	935	33	25	12	11	81	38		1,082
Female	50	237	141	176	162	98	120	87	1,021	56	46	26	27	155	43		1,269
Total	78	498	286	333	309	206	193	131	1,956	89	71	38	38	236	81		2,351
Indian—																	
Male																	
Female						1							1	1			1
Total						1							1	1			1
Total native-born—																	
Male	442	1,846	1,200	1,345	1,494	1,174	934	661	8,654	504	314	231	174	1,223	38		10,357
Female	418	1,677	1,125	1,390	1,423	1,193	1,046	922	8,776	658	456	349	309	1,772	43	4	11,013
Total	860	3,523	2,325	2,735	2,917	2,367	1,980	1,583	17,430	1,162	770	580	483	2,995	81	4	21,370
Foreign-born:																	
Bohemian and Moravian—																	
Male	1	2	1	2	1	1	2	1	6	2	1			1			8
Female	1	2	1	2	1	1	2	1	9								10
Total	2	4	2	4	2	2	4	1	15	2	1			1			18
Canadian, French—																	
Male	1	2	4	2	2	3	4	1	11		1			2			14
Female				4				1	11		1			4			15
Total	1	2	4	6	2	3	4	1	22		1			6			29
Canadian, Other—																	
Male	4	11	14	26	16	17	25	11	120	6	5	5	2	18			142
Female	1	14	12	12	14	9	19	10	90	18	1	8	7	34			125
Total	5	25	26	38	30	26	44	21	210	24	6	13	9	52			267
Danish—																	
Male	4	13	1	3	5	8	2	3	35	1	2	1	2	4			43
Female	1	9	7	9	6	2	9	3	45		7			9			55
Total	5	22	8	12	11	10	11	6	80	1	9	1	2	13			98
Dutch—																	
Male	1	5	6	4	6	6		2	29	2	1	1	1	3			32
Female		2	1	1	3	4	1	2	14		1		1	3			18
Total	1	7	7	5	9	10	1	4	43	2	2	1	1	6			50

English—																	
Male	12	38	27	32	31	32	17	17	194	8	6	4	4	22			228
Female	14	27	29	19	27	30	16	21	169	16	14	5	9	44			227
Total	26	65	56	51	58	62	33	38	363	24	20	9	13	66			455
Finnish—																	
Male				2		1			3								3
Female		3	1		2		1		7								7
Total		3	1	2	2	1	1		10								10
French—																	
Male	2	4	3	3	6	7	2	4	29	1	2	1		4			35
Female		5	5	4	1	6	4	5	30	6	2	1		9			39
Total	2	9	8	7	7	13	6	9	59	7	4	2		13			74
German—																	
Male	31	93	69	87	92	90	59	40	530	35	31	7	11	84			645
Female	20	66	59	88	100	89	81	62	545	44	29	15	20	108			673
Total	51	159	128	175	192	179	140	102	1,075	79	60	22	31	192			1,318
Hebrew, German—																	
Male	8	19	11	19	20	19	14	17	119	6	7	6	3	22			149
Female	4	19	13	16	27	23	10	19	127	7	5	3	4	19			150
Total	12	38	24	35	47	42	24	36	246	13	12	9	7	41			299
Hebrew, Polish—																	
Male	6	25	8	9	14	7	10	9	82	2	1	1	1	5			93
Female	1	22	13	4	12	21	19	10	101	1			1	2			104
Total	7	47	21	13	26	28	29	19	183	3	1	1	2	7			197
Hebrew, Roumanian—																	
Male	1	1	4	4	2	5	1	1	18								19
Female		3	2	1	1	10	3	1	21								21
Total	1	4	6	5	3	15	4	2	39								40
Hebrew, Russian—																	
Male	27	104	35	50	45	34	32	28	328	10	4	2	3	19			374
Female	17	77	36	51	37	30	23	28	282	6	4	7	3	20			319
Total	44	181	71	101	82	64	55	56	610	16	8	9	6	39			693
Hebrew, Other—																	
Male	2	6	8	4	9	4	2	2	35	1	1			2			39
Female		4	3	7	5	6	5	3	33	2		3		5			38
Total	2	10	11	11	14	10	7	5	68	3	1	3		7			77
Irish—																	
Male	10	38	33	30	52	35	23	17	228	12	10	6	7	35			273
Female	9	31	25	29	33	33	26	24	201	32	6	8	11	57			267
Total	19	69	58	59	85	68	49	41	429	44	16	14	18	92			540
Italian, North—																	
Male	4	10	6	10	5	6	2	1	40								44
Female	7	15	14	11	3	6	2	1	52			1		1			60
Total	11	25	20	21	8	12	4	2	92			1		1			104
Italian, South—																	
Male	35	75	77	58	28	13	11	3	265								300
Female	41	107	46	29	43	10	10	4	249			1		1			291
Total	76	182	123	87	71	23	21	7	514			1		1			591

TABLE 2.—*Race, sex, and grade—Number of pupils of each sex in each grade, by general nativity and race of father of pupil*—Continued.

General nativity and race of father of pupil	Kinder-garten	Elementary grades.								High school.					Mixed.	Normal.	Grand total.
		1.	2.	3.	4.	5.	6.	7.	Total.	First year.	Second year.	Third year.	Fourth year.	Total.			
Foreign-born—Continued.																	
Magyar—Male		2						1	3		1		1	2			5
Female			1	1		2	1	1	6								6
Total		2	1	1		2	1	2	9		1		1	2			11
Norwegian—Male		2	3	3	5	2	1	1	17				1	1			18
Female		6	2	1	2	1	4	1	17				2	5			22
Total		8	5	4	7	3	5	2	34				3	6			40
Polish—Male			1				1		2	1	2			3			5
Female		1		1	1	1		1	5								5
Total		1	1	1	1	1	1	1	7	1	2			3			10
Russian—Male		9	2	1	4	1	2	1	20					5			25
Female		11	1	3	6	3	1		25					5			30
Total		20	3	4	10	4	3	1	45					10			55
Ruthenian—Male		11							11								11
Female		14							14								14
Total		25							25								25
Scotch—Male	3	5	5	6	11	14	10	8	59	4	3	4	3	14			76
Female	3	7	6	12	15	14	10	9	73	3	4	4	2	13			89
Total	6	12	11	18	26	28	20	17	132	7	7	8	5	27			165
Syrian—Male	1	1			2				3								4
Female	1	2	3			2			7								8
Total	2	3	3		2	2			10								12
Swedish—Male	14	38	35	39	22	33	35	23	225	4	9	7	1	21			260
Female	11	31	35	35	41	37	35	19	233	8	4	3	4	19			263
Total	25	69	70	74	63	70	70	42	458	12	13	10	5	40			523
Welsh—Male		2	2	4		2	3		13					2			15
Female		2	2	1	1	2	3	2	13					4			17
Total		4	4	5	1	4	6	2	26					6			32

Other races [a]—																
Male	35	3						30	1	3	1	3	6	5	11	2
Female	21	1			1		2	19	2	3	2	2	1	3	6	1
Total	56	4			1	1	2	49	3	6	3	5	7	8	17	3
Total foreign-born—																
Male	2,895	266		39	44	87	96	2,458	192	261	344	380	405	358	518	171
Female	2,894	357	4	66	65	80	146	2,398	228	289	340	387	342	331	481	139
Total	5,789	623	4	105	109	167	242	4,856	420	550	684	767	747	689	999	310
Grand total—																
Male	13,252	1,489	38	213	275	401	600	11,112	853	1,195	1,518	1,874	1,750	1,558	2,364	613
Female	13,907	2,129	43	375	414	536	804	11,174	1,150	1,335	1,533	1,810	1,732	1,456	2,158	557
Total	27,159	3,618	81	588	689	937	1,404	22,286	2,003	2,530	3,051	3,684	3,482	3,014	4,522	1,170

[a] Other races: Arabian, 1; Assyrian, 1; Bulgarian, 1; Chinese, 3; Croatian, 1; Dalmatian, 1; Flemish, 3; Greek, 5; Japanese, 3; Mexican, 4; Negro, 1; Roumanian, 3; Scotch Irish, 3; Spanish-American, 6; and Spanish, 2; races not specified, 12.

TABLE 3.—*Race, sex, and age, by grade—Number of pupils of each age in each grade, by sex and by general nativity and race of father of pupil.*

KINDERGARTEN.

BOYS.

General nativity and race of father of pupil.	Number of pupils of each age.							Total.
	4.	5.	6.	7.	8.	9.	10.	
Native-born:								
White	1	7	382	23	1			414
Negro		10	18					28
Total native-born	1	17	400	23	1			442
Foreign-born:								
Bohemian and Moravian			1					1
Canadian (other than French)			4					4
Danish			4					4
English			11	1				12
French			2					2
German			31					31
Hebrew, German			7	1				8
Hebrew, Polish			5	1				6
Hebrew, Roumanian			1					1
Hebrew, Russian			15	9	2	1		27
Hebrew, Other			2					2
Irish			10					10
Italian, North			3	1				4
Italian, South			25	7	3			35
Russian			4					4
Scotch			3					3
Syrian					1			1
Swedish			13	1				14
Other races *a*			2					2
Total foreign-born			143	21	6	1		171
Grand total	1	17	543	44	7	1		613

GIRLS.

General nativity and race of father of pupil.	4.	5.	6.	7.	8.	9.	10.	Total.
Native-born:								
White		4	356	8				368
Negro		8	40	2				50
Total native-born		12	396	10				418
Foreign-born:								
Bohemian and Moravian			1					1
Canadian, French			1					1
Canadian, Other			1					1
Danish			1					1
Dutch			1					1
English			13	1				41
German			19	1				20
Hebrew, German			4					4
Hebrew, Polish			1					1
Hebrew, Russian		1	12	4				17
Irish			9					9
Italian, North			7					7
Italian, South		1	34	4	2			41
Russian			5					5
Scotch			2	1				3
Syrian					1			1
Swedish			11					11
Other races			1					1
Total foreign-born		2	123	11	3			139
Grand total		14	519	21	3			557

a "Other races" includes races having less than 10 represeneatives in this city and pupils whose race is not reported.

TABLE 3.—*Race, sex, and age, by grade—Number of pupils of each age in each grade, by sex and by general nativity and race of father of pupil—Continued.*

KINDERGARTEN—Continued.

TOTAL.

General nativity and race of father of pupil.	Number of pupils of each age.							Total.
	4.	5.	6.	7.	8.	9.	10.	
Native-born:								
White...........................	1	11	738	31	1	....	....	782
Negro...........................	....	18	58	2	....	....	....	78
Total native-born	1	29	796	33	1	....	....	860
Foreign-born:								
Bohemian and Moravian.........	....	....	2	....	....	....	....	2
Canadian, French...............	....	....	1	....	....	....	....	1
Canadian, Other................	....	....	5	....	....	....	....	5
Danish.........................	....	....	5	....	....	....	....	5
Dutch..........................	....	....	1	....	....	....	....	1
English........................	....	....	24	2	....	....	....	26
French.........................	....	....	2	....	....	....	....	2
German.........................	....	....	50	1	....	....	....	51
Hebrew, German.................	....	....	11	1	....	....	....	12
Hebrew, Polish.................	....	....	6	1	....	....	....	7
Hebrew, Roumanian..............	....	....	1	....	....	....	....	1
Hebrew, Russian................	....	1	27	13	2	1	....	44
Hebrew, Other..................	....	....	2	....	....	....	....	2
Irish..........................	....	....	19	....	....	....	....	19
Italian, North.................	....	....	10	1	....	....	....	11
Italian, South.................	....	1	59	11	5	....	....	76
Russian........................	....	....	9	....	....	....	....	9
Scotch.........................	....	....	5	1	....	....	....	6
Syrian.........................	....	....	....	....	2	....	....	2
Swedish........................	....	....	24	1	....	....	....	25
Other races a	....	....	3	....	....	....	....	3
Total foreign-born.............	....	2	266	32	9	1	....	310
Grand total....................	1	31	1,062	65	10	1	....	1,170

a "Other races" includes races having less than 10 representatives in this city and pupils whose race is not reported.

TABLE 3.—*Race, sex, and age, by grade—Number of pupils of each age in each grade, by sex and by general nativity and race of father of pupil*—Continued.

FIRST GRADE.

BOYS.

General nativity and race of father of pupil.	Number of pupils of each age.														Total.
	4.	5.	6.	7.	8.	9.	10.	11.	12.	13.	14.	15.	16.	17.	
Native-born:															
White		1	484	651	298	88	40	11	7	3	2				1,585
Negro			64	64	56	43	24	7	1	1	1				261
Total native-born		1	548	715	354	131	64	18	8	4	3				1,846
Foreign-born:															
Canadian, French			1		1										2
Canadian, Other			1	9		1									11
Danish			2	5	4	2									13
Dutch			1	3		1									5
English			14	15	6	3									38
French			1	3											4
German		1	34	36	15	6	1								93
Hebrew, German			5	11	3										19
Hebrew, Polish			10	10	3	1	1								25
Hebrew, Roumanian					1										1
Hebrew, Russian			32	43	18	6	3	1	1						104
Hebrew, Other			4	1	1										6
Irish			10	16	8	3									38
Italian, North			2	3	3	1							1		10
Italian, South			16	27	17	9	1	2		2	1				75
Norwegian			1	1											2
Russian				6	1	2									9
Ruthenian															
Swedish			4	6	1										11
Syrian			9	16	11	2									38
Welsh					1										1
Other races a			2		6	1					1		1		11
Total foreign-born		1	150	212	99	38	8	3	1	2	2		2		518
Grand total		2	698	927	453	169	72	21	9	6	5		2		2,364

a "Other races" includes races having less than 10 representatives in this city and pupils whose race is not reported.

TABLE 3.—*Race, sex, and age, by grade—Number of pupils of each age in each grade, by sex and by general nativity and race of father of pupil*—Continued.

FIRST GRADE—Continued.

GIRLS.

General nativity and race of father of pupil.	Number of pupils of each age.														Total.
	4.	5.	6.	7.	8.	9.	10.	11.	12.	13.	14.	15.	16.	17.	
Native-born:															
White		1	480	636	228	64	23	7	1						1,440
Negro			59	72	52	31	18	3	2						237
Total native-born		1	539	708	280	95	41	10	3						1,677
Foreign-born:															
Bohemian and Moravian				1	1										2
Canadian, Other			5	7	1	1									14
Danish			2	4	2	1									9
Dutch			2												2
English			7	11	9										27
Finnish				1	2										3
French			2	1	2										5
German			32	23	7	3	1								66
Hebrew, German			7	8	3	1									19
Hebrew, Polish			8	7	4		1	2							22
Hebrew, Roumanian			2		1										3
Hebrew, Russian			24	22	18	8	4	1							77
Hebrew, Other			1	3											4
Irish			10	15	5		1								31
Italian, North			2	6	3	3				1					15
Italian, South		1	26	40	18	11	7	1	2	1					107
Magyar				2											2
Norwegian			3		3										6
Polish			1												1
Russian			1	7	2		1								11
Ruthenian			5	7	2										14
Swedish			5	17	7	1	1								31
Syrian			1	1											2
Welsh				2											2
Other races a			3	1	1	1									6
Total foreign-born		1	149	186	91	30	16	4	2	2					481
Grand total		2	688	894	371	125	57	14	5	2					2,158

a "Other races" includes races having less than 10 representatives in this city and pupils whose race is not reported.

TABLE 3.—*Race, sex, and age, by grade—Number of pupils of each age in each grade, by sex and by general nativity and race of father of pupil*—Continued.

FIRST GRADE—Continued.

TOTAL.

General nativity and race of father of pupil.	Number of pupils of each age.														Total.
	4.	5.	6.	7.	8.	9.	10.	11.	12.	13.	14.	15.	16.	17.	
Native-born:															
White		2	964	1,287	526	152	63	18	8	3	2				3,025
Negro			123	136	108	74	42	10	3	1	1				498
Total native-born		2	1,087	1,423	634	226	105	28	11	4	3				3,523
Foreign-born:															
Bohemian and Moravian				1	1										2
Canadian, French			1		1										2
Canadian, Other			6	16	1	2									25
Danish			4	9	6	3									22
Dutch			3	3		1									7
English			21	26	15	3									65
Finnish				1	2										3
French			3	4	2										9
German		1	66	59	22	9	2								159
Hebrew, German			12	19	6	1									38
Hebrew, Polish			18	17	7	1	2	2							47
Hebrew, Roumanian			2		2										4
Hebrew, Russian			56	65	36	14	7	2	1						181
Hebrew, Other			5	4	1										10
Irish			20	31	13	3	1							1	69
Italian, North			4	9	6	4	1			1					25
Italian, South		1	42	67	35	20	8	3	2	3	1				182
Magyar				2											2
Norwegian			4	1	3										8
Polish			1												1
Russian			1	13	3	2	1								20
Ruthenian			9	13	3										25
Swedish			14	33	18	3	1								69
Syrian			1	2											3
Welsh			1	2		1									4
Other races a			5	1	7	1	1				1			1	17
Total foreign-born		2	299	398	190	68	24	7	3	4	2			2	999
Grand total		4	1,386	1,821	824	294	129	35	14	8	5			2	4,522

a "Other races" includes races having less than 10 representatives in this city and pupils whose race is not reported.

TABLE 3.—*Race, sex, and age, by grade—Number of pupils of each age in each grade, by sex and by general nativity and race of father of pupil*—Continued.

SECOND GRADE.

BOYS.

General nativity and race of father of pupil.	Number of pupils of each age.											Total.
	5.	6.	7.	8.	9.	10.	11.	12.	13.	14.	15.	
Native-born:												
White		5	204	458	232	98	37	16	5	....	....	1,055
Negro		2	11	37	25	29	17	12	7	4	1	145
Total native-born		7	215	495	257	127	54	28	12	4	1	1,200
Foreign-born:												
Canadian (other than French)			3	5	4	2						14
Danish				1								1
Dutch				3		2	1					6
English			5	9	8	4			1			27
French				2		1						3
German		1	13	28	12	10	3	2				69
Hebrew, German			2	7	2							11
Hebrew, Polish		1	2	3	1	1						8
Hebrew, Roumanian		1		1	1		1					4
Hebrew, Russian			2	12	9	9	1		2			35
Hebrew, Other		1	1	4	2							8
Irish			5	12	10	3	3					33
Italian, North				4		2						6
Italian, South		2	4	21	22	14	8	4	1	1		77
Norwegian						1		2				3
Polish				1								1
Russian				2								2
Scotch			2	3	4		1					10
Swedish			5	15	10	4	1					35
Other races a				1	1	1	1			1		5
Total foreign-born		6	44	134	87	53	22	6	4	2	....	358
Grand total		13	259	629	344	180	76	34	16	6	1	1,558

a "Other races" includes races having less than 10 representatives in this city and pupils whose race is not reported.

TABLE **3.**—*Race, sex, and age, by grade—Number of pupils of each age in each grade, by sex and by general nativity and race of father of pupil*—Continued.

SECOND GRADE—Continued.

GIRLS.

General nativity and race of father of pupil.	Number of pupils of each age.											Total.
	5.	6.	7.	8.	9.	10.	11.	12.	13.	14.	15.	
Native-born:												
White	....	4	221	428	216	69	27	16	2	1	....	984
Negro	....	1	19	34	31	26	13	8	7	1	1	141
Total native-born	....	5	240·	462	247	95	40	24	9	2	1	1,125
Foreign-born:												
Bohemian and Moravian	....	....	....	....	....	1	....	....	....	....	....	1
Canadian, French	....	....	2	2	....	....	....	....	....	....	....	4
Canadian, Other	....	....	2	7	1	2	....	....	....	....	....	12
Danish	....	....	2	2	1	1	....	1	....	....	....	7
Dutch	....	....	....	1	....	....	....	....	....	....	....	1
English	....	....	6	10	10	1	2	....	....	....	....	29
Finnish	....	....	....	1	....	....	....	....	....	....	....	1
French	....	....	1	....	2	2	....	....	....	....	....	5
German	....	1	14	22	14	3	3	1	....	1	....	59
Hebrew, German	....	....	6	3	3	1	....	....	....	....	....	13
Hebrew, Polish	....	....	3	4	2	3	....	....	1	....	....	13
Hebrew, Roumanian	....	....	....	1	1	....	....	....	....	....	....	2
Hebrew, Russian	....	1	5	16	3	6	1	3	1	....	....	36
Hebrew, Other	....	....	....	2	....	1	....	....	....	....	....	3
Irish	....	....	5	10	8	2	....	....	....	....	....	25
Italian, North	....	....	1	3	6	1	1	2	....	....	....	14
Italian, South	....	....	3	11	13	13	3	2	....	1	....	46
Magyar	....	....	1	....	....	....	....	....	....	....	....	1
Norwegian	....	....	....	1	....	1	....	....	....	....	....	2
Russian	....	....	....	....	1	....	....	....	....	....	....	1
Scotch	....	....	5	4	2	2	....	....	....	....	....	13
Swedish	....	....	7	21	5	1	1	....	....	....	....	35
Syrian	1	....	....	....	....	....	....	1	1	....	....	3
Welsh	....	....	1	1	....	....	....	....	....	....	....	2
Other races *a*	....	....	1	....	1	....	....	1	....	....	....	3
Total foreign-born	1	2	65	122	73	41	11	11	3	2	....	331
Grand total	1	7	305	584	320	136	51	35	12	4	1	1,456

a "Other races" includes races having less than 10 representatives in this city and pupils whose race is not reported.

TABLE 3.—*Race, sex, and age, by grade—Number of pupils of each age in each grade, by sex and by general nativity and race of father of pupil*—Continued.

SECOND GRADE—Continued.

TOTAL.

General nativity and race of father of pupil.	Number of pupils of each age.											Total.
	5.	6.	7.	8.	9.	10.	11.	12.	13.	14.	15.	
Native-born:												
White....................		9	425	886	448	167	64	32	7	1	....	2,039
Negro....................		3	30	71	56	55	30	20	14	5	2	286
Total native born.........		12	455	957	504	222	94	52	21	6	2	2,325
Foreign-born:												
Bohemian and Moravian.....						1						1
Canadian, French...........			2	2								4
Canadian, Other............			5	12	5	4						26
Danish....................			2	3	1	1		1				8
Dutch....................				4		2	1					7
English....................			11	19	18	5	2	....	1			56
Finnish....................				1								1
French....................			1	2	2	3						8
German....................		2	27	50	26	13	6	3	....	1		128
Hebrew, German............			8	10	5	1						24
Hebrew, Polish.............		1	5	7	3	4			1			21
Hebrew, Roumanian.........		1		2	2		1					6
Hebrew, Russian............		1	7	28	12	15	2	3	3			71
Hebrew, Other.............		1	1	6	2	1						11
Irish....................			10	22	18	5	3					58
Italian, North.............			1	7	6	3	1	2				20
Italian, South.............		2	7	32	35	27	11	6	1	2		123
Magyar....................			1									1
Norwegian.................				1	1	1	2					5
Polish....................				1								1
Russian....................				2	1							3
Scotch....................			7	7	6	2	1					23
Swedish....................			12	36	15	5	2					70
Syrian....................	1							1	1			3
Welsh....................			1	1								2
Other races *a*............			1	1	2	1	1	1		1		8
Total foreign-born.........	1	8	109	256	160	94	33	17	7	4	....	689
Grand total..............	1	20	564	1,213	664	316	127	69	28	10	2	3,014

a "Other races" includes races having less than 10 representatives in this city and pupils whose race is not reported.

TABLE **3.**—*Race, sex, and age, by grade—Number of pupils of each age in each grade, by sex and by general nativity and race of father of pupil*—Continued.

THIRD GRADE.

BOYS.

General nativity and race of father of pupil.	Number of pupils of each age.															Total.
	6.	7.	8.	9.	10.	11.	12.	13.	14.	15.	16.	17.	18.	19.	20.	
Native-born:																
White		16	189	407	306	142	73	32	19	4						1,188
Negro		2	9	30	35	29	25	12	14	1						157
Total native-born		18	198	437	341	171	98	44	33	5						1,345
Foreign-born:																
Bohemian and Moravian					2											2
Canadian, English			2	12	8	2	2									26
Canadian, French				2												2
Danish				1		1										2
Dutch			1		2		1			1						4
English			4	12	8	6	1	1								32
Finnish			2													2
French					3											3
German		1	20	29	17	12	5	2	1							87
Hebrew, German		1	5	6	7											19
Hebrew, Polish			2	3	2	2										9
Hebrew, Roumanian			2	1		1										4
Hebrew, Russian		1	11	14	13	7	3	1								50
Hebrew, Other		1	1	1		1										4
Irish			8	5	8	6	3									30
Italian, North			1	2	4	2	1									10
Italian, South			3	10	22	11	7	3	2							58
Norwegian			1	1	1											3
Polish			1													1
Russian				1												1
Scotch				2	2	2										6
Swedish			6	17	7	7	2									39
Welsh			1		2	1										4
Other races *a*		1		1	1	1						1		1		6
Total foreign-born		5	71	120	109	62	25	7	3	1		1		1		405
Grand total		23	269	557	450	233	123	51	36	6		1		1		1,750

a "Other races" includes races having less than 10 representatives in this city and pupils whose race is not reported.

TABLE **3.**—*Race, sex, and age, by grade—Number of pupils of each age in each grade, by sex and by general nativity and race of father of pupil*—Continued.

THIRD GRADE—Continued.

GIRLS.

															Total
Native-born:															
White		19	238	426	305	135	60	21	7	2	1					1,214
Negro	1	5	19	29	35	36	27	13	9	2						176
Total native-born	1	24	257	455	340	171	87	34	16	4	1					1,390
Foreign-born:																
Bohemian and Moravian			1		1											2
Canadian, English			3	3	3	1	2									12
Canadian, French				1		3										4
Danish			1	3	2	1	2									9
Dutch					1											1
English			4	4	6	1	3		1							19
French				3	1											4
German		1	16	31	26	8	4	1	1							88
Hebrew, German			5	7	2	1	1									16
Hebrew, Polish		1	3													4
Hebrew, Roumanian					1											1
Hebrew, Russian		2	9	18	9	5	5	2		1						51
Hebrew, Other			2	2	1	1								1		7
Irish			7	7	8	4	2	1								29
Italian, North			1	2	4	4										11
Italian, South			1	8	12	3	3	1	1							29
Magyar			1													1
Norwegian						1										1
Polish					1											1
Russian			1		2											3
Scotch			2	2	7					1						12
Swedish			4	14	12	5										35
Welsh				1												1
Other races *a*				1												1
Total foreign-born		4	61	107	99	38	22	5	3	2					1	342
Grand total	1	28	318	562	439	209	109	39	19	6	1				1	1,732

a "Other races" includes races having less than 10 representatives in this city and pupils whose race is not reported.

TABLE 3.—*Race, sex, and age, by grade—Number of pupils of each age in each grade, by sex and by general nativity and race of father of pupil*—Continued.

THIRD GRADE—Continued.

TOTAL.

General nativity and race of father of pupil.	Number of pupils of each age.															Total.
	6.	7.	8.	9.	10.	11.	12.	13.	14.	15.	16.	17.	18.	19.	20.	
Native-born:																
White		35	427	833	611	277	133	53	26	6	1					2,402
Negro	1	7	28	59	70	65	52	25	23	3						333
Total native-born	1	42	455	892	681	342	185	78	49	9	1					2,735
Foreign-born:																
Bohemian and Moravian			1		3											4
Canadian, English			5	15	11	3	4									38
Canadian, French				3		3										6
Danish			1	4	2		2			1						12
Dutch			1		3		1									5
English			8	16	14	7	4	1	1							51
Finnish			2													2
French				3	4											7
German		2	36	60	43	20	9	3	2							175
Hebrew, German		1	10	13	9	1	1									35
Hebrew, Polish		1	5	3	2	2										13
Hebrew, Roumanian			2	1	1	1										5
Hebrew, Russian		3	20	32	22	12	8	3		1						101
Hebrew, Other		1	3	3	1	2								1		11
Irish			15	12	16	10	5	1								59
Italian, North			2	4	8	6	1									21
Italian, South			4	18	34	14	10	4	3							87
Magyar			1													1
Norwegian			1	1	1	1										4
Polish			1		1											2
Russian			1	1	2											4
Scotch			2	4	9	2					1					18
Swedish			10	31	19	12	2									74
Welsh			1	1	2	1										5
Other races a		1		2	1	1						1		1		7
Total foreign-born		9	132	227	208	100	47	12	6	3		1		1	1	747
Grand total	1	51	587	1,119	889	442	232	90	55	12	1	1		1	1	3,482

a "Other races" includes races having less than 10 representatives in this city and pupils whose race is not reported.

TABLE 3.—*Race, sex, and age, by grade—Number of pupils of each age in each grade, by sex and by general nativity and race of father of pupil—Continued.*

FOURTH GRADE.

BOYS.

General nativity and race of father of pupil.	Number of pupils of each age.												Total.
	7.	8.	9.	10.	11.	12.	13.	14.	15.	16.	17.	18.	
Native-born:													
White		14	156	415	354	234	123	38	10	2	1	....	1,347
Negro		3	11	17	33	34	18	19	12	....	....	....	147
Total native-born		17	167	432	387	268	141	57	22	2	1	....	1,494
Foreign-born:													
Bohemian and Moravian				1									1
Canadian(other than French)			5	2	4	3	1		1				16
Danish					4	1							5
Dutch			1		1	2	1	1					6
English			5	7	12	2	4		1				31
French			1	1	2		1	1					6
German	1		13	26	18	19	11	4					92
Hebrew, German			4	6	4	4	1	1					20
Hebrew, Polish				4	5	3		2					14
Hebrew, Roumanian				2									2
Hebrew, Russian			3	17	7	8	8	1	1				45
Hebrew, Other			2	5	1			1					9
Irish			3	11	17	10	8	3					52
Italian, North				1	1			3					5
Italian, South				3	6	7	6	5	1				28
Norwegian					1	2		1					5
Russian				3		1							4
Scotch			1		7	3							11
Syrian						1	1						2
Swedish			1	11	5	4	1						22
Welsh							1						1
Other races *a*						1	1					1	3
Total foreign-born		1	39	99	97	71	45	23	4			1	380
Grand total		18	206	531	484	339	186	80	26	2	1	1	1,874

a "Other races" includes races having less than 10 representatives in this city and pupils whose race is not reported.

TABLE 3.—*Race, sex, and age, by grade—Number of pupils of each age in each grade, by sex and by general nativity and race of father of pupil*—Continued.

FOURTH GRADE—Continued.

GIRLS.

General nativity and race of father of pupil.	Number of pupils of each age.												Total.
	7.	8.	9.	10.	11.	12.	13.	14.	15.	16.	17.	18.	
Native-born:													
White	....	15	174	383	355	194	109	22	6	2	1	....	1,261
Negro	1	2	10	29	34	31	31	15	6	3	....	....	162
Total native-born	1	17	184	412	389	225	140	37	12	5	1	....	1,423
Foreign-born:													
Bohemian and Moravian	....	....	....	1	....	....	....	....	....	....	....	....	1
Canadian, French	....	....	....	1	1	....	....	....	....	....	....	....	2
Canadian, Other	....	1	6	2	5	....	....	....	....	....	....	....	14
Danish	....	....	1	4	1	....	....	....	....	....	....	....	6
Dutch	....	....	1	2	....	....	....	....	....	....	....	....	3
English	....	....	5	8	3	7	4	....	....	....	....	....	27
Finnish	....	....	....	....	1	1	....	....	....	....	....	....	2
French	....	....	....	....	....	1	....	....	....	....	....	....	1
German	....	....	13	39	25	15	6	1	....	....	1	....	100
Hebrew, German	....	1	3	10	6	4	3	....	....	....	....	....	27
Hebrew, Polish	....	....	5	2	2	2	1	....	....	....	....	....	12
Hebrew, Roumanian	....	....	....	1	....	....	....	....	....	....	....	....	1
Hebrew, Russian	....	....	10	10	9	5	1	1	1	....	....	....	37
Hebrew, Other	....	....	....	....	3	1	....	1	....	....	....	....	5
Irish	....	....	5	9	8	7	4	....	....	....	....	....	33
Italian, North	....	....	....	....	1	1	1	....	....	....	....	....	3
Italian, South	....	....	2	9	15	12	3	2	....	....	....	....	43
Norwegian	....	....	....	....	....	2	....	....	....	....	....	....	2
Polish	....	....	1	....	....	....	....	....	....	....	....	....	1
Russian	....	....	1	3	....	....	....	2	....	....	....	....	6
Scotch	....	....	2	6	4	2	1	....	....	....	....	....	15
Syrian	....	....	....	....	....	....	....	....	....	....	....	....	....
Swedish	....	....	4	18	12	6	1	....	....	....	....	....	41
Welsh	....	....	1	....	....	1	1	....	....	....	....	....	3
Other races *a*	....	....	2	....	....	....	....	....	....	....	....	....	2
Total foreign-born	....	2	54	125	98	73	26	7	1	....	1	....	387
Grand total	1	19	238	537	487	298	166	44	13	5	2	....	1,810

a "Other races" includes races having less than 10 representatives in this city and pupils whose race is not reported.

TABLE 3.—*Race, sex, and age, by grade—Number of pupils of each age in each grade, by sex and by general nativity and race of father of pupil*—Continued.

FOURTH GRADE—Continued.

TOTAL.

General nativity and race of father of pupil.	Number of pupils of each age.												Total.
	7.	8.	9.	10.	12.	13.	14.	15.	16.	16.	17.	18.	
Native-born:													
White		29	330	798	709	428	232	60	16	4	2	....	2,608
Negro	1	5	21	46	67	65	49	34	18	3	....	....	309
Total native-born	1	34	351	844	776	493	281	94	34	7	2	....	2,917
Foreign-born:													
Bohemian and Moravian	....	....	....	2	....	....	....	....	....	....	....	....	2
Canadian, French	....	....	....	1	1	....	....	....	....	....	....	....	2
Canadian, Other	....	1	5	8	6	8	1	....	1	....	....	....	30
Danish	....	....	....	1	8	2	....	....	....	....	....	....	11
Dutch	....	....	1	1	3	2	1	1	....	....	....	....	9
English	....	....	10	15	15	9	8	....	1	....	....	....	58
Finnish	....	....	....	....	1	1	....	....	....	....	....	....	2
French	....	....	1	1	2	1	1	1	....	....	....	....	7
German	....	1	26	65	43	34	17	5	....	....	1	....	192
Hebrew, German	....	1	7	16	10	8	4	1	....	....	....	....	47
Hebrew, Polish	....	....	5	6	7	5	1	2	....	....	....	....	26
Hebrew, Roumanian	....	....	....	1	2	....	....	....	....	....	....	....	3
Hebrew, Russian	....	....	13	27	16	13	9	2	2	....	....	....	82
Hebrew, Other	....	....	2	5	4	1	....	2	....	....	....	....	14
Irish	....	....	8	20	25	17	12	3	....	....	....	....	85
Italian, North	....	....	....	1	2	1	1	3	....	....	....	....	8
Italian, South	....	....	2	12	21	19	9	7	1	....	....	....	71
Norwegian	....	....	....	1	1	4	....	1	....	....	....	....	7
Polish	....	....	1	....	....	....	....	....	....	....	....	....	1
Russian	....	....	1	6	....	1	....	2	....	....	....	....	10
Scotch	....	....	3	6	11	5	1	....	....	....	....	....	26
Syrian	....	....	....	....	....	1	1	....	....	....	....	....	2
Swedish	....	....	5	29	17	10	2	....	....	....	....	....	63
Welsh	....	....	1	....	....	1	2	....	....	....	....	....	4
Other races a	....	....	2	....	....	1	1	....	....	....	....	1	5
Total foreign-born	....	3	93	224	195	144	71	30	5	....	1	1	767
Grand total	1	37	444	1,068	971	637	352	124	39	7	3	1	3,684

a "Other races" includes races having less than 10 representatives in this city and pupils whose race is not reported.

TABLE 3.—*Race, sex, and age, by grade—Number of pupils of each age in each grade, by sex and by general nativity and race of father of pupil—Continued.*

FIFTH GRADE.

BOYS.

General nativity and race of father of pupil.	Number of pupils of each age.													Total.
	8.	9.	10.	11.	12.	13.	14.	15.	16.	17.	18.	19.	20 or over.	
Native-born:														
White		5	107	257	326	230	103	30	8					1,066
Negro			5	12	26	34	16	9	4	1			1	108
Total native-born		5	112	269	352	264	119	39	12	1			1	1,174
Foreign-born:														
Bohemian and Moravian					1									1
Canadian, French					1	2								3
Canadian, Other			3	4	5	4	1							17
Danish			2	1	3	2								8
Dutch			1	2	1	2								6
English			4	11	8	7		2						32
Finnish				1										1
French			2	1	2			2						7
German			13	30	19	19	8	1						90
Hebrew, German			4	7	4	2	1	1						19
Hebrew, Polish			3	2	2									7
Hebrew, Roumanian					2	1	2							5
Hebrew, Russian			4	12	9	8	1							34
Hebrew, Other				3	1									4
Irish	1		4	6	8	9	6	1						35
Italian, North				1		3	1	1						6
Italian, South			1	1	8	1	1	1						13
Magyar				1		1								2
Norwegian				2										2
Polish					1									1
Russian						1								1
Scotch			3	1	3	6	1							14
Swedish			4	11	13	3	1				1			33
Welsh				2										2
Other races *a*					1									1
Total foreign-born	1		48	99	92	69	25	9			1			344
Grand total		6	160	368	444	333	144	48	12	1	1		1	1,518

a "Other races" includes races having less than 10 representatives in this city and pupils whose race is not reported.

TABLE **3.**—*Race, sex, and age, by grade—Number of pupils of each age in each grade, by sex and by general nativity and race of father of pupil*—Continued.

FIFTH GRADE—Continued.

GIRLS.

General nativity and race of father of pupil.	Number of pupils of each age.													Total.
	8.	9.	10.	11.	12.	13.	14.	15.	16.	17.	18.	19.	20 or over.	
Native-born:														
White	....	7	130	248	339	252	97	18	2	1	....	1	....	1,095
Negro	....	1	9	24	13	21	29	6	....	....	....	....	....	98
Total native-born	....	8	139	272	352	273	121	24	2	1	....	1	....	1,193
Foreign-born:														
Bohemian and Moravian	....	....	....	....	....	1	....	....	....	....	....	....	....	1
Canadian (other than French)	....	....	....	4	3	2	....	....	....	....	....	....	....	9
Danish	....	....	....	....	....	2	....	....	....	....	....	....	....	2
Dutch	....	....	....	1	3	....	....	....	....	....	....	....	....	4
English	....	....	4	7	7	10	1	1	....	....	....	....	....	30
French	....	....	....	1	1	2	2	....	....	....	....	....	....	6
German	1	1	8	29	27	14	9	....	....	....	....	....	....	89
Hebrew, German	....	....	....	7	7	6	3	....	....	....	....	....	....	23
Hebrew, Polish	....	2	4	3	9	2	1	....	....	....	....	....	....	21
Hebrew, Roumanian	....	....	....	5	2	2	1	....	....	....	....	....	....	10
Hebrew, Russian	....	1	2	8	9	6	4	....	....	....	....	....	....	30
Hebrew, Other	....	....	1	2	1	....	1	1	....	....	....	....	....	6
Irish	....	....	2	8	13	7	3	....	....	....	....	....	....	33
Italian, North	....	....	1	....	2	2	1	....	....	....	....	....	....	6
Italian, South	....	....	1	....	1	3	5	....	....	....	....	....	....	10
Norwegian	....	....	....	....	1	....	....	....	....	....	....	....	....	1
Polish	....	....	....	1	....	....	....	....	....	....	....	....	....	1
Russian	....	....	1	....	2	....	....	....	....	....	....	....	....	3
Scotch	....	....	2	3	4	5	....	....	....	....	....	....	....	14
Swedish	....	....	4	10	12	11	....	....	....	....	....	....	....	37
Welsh	....	....	....	....	1	1	....	....	....	....	....	....	....	2
Other races a	....	....	....	....	....	2	....	....	....	....	....	....	....	2
Total foreign-born	1	4	30	89	105	78	31	2	....	....	....	....	....	340
Grand total	1	12	169	361	457	351	152	26	2	1	....	1	....	1,533

a "Other races" includes races having less than 10 representatives in this city and pupils whose race is not reported.

TABLE 3.—*Race, sex, and age, by grade—Number of pupils of each age in each grade, by sex and by general nativity and race of father of pupil*—Continued.

FIFTH GRADE—Continued.

TOTAL.

General nativity and race of father of pupil.	Number of pupils of each age.													Total.
	8.	9.	10.	11.	12.	13.	14.	15.	16.	17.	18.	19.	20 or over.	
Native-born:														
White	....	12	237	505	665	482	200	48	10	1	....	1	....	2,161
Negro	....	1	14	36	39	55	40	15	4	1	....	....	1	206
Total native-born	....	13	251	541	704	537	240	63	14	2	....	1	1	2,367
Foreign-born:														
Bohemian and Moravian	....	....	....	....	1	1	....	....						2
Canadian, French	....	....	....	....	....	1	2	....						3
Canadian, Other	....	....	3	8	8	6	1	....						26
Danish	....	....	2	1	3	4	....							10
Dutch	....	....	1	3	4	2								10
English	....	....	8	18	15	17	1	3						62
Finnish	....	....	....	1	....	....								1
French	....	....	2	2	3	2	2	2						13
German	1	1	21	59	46	33	17	1	....	....				179
Hebrew, German	....	....	4	14	11	8	4	1						42
Hebrew, Polish	....	2	7	5	11	2	1	....						28
Hebrew, Roumanian	....	....	5	4	3	3	....							15
Hebrew, Russian	....	1	6	20	18	14	5	....						64
Hebrew, Other	....	....	1	5	2	....	1	1						10
Irish	....	1	6	14	21	16	9	1						68
Italian, North	....	....	1	1	2	5	2	1						12
Italian, South	....	....	2	1	9	4	6	1						23
Magyar	....	....	....	1	1	1	....							2
Norwegian	....	....	....	2	1	....	....							3
Polish	....	....	....	1	1	....								2
Russian	....	....	1	....	3	....	....							4
Scotch	....	....	5	4	7	11	1	....						28
Swedish	....	....	8	21	25	14	1	....	....	....	1			70
Welsh	....	....	....	2	1	1	....							4
Other races *a*	....	....	....	....	1	2	....							3
Total foreign-born	1	5	78	188	197	147	56	11	....	....	1	....	....	684
Grand total	1	18	329	729	901	684	296	74	14	2	1	1	1	3,051

a "Other races" includes races having less than 10 representatives in this city and pupils whose race is not reported.

TABLE **3.**—*Race, sex, and age, by grade*—*Number of pupils of each age in each grade, by sex and by general nativity and race of father of pupil*—Continued.

SIXTH GRADE.

BOYS.

General nativity and race of father of pupil.	Number of pupils of each age.									Total.
	10.	11.	12.	13.	14.	15.	16.	17.	18.	
Native-born:										
White	7	58	226	271	200	84	12	2	1	861
Negro		2	10	25	21	9	4	1	1	73
Total native-born	7	60	236	296	221	93	16	3	2	934
Foreign-born:										
Bohemian and Moravian		1	1							2
Canadian, French				1	2	1				4
Canadian, Other			6	9	8	2				25
Danish					2					2
English		2	5	6	2	1	1			17
French		1	1							2
German		3	13	17	22	3	1			59
Hebrew, German		3	3	4	3	1				14
Hebrew, Polish			2	4	4					10
Hebrew, Roumanian		1								1
Hebrew, Russian		8	8	8	4	2	2			32
Hebrew, Other			2							2
Irish			4	7	10	1	1			23
Italian, North			1		1					2
Italian, South		1	2	7		1				11
Norwegian				1						1
Polish				1						1
Russian				2						2
Scotch			3	4	3					10
Swedish	1	3	6	15	7	3				35
Welsh		1				2				3
Other races *a*			2	1						3
Total foreign-born	1	24	59	87	68	17	5			261
Grand total	8	84	295	383	289	110	21	3	2	1,195

a "Other races" includes races having less than 10 representatives in this city and pupils whose race is not reported.

TABLE 3.—*Race, sex, and age, by grade—Number of pupils of each age in each grade, by sex and by general nativity and race of father of pupil—Continued.*

SIXTH GRADE—Continued.

GIRLS.

General nativity and race of father of pupil.	Number of pupils of each age.									Total.
	10.	11.	12.	13.	14.	15.	16.	17.	18.	
Native-born:										
White	5	107	250	293	192	67	10	2	......	926
Negro	4	16	24	31	18	17	9	1	......	120
Total native-born	9	123	274	324	210	84	19	3	......	1,046
Foreign-born:										
Bohemian and Moravian	......	......	1	1	......	......	......	......	......	2
Canadian (other than French)	......	1	5	8	5	......	......	......	......	19
Danish	......	......	5	1	3	......	......	......	......	9
Dutch	......	......	......	......	......	1	......	......	......	1
English	......	1	4	8	2	1	......	......	......	16
Finnish	......	......	......	1	......	......	......	......	......	1
French	......	......	......	4	......	......	......	......	......	4
German	1	8	27	26	17	2	......	......	......	81
Hebrew, German	......	1	3	5	......	1	......	......	......	10
Hebrew, Polish	......	2	11	2	4	......	......	......	......	19
Hebrew, Roumanian	1	......	......	2	......	......	......	......	......	3
Hebrew, Russian	......	3	9	6	5	......	......	......	......	23
Hebrew, Other	......	......	4	1	......	......	......	......	......	5
Irish	......	3	4	10	7	2	......	......	......	26
Italian, North	......	......	1	......	1	......	......	......	......	2
Italian, South	......	2	2	2	3	......	1	......	......	10
Magyar	......	......	......	1	......	......	......	......	......	1
Norwegian	......	......	1	......	3	......	......	......	......	4
Polish	......	......	1	......	......	......	......	......	......	1
Russian	......	......	......	1	......	......	......	......	......	1
Scotch	......	3	4	2	......	1	......	......	......	10
Swedish	......	4	12	12	5	2	......	......	......	35
Welsh	......	......	......	1	1	1	......	......	......	3
Other races a	......	......	1	2	......	......	......	......	......	3
Total foreign-born	2	28	95	96	56	11	1	......	......	289
Grand total	11	151	369	420	266	95	20	3	......	1,335

a "Other races" includes races having less than 10 representatives in this city and pupils whose race is not reported.

TABLE 3.—*Race, sex, and age, by grade—Number of pupils of each age in each grade, by sex and by general nativity and race of father of pupil—Continued.*

SIXTH GRADE—Continued.

TOTAL.

General nativity and race of father of pupil.	Number of pupils of each age.									Total.
	10.	11.	12.	13.	14.	15.	16.	17.	18.	
Native-born:										
White	12	165	476	564	392	151	22	4	1	1,787
Negro	4	18	34	56	39	26	13	2	1	193
Total native-born	16	183	510	620	431	177	35	6	2	1,980
Foreign-born:										
Bohemian and Moravian		1	2	1						4
Canadian, French				1	2	1				4
Canadian, Other		1	11	17	13	2				44
Danish			5	1	5					11
Dutch						1				1
English		3	9	14	4	2	1			33
Finnish				1						1
French		1	1	4						6
German	1	11	40	43	39	5	1			140
Hebrew, German		4	6	9	3	2				24
Hebrew, Polish		2	13	6	8					29
Hebrew, Roumanian	1	1		2						4
Hebrew, Russian		11	17	14	9	2	2			55
Hebrew, Other			6	1						7
Irish		3	8	17	17	3	1			49
Italian, North			2		2					4
Italian, South		3	4	9	3	1	1			21
Magyar				1						1
Norwegian			1	1	3					5
Polish			1	1						2
Russian				3						3
Scotch		3	7	6	3	1				20
Swedish	1	7	18	27	12	5				70
Welsh		1		1	1	3				6
Other races a			3	3						6
Total foreign-born	3	52	154	183	124	28	6			550
Grand total	19	235	664	803	555	205	41	6	2	2,530

a "Other races" includes races having less than 10 representatives in this city and pupils whose race is not reported.

Table **3.**—*Race, sex, and age, by grade—Number of pupils of each age in each grade, by sex and by general nativity and race of father of pupil*—Continued.

SEVENTH GRADE.

BOYS.

General nativity and race of father of pupil.	Number of pupils of each age.									Total.
	10.	11.	12.	13.	14.	15.	16.	17.	18.	
Native-born:										
White		4	56	176	205	122	48	6		617
Negro	1	1	2	8	13	13	4	1	1	44
Total native-born	1	5	58	184	218	135	52	7	1	661
Foreign-born:										
Canadian (other than French)		1	1	3	2	4				11
Danish				1	1	1				3
Dutch			1	1						2
English			2	4	7	2	1	1		17
French				2	1	1				4
German			4	15	12	7	2			40
Hebrew, German			2	6	7	1	1			17
Hebrew, Polish			1		6	2				9
Hebrew, Roumanian		1								1
Hebrew, Russian		2	4	8	9	4	1			28
Hebrew, Other		1		1						2
Irish			4	8	3	2				17
Italian, North				1						1
Italian, South					2	1				3
Magyar					1					1
Norwegian					1					1
Polish					1					1
Russian					1					1
Scotch				1	4	2	1			8
Swedish			2	4	8	8	1			23
Welsh				1						1
Other races a							1			1
Total foreign-born		5	20	56	67	35	8	1		192
Grand total	1	10	78	240	285	170	60	8	1	853

a "Other races" includes races having less than 10 representatives in this city and pupils whose race is not reported.

TABLE 3.—*Race, sex, and age, by grade—Number of pupils of each age in each grade, by sex and by general nativity and race of father of pupil*—Continued.

SEVENTH GRADE—Continued.

GIRLS.

General nativity and race of father of pupil.	Number of pupils of each age.									Total.
	10.	11.	12.	13.	14.	15.	16.	17.	18.	
Native-born:										
White..............		5	76	257	301	146	43	6	1	835
Negro..............	3	7	24	17	21	9	4	2		87
Total native-born..............		8	83	281	318	167	52	10	3	922
Foreign-born:										
Canadian, French............				1						1
Canadian, Other............			1	2	4	3				10
Danish............					2			1		3
Dutch............				1		1				2
English............			2	7	6	4	1	1		21
French............				3	2					5
German............		1	7	20	19	12	1	2		62
Hebrew, German............		1	2	5	8	3				19
Hebrew, Polish............				3	3	3	1			10
Hebrew, Roumanian............						1				1
Hebrew, Russian............		1	8	11	7	1				28
Hebrew, Other............				1	2					3
Irish............			3	5	8	6	2			24
Italian, North............						1				1
Italian, South............				3	1					4
Magyar............					1					1
Norwegian............						1				1
Scotch............				1	2	3	2	1		9
Syrian............					1	1				2
Swedish............			1	3	8	6	1			19
Welsh............										
Other races *a*............				1	1					2
Total foreign-born............		3	24	67	75	46	8	5		228
Grand total............		11	107	348	393	213	60	15	3	1,150

a "Other races" includes races having less than 10 representatives in this city and pupils whose race is not reported.

TABLE 3.—*Race, sex, and age, by grade—Number of pupils of each age in each grade, by sex and by general nativity and race of father of pupil*—Continued.

SEVENTH GRADE—Continued.

TOTAL.

General nativity and race of father of pupil.	Number of pupils of each age.									Total.
	10.	11.	12.	13.	14.	15.	16.	17.	18.	
Native-born:										
White................		9	132	433	506	268	91	12	1	1,452
Negro................	1	4	9	32	30	34	13	5	3	131
Total native-born......	1	13	141	465	536	302	104	17	4	1,583
Foreign-born:										
Canadian, French........				1						1
Canadian, Other........		1	2	5	6	7				21
Danish................				1	3	1		1		6
Dutch................				2	1	1				4
English................			4	11	13	6	2	2		38
French................				5	3	1				9
German................		1	11	35	31	19	3	2		102
Hebrew, German........		1	4	11	15	4	1			36
Hebrew, Polish........			1	3	9	5	1			19
Hebrew, Roumanian....		1				1				2
Hebrew, Russian........		3	12	19	16	5	1			56
Hebrew, Other........		1		2	2					5
Irish................			7	13	11	8	2			41
Italian, North........				1		1				2
Italian, South........				3	3	1				7
Magyar................					2					2
Norwegian............					1	1				2
Polish................					1					1
Russian................					1					1
Scotch................				2	6	5	3	1		17
Syrian................					1	1				2
Swedish................			3	7	16	14	2			42
Welsh................				1						1
Other races *a*........				1	1		1			3
Total foreign-born......		8	44	123	142	81	16	6		420
Grand total............	1	21	185	588	678	383	120	23	4	2,003

a "Other races" includes races having less than 10 representatives in this city and pupils whose race is not reported.

TABLE 3.—*Race, sex, and age, by grade—Number of pupils of each age in each grade, by sex and by general nativity and race of father of pupil*—Continued.

FIRST YEAR HIGH SCHOOL.

BOYS.

General nativity and race of father of pupil.	Number of pupils of each age.									Total.
	12.	13.	14.	15.	16.	17.	18.	19.	20.	
Native-born:										
White	1	41	133	135	101	45	7	4	4	471
Negro	1	4	8	6	10	2	1	1	......	33
Total native-born	2	45	141	141	111	47	8	5	4	504
Foreign-born:										
Canadian, French				1	1					2
Canadian, Other			1	3	2					6
Danish					1					1
Dutch				2						2
English			2	5	1					8
French				1						1
German		5	13	10	5	1	1			35
Hebrew, German	1	1	1		2	1				6
Hebrew, Polish		1		1						2
Hebrew, Russian	1	1	3	4	1					10
Hebrew, Other				1						1
Irish			6	4	2					12
Scotch				2	1	1				4
Swedish			3	1					2	4
Other races *a*										2
Total foreign-born	2	8	29	35	16	3	1		2	96
Grand total	4	53	170	176	127	50	9	5	6	600

GIRLS.

General nativity and race of father of pupil.	12.	13.	14.	15.	16.	17.	18.	19.	20.	Total.
Native-born:										
White	6	49	179	220	102	31	12	2	1	602
Negro	1	7	6	20	18	2	1	1	......	56
Total native-born	7	56	185	240	120	33	13	3	1	658
Foreign-born:										
Canadian (other than French)		3	7	4	2	2				18
English		1	4	7	3				1	16
French	1		2	1	1	1				6
German		3	15	13	9	1	2		1	44
Hebrew, German		2	1	2	1		1			7
Hebrew, Polish			1							1
Hebrew, Russian			3	2	1					6
Hebrew, Other		1		1						2
Irish		6	12	6	8					32
Norwegian			1							1
Scotch			2	1						3
Swedish		1	4	1	2					8
Welsh			1	1						2
Total foreign-born	1	17	53	39	27	4	3	1	1	146
Grand total	8	73	238	279	147	37	16	4	2	804

a "Other races" includes races having less than 10 representatives in this city and pupils whose race is not reported.

TABLE **3.**—*Race, sex, and age, by grade—Number of pupils of each age in each grade, by sex and by general nativity and race of father of pupil*—Continued.

FIRST YEAR HIGH SCHOOL—Continued.
TOTAL.

General nativity and race of father of pupil.	Number of pupils of each age.									Total.
	12.	13.	14.	15.	16.	17.	18.	19.	20.	
Native-born:										
White	7	90	312	355	203	76	19	6	5	1,073
Negro	2	11	14	26	28	4	2	2		89
Total native-born	9	101	326	381	231	80	21	8	5	1,162
Foreign-born:										
Canadian, French				1	1					2
Canadian, Other		3	8	7	4	2				24
Danish				1						1
Dutch				2						2
English		1	6	12	4			1		24
French	1		2	2	1	1				7
German		8	28	23	14	2	3		1	79
Hebrew, German	1	3	2	2	3	1	1			13
Hebrew, Polish		1	1	1						3
Hebrew, Russian	1	1	6	6	2					16
Hebrew, Other		1		2						3
Irish		6	18	10	10					44
Norwegian			1							1
Scotch			2	2	2	1				7
Swedish		1	7	2	2					12
Welsh			1	1						2
Other races [a]									2	2
Total foreign-born	3	25	82	74	43	7	4	1	3	242
Grand total	12	126	408	455	274	87	25	9	8	1,404

SECOND YEAR HIGH SCHOOL.
BOYS.

General nativity and race of father of pupil.	12.	13.	14.	15.	16.	17.	18.	19.	20.	Total.
Native-born:										
White		2	29	73	106	53	18	6	2	289
Negro			4	4	5	4	5	3		25
Total native-born		2	33	77	111	57	23	9	2	314
Foreign-born:										
Bohemian				1						1
Canadian (other than French)			1	2		1		1		5
Danish					2					2
Dutch								1		1
English					3	2	1			6
French			1	1						2
German			4	15	5	3	4			31
Hebrew, German			1	3		3				7
Hebrew, Polish					1					1
Hebrew, Russian			1	2		1				4
Hebrew, Other				1						1
Irish			4	4		1	1			10
Magyar				1						1
Russian			1							1
Scotch					3					3
Swedish				1	3	2	2	1		9
Welsh				1						1
Other races [a]				1						1
Total foreign-races			13	33	17	13	8	3		87
Grand total		2	46	110	128	70	31	12	2	401

[a] "Other races" includes races having less than 10 representatives in this city and pupils whose race is not reported.

TABLE 3.—*Race, sex, and age, by grade—Number of pupils of each age in each grade, by sex and by general nativity and race of father of pupil*—Continued

SECOND YEAR HIGH SCHOOL—Continued.

GIRLS.

General nativity and race of father of pupil.	Number of pupils of each age.									Total.
	12.	13.	14.	15.	16.	17.	18.	19.	20.	
Native-born:										
White		3	34	125	139	75	21	9	4	410
Negro		1	2	12	16	12	3			46
Total native-born		4	36	137	155	87	24	9	4	456
Foreign-born:										
Canadian, French				1						1
Canadian, Other					1					1
Danish			1	1	4	1				7
Dutch						1				1
English			3	2	4	4	1			14
French			1	1						2
German			2	9	7	9		2		29
Hebrew, German			2	2	1					5
Hebrew, Russian		1	1	2						4
Irish				1	5					6
Norwegian			1		1					2
Scotch				1	2	1				4
Swedish			1		1	1		1		4
Total foreign races		1	12	20	26	17	1	3		80
Grand total		5	48	157	181	104	25	12	4	536

TOTAL.

General nativity and race of father of pupil.	12.	13.	14.	15.	16.	17.	18.	19.	20.	Total.
Native-born:										
White		5	63	198	245	128	39	15	6	699
Negro		1	6	16	21	16	3			71
Total native-born		6	69	214	266	144	47	18	6	770
Foreign-born:										
Bohemian				1						1
Canadian, French				1						1
Canadian, Other			1	2	1	1		1		6
Danish			1	1	6	1				9
Dutch						1	1			2
English			3	2	7	6	1	1		20
French			2	2						4
German			6	24	12	12	4	2		60
Hebrew, German			3	5	1	3				12
Hebrew, Polish					1					1
Hebrew, Russian		1	2	4		1				8
Hebrew, Other				1						1
Irish			4	5	5	1				16
Magyar				1						1
Norwegian			1		1					2
Russian			1							1
Scotch				1	5	1				7
Swedish			1	1	4	3	2	2		13
Welsh				1						1
Other races a				1						1
Total foreign races		1	25	53	43	30	9	6		167
Grand total		7	94	267	309	174	56	24	6	937

a "Other races" includes races having less than 10 representatives in this city and pupils whose race is not reported.

TABLE 3.—*Race, sex, and age, by grade—Number of pupils of each age in each grade, by sex and by general nativity and race of father of pupil*—Continued.

THIRD YEAR HIGH SCHOOL.

BOYS.

General nativity and race of father of pupil.	Number of pupils of each age.							Total.
	14.	15,	16.	17.	18.	19.	20.	
Native-born:								
White	6	14	83	65	35	12	4	219
Negro	1	2	2	3	2		2	12
Total native-born	7	16	85	68	37	12	6	231
Foreign-born:								
Canadian (other than French)			1	2	2			5
Danish			1					1
English			1	1	1	1		4
French			1					1
German		1	4	2				7
Hebrew, German			1	3	2			6
Hebrew, Polish			1					1
Hebrew, Russian			1	1				2
Irish			2	1		3		6
Scotch		1	1	1			1	4
Swedish			6	1				7
Total foreign-born		2	20	12	5	4	1	44
Grand total	7	18	105	80	42	16	7	275

GIRLS.

General nativity and race of father of pupil.	14.	15,	16.	17.	18.	19.	20.	Total.
Native-born:								
White	5	28	111	117	47	12	3	323
Negro	2	5	8	6	2	2	1	26
Total native-born	7	33	119	123	49	14	4	349
Foreign-born:								
Canadian, French				2				2
Canadian, Other		1	1	3	2		1	8
Dutch				1				1
English		1		2	1		1	5
French			1					1
German		4	4	5	2			15
Hebrew, German		1	2					3
Hebrew, Russian		3	3	1				7
Hebrew, Other		1		1	1			3
Irish	1		3	3	1			8
Italian, North			1					1
Italian, South			1					1
Scotch	1	1	1	1				4
Swedish			1	2				3
Welsh			1		1			2
Other races a				1				1
Total foreign-born	2	12	19	22	8		2	65
Grand total	9	45	138	145	57	14	6	414

a "Other races" includes races having less than 10 representatives in this city and pupils whose race is not reported.

TABLE 3.—*Race, sex, and age, by grade—Number of pupils of each age in each grade, by sex and by general nativity and race of father of pupil*—Continued.

THIRD YEAR HIGH SCHOOL—Continued.

TOTAL.

General nativity and race of father of pupil.	Number of pupils of each age.							Total.
	14.	15.	16.	17.	18.	19.	20.	
Native-born:								
White	11	42	194	182	82	24	7	542
Negro	3	7	10	9	4	2	3	38
Total native-born	14	49	204	191	86	26	10	580
Foreign-born:								
Canadian, French				2				2
Canadian, Other		1	2	5	4		1	13
Danish			1					1
Dutch				1				1
English		1	1	3	2	1	1	9
French			2					2
German		5	8	7	2			22
Hebrew, German		1	3	3	2			9
Hebrew, Polish			1					1
Hebrew, Russian		3	4	2				9
Hebrew, Other		1		1	1			3
Irish	1		5	4	1	3		14
Italian, North			1					1
Italian, South			1					1
Scotch	1	2	2	2			1	8
Swedish			7	3				10
Welsh			1		1			2
Other races [a]				1				1
Total foreign-born	2	14	39	34	13	4	3	109
Grand total	16	63	243	225	99	30	13	689

FOURTH YEAR HIGH SCHOOL.

BOYS.

General nativity and race of father of pupil.	Number of pupils of each age.								Total.
	13.	14.	15.	16.	17.	18.	19.	20.	
Native-born									
White		3	6	29	56	45	19	5	163
Negro				3	3	2	1	2	11
Total native-born		3	6	32	59	47	20	7	174
Foreign-born:									
Canadian, French						1			1
Canadian, Other						2			2
English					1	1	2		4
German			1	3	5	1	1		11
Hebrew, German					1	2			3
Hebrew, Polish						1			1
Hebrew, Russian				2	1				3
Irish				3	1	2	1		7
Magyar						1			1
Norwegian						1			1
Scotch					1	1	1		3
Swedish					1				1
Welsh					1				1
Total foreign-born			1	10	12	11	5		39
Grand total		3	7	42	71	58	25	7	213

[a] "Other races" includes races having less than 10 representatives in this city and pupils whose race is not reported.

TABLE **3.**—*Race, sex, and age, by grade—Number of pupils of each age in each grade, by sex and by general nativity and race of father of pupil*—Continued.

FOURTH YEAR HIGH SCHOOL—Continued.

GIRLS.

General nativity and race of father of pupil.	Number of pupils of each age.								Total.
	13.	14.	15.	16.	17.	18.	19.	20.	
Native-born:									
White	1	4	3	48	106	77	37	5	281
Negro			2	4	6	10	5		27
Indian							1		1
Total native-born	1	4	5	52	112	87	43	5	309
Foreign-born:									
Canadian (other than French)				1	3	2		1	7
Danish					1	1			2
Dutch				1					1
English				3	4	2			9
German		1		3	9	4	2	1	20
Hebrew, German			1		2	1			4
Hebrew, Polish			1						1
Hebrew, Russian		1	1	1					3
Irish				3	6		1	1	11
Norwegian					1		1		2
Scotch					1	1			2
Swedish				2		1	1		4
Total foreign-born		2	3	14	27	12	5	3	66
Grand total	1	6	8	66	139	99	48	8	375

TOTAL.

General nativity and race of father of pupil.	13.	14.	15.	16.	17.	18.	19.	20.	Total.
Native-born:									
White	1	7	9	77	162	122	56	10	444
Negro			2	7	9	12	6	2	38
Indian							1		1
Total native-born	1	7	11	84	171	134	63	12	483
Foreign-born:									
Canadian, French						1			1
Canadian, Other				1	3	4		1	9
Danish					1	1			2
Dutch				1					1
English				3	5	3	2		13
German		1	1	6	14	5	3	1	31
Hebrew, German			1	1	4	1			7
Hebrew, Polish			1			1			2
Hebrew, Russian		1	1	3	1				6
Irish				6	7	2	2	1	18
Magyar						1			1
Norwegian					1	1	1		3
Scotch					2	2	1		5
Swedish				2	1	1	1		5
Welsh				1					1
Total foreign-born		2	4	24	39	23	10	3	105
Grand total	1	9	15	108	210	157	73	15	588

a "Other races" includes races having less than 10 representatives in this city and pupils whose race is not reported.

TABLE 3.—*Race, sex, and age, by grade—Number of pupils of each age in each grade, by sex and by general nativity and race of father of pupil*—Continued.

NORMAL SCHOOL.

GIRLS.

General nativity and race of father of pupil.	Number of pupils of each age.										Total.
	11.	12.	13.	14.	15.	16.	17.	18.	19.	20.	
Native-born, White............									3	1	4

MIXED GRADES.

BOYS.

General nativity and race of father of pupil.	Number of pupils of each age.														Total.
	6.	7.	8.	9.	10.	11.	12.	13.	14.	15.	16.	17.	18.	19.	
Native-born, Negro..............	2	4	5	2	3	8	2	3	4	4				1	38

GIRLS.

Native-born, Negro..............	1	3	2	4	5	2	4	7	7	5	2	1			43

TOTAL.

Native-born, Negro..............	3	7	7	6	8	10	6	10	11	9	2	1		1	81

TABLE 4.—*Race and grade, by age—Number of pupils of each specified age in each grade, by general nativity and race of father of pupil.*

BOY: AGE 4 YEARS.

General nativity and race of father of pupil.	Kinder-garten.
Native-born, White..	1

BOYS: AGE 5 YEARS.

General nativity and race of father of pupil.	Kinder-garten.	Elemen-tary grade 5.	Total.
Native-born:			
White...	7	1	8
Negro...	10	....	10
Total native-born..	17	1	18
Foreign-born, Other races *a*....................................	....	1	1
Total foreign-born..	....	1	1
Grand total...	17	2	19

a "Other races" includes races having less than 10 representatives of this sex and age and pupils whose race is not reported.

TABLE 4.—*Race and grade, by age—Number of pupils of each specified age in each grade, by general nativity and race of father of pupil*—Continued.

BOYS: AGE 6 YEARS.

General nativity and race of father of pupil.	Kinder-garten.	Elementary grades.		Mixed school.	Total.
		1.	2.		
Native-born:					
White	382	484	5		871
Negro	18	64	2	2	86
Total native-born	400	548	7	2	957
Foreign-born:					
English	11	14			25
German	31	34	1		66
Hebrew, German	7	5			12
Hebrew, Polish	5	10	1		16
Hebrew, Russian	15	32			47
Irish	10	10			20
Italian, South	25	16	2		43
Swedish	13	9			22
Other races a	26	20	2		48
Total foreign-born	143	150	6		299
Grand total	543	698	13	2	1,256

a "Other races" includes races having less than 10 representatives of this sex and age and pupils whose race is not reported.

BOYS: AGE 7 YEARS.

General nativity and race of father of pupil.	Kinder-garten.	Elementary grades.			Ungraded and special schools.	Total.
		1.	2.	3.		
Native-born:						
White	23	651	204	16		894
Negro		64	11	3	4	82
Total native-born	23	715	215	19	4	976
Foreign-born:						
Canadian (other than French)		9	3			12
English	1	15	5			21
German		36	13	1		50
Hebrew, German	1	11	2	1		15
Hebrew, Polish	1	10	2			13
Hebrew, Russian	9	43	2	1		55
Irish		16	5			21
Italian, South	7	27	4			38
Swedish	1	16	5			22
Other races a	1	29	3	1		34
Total foreign-born	21	212	44	4		281
Grand total	44	927	259	23	4	1,257

a "Other races" includes races having less than 10 representatives of this sex and age and pupils whose race is not reported.

TABLE 4.—*Race and grade, by age—Number of pupils of each specified age in each grade, by general nativity and race of father of pupil*—Continued.

BOYS: AGE 8 YEARS.

General nativity and race of father of pupil.	Kinder-garten.	Elementary grades.				Ungraded and special schools.	Total.
		1.	2.	3.	4.		
Native-born:							
White..................................	1	298	458	189	14	....	960
Negro.................................	....	56	37	9	3	5	110
Total native-born...............	1	354	495	198	17	5	1,070
Foreign-born:							
English............................	....	6	9	4	....	....	19
German............................	....	15	28	20	1	....	64
Hebrew, German...................	....	3	7	5	....	....	15
Hebrew, Russian...................	2	18	12	11	....	....	43
Hebrew, Other.....................	....	5	8	5	....	....	18
Irish...............................	....	8	12	8	....	....	28
Italian, South.....................	3	17	21	3	....	....	44
Swedish............................	....	11	15	6	....	....	32
Other races *a*.....................	1	16	22	9	....	....	48
Total foreign-born...............	6	99	134	71	1	....	311
Grand total......................	7	453	629	269	18	5	1,381

a "Other races" includes races having less than 10 representatives of this sex and age and pupils whose race is not reported.

BOYS: AGE 9 YEARS.

General nativity and race of father of pupil.	Kinder-garten.	Elementary grades.					Un-graded and special schools.	Total.
		1.	2.	3.	4.	5.		
Native-born:								
White............................	....	88	232	407	156	5	....	888
Negro............................	....	43	25	30	11	....	2	111
Total native-born..............	....	131	257	437	167	5	2	999
Foreign-born:								
Canadian (other than French)....	....	1	4	12	5	....	....	22
English..........................	....	3	8	12	5	....	....	28
German..........................	....	6	12	29	13	....	....	60
Hebrew, German..................	....	....	2	6	4	....	....	12
Hebrew, Russian.................	1	6	9	14	3	....	....	33
Hebrew, Other...................	....	1	4	5	2	....	....	12
Irish............................	....	3	10	5	3	1	....	22
Italian, South...................	....	9	22	10	....	....	....	41
Swedish.........................	....	2	10	17	1	....	....	30
Other races *a*...................	....	7	6	10	3	....	....	26
Total foreign-born..............	1	38	87	120	39	1	....	286
Grand total.....................	1	169	344	557	206	6	2	1,285

a "Other races" includes races having less than 10 representatives of this sex and age and pupils whose race is not reported.

TABLE 4.—*Race and grade, by age—Number of pupils of each specified age in each grade, by general nativity and race of father of pupil—Continued.*

BOYS: AGE 10 YAERS.

General nativity and race of father of pupil.	Elementary grades.							Un-graded and special schools.	Total.
	1.	2.	3.	4.	5.	6.	7.		
Native-born:									
White	40	98	306	415	107	7			973
Negro	24	29	35	17	5		1	3	114
Total native-born	64	127	341	432	112	7	1	3	1,087
Foreign-born:									
Canadian (other than French)		2	8	2	3				15
English		4	8	7	4				23
German	1	10	17	26	13				67
Hebrew, German			7	6	4				17
Hebrew, Polish	1	1	2	4	3				11
Hebrew, Russian	3	9	13	17	4				46
Irish		3	8	11	4				26
Italian, South	1	14	22	3	1				41
Swedish		4	7	11	4	1			27
Other races a	2	6	17	12	8				45
Total foreign-born	8	53	109	99	48	1			318
Grand total	72	180	450	531	160	8	1	3	1,405

a "Other races" includes races having less than 10 representatives of this sex and age and pupils whose race is not reported.

BOYS: AGE 11 YEARS.

General nativity and race of father of pupil.	Elementary grades.							Un-graded and special schools.	Total.
	1.	2.	3.	4.	5.	6.	7.		
Native-born:									
White	11	37	142	354	257	58	4		863
Negro	7	17	29	33	12	2	1	8	109
Total native-born	18	54	171	387	269	60	5	8	972
Foreign-born:									
Canadian (other than French)			2	4	4		1		11
English			6	12	11	2			31
German		3	12	18	30	3			66
Hebrew, German				4	7	3			14
Hebrew, Russian	1	1	7	7	12	8	2		38
Hebrew, Other		1	4	8	5	1	2		21
Irish		3	6	17	6				32
Italian, South	2	8	11	6	1	1			29
Scotch		1	2	7	1				11
Swedish		1	7	5	11	3			27
Other races a		4	5	9	11	3			32
Total foreign-born	3	22	62	97	99	24	5		312
Grand total	21	76	233	484	368	84	10	8	1,284

a "Other races" includes races having less than 10 representatives of this sex and age, and pupils whose race is not reported.

TABLE 4.—*Race and grade, by age—Number of pupils of each specified age in each grade, by general nativity and race of father of pupil*—Continued.

BOYS: AGE 12 YEARS.

General nativity and race of father of pupil.	Elementary grades.							High school, first year.	Un-graded and special schools.	Total.
	1.	2.	3.	4.	5.	6.	7.			
Native-born:										
White..........................	7	16	73	234	326	226	56	1	....	939
Negro..........................	1	12	25	34	26	10	2	1	2	113
Total native-born..............	8	28	98	268	352	236	58	2	2	1,052
Foreign-born:										
Canadian (other than French)......	....	....	2	3	5	6	1	....	....	17
English.......................	....	....	1	2	8	5	2	....	....	18
German........................	....	2	5	19	19	13	4	....	....	62
Hebrew, German................	....	....	....	4	4	3	2	1	....	14
Hebrew, Russian...............	1	....	3	8	9	8	4	1	....	34
Hebrew, Other.................	....	....	....	3	5	4	1	....	....	13
Irish.........................	....	....	3	10	8	4	4	....	....	29
Italian, South................	....	4	7	7	8	2	....	....	....	28
Swedish.......................	....	....	2	4	13	6	2	....	....	27
Other races..................	....	....	2	11	13	8	....	....	....	34
Total foreign-born............	1	6	25	71	92	59	20	2	....	276
Grand total...................	9	34	123	339	444	295	78	4	2	1,328

BOYS: AGE 13 YEARS.

General nativity and race of father of pupil.	Elementary grades.							High schools.		Un-graded and special schools.	Total.
	1.	2.	3.	4.	5.	6.	7.	First year.	Second year.		
Native-born:											
White..................	3	5	32	123	230	271	176	41	2	....	883
Negro..................	1	7	12	18	34	25	8	4	....	3	112
Total native-born........	4	12	44	141	264	296	184	45	2	3	995
Foreign-born:											
Canadian (other than French)......	....	....	1	4	9	3	....	....	....	....	17
English...............	....	1	1	4	7	6	4	....	....	....	23
German................	....	....	2	11	19	17	15	5	....	....	69
Hebrew, German........	....	....	....	1	2	4	6	1	....	....	14
Hebrew, Russian.......	....	2	1	8	8	8	8	1	....	....	36
Irish.................	....	....	....	8	9	7	8	....	....	....	32
Italian, South........	2	1	3	6	1	7	....	....	....	....	20
Scotch................	....	....	....	....	6	4	1	....	....	....	11
Swedish...............	....	....	....	1	3	15	4	....	....	....	23
Other races *a*.......	....	....	....	5	10	10	7	1	....	....	33
Total foreign-born........	2	4	7	45	69	86	56	8	....	....	277
Grand total...............	6	16	51	186	333	383	240	53	2	3	1,273

a "Other races" includes races having less than 10 representatives of this sex and age, and pupils whose race is not reported.

TABLE 4.—*Race and grade, by age—Number of puipls of each specified age in each grade, by general nativity and race of father of pupil*—Continued.

BOYS: AGE 14 YEARS.

General nativity and race of father of pupil.	Elementary grades.							High school.				Ungraded and special schools.	Total.
	1.	2.	3.	4.	5.	6.	7.	First year.	Second year.	Third year.	Fourth year.		
Native-born:													
White	2	....	19	38	103	200	205	133	29	6	3	....	738
Negro	1	....	14	19	16	21	13	8	4	1	....	4	105
Total native-born	3	4	33	57	119	221	218	141	33	7	3	4	843
Foreign-born:													
Canadian, (other than French)				1	8	2	1	1					13
English					2	7	2						11
German			1	4	8	22	12	13	4				64
Hebrew, German				1	1	3	7	1	1				14
Hebrew, Polish				2		4	6						12
Hebrew, Russian				1	1	4	9	3	1				1'
Irish				3	6	10	3	6	4				32
Italian, South	1	1	2	5	1		2						12
Swedish				1	7	8	3						19
Other races a	1	1		7	6	8	11		2				36
Total foreign-born	2	2	3	23	25	68	67	29	13				232
Grand total	5	6	36	80	144	289	285	170	46	7	3	4	1,075

a "Other races" includes races having less than 10 representatives of this sex and age, and pupils whose race is not reported.

BOYS: AGE 15 YEARS.

	1.	2.	3.	4.	5.	6.	7.	First year.	Second year.	Third year.	Fourth year.	Ungraded and special schools.	Total.
Native-born:													
White		1	4	10	30	84	122	135	73	14	6	....	479
Negro			1	12	9	9	13	6	4	2	....	4	60
Total native-born		1	5	22	39	93	135	141	77	16	6	4	539
Foreign-born:													
Canadian (other than French)				1		2	4	3	2				12
English				1	2	1	2	5					11
German				1	3	7	10	15	1	1			38
Hebrew, Russian			1		2	4	4	2					13
Hebrew, Other				1	1	3	2	4					11
Irish				1	1	2	4	4					12
Swedish					3	8	1	1					13
Other races a		1	1	4	4	5	6	5	1				27
Total foreign-born		1	4	9	17	35	35	32	2	1			136
Grand total		1	6	26	48	110	170	176	110	18	7	4	676

a "Other races" includes races having less than 10 representatives of this sex and age, and pupils whose race is not reported.

TABLE 4.—*Race and grade, by age—Number of pupils of each specified age in each grade, by general nativity and race of father of pupil*—Continued.

BOYS: AGE 16 YEARS.

General nativity and race of father of pupil.	Elementary grades.				High school.				Total.
	4.	5.	6.	7.	First year.	Second year.	Third year.	Fourth year.	
Native-born:									
White.................................	2	8	12	48	101	106	83	29	389
Negro...............................	....	4	4	4	10	5	2	3	32
Total native-born..................	2	12	16	52	111	111	85	32	421
Foreign-born:									
German.............................	....	....	1	2	5	5	4	3	20
Hebrew (not specified)..............	....	....	2	2	3	1	3	3	14
Swedish............................	....	....	....	1	....	3	6	....	10
Other races a......................	....	....	2	3	8	8	7	4	32
Total foreign-born.................	....	....	5	8	16	17	20	10	76
Grand total......................	2	12	21	60	127	128	105	42	497

a "Other races" includes races having less than 10 representatives of this sex and age, and pupils whose race is not reported.

BOYS: AGE 17 YEARS.

General nativity and race of father of pupil.	Elementary grades.							High school.				Total.
	1.	2.	3.	4.	5.	6.	7.	First year.	Second year.	Third year.	Fourth year.	
Native-born:												
White.....................	....	....	....	1	....	2	6	45	53	65	56	228
Negro.....................	....	....	....	....	1	1	1	2	4	3	3	15
Total native-born.......	....	....	....	1	1	3	7	47	57	68	59	243
Foreign-born:												
German..................	....	....	....	....	....	....	....	1	3	2	5	11
Hebrew (not specified)...	....	....	....	....	....	....	....	1	4	4	3	12
Other races a............	2	....	1	....	....	....	1	1	6	6	4	21
Total foreign-born.......	2	....	1	....	....	....	1	3	13	12	12	44
Grand total.............	2	....	1	1	1	3	8	50	70	80	71	287

a "Other races" includes races having less than 10 representatives of this sex and age, and pupils whose race is not reported.

BOYS: AGE 18 YEARS.

General nativity and race of father of pupil.	Elementary grades.				High school.				Total.
	4.	5.	6.	7.	First year.	Second year.	Third year.	Fourth year.	
Native-born:									
White......................	....	....	1	....	7	18	35	45	106
Negro.....................	....	....	1	1	1	5	2	2	12
Total native-born..........	....	....	2	1	8	23	37	47	118
Foreign-born, Other races a..........	1	1	....	....	1	8	5	11	27
Grand total.................	1	1	2	1	9	31	42	58	145

a "Other races" includes races having less than 10 representatives of this sex and age and pupils whose race is not reported.

The Immigration Commission.

TABLE 4.—*Race and grade, by age—Number of pupils of each specified age in each grade, by general nativity and race of father of pupil*—Continued.

BOYS: AGE 19 YEARS.

General nativity and race of father of pupil.	Elementary grade 3.	High school.				Ungraded and special schools.	Total.
		First year.	Second year.	Third year.	Fourth year.		
Native-born:							
White...............................	....	4	6	12	19	....	41
Negro...............................	....	1	3	....	1	1	6
Total native-born...............	....	5	9	12	20	1	47
Foreign-born, Other races a........	1	....	3	4	5	....	13
Grand total.....................	1	5	12	16	25	1	60

a "Other races" includes races having less than 10 representatives of this sex and age and pupils whose race is not reported.

BOYS: AGE 20 YEARS.

General nativity and race of father of pupil.	High school.					Total.
	First year.	Second year.	Third year.	Fourth year.	Fifth year.	
Native-born:						
White...............................	4	2	4	5	....	15
Negro...............................	....	....	2	2	1	5
Total native-born...............	4	2	6	7	1	20
Foreign-born, Other races a........	2	....	1	....	....	3
Grand total.....................	6	2	7	7	1	23

a "Other races" includes races having less than 10 representatives of this sex and age and pupils whose race is not reported.

GIRLS: AGE 5 YEARS.

General nativity and race of father of pupil.	Kindergarten.	Elementary grades.		Total.
		1.	2.	
Native-born:				
White...............................	4	1	....	5
Negro...............................	8	....	....	8
Total native-born...............	12	1	....	13
Foreign-born, Other races a........	2	1	1	4
Grand total.....................	14	2	1	17

a "Other races" includes races having less than 10 representatives of this sex and age and pupils whose race is not reported.

TABLE 4.—*Race and grade, by age—Number of pupils of each specified age in each grade, by general nativity and race of father of pupil—Continued.*

GIRLS: AGE 6 YEARS.

General nativity and race of father of pupil.	Kinder-garten.	Elementary grades.			Total.
		1.	2.	3.	
Native-born:					
White..................................	356	480	4	....	840
Negro..................................	40	59	1	1	102
Total native-born....................	396	539	5	1	942
Foreign-born:					
English................................	13	7	....	....	20
German................................	19	32	1	....	52
Hebrew, German.......................	4	7	....	....	11
Hebrew, Russian......................	12	24	1	....	37
Hebrew, Other.........................	1	11	....	....	12
Irish..................................	9	10	....	....	19
Italian, South.........................	34	26	....	....	60
Swedish................................	11	5	....	....	16
Other races a.........................	20	27	....	....	47
Total foreign-born....................	123	148	2	....	274
Grand total..........................	519	688	7	1	1,216

a "Other races" includes races having less than 10 representatives of this sex and age and pupils whose race is not reported.

GIRLS: AGE 7 YEARS.

General nativity and race of father of pupil.	Kinder-garten.	Elementary grades.					Un-graded and special schools.	Total.
		1.	2.	3.	4.			
Native-born:								
White..................................	8	636	221	19	....		....	884
Negro..................................	2	72	19	5	1		3	102
Total native-born....................	10	708	240	24	1		3	986
Foreign-born:								
English................................	1	11	6	....	....		....	18
German................................	1	23	14	1	....		....	39
Hebrew, German.......................	....	8	6	....	....		....	14
Hebrew, Polish........................	....	7	3	1	....		....	11
Hebrew, Russian......................	4	22	5	2	....		....	33
Irish..................................	....	15	5	....	....		....	20
Italian, South.........................	4	40	3	....	....		....	47
Swedish................................	....	17	7	....	....		....	24
Other races a.........................	1	43	16	....	....		....	60
Total foreign-born....................	11	186	64	4	....		....	265
Grand total..........................	21	894	305	28	1		3	1,252

a "Other races" includes races having less than 10 representatives of this sex and age and pupils whose race is not reported.

TABLE **4.**—*Race and grade, by age—Number of pupils of each specified age in each grade, by general nativity and race of father of pupil*—Continued.

GIRLS: AGE 8 YEARS.

General nativity and race of father of pupil.	Kinder-garten.	Elementary grades.					Un-graded and special schools.	Total.
		1.	2.	3.	4.	5.		
Native-born:								
White		228	428	238	15			909
Negro		52	34	19	2		2	109
Total native-born		280	462	257	17		2	1,018
Foreign-born:								
Canadian (other than French)		1	7	3	1			12
English		9	10	4				23
Germany		7	22	16		1		46
Hebrew, German		3	3	5	1			12
Hebrew, Polish		4	4	3				11
Hebrew, Russian		18	16	9				43
Irish		5	10	7				22
Italian, South	2	18	11	1				32
Swedish		7	21	4				32
Other races a	1	19	18	9				47
Total foreign-born	3	91	122	61	2	1		280
Grand total	3	371	584	318	19	1	2	1,298

a "Other races" includes races having less than 10 representatives of this sex and age and pupils whose race is not reported.

GIRLS: AGE 9 YEARS.

General nativity and race of father of pupil.	Elementary grades.					Un-graded and special schools.	Total.
	1.	2.	3.	4.	5.		
Native-born:							
White	64	216	426	174	7		887
Negro	31	31	29	10	1	4	106
Total native-born	95	247	455	184	8	4	993
Foreign-born:							
English		10	4	5			19
German	3	14	31	13	1		62
Hebrew, German	1	3	7	3			14
Hebrew, Russian	8	3	18	10	1		40
Hebrew, Other		3	2	5	2		12
Irish		8	7	5			20
Italian, North	3	6	2				11
Italian, South	11	13	8	2			34
Swedish	1	5	14	4			24
Other races a	3	8	14	7			32
Total foreign-born	30	73	107	54	4		268
Grand total	125	320	562	238	12	4	1,261

a "Other races" includes races having less than 10 representatives of this sex and age and pupils whose race is not reported.

TABLE 4.—*Race and grade, by age—Number of pupils of each specified age in each grade, by general nativity and race of father of pupil*—Continued.

GIRLS: AGE 10 YEARS.

General nativity and race of father of pupil.	Elementary grades.						Ungraded and special schools.	Total.
	1.	2.	3.	4.	5.	6.		
Native-born:								
White	23	69	305	383	130	5		915
Negro	18	26	35	29	9	4	5	126
Total native-born	41	95	340	412	139	9	5	1,041
Foreign-born:								
Canadian (other than French)		2	3	6				11
English		1	6	8	4			19
German	1	3	26	39	8	1		78
Hebrew, German		1	2	10				13
Hebrew, Polish	1	3		2	4			10
Hebrew, Russian	4	6	9	10	2			31
Irish	1	2	8	9	2			22
Italian, South	7	13	12	9	1			42
Scotch		2	7	6	2			17
Swedish	1	1	12	18	4			36
Other races *a*	1	7	14	8	3	1		34
Total foreign-born	16	41	99	125	30	2		313
Grand total	57	136	439	537	169	11	5	1,354

a "Other races" includes races having less than 10 representatives of this sex and age and pupils whose race is not reported.

GIRLS: AGE 11 YEARS.

General nativity and race of father of pupil.	Elementary grades.							Ungraded and special schools.	Total.
	1.	2.	3.	4.	5.	6.	7.		
Native-born:									
White	7	27	135	355	248	107	5		884
Negro	3	13	36	34	24	16	3	2	131
Total native-born	10	40	171	389	272	123	8	2	1,015
Foreign-born:									
English		2	1	3	7	1			14
German		3	8	25	29	8	1		74
Hebrew, German			1	6	7	1	1		16
Hebrew, Russian	1		5	9	8	4	1		28
Hebrew, Other	2	1	1	5	9	2			20
Irish			4	9	9	1			23
Italian, South	1	3	3	15		2			24
Scotch				3	3	4			10
Swedish		1	5	12	10	4			32
Other races *a*		1	10	11	7	1			30
Total foreign-born	4	11	38	98	89	28	3		271
Grand total	14	51	209	487	361	151	11	2	1,286

a "Other races" includes races having less than 10 representatives of this sex and age and pupils whose race is not reported.

TABLE 4.—*Race and grade, by age—Number of pupils of each specified age in each grade, by general nativity and race of father of pupil—Continued.*

GIRLS: AGE 12 YEARS.

General nativity and race of father of pupil.	Elementary grades.							High school, first year.	Ungraded and special schools.	Total.
	1.	2.	3.	4.	5.	6.	7.			
Native-born:										
White	1	16	60	194	339	250	76	6	....	942
Negro	2	8	27	31	13	24	7	1	4	117
Total native-born	3	24	87	225	352	274	83	7	4	1,059
Foreign-born:										
Canadian, (other than French)			2	5	3	5	1			16
English			3	7	7	4	2			23
German		1	4	15	27	27	7			81
Hebrew, German			1	4	7	3	2			17
Hebrew, Polish				2	9	11				22
Hebrew, Russian		3	5	5	9	9	8			39
Irish			2	7	13	4	3			29
Italian, South	2		3	12	1	2				22
Scotch				2	4	4				10
Swedish				6	12	12	1			31
Other races *a*		5	2	8	13	14			1	43
Total foreign-born	2	11	22	73	105	95	24	1		333
Grand total	5	35	109	298	457	369	107	8	4	1,392

a "Other races" includes races having less than 10 representatives of this sex and age and pupils whose race is not reported.

GIRLS: AGE 13 YEARS.

General nativity and race of father of pupil.	Elementary grades.							High school.				Ungraded and special schools.	Total.
	1.	2.	3.	4.	5.	6.	7.	First year.	Second year.	Third year.	Fourth year.		
Native-born:													
White		2	21	109	252	293	257	49	3		1		987
Negro		7	13	31	21	31	24	7	1			7	142
Total native-born		9	34	140	273	324	281	56	4		1	7	1,129
Foreign-born:													
Canadian (other than French)					2	8	2	3					15
English				4	10	8	7	1					30
German			1	6	14	26	20	3					70
Hebrew, German				3	6	5	5	2					21
Hebrew, Russian		1	2	1	6	6	11		1				28
Hebrew, Other		1		1	4	5	4	1					16
Irish			1	4	7	10	5	6					33
Italian, South	1		1	3	3	2	3						13
Swedish				1	11	12	3	1					28
Other races *a*	1	1		3	15	14	7						41
Total foreign-born	2	3	5	26	78	95	67	17	1				294
Grand total	2	12	39	166	351	420	348	73	5		1	7	1,424

a "Other races" includes races having less than 10 representatives of this sex and age and pupils whose race is not reported.

TABLE **4.**—*Race and grade, by age—Number of pupils of each specified age in each grade, by general nativity and race of father of pupil*—Continued.

GIRLS: AGE 14 YEARS.

General nativity and race of father of pupil.	Elementary grades.						High school.				Un-graded and special schools.	Total.
	2.	3.	4.	5.	6.	7.	First year.	Second year.	Third year.	Fourth year.		
Native-born:												
White	1	7	22	97	192	301	179	34	5	4	......	842
Negro	1	9	15	24	18	17	6	2	2	......	7	101
Total native-born	2	16	37	121	210	318	185	36	7	4	7	943
Foreign-born:												
Canadian (other than French)	......	......	......	......	5	4	7	......	......	......	......	16
English	......	1	......	1	2	6	4	3	......	......	......	17
German	1	1	1	9	17	19	15	2	......	1	......	66
Hebrew, German	......	......	......	3	......	8	1	2	......	......	......	14
Hebrew, Russian	......	......	1	4	5	7	3	1	......	1	......	22
Hebrew, Other	......	......	1	3	4	5	1	......	......	......	......	14
Irish	......	......	......	3	7	8	12	......	1	......	......	31
Italian, South	1	1	2	5	3	1	......	......	......	......	......	13
Swedish	......	......	......	......	5	8	4	1	......	......	......	18
Other races a	......	......	2	3	8	9	6	3	1	......	......	32
Total foreign-born	2	3	7	31	56	75	53	12	2	2	......	243
Grand total	4	19	44	152	266	393	238	48	9	6	7	1,186

GIRLS: AGE 15 YEARS.

General nativity and race of father of pupil.	2.	3.	4.	5.	6.	7.	First year.	Second year.	Third year.	Fourth year.	Ungraded.	Total.
Native-born:												
White	......	2	6	18	67	146	220	125	28	3	......	618
Negro	1	2	6	6	17	21	20	12	5	2	5	97
Total native-born	1	4	12	24	84	167	240	137	33	5	5	712
Foreign-born:												
English	......	......	......	1	1	4	7	2	1	......	......	16
German	......	......	......	......	2	12	13	9	4	......	......	40
Hebrew, German	......	......	......	1	3	2	2	1	1	......	......	10
Hebrew, Russian	......	1	1	......	......	1	2	2	3	1	......	11
Irish	......	......	......	......	2	6	6	1	......	......	......	15
Other races a	......	1	......	1	5	20	9	4	3	1	......	44
Total foreign-born	......	2	1	2	11	46	39	20	12	3	......	136
Grand total	1	6	13	26	95	213	279	157	45	8	5	848

a "Other races" includes races having less than 10 representatives of this sex and age and pupils whose race is not reported.

TABLE 4.—*Race and grade, by age—Number of pupils of each specified age in each grade, by general nativity and race of father of pupil*—Continued.

GIRLS: AGE 16 YEARS.

General nativity and race of father of pupil.	Elementary grades.					High school.				Un-graded and special schools.	Total.
	3.	4.	5.	6.	7.	First year.	Second year.	Third year.	Fourth year.		
Native-born:											
White	1	2	2	10	43	102	139	111	48	......	458
Negro	....	3	....	9	9	18	16	8	4	2	69
Total native-born	1	5	2	19	52	120	155	119	52	2	527
Foreign-born:											
English					1	3	4	......	3	....	11
German					1	9	7	4	3	....	24
Hebrew, other					1	2	1	5	1	....	10
Irish					2	8	5	3	3	....	21
Other races a				1	3	5	9	7	4		29
Total foreign-born				1	8	27	26	19	14	....	95
Grand total	1	5	2	20	60	147	181	138	66	2	622

a "Other races" includes races having less than 10 representatives of this sex and age and pupils whose race is not reported.

GIRLS: AGE 17 YEARS.

General nativity and race of father of pupil	Elementary grades.				High school.				Un-graded and special schools.	Total.
	4.	5.	6.	7.	First year.	Second year.	Third year.	Fourth year.		
Native-born:										
White	1	1	2	6	31	75	117	106	....	339
Negro	....	....	1	4	2	12	6	6	1	32
Total native-born	1	1	3	10	33	87	123	112	1	371
Foreign-born:										
English				1	......	4	2	4	....	11
German	1			2	1	9	5	9	....	27
Other races a				2	3	4	15	14	....	38
Total foreign-born	1			5	4	17	21	27	....	75
Grand total	2	1	3	15	37	104	145	139	1	447

a "Other races" includes races having less than 10 representatives of this sex and age and pupils whose race is not reported.

GIRLS: AGE 18 YEARS.

General nativity and race of father of pupil.	Elementary grade 7.	High school.				Total.
		First year	Second year.	Third year.	Fourth year.	
Native-born:						
White	1	12	21	47	77	168
Negro	2	1	3	2	10	8
Total native-born	3	13	24	49	87	176
Foreign-born, other races a	....	3	1	8	12	24
Grand total	3	16	25	57	99	200

a "Other races" includes races having less than 10 representatives of this sex and age and pupils whose race is not reported.

TABLE 4.—*Race and grade, by age—Number of pupils of each specified age in each grade, by general nativity and race of father of pupil*—Continued.

GIRLS: AGE 19 YEARS.

General nativity and race of father of pupil.	Elementary grade 5.	High school.				Ungraded.	Normal school.	Total.
		First year.	Second year.	Third year.	Fourth year.			
Native-born:								
White............................	1	2	9	12	37	....	3	64
Negro.............................	....	1	....	2	5	....	....	8
Indian............................	....	....	....	....	1	....	....	1
Total native-born..............	1	3	9	14	43	....	3	73
Foreign-born, other races *a*..........	....	1	3	....	5	....	....	9
Grand total.....................	1	4	12	14	48	....	3	82

a "Other races" includes races having less than 10 representatives of this sex and age and pupils whose race is not reported.

GIRLS: AGE 20 YEARS.

General nativity and race of father of pupil.	Elementary grade 3.	High school.				Normal school.	Total.
		First year.	Second year.	Third year.	Fourth year.		
Native-born:							
White..............................	....	1	4	3	5	1	14
Negro.............................	....	....	....	1	....	....	1
Total native-born..................	....	1	4	4	5	1	15
Foreign-born, other races *a*..................	1	1	....	2	3	....	7
Grand total........................	1	2	4	6	8	1	22

a "Other races" includes races having less than 10 representatives of this sex and age and pupils whose race is not reported.

TABLE 5.—Race distribution in each grade—Percentages.

[This table shows in detail only races with 100 or more pupils reporting. The totals, however, are for all races.]

General nativity and race of father of pupil.	Kindergarten.	Elementary grades.								High school.					Ungraded school.	Normal school.	Grand total.
		1.	2.	3.	4.	5.	6.	7.	Total.	First year.	Second year.	Third year.	Fourth year.	Total.			
Native-born:																	
White	66.8	66.9	67.7	69.0	70.8	70.8	70.6	72.5	69.4	76.4	74.6	78.7	75.5	76.2		100.0	70.0
Negro	6.7	11.0	9.5	9.6	8.4	6.8	7.6	6.5	8.8	6.3	7.6	5.5	6.5	6.5			8.7
Indian													.2		100.0		
Total native-born	73.5	77.9	77.1	78.5	79.2	77.6	78.3	79.0	78.2	82.8	82.2	84.2	82.1	82.8	100.0	100.0	78.7
Foreign-born:																	
Canadian, other than French	.4	.6	.9	1.1	.8	.9	1.7	1.0	.9	1.7	.6	1.9	1.5	1.4			1.0
English	2.2	1.4	1.9	1.5	1.6	2.0	1.3	1.9	1.6	1.7	2.1	1.3	2.2	1.8			1.7
German	4.4	3.5	4.2	5.0	5.2	5.9	5.5	5.1	4.8	5.6	6.4	3.2	5.3	5.3			4.9
Hebrew, German	1.0	.8	.8	1.0	1.3	1.4	.9	1.8	1.1		1.3	1.1	1.2	1.1			1.1
Hebrew, Polish	.6	1.0		.4	.7	.9	1.1	.9	.8	.9	.9	.1	.3				.7
Hebrew, Russian	3.8	4.0	2.4	2.9	2.2	2.1	2.2	2.8	2.7	1.1		1.3	1.0	1.1			2.6
Irish	1.6	1.5	1.9	1.7	2.3	2.2	1.9	2.0	1.9	3.1	1.7	2.0	3.1	2.5			2.0
Italian, North	.9	.6	.7	.6	.8	.4	.8	.3	.4			.1		(a)			.4
Italian, South	6.5	4.0	4.1	2.5	1.1	.9	.8	.8	2.3		.7	1.2		(a)			2.2
Scotch	.5			.5	.7	.9	.8		.6	.5		.1	.9	.7			.6
Swedish	2.1	1.5	2.3	2.1	1.7	2.3	2.8	2.1	2.1	.9	1.4	1.2	.9	1.1			1.9
Other races	2.4	3.1	2.3	2.2	2.1	2.7	2.4	1.9	2.4	1.4	2.6	1.7	1.5	1.8			2.3
Total foreign-born	26.5	22.1	22.9	21.5	20.8	22.4	21.7	21.0	21.8	17.2	17.8	15.8	17.9	17.2			21.3
Grand total	100.0	100.0	100.0	100.0	100.0	100.0	100.0	100.0	100.0	100.0	100.0	100.0	100.0	100.0	100.0	100.0	100.0

a Less than 0.05 per cent.

TABLE 6.—*Grade distribution of each race—Percentages.*

[This table shows in detail only races with 100 or more pupils reporting. The totals, however, are for all races.]

	Kinder-garten.	Elementary grades.								High school.					Un-graded school.	Normal school.	Grand total.
		1.	2.	3.	4.	5.	6.	7.	Total.	First year.	Second year.	Third year.	Fourth year.	Total.			
Native-born:																	
White	4.1	15.9	10.7	12.6	13.7	11.4	9.4	7.6	81.4	5.6	3.7	2.8	2.3	14.5	.....	(b)	100.0
Negro	3.3	21.2	12.2	14.2	13.1	8.8	8.2	5.6	83.2	3.8	3.0	1.6	1.6	10.0	3.4	.....	100.0
Indian	(a)	(a)	(a)	(a)	(a)	(a)	(a)	(a)	(a)	(a)	(a)	(a)	(a)	(a)	(a)	(a)	(a)
Total native-born	4.0	16.5	10.9	12.8	13.6	11.1	9.3	7.4	81.6	5.4	3.6	2.0	2.3	14.0	.4	(b)	100.0
Foreign-born:																	
Canadian (other than French)	1.9	9.4	9.7	14.2	11.2	9.7	16.5	7.9	78.7	9.0	2.2	4.9	3.4	19.5			100.0
English	5.7	14.3	12.3	11.2	12.7	13.6	7.3	8.4	79.8	5.3	4.4	2.0	2.9	14.5			100.0
German	3.9	12.1	9.7	13.3	14.6	13.6	10.6	8.7	81.6	6.0	4.6	1.7	2.4	14.6			100.0
Hebrew, German	4.0	12.7	8.0	11.7	15.7	14.0	8.0	12.0	82.3	4.3	4.0	3.0	2.3	13.7			100.0
Hebrew, Polish	3.6	23.9	10.7	6.6	15.2	14.2	14.7	9.6	92.9	1.5	.5	.5	1.0	3.6			100.0
Hebrew, Russian	6.3	26.1	10.2	14.6	11.8	9.2	7.9	8.1	88.0	2.3	1.2	1.3	.9	5.6			100.0
Irish	3.5	12.8	10.7	10.9	15.7	12.6	9.1	7.6	79.4	8.1	3.0	2.6	3.3	17.0			100.0
Italian, North	10.6	24.0	19.2	20.2	12.0	11.5	3.8	1.9	88.5			1.0		1.0			100.0
Italian, South	12.9	30.8	20.8	14.7	15.8	3.9	3.6	1.2	87.0								100.0
Scotch	3.6	13.2	13.9	10.9	12.0	17.0	12.1	8.0	80.0	4.2	4.2	4.8	3.0	16.4			100.0
Swedish	4.8	21.8	13.4	14.1	12.4	12.0	13.4	6.1	87.6	2.3	2.5	1.9	1.1	7.6			100.0
Other races	4.4	21.8	10.8	11.8	12.4	12.9	9.6	6.1	85.4	3.1	3.8	1.9	1.4	10.2			100.0
Total foreign-born	5.4	17.3	11.9	12.9	13.2	11.8	9.5	7.3	83.9	4.2	2.9	1.9	1.8	10.8			100.0
Grand total	4.3	16.7	11.1	12.8	13.6	11.2	9.3	7.4	82.1	5.2	3.5	2.5	2.2	13.3			100.0

a Not computed, owing to small number involved. b Less than 0.05 per cent.

PUBLIC SCHOOL TEACHERS IN ELEMENTARY GRADES AND KINDERGARTEN.

TABLE 1.—*Number of teachers in each grade, by sex and general nativity and race.*

MALE.

[This table does not include 20 teachers not reporting complete data.]

General nativity and race.	Kinder-garten.	Elementary grades. 1.	2.	3.	4.	5.	6.	7.	Un-graded and special.	Total.	Total kinder-garten and elementary.
Native-born of native father:											
White		1		1	2					4	4
Negro			2		2	5	1		2	12	12
Grand total		1	2	1	4	5	1		2	16	16

FEMALE.

General nativity and race.	Kinder-garten.	Elementary grades. 1.	2.	3.	4.	5.	6.	7.	Un-graded and special.	Total.	Total kinder-garten and elementary.
Native-born of native father:											
White	26	80	57	69	75	63	56	47	1	448	474
Negro	2	10	7	6	7	4	2	3	2	41	43
Total	28	90	64	75	82	67	58	50	3	489	517
Native-born of foreign father, by race of father:											
Canadian (other than French)	1	2		3	4		1	1		11	12
Danish		1								1	1
Dutch					1					1	1
English				1						1	1
French		3	1	1	2	4		2		13	13
German	1	6	6	4	5	6	5	2		34	35
Hebrew, German				1	1		1	1		4	4
Irish	2	5	6	3	4	3	2	4		27	29
Mexican							1			1	1
Negro			1							1	1
Norwegian		1	1					2		4	4
Scotch		1	1			1	3	1		7	7
Scotch-Irish							3			3	3
Swedish		4	2	1	2	1	1			11	11
Welsh				2	1					3	3
Total	4	23	18	17	21	15	18	13		125	129
Total native-born	32	113	82	92	103	82	76	63	3	614	646
Foreign-born:											
English							1			1	1
Hebrew, Polish								1		1	1
Irish					1					1	1
Scotch					1		1			2	2
Scotch-Irish		1				2				3	3
Swedish				1	1					2	2
Total foreign-born		1		1	3	2	2	1		10	10
Grand total	32	114	82	93	106	84	78	64	3	624	656

TABLE 1.—*Number of teachers in each grade, by sex and general nativity and race*—Contd.

TOTAL.

General nativity and race.	Kindergarten	Elementary grades. 1.	2.	3.	4.	5.	6.	7.	Ungraded and special.	Total.	Total kindergarten and elementary.	Race distribution. Percentages. Elementary.	Elementary and kindergarten.
Native-born of native father:													
White	26	80	58	69	76	65	56	47	1	452	478	70.6	71.1
Negro	2	10	7	8	7	6	7	4	4	53	55	8.3	8.2
Total	28	90	65	77	83	71	63	51	5	505	533	78.9	79.3
Native-born of foreign father, by race of father:													
Canadian (other than French)	1	2	....	3	4	....	1	1	....	11	12	1.7	1.8
Danish	....	1	....	....	....	....	....	....	....	1	1	.2	.1
Dutch	....	....	....	....	1	....	....	....	....	1	1	.2	.1
English	....	3	1	1	2	4	....	2	....	13	13	2.0	1.9
French	....	....	1	1	1	....	1	....	....	4	4	.6	.6
German	1	6	6	4	5	6	5	2	....	34	35	5.3	5.2
Hebrew, German	....	....	....	1	1	....	1	1	....	4	4	.6	.6
Irish	2	5	6	3	4	3	2	4	....	27	29	4.2	4.3
Mexican	....	....	....	....	....	....	1	....	....	1	1	.2	.1
Negro	....	....	....	1	....	....	....	....	....	1	1	.2	.1
Norwegian	....	1	1	....	....	....	....	2	....	4	4	.6	.6
Scotch	....	1	1	....	....	1	3	1	....	7	7	1.1	1.0
Scotch-Irish	....	....	....	....	....	....	3	....	....	3	3	.5	.4
Swedish	....	4	2	1	2	1	1	....	....	11	11	1.7	1.6
Welsh	....	....	....	2	1	....	....	....	....	3	3	.5	.4
Total	4	23	18	17	21	15	18	13	....	125	129	19.5	19.2
Total native-born	32	113	83	94	104	86	81	64	5	630	662	98.4	98.5
Foreign-born:													
English	....	....	....	....	....	....	....	1	....	1	1	.2	.1
Hebrew, Polish	....	....	....	....	1	....	....	....	....	1	1	.2	.1
Irish	....	....	....	....	....	....	2	....	....	2	2	.3	.3
Scotch	....	1	....	1	....	1	....	....	....	3	3	.5	.4
Scotch-Irish	....	....	....	....	1	1	....	....	....	2	2	.3	.3
Swedish	....	....	....	....	1	....	....	....	....	1	1	.2	.1
Total foreign-born	....	1	....	1	3	2	2	1	....	10	10	1.6	1.5
Grand total	32	114	83	95	107	88	83	65	5	640	672	100.0	100.0

TABLE 2.—*Number of teachers engaged in teaching each specified number of years, by sex and general nativity and race.*

MALE.

[This table does not include 24 teachers not reporting complete data.]

General nativity and race.	Under 5 years.	5 to 9 years.	10 to 14 years.	15 to 19 years.	20 to 24 years.	25 to 29 years.	30 years or over.	Total.
Native-born of native father:								
White			3					3
Negro		3	2	2	1		4	12
Grand total		3	5	2	1		4	15

FEMALE.

General nativity and race.	Under 5 years.	5 to 9 years.	10 to 14 years.	15 to 19 years.	20 to 24 years.	25 to 29 years.	30 years or over.	Total.
Native-born of native father:								
White	73	103	130	87	51	17	12	473
Negro	4	12	13	5	5	4		43
Total	77	115	143	92	56	21	12	516
Native-born of foreign father, by race of father:								
Canadian (other than French)	2	5	3	1	1			12
Danish		1						1
Dutch						1		1
English	1	3	2	4		1	2	13
French		2			2			4
German	7	4	10	8	4			33
Hebrew, German		2	2					4
Irish	3	10	3	4	6	2	1	29
Mexican			1					1
Negro			1					1
Norwegian		2		2				4
Scotch	1	2	3		1			7
Scotch-Irish				3				3
Swedish	5	2	4					11
Welsh			2	1				3
Total	19	33	31	23	14	4	3	127
Total native-born	96	148	174	115	70	25	15	643
Foreign-born:								
English					1			1
Hebrew, Polish		1						1
Irish			1					1
Scotch		1			1			2
Scotch-Irish					3			3
Swedish		1	1					2
Total foreign-born		3	2		5			10
Grand total	96	151	176	115	75	25	15	653

TABLE 2.—*Number of teachers engaged in teaching each specified number of years, by sex and general nativity and race*—Continued.

TOTAL.

General nativity and race.	Under 5 years.	5 to 9 years.	10 to 14 years.	15 to 19 years.	20 to 24 years.	25 to 29 years.	30 years or over.	Total.
Native-born of native father:								
White...........................	73	103	133	87	51	17	12	476
Negro...........................	4	15	15	7	6	4	4	55
Total.....................	77	118	148	94	57	21	16	531
Native-born of foreign father, by race of father:								
Canadian (other than French) ...	2	5	3	1	1	....	....	12
Danish..........................		1						1
Dutch...........................						1	....	1
English..........................	1	3	2	4	....	1	2	13
French..........................		2			2			4
German..........................	7	4	10	8	4			33
Hebrew, German..................		2	2					4
Irish.............................	3	10	3	4	6	2	1	29
Mexican.........................			1					1
Negro...........................			1					1
Norwegian.......................		2	....	2				4
Scotch...........................	1	2	3		1			7
Scotch-Irish......................				3				3
Swedish..........................	5	2	4					11
Welsh...........................			2	1				3
Total.....................	19	33	31	23	14	4	3	127
Total native-born	96	151	179	117	71	25	19	658
Foreign-born:								
English..........................						1	....	1
Hebrew, Polish...................		1				....	....	1
Irish.............................			1					1
Scotch...........................		1				1		2
Scotch-Irish......................						3		3
Swedish..........................		1	1					2
Total foreign-born.............	....	3	2	....		5	....	10
Grand total...................	96	154	181	117	76	25	19	668

PAROCHIAL SCHOOL PUPILS: GENERAL INVESTIGATION.

TABLE 1.—*Grade and age—Number of pupils of each age in each grade, by sex.*

BOYS.

Age.	Kindergarten.	Elementary.									High school.					Grand total.
		1.	2.	3.	4.	5.	6.	7.	8.	Total.	First year.	Second year.	Third year.	Fourth year.	Total.	
5 years	3	4								4						7
6 years	5	23	1							24						29
7 years	1	46	6	1						53						54
8 years		15	28	8	1					52						52
9 years		4	38	24	10					76						76
10 years		1	4	26	27	5				63						63
11 years			4	10	24	13	5	1		57						57
12 years				1	15	33	13	4	1	67						67
13 years				1	3	11	12	10	2	39						39
14 years						5	8	7	3	23						23
15 years									1	1						1
17 years					1					1						1
Total	9	93	81	71	81	67	38	22	7	460						469

GIRLS.

Age.	Kindergarten.	Elementary.									High school.					Grand total.
		1.	2.	3.	4.	5.	6.	7.	8.	Total.	First year.	Second year.	Third year.	Fourth year.	Total.	
5 years	8	4								4						12
6 years	4	31	1							32						36
7 years	2	46	13							59						61
8 years		13	23	3	1					40						40
9 years		4	23	30	6					63						63
10 years			4	35	33	4				76						76
11 years				10	19	6	2			37						37
12 years				2	7	23	19	3	1	55						55
13 years			1		4	11	20	9	6	51	3				3	54
14 years						19	9	7	11	46	1	1			2	48
15 years							2	6	1	9	2	5	1		8	17
16 years								2		2	2	4	1		7	9
17 years											1	1	1	2	5	5
18 years												1			1	1
Total	14	98	65	80	70	63	52	27	19	474	9	12	3	2	26	514

TOTAL.

Age.	Kindergarten.	Elementary.									High school.					Grand total.
		1.	2.	3.	4.	5.	6.	7.	8.	Total.	First year.	Second year.	Third year.	Fourth year.	Total.	
5 years	11	8								8						19
6 years	9	54	2							56						65
7 years	3	92	19	1						112						115
8 years		28	51	11	2					92						92
9 years		8	61	54	16					139						139
10 years		1	8	61	60	9				139						139
11 years			4	20	43	19	7	1		94						94
12 years				3	22	56	32	7	2	122						122
13 years			1	1	7	22	32	19	8	90	3				3	93
14 years						24	17	14	14	69	1	1			2	71
15 years							2	6	2	10	2	5	1		8	18
16 years								2		2	2	4	1		7	9
17 years					1					1	1	1	1	2	5	6
18 years												1			1	1
Total	23	191	146	151	151	130	90	49	26	934	9	12	3	2	26	983

TABLE 2.—Race, sex, and grade—Number of pupils of each sex in each grade, by general nativity and race of father of pupil.

General nativity and race of father of pupil.	Kindergarten.	Elementary grades.									High school.					Grand total.
		1.	2.	3.	4.	5.	6.	7.	8.	Total.	First year.	Second year.	Third year.	Fourth year.	Total.	
Native-born:																
White:																
Male	7	58	37	39	30	33	18	9	6	230						237
Female	11	59	37	25	34	27	26	16	11	235	5	8	3	1	17	263
Total	18	117	74	64	64	60	44	25	17	465	5	8	3	1	17	500
Negro, Female				7						7						7
Total native-born:																
Male	7	58	37	39	30	33	18	9	6	230						237
Female	11	59	37	32	34	27	26	16	11	242	5	8	3	1	17	270
Total	18	117	74	71	64	60	44	25	17	472	5	8	3	1	17	507
Foreign-born:																
English—																
Male						2				4						4
Female		3			1	2	3			8						8
Total		3			1	2	3			12						12
Flemish—																
Male		3	1		3					7						7
Female		3	1	5	1					13						13
Total		6	2	5	4					20						20
German—																
Male		19	33	23	32	25	15	6		153						153
Female	3	26	20		20	13	16	5	6	106	2	1			3	112
Total	3	45	53	23	52	38	31	11	6	259	2	1			3	265
Hebrew, German—																
Female										20						20
Total										20						20
Irish—																
Male	2	8	8	5	15	7	5	7	1	56						58
Female		4	5	21	7	20	6	5	1	69	2	2		1	5	74
Total	2	12	13	26	22	27	11	12	2	125	2	2		1	5	132
Other races a—																
Male			2	2	1	1				10						10
Female			2	1	7		1	1		16		1			1	17
Total			4	3	8	1	1	1		26		1			1	27
Total foreign-born:																
Male	2	35	44	32	51	34	20	13	7	230						232
Female	3	39	28	48	36	36	26	11	19	232	4	4		1	9	244
Total	5	74	72	80	87	70	46	24	7	462	4	4		1	9	476
Grand total—																
Male	9	93	81	81	81	67	38	22	7	460						469
Female	14	98	65	70	70	63	52	27	19	474	9	12	3	2	26	514
Total	23	191	146	151	151	130	90	49	26	934	9	12	3	2	26	983

a "Other races" include Belgian, 2; Bohemian, 1; Canadian, French, 1; Canadian, Other, 3; Dutch Hollander, 3; French, 5; Italian, North, 8; Magyar, 1; Polish, 1; Swedish, 2.

TABLE 3.—*Race, sex, and age, by grade—Number of pupils of each age in each grade, by sex and by general nativity and race of father of pupil.*

KINDERGARTEN.

BOYS.

General nativity and race of father of pupil.	Number of pupils of each age.			Total.
	5.	6.	7.	
Native-born, White	2	4	1	7
Foreign-born, Irish	1	1		2
Grand total	3	5	1	9

GIRLS.

	5.	6.	7.	Total.
Native-born, White	6	3	2	11
Foreign-born, German	2	1		3
Grand total	8	4	2	14

TOTAL.

	5.	6.	7.	Total.
Native-born, White	8	7	3	18
Foreign-born:				
German	2	1		3
Irish	1	1		2
Total	3	2		5
Grand total	11	9	3	23

FIRST GRADE.

BOYS.

General nativity and race of father of pupil.	Number of pupils of each age.						Total.
	5.	6.	7.	8.	9.	10.	
Native-born, White	2	15	28	11	1	1	58
Foreign-born:							
Flemish	1	2					3
German		3	14	1	1		19
Irish		2	3	1	2		8
Other races *a*	1	1	1	2			5
Total foreign-born	2	8	18	4	3		35
Grand total	4	23	46	15	4	1	93

GIRLS.

	5.	6.	7.	8.	9.	10.	Total.
Native-born, White		19	26	12	2		59
Foreign-born:							
English	1	2			1		3
Flemish			2		1		3
German	3	9	13		1		26
Irish		1	2	1			4
Other races *a*			3				3
Total foreign-born	4	12	20	1	2		39
Grand total	4	31	46	13	4		98

a "Other races" includes races having less than 10 representatives in this city and pupils whose race is not reported.

TABLE 3.—*Race, sex, and age, by grade—Number of pupils of each age in each grade, by sex and by general nativity and race of father of pupil.*

FIRST GRADE—Continued.

TOTAL.

General nativity and race of father of pupil.	Number of pupils of each age.						Total.
	5.	6.	7.	8.	9.	10.	
Native-born, White......................	2	34	54	23	3	1	117
Foreign-born:							
English..............	1	2	....	....	....	....	3
Flemish.............	1	2	2	....	1	....	6
German.............	3	12	27	1	2	....	45
Irish................	....	3	5	2	2	....	12
Other races *a*	1	1	4	2	....	....	8
Total foreign-born.......	6	20	38	5	5	....	74
Grand total..........	8	54	92	28	8	1	191

a " Other races" includes races having less than 10 representatives in this city and pupils whose race is not reported.

SECOND GRADE.

BOYS.

General nativity and race of father of pupil.	Number of pupils of each age.							Total.
	6.	7.	8.	9.	10.	11.	13.	
Native-born, White..............	....	1	17	17	1	1	....	37
Foreign-born:								
Flemish............	....	....	....	....	....	1	....	1
German............	1	4	9	15	3	1	....	33
Irish...............	....	1	2	5	....	....	....	8
Other races *a*	....	....	....	1	....	1	....	2
Total............	1	5	11	21	3	3	....	44
Grand total........	1	6	28	38	4	4	....	81

GIRLS.

Native-born, White..............	1	3	17	13	3	....	....	37
Foreign-born:								
Flemish............	....	....	....	....	1	....	....	1
German............	....	8	5	7	....	....	....	20
Irish...............	....	1	1	2	....	....	1	5
Other races *a*	....	1	....	1	....	....	....	2
Total............	....	10	6	10	1	....	1	28
Grand total........	1	13	23	23	4	....	1	65

TOTAL.

Native-born, White..............	1	4	34	30	4	1	....	74
Foreign-born:								
Flemish............	....	....	....	....	1	1	....	2
German............	1	12	14	22	3	1	....	53
Irish...............	....	2	3	7	....	....	1	13
Other races *a*	....	1	....	2	....	1	....	4
Total............	1	15	17	31	4	3	1	72
Grand total........	2	19	51	61	8	4	1	146

a "Other races" includes races having less than 10 representatives in this city and pupils whose race is not reported.

TABLE **3.**—*Race, sex, and age, by grade—Number of pupils of each age in each grade, by sex and by general nativity and race of father of pupil*—Continued.

THIRD GRADE.

BOYS.

General nativity and race of father of pupil.	Number of pupils of each age.							Total.
	7.	8.	9.	10.	11.	12.	13.	
Native-born, White		2	12	19	4	1	1	39
Foreign-born:								
English				1	1			2
German	1	6	8	4	4			23
Irish			3	1	1			5
Other races a			1	1				2
Total foreign-born	1	6	12	7	6			32
Grand total	1	8	24	26	10	1	1	71

GIRLS.

General nativity and race of father of pupil.	7.	8.	9.	10.	11.	12.	13.	Total.
Native-born:								
White		2	8	12	3			25
Negro			2	5				7
Total native-born		2	10	17	3			32
Foreign-born:								
English				1				1
Flemish			1	3	1			5
Hebrew, German		1	10	6	2	1		20
Irish			8	8	4	1		21
Other races a			1					1
Total foreign-born		1	20	18	7	2		48
Grand total		3	30	35	10	2		80

TOTAL.

General nativity and race of father of pupil.	7.	8.	9.	10.	11.	12.	13.	Total.
Native-born:								
White		4	20	31	7	1	1	64
Negro			2	5				7
Total native-born		4	22	36	7	1	1	71
Foreign-born:								
English				2	1			3
Flemish			1	3	1			5
German	1	6	8	4	4			23
Hebrew, German		1	10	6	2	1		20
Irish			11	9	5	1		26
Other races a			2	1				3
Total foreign-born	1	7	32	25	13	2		80
Grand total	1	11	54	61	20	3	1	151

a "Other races" includes races having less than 10 representatives in this city and pupils whose race is not reported.

TABLE 3.—*Race, sex, and age, by grade—Number of pupils of each age in each grade, by sex and by general nativity and race of father of pupil*—Continued.

FOURTH GRADE.

BOYS.

General nativity and race of father of pupil.	Number of pupils of each age.										Total.
	8.	9.	10.	11.	12.	13.	14.	15.	16.	17.	
Native-born, White		4	8	11	6						1	30
Foreign-born:											
Flemish				2	1						3
German		6	13	7	4	2					32
Irish	1		6	3	4	1					15
Other races a				1							1
Total foreign-born	1	6	19	13	9	3					51
Grand total	1	10	27	24	15	3				1	81

GIRLS.

General nativity and race of father of pupil.	8.	9.	10.	11.	12.	13.	14.	15.	16.	17.	Total.
Native-born, White		3	16	9	5	1					34
Foreign-born:											
English		1									1
Flemish						1					1
German		1	11	4	2	2					20
Irish	1		1	5							7
Other races a		1	5	1							7
Total foreign-born	1	3	17	10	2	3					36
Grand total	1	6	33	19	7	4					70

TOTAL.

General nativity and race of father of pupil.	8.	9.	10.	11.	12.	13.	14.	15.	16.	17.	Total.
Native-born, White		7	24	20	11	1				1	64
Foreign-born:											
English		1									1
Flemish				2	1	1					4
German		7	24	11	6	4					52
Irish	2		7	8	4	1					22
Other races a		1	5	2							8
Total foreign-born	2	9	36	23	11	6					87
Grand total	2	16	60	43	22	7				1	151

a "Other races" includes races having less than 10 representatives in this city and pupils whose race is not reported.

TABLE 3.—*Race, sex, and age, by grade—Number of pupils of each age in each grade, by sex and by general nativity and race of father of pupil*—Continued.

FIFTH GRADE.

BOYS.

General nativity and race of father of pupil.	Number of pupils of each age.					Total.
	10.	11.	12.	13.	14.	
Native-born, White........................	2	7	19	4	1	33
Foreign-born:						
English................................		1	1	....		2
German................................	3	3	10	6	3	25
Irish..................................		2	3	1	1	7
Total foreign-born................	3	6	14	7	4	34
Grand total.....................	5	13	33	11	5	67

GIRLS.

Native-born, White........................	3	4	14	4	2	27
Foreign-born:						
Flemish...............................			1		1	2
German................................	1	1	5	4	2	13
Irish.................................		1	2	3	14	20
Other races a........................			1	....		1
Total foreign-born................	1	2	9	7	17	36
Grand total.....................	4	6	23	11	19	63

TOTAL.

Native-born, White........................	5	11	33	8	3	60
Foreign-born:						
English................................		1	1	....	....	2
Flemish...............................			1		1	2
German................................	4	4	15	10	5	38
Irish.................................		3	5	4	15	27
Other races a........................			1	....	....	1
Total foreign-born................	4	8	23	14	21	70
Grand total.....................	9	19	56	22	24	130

a "Other races" includes races having less than 10 representatives in this city and pupils whose race is not reported.

SIXTH GRADE.

BOYS.

General nativity and race of father of pupil.	Number of pupils of each age.					Total.
	11.	12.	13.	14.	15.	
Native-born, White........................	3	9	5	1	....	18
Foreign-born:						
German................................		4	6	5	....	15
Irish..................................	2	....	1	2	....	5
Total foreign-born.............	2	4	7	7	....	20
Grand total.....................	5	13	12	8	....	38

a "Other races" includes races having less than 10 representatives in this city and pupils whose race is not reported.

TABLE 3.—*Race, sex, and age, by grade—Number of pupils of each age in each grade, by sex and by general nativity and race of father of pupil*—Continued.

SIXTH GRADE—Continued.

GIRLS.

General nativity and race of father of pupil.	Number of pupils of each age.					Total.
	11.	12.	13.	14.	15.	
Native-born, White...............	1	12	9	4	....	26
Foreign-born:						
English........................	....	....	2	1	....	3
Flemish........................	....	1	....	....	....	1
German........................	1	4	8	3	....	16
Irish..........................	....	2	1	1	2	6
Total foreign-born.............	1	7	11	5	2	26
Grand total...................	2	19	20	9	2	52

TOTAL.

General nativity and race of father of pupil.	Number of pupils of each age.					Total.
	11.	12.	13.	14.	15.	
Native-born, White...............	4	21	14	5	....	44
Foreign-born:						
English........................	....	....	2	1	....	3
Flemish........................	....	1	....	....	....	1
German........................	1	8	14	8	....	31
Irish..........................	2	2	2	3	2	11
Total foreign-born.............	3	11	18	12	2	46
Grand total...................	7	32	32	17	2	90

SEVENTH GRADE.

BOYS.

General nativity and race of father of pupil.	Number of pupils of each age.							Total.
	11.	12.	13.	14.	15.	16.	17.	
Native-born, White..............	....	2	4	3	....	....	....	9
Foreign-born:								
German......................	1	1	2	2	....	....	....	6
Irish.......................	....	1	4	2	....	....	....	7
Total foreign-born..........	1	2	6	4	....	....	....	13
Grand total.................	1	4	10	7	....	....	....	22

GIRLS.

General nativity and race of father of pupil.	Number of pupils of each age.							Total.
	11.	12.	13.	14.	15.	16.	17.	
Native-born, White..............	....	2	4	5	4	1	....	16
Foreign-born:								
German......................	....	....	2	1	2	....	....	5
Irish.......................	....	1	3	1	....	....	....	5
Other races *a*...............	....	....	....	....	....	1	....	1
Total foreign-born..........	....	1	5	2	2	1	....	11
Grand total.................	....	3	9	7	6	2	....	27

a "Other races" includes races having less than 10 representatives in this city and pupils whose race is not reported.

TABLE 3.—*Race, sex, and age, by grade—Number of pupils of each age in each grade, by sex and by general nativity and race of father of pupil*—Continued.

SEVENTH GRADE—Continued.

TOTAL.

General nativity and race of father of pupil.	Number of pupils of each age.							Total.
	11.	12.	13.	14.	15.	16.	17.	
Native-born, White		4	8	8	4	1		25
Foreign-born:								
German	1	1	4	3	2			11
Irish		2	7	3				12
Other races a						1		1
Total foreign-born	1	3	11	6	2	1		24
Grand total	1	7	19	14	6	2		49

a "Other races" includes races having less than 10 representatives in this city and pupils whose race is not reported.

EIGHTH GRADE.

BOYS.

General nativity and race of father of pupil.	Number of pupils of each age.				Total.
	12.	13.	14.	15.	
Native-born, White	1	2	3		6
Foreign-born, Irish				1	1
Grand total	1	2	3	1	7

GIRLS.

General nativity and race of father of pupil.	Number of pupils of each age.				Total.
Native-born, White		4	6	1	11
Foreign-born:					
German	1	2	3		6
Irish			1		1
Other races a			1		1
Total foreign-born	1	2	5		8
Grand total	1	6	11	1	19

TOTAL.

General nativity and race of father of pupil.	Number of pupils of each age.				Total.
Native-born, White	1	6	9	1	17
Foreign-born:					
German	1	2	3		6
Irish			1	1	2
Other races a			1		1
Total foreign-born	1	2	5	1	9
Grand total	2	8	14	2	26

a "Other races" includes races having less than 10 representatives in this city and pupils whose race is not reported.

TABLE 3.—*Race, sex, and age, by grade—Number of pupils of each age in each grade, by sex and by general nativity and race of father of pupil—Continued.*

FIRST YEAR HIGH SCHOOL.

GIRLS.

General nativity and race of father of pupil.	Number of pupils of each age.					Total.
	13.	14.	15.	16.	17.	
Native-born, White		1	1	2	1	5
Foreign-born:						
German	2					2
Irish	1		1			2
Total foreign-born	3		1			4
Grand total	3	1	2	2	1	9

SECOND YEAR HIGH SCHOOL.

GIRLS.

General nativity and race of father of pupil.	Number of pupils of each age.					Total.
	14.	15.	16.	17.	18.	
Native-born, White	1	2	4		1	8
Foreign-born:						
German				1		1
Irish		2				2
Other races a		1				1
Total foreign-born		3		1		4
Grand total	1	5	4	1	1	12

a "Other races" includes races having less than 10 representatives in this city and pupils whose race is not reported.

THIRD YEAR HIGH SCHOOL.

GIRLS.

General nativity and race of father of pupil.	Number of pupils of each age.			Total.
	15.	16.	17.	
Native-born, White	1	1	1	3

FOURTH YEAR HIGH SCHOOL.

GIRLS.

General nativity and race of father of pupil.	Number of pupils of each age.	
	17.	Total.
Native-born, White	1	1
Foreign-born, Irish	1	1
Total	2	2

TABLE 4.—Race distribution in each grade—Percentages.

[This table shows in detail only races with 100 or more pupils reporting. The totals, however, are for all races.]

General nativity and race of father of pupil.	Kindergarten.	Elementary grades.									High school.					Grand total.
		1.	2.	3.	4.	5.	6.	7.	8.	Total.	First year.	Second year.	Third year.	Fourth year.	Total.	
Native-born:																
White	78.3	61.3	50.7	42.4	42.4	46.2	48.9	51.0	65.4	49.8	55.6	66.7	100.0	50.0	65.4	50.9
Negro	.0	.0	.0	.6	.0	.0	.0	.0	.0	.7	.0	.0	.0	.0	.0	.7
Total native-born	78.3	61.3	50.7	47.0	42.4	46.2	48.9	51.0	65.4	50.5	55.6	66.7	100.0	50.0	65.4	51.6
Foreign-born:																
German	13.0	23.6	36.3	15.2	34.4	29.2	34.4	22.4	23.1	27.7	22.2	8.3	.0	.0	11.5	27.0
Irish	8.7	6.3	8.9	17.2	14.6	20.8	12.2	24.5	7.7	13.4	22.2	16.7	.0	50.0	19.2	13.4
Other races	.0	8.9	4.1	20.5	8.6	3.8	4.4	2.0	3.8	8.4	.0	8.3	.0	.0	3.8	8.0
Total foreign-born	21.7	38.7	49.3	53.0	57.6	53.8	51.1	49.0	34.6	49.5	44.4	33.3	.0	50.0	34.6	48.4
Grand total	100.0	100.0	100.0	100.0	100.0	100.0	100.0	100.0	100.0	100.0	100.0	100.0	100.0	100.0	100.0	100.0

TABLE 5.—*Grade distribution of each race—Percentages.*

[This table shows in detail only races with 100 or more pupils reporting. The totals, however, are for all races.]

General nativity and race of father of pupil.	Kindergarten.	Elementary grades.									High school.					Grand total.
		1.	2.	3.	4.	5.	6.	7.	8.	Total.	First year.	Second year.	Third year.	Fourth year.	Total.	
Native-born:																
White..........	3.6	23.4	14.8	12.8	12.8	12.0	8.8	5.0	3.4	93.0	1.0	1.6	.6	.2	3.4	100.0
Negro..........	(a)	(a)	(a)	(a)	(a)	(a)	(a)	(a)	(a)	(a)	(a)	(a)	(a)	(a)	(a)	(a)
Total native-born....	3.6	23.1	14.6	14.0	12.6	11.8	8.7	4.9	3.4	93.1	1.0	1.6	.6	.2	3.4	100.0
Foreign-born:																
German........	1.1	17.0	20.0	8.7	19.6	14.3	11.7	4.2	2.3	97.7	.8	.4	.0	.0	1.1	100.0
Irish..........	1.5	9.1	9.8	19.7	16.7	20.5	8.3	9.1	1.5	94.7	1.5	1.5	.0	.8	3.8	100.0
Other races....	.0	21.5	7.6	39.2	16.5	6.3	5.1	1.3	1.3	98.7	.0	1.3	.0	.0	1.3	100.0
Total foreign-born....	1.1	15.5	15.1	16.8	18.3	14.7	9.7	5.0	1.9	97.1	.8	.8	.0	.2	1.9	100.0
Grand total.........	2.3	19.4	14.9	15.4	15.4	13.2	9.2	5.0	2.6	95.0	.9	1.2	.3	.2	2.6	100.0

a Not computed, owing to small number involved.

LOS ANGELES, CALIFORNIA.

545

LIST OF TABLES.

LOS ANGELES.

The general tables here presented for the city of Los Angeles concern the pupils in both the public and parochial schools of the city. At the same time that the information was gathered in regard to the pupils in the public schools certain data relating to the public school teachers were also obtained. The information here presented was gathered in Los Angeles by means of a record made by each grade teacher, giving the grade and the number of pupils of each sex, divided by ages and by the several racial groups to which they belonged, race being distinguished by that of the father of the pupil. The general introduction to this volume explains the method by which these class or grade records were summarized into general tables and gives an account of those general tables, and explains the purpose which they serve.[a]

PUBLIC SCHOOL PUPILS.

The whole number of pupils reported to the Immigration Commission as being in attendance on a given day early in December, 1908, was 33,422. In confining the enumeration to attendance on a single day the purpose was to avoid any difficulties which might arise from absent pupils. It was felt that attendance would give a more correct picture of actual conditions than enrollment. While this standpoint was undoubtedly correct, it is obvious that the date for the enumeration must be selected in advance, and that unforeseen circumstances or inclemency of the weather might reduce the attendance on that day below the general average. It seems well to point out these circumstances in view of the fact that the annual average attendance in the Los Angeles public schools for 1908–9 was 36,618. Compared with this figure the numbers reported to the Commission are somewhat smaller, constituting only 91.3 per cent of the former. How far this attendance might differ from that of the month of December is not known. The month of December is not always that of the best attendance, and in some cases its average falls below that of the year. Whatever combination of circumstances may have been at work to depress the number of pupils reported somewhat below the annual average, there is no reason to suppose that these circumstances worked with particular force on any age or other group of the school children, and that therefore the proportions which are found to exist among the children reported may be accepted as a truthful and representative picture of conditions generally prevailing within the school system.

The division of these 33,422 pupils by grades was as follows:

Kindergarten	2,129	Eighth grade	2,216
First grade	4,765	First year high school	1,794
Second grade	3,536	Second year high school	744
Third grade	3,748	Third year high school	461
Fourth grade	3,732	Fourth year high school	391
Fifth grade	3,552	Ungraded and special	279
Sixth grade	3,304		
Seventh grade	2,771	Total	33,422

[a] See pp. VII to XVII.

An examination of this table shows that the first grade is very large, more numerous than any of those that follow it. It shows, however, that grades 2 to 6 form a group in which the numbers are approximately equal, there being an average of about 3,500 for this group, with a variation in three cases of about 200 from the average. From this average of approximately 3,500 in this group of grades, there is a loss of 500 in the seventh and a further loss of like amount in the eighth grade. So that the eighth grade is therefore approximately about two-thirds as numerous as grades 2 to 6 on the average.

The distribution of pupils between the upper and lower schools is shown in condensed form in the following statement, where the elementary schools are divided into main groups, grades 1 to 4 designated as primary, and grades 5 to 8 designated as grammar grades:

Class of school.	Number.	Per cent.
Kindergarten	2,129	6.4
Primary, grades 1 to 4	15,781	47.6
Grammar, grades 5 to 8	11,843	35.7
High school	3,390	10.2
Total	33,143	100.0

This table shows that the grammar grades and the high school, constituting the last eight years of school life, have together just about as many pupils ·as the primary grades, which constitute the first four years of the regular school course. The number of pupils in the kindergarten is considerable.

Table 1 gives information also in regard to the distribution of pupils by age. Corresponding to the relatively large number of children in the kindergarten, we find in the schools a considerable number of children of 5 years of age and under, namely, 1,867. At 6 years of age there are 2,727 children, and in the ages immediately following there are about the same number, the maximum being found at 11 years of age, where 3,065 are recorded. At the age of 14, when in many school systems a rather conspicuous dropping off is noticed, the number of pupils in the Los Angeles schools is 2,984, showing little change from the figures observed between 8 and 13 years. With the fifteenth year, however, a diminution is observed, the number falling off about 1,000. At 16 there are still 1,300 pupils in the Los Angeles schools, and it is only after this year of age that the figures become much smaller.

Table 1 is so arranged as to give the view not only of the distribution by grades and the distribution by ages of the pupils in the schools as a whole, but also the distribution of the ages within each grade. This table offers, therefore, a considerable amount of detail, as a cursory examination shows that for each grade there is a wide variety of ages, and conversely for each age a considerable number of grades represented. A concise statement of the general tendencies of this table can only be shown by a resort to the concept of retardation familiar in current educational discussion. This assumes that for each grade there is an appropriate age and conversely for each age an appropriate grade. Hence the pupils of a given grade who are older than the age appropriate to that grade are considered as retarded and in the same way the pupils of a given age who have not attained the grade appropriate to their age can be considered as retarded pupils. The most familiar form of statement is that which shows in the several grades the number of pupils who are overage for their respective grades. The table following shows for the schools of Los Angeles the number of pupils in each grade and the number of pupils in each grade who are older than the standard for the grade.

Grade.	Number in grade.	Retarded pupils.		
		Age.	Number.	Per cent of all pupils.
First............	4,765	8 years and over.....	836	17.5
Second..........	3,536	9 years and over.....	982	27.8
Third...........	3,748	10 years and over.....	1,390	37.1
Fourth..........	3,732	11 years and over.....	1,673	44.8
Fifth............	3,552	12 years and over.....	1,723	48.5
Sixth............	3,304	13 years and over.....	1,658	50.2
Seventh.........	2,771	14 years and over.....	1,342	48.4
Eighth..........	2,216	15 years and over.....	941	42.5
Total........	27,624		10,545	38.2

The comparison of the whole number of overage pupils with the total attendance shows that 38.2 per cent of the pupils are retarded. The grades, however, show considerable difference. The first and second grades have ratios which are below the general average. But from the first to the sixth grade, when retardation reaches its maximum with 50.2 per cent of all the pupils, the proportion of retarded pupils steadily advances. In the seventh and eighth grades there is a slight falling off in the percentages, which remain, however, above the level of the general average.

The method of estimating retardation by a reference to the pupils of a given age instead of a given grade is exemplified in the following table for the pupils 10, 11, and 12 years of age:

Age.	Number of pupils of this age.	Normal grade.	Retarded, or below normal grade.	
			Number.	Per cent.
10 years............	3,038	4	1,048	34.5
11 years............	3,052	5	1,357	44.5
12 years............	3,221	6	1,668	51.7
Total............	9,311	....	4,073	43.7

At 10 years of age somewhat more than one-third of all the pupils are in the backward or retarded class. This proportion increases as the age of the pupils advances, and at 12 years more than one-half of them are retarded. The average for these three years is 43.7 per cent. It is calculated here in order that it may hereafter serve as a measure of comparison with corresponding calculations for smaller groups comprised in the school population. In some of these smaller groups the numbers for a given year are so small that in order to establish relationships it is necessary to consider the three years in combination.

The main object of the researches of the Immigration Commission was to establish whether, as respects participation in the public schools and the progress of children within them, there were any marked differences among the children of different racial origin. The bulk of the general tables is therefore devoted to an exhibit of school conditions with distinctions of the races of the pupils. Some of the more important results can be briefly noted.

The racial composition of the school population is revealed in the following table, which shows the pupils of native and of foreign born fathers, and among the latter those races separately which had a representation of at least 200 pupils in the schools of the city:

General nativity and race of father of pupil.	Pupils.		General nativity and race of father of pupil.	Pupils.	
	Number.	Per cent.		Number.	Per cent.
Native-born:			Foreign-born—Continued.		
White.....................	21,673	64.8	Irish.....................	498	1.5
Negro and Indian.........	1,069	3.2	Italian, North...........	448	1.3
			Italian, South...........	392	1.2
Total native-born.......	22,742	68.0	Mexican.................	642	1.9
			Russian.................	418	1.3
Foreign-born:			Scotch..................	329	1.0
Canadian (other than French).................	988	3.0	Spanish-American........	320	1.0
Danish..................	202	.6	Swedish.................	509	1.5
English.................	1,282	3.8	All other...............	1,318	3.9
French..................	388	1.2	Total foreign-born.......	10,680	32.0
German..................	2,025	6.1			
Hebrew, German..........	406	1.2	Grand total.............	33,422	100.0
Hebrew, Russian.........	515	1.5			

An examination of this table shows that 3.2 per cent of the pupils were of negro and Indian fathers and that the remainder were so divided that a little short of two-thirds of all the pupils were of native white fathers and a little less than one-third of all the pupils had foreign-born fathers. The table shows, moreover, that the latter element is remarkably varied, there being no less than 15 distinct races, with a representation of at least 200 pupils each. Among so many races none can be dominant. The most numerous are the German, with 6.1 per cent of the whole school population; the English, with 3.8 per cent; and the English Canadian, with 3 per cent. No other individual race has as many as 2 per cent of the entire population. At the end of the table there is a collective group designated as "All other." It forms only 3.9 per cent of the aggregate population, but it also comprises a very remarkable variety of races. They are: Arabian (1), Armenian (37), Bohemian and Moravian (33), Bosnian (2), Bulgarian (10), Canadian, French (100), Chinese (80), Croatian (4), Cuban (2), Dalmatian (7), Dutch (63), Egyptian (1), Filipino (3), Finnish (14), Flemish (7), Greek (10), Hebrew, Polish (66), Hebrew, Roumanian (70), Hebrew, Other (105), Herzegovinian (1), Hindu (2), Indian, South American (1), Japanese (114), Korean (5), Lithuanian (6), Magyar (58), Negro (5), Norwegian (120), Persian (1), Polish (58), Portuguese (27), Roumanian (25), Ruthenian (3), Scotch-Irish (6), Servian (1), Slovak (15), Slovenian (25), Spanish (45), Syrian (20), Turkish (8), Welsh (89), and West Indian (2).

The consideration of so many races by their distribution into the various grades would lead into endless detail. A summary is therefore given in the following table by grade groups:

General nativity and race of father of pupil.	Number of pupils.					Per cent.			
	Kinder-garten.	Pri-mary.	Gram-mar.	High.	Total.	Kinder-garten.	Pri-mary.	Gram-mar.	High.
Native-born:									
White..................	1,377	9,707	7,931	2,494	21,509	6.4	45.1	36.9	11.6
Negro and Indian.......	61	593	355	50	1,059	5.8	56.0	33.5	4.7
Total native-born.....	1,438	10,300	8,286	2,544	22,568	6.4	45.6	36.7	11.3
Foreign-born:									
Canadian (other than French)...............	43	407	412	116	978	4.4	41.6	42.1	11.9
Danish.................	4	91	98	9	202	2.0	45.0	48.5	4.5
English................	83	554	496	143	1,276	6.5	43.4	38.9	11.2
French.................	13	185	157	31	386	3.4	47.9	40.7	8.0
German................	106	910	796	194	2,006	5.3	45.4	39.7	9.7
Hebrew, German.......	17	187	167	32	403	4.2	46.4	41.4	7.9
Hebrew, Russian.......	71	262	165	13	511	13.9	51.3	32.3	2.5
Irish..................	16	212	194	70	492	3.3	43.1	39.4	14.2
Italian, North..........	55	270	108	6	439	12.5	61.5	24.6	1.4
Italian, South..........	35	281	67	6	389	9.0	72.2	17.2	1.5
Mexican...............	51	528	43	......	622	8.2	84.9	6.9	......
Russian................	41	350	25	1	417	9.8	83.9	6.0	.2
Scotch.................	13	105	155	55	328	4.0	32.0	47.3	16.8
Spanish-American.......	31	215	59	8	313	9.9	68.7	18.8	2.6
Swedish...............	29	244	199	34	506	5.7	48.2	39.3	6.7
All others.............	83	680	416	128	1,307	6.4	52.0	31.8	9.8
Total foreign-born.....	691	5,481	3,557	846	10,575	6.5	51.8	33.6	8.0
Grand total...........	2,129	15,781	11,843	3,390	33,143	6.4	47.6	35.7	10.2

The lower or primary grades 1 to 4 are distinguished from the upper or grammar grades 5 to 8. A consideration of this table shows that in the kindergarten there is about the same proportion of pupils of native as of foreign parentage. There are, however, two races—the Russian Hebrew and Italian—which have a conspicuously large representation in this group of schools. In the primary grades there is a larger representation of pupils of foreign parentage than of native parentage. Particular attention might be directed to the large proportions in these grades which are exhibited by the Mexicans, Russians, Italians, and Spanish Americans. The grammar grades present a picture which, so far as proportions are concerned, is usually converse of the primary grades. Here there is a larger proportion of children of native than of foreign parents, while those races which are conspicuous in the kindergarten and grammar grades have naturally a smaller representation in the grammar grades. Still more marked is the difference between native and foreign in the high school; of the native children 11.6 per cent are in the high school, of the foreign 8 per cent. Particularly weak is the representation in the high school of the Russians, Mexicans, Spanish Americans, Italians, and Russian Hebrews. Such a meager representation may be due to two things—either the children of a given race do not pursue their studies to an advanced point, or in exceptional cases the children of the high school age are distinctly less numerous than those of the ages appropriate to the lower schools. In considering races of recent migration the latter explanation must always be kept in mind. It will be seen, for instance, that while the Russian Hebrews have a small representation in the high school, in the schools in which they are more numerously represented they make good progress.

The following table presents for the same races a statement in two sections in regard to school progress in the elementary grades, as measured negatively by the percentage of retardation.

General nativity and race of father of pupil.	All elementary pupils.			Pupils 10, 11, and 12 years of age.		
	Number.	Retarded, overage.	Per cent retarded.	Number.	Retarded, undergrade.	Per cent retarded.
Native-born:						
White	17,638	6,228	35.3	5,897	2,319	39.3
Negro and Indian	948	561	59.2	309	218	70.6
Total native-born	18,586	6,789	36.5	6,206	2,537	40.9
Foreign-born:						
Canadian (other than French)	819	315	38.5	286	120	42.0
Danish	189	87	46.0	35	30	85.7
English	1,050	405	38.6	339	129	38.1
French	342	168	49.1	132	75	56.8
German	1,706	570	33.4	621	247	39.8
Hebrew, German	354	101	28.5	130	44	33.8
Hebrew, Russian	427	126	29.5	151	50	33.1
Irish	406	162	39.9	133	58	43.6
Italian, North	378	173	45.8	123	74	60.2
Italian, South	348	148	42.5	104	69	66.3
Mexican	571	377	66.0	198	161	81.3
Russian	375	190	50.7	122	108	88.5
Scotch	260	86	33.1	107	34	31.8
Spanish-American	274	175	63.9	83	70	84.3
Swedish	443	164	37.0	155	72	46.5
All others	1,096	509	46.4	386	195	50.5
Total foreign-born	9,038	3,756	41.6	3,105	1,536	49.5
Grand total	27,624	10,545	38.2	9,311	4,073	43.7

The first three columns in the table refer to all elementary pupils. They show that the retardation of the comparatively small number of negro and Indian pupils is very much greater than the general average. Comparing the children of native white parents and those of foreign-born parents, it is observed that the retardation for the former is not a little less than for the latter. Children of foreign parents are composed of many and very diverse races as already noted. Some of these races show a less retardation than the children of native parents. These are the Germans, the German Hebrews, the Russian Hebrews, and the Scotch. Contrasted with these races others, notably the Mexicans, the Russians, and Spanish Americans, show a degree of retardation which is high above the average for the foreign-born.

In the part of the table referring to the selected group of pupils of 10, 11, and 12 years of age, the rates of retardation observed are higher, but by reason of the age uniformity the comparison between the groups is perhaps more exact. Among children of native-born parents retardation is 39.3 per cent, among those of foreign-born parents 49.5 per cent. Races which show among these selected pupils less retardation than the children of native parents are the English, German Hebrews, Russian Hebrews, and Scotch. The Spanish Americans, Russians, and Mexicans show here also a high degree of retardation.

PUBLIC SCHOOL TEACHERS.

In the kindergarten and elementary grades of the public schools of Los Angeles 1,147 teachers were employed. Of these teachers 48 were men, 6 of whom were employed in the primary grades and the remainder in the grammar and special grades.

Divided by race, the teachers were as follows:

	Number.	Per cent.
Native white of native fathers	840	73.2
Native white of foreign fathers	245	21.4
Foreign white	62	5.4
Total	1,147	100.0

Nearly three-fourths of all the teachers were of native fathers. The group native of foreign fathers comprised 21.4 per cent of all the teachers, and among them the prominent races were the Germans with 5 per cent of all teachers, English with 3.8 per cent, Irish with 3.7 per cent, English Canadian with 2.4 per cent, and Scotch with 2.7 per cent. It will be noted that the teachers of English-speaking races form a large proportion of those having native birth and foreign parentage. Among the much smaller number of foreign birth, as well as parentage, about one-half were English Canadians. Classified by grades, the distribution of these teachers by racial groups was as follows:

	Kindergarten and primary.	Grammar and special.	Total.	Per cent in grammar grades.
Native white of native fathers	472	368	840	43.8
Native white of foreign fathers	154	91	245	37.1
Foreign white	40	22	62	35.5
Total	666	481	1,147	41.9

It appears on the average that some 42 per cent of the teachers were in the grammar and special grades. This percentage is slightly larger for the teachers of purely native antecedents and slightly less for those having foreign antecedents.

Of these teachers 1,141 reported length of service, as follows:

Under 5 years	114	From 25 to 29 years	34
From 5 to 9 years	351	30 years and over	14
From 10 to 14 years	334		
From 15 to 19 years	196	Total	1,141
From 20 to 24 years	98		

While the teachers of relatively short experience—that is, of less than ten years—are a considerable number, those of an experience of from ten to twenty years are quite a little more numerous. On the other hand, the group of teachers having an experience of twenty years or more is about one-eighth of the total number of teachers.

Length of service is summarized by race in the following statement:

Race and nativity of teachers.	Length of service, in years.			
	Under 10.	10 to 19.	20 and over.	Total.
Native white of native fathers...................................	348	383	109	840
Native white of foreign fathers..................................	90	118	32	240
Foreign white...	27	29	5	61
Total...	465	530	146	1,141
Percentages: All teachers..	40.8	46.5	12.8	100.0

It will be noted that for each racial group the largest number of teachers is found in the group having from ten to nineteen years' experience, approximately the same proportion being observed in each racial group.

PUPILS OF THE PAROCHIAL SCHOOLS.

Through the courtesy of the authorities of the Roman Catholic Church, information was collected in Los Angeles concerning 2,200 pupils in attendance in the parochial schools in December, 1908. The official directory of the Roman Catholic Church gives the total enrollment of pupils in the parochial schools as 2,211, practically the same number as were recorded for the statistics of the Commission. The division of pupils in the grades is as follows:

Kindergarten......................	38	Seventh grade......................	278
First grade.........................	399	Eighth grade.......................	126
Second grade......................	229	First year high school.............	41
Third grade........................	283	Second year high school..........	8
Fourth grade.......................	181	Mixed..............................	149
Fifth grade.........................	263		
Sixth grade........................	205	Total......................	2,200

In common with school systems generally, the first grade is considerably more numerous than those that follow. From the second to the seventh the grades are approximately equal in number, except that the fourth is small in comparison with the others. There is, however, a marked distinction between the seventh and the eighth grades, the number in the latter sinking to one-half that found in the former.

If the elementary grades be divided into two groups we find that in round numbers 55 per cent of the pupils are below and 45 above the fifth grade.

The ages of pupils in the parochial schools as given in Table 1 show from the sixth year of age, when there are 157 pupils, an increasing number until the tenth year is reached, when there are 320 pupils. The number then diminishes, reaching 202 at the age of 13. Compared with the number at the age 13, that at the age of 14 years (129) is well maintained, but at the age of 15 there is a drop to 107.

Comparing the ages of the pupils with the grades in which they are found, we find for all pupils in the parochial schools the following results, by grades:

Class of school.	Number.	Per cent.
Kindergarten	38	1.9
Grades 1 to 4	1,092	53.2
Grades 5 to 8	872	42.5
High school	49	2.3
Total	2,051	100.0

A statement of the retardation of pupils, by grades, showing in each grade the number of retarded pupils and the proportion which this number bears to the whole number of pupils, follows:

Grade.	Number in grade.	Retarded pupils.		
		Age.	Number.	Per cent of all pupils.
First	399	8 years and over	87	21.8
Second	229	9 years and over	137	59.8
Third	283	10 years and over	154	54.4
Fourth	181	11 years and over	96	53.0
Fifth	263	12 years and over	118	44.9
Sixth	205	13 years and over	106	51.7
Seventh	278	14 years and over	94	33.8
Eighth	126	15 years and over	55	43.7
Total	1,964		847	43.1

The retarded pupils are 43.1 per cent of the whole number of pupils. The figures for the grades show considerable variation, the maximum, which singularly enough occurs in the second grade, being 59.8.

A computation for the special class of pupils of 10 to 12 years of age is presented in the table following:

Age.	Number of pupils of this age.	Normal grade.	Retarded, or below normal grade.	
			Number.	Per cent.
10 years	298	4	128	43.0
11 years	220	5	83	37.7
12 years	196	6	116	59.2
Total	714		327	45.8

Among these pupils, who are, of course, somewhat older than the average, there is a somewhat greater percentage of retardation, the average for the three years being 45.8.

A summary of the children in the parochial schools, distributed by race, is given in the following table:

General nativity and race of father of pupil.	Pupils.	
	Number.	Per cent.
Native-born:		
White	1,112	50.5
Negro	7	.3
Total native-born	1,119	50.9
Foreign-born:		
German	257	11.7
Irish	253	11.5
All others	571	25.9
Total foreign-born	1,081	49.1
Grand total	2,200	100.0

It will be noted that practically one-half of the children in the parochial schools have native-born fathers and one-half have foreign parents. Very nearly one-fourth of all the pupils consist of the two races, German and Irish, in almost equal numbers. A remaining quarter of the pupils is made up of a large number of miscellaneous races, as follows: Bohemian and Moravian (12), Bulgarian (2), Canadian, French (33), Canadian, other than French (45), Chinese (2), Croatian (1), Dalmatian (40), Danish (2), Dutch (6), English (33), Finnish (2), Flemish (1), French (87), Hebrew, not specified (9), Italian, North (85), Italian, South (59), Magyar (3), Mexican (68), Polish (12), Portuguese (1), Roumanian (9), Russian (1), Scotch (9), Slovak (1), Slovenian (1), Spanish (1), Spanish-American (35), Swedish (4), Syrian (3), and Welsh (4).

PUBLIC AND PAROCHIAL SCHOOL PUPILS COMBINED.

The combination of the figures which have heretofore been presented for public and parochial schools separately gives a picture of the distribution of races among the school children of the community as a whole, and at the same time affords certain interesting contrasts between the two school systems.

General nativity and race of father of pupil.	Pupils by schools.			Per cent of all pupils.
	Public schools.	Parochial schools.	Total.	
Native-born:				
White	21,673	1,112	22,785	64.0
Negro and Indian	1,069	7	1,076	3.0
Total native-born	22,742	1,119	23,861	67.0
Foreign-born:				
Canadian (other than French)	988	45	1,033	2.9
Danish	202	2	204	.6
English	1,282	33	1,315	3.7
French	388	87	475	1.3
German	2,025	257	2,282	6.4
Hebrew, German	406		406	1.1
Hebrew, Russian	515		515	1.4
Irish	498	253	751	2.1
Italian, North	448	85	533	1.5
Italian, South	392	59	451	1.3
Mexican	642	68	710	2.0
Russian	418	1	419	1.2
Scotch	329	9	338	1.0
Spanish-American	320	35	355	1.0
Swedish	509	4	513	1.4
All others	1,318	143	1,461	4.1
Total foreign-born	10,680	1,081	11,761	33.0
Grand total	33,422	2,200	35,622	100.0

In round numbers two-thirds of the children are of native origin and one-third are of foreign origin. Among the latter are represented various races, few of which stand out conspicuously. The most important is the German, which has 6.4 per cent of the entire number of school children. In the aggregate the parochial system is very much smaller than the public school system, yet it contains a not inconsiderable proportion of at least one of the distinct races, the Irish.

GENERAL TABLES.

PUBLIC SCHOOL PUPILS: GENERAL INVESTIGATION.

TABLE **1.**—*Grade and age—Number of pupils of each age in each grade, by sex.*

BOYS.

Age.	Kinder-garten.	Elementary grades.								
		1.	2.	3.	4.	5.	6.	7.	8.	Total.
4 years	143									
5 years	722	2								2
6 years	139	1,237	24							1,261
7 years		835	524	46	2					1,407
8 years		328	726	418	50	1	1			1,524
9 years		95	355	622	336	36	1			1,445
10 years		49	125	407	569	320	31	3	3	1,507
11 years		19	52	216	486	513	253	41	2	1,582
12 years		8	34	107	287	504	472	243	33	1,688
13 years		4	11	44	130	293	436	375	186	1,479
14 years		2	9	25	51	127	306	430	381	1,331
15 years		1	3	9	12	33	97	205	276	636
16 years				2	7	5	15	41	139	209
17 years				1	3	5	4	5	28	46
18 years				2	1	1	3	4	6	17
19 years		1		2		2		1	1	7
20 years or over						2	1			3
Total	1,004	2,581	1,863	1,901	1,934	1,842	1,620	1,348	1,055	14,144

Age.	High school.					Un-graded and special schools.	Grand total.
	First year.	Second year.	Third year.	Fourth year.	Total.		
4 years						1	144
5 years						2	726
6 years						2	1,402
7 years						7	1,414
8 years						3	1,527
9 years						7	1,452
10 years						7	1,514
11 years						5	1,587
12 years						21	1,709
13 years	19		1		20	23	1,522
14 years	153	14	3		170	43	1,544
15 years	246	49	13		308	32	976
16 years	265	95	38	6	404	24	637
17 years	159	123	49	44	375	4	425
18 years	68	50	53	48	219	1	237
19 years	18	22	29	35	104	1	112
20 years or over	8	4	12	32	56	3	62
Total	936	357	198	165	1,656	186	16,990

TABLE 1.—*Grade and age—Number of pupils of each age in each grade, by sex*—Contd.

GIRLS.

Age.	Kindergarten.	Elementary grades.								
		1.	2.	3.	4.	5.	6.	7.	8.	Total.
4 years	152									
5 years	842	1								1
6 years	131	1,153	39							1,192
7 years		701	624	59	1					1,385
8 years		206	617	584	54	1				1,462
9 years		52	231	629	426	45				1,383
10 years		35	101	331	621	383	57	2	1	1,531
11 years		13	28	134	409	530	321	31	1	1,531
12 years		12	18	72	188	438	510	265	4	1,470
13 years		6	9	23	66	204	453	469	30	1,533
14 years		4	5	9	26	85	254	424	211	1,441
15 years		1		5	6	21	70	187	424	1,231
16 years			1	1	1	3	15	40	324	614
17 years							3	3	140	201
18 years							1	1	24	30
19 years								1	3	5
20 years or over									1	1
Total	1,125	2,184	1,673	1,847	1,798	1,710	1,684	1,423	1,161	13,480

Age.	High school.					Ungraded and special schools.	Grand total.
	First year.	Second year.	Third year.	Fourth year.	Total.		
4 years							152
5 years						2	845
6 years						2	1,325
7 years						2	1,387
8 years						2	1,464
9 years						5	1,388
10 years						1	1,532
11 years						7	1,477
12 years						5	1,538
13 years	25		1		26	5	1,472
14 years	181	11	4		196	13	1,440
15 years	269	86	19	2	376	25	1,015
16 years	230	134	70	11	445	17	663
17 years	118	96	106	81	401	7	438
18 years	27	43	44	77	191		196
19 years	6	11	13	39	69		70
20 years or over	2	6	6	16	30		30
Total	858	387	263	226	1,734	93	16,432

TABLE 1.—*Grade and age—Number of pupils of each age in each grade, by sex*—Contd.

TOTAL.

Age.	Kinder-garten.	Elementary grades.								
		1.	2.	3.	4.	5.	6.	7.	8.	Total.
4 years	295									
5 years	1,564	3								3
6 years	270	2,390	63							2,453
7 years		1,536	1,148	105	3					2,792
8 years		534	1,343	1,002	104	2	1			2,986
9 years		147	586	1,251	762	81	1			2,828
10 years		84	226	738	1,190	703	88	5	4	3,038
11 years		32	80	350	895	1,043	574	72	6	3,052
12 years		20	52	179	475	942	982	508	63	3,221
13 years		10	20	67	196	497	889	844	397	2,920
14 years		6	14	34	77	212	560	854	805	2,562
15 years		2	3	14	18	54	167	392	600	1,250
16 years			1	3	8	8	30	81	279	410
17 years				1	3	5	7	8	52	76
18 years				2	1	1	4	5	9	22
19 years		1		2		2		2	1	8
20 years or over						2	1			3
Total	2,129	4,765	3,536	3,748	3,732	3,552	3,304	2,771	2,216	27,624

Age.	High school.					Un-graded and special schools.	Grand total.
	First year.	Second year.	Third year.	Fourth year.	Total.		
4 years						1	296
5 years						4	1,571
6 years						4	2,727
7 years						9	2,801
8 years						5	2,991
9 years						12	2,840
10 years						8	3,046
11 years						12	3,064
12 years						26	3,247
13 years	44		2		46	28	2,994
14 years	334	25	7		366	56	2,984
15 years	515	135	32	2	684	57	1,991
16 years	495	229	108	17	849	41	1,300
17 years	277	219	155	125	776	11	863
18 years	95	93	97	125	410	1	433
19 years	24	33	42	74	173	1	182
20 years or over	10	10	18	48	86	3	92
Total	1,794	744	461	391	3,390	279	33,422

TABLE 2.—*Race, sex, and grade—Number of pupils of each sex in each grade, by general nativity and race of father of pupil.*

General nativity and race of father of pupil	Elementary grades.										High school.					Un-graded and special schools.	Grand total.
	Kindergarten.	1.	2.	3.	4.	5.	6.	7.	8.	Total.	First year.	Second year.	Third year.	Fourth year.	Total.		
Native-born:																	
White—																	
Male	646	1,511	1,177	1,178	1,223	1,177	1,097	932	741	9,036	700	261	146	108	1,215	108	11,005
Female	731	1,280	1,048	1,139	1,151	1,076	1,125	1,002	781	8,602	617	286	202	174	1,279	56	10,668
Total	1,377	2,791	2,225	2,317	2,374	2,253	2,222	1,934	1,522	17,638	1,317	547	348	282	2,494	164	21,673
Negro—																	
Male	26	97	64	65	72	66	42	26	14	446	11	2		1	14	9	495
Female	34	77	61	75	79	68	62	35	38	495	22	8	3	2	35		564
Total	60	174	125	140	151	134	104	61	52	941	33	10	3	3	49	9	1,059
Indian—																	
Male	1				1			1		2	1				1	1	5
Female					2				3	5							5
Total	1				3			1	3	7	1				1	1	10
Total native-born:																	
Male	673	1,608	1,241	1,243	1,296	1,243	1,139	959	755	9,484	712	263	146	109	1,230	118	11,505
Female	765	1,357	1,109	1,214	1,232	1,144	1,187	1,037	822	9,102	639	294	205	176	1,314	56	11,237
Total	1,438	2,965	2,350	2,457	2,528	2,387	2,326	1,996	1,577	18,586	1,351	557	351	285	2,544	174	22,742
Foreign-born:																	
Armenian—																	
Male	1	3	3	3	4					13							14
Female	5	4	4	6	1	1				16		2			2		23
Total	6	7	7	9	5	1				29		2			2		37
Bohemian and Moravian—																	
Male	1	3		1	3	4		3	1	15	1				1		17
Female		4		5	2	3			2	16							16
Total	1	7		6	5	7		3	3	31	1				1		33
Bulgarian—																	
Male	1				2					2							3
Female				2	3				2	7							7
Total	1			2	5				2	9							10
Canadian, French—																	
Male	5	7	3	4	6	7	6	3	5	41	3	2			5		51
Female	3	3	7	4	4	8	6	5	2	39	3	3		1	7		49
Total	8	10	10	8	10	15	12	8	7	80	6	5		1	12		100
Canadian, Other—																	
Male	25	57	44	57	63	58	53	49	50	431	24	23	7	5	59	7	522
Female	18	49	43	47	47	58	48	48	48	388	29	12	7	9	57	3	466
Total	43	106	87	104	110	116	101	97	98	819	53	35	14	14	116	10	988

Chinese—																	
Male	3	5	7	3	9	4	5	4		37	3		2	1	6	1	47
Female	7	5	4	6	2	3		1	1	22	1				1	3	33
Total	10	10	11	9	11	7	5	5	1	59	4		2	1	7	4	80
Danish—																	
Male	2	19	14	5	11	20	9	10	8	96	2	1			3		101
Female	2	7	7	17	11	15	14	12	10	93	3	2	1		6		101
Total	4	26	21	22	22	35	23	22	18	189	5	3	1		9		202
Dutch—																	
Male	1	5	5	6	3	1	3	3		26		2			2		29
Female	2	2	7	5	1	4	1	3	5	28	1	1		1	3	1	34
Total	3	7	12	11	4	5	4	6	5	54	1	3		1	5	1	63
English—																	
Male	40	93	54	72	75	70	69	54	41	528	39	7	10	10	66	4	638
Female	43	64	52	63	81	64	79	67	52	522	47	13	9	8	77	2	644
Total	83	157	106	135	156	134	148	121	93	1,050	86	20	19	18	143	6	1,282
Finnish—																	
Male	1	1		1	2					4							5
Female		2	1	1	2	1		1		8	1				1		9
Total	1	3	1	2	4	1		1		12	1				1		14
French—																	
Male	5	32	18	23	16	25	24	11	12	161	8	2	1	2	13		179
Female	8	26	20	28	22	36	16	16	17	181	10	3	3	2	18	2	209
Total	13	58	38	51	38	61	40	27	29	342	18	5	4	4	31	2	388
German—																	
Male	48	135	105	103	128	128	106	85	60	850	44	15	12	18	89	16	1,003
Female	58	103	76	122	138	132	119	87	79	856	57	19	15	14	105	3	1,022
Total	106	238	181	225	266	260	225	172	139	1,706	101	34	27	32	194	19	2,025
Greek—																	
Male		1	2	1		1				5							5
Female			2	1				1		4		1			1		5
Total		1	4	2		1		1		9		1			1		10
Hebrew, German—																	
Male	10	20	21	25	27	14	26	17	16	166	8	5	3	1	17	2	195
Female	7	23	24	15	32	29	29	20	16	188	7	5	1	2	15	1	211
Total	17	43	45	40	59	43	55	37	32	354	15	10	4	3	32	3	406
Hebrew, Polish—																	
Male		4		4	3	5	5	4	4	29	2	1			3		32
Female	2	5	5	8		7	5	1	1	32							34
Total	2	9	5	12	3	12	10	5	5	61	2	1			3		66
Hebrew, Roumanian—																	
Male		9	4	5	6	4	2	3		33	1	1			2	1	36
Female	2	5	5	7	3	3	3	1	2	29		1	1	1	3		34
Total	2	14	9	12	9	7	5	4	2	62	1	2	1	1	5	1	70
Hebrew, Russian—																	
Male	38	36	24	42	28	37	28	13	13	221	2	2	1	1	6	3	268
Female	33	49	26	29	28	30	19	15	10	206	3	3		1	7	1	247
Total	71	85	50	71	56	67	47	28	23	427	5	5	1	2	13	4	515
Hebrew, Other—																	
Male	8	5	5	5	5	6	4	5	6	41			2		2	1	52
Female	2	10	5	6	8	4	5	8	2	48	3				3		53
Total	10	15	10	11	13	10	9	13	8	89	3		2		5	1	105

TABLE 2.—Race, age, and grade—Number of pupils of each sex in each grade, by general nativity and race of father of pupil—Continued.

General nativity and race of father of pupil	Kindergarten	Elementary grades									High school					Ungraded and special schools	Grand total
		1.	2.	3.	4.	5.	6.	7.	8.	Total.	First year.	Second year.	Third year.	Fourth year.	Total.		
Foreign-born—Continued.																	
Irish—																	
Male	9	27	25	30	31	32	25	25	14	209	16	7	2	6	31	4	253
Female	7	19	22	28	30	38	27	16	17	197	14	13	6	6	39	2	245
Total	16	46	47	58	61	70	52	41	31	406	30	20	8	12	70	6	498
Italian, North—																	
Male	25	58	34	36	29	7	20	18	2	204	3				4	4	237
Female	30	33	24	35	21	22	25	10	4	174	2				2	5	211
Total	55	91	58	71	50	29	45	28	6	378	5				6	9	448
Italian, South—																	
Male	19	69	37	36	26	23	10	3	4	208	1				1	3	231
Female	16	42	27	23	21	14	8	3	2	140	4		1		5		161
Total	35	111	64	59	47	37	18	6	6	348	5		1		6	3	392
Japanese—																	
Male	1	9	4	12	8	9	6	4	6	58	12	7	7	3	29		88
Female	1	9	4	5	4		1		1	24	1				1		26
Total	2	18	8	17	12	9	7	4	7	82	13	7	7	3	30		114
Magyar—																	
Male	4	11	2	2	5		1	1	2	24	2				2		30
Female	2	10	1	1	3	7	1		1	25					1		28
Total	6	21	3	3	8	7	2	1	3	49	2				3		58
Mexican—																	
Male	19	158	45	59	33	19	6	5	2	327						12	358
Female	32	137	41	40	15	7	4	4	2	244						8	284
Total	51	295	86	99	48	26	10	9	4	571						20	642
Norwegian—																	
Male	1	13	8	5	9	8	4	6	8	61	2	1			3		65
Female	8	6	7	7	5	6	4	4	6	43	2	1	1		3		55
Total	9	19	15	12	14	14	8	10	14	104	4	2	1		6		120
Polish—																	
Male	4	7		5	4	3		1	3	25	2				2		31
Female	1	7	3	5			1		2	26							27
Total	5	14	3	10	4	3	1	1	5	51	2				2		58
Portuguese—																	
Male		4	2	4		1	1	2	1	15							15
Female		1	2	6		1		2		12							12
Total		5	4	10		2	1	4	1	27							27
Roumanian—																	
Male	2	2	1	1	1	1	1	3	2	10	1				1		12
Female	3	1	2	1		1		2	2	9							13
Total	5	3	3	2	1	2	1	5		19	1				1		25

Race and sex	1	2	3	4	5	6	7	8	9	10	11	12	13	14	15	16	Total
Russian— Male	22	72	62	32	8	5	3	4	—	186	—	—	—	4	27	—	208
Female	19	97	56	21	2	5	3	4	1	189	1	1	—	2	28	1	210
Total	41	169	118	53	10	10	6	8	1	375	1	1	—	6	55	1	418
Scotch— Male	4	15	11	11	19	34	18	21	9	138	14	7	2	—	1	1	170
Female	9	8	7	20	14	16	15	21	21	122	17	4	5	—	—	—	159
Total	13	23	18	31	33	50	33	42	30	260	31	11	7	—	1	1	329
Slovak— Male	—	—	—	—	—	1	—	—	1	2	1	—	—	—	—	—	3
Female	—	—	5	—	2	2	—	—	—	11	—	—	—	—	—	—	12
Total	—	—	5	—	2	3	—	—	1	13	1	—	—	—	—	—	15
Slovenian— Male	1	1	2	1	2	1	2	1	3	15	—	1	—	—	1	—	16
Female	—	—	—	—	1	2	1	—	1	9	—	—	1	—	—	—	9
Total	1	1	2	1	3	3	3	1	4	24	—	1	1	—	1	—	25
Spanish— Male	1	2	3	2	4	1	1	1	5	22	1	—	—	4	—	—	24
Female	—	1	2	3	1	3	2	1	2	21	4	—	—	2	—	—	21
Total	1	3	5	5	5	4	3	2	7	43	5	—	—	6	—	—	45
Spanish-American— Male	1	2	3	5	20	14	9	5	3	152	13	6	—	—	1	—	173
Female	—	6	2	4	11	8	13	6	1	122	3	4	1	—	—	—	147
Total	1	8	5	9	31	22	22	11	4	274	16	10	1	—	1	—	320
Swedish— Male	14	50	35	14	25	31	26	24	15	211	7	13	—	4	2	—	251
Female	17	32	35	18	36	23	36	25	19	232	2	3	2	—	6	—	258
Total	31	82	70	32	61	54	62	49	34	443	9	16	2	4	8	—	509
Syrian— Male	16	27	30	33	1	2	—	—	2	11	—	—	—	1	—	—	11
Female	13	36	22	35	—	—	—	—	—	7	—	—	—	1	—	—	9
Total	29	63	52	68	1	2	—	—	2	18	—	—	—	2	—	—	20
Welsh— Male	2	1	5	1	7	10	3	1	2	32	12	2	2	—	23	—	44
Female	—	5	5	1	—	6	4	3	5	36	1	2	2	—	11	—	45
Total	2	6	10	2	7	16	7	4	7	68	13	4	4	—	34	—	89
Other races a— Male	2	10	5	9	10	8	5	3	1	51	—	1	4	—	12	13	68
Female	2	11	10	8	7	4	8	1	3	52	—	4	—	—	7	9	66
Total	4	21	15	17	17	12	13	4	4	103	—	5	4	—	19	22	134
Total foreign-born— Male	331	973	622	658	638	599	481	389	300	4,660	224	94	52	56	426	68	5,485
Female	360	827	564	633	566	566	497	386	339	4,378	219	93	58	50	420	37	5,195
Total	691	1,800	1,186	1,291	1,204	1,165	978	775	639	9,038	443	187	110	106	846	105	10,680
Grand total— Male	1,004	2,581	1,863	1,901	1,934	1,842	1,620	1,348	1,055	14,144	936	357	198	165	1,656	186	16,990
Female	1,125	2,184	1,673	1,847	1,798	1,710	1,684	1,423	1,161	13,480	858	387	263	226	1,734	93	16,432
Total	2,129	4,765	3,536	3,748	3,732	3,552	3,304	2,771	2,216	27,624	1,794	744	461	391	3,390	279	33,422

a "Other races" includes 1 Arabian, 2 Bosnian, 4 Croatian, 2 Cuban, 7 Dalmatian, 1 Egyptian, 3 Filipino, 7 Flemish, 1 Herzegovinian, 2 Hindu, 5 Korean, 6 Lithuanian, 5 Negro, 1 Persian, 3 Ruthenian, 6 Scotch-Irish, 1 Servian, 1 South American Indian, 8 Turkish, 2 West Indian, and 66 race not specified.

TABLE 3.—*Race, sex, and age, by grade—Number of pupils of each age in each grade, by sex and by general nativity and race of father of pupil.*

KINDERGARTEN.

BOYS.

General nativity and race of father of pupil.	Number of pupils of each age.			Total.
	4.	5.	6.	
Native-born:				
White.........	84	477	85	646
Negro.........	5	14	7	26
Indian.........		1		1
Total native-born.........	89	492	92	673
Foreign-born:				
Armenian.........	1			1
Bohemian and Moravian.........		1		1
Canadian, French.........	2	3		5
Canadian, Other.........	3	16	6	25
Chinese.........		3		3
Danish.........			2	2
Dutch.........		1		1
English.........	11	23	6	40
Finnish.........			1	1
French.........		5		5
German.........	5	36	7	48
Hebrew, German.........	2	7	1	10
Hebrew, Russian.........	2	30	6	38
Hebrew, Other.........	1	6	1	8
Irish.........		8	1	9
Italian, North.........	3	17	5	25
Italian, South.........	2	15	2	19
Japanese.........		1		1
Magyar.........	1	3		4
Mexican.........	5	13	1	19
Norwegian.........		1		1
Polish.........		3	1	4
Roumanian.........	1		1	2
Russian.........	7	15		22
Scotch.........		3	1	4
Slovenian.........		1		1
Spanish-American.........	6	7	1	14
Spanish.........		1		1
Swedish.........	2	10	4	16
Other races a.........		1		1
Total foreign-born.........	54	230	47	331
Grand total.........	143	722	139	1,004

a "Other races" includes races having less than 10 representatives in this city and pupils whose race is not reported.

TABLE 3.—*Race, sex, and age, by grade—Number of pupils of each age in each grade, by sex and by general nativity and race of father of pupil*—Continued.

KINDERGARTEN—Continued.

GIRLS.

General nativity and race of father of pupil.	Number of pupils of each age.			Total.
	4.	5.	6.	
Native-born:				
White..................................	97	542	92	731
Negro..................................	7	24	3	34
Total native-born....................	104	566	95	765
Foreign-born:				
Armenian..............................		4	1	5
Canadian, French......................		3		3
Canadian, Other.......................	3	14	1	18
Chinese...............................	1	5	1	7
Danish................................		2		2
Dutch.................................		2		2
English...............................	6	33	4	43
French................................	1	5	2	8
German................................	8	45	5	58
Hebrew, German........................	1	5	1	7
Hebrew, Polish........................	1	1		2
Hebrew, Roumanian.....................		2		2
Hebrew, Russian.......................	1	28	4	33
Hebrew, Other.........................	1		1	2
Irish.................................		6	1	7
Italian, North........................	5	25		30
Italian, South........................	6	8	2	16
Japanese..............................		1		1
Magyar................................	1	1		2
Mexican...............................	1	30	1	32
Norwegian.............................	2	6		8
Polish................................			1	1
Roumanian.............................		2	1	3
Russian...............................	5	13	1	19
Scotch................................	2	6	1	9
Slovak................................		1		1
Spanish-American......................	1	11	5	17
Swedish...............................	1	10	2	13
Syrian................................		2		2
Welsh.................................		2		2
Other races a.........................	1	3	1	5
Total foreign-born...................	48	276	36	360
Grand total..........................	152	842	131	1,125

a "Other races" includes races having less than 10 representatives in this city and pupils whose race is not reported.

TABLE 3.—*Race, sex, and age, by grade—Number of pupils of each age in each grade,
by sex and by general nativity and race of father of pupil*—Continued.

KINDERGARTEN.

TOTAL.

General nativity and race of father of pupil.	Number of pupils of each age.			Total.
	4.	5.	6.	
Native-born:				
White	181	1,019	177	1,377
Negro	12	38	10	60
Indian		1		1
Total native-born	193	1,058	187	1,438
Foreign-born:				
Armenian	1	4	1	6
Bohemian and Moravian		1		1
Canadian, French	2	6		8
Canadian, Other	6	30	7	43
Chinese	1	8	1	10
Danish		2	2	4
Dutch		3		3
English	17	56	10	83
Finnish			1	1
French	1	10	2	13
German	13	81	12	106
Hebrew, German	3	12	2	17
Hebrew, Polish	1	1		2
Hebrew, Roumanian		2		2
Hebrew, Russian	3	58	10	71
Hebrew, Other	2	6	2	10
Irish		14	2	16
Italian, North	8	42	5	55
Italian, South	8	23	4	35
Japanese		2		2
Magyar	2	4		6
Mexican	6	43	2	51
Norwegian	2	7		9
Polish		3	2	5
Roumanian	1	2	2	5
Russian	12	28	1	41
Scotch	2	9	2	13
Slovak		1		1
Slovenian		1		1
Spanish-American	7	18	6	31
Spanish		1		1
Swedish	3	20	6	29
Syrian		2		2
Welsh		2		2
Other races a	1	4	1	6
Total foreign-born	102	506	83	691
Grand total	295	1,564	270	2,129

a "Other races" includes races having less than 10 representatives in this city and pupils whose race is not reported.

TABLE **3.**—*Race, sex, and age, by grade—Number of pupils of each age in each grade, by sex and by general nativity and race of father of pupil*—Continued.

FIRST GRADE.

BOYS.

General nativity and race of father of pupil.	Number of pupils of each age.															Total.
	5.	6.	7.	8.	9.	10.	11.	12.	13.	14.	15.	16.	17.	18.	19.	
Native-born:																
White	2	754	523	186	31	12	....	1	1	...	1	...	...	...	...	1,511
Negro	...	42	30	15	5	5	....	...	...	...	...	...	...	...	...	97
Total native-born	2	796	553	201	36	17	....	1	1	...	1	...	...	...	...	1,608
Foreign-born:																
Armenian	...	3	...	...	...	...	...	...	...	...	...	...	...	...	...	3
Bohemian and Moravian	...	3	...	...	...	...	...	...	...	...	...	...	...	...	...	3
Canadian, French	...	3	2	1	...	...	1	...	...	...	...	...	...	...	...	7
Canadian, Other	...	37	11	7	1	1	...	...	...	...	...	...	...	...	...	57
Chinese	...	2	...	2	...	...	1	...	...	...	...	...	...	...	...	5
Danish	...	10	8	1	...	...	...	...	...	...	...	...	...	...	...	19
Dutch	...	3	1	1	...	...	...	...	...	...	...	...	...	...	...	5
English	...	39	40	9	3	2	...	...	...	...	...	...	...	...	...	93
Finnish	...	1	...	...	...	...	...	...	...	...	...	...	...	...	...	1
French	...	15	8	3	4	2	...	...	...	...	...	...	...	...	...	32
German	...	72	47	13	3	...	...	...	...	...	...	...	...	...	...	135
Greek	...	1	...	...	...	...	...	...	...	...	...	...	...	...	...	1
Hebrew, German	...	12	6	1	1	...	...	...	...	...	...	...	...	...	...	20
Hebrew, Polish	...	2	2	...	...	...	...	...	...	...	...	...	...	...	...	4
Hebrew, Roumanian	...	8	1	...	...	...	...	...	...	...	...	...	...	...	...	9
Hebrew, Russian	...	20	11	3	1	...	...	1	...	...	...	...	...	...	...	36
Hebrew, Other	...	3	1	...	1	...	...	...	...	...	...	...	...	...	...	5
Irish	...	18	7	1	1	...	...	...	...	...	...	...	...	...	...	27
Italian, North	...	23	20	11	1	3	...	...	...	...	...	...	...	...	...	58
Italian, South	...	37	19	5	6	2	...	...	...	...	...	...	...	...	...	69
Japanese	...	3	3	1	1	...	...	...	...	...	...	...	...	...	1	9
Magyar	...	3	5	1	1	1	...	...	...	...	...	...	...	...	...	11
Mexican	...	37	30	37	23	11	15	3	1	1	...	...	...	...	...	158
Norwegian	...	6	4	1	1	...	...	...	1	...	...	...	...	...	...	13
Polish	...	3	2	1	...	1	...	...	...	...	...	...	...	...	...	7
Portuguese	...	1	1	...	...	...	...	...	...	...	...	...	...	...	...	2
Roumanian	...	...	2	...	...	...	...	...	...	...	...	...	...	...	...	2
Russian	...	35	17	11	5	2	...	1	1	...	...	...	...	...	...	72
Scotch	...	3	9	3	...	...	...	...	...	...	...	...	...	...	...	15
Slovenian	...	1	1	...	...	...	...	...	...	...	...	...	...	...	...	2
Spanish	...	...	1	...	...	...	1	...	...	...	...	...	...	...	...	2
Spanish-American	...	15	11	11	6	5	2	1	1	...	...	...	...	...	...	52
Swedish	...	16	8	2	...	1	...	...	...	...	...	...	...	...	...	27
Syrian	...	1	...	...	...	...	...	...	...	...	...	...	...	...	...	1
Welsh	...	...	1	...	...	...	...	...	...	...	...	...	...	...	...	1
Other races a	...	5	3	1	...	1	...	...	...	...	...	...	...	...	...	10
Total foreign-born	...	441	282	127	59	32	19	7	3	2	...	...	...	...	1	973
Grand total	2	1,237	835	328	95	49	19	8	4	2	1	...	...	...	1	2,581

a "Other races" includes races having less than 10 representatives in this city and pupils whose race is not reported.

TABLE 3.—*Race, sex, and age, by grade—Number of pupils of each age in each grade, by sex and by general nativity and race of father of pupil—Continued.*

FIRST GRADE—Continued.

GIRLS.

General nativity and race of father of pupil.	Number of pupils of each age.															Total.
	5.	6.	7.	8.	9.	10.	11.	12.	13.	14.	15.	16.	17.	18.	19.	
Native-born:																
White	1	716	437	108	10	2	3	2	....	1						1,280
Negro	...	38	29	8	....	1	...	1								77
Total native-born	1	754	466	116	10	3	3	3	....	1						1,357
Foreign-born:																
Armenian	...	4														4
Bohemian and Moravian	...	2	2													4
Canadian, French	...	2	1													3
Canadian, Other	...	31	13	4	....	1										49
Chinese	...	3	2													5
Danish	...	3	2	1	1											7
Dutch	...	2														2
English	...	34	24	5	1											64
Finnish	...	1	1													2
French	...	16	8	....	1	1										26
German	...	58	32	9	4											103
Hebrew, German	...	19	3	1												23
Hebrew, Polish	...	4	....	1												5
Hebrew, Roumanian	...	5														5
Hebrew, Russian	...	26	12	5	3	...	2	...	1							49
Hebrew, Other	...	2	5	3												10
Irish	...	13	6													19
Italian, North	...	17	13	3												33
Italian, South	...	22	14	4	1	1										42
Japanese	...	1	3	3	1	...	1									9
Magyar	...	4	4	1	...	1										10
Mexican	...	42	31	23	14	17	4	2	2	2						137
Norwegian	...	3	1	2												6
Polish	...	5	1	1												7
Portuguese	...	....	1													1
Roumanian	...	1														1
Russian	...	25	26	14	10	9	4	4	4	...	1					97
Scotch	...	6	1	1												8
Slovak	...	1														1
Slovenian	...	1														1
Spanish	...	2	2	...	1	...	1									6
Spanish-American	...	8	9	7	4	1	1									30
Swedish	...	27	8	1												36
Syrian	...	3	....	1	...	1										5
Welsh	...	4	2													6
Other races a	...	7	3	1												11
Total foreign-born	...	399	235	90	42	32	10	9	6	3	1					827
Grand total	1	1,153	701	206	52	35	13	12	6	4	1					2,184

a "Other races" includes races having less than 10 representatives in this city and pupils whose race is not reported.

TABLE 3.—*Race, sex, and age, by grade—Number of pupils of each age in each grade, by sex and by general nativity and race of father of pupil*—Continued.

FIRST GRADE—Continued.

TOTAL.

General nativity and race of father of pupil.	Number of pupils of each age.															Total.
	5.	6.	7.	8.	9.	10.	11.	12.	13.	14.	15.	16.	17.	18.	19.	
Native-born:																
White	3	1,470	960	294	41	14	3	3	1	1	1					2,791
Negro		80	59	23	5	6		1								174
Total native-born	3	1,550	1,019	317	46	20	3	4	1	1	1					2,965
Foreign-born:																
Armenian		7														7
Bohemian and Moravian		5	2													7
Canadian, French		5	3	1		1										10
Canadian, Other		68	24	11	1	2										106
Chinese		5	2	2			1									10
Danish		13	10	2	1											26
Dutch		5	1	1												7
English		73	64	14	4	2										157
Finnish		2	1													3
French		31	16	3	5	3										58
German		130	79	22	7											238
Greek		1														1
Hebrew, German		31	9	2	1											43
Hebrew, Polish		2	6		1											9
Hebrew, Roumanian		13	1													14
Hebrew, Russian		46	23	8	4			3		1						85
Hebrew, Other		5	6	3	1											15
Irish		31	13	1	1											46
Italian, North		40	33	14	1	3										91
Italian, South		59	33	9	7	3										111
Japanese		4	6	4	2			1							1	18
Magyar		7	9	2	1	2										21
Mexican		79	61	60	37	28	19	5	3	3						295
Norwegian		9	5	3	1					1						19
Polish		8	3	2		1										14
Portuguese		1	2													3
Roumanian		1	2													3
Russian		60	43	25	15	11	4	5	5		1					169
Scotch		9	10	4												23
Slovak		1														1
Slovenian		1	2													3
Spanish		2	3		1		1	1								8
Spanish-American		23	20	18	10	6	3	1	1							82
Swedish		43	16	3		1										63
Syrian		4		1		1										6
Welsh		4	3													7
Other races[a]		12	6	2		1										21
Total foreign-born		840	517	217	101	64	29	16	9	5	1				1	1,800
Grand total	3	2,390	1,536	534	147	84	32	20	10	6	2				1	4,765

[a] "Other races" includes races having less than 10 representatives in this city and pupils whose race is not reported.

TABLE 3.—*Race, sex, and age, by grade—Number of pupils of each age in each grade, by sex and by general nativity and race of father of pupil*—Continued.

SECOND GRADE.

BOYS.

General nativity and race of father of pupil.	Number of pupils of each age.															Total.
	6.	7.	8.	9.	10.	11.	12.	13.	14.	15.	16.	17.	18.	19.	20.	
Native-born:																
White	14	348	512	207	58	21	14	2	....	1						1,177
Negro	....	11	22	16	8	4	1	2								64
Total native-born	14	359	534	223	66	25	15	4	....	1						1,241
Foreign-born:																
Armenian	1	2														3
Canadian, French		1				2										3
Canadian, Other	1	15	17	9	1	1										44
Chinese			2	2	1		1		1							7
Danish		3	6	4		1										14
Dutch		3	1				1									5
English	1	18	20	12	2	1										54
French		7	5	3	1	1	1									18
German	1	33	41	23	6		1									105
Greek				1	1											2
Hebrew, German		6	9	5	1											21
Hebrew, Roumanian		2	1	1												4
Hebrew, Russian	1	6	8	9												24
Hebrew, Other		4	1													5
Irish	1	8	10	6												25
Italian, North		8	12	10	3			1								34
Italian, South	1	8	15	8	3	2										37
Japanese		1	1	1					1							4
Magyar		1	1													2
Mexican		2	6	6	8	11	5	2	4	1						45
Norwegian		4	3		1											8
Roumanian				1												1
Russian	3	7	10	9	15	3	10	3	2							62
Scotch		7	2	1	1											11
Slovenian				1	1											2
Spanish		1		1	1											3
Spanish-American		2	6	10	10	4	1	1	1							35
Swedish		10	11	6	2	1										30
Syrian			3	1												4
Welsh		4	1													5
Other foreign a		2		2	1											5
Total foreign-born	10	165	192	132	59	27	19	7	9	2						622
Grand total	24	524	726	355	125	52	34	11	9	3						1,863

a "Other races" includes races having less than 10 representatives in this city and pupils whose race is not reported.

TABLE 3.—*Race, sex, and age, by grade—Number of pupils of each age in each grade, by sex and by general nativity and race of father of pupil*—Continued.

SECOND GRADE—Continued.

GIRLS.

General nativity and race of father of pupil.	Number of pupils of each age.															Total.
	6.	7.	8.	9.	10.	11.	12.	13.	14.	15.	16.	17.	18.	19.	20.	
Native-born:																
White	25	444	394	142	33	7	3									1,048
Negro		16	25	11	6	1	1		1							61
Total native-born	25	460	419	153	39	8	4		1							1,109
Foreign-born:																
Armenian			2	1	1											4
Canadian, French		1	2	1	2		1									7
Canadian, Other	1	22	14	4	1	1										43
Chinese		1	1	2												4
Danish		3	3	1												7
Dutch		3	4													7
English		23	20	7			1		1							52
Finnish			1													1
French	2	3	8	2	3	2										20
German	2	29	28	13	4											76
Greek			1				1									2
Hebrew, German	2	11	8	2	1											24
Hebrew, Polish		3	2													5
Hebrew, Roumanian		5														5
Hebrew, Russian	3	6	11	2	3	1										26
Hebrew, Other		1	3		1											5
Irish	1	6	13	2												22
Italian, North	1	3	7	8	1	2	2									24
Italian, South	1	5	10	4	5	1	1									27
Japanese			3		1											4
Magyar			1													1
Mexican		2	8	4	10	5	5	4	2		1					41
Norwegian		2	2	2	1											L
Polish	1		2													3
Portuguese			1	1												2
Roumanian		1	1													2
Russian		7	10	10	15	7	1	5	1							56
Scotch		3	2	1	1											7
Slovak		2	1	1	1											5
Spanish		1	1													2
Spanish-American		3	12	9	8	1	2									35
Swedish		9	11		2											22
Syrian		1														1
Welsh		5														5
Other foreign *a*		3	5	1	1											10
Total foreign-born	14	164	198	78	62	20	14	9	4		1					564
Grand total	39	624	617	231	101	28	18	9	5		1					1,673

a "Other races" includes races having less than 10 representatives in this city and pupils whose race is not reported.

TABLE 3.—*Race, sex, and age, by grade—Number of pupils of each age in each grade, by sex and by general nativity and race of father of pupil*—Continued.

SECOND GRADE—Continued.

TOTAL.

General nativity and race of father of pupil.	Number of pupils of each age.															Total.
	6.	7.	8.	9.	10.	11.	12.	13.	14.	15.	16.	17.	18.	19.	20.	
Native-born:																
White	39	792	906	349	91	28	17	2	...	1						2,225
Negro	....	27	47	27	14	5	2	2	1							125
Total native-born	39	819	953	376	105	33	19	4	1	1						2,350
Foreign-born:																
Armenian	1	2	2	1	1											7
Canadian, French	....	2	2	1	2	2	1									10
Canadian, Other	2	37	31	13	2	2										87
Chinese	....	1	3	4	1			1		1						11
Danish	....	6	9	5		1										21
Dutch	....	6	5			1										12
English	1	41	40	19	2	1	1		1							106
Finnish	....	1														1
French	2	10	13	5	4	3	1									38
German	3	62	69	36	10		1									181
Greek	....		1	1	1		1									4
Hebrew, German	2	17	17	7	2											45
Hebrew, Polish	....	3	2													5
Hebrew, Roumanian	....	7	1	1												9
Hebrew, Russian	4	12	19	11	3	1										50
Hebrew, Other	....	5	4		1											10
Irish	2	14	23	8												47
Italian, North	1	11	19	18	4	2	2		1							58
Italian, South	2	13	25	12	8	3	1									64
Japanese	....	1	4	1	1				1							8
Magyar	....	1	2													3
Mexican	....	4	14	10	18	16	10	6	6	1	1					86
Norwegian	....	6	5	2	2											15
Polish	1		2													3
Portuguese	....		1	1												2
Roumanian	....	1	1	1												3
Russian	3	14	20	19	30	10	11	8	3							118
Scotch	....	10	4	2	2											18
Slovak	....	2	1	1	1											5
Slovenian	....		1	1												2
Spanish	....	2	1	1	1											5
Spanish-American	....	5	18	19	18	5	3	1	1							70
Swedish	....	19	22	6	4	1										52
Syrian	....	1	3	1												5
Welsh	....	9	1													10
Other foreign *a*	....	5	5	3	2											15
Total foreign-born	24	329	390	210	121	47	33	16	13	2	1					1,186
Grand total	63	1,148	1,343	586	226	80	52	20	14	3	1					3,536

a "Other races" includes races having less than 10 representatives in this city and pupils whose race is not reported.

TABLE 3.—*Race, sex, and age, by grade—Number of pupils of each age in each grade, by sex and by general nativity and race of father of pupil*—Continued.

THIRD GRADE.

BOYS.

General nativity and race of father of pupil.	Number of pupils of each age.															Total.
	6.	7.	8.	9.	10.	11.	12.	13.	14.	15.	16.	17.	18.	19.	20.	
Native-born:																
White		28	307	398	259	121	47	11	4	2	1					1,178
Negro			5	15	17	13	9	3		3						65
Total native-born		28	312	413	276	134	56	14	4	5	1					1,243
Foreign-born:																
Armenian			1	1	1											3
Bohemian and Moravian			1													1
Canadian, French	1	1	1		1											4
Canadian, Other	1		13	23	14	4	2									57
Chinese				2		1										3
Danish					3	2										5
Dutch			4	1		1										6
English		3	11	35	9	9	3	1	1							72
Finnish				1												1
French			2	8	6	3	2	1								23
German		4	24	32	24	12	5	1	1							103
Greek						1										1
Hebrew, German		2	8	9	4		1	1								25
Hebrew, Polish			2	1			1									4
Hebrew, Roumanian			2	3												5
Hebrew, Russian		4	6	18	7	2		4	1							42
Hebrew, Other				1		3		1								5
Irish			8	12	5	3	1		1							30
Italian, North		2	6	5	13	6	3	1								36
Italian, South			4	9	7	5	4	3	3	1						36
Japanese				3		1	1			1	1	1	2	2		12
Magyar				1	1											2
Mexican				7	12	12	14	8	5	1						59
Norwegian			1	3	1											5
Polish			1	3												4
Portuguese				1	1	1										3
Roumanian							1									1
Russian				1	4	5	8	6	8							32
Scotch		1	4	3	1	2										11
Slovenian			1		1											2
Spanish			1	1	1	1					1					5
Spanish-American				3	4	2	3	1	1							14
Swedish			3	16	9	3	2									33
Syrian								1								1
Welsh				3												3
Other races[a]			2	4	1	2										9
Total foreign-born		18	106	209	131	82	51	30	21	4	1	1	2	2		658
Grand total		46	418	622	407	216	107	44	25	9	2	1	2	2		1,901

a "Other races" includes races having less than 10 representatives in this city and pupils whose race is not reported.

TABLE 3.—*Race, sex, and age, by grade—Number of pupils of each age in each grade, by sex and by general nativity and race of father of pupil—Continued.*

THIRD GRADE—Continued.

GIRLS.

General nativity and race of father of pupil	Number of pupils of each age.															Total.
	6.	7.	8.	9.	10.	11.	12.	13.	14.	15.	16.	17.	18.	19.	20.	
Native-born:																
White		30	396	408	199	69	26	7	1	2	1					1,139
Negro			10	18	19	11	10	6	1							75
Total native-born		30	406	426	218	80	36	13	2	2	1					1,214
Foreign-born:																
Armenian																
Bohemian and Moravian					2	3	1									6
Bulgarian				2	2											5
Canadian, French			1	1												2
Canadian, Other				2	1	1										4
Chinese		1	20	16	7	3										47
Danish																6
Dutch			5	8	2	2										17
English			1	1	2		1									5
Finnish		4	23	20	7	3	6									63
French			1													1
German		6	39	43	23	6	2	3								122
Greek				1												1
Hebrew, German			2	6	6		1									15
Hebrew, Polish			4	3		1										8
Hebrew, Roumanian			4	2		1										7
Hebrew, Russian		5	10	9	2		2		1							29
Hebrew, Other			3	3												6
Irish		3	4	12	5	1	1		1	1						28
Italian, North			10	10	10	2	3									35
Italian, South	1		5	7	6	1	3									23
Japanese	1			1	1	1	1									5
Magyar				1												1
Mexican			4	5	9	10	4	3	5							40
Norwegian			1	1												2
Polish			3	2			1									6
Portuguese			2													2
Roumanian				1												1
Russian			1	4	4	8	2	2								21
Scotch		1	7	7	3		2									20
Slovak				1	1											1
Slovenian				1	1		1									3
Spanish			1	2	1		1				1					4
Spanish-American											1					7
Swedish		3	13	13	5	1	2		1							35
Syrian			5	5	5	2	1									18
Welsh					1	1										1
Other races a	1		2	4	2	1	1	3								8
Total foreign-born		29	178	203	113	54	36	10	7	3						633
Grand total		59	584	629	331	134	72	23	9	5	1					1,847

a "Other races" includes races having less than 10 representatives in this city and pupils whose race is not reported.

TABLE 3.—*Race, sex, and age, by grade—Number of pupils of each age in each grade, by sex and by general nativity and race of father of pupil*—Continued.

THIRD GRADE—Continued.

TOTAL.

General nativity and race of father of pupil.	6.	7.	8.	9.	10.	11.	12.	13.	14.	15.	16.	17.	18.	19.	20.	Total.
Native-born:																
White		58	703	806	458	190	73	18	5	4	2					2,317
Negro			15	33	36	24	19	9	1	3						140
Total native-born		58	718	839	494	214	92	27	6	7	2					2,457
Foreign-born:																
Armenian			1	1	3	3	1									9
Bohemian and Moravian			3	1	2											6
Bulgarian			1	1												2
Canadian, French	1		2	3	1	1										8
Canadian, Other	1		33	39	21	7	3									104
Chinese	1		2	4		2										9
Danish			5	8	5	4										22
Dutch			5	2	1	1										11
English		7	34	55	16	12	9	1	1							135
Finnish			1	1												2
French	3		7	14	12	9	4	2								51
German	10		63	75	47	18	7	4	1							225
Greek			1			1										2
Hebrew, German	2		10	15	10		2	1								40
Hebrew, Polish			6	3	2		1									12
Hebrew, Roumanian			6	5		1										12
Hebrew, Russian	9		16	27	9	2	2	4	2							71
Hebrew, Other			3	3		3		1								11
Irish	3		12	24	10	4	2		2	1						58
Italian, North	2		16	15	23	8	6	1								71
Italian, South	1		9	16	13	6	7	3	3	1						59
Japanese	1			4	1	2	2			1	1	1	2	2		17
Magyar				2	1											3
Mexican			4	12	21	22	18	11	10	1						99
Norwegian			2	4	1											7
Polish			4	5			1									10
Portuguese			2	1	1	1										5
Roumanian				1			1									2
Russian			1	5	8	13	10	8	8							53
Sctoch		2	11	10	4	4										31
Slovak				1												1
Slovenian			1	1	2		1									5
Spanish			2	3	1	1				2						9
Spanish-American			2	8	9	4	4	3	1	1						32
Swedish	3		16	29	14	4	2									68
Syrian					1			1								2
Welsh			2	7	1											10
Other races [a]	1		2	6	2	3	3									17
Total foreign-born		47	284	412	244	136	87	40	28	7	1	1	2	2		1,291
Grand total		105	1,002	1,251	738	350	179	67	34	14	3	1	2	2		3,748

[a] "Other races" includes races having less than 10 representatives in this city and pupils whose race is not reported.

TABLE 3.—*Race, sex, and age, by grade—Number of pupils of each age in each grade, by sex and by general nativity and race of father of pupil*—Continued.

FOURTH GRADE.

BOYS.

General nativity and race of father of pupil.	Number of pupils of each age.												Total.
	7.	8.	9.	10.	11.	12.	13.	14.	15.	16.	17.	18.	
Native-born of native father:													
White	1	32	237	380	318	174	62	13	5	1	....	....	1,223
Negro	....	....	5	7	18	17	13	9	1	2	....	....	72
Indian	....	....	....	....	....	....	....	....	1	....	....	....	1
Total native-born	1	32	242	387	336	191	75	22	7	3	....	....	1,296
Foreign-born:													
Armenian	....	1	....	1	1	....	....	1	....	....	....	....	4
Bohemian and Moravian	....	....	1	2	....	....	....	....	....	....	....	....	3
Bulgarian	....	....	....	....	1	1	....	....	....	....	....	....	2
Canadian, French	....	....	1	3	....	....	....	1	....	....	....	....	6
Canadian, Other	....	....	13	24	16	8	2	....	....	....	....	....	63
Chinese	....	....	1	3	1	....	1	1	1	1	....	....	9
Danish	....	1	1	2	6	....	....	1	....	....	....	....	11
Dutch	....	....	....	2	1	....	....	....	....	....	....	....	3
English	....	2	9	25	13	14	7	4	1	....	....	....	75
Finnish	....	....	1	1	....	....	....	....	....	....	....	....	2
French	....	....	....	5	4	5	....	2	....	....	....	....	16
German	1	5	18	40	34	23	5	2	....	....	....	....	128
Hebrew, German	....	4	3	12	6	2	....	....	....	....	....	....	27
Hebrew, Polish	....	1	....	1	1	....	....	....	....	....	....	....	3
Hebrew, Roumanian	....	....	....	2	2	....	2	....	....	....	....	....	6
Hebrew, Russian	....	3	5	8	8	2	2	....	....	....	....	....	28
Hebrew, Other	....	....	2	....	2	1	....	....	....	....	....	....	5
Irish	....	1	7	6	9	4	2	2	....	....	....	....	31
Italian, North	....	....	4	12	4	3	5	1	....	....	....	....	29
Italian, South	....	....	2	4	4	6	2	5	....	....	3	....	26
Japanese	....	....	....	....	1	1	1	....	1	3	....	1	8
Magyar	....	....	1	2	....	2	....	....	....	....	....	....	5
Mexican	....	....	3	3	5	7	8	7	....	....	....	....	33
Norwegian	....	....	1	4	3	1	....	....	....	....	....	....	9
Polish	....	....	1	2	....	2	....	....	....	....	....	....	5
Portuguese	....	....	1	....	1	1	....	1	....	....	....	....	4
Roumanian	....	....	....	....	....	1	....	....	....	....	....	....	1
Russian	....	....	....	2	1	1	3	1	....	....	....	....	8
Scotch	....	....	6	4	7	1	1	....	....	....	....	....	19
Slovenian	....	....	....	....	....	1	1	....	....	....	....	....	2
Spanish	....	....	1	2	1	....	....	....	....	....	....	....	4
Spanish-American	....	....	2	2	2	6	7	1	....	....	....	....	20
Swedish	....	....	5	5	8	3	3	1	....	....	....	....	25
Syrian	....	....	1	....	....	....	....	....	....	....	....	....	1
Welsh	....	....	1	2	2	....	2	....	....	....	....	....	7
Other races a	....	....	3	3	3	....	1	....	....	....	....	....	10
Total foreign-born	1	18	94	182	150	96	55	29	5	4	3	1	638
Grand total	2	50	336	569	486	287	130	51	12	7	3	1	1,934

a "Other races" includes races having less than 10 representatives in this city and pupils whose race is not reported.

TABLE **3.**—*Race, sex, and age, by grade—Number of pupils of each age in each grade, by sex and by general nativity and race of father of pupil—Continued.*

FOURTH GRADE—Continued.

GIRLS.

General nativity and race of father of pupil.	Number of pupils of each age.												Total.
	7.	8.	9.	10.	11.	12.	13.	14.	15.	16.	17.	18.	
Native-born of native father:													
White		39	304	407	253	100	33	10	5				1,151
Negro		1	10	18	24	16	6	4					79
Indian					1	1							2
Total native-born		40	314	425	278	117	39	14	5				1,232
Foreign-born:													
Armenian					1								1
Bohemian and Moravian							1			1			2
Bulgarian				2		1							3
Canadian, French		1	1			1	1						4
Canadian, Other		3	9	18	12	5							47
Chinese			1	1									2
Danish			2	2	3	2	1	1					11
Dutch			1										1
English		3	18	26	21	10	2	1					81
Finnish						1	1						2
French			3	8	5	5			1				22
German		1	32	54	29	12	6	4					138
Hebrew, German		1	8	12	6	4	1						32
Hebrew, Roumanian					2	1							3
Hebrew, Russian	1	1	7	8	6	2	2	1					28
Hebrew, Other		1	2	3	2								8
Irish		2	8	10	7	2		1					30
Italian, North		1	3	5	6	3	3						21
Italian, South			1	8	5	3	3	1					21
Japanese			1	1	1	1							4
Magyar				1	2								3
Mexican				5	2	3	3	2					15
Norwegian				3	1	1							5
Polish			1	3	2								6
Portuguese				1		1							2
Russian					1	1							2
Scotch			3	10	1								14
Slovak				1	1								2
Slovenian						1							1
Spanish						1							1
Spanish-American				4	1	3	3						11
Swedish			10	9	11	6							36
Other races a			1	1	3	1		1					7
Total foreign-born	1	14	112	196	131	71	27	12	1	1			566
Grand total	1	54	426	621	409	188	66	26	6	1			1,798

a "Other races" includes races having less than 10 representatives in this city and pupils whose race is not reported.

TABLE 3.—*Race, sex, and age, by grade—Number of pupils of each age in each grade, by sex and by general nativity of race of father of pupil*—Continued.

FOURTH GRADE—Continued.

TOTAL.

General nativity and race of father of pupil.	Number of pupils of each age.												Total.
	7.	8.	9.	10.	11.	12.	13.	14.	15.	16.	17.	18.	
Native-born of native father:													
White	1	71	541	787	571	274	95	23	10	1			2,374
Negro		1	15	25	42	33	19	13	1	2			151
Indian					1	1			1				3
Total native-born	1	72	556	812	614	308	114	36	12	3			2,528
Foreign-born:													
Armenian		1		1	2			1					5
Bohemian and Moravian			1	2			1			1			5
Bulgarian				2	1	1				1			5
Canadian, French			1	2	1	3	1	1	1				10
Canadian, Other		3	22	42	28	13	2						110
Chinese			2	4	1		1	1	1	1			11
Danish		1	3	4	9	2	1	1	1				22
Dutch			1	2	1								4
English		5	27	51	34	24	9	5	1				156
Finnish			1	1		1	1						4
French			3	13	9	10		2	1				38
German	1	6	50	94	63	35	11	6					266
Hebrew, German		5	11	24	12	6	1						59
Hebrew, Polish		1		1	1								3
Hebrew, Roumanian				2	4	1	2						9
Hebrew, Russian	1	4	12	16	14	4	4	1					56
Hebrew, Other		1	4	3	4	1							13
Irish		3	15	16	16	6	2	3					61
Italian, North		1	7	17	10	6	8	1					50
Italian, South			3	12	9	9	5	6					47
Japanese			1	1	2	1			1	2	3	1	12
Magyar			1	3	2	2							8
Mexican			3	8	7	10	11	9					48
Norwegian			1	7	4	2							14
Polish			2	5	2	2							11
Portuguese			1	1	1	2		1					6
Roumanian						1							1
Russian				2	2	2	3	1					10
Scotch			9	14	8	1	1						33
Slovak					1	1							2
Slovenian						2	1						3
Spanish			1	2	1	1							5
Spanish-American			2	6	3	9	10	1					31
Swedish			15	14	19	9	3	1					61
Syrian			1										1
Welsh			1	2	2		2						7
Other races *a*			4	4	6	1	1	1					17
Total foreign-born	2	32	206	378	281	167	82	41	6	5	3	1	1,204
Grand total	3	104	762	1,190	895	475	196	77	18	8	3	1	3,732

a "Other races" includes races having less than 10 representatives in this city and pupils whose race is not reported.

TABLE 3.—*Race, sex, and age, by grade—Number of pupils of each age in each grade, by sex and by general nativity and race of father of pupil*—Continued.

FIFTH GRADE.

BOYS.

General nativity and race of father of pupil.	Number of pupils of each age.													Total.
	8.	9.	10.	11.	12.	13.	14.	15.	16.	17.	18.	19.	20 or over.	
Native-born:														
White		18	236	345	321	171	73	13						1,177
Negro		2	4	6	17	15	16	5	1					66
Total native-born		20	240	351	338	186	89	18	1					1,243
Foreign-born:														
Bohemian and Moravian				2	1	1								4
Canadian, French				4	1	1	1							7
Canadian, Other			7	15	23	10	3							58
Chinese								1	1	1	1			4
Danish			4	5	5	6								20
Dutch						1								1
English		2	11	20	14	18	3	2						70
French				6	10	6	3							25
German		3	11	33	46	25	9	1						128
Greek				1										1
Hebrew, German		3	1	1	7	1	1							14
Hebrew, Polish		1	1	1	1	1								5
Hebrew, Roumanian			2	1		1								4
Hebrew, Russian		1	10	15	7	3	1							37
Hebrew, Other			2	1	2	1								6
Irish		2	6	8	6	6	3						1	32
Italian, North			1	2	2	2								7
Italian, South			1	6	5	5	4	2						23
Japanese							2	1	2	3		1		9
Magyar													1	1
Mexican		1	1	1	3	5	3	2	2				1	19
Norwegian		1			3	3	1							8
Polish			1	1	2		1							5
Portuguese	1			1	1									3
Roumanian				1										1
Russian			1	1	1	2								5
Scotch		1	9	11	8	4	1							34
Slovak				1										1
Slovenian							1							1
Spanish				1										1
Spanish-American			1	4	2	1	4	2						14
Swedish		1	5	8	12	3	2							31
Syrian			1	1										2
Welsh				3	4	2		2		1			1	10
Other races *a*					2		2			2		1	1	8
Total foreign-born	1	16	80	162	166	107	38	15	4	5	1	2	2	599
Grand total	1	36	320	513	504	293	127	33	5	5	1	2	2	1,842

a "Other races" includes races having less than 10 representatives in this city and pupils whose race is not reported.

TABLE 3.—*Race, sex, and age, by grade—Number of pupils of each age in each grade, by sex and by general nativity and race of father of pupil—Continued.*

FIFTH GRADE—Continued.

GIRLS.

General nativity and race of father of pupil.	Number of pupils of each age.													Total.
	8.	9.	10.	11.	12.	13.	14.	15.	16.	17.	18.	19.	20 or over.	
Native-born:														
White	1	33	254	347	276	110	43	11	1					1,076
Negro			6	15	17	17	12	1						68
Total native-born	1	33	260	362	293	127	55	12	1					1,144
Foreign-born:														
Armenian				1										1
Bohemian and Moravian				3										3
Canadian, French			4	1	3									8
Canadian, Other		1	14	18	19	5	1							58
Chinese			2	1										3
Danish		1	6	2	4	1	1							15
Dutch			1		2	1								4
English		1	12	23	14	11	2		1					64
Finnish				1										1
French			4	13	10	2	3	3	1					36
German		4	35	44	20	19	9	1						132
Hebrew, German		3	7	10	5	3		1						29
Hebrew, Polish			2	3	2									7
Hebrew, Roumanian			1	1	1									3
Hebrew, Russian		1	10	8	5	3	2	1						30
Hebrew, Other			1		2	1								4
Irish			5	11	14	5	1	2						38
Italian, North			3	6	8	3	2							22
Italian, South			1	4	5	4								14
Magyar			1	2	2	2								7
Mexican				1	1	2	3							7
Norwegian			1	1	3	1								6
Polish			1	2										3
Portuguese					1									1
Roumanian				1										1
Russian			2		1	2								5
Scotch		1	4	3	7	1								16
Slovak					2									2
Slovenian					1	1								2
Spanish						1	1	1						3
Spanish-American			1		3	1	3							8
Swedish			5	6	6	4	2							23
Welsh				2	2	2								6
Other races *a*				1	3									4
Total foreign-born		12	123	168	145	77	30	9	2					566
Grand total	1	45	383	530	438	204	85	21	3					1,710

a "Other races" includes races having less than 10 representatives in this city and pupils whose race is not reported.

TABLE 3.—*Race, sex, and age, by grade—Number of pupils of each age in each grade, by sex and by general nativity and race of father of pupil—Continued.*

FIFTH GRADE—Continued.

TOTAL.

General nativity and race of father of pupil.	Number of pupils of each age.													Total.
	8.	9.	10.	11.	12.	13.	14.	15.	16.	17.	18.	19.	20 or over.	
Native-born:														
White	1	51	490	692	597	281	116	24	1					2,253
Negro		2	10	21	34	32	28	6	1					134
Total native-born	1	53	500	713	631	313	144	30	2					2,387
Foreign-born:														
Armenian				1										1
Bohemian and Moravian				5	1	1								7
Canadian, French			4	5	4	1	1							15
Canadian, Other		1	21	33	42	15	4							116
Chinese			2	2				1		1	1			7
Danish		1	10	7	9	7	1							35
Dutch			1		2	2								5
English		3	23	43	28	29	5	2	1					134
Finnish				1										1
French			4	19	20	8	6	3	1					61
German		7	46	77	66	44	18	2						260
Greek				1										1
Hebrew, German		6	8	12	12	3		2						43
Hebrew, Polish		1	3	4	3	1								12
Hebrew, Roumanian			3	1	1	2								7
Hebrew, Russian		2	20	23	12	6	3	1						67
Hebrew, Other			3	1	4	2								10
Irish		2	11	19	20	11	4	2				1		70
Italian, North			4	8	10	5	2							29
Italian, South			2	10	10	9	4	2						37
Japanese					1	1		1	2	3		1		9
Magyar			1	3	2	2								8
Mexican		1	1	2	4	7	6	2	2				1	26
Norwegian		1	1	4	6	1		1						14
Polish			2	3	2		1							8
Portuguese	1				2	1								4
Roumanian			1	1										2
Russian			3	1	2	4								10
Scotch		2	13	14	15	5	1							50
Slovak				1	2									3
Slovenian					1	2	1	1						3
Spanish						1	1	1						4
Spanish-American			2	4	5	2	7	2						22
Swedish		1	10	14	18	7	4							54
Syrian			1	1										2
Welsh			3	6	4	3								16
Other races a				3	3	2		2		1			1	12
Total foreign-born	1	28	203	330	311	184	68	24	6	5	1	2	2	1,165
Grand total	2	81	703	1,043	942	497	212	54	8	5	1	2	2	3,552

a "Other races" includes races having less than 10 representatives in this city and pupils whose race is not reported.

TABLE 3.—*Race, sex, and age, by grade—Number of pupils of each age in each grade, by sex and by general nativity and race of father of pupil*—Continued.

SIXTH GRADE.

BOYS.

General nativity and race of father of pupil.	Number of pupils of each age.													Total.
	8.	9.	10.	11.	12.	13.	14.	15.	16.	17.	18.	19.	20 or over	
Native-born:														
White	1	1	19	180	322	304	195	65	8	2				1,097
Negro				3	6	15	12	4	2					42
Total native-born	1	1	19	183	328	319	207	69	10	2				1,139
Foreign-born:														
Canadian, French				1		2	3							6
Canadian, Other			2	6	16	16	11	1		1				53
Chinese				1	2	1		1						5
Danish					2	4	2	1						9
Dutch					2		1							3
English			1	6	19	18	18	6	1					69
French				1	6	6	8	3						24
German			2	21	35	22	20	5	1					106
Hebrew, German			3	5	9	6	3							26
Hebrew, Polish			1	1	1		2							5
Hebrew, Roumanian			1				1							2
Hebrew, Russian			1	8	11	7	1							28
Hebrew, Other				1	3									4
Irish				3	5	6	8	3						25
Italian, North				4	1	9	5	1						20
Italian, South				2	5	1	1	1						10
Japanese					1	1		1	1		2			6
Magyar					1									1
Mexican						1	3	2						6
Norwegian							2	1		1				4
Portuguese								1						1
Roumanian						1								1
Russian				1	2									3
Scotch				1	9	3	4	1						18
Slovenian						1	1							2
Spanish						1								1
Spanish-American				5	1	3								9
Swedish			1	5	10	7	2	1						26
Welsh					1	1	1							3
Other foreign a					1	1	1				1		1	5
Total foreign-born			12	70	144	117	99	28	5	2	3		1	481
Grand total	1	1	31	253	472	436	306	97	15	4	3		1	1,620

a "Other races" includes races having less than 10 representatives in this city and pupils whose race is not reported.

TABLE 3.—*Race, sex, and age, by grade—Number of pupils of each age in each grade, by sex and by general nativity and race of father of pupil*—Continued.

SIXTH GRADE—Continued.

GIRLS.

General nativity and race of father of pupil.	Number of pupils of each age.													Total.
	8.	9.	10.	11.	12.	13.	14.	15.	16.	17.	18.	19.	20 or over.	
Native-born:														
White			30	228	356	300	162	39	10					1,125
Negro				5	15	14	11	12	3	2				62
Total native-born			30	233	371	314	173	51	13	2				1,187
Foreign-born:														
Canadian, French			1	1	3			1						6
Canadian, Other			4	9	12	15	6	2						48
Danish				3		7	3	1						14
Dutch					1									1
English			4	13	22	21	13	1						79
French			1	3	2	6	2	2						16
German			6	18	38	38	15	3	1					119
Hebrew, German			1	7	6	11	4							29
Hebrew, Polish				2	1	1	1							5
Hebrew, Roumanian			1	1	1									3
Hebrew, Russian			2	6	6	5								19
Hebrew, Other			1	2	1	1								5
Irish				5	7	8	4	3						27
Italian, North				1	5	5	10	3		1				25
Italian, South			1	1	2	1	2	1						8
Japanese						1								1
Magyar							1							1
Mexican						1								1
Norwegian					4	3								7
Polish							1							1
Russian				1	1	1								3
Scotch			2	5	6	1	1							15
Slovenian					1									1
Spanish				1	1									2
Spanish-American			1		2	4	3	1	1		1			13
Swedish			1	9	12	7	7							36
Welsh					2		1	1						4
Other foreign a			1		3	2	2							8
Total foreign-born			27	88	139	139	81	19	2	1	1			497
Grand total			57	321	510	453	254	70	15	3	1			1,684

a "Other races" includes races having less than 10 representatives in this city and pupils whose race is not reported.

TABLE 3.—*Race, sex, and age, by grade—Number of pupils of each age in each grade, by sex and by general nativity and race of father of pupil*—Continued.

SIXTH GRADE—Continued.

TOTAL.

General nativity and race of father of pupil.	Number of pupils of each age.													Total.
	8.	9.	10.	11.	12.	13.	14.	15.	16.	17.	18.	19.	20 or over.	
Native-born:														
White	1	1	49	408	678	604	357	104	18	2				2,222
Negro				8	21	29	23	16	5	2				104
Total native-born	1	1	49	416	699	633	380	120	23	4				2,326
Foreign-born:														
Canadian, French			1	2	3	2	3	1						12
Canadian, Other			6	15	28	31	17	3		1				101
Chinese				1	2	1			1					5
Danish				3	2	11	5	2						23
Dutch					3			1						4
English			5	19	41	39	36	7	1					148
French			1	4	8	12	10	5						40
German			8	39	73	60	35	8	2					225
Hebrew, German			4	12	15	17	7							55
Hebrew, Polish			1	3	2	1	3							10
Hebrew, Roumanian			2	1	1									5
Hebrew, Russian			3	14	17	12	1							47
Hebrew, Other			1	3	4	1								9
Irish				8	12	14	12	6						52
Italian, North				5	6	14	15	4		1				45
Italian, South			1	3	7	2	3	2						18
Japanese					1	2		1	1		2			7
Magyar					1		1							2
Mexican					1	1	2	2		1				7
Norwegian					4	3	3	1						11
Polish							1							1
Portuguese					1									1
Roumanian						1								1
Russian				2	3	1								6
Scotch			2	6	15	4	5	1						33
Slovenian				1	1	1								3
Spanish				1	1	1								3
Spanish-American			1	1	3	7	5	3	1		1			22
Swedish			2	14	22	14	10							62
Welsh				1	2	1	2	1						7
Other foreign a			1		4	3	3				1		1	13
Total foreign-born			39	158	283	256	180	47	7	3	4		1	978
Grand total	1	1	88	574	982	889	560	167	30	7	4		1	3,304

a "Other races" includes races having less than 10 representatives in this city and pupils whose race is not reported.

TABLE 3.—*Race, sex, and age, by grade—Number of pupils of each age in each grade, by sex and by general nativity and race of father of pupil*—Continued.

SEVENTH GRADE.

BOYS.

General nativity and race of father of pupil.	Number of pupils of each age.										
	10.	11.	12.	13.	14.	15.	16.	17.	18.	19.	Total.
Native-born:											
White	1	33	179	257	290	142	25	3	2		932
Negro			1	4	10	6	5				26
Indian				1							1
Total native-born	1	33	180	262	300	148	30	3	2		959
Foreign-born:											
Bohemian and Moravian				1	1	1					3
Canadian, French				1	1	1					3
Canadian, Other	1		8	14	17	8	1				49
Chinese			1			1	1				4
Danish		1	1	2	3	3					10
Dutch				1	1	1					3
English		1	9	15	19	9	1				54
French			2	1	5	3					11
German		2	18	21	34	9	1				85
Hebrew, German			3	9	4	1					17
Hebrew, Polish			1	1		2					4
Hebrew, Roumanian	1		1	1							3
Hebrew, Russian		1	1	7	3	1					13
Hebrew, Other		1		2	1	1					5
Irish			4	7	9	3	2				25
Italian, North		1	5	6	5	1					18
Italian, South				1	1	1					3
Japanese							1	2	1		4
Mexican				1	1	1	2				5
Norwegian				2	3	1					6
Polish				1							1
Roumanian				1	1	1					3
Russian			1	2		1					4
Scotch			3	7	8	2	1				21
Slovenian				1							1
Spanish					1						1
Spanish-American			1	2	1				1		5
Swedish			3	6	10	5					24
Welsh					1						1
Other races a			1				1			1	3
Total foreign-born	2	8	63	113	130	57	11	2	2	1	389
Grand total	3	41	243	375	430	205	41	5	4	1	1,348

a " Other races " includes races having less than 10 representatives in this city and pupils whose race is not reported.

TABLE 3.—*Race, sex, and age, by grade—Number of pupils of eaeh age in each grade, by sex and by general nativity aud race of father of pupil*—Continued.

SEVENTH GRADE—Continued.

GIRLS.

General nativity and race of father of pupil.	Number of pupils of each age.										
	10.	11.	12.	13.	14.	15.	16.	17.	18.	19.	Total.
Native-born:											
White	2	20	191	337	294	135	23	....	....	....	1,002
Negro	....	1	3	5	9	9	7	1	....	....	35
Total native-born	2	21	194	342	303	144	30	1	....	....	1,037
Foreign-born:											
Canadian, French	....	....	1	2	2	....	....	....	....	....	5
Canadian, Other	....	1	10	15	16	6	....	....	....	....	48
Chinese	....	....	1	....	....	....	....	....	....	....	1
Danish	....	....	2	3	6	....	1	....	....	....	12
Dutch	....	....	....	3	....	....	....	....	....	....	3
English	....	....	15	22	18	8	4	....	....	....	67
Finnish	....	....	....	....	1	....	....	....	....	....	1
French	....	....	6	....	7	2	....	....	1	....	16
German	....	4	8	32	29	9	3	2	....	....	87
Greek	....	....	1	....	....	....	....	....	....	....	1
Hebrew, German	....	....	6	10	3	1	....	....	....	....	20
Hebrew, Polish	....	....	....	1	....	....	....	....	....	....	1
Hebrew, Roumanian	....	....	....	....	1	....	....	....	....	....	1
Hebrew, Russian	....	....	3	6	6	....	....	....	....	....	15
Hebrew, Other	....	2	2	....	4	....	....	....	....	....	8
Irish	....	....	3	7	5	1	....	....	....	....	16
Italian, North	....	1	2	2	2	2	1	....	....	....	10
Italian, South	....	....	....	....	2	....	....	....	1	....	3
Magyar	....	....	....	1	....	....	....	....	....	....	1
Mexican	....	....	....	1	....	....	....	....	....	....	1
Norwegian	....	....	1	2	1	....	....	....	....	....	4
Portuguese	....	....	....	....	2	....	....	....	....	....	2
Roumanian	....	....	2	....	....	....	....	....	....	....	2
Russian	....	....	2	2	....	....	....	....	....	....	4
Scotch	....	1	2	10	5	3	....	....	....	....	21
Spanish	....	....	....	....	1	....	....	....	....	....	1
Spanish-American	....	....	....	3	2	1	....	....	....	....	6
Swedish	....	....	4	8	10	3	....	....	....	....	25
Welsh	....	1	1	1	....	....	....	....	....	....	3
Other races a	....	....	....	1	....	....	....	....	....	....	1
Total foreign-born	....	10	71	127	121	43	10	2	1	1	386
Grand total	2	31	265	469	424	187	40	3	1	1	1,423

a "Other races" includes races having less than 10 representatives in this city and pupils whose race is not reported.

TABLE **3.**—*Race, sex, and age, by grade—Number of pupils of each age in each grade, by sex and by general nativity and race of father of pupil*—Continued.

SEVENTH GRADE—Continued.

TOTAL.

General nativity and race of father of pupil.	Number of pupils of each age.										
	10.	11.	12.	13.	14.	15.	16.	17.	18.	19.	Total.
Native-born:											
White....................	3	53	370	594	584	277	48	3	2	......	1,934
Negro....................	......	1	4	9	19	15	12	1	......	......	61
Indian....................	......	......	......	1	......	......	......	......	......	......	1
Total native-born........	3	54	374	604	603	292	60	4	2	......	1,996
Foreign-born:											
Bohemian and Moravian...	......	......	......	1	1	1	......	......	......	......	3
Canadian, French.........	......	......	1	3	3	1	......	......	......	......	8
Canadian, Other..........	1	1	18	29	33	14	1	......	......	......	97
Chinese..................	......	1	2	......	......	1	1	......	......	......	5
Danish...................	......	1	3	5	9	3	1	......	......	......	22
Dutch....................	......	......	......	4	1	1	......	......	......	......	6
English..................	......	1	24	37	37	17	5	......	......	......	121
Finnish..................	......	......	......	......	1	......	......	......	......	......	1
French...................	......	......	8	1	12	5	......	......	1	......	27
German...................	......	6	26	53	63	18	4	2	......	......	172
Greek....................	......	......	1	......	......	......	......	......	......	......	1
Hebrew, German...........	......	......	9	19	7	2	......	......	......	......	37
Hebrew, Polish...........	......	......	1	2	......	2	......	......	......	......	5
Hebrew, Roumanian........	1	......	1	1	1	......	......	......	......	......	4
Hebrew, Russian..........	......	1	4	13	9	1	......	......	......	......	28
Hebrew, Other............	......	3	2	2	5	1	......	......	......	......	13
Irish....................	......	......	7	14	14	4	2	......	......	......	41
Italian, North...........	......	2	7	8	7	3	1	......	......	......	28
Italian, South...........	......	......	......	1	1	3	......	......	......	1	6
Japanese.................	......	......	......	......	......	......	1	2	1	......	4
Magyar...................	......	......	......	......	1	......	......	......	......	......	1
Mexican..................	......	......	......	1	2	1	2	......	......	......	6
Norwegian................	......	......	1	4	4	1	......	......	......	......	10
Polish...................	......	......	......	1	......	......	......	......	......	......	1
Portuguese...............	......	......	......	......	......	2	......	......	......	......	2
Roumanian................	......	......	2	1	1	1	......	......	......	......	5
Russian..................	......	......	3	4	......	1	......	......	......	......	8
Scotch...................	......	1	5	17	13	5	1	......	......	......	42
Slovenian................	......	......	......	1	......	......	......	......	......	......	1
Spanish..................	......	......	......	......	1	1	......	......	......	......	2
Spanish-American.........	......	......	1	2	4	2	1	......	1	......	11
Swedish..................	......	......	7	14	20	8	......	......	......	......	49
Welsh....................	......	1	......	1	1	1	......	......	......	......	4
Other races *a*..........	......	......	1	1	......	......	1	......	......	1	4
Total foreign-born........	2	18	134	240	251	100	21	4	3	2	775
Grand total..............	5	72	508	844	854	392	81	8	5	2	2,771

a "Other races includes races having less than 10 representatives in this city and pupils whose race is not reported.

TABLE 3.—*Race, sex, and age, by grade—Number of pupils of each age in each grade, by sex and by general nativity and race of father of pupil*—Continued.

EIGHTH GRADE.

BOYS.

General nativity and race of father of pupil.	Number of pupils of each age.										Total.
	10.	11.	12.	13.	14.	15.	16.	17.	18.	19.	
Native-born:											
White	1	1	22	128	269	200	96	20	4		741
Negro					1	7	5	1			14
Total native-born	1	1	22	128	270	207	101	21	4		755
Foreign-born:											
Bohemian and Moravian					1						1
Canadian, French					1	1	3				5
Canadian, Other			1	9	17	15	6	2			50
Danish					4	3	1				8
English		1	1	6	13	12	6	2			41
French				4	4	3	1				12
German			2	15	23	12	8				60
Hebrew, German					3	9	4				16
Hebrew, Polish				3	1						4
Hebrew, Russian	1		2	3	2	4		1			13
Hebrew, Other			1	4		1					6
Irish			2	3	2	3	3	1			14
Italian, North				1	1						2
Italian, South					3						4
Japanese					2		1	1	1	1	6
Magyar					2						2
Mexican	1				1						2
Norwegian				1	4	1	2				8
Polish				1		1	1				3
Portuguese					1	1					2
Scotch			2		6	1					9
Slovak					1						1
Slovenian					1	2					3
Spanish				1	2		2				5
Spanish-American					1	1	1				3
Swedish				4	5	3	3				15
Syrian					2						2
Welsh					1	1					2
Other races a					1						1
Total foreign-born	2	1	11	58	111	69	38	7	2	1	300
Grand total	3	2	33	186	381	276	139	28	6	1	1,055

a "Other races" includes races having less than 10 representatives in this city and pupils whose race is not reported.

TABLE 3.—*Race, sex, and age, by grade—Number of pupils of each age in each grade, by sex and by general nativity and race of father of pupil*—Continued.

EIGHTH GRADE—Continued.

GIRLS.

General nativity and race of father of pupil.	Number of pupils of each age.										Total.
	10.	11.	12.	13.	14.	15.	16.	17.	18.	19.	
Native-born:											
White		1	23	145	292	214	90	14	2		781
Negro		1		1	4	20	10	2			38
Indian					1	1			1		3
Total native-born		1	24	146	297	235	100	16	3		822
Foreign-born:											
Bohemian and Moravian					1	1					2
Bulgarian						1		1			2
Canadian, French				1		1					2
Canadian, Other				8	13	20	5	2			48
Chinese					1						1
Danish				2	5	3					10
Dutch				1	2		2				5
English			1	7	22	14	7	1			52
French				2	7	7	1				17
German		1	2	18	35	13	8	2			79
Hebrew, German	1		1	3	8	1	2				16
Hebrew, Polish						1					1
Hebrew, Roumanian				1	1						2
Hebrew, Russian				5	2	1	2				10
Hebrew, Other				1	1						2
Irish				2	6	6	3				17
Italian, North				1		2		1			4
Italian, South						2					2
Japanese			1								1
Magyar				1							1
Mexican			1				1				2
Norwegian				1	2	2	1				6
Portuguese					1	1					2
Roumanian						2					2
Russian					1						1
Scotch			1	4	7	7	2				21
Slovenian					1						1
Spanish					1		1				2
Spanish-American							1				1
Swedish				6	5	3	4	1			19
Welsh			1	1	2	1					5
Other races a					3						3
Total foreign-born	1	3	6	65	127	89	40	8			339
Grand total	1	4	30	211	424	324	140	24	3		1,161

a "Other races" includes races having less than 10 representatives in this city and pupils whose race is not reported.

TABLE 3.—*Race, sex, and age, by grade—Number of pupils of each age in each grade, by sex and by general nativity and race of father of pupil*—Continued.

EIGHTH GRADE—Continued.

TOTAL.

General nativity and race of father of pupil.	Number of pupils of each age.										Total.
	10.	11.	12.	13.	14.	15.	16.	17.	18.	19.	
Native-born:											
White	1	2	45	273	561	414	186	34	6		1,522
Negro			1	1	5	27	15	3			52
Indian					1	1			1		3
Total native-born	1	2	46	274	567	442	201	37	7		1,577
Foreign-born:											
Bohemian and Moravian					2	1					3
Bulgarian						1		1			2
Canadian, French				1	1	2	3				7
Canadian, Other			1	17	30	35	11	4			98
Chinese					1						1
Danish				2	9	6	1				18
Dutch				1	2		2				5
English		1	2	13	35	26	13	3			93
French				6	11	10	2				29
German		1	4	33	58	25	16	2			139
Hebrew, German	1		1	6	17	5	2				32
Hebrew, Polish				3	1	1					5
Hebrew, Roumanian				1	1						2
Hebrew, Russian	1		2	8	4	5	2		1		23
Hebrew, Other			1	5	1	1					8
Irish			2	5	8	9	6	1			31
Italian, North				2	1	2		1			6
Italian, South					3	2		1			6
Japanese		1			2		1	1	1	1	7
Magyar				1	2						3
Mexican	1		1		1		1				4
Norwegian				2	6	3	3				14
Polish				1		1	1				3
Portuguese					2	2					4
Roumanian						2					2
Russian					1						1
Scotch		1	2	4	13	8	2				30
Slovak					1						1
Slovenian					2	2					4
Spanish				1	3		3				7
Spanish-American					1	1	2				4
Swedish				10	10	6	7	1			34
Syrian					2						2
Welsh			1	1	3	2					7
Other races *a*					4						4
Total foreign-born	3	4	17	123	238	158	78	15	2	1	639
Grand total	4	6	63	397	805	600	279	52	9	1	2,216

a "Other races" includes races having less than 10 representatives in this city and pupils whose race is not reported.

TABLE 3.—*Race, sex, and age, by grade—Number of pupils of each age in each grade, by sex and by general nativity and race of father of pupil—Continued.*

FIRST YEAR HIGH SCHOOL.

BOYS.

General nativity and race of father of pupil.	Number of pupils of each age.								Total.
	13.	14.	15.	16.	17.	18.	19.	20.	
Native-born:									
White..........................	16	116	179	207	114	57	8	3	700
Negro........................			5	2	3		1		11
Indian........................				1					1
Total native-born..........	16	116	184	210	117	57	9	3	712
Foreign-born:									
Bohemian and Moravian.........				1					1
Bulgarian.....................				1					1
Canadian, French.............			1	1	1				3
Canadian, Other..............		5	7	4	6	1	1		24
Chinese......................					1		1	1	3
Danish.......................			1	1					2
English......................		7	13	10	4	3	2		39
French.......................			1	2	5				8
German.......................	1	8	13	10	10	1		1	44
Hebrew, German...............	1	3	1	3					8
Hebrew, Polish...............			2						2
Hebrew, Roumanian............			1						1
Hebrew, Russian..............	1		1						2
Irish........................		3	4	7	1	1			16
Italian, North...............			2	1					3
Italian, South...............					1				1
Japanese.....................				1	2	2	4	3	12
Magyar.......................			1	1					2
Norwegian....................		1	1						2
Polish.......................			1		1				2
Scotch.......................		5	2	4	2	1			14
Slovak.......................					1				1
Spanish-American.............					1				1
Swedish......................		2	5	2	2	2			13
Welsh........................		2		3	1		1		7
Other foreign a..............		1	5	3	3				12
Total foreign-born..........	3	37	62	55	42	11	9	5	224
Grand total.................	19	153	246	265	159	68	18	8	936

a "Other races" includes races having less than 10 representatives in this city and pupils whose race is not reported.

TABLE 3.—*Race, sex, and age, by grade—Number of pupils of each age in each grade, by sex and by general nativity and race of father of pupil*—Continued.

FIRST YEAR HIGH SCHOOL—Continued.

GIRLS.

General nativity and race of father of pupil.	Number of pupils of each age.								Total.
	13.	14.	15.	16.	17.	18.	19.	20.	
Native-born:									
White...............	17	125	193	174	82	21	4	1	617
Negro...............	......	3	6	4	8	1	......	......	22
Total native-born........	17	128	199	178	90	22	4	1	639
Foreign-born:									
Armenian...............	......	......	1	......	......	......	......	1	2
Canadian, French........	......	2	......	1	......	......	......	......	3
Canadian, Other.........	......	6	10	9	2	2	......	......	29
Chinese.................	......	......	......	1	......	......	......	......	1
Danish.................	......	1	1	1	......	......	......	......	3
Dutch..................	......	......	......	......	1	......	......	......	1
English................	1	10	14	15	6	1	......	......	47
Finnish................	......	......	1	......	......	......	......	......	1
French.................	......	2	4	3	1	......	......	......	10
German................	1	19	18	11	7	......	1	......	57
Hebrew, German.........	1	2	3	1	......	......	......	......	7
Hebrew, Russian........	2	1	......	......	......	......	......	......	3
Hebrew, Other..........	......	......	2	......	1	......	......	......	3
Irish..................	2	5	3	3	......	1	......	......	14
Italian, North..........	......	1	......	......	1	......	......	......	2
Italian, South..........	......	......	2	......	1	......	1	......	4
Japanese...............	......	......	......	......	1	......	......	......	1
Norwegian..............	......	......	1	1	......	......	......	......	2
Roumanian.............	......	......	1	......	......	......	......	......	1
Russian................	......	......	1	......	......	......	......	......	1
Scotch.................	......	2	6	3	5	1	......	......	17
Spanish-American.......	1	......	......	3	......	......	......	......	4
Swedish................	......	1	1	......	1	......	......	......	3
Welsh.................	......	1	1	......	......	......	......	......	2
Other foreign a........	......	......	......	......	1	......	......	......	1
Total foreign-born........	8	53	70	52	28	5	2	1	219
Grand total............	25	181	269	230	118	27	6	2	858

a "Other races" includes races having less than 10 representatives in this city and pupils whse race is not reported.

TABLE **3.**—*Race, sex, and age, by grade—Number of pupils of each age in each grade, by sex and by general nativity and race of father of pupil—Continued.*

FIRST YEAR HIGH SCHOOL—Continued.

TOTAL.

General nativity and race of father of pupil.	Number of pupils of each age.								Total.
	13.	14.	15.	16.	17.	18.	19.	20.	
Native-born:									
White	33	241	372	381	196	78	12	4	1,317
Negro		3	11	6	11	1	1		33
Indian				1					1
Total native-born	33	244	383	388	207	79	13	4	1,351
Foreign-born:									
Armenian			1					1	2
Bohemian and Moravian				1					1
Bulgarian				1					1
Canadian, French		2	1	2	1				6
Canadian, Other		11	17	13	8	3	1		53
Chinese				1	1		1	1	4
Danish		1	2	2					5
Dutch					1				1
English	1	17	27	25	10	4	2		86
Finnish			1						1
French		2	5	5	6				18
German	2	27	31	21	17	1	1	1	101
Hebrew, German	2	5	4	4					15
Hebrew, Polish			2						2
Hebrew, Roumanian			1						1
Hebrew, Russian	3	1	1						5
Hebrew, Other			2		1				3
Irish	2	8	7	10	1	2			30
Italian, North		1	2	1	1				5
Italian, South			2		2		1		5
Japanese				1	3	2	4	3	13
Magyar			1	1					2
Norwegian		1	2	1					4
Polish			1		1				2
Roumanian			1						1
Russian			1						1
Scotch		7	8	7	7	2			31
Slovak					1				1
Spanish-American	1			3	1				5
Swedish		3	6	2	3	2			16
Welsh		3	1	3	1		1		9
Other foreign *a*		1	5	3	4				13
Total foreign-born	11	90	132	197	70	16	11	6	443
Grand total	44	334	515	495	277	95	24	10	1,794

a "Other races" includes races having less than 10 representatives in this city and pupils whose race is not reported.

TABLE 3.—*Race, sex, and age, by grade—Number of pupils of each age in each grade, by sex and by general nativity and race of father of pupil*—Continued.

SECOND YEAR HIGH SCHOOL.

BOYS.

General nativity and race of father of pupil.	Number of pupils of each age.							Total.
	14.	15.	16.	17.	18.	19.	20 or over.	
Native-born:								
White..........................	10	38	73	93	35	12	....	261
Negro............................	......	......	......	1	....	1	....	2
Total native-born.............	10	38	73	94	35	13	....	263
Foreign-born:								
Canadian, French.............	......	......	1	1	....	......	....	2
Canadian, Other...............	......	1	7	9	6	......	....	23
Danish..........................	......	......	......	......	....	1	....	1
Dutch...........................	......	1	......	......	....	1	....	2
English.........................	2	1	1	1	1	1	....	7
French..........................	......	......	2	......	....	......	....	2
German..........................	1	5	3	4	1	1	....	15
Hebrew, German.................	1	1	......	2	....	......	1	5
Hebrew, Polish.................	......	......	......	1	....	......	....	1
Hebrew, Roumanian..............	......	......	1	......	....	......	....	1
Hebrew, Russian................	......	1	1	......	....	......	....	2
Irish...........................	......	......	2	3	2	......	....	7
Japanese........................	......	......	1	2	1	1	2	7
Norwegian.......................	......	......	......	......	1	......	....	1
Scotch..........................	......	......	......	3	1	2	1	7
Spanish.........................	......	......	......	1	....	......	....	1
Spanish-American................	......	......	......	......	1	......	....	1
Swedish.........................	......	......	2	1	1	2	....	6
Welsh...........................	......	1	1	......	....	......	....	2
Other races a...................	......	......	......	1	....	......	....	1
Total foreign-born.............	4	11	22	29	15	9	4	94
Grand total....................	14	49	95	123	50	22	4	357

a "Other races" includes races having less than 10 representatives in this city and pupils whose race is not reported.

TABLE 3.—*Race, sex, and age, by grade—Number of pupils of each age in each grade, by sex and by general nativity and race of father of pupil*—Continued.

SECOND YEAR HIGH SCHOOL—Continued.

GIRLS.

General nativity and race of father of pupil.	Number of pupils of each age.							Total.
	14.	15.	16.	17.	18.	19.	20 or over.	
Native-born:								
White..........................	8	59	101	75	31	8	4	286
Negro...........................	1	1	4	2	......	......	......	8
Total native-born.............	9	60	105	77	31	8	4	294
Foreign-born:								
Canadian, French..............	......	......	1	......	......	......	2	3
Canadian, Other...............	......	3	3	6	......	......	......	12
Danish.........................	......	......	......	......	1	1	......	2
Dutch..........................	......	1	......	......	......	......	......	1
English........................	......	8	3	......	2	......	......	13
French.........................	......	......	......	2	......	1	......	3
German.........................	......	5	8	2	3	1	......	19
Greek..........................	......	......	1	......	......	......	......	1
Hebrew, German.................	......	3	1	1	......	......	......	5
Hebrew, Roumanian..............	......	......	......	1	......	......	......	1
Hebrew, Russian................	......	2	1	......	......	......	......	3
Irish..........................	......	2	4	3	4	......	......	13
Italian, South.................	......	......	......	1	......	......	......	1
Norwegian......................	......	......	1	......	......	......	......	1
Scotch.........................	1	1	......	1	1	......	......	4
Spanish-American...............	......	......	1	......	......	......	......	1
Swedish........................	......	1	2	1	......	......	......	4
Welsh..........................	......	......	1	......	1	......	......	2
Other races a..................	1	......	2	1	......	......	......	4
Total foreign-born.............	2	26	29	19	12	3	2	93
Grand total....................	11	86	134	96	43	11	6	387

a "Other races" includes races having less than 10 representatives in this city and pupils whose race is not reported.

TABLE 3.—*Race, sex, and age, by grade—Number of pupils of each age in each grade, by sex and by general nativity and race of father of pupil*—Continued.

SECOND YEAR HIGH SCHOOL—Continued.

TOTAL.

General nativity and race of father of pupil.	Number of pupils of each age.							Total.
	14.	15.	16.	17.	18.	19.	20 or over.	
Native-born:								
White	18	97	174	168	66	20	4	547
Negro	1	1	4	3		1		10
Total native-born	19	98	178	171	66	21	4	557
Foreign-born:								
Canadian, French			2	1			2	5
Canadian, Other		4	10	15	6			35
Danish					1	2		3
Dutch		2				1		3
English	2	9	4	1	3	1		20
French			2	2		1		5
German	1	10	11	6	4	2		34
Greek			1					1
Hebrew, German	1	4	1	3			1	10
Hebrew, Polish				1				1
Hebrew, Roumanian			1	1				2
Hebrew, Russian		3	2					5
Irish		2	6	6	6			20
Italian, South				1				1
Japanese			1	2	1	1	2	7
Norwegian			1		1			2
Scotch	1	1		4	2	2	1	11
Spanish				1				1
Spanish-American			1		1			2
Swedish		1	4	2	1	2		10
Welsh		1	2		1			4
Other races a	1		2	2				5
Total foreign-born	6	37	51	48	27	12	6	187
Grand total	25	135	229	219	93	33	10	744

a "Other races" includes races having less than 10 representatives in this city and pupils whose race is not reported.

TABLE 3.—*Race, sex, and age, by grade—Number of pupils of each age in each grade, by sex and by general nativity and race of father of pupil*—Continued.

THIRD YEAR HIGH SCHOOL.

BOYS.

General nativity and race of father of pupil.	Number of pupils of each age.								Total.
	13.	14.	15.	16.	17.	18.	19.	20.	
Native-born, White		3	13	26	35	43	18	8	146
Foreign-born:									
Canadian (other than French)				2	2		2	1	7
Chinese						1	1		2
English				3	3	4			10
French					1				1
German				5	3	1	3		12
Hebrew, German					3				3
Hebrew, Russian								1	1
Hebrew, Other				1			1		2
Irish							2		2
Italian, North					1				1
Japanese						4	1	2	7
Scotch	1				1				2
Welsh				1			1		2
Total foreign-born	1			12	14	10	11	4	52
Grand total	1	3	13	38	49	53	29	12	198

GIRLS.

General nativity and race of father of pupil.	13.	14.	15.	16.	17.	18.	19.	20.	Total.
Native-born:									
White	1	4	14	54	79	33	12	5	202
Negro					2	1			3
Total native-born	1	4	14	54	81	34	12	5	205
Foreign-born:									
Canadian (other than French)			1	1	3	2			7
Danish			1						1
English				2	5	2			9
French				2		1			3
German			2	3	5	4	1		15
Hebrew, German					1				1
Hebrew, Roumanian					1				1
Irish				2	4				6
Magyar						1			1
Scotch			1	1	3				5
Spanish-American					1				1
Swedish						2			2
Welsh					1	1			2
Other races *a*					1	1	1	1	4
Total foreign-born			5	16	25	10	1	1	58
Grand total	1	4	19	70	106	44	13	6	263

a "Other races" includes races having less than 10 representatives in this city and pupils whose race is not reported.

TABLE 3.—*Race, sex, and age, by grade—Number of pupils of each age in each grade, by sex and by general nativity and race of father of pupil*—Continued.

THIRD YEAR HIGH SCHOOL—Continued.

TOTAL.

General nativity and race of father of pupil.	Number of pupils of each age.								Total.
	13.	14.	15.	16.	17.	18.	19.	20.	
Native-born:									
White	1	7	27	80	114	76	30	13	348
Negro					2	1			3
Total native-born	1	7	27	80	116	77	30	13	351
Foreign-born:									
Canadian (other than French)			1	3	5	2	2	1	14
Chinese						1	1		2
Danish			1						1
English				5	8	6			19
French				2	1	1			4
German			2	8	8	5	4		27
Hebrew, German				1	3				4
Hebrew, Roumanian				1					1
Hebrew, Russian								1	1
Hebrew, Other				1			1		2
Irish				2	4		2		8
Italian, North					1				1
Japanese						4	1	2	7
Magyar					1				1
Scotch	1		1	1	4				7
Spanish-American				1					1
Swedish					2				2
Welsh				2	1		1		4
Other races a				1	1	1		1	4
Total foreign-born	1		5	28	39	20	12	5	110
Grand total	2	7	32	108	155	97	42	18	461

a "Other races" includes races having less than 10 representatives in this city and pupils whose race is not reported.

FOURTH YEAR HIGH SCHOOL.

BOYS.

General nativity and race of father of pupil.	Number of pupils of each age.						Total.
	15.	16.	17.	18.	19.	20 or over.	
Native-born:							
White		2	26	32	25	23	108
Negro				1			1
Total native-born		2	26	33	25	23	109
Foreign-born:							
Canadian (other than French			1	1	2	1	5
Chinese					1		1
English			3	4	2	1	10
French			1		1		2
German		3	8	5	1	1	18
Hebrew, German			1				1
Hebrew, Russian		1					1
Irish			1	2		3	6
Japanese			1		1	1	3
Scotch			2	1		1	4
Swedish				2	1	1	4
Welsh					1		1
Total foreign-born		4	18	15	10	9	56
Grand total		6	44	48	35	32	165

TABLE 3.—*Race, sex, and age, by grade—Number of pupils of each age in each grade, by sex and by general nativity and race of father of pupil*—Continued.

FOURTH YEAR HIGH SCHOOL—Continued.

GIRLS.

General nativity and race of father of pupil.	Number of pupils of each age.						Total.
	15.	16.	17.	18.	19.	20 or over.	
Native-born:							
White		8	62	60	32	12	174
Negro				2			2
Total native-born		8	62	62	32	12	176
Foreign-born:							
Canadian, French	1		2	2	1	3	9
Canadian, Other						1	1
Dutch			5	1	2		8
English				1	1		2
French		2	6	3	3		14
German			1	1			2
Hebrew, German			1				1
Hebrew, Roumanian	1						1
Hebrew, Russian				1			1
Irish		1	2	3			6
Scotch			1	1			2
Swedish			1	1			2
Welsh				1			1
Total foreign-born	2	3	19	15	7	4	50
Grand total	2	11	81	77	39	16	226

TOTAL.

General nativity and race of father of pupil.	Number of pupils of each age.						Total.
	15.	16.	17.	18.	19.	20 or over.	
Native-born:							
White		10	88	92	57	35	282
Negro				3			3
Total native-born		10	88	95	57	35	285
Foreign-born:							
Canadian, French	1		3	3	3	4	14
Canadian, Other						1	1
Chinese						1	1
Dutch			8	5	4	1	18
English			1	2	1		4
French		5	14	8	4	1	32
German			2	1			3
Hebrew, German	1						1
Hebrew, Roumanian		1	1				2
Hebrew, Russian			1				1
Irish			3	5	1	3	12
Japanese				1	1	1	3
Scotch			2	2	1	1	6
Swedish		1	2	2	1		6
Welsh				1	1		2
Total foreign-born	2	7	37	30	17	13	106
Grand total	2	17	125	125	74	48	391

a "Other races" includes races having less than 10 representatives in this city and pupils whose race is not reported.

TABLE 3.—*Race, sex, and age, by grade—Number of pupils of each age in each grade, by sex and by general nativity and race of father of pupil—Continued.*

UNGRADED SCHOOL.

BOYS.

General nativity and race of father of pupil.	Number of pupils of each age.															Total.
	6.	7.	8.	9.	10.	11.	12.	13.	14.	15.	16.	17.	18.	19.	20.	
Native-born:																
White		2	1			3	7	7	20	19	12	3	1	1	1	77
Negro		1		1				1		1						4
Indian									1							1
Total		3	1	1		3	7	8	21	20	12	3	1	1	1	82
Foreign-born:																
Canadian (other than French)									3		3				1	7
Chinese											1					1
English									2	1						3
German								1	5		5					11
Hebrew, German										1	1					2
Hebrew, Russian				1							1					2
Hebrew, Roumanian									1							1
Hebrew, Other									1							1
Irish									1	1						2
Italian, North					1			1		2						4
Italian, South								1								1
Mexican	1	1		3	2		1	1	1							10
Scotch										1						1
Spanish-American	1	1			1			1		1						5
Swedish										1						1
Other races *a*			1												1	2
Total foreign-born	2	2	1	4	4		1	5	14	8	11				2	54
Grand total	2	5	2	5	4	3	8	13	35	28	23	3	1	1	3	136

GIRLS.

General nativity and race of father of pupil.	6.	7.	8.	9.	10.	11.	12.	13.	14.	15.	16.	17.	18.	19.	20.	Total.
Native-born, White					1		1	2	10	13	10	4				41
Foreign-born:																
Canadian (other than French)																
Chinese			1							1	1					3
Dutch				1						1	1					3
English								1								1
French										1	1					2
German									1	1						2
Hebrew, German											1					1
Hebrew, Russian										1						1
Irish										1	1					2
Italian, North				1		2		1		3						7
Mexican		1	1	2		2	1		1							8
Norwegian											1					1
Russian											1					1
Spanish-American		1								1						2
Swedish												2				2
Total foreign-born		2	2	4		4	1	2	2	10	7	2				36
Grand total		2	2	4	1	4	2	4	12	23	17	6				77

a "Other races" includes races having less than 10 representatives in this city and pupils whose race is not reported.

TABLE 3.—*Race, sex, and age, by grade—Number of pupils of each age in each grade, by sex and by general nativity and race of father of pupil*—Continued.

UNGRADED SCHOOL—Continued.

TOTAL.

General nativity and race of father of pupil.	Number of pupils of each age.															Total.
	6.	7.	8.	9.	10.	11.	12.	13.	14.	15.	16.	17.	18.	19.	20.	
Native-born:																
White		2	1		1	3	8	9	30	32	22	7	1	1	1	118
Negro		1		1				1		1						4
Indian									1							1
Total native-born		3	1	1	1	3	8	10	31	33	22	7	1	1	1	123
Foreign-born:																
Canadian (other than French)									4		4	1			1	10
Chinese			1						1		2					4
Dutch							1									1
English									2	1	1	1				5
French										1	1					2
German								1	5	2	5					13
Hebrew, German								1			2					3
Hebrew, Russian				1						2						3
Hebrew, Roumanian									1							1
Hebrew, Other									1							1
Irish						1					3					4
Italian, North					1	1		2	1	4						9
Italian, South								1								1
Mexican	1	2	1	7	2	1	1	1	1	1						18
Norwegian										1						1
Russian										1						1
Scotch										1						1
Spanish-American	1	2			1	1		1		1						7
Swedish										3						3
Other races *a*			1												1	2
Total foreign-born	2	4	3	8	4	4	2	7	16	18	18	2			2	90
Grand total	2	7	4	9	5	7	10	17	47	51	40	9	1	1	3	213

a "Other races" includes races having less than 10 representatives in this city and pupils whose race is not reported.

SPECIAL.

BOYS.

General nativity and race of father of pupil.	Number of pupils of each age.														Total.
	4.	5.	6.	7.	8.	9.	10.	11.	12.	13.	14.	15.	16.	17.	
Native-born:															
White	1	1		2	1	2	1	2	8	6	4	2		1	31
Negro									2	3					5
Total native-born	1	1		2	1	2	1	2	10	9	4	2		1	36
Foreign-born:															
English		1													1
German										1	2	1	1		5
Hebrew, Russian												1			1
Irish											2				2
Italian, South							1		1						2
Mexican							1		1						2
Other races *a*									1						1
Total foreign-born		1					2		3	1	4	2	1		14
Grand total	1	2		2	1	2	3	2	13	10	8	4	1	1	50

a "Other races" includes races having less than 10 representatives in this city and pupils whose race is not reported.

TABLE 3.—*Race, sex, and age, by grade—Number of pupils of each age in each grade, by sex and by general nativity and race of father of pupil*—Continued.

SPECIAL—Continued.

GIRLS.

General nativity and race of father of pupil.	Number of pupils of each age.														Total.
	4.	5.	6.	7.	8.	9.	10.	11.	12.	13.	14.	15.	16.	17.	
Native-born, White	....	2	2	....	....	1	....	3	3	1	1	2	....	....	15
Foreign-born, German	....	....	....	....	....	....	....	....	....	....	....	....	....	1	1
Total	....	2	2	....	....	1	....	3	3	1	1	2	....	1	16

TOTAL.

General nativity and race of father of pupil.	4.	5.	6.	7.	8.	9.	10.	11.	12.	13.	14.	15.	16.	17.	Total.
Native-born:															
White	1	3	2	2	1	3	1	5	11	7	5	4	....	1	46
Negro	....	....	....	....	....	....	....	....	2	3	....	....	....	....	5
Total native-born	1	3	2	2	1	3	1	5	13	10	5	4	....	1	51
Foreign-born:															
English	....	1	....	....	....	....	....	....	....	....	....	....	....	....	1
German	....	....	....	....	....	....	1	....	....	1	2	1	1	....	6
Hebrew, Russian	....	....	....	....	....	....	....	....	....	....	....	1	....	....	1
Irish	....	....	....	....	....	....	....	....	1	....	....	1	....	....	2
Italian, South	....	....	....	....	....	....	....	....	....	2	....	....	....	....	2
Mexican	....	....	....	....	....	....	1	....	1	....	....	....	....	....	2
Other races a	....	....	....	....	....	....	....	....	1	....	....	....	....	....	1
Total foreign-born	....	1	....	....	....	....	2	....	3	1	4	2	1	1	15
Grand total	1	4	2	2	1	3	3	5	16	11	9	6	1	2	66

a "Other races" includes races having less than 10 representatives in this city and pupils whose race is not reported.

TABLE 4.—*Race and grade, by age—Number of pupils of each specified age in each grade, by general nativity and race of father of pupil.*

BOYS: AGE 4 YEARS.

General nativity and race of father of pupil.	Kindergarten.	Ungraded and special schools.	Grand total.
Native-born:			
White	84	1	85
Negro	5	....	5
Total native-born	89	1	90
Foreign-born:			
English	11	....	11
Other races a	43	....	43
Total foreign-born	54	....	54
Grand total	143	1	144

a "Other races" includes races having less than 10 representatives of this sex and age and pupils whose race is not reported.

TABLE **4.**—*Race and grade, by age—Number of pupils of each specified age in each grade, by general nativity and race of father of pupil*—Continued.

BOYS: AGE 5 YEARS.

General nativity and race of father of pupil.	Kindergarten.	Elementary grade 1.	Ungraded and special schools.	Grand total.
Native-born:				
White	477	2	1	480
Negro	14			14
Indian	1			1
Total native-born	492	2	1	495
Foreign-born:				
Canadian (other than French)	16		1	16
English	23			24
German	36			36
Hebrew, Russian	30			30
Hebrew, Other	13			13
Italian, North	17			17
Italian, South	15			15
Mexican	13			13
Russian	15			15
Swedish	10			10
Other races *a*	42			42
Total foreign-born	230		1	231
Grand total	722	2	2	726

a "Other races" includes races having less than 10 representatives of this sex and age and pupils whose race is not reported.

BOYS: AGE 6 YEARS.

General nativity and race of father of pupil.	Kindergarten.	Elementary grades.			Ungraded schools.	Grand total.
		1.	2.	Total.		
Native-born:						
White	85	754	14	768		853
Negro	7	42		42		49
Total native-born	92	796	14	810		902
Foreign-born:						
Canadian (other than French)	6	37	1	38		44
Danish	2	10		10		12
English	6	39	1	40		46
French		15		15		15
German	7	72	1	73		80
Hebrew, German	1	12		12		13
Hebrew, Russian	6	20	1	21		27
Hebrew, Other	1	13		13		14
Irish	1	18	1	19		20
Italian, North	5	23		23		28
Italian, South	2	37	1	38		40
Mexican	1	37		37	1	39
Russian		35	3	38		38
Spanish-American	1	15		15	1	17
Swedish	4	16		16		20
Other races *a*	4	42	1	43		47
Total foreign-born	47	441	10	451	2	500
Grand total	139	1,237	24	1,261	2	1,402

a "Other races" includes races having less than 10 representatives of this sex and age and pupils whose race is not reported.

TABLE 4.—*Race and grade, by age—Number of pupils of each specified age in each grade, by general nativity and race of father of pupil—Continued.*

BOYS: AGE 7 YEARS.

General nativity and race of father of pupil.	Elementary grades.					Ungraded and special schools.	Grand total.
	1.	2.	3.	4.	Total.		
Native-born:							
White	523	348	28	1	900	4	904
Negro	30	11			41	1	42
Total native-born	553	359	28	1	941	5	946
Foreign-born:							
Canadian (other than French)	11	15	1		27		27
Danish	8	3			11		11
English	40	18	3		61		61
French	8	7			15		15
German	47	33	4	1	85		85
Hebrew, German	6	6	2		14		14
Hebrew, Russian	11	6	4		21		21
Hebrew, Other	4	6			10		10
Irish	7	8			15		15
Italian, North	20	8	2		30		30
Italian, South	19	8			27		27
Mexican	30	2			32	1	33
Russian	17	7			24		24
Scotch	9	7	1		17		17
Spanish-American	11	2			13	1	14
Swedish	8	10			18		18
Other races a	26	19	1		46		46
Total foreign-born	282	165	18	1	466	2	468
Grand total	835	524	46	2	1,407	7	1,414

a "Other races" includes races having less than 10 representatives of this sex and age and pupils whose race is not reported.

BOYS: AGE 8 YEARS.

General nativity and race of father of pupil.	Elementary grades.						Ungraded and special schools.	Grand total.
	1.	2.	3.	4.	5.	6.	Total.		
Native-born:									
White	186	512	307	32		1	1,038	2	1,040
Negro	15	22	5				42		42
Total native-born	201	534	312	32		1	1,080	2	1,082
Foreign-born:									
Canadian (other than French)	7	17	13				37		37
English	9	20	11	2			42		42
French	3	5	2				10		10
German	13	41	24	5			83		83
Hebrew, German	1	9	8	4			22		22
Hebrew, Russian	3	8	6	3			20		20
Irish	1	10	8	1			20		20
Italian, North	11	12	6				29		29
Italian, South	5	15	4				24		24
Mexican	37	6					43		43
Russian	11	10					21		21
Spanish-American	11	6					17		17
Swedish	2	11	3				16		16
Other races a	13	22	21	3	1		60	1	61
Total foreign-born	127	192	106	18	1		444	1	445
Grand total	328	726	418	50	1	1	1,524	3	1,527

a "Other races" includes races having less than 10 representatives of this sex and age and pupils whose race is not reported.

TABLE 4.—*Race, sex, and age, by grade—Number of pupils of each age in each grade, by sex and by general nativity and race of father of pupil*—Continued.

BOYS: AGE 9 YEARS.

General nativity and race of father of pupil.	Elementary grades.							Un-graded and special school.	Grand total.
	1.	2.	3.	4.	5.	6.	Total.		
Native-born:									
White....................	31	207	398	237	18	1	892	2	894
Negro....................	5	16	15	5	2		43	1	44
Total native-born........	36	223	413	242	20	1	935	3	938
Foreign-born:									
Canadian (other than French)........	1	9	23	13			46		46
English..................	3	12	35	9	2		61		61
French...................	4	3	8				15		15
German...................	3	23	32	18	3		79		79
Hebrew, German...........	1	5	9	3	3		21		21
Hebrew, Russian..........	1	9	18	5	1		34	1	35
Irish....................	1	6	12	7	2		28		28
Italian, North...........	1	10	5	4			20		20
Italian, South	6	8	9	2			25		25
Mexican..................	23	6	7	3	1		40	3	43
Russian..................	5	9	1				15		15
Scotch...................		1	3	6	1		11		11
Spanish-American.........	6	10	3	2			21		21
Swedish..................		6	16	5	1		28		28
Other races *a*..........	4	15	28	17	2		66		66
Total foreign-born.......	59	132	209	94	16		510	4	514
Grand total.............	95	355	622	336	36	1	1,445	7	1,452

a "Other races" includes races having less than 10 representatives of this sex and age and pupils whose race is not reported.

BOYS: AGE 10 YEARS.

General nativity and race of father of pupil.	Elementary grades.									Un-graded and special schools.	Grand total.
	1.	2.	3.	4.	5.	6.	7.	8.	Total.		
Native-born:											
White....................	12	58	259	380	236	19	1	1	966	1	967
Negro....................	5	8	17	7	4				41		41
Total native-born.......	17	66	276	387	240	19	1	1	1,007	1	1,008
Foreign-born:											
Canadian (other than French)..	1	1	14	24	7	2	1		50		50
English..................	2	2	9	25	11	1			50		50
French..................	2	1	6	5					14		14
German..................		6	24	40	11	2			83	1	84
Hebrew, German..........		1	4	12	1	3			21		21
Hebrew, Russian.........			7	8	10	1	1		27		27
Hebrew, Other...........			2	3	5	2		1	13		13
Irish...................	3	3	13	12	1				32	1	33
Italian, North..........	2	3	7	4	1				17		17
Italian, South..........	11	8	12	3	2				36	3	39
Mexican.................	2	15	4	3					24		24
Russian.................			4	5	6				15		15
Scotch..................		1	1	4	9				15		15
Spanish-American........	5	10	4	2	1				22	1	23
Swedish.................	1	2	9	5	5	1			23		23
Other races *a*.........	3	6	10	27	10				56		56
Total foreign-born.....	32	59	130	182	80	12	2	2	499	6	505
Grand total...........	49	125	407	569	320	31	3	3	1,507	7	1,504

a "Other races" includes races having less than 10 representatives of this sex and age and pupils whose race is not reported.

TABLE 4.—*Race, sex, and age, by grade—Number of pupils of each age in each grade, by sex and by general nativity and race of father of pupil*—Continued.

BOYS: AGE 11 YEARS.

General nativity and race of father of pupil.	Elementary grades.									Ungraded and special schools.	Grand total.
	1.	2.	3.	4.	5.	6.	7.	8.	Total.		
Native-born:											
White		21	121	318	345	180	33	1	1,019	5	1,024
Negro		4	13	18	6	3			44		44
Total native-born		25	134	336	351	183	33	1	1,063	5	1,068
Foreign-born:											
Canadian (other than French)		1	4	16	15	6			42		42
Canadian, French	1	2	1	3	4	1			12		12
Danish		1	2	6	5		1		15		15
English		1	9	13	20	6	1	1	51		51
French		1	3	4	6	1			15		15
German			12	34	33	21	2		102		102
Hebrew, German				6	2	5			13		13
Hebrew, Russian			2	8	15	8	1		34		34
Hebrew, Other			3	5	3	2	1		14		14
Irish			3	9	8	3			23		23
Italian, North			6	4	2	4	1		17		17
Italian, South		2	5	4	6	2			19		19
Mexican	15	11	12	5	1				44		44
Russian		3	5	1	1	1			11		11
Scotch			2	7	11	1			21		21
Spanish-American	2	4	2	2	4	1			15		15
Swedish		1	3	8	8	5			25		25
Other races *a*	1		8	15	18	3	1		46		46
Total foreign-born	19	27	82	150	162	70	8	1	519		519
Grand total	19	52	216	486	513	253	41	2	1,582	5	1,587

a "Other races" includes races having less than 10 representatives of this sex and age and pupils whose race is not reported.

TABLE 4.—*Race and grade, by age—Number of pupils of each specified age in each grade, by general nativity and race of father of pupil*—Continued.

BOYS: AGE 12 YEARS.

General nativity and race of father of pupil.	Elementary grades.									Ungraded and special schools.	Grand total.
	1.	2.	3.	4.	5.	6.	7.	8.	Total.		
Native-born:											
White	1	14	47	174	321	322	179	22	1,080	15	1,095
Negro		1	9	17	17	6	1	....	51	2	53
Total native-born	1	15	56	191	338	328	180	22	1,131	17	1,148
Foreign-born:											
Canadian (other than French)	....	....	2	8	23	16	8	1	58	....	58
English	....	....	3	14	14	19	9	1	60	....	60
French	....	1	2	5	10	6	2	....	26	....	26
German	....	1	5	23	46	35	18	2	130	....	130
Hebrew, German	....	....	1	2	7	9	3	....	22	....	22
Hebrew, Russian	1	....	....	2	7	11	1	2	24	....	24
Hebrew, Other	....	....	1	1	3	4	2	1	12	....	12
Irish	....	....	1	4	6	5	4	2	22	1	23
Italian, North	....	....	3	3	2	1	5	....	14	....	14
Italian, South	....	....	4	6	5	5	....	....	20	....	20
Mexican	3	5	14	7	3	1	....	....	33	2	35
Russian	1	10	8	1	1	2	1	....	24	....	24
Scotch	....	....	....	1	8	9	3	2	23	....	23
Spanish-American	1	1	3	6	2	1	1	....	15	....	15
Swedish	....	....	2	3	12	10	3	....	30	....	30
Other races a	1	1	2	10	17	10	3	....	44	1	45
Total foreign-born	7	19	51	96	166	144	63	11	557	4	561
Grand total	8	34	107	287	504	472	243	33	1,688	21	1,709

a "Other races" includes races having less than 10 representatives of this sex and age and pupils whose race is not reported.

TABLE 4.—*Race and grade, by age—Number of pupils of each specified age in each grade, by general nativity and race of father of pupil—Continued.*

BOYS: AGE 13 YEARS.

General nativity and race of father of pupil	__Elementary grades.__ 1.	2.	3.	4.	5.	6.	7.	8.	Total.	__High school.__ First year.	Second year.	Third year.	Total.	Ungraded and special schools.	Grand total.
Native-born:															
White	1	2	11	62	171	304	257	128	936	16			16	13	965
Negro		2	3	13	15	15	4		52					4	56
Indian							1		1						1
Total native-born	1	4	14	75	186	319	262	128	989	16			16	17	1,022
Foreign-born:															
Canadian (other than French)				2	10	16	14	9	51						51
Danish					6	4	2		12						12
English			1	7	18	18	15	6	65						65
French			2		6	6	1	4	19						19
German			1	5	25	22	21	15	89	1			1	2	92
Hebrew, German			1		6	9	3		19	1		1	2		21
Hebrew, Russian			4	2	3	7	7	3	26	1			1		27
Hebrew, Other			1	2	3	4	7		17						17
Irish				2	6	6	7	3	24						24
Italian, North			1	5	2	9	6	1	24					1	25
Italian, South			3	2	5	1	1		12						12
Mexican	1	2	8	8	5		1		25					1	26
Russian	1	3	6	3	2		2		17						17
Scotch				1	4	3	7		15					2	17
Spanish-American	1	1	1	7	1	3	2		16						16
Swedish				3	3	7	6	4	23						23
Other races a		1	1	6	8	9	8	3	36						36
Total foreign-born	3	7	30	55	106	117	113	58	489	3		1	4	6	499
Grand total	4	11	44	130	293	436	375	186	1,479	19		1	20	23	1,522

a "Other races" includes races having less than 10 representatives of this sex and age and pupils whose race is not reported.

TABLE 4.—*Race and grade, by age—Number of pupils of each specified age in each grade, by general nativity and race of father of pupil—Continued.*

BOYS: AGE 14 YEARS.

General nativity and race of father of pupil.	Elementary grades.									High school.				Un-graded and special schools.	Grand total.
	1.	2.	3.	4.	5.	6.	7.	8.	Total.	First year.	Second year.	Third year.	Total.		
Native-born:															
White			4	13	73	195	290	269	844	116	10	3	129	24	997
Negro				9	16	12	10	1	48						48
Indian														1	1
Total native-born			4	22	89	207	300	270	892	116	10	3	129	25	1,046
Foreign-born:															
Canadian (other than French)					3	11	17	17	48	5			5	3	56
English			1	4	3	18	19	13	58	7	2		9	2	69
French				2	3	8	5	4	22						22
German			1	2	9	20	34	23	89	8	1		9	7	105
Hebrew, German						3	4	9	16	3	1		4		20
Hebrew, Other			1		1	4	4	3	13					2	15
Irish			1	2	3	8	9	2	25	3			3		28
Italian, North		1	1			5	5	1	13					1	14
Italian, South			3	5	4	1	1	3	17					2	19
Mexican	1	4	5	7	3	2	1	1	24					1	25
Norwegian	1					3	3	4	11	1			1		12
Russian		2	8	1					11						11
Scotch				1		4	8	6	19	5			5		24
Spanish-American				1		2	3	3	9	2			2		11
Swedish				1	2	3	7	7	20	3			3		23
Other races *a*		2		3	6	7	10	16	44						44
Total foreign-born	2	9	21	29	38	99	130	111	439	37	4		41	18	498
Grand total	2	9	25	51	127	306	430	381	1,331	153	14	3	170	43	1,544

a "Other races" includes races having less than 10 representatives of this sex and age and pupils whose race is not reported.

TABLE **4.**—*Race and grade, by age—Number of pupils of each specified age in each grade, by general nativity and race of father of pupil*—Continued.

BOYS: AGE 15 YEARS.

General nativity and race of father of pupil.	Elementary grades.								High school.			Un-graded and special schools.	Total.
	1.	2.	3.	4.	5.	6.	7.	8.	First year.	Second year.	Third year.		
Native-born:													
White	1	1	2	5	13	65	142	200	179	38	13	21	680
Negro			3	1	5	4	6	7	5			1	32
Indian				1									1
Total native-born	1	1	5	7	18	69	148	207	184	38	13	22	713
Foreign-born:													
Canadian (other than French)													
English						1	8	15	7	1			32
French				1	2	6	9	12	13	1		1	45
German					1	3	3	3	1				10
Hebrew, Other					1	5	9	12	13	5		1	46
Irish							5	9	5	2			22
Swedish						3	3	3	4			3	16
Other races a		2	4	4	11	10	15	12	5	2		1	14
Total foreign-born		2	4	5	15	28	57	68	62	11		10	263
Grand total	1	3	9	12	33	97	205	275	246	49	13	32	976

a "Other races" includes races having less than 10 representatives of this sex and age and pupils whose race is not reported.

BOYS: AGE 16 YEARS.

General nativity and race of father of pupil.	Elementary grades.						High school.				Un-graded and special schools.	Total.
	3.	4.	5.	6.	7.	8.	First year.	Second year.	Third year.	Fourth year.		
Native-born:												
White	1	1		8	25	96	207	73	26	2	12	451
Negro		2	1	2	5	5	2					17
Indian						1						1
Total native-born	1	3	1	10	30	101	210	73	26	2	12	469
Foreign-born:												
Canadian (other than French)												
English				1	1	6	4	7	2		3	23
German			1	1	1	6	10	1	3			22
Hebrew, Other				1	1	8	10	3	5	3	5	36
Irish						3	7	2	1	1	3	10
Japanese	1	3	2	1	1	1	1	1				14
Other races a		1	2	2	5	14	20	6	1		1	11
Total foreign-born	1	4	4	5	11	38	55	22	12	4	12	168
Grand total	2	7	5	15	41	139	265	95	38	6	24	637

a "Other races" includes races having less than 10 representatives of this sex and age and pupils whose race is not reported.

TABLE 4.—*Race and grade, by age—Number of pupils of each specified age in each grade, by general nativity and race of father of pupil*—Continued.

BOYS: AGE 17 YEARS.

General nativity and race of father of pupil.	Elementary grades.						High school.				Un-graded and special schools.	Total.
	3.	4.	5.	6.	7.	8.	First year.	Second year.	Third year.	Fourth year.		
Native-born:												
White..................				2	3	20	114	93	35	26	4	297
Negro..................						1	3	1				5
Total native-born....				2	3	21	117	94	35	26	4	302
Foreign-born:												
Canadian (other than French).................				1	....	2	6	9	2	1	....	21
English................						2	4	1	3	3	....	13
German................			3		....	....	10	4	3	8	....	25
Japanese..............	1	....	2	1	2	1	2	2	....	1	....	12
Other races a.........	....	3	2	1	....	2	20	13	6	5	....	52
Total foreign-born....	1	3	5	2	2	7	42	29	14	18	....	123
Grand total..........	1	3	5	4	5	28	159	123	49	44	4	425

a "Other races" includes races having less than 10 representatives of this sex and age and pupils whose race is not reported.

BOYS: AGE 18 YEARS.

General nativity and race of father of pupil.	Elementary grades.						High school.				Un-graded school.	Total.
	3.	4.	5.	6.	7.	8.	First year.	Second year.	Third year.	Fourth year.		
Native-born:												
White..................					2	4	57	35	43	32	1	174
Negro..................										1	....	1
Total native-born....					2	4	57	35	43	33	1	175
Foreign-born:												
English................							3	1	4	4	....	12
Japanese..............	2	1	....	2	1	1	2	1	4	....	....	14
Other races a.........			1	1	1	1	6	13	2	11	....	36
Total foreign-born....	2	1	1	3	2	2	11	15	10	15	....	62
Grand total..........	2	1	1	3	4	6	68	50	53	48	1	237

a "Other races" includes races having less than 10 representatives of this sex and age and pupils whose race is not reported.

TABLE **4.**—*Race and grade, by age—Number of pupils of each specified age in each grade, by general nativity and race of father of pupil*—Continued.

BOYS: AGE 19 YEARS.

General nativity and race of father of pupil.	Elementary grades.								High school.				Un-graded school.	Total.
	1.	2.	3.	4.	5.	6.	7.	8.	First year.	Second year.	Third year.	Fourth year.		
Native-born:														
White.............	...	...	...	...	...	...	...	...	8	12	18	25	1	64
Negro.............	...	...	...	...	...	...	...	...	1	1	.....	.....	....	2
Total native-born...	...	...	...	...	...	...	...	...	9	13	18	25	1	66
Foreign-born:														
Japanese.............	1	...	2	...	1	...	...	1	4	1	1	1	....	12
Other races *a*........	...	...	...	...	1	...	1	...	5	8	10	9	....	34
Total foreign-born...	1	...	2	...	2	...	1	1	9	9	11	10	....	46
Grand total.........	1	...	2	...	2	...	1	1	18	22	29	35	1	112

a "Other races" includes races having less than 10 representatives of this sex and age and pupils whose race is not reported.

BOYS: AGE 20 YEARS.

General nativity and race of father of pupil.	Elementary grades.		High school.				Un-graded school.	Total.
	5.	6.	First year.	Second year.	Third year.	Fourth year.		
Native-born, White.........................	...	...	3	....	8	23	1	35
Foreign-born, other races *a*.................	2	1	5	4	4	9	2	27
Grand total.............................	2	1	8	4	12	32	3	62

a "Other races" includes races having less than 10 representatives of this sex and age and pupils whose race is not reported.

GIRLS: AGE 4 YEARS.

General nativity and race of father of pupil.	Kinder-garten.
Native-born:	
White...	97
Negro...	7
Total native-born...	104
Foreign-born, other races *a*..	48
Grand total...	152

a "Other races" includes races having less than 10 representatives of this sex and age and pupils whose race is not reported.

TABLE 4.—*Race and grade, by age—Number of pupils of each specified age in each grade, by general nativity and race of father of pupil—Continued.*

GIRLS: AGE 5 YEARS.

General nativity and race of father of pupil.	Kindergarten.	Elementary grade 1.	Special school.	Grand total.
Native-born:				
White	542	1	2	545
Negro	24			24
Total native-born	566	1	2	569
Foreign-born:				
Canadian (other than French)	14			14
English	33			33
German	45			45
Hebrew, Russian	28			28
Italian, North	25			25
Mexican	30			30
Russian	13			13
Spanish-American	11			11
Swedish	10			10
Other races a	67			67
Total foreign-born	276			276
Grand total	842	1	2	845

a "Other races" includes races having less than 10 representatives of this sex and age and pupils whose race is not reported.

GIRLS: AGE 6 YEARS.

General nativity and race of father of pupil.	Kindergarten.	Elementary grades. 1.	Elementary grades. 2.	Special school.	Total.
Native-born:					
White	92	716	25	2	835
Negro	3	38			41
Total native-born	95	754	25	2	876
Foreign-born:					
Canadian (other than French)	1	31	1		33
English	4	34			38
French	2	16	2		20
German	5	58	2		64
Hebrew, German	1	19	2		22
Hebrew, Russian	4	26	3		33
Irish	1	13	1		15
Italian, North		17	1		18
Italian, South	2	22	1		25
Mexican	1	42			43
Russian	1	25			26
Spanish-American	5	8			13
Swedish	2	27			29
Other races a	7	61	1		70
Total foreign-born	36	399	14		449
Grand total	131	1,153	39	2	1,325

a "Other races" includes races having less than 10 representatives of this sex and age and pupils whose race is not reported.

TABLE 4.—*Race and grade, by age—Number of pupils of each specified age in each grade, by general nativity and race of father of pupil*—Continued.

GIRLS: AGE 7 YEARS.

General nativity and race of father of pupil.	Elementary grades.				Ungraded schools.	Total.
	1.	2.	3.	4.		
Native-born:						
White................................	437	444	30	....	....	911
Negro................................	29	16	....	....	....	45
Total native-born................	466	460	30	....	....	956
Foreign-born:						
Canadian (other than French).........	13	22	....	4	....	35
English.............................	24	23	4	....	....	51
French..............................	8	3	3	....	....	14
German..............................	32	29	6	....	....	67
Hebrew, German......................	3	11	....	....	....	14
Hebrew, Russian.....................	12	6	5	1	....	24
Hebrew, Other.......................	9	9	....	....	....	18
Irish...............................	6	6	3	....	....	15
Italian, North......................	13	3	....	....	....	16
Italian, South......................	14	5	1	....	....	20
Mexican.............................	31	2	....	....	1	34
Russian.............................	26	7	....	....	....	33
Spanish-American....................	9	3	....	....	1	13
Swedish.............................	8	9	3	....	....	20
Other races a......................	27	26	4	....	....	57
Total foreign-born...............	235	164	29	1	2	431
Grand total.....................	701	624	59	1	2	1,387

a "Other races" includes races having less than 10 representatives of this sex and age and pupils whose race is not reported.

GIRLS: AGE 8 YEARS.

General nativity and race of father of pupil.	Elementary grades.					Ungraded schools.	Total.
	1.	2.	3.	4.	5.		
Native-born:							
White....	108	394	396	39	1	....	938
Negro....	8	25	10	1	....	....	44
Total native-born....	116	419	406	40	1	....	982
Foreign-born:							
Canadian (other than French).............	4	14	20	3	....	....	41
English....	5	20	23	3	....	....	51
French....	....	8	5	....	....	....	13
German....	9	28	39	1	....	....	77
Hebrew, German....	1	8	2	1	....	....	12
Hebrew, Russian....	5	11	10	1	....	....	27
Hebrew, Other....	3	5	11	1	....	....	20
Irish....	....	13	4	2	....	....	19
Italian, North....	3	7	10	1	....	....	21
Italian, South....	4	10	5	....	....	....	19
Mexican....	23	8	4	....	....	1	36
Russian....	14	10	1	....	....	....	25
Scotch....	1	2	7	....	....	....	10
Spanish-American....	7	12	2	....	....	....	21
Swedish....	1	11	13	....	....	....	25
Other races a....	10	31	22	1	....	1	65
Total foreign-born....	90	198	178	14	....	2	482
Grand total....	206	617	584	54	1	2	1,464

a "Other races" includes races having less than 10 representatives of this sex and age and pupils whose race is not reported.

TABLE 4.—*Race and grade, by age—Number of pupils of each specified age in each grade, by general nativity and race of father of pupil*—Continued.

GIRLS: AGE 9 YEARS.

General nativity and race of father of pupil.	Elementary grades.					Un-graded and special schools.	Total.
	1.	2.	3.	4.	5.		
Native-born:							
White....................	10	142	408	304	33	1	898
Negro....................	....	11	18	10	....	....	39
Total native-born..........	10	153	426	314	33	1	937
Foreign-born:							
Canadian (other than French).............	....	4	16	9	1	...:....	30
Danish....................	1	1	8	2	....	....	12
English....................	1	7	20	18	....	....	46
French....................	1	2	6	3	....	....	12
German....................	4	13	43	32	4	....	96
Hebrew, German....................	....	2	6	8	3	....	19
Hebrew, Russian....................	3	2	9	7	1	....	22
Hebrew, Other....................	1	....	8	2	....	....	11
Irish....................	....	2	12	8	....	....	22
Italian, North....................	....	8	10	3	....	....	21
Italian, South....................	1	4	7	1	....	....	13
Mexican....................	14	4	5	....	....	4	27
Russian....................	10	10	4	....	....	....	24
Scotch....................	....	1	7	3	1	....	12
Spanish-American....................	4	9	5	....	....	....	18
Swedish....................	....	....	13	10	....	....	23
Other races *a*....................	2	9	24	6	2	....	43
Total foreign-born....................	42	78	203	112	12	4	451
Grand total....'....................	52	231	629	426	45	5	1,388

a "Other races" includes races having less than 10 representatives of this sex and age and pupils whose ace is not reported.

TABLE 4.—*Race and grade, by age—Number of pupils of each specified age in each grade, by general nativity and race of father of pupil*—Continued.

GIRLS: AGE 10 YEARS.

General nativity and race of father of pupil.	Elementary grades.								Un-graded schools.	Total.
	1.	2.	3.	4.	5.	6.	7.	8.		
Native-born:										
White	2	33	199	407	254	30	2		1	928
Negro	1	6	19	18	6					50
Total native-born	3	39	218	425	260	30	2	1	1	978
Foreign-born:										
Canadian (other than French)	1	1	7	18	14	4				45
Danish			2	2	6					10
English			7	26	12	4				49
French	1	3	6	8	4	1				23
German		4	23	54	35	6				122
Hebrew, German		1	6	12	7	1		1		28
Hebrew, Russian		3	2	8	10	2				25
Hebrew, Other		1	1	3	4	2				11
Irish			5	10	5					20
Italian, North		1	10	5	3					19
Italian, South	1	5	6	8	1	1				21
Mexican	17	10	9	5						41
Russian	9	15	4		2					30
Scotch		1	3	10	4	2				20
Spanish-American	1	8	5	4	1	1				19
Swedish		2	5	9	5	1				22
Other races a	2	7	12	14	10	2				49
Total foreign-born	32	62	113	196	123	27		1		554
Grand total	35	101	331	621	383	57	2	1	1	1,532

a "Other races" includes races having less than 10 representatives of this sex and age and pupils whose race is not reported.

TABLE 4.—*Race and grade, by age—Number of pupils of each specified age in each grade, by general nativity and race of father of pupil*—Continued.

GIRLS: AGE 11 YEARS.

General nativity and race of father of pupil.	Elementary grades.								Ungraded and special schools.	Total.
	1.	2.	3.	4.	5.	6.	7.	8.		
Native-born:										
White	3	7	69	253	347	228	20	1	3	931
Negro		1	11	24	15	5	1			57
Indian				1						1
Total native-born	3	8	80	278	362	233	21	1	3	989
Foreign-born:										
Canadian (other than French)		1	3	12	18	9	1			44
Danish			2	3	2	3				10
English			3	21	23	13				60
French		2	6	5	13	3				29
German			6	29	44	18	4	1		102
Hebrew, German				6	10	7				23
Hebrew, Russian		1		6	8	6				21
Hebrew, Other			1	4	3	5	2			15
Irish			1	7	11	5			1	25
Italian, North		2	2	6	6	1	1		1	19
Italian, South		1	1	5	4	1				12
Mexican	4	5	10	2	1				1	23
Russian	4	7	8	1		1				20
Scotch			2	1	3	5	1	1		13
Swedish			1	11	6	9		1		27
Other races a	2	1	8	12	16	2	1	1	1	43
Total foreign-born	10	20	54	131	168	88	10	3	4	488
Grand total	13	28	134	409	530	321	31	4	7	1,477

a "Other races" includes races having less than 10 representatives of this sex and age and pupils whose race is not reported.

TABLE 4.—*Race and grade, by age—Number of pupils of each specified age in each grade, by general nativity and race of father of pupil—Continued.*

GIRLS: AGE 12 YEARS.

General nativity and race of father of pupil.	Elementary grades.								Un-graded and special schools.	Total.
	1.	2.	3.	4.	5.	6.	7.	8.		
Native-born:										
White	2	3	26	100	276	356	191	23	4	981
Negro	1	1	10	16	17	15	3	1	....	64
Indian	....	....	....	1	....	....	....	....	....	1
Total native-born	3	4	36	117	293	371	194	24	4	1,046
Foreign-born:										
Canadian (other than French)	....	....	1	5	19	12	10	....	....	47
English	....	1	6	10	14	22	15	1	....	69
French	....	....	2	5	10	2	6	....	....	25
German	....	....	2	12	20	38	8	2	....	82
Hebrew, German	....	....	1	4	5	6	6	1	....	23
Hebrew, Russian	2	....	2	2	5	6	3	....	....	20
Hebrew, Other	....	....	....	1	5	3	2	....	....	11
Irish	....	....	1	2	14	7	3	....	....	27
Italian, North	....	2	3	3	8	5	2	....	....	23
Italian, South	....	1	3	3	5	2	....	....	....	14
Mexican	2	5	4	3	1	....	....	1	....	16
Russian	4	1	2	1	1	1	2	....	....	12
Scotch	....	....	....	....	7	6	2	....	....	15
Spanish-American	....	2	1	3	3	2	....	....	....	11
Swedish	....	....	....	6	6	12	4	....	....	28
Other races a	1	2	8	11	22	15	8	1	1	69
Total foreign-born	9	14	36	71	145	139	71	6	1	492
Grand total	12	18	72	188	438	510	265	30	5	1,538

a "Other races" includes races having less than 10 representatives of this sex and age and pupils whose race is not reported.

GIRLS: AGE 13 YEARS.

General nativity and race of father of pupil.	Elementary grades.								High school.			Un-graded and special schools.	Total.
	1.	2.	3.	4.	5.	6.	7.	8.	First year.	Second year.	Third year.		
Native-born:													
White	....	....	7	33	110	300	337	145	17	....	1	3	953
Negro	....	....	6	6	17	14	5	1	....	....	....	....	49
Total native-born	....	....	13	39	127	314	342	146	17	....	1	3	1,002
Foreign-born:													
Canadian (other than French)	....	....	....	1	5	15	15	8	....	....	....	.....	43
Danish	....	....	1	1	1	7	3	2	....	....	....	....	14
English	....	....	2	11	21	22	7	1	....	....	....	64
French	....	....	....	2	6	....	2	....	....	....	....	10
German	....	....	3	6	19	38	32	18	1	....	....	....	117
Hebrew, German	....	....	....	1	3	11	10	3	1	....	....	....	29
Hebrew, Russian	....	....	2	3	5	6	5	2	....	....	....	23
Irish	....	....	....	5	8	7	2	2	....	....	....	24
Italian, North	....	....	3	3	5	2	1	....	....	....	1	15
Mexican	2	4	3	3	2	1	....	....	....	....	....	15
Russian	4	5	2	....	2	1	2	....	....	....	1	18
Scotch	....	....	....	....	1	1	10	4	....	....	....	16
Spanish-American	....	....	2	3	1	4	....	1	....	....	....	11
Swedish	....	....	....	....	4	7	8	6	1	....	....	....	25
Other races a	....	....	....	6	15	9	10	7	....	....	....	42
Total foreign-born	6	9	10	27	77	139	127	65	8	....	....	2	470
Grand total	6	9	23	66	204	453	469	211	25	....	1	5	1,472

a "Other races" includes races having less than 10 representatives of this sex and age and pupils whose race is not reported.

TABLE 4.—*Race and grade, by age—Number of pupils of each specified age in each grade, by general nativity and race of father of pupil*—Continued.

GIRLS: AGE 14 YEARS.

General nativity and race of father of pupil.	Elementary grades.								High school.			Ungraded and special schools.	Total.
	1.	2.	3.	4.	5.	6.	7.	8.	First year.	Second year.	Third year.		
Native-born:													
White	1		1	10	43	162	294	292	125	8	4	11	951
Negro		1	1	4	12	11	9	4	3	1			46
Indian								1					1
Total native-born	1	1	2	14	55	173	303	297	128	9	4	11	998
Foreign-born:													
Canadian (other than French)					1	6	16	13	6			1	43
Danish				1	1	3	6	5	1				17
English		1		1	2	18	18	22	10				71
French					3	2	7	7	2				21
German				4	9	15	29	35	19				111
Hebrew, German						4	3	8	2				17
Hebrew, Russian	1		1	1	2		6	2	1				14
Irish			1	1	1	4	5	6	5				23
Italian, North					2	10	2		1				15
Mexican	2	2	5	2	3		1						15
Scotch						1	5	7	2	1			16
Swedish					2	7	10	5	1				25
Other races a		1		2	4	11	13	17	3	2		1	54
Total foreign-born	3	4	7	12	30	81	121	127	53	2		2	442
Grand total	4	5	9	26	85	254	424	424	181	11	4	13	1,440

a "Other races" includes races having less than 10 representatives of this sex and age and pupils whose race is not reported.

GIRLS: AGE 15 YEARS.

General nativity and race of father of pupil.	Elementary grades.								High school.				Ungraded and special schools.	Total.
	1.	2.	3.	4.	5.	6.	7.	8.	First year.	Second year.	Third year.	Fourth year.		
Native-born:														
White			2	5	11	39	135	214	193	59	14		15	687
Negro					1	12	9	20	6	1				49
Indian								1						1
Total native-born			2	5	12	51	144	235	199	60	14		15	737
Foreign-born:														
Canadian (other than French)						2	6	20	10	3	1	1		43
English						1	8	14	14	8				44
French				1	3	2	7		4		1		2	20
German					1	3	9	13	18	5	2	1	1	53
Hebrew (not specified)					2	1	3	5	5				2	18
Irish							2	3	6	3	2		3	19
Italian, North							3	2	2				3	10
Scotch								3	7	6	1			17
Other races a	1		2	1	5	11	17		10	3	1		2	53
Total foreign-born	1		3	1	9	19	43	89	70	26	5	2	10	278
Grand total	1		5	6	21	70	187	324	269	86	19	2	25	1,015

a "Other races" includes races having less than 10 representatives of this sex and age and pupils whose race is not reported.

TABLE **4.**—*Race and grade, by age—Number of pupils of each specified age in each grade, by general nativity and race of father of pupil*—Continued.

GIRLS: AGE 16 YEARS.

General nativity and race of father of pupil.	Elementary grades.								High school.				Un-graded school.	Total.
	1.	2.	3.	4.	5.	6.	7.	8.	First year.	Second year.	Third year.	Fourth year.		
Native-born:														
White.............	...	...	1	...	1	10	23	90	174	101	54	8	10	472
Negro.............	...	...	..	...	...	...	3	7	10	4	4	......	......	28
Total native-born.....	...	...	1	...	1	13	30	100	178	105	54	8	10	500
Foreign-born:														
Canadian (other than French).............									5	9	3	1	......	1	19
English.............	...	...	...	...	1	...	...	4	7	15	3	2	......	1	33
German.............	...	...	...	...	...	1	3	8	11	8	3	2	......		36
Hebrew (not specified)...								4	1	2	2	......	1		10
Irish.............								3	3	4	2	1	......		13
Other races a.............	...	1	...	1	1	1	3	30	27	9	6	......	4	52
Total foreign-born.....	...	...	...	1	2	2	10	40	52	29	16	3	7	163
Grand total.............	...	1	1	1	3	15	40	140	230	134	70	11	17	663

a "Other races" includes races having less than 10 representat ves of this sex and age and pupils whose race is not reported.

GIRLS: AGE 17 YEARS.

General nativity and race of father of pupil.	Elementary grades.			High school.				Un-graded and special schools.	Total.
	6.	7.	8.	First year.	Second year.	Third year.	Fourth year.		
Native-born:									
White.............			14	82	75	79	62	4	316
Negro.............	2	1	2	8	2	2	......	......	17
Total native-born.............	2	1	16	90	77	81	62	4	333
Foreign-born:									
Canadian (other than French).............	...	...	2	2	6	3	2	1	16
English.............	...	...	1	6	......	5	5	1	18
German.............	...	2	2	7	2	5	6	1	25
Other races a.............	1	...	3	13	11	12	6	......	46
Total foreign-born.............	1	2	8	28	19	25	19	3	105
Grand total.............	3	3	24	118	96	106	81	7	438

a "Other races" includes races having less than 10 representatives of this sex and age and pupils whose race is not reported.

TABLE 4.—*Race and grade, by age—Number of pupils of each specified age in each grade, by general nativity and race of father of pupil*—Continued.

GIRLS: AGE 18 YEARS.

General nativity and race of father of pupil.	Elementary grades.			High school.					Grand total.
	6.	7.	8.	First year.	Second year.	Third year.	Fourth year.	Total.	
Native-born:									
White			2	21	31	33	60	145	147
Negro				1		1	2	4	4
Indian			1						1
Total native-born			3	22	31	34	62	149	152
Foreign-born:									
German					3	4	3	10	10
Other races a	1	1		5	9	6	12	32	34
Total foreign-born	1	1		5	12	10	15	42	44
Grand total	1	1	3	27	43	44	77	191	196

a "Other races" includes races having less than 10 representatives of this sex and age and pupils whose race is not reported.

GIRLS: AGE 19 YEARS.

General nativity and race of father of pupil.	Elementary grades.		High school.				Total.
	7.	8.	First year.	Second year.	Third year.	Fourth year.	
Native-born, White			4	8	12	32	56
Foreign-born, Other races a	1		2	3	1	7	14
Grand total	1		6	11	13	39	70

a "Other races" includes races having less than 10 representatives of this sex and age and pupils whose race is not reported.

GIRLS: AGE 20 YEARS.

General nativity and race of father of pupil.	High school.				Total.
	First year.	Second year.	Third year.	Fourth year.	
Native-born, White	1	4	5	12	22
Foreign-born, Other races a	1	2	1	4	8
Grand total	2	6	6	16	30

a "Other races" includes races having less than 10 representatives of this sex and age and pupils whose race is not reported.

TABLE 5.—*Race distribution in each grade—Percentages.*

[This table shows in detail only races with 100 or more pupils reporting. The totals, however, are for all races.]

General nativity and race of father of pupil	Kindergarten	Elementary grades									High school					Ungraded and special schools	Grand total
		1.	2.	3.	4.	5.	6.	7.	8.	Total.	First year.	Second year.	Third year.	Fourth year.	Total.		
Native-born:																	
White	64.7	58.6	62.9	61.8	63.6	63.4	67.3	69.8	68.7	63.9	73.4	73.5	75.5	72.1	73.6	58.8	64.8
Negro	2.8	3.7	3.5	3.7	4.0	3.8	3.1	2.2	2.3	3.4	1.8	1.3	.0	.8	1.4	3.2	3.2
Indian	(a)	.0	.0	.0	(a)			(a)	(a)	(a)	(a)			.0	(a)	(a)	(a)
Total native-born	67.5	62.2	66.5	65.6	67.7	67.2	70.4	72.0	71.2	67.3	75.3	74.9	76.1	72.9	75.0	62.4	68.0
Foreign-born:																	
Canadian, French	.4	.2	.3	.2	.3	.4	.3	.3	.3	.3	.3	.7	.0	.3	.4	.0	.3
Canadian, Other	2.0	2.2	2.5	2.8	2.9	3.3	3.1	3.5	4.4	3.0	3.0	4.7	3.0	3.6	3.4	3.6	3.6
Danish	.9	.5	.6	.6	.6	1.0	.7	1.0	.8	.7	.3	.4	.2	.5	.2	.0	.6
English	3.9	3.3	3.0	3.6	4.2	3.8	4.5	4.4	4.2	3.8	4.8	4.4	4.1	4.6	4.2	2.2	3.8
French	3.6	1.2	1.1	1.4	1.0	1.7	1.2	1.0	1.3	1.2	1.0	2.7	.9	1.0	.9	.7	1.2
German	5.0	5.0	5.1	6.0	7.1	7.3	6.8	6.2	6.3	6.2	5.6	4.6	5.9	8.2	5.7	6.8	6.1
Hebrew, German	.8	.9	1.4	1.1	1.6	1.9	1.7	1.3	1.3	1.3	.8	.9	.9	.5	.9	1.1	1.2
Hebrew, Russian	3.3	1.8	1.4	1.5	1.5	1.9	1.4	1.0	1.0	1.5	.8	.7	.2	.5	.4	1.4	1.5
Hebrew, Other	.8	1.0	1.3	.3	.3	1.3	1.3	1.3	1.0	1.5	.2	.0	.2	.0	.4	2.2	1.9
Irish	.8	1.0	1.3	1.5	1.6	2.0	1.6	1.5	1.4	1.5	1.7	2.7	1.7	3.1	2.1	2.2	1.5
Italian, North	2.6	1.9	1.6	1.9	1.3	.8	1.4	1.0	.3	1.4	.3	.0	.2	.0	.2	3.2	1.3
Italian, South	1.6	2.3	1.6	1.6	1.3	1.0	1.7	1.0	1.1	1.3	.3	.9	1.5	.0	.9	1.1	1.3
Japanese	2.1	.4	.2	.5	.3	.3	.2	.1	.3	.3	.7	.9	.0	.8	.0	.0	1.3
Mexican	2.4	6.2	2.4	2.6	1.3	.7	.1	.1	.3	2.1	.2	.3	.0	.0	.0	7.2	1.9
Norwegian	.4	.4	.4	.2	.4	.4	.4	.4	.6	.4	.2	.3	.0	.0	.2	.4	.4
Russian	1.9	3.5	3.3	1.4	.3	.3	.2	.3	(a)	1.4	1.7	1.5	1.0	.0	1.6	.4	1.3
Scotch	.6	.5	.5	.8	.9	1.4	1.0	1.5	1.4	1.3	.3	1.3	1.5	1.5	1.6	.4	1.0
Spanish-American	1.5	1.7	2.0	.9	.8	.6	.7	.4	1.2	1.0	.9	1.3	1.2	1.0	1.2	2.5	1.0
Swedish	1.4	1.3	1.5	1.6	1.6	1.5	1.9	1.8	1.5	1.0	2.3	2.3	2.6	1.5	2.2	3.2	1.5
Other races	2.5	3.0	2.9	3.4	2.9	2.9	1.7	1.6	2.5	2.7	2.3	2.3	2.6	1.3	2.2	3.2	2.6
Total foreign-born	32.5	37.8	33.5	34.4	32.3	32.8	29.6	28.0	28.8	32.7	24.7	25.1	23.9	27.1	25.0	37.6	32.0
Grand total	100.0	100.0	100.0	100.0	100.0	100.0	100.0	100.0	100.0	100.0	100.0	100.0	100.0	100.0	100.0	100.0	100.0

a Less than 0.05 per cent.

TABLE 6.—*Grade distribution of each race—Percentages.*

[This table shows in detail only races with 100 or more pupils reporting. The totals, however, are for all races.]

General nativity and race of father of pupil	Kinder-garten	Elementary grades										High school					Ungraded and special schools	Grand total
		1	2	3	4	5	6	7	8	Total	First year	Second year	Third year	Fourth year	Total		
Native-born:																		
White	6.4	12.9	10.3	10.7	11.0	10.4	10.3	8.9	7.0	81.4	6.1	2.5	1.6	1.3	11.5	0.8	100.0
Negro	5.7	16.4	11.8	13.2	14.3	12.7	9.8	5.8	4.9	88.9	3.1	.9	.3	.3	4.6	.8	100.0
Indian	(a)	(a)	(a)	(a)	(a)	(a)	(a)	(a)	(a)	(a)	(a)	(a)	(a)	(a)	(a)	(a)	100.0
Total native-born	6.3	13.0	10.3	10.8	11.1	10.5	10.2	8.8	6.9	81.7	5.9	2.4	1.5	1.3	11.2	.8	100.0
Foreign-born:																		
Canadian, French	8.0	10.7	10.0	8.0	10.1	15.7	12.0	8.0	7.0	80.0	6.4	5.0	.4	1.0	12.0	.0	100.0
Canadian, Other	4.4	10.7	8.8	10.5	11.1	11.7	13.5	9.8	9.9	82.9	5.4	3.5	1.4	1.4	11.7	1.0	100.0
Danish	2.0	12.9	10.4	10.9	10.9	17.3	11.4	10.9	8.9	93.6	2.5	1.5	1.5	.0	4.5	.5	100.0
English	2.5	12.2	8.3	10.5	12.2	10.5	11.5	9.4	7.3	81.9	6.7	1.6	1.5	1.4	11.2	.5	100.0
French	3.4	14.9	9.8	13.1	9.8	13.7	10.3	7.0	7.5	88.1	4.6	1.3	1.0	1.0	8.0	.5	100.0
German	5.2	11.8	8.9	11.1	13.1	12.8	11.1	8.5	6.9	84.2	5.0	1.7	1.3	1.6	9.6	.9	100.0
Hebrew, German	4.4	10.6	11.1	11.1	14.5	10.6	13.5	9.1	7.9	87.2	3.7	2.5	1.0	.7	7.9	.7	100.0
Hebrew, Russian	13.8	16.5	9.7	13.8	10.4	13.0	9.1	5.4	4.5	82.9	1.0	1.0	.2	.4	2.5	.5	100.0
Hebrew, Other	9.5	14.3	9.5	10.5	10.4	9.5	8.6	7.6	7.6	84.8	2.9	.0	1.9	.0	4.8	1.0	100.0
Irish	3.2	9.2	9.4	11.6	12.2	14.1	10.4	8.2	6.2	81.5	6.0	4.0	1.6	2.4	14.1	1.2	100.0
Italian, North	12.3	20.3	12.9	15.8	11.2	6.5	10.0	6.3	1.3	84.4	1.1	.0	.2	.0	1.3	2.0	100.0
Italian, South	8.9	28.3	16.3	14.9	12.5	9.4	4.6	1.5	1.5	88.8	1.3	.3	.0	.0	1.5	.8	100.0
Japanese	1.8	1.8	7.0	14.3	10.5	7.9	6.1	3.5	6.1	71.9	11.4	6.1	6.1	2.6	26.3	.0	100.0
Mexican	7.9	46.0	13.4	15.4	7.5	4.0	1.1	.9	1.6	88.9	.1	.0	.0	.0	.1	3.1	100.0
Norwegian	7.5	5.8	12.5	15.8	11.7	11.7	9.2	8.3	11.7	86.7	3.3	1.7	.0	.0	5.0	.8	100.0
Russian	9.8	40.4	28.2	12.7	2.4	2.4	1.4	1.9	.2	89.7	.2	.0	.0	.0	.2	.2	100.0
Scotch	4.0	7.0	5.5	9.4	10.7	15.2	10.0	12.8	9.1	79.0	9.4	3.3	2.1	1.8	16.7	.3	100.0
Spanish-American	9.7	25.6	21.9	9.0	9.7	6.9	6.9	3.4	1.3	85.6	1.6	.6	.4	.0	2.5	2.2	100.0
Swedish	5.7	12.4	10.2	13.4	12.0	10.6	12.2	9.6	6.7	87.0	3.1	2.0	1.0	.6	6.7	.6	100.0
Other races	5.1	16.5	11.6	14.7	12.2	11.7	6.3	5.1	6.3	84.3	4.7	1.9	1.4	.6	8.5	1.0	100.0
Total foreign-born	6.5	16.9	11.1	12.1	11.3	10.9	9.2	7.3	6.0	84.6	4.1	1.8	1.0	1.0	7.9	1.0	100.0
Grand total	6.4	14.3	10.6	11.2	11.2	10.6	9.9	8.3	6.6	82.7	5.4	2.2	1.4	1.2	10.1	.8	100.0

a Not computed, owing to small number involved.

PUBLIC SCHOOL TEACHERS IN ELEMENTARY GRADES AND KINDERGARTEN.

TABLE 1.—*Number of teachers in each grade, by sex and general nativity and race.*

MALE.

[This table does not include 13 teachers not reporting complete data.]

General nativity and race	Kindergarten	1.	2.	3.	4.	5.	6.	7.	8.	Ungraded and special	Total	Total elementary and kindergarten
Native-born of native father, White				1	4	2	12	8	14	2	43	43
Native-born of foreign father, by race of father:												
French										1	1	1
Irish							1	1			2	2
Scotch-Irish								1	1		2	2
Total							1	2	1	1	5	5
Total native-born				1	4	2	13	10	15	3	48	48
Foreign-born:												
Canadian, Other						1			1		2	2
English			1								1	1
Total foreign-born			1			1			1		3	3
Grand total			1	1	4	3	13	10	16	3	51	51

FEMALE.

General nativity and race	Kindergarten	1.	2.	3.	4.	5.	6.	7.	8.	Ungraded and special	Total	Total elementary and kindergarten
Native-born of native father, White	47	110	106	104	100	95	81	73	69	12	750	797
Native-born of foreign father, by race of father:												
Bohemian and Moravian					1						1	1
Canadian, French		1	1		1						3	3
Canadian, Other	1	5	3	6	1	2	3	7			27	28
Danish						1		3			4	4
English	3	6	7	5	5	8	4	3		3	41	44
French		1									1	1
German	4	9	15	4	11	5	8	1			53	57
Irish	1	5	6	10	2	3	2	6	2	4	40	41
Mexican										1	1	1
Norwegian			1				2			3	6	6
Scotch	1	9	2	8	1	2	5		3		30	31
Scotch-Irish		3	4		1	1				1	10	10
Swedish		1			1	1					3	3
Welsh		1	2	2	3	2					10	10
Total	10	41	41	35	27	25	24	20	5	12	230	240
Total native-born	57	151	147	139	127	120	105	93	74	24	980	1,037
Foreign-born:												
Canadian, French	1					1		1			2	3
Canadian, Other	3	4	2	4	5	4		3			22	25
Dutch								2			2	2
English		1		1	1		1	1			5	5
German		3	1	1	1	3					9	9
Irish			1	2	1					1	5	5
Norwegian					1						1	1
Scotch	1			2	1				2		5	6
Scotch-Irish						1					1	1
Swedish		2									2	2
Total foreign-born	5	10	4	10	10	9	1	7	2	1	54	59
Grand total	62	161	151	149	137	129	106	100	76	25	1,034	1,096

TABLE 1.—*Number of teachers in each grade, by sex and general nativity and race*—Contd.

TOTAL.

General nativity and race.	Kindergarten.	Elementary grades.									Total elementary.	Total kindergarten and elementary.	Race distribution (percentages).	
		1.	2.	3.	4.	5.	6.	7.	8.	Ungraded and special.			Elementary.	Elementary and kindergarten.
Native-born of native father, White........	47	110	106	105	104	97	93	81	83	14	793	840	73.1	73.2
Native-born of foreign father, by race of father:														
Bohemian and Moravian...				1							1	1	.1	.1
Canadian, French..		1	1		1						3	3	.3	.3
Canadian, Other...	1	5	3	6	1	2	3	7			27	28	2.5	2.4
Danish..............						1		3			4	4	.4	.3
English.............	3	6	7	5	5	8	4	3		3	41	44	3.8	3.8
French.............		1								1	2	2	.2	.2
German............	4	9	15	4	11	5	8	1			53	57	4.9	5.0
Irish..............	1	5	6	10	2	3	3	7	2	4	42	43	3.9	3.7
Mexican............										1	1	1	.1	.1
Norwegian.........			1				2			3	6	6	.6	.5
Scotch	1	9	2	8	1	2	5		3		30	31	2.8	2.7
Scotch-Irish........		3	4		1		1	1		1	12	12	1.1	1.0
Swedish............		1			1	1					3	3	.3	.3
Welsh..............		1	2	2	3	2					10	10	.9	.9
Total............	10	41	41	35	27	25	25	22	6	13	235	245	21.7	21.4
Total native-born	57	151	147	140	131	122	118	103	89	27	1,028	1,085	94.7	94.6
Foreign-born:														
Canadian, French..	1					1		1			2	3	.2	.3
Canadian, Other...	3	4	2	4	5	5		3	1		24	27	2.2	2.4
Dutch..............								2			2	2	.2	.2
English.............		1	1	1	1		1	1			6	6	.6	.5
German............		3	1	1	1	3					9	9	.8	.8
Irish..............			1	2	1					1	5	5	.5	.4
Norwegian.........					1						1	1	.1	.1
Scotch	1			2	1				2		5	6	.5	.5
Scotch-Irish........					1						1	1	.1	.1
Swedish............		2									2	2	.2	.2
Total foreign-born.	5	10	5	10	10	10	1	7	3	1	57	62	5.3	5.4
Grand total	62	161	152	150	141	132	119	110	92	28	1,085	1,147	100.0	100.0

TABLE 2.—*Number of teachers engaged in teaching each specified number of years, by sex and general nativity and race.*

MALE.

[This table does not include 19 teachers not reporting complete data.]

General nativity and race.	Under 5 years.	5 to 9 years.	10 to 14 years.	15 to 19 years.	20 to 24 years.	25 to 29 years.	30 years or over.	Total.
Native-born of native father, White..	1	17	9	9	5	1	1	43
Native-born of foreign father, by race of father:								
French....				1				1
Irish....		2						2
Scotch-Irish....		2						2
Total....		4		1				5
Total native-born....	1	21	9	10	5	1	1	48
Foreign-born:								
Canadian (other than French)...		1	1					2
English....		1						1
Total foreign-born....		2	1					3
Grand total....	1	23	10	10	5	1	1	51

FEMALE.

General nativity and race.	Under 5 years.	5 to 9 years.	10 to 14 years.	15 to 19 years.	20 to 24 years.	25 to 29 years.	30 years or over.	Total.
Native-born of native father: White..	86	244	225	140	70	21	11	797
Native-born of foreign father, by race of father:								
Bohemian and Moravian....		1						1
Canadian, French....			2	1				3
Canadian, Other....	4	10	9	2	3			28
Danish....	2	2						4
English....	3	16	14	3	7			43
French....								
German....	7	16	16	12	4	2		57
Irish....	4	5	20	5	3	3	1	41
Mexican....	1							1
Norwegian....			2	1				3
Scotch....	1	7	8	9	2	4		31
Scotch-Irish....		3	4	1	1		1	10
Swedish....		1	1		1			3
Welsh....		3	7					10
Total....	22	64	83	34	21	9	2	235
Total native-born....	108	308	308	174	91	30	13	1,032
Foreign-born:								
Canadian, French....			2	1				3
Canadian, Other....	2	4	10	7		2		25
Dutch....		2						2
English....	2		1	1	1			5
German....		5	2	2				9
Irish....		3		1	1			5
Norwegian....						1		1
Scotch....		5	1					6
Scotch-Irish....	1							1
Swedish....		1						1
Total foreign-born....	5	20	16	12	2	3		58
Grand total....	113	328	324	186	93	33	13	1,090

TABLE 2.—*Number of teachers engaged in teaching each specified number of years, by sex and general nativity and race*—Continued.

TOTAL.

General nativity and race.	Under 5 years.	5 to 9 years.	10 to 14 years.	15 to 19 years.	20 to 24 years.	25 to 29 years.	30 years or over.	Total.
Native-born of native father: White..	87	261	234	149	75	22	12	840
Native-born of foreign father, by race of father:								
Bohemian and Moravian		1						1
Canadian, French			2	1				3
Canadian, Other	4	10	9	2	3			28
Danish	2	2						4
English	3	16	14	3	7			43
French				1				1
German	7	16	16	12	4	2		57
Irish	4	7	20	5	3	3	1	43
Mexican	1							1
Norwegian			2	1				3
Scotch	1	7	8	9	2	4		31
Scotch-Irish		5	4	1	1		1	12
Swedish		1	1		1			3
Welsh		3	7					10
Total	22	68	83	35	21	9	2	240
Total native-born	109	329	317	184	96	31	14	1,080
Foreign-born:								
Canadian, French			2	1				3
Canadian, Other	2	5	11	7		2		27
Dutch		2						2
English	2	1	1	1	1			6
German		5	2	2				9
Irish		3		1	1			5
Norwegian						1		1
Scotch		5	1					6
Scotch-Irish	1							1
Swedish		1						1
Total foreign-born	5	22	17	12	2	3		61
Grand total	114	351	334	196	98	34	14	1,141

PAROCHIAL SCHOOL PUPILS: GENERAL INVESTIGATION.

TABLE 1.—*Grade and age—Number of pupils of each age in each grade, by sex.*

BOYS.

Age.	Kindergarten.	Elementary grades.									High school.			Mixed school.	Grand total.
		1.	2.	3.	4.	5.	6.	7.	8.	Total.	1.	2.	Total.		
4 years	9													1	10
5 years	9	4								4				3	16
6 years		63								63				8	71
7 years		87	9	4						100				6	106
8 years		22	31	8				2		63				4	67
9 years		12	40	44	11	3		15		125				6	131
10 years		7	15	34	24	25		20		125				11	136
11 years		6	14	13	12	43	6	6		100				2	102
12 years			3	5	18	17	40	4		87				9	96
13 years			2	3	14	14	28	22	3	86				5	91
14 years			1	1	2	2	20	25	14	65				2	67
15 years				2		1	3	13	3	22				2	24
16 years				4		4	2	3	3	16					16
17 years								1		1					1
18 years								1		1					1
Total	18	201	115	118	81	109	99	112	23	858				59	935

GIRLS.

Age.	Kindergarten.	Elementary grades.									High school.			Mixed school.	Grand total.
		1.	2.	3.	4.	5.	6.	7.	8.	Total.	1.	2.	Total.		
4 years	10														10
5 years	10	2								2				3	15
6 years		75	1							76				10	86
7 years		81	13	1						95				10	105
8 years		24	38	23	1					86				7	93
9 years		11	37	49	16			29		142				11	153
10 years		1	18	53	33	23	11	34		173				11	184
11 years		1	2	16	19	51	13	18		120				11	131
12 years		1	4	5	15	48	29	7		109				13	122
13 years				11	10	20	26	27	11	105				6	111
14 years		2		4	3	5	21	33	43	111	6	1	7	4	122
15 years				3	1	4	4	11	37	60	19	3	22	1	83
16 years			1		2	3	1	6	11	24	10	2	12	2	38
17 years								1	1	2	4	2	6	1	9
18 years							1			1	2		2		3
Total	20	198	114	165	100	154	106	166	103	1,106	41	8	49	90	1,265

TOTAL.

Age.	Kindergarten.	Elementary grades.									High school.			Mixed school.	Grand total.
		1.	2.	3.	4.	5.	6.	7.	8.	Total.	1.	2.	Total.		
4 years	19													1	20
5 years	19	6								6				6	31
6 years		138	1							139				18	157
7 years		168	22	5						195				16	211
8 years		46	69	31	1			2		149				11	160
9 years		23	77	93	27	3		44		267				17	284
10 years		8	33	87	57	48	11	54		298				22	320
11 years		7	16	29	31	94	19	24		220				13	233
12 years		1	7	10	33	65	69	11		196				22	218
13 years			2	14	24	34	54	49	14	191				11	202
14 years		2	1	5	5	7	41	58	57	176	6	1	7	6	189
15 years				5	1	5	7	24	40	82	19	3	22	3	107
16 years			1	4	2	7	3	9	14	40	10	2	12	2	54
17 years								2	1	3	4	2	6	1	10
18 years							1	1		2	2		2		4
Total	38	399	229	283	181	263	205	278	126	1,964	41	8	49	149	2,200

TABLE 2.—Race, sex, and grade—Number of pupils of each sex in each grade, by general nativity and race of father of pupil.

General nativity and race of father of pupil	Kinder-garten	Elem. 1	Elem. 2	Elem. 3	Elem. 4	Elem. 5	Elem. 6	Elem. 7	Elem. 8	Elem. Total	H.S. First year	H.S. Second year	H.S. Total	Mixed school	Grand total
Native-born:															
White—															
Male	4	95	41	66	31	62	49	70	15	429				31	464
Female	3	91	44	86	47	76	59	117	63	583	12	5	17	45	648
Total	7	186	85	152	78	138	108	187	78	1,012	12	5	17	76	1,112
Negro—															
Male		1						5		6				1	7
Female															
Total		1						5		6				1	7
Total native-born—															
Male	4	96	41	66	31	62	49	75	15	435				32	471
Female	3	91	44	86	47	76	59	117	63	583	12	5	17	45	648
Total	7	187	85	152	78	138	108	192	78	1,018	12	5	17	77	1,119
Foreign-born:															
Canadian, French—															
Male		1		2	3	1	1	4		12					12
Female		2			4	5	2	4	1	18	3		3		21
Total		3		2	7	6	3	8	1	30	3		3		33
Canadian, Other—															
Male				3		4	2	4		13					13
Female	1	1		13	6	2	2	1	4	29	2		2		32
Total	1	1		16	6	6	4	5	4	42	2		2		45
Dalmatian—															
Male	4	6	7	5	1					19					23
Female	4	4	4	4	1					13					17
Total	8	10	11	9	2					32					40
English—															
Male			3		4		1			8				1	9
Female		1	1		1	5	8	4		20	1		1	3	24
Total		1	4		5	5	9	4		28	1		1	4	33
French—															
Male	2	17	1	2	2	5	1	3		31					33
Female	2	4	5	3	3	8	5	10	4	42	2		2	8	54
Total	4	21	6	5	5	13	6	13	4	73	2		2	8	87
German—															
Male	1	21	19	13	8	16	21	11	2	111				7	119
Female	1	23	16	7	15	16	12	21	8	118	6		6	9	134
Total	2	44	35	20	23	32	33	32	10	229	6		6	16	253
Irish—															
Male	1	26	16	5	9	4	15	11	3	89				12	102
Female	1	29	18	10	13	19	13	6	18	126	6	2	8	16	151
Total	2	55	34	15	22	23	28	17	21	215	6	2	8	28	253

Table 2.—Race, sex, and grade—Number of pupils of each sex in each grade, by general nativity and race of father of pupil—Continued.

General nativity and race of father of pupil	Kindergarten	Elementary grades.									High school.			Mixed school.	Grand total.
		1.	2.	3.	4.	5.	6.	7.	8.	Total.	First year.	Second year.	Total.		
Foreign-born—Continued.															
Italian, North—															
Male	2	5	9	4	1	5	4	2		30				1	33
Female	3	13	7	12	3	9	2	1	1	48				1	52
Total	5	18	16	16	4	14	6	3	1	78				2	85
Italian, South—															
Male	1	8	6	3	6	2	1	1	1	28					29
Female	2	8	3	9	1	5	1		1	28					30
Total	3	16	9	12	7	7	2	1	2	56					59
Mexican—															
Male	2	16	9	7	1			1		34					36
Female	3	12	7	5	2	2	1			29					32
Total	5	28	16	12	3	2	1	1		63					68
Polish—															
Male		1	1		1					3				3	6
Female		2	1	1	1	1				6					6
Total		3	2	1	2	1				9				3	12
Spanish-American—															
Male		1	1	3	6	9				20				1	21
Female		2	1	1	3	3				10	1	1	2	2	14
Total		3	2	4	9	12				30	1	1	2	3	35
Welsh—															
Male		4								4					4
Female															
Total		4								4					4
Other races a—															
Male	1	3	3	5	8	1	2	1	2	25				2	28
Female	1	2	7	14		3	2	2	2	32	8		8	5	46
Total	2	5	10	19	8	4	6	3	4	57	8		8	7	74
Total foreign-born—															
Male	14	105	74	52	50	47	50	37	8	423				27	464
Female	17	107	70	79	53	78	47	49	40	523	29	3	32	45	617
Total	31	212	144	131	103	125	97	86	48	946	29	3	32	72	1,081
Grand total—															
Male	18	201	115	118	81	109	99	112	23	858				59	935
Female	20	198	114	165	100	154	106	166	103	1,106	41	8	49	90	1,265
Total	38	399	229	283	181	263	205	278	126	1,964	41	8	49	149	2,200

a "Other races" includes races having less than 10 representatives in this city and pupils whose race is not reported.

TABLE 3.—*Race, sex, and age, by grade—Number of pupils of each age in each grade, by sex and by general nativity and race of father of pupil.*

KINDERGARTEN.

BOYS.

General nativity and race of father of pupil.	Number of pupils of each age.			Total.
	4.	5.	6.	
Native-born, White............................	3	1	....	4
Foreign-born:				
Dalmatian...........................	....	4	....	4
French..............................	2	....	....	2
German.............................	....	1	....	1
Irish...............................	....	1	....	1
Italian, North.......................	2	....	....	2
Italian, South.......................	....	1	....	1
Mexican............................	2	....	....	2
Other races *a*......................	....	1	....	1
Total foreign born...............	6	8	....	14
Grand total......................	9	9	....	18

GIRLS.

	4.	5.	6.	Total.
Native-born, White............................	2	1	....	3
Foreign-born:				
Dalmatian...........................	4	....	....	4
French..............................	....	2	....	2
German.............................	1	....	....	1
Irish...............................	....	1	....	1
Italian, North.......................	3	....	....	3
Italian, South.......................	....	2	....	2
Mexican............................	....	3	....	3
Other races *a*......................	....	1	....	1
Total foreign born...............	8	9	....	17
Grand total......................	10	10	....	20

TOTAL.

	4.	5.	6.	Total.
Native-born, White............................	5	2	....	7
Foreign-born:				
Dalmatian...........................	4	4	....	8
French..............................	2	2	....	4
German.............................	1	1	....	2
Irish...............................	....	2	....	2
Italian, North.......................	5	....	....	5
Italian, South.......................	....	3	....	3
Mexican............................	2	3	....	5
Other races *a*......................	....	2	....	2
Total foreign born...............	14	17	....	31
Grand total......................	19	19	....	38

a "Other races" includes races having less than 10 representatives in this city and pupils whose race is not reported.

TABLE 3.—*Race, sex, and age, by grade—Number of pupils of each age in each grade, by sex and by general nativity and race of father of pupil—Continued.*

FIRST GRADE.

BOYS.

General nativity and race of father of pupil.	Number of pupils of each age.										Total.
	5.	6.	7.	8.	9.	10.	11.	12.	13.	14.	
Native-born:											
White	3	38	38	9	4	3					95
Negro			1								1
Total native-born	3	38	39	9	4	3					96
Foreign-born:,											
Canadian, French			1								1
Dalmatian		3	1								6
French		3	9		2		3				17
German	1	2	15	2	1						21
Irish		7	12	4	3						26
Italian, North		2	1			2					5
Italian, South		2	3				3				8
Mexican		4	4	6		2					16
Polish			1								1
Spanish-American				1							1
Other races a		2	1								3
Total foreign-born	1	25	48	13	8	4	6				105
Grand total	4	63	87	22	12	7	6				201

GIRLS.

General nativity and race of father of pupil.	5.	6.	7.	8.	9.	10.	11.	12.	13.	14.	Total.
Native-born, White	2	43	35	9	1	1					91
Foreign-born:											
Canadian, French			2								2
Canadian, Other				1							1
Dalmatian			4								4
English			1								1
French			2	1	1						4
German		7	14	1	1						23
Irish		13	9	6	1						29
Italian, North		4	2	4	3						13
Italian, South		2	1	1	2		1			1	8
Mexican		2	6		2			1		1	12
Polish		1	1								2
Spanish-American			1	1							2
Welsh		3	1								4
Other races a			2								2
Total foreign-born		32	46	15	10		1	1		2	107
Grand total	2	75	81	24	11	1	1	1		2	198

a "Other races" includes races having less than 10 representatives in this city and pupils whose race is not reported.

TABLE 3.—*Race, sex, and age, by grade—Number of pupils of each age in each grade, by sex and by general nativity and race of father of pupil—Continued.*

FIRST GRADE—Continued.

TOTAL.

General nativity and race of father of pupil.	**Number of pupils of each age.**										Total.
	5.	6.	7.	8.	9.	10.	11.	12.	13.	14.	
Native-born:											
White	5	81	73	18	5	4					186
Negro			1								1
Total native-born	5	81	74	18	5	4					187
Foreign-born:											
Canadian, French			3								3
Canadian, Other				1							1
Dalmatian		3	5		2						10
English			1								1
French		3	11	1	3		3				21
German	1	9	29	3	2						44
Irish		20	21	10	4						55
Italian, North		6	3	4	3	2					18
Italian, South		4	4	1	2		4			1	16
Mexican		6	10	6	2	2		1		1	28
Polish		1	2								3
Spanish-American			1	2							3
Welsh		3	1								4
Other races a		2	3								5
Total foreign-born	1	57	94	28	18	4	7	1		2	212
Grand total	6	138	168	46	23	8	7	1		2	399

a "Other races" includes races having less than 10 representatives in this city and pupils whose race is not reported.

SECOND GRADE.

BOYS.

General nativity and race of father of pupil.	**Number of pupils of each age.**											Total.
	6.	7.	8.	9.	10.	11.	12.	13.	14.	15.	16.	
Native-born, White		2	11	23	5							41
Foreign-born:												
Dalmatian					2	3		2				7
English				1	2							3
French			1									1
German		5	6	4	2	2						19
Irish		1	10	5								16
Italian, North			2	2		2	2		1			9
Italian, South				1	2	2	1					6
Mexican			1	4	2	2						9
Polish						1						1
Other races a		1				2						3
Total		7	20	17	10	14	3	2	1			74
Grand total		9	31	40	15	14	3	2	1			115

a "Other races" includes races having less than 10 representatives in this city and pupils whose race is not reported.

TABLE 3.—*Race, sex, and age, by grade—Number of pupils of each age in each grade, by sex and by general nativity and race of father of pupil*—Continued.

SECOND GRADE—Continued.

GIRLS.

General nativity and race of father of pupil.	6.	7.	8.	9.	10.	11.	12.	13.	14.	15.	16.	Total.
Native-born, White		7	8	18	10	1						44
Foreign-born:												
Dalmatian					2	1	1					4
English				1								1
French			2	3								5
German		4	10	1	1							16
Irish	1	2	9	4	2							18
Italian, North			5	1						1		7
Italian, South				2	1							3
Mexican				3	2		2					7
Polish			1									1
Spanish-American				1								1
Other races a			3	3			1					7
Total	1	6	30	19	8	1	4				1	70
Grand total	1	13	38	37	18	2	4				1	114

TOTAL.

General nativity and race of father of pupil.	6.	7.	8.	9.	10.	11.	12.	13.	14.	15.	16.	Total.
Native-born, White		9	19	41	15	1						85
Foreign-born:												
Dalmatian					4	4	1	2				11
English				2	2							4
French			3	3								6
German		9	16	5	3	2						35
Irish	1	3	19	9	2							34
Italian, North			7	3	2	3				1		16
Italian, South			1	2	3	2	1					9
Mexican				7	2	2	4		1			16
Polish			1	1								2
Spanish-American				1								1
Other races a		1	3	3		2	1					10
Total	1	13	50	36	18	15	7	2	1		1	144
Grand total	1	22	69	77	33	16	7	2	1		1	229

a "Other races" includes races having less than 10 representatives in this city and pupils whose race is not reported.

TABLE 3.—*Race, sex, and age, by grade—Number of pupils of each age in each grade, by sex and by general nativity and race of father of pupil*—Continued.

THIRD GRADE.

BOYS.

General nativity and race of father of pupil	Number of pupils of each age.										Total.
	7.	8.	9.	10.	11.	12.	13.	14.	15.	16.	
Native-born, White	2	7	31	22	2		2				66
Foreign-born:											
Canadian, French			2								2
Canadian, Other			1	1		1					3
Dalmatian					1				2	2	5
French	2										2
German		1	5	5	2						13
Irish			2	1	2						5
Italian, North				1	2		1				4
Italian, South						2		1			3
Mexican				1	2	2				2	7
Spanish-American				1	2						3
Other races a			3	2							5
Total foreign-born	2	1	13	12	11	5	1	1	2	4	52
Grand total	4	8	44	34	13	5	3	1	2	4	118

GIRLS.

General nativity and race of father of pupil	7.	8.	9.	10.	11.	12.	13.	14.	15.	16.	Total.
Native-born, White	1	20	26	26	11	1	1				86
Foreign-born:											
Canadian (other than French)			2	11							13
Dalmatian			1	1			1	1			4
French			1	1		1					3
German		1	2	3				1			7
Irish		2	4	1	3						10
Italian, North			2	3	1	1	3	2			12
Italian, South			2	3		1	3				9
Mexican					1		1		3		5
Polish				1							1
Spanish-American							1				1
Other races a			9	3		1	1				14
Total foreign-born		3	23	27	5	4	10	4	3		79
Grand total	1	23	49	53	16	5	11	4	3		165

a "Other races" includes races having less than 10 representatives in this city and pupils whose race is not reported.

TABLE 3.—*Race, sex, and age, by grade—Number of pupils of each age in each grade, by sex and by general nativity and race of father of pupil*—Continued.

THIRD GRADE—Continued.

TOTAL.

General nativity and race of father of pupil.	7.	8.	9.	10.	11.	12.	13.	14.	15.	16.	Total.
Native-born, White	3	27	57	48	13	1	3	......	......	......	152
Foreign-born:											
Canadian, French	......	......	2	......	......	......	......	......	......	......	2
Canadian, Other	......	......	3	12	......	1	......	......	......	......	16
Dalmatian	......	......	......	1	1	......	......	3	2	2	9
French	2	......	1	1	......	1	......	......	......	......	5
German	......	2	7	8	2	......	1	......	......	......	20
Irish	......	2	6	2	5	......	......	......	......	......	15
Italian, North	......	......	2	4	2	2	5	1	......	......	16
Italian, South	......	......	2	3	2	3	2	......	......	......	12
Mexican	......	......	......	1	2	2	1	1	3	2	12
Polish	......	......	......	1	......	......	......	......	......	......	1
Spanish-American	......	......	1	1	2	......	......	......	......	......	4
Other races a	......	......	12	5	......	......	2	......	......	......	19
Total foreign-born	2	4	36	39	16	9	11	5	5	4	131
Grand total	5	31	93	87	29	10	14	5	5	4	283

a "Other races" includes races having less than 10 representatives in this city and pupils whose race is not reported.

FOURTH GRADE.

BOYS.

General nativity and race of father of pupil.	8.	9.	10.	11.	12.	13.	14.	15.	16.	Total.
Native-born, White	......	4	9	7	7	4	......	......	......	31
Foreign-born:										
Canadian, French	......	2	1	......	......	......	......	......	......	3
Canadian, Other	......	......	......	......	......	......	......	......	......	......
Dalmatian	......	......	......	......	......	1	......	......	......	1
English	......	1	......	1	2	......	......	......	......	4
French	......	......	1	......	1	......	......	......	......	2
German	......	2	4	2	......	......	......	......	......	8
Irish	......	1	5	1	1	1	......	......	......	9
Italian, North	......	......	......	......	1	......	......	......	......	1
Italian, South	......	......	3	......	......	1	2	......	......	6
Mexican	......	......	......	......	1	......	......	......	......	1
Polish	......	1	......	......	......	......	......	......	......	1
Spanish-American	......	......	......	1	1	4	......	......	......	6
Other races a	......	......	1	......	4	3	......	......	......	8
Total foreign-born	......	7	15	5	11	10	2	......	......	50
Grand total	......	11	24	12	18	14	2	......	......	81

a "Other races" includes races having less than 10 representatives in this city and pupils whose race is not reported.

TABLE 3.—*Race, sex, and age, by grade—Number of pupils of each age in each grade, by sex and by general nativity and race of father of pupil*—Continued.

FOURTH GRADE—Continued.

GIRLS.

General nativity and race of father of pupil.	Number of pupils of each age.									Total.
	8.	9.	10.	11.	12.	13.	14.	15.	16.	
Native-born, White		7	18	10	6	4	1		1	47
Foreign-born:										
Canadian, French	1	2	1							4
Canadian, Other		1	1	2		2				6
Dalmatian									1	1
English						1				1
French		1	1			1				3
German		3	5	2	4	1				15
Irish			4	3	4		2			13
Italian, North			1	1	1					3
Italian, South		1								1
Mexican						1		1		2
Polish			1							1
Spanish-American			2			1				3
Total foreign-born	1	9	15	9	9	6	2	1	1	53
Grand total	1	16	33	19	15	10	3	1	2	100

TOTAL.

	8.	9.	10.	11.	12.	13.	14.	15.	16.	Total.
Native-born, White		11	27	17	13	8	1		1	78
Foreign-born:										
Canadian, French	1	4	2			2				7
Canadian, Other		1	1	2		2				6
Dalmatian				1					1	2
English		1			2		1			5
French		1	2			1	1			5
German		5	9	4	4	1		2		23
Irish		1	9	4	5	2				22
Italian, North		1	1	1			1	2		7
Italian, South		1	3			1				4
Mexican					1	1		1		3
Polish	1		1							2
Spanish-American			2	1	1	5				9
Other races a			1		4	3				8
Total foreign-born	1	16	30	14	20	16	4	1	1	103
Grand total	1	27	57	31	33	24	5	1	2	181

a "Other races" includes races having less than 10 representatives in this city and pupils whose race is not reported.

TABLE 3.—*Race, sex, and age, by grade—Number of pupils of each age in each grade, by sex and by general nativity and race of father of pupil*—Continued.

FIFTH GRADE.

BOYS.

General nativity and race of father of pupil.	Number of pupils of each age.									Total.
	9.	10.	11.	12.	13.	14.	15.	16.	17.	
Native-born, White	3	13	28	10	6	1	1			62
Foreign-born:										
Canadian, French			1							1
Canadian, Other			3		1					4
French		4	1							5
German		5	9	1	1					16
Irish		3	1							4
Italian, North					1			4		5
Italian, South				1	1					2
Spanish-American				4	4	1				9
Other races a				1						1
Total foreign-born		12	15	7	8	1		4		47
Grand total	3	25	43	17	14	2	1	4		109

GIRLS.

General nativity and race of father of pupil.	9.	10.	11.	12.	13.	14.	15.	16.	17.	Total.
Native-born, White		16	31	17	6	3	2	1		76
Foreign-born:										
Canadian, French		1	2	2						5
Canadian, Other			1	1						2
English			1	2	2					5
French			3	5						8
German			3	7	4	2				16
Irish		2	4	6	5		1	1		19
Italian, North		2	3	3			1			9
Italian, South		1		3				1		5
Mexican			1	1						2
Polish					1					1
Spanish-American				1	2					3
Other races a		1	2							3
Total foreign-born		7	20	31	14	2	2	2		78
Grand total		23	51	48	20	5	4	3		154

TOTAL.

General nativity and race of father of pupil.	9.	10.	11.	12.	13.	14.	15.	16.	17.	Total.
Native-born, White	3	29	59	27	12	4	3	1		138
Foreign-born:										
Canadian, French		1	3	2						6
Canadian, Other			4	1	1					6
English			1	2	2					5
French		4	4	5						13
German		5	12	8	5	2				32
Irish		5	5	6	5		1	1		23
Italian, North		2	3	3	1		1	4		14
Italian, South		1		4	1			1		7
Mexican			1	1						2
Polish					1					1
Spanish-American				5	6	1				12
Other races a		1	2	1						4
Total foreign-born		19	35	38	22	3	2	6		125
Grand total	3	48	94	65	34	7	5	7		263

a "Other races" includes races having less than 10 representatives in this city and pupils whose race is not reported.

TABLE 3.—*Race, sex, and age, by grade—Number of pupils of each age in each grade, by sex and by general nativity and race of father of pupil*—Continued.

SIXTH GRADE.

BOYS.

General nativity and race of father of pupil.	Number of pupils of each age.									Total.
	10.	11.	12.	13.	14.	15.	16.	17.	18.	
Native-born, White		1	19	14	14		1			49
Foreign-born:										
Canadian, French				1						1
Canadian, Other				2						2
English		1								1
French			1							1
German		2	9	6	2	1	1			21
Irish		1	5	5	3	1				15
Italian, North		1	3							4
Italian, South			1							1
Mexican					1					1
Spanish-American						1				1
Other races *a*			2							2
Total foreign-born		5	21	14	6	3	1			50
Grand total		6	40	28	20	3	2			99

GIRLS.

General nativity and race of father of pupil.	Number of pupils of each age.									Total.
	10.	11.	12.	13.	14.	15.	16.	17.	18.	
Native-born, White	9	8	14	14	11	1	1		1	59
Foreign-born:										
Canadian, French			2							2
Canadian, Other				2						2
English		1	5	1		1				8
French	1		1		2	1				5
German		3	3	3	3					12
Irish	1	1	3	4	3	1				13
Italian, North					2					2
Italian, South				1						1
Other races *a*			1	1						2
Total foreign-born	2	5	15	12	10	3				47
Grand total	11	13	29	26	21	4	1		1	106

TOTAL.

General nativity and race of father of pupil.	Number of pupils of each age.									Total.
	10.	11.	12.	13.	14.	15.	16.	17.	18.	
Native-born, White	9	9	33	28	25	1	2		1	108
Foreign-born:										
Canadian, French			2	1						3
Canadian, Other				4						4
English		2	5	1		1				9
French	1		2		2	1				6
German		5	12	9	5	1	1			33
Irish	1	2	8	9	6	2				28
Italian, North		1	3		2					6
Italian, South			1	1						2
Mexican					1					1
Spanish-American						1				1
Other races *a*			3	1						4
Total foreign-born	2	10	36	26	16	6	1			97
Grand total	11	19	69	54	41	7	3		1	205

a "Other races" includes races having less than 10 representatives in this city and pupils whose race is not reported.

TABLE 3.—*Race, sex, and age, by grade—Number of pupils of each age in each grade, by sex and by general nativity and race of father of pupil*—Continued.

SEVENTH GRADE.

BOYS.

General nativity and race of father of pupil.	Number of pupils of each age.											Total.
	8.	9.	10.	11.	12.	13.	14.	15.	16.	17.	18.	
Native-born:												
White		10	19	5	1	9	16	8	1		1	70
Negro						2	3					5
Total native-born		10	19	5	1	11	19	8	1		1	75
Foreign-born:												
Canadian, French						1	1	2				4
Canadian, Other					1	2		1				4
French							2		1			3
German			1	1	1	5	2	1				11
Irish	2	5			1	1	1	1				11
Italian, North							1			1		2
Italian, South							1					1
Other races a									1			1
Total foreign-born	2	5	1	1	3	11	6	5	2	1		37
Grand total	2	15	20	6	4	22	25	13	3	1	1	112

GIRLS.

General nativity and race of father of pupil.	8.	9.	10.	11.	12.	13.	14.	15.	16.	17.	18.	Total.
Native-born, White		29	26	7	4	15	25	4	6	1		117
Foreign-born:												
Canadian, French			1			1		2				4
Canadian, Other						1						1
English			2		1	1						4
French			4	5				1				10
German			2	3	1	5	7	3				21
Irish				1		4	1					6
Italian, North								1				1
Other races a			1	1								2
Total foreign-born			8	11	3	12	8	7				49
Grand total		29	34	18	7	27	33	11	6	1		166

TOTAL.

General nativity and race of father of pupil.	8.	9.	10.	11.	12.	13.	14.	15.	16.	17.	18.	Total.
Native-born:												
White		39	45	12	5	24	41	12	7	1	1	187
Negro						2	3					5
Total native-born		39	45	12	5	26	44	12	7	1	1	192
Foreign-born:												
Canadian, French			1			2	1	4				8
Canadian, Other					1	3		1				5
English			2		1	1						4
French			4	5			2	1	1			13
German			3	4	2	10	9	4				32
Irish	2	5		1	1	5	2	1				17
Italian, North							1	1		1		3
Italian, South							1					1
Other races a			1	1					1			3
Total foreign-born	2	5	9	12	6	23	14	12	2	1		86
Grand total	2	44	54	24	11	49	58	24	9	2	1	278

a "Other races" includes races having less than 10 representatives in this city and pupils whose race is not reported.

TABLE 3.—*Race, sex, and age, by grade—Number of pupils of each age in each grade, by sex and by general nativity and race of father of pupil—Continued.*

EIGHTH GRADE.

BOYS.

General nativity and race of father of pupil.	Number of pupils of each age.						Total.
	13.	14.	15.	16.	17.	18.	
Native-born, White...............	2	10	....	3	....	....	15
Foreign-born:							
German....................	1	1	....				2
Irish........................	....	2	1				3
Italian, South.............	....	1	....				1
Other races *a*.............	....	....	2				2
Total foreign-born........	1	4	3	....	....	....	8
Grand total...............	3	14	3	3	....	....	23

GIRLS.

General nativity and race of father of pupil.	13.	14.	15.	16.	17.	18.	Total.
Native-born, White...............	7	26	25	5	....	....	63
Foreign-born:							
Canadian, French.............	....	1	....	....	....	....	1
Canadian, Other.............	....	4	....	....	....	....	4
French......................	....	1	....	3	....	....	4
German.....................	2	2	3	1	....	....	8
Irish........................	2	8	7	1	....	....	18
Italian, North...............	....	....	1	....	....	....	1
Italian, South...............	....	1	....	....	....	....	1
Mexican.....................	....	....	....	1	....	....	1
Other races *a*.............	....	....	1	....	1	....	2
Total foreign-born........	4	17	12	6	1	....	40
Grand total...............	11	43	37	11	1	....	103

TOTAL.

General nativity and race of father of pupil.	13.	14.	15.	16.	17.	18.	Total.
Native-born, White...............	9	36	25	8	....	....	78
Foreign-born:							
Canadian, French.............	....	1	....	....	....	....	1
Canadian, Other.............	....	4	....	....	....	....	4
French......................	....	1	....	3	....	....	4
German.....................	3	3	3	1	....	....	10
Irish........................	2	10	8	1	....	....	21
Italian, North...............	....	....	1	....	....	....	1
Italian, South...............	....	2	....	....	....	....	2
Mexican.....................	....	....	....	1	....	....	1
Other races *a*.............	....	....	3	....	1	....	4
Total foreign-born........	5	21	15	6	1	....	48
Grand total...............	14	57	40	14	1	....	126

a "Other races" includes races having less than 10 representatives in this city and pupils whose race is not reported.

TABLE 3.—*Race, sex, and age, by grade—Number of pupils of each age in each grade, by sex and by general nativity and race of father of pupil—Continued.*

FIRST YEAR HIGH SCHOOL.

GIRLS.

General nativity and race of father of pupil.	Number of pupils of each age.					Total.
	14.	15.	16.	17.	18.	
Native-born, White	1	7	2	1	1	12
Foreign-born:						
Canadian, French		3				3
Canadian, Other			2			2
English					1	1
French	1	1				2
German	1	2	3			6
Irish	2		2	2		6
Spanish-American	1					1
Other races a		6	1	1		8
Total foreign-born	5	12	8	3	1	29
Grand total	6	19	10	4	2	41

a "Other races" includes races having less than 10 representatives in this city and pupils whose race is not reported.

SECOND YEAR HIGH SCHOOL.

GIRLS.

General nativity and race of father of pupil.	Number of pupils of each age.				Total.
	14.	15.	16.	17.	
Native-born, White	1	2		2	5
Foreign-born:					
Irish		1	1		2
Spanish-American			1		1
Total foreign-born		1	2		3
Grand total	1	3	2	2	8

a "Other races" includes races having less than 10 representatives in this city and pupils whose race is not reported.

TABLE 3.—*Race, sex, and age, by grade—Number of pupils of each age in each grade, by sex and by general nativity and race of father of pupil—*Continued.

MIXED GRADES.

BOYS.

General nativity and race of father of pupil.	Number of pupils of each age.														Total.
	4.	5.	6.	7.	8.	9.	10.	11.	12.	13.	14.	15.	16.	17.	
Native-born:															
White	1	1	3	2	4	3	6	....	4	4	1	2	....	....	31
Negro			1												1
Total native-born	1	1	4	2	4	3	6	....	4	4	1	2	....	....	32
Foreign-born:															
English						1									1
German		1	1	1		1		1	2						7
Irish		1	1	3			4		2		1				12
Italian, North								1							1
Polish							1		1	1					3
Spanish-American			1												1
Other races a		2	1			1									2
Total foreign-born		2	4	4	....	3	5	2	5	1	1				27
Grand total	1	3	8	6	4	6	11	2	9	5	2	2	....	....	59

GIRLS.

General nativity and race of father of pupil.	4.	5.	6.	7.	8.	9.	10.	11.	12.	13.	14.	15.	16.	17.	Total.
Native-born:															
White		3	6	4	2	5	7	5	7	2	1	....	2	1	45
Negro															
Total native-born		3	6	4	2	5	7	5	7	2	1	....	2	1	45
Foreign-born:															
Canadian (other than French)											1				1
English			1												3
French				2		1	1	1	1	1					8
German			2		1	2	1	1	2						9
Irish			1	3	3	1	....	3	2	2	1				16
Italian, North									1						1
Spanish-American				1						1					2
Other races a							1	1	1			1	1		5
Total foreign-born		....	4	6	5	6	4	6	6	4	3	1	....	....	45
Grand total		3	10	10	7	11	11	11	13	6	4	1	2	1	90

TOTAL.

General nativity and race of father of pupil.	4.	5.	6.	7.	8.	9.	10.	11.	12.	13.	14.	15.	16.	17.	Total.
Native-born:															
White	1	4	9	6	6	8	13	5	11	6	2	2	2	1	76
Negro			1												1
Total native-born	1	4	10	6	6	8	13	5	11	6	2	2	2	1	77
Foreign-born:															
Canadian (other than French)											1				1
English			1			2	1								4
French				2	1	1	1	1	1	1					8
German		1	3	1	1	3	1	2	4						16
Irish		1	2	6	3	1	4	3	4	2	2				28
Italian, North								1	1						2
Polish							1	....	1	1					3
Spanish-American			1	1						1					3
Other races a			1			2	1	1	....			1	1		7
Total foreign-born		2	8	10	5	9	9	8	11	5	4	1	....	....	72
Grand total	1	6	18	16	11	17	22	13	22	11	6	3	2	1	149

a "Other races" includes races having less than 10 representatives in this city and pupils whose race is not reported.

TABLE 5.—*Race distribution in each grade—Percentages.*

[This table shows in detail only races with 100 or more pupils reporting. The totals, however, are for all races.]

General nativity and race of father of pupil	Kindergarten	Elementary grades									High school			Mixed school.	Grand total.
		1.	2.	3.	4.	5.	6.	7.	8.	Total.	First year.	Second year.	Total.		
Native-born:															
White	18.4	46.6	37.1	53.7	43.1	52.5	52.7	67.3	61.9	51.5	29.3	62.5	34.7	51.0	50.5
Negro	.0	.3	.0	.0	.0	.0	.0	1.8	.0	.3	.0	.0	.0	.7	.3
Total native-born	18.4	46.9	37.1	53.7	43.1	52.5	52.7	69.1	61.9	51.8	29.3	62.5	34.7	51.7	50.9
Foreign-born:															
German	5.3	11.0	15.3	7.1	12.7	12.2	16.1	11.5	7.9	11.7	14.6	.0	12.2	10.7	11.5
Irish	5.3	13.8	14.8	5.3	12.2	8.7	13.7	6.1	16.7	10.9	14.6	25.0	16.3	18.8	11.5
Other races	71.1	28.3	32.8	33.9	32.0	26.6	17.6	13.3	13.5	25.6	41.5	12.5	36.7	18.8	26.1
Total foreign-born	81.6	53.1	62.9	46.3	56.9	47.5	47.3	30.9	38.1	48.2	70.7	37.5	65.3	48.3	49.1
Grand total	100.0	100.0	100.0	100.0	100.0	100.0	100.0	100.0	100.0	100.0	100.0	100.0	100.0	100.0	100.0

TABLE 6.—*Grade distribution of each race—Percentages.*

[This table shows in detail only races with 100 or more pupils reporting. The totals, however, are for all races.]

General nativity and race of father of pupil.	Kindergarten.	Elementary grades.									High school.			Mixed school.	Grand total.
		1.	2.	3.	4.	5.	6.	7.	8.	Total.	First year.	Second year.	Total.		
Native-born:															
White............	0.6 (a)	16.7	7.6 (a)	13.7	7.0 (a)	12.4 (a)	9.7 (a)	16.8 (a)	7.0 (a)	91.0 (a)	1.1 (a)	0.4 (a)	1.5 (a)	6.8 (a)	100.0 (a)
Negro............															
Total native-born......	.6	16.7	7.6	13.6	7.0	12.3	9.7	17.2	7.0	91.0	1.1	.4	1.5	6.9	100.0
Foreign-born:															
German..........	.8	17.4	13.8	7.9	9.1	12.6	13.0	12.6	4.0	90.5	2.4		2.4	6.3	100.0
Irish............	.8	21.7	13.4	5.9	8.7	9.1	11.1	6.7	8.3	85.0	2.4	.8	3.2	11.1	100.0
Other races......	4.7	19.7	13.0	16.7	10.1	12.2	6.3	6.4	3.0	87.3	3.0	.2	3.1	4.9	100.0
Total foreign-born......	2.9	19.6	13.3	12.1	9.5	11.6	9.0	8.0	4.4	87.5	2.7	.3	3.0	6.7	100.0
Grand total......	1.7	18.1	10.4	12.9	8.2	12.0	9.3	12.6	5.7	89.3	1.9	.4	2.2	6.8	100.0

a Not computed, owing to small number involved.

LOWELL, MASSACHUSETTS.

651

LIST OF TABLES.

LOWELL.

The investigations of the Immigration Commission concerning the school children in the city of Lowell relate to the children of the public schools, the teachers of those schools, and the pupils in the parochial schools. Each of these more or less distinct investigations gave rise to a series of general tables, which are presented herewith. Information concerning the method of collecting the data, tabulating the same, and constructing the general tables, is given in the introduction to this volume.[a] A reference to this introduction will explain these matters in detail and will also give the reader a general idea of the purpose which the several tables serve. This note is concerned not so much with the methods of investigation as with the result in the city of Lowell.

PUBLIC SCHOOL PUPILS.

The reports made to the Immigration Commission indicate the attendance on a day early in December, 1908, of 11,009 children in the public schools of the city of Lowell. During the school year of 1908–9 the average daily attendance in the Lowell schools was 10,539, a figure which, it will be noted, is below the actual attendance on the day of the enumeration. These relative numbers afford gratifying evidence that the enumeration of pupils in the schools of the city was comprehensive and complete. The resulting figures can therefore be accepted without hesitation as a correct picture of the conditions generally prevailing in the schools.

The division of these pupils among the several classes of schools was as follows:

Kindergarten	357	Ninth grade	547
First grade	1,693	First-year high school	382
Second grade	1,445	Second-year high school	310
Third grade	1,144	Third-year high school	263
Fourth grade	1,188	Fourth-year high school	161
Fifth grade	1,085	Illiterate and ungraded	78
Sixth grade	950		
Seventh grade	764	Total	11,009
Eighth grade	642		

A striking fact in this table is not so much the large number of pupils in the first grade as the number of pupils in the first and second grades combined in comparison with those which follow. There is here a greater difference between the second grade and the third than is commonly the case. The numbers in the third and fourth grades are approximately equal. Those in the fifth and sixth do not greatly vary from one another, but are somewhat less than in the third and fourth. With the seventh grade there is a marked diminution in numbers, which continues throughout the remainder of the

---

[a] See pp. VII to XVII.

grades. In the Lowell system the ninth is the final elementary grade. This grade contains 547 pupils, or about one-half as many as are found in the fifth grade.

In order to display more clearly the concentration of pupils in the lower grades, the elementary grades are in the following table divided into two groups, the primary, consisting of grades 1 to 4, and the grammer, consisting of grades 5 to 9, and these two groups are contrasted with the kindergarten and with high schools.

Class of school.	Number.	Per cent.
Kindergarten	357	3.3
Primary, grades 1 to 4	5,470	50.0
Grammar, grades 5 to 9	3,988	36.5
High school	1,116	10.2
Total	10,931	100.0

It appears that exactly one-half of the pupils in the Lowell schools are in the primary grades. The ratio of 10 per cent in the high schools is noteworthy, especially in view of the fact that the grammar grades cover five years instead of four, as in most cities.

Table 1 contains not only a statement of the distribution of pupils by grades, but also by ages. One of the noteworthy facts of this table is the presence in the schools of 694 children of the age of 5 years, of whom not more than 50 are in the kindergarten, the rest being in the first grade. At the age of 6 years there are 962 children. This number is fairly well maintained until the age of 11 years is reached, when the number rises to 1,002 and reaches a maximum at the age of 13 years with 1,173. At the age of 14 years there is a conspicuous falling off of the number of pupils, 800 being recorded at this age, while at the age of 15, with 533 pupils, the number is only about one-half as great as for children two and three years younger.

In the same general table (1) will be found information regarding the number of pupils of each age in each grade, which shows that for any given grade there is a wide variety of ages and conversely for any given age a wide variety of grades represented. The voluminous details of this table find a compact expression through the division in each grade of the pupils who are of the age appropriate to the grade, or under it, and those who are older than the appropriate age. The latter are designated as overage children, and in current educational discussion are noted as retarded or backward children. The retardation can also be measured by ascertaining for the pupils of a given age how many are in appropriate grades and how many have not attained the grades appropriate to that age. The form of expression which states the number of overage children is the most usual.

In the following table a statement is made for each grade of the number and percentage of the pupils who are older than the normal age for the grade. By a comparison of the whole number of such children with all of the children in the elementary grades an average for the entire school system is obtained.

Grade.	Number in grade.	Retarded pupils.		
		Age.	Number.	Per cent of all pupils.
First	1,693	8 years and over	159	9.4
Second	1,445	9 years and over	329	22.8
Third	1,144	10 years and over	287	25.1
Fourth	1,188	11 years and over	437	36.8
Fifth	1,085	12 years and over	383	35.3
Sixth	950	13 years and over	283	29.8
Seventh	764	14 years and over	100	13.1
Eighth	642	15 years and over	54	8.4
Ninth	547	16 years and over	36	6.6
Total	9,458		2,068	21.9

The average retardation for the Lowell schools is a little over one-fifth of all the pupils, or, precisely, 21.9 per cent. In the grades this average is exceeded from the second to the sixth grades, inclusive. In the first grade the average is not attained, and the divergence between the figures for the first grade and those for subsequent grades is in part explained by the fact that the children in Lowell begin school very young, and may in such cases fail to be promoted two or three times before; in accord with the definition stated, they would be rated as retarded pupils. In the upper grades, from the seventh to the ninth, inclusive, the ratio of retardation diminishes by reason of the fact that the backward children leave school more rapidly than do those who make normal progress. If we compare the figures for the fifth and for the ninth grades, as given in the foregoing table, we observe that among the pupils, as a whole, there is a diminution of about one-half, but with the group of retarded pupils the diminution is over nine-tenths. There are in the fifth grade 702 pupils of normal age and in the ninth grade 511. On the other hand, there are in the fifth grade 383 retarded pupils, and in the ninth grade only 36.

A computation of the retardation of pupils, showing the number who are below the proper grade for their age, is shown for the ages 10, 11, and 12 years in the following table:

Age.	Number of pupils of this age.	Normal grade.	Retarded, or below normal grade.	
			Number.	Per cent.
10 years	921	4	238	25.8
11 years	1,001	5	295	29.5
12 years	1,080	6	383	35.5
Total	3,002		916	30.5

The pupils recorded in this table are older than the general average of those who figured in the table given for retardation for all elementary pupils, hence the average rate for retardation for this special group, 30.5 per cent, is higher than for the pupils as a whole. It will be noted that at the age of 10 years over one-fourth of the pupils are retarded, and that as the years advance there is a steady increase in the percentage of retarded pupils. The average for the three years is computed for purposes of comparison. In a later study of individual races we shall find in some cases the numbers so small that it would be improper to compute the relationship on the basis of a single year of age. In such cases the average of the years 10 to 12 is a necessity, and for comparative purposes the same average for all pupils is necessary.

The main object of the researches of the Immigration Commission was to determine what differences, if any, exist respecting school attendance and school progress among the different races which compose the school population. The materials for such a study are presented in the general tables, where information is given for each of the prominent races, the race being distinguished by that of the father of the pupil.

The following table gives a general view of the distribution of races among Lowell school children:

General nativity and race of father of pupil.	Pupils.		General nativity and race of father of pupil.	Pupils.	
	Number.	Per cent.		Number.	Per cent.
Native-born:			Foreign-born—Continued.		
White	4,427	40.2	Hebrew, Russian	290	2.6
Negro and Indian	14	.1	Irish	1,912	17.4
			Portuguese	322	2.9
Total native-born	4,441	40.3	Scotch	315	2.9
			Swedish	208	1.9
Foreign-born:			All others	711	6.5
Canadian, French	1,078	9.8			
Canadian (other than French)	684	6.2	Total foreign-born	6,570	59.7
English	1,050	9.5	Grand total	11,011	100.0

It will be noted that in round numbers four-tenths of the children have native parents and six-tenths have foreign parents. Among the children having foreign-born parents by far the most important numerically are those with Irish parents, these constituting 17.4 per cent of the entire number of school children in the community. Next in order come the Canadian, represented by 16 per cent of the school children. Of these the greater part, nearly 10 per cent of the whole number of children in the schools, are of French Canadian extraction. There is also a considerable contingent of children of English parents, amounting to nearly 10 per cent of all the children in the community. The group "All others" contains races having less than 200 representatives in the schools. They are omitted by name from the table because the small numbers in each individual case would have made it difficult to calculate per cents with much precision. A mention of them, however, adds somewhat to the view already given of the diversity of races in the Lowell schools. They are: Armenian (29), Bulgarian (1), Chinese (3), Danish (7), Dutch (6), Egyptian (2), Finnish (7), Flemish (17), French (31), German (88), Greek (52), Hebrew, German (16), Hebrew, Polish (35), Hebrew, Other (86), Italian, North (32), Italian, South (43), Japanese (1), Lithuanian (12), Magyar (4), Norwegian (33), Polish (133), Roumanian (4), Russian (8), Scotch-Irish (7), Slovak (8), Spanish-American (3), Syrian (28), and Welsh (13).

For each of the racial groups, native and foreign, as well as for the important races among the latter, it is possible to study the same features of grade and age distribution as received attention in the discussion of the whole number of children in the schools. As grades are numerous, the examination of grade distribution can be most conveniently made by means of a group of the elementary grades. Such a group of elementary grades, showing the number and per cent in each group of schools, is given in the following table:

General nativity and race of father of pupil.	Number of pupils.					Per cent.			
	Kinder- garten.	Pri- mary.	Gram- mar.	High.	Total.	Kinder- garten.	Pri- mary.	Gram- mar.	High.
Native-born:									
White.................	132	1,945	1,666	674	4,417	3.0	44.0	37.7	15.3
Negro and Indian.......	2	3	7	1	13	15.4	23.1	53.8	7.7
Total native-born......	134	1,948	1,673	675	4,430	3.0	44.0	37.8	15.2
Foreign-born:									
Canadian, French.......	16	622	350	40	1,028	1.6	60.5	34.0	3.9
Canadian (other than French)................	13	336	222	67	638	2.0	52.7	34.8	10.5
English.................	40	513	411	85	1,049	3.8	48.9	39.2	8.1
Hebrew, Russian........	24	160	92	14	290	8.3	55.2	31.7	4.8
Irish..................	53	959	795	97	1,904	2.8	50.4	41.8	5.1
Portuguese.............	16	262	43	1	322	5.0	81.4	13.4	0.3
Scotch.................	11	156	120	27	314	3.5	49.7	38.2	8.6
Swedish................	12	93	85	17	207	5.8	44.9	41.1	8.2
All other..............	38	421	197	93	749	5.1	56.2	26.3	12.4
Total foreign-born.....	223	3,522	2,315	441	6,501	3.4	54.2	35.6	6.8
Grand total...........	357	5,470	3,988	1,116	10,931	3.3	50.0	36.5	10.2

In the primary schools there is a considerably smaller percentage of children of native white parents than of those of foreign-born parents. Among the individual races there are some which approximate the same proportion as is observed for children of native parents, but no race which has quite so low a proportion of children in these schools. On the other hand certain races, among which the Portuguese and the French Canadians are the most conspicuous, have a very large proportion of their children in the primary grades.

In the grammer grades less difference is observed between the children of native parents and those of foreign-born parents. A marked deviation from the average can be noted only among the Irish and Swedish, who have a larger proportion of pupils in this grade than the average, and among the Portuguese, who have a much smaller proportion. In high schools there is a very marked contrast among the children of various races. Children of native fathers are represented in these schools by 15.3 per cent of their number, while pupils of foreign parents are represented by only 6.8 per cent of the whole number. The general average for the pupils of foreign parents is greatly lowered by the French Canadians and the Portuguese, of whom only a very small proportion are found in the high school, while other races among the foreigners range generally higher than the average. There is none which approximates the proportions found among children of native parents, the maximum being among the English Canadians, who have 10.5 per cent of the children in the high schools.　The relationship of age and grade is exhibited for the different races in the following table on retardation:

General nativity and race of father of pupil.	All elementary pupils.			Pupils 10, 11, and 12 years of of age.		
	Number.	Retarded, overage.	Per cent retarded.	Number.	Retarded, under-grade.	Per cent retarded.
Native-born:						
White	3,611	584	16.2	1,153	260	22.5
Negro and Indian	10	5	50.0	5	1	20.0
Total native-born	3,621	589	16.3	1,158	261	22.5
Foreign-born:						
Canadian, French	972	451	46.4	242	146	60.3
Canadian (other than French)	558	93	16.7	180	46	25.6
English	924	164	17.7	334	89	26.6
Hebrew, Russian	252	57	22.6	74	23	31.1
Irish	1,754	314	17.9	583	159	27.3
Portuguese	305	151	49.5	94	77	81.9
Scotch	276	47	17.0	85	23	27.1
Swedish	178	19	10.7	67	11	16.4
All others	618	183	29.6	185	81	43.8
Total foreign-born	5,837	1,479	25.3	1,844	655	35.5
Grand total	9,458	2,068	21.9	3,002	916	30.5

This table is in two sections; the first refers to all elementary pupils, the second to a selected group of pupils, smaller in number, but uniform as to age and therefore more strictly comparable.　The first section, measuring general retardation, indicates a wide difference between children of native and those of foreign origin.　Among the former, 16.2 per cent are retarded; among the latter as many as 25.3 per cent.　Wide variations exist among the different races which constitute the foreign groups.　One of them, the Swedish, has a percentage of retardation considerably lower than that of children of native parents.　Scotch, Irish, English, and English Canadians approximate the same proportions as are noted for children of native parents.　On the other hand, French Canadians, and especially Portuguese, show high percentages of retarded children.

In the second section of the table, relating to the ages 10, 11, and 12 years, the average for children of native white fathers is 22.5 per cent, while that for children of foreign fathers is 35.5 per cent.　In this special group the Swedish again show smaller percentages of retardation than the natives.　Excessive retardation is indicated among the French Canadians, and especially among the Portuguese.

PUBLIC SCHOOL TEACHERS.

In the kindergarten and the elementary grades of the Lowell public schools there were employed 285 teachers, all of whom were women.　The distribution of these teachers by racial groups was as follows:

	Number.	Per cent.
Native white of native fathers	167	
Native white of foreign fathers	109	38.2
Foreign white	9	3.2
Total	285	100.0

It will be noted that the percentage of teachers with wholly native antecedents, 58.6, is greater than the corresponding percentage of pupils. Nearly four-tenths of the teachers were native-born of foreign fathers. This group consisted of 109 teachers, of whom 84 were Irish. The entire group contains one teacher of German and two of French Canadian extraction, but apart from these three teachers all of the others, though of foreign parentage, were of English-speaking antecedents.

The division of the teachers among the several grades of schools by racial groups was as follows:

	Kindergarten and primary.	Grammar and special.	Total.	Per cent in grammar grades.
Native white of native fathers...	104	63	167	37.7
Native white of foreign fathers...	69	40	109	36.7
Foreign white...	6	3	9	33.3
Total...	179	106	285	37.2

The proportion of teachers engaged in the upper grades, which are commonly considered the more important positions, is about the same for each racial group.

Of these teachers, 282 reported length of service, as follows:

Under 5 years...	34	From 25 to 29 years...	23
From 5 to 9 years...	55	30 years and over...	48
From 10 to 14 years...	57		
From 15 to 19 years...	35	Total...	282
From 20 to 24 years...	30		

In this list, which gives the teachers by five-year groups, it will be noted that the largest group of teachers is that having from ten to fourteen years' experience. If we divide the teachers according to experience into three groups, of those having less than ten, those having ten to nineteen, and those having twenty years' experience or more, we find that the last is the largest class. Dividing the teachers by length of experience and by racial groups, we have the following results:

Race and nativity of teachers.	Length of service, in years.			
	Under 10.	10 to 19.	20 and over.	Total.
Native white of native fathers...	55	43	67	165
Native white of foreign fathers...	32	45	31	108
Foreign white...	2	4	3	9
Total...	89	92	101	282
Percentages: All teachers...	31.6	32.6	35.8	100.0

It will be noted in this table that among the teachers of native birth and foreign parentage the older teachers are the most numerous. Among those of native birth by foreign parentage the most numerous group is found among those who had served from ten to nineteen years.

PUPILS OF THE PAROCHIAL SCHOOLS.

Through the courtesy of the authorities of the Roman Catholic Church, information was collected in Lowell concerning 4,412 pupils attending the parochial schools. For the school year the official directory of the Roman Catholic Church gives an enrollment in the Lowell schools of 5,029. The divergence between the figures is not greater than that which is frequently observed between the total enrollment of a school system and its average attendance. We may therefore assume that the figures reported to the Commission are fairly comprehensive and that no schools or pupils have been omitted. The division of these pupils among the grades was as follows:

Kindergarten	89	Eighth grade	147
First grade	1,225	Ninth grade	79
Second grade	629	First year high school	13
Third grade	515	Commercial school	12
Fourth grade	475	Ungraded and mixed schools	343
Fifth grade	382		
Sixth grade	287	Total	4,412
Seventh grade	216		

The characteristic of this table is, in the first instance, the numerical preponderance of the first grade, which is about twice as numerous as the second. After the first grade the numbers decrease with the advancing grades at a somewhat rapid rate. In the ninth or final grade of the elementary system there are only 79 pupils, or about one-eighth as many as in the second grade. The concentration of pupils in the lower grades is even more strikingly evident by a grouping of the elementary grades into primary and grammar groups, as in the statement following:

Class of school.	Number.	Per cent.
Kindergarten	89	2.2
Grades 1 to 4	2,844	70.1
Grades 5 to 9	1,111	27.4
High school	13	.3
Total	4,057	100.0

It here appears that 70 per cent of the pupils are in the primary grades and a little more than one-fourth are in the grammar grades.

Table 1 gives us information with respect to the ages of pupils. Starting with 206 pupils at the age of 5 years, we find in the following year as many as 362, and thereafter an increase until a maximum of 594 is reached at the age of 11 years. At the age of 12 years there are 526 pupils, but at 13 this number drops to 271, and at 14 to 208. These schools being mainly elementary schools, they contain only 89 children of 15 years of age and over. The relation between age and grade is exhibited in the table next presented, which states the number of retarded pupils in each grade.

Grade.	Number in grade.	Retarded pupils.		
		Age.	Number.	Per cent of all pupils.
First...............	1,225	8 years and over........................	402	32.8
Second.............	629	9 years and over........................	331	52.6
Third..............	515	10 years and over.......................	257	49.9
Fourth............	475	11 years and over.......................	290	61.1
Fifth..............	382	12 years and over.......................	192	50.3
Sixth..............	287	13 years and over.......................	92	32.1
Seventh...........	216	14 years and over.......................	44	20.4
Eighth............	147	15 years and over.......................	18	12.2
Ninth.............	79	16 years and over.......................	7	8.9
Total........	3,955		1,633	41.3

The proportion of retarded pupils for the schools as a whole is 41.3
per cent. The percentage is high in the first grade, with 38.8 per
cent, and reaches the maximum in the fourth grade, with 61.1 per
cent, grades 6 to 9, by reason of the elimination of backward pupils
in the upper grades, showing percentages of retardation considerably
less than the average. A further expression of retardation for the
special class of pupils from 10 to 12 years of age is found in the following statement, giving for each of these ages the number and
percentage of pupils who are below the normal grade for the respective
ages:

Age.	Number of pupils of this age.	Normal grade.	Retarded, or below normal grade.	
			Number.	Per cent.
10 years..........	444	4	239	53.8
11 years..........	481	5	271	56.3
12 years..........	463	6	282	60.9
Total.........	1,398		792	56.7

This table shows that more than half of the pupils of these ages are
in the retarded class, and that the percentage of retardation grows
with advancing years.

The distribution of the pupils of the parochial schools according to
racial groups is found in the table next presented.

General nativity and race of father of pupil.	Pupils.	
	Number.	Per cent.
Native-born, White...........	476	10.8
Foreign-born:		
Canadian, French...........	2,340	53.0
English............	104	2.4
Irish...........	1,347	30.5
All others..........	145	3.3
Total foreign-born........	3,936	89.2
Grand total.........	4,412	100.0

In the total number of pupils only 10.8 per cent have native antecedents. Nearly 90 per cent have fathers of foreign birth. The
most numerous among the latter are the French Canadian, which
constitutes somewhat more than one-half of the whole number of
pupils in the parochial schools. The Irish form considerably more
than one-fourth of the pupils in these schools. The other races
here grouped under "All others" are not numerous. They are:
Canadian, other than French (20), Dutch (2), French (8), German
(3), Greek (2), Italian, North (3), Italian, South (1), Polish (89),
Portuguese (2), Russian (1), Scotch (11), and Syrian (3).

PUBLIC AND PAROCHIAL SCHOOL PUPILS COMBINED.

A combination of the facts recorded in our tables for the public
school pupils and for the parochial school pupils has an interest in
displaying somewhat more accurately the racial composition of the
school children of the city as a whole, as well as suggesting a
contrast between the two systems of schools. Such a combination
follows:

General nativity and race of father of pupil.	Pupils by schools.			Per cent of all pupils.
	Public schools.	Parochial schools.	Total.	
Native-born:				
White..	4,427	476	4,903	31.8
Negro and Indian................................	14	....	14	.1
Total native-born...........................	4,441	476	4,917	31.9
Foreign-born:				
Canadian, French................................	1,078	2,340	3,418	22.2
Canadian (other than French)..................	684	20	704	4.6
English...	1,050	104	1,154	7.5
Hebrew, Russian.................................	290	....	290	1.9
Irish...	1,912	1,347	3,259	21.1
Portuguese.......................................	322	2	324	2.1
Scotch...	315	11	326	2.1
Swedish..	208	....	208	1.3
All others.......................................	711	112	823	5.3
Total foreign-born..........................	6,570	3,936	10,506	68.1
Grand total.................................	11,011	4,412	15,423	100.0

From the figures here given it appears that somewhat less
than one-third of the children have native parents, while a little
more than two-thirds have foreign fathers. Moreover, the children
of French Canadian fathers are rather more than half as numerous
as those of native fathers, and the same is true of the Irish. These
two races together constitute 42.3 per cent of all the school children
in the city.

It is interesting to note that the smaller parochial school system
contains a large proportion of the children of Irish parentage, over
one-third of the whole number, and that these schools contain more
than twice as many French Canadian school children as do the
public schools.

GENERAL TABLES.

PUBLIC SCHOOL PUPILS: GENERAL INVESTIGATION.

TABLE **1.**—*Grade and age—Number of pupils of each age in each grade, by sex.*

BOYS.

Age.	Kinder-garten.	Elementary grades.									
		1.	2.	3.	4.	5.	6.	7.	8.	9.	Total.
3 years....	5										
4 years....	155	5									5
5 years....	23	296	14								310
6 years....	3	334	163	2							499
7 years....		133	254	118	9						514
8 years....		61	186	183	62	5	1				498
9 years....		20	79	129	156	80	9				473
10 years....		8	52	72	128	145	46	11	1		463
11 years....		6	17	33	101	140	125	73	19		514
12 years....		2	9	26	69	96	120	115	72	18	527
13 years....			13	18	54	70	101	141	105	74	576
14 years....			4	8	16	27	51	44	87	78	315
15 years....			5	2	4	4	7	14	27	67	130
16 years....			1		1			1	6	19	28
17 years....							1			1	2
18 years....											
19 years....										1	1
20 years or over.											
Total.	186	865	797	591	600	a 567	461	b 399	317	258	4,855

Age.	High school.					Illiter-ate and un-graded.	Grand total.
	First year.	Second year.	Third year.	Fourth year.	Total.		
3 years							5
4 years							160
5 years						3	336
6 years						4	506
7 years						1	515
8 years						2	500
9 years						1	474
10 years						1	464
11 years						1	515
12 years	3				3		530
13 years	22	3			25	4	605
14 years	62	16	3		81	26	422
15 years	57	57	17	2	133	8	271
16 years	31	44	41	9	125		153
17 years	8	20	30	31	89		91
18 years	3	6	13	12	34		34
19 years			4	11	15		16
20 years or over		1	2	3	6		6
Total	186	147	110	68	511	51	c 5,603

a Not including 1 American Indian not reporting age.
b Not including 1 Japanese not reporting age.
c Not including 1 American Indian and 1 Japanese not reporting age.

TABLE 1.—*Grade and age—Number of pupils of each age in each grade, by sex*—Contd.

GIRLS.

Age	Kinder-garten.	Elementary grades.									
		1.	2.	3.	4.	5.	6.	7.	8.	9.	Total.
3 years											
4 years	4										
5 years	142	6									6
6 years	24	325	8								333
7 years	1	312	139	3							454
		123	229	112	6						470
8 years											
9 years		33	123	183	91	5	3				438
10 years ...		15	71	127	178	63	16	2			472
11 years ...		9	41	56	121	138	81	12			458
12 years ...		2	20	29	87	126	137	68	16	2	487
		1	8	17	45	110	129	130	86	22	548
13 years											
14 years ...		2	3	19	37	64	93	112	121	86	537
15 years ...			4	6	19	11	26	33	81	99	279
16 years ...			2	1	1	1	4	7	19	65	100
					3			1	2	12	17
17 years											
18 years ...										3	4
19 years											
20 years or over.											
Total.	171	828	648	553	588	518	489	365	325	289	4,603

Age	High school.					Illiter-ate and un-graded.	Grand total.
	First year.	Second year.	Third year.	Fourth year.	Total.		
3 years							4
4 years							148
5 years						1	358
6 years						1	456
7 years						2	472
8 years						5	443
9 years						2	474
10 years						1	459
11 years							487
12 years	2				2		550
13 years	27	2			29	2	568
14 years	68	18	1		87	12	378
15 years	69	64	28		161	1	262
16 years	22	43	36	20	121		138
17 years	8	32	54	37	131		135
18 years		4	28	30	62		62
19 years			5	6	11		11
20 years or over			1		1		1
Total	196	163	153	93	605	27	5,406

TABLE 1.—*Grade and age—Number of pupils of each age in each grade, by sex*—Contd.

TOTAL.

Age.	Kinder-garten.	Elementary grades.									
		1.	2.	3.	4.	5.	6.	7.	8.	9.	Total.
3 years	9										11
4 years	297	11									643
5 years	47	621	22								953
6 years	4	646	302	5							984
7 years		256	483	230	15						936
8 years		94	309	366	153	10	4	2			945
9 years		35	150	256	334	143	25	23	1		921
10 years		17	93	128	249	283	127	141	35	2	1,001
11 years		8	37	62	188	266	262	245	158	40	1,075
12 years		3	17	43	114	206	249	226	160		1,113
13 years		2	16	37	91	134	194	253	168	177	594
14 years			8	14	35	38	77	77	46	132	230
15 years			7	3	5	5	11	21	8	31	45
16 years			1		4		1	1		4	6
17 years							1	1		1	1
18 years										1	1
19 years											
20 years or over......											
Total.	357	1,693	1,445	1,144	1,188	1,085	950	764	642	547	9,458

Age.	High schools.					Illiter-ate and un-graded.	Grand total.
	First year.	Second year.	Third year.	Fourth year.	Total.		
3 years							9
4 years						4	308
5 years						5	694
6 years						3	962
7 years							987
8 years						7	943
9 years						3	948
10 years						2	923
11 years						1	1,002
12 years	5				5		1,080
13 years	49	5			54	6	1,173
14 years	130	34	4		168	38	800
15 years	126	121	45	2	294	9	533
16 years	53	87	77	29	246		291
17 years	16	52	84	68	220		226
18 years	3	10	41	42	96		96
19 years			9	17	26		27
20 years or over		1	3	3	7		7
Total	382	310	263	161	1,116	78	11,009

TABLE 2.—*Race, sex, and grade—Number of pupils of each sex in each grade, by general nativity and race of father of pupil.*

General nativity and race of father of pupil	Kindergarten	Elementary grades											High school					Illiterate and ungraded.	Grand total.
		1.	2.	3.	4.	5.	6.	7.	8.	9.	Total.	First year.	Second year.	Third year.	Fourth year.	Total.		
Native-born:																		
White—																		
Male	67	304	264	204	231	207	182	166	145	136	1,839	98	83	62	50	293	6	2,205
Female	65	295	238	204	205	207	182	143	154	144	1,772	111	103	95	72	381	4	2,222
Total	132	599	502	408	436	414	364	309	299	280	3,611	209	186	157	122	674	10	4,427
Negro—																		
Male	1	1	1			1		1			4							5
Female	1				1	2					3	1				1		5
Total	2	1	1		1	3		1			7	1				1		10
Indian—																		
Male						2	1				3							3
Female						1					1							1
Total						3	1				4							4
Total native-born—																		
Male	68	305	265	204	231	210	183	167	145	136	1,846	98	83	62	50	293	6	2,213
Female	66	295	238	204	206	210	182	143	154	144	1,776	112	103	95	72	382	4	2,228
Total	134	600	503	408	437	420	365	310	299	280	3,622	210	186	157	122	675	10	4,441
Foreign-born:																		
Armenian—																		
Male	2	3	6		1	1					11	2				2		15
Female	3	2	5		2	2					11							14
Total	5	5	11		3	3					22	2				2		29
Canadian, French—																		
Male	10	128	71	60	72	67	53	31	15	4	501	7	7	6	1	21	34	566
Female	6	112	42	69	68	52	54	36	15	23	471	6	5	6	2	19	16	512
Total	16	240	113	129	140	119	107	67	30	27	972	13	12	12	3	40	50	1,078
Canadian, Other—																		
Male	7	40	54	36	27	33	28	23	15	21	277	15	5	8	5	33	1	318
Female	6	52	44	32	51	34	44	28	24	17	326	14	9	7	4	34		366
Total	13	92	98	68	78	67	72	51	39	38	603	29	14	15	9	67	1	684
English—																		
Male	22	72	78	70	65	65	50	48	28	19	495	14	14	8	2	38	1	556
Female	18	67	50	50	61	57	44	37	32	31	429	19	9	13	6	47		494
Total	40	139	128	120	126	122	94	85	60	50	924	33	23	21	8	85	1	1,050
Flemish—																		
Male		2	3			1					5							5
Female		2	3			1					12							12
Total		4	6			2					17							17

Race or nativity		Male	Female	Total
French	Male	19		
	Female		12	
	Total			31
German	Male	41		
	Female		47	
	Total			88
Greek	Male	30		
	Female		22	
	Total			52
Hebrew, German	Male	10		
	Female		6	
	Total			16
Hebrew, Polish	Male	15		
	Female		20	
	Total			35
Hebrew, Russian	Male	154		
	Female		136	
	Total			290
Hebrew, Other	Male	45		
	Female		41	
	Total			86
Irish	Male	1,004		
	Female		908	
	Total			1,912
Italian, North	Male	14		
	Female		18	
	Total			32
Italian, South	Male	20		
	Female		23	
	Total			43
Lithuanian	Male	6		
	Female		6	
	Total			12
Norwegian	Male	21		
	Female		12	
	Total			33
Polish	Male	65		
	Female		68	
	Total			133

TABLE 2.—Race, sex, and grade—Number of pupils of each sex in each grade, by general nativity and race of father of pupil—Continued.

General nativity and race of father of pupil.	Kindergarten.	Elementary grades.										High school.					Illiterate and ungraded.	Grand total.
		1.	2.	3.	4.	5.	6.	7.	8.	9.	Total.	First year.	Second year.	Third year.	Fourth year.	Total.		
Foreign-born—Continued.																		
Portuguese—																		
Male........	6	34	75	20	15	14	9	2	2		171							178
Female......	10	50	44	18	6	6	6	3	1		134						1	144
Total........	16	84	119	38	21	20	15	5	3		305			1		1	1	322
Scotch—																		
Male........	6	21	24	25	13	12	12	14	12	11	144	3	3	3	1	10		161
Female......	5	23	21	18	11	16	16	7	10	10	132	7	5	4	1	17	1	154
Total........	11	44	45	43	24	28	28	21	22	21	276	10	8	7	2	27	1	315
Swedish—																		
Male........	7	13	14	5	12	7	7	11	5	7	81	4	3	1	1	8		96
Female......	5	9	14	13	13	9	12	11	9	7	97	3	1	4		9		112
Total........	12	22	28	18	25	16	19	22	14	14	178	7	4	5	1	17		208
Syrian—																		
Male........	3	5	1	1	4	1	1	2			13						1	16
Female......	2	2	1	2	3	1		1			10						1	12
Total........	5	7	2	3	7	2	1	3			23						1	28
Welsh—																		
Male........		2	1						1	1	7		1	1		1		7
Female......		1		1			1		1		5					1		6
Total........		3	1	1			1		2	1	12		1	1		1		13
Other races a—																		
Male........	2	8	3	2	3	3	2	2	1		24	3	3			3	1	30
Female......	1	9	4	2		3	3	2	5		28	3		1		4	1	33
Total........	3	17	7	4	3	6	5	4	6		52	3	3	1		7	1	63
Total foreign-born—																		
Male........	118	560	532	387	369	358	278	233	172	122	3,011	88	64	48	18	218	45	3,392
Female......	105	533	410	349	382	308	307	222	171	145	2,827	84	60	58	21	223	23	3,178
Total........	223	1,093	942	736	751	666	585	455	343	267	5,838	172	124	106	39	441	68	6,570
Grand total—																		
Male........	186	865	797	591	600	b 568	461	c 400	317	258	4,857	186	147	110	68	511	51	5,605
Female......	171	828	648	553	588	518	489	c 365	325	289	4,603	196	163	153	93	605	27	5,406
Total........	357	1,693	1,445	1,144	1,188	b 1,086	950	c 765	642	547	9,460	382	310	263	161	1,116	78	11,011

a "Other races" include: 1 Bulgarian, 3 Chinese, 7 Danish, 7 Dutch, 2 Egyptian, 7 Finnish, 4 Magyar, 4 Roumanian, 8 Russian, 7 Scotch-Irish, 8 Slovak, 3 Spanish-American, 2 race not specified.
b 1 American Indian not reporting age.
• 1 Japanese not reporting age.

TABLE **3.**—*Race, sex, and age, by grade—Number of pupils of each age in each grade, by sex and by general nativity and race of father of pupil.*

KINDERGARTEN.

BOYS.

General nativity and race of father of pupil.	Number of pupils of each age.				Total.
	3.	4.	5.	6.	
Native-born:					
White	1	50	14	2	67
Negro		1			1
Total native-born	1	51	14	2	68
Foreign-born:					
Armenian		2			2
Canadian, French		8	2		10
Canadian, Other		6	1		7
English		20	2		22
French		2			2
German		1			1
Hebrew, Polish		2			2
Hebrew, Russian		14			14
Irish	4	21	2		27
Italian, South		3			3
Norwegian		3			3
Polish		1			1
Portuguese		6			6
Scotch		5	1		6
Syrian		1	1	1	3
Swedish		7			7
Other races *a*		2			2
Total foreign-born	4	104	9	1	118
Grand total	5	155	23	3	186

GIRLS.

General nativity and race of father of pupil.	Number of pupils of each age.				Total.
	3.	4.	5.	6.	
Native-born:					
White	2	52	11		65
Negro			1		1
Total native-born	2	52	12		66
Foreign-born:					
Armenian		2	1		3
Canadian, French		6			6
Canadian, Other		4	2		6
English		18			18
French		2	1		3
German		3	1		4
Greek		1			1
Hebrew, Russian		10			10
Hebrew, Other		1			1
Irish	2	18	6		26
Italian, South		1	1		2
Norwegian		1			1
Polish		1			1
Portuguese		10			10
Scotch		4		1	5
Syrian		2			2
Swedish		5			5
Other races *a*		1			1
Total foreign-born	2	90	12	1	105
Grand total	4	142	24	1	171

a "Other races" includes races having less than 10 representatives in this city and pupils whose race is not reported.

TABLE 3.—*Race, sex, and age, by grade—Number of pupils of each age in each grade, by sex and by general nativity and race of father of pupil—Continued.*

KINDERGARTEN—Continued.

TOTAL.

General nativity and race of father of pupil.	Number of pupils of each age.				Total.
	3.	4.	5.	6.	
Native-born:					
White.............................	3	102	25	2	132
Negro.............................	......	1	1	....	2
Total native-born..............	3	103	26	2	134
Foreign-born:					
Armenian.........................	......	4	1	....	5
Canadian, French................	......	14	2	....	16
Canadian, Other.................	......	10	3	....	13
English..........................	......	38	2	....	40
French...........................	......	4	1	....	5
German...........................	......	4	1	....	5
Greek............................	......	1	....	....	1
Hebrew, Polish...................	......	2	....	....	2
Hebrew, Russian..................	......	24	....	....	24
Hebrew, Other....................	......	1	....	....	1
Irish............................	6	39	8	....	53
Italian, South...................	......	4	1	....	5
Norwegian........................	......	4	....	....	4
Polish...........................	......	2	....	....	2
Portuguese.......................	......	16	....	....	16
Scotch...........................	......	9	1	1	11
Syrian...........................	......	3	1	1	5
Swedish..........................	......	12	....	....	12
Other races a....................	......	3	....	....	3
Total foreign-born.............	6	194	21	2	223
Grand total...................	9	297	47	4	357

a "Other races" includes races having less than 10 representatives in this city and pupils whose race is not reported.

TABLE 3.—*Race, sex, and age, by grade—Number of pupils of each age in each grade, by sex and by general nativity and race of father of pupil*—Continued.

FIRST GRADE.

BOYS.

General nativity and race of father of pupil.	Number of pupils of each age.										Total.
	4.	5.	6.	7.	8.	9.	10.	11.	12.	13.	
Native-born:											
White....................	1	115	133	35	14	3	2	1			304
Negro.................:			1								1
Total native-born........	1	115	134	35	14	3	2	1			305
Foreign-born:											
Armenian.................			2	1							3
Canadian, French..........	1	39	40	24	17	4	1	2			128
Canadian, Other	1	12	15	6	2	2	1	1			40
English.................		30	26	11	5						72
French.................			1	1							2
German.................		2	1	1							4
Greek....................		3	2	1	3		1				10
Hebrew, German..........		2									2
Hebrew, Polish..........			1								1
Hebrew, Russian..........		9	10	6	3						28
Hebrew, Other..........		1									1
Irish...................	2	51	55	24	6	5		1			144
Italian, North...........			2		1						3
Italian, South...........		2									2
Lithuanian..............				1							1
Norwegian..............		1	1								2
Polish.................		6	15	6	3	1	1				32
Portuguese.............		7	8	7	5	3	2	1	1		34
Scotch.................		10	7	4							21
Swedish................		4	6	3							13
Syrian................			3	2							5
Welsh.................			2								2
Other races *a*.............		2	3		2	2			1		10
Total foreign-born........	4	181	200	98	47	17	6	5	2		560
Grand total..............	5	296	334	133	61	20	8	6	2		860

a "Other races" includes races having less than 10 representatives in this city and pupils whose race is not reported.

TABLE 3.—*Race, sex, and age, by grade—Number of pupils of each age in each grade, by sex and by general nativity and race of father of pupil—Continued.*

FIRST GRADE—Continued.

GIRLS.

General nativity and race of father of pupil.	Number of pupils of each grade.										Total.
	4.	5.	6.	7.	8.	9.	10.	11.	12.	13.	
Native-born, White	3	131	118	26	8	6	3				295
Foreign-born:											
Armenian				1		1					2
Canadian, French		29	47	25	8	2	1				112
Canadian, Other		19	21	8	2	1	1				52
English	1	30	21	13	2						67
French		1	1								2
German		4	3	1	1						9
Greek		2	2	1		1	1				7
Hebrew, German		1									1
Hebrew, Polish			1								1
Hebrew, Russian		12	14	1		1					28
Hebrew, Other			2								2
Irish	2	63	39	14	2		1			1	122
Italian, North		1	2							1	4
Italian, South				1							1
Lithuanian				1					1		2
Norwegian			1								1
Polish		6	8	8	1		1				24
Portuguese		10	19	12	4	3	1	1			50
Scotch		7	7	6	3						23
Swedish		5	3	1							9
Syrian			1	1							2
Welsh		1									1
Other races *a*		3	2	3	2			1			11
Total foreign-born	3	194	194	97	25	9	6	2	1	2	533
Grand total	6	325	312	123	33	15	9	2	1	2	828

a "Other races" includes races having less than 10 representatives in this city and pupils whose race is not reported.

TABLE 3.—*Race, sex, and age, by grade—Number of pupils of each age in each grade, by sex and by general nativity and race of father of pupil*—Continued.

FIRST GRADE—Continued.

TOTAL.

General nativity and race of father of pupil.	Number of pupils of each age.										Total.
	4.	5.	6.	7.	8.	9.	10.	11.	12.	13.	
Native-born:											
White	4	246	251	61	22	9	5	1			599
Negro			1								1
Total native-born	4	246	252	61	22	9	5	1			600
Foreign-born:											
Armenian			2	2		1					5
Canadian, French	1	68	87	49	25	6	2	2			240
Canadian, Other	1	31	36	14	4	3	2	1			92
English	1	60	47	24	7						139
French		1	2	1							4
German		6	4	2	1						13
Greek		5	4	2	3	1	2				17
Hebrew, German		3									3
Hebrew, Polish			2								2
Hebrew, Russian		21	24	7	3	1					56
Hebrew, Other		1	2								3
Irish	4	114	94	38	8	5	1	1		1	266
Italian, North		1	4		1					1	7
Italian, South		2		1							3
Lithuanian				2					1		3
Norwegian		1	2								3
Polish		12	23	14	4	1	2				56
Portuguese		17	27	19	9	6	3	2	1		84
Scotch		17	14	10	3						44
Swedish		9	9	4							22
Syrian			4	3							7
Welsh		1	2								3
Other races *a*		5	5	3	4	2		1	1		21
Total foreign-born	7	375	394	195	72	26	12	7	3	1	1,093
Grand total	11	621	646	256	94	35	17	8	3	2	1,693

a "Other races" includes races having less than 10 representatives in this city and pupils whose race is not reported.

TABLE **3.**—*Race, sex, and age, by grade—Number of pupils of each age in each grade, by sex and by general nativity and race of father of pupil—Continued.*

SECOND GRADE.

BOYS.

General nativity and race of father of pupil.	Number of pupils of each age.												Total.
	5.	6.	7.	8.	9.	10.	11.	12.	13.	14.	15.	16.	
Native-born:													
White	6	64	105	50	24	11	1	2	....	1	....	....	264
Negro	....	....	....	1	....	....	....	....	....	....	....	....	1
Total native-born	6	64	105	51	24	11	1	2	....	1	....	....	265
Foreign-born:													
Armenian	....	3	....	1	1	....	....	1	....	....	....	....	6
Canadian, French	....	11	12	20	11	6	1	3	5	1	1	....	71
Canadian, Other	2	12	17	14	5	3	1	....	....	....	....	....	54
English	3	17	24	19	6	8	1	....	....	....	....	....	78
French	....	....	....	2	....	....	....	....	....	....	....	....	2
German	....	....	....	1	1	....	....	....	....	....	....	....	2
Greek	....	....	....	1	....	1	1	....	....	....	....	....	3
Hebrew, German	....	1	....	....	....	....	....	....	....	....	....	....	1
Hebrew, Polish	....	....	3	....	....	....	....	....	....	....	....	....	3
Hebrew, Russian	....	4	4	9	3	1	....	1	....	....	....	....	22
Hebrew, Other	....	1	....	....	....	....	....	....	....	....	....	....	1
Irish	2	27	50	41	13	5	2	1	....	1	....	....	142
Italian, North	....	2	2	....	2	....	....	....	....	....	....	....	6
Italian, South	....	1	5	1	....	....	....	1	....	....	....	....	8
Lithuanian	....	1	1	2	1	....	1	....	....	....	....	....	5
Polish	....	3	2	3	1	1	....	....	....	....	....	....	10
Portuguese	....	4	13	14	8	14	8	....	8	1	4	1	75
Scotch	1	9	5	5	2	1	1	....	....	....	....	....	24
Swedish	....	3	8	2	....	1	....	....	....	....	....	....	14
Syrian	....	....	....	....	1	....	....	....	....	....	....	....	1
Welsh	....	....	1	....	....	....	....	....	....	....	....	....	1
Other races *a*	....	....	2	....	1	....	....	....	....	....	....	....	3
Total foreign-born	8	99	149	135	55	41	16	7	13	3	5	1	532
Grand total	14	163	254	186	79	52	17	9	13	4	5	1	797

a "Other races" includes races having less than 10 representatives in this city and pupils whose race is not reported.

TABLE 3.—*Race, sex, and age, by grade—Number of pupils of each age in each grade, by sex and by general nativity and race of father of pupil*—Continued.

SECOND GRADE—Continued.

GIRLS.

General nativity and race of father of pupil.	Number of pupils of each age.												Total.
	5.	6.	7.	8.	9.	10.	11.	12.	13.	14.	15.	16.	
Native-born, White	3	70	87	39	22	9	6	1	....	1	....	....	238
Foreign-born:													
Armenian	....	1	1	1	....	2	....	....	....	....	....	....	5
Canadian, French	....	3	11	7	9	5	4	1	1	1	....	....	42
Canadian, Other	1	12	18	2	8	2	....	1	....	....	....	....	44
English	....	8	29	10	3	....	....	....	....	....	....	....	50
Flemish	....	....	3	....	....	....	....	....	....	....	....	....	3
French	....	....	2	....	....	....	....	....	....	....	....	....	2
German	....	....	1	1	....	....	....	....	....	....	....	....	2
Greek	....	....	....	1	2	1	....	1	....	2	....	....	7
Hebrew, German	....	....	2	....	....	....	....	....	....	....	....	....	2
Hebrew, Polish	....	....	1	2	....	1	....	....	....	....	....	....	4
Hebrew, Russian	....	6	13	3	3	2	3	....	....	....	....	....	30
Hebrew, Other	....	....	1	2	....	....	....	....	....	....	....	....	3
Irish	3	20	40	23	8	3	2	1	....	....	....	....	100
Italian, North	....	....	1	1	1	....	....	....	....	....	....	....	3
Italian, South	1	2	2	2	....	....	....	....	....	....	....	....	7
Lithuanian	....	....	....	3	....	....	....	....	....	....	....	....	3
Norwegian	....	1	....	....	1	....	....	....	....	....	....	....	2
Polish	....	4	1	3	4	2	2	1	....	....	....	....	17
Portuguese	....	2	2	13	8	10	3	2	2	....	2	....	44
Scotch	....	4	6	5	2	4	....	....	....	....	....	....	21
Swedish	....	4	6	4	....	....	....	....	....	....	....	....	14
Syrian	....	1	....	....	....	....	....	....	....	....	....	....	1
Other races *a*	....	1	2	1	....	....	....	....	....	....	....	....	4
Total foreign-born	5	69	142	84	49	32	14	7	3	3	2	....	410
Grand total	8	139	229	123	71	41	20	8	3	4	2	....	648

a "Other races" includes races having less than 10 representatives in this city and pupils whose race is not reported.

TABLE 3.—*Race, sex, and age, by grade—Number of pupils of each age in each grade, by sex and by general nativity and race of father of pupil*—Continued.

SECOND GRADE—Continued.

TOTAL.

General nativity and race of father of pupil.	Number of pupils of each age.												Total.
	5.	6.	7.	8.	9.	10.	11.	12.	13.	14.	15.	16.	
Native-born:													
White	9	134	192	89	46	20	7	3	....	2	....	....	502
Negro				1									1
Total native-born	9	134	192	90	46	20	7	3	....	2	....	....	503
Foreign-born:													
Armenian	....	4	1	2	1	2		1					11
Canadian, French	....	14	23	27	20	11	5	4	6	2	1	....	113
Canadian, Other	3	24	35	16	13	5	1	1					98
English	3	25	53	29	9	8	1						128
Flemish			3										3
French			2	2									4
German			1	2	1								4
Greek				2	2	2	1	1		2			10
Hebrew, German		1	2										3
Hebrew, Polish			4	2		1							7
Hebrew, Russian		10	17	12	6	3	3	1					52
Hebrew, Other		1	1	2									4
Irish	5	47	90	64	21	8	4	2		1			242
Italian, North		2	3	1	3								9
Italian, South	1	3	7	3				1					15
Lithuanian		1	1	5			1	..					8
Norwegian		1			1								2
Polish		7	3	6	5	3	2	1					27
Portuguese	....	6	15	27	16	24	11	2	10	1	6	1	119
Scotch	1	13	11	10	4	5	1						45
Swedish		7	14	6		1							28
Syrian		1			1								2
Welsh			1										1
Other races a		1	4	1	1								7
Total foreign-born	13	168	291	219	104	73	30	14	16	6	7	1	942
Grand total	22	302	483	309	150	93	37	17	16	8	7	1	1,445

a "Other races" includes races having less than 10 representatives in this city and pupils whose race is not reported.

TABLE 3.—*Race, sex, and age, by grade—Number of pupils of each age in each grade, by sex and by general nativity and race of father of pupil*—Continued.

THIRD GRADE.

BOYS.

General nativity and race of father of pupil.	Number of pupils of each age.										Total.
	6.	7.	8.	9.	10.	11.	12.	13.	14.	15.	
Native-born, White	1	46	81	42	22	9	2	......	1	......	204
Foreign-born:											
Canadian, French	......	9	6	5	6	4	11	15	2	2	60
Canadian, Other	......	12	12	7	3	2	......	......	......	......	36
English	......	13	25	18	8	4	2	......	......	......	70
French	......	......	......	1	......	......	1	......	......	......	2
German	......	......	3	1	1	......	1	......	......	......	5
Greek	......	......	......	......	......	1	1	2	2	......	6
Hebrew, German	......	1	1	1	......	......	......	......	......	......	3
Hebrew, Polish	......	2	......	......	2	......	1	......	......	......	4
Hebrew, Russian	......	1	3	5	4	......	1	......	......	......	14
Hebrew, Other	......	1	......	1	......	......	......	......	......	......	2
Irish	1	23	36	35	13	8	6	......	1	......	123
Italian, North	......	......	......	......	1	......	......	......	......	......	1
Italian, South	......	......	......	1	1	......	......	......	......	......	2
Norwegian	......	2	1	......	......	......	......	......	......	......	3
Polish	......	......	1	......	......	......	......	......	......	......	1
Portuguese	......	......	5	5	4	3	2	......	1	......	20
Scotch	......	5	8	5	4	2	......	1	1	......	25
Swedish	......	3	1	......	1	......	......	......	......	......	5
Syrian	......	......	......	1	......	......	......	......	......	......	1
Welsh	......	......	......	......	1	......	......	......	......	......	1
Other races *a*	......	......	1	......	1	......	......	1	......	......	3
Total foreign-born	1	72	102	87	50	24	24	18	7	2	387
Grand total	2	118	183	129	72	33	26	18	8	2	591

a "Other races" includes races having less than 10 representatives in this city and pupils whose race is not reported.

TABLE **3.**—*Race, sex, and age, by grade—Number of pupils of each age in each grade, by sex and by general nativity and race of father of pupil*—Continued.

THIRD GRADE—Continued.

GIRLS.

General nativity and race of father and pupil.	Number of pupils of each age.										Total.
	6.	7.	8.	9.	10.	11.	12.	13.	14.	15.	
Native-born, White	1	53	80	37	21	9	2	1			204
Foreign-born:											
Canadian, French		8	11	16	2	8	7	12	4	1	69
Canadian, Other		6	13	11	1	1					32
English	1	11	14	12	5	2	2	3			50
Flemish		1		1							2
French				1							1
German		2		1	3						6
Greek					1		1				2
Hebrew, German			1								1
Hebrew, Polish			2	3	1						6
Hebrew, Russian			2	2					1		5
Hebrew, Other		1	1	1							3
Irish	1	20	43	27	10	3	1		1		106
Italian, North			2					1			3
Italian, South				1							1
Lithuanian		1									1
Norwegian			1								1
Polish		3	1	2		1					7
Portuguese				4	5	3	4	2			18
Scotch		4	7	4	3						18
Swedish		2	5	4	2						13
Syrian					1	1					2
Other races *a*					1	1					2
Total foreign-born	2	59	103	90	35	20	15	18	6	1	349
Grand total	3	112	183	127	56	29	17	19	6	1	553

a "Other races" includes races having less than 10 representatives of this sex and age and pupils whose race is not reported.

TABLE 3.—*Race, sex, and age, by grade—Number of pupils of each age in each grade, by sex and by general nativity and race of father of pupil—Continued.*

THIRD GRADE—Continued.

TOTAL.

General nativity and race of father of pupil.	Number of pupils of each age.										Total.
	6.	7.	8.	9.	10.	11.	12.	13.	14.	15.	
Native-born, White	2	99	161	79	43	18	4	1	1	......	408
Foreign-born:											
Canadian, French	......	17	17	21	8	12	18	27	6	3	129
Canadian, Other	......	18	25	18	4	3	......	......	......	......	68
English	1	24	39	30	13	6	4	3	......	......	120
Flemish	......	1	......	......	......	......	......	......	......	......	2
French	......	......	......	2	......	......	1	......	......	......	3
German	......	2	3	2	4	......	......	......	......	......	11
Greek	......	......	......	......	1	1	2	2	2	......	8
Hebrew, German	......	1	2	1	......	......	......	......	......	......	4
Hebrew, Polish	......	2	2	3	3	......	......	......	......	......	10
Hebrew, Russian	......	1	5	7	4	......	1	......	1	......	19
Hebrew, Other	......	2	1	2	......	......	......	......	......	......	5
Irish	2	43	79	62	23	11	7	......	2	......	229
Italian, North	......	......	2	......	1	......	......	1	......	......	4
Italian, South	......	......	......	2	1	......	......	......	......	......	3
Lithuanian	......	1	......	......	......	......	......	......	......	......	1
Norwegian	......	2	2	......	......	......	......	......	......	......	4
Polish	......	3	2	2	......	1	......	......	......	......	8
Portuguese	......	......	5	9	9	6	6	2	1	......	38
Scotch	......	9	15	9	7	2	......	......	1	......	43
Swedish	......	5	6	4	3	......	......	......	......	......	18
Syrian	......	......	......	1	1	1	......	......	......	......	3
Welsh	......	......	......	......	1	......	......	......	......	......	1
Other races a	......	......	......	1	2	1	......	1	......	......	5
Total foreign-born	3	131	205	177	85	44	39	36	13	3	736
Grand total	5	230	366	256	128	62	43	37	14	3	1,144

a "Other races" includes races having less than 10 representatives in this city and pupils whose race is not reported.

TABLE 3.—*Race, sex, and age, by grade—Number of pupils of each age in each grade, by sex and by general nativity and race of father of pupil—*Continued.

FOURTH GRADE.

BOYS.

General nativity and race of father of pupil.	7.	8.	9.	10.	11.	12.	13.	14.	15.	16.	Total.
Native-born, White	5	31	80	50	39	16	5	3	1	1	231
Foreign-born:											
Armenian							1				1
Canadian, French		3	6	4	6	18	27	8			72
Canadian, Other	1	2	9	7	5	3					27
English	1	7	16	16	6	12	6	1			65
Flemish						1					1
French			1	1		1	1				4
German		1		3	2	1					7
Greek	1		1	1		1		1	1		6
Hebrew, Polish				1							1
Hebrew, Russian	1	1	3	4	2	1	2	1			15
Hebrew, Other					1						1
Irish		11	26	30	24	8	6	1			106
Italian, North				1							1
Italian, South							1				1
Norwegian		1	2								3
Polish			3	1	3	3	1				11
Portuguese			3	1	4	2	2	1	2		15
Scotch		2	4	3	3	1					13
Swedish		3	2	4	3						12
Syrian				1	2		2				4
Other races a				1	1	1					3
Total foreign-born	4	31	76	78	62	53	49	13	3		369
Grand total	9	62	156	128	101	69	54	16	4	1	600

a "Other races" includes races having less than 10 representatives in this city and pupils whose race is not reported.

TABLE 3.—*Race, sex, and age, by grade—Number of pupils of each age in each grade, by sex and by general nativity and race of father of pupil—Continued.*

FOURTH GRADE—Continued.

GIRLS.

General nativity and race of father of pupil.	Number of pupils of each age.										Total.
	7.	8.	9.	10.	11.	12.	13.	14.	15.	16.	
Native-born:											
White	1	37	76	49	25	11	5	1			205
Negro				1							1
Total native-born	1	37	76	50	25	11	5	1			206
Foreign-born:											
Armenian			1	1							2
Canadian, French		5	10	4	11	11	16	11			68
Canadian, Other		11	18	10	7	3	1	1			51
English	2	9	17	12	11	6	3	1			61
Flemish				1							1
French			1								1
German	1	1	1	1	2		1				7
Greek		1								2	3
Hebrew, Polish				2			1				3
Hebrew, Russian		2	4	5	2	1	2	1		1	18
Hebrew, Other			1	1							2
Irish	1	19	38	21	20	8	6	3			116
Italian, North					1	2		1			4
Italian, South				1	3						4
Norwegian				1							1
Polish			3	3	1						7
Portuguese			1	2	1	2					6
Scotch		2	4	2	2		1				11
Swedish	1	4	3	4	1						13
Syrian						1	1		1		3
Other races a											
Total foreign-born	5	54	102	71	62	34	32	18	1	3	382
Grand total	6	91	178	121	87	45	37	19	1	3	588

a "Other races" includes races having less than 10 representatives in this city and pupils whose race is not reported.

TABLE **3.**—*Race, sex, and age, by grade—Number of pupils of each age in each grade, by sex and by general nativity and race of father of pupil*—Continued.

FOURTH GRADE—Continued.

TOTAL.

General nativity and race of father of pupil.	Number of pupils of each age.										Total.
	7.	8.	9.	10.	11.	12.	13.	14.	15.	16.	
Native-born:											
White	6	68	156	99	64	27	10	4	1	1	436
Negro				1							1
Total native-born	6	68	156	100	64	27	10	4	1	1	437
Foreign-born:											
Armenian			1	1			1				3
Canadian, French		8	16	8	17	29	43	19			140
Canadian, Other	1	13	27	17	12	6	1	1			78
English	3	16	33	28	17	18	9	2			126
Flemish				1		1					2
French			2	1		1	1				5
German	1	2	1	4	4	1	1				14
Greek	1	1	1	1		1		1	1	2	9
Hebrew, Polish				3			1				4
Hebrew, Russian	1	3	7	9	4	2	4	2		1	33
Hebrew, Other			1	1	1						3
Irish	1	30	64	51	44	16	12	4			222
Italian, North				1	1	2		1			5
Italian, South				1	3		1				5
Norwegian		1	2	1							4
Polish			6	4	4	3	1				18
Portuguese			4	3	5	4	2	1	2		21
Scotch		4	8	5	5	1	1				24
Swedish	1	7	5	8	4						25
Syrian					2	1	3		1		7
Other races a				1	1	1					3
Total foreign-born	9	85	178	149	124	87	81	31	4	3	751
Grand total	15	153	334	249	188	114	91	35	5	4	1,188

a " Other races" includes races having less than 10 representatives in this city and pupils whose race is not reported.

TABLE 3.—*Race, sex, and age, by grade—Number of pupils of each age in each grade, by sex and by general nativity and race of father of pupil*—Continued.

FIFTH GRADE.

BOYS.

General nativity and race of father of pupil.	Number of pupils of each age.								Total.
	8.	9.	10.	11.	12.	13.	14.	15.	
Native-born:									
White....................	1	35	65	55	25	20	6	......	207
Indian.....................	......	......	1	......	......	......	......	......	a 1
Negro.....................	......	......	......	1	......	......	......	......	1
Total native-born............	1	35	66	56	25	20	6	......	a 209
Foreign-born:									
Canadian, French............	......	1	6	14	19	15	11	1	67
Canadian, Other............	1	2	10	11	4	5	......	......	33
English....................	1	7	17	21	11	7	1	......	65
Flemish....................	......	......	......	......	......	1	......	......	1
French.....................	......	......	......	......	......	1	......	......	1
German....................	......	1	1	1	3	2	......	......	8
Greek.....................	......	......	......	......	......	......	1	2	3
Hebrew, Polish............	......	......	......	2	......	......	......	......	2
Hebrew, Russian...........	......	3	3	4	4	2	3	......	19
Hebrew, Other.............	......	1	......	......	......	......	......	......	1
Irish......................	2	25	33	18	26	6	3	......	113
Italian, South.............	......	......	......	......	......	3	......	......	3
Norwegian.................	......	......	......	......	1	2	......	......	3
Polish.....................	......	......	......	1	......	1	......	......	2
Portuguese.................	......	......	2	5	2	3	1	1	14
Scotch.....................	......	3	5	4	......	......	......	......	12
Swedish....................	......	2	1	3	1	......	......	......	7
Welsh.....................	......	......	......	......	......	1	......	......	1
Other races b..............	......	......	1	......	......	1	1	......	3
Total foreign-born..............	4	45	79	84	71	50	21	4	358
Grand total.................	5	80	145	140	96	70	27	4	a 567

a Not including 1 Indian not reporting age.
b "Other races" includes races having less than 10 representatives in this city and pupils whose race is not reported.

TABLE 3.—*Race, sex, and age, by grade—Number of pupils of each age in each grade, by sex and by general nativity and race of father of pupil—Continued.*

FIFTH GRADE—Continued.

GIRLS.

General nativity and race of father of pupil.	Number of pupils of each age.								Total.
	8.	9.	10.	11.	12.	13.	14.	15.	
Native-born:									
White..................................	......	26	71	50	43	12	4	1	207
Indian.................................	......	......	......	......	1	......	......	......	a 1
Negro..................................	......	1	......	1	......	......	......	......	2
Total native-born..................	......	27	71	51	44	12	4	1	a 210
Foreign-born:									
Canadian, French....................	......	......	1	3	19	26	3	......	52
Canadian, Other.....................	1	7	8	11	7	......	......	......	34
English..............................	2	10	16	15	11	3	......	......	57
Flemish..............................	......	......	......	......	1	......	......	......	1
French...............................	......	......	......	......	......	1	......	......	1
German...............................	......	1	1	1	......	1	......	......	4
Hebrew, Polish.......................	......	......	1	......	1	......	......	......	2
Hebrew, Russian......................	......	1	4	2	1	......	......	......	8
Irish................................	2	12	28	28	16	8	3	......	97
Italian, North.......................	......	......	1	......	......	......	......	......	1
Italian, South.......................	......	......	......	......	4	2	1	......	7
Norwegian............................	......	......	1	2	......	......	......	......	3
Polish...............................	......	......	......	2	......	4	......	......	6
Portuguese...........................	......	......	......	1	2	3	......	......	6
Scotch...............................	......	3	2	6	2	3	......	......	16
Swedish..............................	......	1	4	2	2	......	......	......	9
Welsh................................	......	1	......	......	......	......	......	......	1
Other races b........................	......	......	......	2	......	1	......	......	3
Total foreign-born.................	5	36	67	75	66	52	7	......	308
Grand total........................	5	63	138	126	110	64	11	1	518

a Not including 1 Indian not reporting age.
b "Other races" includes races having less than 10 representatives in this city and pupils whose race is not reported.

TABLE 3.—*Race, sex, and age, by grade—Number of pupils of each age in each grade, by sex and by general nativity and race of father of pupil*—Continued.

TOTAL.

General nativity and race of father of pupil.	Number of pupils of each age.								Total.
	8.	9.	10.	11.	12.	13.	14.	15.	
Native-born:									
White	1	61	136	105	68	32	10	1	414
Indian			1		1				3
Negro		1		2					3
Total native-born	1	62	137	107	69	32	10	1	420
Foreign-born:									
Canadian, French		1	7	17	38	41	14	1	119
Canadian, Other	2	9	18	22	11	5			67
English	3	17	33	36	22	10	1		122
Flemish					1	1			2
French						2			2
German		2	2	2	3	3			12
Greek							1	2	3
Hebrew, Polish			1	2	1				4
Hebrew, Russian		4	7	6	5	2	3		27
Hebrew, Other		1							1
Irish	4	37	61	46	42	14	6		210
Italian, North			1						1
Italian, South					4	5	1		10
Norwegian			1	2	1	2			6
Polish				3		5			8
Portuguese			2	6	4	6	1	1	20
Scotch		6	7	10	2	3			28
Swedish		3	5	5	3				16
Welsh		1				1			2
Other races a			1	2		2	1		6
Total foreign-born	9	81	146	159	137	102	28	4	666
Grand total	10	143	283	266	206	134	38	5	b 1,085

a "Other races" includes races having less than 10 representatives in the city and pupils whose race is not reported.
b Not including 1 Indian not reporting age.

TABLE 3.—*Race, sex, and age, by grade—Number of pupils of each age in each grade, by sex and by general nativity and race of father of pupil*—Continued.

SIXTH GRADE.

BOYS.

General nativity and race of father of pupil.	Number of pupils of each age.								Total.
	8.	9.	10.	11.	12.	13.	14.	15.	
Native-born:									
White		3	22	56	53	32	15	1	182
Negro							1		1
Total native-born		3	22	56	53	32	16	1	183
Foreign-born:									
Canadian, French				6	14	22	9	2	53
Canadian, Other		2	4	7	7	4	4		28
English			6	17	13	8	5	1	50
French			2						2
German			1	1	1				3
Hebrew, Russian			1	4		2			7
Hebrew, Other				2		1			3
Irish	1	3	8	24	24	23	12	2	97
Norwegian				1		1			2
Polish					1	1	1		3
Portuguese				2	3	3	1		9
Scotch			1	3	3	4	1		12
Swedish		1	1	2	1		2		7
Other races *a*								1	2
Total foreign-born	1	6	24	69	67	69	35	6	278
Grand total	1	9	46	125	120	101	51	7	461

GIRLS.

General nativity and race of father of pupil.	8.	9.	10.	11.	12.	13.	14.	15.	Total.
Native-born, White		7	38	62	39	26	8	2	182
Foreign-born:									
Armenian						1			1
Canadian, French			3	6	13	22	10		54
Canadian, Other			11	12	15	5	1		44
English	1	1	6	15	14	6	1		44
German		1		1	2	1			5
Hebrew, Polish				1	1				2
Hebrew, Russian			2	2	2	2	1	1	10
Irish	1	6	12	27	33	20	2	1	102
Italian, North					1				1
Italian, South						1			1
Polish				2		1			3
Portuguese				1		4	1		6
Scotch	1	1	4	5	4	1			16
Swedish			4	3	3	1	1		12
Syrian							1		1
Welsh					2				2
Other races *a*			1			2			3
Total foreign-born	3	9	43	75	90	67	18	2	307
Grand total	3	16	81	137	129	93	26	4	489

a "Other races" includes races having less than 10 representatives in the city and pupils whose race is not reported.

TABLE 3.—*Race, sex, and age, by grade—Number of pupils of each age in each grade, by sex and by general nativity and race of father of pupil*—Continued.

SIXTH GRADE—Continued.

TOTAL.

General nativity and race of father of pupil.	Number of pupils of each age.								Total.
	8.	9.	10.	11.	12.	13.	14.	15.	
Native-born:									
White..........		10	60	118	92	58	23	3	364
Negro..........							1		1
Total native-born..........		10	60	118	92	58	24	3	365
Foreign-born:									
Armenian..........						1			1
Canadian, French..........			3	12	27	44	19	2	107
Canadian, Other..........		2	15	19	22	9	5		72
English..........	1	1	12	32	27	14	6	1	94
French..........			2						2
German..........		1	1	2	3	1			8
Hebrew, Polish..........				1	1				2
Hebrew, Russian..........			3	6	2	4	1	1	17
Hebrew, Other..........				2		1			3
Irish..........	2	9	20	51	57	43	14	3	199
Italian, North..........					1				1
Italian, South..........						1			1
Norwegian..........				1		1			2
Polish..........				2	1	2	1		6
Portuguese..........				3	3	7	2		15
Scotch..........	1	1	5	8	7	5	1		28
Swedish..........		1	5	5	4	1	3		19
Syrian..........							1		1
Welsh..........					2				2
Other races *a*..........			1			2		1	5
Total foreign-born..........	4	15	67	144	157	136	53	8	585
Grand total..........	4	25	127	262	249	194	77	11	950

a "Other races" includes races having less than 10 representatives in this city and pupils whose race is not reported.

TABLE 3.—*Race, sex, and age, by grade—Number of pupils of each age in each grade, by sex and by general nativity and race of father of pupil*—Continued.

SEVENTH GRADE.

BOYS.

General nativity and race of father of pupil.	Number of pupils of each age.									Total.
	9.	10.	11.	12.	13.	14.	15.	16.	17.	
Native-born:										
White		5	37	41	49	26	7	1		166
Indian						1				1
Total native-born		5	37	41	49	27	7	1		167
Foreign-born:										
Canadian, French			2	4	15	5	5			31
Canadian, Other			2	8	11	2				23
English		1	10	18	17	2				48
French							1			1
German						2				2
Greek				1						1
Hebrew, Russian		1	2	4	3	1				11
Irish		3	9	25	33	6	1			77
Italian, South				1						1
Norwegian			3	1						4
Polish			1	2						3
Portuguese					2					2
Scotch		1	5	4	4					14
Swedish			2	5	4					11
Syrian					1	1				2
Other races *a*				1						1
Total foreign-born		6	36	74	92	17	7			232
Grand total		11	73	115	141	44	14	1		399

GIRLS.

General nativity and race of father of pupil.	Number of pupils of each age.									Total.
	9.	10.	11.	12.	13.	14.	15.	16.	17.	
Native-born, White		4	34	55	33	12	5			143
Total native-born		4	34	55	33	12	5			143
Foreign-born:										
Armenian					1					1
Canadian, French		1	1	10	16	6	2			36
Canadian, Other	1	1	6	12	7	1				28
English		1	8	12	13	3				37
Flemish				1						1
German					2	1				3
Hebrew, Russian			1	4	3	3				11
Hebrew, Other			1							1
Irish		3	13	29	28	5				78
Italian, North			1		1					2
Portuguese					3					3
Scotch			1	3	2				1	7
Swedish	1	2	2	3	1	2				11
Syrian					1					1
Other races *a*				1	1					2
Total foreign-born	2	8	34	75	79	21	2		1	222
Grand total	2	12	68	130	112	33	7		1	365

a "Other races" includes races having less than 10 representatives in this city and pupils whose race is not reported.

TABLE 3.—*Race, sex, and age, by grade—Number of pupils of each age in each grade, by sex and by general nativity and race of father of pupil*—Continued.

SEVENTH GRADE—Continued.

TOTAL.

General nativity and race of father of pupil.	Number of pupils of each age.									Total.
	9.	10.	11.	12.	13.	14.	15.	16.	17.	
Native-born:										
White		9	71	96	82	38	12	1		309
Indian						1				1
Total native-born		9	71	96	82	39	12	1		310
Foreign-born:										
Armenian					1					1
Canadian, French		1	3	14	31	11	7			67
Canadian, Other	1	1	8	20	18	3				51
English		2	18	30	30	5				85
Flemish				1						1
French								1		1
German					4	1				5
Greek				1						1
Hebrew, Russian		1	3	8	6	4				22
Hebrew, Other			1							1
Irish		6	22	54	61	11	1			155
Italian, North			1		1					2
Italian, South				1						1
Norwegian			3	1						4
Polish			1	2						3
Portuguese					5					5
Scotch		1	6	7	6				1	21
Swedish	1	2	4	8	5	2				22
Syrian					2	1				3
Other races *a*				2	1					4
Total foreign-born	2	14	70	149	171	38	9		1	454
Grand total	2	23	141	245	253	77	21	1	1	764

a "Other races" includes races having less than 10 representatives in this city and pupils whose race is not reported.

TABLE 3.—*Race, sex, and age, by grade—Number of pupils of each age in each grade, by sex and by general nativity and race of father of pupil*—Continued.

EIGHTH GRADE.

BOYS.

General nativity and race of father of pupil.	Number of pupils of each age.							Total.
	10.	11.	12.	13.	14.	15.	16.	
Native-born, White	1	10	26	41	48	17	2	145
Foreign-born:								
Canadian, French		2		2	6	4	1	15
Canadian, Other			5	4	4	1	1	15
English		3	8	11	3	2	1	28
French				1				1
German			1		1			2
Hebrew, German					1			1
Hebrew, Russian		1	1	2	1			5
Irish		1	26	33	20	3		83
Polish		1						1
Portuguese				1	1			2
Scotch			2	8	1		1	12
Swedish		1	3	1				5
Welsh				1				1
Other races *a*					1			1
Total foreign-born		9	46	64	39	10	4	172
Grand total	1	19	72	105	87	27	6	317

GIRLS.

General nativity and race of father of pupil.	10.	11.	12.	13.	14.	15.	16.	Total.
Native-born, White		8	37	60	38	9	2	154
Foreign-born:								
Canadian, French			2	4	6	3		15
Canadian, Other		1	9	5	7	2		24
English		3	9	13	7			32
French				1				1
Hebrew, German				1				1
Hebrew, Russian			1	2	2	1		6
Irish		3	17	28	14	3		65
Polish			1					1
Portuguese					1			1
Scotch			4	2	3	1		10
Swedish		1	3	3	2			9
Welsh					1			1
Other races *a*			3	2				5
Total foreign-born		8	49	61	43	10		171
Grand total		16	86	121	81	19	2	325

a "Other races" includes races having less than 10 representatives in this city and pupils whose race is not reported.

TABLE 3.—*Race, sex, and age, by grade—Number of pupils of each age in each grade, by sex and by general nativity and race of father of pupil*—Continued.

EIGHTH GRADE—Continued.

TOTAL.

General nativity and race of father of pupil.	Number of pupils of each age.							Total.
	10.	11.	12.	13.	14.	15.	16.	
Native-born, White	1	18	63	101	86	26	4	299
Foreign-born:								
Canadian, French		2	2	6	12	7	1	30
Canadian, Other		1	14	9	11	3	1	39
English		6	17	24	10	2	1	60
French					2			2
German			1		1			2
Hebrew, German				1	1			2
Hebrew, Russian		1	2	4	3	1		11
Irish		4	43	61	34	6		148
Polish		1	1					2
Portuguese				1	2			3
Scotch			6	10	4	1	1	22
Swedish		2	6	4	2			14
Welsh				1	1			2
Other races a			3	2	1			6
Total foreign-born		17	95	125	82	20	4	343
Grand total	1	35	158	226	168	46	8	642

a "Other races" includes races having less than 10 representatives in this city and pupils whose race is not reported.

NINTH GRADE.

BOYS.

General nativity and race of father of pupil.	Number of pupils of each age.									Total.
	11.	12.	13.	14.	15.	16.	17.	18.	19.	
Native-born, White		14	42	34	35	10	1			136
Foreign-born:										
Armenian					1					1
Canadian, French			1		3					4
Canadian, Other			2	11	4	1				21
English		2	7	3	5	2				19
German			2	1		1				4
Hebrew, Polish				1						1
Hebrew, Russian			4	2	2					8
Irish		2	13	17	9	2				43
Italian, North			1	1						2
Scotch			2	3	3	2			1	11
Swedish			1	4	1	1				7
Welsh					1					1
Total foreign-born		4	32	44	32	9			1	122
Grand total		18	74	78	67	19	1		1	258

TABLE 3.—*Race, sex, and age, by grade—Number of pupils of each age in each grade, by sex and by general nativity and race of father of pupil—Continued.*

NINTH GRADE—Continued.

GIRLS.

General nativity and race of father of pupil.	Number of pupils of each age.									Total.
	11.	12.	13.	14.	15.	16.	17.	18.	19.	
Native-born, White	1	8	47	53	27	6	2			144
Foreign-born:										
Canadian, French			6	11	6					23
Canadian, Other		2	6	5	4					17
English		2	8	12	6	3				31
Flemish				1	1					2
German			2	1		1				4
Hebrew, Russian		1	3	2	1					7
Hebrew, Other		1				1				2
Irish	1	6	8	11	13		1			40
Norwegian				1						1
Polish				1						1
Scotch			3		7					10
Swedish		2	3	1		1				7
Total foreign-born	1	14	39	46	38	6	1			145
Grand total	2	22	86	99	65	12	3			289

TOTAL.

General nativity and race of father of pupil.	11.	12.	13.	14.	15.	16.	17.	18.	19.	Total.
Native-born, White	1	22	89	87	62	16	3			280
Foreign-born:										
Armenian					1					1
Canadian, French			6	12	9					27
Canadian, Other		2	8	16	11	1				38
English		4	15	15	11	5				50
Flemish				1	1					2
German			4	2		2				8
Hebrew, Polish				1						1
Hebrew, Russian		1	7	4	3					15
Hebrew, Other		1				1				2
Irish	1	8	21	28	22	2	1			83
Italian, North			1	1						2
Norwegian				1						1
Polish				1						1
Scotch			5	3	10	2			1	21
Swedish		2	4	5	1	2				14
Welsh					1					1
Other races a										
Total foreign-born	1	18	71	90	70	15	1		1	267
Grand total	2	40	160	177	132	31	4		1	547

a "Other races" includes races having less than 10 representatives in this city and pupils whose race is not reported.

TABLE 3.—*Race, sex, and age, by grade—Number of pupils of each age in each grade, by sex and by general nativity and race of father of pupil*—Continued.

FIRST YEAR HIGH SCHOOL.

BOYS.

General nativity and race of father of pupil.	Number of pupils of each age.							Total.
	12.	13.	14.	15.	16.	17.	18.	
Native-born, White:	1	13	31	30	17	6	....	98
Foreign-born:								
Armenian					2			2
Canadian, French			3	2	1		1	7
Canadian, Other			4	5	5	1		15
English		1	7	5			1	14
Hebrew, German					1			1
Hebrew, Polish			1					1
Hebrew, Russian	2	1	1	1				5
Hebrew, Other		6	13	11	5			35
Norwegian				1				1
Scotch			1	1		1		3
Swedish		1	1	1			1	4
Total foreign-born	2	9	31	27	14	2	3	88
Grand total	3	22	62	57	31	8	3	186

GIRLS.

General nativity and race of father of pupil.	12.	13.	14.	15.	16.	17.	18.	Total.
Native-born:								
White	1	16	34	44	11	5	....	111
Negro			1					1
Total native-born	1	16	35	44	11	5	....	112
Foreign-born:								
Canadian, French		1	1	2	2			6
Canadian, Other		3	4	3	4			14
English		2	7	6	2	2		19
German		1						1
Greek			1					1
Hebrew, Russian			1	1				2
Hebrew, Other	1	3	13	7	2	1	....	27
Norwegian				1				1
Scotch		1	3	2	1			7
Swedish			2	1				3
Other races a			1	2				3
Total foreign-born	1	11	33	25	11	3	....	84
Grand total	2	27	68	69	22	8	....	196

a "Other races" includes races having less than 10 representatives in this city and pupils whose race is not reported.

TABLE 3.—*Race, sex, and age, by grade—Number of pupils of each age in each grade, by sex and by general nativity and race of father of pupil*—Continued.

FIRST YEAR HIGH SCHOOL—Continued.

TOTAL.

General nativity and race of father of pupil.	Number of pupils of each age.							Total.
	12.	13.	14.	15.	16.	17.	18.	
Native-born:								
White	2	29	65	74	28	11		209
Negro			1					1
Total native-born	2	29	66	74	28	11		210
Foreign-born:								
Armenian					2			2
Canadian, French		1	4	4	3		1	13
Canadian, Other		3	8	8	9	1		29
English		3	14	11	2	2	1	33
German		1						1
Greek			1					1
Hebrew, German					1			1
Hebrew, Polish			1					1
Hebrew, Russian	2	1	2	2				7
Hebrew, Other	1	9	26	18	7	1		62
Norwegian				2				2
Scotch		1	4	3	1	1		10
Swedish		1	3	2			1	7
Other races *a*			1	2				3
Total foreign-born	3	20	64	52	25	5	3	172
Grand total	5	49	130	126	53	16	3	382

a "Other races" includes races having less than 10 representatives in this city and pupils whose race is not reported.

SECOND YEAR HIGH SCHOOL.

BOYS.

General nativity and race of father of pupil.	Number of pupils of each age.								Total.
	13.	14.	15.	16.	17.	18.	19.	20.	
Native-born, White	3	12	31	17	14	6			83
Foreign-born:									
Canadian, French			3	3	1				7
Canadian, Other			1	4					5
English		1	5	7	1				14
German			1	1	1				3
Hebrew, German				1					1
Hebrew, Russian			2	2					4
Irish		2	8	8	3				21
Scotch		1	2						3
Swedish			3						3
Other races *a*			1	1				1	3
Total foreign-born		4	26	27	6			1	64
Grand total	3	16	57	44	20	6		1	147

a "Other races" includes races having less than 10 representatives in this city and pupils whose race is not reported.

TABLE 3.—*Race, sex, and age, by grade—Number of pupils of each age in each grade, by sex and by general nativity and race of father of pupil*—Continued.

SECOND YEAR HIGH SCHOOL—Continued.

GIRLS.

General nativity and race of father of pupil.	Number of pupils of each age.								Total.
	13.	14.	15.	16.	17.	18.	19.	20.	
ative-born, White..............	......	10	40	25	25	3	......	......	103
Foreign-born:									
Canadian, French..............		1	1	1	2	......	......	......	5
Canadian, Other..............		2	4	1	2	......	......	......	9
English..............		1	2	5	......	1	......	......	9
German..............		1	......	......	......	......	......	......	1
Hebrew, German..............					1	......	......	......	1
Hebrew, Polish..............			2	......	......	......	......	......	2
Irish..............	2	3	11	8	2	......	......	......	26
Scotch..............			2	2	1	......	......	......	5
Swedish..............			1	......	......	......	......	......	1
Welsh..............			1	......	......	......	......	......	1
Total foreign-born..............	2	8	24	18	7	1	......	......	60
Grand total..............	2	18	64	43	32	4	......	......	163

TOTAL.

	13.	14.	15.	16.	17.	18.	19.	20.	Total.
Native-born, White..............	3	22	71	42	39	9	......	......	186
Foreign-born:									
Canadian, French..............	......	1	4	4	3	......	......	......	12
Canadian, Other..............	......	2	5	5	2	......	......	......	14
English..............	......	2	7	12	1	1	......	......	23
German..............	......	1	1	1	1	......	......	......	4
Hebrew, German..............	......	......	......	2	......	......	......	......	2
Hebrew, Polish..............	......	......	2	......	......	......	......	......	2
Hebrew, Russian..............	......	......	2	2	......	......	......	......	4
Irish..............	2	5	19	16	5	......	......	......	47
Scotch..............	......	1	4	2	1	......	......	......	8
Swedish..............	......	......	4	......	......	......	......	......	4
Welsh..............	......	......	1	......	......	......	......	......	1
Other races a..............	......	......	1	1	......	......	......	1	3
Total foreign-born..............	2	12	50	45	13	1	......	1	124
Grand total..............	5	34	121	87	52	10	......	1	310

a "Other races" includes races having less than 10 representatives in this city and pupils whose race is not reported.

TABLE **3.**—*Race, sex, and age, by grade—Number of pupils of each age in each grade, by sex and by general nativity and race of father of pupil*—Continued.

THIRD YEAR HIGH SCHOOL.

BOYS.

General nativity and race of father of pupil.	Number of pupils of each age.							Total.
	14.	15.	16.	17.	18.	19.	20.	
Native-born, White		10	27	14	7	3	1	62
Foreign-born:								
Canadian, French	1		2	1	1	1		6
Canadian, Other		3	5					8
English		1	3	4				8
French			1		1			2
Hebrew, German					1			1
Hebrew, Russian			1	1				2
Hebrew, Other				1				1
Irish	2	3	2	6	2			15
Portuguese				1				1
Scotch				2			1	3
Swedish					1			1
Total foreign-born	3	7	14	16	6	1	1	48
Grand total	3	17	41	30	13	4	2	110

GIRLS.

General nativity and race of father of pupil.	14.	15.	16.	17.	18.	19.	20.	Total.
Native-born, White	1	13	23	31	21	5	1	95
Foreign-born:								
Canadian, French		1		4	1			6
Canadian, Other		1	2	1	3			7
English		2	4	5	2			13
French			1					1
German			1					1
Hebrew, Russian				1				1
Irish		7	3	8	1			19
Norwegian		1						1
Scotch			2	2				4
Swedish		3		1				4
Other races *a*				1				1
Total foreign-born		15	13	23	7			58
Grand total	1	28	36	54	28	5	1	153

a "Other races" includes races having less than 10 representatives in this city and pupils whose race is not reported.

TABLE 3.—*Race, sex, and age, by grade—Number of pupils of each age in each grade, by sex and by general nativity and race of father of pupil—Continued.*

THIRD YEAR HIGH SCHOOL—Continued.

TOTAL.

General nativity and race of father of pupil.	Number of pupils of each age.							Total.
	14.	15.	16.	17.	18.	19.	20.	
Native-born, White	1	23	50	45	28	8	2	157
Foreign-born:								
Canadian, French	1	1	2	5	2	1		12
Canadian, Other		4	7	1	3			15
English		3	7	9	2			21
French			2		1	3		3
German			1					1
Hebrew, German						1		1
Hebrew, Russian			1	2				3
Hebrew, Other				1				1
Irish	2	10	5	14	3			34
Norwegian		1						1
Portuguese				1				1
Scotch			2	4			1	7
Swedish		3		1	1			5
Other races *a*				1				1
Total foreign-born	3	22	27	39	13	1	1	106
Grand total	4	45	77	84	41	9	3	263

a "Other races" includes races having less than 10 representatives in this city and pupils whose race is not reported.

FOURTH YEAR HIGH SCHOOL.

BOYS.

General nativity and race of father of pupil.	Number of pupils of each age.						Total.
	15.	16.	17.	18.	19.	20.	
Native-born, White	2	7	23	7	9	2	50
Foreign-born:							
Canadian, French				1			1
Canadian, Other		1	2	1	1		5
English			2				2
Irish			4	3	1	1	9
Scotch		1					1
Total foreign-born		2	8	5	2	1	18
Grand total	2	9	31	12	11	3	68

GIRLS.

Native-born, White		14	31	21	6		72
Foreign-born:							
Canadian, French				2			2
Canadian, Other		1		3			4
English		1	2	3			6
Irish		4	2	1			7
Scotch				1			1
Swedish			1				1
Total foreign-born		6	6	9			21
Grand total		20	37	30	6		93

TABLE 3.—*Race, sex, and age, by grade—Number of pupils of each age in each grade, by sex and by general nativity and race of father of pupil*—Continued.

FOURTH YEAR HIGH SCHOOL—Continued.

TOTAL.

General nativity and race of father of pupil.	Number of pupils of each age.						Total.
	15.	16.	17.	18.	19.	20.	
Native-born, White	2	21	54	28	15	2	122
Foreign-born:							
Canadian, French				3			3
Canadian, Other		2	2	4	1		9
English		1	4	3			8
Irish		4	6	4	1	1	16
Scotch		1	1				2
Swedish			1				1
Total foreign-born		8	14	14	2	1	39
Grand total	2	29	68	42	17	3	161

UNGRADED.

BOYS.

General nativity and race of father of pupil.	Number of pupils of each age.											Total.
	5.	6.	7.	8.	9.	10.	11.	12.	13.	14.	15.	
Native-born, White	1	3	1	1								6
Foreign-born:												
Canadian, French									1			1
English		1										1
Greek						1						1
Irish				1	1		1					3
Scotch	1											1
Other races *a*	1											1
Total foreign-born	2	1		1	1	1	1			1		8
Grand total	3	4	1	2	1	1	1			1		14

GIRLS.

General nativity and race of father of pupil.	Number of pupils of each age.											Total.
	5.	6.	7.	8.	9.	10.	11.	12.	13.	14.	15.	
Native-born, White	1		1	1		1						4
Foreign-born:												
Canadian, French				1	1					1		3
Greek				1								1
Irish		1	1	1	1							4
Swedish				1								1
Total foreign-born		1	1	4	2					1		9
Grand total	1	1	2	5	2	1				1		13

a "Other races" includes races having less than 10 representatives in this city and pupils whose race is not reported.

TABLE 3.—*Race, sex, and age, by grade—Number of pupils of each age in each grade, by sex and by general nativity and race of father of pupil—Continued.*

UNGRADED—Continued.

TOTAL.

General nativity and race of father of pupil.	Number of pupils of each age.											Total.
	5.	6.	7.	8.	9.	10.	11.	12.	13.	14.	15.	
Native-born, White........................	2	3	2	2	....	1	....	....	....	....	....	10
Foreign-born:												
Canadian, French..............	....	....	....	1	1	....	....	....	....	1	1	4
English......	....	1	....	....	....	....	....	....	....	....	....	1
Greek........................	....	....	....	1	....	1	....	....	....	....	....	2
Irish....	....	1	1	2	2	....	1	....	....	....	....	7
Scotch........................	1	....	....	....	....	....	....	....	....	....	....	1
Swedish......................	....	....	....	....	1	....	....	....	....	....	....	1
Other races *a*..	1	....	....	....	....	....	....	....	....	....	....	1
Total foreign-born..............	2	2	1	5	3	1	1	....	....	1	1	17
Grand total.....	4	5	3	7	3	2	1	....	....	1	1	27

a "Other races" includes races having less than 10 representatives in this city and pupils whose race is not reported.

ILLITERATE.

BOYS.

General nativity and race of father of pupil.	Number of pupils of each age.			Total.
	13.	14.	15.	
Foreign-born:				
Canadian, French................................	3	25	5	33
Canadian, Other................................	1	....	....	1
Irish..	....	....	1	1
Italian, North.......................	....	....	1	1
Polish..	....	....	1	1
Total..................................	4	25	8	37

GIRLS.

General nativity and race of father of pupil.	13.	14.	15.	Total.
Foreign-born:				
Canadian, French.............................	2	11	....	13
Polish..	....	1	....	1
Total..................................	2	12	....	14

TOTAL.

General nativity and race of father of pupil.	13.	14.	15.	Total.
Foreign-born:				
Canadian, French.............................	5	36	5	46
Canadian, Other.............................	1	....	....	1
Irish..	....	....	1	1
Italian, North...............................	....	....	1	1
Polish..	....	1	1	2
Total..................................	6	37	8	51

TABLE 4.—*Race and grade, by age—Number of pupils of each specified age in each grade,*
by general nativity and race of father of pupil.

BOYS: AGE 3 YEARS.

General nativity and race of father of pupil.	Kinder-garten.
Native-born, White.....	1
Foreign-born, Other races a.....	4
Grand total.....	5

a "Other races" includes races having less than 10 representatives of this sex and age and pupils whose race is not reported.

BOYS: AGE 4 YEARS.

General nativity and race of father of pupil.	Kinder-garten.	Elemen-tary grade 1.	Total.
Native-born:			
White.....	50	1	51
Negro.....	1	.....	1
Total native-born.....	51	1	52
Foreign-born:			
English.....	20	.....	20
Hebrew, Russian.....	14	.....	14
Irish.....	21	2	23
Other races a.....	49	2	51
Total foreign-born.....	104	4	108
Grand total.....	155	5	160

a "Other races" includes races having less than 10 representatives of this sex and age and pupils whose race is not reported.

BOYS: AGE 5 YEARS.

General nativity and race of father of pupil.	Kinder-garten.	Elementary grades.		Un-graded.	Total.
		1.	2.		
Native-born, White.....	14	115	6	1	136
Foreign-born:					
Canadian, French.....	2	39	.....	.....	41
Canadian, Other.....	1	12	2	.....	15
English.....	2	30	3	.....	35
Hebrew (not specified).....	.....	10	.....	.....	10
Irish.....	2	51	2	.....	55
Scotch.....	1	10	1	1	13
Other races a.....	1	29	.....	1	31
Total foreign-born.....	9	181	8	2	200
Grand total.....	23	296	14	3	336

a "Other races" includes races having less than 10 representatives of this sex and age and pupils whose race is not reported.

TABLE 4.—*Race and grade, by age—Number of pupils of each specified age in each grade, by general nativity and race of father of pupil*—Continued.

BOYS: AGE 6 YEARS.

General nativity and race of father of pupil.	Kinder-garten.	Elementary grades.			Un-graded.	Total.
		1.	2.	3.		
Native-born:						
White	2	133	64	1	3	203
Negro		1				1
Total native-born	2	134	64	1	3	204
Foreign-born:						
Canadian, French		40	11			51
Canadian, Other		15	12			27
English		26	17		1	44
Hebrew, Russian		10	4			14
Irish		55	27	1		83
Polish		15	3			18
Portuguese		8	4			12
Scotch		7	9			16
Other races a	1	24	12			37
Total foreign-born	1	200	99	1	1	302
Grand total	3	334	163	2	4	506

a "Other races" includes races having less than 10 representatives of this sex and age and pupils whose race is not reported.

BOYS: AGE 7 YEARS.

General nativity and race of father of pupil.	Elementary grades.				Un-graded.	Total.
	1.	2.	3.	4.		
Native-born, White	35	105	46	5	1	192
Foreign-born:						
Canadian, French	24	12	9			45
Canadian, Other	6	17	12	1		36
English	11	24	13	1		49
Hebrew, Russian	6	4	1	1		12
Irish	24	50	23			97
Portuguese	7	13				20
Scotch	4	5	5			14
Swedish	3	8	3			14
Other races a	13	16	6	1		36
Total foreign-born	98	149	72			323
Grand total	133	254	118		1	15

a "Other races" includes races having less than 10 representatives of this sex and age and pupils whose race is not reported.

66083°—VOL 31—12——46

TABLE 4.—*Race and grade, by age—Number of pupils of each specified age in each grade, by general nativity and race of father of pupil—*Continued.

BOYS: AGE 8 YEARS.

General nativity and race of father of pupil.	Elementary grades.						Un-graded.	Total.
	1.	2.	3.	4.	5.	6.		
Native-born:								
White.................	14	50	81	31	1	....	1	178
Negro.................	....	1	....	....	....	....	....	1
Total native-born..........	14	51	81	31	1	....	1	179
Foreign-born:								
Canadian, French........	17	20	6	3	....	....	....	46
Canadian, Other	2	14	12	2	1	....	....	31
English.................	5	19	25	7	1	....	....	57
Hebrew, Russian........	3	9	3	1	....	....	....	16
Irish..................	6	41	36	11	2	1	1	98
Portuguese.............	5	14	5	....	....	....	....	24
Scotch.................	....	5	8	2	....	....	....	15
Other races a..........	9	13	7	5	....	....	....	34
Total foreign-born..........	47	135	102	31	4	1	1	321
Grand total..........	61	186	183	62	5	1	2	500

BOYS: AGE 9 YEARS.

General nativity and race of father of pupil.	1.	2.	3.	4.	5.	6.	Un-graded.	Total.
Native-born, White.................	3	24	42	80	35	3	....	187
Foreign-born:								
Canadian, French........	4	11	5	6	1	....	....	27
Canadian, Other	2	5	7	9	2	2	....	27
English.................	....	6	18	16	7	....	....	47
Hebrew, Russian........	....	3	5	3	3	....	....	14
Irish..................	5	13	35	26	25	3	1	108
Portuguese.............	3	8	5	3	....	....	....	19
Scotch.................	....	2	5	4	3	....	....	14
Other races a..........	3	7	7	9	4	1	....	31
Total foreign-born..........	17	55	87	76	45	6	1	287
Grand total..........	20	79	129	156	80	9	1	474

a "Other races" includes races having less than 10 representatives of this sex and age and pupils whose race is not reported.

BOYS: AGE 10 YEARS.

General nativity and race of father of pupil.	Elementary grades.								Un-graded.	Total.
	1.	2.	3.	4.	5.	6.	7.	8.		
Native-born:										
White.................	2	11	22	50	65	22	5	1	....	178
Indian.................	....	....	....	....	1	....	....	....	....	1
Total native-born..........	2	11	22	50	66	22	5	1	....	179
Foreign-born:										
Canadian, French	1	6	6	4	6	....	....	....	....	23
Canadian, Other	1	3	3	7	10	4	....	....	....	28
English.................	....	8	8	16	17	6	1	....	....	56
Hebrew, Russian........	....	1	4	4	3	1	1	....	....	14
Irish..................	....	5	13	30	33	8	3	....	....	92
Portuguese.............	2	14	4	1	2	....	....	....	....	23
Scotch.................	....	1	4	3	5	1	1	....	....	15
Other races a..........	2	3	8	13	3	4	....	....	1	34
Total foreign-born..........	6	41	50	78	79	24	6	....	1	285
Grand total..........	8	52	72	128	145	46	11	1	1	464

a "Other races" includes races having less than 10 representatives of this sex and age and pupils whose race is not reported.

TABLE **4.**—*Race and grade, by age—Number of pupils of each specified age in each grade, by general nativity and race of father of pupil*—Continued.

BOYS: AGE 11 YEARS.

General nativity and race of father of pupil.	Elementary grades.								Un-graded school.	Total.
	1.	2.	3.	4.	5.	6.	7.	8.		
Native-born:										
White....................	1	1	9	39	55	56	37	10	....	208
Negro...................					1				....	1
Total native-born...........	1	1	9	39	56	56	37	10	....	209
Foreign-born:										
Canadian, French...............	2	1	4	6	14	6	2	2	....	37
Canadian, Other................	1	1	2	5	11	7	2	....	....	29
English......................		1	4	6	21	17	10	3	....	62
Hebrew, Russian................				2	4	4	2	....	....	12
Irish.......................	1	2	8	24	18	24	9	1	1	88
Portuguese	1	8	3	4	5	2	....	....	....	18
Scotch......................		1	2	3	4	3	5	....	....	11
Swedish.....................				3	3	2	2	1	....	11
Other races *a*................		2	1	9	4	4	4	2	....	26
Total foreign-born............	5	16	24	62	84	69	36	9	1	306
Grand total....................	6	17	33	101	140	125	73	19	1	515

a "Other races" includes races having less than 10 representatives of this sex and age and pupils whose race is not reported.

BOYS: AGE 12 YEARS.

General nativity and race of father of pupil.	Elementary grades.									High school, first year.	Total.
	1.	2.	3.	4.	5.	6.	7.	8.	9.		
Native-born, White...........	....	2	2	16	25	53	41	26	14	1	180
Foreign-born:											
Canadian, French.........	....	3	11	18	19	14	4	....	....	....	69
Canadian, Other..........	....			3	4	7	8	5	....	....	27
English..................	....		2	12	11	13	18	8	2	....	66
Hebrew, Russian..........	....	1	1	1	4	....	4	1	....	2	14
Irish....................	....	1	6	8	26	24	25	26	2	....	118
Portuguese...............	1	....	2	2	2	3	....	....	....	....	10
Swedish.................					1	1	5	3	....	....	10
Other races *a*...........	1	2	2	9	4	5	10	3	....	....	36
Total foreign-born......	2	7	24	53	71	67	74	46	4	2	350
Grand total.............	2	9	26	69	96	120	115	72	18	3	530

a "Other races" includes races having less than 10 representatives of this sex and age and pupils whose race is not reported.

TABLE 4.—*Race and grade, by age—Number of pupils of each specified age in each grade, by general nativity and race of father of pupil—Continued.*

BOYS: AGE 13 YEARS.

General nativity and race of father of pupil.	Elementary grades.								High school.		Illiterate.	Total.
	2.	3.	4.	5.	6.	7.	8.	9.	First year.	Second year.		
Native-born, White..............			5	20	32	49	41	42	13	3	....	205
Foreign-born:												
Canadian, French...........	5	15	27	15	22	15	2	....			3	104
Canadian, Other..........		....	5	4	11	4	2				1	27
English............			6	7	8	17	11	7	1			57
Hebrew, Russian.............			2	2	2	3	2	4	1		....	16
Irish...........			6	6	23	33	33	13				114
Portuguese.................	8	....	2	3	3	2	1	....				19
Scotch..........		....	....	4	4	4	8	2				18
Other races a..............		3	6	12	3	7	3	4	7		....	45
Total foreign-born........	13	18	49	50	69	92	64	32	9	....	4	400
Grand total..............	13	18	54	70	101	141	105	74	22	3	4	605

a "Other races" includes races having less than 10 representatives of this sex and age and pupils whose race is not reported.

BOYS: AGE 14 YEARS.

General nativity and race of father of pupil.	Elementary grades.								High school.			Ungraded and special schools.	Total.
	2.	3.	4.	5.	6.	7.	8.	9.	First year.	Second year.	Third year.		
Native-born:													
White.................	1	1	3	6	15	26	48	34	31	12			177
Negro.................						1	1						2
Total native-born....	1	1	3	6	16	27	48	34	31	12			179
Foreign-born:													
Canadian, French.....	1	2	8	11	9	5	6	1	3	....	1	26	73
Canadian, Other......			....	4	2	4	11	4				25
English............			1	1	5	2	3	3	7	1			23
Hebrew, Russian......			1	3	....	1	1	2	1	....			9
Hebrew, Other.......							1	1	14				16
Irish..........	1	1	1	3	12	6	20	17		2	2		65
Other races a..........	1	4	2	3	5	1	4	9	2	1			32
Total foreign-born...	3	7	13	21	35	17	39	44	31	4	3	26	243
Grand total..........	4	8	16	27	51	44	87	78	62	16	3	26	422

a "Other races" includes races having less than 10 representatives of this sex and age and pupils whose race is not reported.

TABLE 4.—*Race and grade, by age—Number of pupils of each specified age in each grade, by general nativity and race of father of pupil*—Continued.

BOYS: AGE 15 YEARS.

General nativity and race of father of pupil.	Elementary grades.								High school.				Illit-erate.	Total.
	2.	3.	4.	5.	6.	7.	8.	9.	First year.	Second year.	Third year.	Fourth year.		
Native-born, White.......	...	...	1	...	1	7	17	35	30	31	10	2	....	134
Foreign-born:														
Canadian, French.....	1	2	...	1	2	5	4	3	2	3	....	....	5	28
Canadian, Other.......	...	...	...	...	...	...	1	7	5	1	3	....	....	17
English..............	...	...	...	1	...	2	5	5	5	1	....	....	19
Hebrew (not specified).	...	...	...	...	...	...	...	2	12	2	....	....	....	16
Irish................	...	...	...	2	1	3	9	....	8	3	....	1	27
Other races*.........	4	...	3	3	1	1	...	6	3	7	....	....	2	30
Total foreign-born...	5	2	3	4	6	7	10	32	27	26	7	....	8	137
Grand total........	5	2	4	4	7	14	27	67	57	57	17	2	8	271

a "Other races" includes races having less than 10 representatives of this sex and age and pupils whose race is not reported.

BOYS: AGE 16 YEARS.

General nativity and race of father of pupil.	Elementary grades.								High school.				Total.
	2.	3.	4.	5.	6.	7.	8.	9.	First year.	Second year.	Third year.	Fourth year.	
Native-born, White.............	...	...	1	...	...	1	2	10	17	17	27	7	82
Foreign-born:													
Canadian (other than French).	...	...	...	...	...	...	1	1	5	4	5	1	17
English.......................	...	...	...	...	...	...	1	2	....	7	3	....	13
Hebrew (not specified)........	...	...	...	...	...	...	...	...	6	3	1	....	10
Irish.........................	...	...	...	...	...	...	...	2	....	8	2	....	12
Other races*.................	1	...	...	...	...	...	2	4	3	5	3	1	19
Total foreign-born..........	1	...	...	...	...	...	4	9	14	27	14	2	71
Grand total.................	1	...	1	...	...	1	6	19	31	44	41	9	153

a "Other races" includes races having less than 10 representatives of this sex and age and pupils whose race is not reported.

BOYS: AGE 17 YEARS.

General nativity and race of father of pupil.	Elementary grades.				High school.				Total.
	6.	7.	8.	9.	First year.	Second year.	Third year.	Fourth year.	
Native-born, White.............	....	....	....	1	6	14	14	23	58
Foreign-born:									
Irish.........................	....	1	....	....	....	3	6	4	13
Other races*.................	....	1	....	....	2	3	10	4	20
Total foreign-born............	....	1	....	....	2	6	16	8	33
Grand total..................	....	....	....	1	8	20	30	31	91

a "Other races" includes races having less than 10 representatives of this sex and age and pupils whose race is not reported.

TABLE 4.—*Race and grade, by age—Number of pupils of each specified age in each grade,
by general nativity and race of father of pupil*—Continued.

BOYS: AGE 18 YEARS.

General nativity and race of father of pupil.	High school.				Total.
	First year.	Second year.	Third year.	Fourth year.	
Native-born, White....................................	....	6	7	7	20
Foreign-born, Other races *a*	3	....	6	5	14
Grand total....................................	3	6	13	12	34

a "Other races" includes races having less than 10 representatives of this sex and age and pupils whose
race is not reported.

BOYS: AGE 19 YEARS.

General nativity and race of father of pupil.	Elementary grade 9.	High school.		Total.
		Third year.	Fourth year.	
Native-born, White....................................	....	3	9	12
Foreign-born, Other races *a*	1	1	2	4
Grand total....................................	1	4	11	16

a "Other races" includes races having less than 10 representatives of this sex and age and pupils whose
race is not reported.

BOYS: AGE 20 YEARS.

General nativity and race of father of pupil.	High school.			Total.
	Second year.	Third year.	Fourth year.	
Native-born, White....................................	....	1	2	3
Foreign-born, Other races *a*	1	1	1	3
Grand total....................................	1	2	3	6

a "Other races" includes races having less than 10 representatives of this sex and age and pupils whose
race is not reported.

GIRLS: AGE 3 YEARS.

General nativity and race of father of pupil.	Kindergarten.
Native-born, White....................................	2
Foreign-born, Other races *a*	2
Grand total....................................	4

a "Other races" includes races having less than 10 representatives of this sex and age and pupils whose
race is not reported.

TABLE 4.—*Race and grade, by age—Number of pupils of each specified age in each grade, by general nativity and race of father of pupil*—Continued.

GIRLS: AGE 4 YEARS.

General nativity and race of father of pupil.	Kindergarten.	Elementary grade 1.	Total.
Native-born, White....................................	52	3	55
Foreign-born:			
English....................................	18	1	19
Hebrew, Russian....................................	10	....	10
Irish....................................	18	2	20
Portuguese....................................	10	....	10
Other races *a*....................................	34	....	34
Total foreign-born....................................	90	3	93
Grand total....................................	142	6	148

a "Other races" includes races having less than 10 representatives of this sex and age and pupils whose race is not reported.

GIRLS: AGE 5 YEARS.

General nativity and race of father of pupil.	Kindergarten.	Elementary grades.		Ungraded.	Total.
		1.	2.		
Native-born:					
White....................................	11	131	3	1	146
Negro....................................	1	....	....	....	1
Total native-born....................................	12	131	3	1	147
Foreign-born:					
Canadian, French....................................	....	29	....	....	29
Canadian, Other....................................	2	19	1	....	22
English....................................	....	30	....	....	30
Hebrew, Russian....................................	....	12	....	....	12
Irish....................................	6	63	3	....	72
Portuguese....................................	....	10	....	....	10
Other races *a*....................................	4	31	1	....	36
Total foreign-born....................................	12	194	5	....	211
Grand total....................................	24	325	8	1	358

a "Other races" includes races having less than 10 representatives of this sex and age and pupils whose race is not reported.

TABLE **4.**—*Race and grade, by age*—*Number of pupils of each specified age in each grade, by general nativity and race of father of pupil*—Continued.

GIRLS: AGE 6 YEARS.

General nativity and race of father of pupil.	Kinder-garten.	Elementary grades.			Un-graded.	Total.
		1.	2.	3.		
Native-born, White	....	118	70	1	....	189
Foreign-born:						
Canadian, French	....	47	3	....	....	50
Canadian, Other	....	21	12	....	....	33
English	....	21	8	1	....	30
Hebrew, Russian	....	14	6	....	1	21
Irish	....	39	20	1	....	60
Polish	....	8	4	....	....	12
Portuguese	....	19	2	....	....	21
Scotch	1	7	4	....	....	12
Other races [a]	....	18	10	....	....	28
Total foreign-born	1	194	69	2	1	267
Grand total	1	312	139	3	1	456

[a] "Other races" includes races having less than 10 representatives of this sex and age and pupils whose race is not reported.

GIRLS: AGE 7 YEARS.

General nativity and race of father of pupil.	Elementary grades.				Un-graded.	Total.
	1.	2.	3.	4.		
Native-born, White	26	87	53	1	1	168
Foreign-born:						
Canadian, French	25	11	8	....	....	44
Canadian, Other	8	18	6	....	....	32
English	13	29	11	2	....	55
Hebrew, Russian	1	13	....	....	....	14
Irish	14	40	20	1	1	76
Polish	8	1	3	....	....	12
Portuguese	12	2	....	....	....	14
Scotch	6	6	4	....	....	16
Swedish	1	6	2	1	....	10
Other races [a]	9	16	5	1	....	31
Total foreign-born	97	142	59	5	1	304
Grand total	123	229	112	6	2	472

[a] "Other races" includes races having less than 10 representatives of this sex and age and pupils whose race is not reported.

TABLE 4.—*Race and grade, by age—Number of pupils of each specified age in each grade, by general nativity and race of father of pupil—Continued.*

GIRLS: AGE 8 YEARS.

General nativity and race of father of pupil.	Elementary grades.						Un-graded.	Total.
	1.	2.	3.	4.	5.	6.		
Native-born, White..................	8	39	80	37	....	....	1	165
Foreign-born:								
Canadian, French...............	8	7	11	5	....	....	1	32
Canadian, Other................	2	2	13	11	1	....	....	29
English........................	2	10	14	9	2	1	....	38
Hebrew, Other.................	....	7	6	2	....	....	....	15
Irish..........................	2	23	43	19	2	1	1	91
Portuguese....................	4	13	....	....	....	....	....	17
Scotch........................	3	5	7	2	....	1	....	18
Swedish.......................	....	4	5	4	....	....	1	14
Other races *a*	4	13	4	2	....	....	1	24
Total foreign-born..............	25	84	103	54	5	3	4	278
Grand total...................	33	123	183	91	5	3	5	443

a "Other races" includes races having less than 10 representatives of this sex and age and pupils whose race is not reported.

GIRLS: AGE 9 YEARS.

General nativity and race of father of pupil.	Elementary grades.							Un-graded.	Total.
	1.	2.	3.	4.	5.	6.	7.		
Native-born:									
White............................	6	22	37	76	26	7	....	....	174
Negro............................	....	....	....	....	1	....	....	....	1
Total native-born..............	6	22	37	76	27	7	....	....	175
Foreign-born:									
Canadian, French................	2	9	16	10	....	....	....	1	38
Canadian, Other.................	1	8	11	18	7	....	1	....	46
English.........................	....	3	12	17	10	1	....	....	43
Hebrew, Russian.................	1	3	2	4	1	....	....	....	11
Irish...........................	....	8	27	38	12	6	....	1	92
Portuguese......................	3	8	4	1	....	....	....	....	16
Scotch..........................	....	2	4	4	3	1	....	....	14
Other races *a*.................	2	8	14	10	3	1	1	....	39
Total foreign-born..............	9	49	90	102	36	9	2	2	299
Grand total...................	15	71	127	178	63	16	2	2	474

a "Other races" includes races having less than 10 representatives of this sex and age and pupils whose race is not reported.

TABLE 4.—*Race and grade, by age—Number of pupils of each specified age in each grade, by general nativity and race of father of pupil*—Continued.

GIRLS: AGE 10 YEARS.

General nativity and race of father of pupil.	Elementary grades.							Un-graded.	Total.
	1.	2.	3.	4.	5.	6.	7.		
Native-born:									
White	3	9	21	49	71	38	4	1	196
Negro				1					1
Total native-born	3	9	21	50	71	38	4	1	197
Foreign-born:									
Canadian, French	1	5	2	4	1	3	1		17
Canadian, Other	1	2	1	10	8	11	1		34
English			5	12	16	6	1		40
Hebrew, Russian		2		5	4	2			13
Irish	1	3	10	21	28	12	3		78
Portuguese	1	10	5	2					18
Scotch		4	3	2	2	4			15
Swedish			2	4	4	4	2		16
Other races a	2	6	7	11	4	1			31
Total foreign-born	6	32	35	71	67	43	8		262
Grand total	9	41	56	121	138	81	12	1	459

a "Other races" includes races having less than 10 representatives of this sex and age and pupils whose race is not reported.

GIRLS: AGE 11 YEARS.

General nativity and race of father of pupil.	Elementary grades.									Total.
	1.	2.	3.	4.	5.	6.	7.	8.	9.	
Native-born:										
White		6	9	25	50	62	34	8	1	195
Negro					1					1
Total native-born		6	9	25	51	62	34	8	1	196
Foreign-born:										
Canadian, French		4	8	11	3	6	1			33
Canadian, Other			1	7	11	12	6	1		38
English			2	11	15	15	8	3		54
Hebrew, Russian		3		2	2	2	1			10
Irish		2	3	20	28	27	13	3	1	97
Portuguese	1	3	3	1	1	1				10
Scotch				2	6	5	1			14
Other races a	1	2	3	8	9	7	4	1		35
Total foreign-born	2	14	20	62	75	75	34	8	1	291
Grand total	2	20	29	87	126	137	68	16	2	487

a "Other races" includes races having less than 10 representatives of this sex and age and pupils whose race is not reported.

TABLE 4.—*Race and grade, by age—Number of pupils of each specified age in each grade, by general nativity and race of father of pupil*—Continued.

GIRLS: AGE 12 YEARS.

General nativity and race of father of pupil.	Elementary grades.									High school, first year.	Total.
	1.	2.	3.	4.	5.	6.	7.	8.	9.		
Native-born:											
White		1	2	11	43	39	55	37	8	1	197
Indian					1						1
Total native-born		1	2	11	44	39	55	37	8	1	198
Foreign-born:											
Canadian, French		1	7	11	19	13	10	2			63
Canadian, Other		1		3	7	15	12	9	2		49
English			2	6	11	14	12	9	2		56
Hebrew, Russian				1	1	2	4	1	1		10
Irish		1	1	8	16	33	29	17	6		111
Portuguese			2	4	2	2					10
Scotch						2	4	3	4		13
Swedish					2	3	3	3	2		13
Other races *a*	1	2	1	3	6	6	2	4	1	1	27
Total foreign-born	1	7	15	34	66	90	75	49	14	1	352
Grand total	1	8	17	45	110	129	130	86	22	2	550

a "Other races" includes races having less than 10 representatives of this sex and age and pupils whose race is not reported.

GIRLS: AGE 13 YEARS.

General nativity and race of father of pupil.	Elementary grades.									High school.		Illiterate.	Total.
	1.	2.	3.	4.	5.	6.	7.	8.	9.	First year.	Second year.		
Native-born, White			1	5	12	26	33	60	47	16			200
Foreign-born:													
Canadian, French		1	12	16	26	22	16	4	6	1		2	106
Canadian, Other			1		5	7	5	6		3			27
English			3	3	3	6	13	13	8	2			51
Hebrew, Russian				2		2	3	2	3				12
Irish	1			6	8	20	28	28	8		2		101
Portuguese		2	2			3	4	3					14
Scotch			1	3	1	2	2	3		1			13
Other races *a*	1		1	3	9	7	7	7	5	4			44
Total foreign-born	2	3	18	32	52	67	79	61	39	11		2	368
Grand total	2	3	19	37	64	93	112	121	86	27		2	568

a "Other races" includes races having less than 10 representatives of this sex and age and pupils whose race is not reported.

TABLE 4.—*Race and grade, by age—Number of pupils of each specified age in each grade, by general nativity and race of father of pupil*—Continued.

GIRLS: AGE 14 YEARS.

General nativity and race of father of pupil.	Elementary grades.								High school.			Illit-erate.	Total.
	2.	3.	4.	5.	6.	7.	8.	9.	First year.	Second year.	Third year.		
Native-born:													
White	1	...	1	4	8	12	38	53	34	10	1	......	162
Negro	...	...	...	...	...	...	...	...	1	......	......	......	1
Total native-born	1	...	1	4	8	12	38	53	35	10	1	......	163
Foreign-born:													
Canadian, French	1	4	11	3	10	6	6	11	1	1	......	11	65
Canadian, Other	...	...	1	...	1	1	7	5	4	2	......	......	21
English	...	...	1	...	1	3	7	12	7	1	......	......	32
Hebrew, Russian	...	1	1	...	1	3	2	2	1	......	......	......	11
Hebrew, Other	...	...	...	...	...	...	...	...	13	......	......	......	13
Irish	...	1	3	3	2	5	14	11	......	3	......	......	42
Other races a	2	...	1	1	3	3	7	5	7	1	......	1	31
Total foreign-born	3	6	18	7	18	21	43	46	33	8	......	12	215
Grand total	4	6	19	11	26	33	81	99	68	18	1	12	378

a "Other races" includes races having less than 10 representatives of this sex and age and pupils whose race is not reported.

GIRLS: AGE 15 YEARS.

General nativity and race of father of pupil.	Elementary grades.								High school.			Un-graded schools.	Total.
	2.	3.	4.	5.	6.	7.	8.	9.	First year.	Second year.	Third year.		
Native-born, White	...	...	...	1	2	5	9	27	44	40	13	......	141
Foreign-born:													
Canadian, French	...	1	...	...	...	2	3	6	2	1	1	1	17
Canadian, Other	...	...	...	...	...	...	2	4	3	4	1	......	14
English	...	...	...	...	...	...	...	6	6	2	2	......	16
Hebrew (not specified)	...	...	...	...	1	...	1	1	8	2	......	......	13
Irish	...	...	...	...	1	...	3	13	......	11	7	......	35
Scotch	...	...	...	...	...	...	1	7	2	2	......	......	12
Other races a	2	...	1	...	...	...	...	1	4	2	4	......	14
Total foreign-born	2	1	1	...	2	2	10	38	25	24	15	1	121
Grand total	2	1	1	1	4	7	19	65	69	64	28	1	262

a "Other races" includes races having less than 10 representatives of this sex and age and pupils whose race is not reported.

GIRLS: AGE 16 YEARS.

General nativity and race of father of pupil.	Elementary grades.						High school.				Total.
	4.	5.	6.	7.	8.	9.	First year.	Second year.	Third year.	Fourth year.	
Native-born, White	...	...	...	...	2	6	11	25	23	14	81
Foreign-born:											
English	...	...	...	...	...	3	2	5	4	1	15
Irish	...	...	...	...	...	...	......	8	3	4	15
Other races a	3	...	...	...	...	3	9	5	6	1	27
Total foreign-born	3	...	...	...	...	6	11	18	13	6	57
Grand total	3	...	...	...	2	12	22	43	36	20	138

a "Other races" includes races having less than 10 representatives of this sex and age and pupils whose race is not reported.

TABLE 4.—*Race and grade, by age—Number of pupils of each specified age in each grade, by general nativity and race of father of pupil*—Continued.

GIRLS: AGE 17 YEARS.

General nativity and race of father of pupil.	Elementary grades.			High school.				Total.
	7.	8.	9.	First year.	Second year.	Third year.	Fourth year.	
Native-born, White			2	5	25	31	31	94
Foreign-born:								
Irish			1		2	8	2	13
Other races*a*	1			3	5	15	4	28
Total foreign-born	1		1	3	7	23	6	41
Grand total	1		3	8	32	54	37	135

a "Other races" includes races having less than 10 representatives of this sex and age and pupils whose race is not reported.

GIRLS: AGE 18 YEARS.

General nativity and race of father of pupil.	High school.			Total.
	Second year.	Third year.	Fourth year.	
Native-born, White	3	21	21	45
Foreign-born, other races*a*	1	7	9	17
Grand total	4	28	30	62

a "Other races" includes races having less than 10 representatives of this sex and age and pupils whose race is not reported.

GIRLS: AGE 19 YEARS.

General nativity and race of father of pupil.	High school.		Total.
	Third year.	Fourth year.	
Native-born, White	5	6	11

GIRLS: AGE 20 YEARS.

General nativity and race of father of pupil.	High school, third year.
Native-born, White	1

TABLE 5.—*Race distribution in each grade—Percentages.*

[This table shows in detail only races with 100 or more pupils reporting. The totals, however, are for all races.]

General nativity and race of father of pupil	Kinder-garten	Elementary grades										High school					Un-graded	Illiter-ate	Total	Grand total
		1	2	3	4	5	6	7	8	9	Total	First year	Second year	Third year	Fourth year	Total				
Native-born:																				
White	37.0	35.3	34.7	35.7	36.7	38.1	38.3	40.4	46.6	51.2	38.2	54.7	60.0	59.7	75.8	60.4	37.0	0.0	12.8	40.2
Negro and Indian	.0	.1	.1	.0	.1	.5	.1	.1	.0	.0	.1	.3	.0	.0	.0	.1	.0	.0	.0	.2
Total native-born	37.5	35.4	34.8	35.7	36.8	38.6	38.4	40.5	46.6	51.2	38.3	55.0	60.0	59.7	75.8	60.5	37.0	.0	12.8	40.4
Foreign-born:																				
Canadian, French	4.5	14.2	7.8	11.3	11.8	11.0	11.2	8.8	4.6	4.9	10.3	3.4	3.9	4.6	1.9	3.6	14.8	90.2	64.1	9.8
Canadian, Other	3.6	5.4	6.8	5.9	6.6	6.2	7.6	6.7	6.1	6.9	6.4	7.6	4.5	5.7	5.0	6.0		2.0	1.3	6.3
English	11.2	8.2	8.6	10.5	10.6	11.2	9.8	11.1	9.3	9.1	9.8	8.6	7.4	8.1	5.0	7.6	3.7		1.3	9.6
Hebrew, Russian	6.7	3.3	3.6	1.7	2.8	2.5	1.7	2.8	1.7	2.7	2.7	1.8	1.3	1.1		1.3				2.7
Irish	14.8	15.7	16.7	20.0	18.7	19.3	20.9	20.3	23.1	15.2	18.5		15.2	12.9	9.9	8.7	25.9	2.0	10.3	17.4
Polish	.6	3.3	1.9	3.3	1.5	.7	.6	.4	.3	.2	1.4					.1		3.9	2.6	1.2
Portuguese	4.5	5.0	8.2	3.8	1.8	1.8	1.6	.7	.5		3.2	2.6	2.6	.4			3.7			3.0
Scotch	3.1	2.6	3.1	3.8	2.0	2.6	2.9	2.7	3.4	3.8	2.9	1.8	1.3	2.7	1.2	2.4	3.7		1.3	2.9
Swedish	3.4	1.3	1.9	1.6	2.1	2.5	2.9	2.9	2.1	2.6	2.9			1.9	.6	1.5				1.9
Other races	10.1	5.6	6.2	5.6	5.4	4.5	2.9	3.1	2.2	3.3	4.7	19.1	3.9	3.0		8.3	11.1	2.0	5.1	5.2
Total foreign-born	62.5	64.6	65.2	64.3	63.2	61.3	61.5	59.5	53.4	48.8	61.7	45.0	40.0	40.3	24.2	39.5	63.0	100.0	87.2	59.7
Grand total	100.0	100.0	100.0	100.0	100.0	100.0	100.0	100.0	100.0	100.0	100.0	100.0	100.0	100.0	100.0	100.0	100.0	100.0	100.0	100.0

TABLE 6.—*Grade distribution of each race—Percentages.*

[This table shows in detail only races with 100 or more pupils reporting. The totals, however, are for all races.]

General nativity and race of father of pupil.	Kinder-garten.	Elementary grades.										High school.					Illiter-ate.	Un-graded.	Total.	Grand total.
		1.	2.	3.	4.	5.	6.	7.	8.	9.	Total.	First year.	Second year.	Third year.	Fourth year.	Total.				
Native-born:																				
White	3.0	13.5	11.3	9.2	9.8	9.4	8.2	7.0	6.8	6.3	81.6	4.7	4.2	3.5	2.8	15.2	0.2		0.2	100.0
Negro and Indian	(a)	(a)	(a)	(a)	(a)	(a)	(a)	(a)	(a)	(a)	(a)	(a)	(a)	(a)	(a)	(a)	(a)		(a)	(a)
Total native-born	3.0	13.5	11.3	9.2	9.8	9.4	8.2	7.0	6.8	6.3	81.6	4.7	4.2	3.5	2.8	15.2	.2		.2	100.0
Foreign-born:																				
Canadian, French	1.5	22.3	10.5	12.0	13.0	11.0	9.9	6.2	2.8	2.5	90.2	1.2	1.1	1.1	.3	3.7	.4	4.3	4.6	100.0
Canadian, Other	1.9	13.5	14.3	9.9	11.4	9.8	10.5	7.5	5.7	5.6	88.2	4.2	2.0	2.2	1.3	9.8	.1		.1	100.0
English	3.8	13.2	12.2	11.4	12.0	11.6	9.0	8.1	5.7	4.8	88.0	3.1	2.2	2.0	.7	8.0	.1		.1	100.0
Hebrew, Russian	8.3	19.3	17.9	6.6	11.4	9.3	5.9	7.6	3.8	5.2	86.9		2.5	1.0	.8	4.8	.4	.1	.4	100.0
Irish	2.8	13.9	12.7	12.0	11.6	11.0	10.4	8.1	7.7	4.3	91.7		2.5	1.8	.8	5.1		1.5	1.5	100.0
Polish	1.5	42.1	20.3	6.0	13.5	6.0	4.5	2.2	1.5	.8	96.9			.3		.3	.3	1.5	1.5	100.0
Portuguese	5.0	26.1	37.0	11.8	6.5	6.2	4.7	1.6	.9	.7	94.7	3.2	2.5	2.2	.6	8.6	.5		.3	100.0
Scotch	3.5	14.6	14.3	13.7	7.6	8.9	8.9	6.7	7.0	6.7	87.6	3.4	1.9	2.4	.5	8.2			.5	100.0
Swedish	5.8	10.6	13.5	8.7	12.0	7.7	9.1	10.6	6.7	3.1	85.6	12.6	2.1	1.4		16.1	.5	.2	.7	100.0
Other races	6.2	16.3	15.6	11.1	11.1	8.5	4.8	4.2	2.4		77.0						.2		1.1	100.0
Total foreign-born	3.4	16.6	14.3	11.2	11.4	10.1	8.9	6.9	5.2	4.1	88.9	2.6	1.9	1.6	.5	6.7	.3	.8	1.1	100.0
Grand total	3.3	15.4	13.2	10.4	10.8	9.9	8.7	7.0	5.9	5.0	86.0	3.5	2.9	2.4	1.5	10.2	.3	.5	.8	100.0

a Not computed, owing to small number involved.

PUBLIC SCHOOL TEACHERS IN ELEMENTARY GRADES AND KINDERGARTEN.

TABLE 1.—*Number of teachers in each grade, by sex and general nativity and race.*

FEMALE.

[This table does not include 7 teachers not reporting complete data.]

General nativity and race.	Kindergarten.	Elementary grades.										Total.	Total kindergarten and elementary.	Race distribution—percentages.	
		1.	2.	3.	4.	5.	6.	7.	8.	9.	Ungraded and special.			Elementary.	Elementary and kindergarten.
Native-born of native father, White	9	27	30	19	19	16	13	10	14	10	....	158	167	57.9	58.6
Native-born of foreign father, by race of father:															
Canadian, French		1									1	2	2	.7	.7
Canadian, Other			2	1				1				4	4	1.5	1.4
English		4	4		1	2	1	2				14	14	5.1	4.9
German					1							1	1	.4	.4
Irish	2	15	11	14	9	10	9	7	3	3	1	82	84	30.0	29.5
Scotch		1	1									2	2	.7	.7
Scotch-Irish		1										1	1	.4	.4
Welsh					1							1	1	.4	.4
Total	2	22	18	15	12	12	10	10	3	3	2	107	109	39.2	38.2
Total native-born	11	49	48	34	31	28	23	20	17	13	2	265	276	97.1	96.8
Foreign-born:															
Canadian (other than French)			1									1	1	.4	.4
English	1	1		1								2	3	.7	1.1
Irish		1										1	1	.4	.4
Scotch			1						1	1	1	4	4	1.5	1.4
Total foreign-born	1	2	2	1					1	1	1	8	9	2.9	3.2
Grand total	12	51	50	35	31	28	23	21	18	14	2	273	285	100.0	100.0

TABLE 2.—*Number of teachers engaged in teaching each specified number of years, by sex and general nativity and race.*[a]

FEMALE.

[This table does not include 10 teachers not reporting complete data.]

General nativity and race.	Under 5 years.	5 to 9 years.	10 to 14 years.	15 to 19 years.	20 to 24 years.	25 to 29 years.	30 years or over.	Total.
Native-born of native father, White..	23	32	26	17	14	13	40	165
Native-born of foreign father, by race of father:								
Canadian, French.................	1	1	....	....	....	....	....	2
Canadian, Other.................	....	....	1	....	2	1	....	4
English.................	....	....	4	3	5	....	2	14
Irish.................	7	21	22	14	8	8	4	84
Scotch.................	1	....	....	....	....	....	1	2
Scotch-Irish.................	1	....	....	....	....	....	....	1
Welsh.................	....	....	1	....	....	....	....	1
Total.................	10	22	28	17	15	9	7	108
Total native-born.................	33	54	54	34	29	22	47	273
Foreign-born:								
Canadian (other than French)....	....	....	....	....	1	....	....	1
English.................	1	....	1	....	....	....	1	3
Irish.................	....	....	....	1	....	....	....	1
Scotch.................	....	1	2	....	....	1	....	4
Total foreign-born.................	1	1	3	1	1	1	1	9
Grand total.................	34	55	57	35	30	23	48	282

[a] No male teachers reported.

PAROCHIAL SCHOOL PUPILS: GENERAL INVESTIGATION.

TABLE 1.—Grade and age—Number of pupils of each age in each grade, by sex.

BOYS.

Age, in years.	Kindergarten.	\[Elem.\] 1.	2.	3.	4.	5.	6.	7.	8.	9.	Total.	High school, first year.	Commercial school.	Ungraded and mixed schools.	Grand total.
4	4	1									1				5
5	25	64									64				89
6	12	151	3								154				166
7	3	178	56	6							240				243
8		116	111	33	1	1					262				262
9		46	98	74	28	5	1				252			1	253
10		23	63	49	52	32	6	2			227				227
11		3	26	39	60	56	27	13	4		228			61	289
12		1	11	42	42	68	47	39	12	3	265			28	293
13			3	7	25	36	28	41	41	12	193	2		9	204
14			2		5	8	12	19	33	15	94	2	4		100
15			1		2		1	6	8	19	37	2	5	2	46
16							1			3	4	1	3		8
17															
18															
19															
20 or over															
Total	44	583	374	250	215	206	123	120	98	52	2,021	7	12	101	2,185

GIRLS.

Age, in years.	Kindergarten.	\[Elem.\] 1.	2.	3.	4.	5.	6.	7.	8.	9.	Total.	High school, first year.	Commercial school.	Ungraded and mixed schools.	Grand total.
4	6	8									8				14
5	19	98									98				117
6	18	167	11								178				196
7	2	156	37	19							212			7	221
8		130	80	40	4						254			29	283
9		64	50	86	39	7	2				248			49	297
10		17	41	46	61	37	14	1			217			34	251
11		1	32	49	61	52	51	7			253			52	305
12		1	3	21	51	42	47	29	4	4	198			35	233

(Upper table — ages 13 to 20 or over)

Age	Total	2	3	4	5	6	7	8	9	10	11	12	13	14	15
13	167	17			150	5	19	40	31	26	25				
14	108	16			92	13	16	17	18	10	17				
15	28	3		5	20	5	9	2	1	1	2				
16	6			1	5	3	1			1					
17												4			
18	1				1	1							1		
19															
20 or over															
Total	2,227	242		6	1,934	27	49	96	164	176	260	265	255	642	45

(Lower table — TOTAL, ages 4 to 20 or over)

Age	Total	2	3	4	5	6	7	8	9	10	11	12	13	14	15
4	19				9									9	10
5	206				162									162	44
6	362				332								14	318	30
7	464	7			452							25	93	334	5
8	545	29			516					1	5	73	191	246	
9	550	50			500		4	3	3	12	67	160	148	110	
10	478	34			444		16	20	20	69	113	95	104	40	
11	594	113			481		60	68	78	108	121	88	58	4	
12	526	63			463	3	49	81	94	110	93	63	14	2	
13	371	26	4	2	343	17	60	81	59	62	50	11	3		
14	208	16	5	2	186	28	49	36	30	18	22		3		
15	74	5	3	7	57	24	17	8	2	1	4		1		
16	14			2	9	6	1		1	1					
17															
18	1				1	1									
19															
20 or over															
Total	4,412	343	12	13	3,955	79	147	216	287	382	475	515	629	1,225	89

TABLE 2.—Race, sex, and grade—Number of pupils of each sex in each grade, by general nativity and race of father of pupil.

General nativity and race of father of pupil	Kindergarten	1.	2.	3.	4.	5.	6.	7.	8.	9.	Total.	High school, first year.	Commercial school.	Ungraded and mixed schools.	Grand total.
Native-born:															
White—															
Male	4	52	39	16	29	29	19	21	18	8	231	4	5	4	248
Female	9	56	33	26	32	16	22	6	10	2	203	4		12	228
Total	13	108	72	42	61	45	41	27	28	10	434	8	5	16	476
Foreign-born:															
Canadian, French—															
Male		366	205	126	102	69	48	47	37	20	1,020	3		97	1,120
Female	6	388	122	94	153	81	87	49	9	1	984			230	1,220
Total	6	754	327	220	255	150	135	96	46	21	2,004	3		327	2,340
Canadian, Other—															
Male			2	2		5	1		2		12		1		13
Female		1	3	3							7				7
Total		1	5	5		5	1		2		19		1		20
English—															
Male	5	3	20	7	4	6	2	3	3	2	50				55
Female		7	13	11	6	6	3	2		1	49				49
Total	5	10	33	18	10	12	5	5	3	3	99				104
Irish—															
Male	35	140	87	89	78	95	52	47	35	22	645		6		686
Female	29	160	69	120	67	71	52	38	30	23	630	2			661
Total	64	300	156	209	145	166	104	85	65	45	1,275	2	6		1,347
Polish—															
Male		20	18	7		1					46				46
Female		24	14	4				1			43				43
Total		44	32	11		1		1			89				89
Scotch—															
Male					1			2	3		6				6
Female				4							4				5
Total				4	1			2	3		10				11
Other races a—															
Male		2	3	3	1	1	1				11				11
Female		6	1	3	2	2					14				14
Total		8	4	6	3	3	1				25				25
Total foreign-born—															
Male	40	531	335	234	186	177	104	99	80	44	1,790	3	7	97	1,937
Female	36	586	222	239	228	160	142	90	39	25	1,731	2		230	1,999
Total	76	1,117	557	473	414	337	246	189	119	69	3,521	5	7	327	3,936
Grand total—															
Male	44	583	374	250	215	206	123	120	98	52	2,021	7	12	101	2,185
Female	45	642	255	265	260	176	164	96	49	27	1,934	6		242	2,227
Total	89	1,225	629	515	475	382	287	216	147	79	3,955	13	12	343	4,412

a "Other races" includes: Dutch, 2; French, 8; German, 3; Greek, 2; Italian, North, 3; Italian, South, 1; Portuguese, 2; Russian, 2; Syrian, 3.

TABLE 3.—*Race, sex, and age, by grade—Number of pupils of each age in each grade, by sex and by general nativity and race of father of pupil.*

KINDERGARTEN.

BOYS.

General nativity and race of father of pupil.	Number of pupils of each age.				Total.
	4.	5.	6.	7.	
Native-born, White..			4		4
Foreign-born:					
English..		5			5
Irish..	4	20	8	3	35
Total..	4	25	8	3	40
Grand total..	4	25	12	3	44

GIRLS.

	4.	5.	6.	7.	Total.
Native-born, White..	1	6	1	1	9
Foreign-born:					
Canadian, French..			6		6
Irish..	5	13	10	1	29
Scotch..			1		1
Total..	5	13	17	1	36
Grand total..	6	19	18	2	45

TOTAL.

	4.	5.	6.	7.	Total.
Native-born, White..	1	6	5	1	13
Foreign-born:					
Canadian, French..			6		6
English..		5			5
Irish..	9	33	18	4	64
Scotch..			1		1
Total..	9	38	25	4	76
Grand total..	10	44	30	5	89

FIRST GRADE.

BOYS.

General nativity and race of father of pupil.	Number of pupils of each age.									Total.
	4.	5.	6.	7.	8.	9.	10.	11.	12.	
Native-born, White....................		4	17	13	10	5	2	1		52
Foreign-born:										
Canadian, French....................	1	33	81	112	86	32	18	2	1	366
English....................			2		1					3
Irish....................		24	47	43	15	8	3			140
Polish....................		2	4	10	4					20
Other races a....................		1				1				2
Total....................	1	60	134	165	106	41	21	2	1	531
Grand total....................	1	64	151	178	116	46	23	3	1	583

a "Other races" includes races having less than 10 representatives of this city and pupils whose race is not reported.

TABLE 3.—*Race, sex, and age, by grade—Number of pupils of each age in each grade, by sex and by general nativity and race of father of pupil—Continued.*

FIRST GRADE—Continued.

GIRLS.

General nativity and race of father of pupil.	Number of pupils of each age.									Total.
	4.	5.	6.	7.	8.	9.	10.	11.	12.	
Native-born, White		8	14	11	14	8	1			56
Foreign-born:										
Canadian, French	8	42	72	105	95	50	15		1	388
Canadian, Other					1					1
English		3	3	1						7
Irish		44	69	28	12	5	1	1		160
Polish			8	9	6	1				24
Other races a		1	1	2	2					6
Total	8	90	153	145	116	56	16	1	1	586
Grand total	8	98	167	156	130	64	17	1	1	642

TOTAL.

General nativity and race of father of pupil.	Number of pupils of each age.									Total.
	4.	5.	6.	7.	8.	9.	10.	11.	12.	
Native-born, White		12	31	24	24	13	3	1		108
Foreign-born:										
Canadian, French	9	75	153	217	181	82	33	2	2	754
Canadian, Other					1					1
English		3	5	1	1					10
Irish		68	116	71	27	13	4	1		300
Polish		2	12	19	10	1				44
Other races a		2	1	2	2	1				8
Total	9	150	287	310	222	97	37	3	2	1,117
Grand total	9	162	318	334	246	110	40	4	2	1,225

a "Other races" includes races having less than 10 representatives in this city and pupils whose race is not reported.

SECOND GRADE.

BOYS.

General nativity and race of father of pupil.	Number of pupils of each age.										Total.
	6.	7.	8.	9.	10.	11.	12.	13.	14.	15.	
Native-born, White		6	16	8	5	4					39
Foreign-born:											
Canadian, French	2	22	48	64	38	17	9	3	1	1	205
Canadian, Other			1		1						2
English		7	4	2	5	1	1				20
Irish	1	21	36	16	9	3	1				87
Polish			6	7	5						18
Other races a				1		1			1		3
Total	3	50	95	90	58	22	11	3	2	1	335
Grand total	3	56	111	98	63	26	11	3	2	1	374

a "Other races" includes races having less than 10 representatives in this city and pupils whose race is not reported.

TABLE 3.—*Race, sex, and age, by grade—Number of pupils of each age in each grade, by sex and by general nativity and race of father of pupil*—Continued.

SECOND GRADE—Continued.

GIRLS.

General nativity and race of father of pupil.	Number of pupils of each age.										Total.
	6.	7.	8.	9	10.	11.	12.	13.	14.	15.	
Native-born, White	1	6	12	4	5	4	1				33
Foreign-born:											
Canadian, French	2	7	35	23	26	27	1		1		122
Canadian, Other		2				1					3
English		5	1	4	2		1				13
Irish	8	17	27	12	5						69
Polish			4	7	3						14
Other races *a*			1								1
Total	10	31	68	46	36	28	2		1		222
Grand total	11	37	80	50	41	32	3		1		255

TOTAL.

General nativity and race of father of pupil.	Number of pupils of each age.										Total.
	6.	7.	8.	9	10.	11.	12.	13.	14.	15.	
Native-born, White	1	12	28	12	10	8	1				72
Foreign-born:											
Canadian, French	4	29	83	87	64	44	10	3	2	1	327
Canadian, Other		2	1		1	1					5
English		12	5	6	7	1	2				33
Irish	9	38	63	28	14	3	1				156
Polish			10	14	8						32
Other races *a*			1	1		1			1		4
Total	13	81	163	136	94	50	13	3	3	1	557
Grand total	14	93	191	148	104	58	14	3	3	1	629

a "Other races" includes races having less than 10 representatives in this city and pupils whose race is not reported.

THIRD GRADE.

BOYS.

General nativity and race of father of pupil.	Number of pupils of each age.							Total.
	7.	8.	9.	10.	11.	12.	13.	
Native-born, White		2	7	5	2			16
Foreign-born:								
Canadian, French	4	7	23	25	21	39	7	126
Canadian, Other			1	1				2
English		2	4	1				7
Irish	2	22	38	16	10	1		89
Polish					1	5	1	7
Other races *a*			1		1	1		3
Total	6	31	67	44	37	42	7	234
Grand total	6	33	74	49	39	42	7	250

a "Other races" includes races having less than 10 representatives in this city and pupils whose race is not reported.

TABLE 3.—*Race, sex, and age, by grade—Number of pupils of each age in each grade, by sex and by general nativity and race of father of pupil*—Continued.

THIRD GRADE—Continued.

GIRLS.

General nativity and race of father of pupil.	Number of pupils of each age.							Total.
	6.	7.	8.	9.	10.	11.	12.	
Native-born, White.....................	....	4	15	2	4	1	....	26
Foreign-born:								
Canadian, French.................	3	5	21	23	29	12	1	94
Canadian, Other..................	....	....	3	....	....	....	....	3
English...'.......................	1	5	2	....	2	1	....	11
Irish............................	15	26	44	17	13	4	1	120
Polish...........................	....	....	....	1	....	1	2	4
Scotch...........................	....	....	1	2	1	....	....	4
Other races a....................	....	....	....	1	....	2	....	3
Total......................	19	36	71	44	45	20	4	239
Grand total..................	19	40	86	46	49	21	4	265

TOTAL.

General nativity and race of father of pupil.	Number of pupils of each age.							Total.
	6.	7.	8.	9.	10.	11.	12.	
Native-born, White.....................	....	6	22	7	6	1	....	42
Foreign-born:								
Canadian, French.................	7	12	44	48	50	51	8	220
Canadian, Other..................	....	....	4	1	....	....	....	5
English...........................	1	7	6	1	2	1	....	18
Irish............................	17	48	82	33	23	5	1	209
Polish...........................	....	....	....	2	5	2	2	11
Scotch...........................	....	....	1	2	1	....	....	4
Other races a...................	....	....	1	1	1	3	....	6
Total......................	25	67	138	88	82	62	11	473
Grand total..................	25	73	160	95	88	63	11	515

a "Other races" includes races having less than 10 representatives in this city and pupils whose race is not reported.

FOURTH GRADE.

BOYS.

General nativity and race of father of pupil.	Number of pupils of each age.								Total.
	8.	9.	10.	11.	12.	13.	14.	15.	
Native-born, White.....................	......	8	9	8	3	1	......	......	29
Foreign-born:									
Canadian, French.................	1	10	21	33	19	12	4	2	102
English..........................	....	....	1	2	1	....	....	....	4
Irish............................	....	10	21	16	18	12	1	....	78
Polish...........................	....	....	....	1	....	....	....	....	1
Scotch...........................	....	....	....	....	1	....	....	....	1
Total......................	1	20	43	52	39	24	5	2	186
Grand total..................	1	28	52	60	42	25	5	2	215

TABLE **3.**—*Race, sex, and age, by grade—Number of pupils of each age in each grade, by sex and by general nativity and race of father of pupil*—Continued.

FOURTH GRADE—Continued.

GIRLS.

General nativity and race of father of pupil.	Number of pupils of each age.								Total.
	8.	9.	10.	11.	12.	13.	14.	15.	
Native-born, White	......	7	10	9	4	1	1	......	32
Foreign-born:									
Canadian, French	3	19	30	36	30	18	15	2	153
English	......	......	2		3	1	......	......	6
Irish	1	12	19	16	14	4	1	......	67
Other races a	......	1	......	......	......	1	......	......	2
Total	4	32	51	52	47	24	16	2	228
Grand total	4	39	61	61	51·	25	17	2	260

TOTAL.

	8.	9.	10.	11.	12.	13.	14.	15.	Total.
Native-born, White	......	15	19	17	7	2	1	......	61
Foreign-born:									
Canadian, French	4	29	51	69	49	30	19	4	255
English	......	......	3	2	4	1	......	......	10
Irish	1	22	40	32	32	16	2	......	145
Polish				1					1
Scotch	......	......	......	......	1	......	......	......	1
Other races a	......	1	......	......	......	1	......	......	2
Total	5	52	94	104	86	48	21	4	414
Grand total	5	67	113	121	93	50	22	4	475

a "Other races" includes races having less than 10 representatives in this city and pupils whose race is not reported.

FIFTH GRADE.

BOYS.

General nativity and race of father of pupil.	Number of pupils of each age.									Total.
	8.	9.	10.	11.	12.	13.	14.	15.	16.	
Native-born, White	......	......	3	7	11	8	......	......	......	29
Foreign-born:										
Canadian, French	1	3	5	24	22	13	1	......	......	69
Canadian, Other	......	......	2	2	1	......	......	......	......	5
English	......	......	......	5	1	......	......	......	......	6
Irish	......	2	22	18	33	14	6	......	......	95
Other races a	......	......	......	......	......	1	1	......	......	2
Total	1	5	29	49	57	28	8	......	......	177
Grand total	1	5	32	56	68	36	8	......	......	206

a "Other races" includes races having less than 10 representatives in this city and pupils whose race is not reported.

TABLE 3.—*Race, sex, and age, by grade—Number of pupils of each age in each grade, by sex and by general nativity and race of father of pupil*—Continued.

FIFTH GRADE—Continued.

GIRLS.

General nativity and race of father of pupil.	Number of pupils of each age.									Total.
	8.	9.	10.	11.	12.	13.	14.	15.	16.	
Native-born, White	......	1	4	4	5	2	......	......	......	16
Foreign-born:										
Canadian, French		3	17	32	17	7	3	1	1	81
English		......	......	1	4	1	......	......	......	6
Irish		3	16	15	15	16	6	......	......	71
Polish		......	......	......	......	......	1	......	......	1
Other races *a*		......	......	......	1	......	......	......	......	1
Total	......	6	33	48	37	24	10	1	1	160
Grand total	......	7	37	52	42	26	10	1	1	176

TOTAL.

General nativity and race of father of pupil.	8.	9.	10.	11.	12.	13.	14.	15.	16.	Total.
Native-born, White	......	1	7	11	16	10	......	......	......	45
Foreign-born:										
Canadian, French	1	6	22	56	39	20	4	1	1	150
Canadian, Other	......	......	2	2	1	......	......	......	......	5
English	......	......	......	6	5	1	......	......	......	12
Irish	......	5	38	33	48	30	12	......	......	166
Polish	......	......	......	......	......	......	1	......	......	1
Other races *a*	......	......	......	......	1	1	1	......	......	3
Total	1	11	62	97	94	52	18	1	1	337
Grand total	1	12	69	108	110	62	18	1	1	382

a "Other races" includes races having less than 10 representatives in this city and pupils whose race is not reported.

SIXTH GRADE.

BOYS.

General nativity and race of father of pupil.	Number of pupils of each age.								Total.
	9.	10.	11.	12.	13.	14.	15.	16.	
Native-born, White	......	......	5	5	6	2	......	1	19
Foreign-born:									
Canadian, French	1	3	9	19	9	7	......	......	48
Canadian, Other	......	1	......	......	......	......	......	......	1
English	......	......	1	1	......	......	......	......	2
Irish	......	2	12	22	13	3	......	......	52
Other races *a*	......	......	......	......	......	......	1	......	1
Total	1	6	22	42	22	10	1	......	104
Grand total	1	6	27,	47	28	12	1	1	123

a "Other races" includes races having less than 10 representatives in this city and pupils whose race is not reported.

TABLE 3.—*Race, sex, and age, by grade—Number of pupils of each age in each grade, by sex and by general nativity and race of father of pupil*—Continued.

SIXTH GRADE—Continued.

GIRLS.

General nativity and race of father of pupil.	Number of pupils of each age.								Total.
	9.	10.	11.	12.	13.	14.	15.	16.	
Native-born, White		1	7	7	6	1			22
Foreign-born:									
Canadian, French	1	5	29	29	13	10			87
English				2	1				3
Irish	1	8	15	9	11	7	1		52
Total	2	13	44	40	25	17	1		142
Grand total	2	14	51	47	31	18	1		164

TOTAL.

General nativity and race of father of pupil.	9.	10.	11.	12.	13.	14.	15.	16.	Total.
Native-born, White		1	12	12	12	3		1	41
Foreign-born:									
Canadian, French	2	8	38	48	22	17			135
Canadian, Other		1							1
English			1	3	1				5
Irish	1	10	27	31	24	10	1		104
Other races a							1		1
Total	3	19	66	82	47	27	2		246
Grand total	3	20	78	94	59	30	2	1	287

a "Other races" includes races having less than 10 representatives in this city and pupils whose race is not reported.

SEVENTH GRADE.

BOYS.

General nativity and race of father of pupil.	Number of pupils of each age.						Total.
	10.	11.	12.	13.	14.	15.	
Native-born, White		3	4	9	4	1	21
Foreign-born:							
Canadian, French		7	17	15	8		47
English		1	1	1			3
Irish	2	2	17	15	7	4	47
Scotch				1		1	2
Total	2	10	35	32	15	5	99
Grand total	2	13	39	41	19	6	120

GIRLS.

General nativity and race of father of pupil.	10.	11.	12.	13.	14.	15.	Total.
Native-born, White	1		3	2			6
Foreign-born:							
Canadian, French		5	12	22	8	2	49
English		1		1			2
Irish		1	14	14	9		38
Other races a				1			1
Total		7	26	38	17	2	90
Grand total	1	7	29	40	17	2	96

a "Other races" includes races having less than 10 representatives in this city and pupils whose race is not reported.

TABLE **3.**—*Race, sex, and age, by grade—Number of pupils of each age in each grade, by sex and by general nativity and race of father of pupil*—Continued.

SEVENTH GRADE—Continued.

TOTAL.

General nativity and race of father of pupil.	Number of pupils of each age.						Total.
	10.	11.	12.	13.	14.	15.	
Native-born, White	1	3	7	11	4	1	27
Foreign-born:							
Canadian, French		12	29	37	16	2	96
English		2	1	2			5
Irish	2	3	31	29	16	4	85
Scotch				1		1	2
Other races a				1			1
Total	2	17	61	70	32	7	189
Grand total	3	20	68	81	36	8	216

a "Other races" includes races having less than 10 representatives in this city and pupils whose race is not reported.

EIGHTH GRADE.

BOYS.

General nativity and race of father of pupil.	Number of pupils of each age.						Total.
	11.	12.	13.	14.	15.	16.	
Native-born, White		2	5	10	1		18
Foreign-born:							
Canadian, French	3	7	17	7	3		37
Canadian, Other			1		1		2
English		1	1	1			3
Irish	1	2	17	12	3		35
Scotch				3			3
Total	4	10	36	23	7		80
Grand total	4	12	41	33	8		98

GIRLS.

Native-born, White		1	4	2	2	1	10
Foreign-born:							
Canadian, French		1	3	3	2		9
Irish		2	12	11	5		30
Total		3	15	14	7		39
Grand total		4	19	16	9	1	49

TOTAL.

Native-born, White		3	9	12	3	1	28
Foreign-born:							
Canadian, French	3	8	20	10	5		46
Canadian, Other			1		1		2
English		1	1	1			3
Irish	1	4	29	23	8		65
Scotch				3			3
Total	4	13	51	37	14		119
Grand total	4	16	60	49	17	1	147

TABLE 3.—*Race, sex, and age, by grade—Number of pupils of each age in each grade, by sex and by general nativity and race of father of pupil*—Continued.

NINTH GRADE.

BOYS.

General nativity and race of father of pupil.	Number of pupils of each age.						Total.
	12.	13.	14.	15.	16.	17.	
Native-born, White........................	....	....	3	5	....	....	8
Foreign-born:							
Canadian, French.....................	3	6	4	5	2	....	20
English..............................	....	....	2	....	....	....	2
Irish................................	....	6	6	9	1	....	22
Total.............................	3	12	12	14	3	....	44
Grand total.......................	3	12	15	19	3	....	52

GIRLS.

	12.	13.	14.	15.	16.	17.	Total.
Native-born, White........................	....	....	1	1	....	....	2
Foreign-born:							
Canadian, French.....................	....	....	....	....	1	....	1
English..............................	....	....	....	1	....	....	1
Irish................................	....	5	12	3	2	1	23
Total.............................	....	5	12	4	3	1	25
Grand total.......................	....	5	13	5	3	1	27

TOTAL.

	12.	13.	14.	15.	16.	17.	Total.
Native-born, White........................	....	....	4	6	....	....	10
Foreign-born:							
Canadian, French.....................	3	6	4	5	3	....	21
English..............................	....	....	2	1	....	....	3
Irish................................	....	11	18	12	3	1	45
Total.............................	3	17	24	18	6	1	69
Grand total.......................	3	17	28	24	6	1	79

TABLE 3.—*Race, sex, and age, by grade—Number of pupils of each age in each grade, by sex and by general nativity and race of father of pupil*—Continued.

FIRST YEAR HIGH SCHOOL.

BOYS.

General nativity and race of father of pupil.	Number of pupils of each age.				Total.
	13.	14.	15.	16.	
Native-born, White	2	1	....	1	4
Foreign-born, Canadian, French	....	1	2	....	3
Total	2	2	2	1	7

GIRLS.

	13.	14.	15.	16.	Total.
Native-born, White	....	....	3	1	4
Foreign-born, Irish	....	....	2	....	2
Total	....	....	5	1	6

TOTAL.

	13.	14.	15.	16.	Total.
Native-born, White	2	1	3	2	8
Foreign-born:					
Canadian, French	....	1	2	....	3
Irish	....	....	2	....	2
Total foreign-born	....	1	4	....	5
Grand total	2	2	7	2	13

COMMERCIAL SCHOOL.

BOYS.

General nativity and race of father of pupil.	Number of pupils of each age.			Total.
	14.	15.	16.	
Native-born, White	3	....	2	5
Foreign-born:				
Canadian (other than French)	....	....	1	1
Irish	1	5	....	6
Total foreign-born	1	5	1	7
Grand total	4	5	3	12

TABLE 3.—*Race, sex, and age, by grade—Number of pupils of each age in each grade, by sex and by general nativity and race of father of pupil*—Continued.

UNGRADED SCHOOL.

BOYS.

General nativity and race of father of pupil.	Number of pupils of each age.							Total.
	9.	10.	11.	12.	13.	14.	15.	
Native-born, White			1	3				4
Foreign-born, Canadian, French	1		60	25	9		2	97
Total	1		61	28	9		2	101

GIRLS.

Native-born, White			1	3				4
Foreign-born, Canadian, French		3	41	29	10	5		88
Total		3	42	32	10	5		92

TOTAL.

Native-born, White			2	6				8
Foreign-born, Canadian, French	1	3	101	54	19	5	2	185
Total	1	3	103	60	19	5	2	193

MIXED GRADES.

GIRLS.

General nativity and race of father of pupil.	Number of pupils of each age.									Total.
	7.	8.	9.	10.	11.	12.	13.	14.	15.	
Native-born, White	1	2	3	2						8
Foreign-born, Canadian, French	6	27	46	29	10	3	7	11	3	142
Total	7	29	49	31	10	3	7	11	3	150

TABLE 4.—*Race distribution in each grade—Percentages.*

[This table shows in detail only races with 100 or more pupils reporting. The totals, however, are for all races.]

General nativity and race of father of pupil.	Kindergarten.	Elementary grades.										High school, first year.	Commercial school.	Ungraded and mixed schools.	Grand total.
		1.	2.	3.	4.	5.	6.	7.	8.	9.	Total.				
Native-born, White	14.6	8.8	11.4	8.2	12.8	11.8	14.3	12.5	19.0	12.7	11.0	61.5	41.7	4.7	10.8
Foreign-born:															
Canadian, French	6.7	61.6	52.0	42.7	53.7	39.3	47.0	44.4	31.3	26.6	50.7	23.1	.0	95.3	53.0
English	5.6	.8	5.2	3.5	2.1	3.1	1.7	2.3	2.0	3.8	2.5	0	0	.0	2.4
Irish	71.9	24.5	24.8	40.6	30.5	43.5	36.2	39.4	44.2	57.0	32.2	15.4	50.0	.0	30.5
Other races	1.1	4.3	6.5	5.0	.8	2.4	.7	1.4	3.4	.0	3.6	.0	.0	.0	3.3
Total foreign-born	85.4	91.2	88.6	91.8	87.2	88.2	85.7	87.5	81.0	87.3	89.0	38.5	58.3	95.3	89.2
Grand total	100.0	100.0	100.0	100.0	100.0	100.0	100.0	100.0	100.0	100.0	100.0	100.0	100.0	100.0	100.0

TABLE 5.—*Grade distribution of each race—Percentages.*

[This table shows in detail only races with 100 or more pupils reporting. The totals, however, are for all races.]

General nativity and race of father of pupil.	Kindergarten.	Elementary grades.										High school, first year.	Commercial school.	Ungraded and mixed schools.	Grand total.
		1.	2.	3.	4.	5.	6.	7.	8.	9.	Total.				
Native-born, White	2.7	22.7	15.1	8.8	12.8	9.5	8.6	5.7	5.9	2.1	91.2	1.7	1.1	3.4	100.0
Foreign-born:															
Canadian, French	.3	32.2	14.0	9.4	10.9	6.4	5.8	4.1	2.0	.9	85.6	.1	.0	14.0	100.0
English	4.8	9.6	31.7	17.3	9.6	11.5	4.8	4.8	2.9	2.9	95.2	.0	.0	.0	100.0
Irish	4.8	22.3	11.6	15.5	10.8	12.3	7.7	6.3	4.8	3.3	94.7	.0	.4	.0	100.0
Other races	.7	36.6	28.3	17.9	2.8	6.2	1.4	2.1	3.4	3.0	98.6	.1	.0	.0	100.0
Total foreign-born	1.9	28.4	14.2	12.0	10.5	8.6	6.3	4.8	3.0	1.8	89.5	.1	.2	8.3	100.0
Grand total	2.0	27.8	14.3	11.7	10.8	8.7	6.5	4.9	3.3	1.8	89.6	.3	.3	7.8	100.0

LYNN, MASSACHUSETTS.

INTRODUCTORY NOTE.
PUBLIC SCHOOL PUPILS—GENERAL INVESTIGATION.
PUBLIC SCHOOL TEACHERS IN ELEMENTARY GRADES
    AND KINDERGARTEN.
PAROCHIAL SCHOOL PUPILS.

LIST OF TABLES.

737

LYNN.

In the public schools of Lynn information was collected for the Immigration Commission concerning both the pupils and the teachers. A parallel inquiry was conducted concerning the pupils only in the parochial schools of the city. These three more or less distinct investigations gave rise to a series of general tables which are presented herewith. The method of compiling the information, together with the description of the tables and the general statement of the uses which the several tables serve, will be found in the introduction to this volume.[a] This note is concerned not with the processes but with the results for the city of Lynn.

PUBLIC SCHOOL PUPILS.

The number of pupils reported to the Immigration Commission as being in actual attendance in the public schools of Lynn on a day early in December, 1908, was 9,583. The fact that the annual average attendance for the school year 1908–9 was 9,425 is evidence that the enumeration undertaken in December was comprehensive and complete. The attendance for a single day being in such close approximation to the average attendance for the year, it can be accepted as a satisfactory picture of the conditions usually prevailing in the public schools of the city.

Divided among the grades, the number of pupils was as follows:

First grade	1,307	Ninth grade	518
Second grade	1,077	First year high school	354
Third grade	1,038	Second year high school	282
Fourth grade	1,002	Third year high school	191
Fifth grade	1,125	Fourth year high school	166
Sixth grade	996	Special and ungraded	70
Seventh grade	803		
Eighth grade	654	Total	9,583

It will be noted that this city contains no kindergarten and that the first grade has a somewhat larger number of pupils than the second or those which follow. The second to the sixth grades constitute a group in which the numbers are not far from equal. Each of these grades includes in round numbers 1,000 pupils. The drop to 803 in the seventh grade indicates a loss of 20 per cent and to 518 in the ninth grade a loss of nearly one-half of the pupils attending in earlier grades.

---

[a] See pp. VII to XVII.

The relation of the lower to the upper grades is more plainly evident when grades 1 to 4 are grouped as primary and grades 5 to 9 as grammar grades for the purpose of contrasting these two groups with the high school, as shown in the table following.

Class of school.	Number.	Per cent.
Primary grades 1 to 4	4,424	46.5
Grammar grades 5 to 9	4,096	43.1
High school	993	10.4
Total	9,513	100.0

A little less than one-half of the pupils of Lynn are in the primary grades, somewhat more than one-half in the grammar grades and high school. The relative numbers in primary and grammar grades are very close to one another, although it should be remembered that the grammar grades represent five years of school and the primary only four.

The distribution of ages, as shown in ⊥able 1, reveals the fact that there are 372 pupils of 5 years of age in the first grade. At 6 years of age this number has increased to 765 and at 7 years to 849. The number at each age remains between 800 and 900 until the end of the tenth year. In the ages 10 to 13 there are somewhat larger numbers. At the age of 14 slightly less than 800 pupils still remain in the school. But at 15 this drops to 543 and at 16 to 387. After that point the number diminishes rapidly.

In Table 1 will be found also a statement of the number of pupils of each age in each grade. This forms a table of somewhat extensive detail, the significance of which can only be mastered by dividing in each grade the pupils into not more than two groups, the first representing those who are of an age appropriate to the grade, and the second those who are overage for their grade. These overage pupils may be designated as retarded pupils, and the number and percentage of such pupils is a measure of frequent use in recent educational discussion to estimate school conditions in various communities. If we can thus reckon the number of retarded pupils by reference to the grades, it is equally obvious that we can reckon it by reference to the ages. In this case the process is to ascertain for any given age the number of pupils who have not attained the grade which is appropriate to that age, such pupils being designated as undergrade pupils. The commoner form of expression is that which indicates the number of overage pupils.

For the city of Lynn the table following gives for each grade the number of pupils who are overage and the percentage which such pupils bear to the total number of pupils in the grade. The total number of overage pupils in all grades, compared with the whole number of pupils in the grades, gives an average for the city.

| Grade. | Number in grade. | Retarded pupils. | | |
		Age.	Number.	Per cent of all pupils.
First............	1,307	8 years and over......................	88	6.7
Second............	1,077	9 years and over......................	199	18.4
Third............	1,038	10 years and over.....................	253	24.4
Fourth............	1,002	11 years and over.....................	301	30.0
Fifth............	1,125	12 years and over.....................	387	34.4
Sixth............	996	13 years and over.....................	304	30.5
Seventh...........	803	14 years and over.....................	204	25.4
Eighth............	654	15 years and over.....................	144	22.0
Ninth............	518	16 years and over.....................	91	17.6
Total........	8,520		1,971	23.1

A little less than one-fourth of all the pupils—precisely 23.1 per cent—are in the retarded class. In the first grade the number of retarded children is small, and the proportion is only 6.7 per cent. An explanation of this small percentage lies in the fact already noted that many children in Lynn begin the first grade at 5 years of age. It is plain that such children might fail of promotion two or three times before they would be reckoned as retarded pupils. In the second grade the number of retarded pupils is below the average. The average is attained in the third grade. Both the number and proportion of retarded children reaches its maximum in the fifth grade, where 34.4 per cent, or over one-third of all the children, are retarded. After this grade the percentage of retarded children slowly diminishes. This is not necessarily due to the fact that failures to secure promotions are less frequent in these grades, but more especially to the fact that retarded children leave school earlier than those who make normal progress. In this connection comparison of the fifth and ninth grades is instructive. The fifth grade contains 738 children of normal age, the ninth grade 427. On the other hand, the fifth grade contains 387 retarded children, while the ninth grade contains only 91.

A comparison of normal and retarded children by ages is given in the following table for the selected years of age 10, 11, and 12:

| Age. | Number of pupils of this age. | Normal grade. | Retarded, or below normal grade. | |
			Number.	Per cent.
10 years............	852	4	176	20.7
11 years............	921	5	227	24.6
12 years............	1,024	6	369	36.0
Total............	2,797		772	27.6

The children here represented being somewhat older than the average of the earlier table, the percentages of retardation are somewhat higher. Moreover, the per cent of retardation increases considerably between 10 years and 12 years. The average for the group, 27.6 per cent, is computed for the purpose of showing the method of obtaining an average for such group and because it will be useful hereafter in comparison with similar averages for the different races which constitute the school population.

The main object of the researches of the Immigration Commission was to investigate the differences, if any, which exist among the different races constituting the school population. The material for this study is given in extended form in the general tables, but a few of the more important results may be noted here.

The distribution of pupils in the Lynn public schools by race and general nativity is given in the following statement:

General nativity and race of father of pupil.	Pupils.		General nativity and race of father of pupil.	Pupils.	
	Number.	Per cent.		Number.	Per cent.
Native-born:			Foreign-born—Continued.		
White.....................	5,238	54.7	Hebrew, Russia...........	638	6.7
Negro and Indian..........	105	1.1	Irish.....................	653	6.9
			Swedish..................	359	3.7
Total native-born........	5,343	55.8	All others................	1,083	11.3
Foreign-born;					
Canadian (other than French).................	1,007	10.5	Total foreign-born.......	4,240	44.2
English..................	495	5.2	Grand total.............	9,583	100.0

More than one-half of the children of Lynn had native white fathers; 44.2 per cent had foreign-born fathers. Among the children of foreign parentage the most numerous are the English Canadians, who represent one-tenth of all the children in the public schools of Lynn. Other prominent races are the Irish with 6.9 per cent of the total population, the Russian Hebrews with 6.7 per cent, and the English with 5.2 per cent.

The group "All others," consisting of the races which had a less representation than 200 in the public schools of Lynn, is relatively numerous, constituting 11.3 per cent of all the school children. It represents a considerable number of individual races, as follows: Armenian (63), Bohemian and Moravian (9), Bulgarian (1), Canadian, French (179), Chinese (1), Danish (15), Dutch (8), Finnish (4), French (27), German (107), Greek (16), Hebrew, German (44), Hebrew, Polish (46), Hebrew, Other (36), Italian, North (71), Italian, South (126), Japanese (2), Lithuanian (36), Macedonian (1), Magyar (2), Negro (8), Norwegian (31), Polish (42), Portuguese (3), Russian (9), Scotch (169), Scotch-Irish (1), Slovak (3), Spanish-American (4), Turkish (4), and Welsh (13).

The general tables are so constructed that for each racial group and for each of the more important races the same studies with respect to age and grade distribution can be made as for the schools as a whole. Of necessity this information is scattered through many sections of the tables, and it may be of advantage to present here some of the chief results of these inquiries. In order to present a more compact statement and summary, distribution by grade, for each racial group, and for the more important individual races is given in the table next submitted.

General nativity and race of father of pupil.	Number of pupils.				Per cent.		
	Primary.	Gram-mar.	High.	Total.	Primary.	Gram-mar.	High.
Native-born:							
White....................	2,190	2,337	708	5,235	41.8	44.6	13.5
Negro and Indian..........	69	34	2	105	65.7	32.4	1.9
Total native-born.......	2,259	2,371	710	5,340	42.3	44.4	13.3
Foreign-born:							
Canadian (other than French).................	419	497	91	1,007	41.6	49.4	9.0
English....................	227	219	49	495	45.9	44.2	9.9
Hebrew, Russian...........	429	158	8	595	72.1	26.6	1.3
Irish......................	299	298	60	657	45.5	45.4	9.1
Swedish...................	174	170	15	359	48.5	47.4	4.2
All others................	617	383	60	1,060	58.2	36.1	5.7
Total foreign-born........	2,165	1,725	283	4,173	51.9	41.3	6.8
Grand total.............	4,424	4,096	993	9,513	46.5	43.1	10.4

In the primary schools we find 41.8 per cent of all the children of native white parents and 51.9 of all those of foreign parents. The proportion of English Canadians in the primary schools is about the same as that of children of native parentage. There is, however, a conspicuous excess in the proportion of Russian Hebrew children in the primary schools. The grammar schools offer a less marked contrast, the proportions for the two groups approaching each other more closely. Variation from the general average is observed only in the case of the Russian Hebrew. On the other hand, the contrast between races is very marked in the high school. The high school comprises 13.5 per cent of the children of native parents, but only 6.8 per cent of those of foreign parents. The proportion of Russian Hebrew children in the high school is very small, and that of Swedish children falls considerably below the average. In the case of the Russian Hebrews consideration should be given to the fact that the migration of this race is comparatively recent, and the explana on of the very small number in the upper school may very well be tne small number of children in the population at large of the ages appropriate to the high school as contrasted with the younger children.

For the same racial groups the following table gives a statement of school progress measured negatively by the degree of retardation.

General nativity and race of father of pupil.	All elementary pupils.			Pupils 10, 11, and 12 years of age.		
	Number.	Retarded, overage.	Per cent retarded.	Number.	Retarded, under-grade.	Per cent retarded.
Native-born:						
White.....	4,527	916	20.2	1,502	343	22.8
Negro and Indian....................	103	50	48.5	35	22	62.9
Total native-born................	4,630	966	20.8	1,537	365	23.7
Foreign-born:						
Canadian (other than French).........	916	233	25.4	314	76	24.2
English....................	446	91	20.4	139	36	25.9
Hebrew, Russian......................	587	169	28.8	163	79	48.5
Irish...	597	136	22.8	199	54	27.1
Swedish.....	344	66	19.2	139	30	21.6
All others...................	1,000	310	31.0	306	129	42.1
Total foreign-born.....	3,890	1,005	25.8	1,260	407	32.3
Grand total................	8,520	1,971	23.1	2,797	772	27.6

This table is in two sections, the first three columns relating to all elementary pupils and the second three columns relating to the pupils 10, 11, and 12 years of age. The former measures general retardation, the latter that of the selected group.

In the first section of the table it will be noted that one-fifth of the pupils of native parents are retarded as against one-fourth of those of foreign parentage. Low rates of retardation are observed among the Swedish and English pupils.

In the second section of the table, relating to the selected ages, there is a wider difference between the different groups. Among native white children of native parents 22.8 per cent are retarded; among children of foreign parents 32.3 per cent. In the latter group the lowest per cent of retardation is among the Swedish, who show fewer retarded pupils than do the children of native parentage. In connection with the last table it will be noted therefore that the small proportion of Swedes in the high school is not due to their failures in the lower schools. Conspicuously large is the ratio of retardation among the Russian Hebrew pupils, in considering which it must again be borne in mind that this race is of comparatively recent migration and the pupils of these ages probably comprise a larger percentage of pupils who were themselves born abroad than do the figures for other races of the same ages.

PUBLIC SCHOOL TEACHERS.

In the elementary grades of the Lynn public schools 219 teachers are employed. With one exception the teachers are women.

Divided by racial groups, the following numbers and proportions are noted:

	Number.	Per cent.
Native white of native fathers	152	69. 4
Native white of foreign fathers	54	24. 7
Foreign white	13	5. 9
Total	219	100, 0

About seven-tenths of all the teachers are of both native birth and native parentage, and about one-fourth, though of native birth, have foreign parents. Among the latter the Irish are most numerous, and in fact all of these teachers had fathers of English-speaking races.

The distribution of these teachers by racial groups between the primary and grammar grades is shown in the table following.

	Primary.	Grammar.	Total.	Per cent in grammar grade.
Native white of native fathers	72	80	152	52. 6
Native white of foreign fathers	32	22	54	40. 7
Foreign white	9	4	13	30. 8
Total	113	106	219	48. 4

Somewhat more than one-half of the teachers having native fathers were employed in the grammar grades. For the other groups the proportions are somewhat less.

Length of service of these teachers was as follows:

Under 5 years	31	From 25 to 29 years	8.
From 5 to 9 years	51	30 years and over	21
From 10 to 14 years	50		
From 15 to 19 years	27	Total	219
From 20 to 24 years	31		

In the five-year periods here given the most numerous is that of teachers having from five to nine years' experience. If to these we add the teachers of from ten to fourteen years' experience, we have nearly one-half of the whole number of teachers.

The length of service in connection with nativity and parentage is shown in the following table:

Race and nativity of teachers.	Length of service, in years.			
	Under 10.	10 to 19.	20 and over.	Total.
Native white, native fathers	53	57	42	152
Native white, foreign fathers	21	17	16	54
Foreign white	8	3	2	13
Total	82	77	60	219
Percentages: All teachers	37.4	35.2	27.4	100.0

The youngest group of teachers, those who had experience of less than ten years, constitute about one-half of the group having native fathers and two-fifths of those having foreign fathers.

PUPILS IN THE PAROCHIAL SCHOOLS.

Through the courtesy of the church authorities information was collected in Lynn concerning 2,959 pupils in the parochial schools. The official directory of the Roman Catholic Church gives the total enrollment of the parochial schools for the year as 3,279. The difference between the figures reported to the Commission and this record is not greater than is frequently found between the attendance in a school system and the total enrollment of the same. There is, therefore, every reason to believe that we have in the figures reported to the Commission a comprehensive and therefore characteristic statement of the pupils in this class of schools.

Divided by grades, these pupils were as follows:

First grade	574	Eighth grade	178
Second grade	396	Ninth grade	151
Third grade	390	First year high school	25
Fourth grade	371	Second year high school	19
Fifth grade	344	Third year high school	6
Sixth grade	312		
Seventh grade	193	Total	2,959

The first grade is, as commonly the case, much larger than those which follow. The second to the sixth grade have about the same range of numbers. In the seventh there is a noticeable falling off. In the ninth grade there are just about one-half as many pupils as in the sixth.

Dividing these pupils by groups of grades, we have the following contrast between the lower and upper grades:

	Number.	Per cent.
Grades 1 to 4	1,731	58.5
Grades 5 to 9	1,178	39.8
High school	50	1.7
Total	2,959	100.0

In round numbers six-tenths of the pupils are in the lower grades and most of the remainder are in the upper elementary grades, the high school being represented by only a very small number of pupils, and, as indicated in the previous list, by only three years of study.

Table 1 shows the ages of the pupils in the parochial schools. At the age of 5 years there are 138; at the age of 6 years, 282. The number at each age, up to and including 12 years, ranges in the neighborhood of 300. After that the numbers diminish rapidly.

The relation of age and grade is shown in the table following, which exhibits the number and proportion of retarded pupils.

Grade.	Number in grade.	Retarded pupils.		
		Age.	Number.	Per cent of all pupils.
First	574	8 years and over	78	13.6
Second	396	9 years and over	106	26.8
Third	390	10 years and over	75	19.2
Fourth	371	11 years and over	116	31.3
Fifth	344	12 years and over	96	27.9
Sixth	312	13 years and over	69	22.1
Seventh	193	14 years and over	45	23.3
Eighth	178	15 years and over	31	17.4
Ninth	151	16 years and over	19	12.6
Total	2,909		635	21.8

For the schools as a whole 21.8 per cent of the pupils are in the retarded class. In the eighth and ninth grades the proportion is considerably less, due to the elimination of the retarded pupils in these grades.

A further table gives a statement of retardation for the selected class of pupils 10 to 12 years of age.

Age.	Number of pupils of this age.	Normal grade.	Retarded, or below normal grade.	
			Number.	Per cent.
10 years	320	4	84	26.3
11 years	349	5	100	28.7
12 years	306	6	110	35.9
Total	975		294	30.2

In these ages 30.2 per cent of the pupils are retarded. The proportion, which is 26.3 per cent at the age of 10 years, increases to 35.9 per cent at the age of 12.

A summary of the pupils in the parochial schools divided by race follows:

General nativity and race of father of pupil.	Pupils.	
	Number.	Per cent.
Native-born, White	934	31.6
Total native white	934	31.6
Foreign-born:		
Canadian, French	525	17.7
Canadian (other than French)	172	5.8
Irish	1,134	38.3
All others	194	6.6
Total foreign-born	2,025	68.4
Grand total	2,959	100.0

This table shows that somewhat less than one-third of the pupils in these schools have native fathers, while somewhat more than two-thirds have foreign fathers. Among the latter the most numerous are the Irish, represented by 38.3 per cent of the whole number of school children. Next in importance come the French Canadian, who have 17.7 per cent of the whole number. The small group "All others" contains a few children from each of the following races: Dutch (2), English (55), French (2), German (6), Greek (2), Hebrew, Polish (5), Hindu (2), Italian, North (19), Italian, South (22), Lithuanian (3), Norwegian (2), Polish (31), Portuguese (1), Russian (8), and Scotch (31).

PUBLIC AND PAROCHIAL SCHOOL PUPILS COMBINED.

A combination of the facts with regard to race heretofore given separately for the public and parochial school pupils gives a view of the distribution of the population by races in the school ages.

General nativity and race of father of pupil.	Pupils by schools.			Per cent of all pupils.
	Public schools.	Parochial schools.	Total.	
Native-born:				
White	5,238	934	6,172	49.2
Negro and Indian	105	....	105	.8
Total native-born	5,343	934	6,277	50.0
Foreign-born:				
Canadian (other than French)	1,007	172	1,179	9.4
English	495	55	550	4.4
Hebrew, Russian	638	....	638	5.1
Irish	658	1,134	1,792	14.3
Swedish	359	....	359	2.9
All others	1,083	664	1,747	13.9
Total foreign-born	4,240	2,025	6,265	50.0
Grand total	9,583	2,959	12,542	100.0

One-half of the pupils have native and one-half have foreign fathers. Of the whole number of pupils, 14.3 per cent are Irish and nearly 10 per cent are English Canadians.

The table shows also that of the whole number of Irish pupils in the schools considerably more than one-half are in the parochial schools.

GENERAL TABLES.

PUBLIC SCHOOL PUPILS: GENERAL INVESTIGATION.

TABLE 1.—*Grade and age—Number of pupils of each age in each grade, by sex.*

BOYS.

Age.	Elementary grades.									
	1.	2.	3.	4.	5.	6.	7.	8.	9.	Total.
4 years										
5 years	208	1								209
6 years	310	83	1							394
7 years	148	208	68	4						428
8 years	31	135	181	58						405
9 years	6	71	150	172	47	1				447
10 years	5	20	71	138	139	55	2			430
11 years		13	35	87	152	139	43	4		473
12 years		11	21	54	116	139	122	42	5	510
13 years		1	6	20	64	99	116	95	52	453
14 years			5	14	28	56	87	96	79	365
15 years			1	3	12	12	27	53	60	168
16 years				1	3	5	20	29		58
17 years							1		10	11
18 years							1	1	2	4
19 years							1			1
20 years or over										
Total	708	543	539	550	559	504	405	311	237	4,356

Age.	High school.					Special and un-graded schools.	Grand total.
	First year.	Second year.	Third year.	Fourth year.	Total.		
4 years							
5 years							209
6 years						2	396
7 years						4	432
8 years						6	411
9 years						9	456
10 years						4	434
11 years							473
12 years						1	511
13 years	7				7	4	464
14 years	35	1			36	4	405
15 years	63	31	5		99	2	269
16 years	35	55	14	5	109	1	168
17 years	26	31	42	15	114	1	126
18 years	2	6	10	29	47	1	52
19 years	1	2	3	16	22		23
20 years or over		2		4	6		6
Total	169	128	74	69	440	39	4,835

TABLE 1.—*Grade and age—Number of pupils of each age in each grade, by sex*—Contd.

GIRLS.

Age.	Elementary grades.									
	1.	2.	3.	4.	5.	6.	7.	8.	9.	Total.
4 years										
5 years	163									163
6 years	278	88	1							367
7 years	112	224	73	5						414
8 years	33	139	194	62	1					429
9 years	10	54	117	150	83	4				418
10 years	1	14	65	112	168	59	3			422
11 years	1	7	21	63	148	155	52	1		448
12 years	1	5	17	40	104	140	140	65	2	514
13 years		1	7	10	48	89	121	114	52	442
14 years		2	4	8	13	38	64	93	100	322
15 years				2	1	4	13	55	77	152
16 years						3	4	14	38	59
17 years							1		9	10
18 years								1	3	4
19 years										
20 years or over										
Total	599	534	499	452	566	492	398	343	281	4,164

Age.	High school.					Special and un-graded schools.	Grand total.
	First year.	Second year.	Third year.	Fourth year.	Total.		
4 years							
5 years							163
6 years						2	369
7 years						3	417
8 years						2	431
9 years						2	420
10 years						7	429
11 years						4	452
12 years							514
13 years	3				3	3	448
14 years	43	6			49	2	373
15 years	75	40	3		118	4	274
16 years	52	74	31		158	2	219
17 years	11	23	56	23	113		123
18 years	1	11	21	46	79		83
19 years				6	21	27		27
20 years or over				6	6		6
Total	185	154	117	97	553	31	4,748

TABLE 1.—*Grade and age—Number of pupils of each age in each grade, by sex*—Contd.

TOTAL.

Age.	Elementary grades.									
	1.	2.	3.	4.	5.	6.	7.	8.	9.	Total.
4 years										
5 years	371	1								372
6 years	588	171	2							761
7 years	260	432	141	9						842
8 years	64	274	375	120	1					834
9 years	16	125	267	322	130	5				865
10 years	6	34	136	250	307	114	5			852
11 years	1	20	56	150	300	294	95	5		921
12 years	1	16	38	94	220	279	262	107	7	1,024
13 years		2	13	30	112	188	237	209	104	895
14 years		2	9	22	41	94	151	189	179	687
15 years			1	5	13	16	40	108	137	320
16 years					1	6	9	34	67	117
17 years							2		19	21
18 years							1	2	5	8
19 years							1			1
20 years or over										
Total	1,307	1,077	1,038	1,002	1,125	996	803	654	518	8,520

Age.	High school.					Special and un-graded schools.	Grand total.
	First year.	Second year.	Third year.	Fourth year.	Total.		
4 years							
5 years							372
6 years						4	765
7 years						7	849
8 years						8	842
9 years						11	876
10 years						11	863
11 years						4	925
12 years						1	1,025
13 years	10				10	7	912
14 years	78	7			85	6	778
15 years	138	71	8		217	6	543
16 years	87	129	45	6	267	3	387
17 years	37	54	98	38	227	1	249
18 years	3	17	31	75	126	1	135
19 years	1	2	9	37	49		50
20 years		2		10	12		12
Total	354	282	191	166	993	70	9,583

TABLE 2.—*Race, sex, and grade—Number of pupils of each sex in each grade, by general nativity and race of father of pupil.*

General nativity and race of father of pupil	Elementary grades										High school					Special and ungraded schools	Grand total.
	1.	2.	3.	4.	5.	6.	7.	8.	9.	Total.	First year.	Second year.	Third year.	Fourth year.	Total.		
Native-born:																	
White—																	
Male	325	281	285	290	301	280	240	185	139	2,326	107	94	50	52	303	2	2,631
Female	278	252	258	221	300	267	225	220	180	2,201	123	111	84	87	405	1	2,607
Total	603	533	543	511	601	547	465	405	319	4,527	230	205	134	139	708	3	5,238
Negro—																	
Male	16	5	6	6	8	7	1	2		51		1			1		52
Female	10	8	8	9	7	4	1	2	2	51			1		1		52
Total	26	13	14	15	15	11	2	4	2	102		1	1		2		104
Indian—																	
Male																	
Female				1						1							1
Total				1						1							1
Total native-born—																	
Male	341	286	291	296	309	287	241	187	139	2,377	107	95	50	52	304	2	2,683
Female	288	260	266	231	307	271	226	222	182	2,253	123	111	85	87	406	1	2,660
Total	629	546	557	527	616	558	467	409	321	4,630	230	206	135	139	710	3	5,343
Foreign-born:																	
Armenian—																	
Male	5	8	3	7	2	1	2	3	2	33	2		2		4	3	40
Female	4	7	3	1	1	4	1	1		22	1				1		23
Total	9	15	6	8	3	5	3	4	2	55	3		2		5	3	63
Canadian, French—																	
Male	12	5	7	9	10	4	8	11	5	71	4	1	4		9		80
Female	19	7	7	9	16	10	9	10	6	93	2	1	3		6		99
Total	31	12	14	18	26	14	17	21	11	164	6	2	7		15		179
Canadian, Other—																	
Male	64	49	49	48	61	71	46	34	32	454	17	13	5	8	43		497
Female	50	49	54	56	61	65	49	36	42	462	19	15	9	5	48		510
Total	114	98	103	104	122	136	95	70	74	916	36	28	14	13	91		1,007
Danish—																	
Male	2				1	2	1			6	1				1		7
Female				2	2	2	1			7	1				1		8
Total	2			2	3	4	2			13	2				2		15
English—																	
Male	38	30	25	22	24	33	18	19	10	219	11	3	3	2	19		238
Female	28	29	28	27	32	27	20	16	20	227	15	10	3	2	30		257
Total	66	59	53	49	56	60	38	35	30	446	26	13	6	4	49		495

	Male	Female	Total
French—	12	15	27
German—	53	54	107
Greek—	12	4	16
Hebrew, German—	26	18	44
Hebrew, Polish—	23	23	46
Hebrew, Russian—	327	311	638
Hebrew, Other—	19	17	36
Irish—	362	296	658
Italian, North—	39	32	71
Italian, South—	62	64	126
Lithuanian—	20	16	36
Norwegian—	11	20	31
Polish—	21	21	42

TABLE 2.—*Race, sex, and grade—Number of pupils of each sex in each grade, by general nativity and race of father of pupil*—Continued.

General nativity and race of father of pupil.	Elementary grades.										High school.					Special and ungraded schools.	Grand total.
	1.	2.	3.	4.	5.	6.	7.	8.	9.	Total.	First year.	Second year.	Third year.	Fourth year.	Total.		
Foreign-born—Continued.																	
Scotch—																	
Male	14	7	16	11	8	7	3	1	3	70	3	1	3		7	1	78
Female	8	9	12	7	14	10	8	9	5	82	4	1	4		9		91
Total	22	16	28	18	22	17	11	10	8	152	7	2	7		16	1	169
Swedish—																	
Male	26	25	21	16	27	25	15	14	12	181	3	4		3	10		191
Female	19	24	18	25	19	29	19	6	4	163	3	1	1		5		168
Total	45	49	39	41	46	54	34	20	16	344	6	5	1	3	15		359
Welsh—																	
Male												1			1		1
Female					5			5	1	11		1			1		12
Total					5			5	1	11		2			2		13
Other races a—																	
Male	10	6	4	5	3		2		2	32						1	33
Female	7	6	5	1	1	5				25	1	1	1	1	4		29
Total	17	12	9	6	4	5	2		2	57	1	1	1	1	4	1	62
Total foreign-born—																	
Male	367	257	248	254	250	217	164	124	98	1,979	62	33	24	17	136	37	2,152
Female	311	274	233	221	259	221	172	121	99	1,911	62	43	32	10	147	30	2,088
Total	678	531	481	475	509	438	336	245	197	3,890	124	76	56	27	283	67	4,240
Grand total—																	
Male	708	543	539	550	559	504	405	311	237	4,354	169	128	74	69	440	39	4,835
Female	599	534	499	452	566	492	398	343	281	4,164	185	154	117	97	553	31	4,748
Total	1,307	1,077	1,038	1,002	1,125	996	803	654	518	8,520	354	282	191	166	993	70	9,583

a "Other races" includes 9 Bohemian, 1 Bulgarian, 1 Chinese, 8 Dutch, 4 Finnish, 2 Japanese, 1 Macedonian, 2 Magyar, 8 Negroes, 3 Portuguese, 9 Russian, 1 Scotch-Irish, 3 Slovak, 4 Spanish-Americans, 4 Turkish, 2 not reporting.

TABLE 3.—*Race, sex, and age, by grade—Number of pupils of each age in each grade, by sex and by general nativity and race of father of pupil.*

FIRST GRADE.

BOYS.

General nativity and race of father of pupil.	Number of pupils of each age.								Total.
	5.	6.	7.	8.	9.	10.	11.	12.	
Native-born:									
White....................................	115	134	60	11	3	2			325
Negro....................................	1	7	3	2	1	2			16
Total native-born.....................	116	141	63	13	4	4			341
Foreign-born:									
Armenian...............................		2	3						5
Canadian, French.....................	4	3	4	1					12
Canadian, Other.......................	13	34	13	3	1				64
Danish.................................	1	1							2
English.................................	8	22	7	1					38
French..................................	1		1	1					3
German.................................	1	2	2						5
Greek...................................		2	3						5
Hebrew, German.......................	1	2							3
Hebrew, Polish........................	2	1							3
Hebrew, Roumanian..................	1								1
Hebrew, Russian......................	25	39	14	1					79
Irish....................................	11	28	9	2					50
Italian, North.........................	2	1	4	2					9
Italian, South.........................	3	5	5	2					15
Lithuanian.............................		6	3						9
Norwegian.............................	2	1	1						4
Polish...................................		3	5	2					10
Scotch...................................	3	6	2	2	1				14
Swedish.................................	9	9	7			1			26
Other races *a*.......................	5	2	2	1					10
Total foreign-born....................	92	169	85	18	2	1			367
Grand total...........................	208	310	148	31	6	5			708

a "Other races" includes races having less than 10 representatives in this city and pupils whose race is not reported.

Table 3.—*Race, sex, and age, by grade—Number of pupils of each age in each grade by sex and by general nativity and race of father of pupil—Continued.*

FIRST GRADE—Continued.

GIRLS.

General nativity and race of father of pupil.	Number of pupils of each age.								Total.
	5.	6.	7.	8.	9.	10.	11.	12.	
Native-born:									
White	94	129	47	5	2			1	278
Negro	3	1	3	3					10
Total native-born	97	130	50	8	2			1	288
Foreign-born:									
Armenian		1	2	1					4
Canadian, French	1	9	8	1					19
Canadian, Other	10	23	10	6	1				50
English	9	15	3	1					28
French		2	1						3
German	1	2	1	1	1				6
Hebrew, German		1		1					2
Hebrew, Polish		2							2
Hebrew, Russian	21	34	9	6	4				74
Hebrew, Other			1	1					2
Irish	10	16	6						32
Italian, North	2	10	1	1		1			15
Italian, South	4	3	5	1	1				14
Lithuanian		3	4						7
Norwegian		3		1					4
Polish	1	7	5	1			1		15
Scotch	4	3			1				8
Swedish	3	9	5	2					19
Other races a		5	1	1					7
Total foreign-born	66	148	62	25	8	1	1		311
Grand total	163	278	112	33	10	1	1	1	599

a "Other races" includes races having less than 10 representatives in this city and pupils whose race is not reported.

TABLE **3.**—*Race, sex, and age, by grade—Number of pupils of each age in each grade, by sex and by general nativity and race of father of pupil*—Continued.

FIRS'.' GRADE—Continued.

TOTAL.

General nativity and race of father of pupil.	Number of pupils of each age.								Total.
	5.	6.	7.	8.	9.	10.	11.	12.	
Native-born:									
White	209	263	107	16	5	2	......	1	602
Negro.................................	4	8	6	5	1	2			26
Total native-born..................	213	271	113	21	6	4	......	1	629
Foreign-born:									
Armenian.............................	......	3	5	1					9
Canadian, French....................	5	12	12	2					31
Canadian, Other.....................	23	57	23	9	2				114
Danish...............................	1	1							2
English...............................	17	37	10	2					66
French...............................	1	2	2	1					6
German..............................	2	4	3	1	1				11
Greek................................	......	2	3						5
Hebrew, German.....................	1	3	......	1					5
Hebrew, Polish......................	2	3							5
Hebrew, Roumanian..................	1								1
Hebrew, Russian.....................	46	73	23	7	4				153
Hebrew, Other.......................	......	......	1	1					2
Irish.................................	21	44	15	2					82
Italian, North.......................	4	11	5	3	......	1			24
Italian, South.......................	7	8	10	3	1				29
Lithuanian...........................	......	9	7						16
Norwegian...........................	2	4	1	1					8
Polish................................	1	10	10	3	......	......	1		25
Scotch...............................	7	9	2	2	2	......			22
Swedish..............................	12	18	12	2	......	1			45
Other races a	5	7	3	2					17
Total foreign-born..................	158	317	147	43	10	2	1	......	678
Grand total......................	371	588	260	64	16	6	1	1	1,307

a "Other races" includes races having less than 10 representatives in this city and pupils whose race is not reported.

TABLE 3.—*Race, sex, and age, by grade—Number of pupils of each age in each grade, by sex and by general nativity and race of father of pupil*—Continued.

SECOND GRADE.

BOYS.

General nativity and race of father of pupil.	Number of pupils of each age.														Total.
	5.	6.	7.	8.	9.	10.	11.	12.	13.	14.	15.	16.	17.	18.	
Native-born:															
White		58	114	68	28	6	4	3							281
Negro		1		2	1	1									5
Total native-born		59	114	70	29	7	4	3							286
Foreign-born:															
Armenian		3		1	2	1	1								8
Canadian, French		2	2	1											5
Canadian, Other		6	23	12	8										49
Danish			1												1
English		2	15	9	1	2	1								30
French			1		1										2
German		2	1	3	1										7
Greek		1					1								2
Hebrew, German		1	1	4		1									7
Hebrew, Polish		2		1			1								4
Hebrew, Russian		2	12	11	13	1	2	4							45
Hebrew, Other			2	2	1					1					6
Irish		3	11	9	5	3		1							32
Italian, North		3	1	1	2	1									8
Italian, South			3	1	2	1	1	1							9
Lithuanian			1												1
Norwegian				1											1
Polish			1	1											2
Scotch	1		4	1		1									7
Swedish		2	10	6	6	1									25
Other races *a*			2	1			2	1							6
Total foreign-born	1	24	94	65	42	13	9	8	1						257
Grand total	1	83	208	135	71	20	13	11	1						543

a "Other races" includes races having less than 10 representatives in this city and pupils whose race is not reported.

TABLE **3.**—*Race, sex, and age, by grade—Number of pupils of each age in each grade, by sex and by general nativity and race of father of pupil*—Continued.

SECOND GRADE—Continued.

GIRLS.

General nativity and race of father of pupil.	Number of pupils of each age.														Total.
	5.	6.	7.	8.	9.	10.	11.	12.	13.	14.	15.	16.	17.	18.	
Native-born:															
White........................	....	52	115	55	21	6	3	....	....	....	....	....	....	....	252
Negro........................	....	2	2	3	1	....	....	....	....	....	....	....	....	....	8
Total native-born.........	....	54	117	58	22	6	3	....	....	....	....	....	....	....	260
Foreign-born:															
Armenian....................	....	1	1	2	1	....	....	1	....	1	....	....	....	....	7
Canadian, French..........	....	1	4	2	....	....	....	....	....	....	....	....	....	....	7
Canadian, Other...........	....	9	22	11	6	....	....	1	....	....	....	....	....	....	49
Danish.......................	....	....	1	....	....	....	....	....	....	....	....	....	....	....	1
English.......................	....	2	9	15	3	....	....	....	....	....	....	....	....	....	29
French........................	....	....	1	....	....	....	....	....	....	....	....	....	....	....	1
German.......................	....	3	3	....	3	....	....	1	....	....	....	....	....	....	10
Greek.........................	....	....	1	....	....	....	....	....	....	....	....	....	....	....	1
Hebrew, German............	....	....	....	2	....	....	1	....	....	....	....	....	....	....	3
Hebrew, Polish.............	....	....	3	1	....	....	1	....	....	....	....	....	....	....	5
Hebrew, Russian...........	....	5	24	19	7	4	....	1	1	....	....	....	....	....	61
Hebrew, Other..............	....	....	2	1	1	....	....	....	....	....	....	....	....	....	4
Irish..........................	....	7	13	9	2	2	....	....	....	....	....	....	....	....	33
Italian, North..............	....	....	....	2	2	2	....	....	....	....	....	....	....	....	6
Italian, South..............	....	1	3	3	2	....	1	....	....	....	....	....	....	....	10
Lithuanian..................	....	....	1	....	....	....	....	....	....	....	....	....	....	....	1
Norwegian...................	....	1	1	3	....	....	....	....	....	....	....	....	....	....	5
Polish........................	....	....	....	....	....	....	1	....	....	1	....	....	....	....	2
Scotch........................	....	1	5	1	2	....	....	....	....	....	....	....	....	....	9
Swedish......................	....	3	11	8	1	....	1	....	....	....	....	....	....	....	24
Other races a...............	....	....	2	2	2	....	....	....	....	....	....	....	....	....	6
Total foreign-born.........	....	34	107	81	32	8	4	5	1	2	....	....	....	....	274
Grand total................	....	88	224	139	54	14	7	5	1	2	....	....	....	....	534

a "Other races" includes races having less than 10 representatives in this city and pupils whose race is not reported.

TABLE **3.**—*Race, sex, and age, by grade—Number of pupils of each age in each grade, by sex and by general nativity and race of father of pupil*—Continued.

SECOND GRADE—Continued.

TOTAL.

General nativity and race of father of pupil.	Number of pupils of each age.														Total.
	5.	6.	7.	8.	9.	10.	11.	12.	13.	14.	15.	16.	17.	18.	
Native-born:															
White		110	229	123	49	12	7	3							533
Negro		3	2	5	2	1									13
Total native-born		113	231	128	51	13	7	3							546
Foreign-born:															
Armenian		1	4	2	2	2	1	2		1					15
Canadian, French		1	6	4	1										12
Canadian, Other		15	45	23	14			1							98
Danish			2												2
English		4	24	24	4	2	1								59
French			2		1										3
German		5	4	3	4				1						17
Greek		1	1				1								3
Hebrew, German		1	1	6		1	1								10
Hebrew, Polish		2	3	2			2								9
Hebrew, Russian		7	36	30	20	5	2	5	1						106
Hebrew, Other			4	3	2					1					10
Irish		10	24	18	7	5		1							65
Italian, North		3	1	3	4	3									14
Italian, South		1	6	4	4	1	2	1							19
Lithuanian			2												2
Norwegian		1	1	4											6
Polish			1	1			1		1						4
Scotch	1	1	9	2	2	1									16
Swedish		5	21	14	7	1		1							49
Welsh															
Other races*a*			4	3	2		2	1							12
Total foreign-born	1	58	201	146	74	21	13	13	2	2					531
Grand total	1	171	432	274	125	34	20	16	2	2					1,077

a "Other races" includes races having less than 10 representatives in this city and pupils whose race is not reported.

TABLE 3.—*Race, sex, and age, by grade—Number of pupils of each age in each grade, by sex and by general nativity and race of father of pupil*—Continued.

THIRD GRADE.

BOYS.

General nativity and race of father of pupil.	Number of pupils of each age.										Total.
	6.	7.	8.	9.	10.	11.	12.	13.	14.	15.	
Native-born:											
White	1	44	101	71	40	17	9		2		285
Negro				2	2	1	1				6
Total native-born	1	44	101	73	42	18	10		2		291
Foreign-born:											
Armenian			2							1	3
Canadian, French		1	2	2	1			1			7
Canadian, Other		8	19	12	4	2	2	2			49
English		4	11	5	4	1					25
French				1							1
German				1	1						2
Greek						1					1
Hebrew, Polish					2						2
Hebrew, Russian		2	16	19	3	6	5		1		52
Hebrew, Other				1	1	1					3
Irish		6	12	18	5			1			42
Italian, North			1	1							2
Italian, South			2	5	1	3		1			12
Lithuanian				1			1	1			3
Norwegian					1						1
Polish				1					1		2
Scotch		3	4	3	4	1	1				16
Swedish			10	7	2	1	1				21
Other races a			1			1	1		1		4
Total foreign-born		24	80	77	29	17	11	6	3	1	248
Grand total	1	68	181	150	71	35	21	6	5	1	539

a "Other races" includes races having less than 10 representatives in this city and pupils whose race is not reported.

TABLE **3.**—*Race, sex, and age, by grade—Number of pupils of each age in each grade, by sex and by general nativity and race of father of pupil—Continued.*

THIRD GRADE—Continued.

GIRLS.

General nativity and race of father of pupil.	Number of pupils of each age.										Total.
	6.	7.	8.	9.	10.	11.	12.	13.	14.	15.	
Native-born:											
White	1	49	123	51	20	10	2	1	1		258
Negro		1	1	1		3	1		1		8
Total native-born	1	50	124	52	20	13	3	1	2		266
Foreign-born:											
Armenian			3								3
Canadian, French		1	3	1	2						7
Canadian, Other		4	20	15	9	2	4				54
Danish				1							1
English		5	8	8	5	2					28
French				1							1
German			1	3							4
Greek								1			1
Hebrew, German			1	1							2
Hebrew, Polish								1			1
Hebrew, Roumanian					1						1
Hebrew, Russian		5	13	12	7	1	5	3	2		48
Hebrew, Other			1	1	1		1				4
Irish		4	5	6	6		2				23
Italian, North			1	2							3
Italian, South		1		2	7	1					11
Lithuanian					1						1
Norwegian			1	1							2
Polish			2		1						3
Scotch		1	4	3	3		1				12
Swedish		1	7	7	2			1			18
Other races *a*		1		1		2	1				5
Total foreign-born		23	70	65	45	8	14	6	2		233
Grand total	1	73	194	117	65	21	17	7	4		499

a "Other races" includes races having less than 10 representatives in this city and pupils whose race is not reported.

TABLE 3.—*Race, sex, and age, by grade—Number of pupils of each age in each grade, by sex and by general nativity and race of father of pupil*—Continued.

THIRD GRADE—Continued.

TOTAL.

General nativity and race of father of pupil.	Number of pupils of each age.										Total.
	6.	7.	8.	9.	10.	11.	12.	13.	14.	15.	
Native-born:											
White....................	2	93	224	122	60	27	11	1	3	......	543
Negro....................	......	1	1	3	2	4	2	......	1	......	14
Total native-born........	2	94	225	125	62	31	13	1	4	......	557
Foreign-born:											
Armenian................	......	......	5	......	......	......	......	......	......	1	6
Canadian, French........	......	2	5	3	3	......	......	1	......	......	14
Canadian, Other.........	......	12	39	27	13	4	6	2	......	......	103
Danish..................	......	......	......	1	......	......	......	......	......	......	1
English.................	......	9	19	13	9	3	......	......	......	......	53
French..................	......	......	......	2	......	......	......	......	......	......	2
German.................	......	......	1	4	1	......	......	......	......	......	6
Greek..................	......	......	......	......	......	1	......	1	......	......	2
Hebrew, German........	......	......	1	1	......	......	......	......	......	......	2
Hebrew, Polish.........	......	......	......	......	2	......	......	1	......	......	3
Hebrew, Roumanian.....	......	......	......	......	1	......	......	......	......	......	1
Hebrew, Russian........	......	7	29	31	10	7	10	3	3	......	100
Hebrew, Other.........	......	......	1	2	2	1	1	......	......	......	7
Irish...................	......	10	17	24	11	......	2	1	......	......	65
Italian, North.........	......	......	2	3	......	......	......	......	......	......	5
Italian, South.........	......	1	2	7	8	4	......	1	......	......	23
Lithuanian.............	......	......	......	1	1	......	1	1	......	......	4
Norwegian.............	......	......	1	1	1	......	......	......	......	......	3
Polish.................	......	......	2	1	1	......	......	......	1	......	5
Scotch................	......	4	8	6	7	1	2	......	......	......	28
Swedish...............	......	1	17	14	4	1	1	1	......	......	39
Other races a.........	......	1	1	1	......	3	2	......	1	......	9
Total foreign-born.......	......	47	150	142	74	25	25	12	5	1	481
Grand total.............	2	141	375	267	136	56	38	13	9	1	1,038

a "Other races" includes races having less than 10 representatives in this city and pupils whose race is not reported.

TABLE **3.**—*Race, sex, and age, by grade—Number of pupils of each age in each grade, by sex and by general nativity and race of father of pupil*—Continued.

FOURTH GRADE.

BOYS.

General nativity and race of father of pupil.	Number of pupils of each age.									Total.
	7.	8.	9.	10.	11.	12.	13.	14.	15.	
Native-born:										
White	3	38	104	68	44	25	5	2	1	290
Negro		1	2	1	2					6
Total native-born	3	39	106	69	46	25	5	2	1	296
Foreign-born:										
Armenian			3		1	1		2		7
Canadian, French		1	2	3	1			2		9
Canadian, Other		4	11	16	11	4	1	1		48
English			9	8	2	2		1		22
French					1					1
German		1	2	3	1	1		1		9
Hebrew, German		1	1	2			1			5
Hebrew, Polish			1	1				1		3
Hebrew, Russian		6	6	8	8	7	4	3		42
Irish	1	3	19	11	7	6	1	1		49
Italian, North			1	2	3	1	1			8
Italian, South			2	2	1	4				9
Lithuanian				1	2	1	1			5
Norwegian		1								1
Polish			2			1			1	4
Scotch		1	2	3	2		3			11
Swedish		1	4	9	1	1				16
Other races a			1				3		1	5
Total foreign-born	1	19	66	69	41	29	15	12	2	254
Grand total	4	58	172	138	87	54	20	14	3	550

a "Other races" includes races having less than 10 representatives in this city and pupils whose race is not reported.

TABLE 3.—*Race, sex, and age, by grade—Number of pupils of each age in each grade, by sex and by general nativity and race of father of pupil*—Continued.

FOURTH GRADE—Continued.

GIRLS.

General nativity and race of father of pupil.	Number of pupils of each age.									Total.
	7.	8.	9.	10.	11.	12.	13.	14.	15.	
Native-born:										
White....................	3	36	71	54	34	17	4	1	1	221
Negro...................			2	2	1	2	1	1		9
Indian..................						1				1
Total native-born........	3	36	73	56	35	20	5	2	1	231
Foreign-born:										
Armenian................							1			1
Canadian, French........			3	3	1	2				9
Canadian, Other.........	1	6	16	16	7	7	1	2		56
Danish..................				2						2
English.................		3	14	5	5					27
French..................		1	1		1					3
German.................			3	1	2	1				7
Hebrew, Polish..........			1	1		1				3
Hebrew, Russian.........		5	8	6	1	3		4	1	28
Irish...................	1	4	15	11	4	1	2			38
Italian, North..........					1					1
Italian, South..........		2	3	3		1				9
Lithuanian..............				1			1			2
Norwegian...............			2							2
Scotch..................		2	1	2	2					7
Swedish.................		3	9	5	4	4				25
Other races *a*.........			1							1
Total foreign-born......	2	26	77	56	28	20	5	6	1	221
Grand total.............	5	62	150	112	63	40	10	8	2	452

a "Other races" includes races having less than 10 representatives in this city and pupils whose race is not reported.

TABLE **3.**—*Race, sex, and age, by grade—Number of pupils of each age in each grade, by sex and by general nativity and race of father of pupil—*Continued.

FOURTH GRADE—Continued.

TOTAL.

General nativity and race of father of pupil.	Number of pupils of each age.									Total.
	7.	8.	9.	10.	11.	12.	13.	14.	15.	
Native-born:										
White	6	74	175	122	78	42	9	3	2	511
Negro		1	4	3	3	2	1	1		15
Indian						1				1
Total native-born	6	75	179	125	81	45	10	4	2	527
Foreign-born:										
Armenian			3		1	1	1	2		8
Canadian, French		1	5	6	2	2		2		18
Canadian, Other	1	10	27	32	18	11	2	3		104
Danish				2						2
English		3	23	13	7	2		1		49
French		1	1		2					4
German		1	5	4	3	2		1		16
Hebrew, German		1	1	2			1			5
Hebrew, Polish			2	2		1		1		6
Hebrew, Russian		11	14	14	9	10	4	7	1	70
Irish	2	7	34	22	11	7	3	1		87
Italian, North			1	2	4	1	1			9
Italian, South		2	5	5	1	5				18
Lithuanian				2	2	1	2			7
Norwegian		1	2							3
Polish			2			1			1	4
Scotch		3	3	5	4		3			18
Swedish		4	13	14	5	5				41
Other races *a*			2				3		1	6
Total foreign-born	3	45	143	125	69	49	20	18	3	475
Grand total	9	120	322	250	150	94	30	22	5	1,002

a "Other races" includes races having less than 10 representatives in this city and pupils whose race is not reported.

TABLE **3.**—*Race, sex, and age, by grade—Number of pupils of each age in each grade, by sex and by general nativity and race of father of pupil*—Continued.

FIFTH GRADE.

BOYS.

General nativity and race of father of pupil.	Number of pupils of each age.												Total.
	5.	6.	7.	8.	9.	10.	11.	12.	13.	14.	15.	16.	
Native-born:													
White					35	85	76	59	31	12	3	....	301
Negro							3	2	1	1	1	....	8
Total native-born					35	85	79	61	32	13	4	....	309
Foreign-born:													
Armenian						1	1	....	....	....	....	....	2
Canadian, French						1	2	3	3	....	1	....	10
Canadian, Other					5	15	18	11	6	2	4	....	61
Danish							1	....	....	....	....	....	1
English					3	4	7	5	4	1	....	....	24
French						1	....	1	....	....	....	....	2
German						4	3	2	....	1	....	....	10
Greek								1	....	....	1	....	2
Hebrew, German							2	....	....	....	....	....	2
Hebrew, Polish						3	1	....	2	....	....	....	6
Hebrew, Russian					2	5	4	10	3	4	1	....	29
Hebrew, Other						1	2	....	1	1	....	....	5
Irish					1	9	15	8	9	1	1	1	45
Italian, North							2	....	1	....	....	....	3
Italian, South							....	4	1	1	....	....	6
Lithuanian							....	....	1	....	....	1
Norwegian							1	....	....	....	....	....	1
Polish										2	....	....	2
Scotch						1	4	....	3	....	....	....	8
Swedish						6	13	7	....	1	....	....	27
Other races *a*							1	....	2	....	....	....	3
Total foreign-born					12	54	73	55	32	15	8	1	250
Grand total					47	139	152	116	64	28	12	1	559

a "Other races" includes races having less than 10 representatives in this city and pupils whose race is not reported.

66083°—VOL 31—12——50

TABLE 3.—*Race, sex, and age, by grade—Number of pupils of each age in each grade, by sex and by general nativity and race of father of pupil*—Continued.

FIFTH GRADE—Continued.

GIRLS.

General nativity and race of father of pupil.	Number of pupils of each age.												Total.
	5.	6.	7.	8.	9.	10.	11.	12.	13.	14.	15.	16.	
Native-born:													
White				1	46	103	83	41	21	5			300
Negro								3	3	1			7
Total native-born				1	46	103	83	44	24	6			307
Foreign-born:													
Armenian							1						1
Canadian, French					2	3	4	3	2	2			16
Canadian, Other					9	18	14	12	7	1			61
Danish						2							2
English					6	9	9	7	1				32
French					1		1						2
German					3	1	1	4	1				10
Hebrew, German					1	2	1						4
Hebrew, Polish						1		1	1				3
Hebrew, Russian					2	9	7	11	1	2			32
Hebrew, Other					1			1	1				3
Irish					6	8	10	9	4				37
Italian, North					1			1					2
Italian, South							3	3	1		1		8
Lithuanian						1	2		2				5
Norwegian							1	1					2
Scotch					1	4	3	3	1	2			14
Swedish					2	7	5	4	1				19
Welsh					1		3		1				5
Other races a					1								1
Total foreign-born					37	65	65	60	24	7	1		259
Grand total				1	83	168	148	104	48	13	1		566

a "Other races" includes races having less than 10 representatives in this city and pupils whose race is not reported.

TABLE 3.—*Race, sex, and age, by grade—Number of pupils of each age in each grade, by sex and by general nativity and race of father of pupil*—Continued.

FIFTH GRADE—Continued.

TOTAL.

General nativity and race of father of pupil.	Number of pupils of each age.												Total.
	5.	6.	7.	8.	9.	10.	11.	12.	13.	14.	15.	16.	
Native-born:													
White			1	81	188	159	100	52	17	3			601
Negro						3	5	4	2	1			15
Total native-born			1	81	188	162	105	56	19	4			616
Foreign-born:													
Armenian					1	2							3
Canadian, French				2	4	6	6	5	2	1			26
Canadian, Other				14	33	32	23	13	3	4			122
Danish					2	1							3
English				9	13	16	12	5	1				56
French				1	1	1	1						4
German				3	5	4	6	1	1				20
Greek							1			1			2
Hebrew, German				1	2	3							6
Hebrew, Polish					4	1	1	3					9
Hebrew, Russian				4	14	11	21	4	6	1			61
Hebrew, Other				1	1	2	1	2	1				8
Irish				7	17	25	17	13	1	1	1		82
Italian, North					1		2	1	1				5
Italian, South						3	7	2	1	1			14
Lithuanian						1	2	2	1				6
Norwegian							2	1					3
Polish										2			2
Scotch				2	8	3	6	1	2				22
Swedish				2	13	18	11	1	1				46
Welsh				1		3		1					5
Other races *a*				1		1				2			4
Total foreign-born				49	119	138	115	56	22	9	1		509
Grand total			1	130	307	300	220	112	41	13	1		1,125

a "Other races" includes races having less than 10 representatives in this city and pupils whose race is not reported.

TABLE **3.**—*Race, sex, and age, by grade—Number of pupils of each age in each grade, by sex and by general nativity and race of father of pupil*—Continued.

SIXTH GRADE.

BOYS.

General nativity and race of father of pupil.	Number of pupils of each age.								Total.
	9.	10.	11.	12.	13.	14.	15.	16.	
Native-born:									
White		39	79	71	51	31	9		280
Negro			1	3	1	2			7
Total native-born		39	80	74	52	33	9		287
Foreign-born:									
Armenian					1				1
Canadian, French		1	1		1	1			4
Canadian, Other	1	4	23	22	14	5	1	1	71
Danish				1	1				2
English		2	6	12	9	4			33
German			2		3	1			6
Hebrew, German			1						1
Hebrew, Russian		1	4	8	4	5		1	23
Hebrew, Other		1							1
Irish		4	8	10	7	3	2	1	35
Italian, North			1		1				2
Italian, South			1	2					3
Lithuanian						1			1
Norwegian			1			1			2
Scotch		1	1	2	2	1			7
Swedish		2	10	8	4	1			25
Other races *a*									
Total foreign-born	1	16	59	65	47	23	3	3	217
Grand total	1	55	139	139	99	56	12	3	504

a "Other races" includes races having less than 10 representatives in this city and pupils whose race is not reported.

TABLE 3.—*Race, sex, and age, by grade—Number of pupils of each age in each grade, by sex and by general nativity and race of father of pupil*—Continued.

SIXTH GRADE—Continued.

GIRLS.

General nativity and race of father of pupil.	Number of pupils of each age.								Total.
	9.	10.	11.	12.	13.	14.	15.	16.	
Native-born:									
White...............................	3	36	90	77	41	16	1	3	267
Negro..............................			1	1	1	1			4
Total native-born..................	3	36	91	78	42	17	1	3	271
Foreign-born:									
Armenian...........................				2		2			4
Canadian, French...................			2	4	4				10
Canadian, Other....................		7	19	21	4	12	2		65
English............................		3	9		13	2			27
French.............................			1						1
German.............................		1			3				4
Hebrew, Polish.....................		1	1	1					3
Hebrew, Russian....................	1	4	7	5	5	1	1		24
Hebrew, Other......................					2				2
Irish..............................		1	9	13	8	1			32
Italian, South.....................		1	1		1				3
Norwegian..........................				1	1				2
Scotch.............................		3	3	1	3				10
Swedish............................		2	10	11	3	3			29
Other races *a*....................			2	3					5
Total foreign-born.................	1	23	64	62	47	21	3		221
Grand total.......................	4	59	155	140	89	38	4	3	492

a "Other races" includes races having less than 10 representatives in this city and pupils whose race is not reported.

TABLE 3.—*Race, sex, and age, by grade—Number of pupils of each age in each grade, by sex and by general nativity and race of father of pupil*—Continued.

SIXTH GRADE—Continued.

TOTAL.

General nativity and race of father of pupil.	Number of pupils of each age.								Total.
	9.	10.	11.	12.	13.	14.	15.	16.	
Native-born:									
White	3	75	169	148	92	47	10	3	547
Negro			2	4	2	3			11
Total native-born	3	75	171	152	94	50	10	3	558
Foreign-born:									
Armenian				2	1	2			5
Canadian, French		1	3	4	5	1			14
Canadian, Other	1	11	42	43	18	17	3	1	136
Danish				1	1				2
English		5	15	12	22	6			60
French			1						1
German		1	2		6	1			10
Hebrew, German			1						1
Hebrew, Polish		1	1	1					3
Hebrew, Russian	1	5	11	13	9	6	1	1	47
Hebrew, Other		1			2				3
Irish		5	17	23	15	4	2	1	67
Italian, North			1		1				2
Italian, South		1	2	2	1				6
Lithuanian						1			1
Norwegian			1	1	1	1			4
Scotch		4	4	3	5	1			17
Swedish		4	20	19	7	4			54
Other races *a*			2	3					5
Total foreign-born	2	39	123	127	94	44	6	3	438
Grand total	5	114	294	279	188	94	16	6	996

a "Other races" includes races having less than 10 representatives in this city and pupils whose race is not reported.

TABLE **3.**—*Race, sex, and age, by grade—Number of pupils of each age in each grade, by sex and by general nativity and race of father of pupil*—Continued.

SEVENTH GRADE.

BOYS.

General nativity and race of father of pupil.	Number of pupils of each age.										Total.
	10.	11.	12.	13.	14.	15.	16.	17.	18.	19.	
Native-born:											
White	1	25	73	65	54	19	2			1	240
Negro		1									1
Total native-born	1	26	73	65	54	19	2			1	241
Foreign-born:											
Armenian					1			1			2
Canadian, French	1	1	3	1	1	1					8
Canadian, Other		3	13	14	13	3					46
Danish		1									1
English		2	5	6	4			1			18
French			1								1
German			3	2							5
Hebrew, German		1	2	2							5
Hebrew, Polish			1		1						2
Hebrew, Russian		2	4	2	4	1			1		14
Irish		4	11	15	5	1	1				37
Italian, North			1	2		1					4
Italian, South							1				1
Scotch				2	1						3
Swedish		3	5	4	3						15
Other races a			1		1						2
Total foreign-born	1	17	49	51	33	8	3	1	1		164
Grand total	2	43	122	116	87	27	5	1	1	1	405

a "Other races" includes races having less than 10 representatives in this city and pupils whose race is not reported.

TABLE **3.**—*Race, sex, and age, by grade—Number of pupils of each age in each grade, by sex and by general nativity and race of father of pupil*—Continued.

SEVENTH GRADE—Continued.

GIRLS.

General nativity and race of father of pupil.	Number of pupils of each age.										Total.
	10.	11.	12.	13.	14.	15.	16.	17.	18.	19.	
Native-born:											
White...............	1	34	86	61	33	7	2	1			225
Negro...............						1					1
Total native-born.......	1	34	86	61	33	8	2	1			226
Foreign-born:											
Armenian...............			1								1
Canadian, French...........		1	2	4	1	1					9
Canadian, Other...........		4	11	19	14		1				49
nglish...............	1	4	8	4	3						20
French...............					1						1
German...............		1	1	2	1						5
Hebrew, German...........		1	1								2
Hebrew, Polish...........		1		3							4
Hebrew, Russian...........	1	1	7	5		2					16
Hebrew, Other...............			1								1
Irish...............		2	11	12	5						30
Italian, North...............			2		1						3
Italian, South...............				1			1				2
Norwegian...............				1							1
Polish...............		1									1
Scotch...............			3	2	2	1					8
Swedish...............		2	6	7	3	1					19
Total foreign-born........	2	18	54	60	31	5	2				172
Grand total...............	3	52	140	121	64	13	4	1			398

a " Other races " includes races having less than 10 representatives in this city and pupils whose race is not reported.

TABLE 3.—*Race, sex, and age, by grade—Number of pupils of each age in each grade, by sex and by general nativity and race of father of pupil*—Continued.

SEVENTH GRADE—Continued.

TOTAL.

General nativity and race of father of pupil.	Number of pupils of each age.										Total.
	10.	11.	12.	13.	14.	15.	16.	17.	18.	19.	
Native-born:											
White	2	59	159	126	87	26	4	1	......	1	465
Negro	......	1	......	......	......	1	......	......	......	......	2
Total native-born	2	60	159	126	87	27	4	1	......	1	467
Foreign-born:											
Armenian	......	......	1	......	1	......	......	1	......	......	3
Canadian, French	1	2	5	5	2	2	......	......	......	......	17
Canadian, Other	......	7	24	33	27	3	1	......	......	......	95
Danish	......	1	......	......	......	......	......	......	......	......	1
English	1	6	13	10	7	......	1	......	......	......	38
French	......	......	1	......	1	......	......	......	......	......	2
German	......	1	4	4	1	......	......	......	......	......	10
Hebrew, German	......	2	3	2	......	......	......	......	......	......	7
Hebrew, Polish	......	1	......	4	......	1	......	......	......	......	6
Hebrew, Russian	1	3	11	7	4	3	......	......	1	......	30
Hebrew, Other	......	......	1	......	......	......	......	......	......	......	1
Irish	......	6	22	27	10	1	1	......	......	......	67
Italian, North	......	......	3	2	1	1	......	......	......	......	7
Italian, South	......	......	......	1	......	......	2	......	......	......	3
Norwegian	......	......	......	1	......	......	......	......	......	......	1
Polish	......	1	......	......	......	......	......	......	......	......	1
Scotch	......	......	3	4	3	1	......	......	......	......	11
Swedish	......	5	11	11	6	1	......	......	......	......	34
Other races *a*	......	......	1	......	1	......	......	......	......	......	2
Total foreign-born	3	35	103	111	64	13	5	1	1	......	336
Grand total	5	95	262	237	151	40	9	2	1	1	803

a "Other races" includes races having less than 10 representatives in this city and pupils whose race is not reported.

TABLE 3.—*Race, sex, and age, by grade—Number of pupils of each age in each grade, by sex and by general nativity and race of father of pupil*—Continued.

EIGHTH GRADE.

BOYS.

General nativity and race of father of pupil.	Number of pupils of each age.							Total.
	11.	12.	13.	14.	15.	16.	18.	
Native-born:								
White	3	25	56	58	34	8	1	185
Negro				1		1		2
Total native-born	3	25	56	59	34	9	1	187
Foreign-born:								
Armenian				1		2		3
Canadian, French		2		7	1	1		11
Canadian, Other		4	9	10	8	3		34
English		2	9	7	1			19
French				1				1
German				3	1			4
Hebrew, German			1	1				2
Hebrew, Polish			1					1
Hebrew, Russian		1	3	1	1	2		8
Irish	1	4	8	5	6	2		26
Scotch						1		1
Swedish		4	8	1	1			14
Total foreign-born	1	17	39	37	19	11		124
Grand total	4	42	95	96	53	20	1	311

GIRLS.

General nativity and race of father of pupil.	Number of pupils of each age.							Total.
	11.	12.	13.	14.	15.	16.	18.	
Native-born:								
White	1	45	76	54	31	12	1	220
Negro					2			2
Total native-born	1	45	76	54	33	12	1	222
Foreign-born:								
Armenian			1					1
Canadian, French		1	3	3	3			10
Canadian, Other		9	12	7	7	1		36
English		6	3	4	3			16
French			1					1
German				2				2
Hebrew, German			3		1			4
Hebrew, Russian			1	3				4
Irish		3	3	13	4			23
Italian, North				1				1
Italian, South				1				1
Norwegian			1			1		2
Scotch			5	2	2			9
Swedish		1	2	1	2			6
Welsh			3	2				5
Total foreign-born		20	38	39	22	2		121
Grand total	1	65	114	93	55	14	1	343

TABLE 3.—*Race, sex, and age, by grade—Number of pupils of each age in each grade, by sex and by general nativity and race of father of pupil*—Continued.

EIGHTH GRADE—Continued.

TOTAL.

General nativity and race of father of pupil.	Number of pupils of each age.							Total.
	11.	12.	13.	14.	15.	16.	18.	
Native-born:								
White	4	70	132	112	65	20	2	405
Negro				1	2	1		4
Total native-born	4	70	132	113	67	21	2	409
Foreign-born:								
Armenian			1	1		2		4
Canadian, French		3	3	10	4	1		21
Canadian, Other		13	21	17	15	4		70
English		8	12	11	4			35
French			1	1				2
German				5	1			6
Hebrew, German			4	1	1			6
Hebrew, Polish			1					1
Hebrew, Russian		1	4	4	1	2		12
Irish	1	7	11	18	10	2		49
Italian, North				1				1
Italian, South				1				1
Norwegian			1			1		2
Scotch			5	2	2	1		10
Swedish		5	10	2	3			20
Welsh			3	2				5
Other races [a]								
Total foreign-born	1	37	77	76	41	13		245
Grand total	5	107	209	189	108	34	2	654

[a] "Other races" includes races having less than 10 representatives in this city and pupils whose race is not reported.

NINTH GRADE.

BOYS.

General nativity and race of father of pupil.	Number of pupils of each age.							Total.
	12.	13.	14.	15.	16.	17.	18.	
Native-born:								
White	4	32	45	35	17	5	1	139
Negro								
Total native-born	4	32	45	35	17	5	1	139
Foreign-born:								
Armenian					1	1		2
Canadian, French			3	2				5
Canadian, Other		5	10	10	5	1	1	32
English		3	4	3				10
German		1	1	1				3
Hebrew, Polish					1			1
Hebrew, Russian		3	2	1				6
Irish		4	6	6	3	2		21
Italian, North		1						1
Scotch	1				1	1		3
Swedish		3	6	2	1			12
Other races [a]			2					2
Total foreign-born	1	20	34	25	12	5	1	98
Grand total	5	52	79	60	29	10	2	237

[a] "Other races" includes races having less than 10 representatives in this city and pupils whose race is not reported.

TABLE 3.—*Race, sex, and age, by grade—Number of pupils of each age in each grade, by sex and by general nativity and race of father of pupil*—Continued.

NINTH GRADE—Continued.

GIRLS.

General nativity and race of father of pupil.	Number of pupils of each age.							Total.
	12.	13.	14.	15.	16.	17.	18.	
Native-born:								
White		40	69	39	24	5	3	180
Negro				1	1			2
Total native-born		40	69	40	25	5	3	182
Foreign-born:								
Canadian, French		1	2	2	1			6
Canadian, Other	1	3	16	13	8	1		42
English	1	3	5	9		2		20
French					1			1
German		2		2				4
Hebrew, Polish		1	1					2
Hebrew, Russian			1			1		2
Irish			5	6	1			12
Scotch		2	1	2				5
Swedish				2	2			4
Welsh				1				1
Total foreign-born	2	12	31	37	13	4		99
Grand total	2	52	100	77	38	9	3	281

TOTAL.

General nativity and race of father of pupil.	12.	13.	14.	15.	16.	17.	18.	Total.
Native-born:								
White	4	72	114	74	41	10	4	319
Negro				1	1			2
Total native-born	4	72	114	75	42	10	4	321
Foreign-born:								
Armenian					1	1		2
Canadian, French		1	5	4	1			11
Canadian, Other	1	8	26	23	13	2	1	74
English	1	6	9	12		2		30
French					1			1
German		3	1	3				7
Hebrew, Polish		1	1		1			3
Hebrew, Russian		3	3	1		1		8
Irish		4	11	12	4	2		33
Italian, North		1						1
Scotch	1	2	1	2	1	1		8
Swedish		3	6	4	3			16
Welsh				1				1
Other races a			2					2
Total foreign-born	3	32	65	62	25	9	1	197
Grand total	7	104	179	137	67	19	5	518

a "Other races" includes races having less than 10 representatives in this city and pupils whose race is not reported.

TABLE **3.**—*Race, sex, and age, by grade—Number of pupils of each age in each grade, by sex and by general nativity and race of father of pupil*—Continued.

FIRST YEAR HIGH SCHOOL.

BOYS.

General nativity and race of father of pupil.	Number of pupils of each age.							Total.
	13.	14.	15.	16.	17.	18.	19.	
Native-born, White	6	24	35	25	17			107
Foreign-born:								
Armenian					2			2
Canadian, French		1	1	2				4
Canadian, Other		4	7	2	3		1	17
English		1	5	4		1		11
French					1			1
German			2					2
Hebrew, Russian			3		1	1		5
Hebrew, Other			2					2
Irish	1	4	4	1	1			11
Italian, North					1			1
Scotch		1	2					3
Swedish			2	1				3
Total	1	11	28	10	9	2	1	62
Grand total	7	35	63	35	26	2	1	169

GIRLS.

General nativity and race of father of pupil.	13.	14.	15.	16.	17.	18.	19.	Total.
Native-born, White	3	34	45	35	5	1		123
Foreign-born:								
Armenian			1					1
Canadian, French			1	1				2
Canadian, Other		4	7	5	3			19
Danish					1			1
English		1	7	5	2			15
Hebrew, German			1					1
Irish		2	10	2				14
Italian, North			1					1
Scotch		1	2	1				4
Swedish		1		2				3
Other races *a*				1				1
Total		9	30	17	6			62
Grand total	3	43	75	52	11	1		185

a "Other races" includes races having less than 10 representatives in this city and pupils whose race is not reported.

TABLE 3.—*Race, sex, and age, by grade—Number of pupils of each age in each grade, by sex and by general nativity and race of father of pupil—Continued.*

FIRST YEAR HIGH SCHOOL.—Continued.

TOTAL.

General nativity and race of father of pupil.	Number of pupils of each age.							Total.
	13.	14.	15.	16.	17.	18.	19.	
Native-born, White	9	58	80	60	22	1		230
Foreign-born:								
Armenian			1		2			3
Canadian, French		1	2	3				6
Canadian, Other		8	14	7	6		1	36
Danish					1			1
English		2	12	9	2	1		26
French					1			1
German			2					2
Hebrew, German			1					1
Hebrew, Russian			3		1	1		5
Hebrew, Other			2					2
Irish	1	6	14	3	1			25
Italian, North			1		1			2
Scotch		2	4	1				7
Swedish		1	2	3				6
Other races *a*				1				1
Total	1	20	58	27	15	2	1	124
Grand total	10	78	138	87	37	3	1	354

a "Other races" includes races having less than 10 representatives in this city and pupils whose race is not reported.

SECOND YEAR HIGH SCHOOL.

BOYS.

General nativity and race of father of pupil.	Number of pupils of each age.							Total.
	14.	15.	16.	17.	18.	19.	20.	
Native-born:								
White	1	23	38	26	4	1	1	94
Negro					1			1
Total native-born	1	23	38	26	5	1	1	95
Foreign-born:								
Canadian, French			1					1
Canadian, Other		3	6	1	1	1	1	13
English			2	1				3
Hebrew, German				1				1
Hebrew, Other			1					1
Irish		2	3	1				6
Italian, North			1					1
Norwegian		1						1
Scotch			1					1
Swedish		1	2	1				4
Welsh		1						1
Total foreign-born		8	17	5	1	1	1	33
Grand total	1	31	55	31	6	2	2	128

TABLE 3.—*Race, sex, and age, by grade—Number of pupils of each age in each grade, by sex and by general nativity and race of father of pupil—Continued.*

SECOND YEAR HIGH SCHOOL—Continued.

GIRLS.

General nativity and race of father of pupil.	Number of pupils of each age.							Total.
	14.	15.	16.	17.	18.	19.	20.	
Native-born, White..............	5	27	53	19	7	....	....	111
Foreign-born:								
Canadian, French............	....	......	......	1	......	....	....	1
Canadian, Other.............	1	6	6	......	2	....	....	15
English.....................	......	3	5	1	1	....	....	10
French......................	......	......	......	1	......	....	....	1
German.....................	......	......	1	......	......	....	....	1
Irish.......................	......	2	7	1	1	....	....	11
Scotch.....................	......	......	1	......	......	....	....	1
Swedish....................	......	1	......	......	......	....	....	1
Welsh......................	......	1	......	......	......	....	....	1
Other races *a*.............	......	......	1	......	......	....	....	1
Total foreign-born...........	1	13	21	4	4	....	....	43
Grand total..................	6	40	74	23	11	....	....	154

TOTAL.

General nativity and race of father of pupil.	Number of pupils of each age.							Total.
	14.	15.	16.	17.	18.	19.	20.	
Native-born:								
White.......................	6	50	91	45	11	1	1	205
Negro......................	......	......	......	......	1	......	......	1
Total native-born.............	6	50	91	45	12	....	....	206
Foreign-born:								
Canadian, French............	......	......	1	1	......	......	......	2
Canadian, Other.............	1	9	12	1	3	1	1	28
English.....................	......	3	7	2	1	......	......	13
French......................	......	......	......	1	......	......	......	1
German.....................	......	......	1	......	......	......	......	1
Hebrew, German.............	......	......	......	1	......	......	......	1
Hebrew, Other..............	......	......	1	......	......	......	......	1
Irish.......................	......	4	10	2	1	......	......	17
Italian, North..............	......	......	1	......	......	......	......	1
Norwegian..................	......	1	......	......	......	......	......	1
Scotch.....................	......	......	2	......	......	......	......	2
Swedish....................	......	2	2	1	......	......	......	5
Welsh......................	......	2	......	......	......	......	......	2
Other races *a*.............	......	......	1	......	......	......	......	1
Total foreign-born...........	1	21	38	9	5	1	1	76
Grand total..................	7	71	129	54	17	2	2	282

a "Other races" includes races having less than 10 representatives in this city and pupils whose race is not reported.

TABLE 3.—*Race, sex, and age, by grade—Number of pupils of each age in each grade, by sex and by general nativity and race of father of pupil*—Continued.

THIRD YEAR HIGH SCHOOL.

BOYS.

General nativity and race of father of pupil.	Number of pupils of each age.					Total.
	15.	16.	17.	18.	19.	
Native-born, White....................	3	9	28	7	3	50
Foreign-born:						
Armenian......................				2	....	2
Canadian, French..................	1	1	2	....	....	4
Canadian, Other..................		2	3	....	....	5
English......................		1	2	....	....	3
Hebrew, Polish..................		1		....	....	1
Irish........................	1		5	....	....	6
Scotch.......................			2	1	....	3
Total foreign-born...........	2	5	14	3	....	24
Grand total..................	5	14	42	10	3	74

GIRLS.

General nativity and race of father of pupil.	15.	16.	17.	18.	19.	Total.
Native-born:						
White........................	2	26	37	15	4	84
Negro........................			1			1
Total native-born...........	2	26	38	15	4	85
Foreign-born:						
Canadian, French..................			3			3
Canadian, Other..................		1	6	2	....	9
English......................		1		2	....	3
German......................			1			1
Hebrew, Russian.................		1				1
Irish........................	1	1	4	2	1	9
Scotch.......................		1	2	....	1	4
Swedish......................			1			1
Other races a..................			1			1
Total foreign-born...........	1	5	18	6	2	32
Grand total..................	3	31	56	21	6	117

TOTAL.

General nativity and race of father of pupil.	15.	16.	17.	18.	19.	Total.
Native-born:						
White........................	5	35	65	22	7	134
Negro........................			1			1
Total native-born...........	5	35	66	22	7	135
Foreign-born:						
Armenian......................				2	....	2
Canadian, French..................	1	1	5	....	....	7
Canadian, Other..................		3	9	2	....	14
English......................		2	2	2	....	6
German......................			1			1
Hebrew, Polish..................		1				1
Hebrew, Russian.................		1				1
Irish........................	2	1	9	2	1	15
Scotch.......................		1	4	1	1	7
Swedish......................			1			1
Other races a..................			1			1
Total foreign-born...........	3	10	32	9	2	56
Grand total..................	8	45	98	31	9	191

a "Other races" includes races having less than 10 representatives in this city and pupils whose race is not reported.

TABLE 3.—*Race, sex, and age, by grade—Number of pupils of each age in each grade, by sex and by general nativity and race of father of pupil*—Continued.

FOURTH YEAR HIGH SCHOOL.

BOYS.

General nativity and race of father of pupil.	Number of pupils of each age.					Total.
	16.	17.	18.	19.	20 or over.	
Native-born, White................................	3	13	20	13	3	52
Foreign-born:						
Canadian (other than French).....................	1	2	5	....	....	8
Hebrew, Russian.................................	1	....	....	1	....	2
English...	....	....	1	1	....	2
Irish...	....	....	1	1	....	2
Swedish...	....	....	2	....	1	3
Total...	2	2	9	3	1	17
Grand total...................................	5	15	29	16	4	69

GIRLS.

	16.	17.	18.	19.	20 or over.	Total.
Native-born, White................................	1	19	44	18	5	87
Foreign-born:						
Canadian (other than French).....................	....	1	2	1	1	5
Danish...	....	1	....	....	....	1
English...	....	1	....	1	....	2
Irish...	....	1	....	....	....	1
Other races *a*.................................	....	....	....	1	....	1
Total...	....	4	2	3	1	10
Grand total...................................	1	23	46	21	6	97

TOTAL.

	16.	17.	18.	19.	20 or over.	Total.
Native-born, White................................	4	32	64	31	8	139
Foreign-born:						
Canadian (other than French).....................	1	3	7	1	1	13
Danish...	....	1	....	....	....	1
Hebrew, Russian.................................	1	....	....	1	....	2
English...	....	1	1	2	....	4
Irish...	....	1	1	1	....	3
Swedish...	....	....	2	....	1	3
Other races *a*.................................	....	....	....	1	....	1
Total...	2	6	11	6	2	27
Grand total...................................	6	38	75	37	10	166

a "Other races" includes races having less than 10 representatives in this city and pupils whose race is not reported.

TABLE 3.—*Race, sex, and age, by grade—Number of pupils of each age in each grade, by sex and by general nativity and race of father of pupil*—Continued.

SPECIAL SCHOOL.

BOYS.

General nativity and race of father of pupil.	Number of pupils of each age.								Total.
	11.	12.	13.	14.	15.	16.	17.	18.	
Foreign-born:									
Armenian...		1					1	1	3
Hebrew, Russian...			4	2	1				7
Italian, South...				1					1
Polish...						1			1
Greek...				1	1				2
Total...		1	4	4	2	1	1	1	14

GIRLS.

General nativity and race of father of pupil.	11.	12.	13.	14.	15.	16.	17.	18.	Total.
Foreign-born:									
Hebrew, Russian...	2		3	1	4	2			12
Italian, South...				1					1
Total...	2		3	2	4	2			13

TOTAL.

General nativity and race of father of pupil.	11.	12.	13.	14.	15.	16.	17.	18.	Total.
Foreign-born:									
Armenian...		1					1	1	3
Hebrew, Russian...	2		7	3	5	2			19
Italian, South...				2					2
Polish...						1			1
Greek...				1	1				2
Total...	2	1	7	6	6	3	1	1	27

UNGRADED SCHOOL.

BOYS.

General nativity and race of father of pupil.	Number of pupils of each age.						Total.
	6.	7.	8.	9.	10.	11.	
Native-born, White...			1		1		2
Foreign-born:							
Hebrew, Russian...		4	4	6	1		15
Italian, South...	1		1	2	2		6
Scotch...	1						1
Other races a...				1			1
Total...	2	4	5	9	3		23
Grand total...	2	4	6	9	4		25

a "Other races" includes races having less than 10 representatives in this city and pupils whose race is not reported.

TABLE 3.—*Race, sex, and age, by grade—Number of pupils of each age in each grade, by sex and by general nativity and race of father of pupil*—Continued.

UNGRADED SCHOOL—Continued.

GIRLS.

General nativity and race of father of pupil.	Number of pupils of each age.						Total.
	6.	7.	8.	9.	10.	11.	
Native-born, White		1					1
Foreign-born:							
Greek		1	1				2
Hebrew, Russian	1	1		2	3	2	9
Irish			1				1
Italian, South	1				4		5
Total	2	2	2	2	7	2	17
Grand total	2	3	2	2	7	2	18

TOTAL.

General nativity and race of father of pupil.	Number of pupils of each age.						Total.
	6.	7.	8.	9.	10.	11.	
Native-born, White		1	1		1		3
Foreign-born:							
Greek		1	1				2
Hebrew, Russian	1	5	4	8	4	2	24
Irish			1				1
Italian, South	2		1	2	6		11
Scotch	1						1
Other races a				1			1
Total	4	6	7	11	10	2	40
Grand total	4	7	8	11	11	2	43

a "Other races" includes races having less than 10 representatives in this city and pupils whose race is not reported.

TABLE 4.—*Race and grade, by age—Number of pupils of each specified age in each grade, by general nativity and race of father of pupil.*

BOYS: AGE 5 YEARS.

General nativity and race of father of pupil.	Elementary grades.		Total.
	1.	2.	
Native-born:			
White	115		115
Negro	1		1
Total native-born	116		116
Foreign-born:			
Canadian (other than French)	13		13
Hebrew, Russian	25		25
Irish	11		11
Other races a	43	1	44
Total foreign-born	92	1	93
Grand total	208	1	209

a "Other races" includes races having less than 10 representatives of this sex and age and pupils whose race is not reported.

TABLE 4.—*Race and grade, by age—Number of pupils of each specified age in each grade, by general nativity and race of father of pupil*—Continued.

BOYS: AGE 6 YEARS.

General nativity and race of father of pupil.	Elementary grades.			Un-graded school.	Total.
	1.	2.	3.		
Native-born:					
White..	134	58	1	....	193
Negro...	7	1	....	....	8
Total native-born.............................	141	59	1	....	201
Foreign-born:					
Canadian (other than French).....................	34	6	....	....	40
English..	22	2	....	....	24
Hebrew, Russian...................................	39	2	....	....	41
Irish..	28	3	....	....	31
Swedish...	9	2	....	....	11
Other races *a*....................................	37	9	....	2	48
Total foreign-born.............................	169	24	....	2	195
Grand total....................................	310	83	1	2	396

a "Other races" includes races having less than 10 representatives of this sex and age and pupils whose race is not reported.

BOYS: AGE 7 YEARS.

General nativity and race of father of pupil.	Elementary grades.				Ungraded school.	Total.
	1.	2.	3.	4.		
Native-born:						
White..	60	114	44	3	....	221
Negro...	3	....	....	....	....	3
Total native-born.............................	63	114	44	3	....	224
Foreign-born:						
Canadian (other than French)..........	13	23	8	....	....	44
English..	7	15	4	....	....	26
Hebrew, Russian......................	14	12	2	....	4	32
Irish..	9	11	6	1	....	27
Swedish...	7	10	....	....	....	17
Other races *a*....................................	35	22	4	....	....	61
Total foreign-born.............................	85	93	24	1	4	207
Grand total....................................	148	207	68	4	4	431

a "Other races" includes races having less than 10 representatives of this sex and age and pupils whose race is not reported.

TABLE 4.—*Race and grade, by age—Number of pupils of each specified age in each grade, by general nativity and race of father of pupil*—Continued.

BOYS: AGE 8 YEARS.

General nativity and race of father of pupil.	Elementary grades.				Un-graded school.	Total.
	1.	2.	3.	4.		
Native-born:						
White...	11	68	101	38	1	219
Negro...	2	2	....	1	....	5
Total native-born........................	13	70	101	39	1	224
Foreign-born:						
Canadian (other than French)............	3	12	19	4	....	38
English......................................	1	9	11	....	....	21
Hebrew, Russian............................	1	11	16	6	4	38
Irish...	2	9	12	3	....	26
Swedish......................................	....	6	10	1	....	17
Other races a................................	11	18	12	5	1	47
Total foreign-born........................	18	65	80	19	5	187
Grand total................................	31	135	181	58	6	411

a "Other races" includes races having less than 10 representatives of this sex and age and pupils whose race is not reported.

BOYS: AGE 9 YEARS.

General nativity and race of father of pupil.	Elementary grades.						Un-graded school.	Total.
	1.	2.	3.	4.	5.	6.		
Native-born:								
White.........................	3	28	71	104	35	....	....	241
Negro.........................	1	1	2	2	....	....	....	6
Total native-born........	4	29	73	106	35	....	....	247
Foreign-born:								
Canadian (other than French)...	1	8	12	11	5	1	....	38
English........................	....	1	5	9	3	....	....	18
Hebrew, Russian..............	....	13	19	6	2	....	6	46
Irish..........................	....	5	18	19	1	....	....	43
Italian, South................	....	2	5	2	....	....	2	11
Swedish.......................	....	6	7	4	....	....	....	17
Other races a.................	1	7	11	15	1	....	1	36
Total foreign-born........	2	42	77	66	12	1	9	209
Grand total................	6	71	150	172	47	1	9	456

a "Other races" includes races having less than 10 representatives of this sex and age and pupils whose race is not reported.

TABLE 4.—*Race and grade, by age—Number of pupils of each specified age in each grade, by general nativity and race of father of pupil*—Continued.

BOYS: AGE 10 YEARS.

General nativity and race of father of pupil.	Elementary grades.								Total.
	1.	2.	3.	4.	5.	6.	7.	8.	
Native-born:									
White.........................	2	6	40	68	85	39	1	1	242
Negro.........................	2	1	2	1					6
Total native-born.........	4	7	42	69	85	39	1	1	248
Foreign-born:									
Canadian (other than French).........			4	15	15	4			38
English.........................		2	4	8	4	2			20
Hebrew, Russian.................		1	3	8	5	1		1	19
Hebrew, Other.................		1	3	3	4	1			12
Irish.........................		3	5	11	9	4			32
Scotch.........................		1	4	3	4	1			13
Swedish.........................	1	1	2	9	6	2			21
Other races *a*.................		4	4	12	7	1	1	2	31
Total foreign-born.........	1	13	29	69	54	16	1	3	186
Grand total.................	5	20	71	138	139	55	2	4	434

a "Other races" includes races having less than 10 representatives of this sex and age and pupils whose race is not reported.

BOYS: AGE 11 YEARS.

General nativity and race of father of pupil.	Elementary grades.							Total.
	2.	3.	4.	5.	6.	7.	8.	
Native-born:								
White.........................	4	17	44	76	79	25	3	248
Negro.........................		1	2	3	1	1		8
Total native-born.........	4	18	46	79	80	26	3	256
Foreign-born:								
Canadian (other than French)....		2	11	18	23	3		57
English.........................	1	1	2	7	6	2		19
Hebrew, Russian.................	2	6	8	4	4	2		26
Irish.........................			7	15	8	4	1	35
Swedish.........................		1	1	13	10	3		28
Other races *a*.................	6	7	12	16	8	3		52
Total foreign-born.........	9	17	41	73	59	17	1	217
Grand total.................	13	35	87	152	159	43	4	473

a "Other races" includes races having less than 10 representatives of this sex and age and pupils whose race is not reported.

TABLE 4.—*Race and grade, by age—Number of pupils of each specified age in each grade, by general nativity and race of father of pupil—Continued.*

BOYS: AGE 12 YEARS.

General nativity and race of father of pupil.	Elementary grades.								Special school.	Total.
	2.	3.	4.	5.	6.	7.	8.	9.		
Native-born:										
White	3	9	25	59	71	73	25	4		269
Negro		1		2	3					6
Total native-born	3	10	25	61	74	73	25	4		275
Foreign-born:										
Canadian (other than French)		2	4	11	22	13	4			56
English			2	5	12	5	2			26
Hebrew, Russian	4	5	7	10	8	4	1			39
Irish	1		6	8	10	11	4			40
Italian, South	1		4	4	2					11
Swedish		1	1	7	8	5	4			26
Other races a	2	3	5	10	3	11	2	1	1	38
Total foreign-born	8	11	29	55	65	49	17	1	1	236
Grand total	11	21	54	116	139	122	42	5	1	511

a "Other races" includes races having less than 10 representatives of this sex and age and pupils whose race is not reported.

BOYS: AGE 13 YEARS.

General nativity and race of father of pupil.	Elementary grades.								High school, first year.	Special school.	Total.
	2.	3.	4.	5.	6.	7.	8.	9.			
Native-born:											
White			5	31	51	65	56	32	6		246
Negro				1	1						2
Total native-born			5	32	52	65	56	32	6		248
Foreign-born:											
Canadian (other than French)		2	1	6	13	14	8	5			49
English				4	9	6	9	3			31
Hebrew, Russian			4	3	4	2	3	3		4	23
Hebrew, Other	1		1	3		3	2				10
Irish		1	1	9	7	15	8	4	1		46
Swedish					4	4	8	3			19
Other races a		3	8	7	10	7	1	2			38
Total foreign-born	1	6	15	32	47	51	39	20	1	4	216
Grand total	1	6	20	64	99	116	95	52	7	4	464

a "Other races" includes races having less than 10 representatives of this sex and age and pupils whose race is not reported.

TABLE **4.**—*Race and grade, by age—Number of pupils of each specified age in each grade, by general nativity and race of father of pupil*—Continued.

BOYS: AGE 14 YEARS.

General nativity and race of father of pupil.	Elementary grades.							High school.		Special school.	Total.
	3.	4.	5.	6.	7.	8.	9.	First year.	Second year.		
Native-born:											
White	2	2	12	31	54	58	45	24	1	....	229
Negro	....	....	1	2	....	1	....	....	....	....	4
Total native-born	2	2	13	33	54	59	45	24	1	....	233
Foreign-born:											
Canadian, French	....	2	....	1	1	7	3	1	......	....	15
Canadian, Other	....	1	2	5	13	10	10	4	......	....	45
English	....	1	1	4	4	7	4	1	......	....	22
Hebrew, Russian	1	3	4	5	4	1	2	......	......	2	22
Irish	....	1	1	3	5	5	6	4	......	....	25
Swedish	....	....	1	1	3	1	6	......	......	....	12
Other races a	2	4	6	4	3	6	3	1	......	2	31
Total foreign-born	3	12	15	23	33	37	34	11	......	4	172
Grand total	5	14	28	56	87	96	79	35	1	4	405

a "Other races" includes races having less than 10 representatives of this sex and age and pupils whose race is not reported.

BOYS: AGE 15 YEARS.

General nativity and race of father of pupil.	Elementary grades.							High school.			Special school.	Total.
	3.	4.	5.	6.	7.	8.	9.	First year.	Second year.	Third year.		
Native-born:												
White	....	1	3	9	19	34	35	35	23	3	....	162
Negro	....	....	1	....	....	....	....	....	....	....	....	1
Total native-born	....	1	4	9	19	34	35	35	23	3	....	163
Foreign-born:												
Canadian (other than French)	....	....	4	1	3	8	10	7	3	......	....	36
Hebrew, Other	....	....	1	....	2	1	1	5	......	......	1	11
Irish	....	....	1	2	1	6	6	4	2	1	....	23
Other races a	1	2	2	....	2	4	8	12	3	1	1	36
Total foreign-born	1	2	8	3	8	19	25	28	8	2	2	106
Grand total	1	3	12	12	27	53	60	63	31	5	2	269

a "Other races" includes races having less than 10 representatives of this sex and age and pupils whose race is not reported.

TABLE **4.**—*Race and grade, by age—Number of puipls of each specified age in each grade, by general nativity and race of father of pupil*—Continued.

BOYS: AGE 16 YEARS.

General nativity and race of father of pupil.	Elementary grades.					High school.				Special school.	Total.
	5.	6.	7.	8.	9.	First year.	Second year.	Third year.	Fourth year.		
Native-born:											
White			2	8	17	25	38	9	3		102
Negro				1							1
Total native-born			2	9	17	25	38	9	3		103
Foreign-born:											
Canadian (other than French)		1		3	5	2	6	2	1		20
Irish	1	1	1	2	3	1	3				12
Other races *a*		1	2	6	4	7	8	3	1	1	33
Total foreign-born	1	3	3	11	12	10	17	5	2	1	65
Grand total	1	3	5	20	29	35	55	14	5	1	168

a "Other races" includes races having less than 10 representatives of this sex and age and pupils whose race is not reported.

BOYS: AGE 17 YEARS.

General nativity and race of father of pupil.	Elementary grades.			High school.				Special school.	Total.
	7.	8.	9.	First year.	Second year.	Third year.	Fourth year.		
Native-born, White			5	17	26	28	13		89
Foreign-born:									
Canadian (other than French)			1	3	1	3	2		10
Other races *a*	1		4	6	4	11		1	27
Total	1		5	9	5	14	2	1	37
Grand total	1		10	26	31	42	15	1	126

BOYS: AGE 18 YEARS.

Native-born:									
White		1	1		4	7	20		33
Negro					1				1
Total native-born		1	1		5	7	20		34
Foreign-born, other races *a*	1		1	2	1	3	9	1	18
Grand total	1	1	2	2	6	10	29	1	52

a "Other races" includes races having less than 10 representatives of this sex and age and pupils whose race is not reported.

TABLE 4.—*Race and grade, by age—Number of pupils of each specified age in each grade, by general nativity and race of father of pupil*—Continued.

BOYS: AGE 19 YEARS.

General nativity and race of father of pupil.	Elementary grades.			High school.				Total.
	7.	8.	9.	First year.	Second year.	Third year.	Fourth year.	
Native-born, White	1	....	....	....	1	3	13	18
Foreign-born, other races *a*	....	....	....	1	1	....	3	5
Total	1	....	....	1	2	3	16	23

a "Other races" includes races having less than 10 representatives of this sex and age and pupils whose race is not reported.

BOYS: AGE 20 YEARS.

General nativity and race of father of pupil.	High school.			Total.
	Second year.	Third year.	Fourth year.	
Native-born, White	1	....	3	4
Foreign-born, other races *a*	1	....	1	2
Total	2	....	4	6

a "Other races" includes races having less than 10 representatives of this sex and age and pupils whose race is not reported.

GIRLS: AGE 5 YEARS.

General nativity and race of father of pupil.	Elementary grade 1.
Native-born:	
White	94
Negro	3
Total native-born	97
Foreign-born:	
Canadian (other than French)	10
Hebrew, Russian	21
Irish	10
Other races *a*	25
Total foreign-born	66
Grand total	163

a "Other races" includes races having less than 10 representatives of this sex and age and pupils whose race is not reported.

TABLE 4.—*Race and grade, by age—Number of pupils of each specified age in each grade, by general nativity and race of father of pupil*—Continued.

GIRLS: AGE 6 YEARS.

General nativity and race of father of pupil.	Elementary grades.			Un-graded schools.	Total.
	1.	2.	3.		
Native-born:					
White..	129	52	1	....	182
Negro...	1	2	....	....	3
Total native-born.........................	130	54	1	....	185
Foreign-born:					
Canadian, French............................	9	1	....	....	10
Canadian, Other..............................	23	9	....	....	32
English..	15	2	....	....	17
Hebrew, Roumanian...........................	34	....	....	....	34
Irish..	16	7	....	....	23
Italian, North................................	10	....	....	....	10
Swedish..	9	3	....	....	12
Other races a	32	12	....	2	46
Total foreign-born.........................	148	34	....	2	184
Grand total.................................	278	88	1	2	369

a "Other races" includes races having less than 10 representatives of this sex and age and pupils whose race is not reported.

GIRLS; AGE 7 YEARS.

General nativity and race of father of pupil.	Elementary grades.				Un-graded schools.	Total.
	1.	2.	3.	4.		
Native-born:						
White..	47	115	49	3	1	215
Negro..	3	2	1	....	....	6
Total native-born.........................	50	117	50	3	1	221
Foreign-born:						
Canadian, French............................	8	4	1	....	....	13
Canadian, Other..............................	10	22	4	1	....	37
English..	3	9	5	....	....	17
Hebrew, Russian..............................	9	24	5	....	1	39
Irish...	6	13	4	1	....	24
Swedish..	5	11	1	....	....	17
Other races a	21	24	3	....	1	49
Total foreign-born.........................	52	107	23	2	2	186
Grand total.................................	102	224	73	5	3	417

a "Other races" includes races having less than 10 representatives of this sex and age and pupils whose race is not reported.

TABLE 4.—*Race and grade, by age—Number of pupils of each specified age in each grade, by general nativity and race of father of pupil—Continued.*

GIRLS: AGE 8 YEARS.

General nativity and race of father of pupil.	Elementary grades.					Un-graded schools.	Total.
	1.	2.	3.	4.	5.		
Native-born:							
White	5	55	123	36	1		220
Negro	3	3	1				7
Total native-born	8	58	124	36	1		227
Foreign-born:							
Canadian (other than French)	6	11	20	6			43
English	1	15	8	3			27
Hebrew, Russian	6	19	13	5			43
Irish		9	5	4		1	19
Swedish	2	8	7	3			20
Other races a	10	19	17	5		1	52
Total foreign-born	25	81	70	26		2	204
Grand total	33	139	194	62	1	2	431

a "Other races" includes races having less than 10 representatives of this sex and age and pupils whose race is not reported.

GIRLS: AGE 9 YEARS.

General nativity and race of father of pupil.	Elementary grades.						Un-graded schools.	Total.
	1.	2.	3.	4.	5.	6.		
Native-born:								
White	2	21	51	71	46	3		194
Negro		1	1	2				4
Total native-born	2	22	52	73	46	3		198
Foreign-born:								
Canadian (other than French)	1	6	15	16	9			47
English		3	8	14	6			31
German	1	3	3	3	3			13
Hebrew, Russian	4	7	12	8	2	1	2	36
Irish		2	6	15	6			29
Swedish		1	7	9	2			19
Other races a	2	10	14	12	9			47
Total foreign-born	8	32	65	77	37	1	2	222
Grand total	10	54	117	150	83	4	2	420

a "Other races" includes races having less than 10 representatives of this sex and age and pupils whose race is not reported.

TABLE **4.**—*Race and grade, by age—Number of pupils of each specified age in each grade, by general nativity and race of father of pupil*—Continued.

GIRLS: AGE 10 YEARS.

General nativity and race of father of pupil.	Elementary grades.							Un-graded schools.	Total.
	1.	2.	3.	4.	5.	6.	7.		
Native-born:									
White...................	......	6	20	54	103	36	1	....	220
Negro....................	......	......	......	2	......	......	......	....	2
Total native-born...............	......	6	20	56	103	36	1	....	222
Foreign-born:									
Canadian (other than French)....	......	......	9	16	18	7	......	....	50
English..................	......	......	5	5	9	3	1	....	23
Hebrew, Russian.................	......	4	7	6	9	4	1	3	34
Irish....................	......	2	6	11	8	1	......	....	28
Italian, South...............	......	......	7	3	......	1	......	4	15
Scotch....................	......	......	3	2	4	3	......	....	12
Swedish..................	......	......	2	5	7	2	......	....	16
Other races *a*...................	1	3	6	8	10	2	......	....	30
Total foreign-born.............	1	9	45	56	65	23	2	7	208
Grand total....................	1	15	65	112	.168	59	3	7	430

a "Other races" includes races having less than 10 representatives of this sex and age and pupils whose race is not reported.

GIRLS: AGE 11 YEARS.

General nativity and race of father of pupil.	Elementary grades.								English class.	Un-graded schools.	Total.
	1.	2.	3.	4.	5.	6.	7.	8.			
Native-born:											
White...................	......	3	10	34	83	90	34	1	......	......	255
Negro....................	......	......	3	1	......	1	......	......	......	......	5
Total native-born.....	......	3	13	35	83	91	34	1	......	......	260
Foreign-born:											
Canadian (other than French)...............	......	......	2	7	14	19	4	......	......	......	46
English.................	......	......	2	5	9	9	4	......	......	......	29
Hebrew, Russian.......	......	......	1	1	7	7	1	......	2	2	21
Irish...................	......	......	......	4	10	9	2	......	......	......	25
Swedish................	......	......	......	4	5	10	2	......	......	......	21
Other races *a*............	1	4	3	7	20	10	5	......	......	......	50
Total foreign-born....	1	4	8	28	65	64	18	......	2	2	192
Grand total..........	1	7	21	63	148	155	52	1	2	2	452

a "Other races" includes races having less than 10 representatives of this sex and age and pupils whose race is not reported.

TABLE **4.**—*Race and grade, by age—Number of pupils of each specified age in each grade, by general nativity and race of father of pupil*—Continued.

GIRLS: AGE 12 YEARS.

General nativity and race of father of pupil.	Elementary grades.									Total.
	1.	2.	3.	4.	5.	6.	7.	8.	9.	
Native-born:										
White	1	......	2	17	41	77	86	45	......	269
Negro			1	2	3	1				7
Indian				1						1
Total native-born	1	......	3	20	44	78	86	45	......	277
Foreign-born:										
Canadian, French				2	3	4	2	1		12
Canadian, Other		1	4	7	12	21	11	9	1	66
English					7		8	6	1	22
Hebrew, Russian		1	5	3	11	5	7			32
Irish			2	1	9	13	11	3		39
Swedish		1		4	4	11	6	1		27
Other races a		2	3	3	14	8	9			39
Total foreign-born	......	5	14	20	60	62	54	20	2	237
Grand total	1	5	17	40	104	140	140	65	2	514

a "Other races" includes races having less than 10 representatives of this sex and age and pupils whose race is not reported.

GIRLS: AGE 13 YEARS.

General nativity and race of father of pupil.	Elementary grades.								High school, first year.	Special school.	Total.
	2.	3.	4.	5.	6.	7.	8.	9.			
Native-born:											
White	....	1	4	21	41	61	76	40	3	....	247
Negro			1	3	1						5
Total native-born	....	1	5	24	42	61	76	40	3	....	252
Foreign-born:											
Canadian, French				2	4	4	3	1			14
Canadian, Other			1	7	4	19	12	3			46
English				1	13	4	3	3			24
Hebrew, Russian	1	3	....	1	5	5	1			3	19
Hebrew, Other		1	....	2	2	3	3	1			12
Irish			2	4	8	12	3				29
Scotch				1	3	2	5	2			13
Swedish		1	....	1	3	7	2				14
Other races a		1	2	5	5	4	6	2			25
Total foreign-born	1	6	5	24	47	60	38	12	....	3	196
Grand total	1	7	10	48	89	121	114	52	3	3	448

a "Other races" includes races having less than 10 representatives of this sex and age and pupils whose race is not reported.

TABLE 4.—*Race and grade, by age—Number of pupils of each specified age in each grade, by general nativity and race of father of pupil—*Continued.

GIRLS: AGE 14 YEARS.

General nativity and race of father of pupil.	Elementary grades.								High school.		Special school.	Total.
	2.	3.	4.	5.	6.	7.	8.	9.	First year.	Second year.		
Native-born:												
White	....	1	1	5	16	33	54	69	34	5	....	218
Negro	....	1	1	1	1	....	....	....	....	....	....	4
Total native-born	....	2	2	6	17	33	54	69	34	5	....	222
Foreign-born:												
Canadian (other than French)	....	....	2	1	11	14	7	16	4	1	....	56
English	....	....	....	....	2	3	4	5	1	....	....	15
Hebrew, Russian	....	2	4	2	1	....	3	1	....	....	1	14
Irish	....	....	....	....	1	5	13	5	2	....	....	26
Other races a	2	....	....	4	6	9	12	4	2	....	1	40
Total foreign-born	2	2	6	7	21	31	39	31	9	1	2	151
Grand total	2	4	8	13	38	64	93	100	43	6	2	373

a "Other races" includes races having less than 10 representatives of this sex and age and pupils whose race is not reported.

GIRLS: AGE 15 YEARS.

General nativity and race of father of pupil.	Elementary grades.						High school.			Special school.	Total.
	4.	5.	6.	7.	8.	9.	First year.	Second year.	Third year.		
Native-born:											
White	1	....	1	7	31	39	45	27	2	....	153
Negro	....	....	....	1	2	1	....	....	....	....	4
Total native-born	1	....	1	8	33	40	45	27	2	....	157
Foreign-born:											
Canadian (other than French)	....	....	2	....	7	12	7	6	....	....	84
English	....	....	....	....	3	9	7	3	....	....	22
Hebrew (not specified)	1	....	1	2	1	....	1	....	....	4	10
Irish	....	....	....	....	4	6	10	2	1	....	23
Other races a	....	1	....	3	7	10	5	2	....	....	28
Total foreign-born	1	1	3	5	22	37	30	13	1	4	117
Grand total	2	1	4	13	55	77	75	40	3	4	274

a "Other races" includes races having less than 10 representatives of this sex and age and pupils whose race is not reported.

TABLE 4.—*Race and grade, by age—Number of pupils of each specified age in each grade, by general nativity and race of father of pupil*—Continued.

GIRLS: AGE 16 YEARS.

General nativity and race of father of pupil.	Elementary grades.				High school.				Special school.	Total.
	6.	7.	8.	9.	First year.	Second year.	Third year.	Fourth year.		
Native-born:										
White....................	3	2	12	24	35	53	26	1	....	156
Negro....................	....	....	....	1	......	......	......	......	....	1
Total native-born.............	3	2	12	25	35	53	26	1	....	157
Foreign-born:										
Canadian (other than French)...	....	1	1	8	5	6	1	......	......	22
English....................	....	....	....	....	5	5	1	......	......	11
Irish....................	....	....	....	1	2	7	1	......	......	11
Other races *....................	....	1	1	4	5	3	2	......	2	18
Total foreign-born.............	....	2	2	13	17	21	5	....	2	62
Grand total....................	3	4	14	38	52	74	31	1	2	219

a "Other races" includes races having less than 10 representatives of this sex and age and pupils whose race is not reported.

GIRLS: AGE 17 YEARS.

General nativity and race of father of pupil.	Elementary grades.			High school.				Special school.	Total.
	7.	8.	9.	First year.	Second year.	Third year.	Fourth year.		
Native-born:									
White....................	1	......	5	5	19	37	19	....	86
Negro....................	......	......	......	......	......	1	......	....	1
Total native-born.............	1	......	5	5	19	38	19	....	87
Foreign-born:									
Canadian (other than French).	......	......	1	3	......	6	1	....	11
Other races *....................	......	......	3	3	4	12	3	....	25
Total foreign-born.............	......	......	4	6	4	18	4	....	36
Grand total....................	1	......	9	11	23	56	23	....	123

GIRLS: AGE 18 YEARS.

General nativity and race of father of pupil.	Elementary grades.		High school.				Total.
	8.	9.	First year.	Second year.	Third year.	Fourth year.	
Native-born, White....................	1	3	1	7	15	44	71
Foreign-born, Other races *....................	......	......	......	4	6	2	12
Total.....................	1	3	1	11	21	46	83

a "Other races" includes races having less than 10 representatives of this sex and age and pupils whose race is not reported.

TABLE 4.—*Race and grade, by age—Number of pupils of each specified age in each grade, by general nativity and race of father of pupil*—Continued.

GIRLS: AGE 19 YEARS.

General nativity and race of father of pupil.	High school.		Total.
	Third year.	Fourth year.	
Native-born, White	4	18	22
Foreign-born, Other races *a*	2	3	5
Total	6	21	27

GIRLS: AGE 20 YEARS.

General nativity and race of father of pupil.	High school, fourth year.	Total.
Native-born, White	5	5
Foreign-born, Other races *a*	1	1
Total	6	6

a "Other races" includes races having less than 10 representatives of this sex and age and pupils whose race is not reported.

TABLE 5.—*Race distribution in each grade—Percentages.*

[This table shows in detail only races with 100 or more pupils reporting. The totals, however, are for all races.]

General nativity and race of father of pupil	Elementary grades.										High school.					Special and un-graded schools.	Grand total.
	1.	2.	3.	4.	5.	6.	7.	8.	9.	Total.	1.	2.	3.	4.	Total.		
Native-born:																	
White	46.1	49.5	52.3	51.0	53.4	54.9	57.9	61.9	61.6	53.1	65.0	72.7	70.2	83.7	71.3	4.3	54.7
Negro	2.0	1.2	1.3	1.5	1.3	1.1	.2	.6	.4	1.2	(a)	.4	.5	(a)	.2	(a)	1.1
Indian	.0	.0	.0	.0	.0	.0	.0	.0	.0	.0	(a)	(a)	(a)	(a)	(a)		(a)
Total native-born	48.1	50.7	53.7	52.6	54.8	56.0	58.2	62.5	62.0	54.3	65.0	73.0	70.7	83.7	71.5	4.3	55.8
Foreign-born:																	
Canadian, French	2.4	1.1	1.3	1.8	2.3	1.4	2.1	3.2	2.1	1.9	1.7	.7	3.7	—	1.5		1.9
Canadian, Other	8.7	9.1	9.9	10.4	10.8	13.7	11.8	10.7	14.3	10.8	10.2	9.9	7.3	7.8	9.2		10.5
English	5.0	5.5	5.1	4.9	5.0	6.0	4.7	5.4	5.8	5.2	7.3	4.6	3.1	2.4	4.9		5.2
German	.8	1.6	.6	1.6	1.8	1.2	1.2	.9	.4	1.2	.6	.4	.5		.4		1.1
Hebrew, Russian	11.7	9.8	9.6	7.0	5.4	4.7	3.7	1.8	1.5	6.9	1.4	.8	.5	1.2	.8	61.4	6.7
Irish	6.3	6.0	6.3	8.7	7.3	6.7	8.3	7.5	6.4	7.0	7.1	6.0	7.9	1.8	6.0	1.4	6.9
Italian, South	2.2	1.8	2.2	1.8	1.2	.6	.4	.4	1.5	1.3						18.6	1.3
Scotch	1.7	1.5	2.7	1.8	2.0	1.7	1.4	1.5	3.1	1.8	2.0	1.7	3.7		1.6	1.4	1.8
Swedish	3.4	4.5	3.8	4.1	4.1	5.4	4.2	3.1	1.9	4.0	1.7	1.8	.5	1.8	1.5		3.7
Other races	9.6	8.4	4.8	5.4	5.3	2.7	3.9	3.2	1.0	5.5	3.1	2.8	2.1	1.2	2.5	12.9	5.2
Total foreign-born	51.9	49.3	46.3	47.4	45.2	44.0	41.8	37.5	38.0	45.7	35.0	27.0	29.3	16.3	28.5	95.7	44.2
Grand total	100.0	100.0	100.0	100.0	100.0	100.0	100.0	100.0	100.0	100.0	100.0	100.0	100.0	100.0	100.0	100.0	100.0

a Less than 0.05 per cent.

TABLE 6.—*Grade distribution of each race—Percentages.*

[This table shows in detail only races with 100 or more pupils reporting. The totals, however, are for all races.]

General nativity and race of father of pupil	Elementary grades.										High school.					Special and ungraded schools.	Grand total.
	1.	2.	3.	4.	5.	6.	7.	8.	9.	Total.	1.	2.	3.	4.	Total.		
Native-born:																	
White	11.5	10.2	10.4	9.8	11.5	10.4	8.9	7.7	6.1	86.4	4.4	3.9	2.6	2.7	13.5	0.1	100
Negro	25.0	12.5	13.5	14.4	14.4	10.6	1.9	3.8	1.9	98.1	(a)	1.0	1.0	(a)	1.9		100
Indian	(a)	(a)	(a)	(a)	(a)	(a)	(a)	(a)	(a)	(a)	(a)	(a)	(a)	(a)	(a)		(a)
Total native-born	11.8	10.2	10.4	9.9	11.5	10.4	8.7	7.7	6.0	86.7	4.3	3.9	2.5	2.6	13.3	.1	100
Foreign-born:																	
Canadian, French	17.3	6.7	7.8	10.1	14.5	7.8	9.5	11.7	6.1	91.6	3.4	1.1	3.9		8.4		100
Canadian, Other	11.3	9.7	10.2	10.3	12.1	13.5	9.4	7.0	7.3	91.0	3.6	2.8	1.4	1.3	9.0		100
English	13.3	11.9	10.7	9.9	11.3	12.1	7.7	7.1	6.1	90.1	5.3	2.6	1.2	.8	9.9		100
German	10.3	15.9	5.6	15.0	18.7	9.3	9.3	5.6	6.5	96.3	1.9	.9	.9	.3	3.7		100
Hebrew, Russian	24.0	16.6	15.7	11.0	9.6	7.4	4.7	1.9	1.3	92.0	.8	.2	.2		1.3	6.7	100
Irish	12.5	9.9	9.9	13.2	12.5	10.2	10.2	7.4	5.0	90.7	3.8	2.6	2.3	.5	9.1	.2	100
Italian, South	23.0	15.1	18.3	14.3	11.1	4.8	2.4	.8	4.7	89.7	4.1	1.2	4.1		9.5	10.3	100
Scotch	13.0	9.5	16.6	10.7	13.0	10.1	6.5	5.9	4.5	89.9	1.7	1.4	.3	.8	4.2	.6	100
Swedish	12.5	13.6	10.9	11.4	12.8	15.0	9.5	5.6	2.0	95.8	2.2	1.6	.8	.4	5.0	1.8	100
Other races	24.9	17.9	10.0	10.8	12.0	5.4	6.2	4.2	2.0	93.2							100
Total foreign-born	16.0	12.5	11.3	11.2	12.0	10.3	7.9	5.8	4.6	91.7	2.9	1.8	1.3	.6	6.7	1.6	100
Grand total	13.6	11.2	10.8	10.5	11.7	10.4	8.4	6.8	5.4	88.9	3.7	2.9	2.0	1.7	10.4	.7	100

a Not computed, owing to small number involved.

PUBLIC SCHOOL TEACHERS IN ELEMENTARY GRADES AND KINDERGARTEN.

TABLE 1.—*Number of teachers in each grade, by sex and general nativity and race.*

[This table does not include 16 teachers not reporting complete data.]

General nativity and race	Male (Elementary grade)										Female (Elementary grade)										Total (Elementary grade)										Race distribution (percentages), elementary
	1	2	3	4	5	6	7	8	9	Total	1	2	3	4	5	6	7	8	9	Total	1	2	3	4	5	6	7	8	9	Total	
Native-born of native father, White				1						1	20	18	18	15	18	21	19	11	11	151	20	18	18	16	18	21	19	11	11	152	69.4
Native-born of foreign father, by race of father:																															
Canadian (other than French)											1	1	1	1	1				1	6	1	1	1	1	1				1	6	2.7
English											2		1	2	1	1	1	2		10	2		1	2	1	1	1	2		10	4.6
Irish											5	10	4	3	5	1	2	4		34	5	10	4	3	5	1	2	4		34	15.5
Scotch																2				2						2				2	.9
Scotch-Irish																			1	1									1	1	.5
Swedish														1						1				1						1	.5
Total											8	11	6	7	7	4	3	6	2	54	8	11	6	7	7	4	3	6	2	54	24.7
Total native-born				1						1	28	29	24	22	25	25	22	17	13	205	28	29	24	23	25	25	22	17	13	206	94.1
Foreign-born:																															
Canadian (other than French)											4		1		2					7	4		1		2					7	3.2
English												1	1	2	1					5		1	1	2	1					5	2.3
Irish																			1	1									1	1	.5
Total foreign-born											4	1	2	2	3				1	13	4	1	2	2	3				1	13	5.9
Grand total				1						1	32	30	26	24	28	25	22	17	14	218	32	30	26	25	28	25	22	17	14	219	100.0

TABLE 2.—*Number of teachers engaged in teaching each specified number of years, by sex and general nativity and race.*

[This table does not include 16 teachers not reporting complete data.]

General nativity and race	Male								Female								Total							
	Under 5 years	5 to 9 years	10 to 14 years	15 to 19 years	20 to 24 years	25 to 29 years	30 years or over	Total	Under 5 years	5 to 9 years	10 to 14 years	15 to 19 years	20 to 24 years	25 to 29 years	30 years or over	Total	Under 5 years	5 to 9 years	10 to 14 years	15 to 19 years	20 to 24 years	25 to 29 years	30 years or over	Total
Native-born of native father, White			1					1	18	35	31	25	24	6	12	151	18	35	32	25	24	6	12	152
Native-born of foreign father, by race of father:																								
Canadian (other than French)									1	2	2		1			6	1	2	2		1			6
English										2		1			7	10		2		1			7	10
Irish									5	7	13	1	5	2	1	34	5	7	13	1	5	2	1	34
Scotch									2							2	2							2
Scotch-Irish									1							1	1							1
Swedish									1							1	1							1
Total									10	11	15	2	6	2	8	54	10	11	15	2	6	2	8	54
Total native-born			1					1	28	46	46	27	30	8	20	205	28	46	47	27	30	8	20	206
Foreign-born:																								
Canadian (other than French)									2	4	1					7	2	4	1					7
English									1	1	1		1		1	5	1	1	1		1		1	5
Irish											1					1			1					1
Total foreign-born									3	5	3		1		1	13	3	5	3		1		1	13
Grand total			1					1	31	51	49	27	31	8	21	218	31	51	50	27	31	8	21	219

PAROCHIAL SCHOOL PUPILS: GENERAL INVESTIGATION.

TABLE 1.—*Grade and age—Number of pupils of each age in each grade, by sex.*

BOYS.

Age.	Elementary grades. 1.	2.	3.	4.	5.	6.	7.	8.	9.	Total.	High school. First year.	Second year.	Third year.	Fourth year.	Total.	Grand total.
4 years	17									17						17
5 years	67									67						67
6 years	118	21	2							141						141
7 years	52	67	21	12						140						140
8 years	24	51	64	12						151						151
9 years	9	37	65	49	7	5				172						172
10 years	7	17	30	37	40	12				143						143
11 years	3	4	12	35	75	47	8	1		185						185
12 years	1	3	4	20	30	52	12	10	1	133						133
13 years				9	12	22	21	26	11	101						101
14 years				3	4	9	12	27	18	73						73
15 years			1	1		2	4	10	15	33						33
16 years								3	6	9						9
17 years									1	1						1
Total	298	200	199	166	168	149	57	77	52	1,366						1,366

GIRLS.

Age.	Elementary grades. 1.	2.	3.	4.	5.	6.	7.	8.	9.	Total.	High school. First year.	Second year.	Third year.	Fourth year.	Total.	Grand total.
4 years	7									7						7
5 years	70	1								71						71
6 years	112	29								141						141
7 years	53	80	41							174						174
8 years	16	41	61	28						146						146
9 years	13	18	61	63	11	1				167						167
10 years	2	14	14	66	63	18				177						177
11 years	1	8	6	31	52	53	13			164						164
12 years	2	5	6	8	31	55	52	13	1	173						173
13 years			1	6	16	23	42	31	15	134						134

Age	1	2	3	4	5	6	7	8	9	10	11	12	13	14	15
14 years				2	3	10	19	39	44	117	3			3	120
15 years			1			3	8	16	27	55	11	5		16	71
16 years				1			2	2	9	14	10	6	1	17	31
17 years									3	3	1	8	2	11	14
18 years													3	3	3
Total	276	196	191	205	176	163	136	101	99	1,543	25	19	6	50	1,593

TOTAL.

Age	1	2	3	4	5	6	7	8	9	10	11	12	13	14	15
4 years	24									24					24
5 years	137	1								138					138
6 years	229	50	2							282					282
7 years	105	147	62							314					314
8 years	40	92	125	40						297					297
9 years	22	55	126	112	18	6				339					339
10 years	9	31	44	103	103	30				320					320
11 years	4	12	18	66	127	100	21			349					349
12 years	3	8	10	28	61	107	64	23	2	306					306
13 years			1	15	28	45	63	57	26	235					235
14 years			2	5	7	19	31	66	62	190	3			3	193
15 years				1		5	12	26	42	88	11	5		16	104
16 years							2	5	15	23	10	6	1	17	40
17 years								1	4	4	1	8	2	11	15
18 years													3	3	3
Total	574	396	390	371	344	312	193	178	151	2,909	25	19	6	50	2,959

TABLE 2.—*Race, sex, and grade—Number of pupils of each sex in each grade, by general nativity and race of father of pupil.*

General nativity and race of father of pupil.	Elementary grades.										High school.				Grand total.
	1.	2.	3.	4.	5.	6.	7.	8.	9.	Total.	First year.	Second year.	Third year.	Total.	
Native-born:															
White—															
Male	94	71	45	51	56	33	24	31	19	424					424
Female	98	48	55	66	57	46	48	26	44	488	10	9	3	22	510
Total	192	119	100	117	113	79	72	57	63	912	10	9	3	22	934
Foreign-born:															
Canadian, French—															
Male	102	45	32	25	28	21	11	7	1	272					272
Female	82	34	27	32	26	21	11	10	9	252	1			1	253
Total	184	79	59	57	54	42	22	17	10	524	1			1	525
Canadian, Other—															
Male	4	12	23	19	7	9	5	5	3	87					87
Female	6	6	8	6	12	21	15	6	4	84	1			1	85
Total	10	18	31	25	19	30	20	11	7	171	1			1	172
English—															
Male	4	1	10	1	4	2	3	1	1	27					27
Female	3	3	3	1	1	4	3	2	6	26	1	1		2	28
Total	7	4	13	2	5	6	6	3	7	53	1	1		2	55
Hebrew, Polish—															
Male			1							1					1
Female			4							4					4
Total			5							5					5
Irish—															
Male	76	56	80	63	69	79	13	31	28	495					495
Female	68	84	87	87	75	69	56	55	35	616	11	9	3	23	639
Total	144	140	167	150	144	148	69	86	63	1,111	11	9	3	23	1,134
Italian, North—															
Male	1	1	2							4					4
Female	3	6	4	1	1					15					15
Total	4	7	6	1	1					19					19
Italian, South—															
Male	3	5	1	2		2				13					13
Female	6			2	1					9					9
Total	9	5	1	4	1	2				22					22
Polish—															
Male	10	2	1	1	3			1		18					18
Female	4	7		2						13					13
Total	14	9	1	3	3			1		31					31

															Total
Scotch—															
Male	1	4	2	1	—	2	1	—	—	—	—	—	—	—	11
Female	2	5	2	6	1	—	2	—	—	—	1	—	—	1	20
Total	3	9	4	7	1	2	3	—	—	—	1	—	—	1	31
Other races a—															
Male	3	3	2	3	1	1	1	1	—	—	—	—	—	—	14
Female	4	3	1	2	2	2	1	1	1	—	—	—	—	—	17
Total	7	6	3	5	3	3	2	2	1	—	—	—	—	—	31
Total—															
Male	204	129	154	115	112	116	33	46	33	942	—	—	—	—	942
Female	178	148	136	139	119	117	88	75	55	1,055	15	10	3	28	1,083
Total	382	277	290	254	231	233	121	121	88	1,997	15	10	3	28	2,025
Grand total—															
Male	298	200	199	166	168	149	57	77	52	1,366	—	—	—	—	1,366
Female	276	196	191	205	176	163	136	101	99	1,543	25	19	6	50	1,593
Total	574	396	390	371	344	312	193	178	151	2,909	25	19	6	50	2,959

a "Other races" includes Dutch Hollander, 2; French, 2; German, 6; Greek, 2; Hindu 2; Lithuanian, 2; Norwegian, 3; Portuguese, 1; Russian, 8; not specified, 3.

TABLE 3.—*Race, sex, and age, by grade—Number of pupils of each age in each grade, by sex and by general nativity and race of father of pupil.*

FIRST GRADE.

BOYS.

General nativity and race of father of pupil.	Number of pupils of each age.									Total.
	4.	5.	6.	7.	8.	9.	10.	11.	12.	
Native-born, White	13	30	38	11	2					94
Foreign-born:										
Canadian, French		4	37	24	18	8	7	3	1	102
Canadian, Other		1	2	1						4
English			2	1	1					4
Irish	3	27	30	12	3	1				76
Italian, North			1							1
Italian, South		2		1						3
Polish		1	7	1	1					10
Scotch			1							1
Other races *a*	1		1	1						3
Total	4	37	80	41	22	9	7	3	1	204
Grand total	17	67	118	52	24	9	7	3	1	298

GIRLS.

General nativity and race of father of pupil.	4.	5.	6.	7.	8.	9.	10.	11.	12.	Total.
Native-born, White	6	38	41	11	2					98
Foreign-born:										
Canadian, French		7	21	23	13	13	2	1	2	82
Canadian, Other			3	3						6
English			2	1						3
Irish	1	21	34	11	1					68
Italian, North			3							3
Italian, South		1	5							6
Polish			1	3						4
Scotch		2								2
Other races *a*		1	2	1						4
Total	1	32	71	42	14	13	2	1	2	178
Grand total	7	70	112	53	16	13	2	1	2	276

TOTAL.

General nativity and race of father of pupil.	4.	5.	6.	7.	8.	9.	10.	11.	12.	Total.
Native-born, White	19	68	79	22	4					192
Foreign-born:										
Canadian, French		11	58	47	31	21	9	4	3	184
Canadian, Other		1	5	4						10
English			2	3	2					7
Irish	4	48	64	23	4	1				144
Italian, North			4							4
Italian, South		3	5	1						9
Polish		1	8	4	1					14
Scotch			2	1						3
Other races *a*	1	1	3	2						7
Total	5	69	151	83	36	22	9	4	3	382
Grand total	24	137	230	105	40	22	9	4	3	574

a "Other races" includes races having less than 10 representatives in this city and pupils whose race is not reported.

TABLE 3.—*Race, sex, and age, by grade—Number of pupils of each age in eacg grade, by sex and by general nativity and race of father of pupil*—Continued.

SECOND GRADE.

BOYS.

General nativity and race of father of pupil.	Number of pupils of each age.								Total.
	5.	6.	7.	8.	9.	10.	11.	12.	
Native-born, White....................		12	34	17	6	2			71
Foreign-born:									
Canadian, French....................			8	8	12	10	4	3	45
Canadian, Other.....................		1	6	3	1	1			12
English.............................			1						1
Irish...............................		7	13	19	14	3			56
Italian, North......................					1				1
Italian, South......................			3		1	1			5
Polish..............................		1	1						2
Scotch..............................			1	3					4
Other races a.......................				1	2				3
Total..........................		9	33	34	31	15	4	3	129
Grand total.....................		21	67	51	37	17	4	3	200

GIRLS.

General nativity and race of father of pupil.	5.	6.	7.	8.	9.	10.	11.	12.	Total.
Native-born, White....................		16	17	10	2	3			48
Foreign-born:									
Canadian, French....................		1	7	1	10	6	7	2	34
Canadian, Other.....................			3	2	1				6
English.............................			1	2					3
Irish...............................		11	47	22	2	2			84
Italian, North......................		1	1	1	1		1	1	6
Polish..............................			2		2	2		1	7
Scotch..............................	1		1	2		1			5
Other races a.......................			1	1				1	3
Total..........................	1	13	63	31	16	11	8	5	148
Grand total.....................	1	29	80	41	18	14	8	5	196

TOTAL.

General nativity and race of father of pupil.	5.	6.	7.	8.	9.	10.	11.	12.	Total.
Native-born, White........,..........		28	51	27	8	5			119
Foreign-born:									
Canadian, French....................		1	15	9	22	16	11	5	79
Canadian, Other.....................		1	9	5	2	1			18
English.............................			2	2					4
Irish...............................		18	60	41	16	5			140
Italian, North......................		1	1	1	2		1	1	7
Italian, South......................			3		1	1			5
Polish..............................		1	3		2	2		1	9
Scotch..............................	1		2	5		1			9
Other races a.......................			1	2	2			1	6
Total..........................	1	22	96	65	47	26	12	8	277
Grand total.....................	1	50	147	92	55	31	12	8	396

a "Other races" includes races having less than 10 representatives in this city and pupils whose race is not reported.

TABLE 3.—*Race, sex, and age, by grade—Number of pupils of each age in each grade, by sex and by general nativity and race of father of pupil*—Continued.

THIRD GRADE.

BOYS.

General nativity and race of father of pupil.	6.	7.	8.	9.	10.	11.	12.	13.	14.	15.	Total.
Native-born, White		6	28	8	1	2					45
Foreign-born:											
Canadian, French			1	5	14	7	4			1	32
Canadian, Other		1	3	16	2	1					23
English		2	4	4							10
Hebrew, Polish			1								1
Irish	2	12	26	25	13	2					80
Italian, North				2							2
Italian, South				1							1
Polish				1							1
Scotch				2							2
Other races[a]			1	1							2
Total	2	15	36	57	29	10	4			1	154
Grand total	2	21	64	65	30	12	4			1	199

GIRLS.

General nativity and race of father of pupil.	6.	7.	8.	9.	10.	11.	12.	13.	14.	15.	Total.
Native-born, White		13	21	16	2	1	1			1	55
Foreign-born:											
Canadian, French				15	5	3	3	1			27
Canadian, Other		3	3	2							8
English			2	1							3
Hebrew, Polish			1		3						4
Irish		25	33	25	3	1					87
Italian, North				1	1	1	1				4
Italian, South											
Polish											
Scotch			1				1				2
Other races[a]				1							1
Total		28	40	45	12	5	5	1			136
Grand total		41	61	61	14	6	6	1		1	191

TOTAL.

General nativity and race of father of pupil.	6.	7.	8.	9.	10.	11.	12.	13.	14.	15.	Total.
Native-born, White		19	49	24	3	3	1			1	100
Foreign-born:											
Canadian, French			1	20	19	10	7	1		1	59
Canadian, Other		4	6	18	2	1					31
English		2	6	5							13
Hebrew, Polish			2		3						5
Irish	2	37	59	50	16	3					167
Italian, North				3	1	1	1				6
Italian, South				1							1
Polish				1							1
Scotch			1	2			1				4
Other races[a]			1	2							3
Total	2	43	76	102	41	15	9	1		1	290
Grand total	2	62	125	126	44	18	10	1		2	390

[a] "Other races" includes races having less than 10 representatives in this city and pupils whose race is not reported.

TABLE 3.—*Race, sex, and age, by grade—Number of pupils of each age in each grade, by sex and by general nativity and race of father of pupil—Continued.*

FOURTH GRADE.

BOYS.

General nativity and race of father of pupil.	Number of pupils of each age.									Total.
	8.	9.	10.	11.	12.	13.	14.	15.	16.	
Native-born, White	7	17	11	8	8					51
Foreign-born:										
Canadian, French		2	3	7	4	5	3	1		25
Canadian, Other	1	4	7	6	1					19
English				1						1
French		1		1						2
Irish	4	23	15	12	6	3				63
Italian, South					1	1				2
Polish		1								1
Scotch			1							1
Other races *a*		1								1
Total	5	32	26	27	12	9	3	1		115
Grand total	12	49	37	35	20	9	3	1		166

GIRLS.

General nativity and race of father of pupil.	8.	9.	10.	11.	12.	13.	14.	15.	16.	Total.
Native-born, White	13	21	19	7	3	3				66
Foreign-born:										
Canadian, French		4	11	10	2	2	2		1	32
Canadian, Other		3	1	1	1					6
English		1								1
Irish	12	32	29	12	2					87
Italian, North			1							1
Italian, South			2							2
Polish				1		1				2
Scotch	1	2	3							6
Other races *a*	2									2
Total	15	42	47	24	5	3	2		1	139
Grand total	28	63	66	31	8	6	2		1	205

TOTAL.

General nativity and race of father of pupil.	8.	9.	10.	11.	12.	13.	14.	15.	16.	Total.
Native-born, White	20	38	30	15	11	3				117
Foreign-born:										
Canadian, French		6	14	17	6	7	5	1	1	57
Canadian, Other	1	7	8	7	2					25
English		1		1						2
French		1		1						2
Irish	16	55	44	24	8	3				150
Italian, North			1							1
Italian, South			2		1	1				4
Polish		1		1		1				3
Scotch	1	2	4							7
Other races *a*	2	1								3
Total	20	74	73	51	17	12	5	1	1	254
Grand total	40	112	103	66	28	15	5	1	1	371

a "Other races" includes races having less than 10 representatives in this city and pupils whose race is not reported.

TABLE 3.—*Race, sex, and age, by grade—Number of pupils of each age in each grade, by sex and by general nativity and race of father of pupil—Continued.*

FIFTH GRADE.

BOYS.

General nativity and race of father of pupil.	Number of pupils of each age.						Total.
	9.	10.	11.	12.	13.	14.	
Native-born, White	2	18	25	9	1	1	56
Foreign-born:							
Canadian, French	2	....	11	7	5	3	28
Canadian, Other	1	2	2	2	....	....	7
English	....	3	1	....	....	....	4
Irish	2	17	35	9	6	....	69
Polish	....	....	....	3	....	....	3
Other races *a*	....	....	1	....	....	....	1
Total	5	22	50	21	11	3	112
Grand total	7	40	75	30	12	4	168

GIRLS.

General nativity and race of father of pupil.	9.	10.	11.	12.	13.	14.	Total.
Native-born, White	6	30	13	4	3	1	57
Foreign-born:							
Canadian, French	1	1	6	9	8	1	26
Canadian, Other	1	....	5	3	2	1	12
English	....	....	1	....	....	....	1
Irish	3	29	26	14	3	....	75
Italian, North	....	1	....	....	....	....	1
Italian, South	....	....	1	....	....	....	1
Scotch	....	....	....	1	....	....	1
Other races *a*	....	2	....	....	....	....	2
Total	5	33	39	27	13	2	119
Grand total	11	63	52	31	16	2	176

TOTAL.

General nativity and race of father of pupil.	9.	10.	11.	12.	13.	14.	Total.
Native-born, White	8	48	38	13	4	2	113
Foreign-born:							
Canadian, French	3	1	17	16	13	4	54
Canadian, Other	2	2	7	5	2	1	19
English	....	3	2	....	....	....	5
Irish	5	46	61	23	9	....	144
Italian, North	....	1	....	....	....	....	1
Italian, South	....	....	1	....	....	....	1
Polish	....	....	....	3	....	....	3
Scotch	....	....	....	1	....	....	1
Other races *a*	....	2	1	....	....	....	3
Total	10	55	89	48	24	5	231
Grand total	18	103	127	61	28	7	344

a "Other races" includes races having less than 10 representatives in this city and pupils whose race is not reported.

TABLE 3.—*Race, sex, and age, by grade—Number of pupils of each age in each grade, by sex and by general nativity and race of father of pupil*—Continued.

SIXTH GRADE.

BOYS.

General nativity and race of father of pupil.	Number of pupils of each age.							Total.
	9.	10.	11.	12.	13.	14.	15.	
Native-born, White................	....	3	15	7	5	3	....	33
Foreign-born:								
Canadian, French............	....	....	3	7	5	4	2	21
Canadian, Other............	....	....	3	4	1	1	....	9
English....................	....	....	....	1	1	....	....	2
Irish......................	5	9	26	29	9	1	....	79
Italian, South.............	....	....	....	2	....	....	....	2
Scotch....................	....	....	....	1	1	....	....	2
Other races *a*.............	....	....	....	1	....	....	....	1
Total.................	5	9	32	45	17	6	2	116
Grand total..............	5	12	47	52	22	9	2	149

GIRLS.

	9.	10.	11.	12.	13.	14.	15.	Total.
Native-born, White................	....	4	19	16	5	2	....	46
Foreign-born:								
Canadian, French............	....	....	2	7	7	4	1	21
Canadian, Other............	....	3	5	9	3	....	1	21
English....................	....	....	2	....	....	1	1	4
Irish......................	1	10	25	22	8	3	....	69
Other races *a*.............	....	1	....	1	....	....	....	2
Total.................	1	14	34	39	18	8	3	117
Grand total..............	1	18	53	55	23	10	3	163

TOTAL.

	9.	10.	11.	12.	13.	14.	15.	Total.
Native-born, White................	....	7	34	23	10	5	....	79
Foreign-born:								
Canadian, French............	....	....	5	14	12	8	3	42
Canadian, Other............	....	3	8	13	4	1	1	30
English....................	....	....	2	1	1	1	1	6
Irish......................	6	19	51	51	17	4	....	148
Italian, South.............	....	....	....	2	....	....	....	2
Scotch....................	....	....	....	1	1	....	....	2
Other races *a*.............	....	1	....	2	....	....	....	3
Total.................	6	23	66	84	35	14	5	233
Grand total..............	6	30	100	107	45	19	5	312

a "Other races" includes races having less than 10 representatives in the city and pupils whose race is not reported.

TABLE 3.—*Race, sex, and age, by grade—Number of pupils of each age in each grade, by sex and by general nativity and race of father of pupil*—Continued.

SEVENTH GRADE.

BOYS.

General nativity and race of father of pupil.	Number of pupils of each age.						Total.
	11.	12.	13.	14.	15.	16.	
Native-born, White............	4	7	7	4	2	....	24
Foreign-born:							
Canadian, French........	....	1	2	6	2	....	11
Canadian, Other.........	1	1	3	....	....	....	5
English.................	1	....	1	1	....	....	3
Irish..................	2	3	7	1	....	....	13
Scotch................	....	....	1	....	....	....	1
Total............	4	5	14	8	2	....	33
Grand total......	8	12	21	12	4	....	57

GIRLS.

General nativity and race of father of pupil.	11.	12.	13.	14.	15.	16.	Total.
Native-born, white............	2	23	14	4	4	1	48
Foreign-born:							
Canadian, French........	1	2	4	3	....	1	11
Canadian, Other.........	2	4	4	1	4	....	15
English.................	....	....	2	1	....	....	3
Irish..................	7	22	18	9	....	....	56
Scotch................	....	1	....	1	....	....	2
Other races *a*..........	1	....	....	....	....	....	1
Total............	11	29	28	15	4	1	88
Grand total......	13	52	42	19	8	2	136

TOTAL.

General nativity and race of father of pupil.	11.	12.	13.	14.	15.	16.	Total.
Native-born, White............	6	30	21	8	6	1	72
Foreign-born:							
Canadian, French........	1	3	6	9	2	1	22
Canadian, Other.........	3	5	7	1	4	....	20
English.................	1	....	3	2	....	....	6
Irish..................	9	25	25	10	....	....	69
Scotch................	....	1	1	1	....	....	3
Other races *a*..........	1	....	....	....	....	....	1
Total............	15	34	42	23	6	1	121
Grand total......	21	64	63	31	12	2	193

a "Other races" includes races having less than 10 representatives in this city and pupils whose race is not reported.

TABLE 3.—*Race, sex, and age, by grade—Number of pupils of each age in each grade, by sex and by general nativity and race of father of pupil*—Continued.

EIGHTH GRADE.

BOYS.

General nativity and race of father of pupil.	Number of pupils of each age.						Total.
	11.	12.	13.	14.	15.	16.	
Native-born, White....................	....	6	12	8	5	....	31
Foreign-born:							
Canadian, French....................	....	....	....	2	4	1	7
Canadian, Other....................	....	1	2	1	1	....	5
English....................	....	....	....	1	....	....	1
Irish....................	1	3	12	14	....	1	31
Polish....................	....	....	....	....	....	1	1
Other races *a*....................	....	....	....	1	....	....	1
Total....................	1	4	14	19	5	3	46
Grand total....................	1	10	26	27	10	3	77

GIRLS.

General nativity and race of father of pupil.	11.	12.	13.	14.	15.	16.	Total.
Native-born, White....................	....	3	12	8	3	....	26
Foreign-born:							
Canadian, French....................	....	....	1	5	3	1	10
Canadian, Other....................	....	....	3	1	2	....	6
English....................	....	....	....	1	1	....	2
German....................	....	....	....	1	....	....	1
Irish....................	....	10	15	22	7	1	55
Scotch....................	....	....	....	1	....	....	1
Total....................	....	10	19	31	13	2	75
Grand total....................	....	13	31	39	16	2	101

TOTAL.

General nativity and race of father of pupil.	11.	12.	13.	14.	15.	16.	Total.
Native-born, White....................	....	9	24	16	8	....	57
Foreign-born:							
Canadian, French....................	....	....	1	7	7	2	17
Canadian, Other....................	....	1	5	2	3	....	11
English....................	....	....	....	2	1	....	3
German....................	....	....	....	1	....	....	1
Irish....................	1	13	27	36	7	2	86
Polish....................	....	....	....	....	....	1	1
Scotch....................	....	....	....	1	....	....	1
Other races *a*....................	....	....	....	1	....	....	1
Total....................	1	14	33	50	18	5	121
Grand total....................	1	23	57	66	26	5	178

a "Other races" includes races having less than 10 representatives in this city and pupils whose race is not reported.

66083°—VOL 31—12——53

TABLE 3.—*Race, sex, and age, by grade—Number of pupils of each age in each grade, by sex and by general nativity and race of father of pupil*—Continued.

NINTH GRADE.

BOYS.

General nativity and race of father of pupil.	Number of pupils of each age.						Total.
	12.	13.	14.	15.	16.	17.	
Native-born, White............................	....	4	6	7	1	1	19
Foreign-born:							
Canadian, French........................	....	....	....	1	....	....	1
Canadian, Other..........................	....	....	2	1	....	....	3
English..................................	....	....	1	....	....	....	1
Irish....................................	1	7	9	6	5	....	28
Total................................	1	7	12	8	5	....	33
Grand total...........................	1	11	18	15	6	1	52

GIRLS.

General nativity and race of father of pupil.	Number of pupils of each age.						Total.
	12.	13.	14.	15.	16.	17.	
Native-born, White............................	1	8	22	11	2	....	44
Foreign-born:							
Canadian, French........................	....	....	1	3	4	1	9
Canadian, Other..........................	....	....	3	1	....	....	4
English..................................	....	1	3	2	....	....	6
Irish....................................	....	5	15	10	3	2	35
Other races a............................	....	....	1	....	....	....	1
Total................................	....	7	22	16	7	3	55
Grand total...........................	1	15	44	27	9	3	99

TOTAL.

General nativity and race of father of pupil.	Number of pupils of each age.						Total.
	12.	13.	14.	15.	16.	17.	
Native-born, White............................	1	12	28	18	3	1	63
Foreign-born:							
Canadian, French........................	....	....	1	4	4	1	10
Canadian, Other..........................	....	....	5	2	....	....	7
English..................................	....	1	4	2	....	....	7
Irish....................................	1	12	24	16	8	2	63
Other races a............................	....	....	1	....	....	....	1
Total................................	1	14	34	24	12	3	88
Grand total...........................	2	26	62	42	15	4	151

a "Other races" includes races having less than 10 representatives in this city and pupils whose race is not reported.

TABLE 3.—*Race, sex, and age, by grade—Number of pupils of each age in each grade, by sex and by general nativiy and race of father of pupil*—Continued.

FIRST YEAR HIGH SCHOOL.

GIRLS.

General nativity and race of father of pupil.	Number of pupils of each age.				Total.
	14.	15.	16.	17.	
Native-born, White	2	6	1	1	10
Foreign-born:					
Canadian, French	1				1
Canadian, Other		1			1
English			1		1
Irish		4	7		11
Scotch			1		1
Total	1	5	9		15
Grand total	3	11	10	1	25

SECOND YEAR HIGH SCHOOL.

GIRLS.

General nativity and race of father of pupil.	Number of pupils of each age.			Total.
	15.	16.	17.	
Native-born, White	1	4	4	9
Foreign-born:				
English	1			1
Irish	3	2	4	9
Total	4	2	4	10
Grand total	5	6	8	19

THIRD YEAR HIGH SCHOOL.

GIRLS.

General nativity and race of father of pupil.	Number of pupils of each age.			Total.
	16.	17.	18.	
Native-born, White		1	2	3
Foreign-born, Irish	1	1	1	3
Grand total	1	2	3	6

TABLE 4.—*Race distribution in each grade—Percentages.*

[This table shows in detail only races with 100 or more pupils reporting. The totals, however, are for all races.]

General nativity and race of father of pupil.	Elementary grades.										High school.				Grand total.
	1.	2.	3.	4.	5.	6.	7.	8.	9.	Total.	First year.	Second year.	Third year.	Total.	
Native-born, White	33.4	30.1	25.6	31.5	32.8	25.3	37.3	32.0	41.7	31.4	40.0	47.4	50.0	44.0	31.6
Foreign-born:															
Canadian, French	32.1	19.9	15.1	15.4	15.7	13.5	11.4	9.6	6.6	18.0	4.0	.	.	2.0	17.7
Canadian, Other	1.7	4.5	7.9	6.7	5.5	9.6	10.4	6.2	4.6	5.9	4.0	.	.	2.0	5.8
Irish	25.1	35.4	42.8	40.4	41.9	47.4	35.8	48.3	41.7	38.2	44.0	47.4	50.0	46.0	38.3
Other races	7.7	10.1	8.5	5.9	4.1	4.2	5.2	3.9	5.3	6.6	8.0	5.3	.	6.0	6.6
Total	66.5	69.9	74.4	68.5	67.2	74.7	62.7	68.0	58.3	68.6	60.0	52.6	50.0	56.0	68.4
Grand total	100.0	100.0	100.0	100.0	100.0	100.0	100.0	100.0	100.0	100.0	100.0	100.0	100.0	100.0	100.0

TABLE 5.—*Grade distribution of each race—Percentages.*

[This table shows in detail only races with 100 or more pupils reporting. The totals, however, are for all races.]

General nativity and race of father of pupil.	Elementary grades.										High school.				Grand total.
	1.	2.	3.	4.	5.	6.	7.	8.	9.	Total.	First year.	Second year.	Third year.	Total.	
Native-born, White	20.6	12.7	10.7	12.5	12.1	8.5	7.7	6.1	6.7	97.6	1.1	1.0	0.3	2.4	100.0
Foreign-born:															
Canadian, French	35.0	15.0	11.2	10.9	10.3	8.0	4.2	3.2	1.9	99.8	.2	.	.	.2	100.0
Canadian, Other	5.8	10.5	18.0	14.5	11.0	17.4	11.6	6.4	4.1	99.4	.6	.	.3	.6	100.0
Irish	12.7	12.3	14.7	13.2	12.7	13.1	6.1	7.6	5.6	98.0	1.0	.8	.3	2.0	100.0
Other races	22.7	20.6	17.0	11.3	7.2	6.7	5.2	3.6	4.1	98.5	1.0	.5	.	1.5	100.0
Total	18.9	13.7	14.3	12.5	11.4	11.5	6.0	6.0	4.3	98.6	.7	.5	.1	1.4	100.0
Grand total	19.4	13.4	13.2	12.5	11.6	10.5	6.5	6.0	5.1	98.3	.8	.6	.2	1.7	100.0

MANCHESTER, NEW HAMPSHIRE.

LIST OF TABLES.

821

MANCHESTER.

In Manchester, N. H., the Immigration Commission conducted inquiries in regard to the pupils of the public schools and those of parochial schools. At the same time that information was gathered concerning pupils in the public schools, data were collected relative to the teachers employed in the same schools. The results of these inquiries are presented herewith in three groups of general tables, relating, respectively, to pupils in the public schools, teachers in the public schools, and pupils in the parochial schools. The methods employed in collecting and tabulating the material are fully explained in the introduction to this volume.[a] The introduction gives also a description of the resulting general tables, with some indications of the various purposes to which these tables may be put. In the present note brief mention will be made of the principal results in the city of Manchester.

PUPILS IN THE PUBLIC SCHOOLS.

There were enumerated in the public schools of the city of Manchester as being in attendance on a day early in December, 1908, 5,078 pupils. The number thus recorded is somewhat larger than the annual average attendance for the school year 1908–9, which was 4,996. An exact correspondence of these two figures, one of them relating to the entire year and the other to a given day in the middle of the year, is hardly to be expected. The fact that at the midyear enumeration more pupils were recorded than the average annual attendance affords evidence that the enumeration of these schools was complete and comprehensive. The representative attendance on the day of enumeration can therefore be taken as a satisfactory picture of the conditions generally prevailing in the schools of the city. Divided by grades these pupils were as follows:

Kindergarten	118	Ninth grade	213
First grade	952	First year high school	207
Second grade	597	Second year high school	100
Third grade	496	Third year high school	116
Fourth grade	467	Fourth year high school	112
Fifth grade	505	Mixed and ungraded	134
Sixth grade	383		
Seventh grade	407	Total	5,078
Eighth grade	271		

Attention is immediately attracted by the relatively large number of the first grade, which is much greater than that found in the second or any subsequent grade. The second grade in turn is considerably larger than the third, but grades 3 and 5 are approximately equal in

---

[a] See pp. VII to XVII.

number. The same is true of grades 6 and 7, though these are considerably less numerous than the group which immediately precedes them. The eighth grade shows a considerable falling off, and the ninth, the final grade of the elementary school system, contains about one-half as many pupils as the seventh grade. It is a noticeable fact that there is a greater difference between the eighth and ninth elementary grades than between the ninth grade and the first year of the high school.

The division of pupils by grade, and the proportion in the upper and lower grades, can best be seen by a grouping of the elementary pupils into two classes—designating grades 1 to 4 as primary and grades 5 to 9 as grammar grades—and contrasting these two groups with the kindergarten and high school. This is done in the table following:

Class of school.	Number.	Per cent.
Kindergarten	118	2.4
Primary, grades 1 to 4	2,512	50.8
Grammar, grades 5 to 9	1,779	36.0
High school	535	10.8
Total	4,944	100.0

In round numbers one-half of the children of the Manchester public schools are in the primary grades, and nearly one-half are in the grammar grades and high school. The proportion of pupils in the high school is about one-tenth of the whole number of pupils.

An examination of the ages of pupils, as revealed in Table 1, shows a relatively large number of 5-year-old pupils (279), the greater part of whom are in the first grade. At 6 years of age there are 455 pupils, and the number of pupils ranges for the several years of age from 6 to 13 between 410 and 514. At the age of 13 years there are 500 pupils in the Manchester schools, but at 14 years of age there are only 380, and at 15, 250, or precisely one-half as many as at the age of 13.

Table 1 also shows the distribution of the pupils by ages within each grade. We find here a great variety. The second grade, for instance, comprises pupils in every year of life from 5 to 15 years. Pupils of 11 years of age again are found in every grade from the first to the ninth. This great diversity in ages renders a study of the table difficult without a grouping. The most convenient form of grouping is that which divides the children of a given grade into two distinct groups, the first containing the younger children whose age is appropriate to the grade in which they are found, and the second comprising the older children who are beyond the age appropriate to their grade. This grouping divides the children of each grade into those who are of normal age and those overage. The overage pupils are designated as "retarded." If there is an age appropriate to each grade, there is conversely a grade appropriate to each age, and the number of children who are behind in their work in any given age is represented by those who have not attained the proper grade for their age. These pupils can be designated as "undergrade" pupils, or those who are deemed retarded. The common form of expression is that which figures the number and percentage of overage pupils in a given grade.

In the following table a statement is given for each grade, with the number of pupils who are overage and the per cent which they form of the total number of pupils. A comparison of the overage pupils in all the grades, with the total number of pupils in these grades, gives the general average for the city.

Grade.	Number in grade.	Retarded pupils.		
		Age.	Number.	Per cent of all pupils.
First	952	8 years and over	163	17.1
Second	597	9 years and over	174	29.1
Third	496	10 years and over	179	36.1
Fourth	467	11 years and over	183	39.2
Fifth	505	12 years and over	194	38.4
Sixth	383	13 years and over	106	27.7
Seventh	407	14 years and over	85	20.9
Eighth	271	15 years and over	34	12.5
Ninth	213	16 years and over	27	12.7
Total	4,291		1,145	26.7

This table shows that of 4,291 pupils in the elementary grades 1,145, or 26.7 per cent, are overage for their respective grades. Considering the individual grades, we find that the proportion in the first grade, 17.1 per cent, is less than the average, but that in the second grade, 29.1 per cent, it rises above the average. The proportion increases from grade to grade until it reaches a maximum with the fourth grade, where there are 39.2 per cent of all the pupils retarded. After this the proportion diminishes, sinking below the average in the seventh grade and falling to about one-half of the average in the eighth and ninth grades. This diminution in the upper grades in the proportion of retarded pupils is due to the fact that these pupils leave school more rapidly than do those that have made normal progress. If the absolute figures of the foregoing table be considered, it will be noted that while the pupils as a whole diminish from 505 in the fifth grade to 213 in the ninth grade, the retarded pupils diminish at a much more rapid rate, as in the fifth grade there are 194 retarded pupils and in the ninth grade 27 pupils.

The method of stating retardation by a reference to the pupils of a given age is exemplified in the following table for the ages 10, 11, and 12 years:

Age.	Number of pupils of this age.	Normal grade.	Retarded, or below normal grade.	
			Number.	Per cent.
10 years	460	4	138	30.0
11 years	468	5	145	31.0
12 years	492	6	194	39.4
Total	1,420		477	33.6

At the age of 10 years three-tenths of the number of pupils are retarded, and two years later nearly four-tenths, the average for this group of pupils being practically one-third of the whole number of pupils of these ages. If the calculation were carried to pupils of 13 and 14 years of age, higher percentages of retardation might be found, but this method of calculation is inapplicable to the more advanced ages, because the retarded pupils leave the schools and consequently escape record in the school statistics.

The primary purpose of the investigations of the Immigration Commission was to discover the difference, if any, which may exist among the different races which compose the school population. To the division of pupils by race, the greater part of the general tables printed herewith is devoted. A view of the main results may be noted in this introductory note.

The races represented in the Manchester schools are shown in the following table, which divides the pupils according to native or foreign parentage, and among the latter gives those races which are represented in the schools of the city by at least 200 pupils.

General nativity and race of father of pupil.	Pupils.		General nativity and race of father of pupil.	Pupils.	
	Number.	Per cent.		Number.	Per cent.
Native-born:			Foreign-born—Continued.		
White	2,595	51.1	German	414	8.2
Negro	2		Irish	224	4.4
			Swedish	291	5.7
Total native-born	2,597	51.1	All others	71	13.4
Foreign-born:					
Canadian, French	589	11.6	Total foreign-born	2,481	48.9
Canadian (other than French)	282	5.6	Grand total	5,078	100.0

In round numbers, one-half of the children have native white fathers and one-half have foreign-born fathers. The race most numerously represented among the latter is the French Canadian, which comprise 11.5 per cent of all the pupils in the schools. Other important races are the German, with 8.2 per cent of all the children, the Swedish with 5.7 per cent, and the English Canadian, represented by 5.6 per cent of all the pupils. The table is rounded off by the group "All others," which is more numerous than any of the individual races enumerated, and comprises a considerable number of distinct races, as follows: Armenian (2), Bohemian and Moravian (2), Chinese (3), Danish (6), Dutch (25), English (183), Finnish (4), Flemish (15), French (30), Greek (12), Hebrew, German (11), Hebrew, Polish (18), Hebrew, Russian (158), Hebrew, Other (13), Italian, North (10), Negro (1), Norwegian (4), Polish (14), Portuguese (2), Russian (5), Scotch (152), Scotch-Irish (5), Slovak (1), Syrian (1), and Welsh (3).

From the figures printed in Table 3 there can be constructed for each racial group, as well as for each of the more prominent races, a table corresponding in character to Table 1 for the entire school population. A comparison of such tables affords an interesting contrast between the races which compose the school population. A review of the main results of such comparison may be made here.

The numbers of the pupils of different races are too small to consider them in their distribution through each of the grades separately, but the table following gives a statement for the grades by groups.

General nativity and race of father of pupil.	Number of pupils.					Per cent.			
	Kinder-garten.	Pri-mary.	Gram-mar.	High.	Total.	Kinder-garten.	Pri-mary.	Gram-mar.	High.
Native-born:									
White................	53	1,131	919	411	2,514	2.1	45.0	36.6	16.3
Negro................			2		2			100.0	
Total native-born......	53	1,131	921	411	2,516	2.1	45.0	36.6	16.3
Foreign-born:									
Canadian, French........	35	372	129	15	551	6.4	67.5	23.4	2.7
Canadian (other than French)................	6	135	109	31	281	2.1	48.0	38.8	11.0
German................	9	230	167	8	414	2.2	55.6	40.3	1.9
Irish................	1	110	90	17	218	0.5	50.5	41.3	7.8
Swedish................	7	145	129	8	289	2.4	50.2	44.6	2.8
All others................	7	389	234	45	675	1.0	57.6	34.7	6.7
Total foreign-born......	65	1,381	858	124	2,428	2.7	56.9	35.3	5.1
Grand total............	118	2,512	1,779	535	4,944	2.4	50.8	36.0	10.8

In the primary grades there is a smaller proportion of children having native fathers, 45 per cent, and a larger proportion of those having foreign fathers, 56.9 per cent. Among the latter each individual race has a larger proportion of pupils in the primary school than have the children of native parentage. The most conspicuous deviation from the average is in the case of the French Canadian, where 67.5 per cent of the children of this group are in the primary schools. The divergence between the children of native and those of foreign parents in the primary schools is to a certain extent compensated in the grammar school, where the proportions of the two groups are approximately equal. On the other hand, there is a marked contrast in the high schools. Of the children of native parentage, 16.3 per cent are in the high schools, while of those of foreign parentage only 5.1 per cent are in schools of this class. Among the English Canadians there is a fair representation in the high schools, their percentage being 11 per cent. On the other hand, for French Canadians, Germans, and Swedes the proportions found in the high schools are conspicuously small.

The following table gives a view of the relative progress of the pupils of different races as measured by retardation:

General nativity and race of father of pupil.	All elementary pupils.			Pupils 10, 11, and 12 years of age.		
	Number.	Retarded, over-age.	Per cent retarded.	Number.	Retarded, under grade.	Per cent retarded.
Native-born:						
White..................................	2,050	453	22.1	702	190	27.1
Negro..................................	2	2	100.0			
Total native-born....................	2,052	455	22.1	....	190	....
Foreign-born:						
Canadian, French.....................	501	259	51.7	128	94	73.4
Canadian, Other......................	244	45	18.4	74	14	18.9
German...............................	397	108	27.2	135	48	35.6
Irish................................	200	61	30.5	66	28	42.4
Swedish..............................	274	44	16.1	105	25	23.8
All others...........................	623	173	27.8	210	78	37.1
Total foreign-born..................	2,239	690	30.8	718	287	39.9
Grand total.........................	4,291	1,145	26.7	1,420	477	33.6

The foregoing table is in two sections. The first three columns, relating to general retardation, comprise all elementary pupils, while the second three columns, relating to pupils of 10, 11, and 12 years of age, refer to a special class. The figures of the first section of this table referring to general retardation show the percentage of retarded pupils to be 22.1 among the children of white parents and 30.8 among those of foreign parents. If the individual races be studied, it is noticeable that there is less retardation among the English Canadians and the Swedes than among the children of native parents. On the other hand, more than one-half of the children of French Canadian parents are in the retarded class.

If the attention be directed to the pupils of 10, 11, and 12 years of age, it will be noted that in this special group the percentages range higher because of the greater average age of this group as compared with the whole number of pupils. There is, however, an equal disproportion between the degree of retardation among children of native-born and that among those of foreign-born parents. In these selected ages it is noticeable that the Swedes and English Canadians again have a lower ratio than the children of native parents. The retardation among the children of French Canadian origin is still further emphasized by this comparison.

PUBLIC SCHOOL TEACHERS.

In the elementary grades, the kindergarten, and the special grades of the city of Manchester there are employed 268 teachers, of whom only three are men. Divided by racial origin, these teachers are as follows:

	Number.	Per cent.
Native white of native fathers...	207	77.2
Native white of foreign fathers..	50	18.7
Foreign white...	11	4.1
Total.......	268	100.0

More than three-fourths of the teachers are of wholly native ante-cedents.   About one-sixth are of native birth but of foreign parent-age; among the latter, with the exception of three teachers of German parentage, all were of English-speaking races.

The location of the teachers in the several grades, as indicated by the grammar and primary grades, is shown in the following table:

	Kinder-garten and primary.	Gram-mar and special.	Total.	Per cent in gram-mar grades.
Native white, native fathers	121	86	207	41.5
Native white, foreign fathers	26	24	50	48.0
Foreign white	4	7	11	63.6
Total	151	117	268	43.7

In general, 43.7 per cent of all teachers are employed in the gram-mar and special grades.   This percentage is, however, somewhat larger among the teachers having foreign fathers than among those whose fathers were native.

Of these teachers 267 reported length of service, as follows:

Under 5 years	73	From 25 to 29 years	11
From 5 to 9 years	68	30 years and over	9
From 10 to 14 years	47		
From 15 to 19 years	39	Total	267
From 20 to 24 years	20		

It is noteworthy that the largest individual group was the teachers having less than five years' experience.   Indeed, teachers with less than ten years' experience constitute more than one-half of the whole number.

The division of these teachers by race is as follows:

Race and nativity of teachers.	Length of service, in years.			
	Under 10.	10 to 19.	20 and over.	Total.
Native white, native fathers	111	70	26	207
Native white, foreign fathers	27	11	11	49
Foreign white	3	5	3	11
Total	141	86	40	267
Percentages: All teachers	56.5	32.2	11.3	100

Both for those of native parents and those of foreign parents the class of teachers having less than ten years' experience is the most numerous.

PUPILS OF THE PAROCHIAL SCHOOLS.

There were enumerated in the parochial schools of the city of Manchester 1,489 pupils.   This number is far from being a complete record of the pupils in this class of schools, since the official directory of the Roman Catholic Church gives as the enrollment for the year 1908-9 a total of 5,088.   The difference between these figures indi-

cates very clearly an omission of important schools in the city.
Hence the figures relate to a group of schools only, and are not necessarily typical of conditions prevailing in the city generally. It will
therefore be sufficient to indicate some of the results of this enumeration without laying too great stress upon the significance of the
figures quoted. The distribution of this group of pupils among the
several grades was as follows:

Kindergarten	75	Sixth grade	68
First grade	438	Seventh grade	13
Second grade	254	Eighth grade	33
Third grade	211	Special	165
Fourth grade	146		
Fifth grade	86	Total	1,489

Divided by groups of grades, we have the following statement:

Class of schools.	Number.	Per cent.
Kindergarten	75	5.0
Grades 1 to 4	1,049	70.4
Grades 5 to 9	200	13.4
Special school	165	11.1
Total	1,489	100.0

Of the pupils here under consideration, 75 per cent are in the
lower schools and only 25 per cent in the upper grades. It will be
noted here that there are no figures given for high schools.

For this group of pupils two statements of retardation are given,
as follows:

Grade.	Number in grade.	Age.	Retarded pupils.	
			Number.	Per cent of all pupils.
First	438	8 years and over	295	67.4
Second	254	9 years and over	211	83.1
Third	211	10 years and over	164	77.7
Fourth	146	11 years and over	123	84.2
Fifth	86	12 years and over	59	68.6
Sixth	68	13 years and over	54	79.4
Seventh	13	14 years and over	9	69.2
Eighth	33	15 years and over	17	51.5
Total	1,249		932	74.6

Age.	Number of pupils of this age.	Normal grade.	Retarded, or below normal grade.	
			Number.	Per cent.
10 years	184	4	164	89.2
11 years	182	5	158	86.8
12 years	190	6	176	92.6
Total	556		498	89.6

In the first statement it appears that of all elementary pupils 75 per cent in round numbers are in the retarded class, and that in certain grades, the second and the fourth, more than 80 per cent are in this class.

In the second statement, regarding pupils of 10, 11, and 12 years of age, we find that in the schools in question nearly 90 per cent of the pupils belong in the retarded class.

The distribution of this group of pupils by nativity follows:

General nativity and race of father of pupil.	Pupils.	
	Number.	Per cent.
Native-born, White	149	10.0
Foreign-born:		
Canadian, French	923	62.0
Irish	127	8.5
Polish	179	12.0
All others	111	7.5
Total foreign-born	1,340	90.0
Grand total	1,489	100.0

It appears that in these schools one-tenth are of native and nine-tenths are of foreign origin, most of the latter being French Canadians, who constitute nearly two-thirds of this group of pupils. Irish and Polish are also numerous, and the miscellaneous group includes Canadian (other than French), English, French, German, Russian, Scotch, and Italian.

PUPILS IN PUBLIC AND PAROCHIAL SCHOOLS COMBINED.

A combination of the figures gathered in the parochial schools with those heretofore given for the public schools will give a picture of the racial diversity of a large part of the school children in the city of Manchester. This combination follows:

General nativity and race of father of pupil.	Pupils, by schools.			Per cent of all pupils.
	Public schools.	Parochial schools.	Total.	
Native-born:				
White	2,595	149	2,744	41.8
Negro	2		2	
Total native-born	2,597	149	2,746	41.8
Foreign-born:				
Canadian, French	589	923	1,512	23.0
Canadian, Other	282	23	305	4.6
German	414	16	430	6.5
Irish	224	127	351	5.3
Swedish	291		291	4.4
All others	681	251	932	14.2
Total foreign-born	2,481	1,340	3,821	58.2
Grand total	5,078	1,489	6,567	100.0

For the pupils here recorded, it will be noted that about four-tenths have native parents and six-tenths foreign parents, nearly one-fourth of all the pupils here recorded being of French Canadian extraction. While the figures for the parochial schools are incomplete, it can not fail to attract attention that the figures given comprehend about one-third of all the Irish pupils and considerably more than one-half of the French Canadian pupils.

GENERAL TABLES.

PUBLIC SCHOOL PUPILS: GENERAL INVESTIGATION.

TABLE **1.**—*Grade and age—Number of pupils of each age in each grade, by sex.*

BOYS.

Age.	Kindergarten.	Elementary grades.									Total.
		1.	2.	3.	4.	5.	6.	7.	8.	9.	
4 years	32	1									1
5 years	24	118	4									122
6 years	9	181	33									214
7 years	2	108	99	17	2							226
8 years		53	80	58	27	3						221
9 years		20	32	77	46	16	2					193
10 years		9	22	43	57	61	23	6				221
11 years		7	18	18	41	69	56	29	8	1		247
12 years		2	12	14	25	56	60	50	26	1		246
13 years		1	8	13	18	35	30	66	40	28		239
14 years		1	5	6	11	16	20	31	31	30		151
15 years		1	2	2	2	2	6	9	13	23		60
16 years							3	1	2	14		20
17 years								1		1		2
18 years												
19 years												
20 years and over												
Total.	67	502	315	248	229	258	200	193	120	98		2,163

Age.	High school.					Mixed and ungraded schools.	Grand total.
	First year.	Second year.	Third year.	Fourth year.	Total.		
4 years							33
5 years						4	150
6 years						9	232
7 years						10	238
8 years						10	231
9 years						11	204
10 years						4	225
11 years						6	253
12 years		1			1	15	262
13 years	11				11	8	258
14 years	20	6			26	11	188
15 years	39	17	7	1	64		124
16 years	13	17	22	7	59		79
17 years	6	5	19	12	42		44
18 years	1	1	6	17	25		25
19 years	1		2	7	10		10
20 years and over				2	2		2
Total.	91	47	56	46	240	88	2,558

TABLE **1.**—*Grade and age—Number of pupils of each age in each grade, by sex*—Contd.

GIRLS.

Age.	Kinder-garten.	Elementary grades.									
		1.	2.	3.	4.	5	6.	7.	8.	9.	Total.
4 years	27										
5 years	21	105									105
6 years	3	174	41								215
7 years		102	92	26	2						222
8 years		42	74	79	29			1			225
9 years		15	42	60	63	24	2				206
10 years		8	13	43	58	79	33	5			239
11 years		2	11	15	33	59	56	39	5	1	221
12 years		1	5	11	28	40	45	71	30	14	245
13 years		1	3	10	16	34	26	55	56	25	226
14 years				3	5	9	14	31	41	43	146
15 years			1	1	3		5	10	14	20	54
16 years					1	2	1	1	5	10	20
17 years							1	1		2	4
18 years											
19 years											
20 years and over											
Total	51	450	282	248	238	247	183	214	151	115	2,128

Age.	High school.					Mixed and un-graded schools.	Grand total.
	First year.	Second year.	Third year.	Fourth year.	Total.		
4 years							27
5 years						3	129
6 years						5	223
7 years						5	227
8 years						7	232
9 years							206
10 years						7	246
11 years						3	224
12 years						7	252
13 years	11				11	5	242
14 years	35	8			43	3	192
15 years	41	19	11		71	1	126
16 years	22	20	24	9	75		95
17 years	6	4	20	26	56		60
18 years		2	4	25	31		31
19 years	1		1	6	8		8
20 years and over							
Total	116	53	60	66	295	46	2,520

TABLE 1.—*Grade and age—Number of pupils of each age in each grade, by sex*—Contd.

TOTAL.

Age.	Kinder-garten.	Elementary grades.									
		1.	2.	3.	4.	5.	6.	7.	8.	9.	Total.
4 years	59	1									1
5 years	45	223	4								227
6 years	12	355	74								429
7 years	2	210	191	43	4						448
8 years		95	154	137	56	3		1			446
9 years		35	74	137	109	40	4				399
10 years		17	35	86	115	140	56	11			460
11 years		9	29	33	74	128	112	68	13	2	468
12 years		3	17	25	53	96	105	121	56	15	491
13 years		2	11	23	34	69	56	121	96	53	465
14 years		1	5	9	16	25	34	62	72	73	297
15 years		1	3	3	5	2	11	19	27	43	114
16 years					1	2	4	2	7	24	40
17 years							1	2		3	6
18 years											
19 years											
20 years and over											
Total.	118	952	597	496	467	505	383	407	271	213	4,291

Age.	High school.					Mixed and un-graded schools.	Grand total.
	First year.	Second year.	Third year.	Fourth year.	Total.		
4 years							60
5 years						7	279
6 years						14	455
7 years						15	465
8 years						17	463
9 years						11	410
10 years						11	471
11 years						9	477
12 years		1			1	22	514
13 years	22				22	13	500
14 years	55	14			69	14	380
15 years	80	36	18	1	135	1	250
16 years	35	37	46	16	134		174
17 years	12	9	39	38	98		104
18 years	1	3	10	42	56		56
19 years	2		3	13	18		18
20 years and over				2	2		2
Total	207	100	116	112	535	134	5,078

TABLE 2.—*Race, sex, and grade—Number of pupils of each sex in each grade, by general nativity and race of father of pupil.*

General nativity and race of father of pupil	Kindergarten	1.	2.	3.	4.	5.	6.	7.	8.	9.	Total.	First year.	Second year.	Third year.	Fourth year.	Total.	Mixed and ungraded schools.	Grand total.
Native-born:																		
White—																		
Male	33	209	127	110	120	133	101	99	61	63	1,023	70	36	42	40	188	54	1,298
Female	20	211	133	105	116	111	91	101	77	82	1,027	88	38	41	56	223	27	1,297
Total	53	420	260	215	236	244	192	200	138	145	2,050	158	74	83	96	411	81	2,595
Negro, female							2				2							2
Total native-born—																		
Male	33	209	127	110	120	133	101	99	61	63	1,023	70	36	42	40	188	54	1,298
Female	20	211	133	105	116	111	93	101	77	82	1,029	88	38	41	56	223	27	1,299
Total	53	420	260	215	236	244	194	200	138	145	2,052	158	74	83	96	411	81	2,597
Foreign-born:																		
Canadian, French—																		
Male	14	97	45	29	31	30	14	10	7	4	258	3	5	1	3	12	26	310
Female	21	85	30	29	26	21	19	10	13	1	243	1			2	3	12	279
Total	35	182	75	58	57	51	33	20	20	5	501	4	5	1	5	15	38	589
Canadian, Other—																		
Male	5	21	12	18	17	15	15	6	9	10	123	5	1	4	1	11		139
Female	1	18	18	14	16	16	9	10	9	10	120	8	5	7		20	2	143
Total	6	39	30	32	33	31	24	16	18	20	243	13	6	11	1	31	2	282
Dutch—																		
Male		6	4		1	1					12							12
Female	1	7	1	3							12							13
Total	1	13	5	3	1	1		1			24							25
English—																		
Male	4	21	10	11	5	15	10	8	5	2	87	3	3	2			1	93
Female		11	7	9	12	10	8	6	10	2	75	4		1			2	90
Total	4	32	17	20	17	25	18	14	15	4	162	7	3	3			3	183
Flemish—																		
Male			1	2							3							3
Female			5	1							12							12
Total			6	3							15							15
French—																		
Male		6		1	5	1		5		1	9							9
Female		2		3		4					19					1	1	21
Total		8		4	5	5		5		1	28						1	30
German—																		
Male	6	48	41	23	17	26	15	31	11	2	214	1	1	1	1		6	226
Female	3	35	35	27	4	24	14	32	10	2	183	1			1		2	188
Total	9	83	76	50	21	50	29	63	21	4	397	2	1	1	2		8	414
Greek—																		
Male		3	5	1	1						7							7
Female		3		1	1						5							5
Total		3	5	2	2						12							12

Hebrew, German—																		
Male						1	3				4							4
Female					1	2		4			7							7
Total					1	3	3	4			11							11
Hebrew, Polish—																		
Male		5								1	6							6
Female		2	5	4			1				12							12
Total		7	5	4			1			1	18							18
Hebrew, Russian—																		
Male		20	14	3	9	4	3	7	4	2	66	1	1	3	1	6		72
Female		19	11	9	9	8	6	6	7	4	79	1	2	3	1	7		86
Total		39	25	12	18	12	9	13	11	6	145	2	3	6	2	13		158
Hebrew, Other—																		
Male		1		1		1	1				4							4
Female		2	1	3	1	1	1				9							9
Total		3	1	4	1	2	2				13							13
Irish—																		
Male	1	21	18	13	9	12	11	9	7	5	105	1	1	2		4	4	114
Female		21	11	11	7	15	8	8	10	6	97	4	2	4	3	13		110
Total	1	42	29	24	16	27	19	17	17	11	202	5	3	6	3	17	4	224
Italian, North—																		
Male		1		1		1					3							3
Female		2	1		2		2				7							7
Total		3	1	1	2	1	2				10							10
Polish—																		
Male		3	1	4		1			1		10							10
Female		1	1	1	1						4							4
Total		4	2	5	1	1			1		14							10
Scotch—																		
Male	1	7	14	12	6	4	5	10	7	1	66	1	2			3	2	72
Female	1	6	10	11	13	9	7	9	4	1	70	3	1	3	1	8	1	80
Total	2	13	24	23	19	13	12	19	11	2	136	4	3	3	1	11	3	152
Swedish—																		
Male	7	32	20	15	11	22	21	10	8	7	146	1		2		3	1	157
Female		23	10	14	20	14	14	15	11	7	128	4			1	5	1	134
Total	7	55	30	29	31	36	35	25	19	14	274	5		2	1	8	2	291
Other races [a]—																		
Male		4	3	4	2	1	1	2			17	2				2		19
Female		2	3	3	4	1	1	3			17	2	2			4		21
Total		6	6	7	6	2	2	5			34	4	2			5		40
Total foreign-born—																		
Male	34	293	188	138	109	125	99	94	59	35	1,140	21	11	14	6	52	34	1,260
Female	31	239	149	143	122	136	90	113	74	33	1,099	28	15	19	10	72	19	1,221
Total	65	532	337	281	231	261	189	207	133	68	2,239	49	26	33	16	124	53	2,481
Grand total—																		
Male	67	502	315	248	229	258	200	193	120	98	2,163	91	47	56	46	240	88	2,558
Female	51	450	282	248	238	247	183	214	151	115	2,128	116	53	60	66	295	46	2,520
Total	118	952	597	496	467	505	383	407	271	213	4,291	207	100	116	112	535	134	5,078

[a] "Other races" includes Armenian, 2; Bohemian and Moravian, 2; Chinese, 3; Danish, 6; Finnish, 4; negro, 1; Norwegian, 4; Portuguese, 2; Russian, 5; Scotch-Irish, 5; Slovak, 1; Syrian, 1; Welsh, 3; race not specified, 1.

TABLE 3.—*Race, sex, and age, by grade—Number of pupils of each age in each grade, by sex and by general nativity and race of father of pupil.*

KINDERGARTEN.

BOYS.

General nativity and race of father of pupil.	Number of pupils of each age.				Total.
	4.	5.	6.	7.	
Native-born, White	17	14	2	....	33
Foreign-born:					
Canadian, French	3	3	6	2	14
Canadian, Other	4	1	....	....	5
German	2	3	1	....	6
Irish	....	1	....	....	1
Scotch	1	....	....	....	1
Swedish	5	2	....	....	7
Total	15	10	7	2	34
Grand total	32	24	9	2	67

GIRLS.

General nativity and race of father of pupil.	4.	5.	6.	7.	Total.
Native-born, White	11	9	....	....	20
Foreign-born:					
Canadian, French	10	8	3	....	21
Canadian, Other	1	....	....	....	1
Dutch	1	....	....	....	1
English	1	3	....	....	4
German	2	1	....	....	3
Scotch	1	....	....	....	1
Total	16	12	3	....	31
Grand total	27	21	3	....	51

TOTAL.

General nativity and race of father of pupil.	4.	5.	6.	7.	Total.
Native-born, White	28	23	2	....	53
Foreign-born:					
Canadian, French	13	11	9	2	35
Canadian, Other	5	1	....	....	6
Dutch	1	....	....	....	1
English	1	3	....	....	4
German	4	4	1	....	9
Irish	....	1	....	....	1
Scotch	2	....	....	....	2
Swedish	5	2	....	....	7
Total	31	22	10	2	65
Grand total	59	45	12	2	118

TABLE 3.—*Race, sex, and age, by grade—Number of pupils of each age in each grade, by sex and by general nativity and race of father of pupil*—Continued.

FIRST GRADE.

BOYS.

General nativity and race of father of pupil.	Number of pupils of each age.												Total.
	4.	5.	6.	7.	8.	9.	10.	11.	12.	13.	14.	15.	
Native-born, White		50	79	46	22	7	2	2	1				209
Foreign-born:													
Canadian, French		16	32	19	13	7	4	2	1	1	1	1	97
Canadian, Other		4	9	4	2			1	1				21
Dutch		1	3	2									6
English		9	8	4									21
French				5	1								6
German		10	18	13	6	1							48
Hebrew, Polish		2		1	1	1							5
Hebrew, Russian	1	4	7	4	2	1	1						20
Hebrew, Other			1										1
Irish		8	6	1	4		1	1					21
Italian, North						*1*							1
Polish		1		1		1							3
Scotch		2	4		1								7
Swedish		10	9	11		1		1					32
Other races *a*		1		1	2								4
Total	1	68	102	62	31	13	7	5	1	1	1	1	293
Grand total	1	118	181	108	53	20	9	7	2	1	1	1	502

GIRLS.

General nativity and race of father of pupil.	Number of pupils of each age.												Total.
	4.	5.	6.	7.	8.	9.	10.	11.	12.	13.	14.	15.	
Native-born, White		57	80	40	24	5	2	1	1	1			211
Foreign-born:													
Canadian, French		17	25	26	9	4	4						85
Canadian, Other		5	8	4	1								18
Dutch		2	4	1									7
English		1	6	2	1	1							11
French		1		1									2
German		4	17	10	2	2							35
Greek			2					1					3
Hebrew, Polish				1			1						2
Hebrew, Russian		6	5	6		2							19
Hebrew, Other			2										2
Irish		4	8	3	4	1	1						21
Italian, North			1	•1									2
Polish				1									1
Scotch		3	2	1									6
Swedish		5	12	5	1								23
Welsh			1										1
Other races *a*			1										1
Total		48	94	62	18	10	6	1					239
Grand total		105	174	102	42	15	8	2	1	1			450

a "Other races" includes races having less than 10 representatives in this city and pupils whose race is not reported.

TABLE 3.—*Race, sex, and age, by grade—Number of pupils of each age in each grade, by sex and by general nativity and race of father of pupil*—Continued.

FIRST GRADE—Continued.

TOTAL.

General nativity and race of father of pupil.	4.	5.	6.	7.	8.	9.	10.	11.	12.	13.	14.	15.	Total.
Native-born, White	....	107	159	86	46	12	4	3	2	1	....	....	420
Foreign-born:													
Canadian, French	....	33	57	45	22	11	8	2	1	1	1	1	182
Canadian, Other	....	9	17	8	3	....	1	1					39
Dutch	....	3	7	3									13
English	....	10	14	6	1	1							32
French	....	1	5	2									8
German	....	14	35	23	8	3							83
Greek	....		2					1					3
Hebrew, Polish	....	2		2	1	1	1						7
Hebrew, Russian	1	10	12	10	2	3	1						39
Hebrew, Other	....		3										3
Irish	....	12	14	4	8	1	2	1					42
Italian, North	....		1	1		1							3
Polish	....	1		2		1							4
Scotch	....	5	6	1	1								13
Swedish	....	15	21	16	1	1		1					55
Welsh	....		1										1
Other races a	....	1	1	1	2								5
Total	1	116	196	124	49	23	13	6	1	1	1	1	532
Grand total	1	223	355	210	95	35	17	9	3	2	1	1	952

a "Other races" includes races having less than 10 representatives in this city and pupils whose race is not reported.

SECOND GRADE.

BOYS.

General nativity and race of father of pupil.	5.	6.	7.	8.	9.	10.	11.	12.	13.	14.	15.	Total.
Native-born, White	1	16	41	32	14	13	4	3	2	1	....	127
Foreign-born:												
Canadian, French	..	1	6	7	6	3	7	7	4	4	....	45
Canadian, Other	1	5	3	1	2							12
Dutch			1	2	1							4
English			1	7	1		1					10
German	1	5	16	9	4	3	2				1	41
Greek		1	1		1				1		1	5
Hebrew, Russian		1	3	4	1	1	3		1			14
Irish		1	6	7	1			2				17
Polish							1					1
Scotch	1	1	8	3	1							14
Swedish		2	10	6		2						20
Welsh			1									1
Other races a			2	2								4
Total foreign-born	3	17	58	48	18	9	14	9	6	4	2	188
Grand total	4	33	99	80	32	22	18	12	8	5	2	315

a "Other races" includes races having less than 10 representatives in this city and pupils whose race is not reported.

TABLE 3.—*Race, sex, and age, by grade—Number of pupils of each age in each grade, by sex and by general nativity and race of father of pupil—Continued.*

SECOND GRADE—Continued.

GIRLS.

General nativity and race of father of pupil.	Number of pupils of each age.											Total.
	5.	6.	7.	8.	9.	10.	11.	12.	13.	14.	15.	
Native-born, White................	....	21	44	42	17	5	2	2	....	....	....	133
Foreign-born:												
Canadian French....................	....	2	5	5	5	2	5	2	3	....	1	30
Canadian, Other....................	....	2	9	4	2	1	....	....	....	....	....	18
Dutch....	....	....	....	1	....	....	....	....	....	....	....	1
English....	....	....	3	3	1	....	....	....	....	....	....	7
German....	....	6	11	6	8	2	2	....	....	....	....	35
Hebrew, Polish....................	....	1	....	2	....	2	....	....	....	....	....	5
Hebrew, Russian....................	....	1	4	2	1	1	1	1	....	....	....	11
Hebrew, Other....................	....	....	1	....	....	....	....	....	....	....	....	1
Irish....	....	2	4	2	2	....	1	....	....	....	....	11
Italian, North....................	....	....	....	....	1	....	....	....	....	....	....	1
Polish....	....	....	....	....	1	....	....	....	....	....	....	1
Scotch....	....	1	4	3	2	....	....	....	....	....	....	10
Swedish....	....	2	3	4	1	....	....	....	....	....	....	10
Other races a....	....	3	4	1	....	....	....	....	....	....	....	8
Total foreign-born....................	....	20	48	32	25	8	9	3	3	....	1	149
Grand total....................	....	41	92	74	42	13	11	5	3	....	1	282

TOTAL.

General nativity and race of father of pupil.	5.	6.	7.	8.	9.	10.	11.	12.	13.	14.	15.	Total.
Native-born, White....................	1	37	85	74	31	18	6	5	2	1	....	260
Foreign-born:												
Canadian, French....................	....	3	11	12	11	5	12	9	7	4	1	75
Canadian, Other....................	1	7	12	5	4	1	....	....	....	....	....	30
Dutch....	....	....	1	2	2	....	....	....	....	....	....	5
English....	....	....	4	10	2	....	1	....	....	....	....	17
German....	1	11	27	15	12	5	4	....	....	....	1	76
Greek....	....	1	1	....	1	....	....	....	1	....	1	5
Hebrew, Polish....	....	1	....	2	....	2	....	....	....	....	....	5
Hebrew, Russian....	....	2	7	6	2	2	4	1	1	....	....	25
Hebrew, Other....	....	....	1	....	....	....	....	....	....	....	....	1
Irish....	....	3	10	9	3	....	1	2	....	....	....	28
Italian, North....................	....	....	....	....	1	....	....	....	....	....	....	1
Polish....	....	....	....	....	1	....	1	....	....	....	....	2
Scotch....	1	2	12	6	3	....	....	....	....	....	....	24
Swedish....	....	4	13	10	1	2	....	....	....	....	....	30
Welsh....	....	....	1	....	....	....	....	....	....	....	....	1
Other races a....	....	3	6	3	....	....	....	....	....	....	....	12
Total foreign-born....................	3	37	106	80	43	17	23	12	9	4	3	337
Grand total....................	4	74	191	154	74	35	29	17	11	5	3	597

a "Other races" includes races having less than 10 representatives in this city and pupils whose race is not reported.

TABLE **3.**—*Race, sex, and age, by grade*—*Number of pupils of each age in each grade, by sex and by general nativity and race of father of pupil*—Continued.

THIRD GRADE.

BOYS.

General nativity and race of father of pupil.	Number of pupils of each age.									Total.
	7.	8.	9.	10.	11.	12.	13.	14.	15.	
Native-born, White	7	33	38	16	8	2	5	1	......	110
Foreign-born:										
Canadian, French	2	5	6	2	2	3	6	3	......	29
Canadian, Other	5	4	5	3	......	1	......	......	......	18
English	......	5	2	3	1	......	......	......	......	11
French	......	......	......	1	......	......	......	......	......	1
German	......	1	10	7	1	3	......	......	1	23
Greek	......	......	......	......	......	......	......	1	......	1
Hebrew, Russian	......	......	3	......	......	......	......	......	......	3
Hebrew, Other	......	......	......	......	......	......	1	......	......	1
Irish	1	1	4	3	......	3	......	......	1	13
Italian, North	......	......	......	......	......	1	......	......	......	1
Polish	......	......	1	1	......	......	1	1	......	4
Scotch	1	4	2	2	2	1	......	......	......	12
Swedish	......	5	4	3	3	......	......	......	......	15
Welsh	......	......	1	......	......	......	......	......	......	1
Other races *a*	1	......	1	2	1	......	......	......	......	5
Total	10	25	39	27	10	12	8	5	2	138
Grand total	17	58	77	43	18	14	13	6	2	248

GIRLS.

General nativity and race of father of pupil.	7.	8.	9.	10.	11.	12.	13.	14.	15.	Total.
Native-born, White	15	40	25	15	7	1	2	......	......	105
Foreign-born:										
Canadian, French	1	4	5	4	2	5	5	2	1	29
Canadian, Other	2	8	4	......	......	......	......	......	......	14
Dutch	......	......	3	......	......	......	......	......	......	3
English	......	......	......	5	3	......	1	......	......	9
French	......	......	......	......	1	1	1	......	......	3
German	1	7	7	7	3	1	1	......	......	27
Greek	......	......	......	1	......	......	......	......	......	1
Hebrew, Polish	......	2	1	1	......	......	......	......	......	4
Hebrew, Russian	3	2	......	1	2	1	......	......	......	9
Hebrew, Other	......	2	......	1	......	......	......	......	......	3
Irish	......	5	2	3	1	......	......	......	......	11
Polish	......	......	......	1	......	......	......	......	......	1
Scotch	2	3	4	1	......	......	......	1	......	11
Swedish	2	5	3	4	......	......	......	......	......	14
Other races *a*	......	1	1	......	......	1	1	......	......	4
Total	11	39	35	28	8	10	8	3	1	143
Grand total	26	79	60	43	15	11	10	3	1	248

a "Other races" includes races having less than 10 representatives in this city and pupils whose race is not reported.

TABLE 3.—*Race, sex, and age, by grade—Number of pupils of each age in each grade, by sex and by general nativity and race of father of pupil—Continued.*

THIRD GRADE—Continued.

TOTAL.

General nativity and race of father of pupil.	Number of pupils of each age.									Total.
	7.	8.	9.	10.	11.	12.	13.	14.	15.	
Native-born, White	22	73	63	31	15	3	7	1	......	215
Foreign-born:										
Canadian, French	3	9	11	6	4	8	11	5	1	58
Canadian, Other	7	12	9	3	......	1				32
Dutch			3							3
English		5	7	6	1	1				20
French				2		1	1			4
German	1	8	17	14	4	4	1		1	50
Greek					1			1		2
Hebrew, Polish		2	1	1						4
Hebrew, Russian	3	2	3	1	2	1				12
Hebrew, Other		2		1			1			4
Irish	1	6	6	6	1	3			1	24
Italian, North						1				1
Polish			1	2			1	1		5
Scotch	3	7	6	3	2	1		1		23
Swedish	2	10	7	7	3					29
Welsh			1							1
Other races *a*	1	1	2	2	1	1	1			9
Total	21	64	74	55	18	22	16	8	3	281
Grand total	43	137	137	86	33	25	23	9	3	496

a "Other races" includes races having less than 10 representatives in this city and pupils whose race is not reported.

FOURTH GRADE.

BOYS.

General nativity and race of father of pupil.	Number of pupils of each age.										Total.
	7.	8.	9.	10.	11.	12.	13.	14.	15.	16.	
Native-born, White	2	19	28	35	19	10	4	3	......	......	120
Foreign-born:											
Canadian, French			1	1	1	10	10	7	1	......	31
Canadian, Other		3	3	7	2		1	1			17
Dutch			1								1
English					5						5
German		1	4	4	5	2	1				17
Greek					1						1
Hebrew, Russian		1	3		2	1	1		1		9
Irish		1	3	2	3						9
Scotch			1	4		1					6
Swedish		2	2	3	2	1	1				11
Other races *a*			1	1							2
Total		8	18	22	22	15	14	8	2	......	109
Grand total	2	27	46	57	41	25	18	11	2	......	229

a "Other races" includes races having less than 10 representatives in this city and pupils whose race is not reported.

TABLE **3.**—*Race, sex, and age, by grade—Number of pupils of each age in each grade, by sex and by general nativity and race of father of pupil—Continued.*

FOURTH GRADE—Continued.

GIRLS.

General nativity and race of father of pupil.	Number of pupils of each age.										Total.
	7.	8.	9.	10.	11.	12.	13.	14.	15.	16.	
Native-born, White	1	14	39	26	19	10	6	......	1	......	116
Foreign-born:											
Canadian, French		1	.....	1	4	9	6	3	1	1	26
Canadian, Other		5	4	5	2	1					17
English		1	1	8		2					12
French			1			1	2	1			5
German	1			1	1	1					4
Greek							1				1
Hebrew, German				1							1
Hebrew, Russian		2	2	2	1			1	1		9
Hebrew, Other						1					1
Irish		1	4	1	1						7
Italian, North			2								2
Polish					1						1
Scotch		1	4	5	1	2					13
Swedish		4	6	8	1	1					20
Other races a					2		1				3
Total	1	15	24	32	14	18	10	5	2	1	122
Grand total	2	29	63	58	33	28	16	5	3	1	238

TOTAL.

General nativity and race of father of pupil.	7.	8.	9.	10.	11.	12.	13.	14.	15.	16.	Total.
Native-born, White	3	33	67	61	38	20	10	3	1	......	236
Foreign-born:											
Canadian, French		1	1	2	5	19	16	10	2	1	57
Canadian, Other		8	7	12	4	1	1	1			34
Dutch			1								1
English		1	1	8	5	2					17
French			1			1	2	1			5
German	1	1	4	5	6	3	1				21
Greek					1		1				2
Hebrew, German				1							1
Hebrew, Russian		3	5	2	3	1	1	1	2		18
Hebrew, Other						1					1
Irish		2	7	3	4						16
Italian, North			2								2
Polish					1						1
Scotch		1	5	9	1	3					19
Swedish		6	8	11	3	2	1				31
Other races a				1	3		1				5
Total	1	23	42	54	36	33	24	13	4	1	231
Grand total	4	56	109	115	74	53	34	16	5	1	467

a "Other races" includes races having less than 10 representatives in this city and pupils whose race is not reported.

TABLE 3.—*Race, sex, and age, by grade—Number of pupils of each age in each grade, by sex and by general nativity and race of father of pupil*—Continued.

FIFTH GRADE.

BOYS.

General nativity and race of father of pupil.	Number of pupils of each age.									Total.
	8.	9.	10.	11.	12.	13.	14.	15.	16.	
Native-born, White....................	3	10	34	35	29	12	9	1	......	133
Foreign-born:										
Canadian, French....................	......	2	1	4	3	8	2	1	......	21
Canadian, Other.....................	......	......	4	5	1	4	1	......	......	15
English..............................	......	1	4	5	1	2	2	......	......	15
French..............................	......	......	......	1	......	......	......	......	......	1
German..............................	......	......	8	5	7	6	......	......	......	26
Hebrew, German.....................	......	......	......	......	1	......	......	......	......	1
Hebrew, Russian.....................	......	......	......	3	1	......	......	......	......	4
Hebrew, Other.......................	......	......	......	......	......	1	......	......	......	1
Irish................................	......	......	......	3	2	4	1	1	......	11
Italian, North.......................	......	......	1	......	......	......	......	......	......	1
Polish...............................	......	......	......	......	......	1	......	......	......	1
Scotch..............................	......	......	......	2	2	......	......	......	......	4
Swedish.............................	......	3	6	7	6	......	......	......	......	22
Other races a	......	......	......	......	1	......	1	......	......	2
Total......................	......	6	27	34	27	23	7	1	......	125
Grand total..................	3	16	61	69	56	35	16	2	......	258

a "Other races" includes races having less than 10 representatives in this city and pupils whose race is not reported.

GIRLS.

General nativity and race of father of pupil.	8.	9.	10.	11.	12.	13.	14.	15.	16.	Total.
Native-born, White....................	......	15	37	32	16	8	3	......	......	111
Foreign-born:										
Canadian, French....................	......	......	3	3	12	8	2	......	2	30
Canadian, Other.....................	......	2	7	4	1	2	......	......	......	16
Dutch...............................	......	......	......	......	......	......	1	......	......	1
English..............................	......	......	3	2	......	4	1	......	......	10
French..............................	......	......	......	1	1	1	1	......	......	4
German..............................	......	1	11	5	1	6	......	......	......	24
Hebrew, German.....................	......	......	......	1	1	......	......	......	......	2
Hebrew, Russian.....................	......	1	2	......	1	4	......	......	......	8
Hebrew, Other.......................	......	......	......	......	1	......	......	......	......	1
Irish................................	......	2	6	2	4	......	1	......	......	15
Scotch..............................	......	2	2	4	1	......	......	......	......	9
Swedish.............................	......	1	7	4	1	1	......	......	......	14
Other races a	......	......	1	1	......	......	......	......	......	2
Total......................	......	9	42	27	24	26	6	......	2	136
Grand total..................	......	24	79	59	40	34	9	......	2	247

a "Other races" includes races having less than 10 representatives in this city and pupils whose race is not reported.

TABLE 3.—*Race, sex, and age, by grade—Number of pupils of each age in each grade, by sex and by general nativity and race of father of pupil*—Continued.

FIFTH GRADE—Continued.

TOTAL.

[General nativity and race of father of pupil.	Number of pupils of each age.									Total.
	8.	9.	10.	11.	12.	13.	14.	15.	16.	
Native-born, White	3	25	71	67	45	20	12	1	......	244
Foreign-born:										
Canadian, French		2	4	7	15	16	4	1	2	51
Canadian, Other		2	11	9	2	6	1			31
Dutch						1				1
English		1	7	7	1	6	3			25
French				2	1	1	1			5
German		1	19	10	8	12				50
Hebrew, German			1		2					3
Hebrew, Russian		1	2	3	2	4				12
Hebrew, Other					1	1				2
Irish		2	9	4	8	1	2			26
Italian, North			1							1
Polish						1				1
Scotch		2	2	6	3					13
Swedish		4	13	11	7	1				36
Other races a			1	1	1		1			4
Total		15	69	61	51	49	13	1	2	261
Grand total	3	40	140	128	96	69	25	2	2	505

a "Other races" includes races having less than 10 representatives in this city and pupils whose race is not reported.

SIXTH GRADE.

BOYS.

General nativity and race of father of pupil.	Number of pupils of each age.									Total.
	9.	10.	11.	12.	13.	14.	15.	16.	17.	
Native-born, White	1	17	29	26	11	12	2	3	......	101
Foreign-born:										
Canadian, French			4	1	7	1	1			14
Canadian, Other		1	2	8	2	1	1			15
English			2	6	2					10
German			3	5	3	4				15
Hebrew, German			2	1						3
Hebrew, Russian			2	1						3
Hebrew, Other							1			1
Irish			2	2	3	3	1			11
Scotch		1		3	1					5
Swedish	1	2	10	5	1	1	1			21
Other races a				1						1
Total foreign-born	1	6	27	34	19	8	4			99
Grand total	2	23	56	60	30	20	6	3	......	200

a "Other races" includes races having less than 10 representatives in this city and pupils whose race is not reported.

TABLE 3.—*Race, sex, and age, by grade—Number of pupils of each age in each grade, by sex and by general nativity and race of father of pupil—Continued.*

SIXTH GRADE—Continued.

GIRLS.

General nativity and race of father of pupil.	9.	10.	11.	12.	13.	14.	15.	16.	17.	Total.
Native-born:										
White............................	2	19	33	21	9	6			1	91
Negro............................						2				2
Total native-born...........	2	19	33	21	9	8			1	93
Foreign-born:										
Canadian, French............		3	2	2	6	3	3			19
Canadian, Other.............		5	3	1						9
English.......................		2	2	2	1			1		8
German........................			3	7	3	1				14
Hebrew, Polish................			1							1
Hebrew, Russian.............		1		2	1		2			6
Hebrew, Other................				1						1
Irish.........................		1	2	1	3	1				8
Italian, North................				1		1				2
Scotch........................			5	2						7
Swedish.......................		2	4	5	3					14
Other races a................			1							1
Total foreign-born.........		14	23	24	17	6	5	1		90
Grand total.................	2	33	56	45	26	14	5	1	1	183

TOTAL.

	9.	10.	11.	12.	13.	14.	15.	16.	17.	Total.
Native-born:										
White.........................	3	36	62	47	20	18	2	3	1	192
Negro.........................						2				2
Total native-born...........	3	36	62	47	20	20	2	3	1	194
Foreign-born:										
Canadian, French............		3	6	3	13	4	4			33
Canadian, Other.............		6	5	9	2	1	1			24
English.......................		2	4	8	3			1		18
German........................			6	12	6	5				29
Hebrew, German...............			2	1						3
Hebrew, Polish................			1							1
Hebrew, Russian.............		1	2	3	1		2			9
Hebrew, Other................				1			1			2
Irish.........................		3	4	4	6	2				19
Italian, North................				1		1				2
Scotch........................		1	5	5	1					12
Swedish.......................	1	4	14	10	4	1	1			35
Other races a................			1	1						2
Total foreign-born.........	1	20	50	58	36	14	9	1		189
Grand total.................	4	56	112	105	56	34	11	4	1	383

a "Other races" includes races having less than 10 representatives in this city and pupils whose race is not reported.

TABLE 3.—*Race, sex, and age, by grade—Number of pupils of each age in each grade, by sex and by general nativity and race of father of pupil*—Continued.

SEVENTH GRADE.

BOYS.

General nativity and race of father of pupil.	Number of pupils of each age.										Total.
	8.	9.	10.	11.	12.	13.	14.	15.	16.	17.	
Native-born, White			4	16	27	32	15	5			99
Foreign-born:											
Canadian, French					4	1	3	1		1	10
Canadian, Other					1	3	1	1			6
Dutch							1				1
English				2	3	2	1				8
German				4	9	13	4	1			31
Hebrew, Russian				1		4	1	1			7
Irish			2	1	2	1	2		1		9
Scotch				3	1	5	1				10
Swedish				2	2	4	2				10
Other races *a*					1	1					2
Total			2	13	23	34	16	4	1	1	94
Grand total			6	29	50	66	31	9	1	1	193

GIRLS.

General nativity and race of father of pupil.	8.	9.	10.	11.	12.	13.	14.	15.	16.	17.	Total.
Native-born, White			3	24	37	19	13	5			101
Foreign-born:											
Canadian, French				1	2	3	3	1			10
Canadian, Other				1	1	3	3	1	1		10
English				1	1	3	1				6
French				1	1	2		1			5
German				7	11	9	5				32
Hebrew, German						3	1				4
Hebrew, Russian				1	4					1	6
Irish					2	4	2				8
Scotch			1		1	5	2				9
Swedish				3	8	3	1				15
Other races *a*	1		1		3	1		2			8
Total	1		2	15	34	36	18	5	1	1	113
Grand total	1		5	39	71	55	31	10	1	1	214

a "Other races" includes races having less than 10 representatives in this city and pupils whose race is not reported.

TABLE 3.—*Race, sex, and age, by grade—Number of pupils of each age in each grade, by sex and by general nativity and race of father of pupil*—Continued.

SEVENTH GRADE—Continued.

TOTAL.

General nativity and race of father of pupil.	Number of pupils of each age.										Total.
	8.	9.	10.	11.	12.	13.	14.	15.	16.	17.	
Native-born, White............	......	......	7	40	64	51	28	10	......	......	200
Foreign-born:											
Canadian, French...........	......	......	......	1	6	4	6	2	......	1	20
Canadian, Other...........	......	......	......	1	2	6	4	2	1	......	16
Dutch.....................	......	......	......	......	......	......	1	......	......	......	1
English...................	......	......	......	3	4	5	2	......	......	......	14
French....................	......	......	......	1	1	2	......	1	......	......	5
German...................	......	......	......	11	20	22	9	1	......	......	63
Hebrew, German...........	......	......	......	......	......	3	1	......	......	......	4
Hebrew, Russian..........	......	......	......	2	4	4	1	1	......	1	13
Irish.....................	......	......	2	1	4	5	4	......	1	......	17
Scotch....................	......	......	1	3	2	10	3	......	......	......	19
Swedish..................	......	......	......	5	10	7	3	......	......	......	25
Other races a.............	1	......	1	......	4	2	......	2	......	......	10
Total..................	1	......	4	28	57	70	34	9	2	2	207
Grand total............	1	......	11	68	121	121	62	19	2	2	407

a "Other races" includes races having less than 10 representatives in this city and pupils whose race is not reported.

EIGHTH GRADE.

BOYS.

General nativity and race of father of pupil.	Number of pupils of each age.						Total.
	11.	12.	13.	14.	15.	16.	
Native-born, White.....................	5	14	21	16	5	....	61
Foreign-born:							
Canadian, French......................	1	....	1	2	3	....	7
Canadian, Other.......................	1	1	1	3	2	1	9
English...............................	....	1	3	1	....	....	5
German...............................	1	2	6	2	....	....	11
Hebrew, Russian......................	....	....	....	2	2	....	4
Irish.................................	....	3	3	1	....	....	7
Polish................................	....	....	....	....	....	1	1
Scotch................................	....	4	3	....	....	....	7
Swedish..............................	....	1	2	4	1	....	8
Total.............................	3	12	19	15	8	2	59
Grand total.......................	8	26	40	31	13	2	120

TABLE **3.**—*Race, sex, and age, by grade—Number of pupils of each age in each grade, by sex and by general nativity and race of father of pupil*—Continued.

EIGHTH GRADE—Continued.

GIRLS.

General nativity and race of father of pupil.	Elementary grades.						Total.
	11.	12.	13.	14.	15.	16.	
Native-born, White..........................	5	20	27	17	6	2	77
Foreign-born:							
Canadian, French.........................	....	1	2	7	1	2	13
Canadian, Other..........................		2	3	4	....	....	9
English................................	....	2	5	1	2	....	10
German.................................	....	1	7	2	....	....	10
Hebrew, Russian.........................		1	3	3	....	....	7
Irish..................................		1	3	3	2	1	10
Scotch.................................		1	2	....	1	....	4
Swedish................................		1	4	4	2	....	11
Total.............................	....	10	29	24	8	3	74
Grand total......................	5	30	56	41	14	5	151

TOTAL.

Native-born, White..........................	10	34	48	33	11	2	138
Foreign-born:							
Canadian, French.........................	1	1	3	9	4	2	20
Canadian, Other..........................	1	3	4	7	2	1	18
English................................	....	3	8	2	2	....	15
German.................................	1	3	13	4	....	....	21
Hebrew, Russian.........................	....	1	3	5	2	....	11
Irish..................................	....	4	6	4	2	1	17
Polish.................................	....	....	....	....	....	1	1
Scotch.................................	....	5	5	....	1	....	11
Swedish................................	....	2	6	8	3	....	19
Total.............................	3	22	48	39	16	5	133
Grand total......................	13	56	96	72	27	7	271

TABLE 3.—*Race, sex, and age, by grade—Number of pupils of each age in each grade, by sex and by general nativity and race of father of pupil*—Continued.

NINTH GRADE.

BOYS.

General nativity and race of father of pupil.	Number of pupils of each age.							Total.
	11.	12.	13.	14.	15.	16.	17.	
Native-born, White		1	20	16	15	10	1	63
Foreign-born:								
Canadian, French				2	1	1		4
Canadian, Other			3	3	3	1		10
English				1	1			2
French			1					1
German			1	1				2
Hebrew, Polish				1				1
Hebrew, Russian	1					1		2
Irish			2	2	1			5
Scotch				1				1
Swedish			1	3	2	1		7
Total	1		8	14	8	4		35
Grand total	1	1	28	30	23	14	1	98

GIRLS.

General nativity and race of father of pupil.	11.	12.	13.	14.	15.	16.	17.	Total.
Native-born, White	1	10	20	29	13	8	1	82
Foreign-born:								
Canadian, French				1				1
Canadian, Other		1	2	6	1			10
English			1	1				2
German				1	1			2
Hebrew, Russian		2			1		1	4
Irish			2	1	2	1		6
Scotch		1						1
Swedish				4	2	1		7
Total		4	5	14	7	2	1	33
Grand total	1	14	25	43	20	10	2	115

TOTAL.

General nativity and race of father of pupil.	11.	12.	13.	14.	15.	16.	17.	Total.
Native-born, White	1	11	40	45	28	18	2	145
Foreign-born:								
Canadian, French				3	1	1		5
Canadian, Other		1	5	9	4	1		20
English			1	2	1			4
French			1					1
German			1	2	1			4
Hebrew, Polish				1				1
Hebrew, Russian	1	2			1	1	1	6
Irish			4	3	3	1		11
Scotch		1		1				2
Swedish			1	7	4	2		14
Total	1	4	13	28	15	6	1	68
Grand total	2	15	53	73	43	24	3	213

TABLE 3.—*Race, sex, and age, by grade—Number of pupils of each age in eaeh grade, by sex and by general nativity and race of father of pupil*—Continued.

FIRST YEAR HIGH SCHOOL.

BOYS.

General nativity and race of father of pupil.	Number of pupils of each age.							Total.
	13.	14.	15.	16.	17.	18.	19.	
Native-born, White	10	14	32	8	4	1	1	70
Foreign-born:								
Canadian, French			1	2				3
Canadian, Other		2	2		1			5
English			1	2				3
German	1		2	1				4
Hebrew, Russian		1						1
Irish		1						1
Scotch		1						1
Swedish					1			1
Other races a		1	1					2
Total	1	6	7	5	2			21
Grand total	11	20	39	13	6	1	1	91

GIRLS.

General nativity and race of father of pupil.	13.	14.	15.	16.	17.	18.	19.	Total.
Native-born, White	9	26	31	18	3		1	88
Foreign-born:								
Canadian, French				1				1
Canadian, Other		4	4					8
English		2		1	1			4
French				1				1
Hebrew, Russian	1							1
Irish		1	2	1				4
Scotch	1		1		1			3
Swedish		2	1		1			4
Other races a			2					2
Total	2	9	10	4	3			28
Grand total	11	35	41	22	6		1	116

TOTAL.

General nativity and race of father of pupil.	13.	14.	15.	16.	17.	18.	19.	Total.
Native-born, White	19	40	63	26	7	1	2	158
Foreign-born:								
Canadian, French			1	3				4
Canadian, Other		6	6		1			13
English		2	1	3	1			7
French				1				1
German	1		2	1				4
Hebrew, Russian	1	1						2
Irish		2	2	1				5
Scotch	1	1	1		1			4
Swedish		2	1		2			5
Other races a		1	3					4
Total	3	15	17	9	5			49
Grand total	22	55	80	35	12	1	2	207

a "Other races" includes races having less than 10 representatives in this city and pupils whose race is not reported.

TABLE 3.—*Race, sex, and age, by grade—Number of pupils of each age in each grade, by sex and by general nativity and race of father of pupil*—Continued.

SECOND YEAR HIGH SCHOOL.

BOYS.

General nativity and race of father of pupil.	Number of pupils of each age.							Total.
	12.	13.	14.	15.	16.	17.	18.	
Native-born, White	1	....	5	13	13	4	....	36
Foreign-born:								
Canadian, French				2	1	1	1	5
Canadian (other than French)			1					1
German								1
Hebrew, Russian				1	1			1
Irish					1			1
Scotch				1	1			2
Total			1	4	4	1	1	11
Grand total	1	....	6	17	17	5	1	47

GIRLS.

General nativity and race of father of pupil.	12.	13.	14.	15.	16.	17.	18.	Total.
Native-born, White			4	14	16	3	1	38
Foreign-born:								
Canadian (other than French)				3	1	1		5
English			1	1	1			3
Hebrew, Russian			2					2
Irish					2			2
Scotch				1				1
Other races a			1				1	2
Total			4	5	4	1	1	15
Grand total			8	19	20	4	2	53

TOTAL.

General nativity and race of father of pupil.	12.	13.	14.	15.	16.	17.	18.	Total.
Native-born, White	1	....	9	27	29	7	1	74
Foreign-born:								
Canadian, French				2	1	1	1	5
Canadian, Other			1	3	1	1		6
English			1	1	1			3
German			1					1
Hebrew, Russian			2		1			3
Irish					3			3
Scotch				2	1			3
Other races a			1				1	2
Total			5	9	8	2	2	26
Grand total	1	....	14	36	37	9	3	100

a "Other races" includes races having less than 10 representatives in this city and pupils whose race is not reported.

TABLE 3.—*Race, sex, and age, by grade—Number of pupils of each age in each grade, by sex and by general nativity and race of father of pupil*—Continued.

THIRD YEAR HIGH SCHOOL.

BOYS.

General nativity and race of father of pupil.	Number of pupils of each age.					Total.
	15.	16.	17.	18.	19.	
Native-born, White	4	16	16	4	2	42
Foreign-born:						
Canadian, French		1				1
Canadian, Other	1	2		1		4
English		2				2
Hebrew, Russian	2			1		3
Irish			2			2
Swedish		1	1			2
Total	3	6	3	2		14
Grand total	7	22	19	6		56

GIRLS.

General nativity and race of father of pupil.	15.	16.	17.	18.	19.	Total.
Native-born, White	10	16	13	2		41
Foreign-born:						
Canadian (other than French)		3	2	1	1	7
English			1			1
German		1				1
Hebrew, Russian	1		2			3
Irish		1	2	1		4
Scotch		3				3
Total	1	8	7	2	1	19
Grand total	11	24	20	4	1	60

TOTAL.

General nativity and race of father of pupil.	15.	16.	17.	18.	19.	Total.
Native-born, White	14	32	29	6	2	83
Foreign-born:						
Canadian, French		1				1
Canadian, Other	1	5	2	2	1	11
English		2	1			3
German		1				1
Hebrew, Russian	3		2	1		6
Irish		1	4	1		6
Scotch		3				3
Swedish		1	1			2
Total	4	14	10	4	1	33
Grand total	18	46	39	10	3	116

TABLE 3.—*Race, sex, and age, by grade—Number of pupils of each age in each grade, by sex and by general nativity and race of father of pupil*—Continued.

FOURTH YEAR HIGH SCHOOL.

BOYS.

General nativity and race of father of pupil.	Number of pupils of each age.						Total.
	15.	16.	17.	18.	19.	20.	
Native-born, White	1	6	11	15	6	1	40
Foreign-born:							
Canadian, French				1	1	1	3
Canadian, Other				1			1
German		1					1
Hebrew, Russian			1				1
Total		1	1	2	1	1	6
Grand total	1	7	12	17	7	2	46

GIRLS.

General nativity and race of father of pupil.	15.	16.	17.	18.	19.	20.	Total.
Native-born, White		8	21	22	5		56
Foreign-born:							
Canadian, French				2			2
English					1		1
German			1				1
Hebrew, Russian			1				1
Irish		1	2				3
Scotch			1				1
Swedish				1			1
Total		1	5	3	1		10
Grand total		9	26	25	6		66

TOTAL.

General nativity and race of father of pupil.	15.	16.	17.	18.	19.	20.	Total.
Native-born, White	1	14	32	37	11	1	96
Foreign-born:							
Canadian, French				3	1	1	5
Canadian, Other				1			1
English					1		1
German		1	1				2
Hebrew, Russian			2				2
Irish		1	2				3
Scotch			1				1
Swedish				1			1
Total		2	6	5	2	1	16
Grand total	1	16	38	42	13	2	112

TABLE **3.**—*Race, sex, and age, by grade—Number of pupils of each age in each grade, by sex and by general nativity and race of father of pupil—Continued.*

UNGRADED.

BOYS.

General nativity and race of father of pupil.	Number of pupils of each age.											Total.
	5.	6.	7.	8.	9.	10.	11.	12.	13.	14.	15.	
Native-born, White	....	4	6	3	6	2	4	7	2	4	....	38
Foreign-born:												
Canadian, French	1	3	....	3	1	1	....	4	5	6	....	24
Swedish										1	....	1
Total	1	3	....	3	1	1	....	4	5	7	...	25
Grand total	1	7	6	6	7	3	4	11	7	11	....	63

GIRLS.

General nativity and race of father of pupil.	5.	6.	7.	8.	9.	10.	11.	12.	13.	14.	15.	Total.
Native-born, White	1	2	2	2	....	3	2	2	2	....	....	16
Foreign-born:												
Canadian, French	2	1	2	....	....	1	1	....	2	2	....	11
Canadian, Other	....	....	....	1	....	....	....	....	....	....	1	2
English	....	1	....	....	....	....	....	....	....	....	....	1
French	....	....	....	....	....	....	....	1	....	....	....	1
Swedish	....	....	....	....	....	1	....	....	....	....	....	1
Total	2	2	2	1	....	2	1	1	2	2	1	16
Grand total	3	4	4	3	....	5	3	3	4	2	1	32

TOTAL.

General nativity and race of father of pupil.	5.	6.	7.	8.	9.	10.	11.	12.	13.	14.	15.	Total.
Native-born, White	1	6	8	5	6	5	6	9	4	4	....	54
Foreign-born:												
Canadian, French	3	4	2	3	1	2	1	4	7	8	....	35
Canadian, Other	....	....	....	1	....	....	....	....	....	....	1	2
English	....	1	....	....	....	....	....	....	....	....	....	1
French	....	....	....	....	....	....	....	1	....	....	....	1
Swedish	....	....	....	....	....	1	....	....	....	1	....	2
Total	3	5	2	4	1	3	1	5	7	9	1	41
Grand total	4	11	10	9	7	8	7	14	11	13	1	95

TABLE 3.—*Race, sex, and age, by grade—Number of pupils of each age in each grade, by sex and by general nativity and race of father of pupil*—Continued.

MIXED FIRST, SECOND, AND THIRD GRADES.

BOYS.

General nativity and race of father of pupil.	Number of pupils of each age.										Total.
	5.	6.	7.	8.	9.	10.	11.	12.	13.	14.	
Native-born, White............	3	2	2	1	3	......	2	2	1	......	16
Foreign-born:											
Canadian, French..........	......	......	1	1	......	......	......	......	......	......	2
English..................	......	......	......	......	......	......	......	1	......	......	1
Irish....................	......	......	......	2	1	......	......	1	......	......	4
Scotch..................	......	......	1	......	......	1	......	......	......	......	2
Total................	......	......	2	3	1	1	......	2	......	......	9
Grand total.............	3	2	4	4	4	1	2	4	1	......	25

GIRLS.

General nativity and race of father of pupil.	5.	6.	7.	8.	9.	10.	11.	12.	13.	14.	Total.
Native-born, White.............	......	1	1	4	......	1	......	4	......	......	11
Foreign-born:											
Canadian, French..........	......	......	......	......	......	1	......	......	......	......	1
English..................	......	......	......	......	......	......	......	......	......	1	1
Scotch..................	......	......	......	......	......	......	......	1	......	......	1
Total................	......	......	......	......	......	1	......	......	1	1	3
Grand total.............	......	1	1	4	......	2	......	4	1	1	14

TOTAL.

General nativity and race of father of pupil.	5.	6.	7.	8.	9.	10.	11.	12.	13.	14.	Total.
Native-born, White.............	3	3	3	5	3	1	2	6	1	......	27
Foreign-born:											
Canadian, French..........	......	......	1	1	......	1	......	......	......	......	3
English..................	......	......	......	......	......	......	......	1	......	1	2
Irish....................	......	......	......	2	1	......	......	1	......	......	4
Scotch..................	......	......	1	......	......	1	......	......	1	......	3
Total................	......	......	2	3	1	2	......	2	1	1	12
Grand total.............	3	3	5	8	4	3	2	8	2	1	39

TABLE 4.—*Race and grade, by age—Number of pupils of each specified age in each grade, by general nativity and race of father of pupil.*

BOYS: AGE 4 YEARS.

General nativity and race of father of pupil.	Kinder-garten.	Elementary grade 1.	Total.
Native-born, White..	17	....	17
Foreign-born, Other races [a]	15	1	16
Total	32	1	33

[a] "Other races" includes races having less than 10 representatives of this sex and age and pupils whose race is not reported.

TABLE 4.—*Race and grade, by age—Number of pupils of each specified age in each grade, by general nativity and race of father of pupil—Continued.*

BOYS: AGE 5 YEARS.

General nativity and race of father of pupil.	Kinder-garten.	Elementary grades.		Special and un-graded schools.	Total.
		1.	2.		
Native-born, White........................	14	50	1	3	68
Foreign-born:					
Canadian, French.........................	3	16	....	1	20
German................................	3	10	1	....	14
Swedish................................	2	10	....	....	12
Other races *a*..........................	2	32	2	....	36
Total.............................	10	68	3	1	82
Grand total.......................	24	118	4	4	150

BOYS: AGE 6 YEARS.

Native-born, White........................	2	79	16	6	103
Foreign-born:					
Canadian, French.........................	6	32	1	3	42
Canadian, Other.........................	....	9	5	....	14
German................................	1	18	5	....	24
Swedish................................	....	9	2	....	11
Other races *a*..........................	....	34	4	....	38
Total.............................	7	102	17	3	129
Grand total.......................	9	181	33	9	232

a "Other races" includes races having less than 10 representatives of this sex and age and pupils whose race is not reported.

BOYS: AGE 7 YEARS.

General nativity and race of father of pupil.	Kinder-garten.	Elementary grades.				Special and un-graded schools.	Total.
		1.	2.	3.	4.		
Native-born, White........................	....	46	41	7	2	8	104
Foreign-born:							
Canadian, French.........................	2	19	6	2	....	1	30
Canadian, Other.........................	....	4	3	5	....	....	12
German................................	....	13	16	....	....	....	29
Scotch................................	....	....	8	1	....	1	10
Swedish................................	....	11	10	....	....	....	21
Other races *a*..........................	....	15	15	2	....	....	32
Total.............................	2	62	58	10	....	2	134
Grand total.......................	2	108	99	17	2	10	238

a "Other races" includes races having less than 10 representatives of this sex and age and pupils whose race is not reported.

TABLE 4.—*Race and grade, by age—Number of pupils of each specified age in each grade, by general nativity and race of father of pupil*—Continued.

BOYS: AGE 8 YEARS.

General nativity and race of father of pupil.	Elementary grades.					Special and ungraded schools.	Total.
	1.	2.	3.	4.	5.		
Native-born, White	22	32	33	19	3	4	113
Foreign-born:							
Canadian, French	13	7	5			4	29
Canadian, Other	2	1	4	3			10
English		7	5				12
German	6	9	1	1			17
Irish	4	7	1	1		2	15
Swedish		6	5	2			13
Other races a	6	11	4	1			22
Total	31	48	25	8		6	118
Grand total	53	80	58	27	3	10	231

a "Other races" includes races having less than 10 representatives of this sex and age and pupils whose race is not reported.

BOYS: AGE 9 YEARS.

General nativity and race of father of pupil.	Elementary grades.						Special and ungraded schools.	Total.
	1.	2.	3.	4.	5.	6.		
Native-born, White	7	14	38	28	10	1	9	107
Foreign-born:								
Canadian, French	7	6	6	1	2		1	23
Canadian, Other		2	5	3				10
German	1	4	10	4				19
Swedish	1		4	2	3	1		11
Other races a	4	6	14	8	1		1	34
Total	13	18	39	18	6	1	2	97
Grand total	20	32	77	46	16	2	11	204

a "Other races" includes races having less than 10 representatives of this sex and age and pupils whose race is not reported.

BOYS: AGE 10 YEARS.

General nativity and race of father of pupil.	Elementary grades.							Special and ungraded schools.	Total.
	1.	2.	3.	4.	5.	6.	7.		
Native-born, White	2	13	16	35	34	17	4	2	123
Foreign-born:									
Canadian, French	4	3	2	1	1			1	12
Canadian, Other	1		3	7	4	1			16
German		3	7	4	8				22
Irish	1		3	2	3	2	2		13
Swedish		2	3	3	6	2			16
Other races a	1	1	9	5	5	1		1	23
Total	7	9	27	22	27	6	2	2	102
Grand total	9	22	43	57	61	23	6	4	225

a "Other races" includes races having less than 10 representatives of this sex and age and pupils whose race is not reported.

TABLE 4.—*Race and grade, by age—Number of pupils of each specified age in each grade, by general nativity and race of father of pupil*—Continued.

BOYS: AGE 11 YEARS.

General nativity and race of father of pupil.	Elementary grades.									Special and ungraded schools.	Total.
	1.	2.	3.	4.	5.	6.	7.	8.	9.		
Native-born, White	2	4	8	19	35	29	16	5	....	6	124
Foreign-born:											
Canadian, French	2	7	2	1	4	4	....	1	....	....	21
Canadian, Other	1	....	....	2	5	2	....	1	....	....	11
English	....	1	1	5	5	2	2	....	....	....	16
German	....	2	1	5	5	3	4	1	....	....	21
Hebrew, Russian	....	3	....	2	3	2	1	....	1	....	12
Swedish	1	....	3	2	7	10	2	....	....	....	25
Other races *a*	1	1	3	5	5	4	4	....	....	....	23
Total	5	14	10	22	34	27	13	3	1	....	129
Grand total	7	18	18	41	69	56	29	8	1	6	253

a "Other races" includes races having less than 10 representatives of this sex and age and pupils whose race is not reported.

BOYS: AGE 12 YEARS.

General nativity and race of father of pupil.	Elementary grades.									High school, second year.	Special and ungraded schools.	Total.
	1.	2.	3.	4.	5.	6.	7.	8.	9.			
Native-born, White	1	3	2	10	29	26	27	14	1	1	9	123
Foreign-born:												
Canadian, French	1	7	3	10	3	1	4	....	....	....	4	33
Canadian, Other	....	....	1	....	1	8	1	1	....	....	..	12
English	....	....	....	1	6	3	1	....	....	....	1	12
German	....	....	3	2	7	5	9	2	....	....	....	28
Irish	....	2	3	....	4	3	2	3	....	....	1	18
Scotch	....	....	1	1	2	3	1	4	....	....	....	12
Swedish	....	....	....	1	6	5	2	1	....	....	....	15
Other races *a*	....	....	1	1	3	3	1	....	....	....	....	9
Total	1	9	12	15	27	34	23	12	....	....	6	139
Grand total	2	12	14	25	56	60	50	26	1	1	15	262

a "Other races" includes races having less than 10 representatives of this sex and age and pupils whose race is not reported.

BOYS: AGE 13 YEARS.

General nativity and race of father of pupil.	Elementary grades.									High school, first year.	Special and ungraded schools.	Total.
	1.	2.	3.	4.	5.	6.	7.	8.	9.			
Native-born, White	....	2	5	4	12	11	32	21	20	10	3	120
Foreign-born:												
Canadian, French	1	4	6	10	8	7	1	1	....	....	5	43
Canadian, Other	....	....	....	1	4	2	3	1	3	....	....	14
German	....	....	....	1	6	3	13	6	1	1	....	31
Irish	....	....	....	....	1	3	1	3	2	....	....	10
Other races *a*	....	2	2	2	4	4	16	8	2	....	....	40
Total	1	6	8	14	23	19	34	19	8	1	5	138
Grand total	1	8	13	18	35	30	66	40	28	11	8	258

a "Other races" includes races having less than 10 representatives of this sex and age and pupils whose race is not reported.

TABLE 4.—*Race and grade, by age—Number of pupils of each specified age in each grade, by general nativity and race of father of pupil*—Continued.

BOYS: AGE 14 YEARS.

General nativity and race of father of pupil.	Elementary grades.									High school.		Un-graded.	Total.
	1.	2.	3.	4.	5.	6.	7.	8.	9.	First year.	Second year.		
Native-born, White		1	1	3	9	12	15	16	16	14	5	4	96
Foreign-born:													
Canadian, French	1	4	3	7	2	1	3	2	2			6	31
Canadian, Other				1	1	1	1	3	3	2	1		13
German						4	4	2	1				11
Swedish						1	2	4	3			1	11
Other races *a*			2		4	1	6	4	5	4			26
Total	1	4	5	8	7	8	16	15	14	6	1	7	92
Grand total	1	5	6	11	16	20	31	31	30	20	6	11	188

a "Other races" includes races having less than 10 representatives of this sex and age and pupils whose race is not reported.

BOYS: AGE 15 YEARS.

General nativity and race of father of pupil.	Elementary grades.									High school.				Total.
	1.	2.	3.	4.	5.	6.	7.	8.	9.	First year.	Second year.	Third year.	Fourth year.	
Native-born, White					1	2	5	5	15	32	13	4	1	78
Foreign-born:														
Canadian, French	1			1	1	1	1	3	1	1	2			12
Canadian, Other						1	1	2	3	2		1		10
Other races *a*		2	2	1		2	2	3	4	4	2	2		24
Total	1	2	2	2	1	4	4	8	8	7	4	3		46
Grand total	1	2	2	2	2	6	9	13	23	39	17	7	1	124

a "Other races" includes races having less than 10 representatives of this sex and age and pupils whose race is not reported.

BOYS: AGE 16 YEARS.

General nativity and race of father of pupil.	Elementary grades.				High school.				Total.
	6.	7.	8.	9.	First year.	Second year.	Third year.	Fourth year.	
Native-born, White	3			10	8	13	16	6	56
Foreign-born, other races *a*		1	2	4	5	4	6	1	23
Grand total	3	1	2	14	13	17	22	7	79

a "Other races" includes races having less than 10 representatives of this sex and age and pupils whose race is not reported.

TABLE 4.—*Race and grade, by age—Number of pupils of each specified age in each grade, by general nativity and race of father of pupil*—Continued.

BOYS: AGE 17 YEARS.

General nativity and race of father of pupil.	Elementary grades.		High school.				Total.
	7.	9.	First year.	Second year.	Third year.	Fourth year.	
Native-born, White		1	4	4	16	11	36
Foreign-born, other races *a*	1		2	1	3	1	8
Grand total	1	1	6	5	19	12	44

a "Other races" includes races having less than 10 representatives of this sex and age and pupils whose race is not reported.

BOYS: AGE 18 YEARS.

General nativity and race of father of pupil.	High school.				Total.
	First year.	Second year.	Third year.	Fourth year.	
Native-born, White	1		4	15	20
Foreign-born, other races *a*		1	2	2	5
Grand total	1	1	6	17	25

a "Other races" includes races having less than 10 representatives of this sex and age and pupils whose race is not reported.

BOYS: AGE 19 YEARS.

General nativity and race of father of pupil.	High school.			Total.
	First year.	Third year.	Fourth year.	
Native-born, White	1	2	6	9
Foreign-born, other races *a*			1	1
Grand total	1	2	7	10

a "Other races" includes races having less than 10 representatives of this sex and age and pupils whose race is not reported.

BOYS: AGE 20 YEARS.

General nativity and race of father of pupil.	High school fourth year.
Native-born, White	1
Foreign-born, other races *a*	1
Grand total	2

a "Other races" includes races having less than 10 representatives of this sex and age and pupils whose race is not reported.

TABLE 4.—*Race and grade, by age—Number of pupils of each specified age in each grade, by general nativity and race of father of pupil*—Continued.

GIRLS: AGE 4 YEARS.

General nativity and race of father of pupil.	Kinder-garten.
Native-born, White	11
Foreign-born:	
Canadian, French	10
Other races *a*	6
Total	16
Grand total	27

a "Other races" includes races having less than 10 representatives of this sex and age and pupils whose race is not reported.

GIRLS: AGE 5 YEARS.

General nativity and race of father of pupil.	Kinder-garten.	Elemen-tary, grade 1.	Un-graded.	Total.
Native-born, White	9	57	1	67
Foreign-born:				
Canadian, French	8	17	2	27
Other races *a*	4	31	....	35
Total	12	48	2	62
Grand total	21	105	3	129

a "Other races" includes races having less than 10 representatives of this sex and age and pupils whose race is not reported.

GIRLS: AGE 6 YEARS.

General nativity and race of father of pupil.	Kinder-garten.	Elementary grades.		Special and un-graded schools.	Total.
		1.	2.		
Native-born, White	....	80	21	3	104
Foreign-born:					
Canadian, French	3	25	2	1	31
Canadian, Other	....	8	2	....	10
German	....	17	6	....	23
Irish	....	8	2	....	10
Swedish	....	12	2	....	14
Other races *a*	....	24	6	1	31
Total	3	94	20	2	119
Grand total	3	174	41	5	223

a "Other races" includes races having less than 10 representatives of this sex and age and pupils whose race is not reported.

TABLE 4.—*Race and grade, by age—Number of pupils of each specified age in each grade, by general nativity and race of father of pupil—Continued.*

GIRLS: AGE 7 YEARS.

General nativity and race of father of pupil.	Elementary grades.				Special and un-graded schools.	Total.
	1.	2.	3.	4.		
Native-born, White	40	44	15	1	3	103
Foreign-born:						
Canadian, French	26	5	1		2	34
Canadian, Other	4	9	2			15
German	10	11	1	1		23
Hebrew, Russian	6	4	3			13
Swedish	5	3	2			10
Other races *a*	11	16	2			29
Total	62	48	11	1	2	124
Grand total	102	92	26	2	5	227

a "Other races" includes races having less than 10 representatives of this sex and age and pupils whose race is not reported.

GIRLS: AGE 8 YEARS.

General nativity and race of father of pupil.	Elementary grades.					Special and un-graded schools.	Total.
	1.	2.	3.	4.	7.		
Native-born, White	24	42	40	14		6	126
Foreign-born:							
Canadian, French	9	5	4	1			19
Canadian, Other	1	4	8	5			19
German	2	6	7			1	15
Hebrew (not specified)		4	6	2			12
Irish	4	2	5	1			12
Swedish	1	4	5	4			14
Other races *a*	1	7	4	2	1		15
Total	18	32	39	15	1	1	106
Grand total	42	74	79	29	1	7	232

a "Other races" includes races having less than 10 representatives of this sex and age and pupils whose race is not reported.

GIRLS: AGE 9 YEARS.

General nativity and race of father of pupil.	Elementary grades.						Total.
	1.	2.	3.	4.	5.	6.	
Native-born, White	5	17	25	39	15	2	103
Foreign-born:							
Canadian, French	4	5	5				14
Canadian, Other		2	4	4	2		12
German	2	8	7		1		18
Irish	1	2	2	4	2		11
Scotch		2	4	4	2		12
Swedish		1	3	6	1		11
Other races *a*	3	5	10	6	1		25
Total	10	25	35	24	9		103
Grand total	15	42	60	63	24	2	206

a "Other races" includes races having less than 10 representatives of this sex and age and pupils whose race is not reported.

TABLE 4.—*Race and grade, by age—Number of pupils of each specified age in each grade, by general nativity and race of father of pupil*—Continued.

GIRLS: AGE 10 YEARS.

General nativity and race of father of pupil.	Elementary grades.							Special and un-graded schools.	Total.
	1.	2.	3.	4.	5.	6.	7.		
Native-born, White	2	5	15	26	37	19	3	4	111
Foreign-born:									
Canadian, French	4	2	4	1	3	3	......	2	19
Canadian, Other		1		5	7	5			18
English			3	8	3	2			16
German		2	7	1	11				21
Hebrew (not specified)	1	3	3	3	2	1			13
Irish	1		3	1	6	1			12
Swedish			4	8	7	2		1	22
Other races *a*			4	5	3		2		14
Total	6	8	28	32	42	14	2	3	135
Grand total	8	13	43	58	79	33	5	7	246

a "Other races" includes races having less than 10 representatives of this sex and age and pupils whose race is not reported.

GIRLS: AGE 11 YEARS.

General nativity and race of father of pupil.	Elementary grades.									Un-graded schools.	Total.
	1.	2.	3.	4.	5.	6.	7.	8.	9.		
Native-born, White	1	2	7	19	32	33	24	5	1	2	126
Foreign-born:											
Canadian, French		5	2	4	3	2	1			1	18
Canadian, Other				2	4	3	1				10
German		2	3	1	5	3	7				21
Scotch				1	4	5					10
Swedish				1	4	4	3				12
Other races *a*	1	2	3	5	7	6	3				27
Total	1	9	8	14	27	23	15			1	98
Grand total	2	11	15	33	59	56	39	5	1	3	224

a "Other races" includes races having less than 10 representatives of this sex and age and pupils whose race is not reported.

GIRLS: AGE 12 YEARS.

General nativity and race of father of pupil.	Elementary grades.									Special and un-graded schools.	Total.
	1.	2.	3.	4.	5.	6.	7.	8.	9.		
Native-born, White	1	2	1	10	16	21	37	20	10	6	124
Foreign-born:											
Canadian, French		2	5	9	12	2	2	1			33
German			1	1	1	7	11	1			22
Hebrew, Russian		1	1		1	2	4	1	2		12
Swedish				1	1	5	8	1			16
Other races *a*			3	7	9	8	9	6	2	1	45
Total		3	10	18	24	24	34	10	4	1	128
Grand total	1	5	11	28	40	45	71	30	14	7	252

a "Other races" includes races having less than 10 representatives of this sex and age and pupils whose race is not reported.

TABLE 4.—*Race and grade, by age—Number of pupils of each specified age in each grade, by general nativity and race of father of pupil*—Continued.

GIRLS: AGE 13 YEARS.

General nativity and race of father of pupil.	Elementary grades.									High school, first year.	Special and ungraded schools.	Total.
	1.	2.	3.	4.	5.	6.	7.	8.	9.			
Native-born, White	1	....	2	6	8	9	19	27	20	9	2	103
Foreign-born:												
Canadian, French		3	5	6	8	6	3	2			2	35
Canadian, Other				2		3	3	2				10
English				4	1	3	5	1				14
German			1	6	3	9	7					26
Hebrew (not specified)				4	1	3	3			1		12
Irish					3	4	3	2				12
Swedish				1	3	3	4					11
Other races a			2	4	1	....	8	2		1	1	19
Total	....	3	8	10	26	17	36	29	5	2	3	139
Grand total	1	3	10	16	34	26	55	56	25	11	5	242

a "Other races" includes races having less than 10 representatives of this sex and age and pupils whose race is not reported.

GIRLS: AGE 14 YEARS.

General nativity and race of father of pupil.	Elementary grades.							High school.		Special and ungraded schools.	Total.
	3.	4.	5.	6.	7.	8.	9.	First year.	Second year.		
Native-born:											
White			3	6	13	17	29	26	4		98
Negro				2							2
Total native-born			3	8	13	17	29	26	4		100
Foreign-born:											
Canadian, French	2	3	2	3	3	7	1			2	23
Canadian, Other				3	4	6		4			17
Swedish					1	4	4	2			11
Other races a	1	2	4	3	11	9	3	3	4	1	41
Total foreign-born	3	5	6	6	18	24	14	9	4	3	92
Grand total	3	5	9	14	31	41	43	35	8	3	192

a "Other races" includes races having less than 10 representatives of this sex and age and pupils whose race is not reported.

GIRLS: AGE 15 YEARS.

General nativity and race of father of pupil.	Elementary grades.							High school.			Ungraded schools.	Total.
	2.	3.	4.	6.	7.	8.	9.	First year.	Second year.	Third year.		
Native-born, White			1		5	6	13	31	14	10		80
Foreign-born:												
Canadian, other than French					1		1	4	3		1	10
Other races a	1	1	2	5	4	8	6	6	2	1		36
Total foreign-born	1	1	2	5	5	8	7	10	5	1	1	46
Grand total	1	1	3	5	10	14	20	41	19	11	1	126

a "Other races" includes races having less than 10 representatives of this sex and age and pupils whose race is not reported.

TABLE **4.**—*Race and grade, by age—Number of pupils of each specified age in each grade, by general nativity and race of father of pupil*—Continued.

GIRLS: AGE 16 YEARS.

General nativity and race of father of pupil.	Elementary grades.						High school.				Total.
	4.	5.	6.	7.	8.	9.	First year.	Second year.	Third year.	Fourth year.	
Native-born, White............					2	8	18	16	16	8	68
Foreign-born, other races *a*.........	1	2	1	1	3	2	4	4	8	1	27
Total................	1	2	1	1	5	10	22	20	24	9	95

a "Other races" includes races having less than 10 representatives of this sex and age and pupils whose race is not reported.

GIRLS: AGE 17 YEARS.

General nativity and race of father of pupil.	Elementary grades.			High chool.				Total.
	6.	7.	9.	First year.	Second year.	Third year.	Fourth year.	
Native-born, White................	1	......	1	3	3	13	21	42
Foreign-born, other races *a*...............	......	1	1	3	1	7	5	18
Total..................	1	1	2	6	4	20	26	60

a "Other races" includes races having less than 10 representatives of this sex and age and pupils whose race is not reported.

GIRLS: AGE 18 YEARS.

General nativity and race of father of pupil.	High school.			Total.
	Second year.	Third year.	Fourth year.	
Native-born, White...............	1	2	22	25
Foreign-born, other races *a*....................	1	2	3	6
Total..................	2	4	25	31

a "Other races" includes races having less than 10 representatives of this sex and age and pupils whose race is not reported.

GIRLS: AGE 19 YEARS.

General nativity and race of father of pupil.	High school.			Total.
	First year.	Third year.	Fourth year.	
Native-born, White................	1	....	5	6
Foreign-born, other races *a*.................	....	1	1	2
Total.................	1	1	6	8

a "Other races" includes races having less than 10 representatives of this sex and age and pupils whose race is not reported.

TABLE 5.—*Race distribution in each grade—Percentages.*

[This table shows in detail only races with 100 or more pupils reporting. The totals, however, are for all races.]

General nativity and race of father of pupil.	Kindergarten.	Elementary grades.										High school.					Mixed and ungraded schools.	Grand total.
		1.	2.	3.	4.	5.	6.	7.	8.	9.	Total.	First year.	Second year.	Third year.	Fourth year.	Total.		
Native-born:																		
White............	44.9	44.1	43.6	43.3	50.5	48.3	50.1	49.1	50.9	68.1	47.8 (a)	76.3	74.0	71.6	85.7	76.8	60.4	51.1
Negro............	.0	.0	.0	.0	.0	.0	.5	.0	.0	.0	.0	.0	.0	.0	.0	.0	.0	......
Total native-born...	44.9	44.1	43.6	43.3	50.5	48.3	50.7	49.1	50.9	68.1	47.8	76.3	74.0	71.6	85.7	76.8	60.4	51.1
Foreign-born:																		
Canadian, French...	29.7	19.1	12.6	11.7	12.2	10.1	8.6	4.9	7.4	2.3	11.7	1.9	5.0	.9	4.5	2.8	28.4	11.6
Canadian, Other...	5.1	4.1	5.0	6.5	7.1	6.1	6.3	3.9	6.6	9.4	5.7	6.3	6.0	9.5	.9	5.8	1.5	5.6
English.........	3.4	3.4	2.8	4.0	3.6	5.0	4.7	3.4	5.5	1.9	3.8	3.4	3.0	2.6	.9	2.6	2.2	3.6
German.........	7.6	8.7	12.7	10.1	4.5	9.9	7.6	15.5	7.7	2.8	9.3	1.9	3.0	.9	1.8	1.5	.0	8.2
Hebrew, Russian...	.0	4.1	4.2	2.4	3.9	2.4	2.3	3.2	4.1	2.8	3.4	1.0	3.0	5.2	1.8	2.4	.0	3.1
Irish...........	.8	4.4	4.9	4.8	3.4	5.3	5.0	4.2	6.3	5.2	4.7	2.4	3.0	5.2	2.7	3.2	3.0	4.4
Scotch..........	1.7	1.4	4.0	4.6	4.1	2.6	3.1	4.7	6.9	.9	3.2	1.9	3.0	2.6	.9	2.1	2.2	3.0
Swedish.........	5.9	5.8	5.0	5.8	6.6	7.1	9.1	6.1	7.0	6.6	6.4	2.4	3.0	1.7	.9	1.5	1.5	5.7
Other races......	.8	4.9	5.2	6.7	4.1	3.2	2.6	4.9	.4	.9	4.2	2.4	2.0	1.0		1.3	.7	3.7
Total foreign-born...	55.1	55.9	56.4	56.7	49.5	51.7	49.3	50.9	49.1	31.9	52.2	23.7	26.0	28.4	14.3	23.2	39.6	48.9
Grand total......	100.0	100.0	100.0	100.0	100.0	100.0	100.0	100.0	100.0	100.0	100.0	100.0	100.0	100.0	100.0	100.0	100.0	100.0

a Less than 0.05 per cent.

TABLE **6.**—*Grade distribution of each race—Percentages.*

[This table shows in detail only races with 100 or more pupils reporting. The totals, however, are for all races.]

General nativity and race of father of pupil.	Kinder-garten.	Elementary grades.										High school.					Mixed and un-graded schools.	Grand total.
		1.	2.	3.	4.	5.	6.	7.	8.	9.	Total.	First year.	Second year.	Third year.	Fourth year.	Total.		
Native-born:																		
White	2.0	16.2	10.0	8.3	9.1	9.4	7.4	7.7	5.3	5.6	79.0	6.1	2.9	3.2	3.7	15.8	3.1	1)0.
Negro	(a)	(a)	(a)	(a)	(a)	(a)	(a)	(a)	(a)	(a)	(a)	(a)	(a)	(a)	(a)	(a)	(a)	(a)
Total native-born	2.0	16.2	10.0	8.3	9.1	9.4	7.5	7.7	5.3	5.6	79.0	6.1	2.8	3.2	3.7	15.8	3.1	100.0
Foreign-born:																		
Canadian, French	5.9	30.9	12.7	9.9	9.7	8.7	5.6	3.4	3.4	.8	85.1	.7	.8	.2	.8	2.5	6.5	100.0
Canadian, Other	2.1	13.8	10.6	11.3	11.7	11.0	8.5	5.7	6.4	7.1	86.1	4.6	2.1	3.9	.4	11.0	.7	100.0
English	2.2	17.5	9.3	10.9	9.3	13.7	9.8	7.7	8.2	2.2	88.5	3.8	1.6	1.6	.5	7.7	1.6	100.0
German	2.2	20.0	18.4	12.1	5.1	12.1	7.0	15.2	5.1	1.0	95.9	1.0	.2	1.2	.5	1.9	.0	100.0
Hebrew, Russian	.0	24.7	15.8	7.6	11.4	7.6	5.7	8.2	7.0	3.8	91.8	1.3	1.9	3.8	1.3	8.2	.0	100.0
Irish	.4	18.8	12.9	10.7	7.1	13.1	8.5	7.6	7.6	4.9	90.2	2.2	1.3	2.7	1.3	7.6	1.8	100.0
Scotch	1.3	8.6	15.8	15.1	12.5	8.6	7.9	12.5	7.2	1.3	89.5	2.6	2.0	2.0	.7	7.2	2.0	100.0
Swedish	2.4	18.9	10.3	10.0	10.7	12.4	12.0	8.6	6.5	4.8	94.2	1.7	.0	.0	.3	2.7	.5	100.0
Other races	.5	25.0	16.5	17.6	10.1	8.5	5.3	10.6		1.1	95.2	2.7	1.1	.0	.0	3.7	.0	100.0
Total foreign-born	2.6	21.4	13.6	11.3	9.3	10.5	7.6	8.3	5.4	2.7	90.2	2.0	1.0	1.3	.6	4.9	2.1	100.0
Grand total	2.3	18.7	11.8	9.8	9.2	9.9	7.5	8.0	5.3	4.2	84.5	4.1	2.0	2.3	2.2	10.5	2.6	100.0

a Not computed, owing to small number involved.

PUBLIC SCHOOL TEACHERS IN ELEMENTARY GRADES AND KINDERGARTEN.

TABLE 1.—*Number of teachers in each grade, by sex and general nativity and race.*

[This table does not include 1 teacher not reporting complete data.]

General nativity and race	Male K	M 1	M 2	M 3	M 4	M 5	M 6	M 7	M 8	M 9	M Ungr.	M Total	M Total K&E	Female K	F 1	F 2	F 3	F 4	F 5	F 6	F 7	F 8	F 9	F Ungr.	F Total	F Total K&E	Total K	T 1	T 2	T 3	T 4	T 5	T 6	T 7	T 8	T 9	T Ungr.	T Total	T Total K&E	% Elem.	% Elem. & Kind.
Native-born of native father, White									1	2		3	3	3	34	35	26	23	20	16	21	15	6	5	201	204	3	34	35	26	23	20	16	21	16	8	5	204	207	76.8	77.2
Native-born of foreign father, by race of father:																																									
Canadian (other than French)																									2	2												2	2	.8	.7
English																									22	22												22	22	8.5	8.2
German																									3	3												3	3	1.2	1.1
Irish																									16	16												16	16	6.2	6.0
Scotch																									7	7												7	7	2.7	2.6
Total															9	3	8	6	9	7	2	2	4		50	50		9	3	8	6	9	7	2	2	4		50	50	19.3	18.7
Total native-born									1	2		3	3	3	43	38	34	29	29	23	23	17	10	5	251	254	3	43	38	34	29	29	23	23	18	12	5	254	257	96.1	95.9
Foreign-born:																																									
Canadian (other than French)														1											2	3	1											2	3	.8	1.1
English																									2	2												2	2	.8	.7
Irish																									4	4												4	4	1.5	1.5
Scotch																									2	2												2	2	.8	.7
Total foreign-born														1	1	1		1	5	1	1				10	11	1	1	1		1	5	1	1				10	11	3.9	4.1
Grand total									1	2		3	3	4	44	39	34	30	34	24	24	17	10	5	261	265	4	44	39	34	30	34	24	24	18	12	5	264	268	100.0	100.0

TABLE 2.—*Number of teachers engaged in teaching each specified number of years, by sex and general nativity and race.*

[This table does not include 2 teachers not reporting complete data.]

General nativity and race	Male								Female								Total							
	Under 5 years	5 to 9 years	10 to 14 years	15 to 19 years	20 to 24 years	25 to 29 years	30 years or over	Total	Under 5 years	5 to 9 years	10 to 14 years	15 to 19 years	20 to 24 years	25 to 29 years	30 years or over	Total	Under 5 years	5 to 9 years	10 to 14 years	15 to 19 years	20 to 24 years	25 to 29 years	30 years or over	Total
Native-born of native father, White	2			1				3	52	57	38	31	12	5	9	204	54	57	38	32	12	5	9	207
Native-born of foreign father, by race of father:																								
Canadian (other than French)									2							2	2							2
English									5	3	2	3	3	6		22	5	3	2	3	3	6		22
German													2			3					2			3
Irish									5	5	5	1				15	5	5	5	1				15
Scotch									4	3						7	4	3						7
Total									16	11	7	4	5	6		49	16	11	7	4	5	6		49
Total native-born	2			1				3	68	68	45	35	17	11	9	253	70	68	45	36	17	11	9	256
Foreign-born of foreign father:																								
Canadian (other than French)													3			3					3			3
English											2					2			2					2
Irish									2			2				4	2			2				4
Scotch									1			1				2	1			1				2
Total foreign-born									3		2	3	3			11	3		2	3	3			11
Grand total	2			1				3	71	68	47	38	20	11	9	264	73	68	47	39	20	11	9	267

PAROCHIAL SCHOOL PUPILS: GENERAL INVESTIGATION.

TABLE 1.—*Grade and age—Number of pupils by each age in each grade, by sex.*

BOYS.

Age.	Kindergarten.	Elementary grades.									Special school.	Grand total.
		1.	2.	3.	4.	5.	6.	7.	8.	Total.		
4 years												
5 years	1	15								15	10	26
6 years	11	28								28	19	58
7 years	7	32	9							41	19	67
8 years	3	49	12	5						66	23	92
9 years	2	44	16	15	1					76	8	86
10 years		34	27	20	6	2				89	1	90
11 years		17	22	23	12	8				82	3	85
12 years		12	21	30	21	19	4	1		108	3	111
13 years		4	17	11	12	5	15	3	1	68		68
14 years		1	3	3	8	7	8	1	6	37		37
15 years			15		1		2		2	20		20
16 years							1		1	2		2
Total	24	236	142	107	61	41	30	5	10	632	86	742

GIRLS.

Age.	Kindergarten.	Elementary grades.									Special school.	Grand total.
		1.	2.	3.	4.	5.	6.	7.	8.	Total.		
4 years												
5 years	3	10								10	7	20
6 years	14	22								22	30	66
7 years	12	36	8	2						46	16	74
8 years	14	40	14	10						64	17	95
9 years	5	33	18	15	6					72	7	84
10 years	1	34	25	23	10	1	1			94	1	96
11 years	1	21	14	26	22	16				99	1	101
12 years		5	24	11	20	13	9			82		82
13 years	1		8	12	17	9	12		2	60		61
14 years		1	1	4	7	5	10	5	7	40		40
15 years				1	2	1	6	3	7	20		20
16 years					1				6	7		7
17 years									1	1		1
Total	51	202	112	104	85	45	38	8	23	617	79	747

TOTAL.

Age.	Kindergarten.	Elementary grades.									Special school.	Grand total.
		1.	2.	3.	4.	5.	6.	7.	8.	Total.		
4 years												
5 years	4	25								25	17	46
6 years	25	50								50	49	124
7 years	19	68	17	2						87	35	141
8 years	17	89	26	15						130	40	187
9 years	7	77	34	30	7					148	15	170
10 years	1	68	52	43	16	3	1			183	2	186
11 years	1	38	36	49	34	24				181	4	186
12 years		17	45	41	41	32	13	1		190	3	193
13 years	1	4	25	23	29	14	27	3	3	128		129
14 years		2	4	7	15	12	18	6	13	77		77
15 years			15	1	3	1	8	3	9	40		40
16 years					1		1		7	9		9
17 years									1	1		1
Total	75	438	254	211	146	86	68	13	33	1,249	165	1,489

TABLE 2.—*Race, sex, and grade—Number of pupils of each sex in each grade, by general nativity and race of father of pupil.*

General nativity and race of father of pupil.	Kindergarten.	Elementary grades.									Special school.	Grand total.
		1.	2.	3.	4.	5.	6.	7.	8.	Total.		
Native-born:												
White—												
Male	9	25	8	4	8	8	2	1	3	59	1	69
Female	10	27	7	4	16	6	3	2	3	68	2	80
Total	19	52	15	8	24	14	5	3	6	127	3	149
Foreign-born:												
Canadian, French—												
Male	7	156	63	72	19	28	19	....	6	363	85	455
Female	13	139	84	47	34	32	26	....	16	378	77	468
Total	20	295	147	119	53	60	45	....	22	741	162	923
Canadian, Other—												
Male		3	2	1	6	....	....	....	....	12		12
Female		3	....	2	4	....	1	....	1	11		11
Total		6	2	3	10	....	1	....	1	23		23
English—												
Male		3	1	1	1	2	....	1	1	10		10
Female	4	....	1	19	....	2	2	2		26		30
Total	4	3	2	20	1	4	2	3	1	36		40
German—												
Male	1	1	1	....	1	1	2	....		6		7
Female	5	1	1	....	2	....	....	....		4		9
Total	6	2	2	....	3	1	2	....		10		16
Irish—												
Male	7	8	33	6	2	1	6	2	....	58		65
Female	17	7	5	9	7	5	6	4	2	45		62
Total	24	15	38	15	9	6	12	6	2	103		127
Polish—												
Male		35	29	22	20	....	....	....	....	106		106
Female		21	12	20	20	....	....	....	....	73		73
Total		56	41	42	40	....	....	....	....	179		179
Scotch—												
Male		2	2	....	3	....	....	1	....	8		8
Female	1	2	2	1	1	....	....	....	1	7		8
Total	1	4	4	1	4	....	....	1	1	15		16
Russian—												
Male		3	....	....	....	....	....			3		3
Female		2	....	....	....	....	....			2		2
Total		5	....	....	....	....	....			5		5
Other races a—												
Male		....	3	1	1	1	1	....	....	7		7
Female	1	....	....	2	1	....	....	....	....	3		4
Total	1	....	3	3	2	1	1	....	....	10		11
Total—												
Male	15	211	134	103	53	33	28	4	7	573	85	673
Female	41	175	105	100	69	39	35	6	20	549	77	667
Total	56	386	239	203	122	72	63	10	27	1,122	162	1,340
Grand total—												
Male	24	236	142	107	61	41	30	5	10	632	86	742
Female	51	202	112	104	85	45	38	8	23	617	79	747
Total	75	438	254	211	146	86	68	13	33	1,249	165	1,489

a "Other races" includes: French, 6; Italian, North, 2; Russian, 3.

TABLE **3.**—*Race, sex, and age, by grade—Number of pupils of each age in each grade, by sex and by general nativity and race of father of pupil.*

KINDERGARTEN.

BOYS.

General nativity and race of father of pupil.	Number of pupils of each age.								Total.
	5.	6.	7.	8.	9.	10.	11.	13.	
Native-born, White	1	3	5						9
Foreign-born:									
Canadian, French		3	1	2	1				7
German			1						1
Irish		5		1	1				7
Total		8	2	3	2				15
Grand total	1	11	7	3	2				24

GIRLS.

	5.	6.	7.	8.	9.	10.	11.	13.	
Native-born, White	1	1	3	3	1	1			10
Foreign-born:									
Canadian, French	1	4	3	3	2				13
English		2	1	1					4
German	1	1	1		2				5
Irish		5	4	6			1	1	17
Scotch		1							1
Other races a				1					1
Total	2	13	9	11	4		1	1	41
Grand total	3	14	12	14	5	1	1	1	51

TOTAL.

	5.	6.	7.	8.	9.	10.	11.	13.	
Native-born, White	2	4	8	3	1	1			19
Foreign-born:									
Canadian, French	1	7	4	5	3				20
English		2	1	1					4
German	1	1	2		2				6
Irish		10	4	7	1		1	1	24
Scotch		1							1
Other races a				1					1
Total	2	21	11	14	6		1	1	56
Grand total	4	25	19	17	7	1	1	1	75

a "Other races" includes races having less than 10 representatives in this city and pupils whose race is not reported.

TABLE 3.—*Race, sex, and age, by grade—Number of pupils of each age in each grade, by sex and by general nativity and race of father of pupil*—Continued.

FIRST GRADE.

BOYS.

General nativity and race of father of pupil.	Number of pupils of each age.										Total.
	5.	6.	7.	8.	9.	10.	11.	12.	13.	14.	
Native-born, White	1	4	2	9	2	6	1				25
Foreign-born:											
Canadian, French	4	7	15	34	37	26	16	12	4	1	156
Canadian, Other			1	1	1						3
English				1	1	1					3
German				1							1
Irish	2			2	3	1					8
Polish	7	15	13								35
Russian		2	1								3
Scotch	1			1							2
Total	14	24	30	40	42	28	16	12	4	1	211
Grand total	15	28	32	49	44	34	17	12	4	1	236

GIRLS.

General nativity and race of father of pupil.	5.	6.	7.	8.	9.	10.	11.	12.	13.	14.	Total.
Native-born, White	2		2	7	8	6	2				27
Foreign-born:											
Canadian, French		14	24	30	23	25	18	4		1	139
Canadian, Other	1		1			1					3
German							1				1
Irish			2	1	2	1	1				7
Polish	7	7	6	1							21
Russian		1		1							2
Scotch			1			1					2
Total	8	22	34	33	25	28	19	5		1	175
Grand total	10	22	36	40	33	34	21	5		1	202

TOTAL.

General nativity and race of father of pupil.	5.	6.	7.	8.	9.	10.	11.	12.	13.	14.	Total.
Native-born, White	3	4	4	16	10	12	3				52
Foreign-born:											
Canadian, French	4	21	39	64	60	51	34	16	4	2	295
Canadian, Other	1		2	1	1	1					6
English				1	1	1					3
German				1				1			2
Irish	2		2	3	5	2	1				15
Polish	14	22	19	1							56
Russian		3	1	1							5
Scotch	1		1	1		1					4
Total	22	46	64	73	67	56	35	17	4	2	386
Grand total	25	50	68	89	77	68	38	17	4	2	438

TABLE 3.—*Race, sex, and age, by grade—Number of pupils of each age in each grade, by sex and by general nativity and race of father of pupil—Continued.*

SECOND GRADE.

BOYS.

General nativity and race of father of pupil.	Number of pupils of each age.									Total.
	7.	8.	9.	10.	11.	12.	13.	14.	15.	
Native-born, White	1	1	1	1	......	3	......	1	......	8
Foreign-born:										
Canadian, French	......	3	7	15	16	17	4	1	......	63
Canadian, Other	......	......	1	1	......	......	......	......	......	2
English	......	......	......	......	1	......	......	......	......	1
German	......	......	......	......	1	......	......	......	......	1
Irish	......	......	2	3	......	......	13	......	15	33
Polish	7	8	4	6	2	1	......	1	......	29
Scotch	......	......	......	1	1	......	......	......	......	2
Other races *a*	1	......	1	......	1	......	......	......	......	3
Total	8	11	15	26	22	18	17	2	15	134
Grand total	9	12	16	27	22	21	17	3	15	142

GIRLS.

General nativity and race of father of pupil.	7.	8.	9.	10.	11.	12.	13.	14.	15.	Total.
Native-born, White	1	1	3	......	......	1	1	......	......	7
Foreign-born:										
Canadian, French	......	8	10	22	14	22	7	1	......	84
English	......	......	......	......	......	1	......	......	......	1
German	......	......	......	1	......	......	......	......	......	1
Irish	1	......	2	2	......	......	......	......	......	5
Polish	6	4	2	......	......	......	......	......	......	12
Scotch	......	1	1	......	......	......	......	......	......	2
Total	7	13	15	25	14	23	7	1	......	105
Grand total	8	14	18	25	14	24	8	1	......	112

TOTAL.

General nativity and race of father of pupil.	7.	8.	9.	10.	11.	12.	13.	14.	15.	Total.
Native-born, White	2	2	4	1	......	4	1	1	......	15
Foreign-born:										
Canadian, French	......	11	17	37	30	39	11	2	......	147
Canadian, Other	......	......	1	1	......	......	......	......	......	2
English	......	......	......	......	1	1	......	......	......	2
German	......	......	......	1	1	......	......	......	......	2
Irish	1	......	4	5	......	......	13	......	15	38
Polish	13	12	6	6	2	1	......	1	......	41
Scotch	......	1	1	1	......	......	......	......	......	4
Other races *a*	1	......	1	......	1	......	......	......	......	3
Total	15	24	30	51	36	41	24	3	15	239
Grand total	17	26	34	·52	36	45	25	4	15	254

a "Other races ' includes races having less than 10 representatives in this city and pupils whose race is not reported.

TABLE 3.—*Race, sex, and age, by grade—Number of pupils of each age in each grade, by sex and by general nativity and race of father of pupil*—Continued.

THIRD GRADE.

BOYS.

General nativity and race of father of pupil.	Number of pupils of each age.									Total.
	7.	8.	9.	10.	11.	12.	13.	14.	15.	
Native-born, White			2	2						4
Foreign-born:										
Canadian, French		1	8	12	17	24	8	2		72
Canadian, Other					1					1
English						1				1
Irish		3		1	2					6
Polish		1	5	5	3	5	2	1		22
Other races a							1			1
Total		5	13	18	23	30	11	3		103
Grand total		5	15	20	23	30	11	3		107

GIRLS.

General nativity and race of father of pupil.	7.	8.	9.	10.	11.	12.	13.	14.	15.	Total.
Native-born, White			1	1	1	1				4
Foreign-born:										
Canadian, French		3	9	17		6	8	3	1	47
Canadian, Other							1	1		2
English			1		18					19
Irish			1		5	1	2			9
Polish	2	7	3	5	2	1				20
Scotch							1			1
Other races a							1	1		2
Total	2	10	14	22	25	10	12	4	1	100
Grand total	2	10	15	23	26	11	12	4	1	104

TOTAL.

General nativity and race of father of pupil.	7.	8.	9.	10.	11.	12.	13.	14.	15.	Total.
Native-born, White			3	3	1	1				8
Foreign-born:										
Canadian, French		4	17	29	17	30	16	5	1	119
Canadian, Other					1		1	1		3
English			1		18	1				20
Irish		3	1	1	7	1	2			15
Polish	2	8	8	10	5	6	2	1		42
Scotch						1				1
Other races a							1	2		3
Total	2	15	27	40	48	40	23	7	1	203
Grand total	2	15	30	43	49	41	23	7	1	211

a "Other races" includes races having less than 10 representatives in this city and pupils whose race is not reported.

TABLE 3.—*Race, sex, and age, by grade—Number of pupils of each age in each grade, by sex and by general nativity and race of father of pupil*—Continued.

FOURTH GRADE.

BOYS.

General nativity and race of father of pupil.	Number of pupils of each age.								Total.
	9.	10.	11.	12.	13.	14.	15.	16.	
Native-born, White	......	3	3	1	......	1	......	......	8
Foreign-born:									
Canadian, French	1	1	1	10	2	3	1	......	19
Canadian, Other	......	......	3	1	2	......	......	......	6
English	......	......	1	......	......	......	......	......	1
German	......	......	......	1	......	......	......	......	1
Irish	......	......	1	1	......	......	......	......	2
Polish	......	2	2	7	6	3	......	......	20
Scotch	......	......	1	......	2	......	......	......	3
Other races a	......	......	......	......	......	1	......	......	1
Total	1	3	9	20	12	7	1	......	53
Grand total	1	6	12	21	12	8	1	......	61

GIRLS.

General nativity and race of father of pupil.	9.	10.	11.	12.	13.	14.	15.	16.	Total.
Native-born, White	......	1	3	4	4	3	......	1	16
Foreign-born:									
Canadian, French	3	6	8	7	8	2	......	......	34
Canadian, Other	......	1	1	1	......	1	......	......	4
German	......	1	......	1	......	......	......	......	2
Irish	1	......	3	......	2	......	1	......	7
Polish	2	1	7	6	3	1	......	......	20
Scotch	......	......	......	......	......	......	1	......	1
Other races a	......	......	......	1	......	......	......	......	1
Total	6	9	19	16	13	4	2	......	69
Grand total	6	10	22	20	17	7	2	1	85

TOTAL.

General nativity and race of father of pupil.	9.	10.	11.	12.	13.	14.	15.	16.	Total.
Native-born, White	......	4	6	5	4	4	......	1	24
Foreign-born:									
Canadian, French	4	7	9	17	10	5	1	......	53
Canadian, Other	......	1	4	2	2	1	......	......	10
English	......	......	1	......	......	......	......	......	1
German	......	1	......	2	......	......	......	......	3
Irish	1	......	4	1	2	......	1	......	9
Polish	2	3	9	13	9	4	......	......	40
Scotch	......	......	1	......	2	......	1	......	4
Other races a	......	......	......	1	......	1	......	......	2
Total	7	12	28	36	25	11	3	......	122
Grand total	7	16	34	41	29	15	3	1	146

a "Other races" includes races having less than 10 representatives in this city and pupils whose race is not reported.

TABLE 3.—*Race, sex, and age, by grade—Number of pupils of each age in each grade, by sex and by general nativity and race of father of pupil*—Continued.

FIFTH GRADE.

BOYS.

General nativity and race of father of pupil.	Number of pupils of each age.						Total.
	10.	11.	12.	13.	14.	15.	
Native-born, White		2	5	1			8
Foreign-born:							
Canadian, French	2	4	11	4	7		28
English		2					2
German			1				1
Irish			1				1
Other races a			1				1
Total	2	6	14	4	7		33
Grand total	2	8	19	5	7		41

GIRLS.

General nativity and race of father of pupil.	10.	11.	12.	13.	14.	15.	Total.
Native-born, White		3	2	1			6
Foreign-born:							
Canadian, French	1	10	8	7	5	1	32
English		2					2
Irish		1	3	1			5
Total	1	13	11	8	5	1	39
Grand total	1	16	13	9	5	1	45

TOTAL.

General nativity and race of father of pupil.	10.	11.	12.	13.	14.	15.	Total.
Native-born, White		5	7	2			14
Foreign-born:							
Canadian, French	3	14	19	11	12	1	60
English		4					4
German			1				1
Irish		1	4	1			6
Other races a			1				1
Total	3	19	25	12	12	1	72
Grand total	3	24	32	14	12	1	86

a "Other races" includes races having less than 10 representatives in this city and pupils whose race is not reported.

TABLE 3.—*Race, sex, and age, by grade—Number of pupils of each age in each grade, by sex and by general nativity and race of father of pupil*—Continued.

SIXTH GRADE.

BOYS.

General nativity and race of father of pupil.	Number of pupils of each age.						Total.
	10.	12.	13.	14.	15.	16.	
Native-born, White			1	1			2
Foreign-born:							
Canadian, French		4	7	7	1		19
German			1			1	2
Irish			5		1		6
Other races a			1				1
Total		4	14	7	2	1	28
Grand total		4	15	8	2	1	30

GIRLS.

General nativity and race of father of pupil.	Number of pupils of each age.						Total.
	10.	12.	13.	14.	15.	16.	
Native-born, White		1	1		1		3
Foreign-born:							
Canadian, French	1	5	8	7	5		26
Canadian, Other		1					1
English			1	1			2
Irish		2	2	2			6
Total	1	8	11	10	5		35
Grand total	1	9	12	10	6		38

TOTAL.

General nativity and race of father of pupil.	Number of pupils of each age.						Total.
	10.	12.	13.	14.	15.	16.	
Native-born, White		1	2	1	1		5
Foreign-born:							
Canadian, French	1	9	15	14	6		45
Canadian, Other		1					1
English			1	1			2
German			1			1	2
Irish		2	7	2	1		12
Other races a			1				1
Total	1	12	25	17	7	1	63
Grand total	1	13	27	18	8	1	68

a "Other races" includes races having less than 10 representatives in this city and pupils whose race is not reported.

TABLE 3.—*Race, sex, and age, by grade—Number of pupils of each age in each grade, by sex and by general nativity and race of father of pupil*—Continued.

SEVENTH GRADE.

BOYS.

General nativity and race of father of pupil.	Number of pupils of each age.				Total.
	12.	13.	14.	15.	
Native-born, White	....	1	....	....	1
Foreign-born:					
English	....	1	....	....	1
Irish	....	1	1	....	2
Scotch	1	....	....	....	1
Total	1	2	1	....	4
Grand total	1	3	1	....	5

GIRLS.

General nativity and race of father of pupil.	Number of pupils of each age.				Total.
	12.	13.	14.	15.	
Native-born, White	....	....	....	2	2
Foreign-born:					
English	....	....	2	....	2
Irish	....	....	3	1	4
Total	....	....	5	1	6
Grand total	....	....	5	3	8

TOTAL.

General nativity and race of father of pupil.	Number of pupils of each age.				Total.
	12.	13.	14.	15.	
Native-born, White	....	1	....	2	3
Foreign-born:					
English	....	1	2	....	3
Irish	....	1	4	1	6
Scotch	1	....	....	....	1
Total	1	2	6	1	10
Grand total	1	3	6	3	13

TABLE **3.**—*Race, sex, and age, by grade—Number of pupils of each age in each grade, by sex and by general nativity and race of father of pupil*—Continued.

EIGHTH GRADE.

BOYS.

General nativity and race of father of pupil.	Number of pupils of each age.					Total.
	13.	14.	15.	16.	17.	
Native-born, White	1	2				3
Foreign-born:						
Canadian, French		3	2	1		6
English		1				1
Total		4	2	1		7
Grand total	1	6	2	1		10

GIRLS.

Native-born, White		2	1			3
Foreign-born:						
Canadian, French	2	5	3	5	1	16
Canadian, Other				1		1
Irish			2			2
Scotch			1			1
Total	2	5	6	5	1	20
Grand total	2	7	7	6	1	23

TOTAL.

Native-born, White	1	4	1			6
Foreign-born:						
Canadian, French	2	8	5	6	1	22
Canadian, Other				1		1
English		1				1
Irish			2			2
Scotch			1			1
Total	2	9	8	7	1	27
Grand total	3	13	9	7	1	33

SPECIAL GRADE.

BOYS.

General nativity and race of father of pupil.	Number of pupils of each age.								Total.
	5.	6.	7.	8.	9.	10.	11.	12.	
Native-born, White			1						1
Foreign-born, Canadian, French	10	19	18	23	8	1	3	3	85
Total	10	19	19	23	8	1	3	3	86

TABLE 3.—*Race, sex, and age, by grade—Number of pupils of each age in each grade, by sex and by general nativity and race of father of pupil—Continued.*

SPECIAL GRADE—Continued.

GIRLS.

General nativity and race of father of pupil.	Number of pupils of each age.								Total.
	5.	6.	7.	8.	9.	10.	11.	12.	
Native-born, White............		1	1	.....	.....	.....	.....	.....	2
Foreign-born, Canadian, French............	7	29	15	17	7	1	1	.....	77
Total...................	7	30	16	17	7	1	1	.....	79

TOTAL.

General nativity and race of father of pupil.	5.	6.	7.	8.	9.	10.	11.	12.	Total.
Native-born, White......		1	2	.....	.....	.....	.....	.....	3
Foreign-born, Canadian, French............	17	48	33	40	15	2	4	3	162
Total...................	17	49	35	40	15	2	4	3	165

TABLE 4.—*Race distribution in each grade—Percentages.*

[This table shows in detail only races with 100 or more pupils reporting. The totals, however, are for all races.]

General nativity and race of father of pupil.	Kinder-gar-ten.	Elementary grades.									Special school.	Grand total.
		1.	2.	3.	4.	5.	6.	7.	8.	Total.		
Native-born, White...	25.3	11.9	5.9	3.8	16.4	16.3	7.4	23.1	18.2	10.2	1.8	10.0
Foreign-born:												
Canadian, French.	26.7	67.4	57.9	56.4	36.3	69.8	66.2	.....	66.7	59.3	98.2	62.0
Irish...............	32.0	.....	15.0	7.1	6.2	7.0	17.6	46.2	6.1	8.2	.....	8.5
Polish.............	.....	12.8	16.1	19.9	27.4	.....	.....	.....	.....	14.3	.....	12.0
Other races........	16.0	4.6	5.1	12.8	13.7	7.0	8.8	30.8	9.1	7.9	.....	7.5
Total............	74.7	88.1	94.1	96.2	83.6	83.7	92.6	76.9	81.8	89.8	98.2	90.0
Grand total.....	100.0	100.0	100.0	100.0	100.0	100.0	100.0	100.0	100.0	100.0	100.0	100.0

TABLE 5.—*Grade distribution of each race—Percentages.*

[This table shows in detail only races with 100 or more pupils reporting. The totals, however, are for all races.]

General nativity and race of father of pupil.	Kinder-garten.	Elementary grades.									Special school.	Grand total.
		1.	2.	3.	4.	5.	6.	7.	8.	Total.		
Native-born, White.....	12.8	34.9	10.1	5.4	16.1	9.4	3.4	2.0	4.0	85.2	2.0	100.0
Foreign-born:												
Canadian, French...	2.2	32.0	15.9	12.9	5.7	6.5	4.9	.....	2.4	80.3	17.6	100.0
Irish...............	18.9	11.8	29.9	11.8	7.1	4.7	9.4	4.7	1.6	81.1	.....	100.0
Polish.............	.....	31.3	22.9	23.4	22.3	.....	.....	.....	.....	100.0	.....	100.0
Other races........	10.8	18.0	11.7	24.3	18.0	5.4	5.4	3.6	2.7	89.3	.....	100.0
Total............	4.2	28.8	17.8	15.1	9.1	5.4	4.7	.7	2.0	83.7	12.1	100.0
Grand total.......	5.0	29.4	17.1	14.2	9.8	5.8	4.6	.9	2.2	83.9	11.1	100.0

MERIDEN, CONNECTICUT.

885

LIST OF TABLES.

887

MERIDEN.

In the city of Meriden, Conn., the investigations of the Immigration Commission concerned the pupils in the public schools, the teachers in the elementary grades of those schools, and the pupils in the parochial schools. The facts reported are presented in the series of general tables on these three subjects. The method of collecting the information and of tabulating it is explained in the introduction to this volume.[a] That introduction also contains a description of the general tables and an explanation of the purpose which they serve. The present note is concerned not with the methods employed in the investigation but with the principal results obtained in the city of Meriden.

PUPILS IN THE PUBLIC SCHOOLS.

The number of pupils reported to the Commission as being in attendance in the public schools of Meriden on a day in December, 1908, was 4,014. This number is not a little superior to the average annual attendance for the year 1908–9, which is reported as 3,846. An exact correspondence of the two figures, the one an average for the entire year and the other the attendance of a given day in the middle of the year, is not to be expected. The fact, however, that the numbers reported to the Commission are so much in excess of the annual average is conclusive evidence that for the day in question the figures are complete and comprehensive, and there can be no doubt that the figures reported furnish a satisfactory picture of conditions generally prevailing in the schools of the city.

Divided by grades these pupils were as follows:

Kindergarten	409	Ninth grade	187
First grade	469	First year high school	152
Second grade	412	Second year high school	101
Third grade	388	Third year high school	52
Fourth grade	463	Fourth year high school	42
Fifth grade	384	Mixed grades	45
Sixth grade	339		
Seventh grade	347	Total	4,014
Eighth grade	224		

The striking fact in this table is the remarkably even distribution of the numbers in the grades between the kindergarten and the seventh. Variations of course occur, but the standard toward which the figures seem to tend is that of an equality in these grades. In

---

[a] See pp. VII to XVII.

the eighth grade there is a considerable drop in numbers, and in the ninth or final grade of the elementary schools the number of pupils is about one-half as large as in the earlier grades.

In order that the distribution by grades can be more conveniently studied the elementary grades are given in groups in the table following, grades 1 to 4 being designated as primary and grades 5 to 9 as grammar, and these groups being compared with the kindergarten and the high school.

Class of school.	Number.	Per cent.
Kindergarten	409	10.3
Primary, grades 1 to 4	1,732	43.6
Grammar, grades 5 to 9	1,481	37.3
High school	347	8.7
Total	3,969	100.0

A noticeable feature of this table is that one-tenth of the Meriden school pupils are in the kindergarten, and indeed that the kindergarten classes outnumber the high school. As between primary and grammar grades there is a slight numerical advantage in favor of the primary grades. In comparing the groups it should be remembered that the grammar grades comprise five years of school life. A comparison between the two can best be made by an average. The average number of pupils in the four primary grades was 433; in the five grammar grades the average number was 296.

The ages of the children are displayed in Table 1, which shows a large number of pupils (490) of 5 years of age and under, most of whom are in the kindergarten. The 6-year-old children, who are mostly in the elementary grades, number 382. In the succeeding years of life the numbers remain approximately at this level. At 13 years of age there are 351 pupils and at 14 years of age 305 pupils. The number of pupils at 15 and 16 years of age naturally is smaller, there being at the latter age 110 pupils.

Table 1 also shows the number of pupils in each grade distributed by their ages, and exhibits the fact that there is a wide diversity of age in each grade and conversely a wide diversity of grades represented by each age. In order to present in simple form the many facts presented in this table, the pupils of any given grade may be divided into two classes, those who are of the normal or appropriate age for the grade and those who are in excess of the normal age. The latter may be designated as overage pupils, and with reference to their school progress be recorded as retarded or backward. Again, children of a given age who have not attained the grade appropriate to that age and who may be designated as undergrade, can also be regarded as backward and retardation measured by this standard. The most frequent measure is that which determines the number and proportion of overage or retarded pupils in a given grade.

The following table gives for each grade of the public schools of Meriden a statement of the number of pupils who are overage and the proportion of such pupils to the whole number in the grade. A comparison of the overage children in all the grades with the total attendance gives the average for the city.

Grade.	Number in grade.	Retarded pupils.		
		Age.	Number.	Per cent of all pupils.
First	469	8 years and over	46	9. 8
Second	412	9 years and over	54	13. 1
Third	388	10 years and over	86	22. 2
Fourth	463	11 years and over	117	25. 3
Fifth	384	12 years and over	98	25. 5
Sixth	339	13 years and over	90	26. 5
Seventh	347	14 years and over	69	19. 9
Eighth	224	15 years and over	25	11. 2
Ninth	187	16 years and over	17	9. 1
Total	3,213		602	18. 7

The average retardation computed as in the foregoing table indicates that about one-sixth of the pupils of the Meriden schools are retarded. Retardation makes its appearance in the first grade, but the number and percentage of retarded children are small. As the grades advance the proportion of retarded children increases, but even at its maximum in the sixth grade it is only 26.5 per cent of the pupils of that grade. In the eighth and ninth grades, where the numbers are depleted by children dropping out of school, the percentage of retarded children is less than the average.

A computation of the amount of retardation is given in the table following for the special group of children of 10 to 12 years of age.

Age.	Number of pupils of this age.	Normal grade.	Retarded, or below normal grade.	
			Number.	Per cent.
10 years	351	4	60	17. 1
11 years	337	5	90	26. 7
12 years	358	6	100	27. 9
Total	1,046		250	23. 9

It will be noted that among these rather older children the average retardation is somewhat less than one-fourth. At 10 years it is 17.1 per cent, the proportion increasing to 27.9 per cent at 12 years.

The purpose of the Immigration Commission in its school inquiry was to determine if possible whether any differences existed, with respect to school attendance and school progress, among the different races of which school population is composed. This material is exhibited at some length in the general tables which follow. Some of the main results can be here noted.

The distribution of the pupils by racial groups is indicated in the table following.

General nativity and race of father of pupil.	Pupils.	
	Number.	Per cent.
Native-born:		
White......	1,787	44.6
Negro......	22	.5
Total native-born.........	1,809	45.1
Foreign-born:		
English......	303	7.5
German......	671	16.7
All others......	1,231	30.7
Total foreign-born......	2,205	54.9
Grand total......	4,014	100.0

This table makes the distinction between the children of native-born and foreign-born fathers, and among the latter indicates specifically those races which had in the schools of Meriden a representation of at least 200 pupils. It will be noted that 45.1 per cent of the children had native parents; 54.9 per cent foreign parents. The number of races in Meriden is considerable, though only the English and German are indicated in the table as having 200 representatives. The group "Other races" includes more than one-half of the whole number of foreign-born. The specific races included in this group are as follows: Canadian, French (69), Canadian, other than French (18), Danish (15), Dutch (4), Finnish (9), Flemish (1), French (40), Greek (2), Hebrew, German (24), Hebrew, Polish (11), Hebrew, Russian (188), Hebrew, Other (2), Irish (174), Italian, North (137), Italian, South (142), Lithuanian (7), Magyar (12), Norwegian (10), Polish (133), Russian (17), Scotch (51), Slovak (14), Slovenian (9), Swedish (130), and Welsh (3).

The distribution of the children of native and of foreign parents, with a special note of the English and German, as among the different classes of schools, is indicated in the table next presented.

General nativity and race of father of pupil.	Number of pupils.					Per cent.			
	Kinder-garten.	Pri-mary.	Gram-mar.	High.	Total.	Kinder-garten.	Pri-mary.	Gram-mar.	High.
Native-born:									
White......	163	695	687	232	1,777	9.2	39.1	38.7	13.1
Negro......	2	5	11	3	21	9.5	23.8	52.4	14.3
Total native-born......	165	700	698	235	1,798	9.2	38.9	38.8	13.1
Foreign-born:									
English......	27	126	129	21	303	8.9	41.6	42.6	6.9
German......	53	326	261	26	666	8.0	48.9	39.2	3.9
All others......	164	580	393	65	1,202	13.6	48.3	32.7	5.4
Total foreign-born......	244	1,032	783	112	2,171	11.2	47.5	36.1	5.2
Grand total......	409	1,732	1,481	347	3,969	10.3	43.6	37.3	8.7

In the kindergarten there is a slightly larger proportion of the children of foreign-born parents than of those of native parents.

The primary grades include 47.5 per cent of the foreign-born children and 39.1 per cent of the native. In the grammar grades these proportions are reversed, as here there is a larger proportion of children of native white fathers. In the high school the representation of the children of native parents is 13.1 per cent of their entire number, but that of the children of foreign parents is only 5.2 per cent. Throughout this table the two races specifically named—the English and the German—correspond somewhat closely to the general average of the foreign-born, although the English in its proportions approaches the group of children of native parents more closely than the German.

In the following table is presented a statement of the number of retarded children by nativity of parents, both for all pupils and for the selected group of pupils from 10 to 12 years of age.

General nativity and race of father of pupil.	All elementary pupils.			Pupils 10, 11, and 12 years of age.		
	Number.	Retarded, overage.	Per cent retarded.	Number.	Retarded, under-grade.	Per cent retarded.
Native-born:						
White...	1,382	219	15.8	445	84	18.9
Negro...	16	3	18.8	3	1	33.3
Total native-born...	1,398	222	15.9	448	85	19.0
Foreign-born:						
English...	255	58	22.7	79	20	25.3
German...	587	112	19.1	198	50	25.3
All others...	973	210	21.6	321	95	29.6
Total foreign-born...	1,815	380	20.9	598	165	27.6
Grand total...	3,213	602	18.7	1,046	250	23.9

In both sections of the table it will be noted that the percentage of retardation among the children of native-born parents is less than that among the children of foreign-born parents. What is true of the entire group of children of foreign-born parents is equally true, though not always in the same degree, of the two races specifically named—the English and the German.

PUBLIC SCHOOL TEACHERS.

In the kindergarten and elementary grades of the schools of Meriden 99 teachers are employed. Only one of these is a man, teaching in the eighth grade.

Divided by racial groups they are as follows:

	Number.	Per cent.
Native white of native fathers...	48	48.5
Native white of foreign fathers...	47	47.5
Foreign white...	4	4.0
Total...	99	100.0

The teachers of foreign birth number only four. Those of native birth are about equally divided between those of native and those of foreign fathers.

The table following shows the distribution of these teachers by racial groups as between the lower and upper schools.

	Kindergarten and primary.	Grammar and special.	Total.	Per cent in grammar grades.
Native white of native fathers	25	23	48	47.9
Native white of foreign fathers	24	23	47	48.9
Foreign white	2	2	4	50.0
Total	51	48	99	48.5

It will be noted that the division between the two classes of schools is practically identical for each racial group.

Of these teachers 97 reported length of service, as follows:

Under 5 years	18	From 25 to 29 years	2
From 5 to 9 years	24	30 years and over	4
From 10 to 14 years	19		
From 15 to 19 years	21	Total	97
From 20 to 24 years	9		

The largest single group here noted is the group of teachers having from five to nine years' experience. Combining these into larger groups, it will be noted that the number of teachers whose experience ranges from ten to nineteen years is almost identical with that of the younger teachers who have had less than ten years' experience.

The following table summarizes the figures for the length of service as divided among the different racial groups:

Race and nativity of teachers.	Length of service, in years.			
	Under 10.	10 to 19.	20 and over.	Total.
Native white, native fathers	19	16	11	46
Native white, foreign fathers	22	22	3	47
Foreign white	1	2	1	4
Total	4	40	15	97
Percentages: All teachers	43.3	41.2	15.5	100.0

PUPILS OF THE PAROCHIAL SCHOOLS.

Information was furnished the Immigration Commission concerning the grade, age, sex, and race of 1,594 pupils in the parochial schools of the city of Meriden, representing a complete statement of schools of this class. The official directory of the Roman Catholic Church gives as the number of pupils in these schools 1,579.

The distribution of these pupils by grade is as follows:

Kindergarten	53	Seventh grade	108
First grade	258	Eighth grade	85
Second grade	248	Ninth grade	44
Third grade	140	Mixed	340
Fourth grade	126		
Fifth grade	125	Total	1,594
Sixth grade	67		

It will be noted that the first and second grades are almost uniform in size, the third grade being considerably less numerous.

The fourth and fifth grades are also practically identical in number. In the upper grades there is some irregularity, but the final or ninth grade shows a comparatively small number of pupils. Disregarding the number of pupils not reported by grade, we find that of 1,254 pupils 772, or 61.6 per cent, are found in the primary grades 1 to 4. With respect to the ages of the pupils in these schools, Table 1 shows that at the age of 6 years there are 140 pupils, and that this number gradually increases until 12 years is reached, when there are 192 pupils. At 13 years there is a decline in number to 162, and at 14 years, with 88 pupils, the numbers are only half as large as in the preceding ages.

The relation of the ages of the pupils to the grades in which they are found is expressed by the table following, which gives in each grade the number of pupils who are over the appropriate age for their grade and the proportion which this number bears to the whole number of pupils.

Grade.	Number in grade.	Retarded pupils.		
		Age.	Number.	Per cent of all pupils.
First	258	8 years and over	79	30.6
Second	248	9 years and over	121	48.8
Third	140	10 years and over	79	56.4
Fourth	126	11 years and over	64	50.8
Fifth	125	12 years and over	62	49.6
Sixth	67	13 years and over	41	61.2
Seventh	108	14 years and over	16	14.8
Eighth	85	15 years and over	19	22.4
Ninth	44	16 years and over	1	2.3
Total	1,201		482	40.1

It will be noted that among the pupils for whom this information can be obtained—that is to say, those who are distributed by grades, numbering in all 1,201—there are 482, or 40.1 per cent, who are retarded. The percentage varies considerably in the different grades, the middle grades having the largest percentages, the maximum being shown by the sixth grade, where 61.2 per cent of the pupils are retarded. The elimination of the older pupils is shown very clearly in the fact that in the ninth grade, with 44 pupils, only 1 is retarded.

A statement of the amount of retardation expressed by ascertaining the number of undergrade pupils is given for the ages 10 to 12 years in the following table:

Age.	Number of pupils of this age.	Normal grade.	Retarded, or below normal grade.	
			Number.	Per cent.
10 years	140	4	71	50.7
11 years	152	5	81	53.3
12 years	138	6	76	55.1
Total	430		228	53.0

More than one-half of the pupils here represented are in the retarded class, the percentage rising from 50.7 at the age of 10 years to 55.1 at the age of 12.

The distribution, by race, of pupils in the parochial schools of Meriden is shown in the table following.

General nativity and race of father of pupil.	Pupils.	
	Number.	Per cent.
Native-born, White	403	25, 3
Foreign-born:		
Canadian, French	218	13.7
German	209	13.1
Irish	419	26.3
Polish	240	15.1
All others	105	6.6
Total foreign-born	1,191	74.7
Grand total	1,594	100.0

Of all the pupils in the parochial schools, nearly three-fourths had foreign parents. The most numerous race is the Irish, represented by more than one-fourth of the whole number of pupils; next in number come the Poles, who have 15.1 per cent of the pupils. Germans and French Canadian are almost equally numerous. The other races represented in these schools are comparatively few in number and are grouped in the class "All others," which includes: Bohemian and Moravian (1), Canadian, other than French (10), Dalmatian (1), Dutch (2), English (37), French (13), Italian, North (17), Italian, South (4), Magyar (1), Russian (1), Scotch (4), Slovak (6), and Slovenian (6).

THE PUPILS OF THE PUBLIC AND PAROCHIAL SCHOOLS COMBINED.

In the preceding pages the distribution of pupils, by race, has been given separately for the public and parochial schools. A combination of the two kinds of schools gives a more complete picture of the distribution of races among the school children of Meriden. This combination is given in the following table:

General nativity and race of father of pupil.	Pupils by schools.			Per cent of all pupils.
	Public schools.	Parochial schools.	Total.	
Native-born:				
White	1,787	403	2,190	39.1
Negro	22		22	.4
Total native-born	1,809	403	2,212	39.4
Foreign-born:				
English	303	37	340	6.1
German	671	209	880	15.7
Irish	174	419	593	10.6
Polish	133	240	373	6.6
All others	924	286	1,210	21.6
Total foreign-born	2,205	1,191	3,396	60.6
Grand total	4,014	1,594	5,608	100.0

The foregoing table shows that in round numbers two-fifths of the children of Meriden have native fathers and three-fifths have foreign fathers. Among the latter the most numerous race is the Germans, who are represented by 15.7 per cent of all the pupils. The Irish form about 10 per cent of the whole number of school children, and the Polish over 6 per cent. An examination of the table also discloses the fact that the parochial school system contains a majority of all the pupils of the Irish and Polish races.

GENERAL TABLES.

PUBLIC SCHOOL PUPILS: GENERAL INVESTIGATION.

TABLE **1.**—*Grade and age—Number of pupils of each age in each grade, by sex.*

BOYS.

Age.	Kinder-garten.	Elementary grades.									
		1.	2.	3.	4.	5.	6.	7.	8.	9.	Total.
4 years	44										
5 years	128	32									32
6 years	26	139	26								165
7 years		61	113	24							198
8 years	1	17	62	87	35						201
9 years	1	6	20	46	72	30					174
10 years		3	4	28	63	60	19	2			179
11 years		1	1	9	42	57	46	26	2		184
12 years	1		2	6	19	33	55	49	11	1	176
13 years				3	6	20	34	56	50	10	179
14 years					1	5	16	28	32	39	121
15 years				1		1	3	6	14	24	49
16 years								2	2	13	17
17 years				1						1	2
18 years											
19 years											
20 years or over											
Total	201	259	228	204	239	206	173	169	111	88	1,677

Age.	High school.					Mixed grades.	Grand total.
	First year.	Second year.	Third year.	Fourth year.	Total.		
4 years							44
5 years							160
6 years							191
7 years						1	199
8 years						4	206
9 years						8	183
10 years						5	184
11 years						3	187
12 years						1	178
13 years	3				3		182
14 years	13	2			15		136
15 years	29	8	1		38		87
16 years	9	18	4	1	32		49
17 years	8	6	7	4	25		27
18 years	1	4	2	6	13		13
19 years			2	2	4		4
20 years or over				3	3		3
Total	63	38	16	16	133	22	2,033

TABLE **1.**—*Grade and age—Number of pupils of each age in each grade, by sex*—Contd.

GIRLS.

Age.	Kinder-garten.	Elementary grades.									
		1.	2.	3.	4.	5.	6.	7.	8.	9.	Total.
4 years	34										
5 years	135	17									17
6 years	30	134	27								161
7 years	8	40	79	28	1						148
8 years	1	12	51	71	32	1					167
9 years		5	19	46	84	25					179
10 years			5	20	59	65	22	1			172
11 years		1		10	26	48	54	13	1		153
12 years				6	11	22	53	67	19	3	181
13 years		1	3	2	9	13	19	64	38	17	166
14 years			1	1	4	15	29	46	47	143
15 years					1		3	4	7	29	44
16 years									2	2	4
17 years										1	1
18 years											
19 years											
20 years or over											
Total	208	210	184	184	224	178	166	178	113	99	1,536

Age.	High school.					Mixed grades.	Grand total.
	First year.	Second year.	Third year.	Fourth year.	Total.		
4 years							34
5 years							152
6 years							191
7 years						1	157
8 years						7	175
9 years						7	186
10 years						5	177
11 years							153
12 years						2	183
13 years	2				2	1	169
14 years	22	4			26		169
15 years	34	20	3	2	59		103
16 years	18	27	11	1	57		61
17 years	10	10	14	4	38		39
18 years	3	2	7	11	23		23
19 years			1	7	8		8
20 years or over				1	1		1
Total	89	63	36	26	214	23	1,981

TABLE 1.—*Grade and age—Number of pupils of each age in each grade, by sex*—Contd.

TOTAL.

Age.	Kinder-garten.	Elementary grades.									
		1.	2.	3.	4.	5.	6.	7.	8.	9.	Total.
4 years	78										49
5 years	263	49									326
6 years	56	273	53								346
7 years	8	101	192	52	1						368
8 years	2	29	113	158	67	1					
9 years	1	11	39	92	156	55					353
10 years		3	9	48	122	125	41	3			351
11 years		2	1	19	68	105	100	39	3		337
12 years	1		2	12	30	55	108	116	30	4	357
13 years		1	3	5	15	33	53	120	88	27	345
14 years				1	2	9	31	57	78	86	264
15 years					2	1	6	10	21	53	93
16 years								2	4	15	21
17 years				1						2	3
18 years											
19 years											
20 years or over											
Total	409	469	412	388	463	384	339	347	224	187	3,213

Age.	High school.					Mixed grades.	Grand total.
	First year.	Second year.	Third year.	Fourth year.	Total.		
4 years							78
5 years							312
6 years							382
7 years						2	356
8 years						11	381
9 years						15	369
10 years						10	361
11 years						3	340
12 years						3	361
13 years	5				5	1	351
14 years	35	6			41		305
15 years	63	28	4	2	97		190
16 years	27	45	15	2	89		110
17 years	18	16	21	8	63		66
18 years	4	6	9	17	36		36
19 years			3	9	12		12
20 years or over				4	4		4
Total	152	101	52	42	347	45	4,014

TABLE 2.—Race, sex, and grade—Number of pupils of each sex in each grade, by general nativity and race of father of pupil.

General nativity and race of father of pupil.	Kindergarten.	Elementary grades.										High school.					Mixed grades.	Grand total.
		1.	2.	3.	4.	5.	6.	7.	8.	9.	Total.	First year.	Second year.	Third year.	Fourth year.	Total.		
Native-born:																		
White—																		
Male	79	94	94	88	93	75	69	76	54	54	697	48	25	13	10	96	5	877
Female	84	88	76	64	98	80	84	79	54	62	685	61	34	24	17	136	5	910
Total	163	182	170	152	191	155	153	155	108	116	1,382	109	59	37	27	232	10	1,787
Negro—																		
Male					1	1	1		1	2	6						1	7
Female	2	2	1	1			2	3		1	10	1	1	1		3		15
Total	2	2	1	1	1	1	3	3	1	3	16	1	1	1		3	1	22
Total native-born—																		
Male	79	94	94	88	94	76	70	76	55	56	703	48	25	13	10	96	6	884
Female	86	90	77	65	98	80	86	82	54	63	695	62	35	25	17	139	5	925
Total	165	184	171	153	192	156	156	158	109	119	1,398	110	60	38	27	235	11	1,809
Foreign-born:																		
Canadian, French—																		
Male	1	8	4	2	4	5		1	2	1	27	2	1			3	1	32
Female	2	6	5	4	5	3	2	2	4		31	1		1		2	2	37
Total	3	14	9	6	9	8	2	3	6	1	58	3	1	1		5	3	69
Canadian, Other—																		
Male		1	2	1	2			1			7							7
Female	1		1	3	1			2	1	1	9	1				1		11
Total	1	1	3	4	3			3	1	1	16	1				1		18
Danish—																		
Male	1				2	1		1			4	1				1		6
Female		2				1	1	3	1	1	9							9
Total	1	2			2	2	1	4	1	1	13	1				1		15
English—																		
Male	13	21	17	12	15	17	21	16	12	4	135	4	2			6		154
Female	14	13	9	17	22	13	13	18	9	6	120	7	7	1		15		149
Total	27	34	26	29	37	30	34	34	21	10	255	11	9	1		21		303
French—																		
Male	6	5	2	3	2	1		2	1	1	17	1				1		24
Female	2	5		1	1	1	2	4			14							16
Total	8	10	2	4	3	2	2	6	1	1	31	1				1		40
German—																		
Male	28	46	38	47	45	51	34	35	19	13	328	2	4	1	1	8	3	367
Female	25	35	32	43	40	36	21	29	15	8	259	2	7	5	4	18	2	304
Total	53	81	70	90	85	87	55	64	34	21	587	4	11	6	5	26	5	671

Race of individual	Total, Male	Total, Female	Total
Hebrew, German—Male	13		
Female		11	
Total			24
Hebrew, Polish—Male	6		
Female		5	
Total			11
Hebrew, Russian—Male	93		
Female		95	
Total			188
Irish—Male	93		
Female		81	
Total			174
Italian, North—Male	68		
Female		69	
Total			137
Italian, South—Male	64		
Female		78	
Total			142
Magyar—Male	8		
Female		4	
Total			12
Norwegian—Male	5		
Female		5	
Total			10
Polish—Male	68		
Female		65	
Total			133
Russian—Male	11		
Female		6	
Total			17
Scotch—Male	23		
Female		28	
Total			51
Slovak—Male	10		
Female		4	
Total			14
Swedish—Male	76		
Female		54	
Total			130

TABLE 2.—*Race, sex, and grade—Number of pupils of each sex in each grade, by general nativity and race of father of pupil*—Continued.

General nativity and race of father of pupil	Kinder-garten	Elementary grades.										High school.					Mixed grades.	Grand total.
		1.	2.	3.	4.	5.	6.	7.	8.	9.	Total.	First year.	Second year.	Third year.	Fourth year.	Total.		
Foreign-born—Continued.																		
Other races a—																		
Male	1	2	3	1	6	3	2	2	...	...	19	1	...	...	...	1	...	21
Female	4	1	4	1	2	2	2	2	4	1	19	1	1	...	...	2	...	25
Total	5	3	7	2	8	5	4	4	4	1	38	2	1	...	...	3	...	46
Total foreign-born—																		
Male	122	165	134	116	145	130	103	93	56	32	974	15	13	3	6	37	16	1,149
Female	122	120	107	119	126	98	80	96	59	36	841	27	28	11	9	75	18	1,056
Total	244	285	241	235	271	228	183	189	115	68	1,815	42	41	14	15	112	34	2,205
Grand total—																		
Male	201	259	228	204	239	206	173	169	111	88	1,677	63	38	16	16	133	22	2,083
Female	208	210	184	184	224	178	166	178	113	99	1,536	89	63	36	26	214	23	1,981
Total	409	469	412	388	463	384	339	347	224	187	3,213	152	101	52	42	347	45	4,014

a "Other races" includes Dutch, 4; Finnish, 9; Flemish, 1; Greek, 2; Hebrew, Other, 2; Lithuanian, 7; Slovenian, 9; Welsh, 3; race not specified, 9.

TABLE 3.—*Race, sex, and age, by grade—Number of pupils of each age in each grade, by sex and by general nativity and race of father of pupil.*

KINDERGARTEN.

BOYS.

General nativity and race of father of pupil.	Number of pupils of each age.									Total.
	4.	5.	6.	7.	8.	9.	10.	11.	12.	
Native-born, White................	21	49	8	......	......	1	......	......	......	79
Foreign-born:										
Canadian, French............	......	1								1
Danish....................	......	1	......							1
English...................	4	7	2	......						13
French....................	1	2	2	......	1					6
German...................	3	21	4							28
Hebrew, Russian............	1	9	......							10
Irish.....................	2	7								9
Italian, North.............	1	7	1					......		9
Italian, South.............	1	5	5						1	12
Norwegian.................	......	1	......							1
Polish....................	5	7	2	......						14
Russian...................	1	3	1							5
Scotch....................	......	......	1							1
Slovak....................	1	2	......							3
Swedish...................	3	5	......							8
Other races *a*............	......	1								1
Total foreign-born........	23	79	18	......	1	......	......	......	1	122
Grand total...............	44	128	26	......	1	1	......	......	1	201

GIRLS.

	4.	5.	6.	7.	8.	9.	10.	11.	12.	
Native-born:										
White....................	17	56	10	1	......	......	......	......	......	84
Negro....................	1	......	1							2
Total native-born........	18	56	11	1	......	......	......	......	......	86
Foreign-born:										
Canadian, French............	......	2	......							2
Canadian, Other............	......	1	1							2
English...................	3	10	1	......						14
French....................	......	2	......							2
German...................	3	17	5	......						25
Hebrew, Russian............	1	6	1	1						9
Irish.....................	......	6	......							6
Italian, North.............	2	7	3	1	......					13
Italian, South.............	1	11	5	4	1					22
Polish....................	4	12	2	1						19
Swedish...................	1	2	1	......						4
Other races *a*............	1	3	......							4
Total foreign-born........	16	79	19	7	1	......	......	......	......	122
Grand total...............	34	135	30	8	1	......	......	......	......	208

a "Other races" includes races having less than 10 representatives in this city and pupils whose race is not reported.

TABLE 3.—*Race, sex, and age, by grade—Number of pupils of each age in each grade, by sex and by general nativity and race of father of pupil*—Continued.

TOTAL.

General nativity and race of father of pupil.	Number of pupils of each age.									Total.
	4.	5.	6.	7.	8.	9.	10.	11.	12.	
Native-born:										
White	38	105	18	1	......	1	......	......	......	163
Negro	1	......	1		......		......	......	......	2
Total native-born	39	105	19	1	......	1	......	......	......	165
Foreign-born:										
Canadian, French	......	3	......							3
Canadian, Other	......	1	1							2
Danish	......	1	......							1
English	7	17	3							27
French	1	4	2	......	1					8
German	6	38	9	......						53
Hebrew, Russian	2	15	1	1						19
Irish	2	13	......							15
Italian, North	3	14	4	1	......					22
Italian, South	2	16	10	4	1	......	......	......	1	34
Norwegian	......	1	......							1
Polish	9	19	4	1						33
Russian	1	3	1							5
Scotch	......	......	1							1
Slovak	1	2	......							3
Swedish	4	7	1							12
Other races a	1	4	......							5
Total foreign-born	39	158	37	7	2	......	......	......	1	244
Grand total	78	263	56	8	2	1	......	......	1	409

a "Other races" includes races having less than 10 representatives in this city and pupils whose race is not reported.

FIRST GRADE.

BOYS.

General nativity and race of father of pupil.	Number of pupils of each age.									Total.
	5.	6.	7.	8.	9.	10.	11.	12.	13.	
Native-born, White	17	51	19	7	......	......	......	......	......	94
Foreign-born:										
Canadian, French	......	2	6							8
Canadian, Other	......	1	......							1
English	1	10	7	2	1					21
French	1	2	1	1						5
German	6	26	11	2	1					46
Hebrew, German	1	2	1	......						4
Hebrew, Russian	......	8	......	1			1			10
Irish	......	6	4	......	2					12
Italian, North	......	5	1	1	1	1				9
Italian, South	......	7	6	3	......					16
Polish	3	12	1	......	1	1				18
Russian	......	......	1							1
Scotch	1	1	......							2
Slovak	1	1	1							3
Swedish	1	4	1	......		1				7
Other races a	......	1	1							2
Total foreign-born	15	88	42	10	6	3	1	......	......	165
Grand total	32	139	61	17	6	3	1	......	......	259

a "Other races" includes races having less than 10 representatives in this city and pupils whose race is not reported.

TABLE 3.—*Race, sex, and age, by grade—Number of pupils of each age in each grade, by sex and by general nativity and race of father of pupil*—Continued.

FIRST GRADE—Continued.

GIRLS.

General nativity and race of father of pupil.	Number of pupils of each age.									Total.
	5.	6.	7.	8.	9.	10.	11.	12.	13.	
Native-born:										
White	6	62	14	3	2	......	1	......	......	88
Negro	......	1	1	......	......	......	......	......	......	2
Total native-born	6	63	15	3	2	......	1	......	......	90
Foreign-born:										
Canadian, French	......	5	......	1	......	......	......	......	......	6
English	......	12	1	......	......	......	......	......	......	13
French	......	5	......	......	......	......	......	......	......	5
German	5	20	7	3	......	......	......	......	......	35
Hebrew, German	......	......	......	1	......	......	......	......	......	1
Hebrew, Russian	3	4	3	......	......	......	......	......	......	10
Irish	......	2	3	1	......	......	......	......	......	6
Italian, North	......	5	......	1	......	......	......	......	......	6
Italian, South	......	5	9	2	2	......	......	......	......	18
Polish	1	6	......	......	1	......	......	......	......	8
Scotch	1	3	1	......	......	......	......	......	......	5
Slovak	1	......	1	......	......	......	......	......	......	2
Swedish	......	4	......	......	......	......	......	......	......	4
Other races a	......	......	......	......	......	......	......	......	1	1
Total foreign-born	11	71	25	9	3	......	......	......	1	120
Grand total	17	134	40	12	5	......	1	......	1	210

TOTAL.

General nativity and race of father of pupil.	Number of pupils of each age.									Total.
	5.	6.	7.	8.	9.	10.	11.	12.	13.	
Native-born:										
White	23	113	33	10	2	......	1	......	......	182
Negro	......	1	1	......	......	......	......	......	......	2
Total native-born	23	114	34	10	2	......	1	......	......	184
Foreign-born:										
Canadian, French	......	7	6	1	......	......	......	......	......	14
Canadian, Other	......	1	......	......	......	......	......	......	......	1
English	1	22	8	2	1	......	......	......	......	34
French	1	7	1	1	......	......	......	......	......	10
German	11	46	18	5	1	......	......	......	......	81
Hebrew, German	1	2	1	1	......	......	......	......	......	5
Hebrew, Russian	3	12	3	1	......	......	1	......	......	20
Irish	......	8	7	1	2	......	......	......	......	18
Italian, North	......	10	1	2	1	1	......	......	......	15
Italian, South	......	12	15	5	2	......	......	......	......	34
Polish	4	18	1	......	2	1	......	......	......	26
Russian	......	......	1	......	......	......	......	......	......	1
Scotch	2	4	1	......	......	......	......	......	......	7
Slovak	2	1	2	......	......	......	......	......	......	5
Swedish	1	8	1	......	......	1	......	......	......	11
Other races a	......	1	1	......	......	......	......	......	1	3
Total foreign-born	26	159	67	19	9	3	1	......	1	285
Grand total	49	273	101	29	11	3	2	......	1	469

a "Other races" includes races having less than 10 representatives in this city and pupils whose race is not reported.

TABLE **3.**—*Race, sex, and age, by grade—Number of pupils of each age in each grade, by sex and by general nativity and race of father of pupil*—Continued.

SECOND GRADE.

BOYS.

General nativity and race of father of pupil.	Number of pupils of each age.								Total.
	6.	7.	8.	9.	10.	11.	12.	13.	
Native-born, White	12	50	24	7	1				94
Foreign-born:									
Canadian, French	1		1	1	1				4
Canadian, Other		2							2
English		9	7	1					17
French		2							2
German	4	20	10	3		1			38
Hebrew, German			1						1
Hebrew, Russian	3	6	4				1		14
Irish	1	3	2		1				7
Italian, North	2	3	1	2					8
Italian, South		1	4	2					7
Magyar			1						1
Norwegian		1							1
Polish	1	6	1	2			1		11
Russian		1	1						2
Slovak		1		1					2
Swedish	2	7	4		1				14
Other races a		1	1	1					3
Total foreign-born	14	63	38	13	3	1	2		134
Grand total	26	113	62	20	4	1	2		228

GIRLS.

General nativity and race of father of pupil.	Number of pupils of each age.								Total.
	6.	7.	8.	9.	10.	11.	12.	13.	
Native-born:									
White	15	39	13	8	1				76
Negro		1							1
Total native-born	15	40	13	8	1				77
Foreign-born:									
Canadian, French		2	3						5
Canadian, Other			1						1
Danish			1						1
English	1	5	3						9
German	6	10	10	6					32
Hebrew, Russian	1	7	3						11
Irish	2	3	3						8
Italian, North		2	5	1	1			1	10
Italian, South			4	1	2			1	8
Polish	1	1	4	2	1				9
Russian		1	1						2
Scotch		2							2
Slovak				1					1
Swedish	1	3							4
Other races a		3						1	4
Total foreign-born	12	39	38	11	4			3	107
Grand total	27	79	51	19	5			3	184

a "Other races" includes races having less than 10 representatives in this city and pupils whose race is not reported.

TABLE 3.—*Race, sex, and age, by grade—Number of pupils of each age in each grade, by sex and by general nativity and race of father of pupil*—Continued.

SECOND GRADE—Continued.

TOTAL.

General nativity and race of father of pupil.	Number of pupils of each age.								Total.
	6.	7.	8.	9.	10.	11.	12.	13.	
Native-born:									
White	27	89	37	15	2				170
Negro		1							1
Total native-born	27	90	37	15	2				171
Foreign-born:									
Canadian, French	1	2	4	1	1				9
Canadian, Other		2	1						3
Danish			1						1
English	1	14	10	1					26
French		2							2
German	10	30	20	9		1			70
Hebrew, German			1						1
Hebrew, Russian	4	13	7				1		25
Irish	3	6	5		1				15
Italian, North	2	5	6	3	1			1	18
Italian, South		1	8	3	2			1	15
Magyar			1						1
Norwegian		1							1
Polish	2	7	5	4	1		1		20
Russian		2	2						4
Scotch		2							2
Slovak		1		2					3
Swedish	3	10	4		1				18
Other races [a]		4	1	1				1	7
Total foreign-born	26	102	76	24	7	1	2	3	241
Grand total	53	192	113	39	9	1	2	3	412

[a] "Other races" includes races having less than 10 representatives in this city and pupils whose race is not reported.

THIRD GRADE.

BOYS.

General nativity and race of father of pupil.	Number of pupils of each age.											Total.
	7.	8.	9	10.	11.	12.	13.	14.	15.	16.	17.	
Native-born, White	13	42	17	11	3	2						88
Foreign-born:												
Canadian, French		1	1									2
Canadian, Other				1								1
Danish		1										1
English	2	3	4		1	1	1					12
French	1		1								1	3
German	5	23	7	10	2							47
Hebrew, Russian	1	1										2
Irish		2	3	1			1					7
Italian, North		3	5			1						9
Italian, South		2	3	3	3	2	1					14
Magyar			1									1
Polish		1		1								2
Scotch	2	2	1									5
Swedish		5	3	1								9
Other races [a]		1										1
Total foreign-born	11	45	29	17	6	4	3				1	116
Grand total	24	87	46	28	9	6	3				1	204

[a] "Other races" includes races having less than 10 representatives in this city and pupils whose race is not reported.

TABLE 3.—*Race, sex, and age, by grade—Number of pupils of each age in each grade, by sex and by general nativity and race of father of pupil*—Continued.

THIRD GRADE—Continued.

GIRLS.

General nativity and race of father of pupil.	Number of pupils of each age.											Total.
	7.	8.	9.	10.	11.	12.	13.	14.	15.	16.	17.	
Native-born:												
White	12	31	16	4	1							64
Negro		1										1
Total native-born	12	32	16	4	1							65
Foreign-born:												
Canadian, French	1	1	1				1					4
Canadian, Other		1	2									3
English	2	4	7	2	2							17
French			1									1
German	7	19	10	4	1	2						43
Hebrew, Polish			1									1
Hebrew, Russian	1	2			1							4
Irish	1	1	1	2	1							6
Italian, North	2	4		5	3							14
Italian, South		2	1	2	1	2	1	1				10
Magyar			1									1
Norwegian		1										1
Polish		1	1	1								3
Russian		1										1
Scotch		1										1
Swedish	2	3	2			1						8
Other races a						1						1
Total foreign-born	16	39	30	16	9	6	2	1				119
Grand total	28	71	46	20	10	6	2	1				184

TOTAL.

General nativity and race of father of pupil.	7.	8.	9.	10.	11.	12.	13.	14.	15.	16.	17.	Total.
Native-born:												
White	25	73	33	15	4	2						152
Negro		1										1
Total native-born	25	74	33	15	4	2						153
Foreign-born:												
Canadian, French	1	2	2				1					6
Canadian, Other		1	2	1								4
Danish		1										1
English	4	7	11	2	3	1	1					29
French	1		2								1	4
German	12	42	17	14	3	2						90
Hebrew, Polish			1									1
Hebrew, Russian	2	3			1							6
Irish	1	3	4	3	1		1					13
Italian, North	2	7	5	5	3	1						23
Italian, South		4	4	5	4	4	2	1				24
Magyar			2									2
Norwegian		1										1
Polish		2	1	2								5
Russian		1										1
Scotch	2	2	2									6
Swedish	2	8	5	1		1						17
Other races a		1				1						2
Total foreign-born	27	84	59	33	15	10	5	1			1	235
Grand total	52	158	92	48	19	12	5	1			1	388

a "Other races" includes races having less than 10 representatives in this city and pupils whose race is not reported.

TABLE 3.—*Race, sex, and age, by grade—Number of pupils of each age in each grade, by sex and by general nativity and race of father of pupil*—Continued.

FOURTH GRADE.

BOYS.

General nativity and race of father of pupil.	Number of pupils of each age.									Total.
	8.	9.	10.	11.	12.	13.	14.	15.	16.	
Native-born:										
White	17	31	28	10	4	2	1			93
Negro		1								1
Total native-born	17	32	28	10	4	2	1			94
Foreign-born:										
Canadian, French	1	1			2					4
Canadian, Other		2								2
English	1	4	2	7		1				15
French		1		1						2
German	3	12	13	11	6					45
Hebrew, Polish	1			1						2
Hebrew, Russian	2	4	5			1				12
Irish	2	4	5	5	1	1				18
Italian, North	4	4	3	2	2	1				16
Italian, South				3	1					4
Magyar		1								1
Polish	2	1	3		1			1		8
Scotch				1						1
Slovak					1					1
Swedish	1	4	3							8
Other races *a*	1	2	1	1	1					6
Total foreign-born	18	40	35	32	15	4		1		145
Grand total	35	72	63	42	19	6	1	1		239

GIRLS.

General nativity and race of father of pupil.	8.	9.	10.	11.	12.	13.	14.	15.	16.	Total.
Native-born:										
White	1	13	35	23	14	8	3	1		98
Negro										
Total native-born	1	13	35	23	14	8	3	1		98
Foreign-born:										
Canadian, French		2	3							5
Canadian, Other				1						1
Danish				2						2
English		6	7	5	3	1				22
French						1				1
German		6	21	7	3		3			40
Hebrew, Russian		1	3	3	1	1				9
Irish		2	4	1						7
Italian, North			2	2	1		1		1	7
Italian, South		1	4	5			1			11
Magyar				1						1
Polish			3	4	1					8
Scotch		1		4	2					7
Swedish			2	1						3
Other races *a*					1		1			2
Total foreign-born		19	49	36	12	3	6		1	126
Grand total	1	32	84	59	26	11	9	1	1	224

a "Other races" includes races having less then 10 representatives in this city and pupils whose race is not reported.

TABLE 3.—*Race, sex, and age, by grade—Number of pupils of each age in each grade, by sex and by general nativity and race of father of pupil*—Continued.

FOURTH GRADE—Continued.

TOTAL.

General nativity and race of father of pupil.	Number of pupils of each age.									Total.
	8.	9.	10.	11.	12.	13.	14.	15.	16.	
Native-born:										
White	1	30	66	51	24	12	5	2	......	191
Negro	......	......	1	......	......	......	......	......	......	1
Total native-born	1	30	67	51	24	12	5	2	......	192
Foreign-born:										
Canadian, French		3	4	......	......	2	......			9
Canadian, Other		......	2	1	......	......				3
Danish		......	......	2	......					2
English		7	11	7	10	1	1	......		37
French		......	1	......	1	1	......			3
German		9	33	20	14	6	3	......		85
Hebrew, Polish		1	......	......	1	......				2
Hebrew, Russian		3	7	8	1	1	1			21
Irish		4	8	6	5	1	1	......		25
Italian, North		4	6	5	3	2	2	......	1	23
Italian, South		1	4	5	3	1	1	......		15
Magyar		......	1	1	......	......				2
Polish		2	4	7	1	1	......	......	1	16
Scotch		1	......	4	3	......				8
Slovak		......	......	......	......	1				1
Swedish		1	6	4	......	......				11
Other races *a*		1	2	1	2	1	1	......		8
Total foreign-born		37	89	71	44	18	10	......	2	271
Grand total	1	67	156	122	68	30	15	2	2	463

a "Other races" includes races having less than 10 representatives in this city and pupils whose race is not reported.

FIFTH GRADE.

BOYS.

General nativity and race of father of pupil.	Number of pupils of each age.								Total.
	8.	9.	10.	11.	12.	13.	14.	15.	
Native-born:									
White	......	15	25	19	14	2	......	......	75
Negro	......	......	......	1	......	......	......	......	1
Total native-born	......	15	25	20	14	2	......	......	76
Foreign-born:									
Canadian, French	......	......	1	......	......	......	4	......	5
Danish	......	......	......	1	......	......			1
English	......	3	2	8	1	3	......	......	17
French	......	......	......	......	1	......			1
German	......	6	19	14	6	6	......	......	51
Hebrew, German	......	......	......	......	1	1			2
Hebrew, Polish	......	......	1	......	......	......			1
Hebrew, Russian	......	1	2	6	2	......			11
Irish	......	1	2	2	2	2	1	1	11
Italian, North	......	......	1	......	3	1	......	......	5
Italian, South	......	1	......	3	1	2	......		7
Magyar	......	......	......	......	1	......			1
Norwegian	......	......	1	......	......	......			1
Polish	......	......	1	......	......	3	......		4
Scotch	......	1	......	......	1	......			2
Swedish	......	1	4	1	......	1	......		7
Other races *a*	......	1	1	......	1	......			3
Total foreign-born	......	15	35	37	19	18	5	1	130
Grand total	......	30	60	57	33	20	5	1	206

a "Other races" includes races having less than 10 representatives in this city and pupils whose race is not reported.

TABLE 3.—*Race, sex, and age, by grade—Number of pupils of each age in each grade, by sex and by general nativity and race of father of pupil—Continued.*

FIFTH GRADE—Continued.

GIRLS.

General nativity and race of father of pupil.	Number of pupils of each age.								Total.
	8.	9.	10.	11.	12.	13.	14.	15.	
Native-born:									
White		14	29	22	10	3	2		80
Negro									
Total native-born		14	29	22	10	3	2		80
Foreign-born:									
Canadian, French			2	1					3
Canadian, Other					1				1
Danish		1							1
English		2	5	2	2	2			13
French				1					1
German	1	2	14	13	4	2			36
Hebrew, German			1						1
Hebrew, Polish		1							1
Hebrew, Russian			4	3					7
Irish			4	2		2			8
Italian, North			3	3	1	2	1		10
Italian, South		1			2	1			4
Magyar						1			1
Polish		1			2		1		4
Scotch		1							1
Swedish		1	2	1					4
Other races*a*		1	1						2
Total foreign-born	1	11	36	26	12	10	2		98
Grand total	1	25	65	48	22	13	4		178

TOTAL.

General nativity and race of father of pupil.	Number of pupils of each age.								Total.
	8.	9.	10.	11.	12.	13.	14.	15.	
Native-born:									
White		29	54	41	24	5	2		155
Negro				1					1
Total native-born		29	54	42	24	5	2		156
Foreign-born:									
Canadian, French			3	1			4		8
Canadian, Other					1				1
Danish		1		1					2
English		5	7	10	3	5			30
French				1	1				2
German	1	8	33	27	10	8			87
Hebrew, German			1	1		1			3
Hebrew, Polish		1	1						2
Hebrew, Russian		1	6	9	2				18
Irish		1	6	4	2	4	1	1	19
Italian, North			4	3	4	3	1		15
Italian, South		2		3	3	3			11
Magyar				1		1			2
Norwegian			1						1
Polish		1	1		2	3	1		8
Scotch		2			1				3
Swedish		2	6	2	1				11
Other races*a*		2	2		1				5
Total foreign-born	1	26	71	63	31	28	7	1	228
Grand total	1	55	125	105	55	33	9	1	384

a "Other races" includes races having less than 10 representatives in this city and pupils whose race is not reported.

TABLE 3.—*Race, sex, and age, by grade—Number of pupils of each age in each grade by sex and by general nativity and race of father of pupil—Continued.*

SIXTH GRADE.

BOYS.

General nativity and race of father of pupil.	Number of pupils of each age.						Total.
	10.	11.	12.	13.	14.	15.	
Native-born:							
White	10	20	24	10	4	1	69
Negro			1				1
Total native-born	10	20	25	10	4	1	70
Foreign-born:							
English	5	6	1	5	2	2	21
French		2					2
German		9	9	11	5		34
Hebrew, Russian	1	2	4	2			9
Irish	1	1	3	1	3		9
Italian, North	1	2	1	2			6
Italian, South			2	1			3
Magyar		1	2				3
Polish		1	1	2			4
Scotch		1	3		1		5
Slovak			1				1
Swedish	1	1	2				4
Other races *a*			1		1		2
Total foreign-born	9	26	30	24	12	2	103
Grand total	19	46	55	34	16	3	173

GIRLS.

General nativity and race of father of pupil.	10.	11.	12.	13.	14.	15.	Total.
Native-born:							
White	10	26	28	11	8	1	84
Negro			1		1		2
Total native-born	10	26	29	11	9	1	86
Foreign-born:							
Canadian, French		1	1				2
Danish	2						2
English	2	4	1	1	3	2	13
German	3	4	8	5	1		21
Hebrew, German		1					1
Hebrew, Polish		1					1
Hebrew, Russian	2	5	2				9
Irish		3	2				5
Italian, North		1	2		1		4
Italian, South			1				1
Magyar			1				1
Norwegian	1						1
Polish	2		2	2	1		7
Scotch			2				2
Swedish		6	2				8
Other races *a*		2					2
Total foreign-born	12	28	24	8	6	2	80
Grand total	22	54	53	19	15	3	166

a "Other races" includes races having less than 10 representatives in this city and pupils whose race is not reported.

TABLE 3.—*Race, sex, and age, by grade—Number of pupils of each age in each grade, by sex and by general nativity and race of father of pupil*—Continued.

SIXTH GRADE—Continued.

TOTAL.

General nativity and race of father of pupil.	Number of pupils of each age.						Total.
	10.	11.	12.	13.	14.	15.	
Native-born:							
White....	20	46	52	21	12	2	153
Negro....			2		1		3
Total native-born....	20	46	54	21	13	2	156
Foreign-born:							
Canadian, French....		1	1				2
Danish....	2						2
English....	7	10	2	6	5	4	34
French....		2					2
German....	3	13	17	16	6		55
Hebrew, German....		1					1
Hebrew, Polish....		1					1
Hebrew, Russian....	3	7	6	2			18
Irish....	1	4	5	1	3		14
Italian, North....	1	3	3	2	1		10
Italian, South....			3	1			4
Magyar....		1	3				4
Norwegian....	1						1
Polish....	2	1	3	4	1		11
Scotch....		1	5		1		7
Slovak....			1				1
Swedish....	1	7	4				12
Other races *a*....		2	1		1		4
Total foreign-born....	21	54	54	32	18	4	183
Grand total....	41	100	108	53	31	6	339

a "Other races" includes races having less than 10 representatives in this city and pupils whose race is not reported.

SEVENTH GRADE.

BOYS.

General nativity and race of father of pupil.	Number of pupils of each age.							Total.
	10.	11.	12.	13.	14.	15.	16.	
Native-born:								
White....	1	9	25	23	13	4	1	76
Negro....								
Total native-born....	1	9	25	23	13	4	1	76
Foreign-born:								
Canadian, French....					1			1
Canadian, Other....			1					1
Danish....			1					1
English....	1	3	5	4	3			16
French....			1					1
German....		9	7	10	8	1		35
Hebrew, German....				1		1		2
Hebrew, Russian....		2	2	5	1			10
Irish....			1	2	1			4
Magyar....			1					1
Norwegian....			1	1				2
Polish....				1			1	2
Russian....			1	2				3
Scotch....			1					1
Swedish....		3	4	3	1			11
Other races *a*....			1	1				2
Total foreign-born....	1	17	24	33	15	2	1	93
Grand total....	2	26	49	56	28	6	2	169

a "Other races" includes races having less than 10 representatives in this city and pupils whose race is not reported.

TABLE 3.—*Race, sex, and age, by grade—Number of pupils of each age in each grade, by sex and by general nativity and race of father of pupil*—Continued.

SEVENTH GRADE—Continued.

GIRLS.

General nativity and race of father of pupil.	Nativity of pupils of each age.							Total.
	10.	11.	12.	13.	14.	15.	16.	
Native-born:								
White		10	34	22	11	2		79
Negro				3				3
Total native-born		10	34	25	11	2		82
Foreign-born:								
Canadian, French				1	1			2
Canadian, Other			1	1				2
Danish			2	1				3
English		1	3	8	6			18
French			1		3	1		5
German	1	2	8	15	2	1		29
Hebrew, German			5					5
Hebrew, Polish				1				1
Hebrew, Russian				3				3
Irish			2	5	2			9
Italian, South			1	1	1			3
Norwegian				1				1
Polish			2					2
Russian			1					1
Scotch					1			1
Swedish			6	1	2			9
Other races *a*			1	1				2
Total foreign-born	1	3	33	39	18	2		96
Grand total	1	13	67	64	29	4		178

TOTAL.

General nativity and race of father of pupil.	10.	11.	12.	13.	14.	15.	16.	Total.
Native-born:								
White	1	19	59	45	24	6	1	155
Negro				3				3
Total native-born	1	19	59	48	24	6	1	158
Foreign-born:								
Canadian, French				1	2			3
Canadian, Other			1	2				3
Danish			2	2				4
English	1	4	8	12	9			34
French			1	1	3	1		6
German	1	11	15	25	10	2		64
Hebrew, German			5	1		1		7
Hebrew, Polish				1				1
Hebrew, Russian		2	2	8	1			13
Irish			3	7	3			13
Italian, South			1	1	1			3
Magyar			1					1
Norwegian			1	2				3
Polish			2	1			1	4
Russian			2	2				4
Scotch			1		1			2
Swedish		3	10	4	3			20
Other races *a*			2	2				4
Total foreign-born	2	20	57	72	33	4	1	189
Grand total	3	39	116	120	57	10	2	347

a "Other races" includes races having less than 10 representatives in this city and pupils whose race is not reported.

TABLE 3.—*Race, sex, and age, by grade—Number of pupils of each age in each grade, by sex and by general nativity and race of father of pupil*—Continued.

EIGHTH GRADE.

BOYS.

General nativity and race of father of pupil.	Number of pupils of each age.						Total.
	11.	12.	13.	14.	15.	16.	
Native-born:							
White	1	5	24	12	11	1	54
Negro					1		1
Total native-born	1	5	24	12	12	1	55
Foreign-born:							
Canadian, French			1	1			2
Danish			1				1
English		1	4	6	1		12
French		1					1
German	1	3	8	5	1	1	19
Hebrew, German			1				1
Hebrew, Polish			2				2
Hebrew, Russian			2	1			3
Irish			2	4			6
Italian, North		1	2	1			4
Scotch				1			1
Swedish			3	1			4
Total foreign-born	1	6	26	20	2	1	56
Grand total	2	11	50	32	14	2	111

GIRLS.

General nativity and race of father of pupil.	11.	12.	13.	14.	15.	16.	Total.
Native-born, White		9	19	19	5	2	54
Foreign-born:							
Canadian, French			2	1	1		4
English		2	2	5			9
German		3	7	5			15
Hebrew, Russian		2	1	9	1		13
Irish				2			2
Italian, North				1			1
Norwegian			2				2
Polish				1			1
Scotch			2	1			3
Swedish		2	2	1			5
Other races a	1	1	1	1			4
Total foreign-born	1	10	19	27	2		59
Grand total	1	19	38	46	7	2	113

a "Other races" includes races having less than 10 representatives in this city and pupils whose race is not reported.

TABLE 3.—*Race, sex, and age, by grade—Number of pupils of each age in each grade, by sex and by general nativity and race of father of pupil*—Continued.

EIGHTH GRADE—Continued.

TOTAL.

General nativity and race of father of pupil.	Number of pupils of each age.						Total.
	11.	12.	13.	14.	15.	16.	
Native-born:							
White	1	14	43	31	16	3	108
Negro					1		1
Total native-born	1	14	43	31	17	3	109
Foreign-born:							
Canadian, French			3	2	1		6
Danish			1				1
English		3	6	11	1		21
French		1					1
German	1	6	15	10	1	1	34
Hebrew, German			1				1
Hebrew, Polish			2				2
Hebrew, Russian		2	3	10	1		16
Irish			2	6			8
Italian, North		1	2	2			5
Norwegian			2				2
Polish				1			1
Scotch			2	2			4
Swedish		2	5	2			9
Other races a	1	1	1	1			4
Total foreign-born	2	16	45	47	4	1	115
Grand total	3	30	88	78	21	4	224

a "Other races" includes races having less than 10 representatives in this city and pupils whose race is not reported.

NINTH GRADE.

BOYS.

General nativity and race of father of pupil	Number of pupils of each age.						Total.
	12.	13.	14.	15.	16.	17.	
Native-born:							
White	1	8	24	14	6	1	54
Negro				1	1		2
Total native-born	1	8	24	15	7	1	56
Foreign-born:							
Canadian, French					1		1
English			2		1		4
German		1	4	8			13
Hebrew, Russian			2		1		3
Irish					2		2
Italian, North			2				2
Polish				1			1
Scotch			3				3
Swedish			2		1		3
Total foreign-born		2	15	9	6		32
Grand total	1	10	39	24	13	1	88

a "Other races" includes races having less than 10 representatives in this city and pupils whose race is not reported.

TABLE **3.**—*Race, sex, and age, by grade—Number of pupils of each age in each grade, by sex and by general nativity and race of father of pupil*—Continued.

NINTH GRADE—Continued.

GIRLS.

General nativity and race of father of pupil.	Number of pupils of each age.						Total.
	12.	13.	14.	15.	16.	17.	
Native-born:							
White	2	14	28	16	1	1	62
Negro				1			1
Total native-born	2	14	28	17	1	1	63
Foreign-born:							
Canadian (other than French)				1			1
English		1	3	1	1		6
French			1				1
German	1	2	4	1			8
Hebrew, German				1			1
Hebrew, Russian			2	4			6
Irish			2	3			5
Italian, North			2				2
Polish			1				1
Scotch			1				1
Swedish			2	1			3
Other races *a*			1				1
Total foreign-born	1	3	19	12	1		36
Grand total	3	17	47	29	2	1	99

TOTAL.

General nativity and race of father of pupil.	Number of pupils of each age.						Total.
	12.	13.	14.	15.	16.	17.	
Native-born:							
White	3	22	52	30	7	2	116
Negro				2	1		3
Total native-born	3	22	52	32	8	2	119
Foreign-born:							
Canadian, French					1		1
Canadian, Other				1			1
English		2	5	1	2		10
French			1				1
German	1	3	8	9			21
Hebrew, German				1			1
Hebrew, Russian			4	4	1		9
Irish			2	3	2		7
Italian, North			4				4
Polish			1	1			2
Scotch			4				4
Swedish			4	1	1		6
Other races *a*			1				1
Total foreign-born	1	5	34	21	7		68
Grand total	4	27	86	53	15	2	187

a "Other races" includes races having less than 10 representatives in this city and pupils whose race is not reported.

TABLE 3.—*Race, sex, and age, by grade—Number of pupils of each age in each grade, by sex and by general nativity and race of father of pupil*—Continued.

FIRST YEAR HIGH SCHOOL.

BOYS.

General nativity and race of father of pupil.	Number of pupils of each age.						Total.
	13.	14.	15.	16.	17.	18.	
Native-born, White	2	12	21	7	5	1	48
Foreign-born:							
Canadian, French			1		1		2
English	1		1	1	1		4
French			1				1
German			2				2
Hebrew, Russian		1	1				2
Irish			1				1
Scotch				1			,1
Swedish			1				1
Other races a					1		1
Total foreign-born	1	1	8	2	3		15
Grand total	3	13	29	9	8	1	63

GIRLS.

General nativity and race of father of pupil.	13.	14.	15.	16.	17.	18.	Total.
Native-born:							
White	2	14	24	12	8	1	61
Negro						1	1
Total native-born	2	14	24	12	8	2	62
Foreign-born:							
Canadian, French				1			1
English		2	2	2	1		7
German		1	1				2
Hebrew, Russian		1	1	2		1	5
Irish		2	3	1			6
Russian					1		1
Scotch		1	2				3
Swedish			1				1
Other races a		1					1
Total foreign-born		8	10	6	2	1	27
Grand total	2	22	34	18	10	3	89

TOTAL.

General nativity and race of father of pupil.	13.	14.	15.	16.	17.	18.	Total.
Native-born:							
White	4	26	45	19	13	2	109
Negro						1	1
Total native-born	4	26	45	19	13	3	110
Foreign-born:							
Canadian, French			1	1	1		3
English	1	2	3	3	2		11
French			1				1
German		1	3				4
Hebrew, Russian		2	2	2		1	7
Irish		2		1			7
Russian					1		1
Scotch		1	2	1			4
Swedish			2				2
Other races a		,1			1		2
Total foreign-born	1	9	18	8	5	1	42
Grand total	5	35	63	27	18	4	152

a "Other races" includes races having less than 10 representatives in this city and pupils whose race is not reported.

TABLE 3.—*Race, sex, and age, by grade*—*Number of pupils of each age in each grade, by sex and by general nativity and race of father of pupil*—Continued.

SECOND YEAR HIGH SCHOOL.

BOYS.

General nativity and race of father of pupil.	Number of pupils of each age.					Total.
	14.	15.	16.	17.	18.	
Native-born, White		7	13	3	2	25
Foreign-born:						
Canadian, French			1			1
Danish					1	1
English			2			2
German			1	2	1	4
Hebrew, German			1			1
Hebrew, Russian		1				1
Irish	1			1		2
Polish	1					1
Total foreign-born	2	1	5	3	2	13
Grand total	2	8	18	6	4	38

GIRLS.

General nativity and race of father of pupil.	Number of pupils of each age.					Total.
	14.	15.	16.	17.	18.	
Native-born:						
White	1	11	14	7	1	34
Negro				1		1
Total native-born	1	11	14	8	1	35
Foreign-born:						
English	1	2	3	1		7
German		4	3			7
Hebrew, German			1			1
Irish	1	3	3			7
Russian			1			1
Scotch			1		1	2
Slovak	1					1
Swedish			1			1
Other races *a*				1		1
Total foreign-born	3	9	13	2	1	28
Grand total	4	20	27	10	2	63

TOTAL.

General nativity and race of father of pupil.	Number of pupils of each age.					Total.
	14.	15.	16.	17.	18.	
Native-born:						
White	1	18	27	10	3	59
Negro				1		1
Total native-born	1	18	27	11	3	60
Foreign-born:						
Canadian, French			1			1
Danish					1	1
English	1	2	5	1		9
German		4	4	2	1	11
Hebrew, German			2			2
Hebrew, Russian		1				1
Irish	2	3	3	1		9
Polish	1					1
Russian			1			1
Scotch			1		1	2
Slovak	1					1
Swedish			1			1
Other races *a*				1		1
Total foreign-born	5	10	18	5	3	41
Grand total	6	28	45	16	6	101

a "Other races" includes races having less than 10 representatives in this city and pupils whose race is not reported.

TABLE 3.—*Race, sex, and age, by grade—Number of pupils of each age in each grade, by sex and by general nativity and race of father of pupil*—Continued.

THIRD YEAR HIGH SCHOOL.

BOYS.

General nativity and race of father of pupil.	Number of pupils of each age.					Total.
	15.	16.	17.	18.	19.	
Native-born, White	....	3	6	2	2	13
Foreign-born:						
German	1	....	....	....	....	1
Irish	....	1	1	....	....	2
Total foreign-born	1	1	1	....	....	3
Grand total	1	4	7	2	2	16

GIRLS.

General nativity and race of father of pupil.	15.	16.	17.	18.	19.	Total.
Native-born:						
White	2	4	10	7	1	24
Negro	....	1	....	....	....	1
Total native-born	2	5	10	7	1	25
Foreign-born:						
Canadian, French	....	1	....	....	....	1
English	....	1	....	....	....	1
German	1	2	2	....	....	5
Hebrew, Russian	....	....	1	....	....	1
Irish	....	2	1	....	....	3
Total foreign-born	1	6	4	....	....	11
Grand total	3	11	14	7	1	36

TOTAL.

General nativity and race of father of pupil.	15.	16.	17.	18.	19.	Total.
Native-born:						
White	2	7	16	9	3	37
Negro	....	1	....	....	....	1
Total native-born	2	8	16	9	3	38
Foreign-born:						
Canadian, French	....	1	....	....	....	1
English	....	1	....	....	....	1
German	2	2	2	....	....	6
Hebrew, Russian	....	....	1	....	....	1
Irish	....	3	2	....	....	5
Total foreign-born	2	7	5	....	....	14
Grand total	4	15	21	9	3	52

TABLE 3.—*Race, sex, and age, by grade—Number of pupils of each age in each grade, by sex and by general nativity and race of father of pupil*—Continued

FOURTH YEAR HIGH SCHOOL.

BOYS.

General nativity and race of father of pupil.	Number of pupils of each age.						Total.
	15.	16.	17.	18.	19.	20 or over.	
Native-born, White		1	2	4	1	2	10
Foreign-born:							
German				1			1
Irish			1	1	1		3
Polish						1	1
Scotch			1				1
Total			2	2	1	1	6
Grand total		1	4	6	2	3	16

GIRLS.

General nativity and race of father of pupil.	15.	16.	17.	18.	19.	20 or over.	Total.
Native-born, White	1		4	8	3	1	17
Foreign-born:							
German	1			1	2		4
Irish		1		1	1*		3
Italian, North				1	1		2
Total	1	1		3	4		9
Grand total	2	1	4	11	7	1	26

TOTAL.

General nativity and race of father of pupil.	15.	16.	17.	18.	19.	20 or over.	Total.
Native-born, White	1	1	6	12	4	3	27
Foreign-born:							
German	1			2	2		5
Irish		1	1	2	2		6
Italian, North				1	1		2
Polish						1	1
Scotch			1				1
Total	1	1	2	5	5	1	15
Grand total	2	2	8	17	9	4	42

TABLE 3.—*Race, sex, and age, by grade—Number of pupils of each age in each grade, by sex and by general nativity and race of father of pupil*—Continued.

MIXED GRADES.

BOYS.

General nativity and race of father of pupil.	Number of pupils of each age.							Total.
	7.	8.	9.	10.	11.	12.	13.	
Native-born:								
White	1	....	2	1	1	....	....	5
Negro	....	....	....	1	....	....	....	1
Total native-born	1	....	2	2	1	....	....	6
Foreign-born:								
Canadian, French	....	....	....	....	1	....	....	1
German	....	2	....	1	....	....	....	3
Hebrew, German	....	1	1	....	....	....	....	2
Hebrew, Polish	....	....	1	....	....	....	....	1
Hebrew, Russian	....	1	3	1	....	1	....	6
Italian, South	....	....	1	....	....	....	....	1
Polish	....	....	....	1	1	....	....	2
Total foreign-born	....	4	6	3	2	1	....	16
Grand total	1	4	8	5	3	1	....	22

GIRLS.

General nativity and race of father of pupil.	7.	8.	9.	10.	11.	12.	13.	Total.
Native-born, White	....	....	2	2	....	1	....	5
Foreign-born:								
Canadian, French	....	....	....	1	....	....	1	2
German	....	1	....	....	....	1	....	2
Hebrew, German	1	....	....	....	....	....	....	1
Hebrew, Polish	....	1	....	....	....	....	....	1
Hebrew, Russian	....	5	2	1	....	....	....	8
Italian, South	....	....	1	....	....	....	....	1
Polish	....	....	2	1	....	....	....	3
Total foreign-born	1	7	5	3	....	1	1	18
Grand total	1	7	7	5	....	2	1	23

TOTAL.

General nativity and race of father of pupil.	7.	8.	9.	10.	11.	12.	13.	Total.
Native-born:								
White	1	....	4	3	1	1	....	10
Negro	....	....	....	1	....	....	....	1
Total native-born	1	....	4	4	1	1	....	11
Foreign-born:								
Canadian, French	....	....	....	1	1	....	1	3
German	....	3	....	1	....	1	....	5
Hebrew, German	1	1	1	....	....	....	....	3
Hebrew, Polish	....	1	1	....	....	....	....	2
Hebrew, Russian	....	6	5	2	....	1	....	14
Italian, South	....	....	2	....	....	....	....	2
Polish	....	....	2	2	1	....	....	5
Total foreign-born	1	11	11	6	2	2	1	34
Grand total	2	11	15	10	3	3	1	45

TABLE 4.—*Race and grade, by age—Number of pupils of each specified age in each grade, by general nativity and race of father of pupil.*

BOYS: AGE 4 YEARS.

General nativity and race of father of pupil.	Kinder-garten.
Native-born, White...	21
Foreign-born, other races *a*	23
Grand total...	44

a "Other races" includes races having less than 10 representatives of this sex and age and pupils whose race is not reported.

BOYS: AGE 5 YEARS.

General nativity and race of father of pupil.	Kindergar-ten.	Elementary grade 1.	Total.
Native-born, White..	49	17	66
Foreign-born:			
German..	21	6	27
Hebrew (other foreign).................................	9	1	10
Polish...	7	3	10
Other races *a*	42	5	47
Total...	79	15	94
Grand total.......................................	128	32	106

a "Other races" includes races having less than 10 representatives of this sex and age and pupils whose race is not reported.

BOYS: AGE 6 YEARS.

General nativity and race of father of pupil.	Kinder-garten.	Elementary grades.		Total.
		1.	2.	
Native-born, White.............................., ...	8	51	12	71
Foreign-born:				
English...	2	10	....	12
German...	4	26	4	34
Hebrew, Russian...................................	....	8	3	11
Italian, South.....................................	5	7	....	12
Polish...	2	12	1	15
Other races *a*	5	25	6	36
Total...	18	88	14	120
Grand total.....................................	26	139	26	191

a "Other races" includes races having less than 10 representatives of this sex and age and pupils whose race is not reported.

TABLE 4.—*Race and grade, by age—Number of pupils of each specified age in each grade, by general nativity and race of father of pupil*—Continued.

BOYS: AGE 7 YEARS.

General nativity and race of father of pupil.	Elementary grades.			Mixed grades.	Total.
	1.	2.	3.		
Native-born, White..	19	50	13	1	83
Foreign-born:					
English..	7	9	2	....	18
German..	11	21	5	....	36
Other races *a*..	24	34	4	....	62
Total..	42	63	11	....	116
Grand total..	61	113	24	1	199

a "Other races" includes races having less than 10 representatives of this sex and age and pupils whose race is not reported.

BOYS: AGE 8 YEARS.

General nativity and race of father of pupil.	Kinder-garten.	Elementary grades.				Mixed grades.	Total.
		1.	2.	3.	4.		
Native-born, White..	....	7	24	42	17	....	90
Foreign-born:							
English..	....	2	7	3	1	....	13
German..	....	2	10	23	3	2	40
Hebrew (not specified).................................	....	1	5	1	3	2	12
Swedish..	....	....	4	5	1	....	10
Other races *a*..	1	5	12	13	10	....	41
Total..	1	10	38	45	18	4	116
Grand total..	1	17	62	87	35	4	206

a "Other races" includes races having less than 10 representatives of this sex and age and pupils whose race is not reported.

BOYS: AGE 9 YEARS.

General nativity and race of father of pupil.	Kinder-garten.	Elementary grades.					Mixed grades.	Total.
		1.	2.	3.	4.	5.		
Native-born:								
White..	1	....	7	17	31	15	2	73
Negro..	....	....	....	....	1	....	....	1
Total native-born.....................................	1	....	7	17	32	15	2	74
Foreign-born:								
English..	....	1	1	4	4	3	....	13
German..	....	1	3	7	12	6	....	29
Hebrew (not specified).................................	....	....	....	4	4	1	5	10
Irish..	....	2	....	3	4	1	....	10
Italian, North..	....	1	2	5	4	....	....	12
Other races *a*..	....	1	7	10	12	4	1	35
Total foreign-born.....................................	....	6	13	29	40	15	6	109
Grand total..	1	6	20	46	72	30	8	183

a "Other races" includes races having less than 10 representatives of this sex and age and pupils whose race is not reported.

TABLE 4.—*Race and grade, by age—Number of pupils of each specified age in each grade, by general nativity and race of father of pupil*—Continued.

BOYS: AGE 10 YEARS.

General nativity and race of father of pupil.	Elementary grades.							Mixed grades.	Total.
	1.	2.	3.	4.	5.	6.	7.		
Native-born:									
White		1	11	28	25	10	1	1	77
Negro								1	1
Total native-born		1	11	28	25	10	1	2	78
Foreign-born:									
English				2	2	5	1		10
German			10	13	19			1	43
Hebrew (not specified)				5	3	1		1	10
Irish		1	1	5	2	1			10
Swedish	1	1	1	3	4	1			11
Other races a	2	1	5	7	5	1		1	22
Total foreign-born	3	3	17	35	35	9	1	3	106
Grand total	3	4	28	63	60	19	2	5	184

a "Other races" includes races having less than 10 representatives of this sex and age and pupils whose race is not reported.

BOYS: AGE 11 YEARS.

General nativity and race of father of pupil.	Elementary grades.								Mixed grades.	Total.
	1.	2.	3.	4.	5.	6.	7.	8.		
Native-born:										
White			3	10	19	20	9	1	1	63
Negro					1					1
Total native-born			3	10	20	20	9	1	1	64
Foreign-born:										
English			1	7	8	6	3			25
German		1	2	11	14	9	9	1		47
Hebrew (not specified)	1			1	7	2	2			13
Other races a			3	13	8	9	3		2	38
Total foreign-born	1	1	6	32	37	26	17	1	2	123
Grand total	1	1	9	42	57	46	26	2	3	187

a "Other races" includes races having less than 10 representatives of this sex and age and pupils whose race is not reported.

TABLE 4.—*Race and grade, by age—Number of pupils of each specified age in each grade, by general nativity and race of father of pupil*—Continued.

BOYS: AGE 12 YEARS.

General nativity and race of father of pupil.	Kinder-garten.	Elementary grades.								Mixed grades.	Total.
		2.	3.	4.	5.	6.	7.	8.	9.		
Native-born:											
White			2	4	14	24	25	5	1		75
Negro						1					1
Total native-born			2	4	14	25	25	5	1		76
Foreign-born:											
German				6	6	9	7	3			31
Hebrew, Russian		1			2	4	2			1	10
Other races *a*	1	1	4	9	11	17	15	3			61
Total foreign-born	1	2	4	15	19	30	24	6		1	102
Grand total	1	2	6	19	33	55	49	11	1	1	178

a "Other races" includes races having less than 10 representatives of this sex and age and pupils whose race is not reported.

BOYS: AGE 13 YEARS.

General nativity and race of father of pupil.	Elementary grades.							High school, first year.	Total.
	3.	4.	5.	6.	7.	8.	9.		
Native-born, White		2	2	10	23	24	8	2	71
Foreign-born:									
English	1	1	3	5	4	4	1	1	20
German			6	11	10	8	1		36
Hebrew (not specified)		1	1	2	6	5			15
Other races *a*	2	2	8	6	13	9			40
Total	3	4	18	24	33	26	2	1	111
Grand total	3	6	20	34	56	50	10	3	182

a "Other races" includes races having less than 10 representatives of this sex and age and pupils whose race is not reported.

BOYS: AGE 14 YEARS.

General nativity and race of father of pupil.	Elementary grades.						High school.		Total.
	4.	5.	6.	7.	8.	9.	First year.	Second year.	
Native-born, White	1		4	13	12	24	12		66
Foreign-born:									
English			2	3	6	2			13
German			5	8	5	4			22
Irish		1	3	1	4			1	10
Other races *a*		4	2	3	5	9	1	1	25
Total		5	12	15	20	15	1	2	70
Grand total	1	5	16	28	32	39	13	2	136

a "Other races" includes races having less than 10 representatives of this sex and age and pupils whose race is not reported.

TABLE 4.—*Race and grade, by age—Number of pupils of each specified age in each grade, by general nativity and race of father of pupil*—Continued.

BOYS: AGE 15 YEARS.

General nativity and race of father of pupil.	Elementary grades.						High school.			Total.
	4.	5.	6.	7.	8.	9.	First year.	Second year.	Third year.	
Native-born:										
White			1	4	11	14	21	7	....	58
Negro					1	1				2
Total native-born			1	4	12	15	21	7	....	60
Foreign-born:										
German				1	1	8	2	....	1	13
Other races a	1	1	2	1	1	1	6	1	....	14
Total foreign-born	1	1	2	2	2	9	8	1	1	27
Grand total	1	1	3	6	14	24	29	8	1	87

a "Other races" includes races having less than 10 representatives of this sex and age and pupils whose race is not reported.

BOYS: AGE 16 YEARS.

General nativity and race of father of pupil.	Elementary grades.			High school.				Total.
	7.	8.	9.	First year.	Second year.	Third year.	Fourth year.	
Native-born:								
White	1	1	6	7	13	3	1	32
Negro			1				....	1
Total	1	1	7	7	13	3	1	33
Foreign-born, other races a	1	1	6	2	5	1	....	16
Grand total	2	2	13	9	18	4	1	49

a "Other races" includes races having less than 10 representatives of this sex and age and pupils whose race is not reported.

BOYS: AGE 17 YEARS.

General nativity and race of father of pupil.	Elementary grades.		High school.				Total.
	3.	9.	First year.	Second year.	Third year.	Fourth year.	
Native-born, White		1	5	3	6	2	17
Foreign-born, other races a	1		3	3	1	2	10
Grand total	1	1	8	6	7	4	27

a "Other races" includes races having less than 10 representatives of this sex and age and pupils whose race is not reported.

TABLE 4.—*Race and grade, by age—Number of pupils of each specified age in each grade, by general nativity and race of father of pupil*—Continued.

BOYS: AGE 18 YEARS.

General nativity and race of father of pupil.	High school.				Total.
	First year.	Second year.	Third year.	Fourth year.	
Native-born, White..................	1	2	2	4	9
Foreign-born, other races a..........		2		2	4
Grand total......................	1	4	2	6	13

a "Other races" includes races having less than 10 representatives of this sex and age and pupils whose race is not reported.

BOYS: AGE 19 YEARS.

General nativity and race of father of pupil.	High school.		Total.
	Third year.	Fourth year.	
Native-born, White................	2	1	3
Foreign-born, other races...........		1	1
Grand total.....................	2	2	4

a "Other races" includes races having less than 10 representatives of this sex and age and pupils whose race is not reported.

BOYS: AGE 20 YEARS.

General nativity, and race of father of pupil.	High school, fourth year.
Native-born, White..................	2
Foreign-born, other races a	1
Grand total.....................	3

a "Other races" includes races having less than 10 representatives of this sex and age and pupils whose race is not reported.

GIRLS: AGE 4 YEARS.

General nativity and race of father of pupil.	Kinder-garten.
Native-born:	
White....................	17
Negro....................	1
Total....................	18
Foreign-born, other races a............	16
Grand total.....................	34

a "Other races" includes races having less than 10 representatives of this sex and age and pupils whose race is not reported.

TABLE 4.—*Race and grade, by age—Number of pupils of each specified age in each grade, by general nativity and race of father of pupil*—Continued.

GIRLS: AGE 5 YEARS.

General nativity and race of father of pupil.	Kinder-garten.	Elementary grade I.	Total.
Native-born, White.......................	56	6	62
Foreign-born:			
English..............................	10	....	10
German..............................	17	5	22
Italian, South.......................	11	....	11
Polish...............................	12	1	13
Other races *a*......................	29	5	34
Total.............................	79	11	90
Grand total.......................	135	17	152

a "Other races" includes races having less than 10 representatives of this sex and age and pupils whose race is not reported.

GIRLS: AGE 6 YEARS.

General nativity and race of father of pupil.	Kinder-garten.	Elementary grades.		Total.
		1.	2.	
Native-born:				
White.................................	10	62	15	87
Negro.................................	1	1	....	2
Total native-born..................	11	63	15	89
Foreign-born:				
English..............................	1	12	1	14
German..............................	5	20	6	31
Italian, South.......................	5	5	....	10
Other races *a*......................	8	34	5	47
Total foreign-born.................	19	71	12	102
Grand total.......................	30	134	27	191

a "Other races" includes races having less than 10 representatives of this sex and age and pupils whose race is not reported.

GIRLS: AGE 7 YEARS.

General nativity and race of father of pupil.	Kinder-garten.	Elementary grades.				Mixed grades.	Total.
		1.	2.	3.	4.		
Native-born:							
White.................................	1	14	39	12	1	....	67
Negro.................................	....	1	1	....	....	....	2
Total native-born..................	1	15	40	12	1	....	69
Foreign-born:							
German..............................	....	7	10	7	....	....	24
Hebrew, Russian.....................	1	3	7	1	....	....	12
Italian, South.......................	4	9	....	....	....	....	13
Other races *a*......................	2	6	22	8	....	1	39
Total foreign-born.................	7	25	39	16	....	1	88
Grand total.......................	8	40	79	28	1	1	157

a "Other races" includes races having less than 10 representatives of this sex and age and pupils whose race is not reported.

TABLE 4.—*Race and grade, by age—Number of pupils of each specified age in each grade, by general nativity and race of father of pupil*—Continued.

GIRLS: AGE 8 YEARS.

General nativity and race of father of pupil.	Kinder-garten.	Elementary grades.					Mixed grades.	Total.
		1.	2.	3.	4.	5.		
Native-born:								
White...............	....	3	13	31	13	......	......	60
Negro..................	....	......	......	1	......	......	......	1
Total native-born...	....	3	13	32	13	......	......	61
Foreign-born:								
English..............	....	......	3	4	6	......	1	13
German..............	....	3	10	19	6	1	1	40
Hebrew, Russian.......	....	......	3	2	1	......	5	11
Italian, North........	....	1	5	4	......	......	......	10
Italian, South........	1	2	4	2	1	......	......	10
Other races *a*	....	3	13	8	5	......	1	30
Total foreign-born...	1	9	38	39	19	1	7	114
Grand total............	1	12	51	71	32	1	7	175

a "Other races" includes races having less than 10 representatives of this sex and age and pupils whose ace is not reported.

GIRLS: AGE 9 YEARS.

General nativity and race of father of pupil.	Elementary grades.					Mixed grades.	Total.
	1.	2.	3.	4.	5.		
Native-born, White................	2	8	16	35	14	2	77
Foreign-born:							
English..............	......	......	7	7	2	......	16
German..............	......	6	10	21	2	......	39
Italian, South........	2	1	1	4	1	1	10
Polish...............	1	2	1	3	1	2	10
Other races *a*	......	2	11	14	5	2	34
Total.............	3	11	30	49	11	5	109
Grand total............	5	19	46	84	25	7	186

a "Other races" includes races having less than 10 representatives of this sex and age and pupils whose race is not reported.

GIRLS: AGE 10 YEARS.

General nativity and race of father of pupil.	Elementary grades.						Mixed grades.	Total.
	2.	3.	4.	5.	6.	7.		
Native-born, White..............	1	4	23	29	10	......	2	69
Foreign-born:								
English..............	......	2	5	5	2	......	......	14
German..............	......	4	7	14	3	1	......	29
Hebrew, Russian.......	......	......	3	4	2	......	1	10
Italian, North........	1	5	2	3	......	......	......	11
Other races *a*	3	5	19	10	5	......	2	44
Total.............	4	16	36	36	12	1	3	108
Grand total............	5	20	59	65	22	1	5	177

a "Other races" includes races having less than 10 representatives of this sex and age and pupils whose race is not reported.

TABLE 4.—*Race and grade, by age—Number of pupils of each specified age in each grade, by general nativity and race of father of pupil—Continued.*

GIRLS: AGE 11 YEARS.

General nativity and race of father of pupil.	Elementary grades.								Total.
	2.	3.	4.	5.	6.	7.	8.	9.	
Native-born, White...............	1	......	1	14	22	26	10	......	74
Foreign-born:									
English...............	......	......	2	3	2	4	1	......	12
German...............	......	......	1	3	13	4	2	......	23
Hebrew, Russian...............	......	......	1	1	3	5	......	......	10
Other races *a*...............	......	......	5	5	8	15	......	1	34
Total...............	......	......	9	12	26	28	3	1	79
Grand total...............	1	......	10	26	48	54	13	1	153

a "Other races" includes races having less than 10 representatives of this sex and age and pupils whose race is not reported.

GIRLS: AGE 12 YEARS.

General nativity and race of father of pupil.	Elementary grades.							Mixed grades.	Total.
	3.	4.	5.	6.	7.	8.	9.		
Native-born:									
White...............	......	8	10	28	34	9	2	1	92
Negro...............				1					1
Total native-born...............	......	8	10	29	34	9	2	1	93
Foreign-born:									
German...............	2	......	4	8	8	3	1	1	27
Hebrew (not specified)...............	......	1	......	2	5	3	......	......	11
Swedish...............	1	......	......	2	6	2	......	......	11
Other races *a*...............	3	2	8	12	14	2	......	......	41
Total foreign-born...............	6	3	12	24	33	10	1	1	90
Grand total...............	6	11	22	53	67	19	3	2	183

a "Other races" includes races having less than 10 representatives of this sex and age and pupils whose race is not reported.

GIRLS: AGE 13 YEARS.

General nativity and race of father of pupil.	Elementary grades.									High school, first year.	Mixed grades.	Total.
	1.	2.	3.	4.	5.	6.	7.	8.	9.			
Native-born:												
White...............	......	......	......	3	3	11	22	19	14	2	......	74
Negro...............							3					3
Total native-born...............	......	......	......	3	3	11	25	19	14	2	......	77
Foreign-born:												
English...............	......	......	......	......	2	1	8	2	1	......	......	14
German...............	......	......	......	3	2	5	15	7	2	......	......	34
Other races *a*...............	1	3	2	3	6	2	16	10	......	......	1	44
Total foreign-born...............	1	3	2	6	10	8	39	19	3	......	1	92
Grand total...............	1	3	2	9	13	19	64	38	17	2	1	169

a "Other races" includes races having less than 10 representatives of this sex and age and pupils whose race is not reported.

TABLE 4.—*Race and grade, by age—Number of pupils of each specified age in each grade, by general nativity and race of father of pupil*—Continued.

GIRLS: AGE 14 YEARS.

General nativity and race of father of pupil.	Elementary grades.							High school.		Total.
	3.	4.	5.	6.	7.	8.	9.	First year.	Second year.	
Native-born:										
White		1	2	8	11	19	28	14	1	84
Negro				1						1
Total native-born		1	2	9	11	19	28	14	1	85
Foreign-born:										
English				3	6	5	3	2	1	20
German				1	2	5	4	1		13
Hebrew, Russian						9	2	1		12
Other races a	1		2	2	10	8	10	4	2	39
Total foreign-born	1		2	6	18	27	19	8	3	84
Grand total	1	1	4	15	29	46	47	22	4	169

a "Other races" includes races having less than 10 representatives of this sex and age and pupils whose race is not reported.

GIRLS: AGE 15 YEARS.

General nativity and race of father of pupil.	Elementary grades.						High school.				Total.
	4.	5.	6.	7.	8.	9.	First year.	Second year.	Third year.	Fourth year.	
Native-born:											
White			1	2	5	16	24	11	2	1	62
Negro						1					1
Total native-born			1	2	5	17	24	11	2	1	63
Foreign-born, other races a	1		2	2	2	12	10	9	1	1	40
Grand total	1		3	4	7	29	34	20	3	2	103

a "Other races" includes races having less than 10 representatives of this sex and age and pupils whose race is not reported.

GIRLS: AGE 16 YEARS.

General nativity and race of father of pupil.	Elementary grades.		High school.				Total.
	8.	9.	First year.	Second year.	Third year.	Fourth year.	
Native-born:							
White	2	1	12	14	4		33
Negro					1		1
Total native-born	2	1	12	14	5		34
Foreign-born, other races a		1	6	13	6	1	27
Grand total	2	2	18	27	11	1	61

a "Other races" includes races having less than 10 representatives of this sex and age and pupils whose race is not reported.

TABLE 4.—*Race and grade, by age—Number of pupils of each specified age in each grade, by general nativity and race of father of pupil*—Continued.

GIRLS: AGE 17 YEARS.

General nativity and race of father of pupil.	Elementary grade.	High school.				Total.
	9.	First year.	Second year.	Third year.	Fourth year.	
Native-born:						
White..........	1	8	7	10	4	30
Negro..........			1			1
Total native-born..........	1	8	8	10	4	31
Foreign-born, other races *a*..........		2	2	4		8
Grand total..........	1	10	10	14	4	39

a "Other races" includes races having less than 10 representatives of this sex and age, and pupils whose race is not reported.

GIRLS: AGE 18 YEARS.

General nativity and race of father of pupil.	High school.				Total.
	First year	Second year.	Third year.	Fourth year.	
Native-born:					
White..........	1	1	7	8	17
Negro..........	1				1
Total native-born..........	2	1	7	8	18
Foreign-born, other races *a*..........	1	1		3	5
Grand total..........	3	2	7	11	23

a "Other races" includes races having less than 10 representatives of this sex and age and pupils whose race is not reported.

GIRLS: AGE 19 YEARS.

General nativity and race of father of pupil.	High school.		Total.
	Third year.	Fourth year.	
Native-born, White..........	1	3	4
Foreign-born, other races *a*..........		4	4
Grand total..........	1	7	8

a "Other races" includes races having less than 10 representatives of this sex and age and pupils whose race is not reported.

GIRLS: AGE 20 YEARS.

General nativity and race of father of pupil.	High school, fourth year.
Native-born, White..........	1

TABLE 5.—Race distribution in each grade—Percentages.

[This table shows in detail only races with 100 or more pupils reporting. The totals, however, are for all races.]

General nativity and race of father of pupil.	Kindergarten.	Elementary grades.										High school.					Special schools.	Grand total.
		1.	2.	3.	4.	5.	6.	7.	8.	9.	Total.	First year.	Second year.	Third year.	Fourth year.	Total.		
Native-born:																		
White	39.9	38.8	41.3	39.2	41.3	40.4	45.1	44.7	48.2	62.0	43.0	71.7	58.4	71.2	64.3	66.9	22.2	44.5
Negro	.5	.4	.2	.3	.2	.3	.9	.9	.4	1.6	.5	.7	1.0	1.9	.0	.9	2.2	.5
Total native-born	40.3	39.2	41.5	39.4	41.5	40.6	46.0	45.5	48.7	63.6	43.5	72.4	59.4	73.1	64.3	67.7	24.4	45.1
Foreign-born:																		
English	6.6	7.2	6.3	7.5	8.0	7.8	10.0	9.8	9.4	5.3	7.9	7.2	8.9	1.9	.0	6.1	1.0	7.5
German	13.0	17.3	17.0	23.2	18.4	22.7	16.2	18.4	15.2	11.2	18.3	2.6	10.9	11.5	11.9	7.5	11.1	16.7
Hebrew, Russian	4.6	4.3	6.1	1.5	4.5	4.7	5.3	3.7	7.1	4.8	4.5	4.6	.0	1.9	.0	2.6	31.1	4.7
Irish	3.7	3.8	3.6	3.4	5.4	4.9	4.1	3.7	3.6	3.7	4.1	4.6	8.9	9.6	14.3	7.8	1.0	4.3
Italian, North	5.4	3.2	4.4	5.9	5.0	3.9	2.9	.0	2.2	2.1	3.5	.0	.0	.0	4.8	.6	.0	3.4
Italian, South	8.3	7.2	3.6	6.2	3.5	2.9	3.2	.9	.0	.0	3.3	.0	.0	.0	.0	.0	4.4	3.5
Polish	8.1	5.5	4.9	1.3	2.4	2.1	3.5	1.2	.4	1.1	2.9	1.3	1.0	.0	.2	.6	11.1	3.3
Swedish	2.9	2.3	4.4	4.3	2.4	2.6	3.5	5.8	4.0	3.2	3.6	7.2	8.9	.0	2.4	.9	1.0	3.2
Other races	7.1	9.8	8.3	7.2	8.2	7.6	7.4	11.0	9.4	4.8	8.3	7.2	8.9	1.9	2.4	6.3	17.8	8.1
Total foreign-born	59.7	60.8	58.5	60.6	58.5	59.4	54.0	54.5	51.3	36.4	56.5	27.6	40.6	26.9	35.7	32.3	75.6	54.9
Grand total	100.0	100.0	100.0	100.0	100.0	100.0	100.0	100.0	100.0	100.0	100.0	100.0	100.0	100.0	100.0	100.0	100.0	100.0

TABLE 6.—*Grade distribution of each race—Percentages.*

[This table shows in detail only races with 100 or more pupils reporting. The totals, however, are for all races.]

General nativity and race of father of pupil.	Kinder-garten.	Elementary grades.										High school.					Special schools.	Grand total.
		1.	2.	3.	4.	5.	6.	7.	8.	9.	Total.	First year.	Second year.	Third year.	Fourth year.	Total.		
Native-born:																		
White	9.1	10.2	9.5	8.5	10.7	8.7	8.6	8.7	6.0	6.5	77.3	6.1	3.3	2.1	1.5	13.0	0.6	100.0
Negro	9.1	9.1	4.5	4.5	4.5	4.5	13.6	13.6	4.5	13.6	72.7	4.5	4.5	4.5	.0	13.6	4.5	100.0
Total native-born	9.1	10.2	9.5	8.5	10.6	8.6	8.6	8.7	6.0	6.6	77.3	6.1	3.3	2.1	1.5	13.0	.6	100.0
Foreign-born:																		
English	8.9	11.2	8.6	9.6	12.2	9.9	11.2	11.2	6.9	3.3	84.2	3.6	3.0	.3	.0	6.9	.0	100.0
German	7.9	12.1	10.4	13.4	12.7	13.0	8.2	9.5	5.1	3.1	87.5	.0	1.6	.9	.7	3.9	.7	100.0
Hebrew, Russian	10.1	10.6	13.3	3.2	11.2	9.6	9.6	6.9	8.5	4.8	77.7	3.7	.5	.5	.0	4.8	7.4	100.0
Irish	8.6	10.3	8.6	7.5	14.4	10.9	8.0	7.5	4.6	4.0	75.9	4.0	5.2	2.9	3.4	15.5	.0	100.0
Italian, North	16.1	10.9	13.1	16.8	16.8	10.9	7.3	.0	3.6	2.9	82.5	.0	.0	.0	1.5	1.5	.4	100.0
Italian, South	23.9	23.5	10.6	16.9	10.6	7.7	2.8	2.1	.0	.0	74.6					.0	3.8	100.0
Polish	24.8	19.5	15.0	3.8	12.0	6.0	8.3	3.0	.8	1.5	69.9	.0	.8	.0	.0	1.5	.0	100.0
Swedish	9.2	8.5	13.8	13.1	8.5	8.5	9.2	15.4	6.9	4.6	88.5	1.5	.8	.0	.8	2.3		100.0
Other races	8.9	14.1	10.4	8.6	11.6	8.9	7.6	11.6	6.4	2.8	82.0	3.4	2.8	.3	.3	6.7	2.4	100.0
Total foreign-born	11.1	12.9	10.9	10.7	12.3	10.3	8.3	8.6	5.2	3.1	82.3	1.9	1.9	.6	.7	5.1	1.5	100.0
Grand total	10.2	11.7	10.3	9.7	11.5	9.6	8.4	8.6	5.6	4.7	80.0	3.8	2.5	1.3	1.0	8.6	1.1	100.0

PUBLIC SCHOOL TEACHERS IN ELEMENTARY GRADES AND KINDERGARTEN.

TABLE 1.—*Number of teachers in each grade, by sex and general nativity and race.*

[This table does not include 2 teachers not reporting complete data.]

General nativity and race	Male: Elementary grade 8	Female: Kindergarten	1	2	3	4	5	6	7	8	9	Ungraded and special schools	Total	Total kindergarten and elementary
Native-born of native father, White	1	4	6	6	6	3	3	3	4	5	4	3	43	47
Native-born of foreign father, by race of father:														
English		2	1	1		2	1	1	1		1		8	10
French								1					1	1
German							1	1	1			1	4	4
Irish			4	2	4	8	5	2	2	1	1	2	31	31
Scotch-Irish									1				1	1
Total		2	5	3	4	10	7	5	5	1	2	3	45	47
Total native-born	1	6	11	9	10	13	10	8	9	6	6	6	88	94
Foreign-born:														
English							1	1					2	2
Hebrew, Russian		1												1
Scotch				1									1	1
Total foreign-born		1		1			1	1					3	4
Grand total	1	7	11	10	10	13	11	9	9	6	6	6	91	98

General nativity and race	Total: Kindergarten	1	2	3	4	5	6	7	8	9	Ungraded and special	Total	Total kindergarten and elementary	Race distribution (percentages): Elementary	Elementary and kindergarten
Native-born of native father, White	4	6	6	6	3	3	3	4	6	4	3	44	48	47.8	48.5
Native-born of foreign father, by race of father:															
English	2	1	1		2	1	1	1		1		8	10	8.7	10.1
French							1					1	1	1.1	1.0
German						1	1	1			1	4	4	4.3	4.0
Irish		4	2	4	8	5	2	2	1	1	2	31	31	33.7	31.3
Scotch-Irish								1				1	1	1.1	1.0
Total	2	5	3	4	10	7	5	5	1	2	3	45	47	48.9	47.5
Total native-born	6	11	9	10	13	10	8	9	7	6	6	89	95	96.7	96.0
Foreign-born:															
English						1	1					2	2	2.2	2.0
Hebrew, Russian	1												1		1.0
Scotch			1									1	1	1.1	1.0
Total foreign-born	1		1			1	1					3	4	3.3	4.0
Grand total	7	11	10	10	13	11	9	9	7	6	6	92	99	100.0	100.0

TABLE 2.—*Number of teachers engaged in teaching each specified number of years, by sex and general nativity and race.*

[This table does not include 4 teachers not reporting complete data.]

MALE.

General nativity and race.	Under 5 years.	5 to 9 years.	10 to 14 years.	15 to 19 years.	20 to 24 years.	25 to 29 years.	30 years or over.	Total.
Native-born of native father, White..					1			1

FEMALE.

General nativity and race.	Under 5 years.	5 to 9 years.	10 to 14 years.	15 to 19 years.	20 to 24 years.	25 to 29 years.	30 years or over.	Total.
Native-born of native father, White..	11	8	7	9	5	1	4	45
Native-born of foreign father, by race of father:								10
English....	3	3	3	1				1
French....		3			1	1		4
German....	3	10	6	11	1			31
Irish....			1					1
Scotch-Irish....								
Total....	6	16	10	12	2	1		47
Total native-born....	17	24	17	21	7	2	4	92
Foreign-born:			2					2
English....								1
Hebrew, Russian....	1				1			1
Scotch....								
Total foreign-born....	1		2		1			4
Grand total....	18	24	19	21	8	2	4	96

TOTAL.

General nativity and race.	Under 5 years.	5 to 9 years.	10 to 14 years.	15 to 19 years.	20 to 24 years.	25 to 29 years.	30 years or over.	Total.
Native-born of native father, White..	11	8	7	9	6	1	4	46
Native-born of foreign father, by race of father:								10
English....	3	3	3	1				1
French....		3			1	1		4
German....	3	10	6	11	1			31
Irish....			1					1
Scotch-Irish....								
Total....	6	16	10	12	2	1		47
Total native-born....	17	24	17	21	8	2	4	93
Foreign-born:			2					2
English....								1
Hebrew, Russian....	1				1			1
Scotch....								
Total foreign-born....	1		2		1			4
Grand total....	18	24	19	21	9	2	4	97

PAROCHIAL SCHOOL PUPILS: GENERAL INVESTIGATION.

TABLE 1.—*Grade and age—Number of pupils of each age in each grade, by sex.*

BOYS.

Age.	Kindergarten.	Elementary grades.										Mixed grades.	Grand total.
		1.	2.	3.	4.	5.	6.	7.	8.	9.	Total.		
4 years		4									4		4
5 years	6	19	1								20	8	34
6 years	6	32	4								36	23	65
7 years	7	35	14	4							53	8	68
8 years		30	37	7	1						75	11	86
9 years		7	35	23	5	4	1				75	20	95
10 years		4	18	18	16	12	2	3			73	17	90
11 years			13	16	22	15	8	11	1		86	19	105
12 years			8	6	7	24	12	19	5		81	27	108
13 years			1	1	2	8	7	11	14	1	45	23	68
14 years		1			1		6	10	12	11	41	8	49
15 years				1		4	2		10	5	22	6	28
16 years									1	1	2	1	3
Grand total	19	132	131	76	54	67	38	54	43	18	613	171	803

GIRLS.

Age.	Kindergarten.	Elementary grades.										Mixed grades.	Grand total.
		1.	2.	3.	4.	5.	6.	7.	8.	9.	Total.		
4 years		5									5	1	6
5 years	10	22									22	5	37
6 years	16	35	11								46	13	75
7 years	7	27	28	8							63	10	80
8 years	1	21	32	12	1						66	26	93
9 years		10	25	17	15	6	2				75	16	91
10 years		4	13	14	24	8	2	2			67	24	91
11 years		1	3	8	18	18	3	14	1		66	14	80
12 years		1	2	4	9	15	6	15	5		57	27	84
13 years					4	9	12	17	21	8	71	23	94
14 years			3		1	2	4	5	7	10	32	7	39
15 years				1				1	7	8	17	3	20
16 years									1		1		1
Grand total	34	126	117	64	72	58	29	54	42	26	588	169	791

TOTAL.

Age.	Kindergarten.	Elementary grades.										Mixed grades.	Grand total.
		1.	2.	3.	4.	5.	6.	7.	8.	9.	Total.		
4 years		9									9	1	10
5 years	16	41	1								42	13	71
6 years	22	67	15								82	36	140
7 years	14	62	42	12							116	18	148
8 years	1	51	69	19	2						141	37	179
9 years		17	60	40	20	10	3				150	36	186
10 years		8	31	32	40	20	4	5			140	41	181
11 years		1	16	24	40	33	11	25	2		152	33	185
12 years		1	10	10	16	39	18	34	10		138	54	192
13 years			1	1	6	17	19	28	35	9	116	46	162
14 years		1	3		2	2	10	15	19	21	73	15	88
15 years				2		4	2	1	17	13	39	9	48
16 years									2	1	3	1	4
Grand total	53	258	248	140	126	125	67	108	85	44	1,201	340	1,594

TABLE 2.—Race, sex, and grade—Number of pupils of each sex in each grade, by general nativity and race of father of pupil.

General nativity and race of father of pupil	Kindergarten	Elementary grades									Total	Mixed school	Grand total
		1.	2.	3.	4.	5.	6.	7.	8.	9.			
Native-born, White:													
Male	4	34	48	19	17	15	12	15	10	6	176	24	204
Female	8	46	33	17	21	15	9	19	15	7	182	9	199
Total	12	80	81	36	38	30	21	34	25	13	358	33	403
Foreign-born:													
Canadian, French—													
Male	13	19	31	1	2	1		3			54	41	108
Female	23	20	20	1							43	44	110
Total	36	39	51	1	2	1		3			97	85	218
Canadian (other than French)—													
Male		2	1		1				1		4		4
Female		1			1	1	1		1	1	6		6
Total		3	1		1	1	1		2	1	10		10
English—													
Male		1	6	1			3	1	3		20		20
Female		1	8	1	2	2	2				16	1	17
Total		2	14	2	2	2	5	1	3		36	1	37
French—													
Male	2	3					1				4	1	7
Female	1							2		2	2	3	6
Total	3	3					1	2		2	6	4	13
German—													
Male		32	15	19	12	16	6	3	4	3	110		110
Female		29	13	13	12	12	7	5	8		99		99
Total		61	28	32	24	28	13	8	12	3	209		209
Irish—													
Male		28	25	30	18	30	13	28	24	8	204		204
Female	1	24	40	26	34	28	6	22	18	16	214		215
Total	1	52	65	56	52	58	19	50	42	24	418		419
Italian, North—													
Male		1	1		1			4			7		7
Female		1		4		2	2	1			10		10
Total		2	1	4	1	2	2	5			17		17
Polish—													
Male		7	4	2	1	2	4				20	104	124
Female	1			2	1					1	4	111	116
Total	1	7	4	4	2	2	4			1	24	215	240

TABLE 2.—*Race, sex, and grade—Number of pupils of each sex in each grade, by general nativity and race of father of pupil*—Continued.

General nativity and race of father of pupil.	Kindergarten.	Elementary grades.									Total.	Mixed schools.	Grand total.
		1.	2.	3.	4.	5.	6.	7.	8.	9.			
Foreign-born—Continued.													
Other races a—													
Male........	......	5	......	4	1	1	......	2	1	......	14	1	15
Female......	......	4	1	1	3	1	2	......	......	......	12	1	13
Total......	......	9	1	5	4	2	2	2	1	......	26	2	28
Male........	15	98	83	57	37	52	26	39	33	12	437	147	599
Female......	26	80	84	47	51	43	20	35	27	19	406	160	592
Total......	41	178	167	104	88	95	46	74	60	31	843	307	1,191
Grand total—													
Male........	19	132	131	76	54	67	38	54	43	18	613	171	803
Female......	34	126	117	64	72	58	29	54	42	26	588	169	791
Total......	53	258	248	140	126	125	67	108	85	44	1,201	340	1,594

a "Other races" includes races having less than 10 representatives in this city and pupils whose race is not specified.

TABLE 3.—*Race, sex, and age, by grade—Number of pupils of each age in each grade, by sex and by general nativity and race of father of pupil.*

KINDERGARTEN.

BOYS.

General nativity and race of father of pupil.	Number of pupils of each age.				Total.
	5.	6.	7.	8.	
Native-born, White...........................	1	2	1	....	4
Foreign-born:					
Canadian, French...........................	5	2	6	....	13
French....................................	....	2	....	....	2
Irish.....................................	....	....	....	....	
Polish....................................	....	....	....	....	
Total.................................	5	4	6	....	15
Grand total...........................	6	6	7	....	19

GIRLS.

Native-born, White...........................	2	3	2	1	8
Foreign-born:					
Canadian, French...........................	7	11	5	....	23
French....................................	....	1	....	....	1
Irish.....................................	....	1	....	....	1
Polish....................................	1	....	....	....	1
Total.................................	8	13	5	....	26
Grand total...........................	10	16	7	1	34

TOTAL.

Native-born, White...........................	3	5	3	1	12
Foreign-born:					
Canadian, French...........................	12	13	11	....	36
French....................................	....	3	....	....	3
Irish.....................................	....	1	....	....	1
Polish....................................	1	....	....	....	1
Total.................................	13	17	11	....	41
Grand total...........................	16	22	14	1	53

TABLE 3.—*Race, sex, and age, by grade—Number of pupils of each age in each grade, by sex and by general nativity and race of father of pupil*—Continued.

FIRST GRADE.

BOYS.

General nativity and race of father of pupil.	Number of pupils of each age.											Total.
	4.	5.	6.	7.	8.	9.	10.	11.	12.	13.	14.	
Native-born, White	....	3	13	10	8	....	....	....	....	....	....	34
Foreign-born:												
Canadian, French	....	....	4	7	5	2	1	....	....	....	....	19
Canadian, Other	1	....	....	....	....	....	....	....	....	....	1	2
English	....	....	....	1	....	....	....	....	....	....	....	1
French	....	....	....	....	2	....	1	....	....	....	....	3
German	....	....	6	8	12	4	2	....	....	....	....	32
Irish	2	11	7	7	1	....	....	....	....	....	....	28
Italian, North	....	....	....	....	1	....	....	....	....	....	....	1
Polish	....	3	1	1	1	1	....	....	....	....	....	7
Other races *a*	1	2	....	2	....	....	....	....	....	....	....	5
Total	4	16	19	25	22	7	4	....	....	....	1	98
Grand total	4	19	32	35	30	7	4	....	....	....	1	132

GIRLS.

General nativity and race of father of pupil.	4.	5.	6.	7.	8.	9.	10.	11.	12.	13.	14.	Total.
Native-born, White	5	8	19	6	7	....	1	....	....	....	....	46
Foreign-born:												
Canadian, French	....	1	3	6	5	2	1	1	1	....	....	20
Canadian, Other	....	1	....	....	....	....	....	....	....	....	....	1
English	....	....	1	....	....	....	....	....	....	....	....	1
German	....	1	3	9	7	8	1	....	....	....	....	29
Irish	....	11	7	4	1	....	1	....	....	....	....	24
Italian, North	....	....	1	....	....	....	....	....	....	....	....	1
Other races *a*	....	....	1	2	1	....	....	....	....	....	....	4
Total	....	14	16	21	14	10	3	1	1	....	....	80
Grand total	5	22	35	27	21	10	4	1	1	....	....	126

TOTAL.

General nativity and race of father of pupil.	4.	5.	6.	7.	8.	9.	10.	11.	12.	13.	14.	Total.
Native-born, White	5	11	32	16	15	....	1	....	....	....	....	80
Foreign-born:												
Canadian, French	....	1	7	13	10	4	2	1	1	....	....	39
Canadian, Other	1	1	....	....	....	....	....	....	....	....	1	3
English	....	....	2	....	....	....	....	....	....	....	....	2
French	....	....	....	....	2	....	1	....	....	....	....	3
German	....	1	9	17	19	12	3	....	....	....	....	61
Irish	2	22	14	11	2	....	1	....	....	....	....	52
Italian, North	....	....	1	....	1	....	....	....	....	....	....	2
Polish	....	3	1	1	1	1	....	....	....	....	....	7
Other races *a*	1	2	1	4	1	....	....	....	....	....	....	9
Total	4	30	35	46	36	17	7	1	1	....	1	178
Grand total	9	41	67	62	51	17	8	1	1	....	1	258

a "Other races" includes races having less than 10 representatives in this city and pupils whose race is not reported.

TABLE 3.—*Race, sex, and age, by grade—Number of pupils of each age in each grade, by sex and by general nativity and race of father of pupil*—Continued.

SECOND GRADE.

BOYS.

General nativity and race of father of pupil.	Number of pupils of each age.										Total.
	5.	6.	7.	8.	9.	10.	11.	12.	13.	14.	
Native-born, White		2	8	20	13	1	2	2			48
Foreign-born:											
Canadian, French				2	4	9	10	6			31
English			1	1	4						6
French							1				1
German			1	1	6	7					15
Irish	1	2	4	11	5	1			1		25
Italian, North				1							1
Polish				1	3						4
Total	1	2	6	17	22	17	11	6	1		83
Grand total	1	4	14	37	35	18	13	8	1		131

GIRLS.

General nativity and race of father of pupil.	5.	6.	7.	8.	9.	10.	11.	12.	13.	14.	Total.
Native-born, White		4	13	8	4	2	1	1			33
Foreign-born:											
Canadian, French			1	2	9	3	2			3	20
Canadian, Other		1									1
English		1	1	1	4	1					8
French						1					1
German				3	7	2		1			13
Irish		5	13	17	1	4					40
Other races *a*					1						1
Total		7	15	24	21	11	2	1		3	84
Grand total		11	28	32	25	13	3	2		3	117

TOTAL.

General nativity and race of father of pupil.	5.	6.	7.	8.	9.	10.	11.	12.	13.	14.	Total.
Native-born, White		6	21	28	17	3	3	3			81
Foreign-born:											
Canadian, French			1	4	13	12	12	6		3	51
Canadian, Other		1									1
English		1	2	2	8	1					14
French						1	1				2
German			1	4	13	9		1			28
Irish	1	7	17	28	6	5			1		65
Italian, North				1							1
Polish				1	3						4
Other races *a*				1							1
Total	1	9	21	41	48	28	13	7	1	3	167
Grand total	1	15	42	69	60	31	16	10	1	3	248

a"Other races" includes races having less than 10 representatives in this city and pupils whose race is not reported.

TABLE **3.**—*Race, sex, and age, by grade—Number of pupils of each age in each grade, by sex and by general nativity and race of father of pupil*—Continued.

THIRD GRADE.

BOYS.

General nativity and race of father of pupil.	Number of pupils of each age.											Total.
	7.	8.	9.	10.	11.	12.	13.	14.	15.	16.	17.	
Native-born, White	3	1	9	4	1	1						19
Foreign-born:												
Canadian, French	1											1
English					1							1
German		2	3	5	6	1	1		1			19
Irish		4	8	9	6	3						30
Polish					1	1						2
Other races *a*			3		1							4
Total	1	6	14	14	15	5	1		1			57
Grand total	4	7	23	18	16	6	1		1			76

GIRLS.

General nativity and race of father of pupil.	7.	8.	9.	10.	11.	12.	13.	14.	15.	16.	17.	Total.
Native-born, White	3	3	3	4	4							17
Foreign-born:												
English		1										1
German		1	5	3	2	1			1			13
Irish	5	6	6	6		3						26
Italian, North			1	1	2							4
Polish		1	1									2
Other races *a*			1									1
Total	5	9	14	10	4	4			1			47
Grand total	8	12	17	14	8	4			1			64

TOTAL.

General nativity and race of father of pupil.	7.	8.	9.	10.	11.	12.	13.	14.	15.	16.	17.	Total.
Native-born, White	6	4	12	8	5	1						36
Foreign-born:												
Canadian, French	1											1
English		1			1							2
German		3	8	8	8	2	1		2			32
Irish	5	10	14	15	6	6						56
Italian, North			1	1	2							4
Polish		1	1		1	1						4
Other races *a*			4		1							5
Total	6	15	28	24	19	9	1		2			104
Grand total	12	19	40	32	24	10	1		2			140

a "Other races" includes races having less than 10 representatives in this city and pupils whose race is not reported.

TABLE 3.—*Race, sex, and age, by grade—Number of pupils of each age in each grade, by sex and by general nativity and race of father of pupil*—Continued.

FOURTH GRADE.

BOYS.

General nativity and race of father of pupil.	Number of pupils of each age.							Total.
	8.	9.	10.	11.	12.	13.	14.	
Native-born, White....................	....	2	9	6	....	....	....	17
Foreign-born:								
Canadian, French..............				2				2
English......................		2						2
German......................			1	6	4	1		12
Irish.........................	1	1	5	8	2	....	1	18
Italian, North................					1			1
Polish........................						1		1
Other races *a*.................			1					1
Total.....................	1	3	7	16	7	2	1	37
Grand total................	1	5	16	22	7	2	1	54

GIRLS.

General nativity and race of father of pupil.	8.	9.	10.	11.	12.	13.	14.	Total.
Native-born, White....................	....	9	7	4	1	....	....	21
Foreign-born:								
Canadian, Other..............				1				1
German......................			3	4	2	3		12
Irish.........................	1	6	12	9	6			34
Polish........................							1	1
Other races *a*.................			2			1		3
Total.....................	1	6	17	14	8	4	1	51
Grand total................	1	15	24	18	9	4	1	72

TOTAL.

General nativity and race of father of pupil.	8.	9.	10.	11.	12.	13.	14.	Total.
Native-born, White....................	....	11	16	10	1	....	....	38
Foreign-born:								
Canadian, French..............				2				2
Canadian, Other..............				1				1
English......................		2						2
German......................			4	10	6	4		24
Irish.........................	2	7	17	17	8	....	1	52
Italian, North................					1			1
Polish........................						1	1	2
Other races *a*.................			3			1		4
Total.....................	2	9	24	30	15	6	2	88
Grand total................	2	20	40	40	16	6	2	126

a "Other races" includes races having less than 10 representatives in this city and pupils whose race is not reported.

TABLE **3.**—*Race, sex, and age, by grade—Number of pupils of each age in each grade, by sex and by general nativity and race of father of pupil*—Continued.

FIFTH GRADE.

BOYS.

General nativity and race of father of pupil.	Number of pupils of each age.							Total.
	8.	9.	10.	11.	12.	13.	14.	
Native-born, White	2	5	3	4	....	....	1	15
Foreign-born:								
Canadian, French	....	....	....	....	....	....	1	1
English	....	1	1	....	....	....	....	2
German	....	1	1	13	1	....	....	16
Irish	2	5	8	6	7	....	2	30
Polish	....	....	1	1	....	....	....	2
Other races *a*	....	....	1	....	....	....	....	1
Total	2	7	12	20	8	....	3	52
Grand total	4	12	15	24	8	....	4	67

GIRLS.

General nativity and race of father of pupil.	8.	9.	10.	11.	12.	13.	14.	Total.
Native-born, White	3	5	5	....	2	....	....	15
Foreign-born:								
German	....	1	2	6	3	....	....	12
Irish	3	2	10	8	4	1	....	28
Italian, North	....	....	....	1	....	1	....	2
Other races *a*	....	....	1	....	....	....	....	1
Total	3	3	13	15	7	2	....	43
Grand total	6	8	18	15	9	2	....	58

TOTAL.

General nativity and race of father of pupil.	8.	9.	10.	11.	12.	13.	14.	Total.
Native-born, White	5	10	8	4	2	....	1	30
Foreign-born:								
Canadian, French	....	....	....	....	....	....	1	1
English	....	1	1	....	....	....	....	2
German	....	2	3	19	4	....	....	28
Irish	5	7	18	14	11	1	2	58
Italian, North	....	....	....	1	....	1	....	2
Polish	....	....	1	1	....	....	....	2
Other races *a*	....	....	2	....	....	....	....	2
Total	5	10	25	35	15	2	3	95
Grand total	10	20	33	39	17	2	4	125

a "Other races" includes races having less than 10 representatives in this city and pupils whose race is not reported.

TABLE 3.—*Race, sex, and age, by grade—Number of pupils of each age in each grade, by sex and by general nativity and race of father of pupil*—Continued.

SIXTH GRADE.

BOYS.

General nativity and race of father of pupil.	Number of pupils of each age.							Total.
	9.	10.	11.	12.	13.	14.	15.	
Native-born, White..........................	......	......	1	9	......	1	1	12
Foreign-born:								
English..................................	......	1	1	......	1	......	......	3
German..................................	......	......	1	1	2	2	......	6
Irish....................................	1	1	4	2	4	1	......	13
Polish..................................	......	......	1	......	......	2	1	4
Total..............................	1	2	7	3	7	5	1	26
Grand total......................	1	2	8	12	7	6	2	38

GIRLS.

	9.	10.	11.	12.	13.	14.	15.	
Native-born, White..........................	1	1	2	3	2	......	......	9
Foreign-born:								
Canadian (other than French).................	1	......	......	......	......	......	......	1
English..................................	......	......	1	......	1	......	......	2
German..................................	......	......	......	3	3	1	......	7
Irish....................................	......	1	......	......	3	2	......	6
Italian, North..........................	......	......	......	......	1	1	......	2
Other races *a*..........................	......	......	......	......	2	......	......	2
Total..............................	1	1	1	3	10	4	......	20
Grand total......................	2	2	3	6	12	4	......	29

TOTAL.

	9.	10.	11.	12.	13.	14.	15.	
Native-born, White..........................	1	1	3	12	2	1	1	21
Foreign-born:								
Canadian (other than French).................	1	......	......	......	......	......	......	1
English..................................	......	1	2	......	2	......	......	5
German..................................	......	......	1	4	5	3	......	13
Irish....................................	1	2	4	2	7	3	......	19
Italian, North..........................	......	......	......	......	1	1	......	2
Polish..................................	......	......	1	......	......	2	1	4
Other races *a*..........................	......	......	......	......	2	......	......	2
Total..............................	2	3	8	6	17	9	1	46
Grand total......................	3	4	11	18	19	10	2	67

a "Other races" includes races having less than 10 representatives in this city and pupils whose race is not reported.

TABLE 3.—*Race, sex, and age, by grade—Number of pupils of each age in each grade, by sex and by general nativity and race of father of pupil—Continued.*

SEVENTH GRADE.

BOYS.

General nativity and race of father of pupil.	Number of pupils of each age.						Total.
	10.	11.	12.	13.	14.	15.	
Native-born, White	2	5	6	2			15
Foreign-born:							
English			1	1			2
German				2	1		3
Irish	1	5	12	2	8		28
Italian, North		1		2	1		4
Other races a				2			2
Total	1	6	13	9	10		39
Grand total	3	11	19	11	10		54

GIRLS.

General nativity and race of father of pupil.	10.	11.	12.	13.	14.	15.	Total.
Native-born, White	2	6	5	5		1	19
Foreign-born:							
Canadian, French			3				3
Canadian, Other					1		1
English					2		2
French			1				1
German			1	4			5
Irish		7	5	8	2		22
Italian, North		1					1
Total		8	10	12	5		35
Grand total	2	14	15	17	5	1	54

TOTAL.

General nativity and race of father of pupil.	10.	11.	12.	13.	14.	15.	Total.
Native-born, White	4	11	11	7		1	34
Foreign-born:							
Canadian, French			3				3
Canadian, Other					1		1
English			1	1	2		4
French			1				1
German			1	6	1		8
Irish	1	12	17	10	10		50
Italian, North		2		2	1		5
Other races a				2			2
Total	1	14	23	21	15		74
Grand total	5	25	34	28	15	1	108

a "Other races" includes races having less than 10 representatives in this city and pupils whose race is not reported.

TABLE 3.—*Race, sex, and age, by grade—Number of pupils of each age in each grade, by sex and by general nativity and race of father of pupil*—Continued.

EIGHTH GRADE.

BOYS.

General nativity and race of father of pupil.	Number of pupils of each age.						Total.
	11.	12.	13.	14.	15.	16.	
Native-born, White............	1	2	3	2	2	....	10
Foreign-born:							
Canadian (other than French)............	....	....	....	....	1	....	1
English............	....	2	....	1	....	....	3
German............	....	....	2	1	1	....	4
Irish............	....	1	8	8	6	1	24
Other races *a*............	....	....	1	....	....	....	1
Total............	....	3	11	10	8	1	33
Grand total............	1	5	14	12	10	1	43

GIRLS.

Native-born, White............	....	2	9	3	1	....	15
Foreign-born:							
Canadian (other than French)............	....	....	1	....	....	....	1
German............	....	1	7	....	....	....	8
Irish............	1	2	4	4	6	1	18
Total............	1	3	12	4	6	1	27
Grand total............	1	5	21	7	7	1	42

TOTAL.

Native-born, White............	1	4	12	5	3	....	25
Foreign-born:							
Canadian (other than French)............	....	....	1	....	1	....	2
English............	....	2	....	1	....	....	3
German............	....	1	9	1	1	....	12
Irish............	1	3	12	12	12	2	42
Other races *a*............	....	....	1	....	....	....	1
Total............	1	6	23	14	14	2	60
Grand total............	2	10	35	19	17	2	85

a "Other races" includes races having less than 10 representatives in this city and pupils whose race is not reported.

TABLE **3.**—*Race, sex, and age, by grade—Number of pupils of each age in each grade, by sex and by general nativity and race of father of pupil—Continued.*

NINTH GRADE.

BOYS.

General nativity and race of father of pupil.	Number of pupils of each age.				Total.
	13.	14.	15.	16.	
Native-born, White	....	3	3	....	6
Foreign-born:					
Canadian (other than French)	....	....	1	....	1
German	....	3	....	....	3
Irish	1	5	1	1	8
Total	1	8	2	1	12
Grand total	1	11	5	1	18

GIRLS.

General nativity and race of father of pupil.	13.	14.	15.	16.	Total.
Native-born, White	1	4	2	....	7
Foreign-born:					
English	....	2	....	....	2
Irish	7	4	5	....	16
Polish	....	....	1	....	1
Total	7	6	6	....	19
Grand total	8	10	8	....	26

TOTAL.

General nativity and race of father of pupil.	13.	14.	15.	16.	Total.
Native-born, White	1	7	5	....	13
Foreign-born:					
Canadian (other than French)	....	....	1	....	1
English	....	2	....	....	2
German	....	3	....	....	3
Irish	8	9	6	1	24
Polish	....	....	1	....	1
Total	8	14	8	1	31
Grand total	9	21	13	1	44

TABLE 3.—*Race, sex, and age, by grade—Number of pupils of each age in each grade, by sex and by general nativity and race of father of pupil*—Continued.

MIXED GRADES.

BOYS.

General nativity and race of father of pupil.	Number of pupils of each age.													Total.
	4.	5.	6.	7.	8.	9.	10.	11.	12.	13.	14.	15.	16.	
Native-born, White					1	3	4	2	6	5	1	2		24
Foreign-born:														
Canadian, French							3	4	13	11	6	3	1	41
French										1				1
Polish		8	22	8	10	17	10	13	8	6	1	1		104
Other races a			1											1
Total		8	23	8	10	17	13	17	21	18	7	4	1	147
Grand total		8	23	8	11	20	17	19	27	23	8	6	1	171

GIRLS.

General nativity and race of father of pupil.	4.	5.	6.	7.	8.	9.	10.	11.	12.	13.	14.	15.	16.	Total.
Native-born, White						1	1	1	3		2	1		9
Foreign-born:														
Canadian, French					1	1	6	3	12	14	5	2		44
English									1					1
French								2		1				3
Polish	1	5	13	10	25	13	17	8	11	8				111
Other races a						1								1
Total	1	5	13	10	26	15	23	13	24	23	5	2		160
Grand total	1	5	13	10	26	16	24	14	27	23	7	3		169

TOTAL.

General nativity and race of father of pupil.	4.	5.	6.	7.	8.	9.	10.	11.	12.	13.	14.	15.	16.	Total.
Native-born, White					1	4	5	3	9	5	3	3		33
Foreign-born:														
Canadian, French					1	1	9	7	25	25	11	5	1	85
English									1					1
French								2		2				4
Polish	1	13	35	18	35	30	27	21	19	14	1	1		215
Other races a			1			1								2
Total	1	13	36	18	36	32	36	30	45	41	12	6	1	307
Grand total	1	13	36	18	37	36	41	33	54	46	15	9	1	340

a "Other races" includes races having less than 10 representatives in this city and pupils whose race is not reported.

TABLE **5.**—*Race distribution in each grade—Percentages.*

[This table shows in detail only races with 100 or more pupils reporting. The totals, however, are for all races.]

General nativity and race of father of pupil.	Kindergarten.	Elementary grades.										Mixed grades.	Grand total.
		1.	2.	3.	4.	5.	6.	7.	8.	9.	Total.		
Native-born, White	22.6	31.0	32.7	25.7	30.2	24.0	31.3	31.5	29.4	29.5	29.8	9.7	25.3
Foreign-born:													
Canadian, French	67.9	15.1	20.6	.7	1.6	.8	.0	2.8	.0	.0	8.1	25.0	13.7
German	.0	23.6	11.3	22.9	19.0	22.4	19.4	7.4	14.1	6.8	17.4	.0	13.1
Irish	1.9	20.2	26.2	40.0	41.3	46.4	28.4	40.0	49.4	54.5	34.8	.0	26.3
Polish	1.9	2.7	1.6	2.9	1.6	1.6	6.0	12.0	.0	2.3	2.0	63.2	15.1
Other races	5.7	7.4	7.7	7.9	6.3	4.8	14.9	12.0	7.1	6.8	7.9	2.1	6.6
Total	77.4	69.0	67.3	74.3	69.8	76.0	68.7	68.5	70.6	70.5	70.2	90.3	74.7
Grand total	100.0	100.0	100.0	100.0	100.0	100.0	100.0	100.0	100.0	100.0	100.0	100.0	100.0

TABLE **6.**—*Grade distribution of each race—Percentages.*

[This table shows in detail only races with 100 or more pupils reporting. The totals, however, are for all races.]

General nativity and race of father of pupil.	Kindergarten.	Elementary grades.										Mixed schools.	Grand total.
		1.	2.	3.	4.	5.	6.	7.	8.	9.	Total.		
Native-born, White	3.0	19.9	20.1	8.9	9.4	7.4	5.2	8.4	6.2	3.2	88.8	8.2	100.0
Foreign-born:													
Canadian, French	16.5	17.9	23.4	.5	.9	.5	.0	1.4	.7	.0	44.5	39.0	100.0
German	.0	29.2	13.4	15.3	11.5	13.4	6.2	3.8	5.7	1.4	100.0	.0	100.0
Irish	.2	12.4	15.5	13.4	12.4	13.8	4.5	11.9	10.0	5.7	99.8	.0	100.0
Polish	.4	2.9	1.7	1.7	7.6	.8	1.7	.4	.0	.4	10.0	89.6	100.0
Other races	2.9	18.1	18.1	10.5	7.6	5.7	9.5	12.4	5.7	2.9	90.5	6.7	100.0
Total	3.4	14.9	14.0	8.7	7.4	8.0	3.9	6.2	5.0	2.6	70.8	25.8	100.0
Grand total	3.3	16.2	15.6	8.8	7.9	7.8	4.2	6.8	5.3	2.8	75.3	21.3	100.0

DATE DUE
